A Review of the Events of 1984

The 1985 World Book Year Book

The Annual Supplement to The World Book Encyclopedia

World Book, Inc.
a Scott Fetzer company

Chicago London Sydney Toronto

Staff

Publisher
William H. Nault

Editor in Chief
Robert O. Zeleny

Editorial Staff
Executive Editor
A. Richard Harmet

Managing Editor
Wayne Wille

Associate Editor
Sara Dreyfuss

Senior Editors
David L. Dreier
Barbara A. Mayes
Jay Myers
Rod Such

Contributing Editors
Robie Liscomb
Karin C. Rosenberg
Darlene R. Stille

Research Editor
Irene B. Keller

Index Editor
Claire Bolton

Statistical Editor
Katherine Norgel

Editorial Assistant
Ethel Matthews

Art Staff
Executive Art Director
William Hammond

Art Director
Roberta Dimmer

Senior Artist
Nikki Conner

Artists
Alice F. Dole
Alexandra Kalantzis
Lucy Smith

Photography Director
John S. Marshall

Senior Photographs Editor
Sandra M. Ozanick

Photographs Editor
Karen M. Koblik

Research and Services
Director of Research Services
Mary Norton

Director of Educational Services
Susan C. Kilburg

Library Services
Mary Kayaian, Head
Susan O'Donnell

Cartographic Services
H. George Stoll, Head

Product Production
Executive Director
Peter Mollman

Director of Manufacturing
Joseph C. LaCount

Director of Pre-Press
J. J. Stack

Production Control Manager
Barbara Podczerwinski

Assistant Product Manager
Madelyn Krzak

Film Separations Manager
Alfred J. Mozdzen

Film Separations Assistant Manager
Barbara J. McDonald

Research and Development Manager
Henry Koval

Copyright © 1985 by World Book, Inc., Chicago, Illinois 60654. Portions of the material contained in this volume are taken from The World Book Encyclopedia, Copyright © 1985 by World Book, Inc., and from The World Book Dictionary, Copyright © 1984 by Doubleday & Company, Inc. All rights reserved. This volume may not be reproduced in whole or in part in any form without written permission from the publishers.

Printed in the United States of America.
ISBN 0-7166-0485-X
ISSN 0084-1439
Library of Congress Catalog Card Number: 62-4818

Preface

The contrast between humankind's triumphs and failures in 1984 is shown dramatically in the two pictures below. At the left is a scene we take almost for granted these days — a picture of an astronaut in space. Joseph Allen is preparing to stow away in the space shuttle *Discovery* the malfunctioning *Westar 6* communications satellite that was retrieved from orbit and returned to Earth for repair. *Time* magazine called this operation "the most spectacular . . . ever attempted in the increasingly workaday world of space."

At the right is another scene that, tragically, many took for granted in 1984 because we have seen it often before — a picture of starvation. Throughout much of Africa, millions of people were starving in 1984, and hundreds of thousands were dying.

Modern technology sent people into space, but the problem of hunger in Africa and throughout the world does not lend itself to a "technological fix." It is a complex problem, with drought, growing populations, economic mismanagement, politics, and wars all contributing to it. How such factors have been at work in Africa for the past quarter-century is detailed in a Special Report, "Africa — The Troubled Continent," which begins on page 30 of this YEAR BOOK. The story of Africa during 1984 can be found in the Year on File section — in the "Africa" article and articles on individual countries. The File's "Space Exploration" article tells the story of the shuttle missions, and other File articles complete the story of the triumphs, failures, and less momentous events that made the year 1984 what it was. WAYNE WILLE

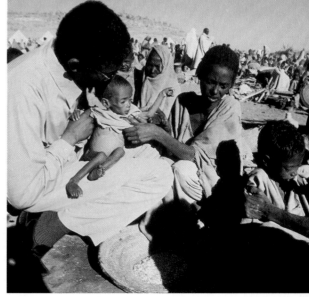

Contents

A tear-out page of cross-reference tabs for insertion in THE WORLD BOOK ENCYCLOPEDIA appears after page 16.

Contributors

Contributors not listed on these pages are members of THE WORLD BOOK YEAR BOOK editorial staff.

Adachi, Ken, B.A., M.A.; Literary Critic, *The Toronto Star*. [LITERATURE, CANADIAN]

Alexiou, Arthur G., B.S.E.E., M.S.E.E.; Associate Director, Office of Sea Grant. [OCEAN]

Andrews, Peter J., B.A., M.S.; Free-Lance Writer; Biochemist. [CHEMISTRY]

Apseloff, Marilyn Fain, B.A., M.A.; Assistant Professor of English, Kent State University. [LITERATURE FOR CHILDREN]

Barber, Peggy, B.A., M.L.S.; Associate Executive Director-Communications, American Library Association. [AMERICAN LIBRARY ASSOCIATION]

Beckwith, David C., A.B., M.S., J.D.; Correspondent, *Time* magazine. [COURTS AND LAWS; CRIME; PRISON; SUPREME COURT OF THE UNITED STATES]

Bednarski, P. J., Television/Radio Critic, Chicago *Sun-Times*. [RADIO; TELEVISION]

Berman, Howard A., M.H.L.; Rabbi, Chicago Sinai Congregation. [JEWS AND JUDAISM]

Biggar, Jeanne C., Ph.D.; Associate Professor of Sociology, University of Virginia. [POPULATION]

Blackadar, Alfred K., A.B., Ph.D.; Professor of Meteorology, The Pennsylvania State University. [WEATHER]

Bradsher, Henry S., A.B., B.J.; Foreign Affairs Analyst; Author. [ASIA and Asian Country Articles]

Brown, Kenneth, former Editor, *United Kingdom Press Gazette*. [EUROPE and European Country Articles]

Brown, Merrill, B.A.; Director of Business Development, The Washington Post Company. [COMMUNICATIONS]

Campbell, Robert, B.A., M.S., M. Arch.; Architect and Critic. [ARCHITECTURE]

Campion, Owen F., B.A.; Editor in Chief, *Tennessee Register*. [ROMAN CATHOLIC CHURCH]

Chandler, David P., B.A., M.A., Ph.D.; Research Director, Center of Southeast Asian Studies, Monash University. [WORLD BOOK SUPPLEMENT: BRUNEI]

Clark, Phil, M.A.; Free-Lance Garden Writer and Photographer. [GARDENING]

Cohn, Anne Harris, D.P.H.; Executive Director, National Committee for Prevention of Child Abuse. [CHILD WELFARE: (Close-Up)]

Cormier, Frank, B.S.J., M.S.J.; former White House Correspondent, Associated Press. [U.S. Government Articles; Special Report: LOBBYING THE LAWMAKERS]

Cormier, Margot, B.A., M.S.; Free-Lance Writer. [U.S. Government Articles]

Crespi, Irving, B.S.S., M.A., Ph.D.; Polling Consultant; past President, American Association for Public Opinion Research. [DEATHS (Close-Up)]

Cromie, William J., B.S.; Executive Director, Council for the Advancement of Science Writing. [BUILDING AND CONSTRUCTION; SPACE EXPLORATION]

Cviic, Chris, B.A., B.S.; Eastern European Specialist, *The Economist*. [Eastern European Country Articles; RUSSIA (Close-Up)]

Datre, Donna M., B.A.; Public Information Manager, Toy Manufacturers of America, Inc. [GAMES AND TOYS]

DeFrank, Thomas M., B.A., M.A.; Correspondent, *Newsweek* magazine. [ARMED FORCES]

Dent, Thomas H., Executive Director, The Cat Fanciers' Association, Inc. [CAT]

Dewey, Russell A., B.A., Ph.D.; Assistant Professor of Psychology, Georgia Southern College. [PSYCHOLOGY]

Dixon, Gloria Ricks, A.B.J.; Vice President/Communications, Magazine Publishers Association. [MAGAZINE]

Duncan, Patricia D., B.F.A.; Writer; Photographer; Author of *Tallgrass Prairie: The Inland Sea*. [Special Report: PRESERVING OUR PRAIRIE HERITAGE]

Esseks, J. Dixon, A.B., A.M., Ph.D.; Associate Professor, Department of Political Science, Northern Illinois University. [AFRICA and African Country Articles]

Evans, Sandra, B.S.J.; Staff Writer, *The Washington Post*. [WASHINGTON, D.C.]

Farr, David M. L., M.A., D.Phil.; Professor of History and Director, Paterson Centre for International Programs, Carleton University, Ottawa. [CANADA; CANADA (Close-Up); Canadian Province Articles; SCHREYER, EDWARD RICHARD; TRUDEAU, PIERRE ELLIOTT]

Fisher, Robert W., B.A., M.A.; Supervisory Economist; U.S. Bureau of Labor Statistics. [LABOR]

Fitzgerald, Mark, B.A.; Midwest Editor, *Editor & Publisher* magazine. [NEWSPAPER; PUBLISHING]

Francis, Henry G., B.S.; Executive Editor, American Contract Bridge League. [BRIDGE]

French, Charles E., B.S., A.M., Ph.D.; Director, Institute of Agribusiness, University of Santa Clara. [FARM AND FARMING]

Gaur, Krishna Kumar, B.A., M.A., M.S.J., J.D.; Editor of the Editorial Pages, Chicago *Sun-Times*. [ASIA (Close-Up)]

Goldner, Nancy, B.A.; Dance Critic, *The Philadelphia Inquirer, Saturday Review*. [DANCING]

Goldstein, Jane, B.A.; Director of Publicity, Santa Anita Park. [HORSE RACING]

Gordon, Margaret T., B.S.J., M.S.J., Ph.D.; Director, Center for Urban Affairs and Policy Research, and Professor, Medill School of Journalism, Northwestern University. [CITY]

Gould, William James, B.A.; Free-Lance Editor, England. [ENGLAND]

Graham, Jarlath J., B.A.; Director of External Relations, *Advertising Age*. [ADVERTISING]

Grigadean, Jerry, B.S., M.Mus., Ph.D.; Music and Video Producer. [MUSIC, POPULAR]

Hannan, Patrick, B.A.; Producer/Presenter, BBC Wales. [WALES]

Harakas, Stanley Samuel, B.A., B.D., Th.D.; Professor of Orthodox Christian Ethics, Holy Cross Greek Orthodox School of Theology. [EASTERN ORTHODOX CHURCHES]

Haverstock, Nathan A., A.B.; Director, The Latin American Service. [LATIN AMERICA and Latin-American Country Articles]

Heller, Walter H., B.A.; Director of Research, *Progressive Grocer Magazine*. [FOOD]

Herreid, Clyde Freeman, II, B.A., M.Sc., Ph.D.; Professor of Biological Sciences, State University of New York at Buffalo. [ZOOLOGY]

Higgins, James V., B.A.; Automotive Industry Reporter, *The Detroit News*. [AUTOMOBILE]

Hornsby, Alton, Jr., B.A., M.A., Ph.D.; Chairman, Department of History, Morehouse College. [WORLD BOOK SUPPLEMENT: BLACK AMERICANS]

Hunzeker, Jeanne M., D.S.W.; Associate Director, Child Welfare League of America, Inc. [CHILD WELFARE]

Jacobi, Peter P., B.S.J., M.S.J.; Vice President and Director of Instructional Services, Jack Hilton, Inc. [MUSIC, CLASSICAL]

Johanson, Donald C., M.A., Ph.D.; Director, Institute of Human Origins. [ANTHROPOLOGY]

Joseph, Lou, B.A.; Senior Science Writer, Hill and Knowlton. [DENTISTRY]

Karr, Albert R., M.S.; Staff Reporter, *The Wall Street Journal*. [TRANSPORTATION and Transportation Articles]

Kelso, William M., B.A., M.A., Ph.D.; Resident Archaeologist, Thomas Jefferson Memorial Foundation. [Special Report: DIGGING ON JEFFERSON'S MOUNTAIN]

Kennedy, Floyd D., Jr., A.B., M.A.; Author, *World Combat Aircraft Directory; Military Helicopters of the World: Military Rotary-Wing Aircraft Since 1917*. [WORLD BOOK SUPPLEMENT: HELICOPTER]

Kind, Joshua B., B.A., Ph.D.; Professor of Art History, Northern Illinois University. [VISUAL ARTS]

Kisor, Henry, B.A., M.S.J.; Book Editor, Chicago *Sun-Times*. [LITERATURE]

Kitchen, Paul, B.A., B.L.S.; Executive Director, Canadian Library Association. [CANADIAN LIBRARY ASSOCIATION]

Knapp, Elaine Stuart, B.A.; Editor, Council of State Governments. [STATE GOVERNMENT]

Koenig, Louis W., B.A., M.A., Ph.D., L.H.D.; Professor of Government, New York University. [CIVIL RIGHTS]

Kolgraf, Ronald, B.A., M.A.; Publisher, Morgan-Grampian Publishing Company. [MANUFACTURING]

Kuersten, Joan M., B.A.; Assistant Editor, *PTA Magazine,* National PTA. [NATIONAL PTA (NATIONAL CONGRESS OF PARENTS AND TEACHERS)]

Kushma, David, B.A., M.A.; City-County Bureau Chief, *Detroit Free Press.* [DETROIT]

Landwehr, Michael E., Director, Information and Referral Services, Schwab Rehabilitation Center. [HANDICAPPED]

Langdon, Robert, Executive Officer, Pacific Manuscripts Bureau, Australian National University. [PACIFIC ISLANDS]

Larsen, Paul A., P.E., B.S., Ch.E.; Member: American Philatelic Society; Collectors Club of Chicago; Fellow, Royal Philatelic Society, London. Past President, British Caribbean Philatelic Study Group. [STAMP COLLECTING]

Lawrence, Al, A.B., M.Ed., M.A.; Associate Director, United States Chess Federation. [CHESS]

Lawrence, Richard, B.E.E.; Correspondent, International Economic Affairs, *Journal of Commerce.* [INTERNATIONAL TRADE AND FINANCE]

Levine, Ed, B.A.; Free-Lance Writer. [Special Report: THE SIGHTS AND SOUNDS OF MUSIC VIDEOS]

Levy, Emanuel, B.A.; Editor, *Insurance Advocate.* [INSURANCE]

Litsky, Frank, B.S.; Sports Writer, *The New York Times.* [Sports Articles]

Maki, John M., B.A., M.A., Ph.D.; Professor Emeritus, University of Massachusetts. [JAPAN]

Mandile, Tony, Free-Lance Writer and Photographer. [FISHING; HUNTING]

Maran, Stephen P., B.S., M.A., Ph.D.; Senior Staff Scientist, National Aeronautics and Space Administration-Goddard Space Flight Center. [ASTRONOMY]

Martin, Lee, Former Associate Editor, Miller Magazines. [COIN COLLECTING]

Marty, Martin E., Ph.D.; Fairfax M. Cone Distinguished Service Professor, University of Chicago. [PROTESTANTISM; RELIGION]

Mather, Ian J., M.A.; Defense Correspondent, *The Observer,* London. [GREAT BRITAIN; IRELAND; NORTHERN IRELAND]

Mathews, Thomas G., B.A., M.A., Ph.D.; Secretary-General, Association of Caribbean Universities. [WORLD BOOK SUPPLEMENT: SAINT CHRISTOPHER AND NEVIS]

Maugh, Thomas H., II, Ph.D.; Senior Science Writer, *Science.* [BIOCHEMISTRY; Special Report: CHANGING LIFE'S BLUEPRINT]

McCall-Newman, Christina, B.A.; Author; Editor, *Saturday Night Magazine,* Toronto. [WORLD BOOK SUPPLEMENT: TURNER, JOHN NAPIER]

McCarron, John, M.S.J.; Urban Affairs Editor, *Chicago Tribune.* [CHICAGO]

Merina, Victor, A.A., B.A., M.S.; Staff Writer, *Los Angeles Times.* [LOS ANGELES]

Miller, J. D. B., M.Ec., M.A.; Professor of International Relations, Australian National University, Canberra. [AUSTRALIA]

Mintz, William A., Assistant Metropolitan Editor, *Houston Chronicle.* [HOUSTON]

Molho, Anthony, Ph.D.; Chairman, Department of History, Brown University. [WORLD BOOK SUPPLEMENT: RENAISSANCE]

Moores, Eldridge M., B.S., Ph.D.; Professor of Geology, University of California at Davis. [GEOLOGY]

Moritz, Owen, B.A.; Urban Affairs Editor, *New York Daily News.* [NEW YORK CITY]

Morris, Bernadine, B.A., M.A.; Chief Fashion Writer, *The New York Times.* [FASHION]

Murray, G. E., B.A., M.A.; Poetry Critic, Chicago *Sun-Times.* [POETRY]

Newcomb, Eldon H., A.B., A.M., Ph.D.; Professor and Chairman, Department of Botany, University of Wisconsin-Madison. [BOTANY]

Newman, Andrew L., A.B., M.A.; former Senior Information Officer, U.S. Department of the Interior. [CONSERVATION; ENVIRONMENT; FISHING INDUSTRY; FOREST AND FOREST PRODUCTS; INDIAN, AMERICAN; WATER]

Oatis, William N., former United Nations Correspondent, Associated Press. [UNITED NATIONS]

Parsons, Cynthia, B.A., M.A.; Education Consultant. [EDUCATION]

Pollock, Steve, B.A.; Features Editor, *Popular Photography.* [PHOTOGRAPHY]

Price, Frederick C., B.S., Ch.E.; Manager of Proposals, Lammas Crest, Inc. [CHEMICAL INDUSTRY]

Rowse, Arthur E., I.A., M.B.A.; Associate Editor, Washington Letter, *U.S. News & World Report.* [CONSUMERISM; SAFETY]

Schaffer, Jan, B.S.J., M.S.J.; Business Reporter, *The Philadelphia Inquirer.* [PHILADELPHIA]

Shand, David A., B.C.A., B.Com.; Chief Director, Auditor-General of Victoria, Melbourne, Australia. [NEW ZEALAND]

Shaw, Robert J., B.S., B.A.; former Editor, *Library Technology Reports,* American Library Association. [LIBRARY]

Shearer, Warren W., A.B., A.M., Ph.D., J.D.; Attorney; former Chairman, Department of Economics, Wabash College. [ECONOMICS]

Simpson, Peggy A., B.A.; Economic Correspondent, Hearst Newspapers; Washington (D.C.) Columnist, *Working Woman* magazine. [Special Report: A REVOLUTION IN THE WORKPLACE]

Spencer, William, A.B., A.M., Ph.D.; Writer; Visiting Professor of Political Science, Rollins College. [MIDDLE EAST and Middle Eastern Country Articles; North Africa Country Articles]

Stasio, Marilyn, B.A., M.A.; Theater Critic, *New York Post.* [THEATER]

Swanton, Donald, B.S., M.S., Ph.D., M.B.A.; Chairman, Department of Finance, Roosevelt University. [BANK; STOCKS AND BONDS]

Taylor, Doreen, Free-Lance Journalist, Writer, and Broadcaster, Scotland. [SCOTLAND]

Thompson, Ida, A.B., M.S., Ph.D.; Associate Research Professor, Center for Coastal and Environmental Studies, Rutgers University. [PALEONTOLOGY]

Thompson, John R., Jr., B.S., M.A., Ph.D.; Head Basketball Coach, Georgetown University. [WORLD BOOK SUPPLEMENT: BASKETBALL]

Vesley, Roberta, A.B., M.L.S.; Library Director, American Kennel Club. [DOG]

Voorhies, Barbara, B.S., Ph.D.; Associate Professor, Department of Anthropology, University of California at Santa Barbara. [ARCHAEOLOGY]

Walter, Eugene J., Jr., B.A.; Editor in Chief, *Animal Kingdom* magazine, and Curator of Publications, New York Zoological Society. [ZOOS]

Weininger, Jean, A.B., M.S., Ph.D.; Research Fellow, Department of Nutritional Sciences, University of California at Berkeley. [NUTRITION]

White, Thomas O., B.S., Ph.D.; Lecturer in Physics and Fellow of King's College, Cambridge University, Cambridge, England. [PHYSICS]

Windeyer, Kendal, Free-Lance Writer and Broadcaster. [MONTREAL; WORLD BOOK SUPPLEMENT: MULRONEY, MARTIN BRIAN]

Wolff, Howard, B.S.; Associate Managing Editor, *Electronics.* [COMPUTER; ELECTRONICS]

Woods, Michael, B.S.; Science Editor, *The Toledo Blade.* [Energy, Mining, and Health Articles]

Wuntch, Philip, B.A.; Film Critic, *Dallas Morning News.* [MOTION PICTURES]

Young, Crawford, B.A., Ph.D.; Professor of Political Science, University of Wisconsin-Madison. [Special Report: AFRICA — THE TROUBLED CONTINENT]

The Year
in Brief

A short essay captures the spirit
of 1984, and a month-by-month
listing highlights some of the
year's significant events.

See February 7, page 17.

The Year in Brief

A review of some of the major trends and events that touched many of our lives during 1984.

The leadership of four — and very nearly five — major nations dominated world news in 1984. Elections in the United States and Canada produced landslides that retained one head of government and turned out another, while in the Soviet Union, one ailing leader died and was replaced by another. Terrorists assassinated India's leader and almost killed the prime minister of Great Britain.

Also during the year, bloody wars and civil wars raged in several parts of the world; famine ravaged Africa; terrorists in Lebanon again lashed out at the United States; and East and West failed to meet at the negotiating table to talk about nuclear disarmament — and also failed to meet on the athletic field. There were, in addition, other big events and many little ones, the important and the unimportant, that made 1984 what it was.

The reelection of United States President Ronald Reagan on November 6 came as no surprise. Nor were many political observers surprised by the nomination of his Democratic challenger, former Vice President Walter F. Mondale.

However, one of Mondale's challengers, Colorado Senator Gary W. Hart, had scored a surprising victory in the New Hampshire primary election, traditionally the nation's first, on February 28. And on March 13, Hart won three primaries to Mondale's two. But by the end of April, Mondale had a lead over Hart of almost 600 delegates, with black candidate Jesse L. Jackson a distant third. On June 6, Mondale announced that he had enough delegates to secure the nomination.

In late June and early July, Mondale interviewed seven prospective vice presidential candidates. The composition of the group indicated that Mondale almost certainly was about to do something unusual. Since the birth of the nation, all previous major party candidates for Vice President — as well as President — had been white, non-Hispanic men, but Mondale interviewed only one such individual. The other prospective candidates were a Hispanic man, two black men, and three white women. On July 12, Mondale announced that he intended to share the ticket with Geraldine A. Fer-

Opposite page: Rafer Johnson, 1960 decathlon gold medalist, carries a torch aloft in Los Angeles Memorial Coliseum on July 28 to light the ceremonial flame that will burn throughout the XXIII Summer Olympic Games.

raro, congresswoman from New York City. Mondale and Ferraro were both nominated by acclamation at the Democratic National Convention in July in San Francisco.

A month later, the Republican Party convened in Dallas and renominated Reagan and Vice President George H. W. Bush. "We're in the midst of a springtime of hope for America," said Reagan in accepting the nomination.

Hope seemed about all that the Mondale/Ferraro team had. On July 8, a public opinion poll conducted by American Broadcasting Companies and *The Washington* (D.C.) *Post* had indicated that Reagan led Mondale by 51 to 44 per cent. By September 12, the lead was 56-40. And in mid-October, after two debates between Reagan and Mondale and one between Bush and Ferraro, both political parties agreed that the Republicans led by about 10 points.

Reagan won the November election with about 59 per cent of the popular vote, capturing all the electoral votes except those of Minnesota and the District of Columbia. Overwhelming as Reagan's victory was, it did not lead to a Republican sweep of federal offices. In fact, although the Democrats lost 15 seats, they retained control of the House of Representatives 252 seats to 182, with 1 seat being contested. The Democrats gained 2 Senate seats, but the Republicans still had a majority there, 53 seats to 47.

Canada's national election on September 4 produced a landslide victory for the Progressive Conservatives. Of the 282 seats in the

The Democrats break tradition in July by nominating Geraldine A. Ferraro to share the ticket with presidential candidate Walter F. Mondale, *above*. In August, the Republicans, *right*, renominate President Ronald Reagan and Vice President George H. W. Bush.

House of Commons, they won 211 — the largest number of seats ever captured by a single party. Their leader, Brian Mulroney, became prime minister on September 17, replacing John N. Turner of the defeated Liberal Party. Turner had become prime minister on June 30, succeeding Pierre Elliott Trudeau, who retired after more than 15 years as prime minister.

Soviet leader Yuri V. Andropov died at the age of 69 on February 9, after only 15 months in office. He had suffered from kidney disease and was not seen in public for the last six months of his life. Andropov's successor, Konstantin U. Chernenko, 72, was thought to be in poor health during much of 1984. He made no public appearances for seven weeks during the summer, finally reappearing on September 5.

Terrorism entered the political scene in India and Great Britain. India's Prime Minister Indira Gandhi was a victim of assassins' bullets on October 31. Her killers — two of her bodyguards — were members of the Sikh religion. The assassination was viewed as a retaliation for the Indian army's June assault on the Golden Temple in Amritsar, which the Sikhs consider to be their holiest shrine. The assault on the temple was part of an effort to crush a campaign by militant Sikhs to expand the state of Punjab and to make it into a semi-independent nation. Indira Gandhi's son, Rajiv, succeeded her as prime minister.

Great Britain's Prime Minister Margaret Thatcher narrowly escaped death at the hands of terrorists early on the morning of October 12. A bomb exploded in a hotel in Brighton, England, where she and virtually the entire British Cabinet were staying during the annual conference of the Conservative Party. The blast killed five people, including one member of Parliament. The Provisional Irish Republican Army, a guerrilla group, claimed responsibility.

The United States presence in Lebanon was the target of terror-

Brian Mulroney greets well-wishers as his Progressive Conservative Party sweeps to victory in Canada's national elections on September 4, assuring Mulroney the post of prime minister.

The year 1984 brought famine in Africa, *above*, where an estimated 500,000 people starved to death; terrorism in Lebanon, *top*, where a bomb killed at least 14 people at the U.S. Embassy; and political assassination in India, where Prime Minister Indira Gandhi, *top right*, was felled by bullets fired by two of her own bodyguards.

ists again in 1984. On September 20, a terrorist steered a station wagon loaded with explosives around concrete barriers amid a hail of bullets at the U.S. Embassy annex in Aukar, near Beirut, Lebanon. The explosives went off when the vehicle reached the front of the annex, killing at least 14 people. This was the third vehicle bombing of a U.S. facility in Lebanon. The first had occurred in April 1983 at the embassy in Beirut, killing 63 people, and the second at a Marine Corps headquarters in Beirut in October 1983, when 241 Americans were killed.

Other trouble spots remained troubled. Iran and Iraq continued their bloody war, but neither nation gained an advantage. In Afghanistan, the Soviets stepped up their military effort against Afghan rebels. And in Kampuchea (Cambodia), government troops and their Vietnamese allies continued to battle Kampuchean rebels.

In Africa a continuing problem worsened — famine. The immediate cause of the famine was a prolonged drought, but there were other important causes, including economic mismanagement and civil wars. By mid-November, according to estimates, 300,000 men, women, and children may have died of hunger in Ethiopia and another 200,000 in Mozambique. Millions more were starving in those two countries and others, and massive relief shipments from outside the troubled continent began to arrive. For many, the help would be too late.

In Central America, El Salvador elected a president who met with rebel leaders, but guerrilla warfare continued in that country. Nicaragua dug in for a U.S. invasion it said was coming — but it never came. And the United States watched a Nicaraguan port for a shipment of Soviet aircraft that failed to materialize.

Although there were worldwide demonstrations in favor of nuclear disarmament throughout 1984, Soviet diplomats failed to appear at negotiating tables in Geneva, Switzerland. The Soviets and their American counterparts had discussed the control of both intermediate range and strategic nuclear missiles there until late 1983, when the North Atlantic Treaty Organization (NATO) began to install intermediate missiles in Western Europe. The Soviets ended the talks abruptly in 1983. On Nov. 22, 1984, however, the Soviet Union and the United States agreed to return to the table for arms talks in 1985.

In 1984, the Soviet Union turned the tables on the United States as far as the Summer Olympic Games were concerned. The United States and several other nations had boycotted the 1980 Summer Games, held in Moscow, to protest the Soviet invasion of Afghanistan in December 1979. In 1984, it was the Soviets' turn to boycott. On May 8, the Soviet Union announced that it would skip the Summer Games because the U.S. government "did not intend to ensure the security of all sportsmen, respect their rights and human dignity, and create normal conditions for holding the games." Eventually, most of the Soviet Union's close allies also withdrew.

Even without the Soviets and their satellites, the Summer Games provided plenty of excitement for television viewers throughout the world. United States track and field star Carl Lewis won four gold medals, matching U.S. athlete Jesse Owens' accomplishment in the 1936 games. Edwin Moses of the United States repeated his 1976 win in the 400-meter hurdles. Great Britain had two winners who duplicated their 1980 gold-medal triumphs, Sebastian Coe in the 1,500-meter run and Daley Thompson in the decathlon. Mary Lou Retton of the U.S. won five medals, including the gold in women's all-around gymnastics, while the U.S. women gymnasts surprisingly won the team silver medal. But a long-awaited showdown between Mary Decker of the United States and Zola Budd of Great Britain in the 3,000-meter run ended disastrously as the two athletes collided on the track.

The year 1984 also brought a Nobel Prize to two physicists for their discovery of subatomic particles, proving that little things are worth pursuing; and riches to a manufacturer of board games, proving that trivial things are worth pursuing. Young padres from southern California wearing leather gloves captured some cubs but then were run off by some fierce tigers. A young man wearing a sequined glove sang his way to financial security while U.S. politicians debated some sharp ways to flatten the deficit and bring the nation's economy into tune.

With some of its leadership questions resolved in 1984, the world looked forward to 1985 in the hope that new leaders — and old — would advance in their pursuit of global harmony.   THE EDITORS

For details about 1984:

The Year on File section — which begins on page 170 — describes events of 1984 according to the country, field, or general subject area in which they occurred. The Chronology, which starts on page 16, lists major events month by month.

Jan. 7-17

Jan. 11

Jan. 22

January

1	2	3	4	5	6	7
8	9	10	11	12	13	14
15	16	17	18	19	20	21
22	23	24	25	26	27	28
29	30	31				

3   **Syria frees** Lieutenant Robert O. Goodman, Jr., a United States Navy flier shot down in Lebanon in December 1983.
Tunisia declares a state of emergency after several days of rioting over food prices.

7-17   **Premier Zhao Ziyang** of China becomes the first Chinese premier to visit the United States.

8   **Suriname's military dictator,** Desi Bouterse, dismisses the government's civilian cabinet.

10   **The United States and the Vatican** establish full diplomatic ties for the first time in 117 years.
Denmark's ruling conservative coalition wins more seats in parliamentary elections but falls short of a majority.

11   **A U.S. Army helicopter pilot** becomes the first American serviceman killed by hostile fire in Honduras.
A presidential commission headed by former U.S. Secretary of State Henry A. Kissinger recommends $8 billion in aid for

Central America over the next five years.

12   **Business executives** on a presidential commission report that the U.S. government could save more than $400 billion over three years by reducing waste and inefficiency.

13   **Television newswoman Christine Craft** wins $325,000 in damages in a retrial of her 1983 suit against her former employer for fraud.

17   **A 35-nation East-West conference** on European security opens in Stockholm, Sweden.
The Supreme Court of the United States rules that home videotaping of television programs for private use does not violate copyright laws.

22   **The Los Angeles Raiders** beat the Washington Redskins 38-9 in U.S. professional football's Super Bowl XVIII.
William French Smith resigns as attorney general of the United States but stays on for the rest of the year. Confirmation hearings on his appointed successor, White House counselor Edwin Meese III are suspended in March pending a probe of Meese's financial dealings.
King Hassan II of Morocco cancels food price increases that triggered four days of rioting.

24   **Roman Catholic Bishop Bernard F. Law** of Springfield-Cape Girardeau, Mo., is appointed archbishop of Boston.

29   **President Ronald Reagan** formally announces his candidacy for reelection.

31   **Roman Catholic Bishop John J. O'Connor** of Scranton, Pa., is appointed archbishop of New York City.

Here are your

1985 YEAR BOOK
Cross-Reference Tabs

For insertion in your WORLD BOOK

Each year, THE WORLD BOOK YEAR BOOK adds a valuable dimension to your WORLD BOOK set. The Cross-Reference Tab System is designed especially to help youngsters and parents alike *link* THE YEAR BOOK's new and revised WORLD BOOK articles, its Special Reports, and its Close-Ups to the related WORLD BOOK articles they update.

How to Use These Tabs

First, remove this page from THE YEAR BOOK.
Begin with the top Tab, AFRICA.

Turn to the A Volume of your WORLD BOOK set and find the first page of the AFRICA article. Moisten the gummed Tab and affix it to that page.

Your WORLD BOOK set may not contain an article with the same name as every Tab. MUSIC VIDEO is an example. Put that Tab in the M volume in its proper alphabetical sequence.

Feb. 7

Feb. 9

February

			1	2	3	4
5	6	7	8	9	10	11
12	13	14	15	16	17	18
19	20	21	22	23	24	25
26	27	28	29			

2   **Jaime Lusinchi** is inaugurated as president of Venezuela.

3   **The United States Environmental Protection Agency (EPA)** bans the use of ethylene dibromide (EDB), a pesticide suspected of causing cancer, on grain and grain products.

3-6   **Two satellites** launched by the space shuttle *Challenger* misfire and stray off course, and a balloon launched by the shuttle explodes.

5   **Lebanon's Prime Minister Shafiq al-Wazzan** and his entire Cabinet resign.

6-7   **Shiite Muslim and Druse militias** take control of most of West Beirut, Lebanon.

7   ***Challenger* astronauts** Bruce McCandless II, in picture above, and Robert L. Stewart become the first human beings to fly free in space without a lifeline to their spacecraft.

8-19   **The Winter Olympic Games** take place in Sarajevo, Yugoslavia. The Soviets win the most medals — 6 gold, 10 silver, and 9 bronze.

9   **Soviet leader Yuri V. Andropov,** 69, dies of kidney failure. His funeral is held on February 14, shown above.

12   **Chief Justice of the United States** Warren E. Burger, in a speech to the American Bar Association, criticizes the legal profession for shoddy ethics.

13   **Konstantin U. Chernenko** succeeds Andropov in the Soviet Union's most powerful post — general secretary of the Central Committee of the Communist Party.
President Ricardo de la Espriella of Panama resigns.

16-24   **French truckers** blockade major highways to protest a variety of grievances.

20   **Former Vice President Walter F. Mondale** wins 49 per cent of the vote in Iowa's Democratic Party caucuses.

21-26   **U.S. Marines** in Beirut move from the city's airport to U.S. Navy vessels offshore.

28   **Singer Michael Jackson** wins a record eight Grammy Awards.
Senator Gary W. Hart (D., Colo.) wins the New Hampshire Democratic presidential primary, capturing 39 per cent of the vote to Mondale's 27 per cent.
The Supreme Court of the United States rules that the federal government can bar sex discrimination by schools only in programs that receive federal funds, not in the school as a whole.

29   **Canadian Prime Minister Pierre Elliott Trudeau** announces that he will resign after the Liberal Party picks a new leader.
Senator Alan Cranston of California becomes the first Democrat to withdraw from the 1984 presidential campaign.

March 12

March 25

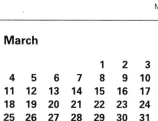

March						
				1	2	3
4	5	6	7	8	9	10
11	12	13	14	15	16	17
18	19	20	21	22	23	24
25	26	27	28	29	30	31

1   **Senator Ernest F. Hollings** of South Carolina and former Florida Governor Reubin O'D. Askew drop out of the Democratic presidential race.

5   **Lebanon** cancels its 1983 troop-withdrawal agreement with Israel.
The Supreme Court rules that a city may sponsor Christmas Nativity displays without violating the constitutional separation of church and state.
Standard Oil Company of California agrees to acquire Gulf Corporation for about $13.2-billion in the largest merger in U.S. history.

6   **The United States** conducts its first flight test of the cruise missile over Canada.

10   **Police in Colombia** carry out the largest drug raid in history, seizing about 13.8 short tons (12.5 metric tons) of cocaine.

12   **British coal miners** strike to protest scheduled layoffs and mine closings.

14   **Former Senator George S. McGovern** of South Dakota withdraws from the Democratic presidential race.

16   **South Africa and Mozambique** sign a nonaggression treaty, one of the first such agreements between South Africa and a black-ruled African country.
Senator John H. Glenn, Jr., of Ohio bows out of the Democratic presidential contest.

17-22   **Four men are found guilty** of the rape of a woman who was assaulted in Big Dan's Tavern in New Bedford, Mass., while other men cheered. Two other defendants are acquitted.

20   **The U.S. Senate** fails to pass a proposed constitutional amendment to allow organized, spoken prayer in public schools.

21   **A federal grand jury** indicts eight Chicago men — five lawyers, two policemen, and a judge — on charges of corruption resulting from the Operation Greylord investigation.
The U.S. Department of Justice announces approval of a proposed merger between LTV Corporation and Republic Steel Corporation.

21-28   **French President François Mitterrand** visits the United States.

24   **Red Brigades terrorists** rob a Rome security company of $21.8 million in the biggest theft in modern Italian history.

25   **Mauna Loa volcano** in Hawaii erupts for the first time since 1975.
El Salvador holds its first presidential election since 1977, but no candidate wins a majority, necessitating a runoff.

28   **Tornadoes** strike North and South Carolina, killing at least 60 people and injuring more than 1,000.

29   **Lynn R. Williams,** a Canadian labor leader, is elected president of the United Steelworkers of America.

April 9

April 11

April 26

April

1	2	3	4	5	6	7
8	9	10	11	12	13	14
15	16	17	18	19	20	21
22	23	24	25	26	27	28
29	30					

3   **A military junta** seizes power in Guinea.

6-9   **Troops** loyal to Cameroon's President Paul Biya put down an attempted coup.

9   *Terms of Endearment,* an American film about a stormy mother-daughter relationship, wins the Academy Award as best picture. Two of the film's stars — Shirley MacLaine and Jack Nicholson, shown above — win Oscars for their performances.

10   **Nearly 1 million Brazilians** demonstrate in Rio de Janeiro to demand direct elections. Similar crowds rally in São Paulo on April 16.

11   **Chernenko** is named president of the Soviet Union, giving him the two top Soviet posts. *Challenger* **astronauts** complete history's first satellite repair in space.

12   **Sandro Mariategui Chiappe** becomes prime minister of Peru, replacing Fernando Schwalb López Aldana, who resigned over economic policy.

13   **President Reagan** by-passes Congress to send $32 million in emergency military aid to El Salvador.

15   **Ten people are shot** to death in a two-family home in New York City in one of the worst mass murders in the city's history.

17   **London police** blockade the Libyan embassy after someone in the building shoots into a crowd of demonstrators, killing a policewoman.

18   **A U.S. Army helicopter** with two U.S. senators aboard is struck by gunfire and forced down in Honduras near the Salvadoran border.
Chrysler Corporation, saved from bankruptcy in 1979 and 1980 by the federal government, announces a record $705.8-million profit for the first quarter of 1984.

19   **Brian Dickson** is sworn in as chief justice of Canada.

22   **Great Britain** breaks formal diplomatic ties with Libya and orders all Libyans in the besieged embassy to leave the country.

23-25   **Riots** over food-price increases kill about 55 people in the Dominican Republic.

25   **David A. Kennedy,** 28-year-old son of the late Senator Robert F. Kennedy (D., N.Y.), is found dead of a drug overdose.

26   **President Reagan** arrives in China for a six-day visit that includes a tour on April 29 of the statue-filled tomb at Xian (Sian), above.
Lebanese President Amin Gemayel appoints Rashid Karami as prime minister.

29   **Sudanese President Gaafar Mohamed Nimeiri** declares a state of emergency because of attacks by guerrillas and strikes by government employees. The state of emergency is lifted on September 29.

May 2-12

May 28

May 15

May						
		1	2	3	4	5
6	7	8	9	10	11	12
13	14	15	16	17	18	19
20	21	22	23	24	25	26
27	28	29	30	31		

2–12   **Pope John Paul II** travels to Alaska, South Korea, Papua New Guinea — shown above — the Solomon Islands, and Thailand.

6   **Three Latin-American countries** hold elections for president. The winners are José Napoleón Duarte, a moderate, in El Salvador; Nicolás Ardito Barletta Vallarina, a military-backed candidate, in Panama; and León Febres-Cordero, a conservative, in Ecuador.

8   **The Soviet Union** withdraws from the 1984 Summer Olympic Games in Los Angeles. Thirteen other countries eventually join the Soviet boycott.

A Canadian soldier opens fire with a submachine gun in Quebec's National Assembly, killing three people.

10   **The World Court** unanimously orders the United States to stop military action aiding Nicaraguan rebels.

12   **The Louisiana World Exposition** opens in New Orleans.

14   **Opponents of Philippine President**

Ferdinand E. Marcos win 62 of 183 seats at stake in parliamentary elections.

Jeanne Sauvé is sworn in as governor general of Canada, replacing Edward R. Schreyer.

West German metalworkers strike for a shorter workweek. The strike eventually idles about 440,000 workers and lasts until July 2.

15   **Archaeologists** find an untouched Maya tomb more than 1,500 years old in Guatemala.

17-28   **Rioting between Hindus and Muslims** in India causes more than 225 deaths.

19   **The Edmonton Oilers** win professional hockey's Stanley Cup, defeating the New York Islanders four games to one.

22   **The U.S. Supreme Court** rules unanimously that federal antidiscrimination laws apply to partnership decisions in law firms.

23   **Richard von Weizsäcker** is elected president of West Germany.

23-29   *Indiana Jones and the Temple of Doom,* an adventure film, grosses a record $45.7-million during its opening week.

24   **Five Salvadoran national guardsmen** are found guilty of murdering four American churchwomen in 1980.

Beatrice Foods Company agrees to buy Esmark Incorporated for more than $2.7-billion, creating one of the largest food and consumer-products companies in the world.

27   **Egyptian President Hosni Mubarak's ruling party** wins 391 of 448 contested seats in parliamentary elections.

28   **An unknown soldier** from the Vietnam War is buried at the Tomb of the Unknowns in Arlington National Cemetery in Virginia.

June 9

June 5-7

June 6

June

					1	2
3	4	5	6	7	8	9
10	11	12	13	14	15	16
17	18	19	20	21	22	23
24	25	26	27	28	29	30

5   **Mondale clinches** the Democratic nomination by winning primaries in New Jersey and West Virginia.

5-7   **Indian troops** seize the Golden Temple in Amritsar, the headquarters of Sikh militants. More than 800 Sikhs and 200 soldiers are killed in the fighting.

6   **President Reagan** and seven other heads of state go to France for ceremonies marking the 40th anniversary of D-Day, the Allied landing in France during World War II.

7-8   **A string of tornadoes** sweeps over the Midwest, killing at least 16 people and demolishing the town of Barneveld, Wis.

7-9   **An economic summit conference** in London is attended by leaders of Canada, France, Great Britain, Italy, Japan, the United States, and West Germany.

9   **Martina Navratilova** becomes the third woman in history to win the grand slam of professional tennis — consecutive victories in the sport's four most important tournaments.

10   **A U.S. missile,** in a test, shoots down an incoming missile in space for the first time.

11   **The U.S. Supreme Court** rules that evidence obtained illegally may be used in criminal trials if police can prove they eventually would have found it legally.

12   **Iran and Iraq** begin a limited cease-fire, halting attacks on each other's cities.

  The Boston Celtics win the National Basketball Association championship, defeating the Los Angeles Lakers four games to three.

  The Supreme Court rules that courts may not order employers to lay off white workers to protect the jobs of minority workers with less seniority.

12-14   **The Council for Mutual Economic Assistance,** an economic union of 10 Communist nations, holds its first summit meeting since the early 1970's, in Moscow.

14   **The MX missile** survives by one vote a Senate attempt to delay its production, with Vice President George H. W. Bush casting the deciding vote.

24   **At least 850,000 demonstrators** in Paris protest a proposal to give the government more control over France's private schools.

27   **Cuban President Fidel Castro** agrees to release 22 American prisoners, most of them held on drug charges, after meeting with Jesse L. Jackson.

28   **Israel and Syria** exchange prisoners of war for the first time in 10 years.

30   **John N. Turner** is sworn in as prime minister of Canada.

  Bolivian President Hernán Siles Zuazo is kidnapped during an attempted coup but released unharmed after 10 hours.

July 16-19

July 23

July 9

July

1	2	3	4	5	6	7
8	9	10	11	12	13	14
15	16	17	18	19	20	21
22	23	24	25	26	27	28
29	30	31				

2 **Anne M. Burford,** who resigned as EPA head in 1983 amid charges of mismanagement, is named by President Reagan to head an advisory panel on the environment. She withdraws on August 1.

4 **Lebanese government troops** begin taking over Muslim and Christian strongholds in Beirut, putting into effect a peace plan aimed at ending the country's civil war.

9 **A fire** severely damages the ancient cathedral of York Minster in York, England.

9-21 **British dockworkers** strike over the use of nonunion labor to unload iron ore.

12 **Representative Geraldine A. Ferraro** (D., N.Y.) is chosen by Mondale as his running mate. On July 19, she becomes the first woman nominated for Vice President by a major party.

14 **New Zealand's Labor Party,** headed by David R. Lange, defeats the conservative National Party of Prime Minister Sir Robert Muldoon. Lange takes office as prime minister on July 26.

16-19 **The Democratic National Convention** meets in San Francisco, nominating Mondale, shown with Ferraro, for President on July 18.

17 **French Prime Minister Pierre Mauroy** and his cabinet resign. President Mitterrand appoints Laurent Fabius to succeed Mauroy. **President Reagan** signs a bill that will cut federal highway funds to states failing to enact a minimum drinking age of 21 years.

18 **James Oliver Huberty** shoots and kills 21 people at a McDonald's restaurant in San Ysidro, near San Diego, before being killed himself in the worst single day's slaughter by an individual in U.S. history. **President Reagan** signs a $63-billion package of tax increases and spending cuts.

23 **Israel's national election** ends indecisively, with the two major political blocs winning nearly equal numbers of seats in the Knesset (parliament). The Labor Party — headed by Shimon Peres, shown above — wins 44 seats to the Likud bloc's 41. **Vanessa Williams** resigns, the first Miss America to do so, after nude photographs of her are published in *Penthouse* magazine.

25 **A Soviet astronaut,** Svetlana Savitskaya, becomes the first woman to walk in space.

26 **Continental Illinois National Bank and Trust Company** receives a $4.5-billion rescue package from the U.S. government, largest federal rescue of a private firm.

28 **The Summer Olympic Games** open in Los Angeles.

30 **A British oil tanker** runs aground in the Gulf of Mexico, creating a huge oil slick that fouls the Texas coast.

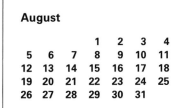

Aug. 20-23

Aug. 12

August						
			1	2	3	4
5	6	7	8	9	10	11
12	13	14	15	16	17	18
19	20	21	22	23	24	25
26	27	28	29	30	31	

1   **Great Britain and China** announce agreement on the terms under which Hong Kong will pass from British to Chinese control in 1997.

6   **The United States** sends Navy minesweeping helicopters to help Egypt search for explosives in the Red Sea.

8   **Congo** names a new prime minister, Ange Edouard Poungui, to replace Louis-Sylvain Goma.
Congress approves legislation strengthening efforts to collect child support payments. Reagan signs the act on August 16.

10   **Costa Rican President** Luis Alberto Monge Alvarez asks his Cabinet to resign.

11   **President Reagan,** during a microphone check before a radio broadcast, jokes about outlawing and bombing Russia.

12   **The Summer Olympic Games** end with the United States winning the most medals — 83 gold, 61 silver, and 30 bronze.

14   **Patti Davis,** daughter of President and Mrs. Reagan, marries Paul Grilley in Los Angeles.

Morocco and Libya announce plans to form an alliance.

15   **A scaffolding collapses** at a ticker-tape parade for Olympic athletes in New York City, injuring about 100 spectators.

15-16   **Protestants in Belfast,** Northern Ireland, hurl gasoline bombs and rocks at police during two nights of rioting.

16   **Automaker John Z. De Lorean** is acquitted of cocaine-dealing charges.
The United States Jaycees approve a resolution allowing women full membership in the formerly all-male organization.
Honduran President Roberto Suazo Córdova asks his Cabinet to resign, the second such shakeup in Central America in less than a week.

20   **Ferraro's husand,** John A. Zaccaro, makes public his income tax returns after initially refusing to do so.

20-23   **The Republican National Convention** meets in Dallas, nominating Reagan and Bush for reelection on August 22, above.

24   **British dockworkers,** in their second strike in six weeks, walk off the job in support of striking coal miners. The dock strike ends on September 18.

25   **A French freighter** collides with a ferry and sinks in the North Sea carrying 30 canisters of radioactive material.

29   **A prototype of the B-1 bomber** crashes in the Mojave Desert of California on a test flight, killing one crew member and injuring two others.

30   **The space shuttle *Discovery*** lifts off on a successful seven-day maiden flight after three postponements.

Sept. 4

Sept. 20

Sept. 15

September

						1
2	3	4	5	6	7	8
9	10	11	12	13	14	15
16	17	18	19	20	21	22
23	24	25	26	27	28	29
30						

2-3 **Typhoon Ike** kills more than 1,360 people in the Philippines.

4 **Canada's Progressive Conservative Party,** led by Brian Mulroney, wins a landslide victory over the Liberal Party in national elections. Mulroney, above, succeeds Turner as prime minister on September 17.
The Zimbabwe government releases former Prime Minister Abel T. Muzorewa after 10 months of detention.
Nestlé S.A., a Swiss food firm, announces that it will buy the Carnation Company, a U.S. dairy company, for about $3 billion in the food industry's largest merger ever.

9 **Pope John Paul II** arrives in Canada for a 12-day visit, the first by any pope.

14 **Peres** takes office as prime minister of Israel, heading a unity government that includes both his Labor Party and Israel's other major political group, the Likud bloc.

14-21 **The United Automobile Workers (UAW)** carries out a selective strike against 13 General Motors Corporation (GM) facilities.

15 **Diana, Princess of Wales,** gives birth to her second son, Prince Henry Charles Albert David.

17 **France and Libya** agree to a simultaneous withdrawal of their troops from Chad.

18 **The 39th UN General Assembly** elects Paul J. F. Lusaka of Zambia as its president.
An American balloonist, Joe W. Kittinger, completes the first solo balloon flight across the Atlantic Ocean.

19 **The Soviet Union** releases five crewmen of an American supply ship who were taken into custody on September 12 when their ship sailed into Soviet waters.

20 **A van packed with explosives** blows up the U.S. Embassy in Aukar, Lebanon, near Beirut, killing at least 14 people.
Edwin Meese III, Reagan's nominee for attorney general, is cleared on charges of financial misdealings.

24 **President Reagan,** addressing the UN General Assembly, proposes renewed arms control talks with the Soviet Union.
Queen Elizabeth II and Prince Philip of Great Britain arrive in Moncton, N.B., to begin a two-week visit to Canada.

26 **Congress** approves a bill requiring stiffer health warnings on cigarette packages and advertising. President Reagan signs it into law on October 13.

27 **Soviet Foreign Minister Andrei A. Gromyko,** in a speech to the UN, blames the United States for world tensions.

28 **Gromyko** meets with President Reagan at the White House.

29-30 **Nearly 10,000 caribous** drown while crossing two rivers in Quebec, Canada.

Oct. 12

Oct. 9

Oct. 15

October

	1	2	3	4	5	6
7	8	9	10	11	12	13
14	15	16	17	18	19	20
21	22	23	24	25	26	27
28	29	30	31			

1   **Secretary of Labor Raymond J. Donovan** confirms that he has been indicted on charges including grand larceny and keeping false records.

2   **Three Soviet cosmonauts** return to earth after a record 237 days in space.

5   **The space shuttle _Challenger_** lifts off from Cape Canaveral, Fla., carrying a crew of seven, the largest in space-flight history.

7   **Reagan and Mondale** meet in Louisville, Ky., for a debate on domestic issues.

9   **Egypt's President Mubarak** — at right in picture above, with Jordan's King Hussein I — makes the first state visit to Jordan by an Egyptian leader since Egypt's 1979 peace treaty with Israel.

10-12   **Pope John Paul II** visits Spain, the Dominican Republic, and Puerto Rico.

11   **Bush and Ferraro** debate in Philadelphia.

12   **A bomb** planted by the Irish Republican Army kills 5 people and injures 33 others at a hotel in Brighton, England, where Prime Minister Margaret Thatcher is staying.

The World Court settles a boundary dispute between the United States and Canada by giving the United States about five-sixths of the Georges Bank fishing area.

President Reagan signs the most extensive revision of federal criminal law in history.

14   **The Detroit Tigers** win the World Series, defeating the San Diego Padres four games to one.

15   **Salvadoran government and rebel leaders** meet in La Palma, El Salvador, in a historic effort to end the country's five-year civil war.

The Roman Catholic Church announces that it will again permit celebration of the old-style Latin Mass, banned in 1963.

17-30   **The UAW's Canadian members** strike General Motors of Canada, Limited.

20   **China** announces major changes in its economic system that will reduce government control of the economy.

21   **Reagan and Mondale** meet in Kansas City, Mo., for a debate on foreign policy.

23   **A panel** investigating the 1983 assassination of Philippine opposition leader Benigno S. Aquino, Jr., blames a military conspiracy.

26   **Surgeons at** Loma Linda University Medical Center in California transplant the heart of a baboon into a baby girl who lives until November 15, becoming the longest surviving human recipient of an animal heart.

30   **A pro-Solidarity Polish priest,** Jerzy Popieluszko, is found murdered after being kidnapped on October 19.

31   **India's Prime Minister Indira Gandhi** is assassinated by two of her own Sikh bodyguards. Her son, Rajiv, succeeds her as prime minister.

Nov. 19

Nov. 12-14

November

				1	2	3
4	5	6	7	8	9	10
11	12	13	14	15	16	17
18	19	20	21	22	23	24
25	26	27	28	29	30	

4   **Nicaragua's ruling Sandinistas** win elections for president, vice president, and a national assembly.

6   **Reagan wins reelection** by a landslide, carrying 49 states for the biggest electoral vote total in U.S. history.
Chile declares a state of siege in response to terrorist violence.
The Louisiana World Exposition in New Orleans files for bankruptcy.

8   **Secretary of Education** Terrel H. Bell says he will resign effective December 31.

11   **A panel** of the National Conference of Catholic Bishops issues a draft document attacking what the bishops see as unjust economic policies.

12-14   *Discovery* **astronauts** retrieve two satellites, misfired into useless orbits in February, to bring them home for repairs.

14   **A federal grand jury** indicts four Chicago lawyers, three policemen, and one judge on corruption charges resulting from Operation Greylord.

14-15   **South African police** round up 2,300 black workers — the biggest mass arrest in years — in raids on a black township.

15   **Chilean troops** raid a Santiago slum and round up at least 3,000 people.
North and South Korea begin talks on economic cooperation, only to break them off on November 27 because of border shootings.

19   **Explosions** at a gas-storage site cause a fire storm that sweeps through a suburb of Mexico City, killing at least 490 people.

22   **The United States and the Soviet Union** announce that they will resume arms control talks in January 1985.

25   **Uruguayan voters** elect Julio María Sanguinetti, a moderate, to replace military rulers in power since 1973.
Surgeons at Humana Heart Institute International in Louisville, Ky., perform the world's second artificial heart implant on a human being.

26   **The United States and Iraq** announce that they will resume diplomatic ties severed in 1967.

28   **New Zealand's National Party** elects James K. McLay as its leader, replacing former Prime Minister Muldoon.
Senator Robert J. Dole (R., Kans.) is elected Senate majority leader.

28-29   **William D. Ruckelshaus** resigns as head of the EPA, effective Jan. 5, 1985. Reagan picks Lee M. Thomas, chief of EPA toxic waste programs, to succeed him.

29   **Chile and Argentina** sign a treaty ending their dispute over the Beagle Channel at the southern tip of South America.

Dec. 3

December

						1
2	3	4	5	6	7	8
9	10	11	12	13	14	15
16	17	18	19	20	21	22
23	24	25	26	27	28	29
30	31					

1   **Australia's Labor Party,** headed by Prime Minister Robert Hawke, wins general elections that are closer than expected.

3   **A poison-gas leak** at a pesticide factory in Bhopal, India, kills at least 2,500 people in the worst industrial accident in history.

Democrats in the House of Representatives reelect Thomas P. (Tip) O'Neill, Jr., of Massachusetts as Speaker and James C. Wright, Jr., of Texas as majority leader. House Republicans keep Robert H. Michel of Illinois as minority leader.

3-16   **Chicago schoolteachers** strike for more pay.

4   **Herbert A. Blaize** becomes prime minister of Grenada — which the United States invaded in 1983 — after his pro-United States party wins elections on December 3.

Bolivian unions end a weeklong general strike that crippled most of Bolivia.

9   **Iranian troops** storm a hijacked Kuwaiti jet in Teheran, Iran, capturing four Arab hijackers who seized the plane on December 4 and killed two American passengers.

10   **Astronomers** announce the first sighting of what appears to be a planet in another solar system.

The UN General Assembly adopts a treaty outlawing torture.

12   **Mauritania's army chief of staff,** Maayouia Ould Sid Ahmed Taya, seizes power in a coup.

Senator Robert C. Byrd (D., W.Va.) is reelected Senate minority leader.

The U.S. Postal Service announces that the price of a first-class stamp will rise from 20 cents to 22 cents on Feb. 17, 1985.

14   **Belize's conservative party,** the United Democratic Party (UDP), sweeps to power in general elections. UDP leader Manuel Esquivel becomes prime minister.

The United States and Cuba announce an agreement for the return to Cuba of 2,746 Cuban criminals and mental patients who came to the United States in 1980.

16   **Polish police** battle about 3,000 Solidarity supporters in Gdansk in the year's worst clash between police and demonstrators.

19   **A fire** at the Wilberg coal mine near Orangeville, Utah, kills 27 people

22   **Reagan and Thatcher** meet at Camp David, Maryland, to discuss Soviet relations and arms talks.

24-28   **India's ruling Congress-I Party,** headed by Prime Minister Rajiv Gandhi, wins a huge majority in parliamentary elections.

27   **The first artificial comet,** a cloud of barium gas, is released in space by American, British, and West German scientists.

31   **Somalia** holds elections for its National Assembly and for local government posts.

Special Reports

Nine articles give special treatment to subjects of current importance and lasting interest.

See "The Sights and Sounds of Music Videos," page 82.

By Crawford Young

Africa — The Troubled Continent

For many African nations, a quarter century of independence has brought endless woes and fading hopes.

On New Year's Eve 1983, soldiers appeared at the residence of Nigerian President Shehu Shagari, who just four months earlier had been elected to a second term, and placed him under arrest. The nation came to a standstill for a day as the army took control of the government and seized many of Shagari's top ministers. Thus, at a time of year normally associated with bright new beginnings, Nigeria's democracy was replaced by military rule — the second time constitutional rule had been set aside by the army since 1960, when the country won its independence from Great Britain.

In the 1960's, as one African nation after another broke free of European rule, the continent was aglow with optimism about the future. With the yoke of colonialism at last removed, all things seemed possible. By the 1980's, however, most of those high hopes had evaporated. Throughout Africa, a quarter century of independence had

Preceding pages: Faces of hope – and of despair: Children celebrate the independence of Swaziland from Great Britain in 1968, *right;* in the 1980's, refugee children from Somalia line up to get food handouts at a refugee camp in Ethiopia, *left.*

brought a seemingly endless series of crises: crop failures, governmental corruption, military coups, civil wars, stumbling economies, and grinding poverty. Edem Kodjo, former secretary-general of the Organization of African Unity (OAU), summed up the prevailing mood when he said, "Our ancient continent is now on the brink of disaster. . . . Gone are the smiles, the joys of life."

Roughly half of the 51 independent African states were battling for their very survival in 1984. Of the 36 poorest countries in the world, 22 were African. The continent's foreign debt, $5 billion in 1970, had jumped to more than $65 billion. Of the world's major regions, Africa alone has had a decline in the amount of food produced per person, so millions of tons of grain have had to be imported. Still, fewer than 40 per cent of its people were getting enough to eat in 1984, and as a result, malnutrition and disease were rampant. Political health has been just as bad. Since the early 1960's, more than 70 African leaders have been overthrown in coups, and hundreds of other coups have been attempted. Contemplating this sad record, Nigerian historian Jacob Ajayi remarked, "This is not what we expected from independence."

Nigeria in many ways typifies all that has gone wrong in Africa. This country of 90 million people is, because of its large deposits of crude oil, the wealthiest black-ruled nation in Africa. When civilian rule was restored in 1979, Nigeria seemed to have everything going for it: democratic institutions, a sizable number of educated citizens, and oil revenues that soon rose to more than $24 billion a year. In 1983, however, with a surplus of petroleum on world markets, Nigeria's oil revenues fell to about $10 billion, and the country found itself saddled with a $15-billion foreign debt. The army, led by Major General Muhammadu Buhari, then stepped in and overthrew the Shagari government, charging it with gross mismanagement and corruption. Although few people disputed those allegations, the coup raised disturbing questions about the ability of African nations to preserve constitutional rule.

Africa's problems varied and hard to solve

The conviction has been growing throughout the world that Africa's troubles will be harder to solve than those confronting any other major geographical region. The reasons for this are many—an often hostile environment; uncontrolled population growth; low prices for African exports, along with the need to pay for vital imports; political situations that have led almost inevitably to coups, dictatorships, and military conflicts; and economic policies that have favored ill-conceived industrialization programs and have neglected agriculture.

The author:
Crawford Young is a professor of political science at the University of Wisconsin in Madison.

Some of these factors have been largely beyond the control of the African states. For one thing, it is nearly impossible for a country to prosper unless it can grow enough food to feed its people, and yet much of Africa is plagued with poor soil and an unfavorable climate. A large portion of the continent is arid or semiarid. Other regions have erratic rainfall, and only a few areas, such as the Nile River Valley, have irrigated farmland. The most common type of soil is *laterite*, a thin, reddish dirt of low fertility. The traditional pattern of land use in Africa was based on rotating crops from year to year and letting depleted soil lie *fallow* (unplanted), allowing it to regain its fertility. However, with hunger on the rise, many countries have found it difficult to let farmland remain idle. Some African nations have tried to maintain soil fertility with artificial fertilizers but have had only limited success.

The parched continent

These problems have been intensified by long periods of punishing drought. From 1968 to 1974, the rains failed in the Sahel, a region stretching across central Africa just south of the Sahara. Hundreds of thousands of people and several million head of cattle died of hunger and thirst in that period.

In the early 1980's, another killer drought struck the continent, this time affecting nearly all of southern Africa, as well as the Sahel. By mid-1984, 25 countries were suffering from parched soil and withered crops. The hardest-hit countries were Cape Verde, Ethiopia, Mauritania, and Mozambique. In Mozambique, where there had been no rain for three years in some parts of the country, officials of international relief agencies estimated that 100,000 people had died. And in Ethiopia the situation was even worse, reaching crisis proportions by fall 1984, when Western nations began a massive airlift of food to the starving country.

Drought is not the only threat to the environmental balance. Other dangers are the cutting down of large stands of forest and the loss of grasslands. Deforestation has been particularly severe in coastal West Africa. For example, 80 per cent of the small West African country of Gambia was covered by trees in 1920, but by 1984 only 10 per cent of the country was still forested. This unrestrained timber cutting has been necessary to clear land for cultivation and also to provide fuel. For the vast majority of Africans, wood is the basic energy source for both cooking and heating.

Not only are Africa's forests being cleared, but some 14 million acres of grasslands are being destroyed each year by the livestock herds of nomads. Trees and grass help to hold moisture in the ground. As forests and grasslands disappear, the land dries out and can no longer hold back the advance of desert, which already covers 20 per cent of the continent. In the Sahel, the Sahara has been edging southward by more than 3 miles a year, and some scientists estimate that 45 per cent of Africa may be desert within 50 years if the trend continues.

These environmental problems are intensified by Africa's skyrocketing population. Excessive population growth is a relatively new phenomenon in most of Africa. In fact, until the 1920's, pop-

Africa's Political Boundaries: A Legacy of Colonialism

Today's African nations inherited the boundaries that were set by the European colonial powers in the 1800's. Only Ethiopia and Liberia were never under foreign rule. Starting in the 1950's, the European rulers began granting independence to their African colonies.

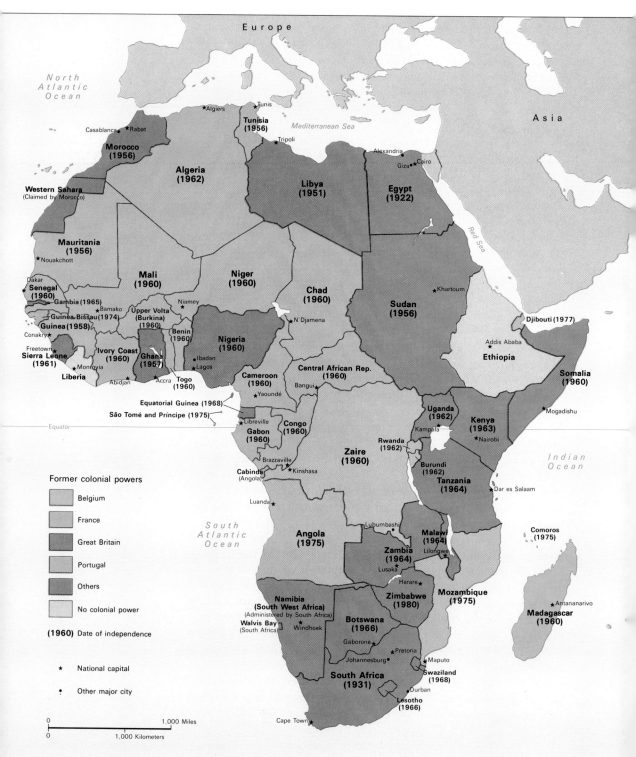

Europe

North Atlantic Ocean

Asia

Mediterranean Sea

★Algiers   •Tunis

Tunisia (1956)

Casablanca• ★Rabat

•Tripoli

Morocco (1956)

Alexandria•

Giza★•Cairo

Algeria (1962)

Libya (1951)

Egypt (1922)

Western Sahara (Claimed by Morocco)

Red Sea

Mauritania (1956)

★Nouakchott

Dakar•   •Khartoum

★**Senegal (1960)**

Mali (1960)

Niger (1960)

Niamey★

Chad (1960)

Sudan (1956)

•Gambia (1965)

Bamako•

Upper Volta (Burkina) (1960)

•N'Djamena

Djibouti (1977)

•Guinea-Bissau (1974)

Benin (1960)

Addis Ababa•

Guinea (1958)

Conakry★

Nigeria (1960)

Central African Rep. (1960)

Ethiopia

Freetown★

Sierra Leone (1961)

Ivory Coast (1960)

Ghana (1957)

•Ibadan

•Lagos

Bangui•

Somalia (1960)

★Monrovia

Liberia

Abidjan•

Accra•

Togo (1960)

Cameroon (1960)

★Yaoundé

Uganda (1962)

•Mogadishu

Equatorial Guinea (1968)

Kenya (1963)

Kampala★

São Tomé and Príncipe (1975)

Equator

•Libreville

Congo (1960)

Gabon (1960)

Rwanda (1962)

★Nairobi

Indian Ocean

Brazzaville•

Zaire (1960)

•Kinshasa

Burundi (1962)

Cabinda (Angola)

Tanzania (1964)

★Dar es Salaam

South Atlantic Ocean

Luanda•

Lubumbashi•

Malawi (1964)

Comoros (1975)

Angola (1975)

Zambia (1964)

Lilongwe•

Lusaka★

Harare★

Mozambique (1975)

Zimbabwe (1980)

Madagascar (1960)

Antananarivo★

Namibia (South West Africa) (Administered by South Africa)

Botswana (1966)

Walvis Bay (South Africa)

Windhoek★

Gaborone•

★Pretoria

•Maputo

Johannesburg•

Swaziland (1968)

South Africa (1931)

•Durban

Lesotho (1966)

Cape Town★

Former colonial powers

- Belgium
- France
- Great Britain
- Portugal
- Others
- No colonial power

(1960) Date of independence

★   National capital

•   Other major city

0 ———— 1,000 Miles

0 ———— 1,000 Kilometers

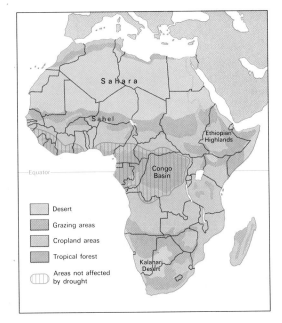

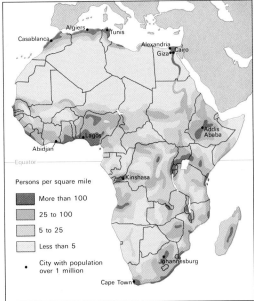

Africa's terrain varies from desert to grassland to rain forest. Nearly all of Africa south of the Sahara except the rain forest areas has been hit by drought, which has brought severe famine to some countries.

The population of Africa is unevenly distributed because much of the continent cannot support large concentrations of people. In recent years, many Africans have moved to the overcrowded cities.

ulation — despite a high birth rate — seemed to be declining in many areas as many blacks died from the harsh treatment they received from their European masters and from diseases the colonists brought with them to the continent. The introduction of public health measures and the elimination of many brutal practices reversed that trend, and by the 1940's Africa's population was increasing at an accelerating pace. The average life expectancy in Africa is still only about 48 years, however, compared with 74 years in the United States.

In recent years, as the rate of population growth has dropped in other underdeveloped parts of the world, Africa's has continued to rise. For the continent as a whole, the population growth rate is about 3 per cent, and in a few countries, such as Kenya and Ivory Coast, it is 4 per cent. In contrast, the worldwide population growth rate is 1.7 per cent and that of the developed nations, 0.6 per cent. With a 3 per cent growth rate, a country's population doubles in 24 years; at 4 per cent, population doubles in just 18 years. With its present population of approximately 530 million, Africa has about 150 million fewer people than Europe on a land area that is nearly three times as large as Europe's. However, much of Africa is desert, semiarid grassland, or tropical rain forest, and the number of people has begun to surpass the ability of the land to support them.

Flimsy shanties huddle together in Lagos, Nigeria, one of Africa's most crowded cities. Since the 1940's, the population of Lagos has zoomed from 165,000 to more than 4 million.

Population pressures have become most severe in the cities, to which millions of rural villagers have moved in search of jobs. Since the 1950's, many once-small towns have mushroomed into sprawling urban centers where people are packed together in filth and poverty. Some cities have annual growth rates as high as 10 per cent, a pace that doubles population in less than a decade. Abidjan, the capital of Ivory Coast, was a sleepy community of 36,000 in 1942, but by the early 1980's, it held more than 1.5 million people. In the same period, the population of Kinshasa, Zaire's capital city, jumped from 47,000 to an estimated 3 million. The population of Lagos, Nigeria, soared from 165,000 to more than 4 million, transforming it into one of the most crowded urban centers in Africa.

A deepening economic crisis

Most African nations have been too financially strapped to improve the living conditions of their citizens. Prices for many African exports, such as copper, iron ore, coffee, and cocoa, were low during the first half of the 1980's. At the same time, these countries had to spend a large portion of their budget to import petroleum and food, causing them to fall ever deeper into debt. By the end of 1983, 23 African states had been forced to seek emergency loans from the International Monetary Fund — a United Nations agency that deals with world trade and helps countries with their economic problems.

Although the outside world has helped the nations of Africa by sending them billions of dollars in food and other forms of aid each year, foreign assistance has not been sufficient to solve the deepening economic crisis. The United States, for example, has contributed about $960 million annually to countries south of the Sahara. When *inflation* — an increase in prices and the resulting decline in the value of money — is taken into account, that total is no more than American aid to Africa in the early 1960's. And Africa's needs are much greater now than they were then. Moreover, an increasing percentage of American assistance in recent years has been in the form of military aid and has been concentrated on a few countries —including Kenya, Liberia, Somalia, and the Sudan — that the United States considers strategically important.

The former colonial powers give substantial amounts of aid to Africa, with France, in particular, continuing to exert a strong influence. When the government of Chad was threatened in 1983 by Libyan-backed rebels, France sent 3,500 troops and 10 combat aircraft to help Chad. There are currently some 300,000 French people living and working in sub-Saharan Africa, more than twice as many as during the colonial era.

Carrying on the traditions of colonialism

The years of colonial rule have left their mark on the economics and politics of today's African states. Economically, the foreign powers forced rural farmers to bear much of the cost of colonial rule by charging them high export taxes and paying them lower prices for their produce than the farmers could have charged in a freely operating market. The colonial governors also encouraged the growing of revenue-producing export crops such as cocoa beans, coffee, and tea rather than the food crops needed to feed a country's own people.

Politically, the foreign rulers imprinted on Africa the tradition of the absolute power of the state over the individual. A black African lived under the colonial state as a subject, not a citizen, and was excluded from sharing in power or influence except at the very lowest levels of governmental administration.

In the 1950's, under the combined pressures of growing African nationalist movements and international criticism, the colonial powers (except for Portugal, which delayed until the 1970's) started preparing for the transfer of power. The Europeans made an effort to transform their colonial governments into constitutional democracies, but the Africans had only a short time to learn the fundamentals of operating these unfamiliar institutions before gaining full independence. It is hardly surprising, therefore, that democracy in its intended form — opposing political parties competing freely for power — has become almost extinct throughout Africa. Only Botswana and the tiny island nation of Mauritius have kept democratic institutions continuously alive since becoming independent.

Ethnic divisions are important in most African countries and have

Africa: Facts and Figures

Country	Type of Government	Major Exports	Infant Mortality Rate (per 1,000 births)	Life Expectancy at Birth
Algeria	Military	petroleum & natural gas	125	57.6
Angola	Civilian	oil & coffee	160	43.5
Benin	Military	palm products & cotton	160	48.3
Botswana	Civilian	diamonds & cattle	88	50.8
Burundi	Military	coffee & tea	127	43.5
Cameroon	Civilian	oil & cocoa	115	48.5
Cape Verde*	Civilian	fish & bananas	87	62.1
Central African Republic	Military	cotton & coffee	154	44.6
Chad	Military	cotton & meat	154	40.8
Comoros	Civilian	perfume oils & vanilla	97	48.0
Congo	Military	oil & lumber	135	48.5
Djibouti	Civilian	hides & skins	N.A.	N.A.
Egypt	Military	oil & raw cotton	76	57.1
Equatorial Guinea	Military	cocoa & coffee	149	48.5
Ethiopia	Military	coffee; hides & skins	150	41.0
Gabon	Civilian	oil & wood	122	46.0
Gambia	Civilian	peanuts & fish	204	42.5
Ghana	Military	cocoa & wood	107	50.8
Guinea	Military	bauxite & alumina	172	46.0
Guinea-Bissau	Military	peanuts & palm kernels	154	43.5
Ivory Coast	Civilian	cocoa & coffee	132	48.5
Kenya	Civilian	petroleum products & coffee	92	55.9
Lesotho	Civilian	wool & mohair	120	52.8
Liberia	Military	iron ore & rubber	160	55.4
Libya	Military	oil	107	57.7
Madagascar	Military	coffee & vanilla	76	48.5
Malawi	Civilian	tobacco & tea	165	48.5
Mali	Military	livestock & peanuts	160	43.4
Mauritania	Military	iron ore & fish	149	43.4
Mauritius*	Civilian	sugar & textiles	29	65.8
Morocco	Monarchy	phosphates	114	57.7
Mozambique	Civilian	cashews & cotton	120	48.5
Namibia†	Civilian	copper; meat & fish	125	51.0
Niger	Military	uranium & livestock	151	43.4
Nigeria	Military	oil & cocoa	141	50.0
Rwanda	Military	coffee & tea	112	48.3
São Tomé & Príncipe	Civilian	cocoa & copra	70	N.A.
Senegal	Civilian	peanuts & phosphate rock	153	43.4
Seychelles*	Civilian	cinnamon & vanilla	17	N.A.
Sierra Leone	Civilian	diamonds & iron ore	215	48.3
Somalia	Military	livestock; hides & skins	150	43.5
South Africa	Civilian	wool & diamonds	101	62.4
Sudan	Military	cotton & gum arabic	131	49.0
Swaziland	Monarchy	sugar & asbestos	140	48.4
Tanzania	Civilian	coffee & cotton	107	53.0
Togo	Military	phosphates & cocoa	115	48.5
Tunisia	Civilian	oil & textiles	107	59.5
Uganda	Civilian	coffee & cotton	101	55.0
Upper Volta (Burkina)	Military	livestock & peanuts	219	43.4
Zaire	Military	copper & cobalt	117	48.5
Zambia	Civilian	copper & zinc	111	50.8
Zimbabwe	Civilian	tobacco & asbestos	79	55.5

N.A. — figure not available.
* Not shown on map on page 34.
† International territory controlled by South Africa.
Sources for Africa chart: International Monetary Fund, United Nations, U.S. Central Intelligence Agency.

% of Population Who Can Read and Write	% of Labor Force in Agriculture
46	30
20	60
20	70
35	79
25	93
65	83
37	55
33	88
20	85
15	87
50	75
20	N.A.
40	45
20	74
15	90
65	65
15	75
30	55
48	82
9	90
24	85
47	17
55	87
24	71
50	24
53	90
25	48
10	80
17	47
61	29
28	50
14	83
33	60
5	90
30	56
37	93
50	N.A.
10	70
60	19
15	96
60	70
50	53
20	78
65	36
66	90
18	78
62	32
52	80
7	83
40	73
54	9
50	35

Workers pick tea on a plantation in Kenya, *top.* An emphasis on export crops over food crops has contributed to Africa's perpetual food shortages, which have made it necessary to import millions of tons of grain — such as the donated Canadian grain being unloaded at a wharf in Somalia, *above.*

A starving child in Uganda squats in the dirt with his empty food bowl, *above*. Besides causing widespread famine, a terrible drought has led to the expansion of desert areas. In Niger, the southward-advancing Sahara engulfs a tree, *below*.

made competitive democratic elections difficult. The struggles between rival ethnic groups have often resulted in conflicts, raising emotion-charged issues of who will dominate in the governing of a country and how national resources will be divided. In most countries, those leaders who acquired power after independence moved quickly to restrict or ban their opponents, arguing that the new nation was too unstable to permit open competition for political office. By the mid-1960's, the great majority of African countries were one-party states. In some cases, such as Guinea, Tanzania, and Tunisia, the ruling party sprang from a nationalistic movement that gained overwhelming support before independence. More often, however, the dominant party after independence used a dual approach to impose single-party rule: inducements to opposition leaders to rally to the party, and intimidation of those who refused.

Especially since 1965, the African political landscape has been altered further by an endless series of military coups. Once-popular heroes of independence movements — Prime Minister Kwame Nkrumah of Ghana and President Mobido Keita of Mali, to name just two — were swept from office, often to the accompaniment of public rejoicing. As of the summer of 1984, 25 African countries were ruled by military leaders.

Many military regimes are no more stable than the civilian governments they replace. Since Nkrumah was ousted in 1966, Ghana has suffered through four more coups. Its current head of state,

Jerry John Rawlings, a former air force lieutenant who seized power in 1981, by mid-1984 had himself been the target of five unsuccessful coup attempts.

The justification given by military leaders for their power seizures is usually that the deposed government was either incompetent or corrupt, and commonly both. Often, the accusation is all too true. Before its overthrow, the Shagari government in Nigeria had gained an international reputation for mismanagement and corruption. Foreign observers estimated that 20 per cent of Nigeria's oil revenues — some $5 billion during the period of peak oil prices — was lost through fraud and smuggling. While the poor went without adequate food, shelter, or health care, many political figures were piling up huge fortunes. By July 1984, more than 500 government officials, including the former vice president and several Cabinet ministers and state governors, were in prison awaiting trial. General Buhari declared a "war on indiscipline," but many observers wondered whether the new regime would itself be able to resist the many temptations that come with power.

Strongmen flex political muscles

A characteristic common to most military regimes and one-party civilian governments is the enormous power in the hands of an individual ruler, or "strongman," who typically claims the right to hold his office for life. For example, in Zaire, where the only political party is the Popular Movement of the Revolution, Mobutu Sese Seko has been president since 1965. Made bold by his firm grasp on power, Mobutu has become the champion treasury looter, reportedly stuffing hundreds of millions of dollars of his nation's wealth into Swiss bank accounts.

Strongman rule can sometimes bring stability to a troubled country, but just as often it leads to a whole new set of problems. Because a ruler with absolute power usually makes all the political and economic decisions of the nation, he can single-handedly lead the country to ruin. Such was the case in Guinea under the 26-year presidency of Ahmed Sékou Touré. Despite its large deposits of diamonds and minerals, Guinea has remained one of the poorest nations in the world. After Touré's death in March 1984, the Guinean Army took over the reins of government, pledging to reverse many of the former ruler's policies.

The excesses of a few African leaders have attracted worldwide attention. Idi Amin Dada, who ruled Uganda from 1971 until his overthrow in 1979, was a tyrant who praised Adolf Hitler and had thousands of Ugandans put to death. Jean-Bédel Bokassa, president of the Central African Republic, became an international laughingstock in 1976 when he renamed his poverty-stricken country the Central African Empire and proclaimed himself its emperor. His coronation ceremony the following year cost $25 million — nearly one-third of the nation's annual budget. In 1979, Bokassa was over-

Many African nations have been afflicted with bad government. Jean-Bédel Bokassa in 1976 proclaimed the Central African Republic an empire and himself its emperor. He was crowned in an elaborate ceremony, *above,* but was overthrown in 1979. Zaire's President Mobutu Sese Seko, *below,* is said to have diverted hundreds of millions of dollars of his nation's wealth to private Swiss bank accounts.

thrown with the help of France, his former patron. Of course, these are extreme examples of the abuse of power by African rulers. In a number of other countries dominated by a single man, the ruler has provided reasonably good leadership. Cameroon and Kenya, for instance, became models of political stability and economic prosperity. But in the 1980's, even those two nations were rocked by coup attempts that exposed underlying currents of discontent. In Kenya, there was growing public anger over one-party rule and a declining economy.

The severe economic problems bedeviling most African countries have been caused in part by the expenditure of large sums of money on grandiose modernization schemes. At the time of independence, there was a widespread conviction in Africa that rapid modernization, and particularly the development of industry, was the key to prosperity. Many African states thus embarked on ambitious building programs, constructing factories, airports, high-rise buildings, hydroelectric plants, and other gleaming symbols of 20th-century technology.

By the 1970's, however, these modernization efforts were running into trouble. Too many projects were excessively costly, poorly designed, and dependent on imported and often unavailable supplies. Furthermore, most African countries have a shortage of skilled technicians able to operate and maintain modern equipment. As a result, many large, expensive facilities have functioned only part of the time or have fallen into disrepair. Throughout much of the continent, one can see idle factories, crumbling highways, skyscrapers made unusable by broken elevators and air-conditioning systems, and electrical-generating plants that frequently wheeze to a stop.

Much of Africa has been wracked by military conflicts that impede economic and political progress. Soldiers fighting in Chad's civil war man an antiaircraft gun, *top*. In Nigeria, Major General Muhammadu Buhari, *above*, center, holds a press conference after leading a successful coup in 1983.

Nairobi, Kenya, *above,* is one of Africa's most attractive, modern cities. Despite some problems in recent years, Kenya has been relatively prosperous and well governed since gaining its independence in 1963. A student at a hospital in Rwanda, *below,* examines a specimen through a microscope. African countries must develop their human resources if they hope to become truly modern, thriving nations.

At the same time that African nations pursued their dreams of modernization, they neglected the most important part of their economy: agriculture. Following the example of the colonial rulers, African governments have emphasized the growing of export crops over food crops. They have also continued the policy of squeezing farmers by controlling the marketing of their crops and paying them artificially low prices. This system provides revenue for the government and cheap food for city residents. It also discourages people from being farmers. The rural farmers have increasingly protested these agricultural policies by growing less food or refusing to sell their produce in official markets. And millions of young people have deserted the countryside to take their chances in the dirty, overcrowded cities, further contributing to the decline of per-capita agricultural production.

The economic vitality of African nations has been eroded further by the unchecked growth of government. The civil service of Kenya, which had 45,000 employees in 1955, had a payroll of 170,000 by 1980. Since 1960, the number of people employed by the government of Senegal has shot up from 10,000 to more than 60,000.

As if African governments didn't have enough to worry about already, much of the continent has been torn by prolonged military conflicts that have produced costly regional arms races. In East Africa, Ethiopia has fought Somalia to retain control of a Somali-speaking area within Ethiopia called Ogaden. An Algerian-supported independence movement in Western Sahara — a former Spanish colony now claimed by Morocco — and a sputtering civil war in Chad have disrupted parts of northern and central Africa. And in the lower part of the continent, white-ruled South Africa since 1981 has conducted military operations and applied ruthless economic pressure against adjacent states that have helped guerrillas struggling against its system of *apartheid* (racial separation).

These conflicts tend to draw in the superpowers and their allies. For example, there are Soviet-backed Cuban troops in Ethiopia and Angola and French troops in Ivory Coast, Gabon, and Djibouti — and until recently in Chad — whose presence heightens regional tensions. Thus, even countries not involved in the fighting often step up their defense by purchasing expensive weaponry. These neighboring countries are burdened further by refugees from the battling states. In 1984, Africa accounted for half the world's refugees — some fleeing war; others, the drought.

A search for new directions

Africa is thus engaged in a struggle for survival. But the situation, grave as it may be, is far from hopeless. Throughout the continent, there is an earnest search for new directions. African leaders are at last recognizing the flaws in their modernization schemes and acknowledging the importance of agriculture.

Furthermore, even the gloomiest pessimist must admit that there have been some notable success stories. A few countries, such as Botswana and Rwanda, have enjoyed political stability while substantially improving the well-being of their populations. Others, including Kenya, Cameroon, and Ivory Coast, are encountering difficulties in the 1980's but have been relatively well governed and economically healthy during most of their postindependence period. Economically, the strongest nation on the continent is South Africa, but that country's prosperity is based on the oppression of its black majority.

Ethnic rivalries, although they have led to power struggles and civil strife, may turn out to be a manageable problem. African states have accepted the borders they inherited from the colonial powers, and many governments are seeking to reconcile rival ethnic groups. Increasingly, Africans are concerned more with a just distribution of wealth — of getting their fair share of what Nigerians call "the national cake" — than with subduing their historical adversaries.

Africa faces its second quarter of a century of independence in a somber mood, knowing that its destiny hangs in the balance. The struggle to make that destiny bright cannot be won by Africa alone. The rest of the world must help — with continued aid, agricultural technology, a plan to ease foreign debt, and an end to superpower meddling. The interdependence of the world's nations is now so great that the survival of Africa is everyone's concern. A more prosperous Africa would be a valuable member of the international community. But if the ancient continent falls over the brink into disaster, the resulting human tragedy would have repercussions throughout the world.

By Patricia D. Duncan

Preserving Our Prairie Heritage

Small parcels of wild land show how beautiful the North American tallgrass prairie was before the plows arrived.

"Grass owned the prairie. The wild grass had its way. The wideness, the delight, the freedom fairly inebriates the spirit.
I do not like to think of the sadness of disappearing grasses dying out for lack of room."

William A. Quayle,
clergyman and educator, 1905

The cowboy boots stood straight and tall in the ranch office, their spurs still strapped to them. They were the fanciest boots I had ever seen, and it was obvious that they were veterans of countless cattle drives. Their owner, Larry Carpenter, foreman of the 29,014-acre H. G. Barnard Ranch in northeastern Oklahoma, was offering me morning coffee before our all-day tour of the ranch. On this June 1984 morning, Larry would not need his cowboy regalia. He was dressed comfortably for driving his crew-cab pickup truck — loaded with my traveling companions, members of the National Audubon Society from several states, led by regional Vice President Ronald D. Klataske. We had been invited by the ranch owners for a firsthand look at this wild, rolling piece of grassland that may represent the last clear chance in this century to preserve and protect a significant and rare parcel of one of North America's greatest historic landscapes — the tallgrass prairie.

This untamed piece of prairie was acquired by Tulsa businessman H. G. Barnard in 1915, when the state of Oklahoma was only eight years old, and it has held almost all forms of civilization at bay ever since. The ranch has been owned by a family trust since Barnard died in 1970, and it is now for sale. Klataske wants the United States government to buy it and make it a *preserve*, or protected area.

The original tallgrass prairie — an enormous carpet of wild grasses and flowers — was part of a vast grassland that extended northward into what are now the Canadian Prairie Provinces of Alberta, Saskatchewan, and Manitoba; eastward, to forestlands in Michigan, Ohio, and Kentucky; southward, through Oklahoma and Texas to the Gulf of Mexico; and westward, to the wall of the Rocky Mountains. This huge prairie was interrupted only occasionally by trees lining the banks of rivers and streams.

In the eastern part of the prairie were the undulating lands of tall grasses called big bluestem, Indian grass, switchgrass, prairie cordgrass, and eastern gama grass — grasses that grow as tall as a man on horseback, with roots as deep. To the west, in areas with less rainfall, the tall grasses mixed with midgrasses — little bluestem and side-oats grama. To the far west, running right into the Rocky Mountains, was the pancake-flat kingdom of the short grass, the 6-inch-tall buffalo grass.

The tallgrass prairie was a bountiful land for the Indians who lived on it. Grasses and flowers and the large creatures that fed upon them — great roaming herds of bison, elk, deer, and antelope — provided the Indians with material for homes, clothing, medicine, and food. The prairie also supported a multitude of birds such as scissor-tailed flycatchers, horned larks, and vesper sparrows; small mammals, including mice, squirrels, and voles; and their predators — coyotes, foxes, wolves, hawks, and eagles.

It was a unique, finely tuned system of living things and environmental factors — the result of millions of years of interaction among soil, climate, fire, changing surface features such as hills and valleys, and a host of plants and animals. When any one of the elements was

The author:
Patricia D. Duncan is a writer, photographer, and painter who specializes in depicting the tallgrass landscape.

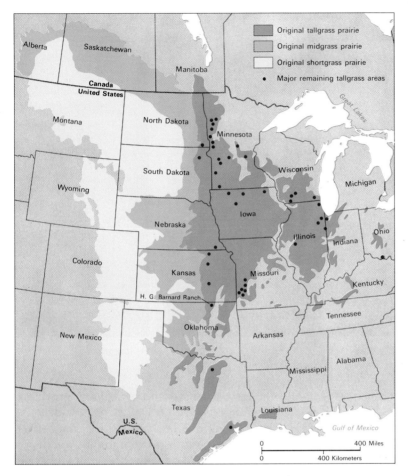

Prairies Past and Present

The tallgrass prairie was once part of a vast grassland covering most of the central United States and a large area in Canada. Today, only a few major parcels of tallgrass land remain as protected tracts in what has become one of the most bountiful agricultural regions in the world.

changed, disturbed, or removed, a ripple effect reverberated from the top of the life chain to the bottom. But eventually the old balance was restored, or a new balance was created, and the complex interdependent life system went on.

Fire prevented the grasslands from becoming forests. At first, the fires were started only by lightning. Later, Indians set fires to drive buffalo herds and other animals over a precipice or into some other trap—a sure improvement over stalking on foot in the days before Spanish explorers brought horses to the Americas.

A prairie fire would roar with deadly fury for miles and miles, consuming all plant life except the deep root systems of the grasses and flowers. The only trees that survived the holocaust were those near rivers, lakes, and small ponds. Many animals perished in a prairie fire. Among those lucky enough to escape were adult birds, burrowing creatures, and surface dwellers that were swift enough to get to water. After the fire, burrowing animals lived on food they had stored underground. Within a few days, new green plants

> *"I saw the prairie, a huge sea of grass spotted with islands of woods, where a series of round hills rise like waves. . . . A vague, sad emotion filled my heart at the sight of this solitude."*
>
> Victor Tixier, explorer, 1840

Preserved remnants of land still support big bluestem, switchgrass, Indian grass, Eastern gama grass, and prairie cordgrass – the major fabrics of the enormous living carpet that was the tallgrass prairie.

Big bluestem

Switchgrass

pushed up from the dense roots beneath the burned soil, providing food for the hungry surface creatures. Scientists suspect that the enormous herds of free-roaming bison had almost the same effect as fire, eating all the grass and young trees down to the ground.

In the late 1970's, I visited a small tallgrass prairie in Ohio that had been discovered recently after an accidental fire. The fire had burned out all the trees and bushes that had suppressed the underlying tallgrass root system for years. The following spring and summer, some 15 species of wild orchids as well as many other tallgrass prairie plants were found.

The first Europeans to see the grasslands — Spanish explorers led by Francisco Vásquez de Coronado in 1541 — could hardly believe their eyes. "The land is in the shape of a ball. Wherever a man stands he is surrounded by the sky," wrote Coronado's diarist.

The explorers would be even more amazed by how the civilization that eventually followed them has transformed the prairie. The big push began shortly after the War of 1812. Thousands upon thousands of plows ripped up the carpet of tall grass for farms as the U.S. population expanded westward out of the forestlands.

The tallgrass prairie was the first to go because it was the most accessible and the most desirable — having the deepest topsoil and the greatest rainfall. Farms filled the tallgrass land quickly, and the open territory was carved into states. By 1890, the American frontier no longer existed. A mosaic of farms and ranches had all but replaced the entire grassland.

Eastern gama grass

Prairie cordgrass

Indian grass

> *"The prairies are beautiful beyond description, yielding prairie grasses, wild sunflowers, small flowers in great variety and color."*
>
> W. W. Phelps, explorer, 1831

Pasqueflower

Purple prairie clover

Tallgrass preserves still contain many of the wild flowers that added bright splashes of color to the underlying greenery of the original prairie.

Today, less than 1 per cent of the original tallgrass prairie remains. It exists only as small preserves that dot the landscape like rare jewels all the way from the Texas coast to Manitoba, Canada, and from Colorado to Ohio. These prairies range in size from less than 1 acre to the 14-square-mile Konza Prairie in Kansas.

Standing in a large parcel of undisturbed prairie such as the Barnard Ranch, one can imagine how it must have felt to stand in the vast grassland before the plows came. In 1918, Nebraska author Willa Cather wrote, in *My Ántonia*, "I felt motion in the landscape, in the fresh, easy blowing morning wind, and in the earth itself, as if the shaggy grass were a sort of loose hide, and underneath it herds of wild buffalo were galloping, galloping. . . ."

Here, one can still watch the grasses, the flowers, and a few of the animals play out the drama of the changing of seasons on the prairie. In late fall, the prairie closes down. November provides a thick-layered, purple cloud-screen of a sky as the first hard freeze rings down the curtain on the dazzling colors of October. The grasses turn to muted browns and tans and stand motionless. It is a quiet time. Migratory birds such as eastern kingbirds, dickcissels, and upland sandpipers have flown south to their winter homes.

In late November, the first snows break the silence, howling down in a fury from the north. During a snowstorm, the horizon is blotted out as earth and sky become one. After a storm, the tall grasses are coated with ice, shimmering and tinkling in the morning sun, looking grander than the finest crystal chandelier.

Prairie smoke

Cardinal flower

53

"The ground was covered with tracks left by wild beasts. One can hardly imagine how numerous they are in these points."

Victor Tixier, explorer, 1840

Prairie chicken

Snow geese and blue geese

Bison

Prairie preserves support a wide variety of animal life. Nearly all species that once inhabited the open prairie also live in the wild on today's farms and ranches. The main exception is the bison, which is raised as a beef animal on a small number of ranches.

Orb weaver

Pronghorn

White-footed mouse

Conservation workers set a field of grass on fire, *above,* imitating a natural process that kept trees and shrubs from establishing a foothold on the open prairie. A raging prairie fire, *below,* burns all grass and woody growth to the ground. Grass roots survive such fires and quickly push up fresh bright green shoots, *right.*

Life goes on in this severe environment. Deer graze through thin layers of ice and snow, or walk to wooded areas to eat bark and twigs. Coyotes search for unwary rodents and birds. Under the ice and snow, insects and mice move about, protected by a layer of fallen vegetation. And beneath the earth's surface, ground squirrels, chipmunks, and snakes hibernate.

Migrating birds announce spring on the prairie. In late February and early March, about 250,000 sandhill cranes stop in central Nebraska on their way from South America and Texas to their summer homes in Canada. In mid-March, snow geese and Canadian geese fly northward.

The prairie slowly turns green again as big bluestem and other tall grasses emerge from the brown of last season's grass. Pasqueflower, verbena, shooting star, bird's-foot violet, wild indigo, and a host of other wild flowers appear. Until the first frost, an average of 17 new species will bloom every week, each with its own splash of color, constantly changing the look of the prairie. In the spring, migratory birds return to the grassland, hibernating animals come out of hiding, insects hatch — and the prairie is back in business.

June is the peak of the prairie growing season. It was a perfect

Tallgrass-prairie restoration projects
are well underway at two vastly different scientific facilities in Illinois.
Near Lisle, a worker at Morton Arboretum – a center for the study of trees
and other plants – waters seedlings of
prairie plants in a greenhouse, *left*.
Outdoors at the arboretum, *below*,
volunteers carefully sow freshly
threshed seeds in a prairie tract. Near
Batavia, *above*, seeds are planted at
Fermi National Accelerator Laboratory, a facility for high-energy physics
research.

time for our tour of the Barnard Ranch. The greenest greens imaginable had taken over the land. As the prairie opened before us, the fluorescent greens waved in row upon row of tall grasses — punctuated by blooming milkweed, penstemon, wild hyacinth, purple poppy mallow, and prairie larkspur — before turning to aquamarine and, finally, to a pale blue before meeting the sky many miles away.

As summer wears into autumn, the tallgrasses begin their most brilliant show. The long bluestem stalks, some of them reaching as high as 12 feet, turn purple, blue, and wine-red. Soon the grass leaves of the other species follow suit, and the prairie is awash in bronze, gold, orange, yellow, and red. The prairie seems to outdo itself in the autumn, reaching its magical climax just before November's curtain brings it all to an end for another year.

To ensure that such cycles of prairie plant and animal life will continue, a growing network of prairie scientists and laymen in public and private organizations has been persuading state legislatures and private landowners to sell, bequeath, or donate prairie land for preservation. Those of us in this network are concerned with how the loss of the prairies may affect human life as well. Many scientists believe that within the community of plants of the original grasslands are undiscovered sources of grain foods and medicines.

In the United States, virtually all tallgrass prairie states have natural heritage programs aimed at restoration and preservation. The Nature Conservancy, the largest privately funded national organization, has been instrumental in saving more than 2 million acres of land, of which 92,245 acres are tallgrass prairie.

The Canadian government took a major step in prairie preservation in May 1984, acquiring about 45 square miles of unplowed shortgrass prairie near Val Marie, Sask., for a national park. The United States, however, has not yet adopted a plan to form a national prairie preserve. The National Audubon Society and other environmental groups are fighting an uphill battle in their effort to persuade the U.S. government to convert the Barnard Ranch into a preserve. If they succeed, people for generations to come will have an irreplaceable preserve in which to experience the beauty of the tallgrass prairie, to feel "motion in the landscape, in the fresh, easy blowing morning wind, and in the earth itself."

For further reading:

Allen, Durward L. *The Life of Prairies and Plains*. McGraw-Hill, 1967.
Costello, David F. *The Prairie World*. Crowell, 1969.
Duncan, Patricia D. *Tallgrass Prairie: The Inland Sea*. Lowell, 1979.
Lerner, Carol. *Seasons of the Tallgrass Prairie*. William Morrow, 1980.
Madson, John. *Where the Sky Began*. Houghton Mifflin, 1982.
Sears, Paul B. *Lands Beyond the Forest*. Prentice-Hall, 1978.
Sigford, Ann E. *Tall Grass and Trouble*. Dillon, 1978.

By Thomas H. Maugh II

Changing Life's Blueprint

The amazing new science of gene-splicing
offers untold benefits for humanity, but
it must be applied with caution and wisdom.

When he is left alone, 7-year-old Charlie often attempts to bite off his fingers and lips. In the company of others, he is overly aggressive and must be forcibly restrained. Charlie is also mentally retarded, suffers from gout, and has the initial symptoms of kidney and heart failure. The unfortunate boy has all these problems because his body cannot produce one relatively simple substance — a protein known as HGPRT.

Charlie has Lesch-Nyhan syndrome, a rare hereditary disorder that is caused by a single malfunctioning gene. Lesch-Nyhan strikes 1 of every 50,000 boys born in the United States, and until now there has been no hope for its victims. But sometime during the next year or so, Charlie may be helped by a radical new approach to the treatment of genetic diseases. Using *gene-splicing*, a technique that enables the insertion of new genes into cells, a team of physicians and scientists at the University of California at San Diego hopes to give the youngster's body a "blueprint" for manufacturing the missing protein. If all goes well, his cells will then begin producing the protein, thereby halting the course of the disease — and perhaps even reversing it. However, other genetic scientists have argued that such an experiment should not be attempted anytime soon because too little is known about the possible side effects.

Meanwhile, researchers at the University of California in Berkeley have been conducting experiments since 1983 that could benefit farmers. They have altered a type of bacteria that lives as a parasite

Opposite page:
A genetics researcher
holds a large flask of cy-
tosine, a substance that
is a major building block
of DNA.

Chromosomes: Structures in the cell nucleus that carry an organism's genes.

DNA: Deoxyribonucleic acid, the complex molecule that genes are made of.

E. coli: A bacterium that is often used in recombinant-DNA procedures.

Enzyme: A protein that speeds up a chemical reaction.

Gene: The basic unit of heredity. Each gene contains coded information for the production of a protein.

Germ cell: An egg or sperm cell or a fertilized egg.

Ligase: An enzyme that can rejoin severed pieces of DNA.

Plasmid: A ring of DNA found in bacteria and yeast.

Proteins: Complex molecules that are essential to the structure and functioning of all living things.

Recombinant DNA: The insertion of DNA from one organism into the DNA of another organism. Also called gene-splicing.

Restriction enzyme: An enzyme that can cut DNA at specific sites.

Retrovirus: A virus that has the ability to insert its genes into the DNA of the cell it has invaded.

The author:
Thomas H. Maugh II is senior science writer for *Science* magazine in Washington, D.C.

on the leaves of many plants and contributes to frost damage. The bacteria ordinarily produce a protein that acts as a "seed" for the formation of ice crystals; in the absence of the bacteria, frost does not form until the thermometer dips to about 25° F. ($-4°$ C). The genetically altered bacteria do not produce the crucial protein and thus do not contribute to ice formation.

When applied to plants in the laboratory, the altered bacteria have successfully displaced the ice-causing bacteria and reduced the possibility of frost damage. The research team wanted to conduct large-scale tests of the bacteria in 1984 by spraying them on a potato field. Outdoor testing was blocked, however, by a court action opposing the release of genetically tailored organisms into the environment. Critics of gene-splicing experiments fear that the altered bacteria may have unforeseen effects on other crops, on the weather, or on animal life — despite the fact that there already exists a naturally occurring strain of the ice-resistant bacteria.

These two examples illustrate both the hoped-for benefits and the possible dangers of the science of *recombinant-DNA technology*, often called genetic engineering or biotechnology. Whatever name it goes by, this remarkable new science has the potential to change the way drugs and industrial chemicals are produced. It may also lead to new methods of growing food and new treatments for diseases — not only genetic diseases but also such common afflictions as cancer, diabetes, and heart disease. But the development of genetic engineering has also provoked a strong debate between scientists and the public — and among scientists themselves — about the possible hazards of genetically altered microorganisms and the ethics of changing the characteristics of human cells.

Biotechnology has developed at a rapid pace, especially considering that the structure of DNA was not even known until 1953. DNA, or *deoxyribonucleic acid*, is a complex molecule that carries the hereditary instructions for all forms of life. It is located in the nucleus of plant and animal cells.

Within the cell nucleus are tiny, threadlike structures called *chromosomes*. Every species of living things has a characteristic number of chromosomes in each of its cells; human beings have 23 pairs, or 46 chromosomes in all. The main component of chromosomes is DNA. The DNA molecule is shaped like a long, twisted ladder, and a gene consists of a section of the ladder. The information in our genes, which is determined by the order of the "rungs" of the DNA ladder, gives us our individual characteristics, such as blue eyes or curly hair. But genes do not actually *code for* (specify the production of) physical features, as such; they code for proteins.

Proteins are complicated, chainlike molecules that are a major component of an organism's body tissues and that carry out many life processes. The regulatory chemicals called *hormones* are proteins, as are *enzymes* — molecules that speed up chemical reactions. Each

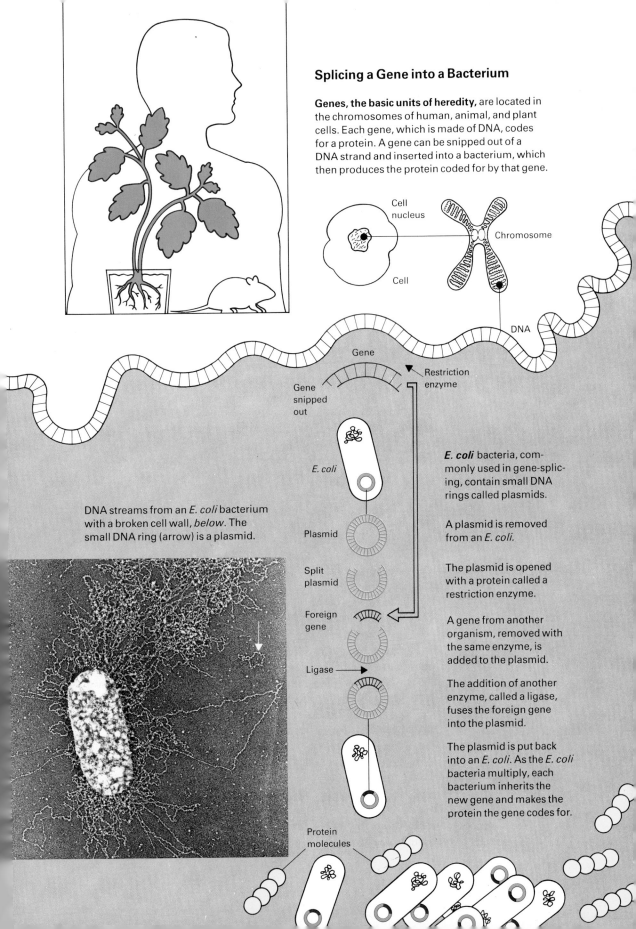

Splicing a Gene into a Bacterium

Genes, the basic units of heredity, are located in the chromosomes of human, animal, and plant cells. Each gene, which is made of DNA, codes for a protein. A gene can be snipped out of a DNA strand and inserted into a bacterium, which then produces the protein coded for by that gene.

Cell nucleus

Chromosome

Cell

DNA

Gene

Gene snipped out

Restriction enzyme

E. coli

Plasmid

Split plasmid

Foreign gene

Ligase

E. coli bacteria, commonly used in gene-splicing, contain small DNA rings called plasmids.

A plasmid is removed from an *E. coli*.

The plasmid is opened with a protein called a restriction enzyme.

A gene from another organism, removed with the same enzyme, is added to the plasmid.

The addition of another enzyme, called a ligase, fuses the foreign gene into the plasmid.

The plasmid is put back into an *E. coli*. As the *E. coli* bacteria multiply, each bacterium inherits the new gene and makes the protein the gene codes for.

DNA streams from an *E. coli* bacterium with a broken cell wall, *below*. The small DNA ring (arrow) is a plasmid.

Protein molecules

Scientists at the 1975 Asilomar Conference in Pacific Grove, Calif., listen to a lecture on gene-splicing. The meeting was held to discuss the possible dangers of experiments with recombinant DNA and to suggest measures to guarantee the safety of such research.

gene codes for just one protein. Higher organisms, such as mammals, are so complex because their cells contain tens of thousands of genes directing the production of a vast array of proteins. Human cells contain about 100,000 genes. In contrast, a bacterium may have just 2,000 to 3,000 genes, and a virus as few as 6.

Genetic engineering got its start in the early 1970's when scientists found that it is possible to take a gene from one organism and splice it into the DNA of another organism. This recombination of genes — from which we get the name recombinant DNA — was first accomplished with viruses and bacteria. The key to the development of this technology was the discovery of two previously unknown groups of enzymes, known as *restriction enzymes* and *ligases*. Restriction enzymes, which are a sort of chemical scissors, can be used to cut DNA at specific sites, making it possible to remove one or more genes. Ligases can be used to rejoin DNA fragments into a continuous, unbroken strand.

Much of the early work on these techniques was done by three California molecular biologists — Paul Berg and Stanley N. Cohen of Stanford University and Herbert Boyer of the University of California at San Francisco. Berg, who is usually credited with being "the father of genetic engineering," in 1973 did the world's first genetic transfer between living organisms of different species. He removed a gene from a monkey virus known as SV40 and, using a laborious procedure, inserted it into the DNA of a virus called lambda phage, which infects bacteria. In 1980, Berg shared the Nobel Prize in chemistry for his research.

At about the same time that Berg was doing his pioneering work, Boyer discovered a restriction enzyme that simplified the gene-splicing operation. Cohen found a way to insert a new gene into a bacterium. The vast majority of a bacterium's genes are contained in a single chromosome. But Cohen observed that a bacterium also possesses small circular strands of DNA, called *plasmids*, that are not connected to the chromosome. He showed that a gene inserted into a plasmid is duplicated along with the plasmid when the bacterium reproduces and that the gene's protein is manufactured in each new bacterial cell. This technique offered the possibility of using bacteria (and other plasmid-containing microorganisms, such as yeast) as tiny "factories" to produce desired proteins, such as the hormone insulin, needed by many diabetics.

The microorganism most commonly used for this sort of recombinant-DNA work is *Escherichia coli*, a bacterium found in the intestines of human beings and many other animals. Berg had originally intended to use lambda phage to insert an SV40 gene into *E. coli*. But SV40 causes cancer in animals and in human cells grown in laboratory culture dishes. Many scientists were concerned that the altered *E. coli* might accidentally escape from the laboratory and find their way to people's intestines, giving rise to an epidemic of cancer. Furthermore, scientists feared that an escaped bacterium might transfer its added genes to other microorganisms and cause an uncontrolled spread in nature of potentially hazardous genes. As recombinant-DNA research grew, with experimenters splicing genes from an ever greater variety of organisms into *E. coli*, a number of scientists thought it would be wise to impose strict controls to ensure that an environmental or public health disaster would not occur.

In July 1974, 11 prominent molecular biologists, including Berg and Cohen, published a letter in *Science* magazine and the British journal *Nature* expressing their concerns about recombinant-DNA research. The biologists, all members of a special committee of the U.S. National Academy of Sciences, called on their colleagues throughout the world to postpone further experiments in what were considered the most hazardous areas of investigation, including cancer research and any experimentation with human DNA. The committee made two other recommendations. First, it asked the National Institutes of Health (NIH) in Bethesda, Md., to devise guidelines for researchers working with potentially dangerous materials. Second, it proposed an international conference of experts to discuss the issues.

After the Asilomar meeting, the National Institutes of Health required scientists doing federally funded gene-splicing research to use specially designed laboratories for all potentially hazardous experimental procedures.

All three recommendations were adopted. Scientists stopped doing experiments thought to be risky, the NIH established the Recombinant-DNA Advisory Committee (RAC), and an international conference was held in February 1975 at the Asilomar Conference Center in Pacific Grove, Calif. Largely as a result of that conference, the RAC in June 1976 issued its first set of guidelines. Those guidelines separated recombinant-DNA research into four general categories, ranging from very safe to exceptionally hazardous, and required scientists engaged in NIH-sponsored research to conduct the highest-risk experiments in expensive, specially constructed laboratories. The guidelines also specified that any potentially hazardous research or release of a genetically altered microorganism into the environment had to be approved by the RAC.

As an added measure of safety, researchers began using microorganisms that had been so weakened that, even if they escaped, they could not live in the environment. *E. coli*, for instance, were altered in a way that prevented them from producing certain proteins vital to their life processes. The bacteria thus could survive only when those substances were provided artificially in the laboratory. Moreover, studies showed that engineered organisms are not able to exchange genetic information with naturally occurring microorganisms. This finding removed the fear of an uncontrolled spread of potentially dangerous genes in the environment.

As a result of such studies and changes in experimental methods, most scientists concluded that recombinant-DNA research was safe. Beginning in 1980, therefore, the NIH guidelines were gradually eased, and many laws that had been passed by state and city govern-

Biotechnology as a Business

The use of recombinant DNA—gene-splicing—on a commercial scale is a complex process. A protein is first made in the laboratory and then produced in large quantities. It must then be tested and approved before being sold. The process is shown below, *left to right.*

   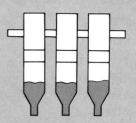

A plasmid with a new gene is inserted into *E. coli* bacteria (or other "host" cells, such as yeast).

The bacteria are first grown in small test batches in the biotechnology company's laboratory.

Great numbers of bacteria, all making the desired protein, are then grown in big fermenting tanks.

The protein coded for by the new gene is then extracted from the bacteria and purified.

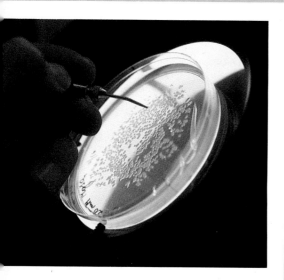

Colonies of *E. coli* bacteria that have been given a gene coding for a desired protein are removed with an instrument from a culture dish, *above.* Vast numbers of the bacteria are later grown in large fermenting tanks, *right,* from which the protein will be "harvested" by technicians.

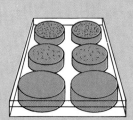  

The protein undergoes various laboratory tests, including experimental tests on animals.

After the protein has been purified, it is formulated into a finished product and then packaged.

The product is clinically tested and, if shown to be safe and effective, receives federal approval.

Finally, the approved brand-name product is placed on the market and goes into widespread use.

Vials of a bacteria-produced protein, *left,* are put through a purification process to separate the protein from other bacterial substances. Working under sterile conditions, production technicians, *below left,* fill syringes with a finished protein product – a medicine that prevents diarrhea in newborn calves. A farmer, *below,* gives a dose of the product to a calf.

ments throughout the United States to restrict gene-splicing research were relaxed or repealed.

By that time, genetic engineering had become an established industry in the United States. Companies such as Genentech in South San Francisco, Calif., and Genex in Rockville, Md., sprang up in the latter half of the 1970's to exploit the new technology. The growth of genetic engineering as a business as well as a science was assured in 1980, when the Supreme Court of the United States ruled that new life forms and gene-splicing techniques can be patented.

In the fermenting tanks of biotechnology companies, bacteria and yeast multiply tirelessly, creating large amounts of the proteins specified by their newly acquired genes. Among the products now being manufactured with recombinant-DNA technology are human insulin, which is already available to diabetics, and several other drugs that are still being tested on human subjects. These drugs include interferons, substances produced in the cells of mammals to ward off viruses; human growth hormone, used to treat individuals who would not otherwise reach normal height; and interleukin-2, a compound manufactured by white blood cells that may prove useful in treating diseases caused by a malfunction of the immune system, such as rheumatoid arthritis.

Genetic-engineering methods can also be used to produce *antigens*, foreign protein molecules on the surface of bacteria and vi-

Above, the potato plant at the right was sprayed with altered bacteria that prevent ice crystals from forming, and survived being exposed to cold weather. The withered plant at left was not sprayed. *Right,* a researcher inspects a tobacco plant containing genes transferred from a bean plant.

ruses that have entered the body. When injected into the bloodstream, an artificially created antigen acts as a vaccine by stimulating the immune system to manufacture *antibodies*, molecules that neutralize invading microbes. Investigators have produced veterinary vaccines for use against the microorganisms that cause hoof-and-mouth disease and diarrhea in farm animals, and a human vaccine against hepatitis B is now being tested.

Researchers at the NIH and the New York State Health Department are experimenting with vaccines made from whole, genetically engineered viruses. They have inserted antigen genes from influenza, herpes, and hepatitis B viruses into the DNA of the vaccinia virus. Vaccinia is a usually harmless virus that has been widely used to immunize people against smallpox. After being genetically altered, the vaccinia virus sprouts new antigens, one for each new antigen gene, on its surface. Studies with animals indicate that the recombinant virus stimulates the production of antibodies to all the disease antigens it carries and thus confers immunity to each of those diseases.

Medicinal drugs are just one of the many kinds of products that can be manufactured with recombinant-DNA techniques. Already, several biotechnology companies are using bacteria to produce *rennins* — enzymes that are normally obtained from the stomachs of calves and that are used to turn milk into cheese. One company has

Using special tools, a scientist inserts a human growth-hormone gene into a fertilized mouse egg, *left.* The eggs are then implanted into foster-mother mice. A mouse that grew from an egg with the human gene grew to twice the size of its normal litter mate that does not have the gene, *below.*

Treating a Genetic Disorder

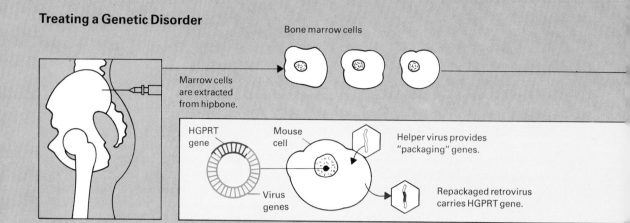

Bone marrow cells

Marrow cells are extracted from hipbone.

HGPRT gene

Mouse cell

Virus genes

Helper virus provides "packaging" genes.

Repackaged retrovirus carries HGPRT gene.

A victim of Lesch-Nyhan syndrome, *below,* whose body cannot make the protein HGPRT, may be helped with a new treatment using retroviruses, *above.* Virus genes, with the HGPRT gene added, are put into a mouse cell. Aided by a "helper" virus, the genes are packaged into new retroviruses. These are added to bone marrow cells from the patient. After picking up the virus genes, the cells are returned to the patient's body, where they will form blood cells. Those blood cells will make HGPRT.

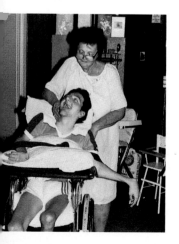

developed a method for producing indigo, a dye used in blue jeans, and another firm is manufacturing an enzyme that dissolves hair caught in drains.

But inserting new genes into bacteria, yeast, and viruses is just the beginning of the possibilities offered by genetic engineering. In the long run, biotechnology's greatest benefits may result from changing the genetic blueprint of farm animals, crop plants, and human beings.

The application of this technology to agriculture is just around the corner. For example, although injectable animal growth hormones produced by genetically engineered bacteria are already being used to raise larger cattle and hogs, it may soon be possible to get the animals' own cells to produce the hormone. This would be done by inserting the growth-hormone gene into the egg cells from which the animals develop.

Scientists at several institutions, working with laboratory mice, have already shown that this approach can work. They inserted the gene for a growth hormone into fertilized mouse eggs and implanted the eggs in foster-mother mice. Not all the eggs incorporated the gene, but some of those that did developed into mice that were twice as large as their normal litter mates. It is not yet possible to insert a gene at a specific site in a cell's DNA, however, so for the time being this is largely a hit-or-miss technique.

Genetic engineering offers great potential for improving crop plants. Corn, for example, is deficient in 2 of the 20 common *amino acids* (building blocks of proteins) that are required in the human diet. Investigators are attempting to insert genes coding for proteins containing more of those two amino acids into new strains of corn to make it a more complete protein source. Other researchers are trying to give food plants such characteristics as increased resistance to insects and greater tolerance to salt in the soil.

Perhaps the greatest impact of genetic engineering will come from the creation of plants that supply their own fertilizer from the

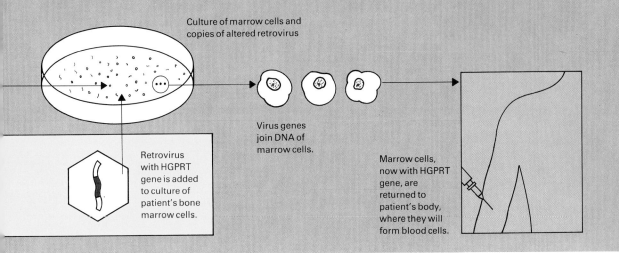

Culture of marrow cells and copies of altered retrovirus

Retrovirus with HGPRT gene is added to culture of patient's bone marrow cells.

Virus genes join DNA of marrow cells.

Marrow cells, now with HGPRT gene, are returned to patient's body, where they will form blood cells.

nitrogen in the air, a process called *nitrogen fixation*. Certain crops called *legumes* — a group that includes peas and beans — are able to do this naturally. These plants have bacteria in their roots that take nitrogen from the air and convert it into a form that can be used by the plants. Researchers at several institutions are attempting to transfer the genes responsible for nitrogen fixation into other varieties of plants. They have not yet succeeded because the task is very difficult, involving at least 17 genes.

There are two major problems in the genetic engineering of plants: getting new genes into a plant's cells and, once they are there, coaxing the plant to produce the proteins coded for by the genes. Scientists have largely solved the first problem with a bacterium called *Agrobacterium tumefaciens*, which ordinarily causes cancerlike growths in plants. The bacterium causes these tumors by entering plant cells and inserting its genes into the plant's DNA. Investigators have succeeded in removing the tumor-producing genes from *A. tumefaciens* and giving it instead genes for desirable plant characteristics. The bacterium is thus converted into a "messenger" that delivers beneficial new genes to plant cells grown in laboratory cultures. In many experiments, however — for reasons that are still unclear — the new genes have failed to function in the plant cells. Scientists still have much to learn about the genetics of plants, which have not been studied as thoroughly as the genetics of microorganisms or animals.

Despite these difficulties, plant geneticists have achieved a few notable successes. For instance, researchers at the University of Wisconsin and Agrigenetics Corporation, both in Madison, have transferred a gene from a bean plant into the cells of sunflower and tobacco plants. In both experiments, which were basic research with no practical results intended, the bean gene functioned normally in its new home.

A current technique for adding genes to human and animal cells also involves a messenger, but in this case it is a virus rather than a bacterium. Like *A. tumefaciens*, the virus, called a *retrovirus*, has the ability to inject its genes into a cell's DNA. Some retroviruses cause various forms of cancer in animals — and perhaps also in human beings — but scientists have removed the harmful genes from the viruses. They hope to use retroviruses to insert genes into people suffering from genetic disorders, such as Lesch-Nyhan syndrome.

The proposed treatment for such disorders is to extract some of the patient's bone marrow cells, which are the source of blood cells. In the laboratory, copies of the altered retrovirus would be added to the marrow cells. After they have taken up the retrovirus genes, the cells would be returned to the patient's body, where they would multiply and release the new gene's protein into the bloodstream.

The San Diego research team, headed by pediatrician Theodore Friedmann, has used an engineered virus to introduce the gene for the human protein HGPRT into cells taken from a Lesch-Nyhan victim. The cells then produced the protein. Experimenters elsewhere have obtained similar results with genes for two other hereditary defects, both of which, like Lesch-Nyhan syndrome, are caused by the lack of a particular protein. Deficiency diseases of this type would be the easiest to treat because the amount of the protein produced by the added gene need not be precisely controlled. Even a small amount of the protein would be helpful to the patient, and a large amount probably would not be harmful, as would be the case if large amounts of another substance, insulin for example, were produced. Since the exact insertion and control of genes is beyond the capability of current technology, the use of gene therapy to treat diseases such as diabetes is much further in the future.

The controversy surrounding genetic engineering never completely died down, and since 1980 it has become increasingly intense. The focus of the debate has shifted to concerns that previously had remained in the background: the intentional release of genetically altered — but presumably safe — microorganisms into the environment and the manipulation of human DNA.

The persons expressing the most anxiety about genetic engineering these days are usually nonscientists, such as Jeremy Rifkin, a social activist who heads a Washington, D.C.-based organization called the Foundation on Economic Trends. It was he who filed suit in federal court to stop genetic scientists Steven Lindow and Nickolas Panopoulos, the leaders of the Berkeley research team, from testing their antifrost bacteria. Rifkin and other opponents of genesplicing usually raise questions that start with "what if." What if, for instance, an organism designed to clean up oil spills got out of control and began consuming petroleum deposits? Or what if an organism engineered to digest the waste from paper mills escaped and started eating entire forests?

Most biotechnologists think such possibilities are extremely unlikely. Microorganisms, they point out, have been *mutating* (undergoing genetic changes) in the environment since life began, and no such catastrophe has occurred. The general opinion among genetic scientists is that all the "what if" horrors belong in the realm of science fiction.

An aspect of genetic engineering that is still science fiction but is well on its way to becoming science fact is the alteration of human *germ cells* (egg or sperm cells, or fertilized egg cells). A genetic change in a germ cell is reproduced in every body cell of the organism that develops from the fertilized egg, and is passed on to succeeding generations. Many geneticists think that by sometime early in the next century, it will be possible to manipulate human germ cells to change or remove dangerous genes — for example, the so-called *oncogenes* that may give rise to cancer — and to add beneficial genes. Science would then, in effect, be guiding human heredity.

Religious leaders, for the most part, have supported the idea of using gene therapy to treat patients with inherited disorders, but many of those same persons oppose any attempts to alter human germ cells. In 1983, 56 prominent church leaders joined Rifkin in issuing a resolution calling for a ban on all such experiments.

Many other theologians, however, have concluded that genetic engineering is a worthwhile endeavor and should proceed — with caution. That was the same conclusion reached by the President's Commission for the Study of Ethical Problems in Medicine and Biomedical and Behavioral Research, a special group named in 1979 by President Jimmy Carter and continued by President Ronald Reagan. In its 1982 report on genetic engineering, *Splicing Life*, the commission stated, "Human beings have not merely the right but the duty to employ their God-given powers to harness nature for human benefit. To turn away from gene-splicing, which may provide a means of curing hereditary diseases, would itself raise serious ethical problems."

With specific regard to changing germ cells, the commission acknowledged that genetic engineering might eventually give humanity the ability to "play God" and attempt to create "perfect" human beings. The commission therefore recommended the establishment of a government-sponsored council that would oversee the continued development and application of gene-splicing and ensure that the technology is not misused. In response to that recommendation, Congress in late 1984 approved legislation setting up a 14-member Biomedical Ethics Advisory Committee. The committee will be appointed by a congressional panel and will include two members from the general public as well as professionals from the sciences and the humanities.

Genetic engineering is an incredible new tool that can be of great benefit to humanity. But like any new technology with the potential for misuse, it must be handled wisely. As the President's commission pointed out, "Great powers imply great responsibility."

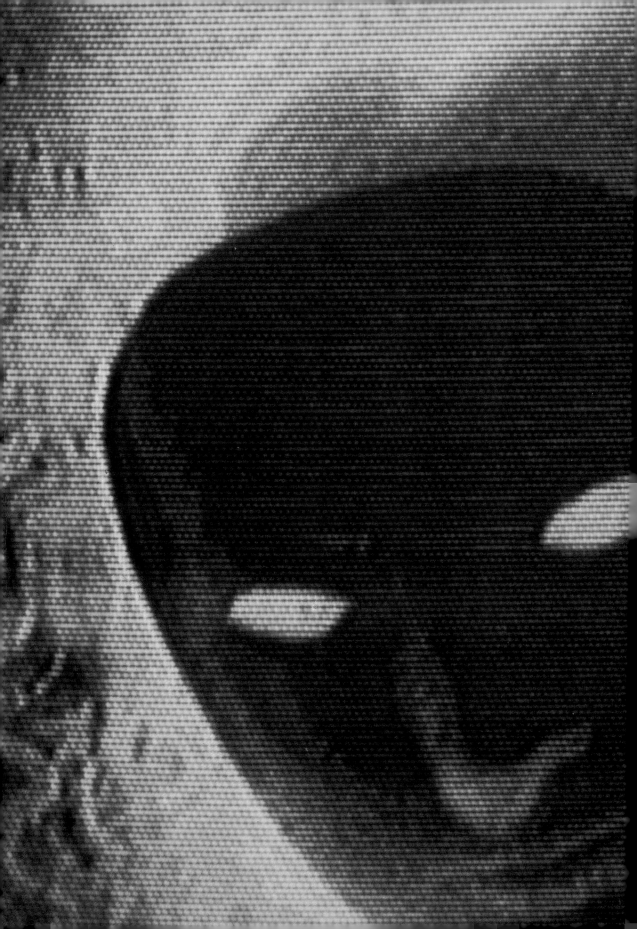

By Ed Levine

The Sights and Sounds of Music Videos

In a brief span of time, music videos have captured the imaginations of millions of people who have found in them a new way of seeing as well as hearing music.

A fire-breathing Satanic figure is the animated cartoon image conjured up by the music of Russian composer Modest Mussorgsky's *A Night on the Bald Mountain* in Walt Disney's film *Fantasia* (1940), which some people regard as the first music video.

The author:
Ed Levine is a free-lance writer based in New York City. He has contributed to *High Fidelity, The New York Times Magazine, Rolling Stone,* and *Video Review.*

A man is standing in the middle of a pasture playing a cello while cows graze around him and a woman works on a computer. An electric guitar comes crashing through a window, a window shade flies up, and the empty eye socket of a mask sheds a tear. What do these images have in common? They are scenes from music videos—the first from "Sweet Dreams" by the Eurythmics and the second from "Miss Me Blind" by Culture Club.

In the living rooms and dens of millions of homes throughout the United States and in other countries, teen-agers and preteens viewed scenes such as this and others even more bizarre on their television screens in 1984. The show they were watching, however, was not an ordinary television program but one of hundreds of new music videos being produced by record companies. With music videos, people can not only hear a new song but also see the recording artists performing the song in a visually imaginative way. In a brief span of time, music videos have captured the imaginations of millions of people.

Teen-agers are not the only people excited by this new phenomenon. Record-industry executives see music videos as the most promising way to help sell phonograph records since the growth of FM rock radio stations in the 1960's. Television programmers see videos as a new source of programs and profits. Finally, a few art museum officials have begun to consider music videos an exciting new art form. The Museum of Modern Art in New York City gave its stamp of approval in 1983 when it acquired three videos for its permanent collection.

What is a music video? At its simplest, it is a visual treatment of a musical work. Music videos can be divided into two broad categories — *concert videos* and *concept videos*. Concert videos are merely filmed or videotaped versions of a musical performance in a studio or concert hall. Concept videos, on the other hand, are dramatic interpretations of a musical work. They may attempt to tell a story, based on a song's lyrics, or they may use some lyric or musical element as a jumping-off point to string together visually stunning images in dreamlike sequences. For example, in Michael Jackson's "Thriller," a young woman's date with Jackson turns into a horror-filled nightmare relieved by tongue-in-cheek touches such as a chorus line of dancing ghouls. In the video "Miss Me Blind" by Culture Club, the visual images appear unrelated to the lyrics or theme of the song. However, they are so startling and vivid — ranging from Oriental masks and flaming guitars to Japanese lettering — that the viewer remains spellbound.

Many of the best videos have the same dazzling look that was characteristic of the "new wave" in television commercials in the mid-1970's. The "new wave" television ads featured such techniques as rapid scene changes and the use of harsh lighting to highlight contrasts in color. With these techniques as a starting point, music video directors have created an impressive array of visual styles, including extreme close-ups, superslow motion, mirror images, and other special effects. This experimental artistic environment has attracted some of Hollywood's most respected movie directors.

Rock star Michael Jackson is surrounded by ghouls in this scene from the music video "Thriller." The professional quality of this and other Jackson videos helped to stimulate popular interest in music videos.

The sinister shadow of a knife in "Eyes Without a Face," a music video by British rock star Billy Idol, is one of the violent images that have stirred controversy about some music videos. Critics charge that much of the violence seen in the videos is directed at women.

Among those who have made music videos are John Landis, who directed *Trading Places* (1983); Brian De Palma, director of *Carrie* (1976); Bob Rafelson, who did *Five Easy Pieces* (1970); and Tobe Hooper, director of *Poltergeist* (1982).

Some people argue that the world's first music video was produced in Hollywood. They point to Walt Disney's 1940 film *Fantasia*, which used animation — motion-picture cartoons — to interpret various works of classical music. Another possible forerunner was "Your Hit Parade," a popular U.S. TV show that featured skits and dance routines accompanying the latest popular songs. The current music video trend, however, can be traced to Great Britain. In the early 1960's, not long after "Your Hit Parade" had gone off the air, a British TV show called "Top of the Pops" became popular in Europe. The show featured rock bands performing their latest songs in a TV studio. Gradually, groups started to videotape their performances to be aired during the program. In 1974, British director

A concert performance by the rock group Judas Priest, *left,* is typical of a concert video, in which a group's song is presented as it was performed on a stage or in a studio. The more imaginative concept video, typified by a scene from Duran Duran's "Rio," *below,* interprets a song in a visually dramatic way.

The rapidly changing frames of a music video create a sequence of bizarre and magical pictures when one image seems to dissolve into another, such as in this music video entitled "Catch Me I'm Falling" by Real Life.

Bruce Gowers made a rock video of a then-unknown group called Queen performing their song "Bohemian Rhapsody." Many people consider this to be the video that was the key to developing the music video trend. After "Bohemian Rhapsody" was shown on TV, Queen's record album featuring the song shot to the top of the best-seller lists. U.S. record companies, needing a way to promote sales in Europe, copied this success story and began to produce music videos for use there.

In the United States, music videos were first seen on large screens in rock dance clubs in the late 1970's. But it wasn't until 1981, when Warner-Amex Satellite Entertainment Corporation founded MTV (Music Television), that music videos began to leave their imprint on U.S. culture. MTV is a cable-programming service that shows virtually nothing but music videos 24 hours a day, seven days a week. MTV's founders felt that a TV station showing music videos could help sell records in much the same way a radio station playing records does—that is, by introducing the record and the recording artist to the public and giving them the exposure needed to make them popular.

Once there was a popular outlet for music videos in the form of MTV, the music video industry grew rapidly. In 1983, record companies in the United States and Europe produced more than 1,200 music videos, twice as many as were produced in 1982. In 1982, MTV was showing music videos through 300 cable outlets that reached into 2.5 million homes. By mid-1984, MTV was beaming more than 300 videos a day into 22 million homes.

MTV's success inspired imitators. By mid-1984, more than 200 music video programs were being shown on cable and broadcast channels. Network television awakened to the trend. The National Broadcasting Company's "Friday Night Videos," network television's first entry into music video programming, was introduced in 1983. In October 1984, MTV had to make room for another music

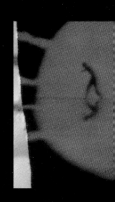

video programming service, the Music Video Network (MVN), part of the Turner Broadcasting Systems, Incorporated. MVN was short-lived, however. By late November, it stopped broadcasting. MTV announced that in January 1985 it would start a second music-programming service designed for a 25- to 49-year-old audience. MTV's original programming is aimed at a 12- to 34-year-old audience. Also in October 1984, Black Entertainment Television (BET), a cable-programming service aimed primarily at blacks, expanded its music video programming to 18 hours a day.

The music video trend has carried over to Hollywood, where movie studios have developed the rock video musical — a new kind of film that puts little emphasis on plot, featuring instead a series of song-and-dance, music video sequences. Two films of this type, *Flashdance* (1983) and *Footloose* (1984), became box-office hits. *Flashdance*, produced at a cost of $9.6 million, earned Paramount Pictures $36 million at U.S. box offices.

Music videos are expensive to make, but apparently the record companies feel they are worth the investment. In 1983, record companies spent approximately $50 million on the production of music videos, with the average cost of each one running between $40,000 and $50,000. However, some videos run into even higher figures. Michael Jackson's "Thriller" cost close to $1 million.

Why are the record companies willing to spend so much money? The answer lies partly in the declining number of record sales that have plagued the industry since the late 1970's. The last good year the record industry had was 1979, when 701 million records and tapes were distributed for sales of $3.6 billion. The number of records and tapes distributed has declined every year since then, but price increases have enabled the industry to keep its sales figures up. For example, in 1983, 578 million records and tapes were distributed, 123 million fewer than were distributed in 1979, but sales figures for 1983 were $3.8 billion, $200 million higher than 1979.

A residential street in New York City, *top,* becomes the setting for a new music video by Kool and the Gang. Stage sets, *right,* are often used to create special effects, such as the illusion of an indoor "sky" in the music video "Separate Ways" by Journey. A film crew checks storyboards, *above,* before shooting an outdoor scene for the Journey video.

Deciding to imitate their experience in Europe, U.S. record companies began to distribute music videos to programming outlets in the United States in the hope that this new type of exposure for recording artists would generate increased record sales. Numerous music video success stories can be found. Britain's Duran Duran, for example, at first had little luck getting U.S. radio stations to play their songs when their records were released. But their dazzling videos were very popular with MTV and other programming outlets, and soon the band's records zoomed to the top of the best-seller lists. Another British import, Billy Idol's album *Rebel Yell*, sold more than 600,000 copies, thanks principally to music video exposure.

Music videos have become so popular that MTV saw an advantage in paying for them in exchange for exclusive rights. Previously, record companies furnished the videos free of charge to programming outlets such as MTV. In June 1984, ever-mindful of the competition from other programmers, MTV signed the first and, as of late 1984, the only contracts agreeing to pay several major record companies a total of $4.6 million in cash and advertising time for the exclusive rights to air videos by those companies' most popular artists. These rights will last 30 days or longer, giving MTV a month-long advantage over its competitors. MTV could afford to pay for these exclusive rights once its advertising revenues grew from $7 million in 1982 to a pace of $1 million a week as of July 1984. In the first half of 1984, MTV took in more than $26 million from such major national advertisers as Levi Strauss & Company; Pepsico, Incorporated; and the Kellogg Company.

However, the money the record companies receive from MTV may seem like small change if the public turns out to have an appetite for purchasing music videos to play on home video cassette

The final touches that may mark the difference between a visually stunning video or a confused jumble of images are made in the control room, where dozens of filmed scenes are assembled to produce the finished video.

Music videos are often at the center of social occasions, such as having friends over to view them on the home television set, *above,* dancing to them under the glare of a giant screen in a video nightclub, *above right,* or watching them on a video jukebox, *right.*

recorders (VCR's). Full-length video albums range in price from $30 to $80, while video singles cost between $16 and $20. In 1983, the Sony Corporation of America began marketing Video 45's, videotapes of three to five songs by such popular artists as David Bowie and Duran Duran. Sales of all but a couple of these cassettes were sluggish, however, with most selling fewer than 20,000 units. Only "Making Michael Jackson's 'Thriller,' " a 60-minute video cassette that shows how the "Thriller" video was made, has sold well, garnering more than 750,000 sales by mid-1984 — an impressive figure considering the $34.95 price tag. That success probably says more about the allure of Michael Jackson than it does about the retail possibilities for music videos. Still, with estimates that 25 million U.S. homes will have VCR's by 1986, with stereo television becoming a reality, and with stereo VCR's providing high-quality sound reproduction, it would seem that there is a potentially huge retail market for music videos.

Music videos have changed the ground rules for performers and the music industry as a whole. Talent scouts searching for the next pop music superstar now have to be almost as concerned with how good a band or a performer looks as with how good they sound. For the newer, younger batch of popular musicians, making videos will come just as naturally as making recordings, if the music video trend persists. They will have grown up watching music videos, so camera angles will be just as important to them as guitar technique. Older musicians may have more difficulty. Like the silent-movie stars who tried to make the transition to "talkies," some will make it, and some will be left behind.

Although music videos appear to be an answer to the prayers of record-industry executives, people outside the music business have criticized the amount of violence in many videos. Women's groups have called record companies and bands to task for the sexist and exploitative way women are portrayed in many videos.

MTV and other video-programming services have also been criticized for showing only a small number of music videos by black and Latino performers. But with the growth of music video programming, the incredible success enjoyed by black artist Michael Jackson, and the growing popularity of other black performers, black artists, at least, are beginning to get a bigger slice of the music video programming pie.

Whether music videos of the less popular forms of music such as jazz, Latin, and classical will be produced and shown remains to be seen. At present, most record companies feel that videos of these forms would not be profitable, considering the great expense of video production. Even that might be changing, however. For example, in 1984, the producers of a movie version of the opera *Carmen*, starring the Spanish tenor Placido Domingo, released a promotional video culled from the film. Columbia Records made an animated video to accompany the release of jazz great Miles Davis' most recent album, *Decoy*; and even nonrockers Frank Sinatra and Dean Martin made videos for recordings in 1984. In what was perhaps the wildest music video scheme yet, rock composer-producer Giorgio Moroder transformed Austrian director Fritz Lang's classic silent film, *Metropolis* (1926), into a feature-length music video in 1984 by giving it a pounding rock score.

Where does the music video phenomenon go from here? It's hard to say. "Rock and roll is here to stay," Danny and the Juniors crooned in the 1950's. Whether the same can be said for music videos is unclear. In 1984, the brokerage house of F. Eberstadt & Company predicted that revenues from sales and rentals of music video cassettes will account for $5 billion by 1988—25 per cent of total home video revenues. If cash registers actually do ring up those kinds of numbers, music videos, like rock and roll, will indeed be here to stay.

By Rod Such

College Sports: Big Money on Campus

Is the education of the college athlete being shoved aside in the scramble for revenues that a winning team can bring?

When Leonard Thompson won his first tournament as a professional golfer, he pocketed the purse of $52,000 and recalled his student days at Wake Forest University in Winston-Salem, N.C. What did he study in college? "Golf," he replied. "If you don't believe me, ask my professors."

When high school basketball star Kevin Ross was recruited to play basketball at Creighton University in Omaha, Nebr., he says, the university was aware that he could barely read or write — but it recruited him anyway. Later, when he was injured in his junior year and could no longer play, his athletic scholarship was taken away, and he had to leave the university. "The college was no longer interested in me," says Ross, who eventually enrolled in Westside Preparatory School, a private elementary school in Chicago, to learn how to read and write.

The experiences of these two student-athletes raise a number of questions about the proper relationship between athletics and education. In October 1984, concern about those questions was being expressed by Walter Byers, executive director of the National Collegiate Athletic Association (NCAA), who called for a special convention of college presidents to discuss abuses in intercollegiate athletics. "We're not keeping up with the chase," said Byers. "I've talked with our representatives and people I respect, and the problem is much worse than I thought."

The problem revolves around such questions as these: In their eagerness to have a winning athletics program, are some colleges taking unfair advantage of student-athletes by putting more emphasis on the students' athletic participation than on their education? Are some colleges allowing student-athletes to take easy courses so that they can maintain the necessary grade-point average that will keep them eligible for athletic scholarships and varsity play? If so, will these students be prepared for a career once their playing days are over? And how many of these student-athletes actually graduate from college? Finally, is the competitiveness of college sports corrupting moral values by involving athletes, alumni, coaches, athletics directors, and other college officials in unethical practices such as tampering with grades, or offering money, jobs, cars, and apartments to student-athletes and their families?

These questions are not new. They are part of a conflict that has troubled educators in the United States since the early 1900's. The conflict arises over whether sports should be pursued as part of a student's education, a training for later life, or as an end in itself — a money-making activity that generates prestige and revenue for the university. The conflict can be traced back to 1906, when the NCAA was formed in response to a public outcry over abuses and injuries in intercollegiate athletics. The NCAA was given the authority to establish rules and policies that would help regulate intercollegiate sports. But abuses continued, and in 1929, the Carnegie Foundation for the Advancement of Teaching issued a landmark report titled *American College Athletics*, the result of a 3½-year study.

The author:
Rod Such is a Senior Editor for THE WORLD BOOK YEAR BOOK and SCIENCE YEAR.

The report appeared at the height of the football season, and it made headlines. In *The New York Times*, the story started on the front page and continued for two full pages inside. The lead headline read, "College Sports Tainted by Bounties, Carnegie Fund Finds in Wide Study." The report might have commanded a bigger headline except for a more prominent story about the crash of stock prices on Wall Street. Nevertheless, the impact of the Carnegie report was not lost on Chick Meehan, football coach at New York University in New York City. He gathered his players and said, "I've already read the report, and you're going to be shocked . . . when you see how little you're getting paid."

Money is at the heart of the conflict. The desire to maintain a successful, winning athletics program that generates valuable revenues through such sources as ticket sales and alumni contributions often runs into conflict with educational values and goals, particularly if star athletes are poor students. In the early 1900's, the amount of money involved was modest compared with the standards of the 1980's, when two television networks and a cable-TV system agreed to pay $281.1 million to televise college football games during the 1982 and 1983 seasons. Television revenues have helped make college sports a big business, and the biggest bonanzas go to the winners. In 1984, the colleges with teams in the Rose Bowl made $5.6 million each, while the Cotton and Orange bowl teams made close to $2 million each. Altogether, the 16 major college football bowl games in 1984 generated $33 million for the schools of the competing teams.

Generally, football is the sport that carries all other college sport activities on its shoulders. The more than 180 colleges with the biggest sports programs in the United States earn 56 per cent of their sports' revenue from football, compared with 13 per cent from basketball. Among the major colleges with football programs, 43 per cent of sports-generated income comes from gate receipts — that is, ticket sales. Because football stadiums seat far more people than basketball arenas and because football is generally a more popular sport, football games produce more money from ticket sales. Among the major colleges, as much as 85 per cent of income from ticket sales comes from football.

The colleges plow most of this revenue back into the money-making sports: 41 per cent is spent on football and 10 per cent on basketball. Few schools — only about 1 per cent — earn enough money from their sports programs to spend it on nonathletic activities. Women's sports also find themselves dependent on the success of men's football. Because they are less popular, the income generated by women's sports covers only about 25 per cent of the expenses incurred.

If there was any doubt that football paid the bills and ran up the bills, it was removed when Jackie Sherrill left his post as head coach

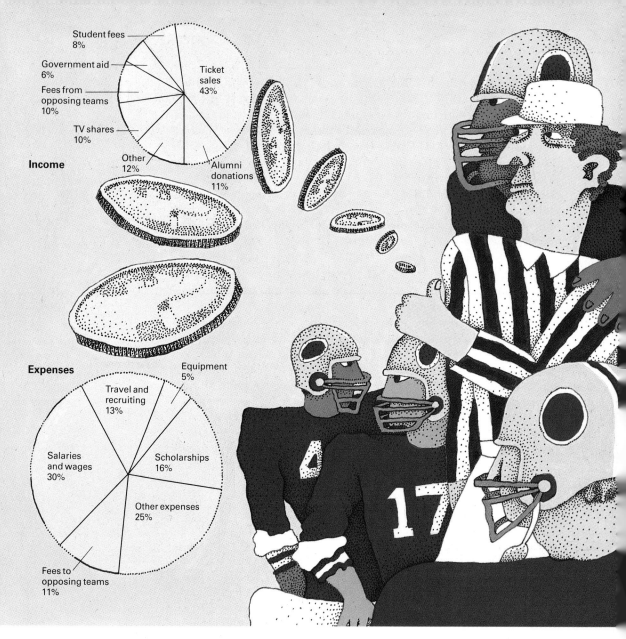

Income

- Student fees 8%
- Government aid 6%
- Fees from opposing teams 10%
- TV shares 10%
- Other 12%
- Ticket sales 43%
- Alumni donations 11%

Expenses

- Equipment 5%
- Travel and recruiting 13%
- Salaries and wages 30%
- Scholarships 16%
- Other expenses 25%
- Fees to opposing teams 11%

A breakdown of income and expenses for the athletics budgets of the top college football powers in the NCAA reveals that ticket sales account for nearly half of their income. This creates pressure to have a winning team to spur the ticket sales.

at the University of Pittsburgh (Pa.) to become head football coach at Texas A&M University in College Station in 1982. Sherrill signed a six-year contract valued at $1.7 million in salary and benefits. Even in this era of big business in sports, people were impressed. Some were even shocked because it was considered the largest financial package ever offered by a U.S. university. It must have left many faculty members, including a number of Nobel Prize winners, wondering how important they really were to the system of higher education. The chairman of Texas A&M's Board of Regents, H. R. Bright, defended the contract: "Higher education is a business, and I think Sherrill's contract is part of that process."

The price of success in this business, however, goes beyond the athletics directors and coaches who stage 32,000 basketball and 3,000 football games during a college year. And it goes beyond the thousands of alumni boosters who join in their alma mater's pursuit of high school stars, and the professional scouts who flock to the college fields and gymnasiums.

The price is usually paid by the student-athlete who becomes part of the system, who is wined and dined and recruited and glorified, and who may in the end get neither a career as a professional athlete nor an education. The NCAA has adopted a number of regulations developed to protect high school athletes from being constantly courted and harassed during the recruitment process. These establish a recruiting season when a college coach is permitted to make personal visits with the athlete he is interested in signing. For football, the recruiting season runs from December 1 to March 1. During the recruitment season, the college coach is permitted only six visits — three at the student's home and three at the student's school. However, there are no limits on the number of contacts by telephone or by letter. The student is also allowed to make five expense-paid visits to the campuses of the colleges he is interested in attending, but there is a limit of one expense-paid visit per school. A second visit must be at the student's own expense. NCAA regulations also restrict the amount of financial aid a college may offer a high school athlete. A student-athlete must not receive more than is required for tuition, room, board, books, and incidental fees.

But none of these regulations can ensure that a student-athlete will end up with either a pro career or an education. And the importance of a college degree to a student-athlete can be seen in statistics that reveal how slim the chances are of making it into professional sports. Of about 200,000 high school seniors who play basketball each year, some 5,700 become college seniors who play basketball. Approximately 200 of these will be drafted by professional teams, and maybe 50 will be signed to a contract. That means about 1 per cent of all college basketball players reach the professional ranks, and 99 per cent do not.

Myles Dorch, a former college basketball player who became a social worker in New York City, recalled how nine of his high school friends had been recruited by a college in Texas. He said the recruiter told them, "You boys can come on down and play basketball — and, if you're lucky, you can get an education." What happened? "Two got pro contracts," Dorch remembered, "but none of those nine kids graduated."

What percentage of student-athletes actually succeed in completing the academic work required to earn a degree? Studies of dropout rates among college athletes have produced varying results. Some colleges encourage their athletes to complete the necessary course work by removing them from the athletics program if it is interfering with their studies. However, Harvard University President Derek Bok, who chaired an American Council on Education committee that studied intercollegiate athletics, has estimated that on some campuses 70 per cent of the varsity athletes fail to graduate. Some of these athletes, he notes, were required to pursue 60 hours of practice a week in their sport, leaving little time for academic work. Several other studies have also shown high dropout rates at various institutions.

However, a study completed for the NCAA in 1984 indicated that the dropout rate for college athletes is comparable to that for nonathletes. Unlike studies that focused on only one or two colleges, the NCAA study was the first done nationwide. It followed the academic careers of student-athletes who entered 206 major colleges in the fall of 1977 and compared their academic achievements with those of all freshman students who entered those colleges in 1977. The study found that 55 per cent of all freshmen who entered in

the fall of 1977 graduated within six years, while 50 per cent of all student-athletes graduated within that period. Because the figures are so similar, it suggests that athletics programs may not be to blame for the 50 per cent who fail to graduate.

Those student-athletes who do graduate may not get the best education, however. Allen L. Sack, a sociologist and a former Notre Dame University football player, surveyed four Connecticut colleges in 1981 and found that 63 per cent of the women and 49 per cent of the men on athletic scholarships feared their financial aid would be lost if they did not meet a coach's demands. Nearly half of the students on athletic scholarships said they had been encouraged to take easy courses to allow more time for their sport.

The NCAA has required only that a student-athlete complete 24 hours of course work during the last semester preceding athletic competition. Also, the student-athlete has had to be in good aca-

The star high school athlete is frequently bombarded with promises of expensive gifts from college recruiters who hope to induce the athlete to attend their college. However, offers of apartments, cars, and cash are violations of NCAA rules, and they are a major reason why the NCAA has placed 55 colleges on probation since 1977.

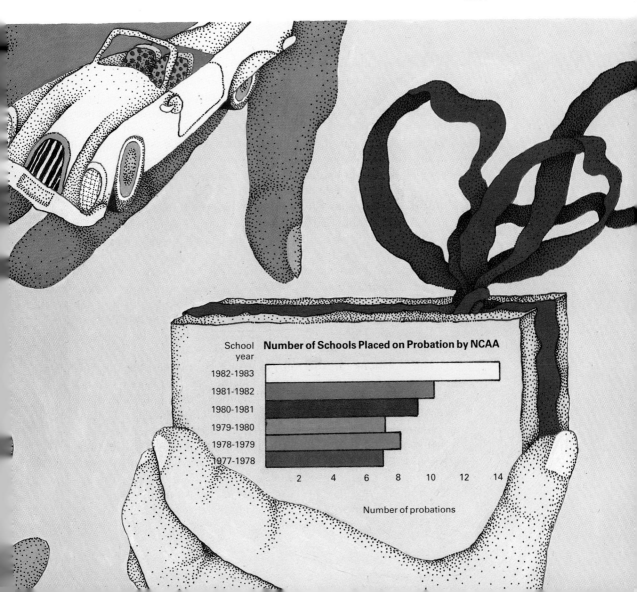

School year — **Number of Schools Placed on Probation by NCAA**

Number of probations

demic standing to remain eligible for athletic aid, practice, and competition. Those 24 semester hours have not had to be in course work leading to a degree, and the NCAA has left it to each college or university to define what was meant by "good academic standing." However, the NCAA planned to revise its requirements so that — beginning in the fall of 1985 — a student-athlete must complete 24 semester hours in a degree program to remain eligible for athletic aid and competition. Presumably, that would make it much more difficult to get through college by taking such courses as basket weaving or sports fiction. It also seemed likely to help solve the problem of athletes graduating without adequate preparation for a career or, as in a few cases, without being able to read.

The new requirement appeared to be the result of a reassessment underway among NCAA officials and college presidents after years of negative publicity concerning recruitment violations and the lowering of academic standards. Throughout the 1970's, reports of abuses and violations of NCAA rules were well publicized, but the publicity seemed to have little impact.

As the colleges entered the 1980's, there appeared to be no slackening in the drive to recruit high school stars and to win at any cost. In the 1982-1983 academic year, the NCAA seemed to be struggling to keep order when it placed 14 schools on probation, including the undefeated and top-ranked football team of Clemson University in Clemson, S.C. During that year, the NCAA imposed three years' probation on the basketball programs of New Mexico State University in Las Cruces and Wichita State University in Wichita, Kans., chiefly for violations in recruiting players. Two years' probation was imposed on the basketball programs of West Texas State University in Canyon; the University of California at Santa Barbara; California State Polytechnic University in Pomona; the University of New Haven in West Haven, Conn.; Arkansas State University in Jonesboro; and the University of California at Los Angeles (UCLA). Two years' probation for violations in their football programs was imposed on the University of Colorado in Boulder, Arizona State University in Tempe, Southern Methodist University in Dallas, the University of Oregon in Eugene, and the University of Miami.

The violations ran the full range of broken rules, but the most common offense was the usual one of giving athletes too much money. Other common violations include tampering with academic grades, giving student-athletes tickets to games to sell at a profit, and offering jobs to student-athletes and their families.

How much was a student-athlete worth to a college? In October 1984, NCAA Executive Director Byers estimated that some star athletes receive more than $20,000 a year in extra financial aid in violation of NCAA rules. Byers said that payments in this range occur much more frequently than he previously believed. David Berst, the

NCAA's director of enforcement, added that an average of 10 of every 12 investigations conducted by his office each year turn up allegations of payments in the $20,000 range.

Violations involving payoffs such as these have continued over the years because the competition for talent has grown steeper, and the financial rewards of winning, as well as the financial risks of losing, have soared. According to a 1977 NCAA study, the average profit margin for a major college with a successful football program was $281,000, while the average financial loss for a college with an unsuccessful football program was a hefty $553,000. The high school athlete being recruited often went along with these rule violations for financial reasons, too: Tuition costs were climbing, and attending a school with a major reputation meant national TV exposure and possibly a highly paid career as a professional.

Probation usually means that a school loses its eligibility for postseason play and the sizable TV money that comes with it. The school also might face a reduction in the number of athletic scholarships it can grant. For example, when the University of Illinois in Urbana-Champaign was placed on probation in 1984, the penalties included a one-year ban on postseason play, a one-year ban on TV appearances, an order prohibiting the head football coach and his top assistant from traveling to the homes of high school athletes to recruit them, and a cut in the number of football scholarships the university could offer from 30 to 20. Also, the salaries of the head coach and his top assistant were frozen for a year.

Men outnumber women by nearly 3 to 1 in intercollegiate athletics programs, and men get the lion's share of the budget, 80 per cent, compared with 20 per cent for women. Because women's sports draw smaller crowds and earn less in ticket sales, women's athletics are often dependent on the success of men's sports, particularly football, for their funding.

Women 20%

Men 80%

But probation and other penalties have failed to solve the problem, and current enforcement efforts apparently are not adequate. (Some schools become repeat offenders. Wichita State, for example, has been punished six times in 30 years, most recently for 42 violations in its basketball program.) The NCAA has increased its staff of enforcement officers from 1 in 1952 to a total of 15 in 1984. Even with the increase, critics charge that the enforcement staff is too small to cover the more than 180 colleges with major sports programs, let alone the more than 790 colleges and universities that belong to the NCAA. The result, they say, is selective enforcement in which some colleges are punished, while others guilty of the same violations get off scot-free.

Jerry Tarkanian was the basketball coach at California State University in Long Beach when it was placed on probation in 1973. "In all my years at Long Beach, my kids were poor ghetto kids," Tarkanian recalled. "They wore old clothes and . . . shoes, and used to play in the summer with UCLA kids. The UCLA kids would pick them up in their new cars and take them to their apartments." Tarkanian said it was an open secret that the cars and apartments were in violation of NCAA rules, but it was Long Beach that was placed on probation, not UCLA.

The future of college sports was further clouded on June 27, 1984, when the Supreme Court of the United States issued a landmark ruling ending NCAA control over the televising of college football. The NCAA had been regulating its members' appearances on television since 1951, when TV first showed signs of becoming a major source of exposure and revenue for college sports. The idea behind controlling TV appearances was to avoid a stampede by the big-time football powers, which might have tried to dominate U.S. television screens and get the lion's share of the money that was certain to come with the televising of games. Instead, the NCAA controlled the division of TV money among the schools.

However, a lawsuit filed in 1981 by two football

Like a lone referee in a heated game, the NCAA was in a difficult situation in 1984, with only 15 people to police more than 790 colleges for rule violations.

powers argued that NCAA control of TV contracts violated federal antitrust laws because it prevented individual schools from arranging their own football telecasts. In a 7 to 2 vote, the Supreme Court justices agreed with the two universities, finding that NCAA control of TV contracts violated the Sherman Antitrust Act. One of the two dissenters was Justice Byron R. White, once renowned as "Whizzer" White, all-America halfback for the University of Colorado in the late 1930's.

Under the decision, the NCAA can still use the withholding of TV appearances to penalize schools in violation of NCAA rules. But there were numerous predictions that the Supreme Court decision would make the monetary stakes even higher and could open the floodgates to more violations. NCAA President John Toner testified in hearings before a subcommittee of the U.S. House of Representatives that he was "dismayed and saddened" that college football was "in disarray because a minority of institutions believe they should have unlimited opportunity to use their property to maximize their profits." He predicted that recruiting violations and other forms of cheating would promptly increase. Justice White appeared to have the same concern in mind when he wrote in his dissenting opinion that NCAA control of TV contracts, like its other regulations, "represents a desirable and legitimate attempt to keep university athletics from becoming professionalized to the extent that profit-making objectives would overshadow educational objectives."

Nevertheless, having been handed the ball by the highest court in the land, the colleges lost absolutely no time running with it. Of the nation's 105 major college football teams that make up Division I-A of the NCAA, 63 formed their own group, the College Football Association, to negotiate with the three national TV networks and the two biggest cable-TV sports systems. The Pacific Ten and Big Ten conferences created their own 20-team TV plan. In 1983, each Big Ten school received about $650,000 from football television revenue. Under the new plan, each team expected to receive about $800,000 from football television revenue. Five other major football universities, including the University of Notre Dame near South Bend, Ind., organized the National Independent Football Network and sold television rights to some of their games.

In the two football seasons before the Supreme Court issued its historic ruling, Notre Dame was permitted six appearances on national TV under the NCAA's TV plan, and the school earned $2.5-million from those games. Gene Corrigan, athletics director at Notre Dame, conceded that the university would probably earn more now that it was free to negotiate its own TV coverage. And that was one of the crowning ironies. Back in 1951, other schools had approved strong controls by the NCAA in part because they feared that Notre Dame would corner the new TV football market.

Fears of another kind brought together a group of college and university presidents in late 1983. They met in an effort to bring sports back into a reasonable perspective in the life of their schools. Led by Harvard's Bok and Georgetown University President Timothy S. Healy, they united behind a proposal put forward by the American Council on Education that would have given a special Presidents' Commission, made up of college presidents, veto power over NCAA rules involving academic standards and financial integrity. Proponents of Proposal 35, as it was called, attended the NCAA's 78th annual convention in January 1984 in Dallas to argue their case.

To some, it seemed a strange case: that the president of a university ought to exert more influence over his athletics director and coaches. But to the presidents, it wasn't so strange. They felt trapped in a runaway system, and they wanted more control over it. The presidents felt powerless because the system had grown bigger than any one university president's ability to buck the tide. Any president might impose strictness on his athletics director, but, of course, he had no power to discipline the athletics directors at rival schools who might still be bending the rules. Everyone tended to be caught up in the compulsion to win — coaches, alumni, trustees, and even local businessmen. The only way to apply presidential pressure, this group reasoned, was by acquiring a stronger voice — even a veto — in NCAA deliberations, in which athletics directors, not presidents, customarily represent their schools.

At Dallas, Georgetown's Healy sounded the alarm, telling the convention: "Within the next two or three years, higher education is going to be belted with exactly the same scrutiny that we have watched the high schools experience. The studies are already started, and we are next . . . ranging from whether or not Johnny can read to whether or not he can read when he has got a degree. Part of the problem we are all going to be facing concerns our athletics and the integrity of the athletics program of kids who are students and athletes." Harvard's Bok added, "In the glow of bowl games and other important victories, there is a large public out there that knows there are things amiss in the world of intercollegiate athletics."

"Let us go out of here," said Paul Hardin of Drew University in Madison, N.J., "with a clear signal that presidents care." Then, the convention voted on Proposal 35. Like a football team without a powerful offensive line, it lost, 328 to 313.

However, the convention did approve the formation of a Presidents' Commission and empowered it to call special conventions to address problems in college sports. By October 1984, there appeared to be a consensus within the NCAA that such a special convention was necessary. A solution to the problems in college sports was not in sight, but one thing was certain — those problems were receiving more serious attention than ever before.

By William M. Kelso

Digging on Jefferson's Mountain

Archaeological excavations at Monticello, Thomas Jefferson's home, are shedding new light on Jefferson and plantation life.

The author:
William M. Kelso is the resident archaeologist for the Thomas Jefferson Memorial Foundation at Monticello.

As I leaned into the raw December wind, I was reminded, once again, that it was much too late in the year to be digging at Monticello, Thomas Jefferson's mountaintop home in Virginia. But as often happens on archaeological excavations, my team of workers and I had made a major discovery late in the summer of 1981, at the end of the digging season. Ordinarily, excavations stop until the warm weather returns. But we believed our discovery would not survive the winter and so kept on digging, even after the snows came.

My destination on that cold, blustery day — and the source of our excitement — was an enormous hole in the ground. Two hundred years ago, that hole was a "dry well," or deep cellar, a place where Jefferson — the third President of the United States — intended to store vegetables and fruit. In a world without refrigerators, a deep cellar was the best way to keep food cool and dry. However, Jefferson's dry well had a short life span. After the well was dug, Jefferson decided to change its location, and so the cellar was filled in.

When I finally reached the cellar site, I was impressed, as usual, by the sheer size of the hole we had dug, which was more than 20 feet wide and 19 feet deep. The last time I had seen the excavation, before leaving on a lecture trip, the crew had nearly reached the bottom. Earlier — before we began excavating — we had dug a 4-inch-wide test hole about 20 feet down into the red-clay soil that filled the dry well. In the soil samples brought up from the test hole, we found many small objects, including pieces of broken pottery and other household artifacts. Evidently, the abandoned dry well had been used as a dump as it was filled in. So we all knew there was a good chance that we might find something really interesting.

And we were right. What I saw when I climbed down into the pit made the months of painstaking digging worthwhile. There in the middle of the floor lay two rows of glass bottles, only their tops poking out of the clay. These "wine bottles" are a dime a dozen on archaeological sites from the American colonial period and were used as storage jars for a variety of liquids from milk to paint. But I knew at a glance that these bottles were different. Most were still tightly corked, and one, partially broken open during discovery, was full of its original contents. "Jefferson's wine" was my first reaction. What a find that would be. A noted expert on winemaking, Jefferson had even planted his own vineyards at Monticello.

However, we discovered that the bottles held other, perhaps more important, surprises. After we carefully removed the rest of the clay surrounding the bottles, I placed a spotlight behind them in order to get a look inside. At that moment, I felt the rare and powerful presence of the past. In the almost clear liquid of one of the bottles, I saw dozens of small, round, red objects. They were in such good condition that there could be no doubt about what they were — cherries. They appeared to be as fresh as they were the day they were picked, more than two centuries ago.

The contents of the other bottles were not so clearly visible. Later we discovered that all but one of them also contained preserved cherries. That one bottle was really a surprise. It was full of cranberries, a rare fruit in colonial Virginia. Where the cranberries came from is a mystery. Today, such cranberries cannot be found growing within 150 miles of Monticello. Perhaps the fruit grew near Monticello in Jefferson's time, though he does not refer to cranberries in any of the voluminous notebooks in which he kept detailed records of the horticultural activity at Monticello. These notebooks were collected in his *Garden Book* and *Farm Book*. Perhaps the cranberries were a gift. We may never know how the cranberries got to Monticello, but finding something as perishable as fruit almost certainly last touched by 18th-century servants, or perhaps even by Jefferson himself, was an unusual and exciting experience.

It may seem that bottles of fruit found in a cellar dug in 1770 could hardly rank among the archaeological prizes of our time, such as an ancient Egyptian king's gold or the splendor of a buried Roman city. But America's own artifacts from its colonial cities, plantations, factories, and even some of its wrecked and abandoned ships are exciting the imagination of American archaeologists as well as that of the general public.

There may be several reasons for this new interest in America's beginnings. First, the United States — a young nation, historically speaking — has now grown old enough to have a relatively distant past. Second, there are surprising gaps in our knowledge of the United States past. Historical records are often incomplete, and much information has been lost in just 300 years. And whenever there are questions about the past that buried objects can answer, no matter how recent that past may be, archaeology can offer important new insights.

Of course, digging to recover the history of the first Americans, the Indians, is the most familiar activity of American archaeology. But now excavations to learn how Americans' early pioneer ancestors lived and worked are going on in practically every state in the country. For example, archaeologists have uncovered New York City's first city hall, a 16th-century Spanish mission in South Carolina, and a Revolutionary War fort in Detroit.

American archaeologists are also turning to the homes of U.S. Presidents, trying to learn more about history's "great men" from another perspective. Excavators have been at work at Mount Vernon, George Washington's home, and Ash Lawn, James Monroe's home near Monticello. So, too, archaeologists have become interested in Thomas Jefferson and Monticello.

Thomas Jefferson began constructing Monticello, which he designed, in 1770 on a 1,000-acre site he inherited at age 14. Monticello, which means *little mountain* in Italian, sits on the top of an 860-foot-high hill that was leveled to make room for the house. Jeffer-

An archaeologist carefully uncovers glass "wine bottles" found at the bottom of Jefferson's dry well, *top.* The uncovered bottles were then placed in front of a spotlight so excavators could see what they contained, *middle.* Inside, *above,* archaeologists found cranberries and cherries that seemed as fresh as the day they were picked.

A Man of Many Talents

Thomas Jefferson in about 1799.

"I think this is the most extraordinary collection of talent, of human knowledge, that has ever been gathered together at the White House," President John F. Kennedy once told a group of Nobel Prize winners, "with the possible exception of when Thomas Jefferson dined alone." Jefferson truly was a man of enormous talent, wide-ranging interests, and remarkable achievements.

During his 60 years of public service, he served as governor of Virginia, minister to France, secretary of state under President George Washington, and Vice President under John Adams. A champion of the rights of the common people, Jefferson was largely responsible for the inclusion of the Bill of Rights in the Constitution. He also devised the decimal system of coinage used in the United States today. Elected President twice, Jefferson doubled the size of the United States by purchasing the Louisiana Territory.

But he always considered himself, first and foremost, a farmer. And he felt his most significant achievements were writing the Declaration of Independence and the Statute of Virginia for Religious Freedom and founding the University of Virginia.

Jefferson was also a surveyor, astronomer, inventor, violinist, and gourmet. Among the foods he introduced to the United States are vanilla, macaroni, olives, almonds, and pistachio nuts. The foremost architect of his time, he designed the Virginia Capitol and the University of Virginia as well as Monticello. His excellent library at Monticello became the nucleus of the Library of Congress.

So it is somehow not surprising to learn that Jefferson is often considered the world's first scientific archaeologist. The methods of digging and recording that he used to excavate an Indian burial mound near Monticello in the 1770's anticipated modern archaeological techniques by more than a century.

Jefferson was intrigued by Indians from the first time he saw them passing along a trail near his boyhood home at Shadwell, Va., and he became a good friend of Jean Baptiste Ducoigne, a Kaskagkia chief. Jefferson, who prepared written vocabularies of Indian languages, also turned the entrance hall at Monticello into a museum filled with an impressive array of Indian weapons, clothing, and cooking utensils. When Jefferson noticed bands of Indians visiting and worshiping at an earthen mound 2 miles up the Rivanna River from Monticello, he determined to learn more about the Indian culture by digging.

The trenches he dug would be considered sound by modern archaeological standards. In addition, Jefferson may have been among the first to grasp the geologic concept that the deeper the layer of soil, the older the artifacts found there.

Jefferson determined from the way the bones of many individuals were mixed together in the mound that the Indians buried the remains of their dead periodically — and only after the flesh had decayed away. Also, because some of the bones were those of children, he concluded that the legend about mounds being burial places for only fallen warriors was not true.

Hoping to verify Jefferson's findings by locating and reopening the trenches he dug, a team of archaeologists tried in 1982 to find the mound. But after two months of searching and digging test trenches, they gave up. More than 200 years of plowing and periodic river flooding had leveled the mound, which, in Jefferson's day, was 7 feet high and 40 feet in diameter. Thankfully, evidence of many of Jefferson's other accomplishments remains.   [W.M.K.]

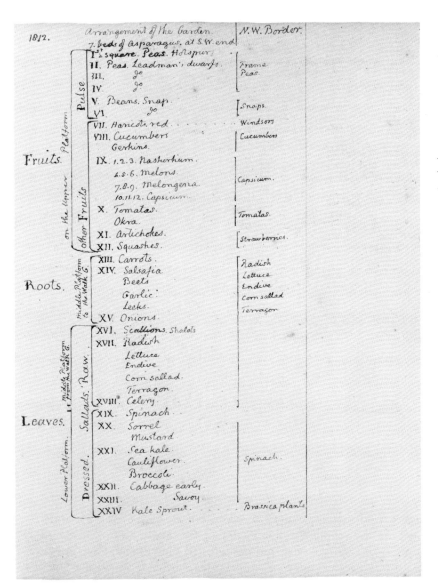

Jefferson's own notes listing the vegetables planted in his garden helped scientists determine the plan of the garden. As the notes indicate, Jefferson organized the vegetables by type, allocating areas for "Fruits," "Roots," and "Leaves."

Soil stains left by decayed fence posts, *below left,* and the remains of posts, *below right,* indicate the location of the garden fence.

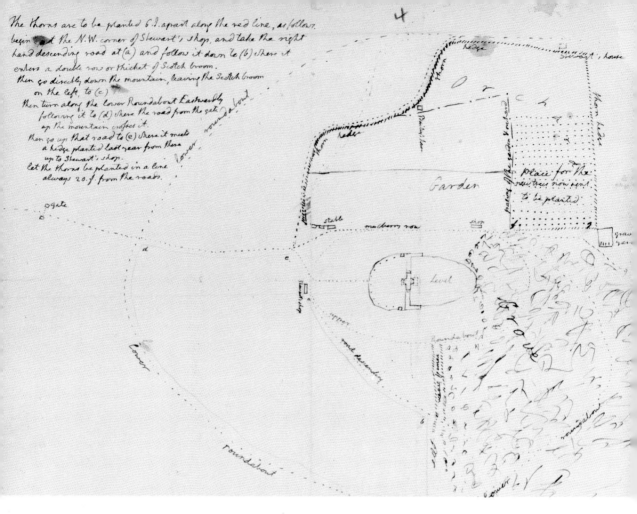

The thorns are to be planted 6.I. apart along the red line, as follows.
begin at the N.W. corner of Stewart's shop, and take the right
hand descending road at (a) and follow it down to (b) where it
enters a double row or thicket of Scotch broom.
then go directly down the mountain, leaving the Scotch broom
on the left, to (c)
then turn along the lower Roundabout Eastwardly
following it to (d) where the road from the gate
up the mountain crosses it.
then go up that road to (e) where it meets
a hedge planted last year from there
up to Stewart's shop.
let the thorns be planted in a line
always 20.f. from the roads.

Detailed plans of Monticello were valuable guides for scientists trying to restore the plantation's landscape. This plan, drawn by Jefferson in 1806 and found in his *Garden Book*, shows the location of the garden, orchard, roundabouts, and several outbuildings, such as the stable and the blacksmith's shop.

son prized the view from his hilltop home. To the east, he could look on the rolling Virginia Piedmont farmlands, and to the west, the city of Charlottesville and the forested Blue Ridge Mountains.

In 1772, Jefferson brought his bride, Martha, to Monticello. But because the main house was still under construction, they moved into the South Pavilion, a small building later used as an office. They moved into the main house in 1775. However, moving in hardly signaled the end of construction. "Architecture is my delight," Jefferson wrote, "and putting up and pulling down, one of my favorite amusements." Jefferson amused himself with Monticello for nearly 40 years, rebuilding, remodeling, and adding on to the house where, he said, "all my wishes end." The 35-room, red-brick house was not really finished until 1809.

The landscape around Monticello was as important to Jefferson as the architectural design of the house. Jefferson himself laid out Monticello's elaborate flower beds, orchard, vineyards, and vegetable garden.

Monticello was more than just a beautiful pleasure garden, however. It was also a working farm. As early as 1770, Jefferson began constructing buildings for the slaves and craftworkers whose labors and skills were needed to make Monticello into his ideal — a self-supporting village. On his plantation, Jefferson built a dairy, a smokehouse, and a blacksmith shop, as well as craft shops where textiles, furniture, nails, and even buttons were produced.

Unfortunately, uncertain economic conditions, along with long absences and incompetent overseers, kept Jefferson from achieving his goal. The plantation was not even to stay in his family. Jefferson was deeply in debt when he died in 1826, and in 1833 his heirs were forced to sell the plantation. Under the new owners, the house deteriorated seriously and Jefferson's carefully planned gardens and orchard, as well as many of the plantation's craft shops and outbuildings, disappeared altogether.

In 1923, however, the Thomas Jefferson Memorial Foundation, a nonprofit group, bought Monticello and 700 surrounding acres. By 1954, the group had renovated the house. Then in 1976, work began on the grounds. One goal of our work is to learn more about the details of day-to-day life on a Virginia plantation. Such information was often reported inaccurately in written records or was ignored altogether. Another goal is the restoration of Jefferson's landscape. Because nearly all traces of the gardens, orchard, and outbuildings had disappeared, we had to search below the surface for clues to their whereabouts. As a result, Monticello has been the scene of intensive digging since 1979.

Our first and most challenging problem was where to dig. There was no way we could dig into the entire mountaintop. Nor did we need to. Fortunately, many of Jefferson's plans for his gardens, orchard, and outbuildings still survive. For example, we have a detailed plan of the vegetable garden and outbuildings as they were

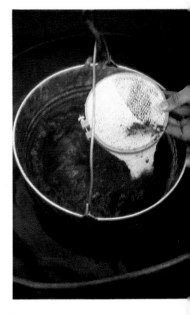

To help determine which vegetables Jefferson planted in his garden, a horticulturist mixes soil from the garden with water. Any seeds left in the soil float to the top and are captured in a strainer.

Jefferson's huge garden was one of the most extensive experimental vegetable gardens of its time in the United States. White dots and X's below the garden indicate where trees once stood in the orchard.

Monticello
1812

1. Monticello (main house)
2. Tree planted by Jefferson still standing today
3. Roundabout
4. Mulberry Row
5. Slave quarters
6. Weaver's cottage
7. Garden gate
8. Workman's house
9. Site of dry well
10. Ruins of smokehouse/dairy
11. Storehouse for nailery
12. Nailery
13. Blacksmith's shop
14. Joinery (carpentry shop)
15. Ha ha (built in 1814)
16. Vegetable garden
17. Pavilion
18. Vineyard
19. Berry patch
20. Garden wall
21. Bean arbor
22. Orchard

Jefferson's passion for vegetables extended even to the unusual arbor he planted at the western end of the garden. To form the green columns of the arbor, Jefferson planted climbing beans that flower in bright red and purple blossoms.

from 1776 to 1778, a 1796 plan of insured buildings, and an 1809 survey of nearly the entire mountaintop showing Monticello's gardens, outbuildings, and road system. We also have Jefferson's notes on his horticultural activities. These documents were invaluable guides in helping us decide where to dig our exploratory trenches. Still, the very richness of the records proved in some ways to be a hindrance. Many of Jefferson's landscape plans vary in detail, so we could never be sure whether a document showed what Jefferson had actually accomplished or what he merely hoped to do.

Another problem was the monotonously bright-red color of the iron-rich clay at Monticello, which disguised the evidence of the gardens and even the remains of the outbuildings. Usually, different layers of soil have different colors. Topsoil, for example, is usually much darker than the subsoil beneath it. Archaeologists can learn a great deal by "reading" these layers. For one thing, they can tell whether the soil in an area has been disturbed — that is, whether the layers have been mixed together — by plowing or building. At first, all the soil layers at Monticello appeared to be the same color. Yet we had to learn to tell these layers apart in order to reclaim Jefferson's lost landscape.

Finally, we had to contend with the curiosity of the more than 500,000 people who visit Monticello each year and who were, naturally enough, full of questions about our work. Eventually, all these hurdles were overcome. We learned to decipher the maps and plans, experience taught us how to read the subtle differences in soil color, and we soon learned the knack of answering questions and working at the same time.

One of our most exciting and ambitious projects was the restoration of Jefferson's vegetable garden. All plantations had a kitchen garden, but Monticello's was something special. In fact, it was one of the most extensive experimental vegetable gardens of its time in the United States.

Jefferson was famous for his lavish dinners, and the garden supplied many of the dishes for his table. However, Jefferson was also an avid botanist and gardener, and the grounds at Monticello, especially the vegetable garden, reflected his passion for horticulture. Jefferson once wrote, "No occupation is so delightful to me as the culture of the earth, and no culture is comparable to that of the garden."

The garden was enormous, measuring about 1,000 feet long — more than the length of three football fields — and 80 feet wide. Even more astounding was the variety of vegetables and herbs grown there — more than 250 in all. Among them were white and purple eggplant, an uncommon vegetable during colonial times; purple broccoli; asparagus beans, a bean like vegetable from Asia with pods 2 feet long; tennis ball lettuce; many-headed cabbage; and sesame, which Jefferson cultivated for its oil. He also grew nearly 20 varieties of his favorite vegetable — the English pea.

Nor was Jefferson content with local varieties. He corresponded widely with people in other parts of the United States and in other countries to obtain specimens. Some of his garden plants even came from unexplored territory. Some of his currants, for example, grew from plants collected by Meriwether Lewis and William Clark, whose government-sponsored exploration of the northwestern wilderness from 1804 to 1806 was planned by then-President Jefferson.

Jefferson first began planting vegetables on the sunny hillside south of the main house in 1774 while a member of Virginia's legislature, the House of Burgesses. But beginning in 1806, workers expanded and terraced the garden, digging into the slope of the mountain and creating three levels that followed the contours of the land. The first terrace was 500 feet long, the sec-

The planting beds of the vegetable garden, seen from above on a fall afternoon, look like a tapestry of color and shadow.

Archaeologists excavate part of the stone retaining wall, *right,* 11 feet high in places, that supported the southern edge of the vegetable garden. Behind the wall, excavators found a remarkable collection of broken bowls, reconstructed *above,* as well as teacups, plates, and serving pieces.

ond and third, 250 feet long each. A thick stone retaining wall ran along the bottom edge of the garden. Jefferson was serving his second term as President while the garden was being constructed and so was living in Washington, D.C. However, he closely supervised the work, writing detailed letters of instruction to his overseer and receiving detailed progress reports in turn.

Guided by Jefferson's correspondence, we began to dig exploratory trenches along the hillside. We were looking for traces of the 10-foot-high fence, or paling, that enclosed the vegetable garden as well as the orchard and vineyards nearby. Jefferson wrote that the fence boards were set so close together "as not to let even a young hare in." (To protect his formally landscaped lawn west of the house, Jefferson constructed a 500-yard-long barrier called a ha ha. This consisted of rails laid over a ditch.)

Our excavations on the hillside soon turned up post stains —

Destroyed by a storm soon after it was built, Jefferson's pavilion has been rebuilt on its original site in the middle of the vegetable garden's southern border. Jefferson liked to read in the pavilion and enjoy the view of the Virginia countryside.

stains in the soil left by the decayed wooden fence posts. In some places, we found the actual remains of the posts. These enabled us to establish the northwestern and southeastern boundaries of the garden. Larger post stains marked the location of the central garden gate.

Once the gate and fence posts had been pinpointed, we turned our attention to the garden itself. Careful digging revealed the soil mixing that marked some of the garden's 27 planting beds.

Once these discoveries were made, it was a relatively easy task for us to apply Jefferson's detailed plans to the land. According to the *Garden Book*, Jefferson organized the vegetables by type, allocating areas for "Roots," such as beets and onions; "Leaves," such as lettuce and spinach; and "Fruits," such as beans and peppers. So after years of neglect, erosion, and overgrowth, the garden has been replanted, almost exactly as it was during Jefferson's time. In fact, many of the vegetables growing there now are the same varieties Jefferson planted. Unfortunately, however, some have become extinct and so have been replaced by modern varieties.

Another part of our garden project was the restoration of the stone retaining wall, 11 feet high in places, that supported the southern edge of the garden. After Jefferson's death, erosion took its toll on the wall. In addition, many of the stones were carted off to line the Monticello exit road. Now, however, these stones have been retrieved and the wall reassembled.

During our excavation of the wall, we discovered a remarkable cache — an abundance of broken teacups, saucers, plates, and serving dishes. Perhaps one of Jefferson's servants took advantage of the wall construction to hide the evidence of his clumsiness.

At the center section of the wall, we made another interesting discovery, a pile of brick rubble and mortar. This was all that remained of Jefferson's pavilion, a small brick building constructed in the middle of the garden's southern border. Jefferson called the pavilion his "temple" and liked to sit there to read and enjoy a breathtaking view of rolling hills and farmland. The original pavilion was destroyed in a storm shortly after it was built, but using information gathered from our excavations and Jefferson's plans, we have reconstructed this charming outpost.

Archaeology also played an important role in the replanting of Jefferson's 18-acre orchard, which lay south of the vegetable garden. There, Jefferson grew more than 150 varieties of fruit, including many types of peaches. Most of the trees in the orchard had long since died or had been uprooted when the land was cleared for farming. But like fence posts, trees leave stains in the soil. Trenches we dug in the area located enough of these soil marks to reveal the original planting pattern. Soil marks also led us to the boundaries of one of Jefferson's vineyards. Jefferson's notebooks told us what types of trees and grapes were planted. And so we have been able to replant both areas. About 75 per cent of the varieties growing in the orchard now are those that grew there during Jefferson's time.

We also uncovered the foundations of 10 of the 19 buildings that once stood on Mulberry Row, Monticello's residential street and center of light industry. When we began excavating, only part of the weaver's cottage, stable, and *joinery* (carpentry shop) remained.

Four of the foundations were those of log cabins that once served as slave quarters. These one-room buildings varied in size from about 12 feet by 14 feet to 42 feet by 18 feet. We found that each cabin had a small cellar, used for the storage of potatoes and other root crops. The cellars also contained numerous artifacts, including usable tools, door locks, and household implements, objects that Jefferson's slaves probably took from the house or storage buildings.

The cellars and some of the surrounding yards were littered with other objects, including some

Amid a tangle of tree roots, archaeologists search for artifacts in the excavated foundation and cellar of a slave cabin on Mulberry Row.

Among the more than 100,000 artifacts uncovered at Monticello are a padlock, forged perhaps by Jefferson himself, *far left;* an ointment or drug jar purchased by Jefferson in Paris, *center;* and a finely engraved Madeira decanter from a French winery, *left.*

pieces of good quality Chinese porcelain tea services, suggesting that some of Monticello's slaves lived better, at least materially, than we might have imagined. Even the butchered bones of cows, pigs, and sheep found on the sites show that a good menu of fine meat might have appeared often on the slave tables. Some of Jefferson's trusted house servants lived in the Mulberry Row cabins, so it should come as no surprise that the quality of the artifacts found in or near some of the structures was so high.

On the other hand, the types of artifacts found in the other excavated slave cabins on Mulberry Row seem to show a life of less elegance. For example, the tableware is of lower quality, and the animal bones are from poorer cuts of meat. Perhaps these differences reflect different levels of social standing and wealth within the slave community itself.

We also uncovered the foundations of a building that was used, at least for a short time, as a smokehouse and dairy, and other buildings that served as a nailery and a storehouse for iron for the nailery. In addition, we excavated the foundations of a workman's house, a stone house that was probably used as a dwelling, and another building not mentioned in any of the records and whose purpose is unknown. Most of the artifacts we found at the nailery site consisted of waste material from manufacturing. That excavation showed that Jefferson's slaves produced a great variety of handmade nail types in the nailery, which at its most active period supplied many of the nails used in central Virginia.

Like its magnificent landscape, Monticello itself has been restored to its former elegance and grandeur. Today, it appears much as it did in Jefferson's time, in stark contrast to its deteriorated condition in about 1870, *inset.*

Rarely can archaeology be expected to discover much about the life of one person. Who made, used, threw away, or lost the artifacts archaeologists uncover is usually unknown to the archaeologist. Rather, artifacts tend to tell a more general story about groups of people or societies. But Jefferson spent his lifetime carefully constructing and collecting the very things archaeologists study best — buildings, furnishings, and the landscape. So digging at Monticello offers not only a means of restoring Jefferson's plantation but also a fresh personal view of Jefferson's accomplishments and values.

The vegetable garden's terraces and planting patterns show how successfully Jefferson harmonized the steep mountain terrain at Monticello with the practical needs of his farming experiments. The discovery that he had more than 20,000 tons of earth moved, wheelbarrow by wheelbarrow, in order to build his garden terrace in itself presents clear proof of the high value Jefferson had for agriculture and landscape design. He was equally dedicated to making Monticello economically independent. The remains of the craft shops and slave quarters along Mulberry Row and the magnitude of the activity there demonstrate how much effort Jefferson put into making self-sufficiency a reality.

The excavations along Mulberry Row also present graphic proof that in the middle of what seems to have been a rather quiet life on a picturesque mountain, Jefferson had to deal with the countless challenges of running a bustling "village." At times, Monticello had a population, including family, craftworkers, servants, and visitors, of more than 100. Laying bare the long-hidden remains of that colorful and busy world paints a more realistic picture of the Monticello that Jefferson really knew.

Some of the more than 100,000 artifacts we've found reveal, in a more personal way, other sides of Jefferson. A wine bottle seal from the Château Lafite French winery found with a wine decanter and fragments of wine glasses in the dry well testify to his interest in and knowledge of winemaking. The extremely fine Chinese porcelain dinnerware discovered in the stone wall help flesh out our knowledge of the mansion's furnishings. Gun parts and a loading wrench for Jefferson's pocket pistols found near the site of the blacksmith's shop give a new view of Jefferson's well-known interest and ability in marksmanship. And seeing where servants lived and uncovering the objects they used adds to our understanding of the complex relationship between master and slave.

Few archaeological projects in the United States are as extensive as this one at Monticello. Those that are study city life. Archaeology at Monticello, on the other hand, is providing a unique and detailed view of plantation life and a new perspective on Thomas Jefferson. As the work expands into other areas of the landscape, Thomas Jefferson and his Virginia plantation world will come into even clearer focus for us all.

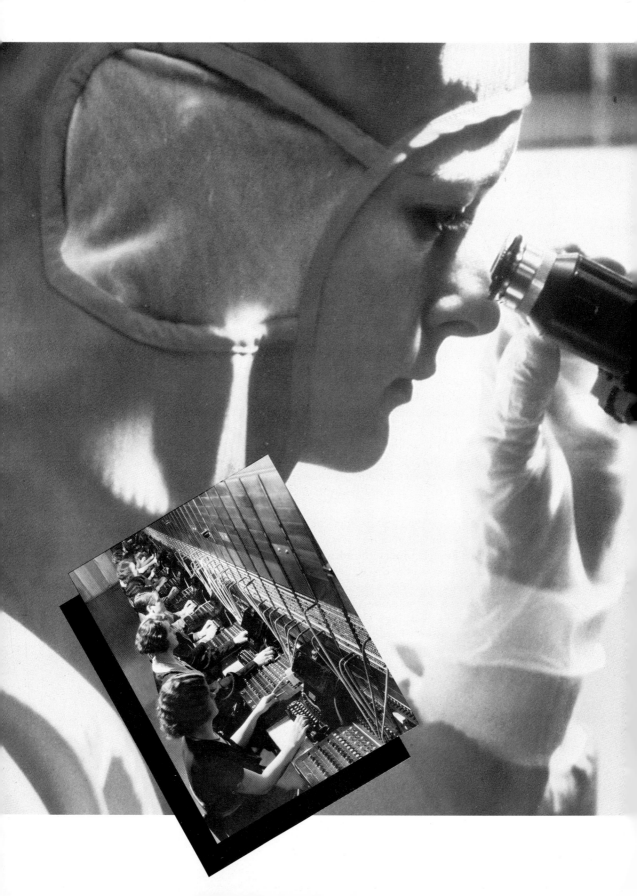

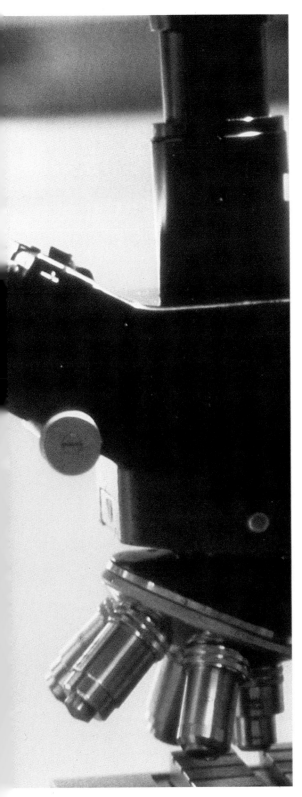

By Peggy A. Simpson

A Revolution in the Workplace

American women are moving into the labor force in ever-increasing numbers — with profound implications for society.

In 1962, on Elizabeth H. Dole's first day at Harvard University law school, a male classmate angrily demanded to know what right she had to take the place of a man who would be able to use such a prestigious education. In 1984, Elizabeth Dole headed the United States Department of Transportation — the first woman to do so — and few people questioned the presence of women in law schools. In fact, women now make up almost one-third of all law students in the United States.

Dole and millions of other women are participants in one of the most remarkable revolutions in modern times — the movement of American women out of the home and into the labor force. In 1950, an estimated 17 million American women — about one-third of American women — worked outside the home. By 1984, that number had nearly tripled, to 50 million, or about 50 per cent of all American women.

In other words, as economics professor Nancy

S. Barrett of American University in Washington, D.C., has reported, "In roughly a generation, since the early 1960's, 20 million workers — comprising 20 per cent of the entire U.S. labor force — have changed their sector of employment" from the home to the workplace. It is a revolution that has had — and continues to have — profound implications not only for the workplace but also for women, men, families, and society.

Many women, of course, continue to work full-time as homemakers, finding satisfaction and rewards in that traditional role. However, because of economic necessity, expanded opportunities, and changing attitudes toward working women, fewer women are able or willing to exercise that option. In fact, in only 13 per cent of American families is the wife a full-time homemaker and the husband the sole financial support.

Accompanying the increase in the number of women working outside the home — full-time or part-time — has been a broadening of job opportunities. Growing numbers of women have moved into fields traditionally dominated by men. Some of the breakthroughs have been historic. In 1981, Sandra Day O'Connor became the first woman justice on the Supreme Court of the United States. In 1983, Sally K. Ride became the first American woman in space. And in 1984, Representative Geraldine A. Ferraro (D., N.Y.) became the first female vice presidential nominee of a major American political party. Significant advances have been occurring out of the limelight, too. For the first time since 1946, women in 1982 earned more than half of the bachelor's degrees granted by American colleges. Changes have also occurred on a more intangible level. For many women, working has provided intellectual stimulation and enhanced their self-esteem as well as their physical and emotional health.

Continuing problems

The changes have not created a paradise for working women, however. Balancing the demands of a career with the responsibilities of marriage and, especially, of motherhood has created special problems for many women. The overwhelming majority of women still work in the types of jobs that have traditionally been held by women, and relatively few women have moved into top-level positions. And despite laws prohibiting sex discrimination and requiring equal pay for equal work, women, for a variety of reasons, earn an average of only 62 cents for every dollar earned by men.

As a result of this wage gap, the battle for economic equality has opened on a new front — comparable pay, or equal pay for work of equal value. Supporters of comparable pay contend that women's jobs have been systematically undervalued and so have paid less than jobs demanding the same skill and responsibility held by men.

The attention currently being paid to the recent movement of women into the workplace sometimes obscures the fact that many American women held paying jobs in the past. In colonial

The author:
Peggy A. Simpson is an economics correspondent for Hearst Newspapers and a columnist for *Working Woman* magazine.

times, for example — during the 1700's — workers were in short supply, so women were expected to work, and their labor was highly valued. In colonial Boston, about 1 out of every 10 merchants and shopkeepers was a woman. Colonial women also worked as butchers, gunsmiths, midwives, and printers.

Early in the 1800's, as Americans became more prosperous and life became more settled, many people came to believe that the ideal woman was the lady of the house, not the woman of business. Thus, economic opportunities for women narrowed. The number of women shopkeepers and retailers dropped. Many professions, such as law and medicine, became closed to women, and the vast majority of middle-class and upper-class women devoted themselves exclusively to domestic concerns.

Opportunity in the factory

At the same time, many poorer women flocked to the factories that sprang up as the Industrial Revolution spread to the United States from Europe. These factory jobs usually paid more than domestic work and other jobs open to women. And the factories, unable to attract large numbers of men, who were still needed on the farm, welcomed — and even sought out — women workers. However, by the 1840's, an influx of immigrant labor and an exodus of men from the farm, where work had become increasingly mechanized, pushed many of the women factory workers into the lower-paying jobs. Nevertheless, factory work — and domestic labor as maids, cooks, and governesses — remained the two chief options for working women throughout the 1800's.

By 1870, women made up 15 per cent of the United States labor force, and a few women had moved into what previously had been an all-male job — clerical work. As business expanded and offices became mechanized, the number of clerical and secretarial jobs grew and women rushed to fill them. Most office work was considered dead-end work, however, with little opportunity for advancement to higher-paying managerial positions.

Women in blue-collar jobs did not fare much better than their sisters in offices. Many trade jobs were completely closed to women. And laws passed to protect women from potentially dangerous working conditions often had an unexpected effect. By limiting the number of hours women could work or by preventing them from working at night, they denied women access to some better-paying, higher-skilled jobs.

Job opportunities for women, especially in industry, increased during World War I as men left the factories to enter military service. After the war, the number of working women continued to climb. By 1920, women made up 21 per cent of the labor force and worked in a wide variety of jobs.

During the Great Depression of the 1930's, as jobs became scarce, disapproval of working women grew along with the unemployment

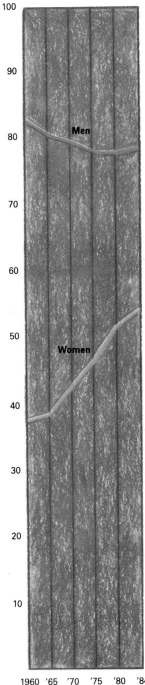

Percentage of Men and Women Who Work

1960 '65 '70 '75 '80 '84

Source: U.S. Bureau of the Census.

The great majority of women who work are still in such traditionally "female" fields as teaching, nursing, and clerical work. In addition, for a variety of reasons, women continue to earn less, on the average, than men at every level of education.

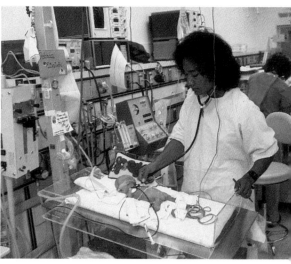

The Wage Gap

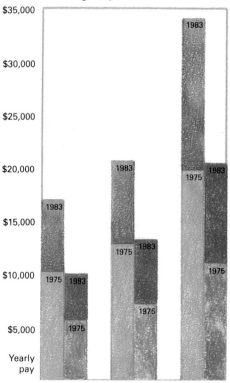

Source: U.S. Bureau of the Census.

rate. Many people felt that women, especially married women, should not take jobs that could be held by men. World War II changed all that as — once again — women replaced men in the factories that supplied the war effort. "Rosie the Riveter" became a national symbol, and women worked as electricians, welders, and drill-press operators.

After the war, many of these women workers were laid off or fired when factories were temporarily shut down. Some lost their jobs because returning servicemen who had been permanently employed before the war were supposed to be given their previous job or an equivalent. However, other women were not rehired in accordance with their seniority when the factories reopened. About this time, attitudes toward working women came full circle as many people came to believe that women should devote themselves totally to their family, a belief furthered by women's magazines of that period that praised the "happy housewife."

The economic boom and the feminist movement

The reality of the 1950's was quite different from the picture painted by the magazines. The number of women, especially married women, working outside the home began to grow again. The economic boom of the 1950's created more jobs, especially jobs — such as clerical positions — traditionally filled by women. In 1940, 17 per cent of married American women worked for pay. By 1950, that number had risen to 24 per cent and by 1959, to 36 per cent. However, women on the average still earned only about half the average wage paid to men.

The movement of women into the work force took off in the mid-1960's, due to a number of social and economic factors. The feminist movement — a movement advocating economic, political, and social equality between women and men — had a major impact on women's attitudes toward employment and the job options available to them. Newly formed women's rights groups began demanding equal employment and educational opportunities, such as admission to professional schools.

Also beginning in the 1960's, women won several powerful legal weapons to help them in their fight. The Equal Pay Act of 1963 mandated equal pay for equal work. The Civil Rights Act of 1964 outlawed discrimination by private employers, unions, and employment agencies on the basis of color, race, national origin, religion, or sex. In 1972, the Equal Employment Opportunity Act extended this coverage to federal, state, and local governments and educational institutions.

Economic necessity also fueled the increase in the number of working women. One-third of all American women are either divorced, separated, or married to men who earn less than $15,000 a year. In addition, many American families, buffeted by inflation and recession, discovered the economic benefits a second paycheck

Women in Some Traditionally Male Jobs		
	Per cent female in	
Job Group	1970	1980
Insurance adjusters, examiners, and investigators	29.6	60.2
Underwriters	0.0	58.3
Bus drivers	28.3	45.8
Chief executives of government agencies	0.0	25.6
Urban planners	12.6	24.1
Professional athletes	11.2	23.8
Photographers	14.8	23.5
Chemists	11.7	20.1
College economics teachers	7.6	20.0
Agricultural inspectors	0.0	17.1
Judges	6.1	17.1
Veterinarians	5.3	13.3
Telephone installers and repairers	2.8	11.5
Hunters and trappers	0.0	11.4
Farmers	4.7	9.8
Metallurgical engineers	0.8	5.2
Police	5.1	8.0
Nuclear engineers	0.0	3.7

Source: U.S. Bureau of the Census.

As job opportunities for women have expanded, increasing numbers of women have moved into fields that have traditionally been dominated by men, such as science, law enforcement, business, and blue-collar jobs such as mining.

can provide. In fact, the influx of women into the labor force has significantly boosted the number of middle- and upper-class families. In 1964, 28 per cent of American families earned more than $25,000 a year (adjusted to today's dollars), compared with 46 per cent in 1984. Also affecting the increase in women working outside the home have been myriad other factors, ranging from better methods of family planning to labor-saving devices for the home.

Explaining the rise in the number of working women, Commissioner of Labor Statistics Janet L. Norwood of the Department of Labor said, "Women are looking at themselves in different ways, and they believe they need to have more identity of their own. I think society has accepted that. Part of the reason women work is

that they need to — we're pushing 10 million women who are supporting families on their own — and husband-wife workers have become accustomed to a standard of living that requires two incomes. But it also is more popular for women to be working."

Norwood says some people expect that since inflation was much lower in 1983 and 1984 than it was in the late 1970's and early 1980's, many women will revert to being full-time homemakers again. She disagrees. "Those who say that with recovery, women will go home again are just crazy. It's not going to happen."

Statistics seem to support Norwood's assertion. According to the U.S. Bureau of the Census, the number of women in the labor force increased by 171 per cent between 1947 and 1980. Most of these new workers took new jobs, created as the U.S. economy shifted from one based on the production of industrial goods, such as steel and automobiles, to one based on providing services, such as data processing and retail sales work.

In the 1970's, women took 57 per cent of all new jobs, and, according to the U.S. Department of Labor, women may fill up to 67 per cent of all new jobs created during the next 10 years. Even poor economic conditions have not slowed the trend. During the recession of the early 1980's, the number of working women grew by more than 3 million. In contrast, only about 200,000 men were added to the employment rolls during that period.

The biggest increase has been among married women, and, especially, women with small children. In 1970, 12.1 million mothers, or 40 per cent, worked for pay. By 1984, that number had jumped to a record 19.5 million, or 60 per cent of mothers. The percentage of working mothers with children under the age of 3 rose from 30 per cent to 50 per cent.

As the number of American working women has risen, so too have the employment opportunities available to them. Many women now work in jobs once considered off-limits. The nomination of Geraldine Ferraro as the Democratic Party's vice presidential candidate has dramatized the remarkable changes that have allowed women to aspire to the highest offices — and have given women a chance to win them. For example, the Census Bureau reported that between 1970 and 1980, the percentage of women lawyers jumped from 4.8 per cent to 13.8 per cent; women physicians, from 9 per cent to 13.4 per cent; and women chief executives of government agencies, from zero to an astonishing 25.6 per cent.

These numbers are certain to continue to rise as women now in school move into the job market. Currently, about one-third of law students and medical students are women. Slightly more than 13 per cent of all bachelor's degrees in engineering went to women in 1983, compared with only 0.4 per cent in 1966.

The largest jump, however, has been in business. The number of women specializing in business in college soared by 300 per cent from 1966 to 1978, compared with only a 66 per cent increase for men. More women are also starting their own businesses.

Women are also moving into blue-collar jobs traditionally held by men. More women are working, for example, as carpenters and miners. However, these increases have been smaller than those in many white-collar jobs because, in part, the recession hit blue-collar jobs harder, slowing hiring and resulting in many layoffs.

Effects on workplace, home, and family

The effects of the revolution in the market place have been profound and wide-ranging. American women, more highly skilled and educated than at any time in the past, have given business and industry a larger talent pool to draw on. In addition, the U.S. economy would be severely damaged if American women left their jobs. The World Bank, an agency of the United Nations, estimates that U.S. women are responsible for 44 per cent of the U.S. gross national product (GNP) — the total amount of goods and services produced — an amount larger than the total GNP of most other countries in the world. In addition, the U.S. Department of Commerce estimates that working women's increased earnings have helped fuel a boom in the fast food, clothing, and entertainment industries.

Opposite page: The rapid rise in the number of mothers working outside the home has led to changes in the way children are cared for. More children are now enrolled in day-care facilities, and more fathers are helping with child-care responsibilities.

Other changes have occurred as well. Many colleges have established new programs or altered existing ones to serve women who want to reenter the job market after years of homemaking. The broader range of occupations open to women and the more lucrative salaries some of the jobs offer have lured women away from some traditionally female professions. For example, between 1970 and 1980, the number of women grade-school teachers dropped from 83.9 per cent to 75.4 per cent.

The increase in working women has also had far-reaching effects on life styles, marriage, and the American family. Economic independence has given women the option of leaving bad marriages, living on their own, or remaining single. American women are also marrying later, having fewer children, and waiting longer to have them. In the past, many career women remained unmarried or, if they did marry, remained childless. Today, many women are trying to have both a career and children. However, it is often difficult to balance the demands of both. Although many husbands now help with household chores, in many cases, working women, even those working full-time, still shoulder most housekeeping responsibilities.

Child care is usually the working wife's responsibility, too. For example, a study of Harvard University medical school graduates revealed that 50 per cent of the women physicians, but none of the male physicians, surveyed had made career adjustments—working fewer hours or taking less demanding positions—because of family demands. In addition, many women may not only feel guilty about spending too little time with their children but also feel guilty about not working harder on the job.

A number of research studies have revealed that working seems to be a tonic for many women, however. For example, in a survey of 2,300 women working in a variety of jobs, health economist Barbara Wolfe of the University of Wisconsin at Madison found that work can actually lead to improvements in health for many women.

The push for comparable pay

But working women continue to face serious obstacles despite the advances, benefits, and breakthroughs. Most women still work in traditionally "female" jobs—such as clerical workers, retail sales clerks, and nurses. About 80 per cent of women workers are clustered into only 20 of the Labor Department's 427 job categories. Only 5 per cent of top executives in U.S. businesses are female. And only 3.6 per cent of women workers earn more than $30,000 a year, in stark contrast to the 25.1 per cent of men who do. In 1982, 60 per cent of all women who worked had earnings below the poverty level—$9,862 for a family of four—compared with 33 per cent of employed men.

On the average, women still earn only 62 cents for every dollar earned by men, a figure that has remained stubbornly constant for more than 30 years. In 1981, the National Academy of Sciences conducted a study of this wage gap. It concluded that the gap resulted from a number of complex factors: Women work in low-paying jobs, they leave the job market to bear and raise children, and they often have less seniority and sometimes less education than men. However, the academy reported that about half the wage gap was probably due to discrimination.

To eliminate the wage gap, some unions and women's groups have turned to *comparable pay*, an approach that goes beyond the issue of equal pay for equal work. This new approach calls instead for equal pay for jobs of comparable worth.

In 1981, the Supreme Court of the United States legitimized comparable worth claims by ruling that women could bring a civil rights suit alleging wage discrimination even though higher-paid men were not doing exactly the same type of work. The case was brought by female prison guards in Oregon who sued the state because they were being paid $200 a month less for guarding women than male guards earned for guarding men. In 1984, comparable pay complaints were pending against many state governments, including

How Some Jobs Compare

Job Title	Monthly Salary	Number of Points
Minnesota		
Registered nurse (Female)	$1,723	275
Vocational education teacher (Male)	2,260	275
Health program representative (F)	$1,590	238
Steam boiler attendant (M)	1,611	156
Data-processing coordinator (F)	$1,423	199
General repair worker (M)	1,564	134
San Jose, California		
Librarian I (F)	$ 750	288
Street sweeper operator (M)	758	124
Senior legal secretary (F)	$ 665	226
Senior carpenter (M)	1,040	226
Senior accounting clerk (F)	$ 638	210
Senior painter (M)	1,040	210
Washington		
Registered nurse (F)	$1,368	348
Highway engineer (M)	1,980	345
Laundry worker (F)	$ 884	105
Truck driver (M)	1,493	97
Secretary (F)	$1,122	197
Maintenance carpenter (M)	1,707	197

Source: National Committee on Pay Equity.

Studies to determine jobs of comparable worth rate positions by awarding points for the knowledge and skills required to do the job. Such studies have revealed that jobs held chiefly by women usually pay less than those held chiefly by men whether they were awarded the same number or even a greater number of points.

The nomination of Geraldine A. Ferraro as the 1984 Democratic vice presidential candidate symbolizes the historic breakthroughs achieved by women in the past 20 years.

Connecticut, Wisconsin, and Hawaii; against a number of cities, including Chicago, Philadelphia, and Los Angeles; and against a number of private employers.

The biggest victory for comparable worth so far has been a case involving employees of the state of Washington. In December 1983, a federal judge ruled that the state was practicing "institutionalized" discrimination against its women employees. He ordered the state to pay the women from $800 million to $1 billion in back pay and to increase wages by 20 per cent in jobs held chiefly by women.

The judge based his ruling on a 1974 job-evaluation study conducted for the state of Washington by a consulting firm. The consultants examined 121 classes of jobs that were dominated chiefly by members of one sex. They rated each job, awarding points for the knowledge and skill required to do the job, the mental effort needed, the level of responsibility involved, and the working conditions. The study revealed that among jobs receiving the same number of points, those held chiefly by women paid an average of 20 to 30 per cent less than jobs held chiefly by men. For example, the jobs of secretary and maintenance carpenter were awarded the same number of points — 197. Yet secretaries earned an average of $1,122 a month, while maintenance carpenters earned an average of $1,707 a month.

Comparable pay — the pros and the cons

Opponents of comparable pay argue that the chief factor determining the wages paid for a particular job is the market place and that wages reflect prevailing market rates. They contend, for example, that some jobs pay more than others because of shortages of workers to fill those positions or because society places a greater value on those kinds of jobs. They contend that many women choose to take low-paying jobs because such jobs are less demanding. For instance, they may require less overtime work. They also argue that upgrading wages in "women's" jobs could cost American business an estimated $150 billion a year, triggering a massive round of inflation, and could lead to federal controls over wages. Finally, they question the legitimacy of job comparison studies, contending that it is impossible to meaningfully equate such diverse jobs as, for example, painter and accounting clerk.

Supporters of comparable pay say adjusting wages on the basis of the skills, training, and responsibility required in a job is the only way to eliminate unfairness in a labor market that remains largely segregated by sex. This segregation, they argue, is the legacy of past discrimination. They point out, for example, that in the past, many companies routinely maintained separate pay scales for men and women. And until the Supreme Court outlawed the practice in 1973, jobs listed in newspaper help-wanted ads were usually classified as "male" or "female."

Supporters of comparable pay argue that wages are determined by a number of factors, such as union contracts and minimum wage laws. They argue that society and industry have consistently under-valued jobs performed chiefly by women simply because they *are* performed by women. Finally, they point out that many large employers already conduct job-evaluation studies, rating diverse jobs in order to determine pay scales.

A look to the future

Issues for working women in the future inevitably will include some of today's most difficult problems — pay equity and trade-offs between career and personal relationships. Many barriers to the working woman have been scaled. But others remain.

Ruth M. Milkman, a professor of sociology at Queens College in New York City who specializes in women and work, believes that despite the advances, working women still have a long way to go. In many ways, she contends, attitudes have outrun behavior.

"The increase in the number of working women has helped change people's attitudes toward working women and their image in the media," Milkman says. "There is now a consensus in the country that women should have equal opportunity in the workplace. But the reality is quite different.

"Women do have more options. But they are still segregated in a relatively few, generally low-level jobs. Although the talents of women in the professions are increasingly being used, those of most women are not. Society does not take child care seriously. The United States still does not provide quality child care for the children of working mothers the way nearly all other industrialized countries do. And most men do not handle their share of domestic responsibility."

Fifteen years ago, the famous anthropologist Margaret Mead wrote, "We are in the midst of a tremendous revolution in the roles of men and women. The only prediction that can be made with certainty is that enormous and continuous readjustment must be made by, and new learning will be demanded of, both sexes in the quarter century ahead." The words were no less true in 1984 than they were in 1969.

For further reading:

Berkin, Carol Ruth, and Norton, M. B. *Women of America: A History*. Houghton, 1979.

Degler, Carl N. *At Odds: Women and the Family in America from the Revolution to the Present*. Oxford, 1980.

Friedan, Betty. *The Feminine Mystique*. Norton, 1963.

Harris, Janet. *Thursday's Daughters: The Story of Women Working in America*. Harper, 1977.

Mitchell, Joyce S. *I Can Be Anything: Careers and Colleges for Young Women*. College Entrance Examination Board, 1978. Also in paperback from Bantam.

Steinem, Gloria. *Outrageous Acts and Everyday Rebellions*. Holt, 1983.

By Jay Myers

Don't Gamble with Your Heart

Bad personal habits can increase your blood
cholesterol level, possibly leading to a heart
attack — but good habits can reduce the level.

"The cholesterol controversy is over!" screamed a magazine headline. Decades of debate climaxed in January 1984, when an agency of the United States government announced evidence that the use of special diets and medication to reduce the amount of a fatty substance called cholesterol circulating in the blood lowers the risk of heart disease.

The evidence came from a 10-year, $150-million investigation conducted by the National Heart, Lung, and Blood Institute (NHLBI), an agency of the Department of Health and Human Services. The NHLBI studied the health of 3,806 men between the ages of 35 and 59. At the beginning of the investigation, all the men were healthy, but their blood contained above-average amounts of cholesterol — more than 265 milligrams per 100 milliliters of blood. NHLBI researchers first put the men on a moderate diet that lowered their blood cholesterol by 3.5 per cent in three months. Half of the group then received daily doses of *cholestyramine* (pronounced KOH leh STYR uh meen), a drug that lowers blood cholesterol. The other half served as a control group, receiving a *placebo* — a substance that resembled the drug but contained no medicine. Neither the men being tested nor the doctors who examined them knew who received the drug. The doctors urged all the men to stay on the diet.

Doctors monitored the men's health for 7 to 10 years. They reported that the men who had been given cholestyramine suffered 155 heart attacks. At the end of 10 years, the men still being moni-

Apolipoprotein,
A puh lihp uh PROH teen:
Any of certain proteins located
on the surfaces of lipoproteins.
Apolipoproteins help to guide
lipoproteins through the body.

Cholesterol,
kuh LEHS tuh rohl:
A fatty substance found in all
animal cells, but in no plant
cells.

Cholesterol count:
The number of milligrams
of cholesterol in 100 milliliters
of blood.

Fat:
　Monounsaturated fat,
　*MAHN oh uhn SATCH uh RAY
　tihd*:
　A fat that seems to reduce
　cholesterol count slightly.

　Polyunsaturated fat,
　*PAHL ee uhn SATCH uh RAY
　tihd*:
　A fat that reduces cholesterol
　count.

　Saturated fat,
　SATCH uh RAY tihd:
　A fat that increases
　cholesterol count.

Lipoprotein,
LIHP uh PROH teen:
　**High-density
　lipoprotein (HDL):**
　A substance that removes
　cholesterol from artery walls.
　**Low-density
　lipoprotein (LDL):**
　A substance that delivers
　cholesterol to cells.

The author:
Jay Myers is a senior
editor of THE WORLD
BOOK YEAR BOOK and
SCIENCE YEAR.

tored had 13.4 per cent less blood cholesterol than at the start of the study. By contrast, the men who had been receiving the placebo had an average drop in blood cholesterol of only 4.9 per cent, and they suffered 187 heart attacks. Furthermore, the men who took the drug had fewer other symptoms of heart disease such as chest pains and poor performance in exercise tests, and they needed fewer coronary by-pass operations than did the control group. In addition, an analysis of the NHLBI data showed that men who lower their cholesterol by 25 per cent cut their risk of heart attack in half.

"The results have implications for millions of Americans," said study director Basil M. Rifkind, a physician specializing in *metabolic diseases*, disorders that affect chemical reactions in the body. Rifkind said that if more Americans went on low-fat, low-cholesterol diets and took cholesterol-reducing drugs when their doctors said it was necessary, about 100,000 fewer Americans might die of heart attacks each year.

Heart disease is the number-one killer in the United States, claiming more than 500,000 lives per year. Particularly at risk are people who smoke, have high blood pressure, or have high blood cholesterol levels.

Women are much less likely than men to have heart attacks. This is why the NHLBI studied men rather than women. In both women and men, however, a high level of cholesterol is literally too much of a good thing, because cholesterol—despite its role in heart disease—is a vital substance. Cholesterol makes up part of the membrane of every cell in the body; the liver uses cholesterol to produce *bile acids*, which aid digestion; and certain other organs use it to manufacture *hormones*, chemical substances that influence many body activities.

The trouble with cholesterol arises when there is too much of it in the blood and it begins to accumulate in artery walls. Fatty deposits called *plaques* form, and the artery walls grow thick and tough. This hardening of the arteries is called *atherosclerosis*, and it can continue for years. The arteries can become so clogged that blood barely squeezes through the narrow passageways. Eventually, a blood clot may form in a clogged coronary artery and prevent blood from reaching the heart, causing a heart attack. In this kind of heart attack, blocked-off blood fails to deliver vital oxygen to a portion of the heart, so the deprived heart tissue dies.

Atherosclerosis often begins in the teen years and can proceed for decades without the victim's knowledge. "You can live with a lot of atherosclerosis," says pathologist Robert W. Wissler of the University of Chicago Medical Center. "You go along feeling fine, not knowing anything is wrong. Then one day, at 55, you die of a heart attack."

Cholesterol travels through the blood in little drops, each surrounded by a ball of protein and fats. This round bundle is called a

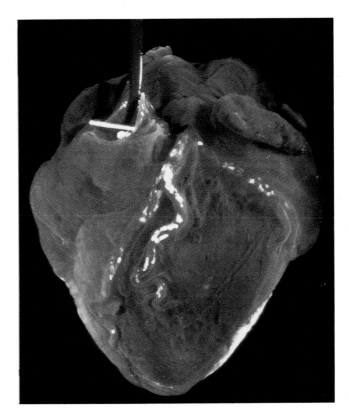

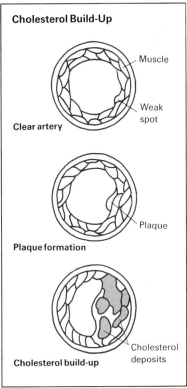

Cholesterol Build-Up

Muscle

Weak spot

Clear artery

Plaque

Plaque formation

Cholesterol deposits

Cholesterol build-up

lipoprotein. There are several types of lipoprotein, but by far the most common are *low-density lipoproteins* (LDL's). Most cholesterol coursing through the blood is in the form of LDL's. It is LDL cholesterol that travels from the liver to other cells to make membranes. And it usually is LDL cholesterol that accumulates on artery walls.

About 20 to 25 per cent of the cholesterol in the blood travels in *high-density lipoproteins* (HDL's). Scientists think that these lipoproteins *remove* cholesterol from artery walls and carry it back to the liver, which can then excrete it in bile. Because they help rid the body of excess cholesterol, HDL's seem to help protect people against heart disease. Thus, HDL cholesterol is called "good cholesterol," while LDL cholesterol is known as "bad cholesterol."

Cholesterol in the blood originates from two sources. Our diets provide some of it. The liver, the body's main chemical factory, produces most of it, however — about 1,000 milligrams per day. This would be enough cholesterol to fill our needs even if we ate none.

But Americans do eat cholesterol — too much of it, perhaps 500 milligrams daily — by dining on such foods as eggs, meat, and dairy products. When we eat too much cholesterol, it builds up in our blood. And when we eat too much *saturated fat* — one of three kinds of fat, the kind in whole milk, butter, and most meats — the liver is stimulated to produce even more cholesterol than it usually does.

Yellow deposits of cholesterol line arteries of a heart, *photo, above left.* Such dangerous deposits are the result of a build-up of matter that begins at a weak spot in the wall of a clear artery, *above, top to bottom.* First, *plaque* — a fibrous substance containing cholesterol — forms in the artery muscle, swelling the wall. Further accumulations then narrow the artery drastically, sometimes blocking it entirely.

What Did the Study Prove?

A laboratory monkey eats large quantities of cholesterol each day and soon develops fatty deposits in its arteries. Scientists have seen this happen for decades in several kinds of laboratory animals, and so they have long linked high levels of blood cholesterol with an increased risk of heart disease. Other evidence pointing to the same conclusion includes the discovery that the material in arterial deposits is mostly cholesterol, studies showing that people with high levels of blood cholesterol have high rates of heart attack, and the high percentage of early heart attacks among individuals who have elevated levels of blood cholesterol because of the disease familial hypercholesterolemia.

Because of such evidence, scientists have long suspected that a lowering of blood cholesterol levels would reduce the risk of heart disease. This suspicion was not proved, however, until the National Heart, Lung, and Blood Institute (NHLBI) conducted a 10-year investigation and announced its results in January 1984.

The study proved that men with very high levels of blood cholesterol benefit from drugs that lower these levels. That in itself was a landmark discovery, yet other questions remain. Would men with moderately high cholesterol levels benefit from such drugs? What about women? And what about people who lower their cholesterol levels with diet instead of drugs?

The NHLBI investigators believe it is scientifically sound to extend their findings to women and men with moderately high cholesterol levels. And they think diets that lower cholesterol benefit many people. "Extensive data suggest that the body doesn't particularly care whether you lower cholesterol by diet or drug," notes Charles Glueck, director of the General Clinical Research Center at the University of Cincinnati Medical School. "You probably get a very similar response." Originally, in fact, the NHLBI investigators considered conducting a study on diet, but decided it would be difficult to carry out effectively and might cost more than $1 billion.

Other experts argue that the study offers no proof that diet helps to reduce the risk of heart disease. Hilarie Hoting, a registered dietitian and director of nutrition and consumer affairs for the American Meat Institute, an industry organization, says "The study was done specifically to test the effects of lowering blood cholesterol by drugs. It was not done to test the diet hypothesis."

The drug used in the NHLBI study does not affect the food in the stomach. Rather, it works in the intestine. Normally, the liver expels cholesterol as part of the bile acids, which travel down the intestinal tract. As the acids flow through the end of the small intestine, they are largely reabsorbed. But when a patient takes the drug, the acids combine chemically with the drug in the intestine, preventing reabsorption.

Allan D. Sniderman, a cardiologist at McGill University in Montreal, Canada, comments, "You cannot extrapolate to women, or to normal cholesterol [levels], or to diet." However, concerning the moderate approach to controlling dietary cholesterol and fat, Sniderman says, "You never argue against a policy of moderation." [J.M.]

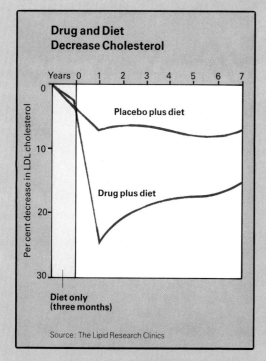

Drug and Diet Decrease Cholesterol

Placebo plus diet

Drug plus diet

Diet only
(three months)

Source: The Lipid Research Clinics

A diet and drug cut LDL cholesterol better than the diet and a placebo – a substance resembling the drug but without medicine.

The typical American diet is rich in saturated fats. This is unfortunate, because the two other types of fat do not stimulate cholesterol production. *Polyunsaturated fats*, including such vegetable oils as corn, cottonseed, and safflower oils, reduce cholesterol levels. *Monounsaturated fats*, such as olive oil and peanut oil, also seem to lower cholesterol levels, but not as much as polyunsaturated fats do.

An investigation called the Seven Countries Study highlighted the danger of a diet that is high in saturated fats. The 1970 study measured the dietary habits and heart attack rates among 12,770 men in Finland, Greece, Italy, Japan, the Netherlands, the United States, and Yugoslavia. The investigators found that in the United States, where men consumed about 18 per cent of their calories in saturated fats, deaths due to heart attack were about four times as common as in Japan, where the typical diet was only 3 per cent saturated fat.

Scientists investigating the causes of excessive cholesterol levels have found that genetic defects can also contribute to cholesterol build-up. For example, geneticist Jan L. Breslow at Rockefeller University in New York City discovered in 1983 that a defect in the gene that makes *apolipoprotein A1* — the main protein in HDL — may prevent some people from having enough HDL cholesterol. Such people do not eliminate cholesterol from the body efficiently, and tend to die of heart attacks when they are young. In the early 1980's, pathologist Robert W. Mahley of the University of California in San Francisco found that defects in another substance, apolipoprotein E, can interfere with the liver's ability to collect and eliminate cholesterol.

And in 1974, geneticists Joseph L. Goldstein and Michael S. Brown at the University of Texas Health Sciences Center in Dallas discovered that people with a disease called *familial hypercholesterolemia* (FH) have a defect in the gene responsible for the production of *LDL receptors*. In healthy individuals, these receptors — large molecules on the surfaces of cells — pluck LDL's out of the bloodstream so that the cells can use them. However, people who have the defective gene make

The Risk of Cholesterol

The risk of heart attack goes up with increases in blood cholesterol, as shown in a United States study of white males aged 30 through 59.

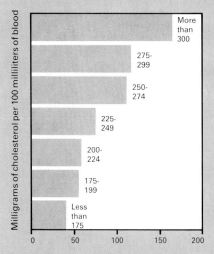

Heart attacks per 1,000 men in 10 years

An international study showed the fatal results of high cholesterol levels among men aged 40 through 59 who had no prior sign of heart disease.

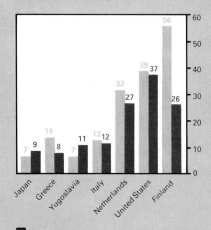

■ Fatal heart attacks per 10,000 men per year

☐ Percentage of men whose cholesterol count was greater than 250

A Safe Bet for Your Heart

Improve your chances of enjoying good coronary health by eating foods with little or no cholesterol and saturated fat — "OK Foods," *below* — and minimizing your intake of "Foods to Avoid," *bottom*.

OK Foods

BREADS	CEREALS, PASTAS, AND DESSERTS	SOUPS	CRACKERS	FATS AND OILS
Bagels; bread; buns; English muffins; pita bread; tortillas; modified* quick breads such as biscuits, cornbread, muffins, pancakes, soft rolls, and waffles	Ready-to-eat and cooked cereals; spaghetti; macaroni; noodles; modified fat* desserts such as layer cakes, sheet cakes, cupcakes, cookies, and pies	Broth; bouillon; clam chowder; minestrone; chicken noodle, onion, split pea, tomato, and vegetarian vegetable soups	Animal crackers; bread sticks; graham crackers; matzos; melba toast; oyster crackers; pretzels; rye crackers; saltines; and zwieback	Margarines listing a vegetable oil as first ingredient†; safflower, corn, sunflower, soybean, and cottonseed oils; salad dressings and mayonnaise made with recommended oil

Foods to Avoid

BREADS	CEREALS, PASTAS, AND DESSERTS	SOUPS	CRACKERS	FATS AND OILS
Bagels made with eggs or cheese; butter rolls; cheese breads; croissants; egg breads; commercial biscuits, doughnuts, muffins, pancakes, sweet rolls, and waffles	Granola-type cereals with coconut or coconut oil; chow mein noodles; cheesecake; sweet rolls; and commercial cakes, cookies, pie crusts, and pies	Chunky soups; cream of potato, mushroom, celery, chicken, and cheese soups; vichyssoise	Butter crackers; cheese crackers; and crackers made with coconut or palm oil	Butter; chocolate; lard; margarines listing animal fat first; coconut, palm, and palm kernel oil; salad dressings made with sour cream or cheese

* Modified to contain such ingredients as skim milk, margarine, vegetable oil, and egg substitute.
† In addition, the nutrition labeling should indicate twice as much polyunsaturated fat as saturated fat.

EGGS, MILK, AND IMITATION MILK	MILK PRODUCTS	VEGETABLES AND FRUITS	BEEF, LAMB, AND PORK	POULTRY, FISH, AND MISC. MEATS
Egg substitute; egg whites; milk, dry milk, and buttermilk with 1% or less butterfat; evaporated skim milk; hot cocoa‡, nondairy creamers made from polyunsaturated fat	Custards‡§; ice milk; puddings‡; sherbet; skim or low-fat yogurt; dry curd or low-fat cottage cheese; cheese with up to 8% butterfat	Most vegetables and fruits	Lean, well-trimmed meat	Chicken and turkey without skin; fish and shellfish, not commercially fried; pheasant; rabbit; venison; wild duck, liver#

EGGS, MILK, AND IMITATION MILK	MILK PRODUCTS	VEGETABLES AND FRUITS	BEEF, LAMB, AND PORK	POULTRY, FISH, AND MISC. MEATS
Egg yolks; whole milk; buttermilk made from whole milk; milk with 1.5% or more butterfat; condensed, dried whole, and evaporated whole milk; nondairy coffee creamers	Ice cream; yogurt made from whole milk; cheese made from cream or whole milk; cream cheese; creamed cottage cheese; sour cream; whipping cream; and nondairy whipped topping	Coconuts; large quantities of avocados and olives	Prime and other heavily marbled meat; ground meat; commercially fried meat; canned and packaged luncheon meat; bacon; chili meat; corned beef; frankfurters; mutton; salami; sausage; spareribs	Poultry skin; commercially fried poultry, fish, and shellfish; domestic duck; goose; opossum; raccoon; venison sausage; brains; chitterlings; gizzard; heart; kidney

‡Mixed or made with milk that contains 1% or less butterfat.
§Made with egg whites or egg substitute.
#Up to 3 ounces per month.

Source: American Heart Association.

Cholesterol in Foods

Milligrams of cholesterol in popular foods. Foods from plants are omitted because they contain no cholesterol.

Meat, 3 ounces

Beef

Eye of round, lean	56
Ground	88
Liver	372
Rib roast, lean and fat	70

Chicken, fried

dark meat	78
light meat	74

Ham, roasted	80

Lamb, loin chop

lean	80
lean and fat	82

Packaged meat

Bacon, 2 slices	11
Bologna, beef and pork, 1 slice	16
Braunschweiger, 1 slice	44
Frankfurters, beef, each	27
Salami, beef and pork, 1 slice	18

Seafood, 3 ounces

Clams, raw	42
Crabmeat, canned	85
Flounder	59
Haddock	51
Oysters, raw	42
Salmon, pink, canned	34
Salmon, red	60
Sardines	85
Shrimp, dry pack	128
Sole	59
Tuna, chunk light	55

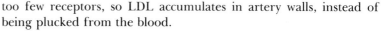

too few receptors, so LDL accumulates in artery walls, instead of being plucked from the blood.

About 1 in 500 Americans has FH. Most of them have inherited a defective gene from one parent and a normal gene from the other parent, so their bodies make some LDL receptors, but not enough. Such people may have double the normal cholesterol levels, and many of them suffer heart attacks in their 30's or 40's.

About 1 person in 1 million inherits a defective gene from each parent. These people cannot make any LDL receptors, so their cholesterol counts may soar above 1,000, making heart disease almost inevitable. Some of these people even have heart attacks during childhood.

Such sky-high counts are obviously dangerous. Not nearly so obvious is what levels of blood cholesterol are safe. The average cholesterol count for middle-aged adults in the United States is 215. However, in a country with more than 500,000 fatal heart attacks annually, average cholesterol levels are not necessarily healthy. A safe level may be closer to that of the average adult in Japan — 170 to 180.

Cholesterol count alone provides only a general indication of danger, however, because not all cholesterol is equally dangerous. "The higher the LDL cholesterol, the greater the risk of coronary disease," says cardiologist Allan D. Sniderman of McGill University in Montreal, Canada. "But the higher the HDL cholesterol, the less the risk."

Some doctors measure the ratio of LDL to HDL cholesterol to assess the patient's risk of heart disease. The average ratio among men aged 40 through 44 in the United States is 3.1 to 1. Women the same ages have an average ratio of 2.2 to 1. Some medical researchers believe that both ratios are too high, and recommend cutting them to 2 to 1.

Some doctors believe that the best way to spot people at risk for heart disease is to measure their apolipoproteins. According to Sniderman, cholesterol measurements uncover only about 10 per cent of people with abnormal coronary arteries, whereas measurements of *apolipoprotein B* — the main protein in LDL (bad) cholesterol — may detect as many as 50 to 65 per cent of those afflicted.

Many doctors also order a measurement of fatty compounds called *triglycerides*. These fats are a major source of energy for the body, and they also travel with lipoproteins through the blood. Scientists do not know whether a high triglyceride level, by itself, increases the risk of heart disease. However, doctors find that triglyceride measurements are useful in rounding out the picture of how a patient's body uses fats, oils, waxes, and *sterols* — solid alcohols, including cholesterol.

The American Medical Association recommends that people have at least their blood cholesterol measured by age 20 — and even ear-

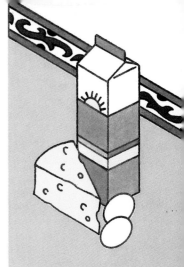

lier in families with FH. In addition, some doctors believe that children should be screened routinely. The American Health Foundation, a nonprofit group, estimates that as many as 25 to 30 per cent of Americans between the ages of 5 and 18 have "dangerously high" levels of cholesterol.

Most people who have high levels of cholesterol can improve their chances of avoiding heart disease by watching what they eat and how they live. They can quit smoking, for example, and exercise regularly. And, if diet and exercise do not lower their cholesterol level enough, their doctors may prescribe special drugs.

If a patient's cholesterol level is in the top 20 per cent of the person's age group, a doctor may recommend a cholesterol-reducing diet published by the American Heart Association (AHA) in May 1984. This diet lowers blood cholesterol by gradually decreasing the consumption of cholesterol and fat.

The diet has three phases. Phase 1 is a moderate diet for people with an above-average level of cholesterol, a family history of excessive blood fat, or other risk factors such as smoking and high blood pressure. In Phase 1, the patient's fat intake is reduced to 30 to 32 per cent of total calories, divided about equally among saturated, monounsaturated, and polyunsaturated fats. Also, the average daily intake of cholesterol is cut to less than 300 milligrams. On the average, people following Phase 1 will experience a 6 to 10 per cent drop in their blood cholesterol, reducing their risk of heart disease by as much as 20 per cent.

Phase 2 is a strict diet designed for patients who do not respond well to Phase 1, and for people with cholesterol counts of 250 and higher. Phase 2 cuts fat intake to 28 per cent of total calories and the consumption of cholesterol to less than 200 milligrams per day. This diet can result in a 10 to 15 per cent reduction in the level of blood cholesterol.

Phase 3 is an extremely strict diet for patients with very high cholesterol or LDL levels, and for people who have moderately high levels combined with a family history of coronary heart disease at an early age. Only 22 per cent of Phase 3 calories come from fat, and cholesterol intake is reduced to about 100 milligrams. Phase 3 usually brings the average cholesterol count down 15 to 20 per cent.

The AHA recommends Phase 1 for the general public, not just for people who are in danger of coronary disease. If you want to follow Phase 1, you will have to plan home meals according to an AHA food list, scrutinize labels for information on fats when shopping for food, and order with extra care when dining out.

Phase 1 calls for eating no more than 5 to 7 ounces of lean meat, poultry, or fish per day, and a maximum of two egg yolks per week. Poultry and fish should be eaten more often than red meat. All poultry, fish, and red meat should be baked, broiled, or roasted, rather than fried. Start exploring alternatives to meat as a main

Dairy Foods and Eggs

Cheese, 1 ounce	
American	27
Blue	21
Camembert	20
Cheddar	30
Cream	31
Swiss	26

Cottage cheese, 1 cup	
Creamed, 4% fat	
large curd	34
small curd	31
Low-fat, 1% fat	10
Uncreamed	10

Cream, 1 tablespoon	
Half-and-half	6
Coffee	10
Whipping	21

Eggs, large, each	274

Ice cream, 1 cup	
Regular	59
Rich	88

Ice milk, 1 cup	
Hardened	18
Soft serve	13
Sherbet	14

Milk, 1 cup	
Low-fat, 1% fat	10
Low-fat, 2% fat	18
Skim	5
Whole, 3.3% fat	33

Fats, 1 tablespoon	
Butter	31
Lard	12
Mayonnaise	8

Source: U.S. Department of Agriculture.

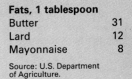

To Buy or Not to Buy?

(1) Soybean oil qualifies this product for the American Heart Association's OK food list (pages 138 and 139) as a dressing made with a recommended oil. Soybean oil is recommended because it has more than twice as much polyunsaturated fat as saturated fat.

NUTRITION INFORMATION PER SERVING
SERVING SIZE 1 TABLESPOON
SERVINGS PER CONTAINER 15 (APPROX.)

CALORIES	100
PROTEIN	0 (2)
CARBOHYDRATE	0
FAT	11 g
SODIUM	3 mg

(2) Eggs are very high in cholesterol, and the label does not say how much egg is in the product. However, eggs are also high in protein, so the "0" listing for protein indicates that the product contains only a small amount of egg and therefore is not high in cholesterol.

*INGREDIENTS: **(1)** SOYBEAN OIL, **(2)** EGGS, VINEGAR, WATER, LEMON JUICE, SPICES, AND POTASSIUM CHLORIDE.

*Soybean oil, vinegar, lemon juice, and spices are foods from plants, and so they have no cholesterol. Potassium chloride is a simple chemical used as a salt substitute.

A food label supplies nutrition information, and it lists ingredients according to their amounts. However, many labels, such as this one – from a low-sodium imitation mayonnaise – do not specify quantities of saturated fat and cholesterol in foods that contain these substances. Reading such a label in the light of a good general knowledge of nutrition can reveal whether the food contains too much of either substance.

course — meatless chili, for example. And when you do eat meat, trim the visible fat from red meat and the skin from chicken. Eat liver no more than once a week. Although nutritious, it is also high in cholesterol. Use margarine instead of butter, and skim or low-fat milk instead of whole milk.

The AHA also encourages people to eat complex carbohydrates — chemicals found in food grains, including wheat, corn, rye, oats, and rice. Pastas such as spaghetti, macaroni, and noodles contain large amounts of complex carbohydrates. In addition, the AHA recommends plenty of fruits and vegetables.

When you are shopping for food, check labels for the amount of fat per serving, the serving size, and the kind of fat. Nutritionists point out that a product "made of 100 per cent vegetable oil" may be high in saturated fats if the oil happens to be coconut or palm oil. On the other hand, a food whose label lists an ingredient containing a saturated fat may not contain much of the fat. A food label lists ingredients in the order of the amounts present in the food, with the main ingredient first. So if the ingredient containing the saturated fat is listed near the end of the label, the product may not have much of this fat in it. As a rule of thumb, you need to check only the first five ingredients listed; the rest will be present in such small amounts that they will not affect your cholesterol level.

Not all experts recommend a low-fat, low-cholesterol diet for the general public, however. Some researchers believe there is not enough proof that lowering dietary cholesterol reduces the average person's risk of heart disease. According to the United Egg Producers, an industry group, "Evidence continues to mount that dietary cholesterol has a minimal and highly variable effect on serum [blood] cholesterol, particularly in . . . the general public." Nevertheless, doctors generally believe cholesterol-reducing diets are appropriate, at least for people with high levels of blood cholesterol.

Certain personal habits also may affect cholesterol levels. Exercise tends to increase the level of HDL — the good cholesterol — and thus reduce the risk of heart disease. Smoking, on the other hand, lowers the HDL level. According to Bryant Stamford, director of the exercise physiology laboratory at the University of Louisville School of Medicine in Kentucky, "Smoking cancels the beneficial effects of running."

If changes in diet and personal habits do not lower a patient's cholesterol enough, the doctor may also prescribe medicine. One drug used for reducing cholesterol is cholestyramine, which was used in the NHLBI study. This drug comes as a yellow powder that is both foul tasting and expensive — a year's supply can cost $1,500 to $2,000.

One way or another, Americans have begun to take better care of their hearts. Millions have stopped smoking. Millions have also started exercising. And, according to the AHA, half the Americans with high blood pressure have had their condition detected and treated — a vast improvement over the 10 to 15 per cent who received treatment a decade ago. Furthermore, Americans are eating so much less cholesterol and saturated fat that, according to Rifkind, "Over the past 10 or 15 years, the average cholesterol count in the United States appears to have dropped from 230 or so to about 215."

As a result of this improvement in care, plus advances in medical treatment, the rate of fatal heart attacks in the United States has dropped some 30 per cent since the mid-1960's. And now that the facts from the NHLBI study are in, doctors hope that Americans will cut their consumption of cholesterol and fat even more sharply. Then, we may see a headline some day announcing that heart disease has lost its ranking as America's number-one killer.

For further reading:

American Heart Association. *AHA Cookbook*, 4th ed. David McKay, 1984.
——. *Heartbook: A Guide to Prevention and Treatment of Cardiovascular Diseases*. E. P. Dutton, 1980.
"Fending Off Cholesterol," *Changing Times*, June 1984.
Kolata, Gina. "Genetics and Cholesterol Metabolism," *Science*, February 1983.

lob|by|ist (lob′ē ist), *n*. a person who tries to influence members of a lawmaking body in their votes, or executives in their administration of laws, especially a member of a group (lobby) having special interests or favoring particular legislation.

By Frank Cormier

Lobbying the Lawmakers

A new breed of professional lobbyists, working
with political action committees, is
generating controversy in Washington, D.C.

In the 1984 elections for the United States Senate and House of
Representatives, organizations called *political action committees* (PAC's)
lavished at least $100 million in campaign contributions on the can-
didates. Set up by corporations, labor unions, and special-interest
groups, PAC's are now being recognized as the cutting edge of a
new type of lobbying because they use campaign contributions to
influence the policies and actions of Congress.

As a result, PAC's — and the lobbyists who advise them — are at
the center of a controversy for the role they are playing in the U.S.
political system. Some critics view them as a threat to representative
democracy, charging that their use of money as a lobbying tool is
corrupting. However, their defenders regard PAC's as a natural extension of the U.S. Constitution's guarantee of free expression. In
the months and years ahead, voters and politicians alike are certain
to give increasing thought to the wisdom of whether or not to restrict — or even outlaw — PAC's.

Evidence of PAC influence on Congress is considerable. Consider
the following examples:
■ By margins of better than 2 to 1, the Senate and House voted in
1982 to veto a Federal Trade Commission (FTC) regulation that
required used-car dealers to disclose to their customers known major defects in their used cars. The used-car dealers' PAC, which had

spent only $14,000 in the 1974 elections, parceled out more than $840,000 to Congress members between 1979 and 1982, while urging the legislators to block the FTC regulation. About 85 per cent of the recipients of that money voted against the FTC rule.

■ In 1981 the House voted down efforts to cut subsidies to dairy producers by $600 million over four years. Three dairy-industry PAC's had contributed $1.2 million to 1980 congressional candidates. During the debate on the subsidies, House Republican leader Robert H. Michel of Illinois noted, "The dairy industry spreads an awful lot of money around, and that gets reflected in votes out here, I'm afraid."

■ Representative Joseph P. Addabbo (D., N.Y.) was among the first in Congress to urge that the U.S. Army buy engines for its new M1 main battle tank from a second supplier. Avco Corporation of Greenwich, Conn., had been the sole supplier of the engines. In early 1983, the Army advertised for competing bids. Avco's PAC, which had given $500 to Addabbo's 1982 campaign, almost immediately gave him another $5,000. A few weeks later, Addabbo voted for legislation that prevented the Army from buying engines from any firm but Avco. He said the PAC money from Avco did not influence his abrupt change of position. He also said he needed campaign funds because his 1984 race for reelection might cost $500,000. Addabbo was not alone in accepting Avco money and supporting Avco's role as monopoly supplier. Of 71 House members who had received $36,540 in contributions from the Avco PAC in 1983, 59 supported the company's position, which prevailed.

Lobbying has probably never been free of controversy since it originated in the 1600's in England. There, the term *lobby-agents* was coined to describe those who approached members of the House of Commons, Great Britain's lower house of Parliament, in the lobby outside the room where voting took place. Although lobbying is often seen in an unfavorable light because of recurrent scandals and excesses, it plays an important and often invaluable role in public affairs. Very little happens in government without some kind of lobbying taking place. It is, after all, simply the act of trying to influence the passage or defeat of legislation or sway the policies or actions of government officials.

"Lobbying," observes Fred Wertheimer, president of Common Cause, a public-affairs lobby, "can provide information and facilitate the exchange of ideas. It can expand citizen participation and encourage government responsiveness and accountability. It can educate and aid in the development of public policy. It can contribute to the building of consensus and help turn theory into reality. It can play an essential role in making our political system work."

Many of the bills introduced in Congress each year are prepared,

The author:
Frank Cormier is a former White House correspondent for the Associated Press.

Lobbying has probably never been free of controversy, as evidenced by this political cartoon from the late 1800's.

in whole or in part, by interest groups and their lobbyists. Lobbyists present much of the testimony heard by congressional committees. Government is so complex that no Congress member can hope to be well informed on every issue that comes to a vote. Lobbyists can provide the information Congress members need to vote intelligently. And, because almost any important issue generates lobbying from opposing sides, legislators can weigh conflicting views.

Still, the popular image of lobbying is often one of bribery and corruption. In the 1800's, lobbyists were known to provide many Congress members, state legislators, and other government officials with "booze, blondes, and boodle" (liquor, women, and bribes) in an effort to sway official actions. Brazen corruption took place. Despite these abuses, the first U.S. law regulating lobbyists was not enacted until 1935. It required lobbyists for the electric power industry to identify their employer, their earnings, and the legislation they sought to influence. Similar provisions were imposed on the maritime industry a year later and, in 1938, a third measure, spawned by the approach of World War II, required the registration of agents and lobbyists for foreign governments.

The first and only comprehensive lobbying law was the Federal Regulation of Lobbying Act, which was passed in 1946. Drafted in haste and vaguely phrased, it requires the registration of anyone who "solicits, collects, or receives money or anything of value to be used principally to aid . . . the passage or defeat of any legislation by the Congress." Those registered are required to make a quarterly public accounting of all receipts of $500 or more and all expenditures of $10 or more.

Many lobbyists refuse to register, however, claiming that lobbying is not their principal activity or that their activities are educational and informational in nature and do not constitute lobbying. The Supreme Court of the United States ruled in 1954 that the lobbying law of 1946 was constitutional. It also held that "one of the main purposes" of a registered lobbyist must be to influence legislation and that this must involve direct communication with members of Congress. This decision has been widely interpreted to mean that indirect lobbying is exempt from the law. For example, a lobbyist

Number of Lobbyists
Registered
with Congress

1976	1977	1978	1979	1980	1981	1982	1983 (est.)
3,420	3,558	4,066	4,627	5,572	5,389	5,808	6,500

can argue that he need not register if he lobbies a senator's legislative assistant but avoids direct communication with the senator.

As a result of such vague registration requirements, the number of lobbyists currently registered with Congress in Washington, D.C. — about 6,500 — is considered low, even though it is four times the number registered in 1969. *Time* magazine has estimated the actual number of lobbyists in Washington to be at least 15,000, and the number continues to grow. In the past decade, the number of corporations with Washington representatives, who are generally recognized as lobbyists, has increased by 500 per cent. Registered lobbyists alone outnumber the 535 members of Congress by a ratio of more than 12 to 1. (Of course, thousands of other lobbyists operate around the country at state and city government levels.)

Who are these lobbyists? Many lobbyists in Washington are former congressional aides, members of Congress, or administration

officials hired because of their inside knowledge of government and their familiarity with lawmakers. Many are lawyers. Perhaps the best-known lobbyist is consumer advocate Ralph Nader. Other notable lobbyists — though not all accept the label — include Democrats Thomas Hale Boggs, Jr., whose late father was a congressman and whose mother is now a member of Congress, and Robert S. Strauss, former national chairman of the Democratic Party, and Republicans Charls E. Walker, whose firm is the registered lobbyist for many major corporations, and William E. Timmons, whose firm represents the National Rifle Association of America (NRA) and dozens of other organizations.

Virtually all major businesses engage in lobbying. So do trade associations such as the American Petroleum Institute, which represents the oil industry; single-issue groups such as the NRA; and broader organizations such as the Chamber of Commerce of the

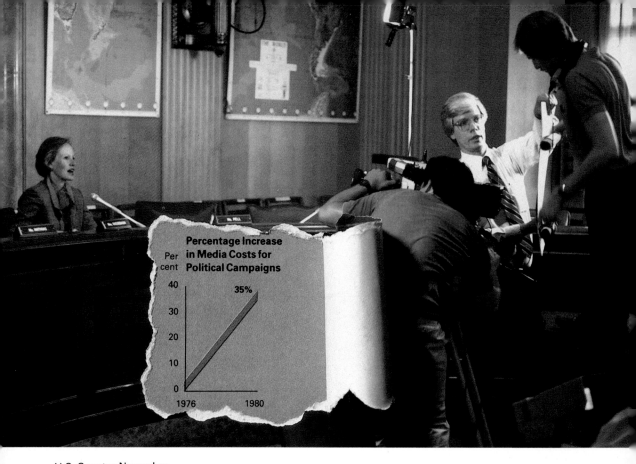

Percentage Increase
Per in Media Costs for
cent Political Campaigns

40
35%
30
20
10
0
1976   1980

U.S. Senator Nancy Landon Kassebaum (R., Kans.) rehearses a television commercial during her 1984 reelection bid. Escalating media advertising costs have contributed to the expense of running an election campaign, thus making contributions from political action committees (PAC's) even more attractive.

United States and the American Federation of Labor and Congress of Industrial Organizations (AFL-CIO).

The daily activities of these lobbyists might vary. Some specialize in cultivating friendly relations with legislators and officials so that they can obtain ready access to present arguments or suggest specific legislative or regulatory language. Others collect information on prospective legislative or administrative actions affecting their clients. Still others try to organize public opinion around a particular issue in order to pressure legislators or perhaps to defeat them in the next election.

Lobbyists have become adept at mobilizing this kind of grass-roots pressure — that is, encouraging large numbers of ordinary citizens to phone, write, or visit Congress members in behalf of a particular course of action. The purpose is to create the impression that a ground swell of public opinion supports that action. Common Cause uses a telephone network, operating something like a chain-letter scheme, to generate letters and phone calls from the public. The NRA once claimed it could inspire 500,000 letters to Congress in three days — and that was before advances in computer technology made such direct mail efforts easier.

The computer has proved invaluable to these grass-roots lobbying efforts. Computerized mailing lists maintained by interest groups can readily be broken down by congressional districts or, sometimes, by the age, sex, race, or business or professional interests of the individuals listed. Using such lists, grass-roots lobbying efforts can be targeted to those likely to be the most responsive. For example, if a bill in Congress is likely to have an adverse impact on a certain profession, the lobbyist can use a computerized mailing list to reach only members of that profession. In this way, the costs of the mailing are lowered, while those most likely to be affected by the bill are alerted to the pending legislation.

Lobbyists know that such grass-roots pressure can be exceptionally effective. "If you get a letter from a constituent, you pay attention," said a House member. "He is not an outsider. He is someone who votes for you or against you."

Some grass-roots lobbying efforts concentrate not on issues but on officeholders themselves. Their aim is not to persuade a legislator to vote a certain way but to punish those legislators who have, in their view, a poor voting record. About 70 special-interest groups try to mobilize public opinion by rating the voting records of Congress members, hoping to persuade the electorate to defeat those who have voted contrary to the groups' interests. Organizations such as Americans for Democratic Action, a liberal group, consider a legislator's overall voting record in making their evaluation, but an increasing number of special-interest groups zero in on how a legislator voted on a single issue. For example, beginning in 1970, Environmental Action, Incorporated, a group with full-time lobbyists devoted to protecting the environment, each election year labeled 12 Congress members who had voted against the environmental movement the "Dirty Dozen." Between 1970 and 1974, the organization claimed a 75 per cent success rate in helping to defeat those on its "Dirty Dozen" list.

These are some of the typical day-to-day activities of lobbyists, but in recent years, more and more of their time has been occupied with fund-raising for congressional candidates. Increasingly, lobbyists see an opportunity to influence law and government policy by raising money for the lawmakers. This has been especially true since 1974, when election law reforms limited the amount of money that individuals could contribute to a congressional campaign but opened the doors for PAC contributions to those campaigns.

The 1974 reforms had their origin in the Watergate scandal that unfolded following the 1972 reelection campaign of President Richard M. Nixon. Individuals later identified as employees of Nixon's campaign organization were apprehended by police while breaking into Democratic National Committee Headquarters at the Watergate Office Building in Washington, D.C. Nixon subsequently tried to cover up the connection between the break-in and his campaign and, facing impeachment proceedings, resigned from the presidency in 1974. During the Watergate inquiry, investigators uncovered nearly $1 million in illegal corporate contributions to Nixon's reelection campaign. Banks and corporations had been barred from contributing to federal campaigns since the Tillman Act of 1907. Even perfectly legal contributions to Nixon's campaign caused concern when it was known that he had received $17 million from just 124 wealthy contributors. The total included $2 million alone from Chicago insurance magnate W. Clement Stone.

As a result, Congress in 1974 passed amendments to the Federal Election Campaign Act (FECA) of 1971, limiting the amount of money an individual or a PAC could contribute to a candidate. The original FECA modified the Tillman Act ban on corporate contributions by allowing corporations to set up PAC's. This provision did not apply to corporations holding government contracts, however, so many companies did not form PAC's. The 1974 amendments to

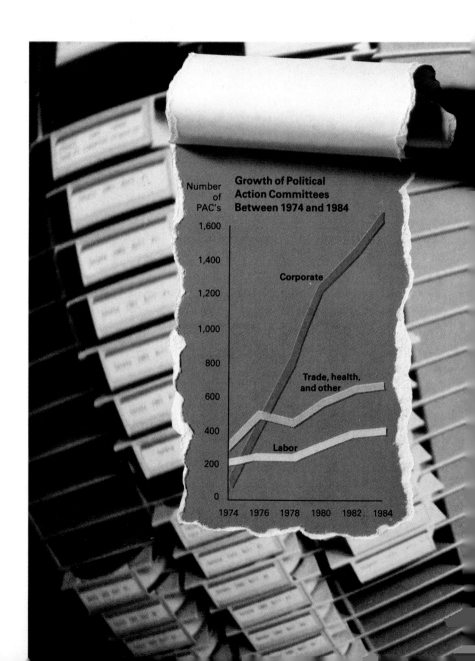

FECA removed this last constraint by permitting government contractors to establish and administer PAC's.

The 1974 reforms allowed PAC's to contribute up to $5,000 to a candidate per election, five times more than the $1,000 limit for individual contributions. Since the contribution is allowed each time a candidate is involved in a primary, runoff, or general election, a PAC could conceivably contribute a total of $15,000 per candidate. Moreover, there is no limit on how much a candidate can receive in combined PAC donations. Ironically, the reforms lessened the influence of wealthy individual contributors but added greatly to the importance of PAC's and the lobbyists who advise them on how to distribute their funds.

Data on the growth of PAC's and their contributions to congressional candidates are stored in a computer's memory at the office of the Federal Election Commission in Washington, D.C. The agency charts the growth of PAC's, which grew from 608 in 1974 to 3,803 in mid-1984.

The new curbs on individual contributions coincided with a sharp inflation in campaign costs, including a marked increase in television advertising outlays. Between 1972 and 1976, media advertising and public opinion polling costs rose by 30 per cent. In 1982 winning a House campaign cost an average of $284,000, while a successful Senate race cost an average of about $2.1 million.

With the curbs on donations from wealthy individuals, a money void was created, but interest groups and their lobbyists stepped forward to fill the gap, using PAC's to make donations to favored candidates. Because some lobbyists control or advise dozens of PAC's, they have replaced wealthy donors as the principal source of campaign contributions. Journalist Elizabeth Drew, in her 1983 study, *Politics and Money: The New Road to Corruption*, quoted a prosperous Washington lawyer-lobbyist as saying, "Ninety-nine per cent of lobbying in this city is now fund-raising."

The results of election-law changes have been dramatic. After the FECA amendments went into effect in 1974, some 600 PAC's gave $12.5 million to congressional candidates. By 1982 the number of PAC's had increased to about 3,400, and their contributions to congressional races had risen to $87.6 million. In 1982 House members received an average of about 28 per cent of campaign financing from PAC's. In contrast, in 1972 PAC's had made only 14 per cent of all contributions to congressional candidates. The PAC spending splurge continued into the 1984 elections as 3,803 PAC's registered with the Federal Election Commission. Common Cause estimated 1984 PAC spending at between $100 million and $120 million.

As PAC contributions swelled steadily during the 1970's, officeholders benefited from the fact that such committees channeled most of their funds to *incumbents* — that is, those already in office. However, in 1980, PAC's gave unprecedented sums to Republican challengers, helping to unseat such liberal Senate Democrats as George S. McGovern of South Dakota, Frank Church of Idaho, and John C. Culver of Iowa. Issue-oriented PAC's, most of them of a conservative ideology, were in the forefront of the effort. Republican Charles E. Grassley, who defeated Culver, was the top PAC beneficiary, receiving more than $700,000. Much of it came from oil and chemical interests who reacted unfavorably to Culver's sponsorship of legislation that mandated an industry-financed cleanup of toxic-waste sites. These developments threw a scare into Democratic survivors and helped trigger a bipartisan clamor for ever-larger PAC contributions.

The often-frantic money chase has led to the growth of Washington fund-raising events where politicians provide lobbyists and PAC's with an opportunity to turn out and contribute. Sprinkling money around at such affairs has become a major activity of top-rank lobbyists, who often attend several fund-raising events in a single evening. The affairs vary widely in scope and social importance,

PAC Contributions to Congressional Candidates

Millions of dollars

	1981-1982	1977-1978
Corporations	1981-1982	1977-1978
Trade, health, and other	1981-1982	1977-1978
Labor	1981-1982	1977-1978

Jerry Falwell, head of the Moral Majority, sits astride a Texas long-horn steer during a fund-raising party at the Republican National Convention in Dallas in August 1984. The party was sponsored by the National Conservative Political Action Commit-tee and was typical of the way PAC's raise campaign funds for fa-vored candidates.

ranging from $50-a-head cocktail receptions at a hotel to $1,000-a-plate sit-down dinners in private mansions.

The money chase has become a game at which both candidates and lobbyists are eager and adept participants. Noting that fund-raising is not a one-sided affair, Bernadette Budde, political education director of the Business-Industry Political Action Committee, observed, "We're not opening the mouths of candidates and forcing dollars down." Lobbyist Robert C. McCandless stressed the importance to him of PAC operations, saying, "I don't even take a client now unless he's willing to set up a political action committee and participate in the [fund-raising] process."

In addition to parceling out PAC money, lobbyists and the interests they represent shower influential Congress members with expense-paid trips to resort areas and with fees for speaking appearances. Federal law limits speaking fees to $2,000 per appearance for a legislator, but some legislators are invited to make multiple appearances before a single group. They might, for example, collect $2,000 for taking part in an afternoon seminar at a convention,

155

then collect another $2,000 for addressing the same group at dinner that evening.

In 1983, speaking fees to Congress members totaled a record $6.1-million, up from $4.5 million a year earlier and nearly triple the 1980 level of $2.2 million. Senator Robert J. Dole (R., Kans.), chairman of the Senate Finance Committee, was the top fee-getter, receiving $188,917, of which he gave $82,000 to charity. Next came Senator Richard G. Lugar (R., Ind.), who received $132,450 and gave $3,385 to charity.

What impact are PAC contributions and speaking fees having on Congress? Former Representative Henry S. Reuss (D., Wis.) is among those who see the quest for PAC contributions as a threat to representative democracy. Laments Reuss: "The corruption and the evil is not only in people seeking to sell access or in some cases their votes; it lies in the preoccupation of legislators, many of them very fine men and women, who have to spend a large part of their lives panhandling, going around to all these groups saying, 'I would just love to have a check from you.' "

Senator Dole told *The Wall Street Journal:* "When these political

As PAC's become an increasingly prominent source of campaign funds, few members of Congress can claim that PAC money is of little importance to their election bids. Are votes given in exchange for contributions, as one former congressman has charged?

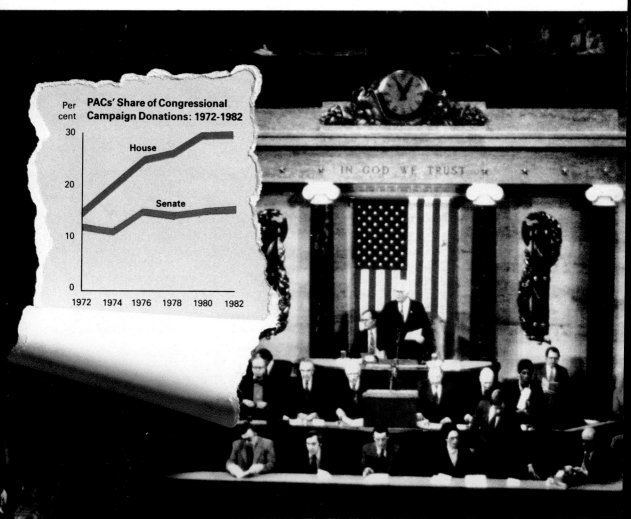

PACs' Share of Congressional Campaign Donations: 1972-1982

Per cent

action committees give money, they expect something in return other than good government. It is making it much more difficult to legislate. We may reach a point where, if everyone is buying something with PAC money, we can't get anything done." Former Representative William M. Brodhead (D., Mich.) cited the money hunt as one reason for his 1982 decision to abandon a promising House career. "It used to be a group would just agree with your philosophical outlook and would be willing to make campaign contributions on that basis," he said. "Now, votes are given in exchange for contributions." Representative Barney Frank (D., Mass.) adds: "We are the only human beings in the world who are expected to take thousands of dollars from perfect strangers on important matters and not be affected by it."

The donors of these dollars argue that they are not buying votes but only access to the legislator. They claim they simply want to present their side of an issue before it comes to a vote. Justin Dart, business magnate and member of President Reagan's informal group of advisers — the "kitchen cabinet" — until his death in January 1984, put it more bluntly. Talking with politicians, he said, "is a fine thing, but with a little money, they hear you better."

The controversy over the role of PAC's has again raised the question of whether or not to impose restrictions on lobbying. The public affairs lobby, Common Cause, has long argued strenuously for stricter regulation of lobbying, contending that more lobbyists should be required to register and that there should be fuller disclosure of sources of lobbying funds. "It is quite clear," Common Cause's Wertheimer told a Senate committee, "that unreported lobbying activities are extensive, and that accurate disclosure is more the exception than the rule. . . . Members [of Congress] and the public should know the source of political pressure, and the amount spent to generate that pressure, in order to evaluate it."

On the other hand, the American Civil Liberties Union (ACLU) has questioned the constitutionality of strict regulation, saying that any legislation must not curb dissent. The ACLU has complained that some proposals favored by Common Cause "are so sweeping in their definitions of 'lobbyists,' and are so onerous in their requirements of record-keeping and reporting, that such legislation would be a real threat to freedom of speech. . . ."

Public financing of congressional campaigns, as exists now for presidential elections, might be one solution. The Senate voted for public financing in 1974, but the House blocked the idea, which would have imposed limitations on PAC spending and, therefore, on their influence. The issue of public financing is emerging anew, however, and is certain to be considered again by Congress, along with proposed new curbs on lobbyists and PAC's. As Common Cause's Wertheimer has said, "The abuses have gotten so bad that we're beginning to see a discernible shift in the climate."

A Year in Perspective

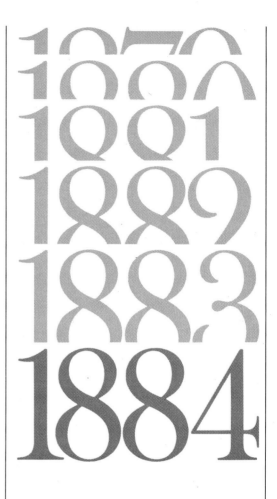

THE YEAR BOOK casts a backward glance at the furors, fancies, and follies of yesteryear. The coincidences of history that are revealed offer substantial proof that the physical world may continually change, but human nature — with all its inventiveness, amiability, and even perversity — remains fairly constant, for better or worse, throughout the years.

See page 163.

In 1884, Pierre Savorgnan de Brazza of France, *top,* explores western Africa; the Ringling brothers, *above,* start their circus in Baraboo, Wis.; American inventor Lewis E. Waterman patents one of the first fountain pens, *above right;* and French chemist Louis Pasteur, *right,* develops a vaccine for rabies.

By Sara Dreyfuss

A Year of Rivalry

A bitter presidential campaign in the United States
and international wrestling for colonies made 1884
a year of widespread struggle and competition.

In 1884, many of the year's major news events involved rivalry.
The United States had a noisy election, with the Democratic and
Republican candidates facing off in a bitter contest for the presidency. The quest for colonies gathered speed as European powers
scrambled to gain control of profitable regions in Africa and Asia.

The 1884 presidential campaign was one of the nastiest in United
States history. The Republican Party's candidate was James G.
Blaine of Maine, former Speaker of the House of Representatives,
making his third bid for the White House. Blaine's first campaign,
in 1876, had been marred by charges that he had used his influence
as Speaker to keep the Little Rock and Fort Smith Railroad from
losing a land grant in 1869. Although Blaine probably had no previous connection with the railroad, the company rewarded him for
the favor with a generous commission to sell the railroad's bonds.

Blaine denied any wrongdoing, but doubts about his honesty lin-
gered. During the summer of 1884, *Harper's Weekly* published correspondence between Blaine and his business associates indicating
that the Speaker had used his position for personal profit. In one
of the most damaging letters, Blaine had written to Warren Fisher,
Jr., an official of the Rock Island Line, asking him to provide a
testimonial to Blaine's innocence. He enclosed a sample statement

for Fisher to copy and wrote on the back, "Burn this letter." Fisher did not destroy the letter, however, and his bookkeeper later found it and made it public.

The Republican Party nominated Blaine for President on June 6, but many reform-minded Republicans felt unable to support him. The reformers included former Secretary of the Interior Carl Schurz; Henry Ward Beecher, a leading clergyman; and George W. Curtis, the influential editor of *Harper's Weekly*. These renegade Republicans were dubbed *Mugwumps*, from an Indian word meaning *chiefs*. The Mugwumps met in New York City on June 16 and voted to support the Democratic candidate if he had a clean record.

The Democrats rose to the occasion and, on July 11, nominated Governor Grover Cleveland of New York, who had a reputation for fierce honesty. The election promised to be close, with an unusual number of minor-party candidates drawing support away from Blaine and Cleveland. The National Greenback-Labor Party and a new group called the Anti-Monopoly Party backed Governor Benjamin F. Butler of Massachusetts. During the Civil War, Butler had been one of the most hated Union generals in the South, resulting in his nickname, Beast Butler. The National Prohibition Party ran John P. St. John, former governor of Kansas. The National Equal Rights Party, formed in San Francisco on September 20, nominated Belva A. Lockwood, a Washington, D.C., lawyer. She was the first woman to appear on a presidential ballot. (A century later, in 1984, Representative Geraldine A. Ferraro [D., N.Y.] became the first woman nominated for Vice President by a major party.)

Belva A. Lockwood, the National Equal Rights Party candidate in 1884, is the first woman whose name appears on the ballot for President of the United States.

The Republicans in 1884 wasted little time in finding a chink in Cleveland's armor. On July 21, the Buffalo (N.Y.) *Evening Telegraph* printed what it called "A Terrible Tale." It charged that Cleveland was the father of an illegitimate child banished to an orphan asylum. Many people considered a man who did such a thing unfit to be mentioned in decent homes, much less elected President.

Cleveland, a bachelor, admitted that he and a young Buffalo widow named Maria Halpin had been lovers. In 1874, she gave birth to a son whom she named Oscar Folsom Cleveland. Cleveland doubted that he was the father, but he agreed to provide for the child. After Halpin began drinking heavily and neglecting her son, Cleveland paid for the boy's care at the Protestant Orphan Asylum in Buffalo until a suitable family adopted him.

A bitter mudslinging contest followed the unsavory revelations. One Mugwump, possibly Massachusetts lawyer Moorfield Storey, assessed the two candidates. "We are told that Mr. Blaine has been delinquent in office but blameless in private life," he said, "while Mr. Cleveland has been a model of official integrity but culpable in his personal relations. We should therefore elect Mr. Cleveland to the public office which he is so well qualified to fill, and remand Mr. Blaine to the private station which he is admirably fitted to adorn."

The author:
Sara Dreyfuss is Associate Editor of THE WORLD BOOK YEAR BOOK.

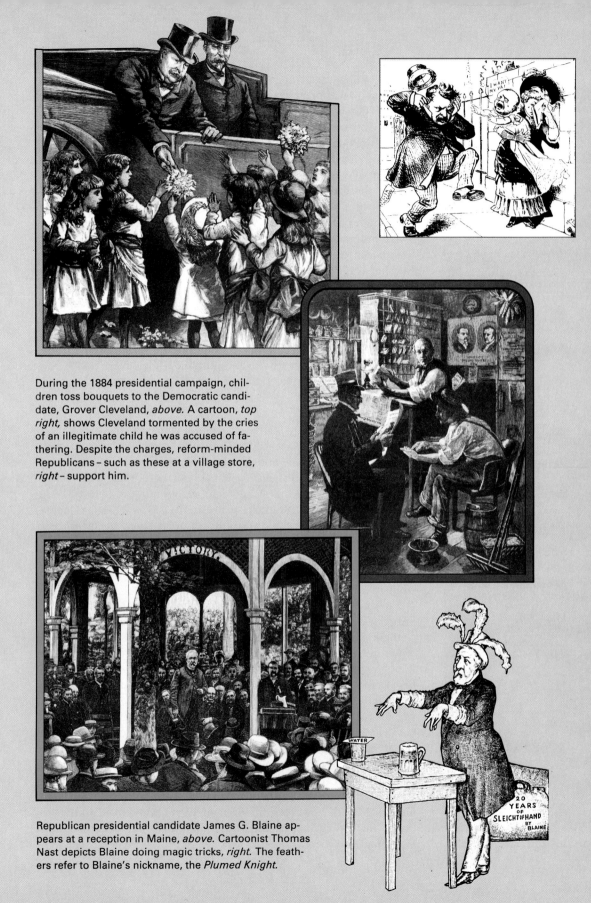

During the 1884 presidential campaign, children toss bouquets to the Democratic candidate, Grover Cleveland, *above.* A cartoon, *top right,* shows Cleveland tormented by the cries of an illegitimate child he was accused of fathering. Despite the charges, reform-minded Republicans – such as these at a village store, *right* – support him.

Republican presidential candidate James G. Blaine appears at a reception in Maine, *above.* Cartoonist Thomas Nast depicts Blaine doing magic tricks, *right.* The feathers refer to Blaine's nickname, the *Plumed Knight.*

The Democrats arranged parades in which the marchers set fire to sheets of paper carried aloft on poles, while chanting, "Blaine, Blaine, James G. Blaine, / The continental liar from the state of Maine, / Burn this letter!" Republicans, in turn, chorused, "Ma! Ma! Where's my pa? / Gone to the White House. / Ha! Ha! Ha!"

As Election Day drew near, *Frank Leslie's Illustrated Newspaper* exclaimed, "For only a few more days need we hold our noses. The filth of the Presidential sewer is about exhausted: the daylight and clear air of November 5th are just ahead."

Then, on October 29, only a week before the election, Blaine made two political blunders in quick succession. At a meeting of Republican clergymen in New York City that morning, Samuel D. Burchard, a Presbyterian minister, called the Democrats the party of "rum, Romanism, and rebellion." Blaine sat quietly in the audience and did not disown Burchard's remark, which linked the Democrats with whiskey, the Roman Catholic Church, and the Confederacy. The Democrats quickly covered the city and other heavily Roman Catholic areas with posters quoting the slogan, which Catholics found deeply offensive. One Catholic leader declared, "I estimate that the remark has changed fifty thousand votes."

That same evening, Blaine attended a dinner gathering of millionaires. The guests included steelmaker Andrew Carnegie, railroad baron Jay Gould, and jeweler Charles L. Tiffany. Financial hardship was widespread in the United States, but the millionaires dined richly at the swank Delmonico's restaurant and heard Blaine make a speech about "Republican prosperity." New York City newspapers the next day carried scathing editorials about the affair. *The World* ran a huge front-page cartoon titled "The Royal Feast of Belshazzar Blaine and the Money Kings." It showed Blaine and the millionaires at a table laden with champagne and other delicacies, while a hungry family begged for crumbs.

For three days after the voting, the election remained in doubt. Largely because of *The World* cartoon and Burchard's insults to Catholics, the key state of New York went Democratic by fewer than 600 votes, giving 36 crucial electoral votes to Cleveland. He beat Blaine by the slim margin of 23,005 popular votes and became the first Democrat elected President since James Buchanan in 1856.

Beyond the noise of the 1884 campaign, an unfolding financial story involving former President Ulysses S. Grant revealed some of both the best and the worst in human nature. Grant had retired to private life with savings of about $100,000, which he invested in the banking firm of Grant & Ward. Grant knew little about finance, but his son Ulysses, Jr., was a partner in the company, and both Grants considered the other partner, Ferdinand Ward, an investment genius. On May 6, however, the younger Grant was forced to tell his father that Ward had cheated them. The firm had collapsed, and Ward had vanished.

The former President and his wife counted their assets, which amounted to $80 in cash in Grant's pocket plus $130 that Mrs. Grant had in the house. To help pay his debts, Grant wrote four magazine articles about his Civil War experiences. The articles proved successful, and Grant began his memoirs, which the famous author Mark Twain agreed to publish. Grant worked on the book through the winter of 1884-1885, though in constant pain from throat cancer. He died in July 1885, shortly after finishing it.

Grant's courage and determination touched many hearts. *Leslie's* newspaper said, "The distress which has been brought suddenly upon General Grant . . . has won for him the sincere sympathy of all classes of citizens . . . . That General Grant was involved in any way in Ward's dishonesties no one believes."

Meanwhile, international attention focused on Africa. There was intense rivalry among several European nations as they staked out claims to valuable parts of what was then called the Dark Continent. Sir Henry Morton Stanley, the British explorer who had won fame for finding Scottish missionary David Livingstone in 1871, returned to London after establishing trading posts along the Congo River for King Leopold II of Belgium. A French explorer, Pierre Savorgnan de Brazza, carried on a similar mission in western Africa, a region later known as French Equatorial Africa. De Brazza established trading stations there and signed treaties with local chiefs, strengthening French control over the area. Great Britain took over what became British Somaliland (now northern Somalia) and assumed direct control of Basutoland (present-day Lesotho), which had been ruled for years by the British Cape Colony.

Britain was less successful in the area that is now Cameroon. For years, British merchants had special trade agreements with the Douala people there. In 1884, the British Parliament decided to acquire Cameroon as a colony and sent a diplomat named Edward Hyde Hewett to make the necessary treaties.

Hewett sailed immediately for Africa, arriving at the city of Douala on July 13. However, a German envoy, Gustav Nachtigal, had beaten him to it. Just six days earlier, Nachtigal had signed treaties with the Douala making Cameroon a German protectorate. Hewett was known from then on by the nickname Too Late Hewett.

Germany acquired several other overseas possessions in 1884, establishing most of its colonial empire that year. Earlier in July, Nachtigal had signed a treaty with a chief in Togo, establishing a German protectorate there. In August, Germany hoisted its flag in present-day Namibia, making it German Southwest Africa.

Karl Peters, the head of a commercial company called the German Colonization Society, traveled to eastern Africa in 1884. By December, he had signed 124 treaties with chiefs for their land. Peters returned to Berlin with the treaties early in 1885 and persuaded his government to claim the area, now Tanzania.

Germany and Britain created colonies in the South Pacific as well. In November, Germany annexed northeastern New Guinea, and Britain proclaimed a protectorate over the southeastern part of the island. The official British proclamation was made on November 6 to a group of local chiefs. The commander of the British warship H.M.S. *Nelson* told them, "Always keep in your minds that the queen guards and watches over you, looks upon you as her children, and will not allow anyone to harm you."

Major strides were made in medicine in 1884. The germ theory of disease had become firmly established by then, largely through the work of Robert Koch, a German physician, and Louis Pasteur, a French chemist. No longer blaming "filth" or "bad air," scientists had discovered the bacteria and other microscopic organisms that cause infectious diseases. In 1884, bacteriologist Friedrich Löffler, one of Koch's assistants, isolated a bacterium from the throats of diphtheria patients and proved that it caused the disease. Another German bacteriologist, Arthur Nicolaier, discovered the tetanus bacillus. Koch himself announced his discovery, made late in 1883, of the organism responsible for cholera.

Pasteur's greatest triumph came with the conquest of rabies, or hydrophobia. He had worked for years to find the organism that caused this dreadful disease, and then to grow it in his laboratory. He finally cultivated the virus in rabbit tissue and prepared a vaccine from dead virus. In 1884, he demonstrated that his vaccine could protect healthy dogs from the bite of a rabid animal. *Leslie's* praised "the brilliant success of M. Pasteur" against "the dreaded malady of hydrophobia," and *Scientific American* said, "French science may indeed claim a new title to the gratitude of humanity."

While some researchers worked to check the spread of disease, others sought to ease pain. Early in 1884, Austrian physician Carl Koller became the first person to use cocaine as a local anesthetic, for operations on the eye. After reading about Koller's work, the American surgeon William S. Halsted sent for a supply of the new drug. Halsted soon discovered that cocaine could also be used to dull the pain of major surgery. When injected into a major nerve, the drug anesthetized the entire area served by that nerve.

Halsted and his colleagues experimented on themselves, as was customary at that time, not knowing that cocaine was habit-forming. They took hundreds of doses in various forms to investigate the drug's possible uses and soon became probably the first cocaine addicts in the United States. Halsted conquered his addiction after a year of hospital treatment and went on to a brilliant surgical career. But three of his fellow experimenters died in misery.

Other people turned their attention to the conquest of poverty. The first settlement house, Toynbee Hall, was founded in London in 1884 by a group of Oxford University students. It was named after Arnold Toynbee, a British social reformer who died in 1883.

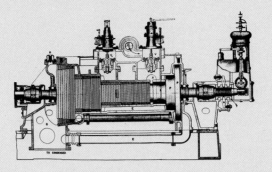

Successful inventors in 1884 include Charles A. Parsons of Great Britain, *far left,* who invents a practical steam turbine, and George Eastman of the United States, *below,* whose picture was taken on his new flexible roll film.

The center's purpose was to attract wealthy young people to move into the city's slums and work with the poor.

Another group of British reformers established a socialist organization called the Fabian Society in London in 1884. They took their name from the ancient Roman general Fabius Cunctator, who triumphed over stronger enemies by patience and elusive tactics, avoiding direct combat. The goal of the Fabian Society was to create a socialist state in Britain, but to do so by education rather than by revolution. Early Fabians included playwright George Bernard Shaw, author H. G. Wells, and historians Sidney and Beatrice Webb.

In October 1884, an international conference of about 25 countries, meeting in Washington, D.C., resolved a major source of confusion in mapmaking. The conference decided that the line of longitude passing through the Greenwich Observatory in London would be the *prime meridian* for mapmakers — that is, the line representing 0 degrees of longitude. All other lines of longitude are numbered east or west of the prime meridian. Before the conference, many countries had decided that the line of longitude passing through their capital city would be the prime meridian. In Spain, for example, longitude was measured from Madrid, and in France, from Paris.

The conference also decided that the line through Greenwich would be the starting point for the world's time zones. The meeting set up 12 time zones west of Greenwich and 12 to the east, each differing from its neighboring zone by one hour.

New inventions came thick and fast during

Ottmar Mergenthaler, a German-born mechanic, demonstrates the Linotype machine he patented in 1884. It uses a keyboard to set type mechanically, eliminating slow typesetting by hand.

The famous American author Mark Twain, *top*, completes his greatest novel, *Adventures of Huckleberry Finn,* in 1884. The book is published in Great Britain, but the United States edition, *above,* does not appear until 1885.

1884. Lewis E. Waterman of the United States patented one of the first workable fountain pens, and Charles A. Parsons of Great Britain invented the first practical steam turbine for generating electricity. George Eastman, an American inventor, revolutionized photography when he patented a flexible, paper-based roll film to replace the bulky glass plates that photographers had been using.

Another major change came in the field of printing. For hundreds of years, printers had set type entirely by hand. Then, in 1884, Ottmar Mergenthaler, a German mechanic in the United States, patented the Linotype machine. The Linotype used a keyboard to set type mechanically, thus speeding the production of newspapers and other printed material.

As new labor-saving inventions provided increased leisure time, people turned more and more to various pastimes for amusement. The first roller coaster in the United States opened on June 16, 1884, in Coney Island in New York City. A pastime that steadily gained popularity was baseball, which had begun in the Eastern United States in the mid-1800's. John A. Hillerich, a Kentucky woodworker, produced the first Louisville Slugger baseball bat in the spring of 1884. The modern breed of statistics-loving sports fan was still an oddity, however. *Leslie's* reported, "There is a man in the Government Hospital for the Insane in Washington who is perfectly sane on every subject except baseball. He knows more about baseball than any other man in America. The authorities have humored him so that he has been able to cover the walls of his large room with intricate schedules of games played since baseball began its career. He has the record of every important club and the individual records of every important player."

That baseball fan probably followed avidly the achievements of Charlie (Old Hoss) Radbourn, a pitcher for the Providence (R.I.) Grays, who compiled the greatest season record in history. Radbourn pitched in 75 games, including 73 complete games, in 1884 and won 60 of them.

Not surprisingly, Radbourn's team won the championship of the National League. The American Association champions, the New York Metropolitans, then challenged the Grays to play the first post-season baseball championship series. The term *World Series* had not been invented, but the two clubs agreed to play a series of three games in October to determine "the championship of the United States." Radbourn pitched the Grays to victory on three successive days, 6-0, 3-1, and 11-2.

Other sports, especially football and tennis, also grew in popularity. The All England Croquet and Lawn Tennis Club, which had sponsored the major men's tennis tournament since 1877 in Wimbledon, a suburb of London, added women's competition in 1884.

Another kind of competition that attracted new attention was the dog show. On Sept. 17, 1884, delegates from dog clubs throughout the United States and Canada founded the American Kennel Club (AKC) to establish uniform rules for dog shows. The AKC has grown into an association of about 10,000 dog clubs.

Dozens of circuses traveled from town to town, the smaller ones in colorful horse-drawn wagons, the larger ones in railroad cars. Colonel Benjamin E. Wallace's traveling circus first took to the road from Peru, Ind., in 1884. It later became the Hagenbeck-Wallace Circus, one of the largest in the United States. The Ringling Brothers' circus also premiered that year, on May 19 in Baraboo, Wis. Because they had little money for equipment or performers, the five Ringling brothers — Albert, Otto, Alfred, Charles, and John — did much of the work themselves. They sewed and pitched the tent, sold tickets, and played in the band. Alfred served as ringmaster, and John was a clown. Their circus grew rapidly and later combined with the Barnum & Bailey circus to form the Ringling Brothers and Barnum & Bailey Circus, the largest circus in history.

Music was another favorite pastime. Many families passed the evening singing ballads around a piano. Some songs of 1884 may still be heard today, including "(Oh My Darling) Clementine," "Love's Old Sweet Song," and "A Fountain in the Park," better known by its first line, "While Strolling Through the Park One Day."

One of the most popular French operas in history, Jules Massenet's *Manon*, premiered on Jan. 19, 1884, in Paris. Enduring classical compositions first heard that year included the Symphony No. 7 and *Te Deum* by Anton Bruckner of Austria.

Mark Twain's *Adventures of Huckleberry Finn*, one of the greatest American novels, was published in Great Britain in 1884 and in the United States in 1885. Other major works of literature published in 1884 included Sarah Orne Jewett's *A Country Doctor*, a novel about a New England woman who chooses a medical career instead of marriage, and *Montcalm and Wolfe* by the great American historian Francis Parkman, a portrait of the French commander and his English counterpart during the French and Indian Wars. Also appearing in 1884 was *The Wild Duck*, a play by the Norwegian dramatist Henrik Ibsen about the importance of illusions to ordinary people. However, the year's major publishing event was the first volume of the *Oxford English Dictionary* (O.E.D.), then called *A New English Dictionary on Historical Principles*. The first installment, "A-Ant," was the result of 25 years of painstaking work by the editors. No other dictionary published since has rivaled the *O.E.D.* for its authority.

The *O.E.D.* is still the standard by which other dictionaries are judged, and it is just one example of how events in 1884 changed the course of history. The creation of Greenwich as the prime meridian, the establishment of colonial boundaries in Africa and the Pacific Islands, even such events as the invention of the fountain pen and roll film shaped the years to come. Things that happened in 1884 were to be felt in 1984, 1985, and beyond.

The Year on File

Contributors to THE WORLD BOOK YEAR BOOK report on the major developments of 1984. The contributors' names appear at the end of the articles they have written, and a complete roster of contributors, listing their professional affiliations and the articles they have written, is on pages 6 and 7.

A quiz on some events of 1984 as reported in various Year on File articles appears on page 172.

Articles in this section are arranged alphabetically by subject matter. In most cases, the article titles are the same as those of the articles in THE WORLD BOOK ENCYCLOPEDIA that they update. The numerous cross-references (in **bold type**) guide the reader to a subject or information that may be in some other article or that may appear under an alternative title. "See" and "See also" cross-references appear within and at the end of articles to direct the reader to related information elsewhere in THE YEAR BOOK. "In WORLD BOOK, see" references point the reader to articles in the encyclopedia that provide background information to the year's events reported in THE YEAR BOOK.

See "Olympic Games," page 427.

THE YEAR BOOK presents a quiz on some events of 1984 as reported in various articles in the Year on File. Answers appear on page 529.

1. What world leader was assassinated in October by the leader's own bodyguards?
2. Why did Yvon Fauconier of France win a yacht race in June despite finishing 10½ hours after the leader?
3. What former President of the United States spent a week in September helping renovate an apartment building in New York City?

4. The woman above in June achieved a sports feat that has been done only four times before in history. Who is she, and what did she do?
5. Vanessa Williams, who in 1983 became the first black Miss America, chalked up another "first" in July 1984. What was it?
6. An October ruling by the International Court of Justice settled a boundary dispute between the United States and Canada. What area was involved in the dispute?
7. An appointee to the U.S. Cabinet was cleared of allegations of financial misdealings in September, and a Cabinet member was indicted on felony charges that same month. Who were the two people?
8. What American singer in February won a record eight Grammy awards?
9. A Canadian became which of these historic "firsts" during 1984?
    a. The first Canadian to head the United Steelworkers of America.
    b. The first Canadian astronaut.
    c. The first woman governor general of Canada.
    d. All of the above.
10. What manufacturer, saved from bankruptcy by the United States government in 1979 and 1980, announced record quarterly profits in the first two quarters of 1984?
11. What African nation changed its name to Burkina in 1984?
12. Two teams of scientists, one American and one French, announced in April that they had found the virus responsible for a deadly disease. What is the disease?
13. What world leader narrowly escaped death in a bomb attack in October?
14. What French postimpressionist painter is the subject of the Broadway musical *Sunday in the Park with George*?
15. A 42-year coaching career ended on a disappointing note in March. Whose career was it, and what happened?
16. Ahmed Sékou Touré, who died in March, was the only president of his nation since it gained independence in 1958. What country was it?
17. What author won a special award from the Pulitzer Prize committee for his lifetime contributions to children's literature?
18. Canada had three prime ministers in 1984. Who were they?
19. What former welterweight boxing champion came out of retirement on May 11 only to retire again hours later?
20. China and Great Britain signed an agreement in December for an event that will not take place until 1997. What event is it?
21. A new edition of a literary masterpiece corrects nearly 5,000 errors in earlier editions. What is the book?
22. What country was suspected of mining the Red Sea and the Gulf of Suez, where underwater explosions damaged vessels during 1984?
23. What is the young man below doing?

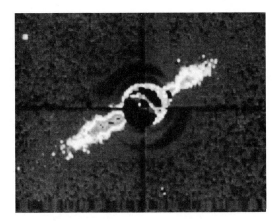

24. What does the photograph above show?
   a. The virus suspected of causing AIDS.
   b. Planets forming a solar system around a sun.
   c. A blazing Frisbee.
   d. A sea animal related to a jellyfish.
25. A diminutive 80-year-old woman uttered one of the most quoted questions of 1984 in commercials for a fast-food chain. What was the question?
26. A National Football League record that had stood since 1965 was broken in October 1984. What record was it, and who broke it?
27. What East European leader decided that going west was not such a good idea after all?
28. At the conclusion of a speech to the United Nations General Assembly in October, President José Napoleón Duarte of El Salvador made a surprising offer. What was it?
29. What did Anatoly Karpov defend in 1984?
30. In January, the United States established diplomatic relations with a political unit, and the action brought protests from some U.S. groups. What unit was it, and why did the groups protest?
31. What took place in Sarajevo, Yugoslavia, in February?
32. In July, a Chicago firm threatened with bankruptcy received the largest federal rescue package in history. What was the firm?
33. What country in Central America had five different armed forces operating within its borders in 1984?
34. What is *ibuprofen*?
35. A battle at the Golden Temple resulted in more than 1,000 deaths in June. Where is the Golden Temple, and who was fighting there?
36. In July, the motion-picture industry added a new category between PG and R. What was it?
37. What athlete won gold medals at the 1984 Summer Olympic Games in the same four track and field events that Jesse Owens won in the 1936 Olympics?

38. In August, doctors announced that skin grafts had saved the lives of two severely burned boys. What was unusual about the grafts?
39. Who in July became the first woman to walk in space?
   a. Sally K. Ride.
   b. Kathryn D. Sullivan.
   c. Roberta L. Crippen.
   d. Svetlana Savitskaya.
40. A seascape by an English artist of the 1800's sold at auction in July for about $10 million, more than had ever been paid for any picture by any artist. Who was the painter?
41. What states did Democratic presidential candidate Walter F. Mondale carry in the 1984 election in November?
42. Why may Chicago lose the nickname *Second City*?
43. What runner won $2.3 million in 1984 at an age when his contemporaries are — literally — out to pasture?
44. What Communist nation in October adopted economic reforms that will reduce government control of the economy?
45. An infant known only as Baby Fae made medical history in October. Why?
46. What newspaper was officially recognized as the third largest daily in the United States in 1984, only its second year of business?
47. Who is Prince Henry Charles Albert David?
48. In May, a team of archaeologists found an untouched tomb built about 1,500 years ago in the jungles of Guatemala. What people built it?
49. What famous lady was in the process of getting a three-year "face-lift" in 1984?
50. The two men below reached an unusual agreement in September. Who are they, and what was it?

ADVERTISING

ADVERTISING. Two of the biggest advertising stories in the United States in 1984 centered on the Olympic Games and the presidential election. The first was really two stories, one about the Winter Games in Sarajevo, Yugoslavia, in February and the other involving the Summer Games in Los Angeles in July and August. American Broadcasting Companies (ABC) paid $91.3 million for exclusive television rights to the Winter Games and $225-million for the Summer Games. Unfortunately for ABC, the Winter Games did not attract nearly as many viewers as the network had guaranteed to advertisers. Reasons given for the low interest included bad weather that caused postponement of some key skiing events, poor timing of some delayed broadcasts, and the fact that the United States had few potential medal winners.

The Summer Games were a smashing advertising success, however. The excellent performance of the U.S. team had a great deal to do with this success. As the games drew to a close, advertisers were competing to sign up U.S. medalists for commercial endorsements of their products and services. Probably the most sought-after Olympian was 16-year-old gold medal gymnast Mary Lou Retton. By September, Retton had signed with McDonald's Corporation; Vidal Sassoon, Incorporated; and General Mills, Incorporated (for Wheaties cereal). The General Mills contract alone was believed worth $400,000 over two or three years.

Even people who were not sports fans agreed that the Summer Games seemed to bring out a patriotic spirit in Americans. Much of that spirit was reflected in political advertising that took over the spotlight before the November 6 election. Once again in 1984, television and radio were the candidates' main advertising media. The campaign to reelect President Ronald Reagan and Vice President George H. W. Bush spent about $25 million to $30 million in all media. The forces of challengers Walter F. Mondale and Geraldine A. Ferraro were believed to have spent much less than that, but their expenditures also were in eight figures. And the campaigns of North Carolina's Republican Senator Jesse A. Helms and his Democratic challenger, Governor James B. Hunt, Jr., spent an estimated $20 million on advertising. The dominance of television and radio in 1984 politics caused a decrease in the use of such traditional campaign tools as campaign buttons and signs.

Where's the Beef? A 1984 television campaign for Wendy's hamburgers featured an elderly woman who, after examining a competitor's product, demanded in a deep, throaty growl, "Where's the beef?" The campaign was a smash hit. The woman, Chicago's Clara Peller, skyrocketed to fame, appearing on major talk shows and in popular magazines, and making more Wendy's commercials. Wendy's International, Incorporated, re-

Clara Peller, the star of Wendy's commercials, poses the most memorable question since "To be or not to be?" — "Where's the beef?"

ported a substantial sales increase as a result of the commercials.

Another highly rated commercial premiered on the telecast of the Super Bowl on January 22. The commercial, for Apple Computer, Incorporated's, Macintosh computer, borrowed the "Big Brother" theme from the George Orwell novel *1984*. Apple used the theme effectively to jab at its archrival, International Business Machines Corporation (IBM). A fresh and imaginative commercial for L'eggs pantyhose was based on the Radio City Music Hall Rockettes, a dancing troupe noted for its synchronized high kicks. Also receiving high marks were new campaigns for J. C. Penney Company, Incorporated, and Montgomery Ward and Company, stressing popular brand names of merchandise; and Beatrice Companies, Incorporated, featuring products and services of many companies in the gigantic firm.

Campaigns Against Pain. *Ibuprofen* was hardly a household word in the United States in 1983, when pharmacists dispensed this nonaspirin pain reliever by prescription only. But when the U.S. Food and Drug Administration approved ibuprofen for sale without a prescription on May 18, 1984, two pharmaceutical firms were prepared to spread the word throughout the land. They launched massive campaigns in all major media — American Home Products Corporation for its Advil brand of ibuprofen, and Bristol-Myers Company, Incorporated, for Nuprin.

Competition in the toothpaste market heated up when pump-dispensed dentifrices began to appear. Minnetonka, Incorporated, began distributing its Check-Up brand in May, and Colgate-Palmolive Company was right behind with Colgate.

Record Year. In 1983, U.S. advertising agencies posted a record gross income of $6.51 billion on worldwide billings of $44.2 billion, according to the annual report published in 1984 by *Advertising Age* magazine. The gross income was 10.7 per cent higher than the $5.88 billion reported in 1982. Billings were up 12.8 per cent from the 1982 total of $39.2 billion. Young & Rubicam was the leader in worldwide income for the fourth straight year with a gross income of $414.0 million on billings of $2.76 billion. Ted Bates Worldwide repeated in the number-two spot with gross income of $388.0-million on billings of $2.59 billion. In third place again was J. Walter Thompson Company with gross income of $378.4 million on billings of $2.52 billion.

The 100 Leading Advertisers in the United States spent $18.9 billion on advertising in 1983, according to *Advertising Age*. This was an 11 per cent increase over the 1982 figure of $17.1 billion. The leader again was Procter & Gamble Company, which spent $773.6 million. 　　　Jarlath J. Graham

In WORLD BOOK, see ADVERTISING.

AFGHANISTAN. The Soviet Union sharply escalated its war with Afghan *mujahedeen* (fighters for the faith) in April 1984 as the Soviet occupation of Afghanistan entered its fifth year with no end in sight. A truce negotiated in 1983 with Ahmad Shah Massoud, the chief mujahedeen commander in the Panjshir Valley north of Kabul, was not renewed after Soviet army leaders rejected his demand for self-government for the Panjshir.

Some 15,000 Soviet and Afghan Army troops supported by tanks, airplanes, and helicopter gunships invaded the valley on April 20. They succeeded in occupying most of the valley in the initial thrust, but Massoud — mistakenly reported killed — regrouped his forces and resumed traditional guerrilla tactics from mountain hideouts. The Soviets were hampered by desertions by soldiers of the Afghan Army. By October, Soviet forces controlled the lower valley from six main bases but were surrounded by mujahedeen lines.

The Soviet Union wanted to gain control of the Panjshir because Massoud had established a "state" there independent of the Soviet-backed government of Revolutionary Council President Babrak Karmal. The Panjshir had its own courts, tax-collection system, schools, and hospital.

U.S. Denounces Soviets. On May 1, United States President Ronald Reagan condemned the escalation of the war in Afghanistan and criticized the Soviet Union for the brutality of its occupation, particularly toward Afghan civilians. Soviet tactics were reported to include the intensive bombing of rural areas, the use of nerve gas, the massacre of villagers suspected of aiding the mujahedeen, and the destruction of crops.

The Soviets gave no sign that they were willing to negotiate a withdrawal of their 105,000 troops from Afghanistan. The Soviet Union's new head of state, Konstantin U. Chernenko, refused to discuss the issue with United Nations mediator Diego Cordóvez when they met in Moscow in April.

The Karmal Regime, already militarily and economically dependent on the Soviet Union, was further hampered by political infighting and inept army leadership. In January, Karmal fired his three top army commanders. The government extended compulsory military service for Afghan men to four years and organized workers' militias to guard state-owned factories and government buildings from sabotage.

Feuding between Karmal's Khalq (Masses) faction and the rival Parcham (Flag) faction of the ruling Afghan Communist Party brought a wave of assassinations of Khalq officials in March. Karmal took several steps toward winning public support, including canceling a forced land redistribution program begun in 1980. 　　　William Spencer

See also ASIA (Facts in Brief Table). In WORLD BOOK, see AFGHANISTAN.

AFRICA

As the terrible drought continued in 1984, famine struck a number of African countries, with Ethiopia and Mozambique reaching a state of crisis. Civil wars persisted in Angola, Chad, Ethiopia, Mozambique, and Uganda, and only in Mozambique was there any significant progress toward peace. Nationalist guerrilla movements continued their efforts to gain control of Namibia from South Africa and of Western Sahara from Morocco. The white-minority government of South Africa strengthened its position by signing non-aggression treaties with black-ruled neighboring states. And Guinea joined the long list of African countries with military governments, but Ethiopia, Ghana, and Liberia took steps toward returning to civilian rule.

Famine. Twenty-seven African countries south of the Sahara had severe food shortages in 1984. In Ethiopia, where the famine was devastating, the government estimated in late October that approximately 6.4 million people out of a total population of 35.3 million were facing starvation. A month later, Ethiopian officials said they expected the 1984 death toll from starvation and malnutrition-related illnesses to reach nearly 1 million. Mozambique was also badly affected by drought and famine. United Nations (UN) officials estimated that, at midyear, about 1.5 million Mozambicans depended on donated food for their survival, and as many as 100,000 people had died. Other countries in every major region of sub-Saharan Africa except the tropical rain forest areas also suffered serious food shortages in 1984.

Drought was the main cause of the food shortages in 1983 and 1984, but another contributing factor was poverty. For example, the estimated 1980 per-capita income in Ethiopia was only $134; in Mozambique, $207; and in Tanzania, $241. Those and other impoverished African countries did not have enough money to import the amount of food they needed to make up for their disastrous harvests.

In the fall of 1984, the United States and other Western nations began transporting massive shipments of grain to Africa — particularly to Ethiopia — but that aid came too late for many starving Africans. The delay in responding to the growing famine resulted partly from the slowness with which some African governments appealed for aid, but delays by donor nations were also to blame. In addition, the long distance between the foreign granaries and the starving Africans was an obstacle to the quick delivery of massive shipments of grain. To speed its response in future crises, the United States government in October selected two grain-storage sites in Africa — one in Niamey, Niger's capital, and the other in Kenya's port city of Mombasa. In each city, 15,000 short tons (13,600 metric tons) of grain from the United States will be held in warehouses, ready for rapid shipment to famine areas.

Armed conflicts in several countries — Angola, Chad, Ethiopia, Mozambique, and Zimbabwe — also contributed to the development of famine by disrupting the distribution of food. Combatants sabotaged roads and railroad tracks, attacked supply trucks, and took food shipments for their own use.

Civil Wars. With French forces continuing to occupy an east-west defensive line across the center of the country, Chad's long-standing civil war settled into a stalemate in 1984. France, the former colonial ruler of Chad, sent some 3,500 troops in 1983 to support President Hissein Habré. The forces of Habré's opponent, former President Goukouni Weddeye, were backed up by about 5,500 Libyan troops. France and Libya agreed in September 1984 to withdraw all their forces. France completed its pullout in November, but about 3,000 Libyan soldiers remained in Chad.

A two-year deadlock in the war in Ethiopia's northern province of Eritrea ended in January as the Eritrean People's Liberation Front (EPLF), a rebel group that seeks to turn Eritrea into an independent country, mounted a strong offensive against the government. Between January and April, the EPLF captured two towns and claimed to have routed the defenders of three government garrisons. Other rebel groups, which sought regional self-rule rather than complete independence, reported successful attacks on government forces in Gondar, Harar, Tigre, and Wollo provinces. Particularly disturbing to the government was the growing military strength of a rebel movement claiming to represent Ethiopia's largest ethnic group, the Oromos.

In Uganda, the National Resistance Army (NRA), the largest of four antigovernment guerrilla movements, made hit-and-run attacks on military and police installations. On February 20, in one of its most dramatic strikes, it raided an army barracks at Masindi, capturing supplies of guns.

Angola's main rebel movement, the National Union for the Total Independence of Angola (UNITA), continued to control most of the country's southeastern region and to attack transportation routes, economic development projects, and military installations elsewhere in Angola. In 1984,

Famine victims who have fled their homes wait for food and medical attention at a relief camp in northern Ethiopia in November.

177

Facts in Brief on African Political Units

Country	Population	Government	Monetary Unit*	Foreign Trade (million U.S. $) Exports†	Imports†
Algeria	22,480,000	President Chadli Bendjedid; Prime Minister Abdelhamid Brahimi	dinar (5 = $1)	13,182	10,754
Angola	8,047,000	President José Eduardo dos Santos	kwanza (29.9 = $1)	2,020	2,082
Benin	3,965,000	President Mathieu Kerekou	CFA franc (462.5 = $1)	368	662
Bophuthatswana	1,036,000	President & Prime Minister Lucas Mangope	rand (1.9 = $1)	no statistics available	
Botswana	1,063,000	President Quett K. J. Masire	pula (1.4 = $1)	582	671
Burundi	4,818,000	President Jean-Baptiste Bagaza	franc (123 = $1)	73	186
Cameroon	9,548,000	President Paul Biya	CFA franc (462.5 = $1)	942	1,217
Cape Verde	365,000	President Aristides Pereira; Prime Minister Pedro Pires	escudo (86.2 = $1)	4	66
Central African Republic	2,672,000	National Recovery Committee President & Prime Minister André-Dieudonné Kolingba	CFA franc (462.5 = $1)	79	95
Chad	4,941,000	President Hissein Habré	CFA franc (462.5 = $1)	58	109
Ciskei	660,000	President Lennox Sebe	rand (1.9 = $1)	no statistics available	
Comoros	411,000	President Ahmed Abdallah Abderemane; Prime Minister Ali Mroudjae	CFA franc (462.5 = $1)	17	33
Congo	1,755,000	President Denis Sassou-Nguesso; Prime Minister Ange Edouard Poungui	CFA franc (462.5 = $1)	977	807
Djibouti	379,000	President Hassan Gouled Aptidon; Prime Minister Barkat Gourad Hamadou	franc (175.4 = $1)	66	152
Egypt	47,395,000	President Hosni Mubarak; Prime Minister Kamal Hasan Ali	pound (1 = $1.27)	3,120	9,078
Equatorial Guinea	411,000	President Teodoro Obiang Nguema Mbasogo; Prime Minister Cristino Seriche Bioko	ekuele (340.1 = $1)	13	37
Ethiopia	35,295,000	Provisional Military Administrative Council & Council of Ministers Chairman Mengistu Haile-Mariam	birr (2 = $1)	404	787
Gabon	688,000	President Omar Bongo; Prime Minister Léon Mébiame	CFA franc (462.5 = $1)	2,113	708
Gambia	686,000	President Sir Dawda Kairaba Jawara	dalasi (3 = $1)	48	115
Ghana	13,736,000	Provisional National Defense Council Chairman Jerry John Rawlings	cedi (38 = $1)	873	705
Guinea	5,726,000	President Lansana Conté; Prime Minister Diarra Traore	syli (24.5 = $1)	385	375
Guinea-Bissau	870,000	President João Bernardo Vieira; Vice President Paulo Correia	peso (78.1 = $1)	12	50
Ivory Coast	9,412,000	President Félix Houphouët-Boigny	CFA franc (462.5 = $1)	2,235	2,090
Kenya	20,373,000	President Daniel T. arap Moi	shilling (13.5 = $1)	979	1,683
Lesotho	1,517,000	King Moshoeshoe II; Prime Minister Leabua Jonathan	loti (1.9 = $1)	35	519
Liberia	2,312,000	President Samuel K. Doe	dollar (1 = $1)	477	428
Libya	3,608,000	Leader of the Revolution Muammar Muhammad al-Qadhafi; General People's Congress General Secretary Muhammad al-Zarruq Rajab; General People's Committee Chairman (Prime Minister) Mohamed el Zarouk Ragab	dinar (1 = $3.37)	11,060	6,514
Madagascar	10,001,000	President Didier Ratsiraka; Prime Minister Désiré Rakotoarijaona	franc (453.1 = $1)	316	540

*Exchange rates as of Dec. 1, 1984, or latest available data. †Latest available data.

Country	Population	Government	Monetary Unit*	Foreign Trade (million U.S. $) Exports†	Imports†
Malawi	6,999,000	President H. Kamuzu Banda	kwacha (1.5 = $1)	230	312
Mali	7,996,000	President Moussa Traoré	CFA franc (462.5 = $1)	167	344
Mauritania	1,812,000	President Maayouia Ould Sid Ahmed Taya	ouguiya (66.2 = $1)	280	218
Mauritius	1,035,000	Governor General Sir Seewoosagur Ramgoolam; Prime Minister Aneerood Jugnauth	rupee (14.6 = $1)	373	438
Morocco	23,418,000	King Hassan II; Prime Minister Mohammed Karim-Lamrani	dirham (9.0 = $1)	1,790	3,192
Mozambique	14,088,000	President Samora Moisés Machel	metical (43.7 = $1)	452	889
Namibia (South West Africa)	1,187,000	Administrator-General Willie van Niekerk	rand (1.9 = $1)	no statistics available	
Niger	6,355,000	Supreme Military Council President Seyni Kountché; Prime Minister Hamid Algabid	CFA franc (462.5 = $1)	333	442
Nigeria	91,081,000	Federal Military Government Head Muhammadu Buhari	naira (1 = $1.30)	19,739	20,846
Rwanda	5,795,000	President Juvénal Habyarimana	franc (98 = $1)	81	279
São Tomé and Príncipe	88,000	President Manuel Pinto da Costa	dobra (44.5 = $1)	9	20
Senegal	6,464,000	President Abdou Diouf; Interim Prime Minister Moustapha Niasse	CFA franc (462.5 = $1)	477	974
Seychelles	69,000	President France Albert René	rupee (7.1 = $1)	19	85
Sierra Leone	3,988,000	President Siaka Stevens	leone (2.5 = $1)	111	298
Somalia	5,661,000	President Mohamed Siad Barre	shilling (16.9 = $1)	185	221
South Africa	32,235,000	State President Pieter Willem Botha	rand (1.9 = $1)	17,256	14,620
Sudan	21,191,000	President & Prime Minister Gaafar Mohamed Nimeiri	pound (1.3 = $1)	624	1,354
Swaziland	639,000	Queen Regent Ntombi; Prime Minister Prince Bhekimpi Dlamani	lilangeni (1.9 = $1)	276	458
Tanzania	21,837,000	President Julius K. Nyerere; Prime Minister Salim Ahmed Salim	shilling (17.3 = $1)	445	1,134
Togo	3,056,000	President Gnassingbe Eyadéma	CFA franc (462.5 = $1)	177	391
Transkei	2,500,000	President Kaiser Matanzima; Prime Minister George Matanzima	rand (1.9 = $1)	no statistics available	
Tunisia	7,161,000	President Habib Bourguiba; Prime Minister Mohamed Mzali	dinar (1 = $1.23)	1,852	3,108
Uganda	15,004,000	President Milton Obote; Prime Minister Erifasi Otema Alimadi	shilling (466.2 = $1)	345	293
Upper Volta (Burkina)	6,889,000	National Council of Revolution President Thomas Sankara	CFA franc (462.5 = $1)	56	346
Venda	343,000	President Patrick Mphephu	rand (1.9 = $1)	no statistics available	
Zaire	30,430,000	President Mobutu Sese Seko; Prime Minister Kengo wa Dondo	zaire (37 = $1)	569	480
Zambia	6,714,000	President Kenneth David Kaunda; Prime Minister Nalumino Mundia	kwacha (2 = $1)	1,059	831
Zimbabwe	8,721,000	President Canaan Banana; Prime Minister Robert Gabriel Mugabe	dollar (1.4 = $1)	1,273	1,430

Beneath a huge portrait of their leader, Jonas Savimbi, rebels of the National Union for the Total Independence of Angola parade in April.

UNITA became active in the far northern region of Cabinda, an oil-producing area of Angola.

Among the continuing civil wars in Africa, only the conflict in Mozambique showed signs of being resolved. On October 3, the Mozambican government announced a cease-fire agreement with the rebel Mozambique National Resistance (MNR).

South Africa, which had been supporting the MNR militarily since 1980, served as an intermediary in the Mozambican negotiations and agreed to participate in policing the cease-fire. Earlier in 1984, South Africa's white-minority government had signed a nonaggression treaty with Mozambique and revealed the existence of a similar pact with Swaziland. Under the terms of the agreements, both black-ruled countries promised not to allow their territory to be used as launching pads for guerrilla attacks on South Africa.

Namibia. In November, Angola offered a plan aimed at encouraging South Africa to complete its withdrawal and grant independence to Namibia. South Africa had insisted since 1981 that it could not agree to Namibian independence until some 23,000 Cuban troops stationed in neighboring Angola were withdrawn. To meet that condition, Angola proposed reducing the Cuban force over a three-year period. During the same time, the UN would supervise elections in Namibia, which would then be granted its freedom by South Africa. Angola wanted 5,000 to 10,000 Cuban troops to remain, presumably to help the government fight the UNITA rebels.

Western Sahara. Another territory fighting for its independence in 1984 was Western Sahara, a former Spanish colony that Morocco annexed in 1976. Since that time, a nationalist movement calling itself the Polisario Front has fought Morocco for possession of the territory, which it has proclaimed to be an independent nation, the Sahara Arab Democratic Republic (SADR). The Polisario Front guerrillas established a government-in-exile that has gained increasing diplomatic recognition in Africa; on March 4, 1984, Upper Volta became the 29th African country to recognize the SADR.

Militarily, however, it was the Moroccans who appeared to strengthen their position in 1984. To protect settled areas against Polisario attacks, Morocco began in 1980 to build a system of earthen defensive walls lined with ditches, barbed wire, and minefields. By late 1984, this system extended in an arc more than 800 miles (1,300 kilometers) long from Algeria to the Atlantic coast.

Organization of African Unity. Since 1981, the Organization of African Unity (OAU) has urged Morocco to hold a referendum in Western Sahara to determine if the majority of its inhabitants want independence. Although no such referendum was held, the OAU voted in 1982 to accept the SADR as its 51st member. Because Morocco protested that action strongly, the annual meeting of OAU leaders scheduled for 1982 was canceled, and the 1983 meeting took place without an SADR delegation. However, when Morocco was unable to prevent SADR participation in the 1984 meeting — held in November in Addis Ababa, Ethiopia — Morocco announced its withdrawal from the OAU.

Name Change. The government of Upper Volta announced on August 3 that the name of the country was being changed to Burkina. Burkina is a general term for the country's people. The full new name is Burkina Faso, which means "land of the honest people."

Military Coups. In an apparently bloodless coup on April 3, a group of military officers seized power in Guinea. The coup came just eight days after the death of Ahmed Sékou Touré, Guinea's president since 1958. The military government named army Colonel Lansana Conté as the country's new president.

Cameroon's civilian government thwarted an attempted military take-over on April 6 and 7. Members of a special presidential palace guard rebelled, but units of the army put down the revolt.

The military government of Upper Volta reported on June 7 that it had uncovered a coup plot involving army officers, civil servants, and the former head of a banned political party, the Vol-

tan Progressive Union. The plot's alleged leader was Colonel Didier Tiendrebeogo, a former military mayor of the capital city, Ouagadougou. He and six other accused conspirators, including two civilians, were executed on June 11.

On December 12, Mauritania's army chief of staff, Maayouia Ould Sid Ahmed Taya, seized power in a bloodless coup. Taya deposed President Mohamed Khouna Ould Haidalla, who was in Burundi.

Ghana's military government reported on March 25 that it had suppressed an attempted coup the day before, the fifth known armed plot against its rule since its own forcible seizure of power in December 1981. In July, the government announced that it was making plans to return the country to civilian rule, and it took a step in that direction by adding civilians to the ruling Provisional National Defense Council.

Also Making Progress toward a return to civilian rule were Ethiopia and Liberia. On September 10, the leaders of Ethiopia, which has been under military rule since 1974, launched the Workers Party of Ethiopia. The party, which would become the ruling body if civilian government is restored, was modeled after the Communist parties in the Soviet-dominated countries of Eastern Europe. Ethiopia's current chief of state, Council of Minis-

Leaders of South Africa and Mozambique shake hands in March over their non-aggression pact, one of the first between South Africa and a black-ruled nation.

ters Chairman Mengistu Haile-Mariam, was selected to head the Politburo, the new party's top policymaking body.

The military government of Liberia, in power since 1980, held a referendum on July 3 on a proposed constitution for civilian rule. Before the vote, the head of government, President Samuel K. Doe, decreed that the constitution needed the approval of at least 67 per cent of the registered voters to be adopted; it received 78 per cent.

On July 21, Doe disbanded the ruling People's Redemption Council (PRC), an all-military body. In its place, he appointed a 57-member interim national assembly, consisting of civilians and the members of the dissolved PRC. Five days later, he ended a four-year ban on political parties in preparation for elections, scheduled for late 1985. The inauguration of a fully civilian government was planned for January 1986.   J. Dixon Esseks

See also articles on individual African countries. In the Special Reports section, see AFRICA — THE TROUBLED CONTINENT. In WORLD BOOK, see AFRICA.

AGRICULTURE. See FARM AND FARMING.

AIR FORCE. See ARMED FORCES.

AIR POLLUTION. See ENVIRONMENT.

AIRPORT. See AVIATION.

ALABAMA. See STATE GOVERNMENT.

ALASKA. See STATE GOVERNMENT.

ALBANIA continued cautiously to strengthen its relations with the West in 1984 against a background of economic difficulties. In January, Albania and Italy signed an agreement on cultural, educational, and scientific cooperation, and the countries' official news agencies agreed to work together. In July, Albanian and Austrian television companies signed a cooperation pact.

Albania signed a transportation agreement with Turkey in February, and Turkey's minister of agriculture visited Albania in May. In August, Franz Josef Strauss, leader of West Germany's Christian Social Union, visited Albania.

Relations with Yugoslavia remained cool. In February, Fadilj Hodža, a Communist Party leader in Yugoslavia and an ethnic Albanian, attacked the Albanian government's "dirty and reactionary intrigues" and criticized it for "chopping people's heads off" and "liquidating opponents." Albania continued to attack Yugoslav trials of ethnic Albanians who had campaigned for the upgrading of Kosovo, a province of the Republic of Serbia in Yugoslavia. Most residents of Kosovo are ethnic Albanians. The defendants at the trials wanted to make Kosovo a republic within Yugoslavia.

In October, Albania and Yugoslavia resumed talks on cultural exchanges. The previous talks had ended in 1981 after ethnic Albanians rioted in Kosovo. The 1984 discussions soon broke down

over Yugoslavia's demands for better treatment of the small Yugoslav minority in Albania and Albania's insistence that its cultural exchanges with Yugoslav republics and provinces, including Kosovo, must be direct.

Other Nations. Albania and Greece quarreled over the rights of ethnic Greeks in Albania. In February, Greece's Prime Minister Andreas Papandreou said that Greece could not remain indifferent to violations of the ethnic Greeks' rights.

Albania discontinued its six-year propaganda campaign against China in May. In October, the Soviet Union made gestures of friendship to Albania, but Albania did not respond.

The Economy. Albania acknowledged that it was having trouble mining chromium ore. Albania was the West's second largest supplier of chromium — after South Africa — but poor mining technology had severely reduced Albania's supply of mined ore. Oil production fell by one-third.

In March, Albania and Italy signed an agreement whereby Albania would send raw materials to Italy in exchange for technology. In May, Albania and France agreed that Albania would export minerals, farm products, and fuels to France in exchange for raw materials, machinery, communications equipment, and chemicals.   Chris Cviic

See also EUROPE (Facts in Brief Table). In WORLD BOOK, see ALBANIA.

ALBERTA. Southern Alberta experienced a hot dry summer in 1984, similar to those of the Dust Bowl years of the 1930's. Crops on nonirrigated land were severely damaged by the drought, and the worst plague of grasshoppers in a decade compounded the problem. On Alberta's vast acreage of irrigated farmland, crop yields were down as hot winds evaporated the moisture.

Budget Problems. For the third year in a row, the Progressive Conservative government of Premier Peter Lougheed was obliged to dip into the province's Heritage Savings Trust Fund to stave off tax increases or cuts in medical and educational services. The fund, accumulated from oil and gas revenues, was drawn on for $1.5 billion (Canadian dollars; $1 = U.S. 76 cents as of Dec. 31, 1984).

The budget, announced on March 27, showed no tax increases, a slight overall reduction in public expenditures, and the elimination of 1,100 civil service jobs. It called for slightly increased spending for hospitals and medical care, social services, and education, and reduced outlays for housing, utilities, and telecommunications.

Economic Growth Plan. Premier Lougheed released a 107-page report on July 11 setting out an optimistic five-year plan for the economic growth of Alberta. The report called for active governmental intervention in the economy to spur busi-

Protesting a U.S. cruise missile test in Canada in early March, members of Greenpeace block the road to a weapons-testing range in Alberta.

ness. This approach was in line with the Lougheed government's actions in recent years, which have included buying a regional airline, constructing a grain terminal in northern British Columbia, financially supporting projects to extract oil from oil sands, and sponsoring sales missions abroad.

The Lougheed government, in power since 1971, also indicated that it was considering establishing a separate personal income tax collection system in Alberta to replace the present arrangement, under which the federal government collects taxes on behalf of the province. This would allow Alberta to provide individual tax concessions for people who invest in Alberta's industries. As part of his economic plan, Lougheed also called for substantial relaxation of the rules for screening investments coming into Canada from other countries and requested increased help from the federal government in selling Alberta's large surplus of natural gas.

Party Leader Dies. Grant Notley, the New Democratic Party leader known as "the conscience of Alberta," was killed in a plane crash in northern Alberta on October 19. One of only four opposition members in the legislature, Notley had been a respected critic of the powerful Lougheed government ever since he was first elected to the legislature in 1971.   David M. L. Farr

In WORLD BOOK, see ALBERTA.

ALGERIA. Chadli Bendjedid was reelected to a second five-year term as Algeria's president on Jan. 12, 1984. He had no opposition, but nevertheless 96 per cent of eligible voters cast their ballots. The ruling National Liberation Front (FLN) had declared that it was the patriotic duty of all eligible Algerians to vote.

Following the election, Bendjedid formed a new cabinet and enlarged the FLN leadership. The moves reflected Bendjedid's intention to continue Algeria's development as a socialist country under his own choice of leaders — task-oriented specialists rather than politicians.

Relations with Morocco, which had improved in 1983, deteriorated again as Algeria continued its backing of the independence movement in Western Sahara. In June, Algerian Army units clashed with Moroccan forces that had crossed the Algerian border in pursuit of guerrillas of the Polisario Front, the military arm of the Saharan nationalists. The Algerians captured 31 Moroccan soldiers, who were later released. Earlier, the government announced closer ties with Upper Volta (Burkina) and Mauritania. Both countries had recognized the Sahara Arab Democratic Republic as an independent state in Western Sahara, which Morocco has annexed.

Friction with Morocco also led Algeria to closer relations with Tunisia. In May, a 1983 friendship pact between the two countries was expanded to set up a joint transport company and integrate their national development plans.

Muslim Fundamentalists. Algeria has been less affected than other Muslim states by Islamic fundamentalism, the movement to bring government and daily life into line with the teachings of Islam. But Algeria had difficulties with the fundamentalists in 1984. In March, the funeral of a prominent Islamic leader, Sheik Solani, who had died while under house arrest, attracted 25,000 chanting mourners. In May, Bendjedid granted amnesty to 91 political prisoners in an effort to defuse Islamic opposition to his socialist policies. But unrest continued. In September, 19 fundamentalist leaders went on trial on charges of provoking riots against the government.

The Algerian Economy slowed down in 1984, largely as a result of overspending on development projects and imports and declining oil exports. The budget, approved on January 8, increased expenditures by 7 per cent over 1983, to $21 billion. The 1985-1989 five-year plan, passed by the National Assembly in May, gave priority to the expansion of domestic production and the streamlining and decentralization of state-owned industries. William Spencer

See also AFRICA (Facts in Brief Table). In WORLD BOOK, see ALGERIA.

AMERICAN LIBRARY ASSOCIATION (ALA). More

than 11,000 ALA members and friends of libraries attended the ALA's annual conference in Dallas, held from June 23 to 27, 1984. Featured speakers included former first lady Rosalynn Carter and Amadou Mahtar M'Bow, director general of the United Nations Educational, Scientific and Cultural Organization (UNESCO). Civil rights leader Coretta Scott King accepted a special citation at the 15th annual award program named for her to honor excellence in books by black authors and illustrators.

Earlier in the year, ALA President Brooke E. Sheldon appointed a task force to respond to the National Commission on Excellence in Education report *A Nation at Risk* — which made no mention of libraries — and to develop ways to involve libraries in improving education. At the Dallas conference, the task force presented its report, *Realities: Educational Reform in a Learning Society.* It stressed the importance of good school libraries and community support for public libraries.

E. J. Josey, chief of the Bureau of Specialist Library Services for the New York State Library in Albany, took office as the new ALA president. Beverly P. Lynch, librarian of the University of Illinois at Chicago, was elected ALA vice president.

Combating Illiteracy. The Coalition for Literacy, a group founded and fostered by the ALA,

launched a major public service campaign in 1984 to combat adult functional illiteracy. More than 23 million adults in the United States are functionally illiterate — that is, unable to read or write well enough to meet the demands of daily life. An individual who is functionally illiterate cannot, for example, read street signs or fill out a job application. The advertising campaign is designed to raise public awareness of the problem and to recruit and train volunteer tutors.

Service Awards. The Minnesota Library Association won the 1984 $5,000 J. Morris Jones-World Book Encyclopedia-ALA Goals Award for a project called "Building Coalitions for the Public Good." The New York Library Association won the $5,000 Bailey K. Howard-World Book Encyclopedia-ALA Goals Award for its efforts in computerizing membership records.

Children's Books. The 1984 Newbery Medal for the most distinguished contribution to American children's literature published in 1983 was awarded to Beverly Cleary for *Dear Mr. Henshaw.* Illustrators Alice Provensen and Martin Provensen received the 1984 Caldecott Medal for the best picture book for *The Glorious Flight: Across the Channel with Louis Blériot.* Peggy Barber

See also CANADIAN LIBRARY ASSOCIATION; LIBRARY; LITERATURE FOR CHILDREN. In WORLD BOOK, see AMERICAN LIBRARY ASSOCIATION.

ANGOLA. The civil war in Angola dragged on for the 10th straight year in 1984 as the main rebel group, the National Union for the Total Independence of Angola (UNITA), mounted hit-and-run attacks in several parts of the country, while maintaining its control over most of the southeastern region. On July 12, the rebels blew up a pipeline owned by Gulf Oil Corporation in Cabinda. And on July 28, UNITA saboteurs damaged two ships in the harbor of Luanda.

The government of President José Eduardo dos Santos was embarrassed by UNITA's continued success in kidnapping foreign specialists working in Angola on economic development projects. In May, UNITA's leader, Jonas Savimbi, said he hoped to pressure the dos Santos government into forming a coalition with UNITA.

In a pact signed on February 16, South Africa agreed to withdraw the approximately 5,000 troops it had stationed in southern Angola. The South African soldiers had operated against Namibian rebels based in Angola who have been fighting to end South African rule in Namibia. At year-end, however, some South African troops still remained in Angola. J. Dixon Esseks

See also AFRICA (Facts in Brief Table); NAMIBIA. In WORLD BOOK, see ANGOLA.

ANIMAL. See CAT; CONSERVATION; DOG; ZOOLOGY; ZOOS.

ANTHROPOLOGY. In October 1984, a team of scientists working in Kenya reported the discovery of the most complete *Homo erectus* skeleton ever found. *Homo erectus*, which lived from 1.6 million to 150,000 years ago, is believed to be the human species that developed into modern human beings.

The scientists, led by anthropologists Alan C. Walker of Johns Hopkins University in Baltimore and Richard E. Leakey of the National Museums of Kenya, found the skeleton, called WT 15000, near the Nariokotome River in northwestern Kenya. It has been dated to approximately 1.6 million years old. The skeleton is nearly complete, lacking only the left arm and hand, the right arm below the elbow, and both feet.

Walker reported that WT 15000 was a boy about 12 years old when he died. His brain was about half the size of a modern human brain.

The most surprising thing about WT 15000, however, is his body size. Walker estimated that, based on the length of the boy's thighbone, he stood about 5 feet 4 inches (163 centimeters) tall and weighed about 150 pounds (68 kilograms). If he had reached adulthood, WT 15000 might have reached a height of 6 feet (183 centimeters). Scientists had previously assumed that *Homo erectus* was smaller than modern human beings.

The newly discovered skeleton promises to pro-

vide more information about the biology of *Homo erectus*. Other *Homo erectus* fossils consist only of portions of skulls, jaws, and other bones. In addition, the discovery of this skeleton, together with other *Homo erectus* fossils also found in northern Kenya, provides strong support for the idea that this early human species originated in Africa.

Oldest Hominid? In April 1984, Andrew P. Hill of Harvard University's Peabody Museum of Archaeology and Ethnology in Cambridge, Mass., announced the discovery in Kenya of a jaw fragment that may be the oldest fossil from a *hominid* (prehuman or human ancestor) found so far. The fossil — a piece of a lower jaw 2 inches (5 centimeters) long containing two molar teeth — was found at Tabarin, near Lake Baringo, about 200 miles (320 kilometers) northwest of Nairobi. Scientists believe the jaw fragment may be 5 million years old. According to David R. Pilbeam of Harvard, who is codirector of the project, the jaw fragment resembles that of the ancient species *Australopithecus afarensis*.

***Proconsul* Family.** In August, Walker and Leakey announced the discovery of five 18-million-year-old partial skeletons from a species thought to be the common ancestor of apes and human beings. The bones, which belong to the species *Proconsul africanus,* were found on Ru-

Anthropologist Richard E. Leakey scrapes soil from the leg bone of a 1.6-million-year-old
Homo erectus skeleton that was found in Kenya in August and September.

A Historic Family Gathering

It was certainly one of the most unusual family gatherings ever. An international affair, it boasted family members from 10 countries, including Egypt, South Africa, the United States, West Germany, and Yugoslavia. The oldest member, represented by a skull, was at least 33 million years old. The youngest, also represented by a skull, was about 9,000 years old. Together, those present provided a once-in-a-lifetime opportunity to see firsthand the evidence of the development of the human family.

The occasion was an extraordinary exhibition called "Ancestors: Four Million Years of Humanity" held at the American Museum of Natural History in New York City from April to September 1984. On display were more than 40 specimens that scientists believe are fossils of our prehuman and human ancestors, fossils described by the curator of the exhibit as "the crown jewels of the human race."

The exhibit was the first time that key hom-inid fossils had ever been gathered together in one place. (Scientists use the word *hominid* to refer to our human and closest prehuman ancestors.) Many of the fossils had never been publicly displayed before. Most of the specimens are considered national treasures and are usually accessible only to scientists.

According to Ian M. Tattersall, the museum's curator of anthropology and the organizer of the exhibit, "The museum wanted to show the actual tangible evidence on which our understanding of human evolution is based."

The fossils represented nearly all the known stages of human development, from very early hominids such as *Australopithecus,* to early advanced human beings, such as *Homo habilis,* and to more recent types, such as Neanderthal man and the Cro-Magnons, the earliest modern inhabitants of Europe. Arranged chronologically, the fossils showed the changes that occurred as early hominids became fully human. Visitors could see that teeth and faces became smaller and brains became larger.

One of the most famous fossils in the exhibit was the skull of a 6-year-old child, probably about 2.25 million years old, known scientifically as *Australopithecus africanus* and commonly as the Taung child. Found in South Africa in 1924, the Taung skull was the first early hominid fossil found in Africa and the first truly ancient human fossil found anywhere.

Another important fossil that made the trip to New York City was the Heidelberg jaw found in Germany in 1907. At 500,000 years old, it is the oldest human fossil found in Europe. Also on display was a 33-million-year-old skull of *Aegyptopithecus zeuxis,* found in Egypt in the 1960's and believed by many scientists to be related to the ancestor of all modern primates, including apes, monkeys, and human beings.

Unfortunately, for a variety of reasons, some important fossils never made the trip. Anthropologist Richard E. Leakey, director of the National Museums of Kenya, refused to let out of Kenya any of the fossils he and his famous parents, Louis and Mary Leakey, discovered. Ethiopia refused to part with "Lucy," the 3.5-million-year-old partial skeleton found in that country in 1974. And Australian fossils stayed at home because Aborigines objected to the public display of the bones of their ancestors. Nevertheless, Tattersall said, the museum got most of the fossils it wanted for the exhibit.

"I think the exhibit had a profound impact on everyone who attended," Tattersall said. Although each fossil had written commentary on its history and significance, the dry bones, our fragile connection to our dim past, spoke most eloquently for themselves.   Barbara A. Mayes

Scientists examine the ancient fossil bones of human ancestors brought to New York City in April for an exhibit on human development.

singa Island in Lake Victoria in Kenya. This unique collection of skeletons, consisting of two adults, a young adult, a youth, and an infant, should provide much new information about this extinct species.

Orang Ancestor? During 1984, anthropologists continued to debate the relationship between orang-utans and modern human beings and the ape's place in evolution. The debate often focused on fossils discovered in August and September 1983 by a team led by Walker and Leakey.

The scientists found the fossilized remains of an apelike creature in Kenya at a site known as Buluk. These specimens, tentatively dated to about 17 million years old, strongly resemble fossils of a creature known as *Sivapithecus*, whose remains have been found in Pakistan. Pilbeam, who has found many of the Asian *Sivapithecus* specimens, believes that because of the creature's close resemblance to modern orang-utans, it was an orang-utan ancestor. The Buluk fossils are particularly exciting because they are twice as old as the 8-million-year-old *Sivapithecus* fossils from Pakistan.

Walker believes the Buluk fossils may represent a species that was an ancestor to all apes as well as to human beings. It is also possible that the fossils represent an ancestor only of orang-utans. Or they may represent a species that was not ancestral to modern apes or to human beings.

Some scientists disagree with Walker's interpretation. They point out that modern orang-utans and the *Sivapithecus* specimens found in Pakistan share a distinctive facial structure different from that of human beings and African apes. As a result, they doubt that the Buluk fossils represent a common ancestor of all apes and human beings.

Orang Cousin. In April 1984, anthropologist Jeffrey H. Schwartz of the University of Pittsburgh in Pennsylvania challenged traditional theories of evolution by arguing that human beings are more closely related to orang-utans than to gorillas and chimpanzees. Traditionally, anthropologists have considered the African apes — chimpanzees and gorillas — as the closest living relatives to human beings. It was also widely accepted that because human beings and African apes share many characteristics, they had a recent common ancestor.

To support his argument, Schwartz pointed to a number of unique features shared by human beings and orang-utans but not by African apes. Many of these features include behavioral traits and physical characteristics that most other scientists do not consider useful for establishing evolutionary relationships. Most scientists contend that such similarities are the result of adaptations to similar environments and do not indicate a common ancestry. Donald C. Johanson

See also ARCHAEOLOGY. In WORLD BOOK, see ANTHROPOLOGY; PREHISTORIC PEOPLE.

ARCHAEOLOGY. On May 15, 1984, a joint team of United States and Guatemalan archaeologists discovered the first painted Maya tomb to be found intact since the early 1960's. Led by Richard E. W. Adams of the University of Texas at San Antonio, the team found the 1,500-year-old tomb containing the remains of a young man at Río Azul in the northern jungle of Guatemala. Adams, the first archaeologist to see the Río Azul site after its discovery in 1962, organized the recent project to salvage historical information from the site, which had been badly looted. Thieves had ransacked at least 28 tombs and crypts for art objects, which they exported and sold illegally.

The tomb discovered in 1984 was hidden within a platform next to a temple pyramid and probably escaped notice for that reason. Tomb 19, as it is officially known, is a cavelike room cut into bedrock approximately 13 feet (4 meters) below ground level. The walls of the tomb are covered with brilliant red *hieroglyphics* — pictures representing words or sounds — that scientists hope will provide a clue to the occupant's identity. Adams speculates that the young man, who was probably in his 30's when he died, may have been a relative of the ruler whose more elaborate tomb, stripped by looters, lay in the nearby pyramid.

The body in the newly found tomb had been reduced to a fragile skeleton, and the clothing had turned to dust. However, archaeologists found decayed fragments of the fabric shroud in which the body was wrapped and remains of the wooden pallet on which it was laid. Bracelets of jade beads were found near the body. Archaeologists also found the spine of a sting ray in the skeleton's pelvic area. The Maya used sting ray spines to draw blood during religious ceremonies.

Beside the body, archaeologists found 15 vessels that originally contained food offerings, including six shallow bowls and six cylindrical jars with lids decorated with animal figures. The most unusual vessel found in the tomb was a pot decorated with designs of Maya writing. It had a curved, hollow handle painted with spots like those of a jaguar and a lid with a locking device resembling modern "childproof" lids.

Human Scavengers. Anthropologists have long known that *hominids* (our human and prehuman ancestors) ate meat. In the past, most scientists believed that early hominids obtained meat by hunting. Now, an increasing number of scholars, led by archaeologists Pat Shipman of Johns Hopkins Medical School in Baltimore and Richard Potts of Yale University in New Haven, Conn., theorize that early hominids may have acquired much of their meat by scavenging.

Since the late 1970's, Shipman and Potts have studied animal bones from Olduvai Gorge in Tanzania. The bones were found in deposits that also

Excavators prepare to lower a ladder into a 1,500-year-old intact
Maya tomb discovered at Río Azul in northern Guatemala in May.

contained early hominid remains dating to almost 2 million years ago. The researchers made the remarkable discovery that some of the animal bones had *cut marks* — nicks and grooves that appeared to have been made by stone tools.

Shipman and Potts found most of the cut marks on those parts of the bones where there would have been little meat, rather than in places where meat would have been abundant. This finding was surprising because butchering marks made by hunters, as well as tooth marks left by *carnivores* (meat-eating animals), tend to be most common in meaty areas of bones. Shipman and Potts concluded from this evidence that the cut marks were not the result of butchering activities by experienced hunters, but, rather, were made by people removing skin and tendons from the animal carcasses, possibly for clothing and other nondietary purposes.

Shipman also found that in more than half of the instances where both carnivore tooth marks and cut marks appear on the Olduvai bones, the cut marks overlap the tooth marks. Such a pattern would occur if the prey had been killed by animal carnivores and then scavenged by hominid tool users. The other bones had the reverse pattern — tooth marks overlap the stone cut marks. This pattern would occur if a hominid hunter's kill was scavenged by carnivores. Because the number of

bones with overlapping marks studied by Shipman and Potts is so small — 13 in all — Shipman's theories are not conclusive. Nevertheless, her analysis provides some support for the scavenger idea.

Bronze Age Treasure. A Greek ship that sank off the coast of Turkey about 3,400 years ago has yielded the most extensive collection of Bronze Age artifacts ever found beneath the sea. (The Bronze Age lasted from about 3600 B.C. to 1000 B.C.) The ship, whose discovery was announced in December 1984, is the oldest ever excavated.

The ship's cargo consisted chiefly of ingots of copper, tin, and glass from at least three cultures: Greek, Cypriot, and Canaanite or Phoenician. George F. Bass, the director of the Institute of Nautical Archaeology at Texas A&M University at College Station and the chief scientist for the project, surmised that the ship, which sank about 1400 B.C., had sailed from Syria. It then stopped to load copper ingots on Cyprus and was headed for Greece or western Turkey when it sank while trying to round Cape Ulu Burun. The ingots were probably raw materials destined for craftworkers and manufacturers. Also found were pottery, glass beads, a gold goblet, bronze daggers, and seeds that scientists have not yet identified. Barbara Voorhies

In the Special Reports section, see DIGGING ON JEFFERSON'S MOUNTAIN. In WORLD BOOK, see ARCHAEOLOGY; MAYA.

ARCHITECTURE served as a festive framework for two public events during 1984: the Louisiana World Exposition, held from May to November in New Orleans, and the Summer Olympic Games, held in July and August in Los Angeles. The New Orleans fair featured a whimsical structure called the Wonderwall — a line of arches, columns, portals, gargoyles, and other architectural elements connecting the fair's two main gates. The Wonderwall was designed by the New Orleans firm of Perez Associates in conjunction with internationally known architects Charles W. Moore of Los Angeles and William Turnbull, Jr., of San Francisco. The artistic design of the Summer Olympics was coordinated by the Jerde Partnership, a Los Angeles architectural firm. They used colorful banners, balloons, signs, and pavilions to tie together the scattered facilities used for the games.

Controversies erupted during 1984 over architects' plans to put modern additions on historical buildings. In London, a proposal for an extension to the National Gallery, a classical building dating from the 1800's, prompted a memorable speech in May by Prince Charles to the Royal Institute of British Architects. The prince compared the proposed new wing to a blemish, calling it "a monstrous carbuncle on the face of a much loved and elegant friend." He added, "It is important in human terms to respect old buildings, street plans, and traditional scales." In September, the British government canceled the proposal.

In Paris, a furor erupted over a government proposal to add a new entrance designed by Chinese-born American architect I. M. Pei to France's national art gallery, the Louvre. Pei's design called for a modern glass pyramid 65 feet (19.8 meters) tall that many people thought inappropriate for the Louvre, the oldest section of which dates from about 1200. The project's fate remained uncertain at year's end, though archaeologists had begun preliminary digging at the site in preparation for construction.

In New York City, controversy continued over a plan to demolish the former Times Tower in Times Square, make its site a plaza, and build four new office towers facing it. The towers were designed by one of the city's leading architectural firms, John Burgee Architects with Philip Johnson. But critics called the towers too big and dull for the lively — if shabby — Times Square area.

The Historic Preservation Movement in architecture continued to grow. The oldest McDonald's hamburger stand, in Downey, Calif., dating from 1953, was nominated to the National Register of Historic Places. Preservationists also saved a neon Citgo sign (trademark of the Cities Service Company oil firm) in Boston.

The New York City Landmarks Preservation Commission in June 1984 rejected an application

The new wing that opened in May at the Museum of Modern Art in New York City includes galleries and an office tower designed by architect Cesar Pelli.

by St. Bartholomew's Church to license a developer to build a new office tower next to the historic Episcopal church. The New York state legislature took no action on a proposal to exempt church property from landmark protection laws. Preservationists hailed both events as major victories. In December, the church submitted a new, revised design to the landmarks commission.

New Buildings. The most publicized building of 1984 was the new American Telephone and Telegraph Company (AT&T) headquarters in New York City, designed by John Burgee Architects with Philip Johnson. Richly clad in granite and marble, the AT&T building featured traditional architectural forms, including a split pediment at the top and an arcade at street level. Most critics considered it a major example of post-modern architecture — the reaction against the glass-box buildings typical of the modern style. John Burgee Architects with Philip Johnson also designed another of 1984's notable buildings, the PPG Industries, Incorporated, headquarters in Pittsburgh, Pa., in a glass version of the Gothic style.

The General Foods Corporation headquarters in Rye, N.Y., a white metal rendering of a Renaissance palace, was another example of the post-modern style. The architects were Kevin Roche, John Dinkeloo and Associates of Hamden, Conn. Still other post-modern structures completed in 1984 included Gordon Wu Hall at Princeton University in New Jersey, a post-modern classroom building by Venturi, Rauch and Scott Brown of Philadelphia; and San Juan Capistrano Public Library in California, in Spanish-style post-modern by Princeton's Michael Graves.

Working in other styles, Edward Larrabee Barnes of New York City designed the International Business Machines Corporation headquarters, an elegant, crisply modern tower across the street from the post-modern AT&T. The Dallas Museum of Art, a long, two-story structure with a limestone facade, was also done by Barnes.

Two firms, Kohn Pederson Fox Associates of New York City and Perkins & Will Group Incorporated of Chicago, collaborated on 333 Wacker Drive in Chicago, a curved glass office tower. Other notable buildings included a new wing for the Museum of Modern Art in New York City by Cesar Pelli of New Haven, Conn.; and an art museum in Stuttgart, West Germany, by James Stirling and Michael Wilford of Great Britain.

Exhibitions. The most notable architecture exhibition of 1984 was "Design in America: The Cranbrook Vision, 1925-1950," which opened in April at the Metropolitan Museum of Art in New York City. The show celebrated the architecture program of the famous Cranbrook Academy of Art in Bloomfield Hills, Mich.   Robert Campbell

In WORLD BOOK, see ARCHITECTURE.

ARDITO BARLETTA VALLARINA, NICOLÁS (1938-), was declared winner of Panama's May 6, 1984, presidential election, amid charges of fraud. Panama's election tribunal made its vote count official on May 16, giving Ardito Barletta a narrow margin of 1,713 votes over his closest opponent, Arnulfo Arias Madrid, who charged the military with stealing the election for Ardito Barletta. See PANAMA.

Ardito Barletta was born on Aug. 21, 1938, in Aguadulce. Ironically, his father was an ardent supporter of Arias, the man Ardito Barletta would later defeat. At 17, Ardito Barletta entered North Carolina State University in Raleigh, where he received a bachelor's and master's degree in economics. After getting a doctorate at the University of Chicago, he returned to Panama to teach economics.

In 1968, Ardito Barletta became a key economic adviser to National Guard Commander Omar Torrijos Herrera, who came to power in a coup that ousted Arias as president after only 11 days in office. From 1973 to 1978, Ardito Barletta was minister of planning and economic policy. In 1978, he became a vice president of the World Bank in charge of projects in Latin America. He lived in Washington, D.C., until February 1984, when he returned to Panama to campaign for the presidency.   Rod Such

ARGENTINA. It was a demanding first full year in office in 1984 for President Raúl Alfonsín of Argentina, who was elected in October 1983 following seven years of military rule. Alfonsín was confronted with a nation ravaged by economic problems, including an enormous debt and one of the highest annual inflation rates in the world at 433.7 per cent in 1983. He inherited a country still suffering from wounded national pride, caused by Argentina's loss to Great Britain during the 1982 Falkland Islands war. And he had to respond to the thousands of Argentines whose friends or family members "disappeared" during the military government's brutal crackdown on civil disorder and terrorism in the late 1970's.

Economic Program. To regain economic stability, Alfonsín took on both the powerful labor unions and the armed forces. His 1984 economic program was designed to reduce the country's $11-billion deficit, curb inflation, raise real wages between 6 and 8 per cent, and stimulate overall economic growth by 5 per cent.

Negative reaction from the unions was not long in coming. On January 27, the day following news of his program, the General Confederation of Labor (CGT) — Argentina's union coalition — called for its repeal. Within the CGT, hard-line and moderate factions joined in opposition to the Alfonsín program after years of internal squabbling.

President Alfonsín, right, and former President Arturo Frondizi look on as former President Isabel Perón signs a unity accord in June.

Curbing the Military. In his first year in office, Alfonsín sought to curb what many Argentines viewed as excessive military power. Dozens of officers responsible for the Falklands war, including former Army Commander and President Leopoldo Galtieri, were stripped of their authority. In February, Galtieri was arrested, and he and two other officers were court-martialed for their conduct of the war.

On July 4, Alfonsín dismissed the army chief of staff and the commander of the Third Army Corps. Both had been outspoken in their opposition to planned cuts in military spending and to investigations of human rights violations. Then, on July 5, President Alfonsín accepted the resignations of two generals who were chief executives of Fabricaciones Militares, an industrial complex controlled by the military that is the nation's largest single employer.

On July 10, Alfonsín issued a decree ordering military officers to collaborate fully with investigations of disappearances under previous military governments. An estimated 6,000 to 30,000 people "disappeared" under these regimes, most of them under that of General Jorge Rafael Videla. On August 2, Videla was indicted and jailed for human rights abuses. Videla led the coup that brought the military to power in 1976, and he was president until 1981.

Foreign Debt. Alfonsín sought to build a national consensus behind his administration's plan for coping with Argentina's foreign debts, which amounted to about $45 billion in September 1984. On June 7, Alfonsín signed a political accord with former President María Estela (Isabel) Martinez de Perón, pledging that they would work together to restore democracy. Fifteen other political parties added their support to the accord.

With the pledges of national unity at hand, Alfonsín on June 11 submitted to the International Monetary Fund (IMF) an economic plan that Argentina would follow in return for IMF help. It was a bold move — the first time that a nation had rejected demands by the IMF in favor of working out its own economic goals based on domestic political realities.

The Alfonsín plan called for an additional $2.1-billion in IMF assistance and the rescheduling of nearly half of Argentina's foreign debts. On September 25, Argentina and the IMF agreed on a program that included a $1.4-billion loan. By late December, Argentina appeared to have made its peace with the IMF as well as with its other creditors.   Nathan A. Haverstock

See also LATIN AMERICA (Facts in Brief Table). In WORLD BOOK, see ARGENTINA.
ARIZONA. See STATE GOVERNMENT.
ARKANSAS. See STATE GOVERNMENT.

ARMED FORCES. Efforts by the Administration of United States President Ronald Reagan to resume talks with the Soviet Union on nuclear arms control remained at a stalemate during much of 1984. In June, the Soviets proposed September talks on banning "the militarization of outer space." The United States agreed but insisted that the agenda also include discussions about limiting strategic and medium-range nuclear weapons. The Soviets rejected the proposal. In November, however, both sides agreed to resume talks in January 1985.

An Aggressive Build-Up of U.S. military strength continued as a result of the stalemate on arms talks. The Department of Defense accelerated research on Reagan's so-called "Star Wars" high-technology program designed to destroy incoming nuclear missiles in space, and it conducted the first test of a missile that could destroy enemy satellites in space. In a June test, an experimental antiballistic missile destroyed an incoming missile with a dummy warhead over the Pacific Ocean.

In other weapons developments, the United States began producing the second generation of a submarine-launched Trident intercontinental ballistic missile (ICBM); *deployed* (installed) the first cruise missiles aboard submarines; and commissioned a fourth Trident submarine designed to carry ballistic missiles. Development proceeded on a single-warhead ICBM and on a Stealth bomber that could escape detection by enemy air defenses.

Two essential components of the Reagan defense build-up — the MX missile and the B-1 strategic bomber — remained controversial. Work continued on the first 21 MX missiles. The MX is a land-based ICBM capable of carrying 10 nuclear warheads. But MX critics in Congress succeeded in blocking funds for 15 additional missiles, at least until a vote could be taken in 1985. The first B-1 bomber rolled off the assembly line on Sept. 4, 1984. A prototype version of the B-1 had crashed in the Mojave Desert in California on August 29, killing the chief test pilot.

In Lebanon, the ill-fated U.S. military presence officially ended on February 26 with the withdrawal of the last group of Marines in the peace-keeping force. The withdrawal came 17 months after 1,600 Marines had been sent to Lebanon and 4 months after an attack by a suicide terrorist on Marine headquarters had killed 241 U.S. troops. The pullback left only 100 Marine guards at the U.S. Embassy outside of Beirut, and they were withdrawn on July 30. That action came under criticism after another suicide attack killed at least 14 people at the embassy on September 20.

Central American Build-Up. The Reagan Administration maintained a sizable military presence in

The last group of U.S. Marines stationed in a multinational peacekeeping force in Lebanon leave Beirut on February 26 and board ships offshore.

Drawing by Dana Fradon; © 1984 The New Yorker Magazine, Inc.

"General Hoskins, I don't care if you *are* in charge of our
star-wars defense. You must wear a regulation uniform."

Central America during 1984. The show of force appeared to stabilize the pro-American government of El Salvador in its civil war against guerrillas who are backed by the left wing government of Nicaragua. Reagan said he had no intention of sending U.S. combat forces to the region, though several thousand U.S. troops participated in exercises in El Salvador and Honduras in 1984.

Reagan sought large increases in military aid to friendly governments in Central America. His Administration engaged in secret operations aimed at undermining Nicaragua's Sandinista regime and shutting off the flow of arms from Nicaragua to rebel forces in El Salvador. The Pentagon in May announced plans to spend $149 million by 1988 to build and upgrade military installations in the region. Major projects included improvements at two air bases in Honduras.

Grenada Aftermath. The October 1983 invasion of Grenada by U.S. troops continued to provoke controversy during 1984. The Army disclosed in March that it had awarded more than 8,600 medals for service in Grenada, though only 6,000 troops had participated in the invasion.

A congressional study released in April charged that the operation suffered from faulty planning and coordination as well as tactical errors. But a Defense Department report denied the charges. The Pentagon also denied charges in October by two former military intelligence officers that combat deaths in Grenada were higher than the number reported officially. The former officers claimed there was a cover-up stemming from military attempts to conceal the existence of a top-secret commando force on the island.

The Readiness of U.S. Armed Forces remained in dispute despite the massive military build-up. In July, a congressional report charged that combat readiness had declined markedly since 1981 and that none of the three services could engage in sustained combat. Pentagon officials, on the other hand, asserted that the military was far more prepared for combat than it had been when Reagan took office. They claimed that U.S. troops could fight an intense war with conventional weapons for at least 30 days with currently available equipment and supplies. Critics of the Pentagon countercharged that the Administration had stressed the purchase of costly weapons systems at the expense of operations and maintenance. The Pentagon conceded that shortages of ammunition and spare parts and reduced training schedules could jeopardize readiness in a sustained conflict.

All the services met their recruitment and reenlistment objectives for 1984. But an improving economic climate began to lure potential enlistees into jobs in private industry and forced the Pentagon to increase enlistment and reenlistment bo-

193

nuses substantially. Troop strength stood at 2,138,303 on October 31, up 17,839 from 1983. About 505,000 troops were stationed abroad, including 344,000 in Western Europe.

Several New Weapons Systems experienced problems during 1984. The Pentagon suspended purchases of the Army's Sergeant York antiaircraft gun after it performed poorly in tests. An internal Pentagon investigation reported in September that the Army had spent millions of dollars in excess payments to the gun's contractor. The Navy grounded its fleet of F-18 Hornet jet fighters in July and said it would refuse delivery of additional planes until the contractor corrected a design flaw causing cracks in the tail assembly. A new air-to-air missile for the Air Force experienced production delays and substantial cost overruns. But the performance of the Navy's Aegis cruiser reportedly improved after poor initial tests.

Efforts to Control Waste, fraud, and other abuses in military purchasing accelerated after several embarrassing revelations about excessive cost and poor quality. The Air Force admitted in September that it had equipped its C-5A cargo planes with coffeemakers costing $7,600, three times the price paid by commercial airlines. In August, the Pentagon suspended payments on three missile systems built by Hughes Aircraft Company on the grounds that they had major defects. The Pentagon reported in September that millions of semiconductors manufactured by Texas Instruments Corporation for use in thousands of sophisticated weapons systems might be faulty.

Defense Budget. On Feb. 1, 1984, Reagan submitted a request to Congress for a $264.4-billion defense budget for the 1985 fiscal year beginning Oct. 1, 1984. The budget request was $33.4 billion higher than fiscal 1984 outlays and reflected a 9.3 per cent increase after adjustment for inflation.

The request included huge jumps in funding for major weapons systems for the third consecutive year. The Pentagon requested $8.2 billion for the B-1 bomber, $5 billion for the MX missile, $4.3 billion for Trident submarines and missiles, $4.2 billion for F-16 jet fighters, $3.2 billion for Aegis cruisers, and $1.9 billion for M-1 tanks. Congress passed a $292.9-billion defense spending bill in September.

Command Change. Pentagon counsel William H. Taft IV was named deputy secretary of defense on January 5. He replaced W. Paul Thayer, who resigned after being charged with illegally passing "insider" stock-trading information to friends before joining the government.   Thomas M. DeFrank

In WORLD BOOK, see the articles on the branches of the armed forces.

ARMY. See ARMED FORCES.

ART. See ARCHITECTURE; DANCING; LITERATURE; MUSIC, CLASSICAL; POETRY; VISUAL ARTS.

ASIA. A traveler in Asia during 1984 would have found most of the continent's more than 2 billion people quietly eking out a living. From villages where too many people tried to wrest enough food from too little good land, to overcrowded cities where some got richer but many barely survived, the people of Asia lived a generally hard but routine life. Beneath this stability and struggle, at least a dozen conflicts sputtered.

Political Changes. The assassination on October 31 of India's Prime Minister Indira Gandhi sent a shock through Asia, which lost one of its best-known figures and a leader of the worldwide nonaligned movement—those nations claiming to be allied with neither the Communist bloc nor the West. Gandhi was shot by two members of her own bodyguard who belonged to the Sikh religion. A campaign of violence by Sikh extremists to back demands for a separate Sikh state in their part of India had led Gandhi in June to order the Indian Army to capture the radicals' headquarters in the Golden Temple in Amritsar, the holiest Sikh shrine. The assault on the temple outraged many Sikhs and led to the murder plot, the extent of which was not immediately clear. See Close-Up.

Gandhi was succeeded as prime minister by her only surviving son, Rajiv, a 40-year-old former airline pilot who had entered politics just four years earlier. His selection emphasized a tendency that had become pronounced in Asia—for political power to be passed down in the same family even in countries not ruled by a monarch.

In addition to monarchies in Bhutan, Brunei Darussalam, and Nepal, Asia had the Chiang family dynasty in Taiwan and was moving toward a Kim family dynasty in North Korea. Taiwan's President Chiang Ching-kuo is the son of the late Nationalist Chinese leader Chiang Kai-shek, and North Korea's President Kim Il-song is grooming his son, Kim Chong Il, as his successor. In Singapore, Prime Minister Lee Kuan Yew's 32-year-old son, Lee Hsien Loong, retired from active duty as the country's youngest brigadier general and entered politics on September 22 amid speculation that he might succeed his father. In the Philippines, Imelda Marcos, the wife of President Ferdinand E. Marcos, kept a Cabinet post despite having said she would relinquish it, also stirring speculation.

In Sri Lanka, where Sirimavo Bandaranaike, the widow of Prime Minister S. W. R. D. Bandaranaike, who was assassinated in 1959, had later held his job, the couple's children became leaders of the political opposition. Widows and children of former leaders also headed opposition parties in Bangladesh and Pakistan.

Mongolia's leader for most of the time since 1952, Yumjaagiyn Tsedenbal, was abruptly fired by the Mongolian People's Revolutionary Party, the country's Communist party, on August 23

Marchers fill the streets of Manila in August to mark the anniversary of the 1983 assassination of Philippine opposition leader Benigno S. Aquino, Jr.

while he was in a Soviet hospital. Council of Ministers Chairman Jambyn Batmonh succeeded him as the party's general secretary. Reasons for the change were unclear. In addition to the official one of Tsedenbal's poor health, the reasons might have included Soviet dissatisfaction with Mongolia's lack of economic progress and political unity. On December 12, Batmonh was also elected Presidium chairman.

One small Asian political unit, the Portuguese territory of Macao on the southeast coast of China, held the first general elections in its 427-year history on August 15. About 56 per cent of the 51,000 voters turned out to choose 6 members of a 17-person assembly. The assembly advises Macao's governor, who is appointed by the president of Portugal.

An even tinier unit, the Cocos Islands — also called the Keeling Islands — in the Indian Ocean 800 miles (1,300 kilometers) southwest of Jakarta, Indonesia, chose integration with Australia. The islanders voted under United Nations (UN) supervision on April 6 to become part of Australia rather than becoming independent or continuing their loose association with Australia.

Military Conflict. Asia's largest wars raged throughout 1984 in Afghanistan and Kampuchea, formerly known as Cambodia. In both countries, modern Communist armies fought lightly equipped guerrillas who sought to drive out foreign invaders: the Soviets in Afghanistan and the Vietnamese in Kampuchea. No peace settlement was in sight in either conflict.

The Soviets in Afghanistan, fighting with little support from dispirited soldiers of their puppet government in the Afghan capital of Kabul, resisted UN efforts to work out a settlement that would end their five-year war. Instead, Moscow increasingly blamed Pakistan for the conflict, charging that its support for Afghan guerrillas had intensified the war. Air and artillery strikes from Afghanistan into border areas of Pakistan killed dozens of people in late 1984. Pakistan did not strike back, but its troops fought several small battles with Indian soldiers on a glacier some 4 miles (6.4 kilometers) high in the Karakoram Range of mountains dividing disputed territory claimed by India and Pakistan.

Vietnam's army, with little help from its puppet regime in Kampuchea's capital city of Phnom Penh, fought in Kampuchea against Communist Khmer Rouge guerrillas and two non-Communist resistance groups. That war occasionally spilled across the border into Thailand, whose army fought several battles with the Vietnamese. Vietnam's forces were also engaged on three other fronts: against resistance to its rule of the highlands of southern Vietnam, against opposition to its regime in Laos, and against limited border at-

Facts in Brief on Asian Countries

Country	Population	Government	Monetary Unit*	Foreign Trade (million U.S. $) Exports†	Imports†
Afghanistan	17,501,000	Revolutionary Council President Babrak Karmal; Prime Minister Sultan Ali Keshtmand	afghani (50.5 = $1)	708	695
Australia	15,661,000	Governor General Sir Ninian Martin Stephen; Prime Minister Robert Hawke	dollar (1.2 = $1)	20,651	19,349
Bangladesh	100,619,000	President Hussain Muhammad Ershad	taka (23.8 = $1)	765	2,284
Bhutan	1,451,000	King Jigme Singye Wangchuck	Indian rupee & ngultrum (12.2 = $1)	21	51
Brunei Darussalam	277,000	Sultan Sir Muda Hassanal Bolkiah	dollar (2 = $1)	4,068	599
Burma	37,875,000	President U San Yu; Prime Minister U Maung Maung Kha	kyat (8.1 = $1)	378	268
China	1,047,800,000	Communist Party General Secretary Hu Yaobang; Communist Party Deputy Chairman Deng Xiaoping; President Li Xiannian; Premier Zhao Ziyang	yuan (2.8 = $1)	22,255	21,267
India	738,759,000	President Zail Singh; Prime Minister Rajiv Gandhi	rupee (12.2 = $1)	7,408	12,839
Indonesia	159,673,000	President Suharto; Vice President Umar Wirahadikusumah	rupiah (1,066 = $1)	21,146	16,352
Iran	44,255,000	President Ali Khamenei; Prime Minister Hosein Musavi-Khamenei	rial (92.6 = $1)	12,587	12,549
Japan	120,494,000	Emperor Hirohito; Prime Minister Yasuhiro Nakasone	yen (247 = $1)	146,676	146,992
Kampuchea (Cambodia)	6,224,000	People's Revolutionary Party Secretary General & Council of State President Heng Samrin (Coalition government: President Norodom Sihanouk; Vice President Khieu Samphan; Prime Minister Son Sann)	riel (4 = $1)	1	20
Korea, North	20,061,000	President Kim Il-song; Premier Yi Chong-ok	won (1 = $1.06)	1,260	1,610
Korea, South	41,371,000	President Chun Doo Hwan; Prime Minister Chin Iee Chong	won (872 = $1)	24,445	26,192
Laos	4,077,00	President Souphanouvong; Prime Minister Kayson Phomvihan	kip (35 = $1)	48	121
Malaysia	15,128,000	Paramount Ruler Tunku Mahmood Iskandar Al-Haj Ibni Almarhum Sultan Ismail; Prime Minister Mahathir bin Mohamed	ringgit (2.4 = $1)	13,917	13,987
Maldives	177,000	President Maumoon Abdul Gayoom	rupee (7.1 = $1)	10	41
Mongolia	1,876,000	People's Revolutionary Party General Secretary & Council of Ministers Chairman Jambyn Batmonh	tughrik (3.4 = $1)	416	566
Nepal	16,450,000	King Birendra Bir Bikram Shah Dev; Prime Minister Lokendra Bahadur Chand	rupee (16.1 = $1)	91	449
New Zealand	3,177,000	Governor General Sir David Stuart Beattie; Prime Minister David R. Lange	dollar (2 = $1)	5,272	5,279
Pakistan	94,650,000	President M. Zia-ul-Haq	rupee (14.8 = $1)	3,075	5,341
Papua New Guinea	3,405,000	Governor General Sir Kingsford Dibela; Prime Minister Michael Thomas Somare	kina (1 = $1.08)	734	974
Philippines	54,759,000	President Ferdinand E. Marcos; Prime Minister César E. A. Virata	peso (20 = $1)	4,781	8,086
Russia	277,465,000	Communist Party General Secretary & Supreme Soviet Presidium Chairman Konstantin U. Chernenko; Council of Ministers Chairman Nikolay Aleksandrovich Tikhonov	ruble (1 = $1.17)	91,331	80,267
Singapore	2,570,000	President Devan Nair; Prime Minister Lee Kuan Yew	dollar (2.2 = $1)	21,833	28,158
Sri Lanka	16,099,000	President J. R. Jayewardene; Prime Minister R. Premadasa	rupee (26 = $1)	1,062	1,786
Taiwan	19,471,000	President Chiang Ching-kuo; Prime Minister Sun Yun-hsuan	new Taiwan dollar (39.5 = $1)	22,204	18,888
Thailand	51,718,000	King Bhumibol Adulyadej; Prime Minister Prem Tinsulanonda	baht (27 = $1)	6,368	10,232
Vietnam	59,967,000	Communist Party General Secretary Le Duan; National Assembly Chairman Nguyen Huu Tho; Prime Minister Pham Van Dong	dong (9.8 = $1)	369	1,080

*Exchange rates as of Dec. 1, 1984, or latest available data.   †Latest available data.

Representatives of Great Britain and China exchange copies in September of an agreement for Hong Kong's transfer from British to Chinese control.

tacks that China made to relieve pressure on Kampuchean guerrillas.

Small-scale guerrilla campaigns, mostly to support separatist demands, smoldered in Bangladesh, Burma, India, Indonesia, the Philippines, and Sri Lanka. Only the New People's Army, a Communist rebel group in the Philippines, seemed to have long-term potential to threaten the government.

Diplomats tried to settle some Asian disputes during 1984. China and Mongolia agreed on defining their border, Bhutan opened negotiations with China on their border, and China and India held another round of border talks without much progress. North Korea and South Korea interrupted their hostility for several talks, and North Korea sent $12 million worth of relief goods to South Korea after floods there in September. China and the Soviet Union held more talks on improving relations. They increased economic contacts but could not agree on reducing troop concentrations along their border or other major issues.

Members of the Association of Southeast Asian Nations (ASEAN) — Brunei Darussalam, Indonesia, Malaysia, the Philippines, Singapore, and Thailand — continued efforts to find a political solution for the Kampuchean conflict. Meeting in Jakarta on July 9 and 10, they called for national reconciliation to end Vietnam's "illegal occupation of Kampuchea."

Refugees continued to flee Indochina during 1984, though at a slower rate than in previous years. About 2,000 refugees per month flew out of Vietnam under a UN program. Another 2,000 per month escaped by boat, though half of them were attacked by pirates before they were able to reach safety. Overland escapes from Laos and Kampuchea into Thailand also continued. Relief officials worried that fewer refugees were being accepted for settlement in other parts of the world, leaving many in temporary camps. Perhaps 5 million Afghans were refugees — in Pakistan, in Iran, and crowded into Kabul and other cities.

Economically, 1984 was a good year for most Asian countries. India, long an importer of food, had such good harvests that it became an exporter. China was able to slash its grain imports. However, the UN's Food and Agriculture Organization (FAO) said in June that seven Asian nations were on its "danger list." The seven were Bangladesh, Bhutan, India, Nepal, Singapore, Sri Lanka, and Vietnam. An FAO official warned that these countries would "be unable to feed their rising populations in coming decades without a major improvement in the level of agricultural technology."

Adverse weather affected crop production in

A Woman of Power

The religious and ethnic hatreds that have long plagued India claimed another victim on Oct. 31, 1984, when Prime Minister Indira Gandhi was killed by members of her bodyguard. The assassins were Sikhs, members of a religious sect whose holiest shrine Gandhi had ordered seized in June (see INDIA).

Born into a prominent Hindu family, Indira Gandhi grew up in an atmosphere of nationalist fervor. Her father, Jawaharlal Nehru — who later became independent India's first prime minister — and her grandfather were leaders in India's struggle for independence from Great Britain.

Her family's involvement in the independence movement deprived Indira of a normal childhood. But her experiences seemed to steel her spirit and make her more self-reliant.

In 1942, after attending Oxford University in England, she married Feroze Gandhi (no relation to independence leader Mohandas K. Gandhi) against the wishes of her family. But the marriage was not a happy one, and after Nehru became prime minister, Indira Gandhi moved into his house with her two sons and became his hostess.

Only days before she was assassinated in October, Indira Gandhi walks with her son Rajiv – who succeeded her as prime minister.

In 1959, the younger members of Nehru's Congress Party engineered Gandhi's election as party president, thinking they could control the inexperienced Indira. But they soon found out that they had underestimated her. She took to the job with skill and relish, and, protected by her father's power and prestige, she streamlined the party. She also became her father's closest adviser and confidante.

In 1964, after Nehru died, Gandhi became minister of information and broadcasting under his successor, Lal Bahadur Shastri. After Shastri died two years later, the party bosses turned to her again as a compromise candidate for prime minister who could be expected to do their bidding. Once again, the bosses were wrong.

Gandhi took office as prime minister in 1966. At first, she seemed unsure how to use her vast powers. But gradually, she consolidated her hold on the party and government. Her policies also turned sharply left.

Gandhi's support in 1971 for the independence movement in what was then East Pakistan (now Bangladesh) won her enormous popularity. But that popularity faded as India's economic situation, damaged by drought and inflation, worsened.

In 1975, an Indian court convicted her of using illegal practices during her 1971 parliamentary election campaign, and her opponents demanded her resignation. Instead, Indira Gandhi declared a nationwide state of emergency, suspended civil rights, and arrested thousands of her opponents.

In 1977, confident of victory, she called elections. But she was routed. The new government's inept performance, however, led a disillusioned electorate to vote her back into office in 1980.

As prime minister, Gandhi made India the dominant power in South Asia, and with India's first explosion of a nuclear device in 1974, she led her country into the nuclear age. But she was much less effective at combating India's centuries-old problems of caste, hunger, poverty, and religious conflict. Her government was often charged with corruption. And in her actions, such as her questionable attempts in 1984 to oust opposition political leaders, she gave every indication of firmly believing that although she was indispensable, democracy was not.

Her murder was a direct result of her attempt to suppress the Sikh secessionist movement in Punjab. As in the case of her bold move in 1975 in proclaiming a state of emergency, this action also backfired. The previous time, the price had been political defeat. This time, she paid with her life.   Krishna Kumar Gaur

several countries as well as causing other hardships. In the Philippines, a tropical storm on August 29 followed by typhoons on September 2 and November 5 killed more than 1,850 people altogether. Flooding around Seoul, South Korea, in September killed about 190 people, and more than 150 others died in September floods that isolated Nepal's capital city of Kathmandu from the rest of the country for a week. Three floods in Bangladesh between May and September killed more than 700 people and aggravated the country's chronic food shortage.

Two Communist countries moved further away from Soviet-style economics in efforts to stimulate their economies. China began the most sweeping changes. Its Communist Party announced on October 20 that centralized control of industry and commerce would be relaxed over the next five years. Vietnam also relaxed its economic controls.

China signed an agreement with Great Britain under which China would assume control of Hong Kong in 1997 but would allow the territory to continue its capitalist ways for at least another 50 years. The agreement, signed on December 19, said Hong Kong's British-style laws would remain "basically unchanged." Henry S. Bradsher

See also the various Asian country articles. In the WORLD BOOK SUPPLEMENT section, see BRUNEI. In WORLD BOOK, see ASIA.

ASTRONOMY. In January 1984, atmospheric scientist Larry W. Esposito of the University of Colorado at Boulder announced that at least one and possibly more of the volcanoes on Venus are active — that is, capable of erupting. When a volcano is inactive, it no longer erupts or has not erupted in a long time. Within the solar system, only Earth and Io, a satellite of Jupiter, were previously known to have active volcanoes.

Studies of Venus. In reaching his findings, Esposito relied on measurements of the atmosphere of Venus obtained by the National Aeronautics and Space Administration (NASA) *Pioneer Venus Orbiter* (*PVO*), which has been orbiting and gathering data around Venus since December 1978. When *PVO* first scanned the planet's atmosphere in 1978, it found that sulfur dioxide gas, a major product of volcanic eruptions, was abundant. Over the next five years, the sulfur dioxide gradually decreased, while *aerosols* — airborne dust particles that produce a measurable haze — increased in Venus' atmosphere. Just such atmospheric changes were observed on Earth after the March and April 1982 eruptions of the Mexican volcano El Chichón. Observations indicated that the same gas-to-dust process has been at work on Venus as a result of a major volcanic eruption that must have occurred shortly before *PVO* reached Venus.

At a March 15, 1984, conference in Houston, astronomers were told that *volcanic landforms* — that is, land that has the physical characteristics of volcanoes — are present all over the surface of Venus. Alexei T. Basilevsky of the V. I. Vernadsky Institute of Geochemistry and Analytical Chemistry in Moscow, presented data from the Soviet Union's *Venera 15* and *16* space probes, which began orbiting Venus in October 1983.

The Soviet scientist also found that unlike the moon and Mercury, which are scarred by thousands of impact craters from meteoroids, only 57 impact craters can be found on Venus. Presumably, most Venusian impact craters have been covered over by lava flows from volcanoes.

Also in March, astronomers at the Arecibo Observatory in Puerto Rico reported using the 1,000-foot (300-meter), dish-shaped radar telescope there to add to the picture of Venus' surface. The scientists obtained sharp images over limited regions of the surface, in contrast to the *Venera* space probes, which scanned a wider area. The Arecibo telescope revealed the presence of what are probably huge solidified lava flows. The radar images also showed long, parallel streaks that might mark a *rift zone* — an area where the planet's surface appears to be cracking. If so, this may signify that the same geologic forces that shaped Earth's surface also operate on Venus.

The First Artificial Comet was created on December 27 when a cloud of barium vapor was released over the Pacific Ocean from a West German satellite 70,000 miles (110,000 kilometers) out in space. The experiment was part of a joint project with the United States and Great Britain. Its purpose was to study how the *solar wind* — a flow of electrically charged gases from the sun — interacts with Earth's magnetic field.

Comet Bombardment. More than 800 years ago, in June 1178, an English monk named Gervase of Canterbury saw a "flame" shoot from the moon. His recorded observation has remained a mystery to this day. However, on June 11, 1984, at an American Astronomical Society meeting in Baltimore, astrophysicist Kenneth Brecher of Boston University suggested that this "flame" might have been debris thrown up from the moon's surface as a result of an impact with a large fragment of a comet. Brecher suggested that this was one of many fragments produced by the breakup of a comet in ancient times, and he has named these fragments "The Canterbury Swarm" after the observation by Gervase. Brecher theorized that the "Swarm" has been responsible for other meteoroid impacts and unexplained events, including the mysterious object that fell from space and exploded in midair over the Tunguska region in Siberia in June 1908.

More recently, dozens of meteoroids struck the moon between June 22 and 26, 1975, when their

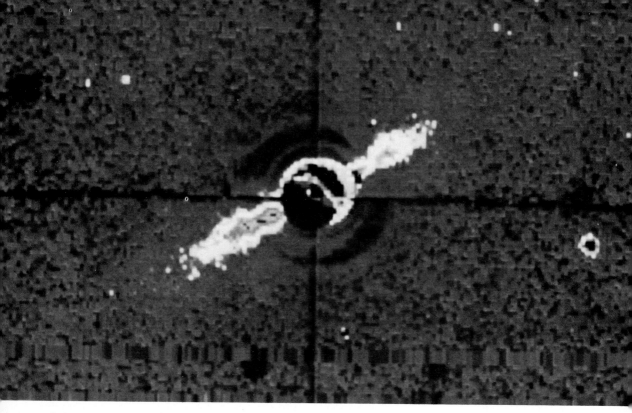

A photograph released in October shows a disk-shaped cloud of material that may be a solar system starting to form around the star Beta Pictoris.

fall was recorded by instruments placed on the lunar surface by Apollo astronauts. Brecher has attributed these impacts also to the "Swarm."

Brecher's key point was that all of these events occurred in June, much like meteor showers that are known to recur on nearly the same date. His ideas have stirred much debate among astronomers. More may be learned in June 1985, when the "Swarm" is expected to come within 30 million kilometers (19 million miles) of Earth.

New Solar System? In October 1984, astronomers Bradford A. Smith of the University of Arizona in Tucson and Richard J. Terrile of NASA's Jet Propulsion Laboratory in Pasadena, Calif., released a photograph showing what may be the first optical view of planets forming around another star. The photograph showed a disk-shaped cloud of solid material, which may range in size from tiny particles to objects the size of the nucleus of a comet, orbiting the star Beta Pictoris. Many scientists believe that the planets of our solar system formed out of a similar disk-shaped cloud of material that surrounded our sun some 4.6 billion years ago.

Beta Pictoris is a star visible to the unaided eye in the constellation Pictor in the southern sky. It is 50 *light-years* from Earth. (A light-year is the distance light travels in one year, about 9.5 trillion kilometers or 5.9 trillion miles.)

The material surrounding Beta Pictoris was first revealed by the *Infrared Astronomical Satellite*, but it was not known that the material was disk-shaped until the two astronomers obtained an optical view of it, using the 2.5-meter (100-inch) optical telescope at the Carnegie Institution's Las Campanas Observatory near La Serena, Chile.

New Planet? On December 10, astronomers announced the detection of what may be the first planet observed outside the solar system. The detection, which confirmed earlier indications that such an object existed, was made by a research team led by Donald W. McCarthy, Jr., of the University of Arizona in Tucson and including colleagues from the University of Arizona and the National Optical Astronomy Observatories in Tucson.

Using an infrared telescope, the astronomers detected the object orbiting a star known as Van Biesbroeck 8 in the constellation Ophiuchus. The star is about 21 light-years from Earth. The astronomers estimated that the object was nine-tenths the size of the planet Jupiter and 30 to 80 times as massive. Other astronomers, however, disagreed with the suggestion that the object is a planet. They argued instead that an object of that mass is probably a small star of a type known as a "brown dwarf."   Stephen P. Maran

See also SPACE EXPLORATION. In WORLD BOOK, see ASTRONOMY.

AUSTRALIA. Australian voters reelected Prime Minister Robert Hawke in national elections on Dec. 1, 1984. Hawke, who had succeeded Malcolm Fraser as prime minister in March 1983, called the new election to take advantage of his popularity and to try to secure for his Labor Party a majority in the Senate. However, Labor received an unexpectedly small margin of victory. Not only did the Labor Party fail to win a Senate majority, but it saw its majority in the House of Representatives trimmed from 25 to 16 seats. After the election, Hawke drastically reshuffled his Cabinet.

Prior to the election, 1984 was a quiet political year. Hawke's government appeared to be in firm control at the federal level. The government's credibility was increased by Hawke's clear domination at the Labor Party's conference in Canberra from July 9 to 13. This had been widely regarded as a trial of strength between Hawke and the left wing of the party. Disagreement centered upon Hawke's policies regarding the United States, the Indonesian occupation of East Timor, uranium mining, and the role of foreign banks and investment capital in the Australian economy. On these issues, Hawke gained support from a majority of the delegates.

The only state election of the year was held in New South Wales on March 24. It resulted in the return of the Labor government led by Neville K. Wran with a reduced but safe majority. Labor governments also held power in Victoria, South Australia, and Western Australia. The Liberal Party was in office in Tasmania, and the National Party in Queensland.

The Economy. The rate of inflation continued to fall, registering about 4 per cent in October. Unemployment fluctuated at around 9 per cent of the work force, but many new jobs were created. Most immigrants, including many refugees from Vietnam, found jobs. However, unemployment among Aborigines continued to be three or four times the national average. Both production and exports rose, and good rains led to higher levels of agricultural production. For the first time in five years, there was a surplus in the balance of trade.

Economic confidence was probably increased by continued industrial peace. Fewer workdays were lost to industrial disputes in 1984 than in any of the preceding 17 years. The Labor government and the unions were in general agreement about the need to curb wage increases as long as efforts also were made to restrain prices.

There was general approval of the federal budget announced by Treasurer Paul Keating on August 21. This budget reduced the existing defi-

Australia's Prime Minister Robert Hawke won reelection on December 1, but his Labor Party's majority in Parliament was unexpectedly trimmed.

cit and cut personal income taxes. Spending on defense, education, foreign aid, and social security was increased. Economic prospects seemed generally bright, especially for investment in such basic industries as oil and coal.

In Foreign Affairs, the government stressed its commitment to ANZUS, a treaty with New Zealand and the United States that is the foundation of Australia's defense policy. Australia also affirmed its wish to see nuclear weapons more tightly controlled, its opposition to nuclear tests, and its view that Asia, rather than Europe, was the part of the world with which Australian economic cooperation would be most fruitful.

At the South Pacific Forum—a meeting of 14 South Pacific nations—in Tuvalu on August 27 and 28, Australia submitted draft proposals for a nuclear-free zone in the area. The conference adopted the proposals. They included freedom from environmental pollution; a ban on the testing, stationing, or use of nuclear weapons in the South Pacific; a refusal by all the member nations to develop or acquire nuclear weapons; support for the nuclear nonproliferation treaty; and the right of individual countries to decide what access they would give to aircraft and naval vessels of other countries that might carry nuclear weapons. This final point had been a matter of dispute in both Australia and New Zealand. The Australian government had announced on February 26 that United States and British ships carrying nuclear weapons could continue to visit Australian ports.

Foreign aid was increased by 6.5 per cent in the budget released in August. A government committee on aid policy recommended that Australia should apply its foreign aid in a more concentrated area of the world and should use such aid to support a more limited range of activities. The committee urged that aid should go, in order of priority, to Papua New Guinea and the small states of the South Pacific and Indian oceans; to Southeast Asia and parts of South Asia; to China, India, Pakistan, and Bangladesh; and finally to other developing countries. The committee also felt that aid should be given mainly in such fields of Australian expertise as education.

Immigration continued to be of concern to both the public and the government in 1984, with some argument about the balance between emigration from Asia and from Europe. On March 7, Minister for Immigration and Ethnic Affairs Stewart West said that Asians accounted for a larger proportion of immigrants in 1984 than in previous years. He attributed this to the falling off of emigration from Great Britain and continental Europe, the continued flow of refugees from Indochina, and the increased interest in moving to Australia among residents of Hong Kong, which will pass from British to Chinese control in 1997.

On May 30, West announced that the immigration target for 1984-1985 would be about 72,000 people.

Other Developments. A tiny addition to the Australian community took place on April 6 when the inhabitants of the Cocos Islands in the Indian Ocean decided by 229 votes out of 261 for integration with Australia. Voters rejected the options of independence or free association with Australia.

In an attempt to settle the controversial question of the Australian national anthem, Prime Minister Hawke announced on April 11 that the new anthem will be a version of "Advance Australia Fair" that had been modified to remove sexist language. The previous national anthem, "God Save the Queen," will be played only during official visits by the royal family. Hawke also announced on April 19 that Australia's official colors will be green and gold. Sporting teams representing Australia have worn these colors for many years.

On February 1, Australia initiated Medicare, a national health insurance scheme. Under this new program, the federal government will pay basic medical and hospital costs.

Australia introduced a $1 coin in 1984. The new coin is intended to replace the $1 note.   J. D. B. Miller

See also ASIA (Facts in Brief Table). In WORLD BOOK, see AUSTRALIA.

AUSTRIA. Chancellor Fred Sinowatz had trouble getting parliament to approve measures to strengthen the economy in 1984. Inflation had almost doubled to 5.8 per cent, and new taxes had increased energy prices by 20 per cent by May 1984, one year after Sinowatz took office. Heavy public spending raised the budget deficit to $2.2-billion by April 1984.

The government took several steps to cope with the deficit. In April, it announced plans to cut civil servants' pensions, which cost Austria $1.7 billion per year. Civil servants retired at 80 per cent of the salary they received when they worked, and widows and widowers received the full amounts of their spouse's pensions. Demonstrations and threats of a general strike by civil service workers followed the announcement. Also in April, the government increased the value-added tax, a tax on purchases and services, from 18 to 20 per cent in some categories and from 30 to 32 per cent in others.

Power Plants. The country's only nuclear power station remained inactive after a 1978 referendum vote against activating it. Sinowatz wanted the power station to be activated. In addition, he proposed to build a hydroelectric plant in a nature preserve at Hainburg on the Danube River.

On May 17, 1984, 50,000 unionized steelworkers and coal miners marched in Vienna to demonstrate their support for the Hainburg project.

The World Wildlife Fund protested against the Hainburg project at a meeting in Vienna in May. The organization's president, Prince Philip of Great Britain, angered Sinowatz by saying that Austria would damage its reputation among conservationists throughout the world if a plant were built in what the prince called "Austria's last Danube forest." Sinowatz said the prince's remarks were "inappropriate." At year's end, however, Sinowatz shelved the project.

Cabinet Changes. In a surprise move, Sinowatz replaced four members of his Cabinet on September 3. The most important changes were the appointment of Leopold Gratz, mayor of Vienna, to succeed Erwin Lanc as foreign minister; and the replacement of Finance Minister Herbert Salcher by Franz Vranitzky, director of Austria's second largest commercial bank.

Social Partnership. The World Bank ranked Austria as the 13th most prosperous country in the world in 1984. The bank said this was largely a result of Austria's *Sozial Partnerschaft* (social partnership), a system that relies on the close cooperation of management, labor, and government to link price hikes to wage increases.   Kenneth Brown

See also EUROPE (Facts in Brief Table). In WORLD BOOK, see AUSTRIA.

AUTOMOBILE. The United States automobile industry recorded another year of solid progress in 1984. At the same time, the industry was dogged by the feeling that the old exuberance of the American car market was gone—perhaps forever.

It was a good sales year, but not as good as several in the past. Despite strikes in September and October against General Motors Corporation (GM), total U.S. new-vehicle sales by U.S. and foreign automakers reached 14.5 million units, including 10.4 million new cars and 4.1 million new trucks. That was up 17.9 per cent from the 1983 total of 12.3 million cars and trucks, but down 5.2 per cent from the 1978 record of 15.4 million vehicles. Auto executives and industry analysts said the failure to set a new record despite the potential demand was due to high prices and high interest rates.

Shrinking U.S. Share. The 1984 sales results looked even less spectacular when sales by U.S. carmakers were separated out. United States automakers were expected to sell only about 7.93 million cars in 1984, far below the 1978 level of 9.3 million. Between 1978 and 1984, sales of imported cars climbed from 2 million to 2.45 million—despite restrictions on Japanese imports. The picture became almost grim when the growing percentage of imported parts in United States-

Car buyers in 1984 snapped up new minivans—such as the Dodge Mini Ram Van above—which offer roominess, fuel efficiency, and easy handling.

built cars was taken into account. Many vehicles included in the count of U.S. vehicles had engines or transmissions built in other countries.

Employment. Nowhere was the impact of this shrinkage felt more strongly than in employment. Rising sales throughout 1983 and 1984 restored the jobs of thousands of blue-collar workers who had been idled during the 1979-1982 auto industry recession. But at year's end, employment at the Big Three U.S. auto companies — GM, Ford Motor Company, and Chrysler Corporation — stood at about 525,000 hourly workers. At the beginning of 1979, Big Three blue-collar employment was 750,000.

Approximately 50,000 laid-off workers were still on the three automakers' recall lists late in 1984. But it seemed likely that the remaining 200,000 production jobs were gone forever because of automation, plant closings, changes allowing fewer workers in certain jobs, and *outsourcing* — the use of auto parts or even complete cars from non-union sources or from other countries.

Profits. There was one area of spectacular success, however — profit making. Industry analysts predicted that U.S. auto industry profits for 1984 would approach $10 billion, far above the previous annual profit record of $6.15 billion set in 1983. Chrysler, saved from bankruptcy by the federal government in 1979 and 1980, announced record profits for the first two quarters of 1984.

The ability to earn record profits at a time of declining sales was a tribute to auto-industry cost efficiencies. Automakers had instituted a variety of cost-cutting measures, including closing marginally profitable plants, streamlining management, cutting white-collar employment, and controlling inventories more carefully.

But buyers cooperated in the profit race by showing a preference for luxury or sporty cars equipped with many profitable options. Because of falling gasoline prices, larger cars sold as fast as the automakers turned them out, and profits on large cars are greater than profits on small cars. Price increases also played a role, though prices in 1984 followed the usual auto-industry pattern of rising just below the level of inflation.

Finally, profitability was aided by U.S. tax laws. The billion-dollar annual losses suffered by U.S. automakers during the recession enabled the carmakers to accumulate tax credits. As a result, Chrysler, for example, used those tax credits to wipe out virtually all of its U.S. corporate income tax bill in 1984. The company expected to resume paying taxes in 1985.

UAW Contract. Progress in sales was matched by new developments in labor relations. Despite a seven-day strike in September that idled about half of GM's U.S. assembly plants and a 13-day walkout in October against the company's Cana-

dian operations, GM and the United Automobile Workers (UAW) negotiated a new three-year contract that both sides hailed as a landmark in labor-management cooperation. In October, the UAW negotiated a nearly identical agreement with Ford.

GM won union promises of cooperation in automating its plants, a move that promised greater productivity in the future. The UAW won important new job-security protection. GM agreed to a $1-billion, six-year program that will provide continued pay for workers idled by automation or outsourcing while they await other jobs at GM. Job-security measures also included extensive retraining programs for displaced workers and job development programs that will help to find — perhaps even create — new jobs for laid-off workers.

GM Reorganization. The drive to become competitive also prompted a major internal reorganization at GM. The company announced plans in January 1984 to merge its five domestic car divisions and GM of Canada into two "super-groups." One — made up of Buick, Oldsmobile, and Cadillac — would design and build only large and luxury cars. The second — made up of Chevrolet, Pontiac, and GM of Canada — would specialize in small, less expensive cars.

Outwardly, there was no visible change. Dealer organizations for the five divisions remained intact, and each continued to offer its traditional range of vehicles. But the reorganization made a big difference internally. Under the new organization, decisions could be made at lower corporate levels, which would save time in bringing new cars to market.

New Operations. The year was also notable for new inroads by foreign carmakers in the U.S. market. Honda Motor Company's carmaking operation in Marysville, Ohio, proved so successful that the company announced in January an expansion of the plant. On May 11, Nissan Motor Company announced it would begin building cars at its truck plant in Smyrna, Tenn., in 1985. And New United Motor Manufacturing Incorporated, the GM-Toyota joint venture in Fremont, Calif., planned to produce its first small car by the end of 1984. On April 11, the U.S. Federal Trade Commission, which enforces antitrust laws, gave final approval to the venture. U.S. carmakers other than GM had opposed the operation, claiming that a joint venture between the world's largest and third-largest automakers would violate U.S. antitrust laws and stifle competition.

Car Recall. On November 26, the Big Three automakers announced that they were recalling more than 4 million autos for the repair of possible safety defects. The defects included faulty rear axle shafts, leakage in fuel hoses, and rear-wheel misalignment.   James V. Higgins

In WORLD BOOK, see AUTOMOBILE.

AUTOMOBILE RACING. In 1984, as always, the high speeds involved in automobile racing meant accidents, injuries, and death. The lone fatality in major United States races in 1984 occurred in stock car racing. Terry Schoonover died on November 11 of massive head and internal injuries following a crash in the Atlanta Journal 500 race at Hampton, Ga. Schoonover, 32, was on the 129th lap when his Chevrolet Monte Carlo SS hit the outside wall coming out of a turn, slid across the speedway, and crashed into the inside wall.

The 16 races in the United States and Canada for Indianapolis-type cars were also marred by accidents that caused leg and foot injuries to several drivers. Only the 16 Formula One Grand Prix races, plagued by accidents in the past, were relatively safe.

The 1985 rules governing Indy cars were changed to help avoid such injuries. The new rules require a 6-inch (15-centimeter) protective partition between the driver's feet and the front of the car so that the pedals cannot be pushed back into the feet in a crash. More protection was created for a driver's head and sides. On the larger and faster oval tracks, a car's chassis must be at least 2 inches (5 centimeters) off the ground, rather than 1 inch (2.5 centimeters), to reduce the ground effects that make higher speeds possible.

Indianapolis 500. Tom Sneva of Paradise Valley, Ariz., set speed records at the Indianapolis 500 for one lap and four laps during qualifying runs. His average speed for one lap was 210.689 miles per hour (mph), or 339.071 kilometers per hour (kph). His average speed for four laps was 210.029 mph (338.009 kph). Another speed record was established for the 500 miles (800 kilometers) of the race itself. Rick Mears of Bakersfield, Calif., won the 500 on May 27 with a record average speed of 163.612 mph (263.308 kph). Mears and the car owners shared $434,060 from a total purse of $2.7 million in the richest automobile race in history.

Mears also won at Indianapolis in 1979. In 1982, he finished only 0.16 second behind Gordon Johncock, the closest Indianapolis finish ever.

Of the 33 Indianapolis starters, 29 had chassis built by the March Engineering factory and 30 had engines built by Cosworth Engineering, both of Great Britain. Mears's car was a March-Cosworth owned by Roger Penske, who usually built his own cars. But the Marches were so good, said Penske, that "in this business, it's a foolish man who will let pride stand in the way."

Formula One Series. Turbocharged cars dominated the 1984 Formula One races in Europe, the United States, Canada, South Africa, and Brazil.

Rick Mears takes the checkered flag, winning the Indianapolis 500 in May with a record average speed of 163.612 miles (263.308 kilometers) per hour.

Niki Lauda of Austria became the world drivers champion for the third time since 1975, accumulating 72 points to 71½ for Alain Prost of France. Both drove turbocharged McLaren-Porsches. Lauda won five races. Prost won seven, equaling Jim Clark's 1963 record.

Nelson Piquet of Brazil and Keke Rosberg of Finland won the three North American Formula One races. Piquet, in a Brabham-BMW, won the Canadian Grand Prix in Montreal, Canada, on June 17 and the Detroit Grand Prix on June 24. Rosberg, in a Williams-Honda, won the Dallas Grand Prix on July 8.

NASCAR. The National Association for Stock Car Auto Racing (NASCAR) ran a 30-race Grand National series for late-model sedans. The highlight was the $1.2-million Daytona 500 on February 19 in Daytona Beach, Fla., won by Cale Yarborough of Timmonsville, S.C. Terry Labonte of Corpus Christi, Tex., won the series title.

Drag Racing. Shirley Muldowney of Mount Clemens, Mich., who has often defeated men in drag racing, is the only driver to have won three world championships in the National Hot Rod Association's top-fuel division. On June 29, outside Montreal, Canada, a front tire blew out, and her car crashed and ripped apart. She suffered multiple fractures and leg wounds.   Frank Litsky

In WORLD BOOK, see AUTOMOBILE RACING.

AVIATION in the United States rebounded smartly in 1984, helped by the economic recovery, firmer fares, and lower labor costs. Many major carriers and new airlines prospered, but others struggled to stay aloft. Passengers endured long runway delays before take-offs as frequent peak-hour flights and the air-traffic-controller shortage strained the system and posed some safety hazards.

Passenger traffic on U.S. domestic airlines through September 1984 rose 3.9 per cent, and air freight climbed 16.1 per cent through August. The International Air Transport Association said that airlines flying the busy North Atlantic Ocean routes carried 10.8 per cent more paying customers in the first seven months of 1984 than in the same period in 1983.

George W. James, the U.S. airline industry's chief economist, estimated in December that U.S. scheduled carriers would have a record operating income of nearly $2 billion in 1984, up from $310 million in 1983.

Under the 1978 Airline Deregulation Act, the Civil Aeronautics Board (CAB) was abolished at the end of 1984. Its powers to regulate international aviation, protect consumers, and control computer reservations systems were transferred to the Department of Transportation.

Ups and Downs. People Express, a three-year-old no-frills carrier, expanded fast, posing stiff competition for major airlines. The newcomer, based in Newark, N.J., extended low-fare service to include Chicago, Detroit, Los Angeles, Miami, and the San Francisco area.

Other newcomers sprang up in the climate of deregulation, and some major established carriers, including United Airlines and American Airlines, scored earnings gains. Earnings improved substantially after big 1983 losses for Trans World Airlines (TWA), Eastern Airlines, Republic Airlines, and Continental Airlines, which had entered bankruptcy in 1983. But Pan American World Airways (PanAm) and Western Airlines had more problems. Air Florida stopped flying on July 3, but it resumed operations on October 16 as Midway Express, after it was bought by Midway Airlines, another "deregulation baby." Several smaller airlines failed. Braniff Incorporated, which reorganized as a slimmed-down carrier after going bankrupt in May 1982, flew again on March 1, 1984. But it had trouble filling seats, sustained new losses, sought a merger partner, and trimmed flights.

Fares Rise and Fall. Airlines boosted many fares and narrowed discounts in the first half of 1984. United capped off increases earlier by boosting most fares 3 to 5 per cent on September 22. Other airlines made similar increases. But not all of the increases were expected to stick as fare cutting broke out again later in the year. Sharp fare decreases by such small airlines as Braniff, Continental, Frontier Airlines, Midway, and People Express prompted some large carriers to make matching reductions.

Transatlantic Fares. Virgin Atlantic Airways, a new London-based airline, offered low-fare flights between London and Newark in June, competing with People Express. British Airways on July 17 drastically lowered its winter fares between the United States and London, and other carriers, including PanAm and TWA, reluctantly followed suit. But the British Department of Transport in October refused to approve the lower fares unless the United States gave British carriers immunity from antitrust complaints in U.S. courts. In December, the U.S. Department of Justice denied any intention of filing antitrust suits because of the fare reductions. In December, British Airways received approval of the fares from both governments. At year's end, both British Airways and PanAm were selling the bargain tickets.

Aircraft Sales competition between U.S. and European producers intensified in 1984. Boeing Company and Airbus Industrie, a European consortium, squared off to fight for an expected aircraft buying surge over the next decade. PanAm and Turkey placed major Airbus orders totaling $1.6 billion. The Saudi national airline ordered $1-billion worth of Boeing 747's. Domestic U.S. air-

Runway rush hour brought travel delays and air-traffic-controller headaches
during the summer as airlines clustered flights at the most popular times.

lines turned from wide bodies to smaller, more economical jets such as Boeing's 737 jetliner. American Airlines in February ordered 67 McDonnell Douglas Corporation MD-80 jets.

Flight and Wage Cuts. Many airlines curbed costs by paring flights from their systems, even as some of them expanded elsewhere. American increased coast-to-coast flights early in the year and then, on October 1, cut them back while adding service in the Midwest.

In 1984, airlines won, or sought, worker concessions, so that they could cut costs and survive deregulation-spurred competition. In return, some carriers allowed union members to sit on their board of directors, or gave workers stock or a share of the profits. Eastern Airlines workers gave up, on average, 18 per cent of their pay, and Republic employees extended a 15 per cent pay cut for three years. Frontier employees agreed to two wage reductions in 1984 and, at year's end, were seeking financing to buy the ailing airline.

Crowded Skies and Air Safety. Flight delays increased in 1984 as traffic rose. Airlines had praised efforts by the Federal Aviation Administration (FAA) to rebuild the air-traffic-control system since the 1981 controllers' strike but in 1984 said that more experienced controllers were needed. In June, the FAA said that it would hire and train more controllers but blamed delays on

airline schedules that clustered many flights at peak hours at large airports. Airlines agreed in September on 1,300 flight-schedule changes, trimming delays at the three airports in the New York City area and those in Atlanta, Ga.; Chicago; and Denver. The CAB on October 25 approved the schedule changes. But, to preserve competition, the CAB required that four new airlines be given take-off and landing slots at Chicago's O'Hare International Airport.

Concerns mounted over rising dangers of midair collisions because of the air-traffic pinch. The National Transportation Safety Board said the FAA was trying to handle too much traffic with inexperienced controllers. Forty-five people died in accidents of scheduled U.S. airline flights in 1984, up from 26 such deaths in 1983.

Skyjacking. Four Arabs forced a Kuwait Airways plane to land in Teheran, Iran, on December 4. They demanded that Kuwait release from jail several terrorists who bombed the United States Embassy in Kuwait in 1983. After a six-day stand-off during which the hijackers killed two United States passengers, Iranian police stormed the plane, freeing the remaining passengers and capturing the hijackers.   Albert R. Karr

See also TRANSPORTATION. In the WORLD BOOK SUPPLEMENT section, see HELICOPTER. In WORLD BOOK, see AVIATION.

AWARDS AND PRIZES presented in 1984 included the following:

Arts Awards

Academy of Motion Picture Arts and Sciences. *"Oscar" Awards: Best Picture,* Terms of Endearment, James L. Brooks, producer. **Best Actor,** Robert Duvall, *Tender Mercies.* **Best Actress,** Shirley MacLaine, *Terms of Endearment.* **Best Supporting Actor,** Jack Nicholson, *Terms of Endearment.* **Best Supporting Actress,** Linda Hunt, *The Year of Living Dangerously.* **Best Director,** James L. Brooks, *Terms of Endearment.* **Best Original Screenplay,** Horton Foote, *Tender Mercies.* **Best Screenplay Adaptation,** James L. Brooks, *Terms of Endearment.* **Best Cinematography,** Sven Nykvist, *Fanny and Alexander.* **Best Film Editing,** Glenn Farr, Lisa Fruchtman, Stephen A. Rotter, Douglas Stewart, and Tom Rolf, *The Right Stuff.* **Best Original Musical Score,** Bill Conti, *The Right Stuff.* **Best Original Song,** "Flashdance . . . What a Feeling," music by Giorgio Moroder, lyrics by Keith Forsey and Irene Cara. **Best Foreign Language Film,** *Fanny and Alexander* (Sweden). See DUVALL, ROBERT; MACLAINE, SHIRLEY.

American Dance Festival. *Samuel H. Scripps-American Dance Festival Award,* Hanya Holm, choreographer.

American Institute of Architects. *Honor Awards,* Bohlin Powell Larkin Cywinski, Pittsburgh, Philadelphia, and Wilkes-Barre, Pa., for Shelly Ridge Girl Scout Center, Miquon, Pa.; Theodore M. Ceraldi, Nyack, N.Y., for Gainesway Farm, Lexington, Ky.; Cooper-Lecky Partnership, Washington, D.C., and Maya Ying Lin, New Haven, Conn., for the Vietnam Veterans Memorial in Washington, D.C.; Croxton Collaborative, New York City, and Hammill-Walter Associates Incorporated, Winston-Salem, N.C., for the R. J. Reynolds Tobacco Company Building in that city; CRS/Caudill Rowlett Scott, Houston, for Carver-Hawkeye Sports Arena, Iowa City, Iowa; Gwathmey Siegel & Associates, New York City, for the Taft residence, Cincinnati, Ohio; Hammond Beeby and Babka Incorporated, Chicago, for an addition to North Shore Congregation Israel, Glencoe, Ill.; Kohn Pederson Fox Associates, New York City, and Perkins & Will Group Incorporated, Chicago, for 333 Wacker Drive, Chicago; Richard Meier & Partners, New York City, for the High Museum of Art, Atlanta, Ga.; Moore Ruble Yudell, Santa Monica, Calif., for St. Matthew's Church, Pacific Palisades, Calif.; I. M. Pei & Partners, New York City, for the Fragrant Hill Hotel, Beijing (Peking), China; Tigerman Fugman McCurry, Chicago, for a weekend house in Michigan; Venturi, Rauch and Scott Brown, Philadelphia, for Gordon Wu Hall, Princeton, N.J.

American Music Awards. *Pop-Rock Awards: Favorite Female Vocalist,* Pat Benatar. **Favorite Male Vocalist,** Michael Jackson. **Favorite Duo or Group,** Daryl Hall and John Oates. **Favorite Single,** "Billie Jean," Michael Jackson. **Favorite Album,** *Thriller,* Michael Jackson. **Favorite Video,** "Beat It," Michael Jackson. *Soul Music Awards: Favorite Female Vocalist,* Aretha Franklin. **Favorite Male Vocalist,** Michael Jackson. **Favorite Duo or Group,** Gladys Knight and the Pips. **Favorite Single,** "All Night Long," Lionel Richie. **Favorite Album,** *Thriller,* Michael Jackson. **Favorite Video,** "Beat It," Michael Jackson. *Country Music Awards: Favorite Female Vocalist,* Barbara Mandrell. **Favorite Male Vocalist,** Willie Nelson. **Favorite Duo or Group,** Alabama. **Favorite Single,** "Islands in the Stream," Kenny Rogers and Dolly Parton. **Favorite Album,** *The Closer You Get,* Alabama. **Favorite Video,** "Dixieland Delight," Alabama.

Cannes International Film Festival. *Golden Palm Grand Prize,* Paris, Texas (West Germany). **Best Actor,** Francisco Rabal and Alfredo Landa, *The Holy Innocents* (Spain). **Best Actress,** Helen Mirren, *Cal* (Ireland). **Best Director,** Bertrand Tavernier, *A Sunday in the Country* (France). **Special Jury Prize,** American director John Huston, for lifetime contributions to film.

Hyatt Foundation. *Pritzker Architecture Prize,* Richard Meier, United States, for lifetime work.

John F. Kennedy Center for the Performing Arts. *Honors,* for contributions to the performing arts, singer Lena Horne; entertainer Danny Kaye; composer Gian Carlo Menotti; playwright Arthur Miller; violinist Isaac Stern.

National Academy of Recording Arts and Sciences. *Grammy Awards: Record of the Year,* "Beat It," Michael Jackson. **Album of the Year,** *Thriller,* Michael Jackson. **Song of the Year,** "Every Breath You Take," Sting. **Best New Artist,** Culture Club. **Producer of the Year (Nonclassical),** Quincy Jones and Michael Jackson. **Best Pop Vocal Performance, Female,** "Flashdance . . . What a Feeling," Irene Cara. **Male,** *Thriller,* Michael Jackson. **Duo or Group with Vocal,** "Every Breath You Take," The Police. **Instrumental,** "Being with You," George Benson. **Best Rock Vocal Performance, Female,** "Love Is a Battlefield," Pat Benatar. **Male,** "Beat It," Michael Jackson. **Duo or Group with Vocal,** Synchronicity, The Police. **Instrumental,** "Brimstone and Treacle," Sting. **Best Rhythm & Blues Vocal Performance, Female,** *Chaka Khan,* Chaka Khan. **Male,** "Billie Jean," Michael Jackson. **Duo or Group with Vocal,** "Ain't Nobody," Rufus and Chaka Khan. **Instrumental,** "Rockit," Herbie Hancock. **Best Rhythm and Blues Song,** "Billie Jean," Michael Jackson. **Best Jazz Fusion Performance, Vocal or Instrumental,** *Travels,* Pat Metheny Group. **Best Country Vocal Performance, Female,** *A Little Good News,* Anne Murray. **Male,** *I.O.U.,* Lee Greenwood. **Duo or Group with Vocal,** *The Closer You Get,* Alabama. **Instrumental,** *Fireball,* The New South. **Best Country Song,** "Stranger in My House," Mike Reed. **Best Jazz Vocal Performance, Female,** *The Best Is Yet to Come,* Ella Fitzgerald. **Male,** *Top Drawer,* Mel Tormé. **Duo or Group,** "Why Not," Manhattan Transfer. **Best Jazz Instrumental Performance, Solo,** *Think of One,* Wynton Marsalis. **Group,** *At the Vanguard,* Phil Woods Quartet. **Big Band,** "All in Good Time," Rob McConnell and the Boss Brass. **Best Classical Album,** *Mahler: Symphony No. 9 in D Major,* Sir Georg Solti, conductor. **Best Classical Orchestra Performance,** *Mahler: Symphony No. 9 in D Major,* Sir Georg Solti, conductor. **Best Opera,** *Mozart: Le Nozze di Figaro,* Sir Georg Solti, conductor; and *Verdi: La Traviata,* James Levine, conductor. **Best Classical Choral Performance,** *Haydn: The Creation,* Sir Georg Solti, conductor.

National Academy of Television Arts and Sciences. *Emmy Awards: Best Comedy Series,* "Cheers." **Best Actor in a Comedy Series,** John Ritter, "Three's Company." **Best Actress in a Comedy Series,** Jane Curtin, "Kate & Allie." **Best Supporting Actor in a Comedy Series,** Pat Harrington, Jr., "One Day at a Time." **Best Supporting Actress in a Comedy Series,** Rhea Perlman, "Cheers." **Best Drama Series,** "Hill Street Blues." **Best Actor in a Drama Series,** Tom Selleck, "Magnum, P. I." **Best Actress in a Drama Series,** Tyne Daly, "Cagney and Lacey." **Best Supporting Actor in a Drama Series,** Bruce Weitz, "Hill Street Blues." **Best Supporting Actress in a Drama Series,** Alfre Woodard, "Hill Street Blues." **Best Drama Special,** Something About Amelia. **Best Limited Series,** "Concealed Enemies." **Best Actor in a Limited Series or Special,** Sir Laurence Olivier, *King Lear.* **Best Actress in a Limited Series or Special,** Jane Fonda, *The Dollmaker.* **Best Variety, Music, or Comedy Program,** *The Sixth Annual Kennedy Center Honors: A Celebration of the Performing Arts.*

National Society of Film Critics Awards. *Best Film,* The Night of the Shooting Stars. **Best Actor,** Gérard Depardieu, *Danton* and *The Return of Martin Guerre*. **Best Actress,** Debra Winger, *Terms of Endearment*. **Best Supporting Actor,** Jack Nicholson, *Terms of Endearment*. **Best Supporting Actress,** Sandra Bernhard, *The King of Comedy*. **Best Director,** Paolo Taviani and Vittorio Taviani, *The Night of the Shooting Stars*.

New York Drama Critics Circle Awards. *Best New Play,* The Real Thing, Tom Stoppard. *Best New American Play,* Glengarry Glen Ross, David Mamet. *Best Musical,* Sunday in the Park with George, Stephen Sondheim and James Lapine.

New York Film Critics Circle Awards. *Best Film,* A Passage to India. *Best Actor,* Steve Martin, All of Me. *Best Actress,* Peggy Ashcroft, A Passage to India. *Best Supporting Actor,* Sir Ralph Richardson, Greystoke. *Best Supporting Actress,* Christine Lahti, Swing Shift. *Best Director,* David Lean, A Passage to India. *Best Screenplay,* Robert Benton, Places in the Heart. *Best Cinematography,* Chris Menges, The Killing Fields.

Antoinette Perry (Tony) Awards. *Drama: Best Play,* The Real Thing, Tom Stoppard. *Best Actor,* Jeremy Irons, The Real Thing. *Best Actress,* Glenn Close, The Real Thing. *Best Featured Actor,* Joe Mantegna, Glengarry Glen Ross. *Best Featured Actress,* Christine Baranski, The Real Thing. *Best Director,* Mike Nichols, The Real Thing. *Musical: Best Musical,* La Cage aux Folles. *Best Actor,* George Hearn, La Cage aux Folles. *Best Actress,* Chita Rivera, The Rink. *Best Featured Actor,* Hinton Battle, The Tap Dance Kid. *Best Featured Actress,* Lila Kedrova, Zorba. *Best Director,* Arthur Laurents, La Cage aux Folles. *Best Choreography,* Danny Daniels, The Tap Dance Kid. *Best Book,* Harvey Fierstein, La Cage aux Folles. *Best Score,* Jerry Herman, La Cage aux Folles. *Best Reproduction of a Play,* Death of a Salesman.

Journalism Awards

American Society of Magazine Editors. *National Magazine Awards: General Excellence, Circulation over 1 Million,* National Geographic; *Circulation of 400,000 to 1 Million,* House & Garden; *Circulation of 100,000 to 400,000,* Outside; *Circulation Under 100,000,* The American Lawyer. *Public Service,* The New Yorker. *Design,* House & Garden. *Fiction,* Seventeen. *Reporting,* Vanity Fair. *Essays and Criticism,* The New Republic. *Single Topic Issue,* Esquire. *Service to Individual,* New York.

Long Island University. *George Polk Memorial Awards: National Reporting,* Rupert R. Frump and Timothy Dwyer, *The Philadelphia Inquirer,* for a series on unsafe vessels in the United States maritime fleet. *Regional Reporting,* Paul Lieberman and Celia Dugger, Atlanta, Ga., *Journal and Constitution,* for "Kaolin: Georgia's Lost Inheritance." *Local Reporting,* Jim McGee, *The Miami* (Fla.) *Herald,* for "The Face of Terror." *Foreign Reporting,* Joseph Lelyveld, *The New York Times,* for reports from South Africa. *Foreign Affairs Reporting,* Philip Taubman, *The New York Times,* for coverage of secret U.S. military operations in Central America. *Economics Reporting,* Dennis Camire and Mark Rohner, Gannett News Service, for a series on corruption in the Farmers Home Administration. *Consumer Reporting,* Marcia Stepanek and Stephen Franklin, *Detroit Free Press,* for a series on unsafe cars. *Medical Reporting,* Benjamin Weiser, *The Washington* (D.C.) *Post.* *Network Television Reporting,* Don McNeill, CBS News correspondent in the Soviet Union. *Television Documentary,* Vietnam: *A Television History,* produced by WGBH, Boston, for the Public Broadcasting System.

The Society of Professional Journalists, Sigma Delta Chi. *Sigma Delta Chi Distinguished Service Awards, Newspaper Awards: General Reporting,* David Ashenfelter and John Castine, *Detroit Free Press,* for a series about the fairness of sentencing for manslaughter in Michigan. *Editorial Writing,* Louis J. Salome, Betsy Willeford, and Ellis Berger, *The Miami* (Fla.) *News,* for

Robert Duvall and Shirley MacLaine won Academy Awards as best actor and best actress in 1984 for *Tender Mercies* and *Terms of Endearment,* respectively.

editorials on capital punishment. *Washington Correspondence,* Michael J. Himowitz, *The* (Baltimore) *Evening Sun,* for a series on defense spending in Maryland. *Foreign Correspondence,* William Branigin, *The Washington* (D.C.) *Post,* for reports from Afghanistan. *Photography,* Rich Lipski, United Press International, for a photograph of President Ronald Reagan with his thumbs in his ears, wiggling his fingers. *Editorial Cartooning,* Rob Lawlor, *Philadelphia Daily News,* for a cartoon about U.S. involvement in Lebanon. *Public Service in Newspaper Journalism,* The Philadelphia Inquirer for a series about the Pennsylvania Supreme Court. *Magazine Awards: Reporting,* Mike Mallowe, *Philadelphia Magazine,* for an investigation of Banco Ambrosiano, an Italian bank. *Public Service in Magazine Journalism,* Memphis Magazine for a report on race relations in that city. *Radio Awards: Reporting,* Howard Berkes, National Public Radio, for a story on mud slides in Farmington, Utah. *Public Service in Radio Journalism,* WMAQ News, Chicago, for a series on schoolchildren mislabeled as mentally handicapped. *Editorializing on Radio,* Gene Slaymaker, WTLC Radio, Indianapolis, for an editorial about the shooting of a university student by police officers. *Television Awards: Reporting,* Peter Arnett, Cable News Network, for a report on a bomb attack on a civilian village in El Salvador. *Public Service in Television Journalism,* WSMV-TV, Nashville, Tenn., for a report on the sexual abuse of children. *Editorializing on Television,* KYW-TV, Philadelphia, for a series on protection of crime victims. *Research About Journalism,* Sig Mickelson for *America's Other Voice.*

University of Georgia. *George Foster Peabody Broadcasting Awards,* WCCO Radio, Minneapolis, Minn., for a series on heart transplants; South Carolina Educational Radio Network for Marion McPartland's "Piano Jazz"; WMAL Radio, Washington, D.C., for *The*

Michael Jackson has an armful in February with just six of his record eight
Grammy Awards from the National Academy of Recording Arts and Sciences.

Jeffersonian World of Dumas Malone; KMOX Radio, St. Louis, for *Times Beach: Born 1925, Died 1983;* Thomas Looker, Montague Center, Mass., for *New England Almanac: Portraits in Sound,* about the people and sounds of New England; WRAL Radio, Cary, N.C., for a series about victims of various social problems; WNBC-TV, New York City, for an examination of the plight of homeless, mentally ill people; CBS News, New York City, for an investigation of the nearly fatal plunge of a jet airliner; WCCO-TV, Minneapolis, for a series on ambulance service; CBS News, New York City, for *Lenell Geter's in Jail,* which resulted in the release from prison of a man convicted of armed robbery despite contradictory evidence; National Broadcasting Company (NBC) and Motown Productions for *Motown 25: Yesterday, Today, Forever;* WTTW, Chicago, for a program about American choreographer Ruth Page; Chrysalis-Yellen Productions and NBC for *Prisoner Without a Name, Cell Without a Number,* about the imprisonment of Argentine journalist Jacobo Timerman; WTTW, Chicago, and the British Broadcasting Corporation for *The Making of a Continent,* about the geologic and other forces that shaped the American West; WTBS, Atlanta, for "Portrait of America," a series about the regional diversity of the United States; WGBH-TV, Boston, Central Independent Television, and Antenne-2 for *Vietnam: A Television History;* Sunbow Productions, New York City, for "The Great Space Coaster," a children's series; CBS Entertainment and Smith-Hemion Productions for *Romeo and Juliet on Ice;* American Broadcasting Companies and Dick Clark Productions for *The Woman Who Willed a Miracle,* the true story of a woman who helped a handicapped child become a musical prodigy; CBS Entertainment and Mendelson-Melendez Productions for *What Have We Learned, Charlie Brown?;* WBBM-TV, Chicago, for a program about the Studebaker Car Company; WBRZ-TV, Baton Rouge,

La., for a program about television evangelists; KRON-TV, San Francisco, for a program about Americans who have died in El Salvador; WGBH-TV, Boston, for "The Miracle of Life," a *Nova* program about human reproduction; NBC and Edgar J. Scherick Associates for *He Makes Me Feel Like Dancin',* a documentary about American dancer Jacques D'Amboise and his work with children; KCTS, Seattle, for *Diagnosis: AIDS;* Cable News Network, Atlanta, for its news and information programming; Don McGannon, Westinghouse Broadcasting Corporation, for lifetime contributions; "The Grand Ole Opry" radio program for nearly 60 years of entertainment.

Literature Awards

Academy of American Poets. *Lamont Poetry Selection,* *Deep Within the Ravine,* Philip Schultz. ***Harold Morton Landon Award for Translation,*** *Virgil: The Aeneid,* Robert Fitzgerald; *The Selected Poetry of Rainer Maria Rilke,* Stephen Mitchell. ***Walt Whitman Award,*** *For the New Year,* Eric Pankey.

American Library Association (ALA). *Bailey K. Howard-World Book Encyclopedia-ALA Goals Award,* New York Library Association. ***J. Morris Jones-World Book Encyclopedia-ALA Goals Award,*** Minnesota Library Association. ***Newbery Medal,*** *Dear Mr. Henshaw,* Beverly Cleary. ***Caldecott Medal,*** *The Glorious Flight: Across the Channel with Louis Blériot.* Alice Provensen and Martin Provensen.

Association of American Publishers. *American Book Awards: Fiction,* *Victory over Japan,* Ellen Gilchrist. ***Nonfiction,*** *Andrew Jackson and the Course of American Democracy, 1833-1845, Volume 3,* Robert V. Remini. ***First Work of Fiction,*** *Stones for Ibarra,* Harriet Doerr. ***National Medal for Literature:*** Mary McCarthy.

Canada Council. *Governor General's Literary Awards, English-Language: Fiction,* *Shakespeare's Dog,*

Leon Rooke. *Poetry, Settlements,* David Donnell. *Drama, Quiet in the Land,* Anne Chislett. *Nonfiction, Byng of Vimy,* Jeffery Williams. *French-Language: Fiction, Laura Laur,* Suzanne Jacob. *Poetry, Un goût de sel,* Suzanne Paradis. *Drama, Syncope,* René Gingras. *Nonfiction, Le contrôle social du crime,* Maurice Cusson.

Canadian Library Association. *Book of the Year for Children Award, Sweetgrass,* Jan Hudson. *Amelia Frances Howard-Gibbon Illustrator's Award, Zoom at Sea,* Ken Nutt.

Ingersoll Foundation. *Ingersoll Prizes: T. S. Eliot Award for Creative Writing,* British novelist Anthony D. Powell; *Richard M. Weaver Award for Scholarly Letters,* American columnist Russell Kirk.

MacDowell Colony. *Edward MacDowell Medal,* American author Mary McCarthy.

National Book Critics Circle. *National Book Critics Circle Awards: Fiction, Ironweed,* by William Kennedy. *General Nonfiction, The Price of Power,* by Seymour M. Hersh. *Biography/Autobiography, Minor Characters,* by Joyce Johnson. *Poetry, The Changing Light at Sandover,* by James Merrill. *Criticism, Hugging the Shore: Essays and Criticism,* by John Updike.

PEN American Center. *Faulkner Award, Sent for You Yesterday,* John E. Wideman.

Royal Society of Canada. *Jason A. Hannah Medal,* Harvey G. Simmons, York University. *Lorne Pierce Medal,* Sheila Watson, University of Alberta. *Tyrrell Medal,* Carl Berger, University of Toronto.

Nobel Prizes. See NOBEL PRIZES.

Public Service Awards

American Institute for Public Service. *Thomas Jefferson Awards,* Maude Callen, nurse who provided health care for the poor in Berkeley County, South Carolina; Virginia Clemmer, Gastonia, N.C., for service to the handicapped; Campbell Cutler and Frances Cutler, Flint, Mich., physician and nurse who helped the needy; J. Peter Grace, chairman of W. R. Grace & Company; Margaret Marshall, Indianapolis, who gave free nursing care to the poor; Sally K. Ride, first American woman in space; Betty Taylor, for helping the needy in Atlanta; Donna Velnick, who runs a home for orphaned and neglected children in Nampa, Ida.; William H. Webster, director of the Federal Bureau of Investigation.

Albert Einstein Peace Prize Foundation. *Albert Einstein Peace Prize,* Pierre Elliott Trudeau, former prime minister of Canada, for efforts to bring disarmament.

National Association for the Advancement of Colored People. *Spingarn Medal,* Los Angeles Mayor Thomas Bradley.

The Templeton Foundation. *Templeton Prize for Progress in Religion,* Michael Bourdeaux, founder and director of Keston College Center for the Study of Religion and Communism, Great Britain.

United States Government. *Presidential Medal of Freedom,* Senator Howard H. Baker, Jr. (R., Tenn.); James Cagney, actor; Whittaker Chambers, journalist (posthumous); Leo Cherne, economist; Denton Cooley, surgeon; Tennessee Ernie Ford, singer; Hector Garcia, founder of a Mexican-American rights group; Andrew J. Goodpaster, retired U.S. Army general; Lincoln E. Kirstein, cofounder of the New York City Ballet; Louis L'Amour, author; Norman Vincent Peale, religious leader; Jackie Robinson, first black baseball player in the major leagues (posthumous); Anwar el-Sadat, president of Egypt (posthumous); Eunice Kennedy Shriver, president of the Special Olympics for the handicapped.

Pulitzer Prizes
Journalism. *Public Service, Los Angeles Times* for its examination of southern California's Hispanic community.

General Local Reporting, Newsday (Long Island, N.Y.) for its coverage of the Baby Jane Doe case. *Special Local Reporting, The Boston Globe,* for its examination of racial tensions in the Boston area. *National Reporting,* John Noble Wilford, *The New York Times,* for science writing. *International Reporting,* Karen Elliott House, *The Wall Street Journal,* for interviews with Jordan's King Hussein I. *Editorial Writing,* Albert Scardino, *The* (Savannah) *Georgia Gazette. Editorial Cartooning,* Paul Conrad, *Los Angeles Times. Spot News Photography,* Stan Grossfeld, *The Boston Globe,* for photographs of the war in Lebanon. *Feature Photography,* Anthony Suau, *The Denver Post,* for photographs of famine in Ethiopia and of a grieving war widow. *Commentary,* Vermont Royster, *The Wall Street Journal. Criticism,* Paul Goldberger, *The New York Times,* for architecture criticism. *Feature Writing,* Peter Mark Rinearson, *The Seattle Times,* for "Making It Fly," about the Boeing 757 jetliner.

Letters. *Biography, Booker T. Washington: The Wizard of Tuskegee, 1901-1915,* Louis R Harlan. *Drama, Glengarry Glen Ross,* David Mamet. *Fiction, Ironweed,* William Kennedy. *General Nonfiction, The Social Transformation of American Medicine,* Paul Starr. *Poetry, American Primitive,* Mary Oliver.

Music. *Music Award,* Canti del Sole, Bernard Rands.
Special Citation. Dr. Seuss (Theodor Seuss Geisel).

Science and Technology Awards
Columbia University. *Louisa Gross Horwitz Prize,* Michael S. Brown and Joseph L. Goldstein, University of Texas.

Gairdner Foundation. *Gairdner Foundation International Awards,* J. Michael Bishop and Harold E. Varmus, University of California at San Francisco; Alfred G. Gilman, University of Texas, and Martin Rodbell, National Institutes of Health; Yuet Wai Kan, University of California at San Francisco; Kresimir I. Krnjevic, McGill University; Robert L. Noble, University of British Columbia; Douglas G. Cameron, McGill University.

Albert and Mary Lasker Foundation. *Albert Lasker Basic Medical Research Award,* César Milstein, Medical Research Council, England; Georges J. F. Köhler, Basel Institute of Immunology, Switzerland; Michael Potter, National Cancer Institute. *Albert Lasker Clinical Medical Research Award,* Paul C. Lauterbur, State University of New York at Stony Brook. *Public Service Award,* Henry J. Heimlich, Xavier University.

National Academy of Sciences (NAS). *Arctowski Medal,* William E. Gordon, Rice University. *John J. Carty Award for the Advancement of Science,* Robert H. Burris, University of Wisconsin, Madison. *Arthur L. Day Prize,* Allan Cox, Stanford University. *Daniel Giraud Elliot Medal,* G. Evelyn Hutchinson, Yale University. *George P. Merrill Award,* Zdeněk Ceplecha, Czechoslovak Academy of Sciences.

Royal Society of Canada. *Bancroft Award,* Jack G. Souther, Geological Society of Canada. *Thomas W. Eadie Medal,* Garry Martin Lindberg and Karl-Heinrich Doetsch, National Research Council; and John D. MacNaughton and Terrence H. Ussher, SPAR Aerospace Limited. *Flavelle Medal,* Robert G. E. Murray, University of Western Ontario. *McLaughlin Medal,* Claude Fortier, Laval University. *Rutherford Memorial Medal in Chemistry,* Robert J. Le Roy, University of Waterloo. *Rutherford Memorial Medal in Physics,* Penny G. Estabrooks, Carleton University.

University of Southern California. *John and Alice Tyler Ecology-Energy Prize,* Roger R. Revelle, University of California at San Diego, and Edward O. Wilson, Harvard University.   Sara Dreyfuss

BAHAMAS. See WEST INDIES.
BAHRAIN. See MIDDLE EAST.
BALLET. See DANCING.

BANGLADESH made several false starts toward returning to an elective system of government during 1984, amid sometimes violent political demonstrations. The weather was sometimes violent as well, causing the worst floods in a century.

President Hussain Muhammad Ershad, who has headed Bangladesh's martial-law government since 1982, announced on Feb. 29, 1984, that elections for president and a 300-seat parliament would be held on May 27.

Opposition Protests. Two political groups agitated against Ershad's plans to combine parliamentary and presidential elections. One of the opposition groups was a coalition of 15 parties led by Sheik Hasina Wajed, the daughter of Bangladesh's first president, Sheik Mujibur Rahman, who was assassinated in 1975. The other was a seven-party coalition led by Begum Khaleda Zia, widow of President Ziaur Rahman, who was assassinated in 1981. The opposition also called for an end to martial law and asked Ershad to yield to a caretaker government that would supervise elections.

Ershad tried to weaken the opposition by making a veteran politician, Ataur Rahman Khan, prime minister on March 30. The two coalitions continued to oppose his election plans, however, and Ershad said on April 20 that he would hold parliamentary voting before presidential elections. He said martial law would be lifted after the new parliament opened, claiming that to end military rule earlier would create a power vacuum. On July 12, the parliamentary elections were scheduled for December 8.

Agitation continued. The opposition called a six-hour general strike on August 27 and a day-long strike on September 27, in which five people died. The groups claimed that more than 2 million people turned out in three separate rallies on October 14 to denounce Ershad's plans. After the opponents said they would boycott the December elections, Ershad announced on October 27 that the voting would be postponed indefinitely. But on November 7, he repeated his pledge to end martial law and restore democracy.

The Economy. Scattered flooding from May to October killed more than 700 people in Bangladesh. Officials estimated that about 1.5 million metric tons (1.7 million short tons) of rice and 900,000 bales of jute, Bangladesh's main export crop, were lost in floods.

Despite flooding, Bangladesh's economy grew at a rate of 4.5 per cent in the year ending on June 30. A group of aid-giving countries said in April that the Bangladesh economy was slowly recovering, "led by excellent progress in the agricultural sector." The group pledged $1.72 billion in aid for 1984-1985.   Henry S. Bradsher

See also ASIA (Facts in Brief Table). In WORLD BOOK, see BANGLADESH.

BANK. The year 1984 was a good one for the United States economy, but it was an uncertain year for the U.S. banking industry. The gross national product (GNP) — the total amount of goods and services produced — grew at an unusually high rate of 12.8 per cent during the first half of the year and slowed to a more sedate 5.7 per cent during the second half. Memories of the 13.9 per cent peak inflation rate of 1979 became less vivid during 1984 as inflation reached about 4 per cent.

This was the first year since 1979 when no major new legislation greatly expanded the scope of the banking business. The slowdown in bank deregulation was generally thought to have resulted from the rising number of bank failures, which set a post-World War II record of 79 in 1984.

Interest Rates remained stubbornly high. The federal funds rate — the rate at which banks lend one another reserves on an overnight basis — began the year at 10.0 per cent and hovered between 9.5 and 10 per cent until the end of March. It rose to more than 11 per cent in June and peaked at 11.8 per cent in the third week of August, before falling to under 9.5 per cent by the end of October and finishing the year at 8.75 per cent.

The interest rate for 90-day certificates of deposit opened the year at 9.6 per cent, fell to 9.4 per cent at the end of January, and rose steadily to a peak of 11.8 per cent in early July. It plunged to under 10 per cent over September and October and ended the year at 8.3 per cent.

The prime rate, which banks charge their best corporate customers, was at 11 per cent from mid-1983 through early April of 1984. It rose to 13 per cent by early July, began to fall in October, and ended December at 10.75 per cent.

In general, short-term rates remained from 5 to 9 percentage points above the inflation rate — a far higher spread than the historical average of only 2 to 3 percentage points. Normally, interest rates that are far higher than the inflation rate slow down business borrowing and depress economic growth, but the GNP remained strong during 1984.

Money and the Fed. The Federal Reserve System (Fed) serves as the central bank of the United States and is responsible for managing the money supply. The Fed increases bank reserves when it wants the supply of money and credit to rise. It drains reserves from the banking system when it wants the supply to fall. Most economists believe that expanding the supply sparks economic activity in the short run and inflation in the long run.

The money supply is commonly measured as either M1 or M2. M1 consists of currency in the hands of the public, plus various kinds of checking and NOW accounts. It represents money to spend, rather than money to hold and, in general, pays little or no interest. M1 was $525 billion at the beginning of January and grew at an annual rate of

The camel bank, a wooden wagon drawn by a camel, travels from village to village and provides banking services in a desert region of northern India.

about 3.5 per cent for the first four months of 1984 to $535 billion. In May, M1 took a big jump to $545 billion. But it flattened out at between $545 billion and $550 billion for much of the rest of 1984 and ended the year at $557.6 billion.

M2 defines money more broadly, adding savings accounts, certificates of deposit, and money market mutual funds to M1. M2 ended 1983 at $2.196-trillion. It grew fairly steadily at about 7 per cent and ended November 1984 at $2.346 trillion.

Bank Failures. The big news in the banking industry in 1984 was the failure of many small banks and the near failure of one large one. From 1946 to 1980, banks averaged only 4.9 failures a year. During 1981, there were 10 failures; in 1982, there were 42; in 1983, 48; and in 1984, 79. But because of deposit insurance, bank failures represented a far smaller danger to the public in 1984 than they once had.

In 1933, Congress created the Federal Deposit Insurance Corporation (FDIC). This agency insures the deposits in about 97 per cent of the banks in the United States and guarantees payment in full to all the depositors of a failed bank up to a legal limit of $100,000.

The FDIC steps in when a member bank is unable to pay off depositors because of too many bad loans. Before 1983, the Fed had always lent extra reserves to a failing bank to cover uninsured deposits in excess of the $100,000 limit. But when the First National Bank of Midland, Tex., failed in October 1983, depositors with more than $100,000 in an account were told they would receive only a share of any remaining bank assets for their uninsured deposits.

The FDIC stated that its purpose was to make large depositors investigate the soundness of their banks. All banks, whether risky or conservative in their loan policies, pay the same deposit-insurance premium. The FDIC wanted banks to make less risky loans or else pay a price for their aggressiveness. At the same time, the FDIC estimated that 80 per cent of all the money deposited at large banks was uninsured — that is, in accounts above the $100,000 limit.

These big banks were the banks that suffered from loans made to the energy industry (when it seemed that the price of oil would continue to rise forever) and to the governments of other countries. Much of 1983 and 1984 saw speculation that some country would default or that bad energy loans would make it impossible for one or more of the large banks to go on without government help.

The Continental Illinois Trouble. The bank that nearly failed was the Continental Illinois National Bank and Trust Company of Chicago. Continental's troubles surfaced in July 1982 after Penn Square Bank in Oklahoma City, Okla., failed.

BARBADOS

Continental announced that it would take large losses on energy-related loans arranged through Penn Square. By the end of 1983, all of Continental's top management had left or been dismissed, and Continental was relying heavily on expensive overnight Eurodollars — that is, on U.S. dollars deposited in foreign banks.

In the second week of May 1984, rumors spread that Continental was in trouble. Foreign investors withdrew $14 billion in deposits in three days with a few telephone calls. By May 17, the collapse was over. The FDIC announced that it was unwilling to let the seventh largest bank in the United States go under and that it had guaranteed all of the bank's deposits, regardless of size. The FDIC had also arranged a rescue package of $5.5 billion in loans from other big banks and $2 billion from the Fed. It was the largest federal bailout of a private enterprise in U.S. history. By the end of July, Continental had in effect been nationalized. Through its infusion of funds, the FDIC owned 80 per cent of Continental's common stock.

The lesson was clear. Small banks could fail. But the FDIC and the Fed had served notice that there would never be a recurrence of the major bank failures of the early 1930's.   Donald W. Swanton

See also ECONOMICS. In WORLD BOOK, see BANK.

BARBADOS. See WEST INDIES.

BASEBALL. The Detroit Tigers made baseball history in 1984 by getting off to the fastest start ever, winning 35 of their first 40 games. The Tigers went on to win the American League's Eastern Division, the American League pennant, and the World Series.

It was a prosperous year for baseball, even though the major-league attendance figure of 44 million was a slight drop from the 1983 record. There was a new commissioner in Peter V. Ueberroth; a new star in 19-year-old New York Mets pitcher Dwight Gooden, the youngest player in the major leagues; and a new player-manager in 43-year-old Pete Rose of the Cincinnati Reds.

The National League beat the American League, 3-1, in the All-Star Game on July 10 in San Francisco. Fernando Valenzuela of the Los Angeles Dodgers struck out the American League batters in order in the fourth inning, and Gooden of the Mets did the same in the fifth inning. The six consecutive strikeouts broke the All-Star Game record of five by Carl Hubbell, which was set 50 years earlier to the day.

American League. The Tigers held first place from opening day. Their record of 104-58, the best in the majors, allowed them to win their division by 15 games over the Toronto Blue Jays.

A week before the season began, the Tigers traded with the Philadelphia Phillies for Willie

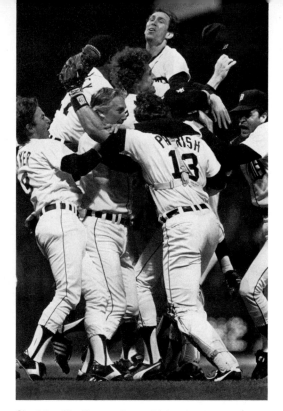

Shortstop Alan Trammell soars higher than his teammates as the Detroit Tigers celebrate their World Series victory over the San Diego Padres.

Hernandez. The left-handed relief pitcher responded with 32 saves in 33 opportunities. He won the Cy Young Award as the American League's outstanding pitcher and was named the league's Most Valuable Player.

Other key Tigers included outfielders Kirk Gibson and Chet Lemon, catcher Lance Parrish, shortstop Alan Trammell, and second baseman Lou Whitaker. Gibson was voted Most Valuable Player in the American League play-offs, and Trammell was voted Most Valuable Player in the World Series.

The Kansas City Royals won the Western Division by three games over the California Angels and the Minnesota Twins, who finished with .500 records. The Royals' record of 84-78 was the poorest ever for an American League play-off team, and the Royals were no match for the Tigers in the play-offs. The Tigers won three straight games, 8-1, 5-3 in 11 innings, and 1-0.

National League. Since 1969, when the team came into existence, the San Diego Padres had never finished higher than fourth place. In 1984, however, the Padres won the Western Division by 12 games over the Atlanta Braves and the Houston Astros.

The Padres blended veterans, such as first baseman Steve Garvey and relief pitcher Rich Gossage, with young stars, such as outfielder Tony Gwynn

Final Standings in Major League Baseball

American League

Eastern Division	W.	L.	Pct.	G.B.
Detroit Tigers	104	58	.642	
Toronto Blue Jays	89	73	.549	15
New York Yankees	87	75	.537	17
Boston Red Sox	86	76	.531	18
Baltimore Orioles	85	77	.525	19
Cleveland Indians	75	87	.463	29
Milwaukee Brewers	67	94	.416	36½

Western Division	W.	L.	Pct.	G.B.
Kansas City Royals	84	78	.519	
California Angels	81	81	.500	3
Minnesota Twins	81	81	.500	3
Oakland Athletics	77	85	.475	7
Chicago White Sox	74	88	.457	10
Seattle Mariners	74	88	.457	10
Texas Rangers	69	92	.429	14½

Offensive Leaders

Batting Average — Don Mattingly, New York	.343
Runs Scored — Dwight Evans, Boston	121
Home Runs — Tony Armas, Boston	43
Runs Batted In — Tony Armas, Boston	123
Hits — Don Mattingly, New York	207
Stolen Bases — Rickey Henderson, Oakland	66

Leading Pitchers

Games Won — Mike Boddicker, Baltimore	20
Win Average — Doyle Alexander, Toronto (17–6)	.739
Earned Run Average — Mike Boddicker, Baltimore	2.79
Strikeouts — Mark Langston, Seattle	204
Saves — Dan Quisenberry, Kansas City	44

Awards*

Most Valuable Player — Willie Hernandez, Detroit
Cy Young — Willie Hernandez, Detroit
Rookie of the Year — Alvin Davis, Seattle
Manager of the Year — George (Sparky) Anderson, Detroit

National League

Eastern Division	W.	L.	Pct.	G.B.
Chicago Cubs	96	65	.596	
New York Mets	90	72	.556	6½
St. Louis Cardinals	84	78	.519	12½
Philadelphia Phillies	81	81	.500	15½
Montreal Expos	78	83	.484	18
Pittsburgh Pirates	75	87	.463	21½

Western Division	W.	L.	Pct.	G.B.
San Diego Padres	92	70	.568	
Atlanta Braves	80	82	.494	12
Houston Astros	80	82	.494	12
Los Angeles Dodgers	79	83	.488	13
Cincinnati Reds	70	92	.432	22
San Francisco Giants	66	96	.407	26

Offensive Leaders

Batting Average — Tony Gwynn, San Diego	.351
Runs Scored — Ryne Sandberg, Chicago	114
Home Runs — Dale Murphy, Atlanta; Mike Schmidt, Philadelphia (tie)	36
Runs Batted In — Gary Carter, Montreal; Mike Schmidt, Philadelphia (tie)	106
Hits — Tony Gwynn, San Diego	213
Stolen Bases — Tim Raines, Montreal	75

Leading Pitchers

Games Won — Joaquin Andujar, St. Louis	20
Win Average — Rick Sutcliffe, Chicago (16–1)	.941
Earned Run Average — Alejandro Peña, Los Angeles	2.48
Strikeouts — Dwight Gooden, New York	276
Saves — Bruce Sutter, St. Louis	45

Awards*

Most Valuable Player — Ryne Sandberg, Chicago
Cy Young — Rick Sutcliffe, Chicago
Rookie of the Year — Dwight Gooden, New York
Manager of the Year — Jim Frey, Chicago

*Selected by Baseball Writers Association of America.

---

and second baseman Alan Wiggins. Gwynn led the major leagues with a .351 batting average, and Wiggins stole 70 bases.

In 1983, the Chicago Cubs finished fifth in the Eastern Division. The Cubs had not had a winning season since 1972 or won a pennant since 1945. In 1984, they finished 6½ games ahead of the Mets to win the division.

Their key player was pitcher Rick Sutcliffe, who had a 4-5 record when the Cubs acquired him on June 13 in a six-player trade with the Cleveland Indians. Sutcliffe went on to post a 16-1 record for the Cubs and was voted the National League Cy Young Award.

The Cubs won the first two games of the play-offs, 13-0 and 4-2. No team had ever won a National League pennant after losing the first two games, but the Padres did it by winning the next three games, 7-1, 7-5, and 6-3.

World Series. The World Series, which ran from October 9 to 14, was the first since 1968 for Detroit. There was little suspense as the Tigers won the first game, 3-2, lost the second, 5-3, and won the next three — 5-2, 4-2, and 8-4 — in the best-of-seven series.

Detroit had to play only eight postseason games, the fewest by a World Series winner since the 1976 Cincinnati Reds swept the National League play-offs and the World Series in seven games.

Leading Players. Starting the final day of the season, outfielder Dave Winfield of the New York Yankees led his teammate, first baseman Don Mattingly, by two points in their battle for the American League batting championship. Mattingly made four hits in the last game to Winfield's one and won the title with a .343 batting average.

Perfect games were pitched by David Palmer of the Montreal Expos and Mike Witt of the Angels. Jack Morris of Detroit threw a no-hitter on April 7. Palmer's 4-0 perfect game against the St. Louis Cardinals came on April 21, but the game lasted only five innings because of rain. Witt pitched a complete, 1-0 perfect game against the Texas Rangers on September 30.

Gooden, the Mets' young right-hander with a blazing fast ball, set a rookie record by striking out 276 batters in 218 innings during the regular season. In September, he struck out 16 players in each of two consecutive games.

Rose, aiming for Ty Cobb's major-league record of 4,191 hits, started the season with the Expos. On April 13, he made his 4,000th hit. On August 16, he was named player-manager at Cincinnati, where he had played most of his career and where he hoped to break Cobb's record. He ended the 1984 season with 4,097 career hits.

Commissioner. On March 3, the major-league club owners, meeting in Tampa, Fla., elected Ueb-

BASKETBALL

erroth to replace Bowie Kuhn as commissioner of baseball. Ueberroth, who was the president of the Los Angeles Olympic Organizing Committee, took over his baseball responsibilities on October 1.

One of Ueberroth's first problems was a strike by umpires during the pennant play-offs. With Ueberroth acting as binding arbitrator, the umpires agreed to work the World Series. The day after the series ended, Ueberroth awarded the umpires $1.4 million for postseason work over the next three years. He also agreed to a demand for postseason money for all major-league umpires, not just for those who work postseason games.

Hall of Fame. Veteran baseball writers elected three former players—shortstop Luis Aparicio, third baseman Harmon Killebrew, and pitcher Don Drysdale—to the Baseball Hall of Fame in Cooperstown, N.Y. Aparicio spent most of his 18-year career with the Chicago White Sox. Killebrew played 14 of his 22 career years with the Twins. Drysdale played all 14 years of his career with the Dodgers. The 16-man veterans committee voted in two former players—shortstop Harold (Pee Wee) Reese and catcher Rick Ferrell. Reese played 16 seasons with the Dodgers, including the legendary teams of the 1950's. Ferrell, who played with several teams, caught 1,805 games, an American League record.   Frank Litsky

In WORLD BOOK, see BASEBALL.

Georgetown's Patrick Ewing pulls in a rebound against Houston's Akeem Olajuwon as Georgetown wins the NCAA championship in April in Seattle.

BASKETBALL. The Boston Celtics won the National Basketball Association (NBA) title in June 1984 for the 15th time by defeating the Los Angeles Lakers, 4 games to 3, in the play-off finals. Georgetown University won the National Collegiate Athletic Association (NCAA) men's basketball championship on April 2 by beating the University of Houston in the final of the 53-team tournament. The University of Southern California defeated the University of Tennessee on April 1 and won the NCAA's 32-team tournament for women for the second straight year.

NBA Season. Each of the NBA's 23 teams played 82 games between October 1983 and April 1984. During the regular season, NBA attendance rose 3.9 per cent to 10,014,543, exceeding 10 million for the first time in the league's history.

The Celtics, under new head coach K. C. Jones, posted the league's best record (62-20) and won the Eastern Conference's Atlantic Division by 10 games. Other division winners were Los Angeles (54-28), the Milwaukee Bucks (50-32), and the Utah Jazz (45-37).

When the finals began, the Celtics used 6-foot 2-inch (188-centimeter) Gerald Henderson to guard the Lakers' all-pro guard, 6-foot 9-inch (206-centimeter) Earvin (Magic) Johnson. The Lakers won two of the first three games. At half-time in the fourth game, the job of stopping Magic John-

son was given to 6-foot 4-inch (193-centimeter) Dennis Johnson. After that, the Celtics controlled the Lakers' running game and went on to win the seventh game on June 12 in Boston. The score was 111-102, as Larry Bird scored 20 points and collected 12 rebounds. The Celtics' star forward was voted the Most Valuable Player of the play-off finals.

Bird was also chosen the league's Most Valuable Player for his regular-season performance. He was joined on the all-pro team by Bernard King of the New York Knicks at forward, Kareem Abdul-Jabbar of Los Angeles at center, and Johnson of Los Angeles and Isiah Thomas of the Detroit Pistons at guard.

On April 5 in Las Vegas, Nev., one of basketball's most towering records was toppled when Abdul-Jabbar sank a 12-foot (3.66-meter) hook shot and became the highest scorer in professional basketball history. He broke the record of 31,419 points, held by Wilt Chamberlain since 1973.

College Men. After the regular season, the final polls of the Associated Press and United Press International had identical rankings for the top six teams. They were, in order of rank, North Carolina (27-2), Georgetown (29-3), Kentucky (26-4), DePaul (26-2), Houston (28-4), and Illinois (24-4).

Then came the NCAA tournament. On March 22, in the East Regional semifinals in Atlanta, Ga.,

National Basketball Association Standings

Eastern Conference

Atlantic Division	W.	L.	Pct.	G.B.
Boston Celtics	62	20	.756	
Philadelphia 76ers	52	30	.634	10
New York Knicks	47	35	.573	15
New Jersey Nets	45	37	.549	.17
Washington Bullets	35	47	.427	27

Central Division				
Milwaukee Bucks	50	32	.610	
Detroit Pistons	49	33	.598	1
Atlanta Hawks	40	42	.488	10
Cleveland Cavaliers	28	54	.341	22
Chicago Bulls	27	55	.329	23
Indiana Pacers	26	56	.317	24

Western Conference

Midwest Division	W.	L.	Pct.	G.B.
Utah Jazz	45	37	.549	
Dallas Mavericks	43	39	.524	2
Denver Nuggets	38	44	.463	7
Kansas City Kings	38	44	.463	7
San Antonio Spurs	37	45	.451	8
Houston Rockets	29	53	.354	16

Pacific Division				
Los Angeles Lakers	54	28	.659	
Portland Trail Blazers	48	34	.585	6
Seattle SuperSonics	42	40	.512	12
Phoenix Suns	41	41	.500	13
Golden State Warriors	37	45	.451	17
San Diego Clippers	30	52	.366	24

Individual Leaders

Scoring	G.	F.G.	F.T.	Pts.	Avg.
Adrian Dantley, Utah	79	802	813	2,418	30.6
Mark Aguirre, Dallas	79	925	465	2,330	29.5
Kiki Vandeweghe, Denver	78	895	494	2,295	29.4
Alex English, Denver	82	907	352	2,167	26.4
Bernard King, New York	77	795	437	2,027	26.3
George Gervin, San Antonio	76	765	427	1,967	25.9
Larry Bird, Boston	79	758	374	1,908	24.2

Rebounding	G.	No.	Avg.
Moses Malone, Philadelphia	71	950	13.4
Buck Williams, New Jersey	81	1,000	12.3
Jeff Ruland, Washington	75	922	12.3
Bill Laimbeer, Detroit	82	1,003	12.2

College Tournament Champions

NCCA (Men) Division I: Georgetown (Washington, D.C.)
    Division II: Central Missouri State
    Division III: Wisconsin-Whitewater
NCAA (Women) Division I: Southern California
    Division II: Central Missouri State
    Division III: Rust (Mississippi)
NAIA (Men): Fort Hays State (Kansas)
    (Women): North Carolina-Asheville
NIT: Michigan
Junior College (Men): San Jacinto (Texas)
    (Women): Roane State (Tennessee)

College Champions

Conference	School
Atlantic Coast	North Carolina (regular season)
	Maryland (conference tournament)
Atlantic Ten	Temple (regular season)
	West Virginia (conference tournament)
Big East	Georgetown*
Big Eight	Oklahoma (regular season)
	Kansas (conference tournament)
Big Sky	Weber State (regular season)
	Nevada-Reno (conference tournament)
Big Ten	Illinois—Purdue (tie)
East Coast	Bucknell (regular season)
	Rider (conference tournament)
Eastern College Athletic-North	Northeastern*
Eastern College Athletic-Metro	Long Island University—Robert Morris (tie; regular season)
	Long Island University (conference tournament)
Eastern College Athletic-South	Richmond*
Ivy League	Princeton
Metro	Memphis State—Louisville (tie; regular season)
	Memphis State (conference tournament)
Metro Atlantic	Iona—St. Peter's—LaSalle (tie; regular season)
	Iona (conference tournament)
Mid-American	Miami*
Mid-Continent	Illinois-Chicago (regular season)
	Western Illinois (conference tournament)
Mid-Eastern	North Carolina A & T*
Midwestern City	Oral Roberts*
Missouri Valley	Tulsa—Illinois State (tie; regular season)
	Tulsa (conference tournament)
Ohio Valley	Morehead State*
Pacific Coast Athletic	Nevada-Las Vegas (regular season)
	Fresno State (conference tournament)
Pacific Ten	Washington—Oregon State (tie)
Southeastern	Kentucky*
Southern	Marshall*
Southland	Lamar (regular season)
	Louisiana Tech (conference tournament)
Southwest	Houston*
Southwestern Athletic	Alabama State—Alcorn State (tie; regular season)
	Alcorn State (conference tournament)
Sun Belt	Virginia Commonwealth (regular season)
	Alabama-Birmingham (conference tournament)
Trans America Athletic	Houston Baptist*
West Coast Athletic	San Diego
Western Athletic	Texas-El Paso*

*Regular season and conference tournament champions.

Indiana upset North Carolina, 72-68. The next night, in the Midwest Regional semifinals in St. Louis, Mo., Wake Forest upset DePaul, 73-71, in overtime. That was the final game for Ray Meyer, who retired at age 70 after 42 years as DePaul's coach. Meyer had a won-lost record of 724-354, the fifth best among NCAA coaches.

In the national semifinals on March 31 in Seattle, Georgetown eliminated Kentucky, 53-40. Houston edged Virginia, 49-47, in overtime, though Virginia held Houston's 7-foot (213-centimeter) center, Akeem Abdul Olajuwon, to 12 points and forced him into eight turnovers.

In the championship game on April 2 in Seattle, Georgetown defeated Houston, 84-75. Michael Graham scored 14 points, and Reggie Williams scored 19 points for Georgetown. Patrick Ewing, Georgetown's 7-foot (213-centimeter) center, was named the tournament's Most Valuable Player.

The players mentioned most frequently on all-America teams were Ewing, Olajuwon, Michael Jordan and Sam Perkins of North Carolina, Wayman Tisdale of Oklahoma, and Chris Mullin of St. John's in New York City. All except Olajuwon, a Nigerian, played on the U.S. team that won the gold medal in men's basketball at the Summer Olympic Games in Los Angeles in August. Olajuwon and Jordan gave up their final season of college eligibility and entered the NBA draft, where Olajuwon was chosen first and Jordan third during the first round. Olajuwon signed with the Houston Rockets for more than $1 million a year. Jordan signed with the Chicago Bulls for almost that much.

College Women. The final regular-season poll showed Texas (30-2) first, Louisiana Tech (27-2) second, Georgia (28-2) third, Old Dominion (22-4) fourth, Southern California (24-4) fifth, and Tennessee (19-9) 15th.

The NCAA tournament ended on April 1 in Los Angeles when Southern California defeated Tennessee, 72-61. Southern California rallied midway through the second half with an 18 to 4 scoring spurt led by Cynthia Cooper, a guard.

Cheryl Miller of Southern California scored 16 points and was chosen the tournament's Most Valuable Player. At the Olympic Games in Los Angeles, she and Pam McGee of Southern California helped the U.S. women's basketball team win a gold medal.

Janice Lawrence, Louisiana Tech's 6-foot 3-inch (191-centimeter) senior center, won the Wade Trophy as the season's outstanding player. She was named to the all-America team with Miller, McGee, Annette Smith of Texas, and Joyce Walker of Louisiana State. Frank Litsky

In the WORLD BOOK SUPPLEMENT section, see BASKETBALL. In WORLD BOOK, see ABDUL-JABBAR, KAREEM.

BELGIUM. Prime Minister Wilfried A. E. Martens announced on March 17, 1984, a drastic three-year austerity plan to stave off Belgium's bankruptcy. Martens was concerned for a number of reasons. The unemployment rate of 15 per cent was one of the highest in Europe. And the national debt was 12.8 per cent of the gross national product, compared with an average of 5 per cent for the European Community (EC or Common Market), to which Belgium belongs. In addition, most Belgian municipalities were insolvent.

The plan took effect immediately. The government did not need to submit the plan to Parliament because, in 1982, Parliament had given the government the power to rule by decree in economic matters.

Martens aimed to cut the national debt in half by the end of 1986 by reducing public employees' wages 3.5 per cent and slashing social security benefits. The plan was to hold increases in the salaries of most Belgians at 2 per cent below the inflation rate until 1986.

Protests and Strikes. Socialists called the plan "the worst frontal assault on workers for half a century," and employers said it did little to improve competition. Scattered strikes followed. On April 9, some 6,000 workers demonstrated in the southern city of Charleroi, and 400 workers marched and exploded firecrackers in Brussels.

But Socialists and union officials conceded that the government was in no mood to compromise.

The Lathe Goes. In the summer of 1984, the government wrestled with the problem of whether to allow a private firm to ship a computerized lathe to the Soviet Union. The machine had taken the company, Pegard, two years to build. The firm was about to ship the lathe, but Foreign Minister Leo Tindemans intervened. He said the Soviets would use the lathe to make parts for SS-20 and SS-21 missiles, and so he would not let Pegard ship it. Pegard was in financial difficulty until Economic Affairs Minister Mark Eyskens ruled that, unless another buyer could be found by August 8, he would allow the machine to go to the Soviet Union. The Belgian Army immediately discovered that it had set aside money for just such a machine. The amount did not match the price, so the United States Department of Defense said it would donate $700,000 to buy the machine. In October, however, the U.S. Embassy learned that the lathe was on its way to the Soviet Union. The United States froze the $700,000, pending an investigation in Washington. Kenneth Brown

See also EUROPE (Facts in Brief Table). In WORLD BOOK, see BELGIUM.

BELIZE. See LATIN AMERICA.

BENIN. See AFRICA.

BHUTAN. See ASIA.

BIOCHEMISTRY. The first evidence of a biochemical abnormality in homosexuals was reported in September 1984 by biologists Brian A. Gladue and Richard Green of the State University of New York in Stony Brook and psychiatrist Ronald E. Hellman of South Beach Psychiatric Center in New York City. They studied the effect of a single dose of estrogen, a female hormone, on *heterosexual* (sexually attracted to the opposite sex) men and women and *homosexual* (sexually attracted to the same sex) men. Hormones are chemicals secreted by one part of the body that affect the function of another part. Estrogen affects the concentration in the body of a substance called *luteinizing hormone* (LH), which plays a role in fertility.

The researchers found that LH production in homosexual men given a dose of estrogen was intermediate between the LH responses of heterosexual men and women. In heterosexual females, for example, the concentration of LH declined by about 25 per cent after administration of estrogen, then increased sharply to a level more than twice as high as the initial concentration. In heterosexual men, however, the concentration of LH declined by about 50 per cent and returned to the normal level slowly. In homosexual males, the concentration of LH declined almost as sharply as it did in heterosexual males but then rose to a level about 40 per cent higher than normal.

These varying reactions may have been caused by differences in the way estrogen binds, or attaches, to cells in males and females. The results suggest that there is an abnormality in estrogen binding in homosexual males, but there is no evidence as yet that this is a cause of homosexuality.

Heart Hormones. The heart has long been thought to be simply a muscle that pumps blood through the body. In the past three years, however, investigators have found that the heart also produces hormones that regulate kidney function and the diameter of blood vessels. The presence of these hormones in the heart was first noted in 1981 by physiologist Adolpho J. deBold of Queens University and Hospital in Kingston, Canada. Not until late 1983 and 1984, however, were deBold and others able to purify and identify them.

One hormone, called *auriculin* by deBold because it is produced in the *auricles* — the upper chambers — of the heart, causes the kidneys to excrete water and salt, a process that lowers blood pressure. Other hormones produced by the heart have been shown to cause blood vessels to relax, which would also lower blood pressure. Each of these substances could thus be useful for the treatment of *hypertension* (high blood pressure) if they could be produced in sufficient quantities.

Magnesium and Hypertension. A shortage of magnesium in the diet can apparently produce hypertension, according to biochemist Burton M. Altura and his colleagues at Downstate Medical Center in New York City. Altura reported in June that rats whose diets contained below-normal quantities of magnesium had blood pressures that were substantially higher than normal.

Most people get enough magnesium from their diet, but two groups of individuals do not: alcoholics and persons taking *diuretics* — drugs that reduce the amount of water in the body by increasing the production of urine. Alcoholics, who typically do not eat properly, often have high blood pressure. Persons on diuretic drugs, on the other hand, may be getting adequate nutrition, but the diuretic causes magnesium to be washed from their bodies.

Manic Depression. Evidence that a form of mental illness known as manic depression may be triggered by a genetic disorder was presented in July by scientists at the National Institute of Mental Health in Bethesda, Md. Manic-depression disorders are characterized by sharp swings in mood.

The researchers, headed by psychiatrist Elliot S. Gershon, compared laboratory-grown skin cells taken from victims of severe manic depression with laboratory-grown cells taken from healthy individuals. They found that the cells from the manic-depressive patients had a greater sensitivity to *acetylcholine*, a chemical that transmits nerve impulses in the brain. Increased sensitivity to acetyl-

A scientist at IGI Biotechnology Incorporated in Columbia, Md., works with bacteria that have been genetically altered to eat agricultural wastes.

choline had been shown by other investigators to produce abnormal behavior. These findings provide strong evidence that manic depression — and perhaps most other kinds of mental illness as well — is biochemical in origin. If so, drugs may largely replace psychotherapy in coming years for the treatment of serious mental disorders.

Chromosome Weak Spots. Scientists at the University of Minnesota in Minneapolis said in November they had discovered 51 previously unknown weak spots on human chromosomes — structures, located in the cell nucleus, that carry the genes. The weak spots, called *fragile sites*, are places where chromosomes are prone to breaking. The investigators found that 20 of these sites were at or near points where chromosomes are known to break in some kinds of cancer cells. The researchers also discovered that chromosomal breakage was inhibited by folic acid, a substance found in leafy vegetables, fruits, and cereal grains. This finding indicated that a diet containing adequate amounts of those foods might help to protect against some cancers — but that was still a supposition. Thomas H. Maugh II

In the Special Reports section, see Changing Life's Blueprint. In World Book, see Biochemistry.

BIOLOGY. See Biochemistry; Botany; Environment; Ocean; Paleontology; Zoology.

BLAIZE, HERBERT AUGUSTUS (1918-   ), was sworn in as prime minister of Grenada on Dec. 4, 1984, after his moderate coalition New National Party swept the December 3 elections. Prime Minister Blaize said he would request United States troops, which had invaded Grenada in 1983, to remain until the island nation was able to maintain its own security.

Blaize was born on Feb. 26, 1918, on the island of Carriacou, about 15 miles (24 kilometers) northeast of Grenada. He began his political career in 1957 when he was elected to represent Carriacou in Grenada's Parliament. He was re-elected repeatedly until 1960, when the British government appointed him to fill a 14-month interim term as chief minister. He was defeated in subsequent elections in 1961 by Sir Eric M. Gairy. After Gairy was forced out of office in 1962 for "financial irregularities," Blaize was elected to a five-year term as leader of the government. He later became an attorney.

Blaize has a reputation for honesty and integrity. He has been described as "a good, solid, respectable fellow," "not flamboyant but sound," and "plodding rather than brilliant." He describes himself as "an ordinary guy."

Blaize and his wife, Venetia, have three daughters and three sons.   Rod Such

BLINDNESS. See HANDICAPPED.

BOATING. In 1984, yachting groups in the United States started a campaign to regain the America's Cup, the sport's most hallowed trophy. The United States had lost the cup to Australia in 1983 after having held it for 132 years.

In August, American yachting groups launched two new 12-Meter sloops, each a candidate for the next America's Cup races in 1987. One contender is *America II,* which has a portable keel, mast, and rigging, with a choice of keels. The other contender, *Courageous II,* has wings rather than a conventional keel, though the wings differ from those on the radically designed winged keel on *Australia II,* the 1983 cup winner.

A record number of 23 yachting organizations from eight nations filed entry fees of $12,000 each for the 1987 challenge. This entitled them to race in the preliminary competition, with the winner challenging the Australian defender.

Distance Races. In June, Yvon Fauconier of France, helped by an unusual ruling, won the Observer Singlehanded Transatlantic Yacht Race from Plymouth, England, to Newport, R.I. In the early stages of the race, Fauconier, in the 53-foot (16-meter) trimaran *Unupro Jardin V,* temporarily abandoned the competition to help rescue Philippe Jeantot of France, whose yacht, *Crédit Agricole II,* had capsized. Philippe Poupon of France, in *Fleury Michon IV,* finished first in the record

The British square-rigger *Marques* leaves Bermuda during a race of tall ships on June 2, one day before it sank in heavy seas, killing 20 people.

time of 16 days 11 hours 56 minutes. Fauconier finished second, 10½ hours later. But race officials gave Fauconier a 16-hour credit for his rescue detour, making him the winner.

The Southern Ocean Racing Conference's annual six-race series was held in February off Florida and the Bahamas. The overall winner was *Diva,* a 39-foot (12-meter) yacht built in France and owned by Berend Beilken of West Germany.

Powerboats. In the U.S. unlimited hydroplane championship, Jim Kropfeld of Cincinnati, Ohio, won his first national title. His *Miss Budweiser* was powered by an old Rolls-Royce aircraft engine. Two boats, *Atlas Van Lines* and *Miller Lite,* using lighter and more powerful turbine engines rather than the traditional engines, made their debuts in the 10-race series.

The 10 races for the U.S. offshore championship included a new division for 45- to 50-foot (14- to 15-meter) superboats. Al Copeland of Metairie, La., in a 50-foot (15-meter) Cougar catamaran named *Popeye's/Diet Coke,* won six of nine races and the series title.   Frank Litsky

In WORLD BOOK, see BOATING; SAILING.

BOLIVIA. See LATIN AMERICA.

BOND. See STOCKS AND BONDS.

BOOKS. See CANADIAN LITERATURE; LITERATURE; LITERATURE FOR CHILDREN; POETRY; PUBLISHING.

BOPHUTHATSWANA. See AFRICA.

BOTANY. Many kinds of trees in the forests of the Eastern United States are growing more slowly than they used to, scientists reported in 1984. The researchers theorized that the cause of the trees' declining growth rate may be *acid rain* — acidic precipitation caused by air pollution.

Arthur H. Johnson, a soil scientist at the University of Pennsylvania in Philadelphia, said his studies showed that the growth rates of evergreen trees in 15 Eastern states have fallen off sharply during the past 20 years. Johnson and his colleagues took core samples — long, thin cylinders of wood drilled from tree trunks — to measure the width of annual tree rings over the past 100 years. They found that tree rings formed since the early 1960's were narrower than rings formed in earlier years. The trees with the thinnest rings were red spruce, pitch pine, and shortleaf pine.

Samuel B. McLaughlin, an investigator at Oak Ridge National Laboratory in Tennessee, reported similar findings in February 1984. But he discovered that several kinds of *deciduous,* or leaf-shedding, trees — such as black oak and hickory — have also suffered declining growth.

Light-Piping in Plants. Researchers reported in 1984 that young, sprouting plants are able to "pipe" light to their roots, thus helping the roots to grow. Botanists Dina F. Mandoli of Stanford University and Winslow R. Briggs of the Carnegie Institution — both in Stanford, Calif. — said young plants contain columns of cells that transmit light, much like the glass strands called *optical fibers*. However, plants transmit only about 1 per cent as much light as do optical fibers.

Gravity-Free Growth. The nodding movements made by the tips of plant shoots as they grow are familiar to many people through time-lapse motion pictures. These movements, called *circumnutation,* are oval paths traced by the plant tip as growth-rate changes occur in parts of the shoot. Plant scientists had long believed that gravity was essential for circumnutation to occur.

In July 1984, however, botanists Allan H. Brown and David K. Chapman of the University of Pennsylvania reported on an experiment that was carried out during the Spacelab mission in late 1983. Sunflower seedlings growing in the weightless condition of earth orbit were automatically videotaped for 10 seconds every 10 minutes. The video images revealed that circumnutation had occurred — proof that it is not dependent on gravity.

Deep Plant. In December 1984, botanists exploring the ocean floor reported the discovery of a new plant growing deeper than any previously known. The plant, a form of coralline algae, was found at a depth of 884 feet (269 meters) in the Atlantic Ocean (see OCEAN).   Eldon H. Newcomb

In WORLD BOOK, see BOTANY.

BOTSWANA. See AFRICA.

BOWLING. Bob Chamberlain, Mike Durbin, Mark Roth, and Earl Anthony won the major bowling tournaments for men in 1984. Aleta Sill and Lisa Rathgeber were the most successful women bowlers.

Chamberlain, of Pontiac, Mich., had never won a tournament on the Professional Bowlers Association (PBA) tour. On March 3, in Toledo, Ohio, he captured the $200,000 PBA championship by defeating Dan Eberl of Tonawanda, N.Y., 219-191. It was the first time anyone had won a major title by beating four opponents in a five-man final.

The 42-year-old Durbin of Chagrin Falls, Ohio, won the $200,000 Firestone Tournament of Champions, held in April in Akron, Ohio. He, too, had to beat four opponents in the final. The last one was Mike Aulby of Indianapolis. Durbin's 246-163 victory gave him his third title in 13 years in this tournament. It came five days after Durbin's induction into the PBA Hall of Fame.

Although Roth, of Spring Lake Heights, N.J., had reached the championship round in nine previous major tournaments, he had never won a title. His fortune changed in the U.S. Open, held from March 12 to 17 in Oak Lawn, Ill. He finished with four strikes and beat Guppy Troup of Jacksonville, Fla., 244-237 in the final match.

Anthony, of Dublin, Calif., had been named PBA Bowler of the Year six times, most recently in 1983. Then, tired of traveling, he retired from the PBA tour at age 45, though he said he might compete occasionally. His only 1984 appearance in a major tournament came in the American Bowling Congress Masters competition, held from May 8 to 12 in Reno, Nev. He defeated Gil Sliker of Washington, N.J., 191-175 in the final for his second Masters title.

Women. The Ladies Pro Bowlers Tour offered a record number of tournaments (23) and record prize money ($768,400). Sill, of Cocoa, Fla., won five tournaments, and Rathgeber of Palmetto, Fla., won four. Sill won the $100,000 Tournament of Champions, held from November 10 to 17 in Las Vegas, Nev., and finished second to Kazue Inahashi of Japan in the $100,000 Queen's tournament, held from May 15 to 19 in Niagara Falls, N.Y. Sill became the first woman bowler to earn more than $50,000 in prize money in one year.

Rathgeber made bowling history while winning the Fairhaven (Mass.) Classic, held from August 22 to 26. In her first 16 games of match play, she totaled 4,030 pins, surpassing the men's record of 4,015 set by Carmen Salvino of Chicago in 1980. For 24 games, she totaled 6,013 pins, exceeding the men's record of 5,825 by Anthony in 1970. In the championship game, Rathgeber continued her strong bowling by defeating Leila Wagner of Dallas, 248-221.   Frank Litsky

In WORLD BOOK, see BOWLING.

World Champion Boxers

World Boxing Association

Division	Champion	Country	Date won
Heavyweight	Gerrie Coetzee	South Africa	1983
	Greg Page	U.S.A.	Dec. '84
Junior heavyweight	Ossie Ocasio	Puerto Rico	1982
	Piet Crous	South Africa	Dec. '84
Light heavyweight	Michael Spinks	U.S.A.	1981
Middleweight	Marvelous Marvin Hagler	U.S.A.	1980
Junior middleweight	Roberto Durán (retired in June)	Panama	1983
	Mike McCallum	Jamaica	Oct. '84
Welterweight	Donald Curry	U.S.A.	1983
Junior welterweight	Aaron Pryor	U.S.A.	1980
	Johnny Bumphus	U.S.A.	Jan. '84
	Gene Hatcher	U.S.A.	June '84
Lightweight	Ray Mancini	U.S.A.	1982
	Livingstone Bramble	Virgin Is.	June '84
Junior lightweight	Roger Mayweather	U.S.A.	1983
	Rocky Lockridge	U.S.A.	Feb. '84
Featherweight	Eusebio Pedroza	Panama	1978
Junior featherweight	Leo Cruz	Dom. Rep.	1982
	Loris Stecca	Italy	Feb. '84
	Victor Callejas	Puerto Rico	May '84
Bantamweight	Jeff Chandler	U.S.A.	1980
	Richard Sandoval	U.S.A.	April '84
Junior bantamweight	Jiro Watanabe	Japan	1982
	Khaosal Galaxy	Thailand	Nov. '84
Flyweight	Santos Laciar	Argentina	1982
Junior flyweight	Lupe Madera	Mexico	1983
	Francisco Quiroz	Dom. Rep.	May '84

World Boxing Council

Division	Champion	Country	Date won
Heavyweight	Tim Witherspoon	U.S.A.	March '84
	Pinklon Thomas	U.S.A.	Aug. '84
Cruiserweight	Carlos DeLeón	Puerto Rico	1983
Light heavyweight	Michael Spinks	U.S.A.	1983
Middleweight	Marvelous Marvin Hagler	U.S.A.	1980
Super welterweight	Thomas Hearns	U.S.A.	1982
Welterweight	Milton McCrory	U.S.A.	1983
Super lightweight	Bruce Curry	U.S.A.	1983
	Billy Costello	U.S.A.	Jan. '84
Lightweight	Edwin Rosario	Puerto Rico	1983
	José Luis Ramirez	Mexico	Nov. '84
Super featherweight	Hector Camacho (resigned in July)	Puerto Rico	1983
	Julio Cesar Chavez	Mexico	Sept. '84
Featherweight	Juan LaPorte	Puerto Rico	1982
	Wilfredo Gomez	Puerto Rico	March '84
	Azumah Nelson	Ghana	Dec. '84
Super bantamweight	Jaime Garza	U.S.A.	1983
	Juan Meza	Mexico	Nov. '84
Bantamweight	Alberto Davila	U.S.A.	1983
Super flyweight	Payao Poontarat	Thailand	1983
	Jiro Watanabe	Japan	July '84
Flyweight	Frank Cedeno	Philippines	1983
	Koji Kobayashi	Japan	Jan. '84
	Gabriel Bernal	Mexico	April '84
	Sot Chitalada	Thailand	Oct. '84
Light flyweight	Jung-Koo Chang	South Korea	1983

BOXING. Greg Page of Louisville, Ky., and Pinklon Thomas of Philadelphia ended 1984 as the heavyweight champions recognized by the world's two most important governing bodies in professional boxing—the World Boxing Association (WBA) and the World Boxing Council (WBC). Both fighters sought to arrange matches with the unbeaten Larry Holmes of Easton, Pa., who was widely regarded as the true heavyweight champion. Disgusted with the politics of boxing, Holmes had resigned the WBC heavyweight title in December 1983. However, the new International Boxing Federation (IBF) immediately named him as its champion.

To fill the title Holmes vacated, the WBC matched Tim Witherspoon of Philadelphia and Page for a title bout on March 9, 1984, in Las Vegas, Nev. Witherspoon won a majority decision, but in his first defense of his new title, on August 31 in Las Vegas, he lost a decision to Thomas.

On December 1 in Johannesburg, South Africa, Page defeated Gerrie Coetzee of South Africa and won the WBA title with a controversial eighth-round knockout. Because of a broken clock or a timekeeper's error, the final round lasted 48 seconds longer than the regulation 3 minutes.

Other Champions. Sugar Ray Leonard of Potomac, Md., and Roberto Durán of Panama both retired in 1984. Leonard's announced retirement was his second. He first retired in 1982 after eye surgery.

In February 1984, Leonard said he missed the excitement of boxing. He ended his retirement by fighting Kevin Howard of Philadelphia on May 11 in Worcester, Mass. In the fourth round, Leonard was knocked down for the first time as a pro. He knocked out Howard in the ninth round, but several hours after the fight, he said that he was retiring again at the age of 27.

Thomas Hearns of Detroit retained his WBC junior middleweight title on June 15 in Las Vegas by knocking out Durán in the second round. It was the first time Durán had been knocked out in 18 years of fighting, and he retired at age 33.

Middleweight champion Marvelous Marvin Hagler of Brockton, Mass., stopped Juan Domingo Roldan of Argentina in 10 rounds on March 30 in Las Vegas and knocked out Mustafa Hamsho of Syria on October 19 in New York City.

Amateur. The United States dominated the world championship challenge bouts in April and the Summer Olympic Games in July and August, both in Los Angeles. U.S. boxers won 6 of the 12 titles in the world championship challenge and 9 of the 12 titles in the Olympics. Frank Litsky

See also OLYMPIC GAMES. In WORLD BOOK, see BOXING.

BOY SCOUTS. See YOUTH ORGANIZATIONS.
BOYS CLUBS. See YOUTH ORGANIZATIONS.

BRAZIL. Brazilians in 1984 impatiently demanded the restoration of direct elections by popular vote for all of Brazil's political leaders. Brazil's leaders are currently chosen by an electoral college. During the first half of 1984, millions of people took to the streets to demonstrate in favor of immediate direct elections to choose their country's first civilian president since 1964.

For a brief time, it appeared that the people might prevail and that Brazil's military rulers might be forced to yield. The demonstrations were the most massive show of support for a political issue in Brazilian history. Public opinion polls indicated that between 80 and 90 per cent of Brazilians favored an immediate return to the full exercise of democracy.

Direct Elections. Faced with the surge in public support for this issue, Brazil's President João Baptista de Oliveira Figueiredo offered a constitutional amendment that would have accelerated the process of restoring direct elections. But on June 28, despite divisions within his own ruling Social Democratic Party, Figueiredo withdrew his offer.

Instead, the military followed a plan under which Brazil's next president was to be chosen by a 686-member electoral college on Jan. 15, 1985. Within the college, the ruling Social Democratic Party enjoys a majority in the number of seats. Due to defections from the party's ranks, however, the opposition candidate, Tancredo Neves, 74, of the Party of the Brazilian Democratic Movement, was expected to win easily on January 15 over Paulo Salim Maluf, 53, the candidate of the Social Democratic Party. Neves is the former governor of Minas Gerais state.

New Energy Sources. On October 25, President Figueiredo joined Paraguay's President Alfredo Stroessner on a bridge over the Paraná River on the common border of the two countries to throw a switch opening the Itaipú Dam, the world's most powerful hydroelectric plant. When fully operational, Itaipú will produce enough energy to meet two-thirds of Brazil's current consumption.

Gold Fever. The discovery of gold in remote areas of the Amazon Region has touched off a gold rush in Brazil. A horde of some 250,000 miners have fanned out over an immense area, hoping to get rich quick with their picks and shovels. At Serra Pelada (Naked Mountain), more than 40,000 miners work the country's largest gold mine, which is ½ mile (0.8 kilometer) long and 250 feet (76 meters) deep.

The rush has accelerated settlement of remote Amazonian areas. The city of Alta Floresta, for example, did not exist eight years ago. Today, it is a bustling city of 140,000 people.   Nathan A. Haverstock

See also LATIN AMERICA (Facts in Brief Table).

In WORLD BOOK, see BRAZIL.

BRIDGE. See BUILDING AND CONSTRUCTION.

BRIDGE. The American Contract Bridge League (ACBL) held its Summer North American Championships in Washington, D.C., in July 1984. The tournament was one of the most eventful in bridge history.

Kidnapping. One of the players, Edith Rosenkranz of Mexico City, was kidnapped at about midnight on July 19 from her hotel. She spent 43 hours in captivity but was released unharmed after her husband and bridge partner, George Rosenkranz, paid a ransom of more than $1 million. George Rosenkranz is the founder of Syntex Corporation, which makes oral contraceptives. The Federal Bureau of Investigation and the Washington, D.C., police arrested three men within minutes after the victim was released and recovered all the ransom money. Arrested were Glenn I. Wright and Orland D. Tolden, both of Houston, and Dennis Moss of Cocoa, Fla. In December, Wright and Moss were convicted of kidnapping. Wright is an expert bridge player who holds the rank of life master, the highest in the ACBL. Tolden pleaded guilty to the lesser charge of conspiracy to kidnap.

George Rosenkranz captained a team at the tournament that won the Spingold Master Team Championship, though he did not play after the kidnapping. His teammates were Marty Bergen of White Plains, N.Y.; Larry Cohen of New York City; Jeff Meckstroth of Pickerington, Ohio; Eric Rodwell of West Lafayette, Ind.; and Edward Wold of Houston.

Suspected Cheating. At the same tournament, a team captained by Moses Ma of Cambridge, Mass., withdrew from the Spingold Knockout Teams competition after being confronted with videotaped evidence that they were using illegal signals. The ACBL expelled Ma and three of his teammates—Rajan Batta and Fadi Farah, also of Cambridge; and Philips Santosa of Boston.

The 1984 World Team Olympiad, held in Seattle from October 25 to November 10, was won by Poland. Poland defeated France in the final round of the 54-nation tournament. In the women's division, the United States beat Great Britain in the final round of the 23-nation competition. On the U.S. women's team were Jacqui Mitchell, Gail Moss, Judi Radin, and Katherine Wei of New York City; Carol Sanders of Nashville, Tenn.; and Betty Ann Kennedy of Shreveport, La.

Winner in the Vanderbilt Knockout Teams division at the Spring North American Championships in San Antonio in March was the powerful California team that won the 1982 and 1983 Grand National Teams. Team members were Chip Martel of Davis, Peter Pender of Guerneville, Hugh Ross of Oakland, and Lew Stansby of Castro Valley.   Henry G. Francis

In WORLD BOOK, see BRIDGE.

BRITISH COLUMBIA

BRITISH COLUMBIA. In 1984, Premier William R. Bennett's governing Social Credit Party advanced toward its goal of establishing a new conservative orientation for Canada's most westerly province. To bring government expenditures more into line with income, Bennett continued the sweeping program of reductions in spending on social programs that he had begun in 1983. During the summer of 1984, the jobless rate was 15.7 per cent, and nearly 20 per cent of the population was collecting unemployment insurance or welfare payments from the provincial government.

The Budget, announced on February 20, further reduced social services and educational payments and increased income taxes by 8 per cent. The civil service suffered an 11 per cent reduction, adding to the 15 per cent cut made in 1983. These measures halved the estimated deficit to $671 million. (All monetary amounts in this article are Canadian dollars, with $1 = U.S. 76 cents as of Dec. 31, 1984.) The total budget was $7.9 billion, a 5.8 per cent decrease from 1983.

Labor Disputes continued to plague British Columbia in 1984 as labor showed its unhappiness with Bennett's restraint measures. At the construction site of Expo 86, the 1986 world's fair to be held in Vancouver, unions had been using a clause in their contracts to reduce nonunion participation in the building of the $1.2-billion project. The clause allowed union workers to refuse to work beside nonunion labor. But a law passed on August 25 declared the fair's location an "economic development site" and prevented union workers from invoking the clause.

A crippling pulp and paper dispute involving a seven-week lockout by the province's 14 pulp and paper companies was ended by legislation forcing strikers back to work on April 10. Almost 13,000 workers reluctantly resumed work, angry because the new law threatened to impose a settlement if the two sides could not reach a voluntary agreement. Paper companies and the unions reached an agreement on June 15 that was similar to one that union members had rejected in April. A three-month strike by Vancouver transit workers in 1984 also ended as a result of back-to-work legislation, and strikers returned to their jobs on September 17.

Undersea Resources Ruling. The Supreme Court of Canada ruled on May 17 that the undersea resources between Vancouver Island and the mainland belonged to British Columbia rather than the federal government. However, there were no immediate plans to lift a 10-year provincial ban on drilling for the oil and gas thought to lie beneath these coastal waters.   David M. L. Farr

In WORLD BOOK, see BRITISH COLUMBIA.

BRUNEI DARUSSALAM. See ASIA. IN the WORLD BOOK SUPPLEMENT section, see BRUNEI.

BUHARI, MUHAMMADU (1942-   ), became Nigeria's head of state after overthrowing Nigeria's President Shehu Shagari in a Dec. 31, 1983, coup. Buhari, a major general in the army, accused the Shagari government of rampant corruption and mishandling of the economy. He instituted a "war against indiscipline," urging Nigerians to be honest and work hard. See NIGERIA.

Buhari was born on Dec. 17, 1942, in the village of Daura in northern Nigeria. He attended the Nigerian Military Training College and later was sent by the British—the rulers of Nigeria until 1960—to the Mons Officer's Cadet School in Aldershot, England.

In 1975, Buhari, then a lieutenant colonel, took part in a coup that overthrew General Yakubu Gowon, who had been head of a military government since 1966. Buhari subsequently served as military governor of Bornu state. He later was appointed federal commissioner for petroleum resources and then chairman of the Nigerian National Petroleum Corporation. From 1976 to 1979, when military rule was replaced by democratic government, Buhari represented Nigeria at meetings of the Organization of Petroleum Exporting Countries.

Buhari has gained a reputation as a tough, self-assured administrator. He promised to improve the "difficult and degrading conditions" existing in Nigeria.   David L. Dreier

BUILDING AND CONSTRUCTION. An increase in construction activity in the United States, begun in 1983, continued in 1984. This recovery paralleled the improved U.S. economy. Spending for new construction, led by a surge in residential building, reached a record $265 billion in 1983 and was expected to top $310 billion by the end of 1984. Contracts for new construction totaled $144.7 billion for the first eight months of 1984, up 10 per cent from the same period in 1983.

Outlays for new private construction reached an estimated annual rate of $255.5 billion in August, compared with a total of $215 billion for the same period in 1983. Spending for private nonresidential construction rose to an estimated annual rate of $76 billion, well above the 1983 rate. The U.S. Department of Commerce estimated that industrial construction would increase to $14.2 billion in 1984 from a 1983 level of $13.1 billion, the lowest in five years. Office-building construction was expected to increase from $21.6 billion in 1983 to $26.7 billion in 1984. Spending for new stores, hospitals, and churches was also up.

Public construction was expected to total $56.2-billion in 1984, compared with $50.8 billion in 1983. The gain was paced by increases in the construction of sewer and water-supply systems, highways, and streets. In a nationwide survey, 46 states said they expected to spend a total of $17.8 billion

224

on highway construction and repair in 1984, a 23 per cent increase from 1983.

More Jobs. The increased building activity produced a steady decline in industry unemployment, from 18.2 per cent in September 1983 to 14.7 per cent in July 1984. In June, about 3.6 million people worked in construction, compared with about 3.1 million in December 1983.

In the same period, competition for available jobs kept wage increases to the lowest levels in decades. The average hourly wage for laborers and skilled workers in the third quarter of 1984 was less than 1.5 per cent higher than 1983 wages. In October 1984, laborers averaged $15.81 per hour; ironworkers, $21.77; and bricklayers, $20.42. Other factors that increased construction costs in 1984 included higher machinery costs and fluctuating materials prices.

Housing. Experts expected 1984 housing starts to reach a level of about 1.5 million units, compared with 1.7 million in 1983. After steadily increasing in the first part of the year, starts declined from May to August, rose in September, and then dropped again in October and November. The rate for apartment buildings of more than five units reached 553,000 starts in September, up from 526,000 during the same period in 1983. The annual rate of building permits issued, a measure of future construction, reached 1.4 million in September, compared with 1.5 million for January through September 1983.

High interest rates slowed sales of new homes from a peak annual rate of 755,000 in December 1983 to 680,000 in October 1984. The situation appeared brighter, however, when compared with the 412,000 rate of home sales in 1982 — the lowest since 1963.

New single-family homes were larger in 1984 and 1983 than in the previous two years. The Urban Land Institute, a Washington, D.C.-based organization involved with city planning, noted that demand was decreasing for no-frills houses with areas of 600 to 900 square feet (56 to 84 square meters). On the other hand, the institute reported that demand was up for houses of more than 1,500 square feet (140 square meters) with such luxury features as skylights, fireplaces, and sunken baths. The improved economy and the higher average age of home buyers were cited as reasons for the change.

Bridges. The repair or replacement of old and structurally deficient bridges in the United States was aided in 1984 by $7 billion from a fund established under the Surface Transportation Assistance Act of 1978. The act has financed work on more than 9,000 failing or inadequate spans. The problem, however, is much larger than the purse. The Federal Highway Administration estimated that another 263,000 bridges in the United States

Scaffolding surrounds the Statue of Liberty, which is being renovated in preparation for its centennial celebration in 1986.

need to be replaced or rehabilitated — a task the agency said would cost $50 billion. State governments will have to make up the difference.

In China, work began on February 18 on what will be that country's longest bridge, a 33,930-foot (10,340-meter) railroad bridge across the Huang Ho (Yellow River) between Henan (Honan) and Shandong (Shantung) provinces. The bridge will be 10,890 feet (3,320 meters) longer than the Yangtze River bridge at Nanjing (Nanking).

Dams. China was ready in 1984 to begin constructing the Three Gorge Dam on the Yangtze River. This flood-control, power, irrigation, and navigation facility may become the world's largest civil engineering project. The plan includes the world's largest-volume concrete dam as well as the largest ship locks and concentration of electrical generating capacity.

The dam will be 541 feet (165 meters) high and will contain 14.4 million cubic yards (11 million cubic meters) of concrete. The Grand Coulee Dam, the largest concrete dam and the largest source of hydroelectric power in the United States, contains about 12 million cubic yards (9.2 million cubic meters) of concrete. The Three Gorge Dam will generate 30 billion watts of power, compared with about 6.5 billion watts for the Grand Coulee Dam.

Black Sea Canal. In Romania, a canal linking the Danube River to the Black Sea was inaugurated on May 26, 1984. The 40-mile (64-kilometer) canal runs from Cernavodă on the Danube to the Black Sea port of Constanța.

Liberty's Overhaul. The renovation of the Statue of Liberty in New York Harbor, begun in October 1983, proceeded in 1984. The restoration task includes replacing the torch and corroded iron at the crown, fixing the shoulder on the torch side, and cleaning and patching the exterior. In addition, the inside framing, or armature, that supports the copper exterior "skin" of the statue will be replaced, and new elevators will be installed in the pedestal on which the statue stands.

The most difficult task is replacing the armature, 1,350 iron ribs that provide a foundation for the 300 sheets of copper that form the robed female figure. A century of condensation and rainwater leakage has caused a corrosive batterylike reaction between the iron and copper connecting bars that link the armature and skin. The damage has caused some of those pieces to pull loose, ripping out rivets and producing small holes in nearly every part of the skin. These holes will be patched, and the iron bars will be replaced by stainless steel bars covered with Teflon. The copper bars will also be replaced. The work was to be completed by July 4, 1986.   William J. Cromie

In WORLD BOOK, see BRIDGE; BUILDING CONSTRUCTION; CANAL; DAM.

BULGARIA. Charges that its secret service was involved in the 1981 attempt to assassinate Pope John Paul II caused Bulgaria's image to suffer internationally in 1984. At home, the government continued to reform the economy.

In July, the United States Senate voted to stop all trade supports for Bulgaria, including credits accompanying trade deals. The Senate said that Bulgaria was involved in "state-sponsored terrorism." In the same month, U.S. officials accused Kintex, a Bulgarian trading agency, of international heroin trafficking.

In October, Ilario Martella, an investigating magistrate in Italy, indicted three Bulgarians and four Turks for complicity in the 1981 attempt on the pope's life. Two of the Bulgarians had left Italy. The third, Sergei Ivanov Antonov, a Bulgarian airline official, was arrested in Italy in 1982.

Trip Canceled. In early September, Bulgarian leader Todor Zhivkov canceled a planned trip to West Germany. Officials and media in the Soviet Union had attacked West Germany during the preceding months for allowing U.S. intermediate-range nuclear missiles to be stationed on its soil.

In February, Bulgaria and Yugoslavia argued about the treatment of ethnic Macedonians living in Bulgaria. Relations between the two countries improved when Yugoslavia's Prime Minister Milka Planinc visited Bulgaria in July. Her visit was the first by a Yugoslav prime minister since the establishment of Communist governments in the two countries in the mid-1940's.

New Leaders. Zhivkov appointed nine new ministers to his Cabinet and made major changes in the Communist Party leadership in January. The moves, which increased Zhivkov's power, were intended to improve the management of the economy. The main change was the elevation of 47-year-old Chudomir Aleksandrov to the post of first deputy prime minister in charge of coordination of economic policy and to full membership in the Politburo, the most powerful part of the Communist Party Central Committee.

Industrial Output increased by 3.8 per cent in the first half of 1984, compared with the first half of 1983. Foreign trade rose 8.4 per cent.

In March, a Communist Party conference on quality control issued a document calling for businesses that make and sell inferior products to bear the financial responsibility for them. The document also recommended pricing that would reward producers of high-quality goods. In April, the government announced financial incentives aimed at increasing Bulgaria's birth rate.   Chris Cviic

See also EUROPE (Facts in Brief Table). In WORLD BOOK, see BULGARIA; MACEDONIA.

BURMA. See ASIA.

BURUNDI. See AFRICA.

BUS. See TRANSIT; TRANSPORTATION.

BUSH, GEORGE H. W. (1924-   ), was reelected for a second term as Vice President of the United States on Nov. 6, 1984. During the vice presidential campaign, Bush's Democratic opponent, Representative Geraldine A. Ferraro of New York, and her husband made public their personal income tax returns and challenged Bush to do likewise. On October 3, Bush released income tax data showing that he and his wife had paid $303,421 in federal taxes during the three-year period of 1981-1983. This was about 37 per cent of their gross income of $810,477. The Bushes also revealed that they were contesting almost $200,000 in back taxes and interest that they had paid in June. On October 11, Bush and Ferraro participated in a televised campaign debate.

Bush traveled widely during 1984. He attended the February 14 funeral in Moscow of Soviet leader Yuri V. Andropov. Bush later met with Konstantin U. Chernenko, Andropov's successor. The Vice President also attended the March 30 funeral of President Ahmed Sékou Touré of Guinea and the August 10 inauguration of León Febres-Cordero as president of Ecuador. Bush also visited Japan, Indonesia, India, Pakistan, and Oman in May.   Frank Cormier and Margot Cormier

In WORLD BOOK, see BUSH, GEORGE H. W.

BUSINESS See BANK; ECONOMICS; LABOR; MANUFACTURING.

CABINET, UNITED STATES. Secretary of Labor Raymond J. Donovan was indicted on Sept. 24, 1984, on charges that, while an officer of a New Jersey construction company in 1979, he had defrauded the New York City Transit Authority of nearly $8 million. Donovan, who took an immediate leave of absence, was the first Cabinet member ever indicted for a crime while in office.

The indictment—handed down by a Bronx County, New York, grand jury—charged Donovan and seven of his former colleagues at the Schiavone Construction Company in Secaucus, N.J., with grand larceny and the falsification of business records. The defendants had allegedly inflated the value of work done by a Schiavone subcontractor, Jopel Contracting and Trucking Corporation, during the construction of a subway tunnel under New York City's East River. All the defendants pleaded not guilty.

The labor secretary had been the subject of investigations since joining the Administration of President Ronald Reagan in 1981. A special Senate prosecutor in 1982 looked into charges that Donovan had made illegal payoffs to union officials and had associated with Mafia figures while with the Schiavone Company, but the prosecutor was unable to substantiate those charges.

Education Secretary Leaves. Secretary of Education Terrel H. Bell, who helped to launch a renaissance in U.S. education, left the Cabinet on Dec. 31, 1984. When Bell joined the Administration, he promised to carry out Reagan's 1980 campaign pledge to abolish the Department of Education. Instead, he established the National Commission on Excellence in Education, which reported in 1983 that American society was being threatened by a "rising tide of mediocrity" in its educational system. That report was instrumental in launching a movement throughout the United States to raise performance standards for both teachers and students. Bell resigned to accept a teaching position at the University of Utah in Salt Lake City.

Meese Cleared. A special investigator reported on September 20 that he could find "no basis" for bringing criminal charges against presidential counselor Edwin Meese III. Meese, nominated by Reagan in January to succeed William French Smith as U.S. attorney general, had been accused of financial misconduct while serving in his White House post. Reagan said he would resubmit Meese's nomination to the Senate in January 1985. While Meese was under investigation, Smith, who had planned to return to private life, stayed on as attorney general.   David L. Dreier

In WORLD BOOK, see CABINET.

CALIFORNIA. See LOS ANGELES; STATE GOV'T.

CAMBODIA. See KAMPUCHEA.

CAMEROON. The government of President Paul Biya survived a 36-hour military uprising in April 1984. On the morning of April 6, units of the 1,500-member presidential guard tried to capture Biya and gain control of the capital city, Yaoundé. Regular army units remained loyal and suppressed the rebellion by the evening of April 7. The army rounded up and imprisoned 1,053 members of the presidential guard.

The coup attempt underscored tensions between Cameroon's predominantly Muslim north and mostly Christian south. Biya is a Christian from the south. His predecessor, Ahmadou Ahidjo, a Muslim northerner, had created the guard and recruited most of its members from the north. A week after the coup attempt, the government said Ahidjo was involved.

When Ahidjo resigned the presidency in 1982, he had selected Biya, then Cameroon's prime minister, to succeed him, but the two men became political enemies. Biya accused Ahidjo of participating in a coup plot that security authorities uncovered in June 1983. Ahidjo avoided arrest by leaving the country before charges were made. On Feb. 24, 1984, a military court found him guilty of treason and sentenced him to death.   J. Dixon Esseks

See also AFRICA (Facts in Brief Table). In WORLD BOOK, see CAMEROON.

CAMP FIRE. See YOUTH ORGANIZATIONS.

CANADA

The face of Canadian politics was changed on Sept. 4, 1984, when the Progressive Conservative Party (PC or Conservatives) won a massive electoral victory. Brian Mulroney, 45, who had been chosen leader of the Progressive Conservative Party in June 1983, became Canada's 18th prime minister on September 17. The election ended the Liberal Party's long domination of Canada's federal government.

Mulroney was the third prime minister in 1984. On June 30, Pierre Elliott Trudeau, after more than 15 years in the post, stepped down. He was succeeded by John N. Turner.

Although Trudeau's unpopularity outside his native province of Quebec was well known, few observers expected the rejection of his party that the lopsided September vote indicated. The Conservatives won a majority of parliamentary seats in every province of Canada, even in Quebec. Capturing 211 of the 282 seats in the House of Commons, the Conservatives achieved one of the most decisive electoral victories in Canadian history.

The Election Campaign. Although Trudeau took almost no part in the election campaign, he bore some of the responsibility for the disaster that overtook the Liberals. Trudeau had served as prime minister almost continuously since 1968, and critics charged he had stayed in the post too long and in recent years had failed to come up with new ideas.

Turner, Trudeau's successor, was unable to distance himself from the Trudeau record before the election. Turner won the leadership of the Liberal Party at a convention in Ottawa, Ont., on June 16. He defeated six other candidates, all of whom were ministers in the Trudeau Cabinet.

Turner formed a new administration on the day Trudeau resigned. Twenty-three of the 29 members of his Cabinet were chosen from among Trudeau's ministers, weakening Turner's attempt to project an image of a new group in power.

On July 9, Turner asked Canada's governor general to dissolve Parliament and call a general election for September 4. This proved to be a mistake, because Turner's party was not ready for a contest. Its candidates had not yet been chosen; the party's campaign strategy had not been worked out; and its platform offered little that was exciting. Turner was unable to arouse the mass enthusiasm that Trudeau had inspired.

Before he resigned, Trudeau obtained a promise from Turner to appoint to important government positions 17 Liberal members of Parliament (MP's) who did not plan to run in the next elec-

tion. In early July, Turner made several such appointments to posts on government boards, the judiciary, the appointed Senate, and the diplomatic service. Voters were outraged at such use of government jobs to reward supporters, and Turner was forced to defend the appointments as best he could throughout the campaign. The appointments, some of which were rescinded later by the Mulroney government, turned many voters away from the Liberals.

Mulroney, the PC leader, ran a confident campaign, strong in the knowledge that polls showed public opinion was swinging behind his party. His message was simple: It was time for a change, time to replace Trudeau's confrontational politics with a search for general agreement, and time to bring fresh faces with new ideas to government.

Mulroney paid much attention to selecting suitable PC candidates to run in Quebec. He gave up the seat in Nova Scotia by which he had entered Parliament in 1983 and decided to run in his hometown, Baie-Comeau, Quebec, on the rugged north shore of the St. Lawrence River.

Turner also took a risk by deciding to run in a district in Vancouver, where he had lived while attending the University of British Columbia. Because no Liberals sat in the House of Commons from any province west of Saskatchewan, Turner ran a risk in trying to put himself forward as a new brand of Liberal leader from the West.

The Voting Results from the September 4 election proved to be disastrous for the Liberals. In the four provinces of Atlantic Canada, the Progressive Conservatives took 25 of the 32 seats. In Quebec, where the Liberals had held all but 1 seat, the Conservatives won 58 of 75. In Ontario, the Conservatives took 67 of 95 seats. In the West and North, they won 61 of 80 seats. The Progressive Conservative total was 211 seats, with an independent conservative elected from Toronto who would undoubtedly throw his support behind the party in the House.

The Liberal Party lost more than 100 seats, dropping from 147 MP's to 40. Their loss in Quebec was particularly painful because that province had been the base of Liberal Party power for a quarter of a century. Fifteen members of the Turner Cabinet were defeated, including experienced ministers who had served in the government for years. Turner managed to win his seat in British Columbia, though other Liberal candidates from the province were defeated. This personal victory allowed Turner to enter Parliament as the official leader of the opposition.

Canada's prime minister-elect, Brian Mulroney, and his wife, Mila, greet supporters as the Progressive Conservatives sweep to victory on September 4.

The Ministry of Canada*
In order of precedence

Martin Brian Mulroney, prime minister
George Harris Hees, minister of veterans affairs
Duff Roblin, leader of the government in the Senate
Charles Joseph Clark, secretary of state for external affairs
Flora Isabel MacDonald, minister of employment and immigration
Erik H. Nielsen, deputy prime minister and president of the Queen's Privy Council for Canada
John Carnell Crosbie, minister of justice and attorney general of Canada
Roch LaSalle, minister of public works
Donald Frank Mazankowski, minister of transport
Elmer MacIntosh MacKay, solicitor general of Canada
Arthur Jacob Epp, minister of national health and welfare
John Allen Fraser, minister of fisheries and oceans
Sinclair McKnight Stevens, minister of regional industrial expansion
John Wise, minister of agriculture
Ramon John Hnatyshyn, minister of state (government House leader)
David Edward Crombie, minister of Indian affairs and northern development
Robert R. de Cotret, president of the Treasury Board
Perrin Beatty, minister of national revenue
Michael Holcombe Wilson, minister of finance
Robert Carman Coates, minister of national defence
Jack Burnett Murta, minister of state (multiculturalism)
Harvie Andre, minister of supply and services
Otto John Jelinek, minister of state (fitness and amateur sport)
Thomas Edward Siddon, minister of state for science and technology
Charles James Mayer, minister of state (Canadian Wheat Board)
William Hunter McKnight, minister of labour
Walter Franklin McLean, secretary of state of Canada
Thomas Michael McMillan, minister of state (tourism)
Patricia Carney, minister of energy, mines, and resources
André Bissonnette, minister of state (small businesses)
Suzanne Blais-Grenier, minister of the environment
Benoit Bouchard, minister of state (transport)
Andrée Champagne, minister of state (youth)
Michel Côté, minister of consumer and corporate affairs
James Francis Kelleher, minister for international trade
Robert E. Layton, minister of state (mines)
Marcel Masse, minister of communications
Barbara Jean McDougall, minister of state (finance)
Gerald S. Merrithew, minister of state (forestry)
Monique Vézina, minister for external relations
*As of Dec. 31, 1984.

Premiers of Canadian Provinces

Province	Premier
Alberta	Peter Lougheed
British Columbia	William R. Bennett
Manitoba	Howard Pawley
New Brunswick	Richard B. Hatfield
Newfoundland	Brian Peckford
Nova Scotia	John Buchanan
Ontario	William G. Davis
Prince Edward Island	James M. Lee
Quebec	René Lévesque
Saskatchewan	Grant Devine

Commissioners of Territories

Northwest Territories	John H. Parker
Yukon Territory	Douglas Bell

The New Democratic Party (NDP) had approached the contest as the underdog. Political observers felt that a strong Conservative showing would sap much NDP support in the West. But NDP leader Edward Broadbent campaigned forcefully on practical policies intended to appeal to "ordinary Canadians." The NDP captured 30 seats in the West and Ontario, down 2 from its previous showing.

The New Democratic Party received 19 per cent of the popular vote—about the same share it had held in 1980 in the last general election. The Progressive Conservative Party won 50 per cent of the vote, gaining the largest share in each region of Canada, something the party had never achieved before. The Liberal Party vote fell from 44 per cent in 1980 to 28 per cent in 1984.

The New Government. The Mulroney administration took over from Turner's government on September 17. The Turner administration had been one of the shortest lived in Canadian history, lasting only 80 days. Mulroney chose an expanded Cabinet, designed to include the most able members of his party's large parliamentary majority and to give representation to all regions of Canada. The new Cabinet was composed of 40 members: 11 each from Ontario and Quebec, 13 from the western provinces, and 5 from the four provinces of Atlantic Canada. The Conservatives had elected 19 women to Parliament, and 6 of them were chosen for Cabinet ministries.

Parliament. The second session of the 32nd Parliament ended on June 29, 1984, having lasted since Dec. 7, 1983. Fifty-one bills were passed in what became a bitter session of strong party feelings reflecting the country's expectation of impending political change.

On June 21, Parliament authorized the creation of the Canadian Security Intelligence Service, a civilian security agency designed to replace the security branch of the Royal Canadian Mounted Police. This new agency will investigate individuals or groups suspected of espionage, sabotage, terrorism, or domestic subversion.

The first amendment to the new Canadian constitution became law on June 21. It gave new rights to American Indians and Inuits (Eskimos), including the promise that their constitutional safeguards could not be altered without their full participation in meetings with both the federal and provincial governments.

Parliament approved on April 9 the Canada Health Act. The act provides for penalizing provinces that permit doctors and hospitals to charge more than fee schedules approved by medical associations. The objective was to ensure that everyone could obtain good health care.

When the 33rd Parliament convened on Nov. 5, 1984, Conservatives, shut out of the federal ad-

Trudeau's Legacy

After more than 15 years in office, Pierre Elliott Trudeau stepped down as Canada's 15th prime minister on June 30, 1984. He had dominated Canada's political life since April 1968, when he succeeded Lester B. Pearson as leader of the Liberal Party and prime minister. Taking office as an enormously popular figure throughout Canada, Trudeau watched that support melt away during his years in power as Canada's economic problems mounted. In February 1984, when Trudeau announced his intention to resign, it was apparent that he had been in power too long. Under his leadership, the Liberals faced certain defeat at the polls.

Trudeau will always be remembered for two passionate concerns. One was his vision of a bilingual, united Canada in which both French- and English-speaking citizens could live, work, and feel at home in every province. This involved protection for the French language outside the mainly French-speaking province of Quebec, guarantees of mobility for French- and English-speaking Canadians, and the opening of federal government employment to French-speaking citizens. Trudeau — a Quebec native who was equally at ease in both languages — helped to achieve these rights and guarantees, particularly through the Official Languages Act of 1969. In so doing, he helped to create a more relaxed atmosphere between the English-speaking majority and the French-speaking minority in Canada. This climate, in turn, helped to defeat a referendum in 1980 on Quebec's separation from Canada. In rejecting separatism, the voters of Trudeau's native province vindicated his belief in a united Canada with a federal form of government.

Trudeau's other passionate concern was in establishing a Canadian constitution. Although an independent nation, Canada had never been totally sovereign. Its constitution was the British North America Act of 1867, which could be amended only by the British Parliament, acting at the request of the Canadian Parliament. Trudeau fashioned an agreement that resulted in the Constitution Act of 1982, which gave Canada complete control over its new constitution and dissolved its last legal tie with Great Britain. Trudeau also succeeded in incorporating into the new constitution a far-reaching Charter of Rights and Freedoms, which set down in writing for the first time 34 basic rights and freedoms for Canadian citizens.

In foreign affairs, Trudeau demonstrated that he was as international in vision as his predecessor, Pearson, who won the Nobel Peace Prize in 1957. Trudeau's decision to reestablish diplomatic relations with China in 1970 helped to end that country's isolation. He argued for greater cooperation and fairness in economic relations between rich and poor nations, sought international protection for fragile environments such as that of the Arctic, and campaigned vigorously for arms control. In November 1984, he was awarded the Albert Einstein Peace Prize for his efforts to promote disarmament.

Trudeau's weaknesses included an obsession with constitutional questions that caused him to pay too little attention to the Canadian economy. Many people thought him arrogant, convinced of the rightness of his course, and more inclined to challenge his opponents than to seek compromises. He paid little attention to provinces other than Quebec and Ontario, an attitude that led to an increasing sense of alienation in the Western provinces. Because he often related poorly to people, he failed to recruit or hold strong-willed individuals in his administration. He seemed cynical about the role of Parliament in the democratic process and on occasion resorted to what was seen by some critics as an outrageous practice of patronage politics.

Yet Trudeau possessed a style and an intellect that set him apart from other politicians and gave him a distinctive standing among world leaders. Canadians could never be neutral toward him. His departure from the Canadian political scene has left a gap that may never be filled.

David M. L. Farr

Trudeau bids farewell at a ceremony in June.

Canada and Provinces Population Estimates

	1983	1984
Alberta	2,353,800	2,348,800
British Columbia	2,826,000	2,870,700
Manitoba	1,046,300	1,056,500
New Brunswick	706,600	713,300
Newfoundland	576,200	579,500
Northwest Territories	48,600	49,400
Nova Scotia	859,300	869,900
Ontario	8,816,000	8,937,400
Prince Edward Island	123,900	125,300
Quebec	6,514,900	6,549,000
Saskatchewan	992,100	1,006,200
Yukon Territory	22,200	21,800
Canada	**24,885,900**	**25,127,800**

City and Metropolitan Population Estimates

	Metropolitan Area June 1, 1983, estimate	City 1981 Census
Toronto	3,067,100	599,217
Montreal	2,862,300	980,354
Vancouver	1,310,600	414,281
Ottawa-Hull	737,600	
Ottawa		295,163
Hull		56,225
Edmonton	698,600	532,246
Calgary	620,500	592,743
Winnipeg	600,700	564,473
Quebec	580,400	166,474
Hamilton	548,100	306,434
St. Catharines-Niagara	304,400	
St. Catharines		124,018
Niagara Falls		17,010
Kitchener	294,400	139,734
London	287,200	254,280
Halifax	280,700	114,594
Windsor	244,800	192,083
Victoria	240,400	64,379
Regina	172,700	162,613
Saskatoon	162,500	154,210
Oshawa	160,000	117,519
St. John's	155,500	83,770
Sudbury	148,400	91,829
Chicoutimi-Jonquière	138,000	
Chicoutimi		60,064
Jonquière		60,354
Thunder Bay	122,200	112,486
Saint John	114,400	80,521
Trois-Rivières	113,400	50,466

ministration in Canada by the Liberals for almost 42 of the previous 50 years, were in a buoyant mood. However, the new parliamentary session promised to be a test of Prime Minister Mulroney's ability to hold together and direct his large and varied army of Conservative MP's. The Conservative legislative program included simplifying the tax system, reducing the budget deficit, improving social programs, and building better relations with the United States.

Canada's Economy grew at an annual rate of 2.8 per cent during the first six months of 1984, then improved to 4 per cent in July. Canada's economic growth was expected to result in a 1984 *gross national product* (GNP) — the total of all goods and services produced — of $387 billion. (All monetary amounts in this article are Canadian dollars, with $1 = U.S. 76 cents as of Dec. 31, 1984.) Exports to the United States, especially automobiles and automobile parts, were strong and led to a healthy merchandise trade surplus for Canada.

The rate of inflation fell steadily, reaching 3.4 per cent in October — the lowest rate since November 1971. Interest rates began to decline in the fourth quarter of 1984; the Bank of Canada rate in December stood at 10.56 per cent, down from 13.5 per cent in July.

Unemployment was still distressingly high, standing at 11.3 per cent of the labor force in October. This followed a year during which the jobless rate had remained remarkably stable, illustrating the deep-seated nature of the problem.

The Budget. The Trudeau government's final budget was presented on February 15 by Finance Minister Marc Lalonde. A deficit of $29.6 billion was predicted for the fiscal year 1984-1985. Lalonde announced that the controls on wages in the public sector imposed in 1982 would be phased out — a move that would allow public servants to resume collective bargaining with their employers.

The Conservative government of Prime Minister Mulroney issued its first major economic policy statement on November 8. Finance Minister Michael Holcombe Wilson, in an address to Parliament, announced that estimates of the federal budget deficit for fiscal year 1984-1985 had grown to $34.6 billion. For fiscal year 1985-1986, Wilson planned to cut government spending by $3.5 billion, projecting a deficit of $34.9 billion. He announced reductions in government grants and in subsidies to the Canadian Broadcasting Corporation and Petro-Canada, the state-owned oil company. Much of the $1.74 billion saved by such cutbacks was to go to job-creation programs. Wilson said that the government had no plans for a tax increase.

Language Rights Ruling. A ruling by the Supreme Court of Canada on July 26 struck down the educational language clause in Quebec's 1977 Charter of the French Language. The clause in question stated that education in English-language schools in Quebec would be available only to children who had at least one parent educated in English in Quebec. The court held that this restriction violated the 1982 federal Charter of Rights and Freedoms, which guarantees that children of parents educated in English or in French should have the right to an English-language or French-language education in any province where numbers warranted.

Foreign Affairs. The new Progressive Conservative government was not expected to depart from the main principles of Canadian foreign policy as they had been applied by Prime Minister Tru-

The New Line-Up in the House of Commons

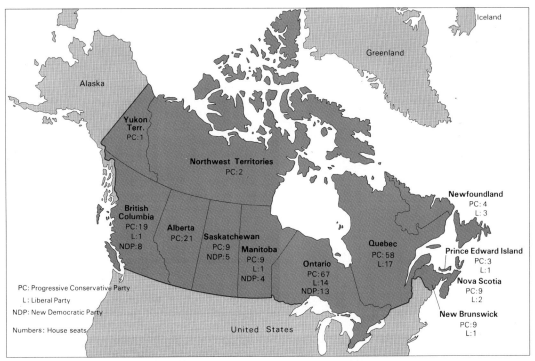

Iceland

Greenland

Alaska

Yukon Terr.
PC:1

Northwest Territories
PC:2

Newfoundland
PC: 4
L: 3

British Columbia
PC:19
L:1
NDP:8

Alberta
PC:21

Saskatchewan
PC:9
NDP:5

Manitoba
PC:9
L:1
NDP:4

Ontario
PC:67
L:14
NDP:13

Quebec
PC:58
L:17

Prince Edward Island
PC:3
L:1

Nova Scotia
PC:9
L:2

New Brunswick
PC:9
L:1

PC: Progressive Conservative Party
L: Liberal Party
NDP: New Democratic Party
Numbers: House seats

United States

deau. However, political observers believed that Canada would align itself more closely with the United States on global and hemispheric issues than had sometimes been the case during the Trudeau years. The Canadian attitude toward troubled Central America was a case in point. Trudeau's Foreign Minister Allan Joseph MacEachen made an 11-day trip to Central America in April. However, he pointedly declined to spend time in El Salvador, where the government, with U.S. military aid, was fighting against leftist guerrillas.

Prime Minister Mulroney paid a courtesy call on United States President Ronald Reagan on September 25, just eight days after Mulroney took office. The two leaders agreed to hold a working meeting at least once a year. Later, in Toronto, on October 15 and 16, Canada's Secretary of State for External Affairs Charles Joseph (Joe) Clark met with U.S. Secretary of State George P. Shultz. The two men discussed the problem of *acid rain* (rain containing sulfuric and nitric acids). Shultz repeated the Reagan government's position that more research was needed before the United States would commit large sums of money to reducing sulfur-dioxide emissions from coalburning factories and power plants.

The testing of a U.S. cruise missile in northern Canada, a controversial topic in 1983, went ahead in March 1984. On March 6, a cruise missile at-

tached to a B-52 bomber guided the aircraft from the Beaufort Sea north of Alaska to an air weapons range on the Saskatchewan-Alberta border. The missile was unarmed, and only its navigation system was being tested.

A historic ocean boundary dispute between Canada and the United States was resolved by a decision handed down on October 12 by the International Court of Justice (World Court) at The Hague in the Netherlands. The dispute involved access to the fisheries and control of the subsea oil and gas resources of the Georges Bank area of the Gulf of Maine. The court drew a maritime boundary across the gulf, dividing the rich fisheries of the Georges Bank between the two countries. Canada received about one-sixth of the fishing area, approximately one-third of what it had claimed, but the area included valuable scallop and lobster beds. See FISHING INDUSTRY.

Visiting Dignitaries. In September, Pope John Paul II became the first pope to visit Canada. The pontiff delivered 34 sermons and speeches in a grueling 12-day tour, emphasizing issues of peace and restating traditional Roman Catholic views on social questions.

On September 24, Queen Elizabeth II and Prince Philip began a royal visit to Canada. The visit had been rescheduled so as not to conflict with the election campaign. For two weeks, the

233

CANADA

Federal Spending in Canada

Estimated Budget for Fiscal 1985*

	Millions of dollars†
Health and welfare	29,586
Public debt	20,350
Economic development and support	11,412
Defense	10,291
Fiscal transfer payments to provinces	5,446
Transportation and communications	4,573
General government services	4,062
Internal overhead expenses	2,563
Education assistance	2,386
Foreign affairs	1.997
Culture and recreation	1,888
Total	94,554

*April 1, 1984, to March 31, 1985.
†Canadian dollars; $1 = U.S. 76 cents as of Dec. 1, 1984.

Spending Since 1979

Billions of dollars†

Fiscal year

Source: Treasury Board of Canada.

queen toured New Brunswick, Ontario, and Manitoba.

Facts in Brief: Population: 25,533,000. Government: Governor General Jeanne M. Sauvé; Prime Minister Martin Brian Mulroney. Monetary unit: the Canadian dollar. Foreign trade (in U.S. dollars): exports, $73,797,000,000; and imports, $61,325,000,000.   David M. L. Farr

See also the Canadian provinces articles; CANADIAN LIBRARY ASSOCIATION (CLA); CANADIAN LITERATURE; MULRONEY, MARTIN B.; SAUVÉ, JEANNE M.; TRUDEAU, PIERRE ELLIOTT; TURNER, JOHN N. In the WORLD BOOK SUPPLEMENT section, see MULRONEY, MARTIN B.; TURNER, JOHN N. In WORLD BOOK, see CANADA; CANADA, GOVERNMENT OF.

CANADIAN LIBRARY ASSOCIATION (CLA) continued its stand against censorship in 1984. On April 6, the CLA presented a report to the Special Committee on Pornography and Prostitution appointed by the federal minister of justice. While deploring the exploitation of children, women, and men by the producers of pornographic publications, the CLA urged the committee to propose no further regulations restricting such publications. The CLA said there is already sufficient legislation that, if wisely applied, could prohibit the distribution and sale of obscene materials.

Also in April, the CLA awarded a contract to the University of Ottawa in Ontario to conduct research on the legal implications of censorship for libraries. The CLA intends to use the findings of that study in its anticensorship program.

Member libraries of the CLA participated in a national Freedom to Read Week held from September 16 to 23. The event was organized by the Book and Periodical Development Council, a national group representing the book industry.

Other Activities. In January, the CLA began a study of whether the library degree programs of Canadian universities should be evaluated by a Canadian accrediting body. All seven Canadian universities offering graduate degrees in library science now apply to the American Library Association's Committee on Accreditation for evaluation of their programs. The CLA study will decide whether it would be economical to have a separate system for this relatively small number of schools, and, if so, what group would serve as the most suitable accrediting agency.

The CLA annual conference was held from June 7 to 12 in Toronto, Ont. Judith McAnanama, chief of the Hamilton, Ont., Public Library, took office as the 39th president, succeeding Lois M. Bewley, a professor at the University of British Columbia's School of Librarianship in Vancouver.

Awards. The winner of the CLA Book of the Year for Children Award was Jan Hudson for *Sweetgrass* (Tree Frog Press). Ken Nutt received the Amelia Frances Howard-Gibbon Illustrator's Award for his illustrations in *Zoom at Sea* (Groundwood Books). The Grolier Award for Research in School Librarianship went to David Jenkinson of the University of Manitoba in Winnipeg, and the CLA Research and Development Award was awarded to Ruth Jellicoe Sheeran of the Bishops University library in Lennoxville, Que.

Scholarships awarded by the CLA in 1984 included the Howard V. Phalin-World Book Graduate Scholarship in Library Science to Kathleen Hogan of Calgary, Alta.; the H. W. Wilson Scholarship to Angela Schmidt of Lethbridge, Alta.; and the CLA-Elizabeth Dafoe scholarship to Angelica Kurtz of Winnipeg, Man.   Paul Kitchen

In WORLD BOOK, see CANADIAN LIBRARY ASSN.

CANADIAN LITERATURE faced threats on several financial fronts in 1984. McClelland and Stewart, Limited, Canada's leading publisher of books for the general public, required $3 million in loans and grants from the provincial government of Ontario to continue its publishing program. Also worrisome was an announcement of substantial cutbacks in the budget of the Canada Council, which awards grants to publishers and writers. Despite these developments, some outstanding books demonstrated that serious writing in Canada remained as fine, varied, and plentiful as ever.

Fiction. The highlight of 1984 was Josef Skvorecky's *The Engineer of Human Souls*. This brilliant, partly autobiographical novel contrasted its protagonist's difficult past in Czechoslovakia with his present comfortable position as a teacher in Toronto, Ont. Timothy Findley contributed another fine novel, *Not Wanted on the Voyage*. This technically adventurous allegory reworked the Biblical story of Noah's ark. Sylvia Fraser brought historical detail to life in *Berlin Solstice*, which traced the rise and fall of Nazi Germany through the differing viewpoints of its characters.

Hugh Hood's *The Scenic Art* was the fifth novel of a projected 12-volume series describing Canada's social and intellectual fabric during the 1900's. The latest novel, which at times tried too hard to educate, explored Canadian theater. The perennially popular W. O. Mitchell wrote *Since Daisy Creek*, a satire about a professor and the university world. Other notable novels included Audrey Thomas' *Intertidal Life*, David Helwig's *The Only Son*, Edward Phillips' *Where There's a Will*, Elizabeth Spencer's *The Salt Line*, and David Lewis Stein's *The Golden Age Hotel*. The best mystery novels of 1984 were Howard Engel's *Murder Sees the Light*, Eric Wright's *Smoke Detector*, and John Reeves's *Murder Before Matins*.

The outstanding work of fiction by a new writer in 1984 was Isabel Huggan's *The Elizabeth Stories*, a series of stories about growing up in a small Ontario town. Other fine short-story collections included Leon Rooke's *A Bolt of White Cloth* and Sandra Birdsell's *Ladies of the House*.

Biographies and Memoirs. Jack Cahill's *John Turner* and Ian MacDonald's *Mulroney* examined the personality and the circumstances that led Turner and Brian Mulroney to seek Canada's highest office. Michael Bliss's *Banting* provided a lively account of the private agonies of Frederick Banting, the controversial scientist credited with discovering insulin.

June Callwood's *Emma* chronicled the bizarre story of Emma Woikin, the Saskatchewan farmer's wife who worked for a Soviet spy ring in Ottawa, Ont. Woikin's story was linked to the revelations of Igor Gouzenko, a Soviet Embassy employee who defected in 1945 and who was the subject of John Sawatsky's 1984 book *Gouzenko: The Inside Story*. *E. H. Norman*, edited by Roger Bowen, traced the life and tragic death of a distinguished Canadian diplomat and historian who leaped to his death in Cairo, Egypt, in 1957, after being accused of having Soviet sympathies.

Two well-known Toronto journalists, Knowlton Nash and Peter Worthington, wrote their memoirs — *History on the Run* and *Looking for Trouble*, respectively. The fascinating personality of Pierre Elliott Trudeau, former Canadian prime minister, came under scrutiny in Larry Zolf's *Just Watch Me*.

History. Pierre Berton completed his best-selling four-volume saga about the opening of the Canadian West with *The Promised Land*, a book that took the reader from 1896 to 1914. Farley Mowat championed conservation in *Sea of Slaughter*, a well-researched but highly personal account of the wanton killing of animals along the northeastern coast of North America. Several books brought out on the occasion of the 40th anniversary of D-Day analyzed Canada's role in the Allied invasion of Europe during World War II. They included Reginald Roy's *1944* and J. L. Granatstein and Desmond Morton's *Bloody Victory*.

George Jonas' *Vengeance* was probably the most controversial book of 1984 because of doubts about the truthfulness of its unnamed sources. The book told of the Israeli counterterrorists who tracked down the killers of 11 Israeli athletes at the 1972 Olympic Games in Munich, West Germany. It claimed that the counterterrorists, in their zeal, came to resemble the terrorists.

Poetry. The most intriguing collection of poetry was Michael Ondaatje's *Secular Love*, which offered striking images of the poet's journey from a broken marriage to community involvement. In her 10th collection, *Interlunar*, Margaret Atwood again tied her poems to an uncompromising vision of humanity. Leonard Cohen's *Book of Mercy* dealt with meditation and religious devotion. Other strong collections came from Roo Borson, David McFadden, Ralph Gustafson, Mary di Michele, Marilyn Bowering, and Judith Fitzgerald.

Other Books. John Robert Colombo, Canada's energetic and widely published editor of reference books, brought out *Canadian Literary Landmarks*. Although the work contained many errors, it provided a useful service in linking some 1,200 entries, mostly of places, with 500 writers. The most provocative collection of essays was Rick Salutin's *Marginal Notes*, an examination of Canadian culture, politics, and society from the viewpoint of the radical left. Mordecai Richler's essays in *Home Sweet Home* were more quirky, if just as acid. Two other essay collections, Paul Stuewe's *Clearing the Ground* and B. W. Powe's *A Climate Charged*, attacked Canadian critics for examining literature on the basis of content rather than technique.

Art and Photography. *A Day in the Life of Canada* was 1984's best-selling book in this category. This lavishly illustrated volume contained 269 photographs taken on June 8, 1984, by 100 outstanding photographers. The most intriguing book was Sally Gibson's *More Than an Island*, which combined a lively text with interesting old photographs of the four islands in Toronto's harbor.

Governor General's Literary Awards for books published in 1983 went to Leon Rooke for *Shakespeare's Dog* (English fiction); Jeffery Williams for *Byng of Vimy* (English nonfiction); David Donnell for *Settlements* (English poetry); Anne Chislett for *Quiet in the Land* (English drama); Suzanne Jacob for *Laura Laur* (French fiction); Maurice Cusson for *Le contrôle social du crime* (French nonfiction); Suzanne Paradis for *Un goût de sel* (French poetry); and René Gingras for *Syncope* (French drama).

Gary Lautens won the Stephen Leacock Memorial Award for his essay collection *No Sex, Please . . . We're Married.* Dorothy Crelinsten received the Canada Council Translation Prize for her English translation of *Délinquants pourquoi?* by Cusson; and Georges Khal won for his French translation of *System and Structure: Essays in Communication* by Anthony Wilden.   Ken Adachi

See also LITERATURE. In WORLD BOOK, see CANADIAN LITERATURE.

CAPE VERDE. See AFRICA.

CARTER, JAMES EARL, JR. (1924-   ), the 39th President of the United States, supported his former Vice President, Walter F. Mondale, for the Democratic presidential nomination in 1984. He campaigned for Mondale in Georgia's Democratic primary, which Mondale won. On July 16, Carter addressed the Democratic convention in San Francisco, at which Mondale was nominated.

Carter also figured prominently, if briefly, in the 1984 presidential campaign when President Ronald Reagan attempted to explain a suicide bomb attack on the U.S. Embassy annex near Beirut, Lebanon, on September 20. Carter reacted angrily when Reagan said the attack had been made possible by "the near destruction of our intelligence capability in recent years before we came here." On September 28, the President telephoned Carter in Plains, Ga., and said he in no way meant to cast blame on his predecessor.

Carter and his wife, Rosalynn, spent a week in early September helping to rehabilitate a burned-out apartment building on New York City's Lower East Side. They were volunteers for Habitat for Humanity, which is a nonprofit Christian organization that builds low-cost housing for the poor. On October 2, Carter participated in the groundbreaking for the Carter presidential library in Atlanta, Ga.   Frank Cormier and Margot Cormier

In WORLD BOOK, see CARTER, JAMES EARL, JR.

In Atlanta, Ga., former President Jimmy Carter leads participants in groundbreaking ceremonies for the Carter presidential library in October.

CAT. The popularity of cats as domestic pets continued to increase in the United States in 1984. The Pet Food Institute estimated that more than $1.7 billion was spent in 1983 to feed the 46 million cats maintained in some 23 million American households. *Cats Magazine* reported that the number of U.S. cat shows in 1983 increased by 12 per cent to a record 575 shows with 110,000 entrants. Registration figures provided by the Cat Fanciers' Association, Incorporated (CFA), showed increases in both individual cats and litters. Persians once again headed the list of registered breeds.

A silver tabby American shorthair male — Grand Champion Hedgewood's Greatest American Hero — was named National Best Cat in 1984 by the CFA. Hero was bred and owned by Gar and Ande DeGeer of Peachtree City, Ga. The title of National Best Kitten went to Grand Champion Simbelair Etcetera of Northbrook, a white Persian female. Simbelair Etcetera was bred by Lois Weston of Mount Hope, Canada, near Toronto, and owned by Peggy and Arnold Blackburn of Winston-Salem, N.C. Grand Champion and Grand Premier Q-T Cats Laurie of Kelley Lane, a blue Persian female, received the title of Best Altered Cat. Laurie was bred by Marcia and Leon Samuels of Elkins Park, near Philadelphia, and owned by Harry Scheeler of Lansdale, Pa.   Thomas H. Dent

In WORLD BOOK, see CAT.

CENSUS. The United States Bureau of the Census continued in 1984 to release information collected during the 1980 census and statistics gathered since then. On Jan. 1, 1985, the population of the United States was about 237.2 million, about 2.3 million more than a year earlier.

New Second City. In April 1984, the Census Bureau announced the results of a computer study of estimated population shifts in the United States between April 1, 1980, and July 2, 1982. The study showed that Los Angeles moved ahead of Chicago to become the second largest city in the United States. New York City remained number one, with an estimated population of 7,086,096.

The population of Los Angeles was estimated at 3,022,247, compared with 2,997,155 for Chicago, which had been the second largest U.S. city since 1890. Houston moved ahead of Philadelphia into fourth place, recording a two-year population gain of 8.2 per cent, the largest for any city.

Women: Gains and Losses. Also in April 1984, the Census Bureau reported that during the 1970's, women increasingly moved into many jobs traditionally dominated by men. According to the 1980 census, the proportion of women in executive, managerial, and administrative occupations increased from 18.5 per cent to 30.5 per cent between 1970 and 1980. The percentage of women judges rose from 6.1 per cent to 17.1 per cent; women architects, from 4 per cent to 8.3 per cent; and mathematical and computer scientists, from 16.7 per cent to 26.1 per cent.

However, in January 1984, the Census Bureau reported that the wage gap between white men and white women widened between 1970 and 1980. White women entering the job market in 1970 earned an average of 86 cents for every dollar earned by white men joining the labor force. In 1980, white women entering the job market earned an average of 83 cents for every dollar earned by men. However, during that same period, the wage gap between white men and black women narrowed, going from a 1970 average of 77 cents earned by black women for every dollar earned by white men to 79 cents per dollar in 1980. In the Special Reports section, see A REVOLUTION IN THE WORKPLACE.

Living Patterns. According to a Census Bureau report issued in July 1984, the number of unmarried couples living together tripled between 1970 and 1983, and the number of young adults living with their parents rose by 85 per cent. In addition, during that period, the number of children under age 18 living with one parent rose from 11.9 per cent to 22 per cent. Frank Cormier and Margot Cormier

See also POPULATION; WELFARE. In WORLD BOOK, see CENSUS; POPULATION.

CENTRAL AFRICAN REPUBLIC. See AFRICA.
CEYLON. See SRI LANKA.

CHAD. In September 1984, France and Libya agreed to pull all of their troops out of Chad. France completed the withdrawal of its forces in early November, but it became evident that Libya was not keeping its side of the bargain.

French and Libyan military units had been in Chad since August 1983. The Libyans entered the country in support of former Chadian President Goukouni Weddeye. To counterbalance the Libyan presence, France — the former colonial ruler of Chad — sent troops and warplanes to back the current president, Hissein Habré.

France and Libya announced their troop-withdrawal agreement on September 17. The simultaneous pullouts were supposed to begin on September 25 and take up to two months. But in late November, when intelligence sources reported that as many as 3,000 of the 5,500-member Libyan force remained in Chad, France made preparations for the possible return of its troops to Chad.

Officials of the Organization of African Unity had invited Weddeye and Habré to meet in Addis Ababa, Ethiopia, on January 9 to discuss peace. But the meeting was aborted because Weddeye refused to treat Habré as Chad's head of state.

Drought caused crop and livestock losses in Chad for the third consecutive year. J. Dixon Esseks

See also AFRICA (Facts in Brief Table). In WORLD BOOK, see CHAD.

CHEMICAL INDUSTRY. The worst chemical accident in history occurred on Dec. 3, 1984, at a Union Carbide Corporation pesticides plant in Bhopal, India. A liquid chemical, methyl isocyanate, overheated in a storage tank, turned into a poison gas, and escaped through a pressure-relief valve. Two safety systems intended to neutralize the gas or to burn it upon release failed for reasons not immediately known. The gas formed a deadly cloud that drifted away from the plant, killing more than 2,500 people. By the end of 1984, the company faced staggering claims for damages.

Industry Sales and Earnings in the United States increased sharply in 1984. Capital spending regained the pace of 1982.

In January, industry experts predicted that the sales revenue of the chemical process industries (CPI's) would be 8 per cent higher in 1984 than in 1983, and that earnings would be 20 per cent higher. The experts predicted a big year for all the industries' major product groups — chemicals, plastics, fibers, specialties such as adhesives, and agricultural chemicals. They also expected the rebuilding of inventories to contribute strongly to the upswing.

As 1984 wore on, encouraging reports rolled in. First-quarter results showed that net earnings for several major companies were up 50 per cent, with some spectacularly higher. Agricultural chemicals blossomed, and plastics sales were up 18 per cent in the first two months. Second-quarter tallies showed that a large segment of the industry had increased profits by an average of 28 per cent.

The Bubble Burst for environmentalists in June 1984, when the Supreme Court of the United States settled a pollution controversy. The Environmental Protection Agency's (EPA's) *bubble* policy allows a company to treat all sources of air pollution in one plant as if they were one source. That is, an individual smokestack can exceed pollution limits as long as the average emission level for all of them does not exceed the limit. In 1982, a United States Court of Appeals ruled that companies could not implement the bubble policy in areas not meeting national clean air standards. The Supreme Court reversed this ruling, 6 votes to 0.

Industry favors the bubble policy, because it allows companies to concentrate on the emission sources that are easiest to control. The EPA estimated that 57 applications of the bubble policy had already saved industry $700 million.

Superfund. In 1980, Congress authorized the EPA to create a *superfund* out of tax money collected from CPI firms and to use the fund to clean up chemical spills and abandoned hazardous-waste sites. By August 1984, the EPA had cleaned

up only 10 of the 542 sites on its national priority list, though work was begun on many other sites in early 1984. The 1980 bill was scheduled to expire in September 1985, so members of Congress from both major political parties strove to reauthorize the superfund during 1984 to gain punch in election campaigns. Congress adjourned before completing action on the superfund.

Agent Orange. In September, U.S. District Judge Jack B. Weinstein tentatively approved a landmark settlement of a case that pitted Vietnam War veterans against seven chemical companies — manufacturers of the *defoliant* (leaf killer) Agent Orange. The issue was whether the spraying of the chemical over jungles and farms in South Vietnam and Laos to defoliate trees and shrubs during the Vietnam War caused cancer, nerve damage, and skin disorders in troops exposed to the defoliant, and birth defects among their children. The companies agreed to provide a fund of $180 million to settle veterans' claims. In August, the Centers for Disease Control in Atlanta, Ga., released a study showing that soldiers exposed to Agent Orange had no greater risk of fathering babies with birth defects than did men in the general population. At the end of 1984, final approval of the settlement was pending while the judge held hearings.   Frederick C. Price

In WORLD BOOK, see CHEMICAL INDUSTRY.

CHEMISTRY. In August 1984, biomedical engineers Robert S. Langer and Howard Bernstein of the Massachusetts Institute of Technology (M.I.T.) in Cambridge reported that they had developed a device for removing heparin, an anticlotting chemical, from the blood of kidney patients undergoing *dialysis* (the cleansing of blood by machine). The device is a small chamber that contains *enzymes* bound chemically to tiny plastic beads. Enzymes are natural substances that speed up chemical reactions. The M.I.T. scientists used certain enzymes produced by bacteria. These enzymes break down heparin into harmless chemicals.

Doctors using the device would mix a patient's blood with heparin, as they do now, before connecting the patient to the dialysis machine. Before the blood returned to the patient's body, it would pass through the chamber, where the enzymes would destroy the heparin. If the heparin were not destroyed, it might cause uncontrolled bleeding.

Heat Pump Clothing. In April 1984, chemists Tyrone L. Vigo and Cynthia M. Frost of the United States Department of Agriculture in Knoxville, Tenn., reported research on plastic crystals that might someday be used in clothing to protect people against extreme cold or extreme heat. The crystals can store and release tremendous amounts of heat.

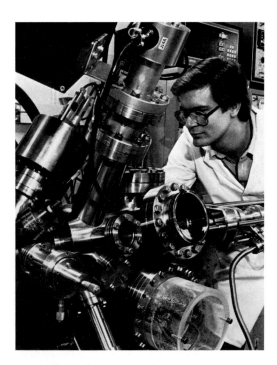
A research chemist operates an instrument that determines how well ceramics and other materials will bond to metals.

The crystals have a high-energy form and a low-energy form. High-energy crystals placed in a cold environment change to the low-energy form, releasing heat. If the crystals were put into clothing, this heat would warm the wearer.

In a hot environment, the reverse process would occur. The clothing would absorb heat, so the wearer would remain relatively cool.

Hot Peppers. In August 1984, researcher Marianne Gillette of McCormick & Company, Incorporated, in Hunt Valley, Md., near Baltimore, announced that she had developed a chemical method for measuring a hot pepper's *pungency*, or sharpness of taste. Finding the "heat" of a pepper is important for two reasons: Growers get more money for "hotter" peppers, and consumers want to be sure of what they are buying. Gillette measured the pungency of peppers by adding up the amounts of the chemicals responsible for it. She measured the individual amounts by *high pressure liquid chromatography* — a technique that separates a substance into its component chemicals. The new method replaces the more costly and less certain determination of "heat" by professional tasters.

Purer Drugs. Chemists at Purdue University in West Lafayette, Ind., announced a breakthrough in synthetic chemistry in March. Herbert C. Brown and Bakthan Singaram developed a way to *synthesize* (manufacture) chemicals that are almost 100 per cent optically pure — a degree of purity almost impossible to obtain previously.

An optically pure chemical is made up of molecules that have one of two mirror-image forms. These forms differ from each other as your right hand differs from your left. The new method should be especially useful in producing drugs, many of which contain one form that offers beneficial effects and another that is less effective or even harmful.

Chemical Transistor. A major step toward making computers that are up to 1,000 times smaller, and many times more powerful, than those in use today was reported in September 1984. Chemists Mark S. Wrighton, Henry S. White, and Gregg P. Kittlesen of M.I.T. built a chemical *transistor*, a device that controls electric currents in computers and other electronic equipment. Ordinary transistors operate through the movement of electrons in solid materials. A chemical transistor controls current by means of chemical reactions. The new transistor is much slower than ordinary transistors in use today.

The development of fast chemical transistors and other electronic devices would lead to computers small enough to replace the optic nerve in a blind person, restoring sight. A computer planted in the body might even control vital chemicals in a person's cells. Peter J. Andrews

In WORLD BOOK, see CHEMISTRY.

CHERNENKO, KONSTANTIN USTINOVICH (1911-), was elected to the Soviet Union's most powerful position, general secretary of the Communist Party Central Committee, on Feb. 13, 1984. He succeeded Yuri V. Andropov, who died on February 9. Andropov's predecessor, Leonid I. Brezhnev, had favored Chernenko rather than Andropov as his successor, but the Communist Party leadership backed Andropov after Brezhnev died in November 1982.

On April 11, Chernenko was elected to the top state post, chairman of the Presidium of the Supreme Soviet, the nation's parliament. The Presidium handles legislation between sessions of the Supreme Soviet.

Chernenko was born on Sept. 24, 1911, in the Siberian village of Bolshaya Tyes. He received little formal education but was active in the Communist Party in his native region. In 1948, the party transferred him to Moldavia, an area on the Romanian border. Brezhnev became party leader in Moldavia in 1950, and Chernenko formed a political alliance with him that lasted until Brezhnev's death. In 1956, Chernenko was transferred to Moscow. He joined the Central Committee in 1971 and became a full member of the Politburo — the party's policymaking body — in 1978.

Chernenko and his wife, Anna Dmitrievna, have a son and a daughter. Jay Myers

CHESS. World champion Anatoly Karpov of the Soviet Union struggled in Moscow against his countryman Gary Kasparov in a title defense that broke a modern record for games played but did not produce a victor in 1984. At year-end, Karpov led, 5 games to 1, with 30 draws. The previous record, established in 1927, was 34 games. (A player must win 6 games to capture a world championship match.)

Meanwhile, Lev Alburt and Maxim Dlugy of New York City; Nick deFirmian of Oakland, Calif.; and Yasser Seirawan of Seattle qualified to compete in the 1985 Interzonal Tournaments leading toward the 1986 world championship match. In October 1984, women's world champion Maya Chiburdanidze of the Soviet Union retained her title by defeating countrywoman Irina Levitina in Volgograd, Soviet Union.

Other Tournaments. In November and December, 18 nations competed at the biennial Chess Olympiad in Salonika, Greece. The Soviet Union won the gold medal. In May, Roman Dzhindzhihashvili of New York City won one of the strongest chess events ever held in the United States, the New York International.

In July, Joel Benjamin of New York City won the World Open in King of Prussia, Pa.; Lev Alburt won the United States Championship in Berkeley, Calif.; and Diane Savereide of Santa

Anatoly Karpov of the Soviet Union, left, defends the world championship of chess against his 21-year-old countryman, Gary Kasparov, in Moscow.

Monica, Calif., won the United States Women's Championship in Berkeley. Savereide had won this tournament four times previously. In August, Dzhindzhihashvili and Sergey Kudrin of Stamford, Conn., were co-winners of the United States Open in Fort Worth, Tex.

Younger Players. In June, 12-year-old Ilya Gurevich of Worcester, Mass., became the second-youngest player in United States history to earn the title of master. Patrick Wolff, 16, of Belmont, Mass., won the Junior Invitational in Ojai, Calif., in June. Dennis Younglove, 18, and defending champion Doug Eckert, 19, both of St. Louis, Mo., tied for first at the 1984 United States Junior Open in St. Louis in July.

Pulaski, Va., schools won an unprecedented triple crown in team play in 1984. Pulaski Middle School and Pojoaque Elementary School near Santa Fe, N. Mex., became national elementary team cochampions. Pulaski Middle School and Orange Grove School of Tucson, Ariz., won the championship for the eighth grade and below. Pulaski County High School and Sunnyside School of Tucson tied for the championship for the ninth grade and below. Stuyvesant High School of New York City and George Washington High School of Philadelphia became the national high school team cochampions.   Al Lawrence

In WORLD BOOK, see CHESS.

CHICAGO. The United States Bureau of the Census made it official in April 1984: Chicago, with a population of 2,997,155, was no longer the nation's "second city," having been surpassed by Los Angeles—population 3,022,247—sometime during 1982. But loss of second-city status ranked low on Chicago's list of problems during 1984.

Council Wars. Political feuding raged throughout the year between Harold Washington, Chicago's first black mayor, and the white majority bloc of the City Council, led by Alderman Edward R. Vrdolyak. The biggest dispute involved city public works contracts that are awarded without competitive bids. Historically, such contracts are awarded by the mayor, but in July 1984 the council voted itself the power to reject the mayor's choice of contractors. Washington then vetoed $826 million worth of public works projects, including continued expansion of O'Hare International Airport.

Work at O'Hare nearly stopped before a compromise was reached on October 1. The council won the right to review nonbid contracts, with disputes to be settled by a new five-member citizens' panel. Meanwhile, the council continued to withhold approval of scores of mayoral appointments to city boards and commissions.

A skirmish over the city's 1985 budget ended on Dec. 31, 1984. Less than five hours before a midnight deadline, the council approved a $1.9 billion budget. The majority bloc forced the mayor to accept a $20 million property tax cut he once described as fiscally irresponsible.

Urban Development. On February 5, majority-bloc aldermen voted to break off negotiations with a private firm for the redevelopment of Navy Pier, a municipal dock that reaches nearly 1 mile (1.6 kilometers) into Lake Michigan. Several other projects remained stalled during 1984, including redevelopment of the North Loop, where the city owns two vacant blocks it condemned in 1980.

A major project that did move ahead, however, was the expansion of the McCormick Place convention center, with groundbreaking for the large annex hall held on October 3. Funds for the $205-million hall were approved in June by the Illinois General Assembly. The legislature refused, however, to give final approval to the proposed 1992 World's Fair on the lakefront. The lawmakers gave that project only a year's planning funds.

Economy. Underscoring Chicago's weak participation in the national economic upswing, U.S. Steel Corporation in 1984 closed all but a small portion of its South Works steel mill, once the city's largest manufacturing plant. In July, the Federal Deposit Insurance Corporation undertook a bailout of Continental Illinois National Bank and Trust Company of Chicago (see BANK).

New School Chief. The Chicago Board of Education voted on September 28 to replace Superintendent of Schools Ruth B. Love in March 1985 with Manford Byrd, Jr., a deputy superintendent. Love filed a federal discrimination complaint against the board, charging that its president, George Munoz, was punishing her for her past support of former Mayor Jane M. Byrne.

Chicago's public-school teachers went on strike on December 3. The Chicago Teachers Union said the city's Board of Education had not met union demands for a new contract that included a salary increase. The strike lasted until December 16, when the union accepted a tentative agreement that included a 4.5 per cent raise and a 2.5 per cent one-time bonus.

Judges Convicted. John A. Murphy and John J. Devine, judges of the Cook County Circuit Court, were convicted in 1984 — in June and October, respectively — of accepting bribes to fix court cases. The judges had been indicted in Operation Greylord, a federal investigation that turned up widespread corruption in the circuit court. On December 18, Devine was sentenced to 15 years in prison. Richard F. LeFevour, the former chief of the Chicago Traffic Court and the highest-ranking judge so far netted by Operation Greylord, was indicted in November.   John McCarron

See also CITY. In WORLD BOOK, see CHICAGO.

CHILD WELFARE. The sexual abuse of children is one of the most common and least understood crimes in the United States, officials of the U.S. Department of Justice said in October 1984. The Justice Department said that as many as 1 out of 4 girls may be sexually molested before the age of 13 and that perhaps only 1 molestation incident in 10 is reported to law enforcement authorities.

Child sexual abuse became an urgent social issue in 1984 after the news media carried several reports about the alleged molestation of children in various parts of the United States. The story that created the greatest public shock and outrage concerned a preschool in Manhattan Beach, Calif., where as many as 300 boys and girls had reportedly been sexually molested over a 10-year period. See Close-Up.

Homeless Children. Some 2.2 million Americans, including at least 750,000 children, were homeless in 1984, according to child-welfare experts. The U.S. Department of Housing and Urban Development in May estimated the homeless total to be far lower, however — between 250,000 and 350,000 people.

Whatever the true figure, homelessness was a problem in both urban and rural areas. In New York City, for example, school officials estimated that about 6,000 children were living with their families in city-financed shelter homes and run-

Chicago Mayor Washington, right, and Alderman Vrdolyak, left, stop feuding in October to meet with Democratic standardbearer Walter Mondale.

Adults Who Prey on Kids

Taking a piece of string, a preschooler in Manhattan Beach, Calif., tied up and gagged a nude female doll. That, she said, is what had been done to her at Manhattan Beach's prestigious Virginia McMartin Pre-School.

As a number of other children revealed their secrets to investigators, the picture grew uglier and uglier. According to the local district attorney, nearly 300 children at the school had been sexually molested by members of the McMartin family and their employees. On March 22, 1984, Virginia McMartin and six other people were indicted on 115 counts of child molestation. The accused persons, all of whom denied any wrongdoing, were still awaiting trial at year-end.

When this story was reported by the news media, Americans were shocked and outraged, and many parents wondered whether their own children had ever been secretly molested. Concern and anger grew during the year as more children — victims of sexual abuse in day-care programs, baby-sitting cooperatives, and other settings, including their own homes — told of their experiences.

Authorities do not know how extensive the problem is in the United States. Nor can they tell whether the problem has grown in recent years or is just being reported with greater frequency. However, several studies suggest that as many as 1 in 4 girls and 1 in 10 boys are molested before the age of 18 — more than half a million children each year.

Hundreds of cases come to light every month in which children under the age of 5, and even as young as 3 to 6 months old, are abused. Typically, though, the victim is 10 to 12 years old and is molested over a period of months or years.

In most cases, the sexual abuse of children is committed by men, but some 20 per cent of male victims and 5 per cent of female victims report being molested by women. And perhaps as often as 90 per cent of the time, the victim knows the abuser.

In a family situation, a girl is more likely than a boy to be molested — in most cases by her father or stepfather or by a boyfriend of the mother. Families in which such abuse occurs tend to be socially isolated, with unhappy or separated parents.

For all the psychological pain and confusion that victims of sexual abuse often feel, few of them ever disclose what has happened to them. The memory of the experience can lead to feelings of shame, fear, and isolation.

However, there are a number of warning signs that can alert parents to the possibility that their child has been sexually molested. In some cases, there are physical symptoms, such as urinary infections, genital irritations, or unexplained bruises. The child may also exhibit unusual behavior — for example, nightmares, difficulty sleeping, fear of a certain person or place, or sexual behavior that is inappropriate for the child's age.

If a child does tell a parent or other adult about being abused, the adult should believe the child, because children rarely lie about such experiences. The adult should stress that the young victim bears no blame for what has happened. The child's accusations should then be reported to law authorities.

Experts agree that a great deal of sexual abuse of children can be prevented if parents warn their children against it. There are several basic principles of self-protection that every child should know:

■ Your body belongs to you. No one — not even a family member — has the right to touch you in ways that make you feel uncomfortable.

■ If this sort of thing ever happens to you, you should tell a parent, teacher, or other adult you trust.

■ If such an incident occurs, it is not your fault.

Children who know these rules, and who have parents they can turn to in trouble, will not be easy prey for child molesters. Anne Harris Cohn

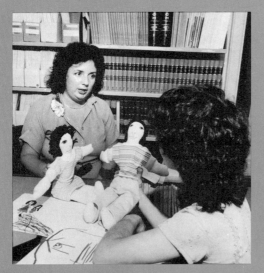

Social workers find it helpful to use dolls to let young abuse victims show them what happened.

down hotels. And in rural Maine, four homeless families were reported to have become so desperate that they gave their children to families who could afford to take care of them.

One reason for the large number of homeless was poverty. An August 1984 report issued by the U.S. Bureau of the Census said that about 35.3 million Americans were living in poverty in 1983. See WELFARE.

Child Support. On August 16, President Ronald Reagan signed into law a bill strengthening efforts to collect child-support payments. The new law would, in many cases, require employers to withhold child support from the paychecks of parents who fall behind in their payments.

On October 9, Reagan signed a so-called "Baby Doe" bill to protect severely handicapped infants, who sometimes have been denied care by hospital personnel. The legislation makes it a crime to withhold treatment from most such infants.

The Department of Justice in April approved a grant of $3.3 million to establish the National Center for Missing and Exploited Children. The privately run center will help find missing children and sponsor education programs on preventing the mistreatment of children.   Jeanne M. Hunzeker

In WORLD BOOK, see CHILD WELFARE.

CHILDREN'S BOOKS. See LITERATURE FOR CHILDREN.

CHILE. Increasingly militant street demonstrations by a broad spectrum of Chileans threatened in 1984 to cut short the dictatorial rule of President Augusto Pinochet Ugarte. Pinochet's military government is empowered to rule until 1989 under a Constitution adopted in 1980, but with unemployment and inflation rampant, opposition groups were demanding an earlier return to civilian rule.

Repression. The government seemed unable to cope with the dire economic situation, and it answered the protests with more repression. Five people were killed and more than 400 were arrested as a result of protests on March 27. The protests came on the heels of a wave of terrorism, including 80 bombings and attacks on radio stations, public utilities, and other targets. Opposition leaders claimed that Chile's secret police were behind some of the bombings, seeking through terrorist acts to justify a crackdown on civil rights.

In early April, following widespread public support for the demonstrations in March, Pinochet dismissed Finance Minister Carlos Cáceres Contreras and Economy Minister Andrés Passicot, who advocated free-market theories. He replaced them with functionaries favoring a larger role for the government in stimulating the economy.

In September, Chileans returned to the streets of Santiago, Concepción, and Valparaíso to demand an end to military rule. During a protest on

September 4, police clubbed the leaders of a group of 300 people who were demonstrating in downtown Santiago. The protesters were singing the national anthem when police rushed in with dogs and water cannons to break up the crowd. Labor leader Rodolfo Seguel was severely beaten. In response, the nation's truckers went on strike the following day. The Pinochet regime censored media reporting of the two days of demonstrations, which left at least nine people dead.

Internal Exile. Other repressive measures included mass arrests during police sweeps of slum areas and sending middle-level political and labor leaders into internal exile. In late October and early November, the government sent 255 people to an internal exile camp at the remote northern fishing village of Pisagua.

State of Siege. On November 5, following another week of political unrest that claimed the lives of 14 people, Pinochet's entire Cabinet resigned, led by Interior Minister Sergio Onofre Jarpa Reyes—the man most prominently responsible for preserving domestic tranquillity. The following day, after Pinochet had decreed a state of siege and a nightly curfew from midnight to 5 A.M., the interior minister and most other Cabinet members resumed their posts.   Nathan A. Haverstock

See also LATIN AMERICA (Facts in Brief Table). In WORLD BOOK, see CHILE.

CHINA, PEOPLE'S REPUBLIC OF. In 1984, China announced major changes in its economic system that would reduce government control over the economy. The changes, to be made gradually over the next five years, were intended to improve living standards and speed up modernization and industrialization. The changes introduced more competition and free enterprise, relaxing the centrally directed economic system China had adapted from the Soviet model in the 1950's. The new policies brought elements of capitalism without giving up Communist theory.

Earlier Changes in Farm Policy. The 1984 changes expanded on earlier reforms made in China's quest for effective economic policies. Mao Zedong (Mao Tse-tung in the traditional Wade-Giles spelling), China's leader from 1949 until his death in 1976, had emphasized collective labor. He believed in equal pay instead of wage differences based on a worker's contributions.

The Communist Party began turning away from Mao's ideas in 1978. It introduced new agricultural policies that allowed farmers to keep more of the fruits of their labor. The party encouraged farmers to plant private plots and permitted village markets to sell produce. The government promised not to raise the quotas for produce that farmers were required to deliver to the state, and to pay 50 per cent more for the rest of the farm-

China's Communist Party Central Committee votes in October to adopt
major changes that will reduce government control of China's economy.

ers' crops after they had met the quotas. Later, farmers were told they could keep the land they worked for at least 15 years, rather than risk losing any improvements they made.

These policies stimulated production. By 1984, China was able to reduce food imports. But rising farm production forced the government to pay premium prices on so much grain and cotton that its deficits were larger than expected.

The 1984 Changes were intended to do for industry what the 1978 changes did for agriculture. Rural incomes had risen 12 per cent per year, and agricultural output went up nearly one-third. But the 20 per cent of China's people living in towns found their income increasing only 7 per cent annually, and industrial production rose by less than one-fourth between 1980 and 1984. Chinese leaders, headed by Deng Xiaoping (Teng Hsiao-p'ing), decided to apply the farm lessons to industry.

On May 15, 1984, Premier Zhao Ziyang told the National People's Congress, China's parliamentary body, that industrial policy would be changed in an effort to obtain "more output with less input." He said a basic problem was that "the pricing system is irrational," but he ruled out immediate changes because tampering with prices could unleash inflation. In China, prices failed to reflect scarcity, quality, or production costs—factors that determine prices in free economies. As a result,

the system used many resources wastefully, and subsidies took up half the government's budget.

Limited changes in May were followed by a 16,000-word "decision on reform of the economic structure" by the Communist Party's Central Committee on October 20. The decision said a rigid economic structure had failed to meet China's needs and had dampened the enthusiasm, initiative, and creativity of workers. To instill vitality, each enterprise should be "a relatively independent economic entity . . . responsible for its own profit and loss" instead of depending on the state.

The decision cut in half the number of products subject to production quotas and price controls. As a result, the supply of many more goods would fluctuate according to demand. Such changes threatened the jobs of about 40 per cent of the bosses at China's 3,000 largest factories and 70 per cent of the factories' party secretaries, suggesting possible future resistance by long-time officials.

The state would keep direct control of such basic industries as oil and steel. But for the most part, government would try to direct the economy merely by use of such tools as price controls, taxes, and interest rates. The value of China's basic unit of money, the yuan, was lowered by 37 per cent against the United States dollar so that internal prices for grain and other products would not exceed world prices.

Mao's concept of nearly equal pay was abandoned. The party said wages and bonuses would be better linked to performance. New rules would "reward the diligent and good, and punish the lazy and bad; give more pay for more work and less pay for less work; and fully reflect the differences between mental and manual, complex and simple, skilled and unskilled, and heavy and light work." Mental work deserved higher pay, the party added. Such concepts reversed Mao's teachings that all work was of equal value and that rewarding good work was uncommunist.

International Trade. China sought more joint ventures with foreign companies to expand its industrial base and gain access to advanced technology. Foreign investment, first permitted in 1978, ran below planned levels, however, so China relaxed some rules. It allowed an American company to wholly own a telecommunications factory in Shanghai, for instance.

China opened more *special economic zones* in 1984 — coastal areas where foreign investors may operate with Chinese labor outside of normal customs duties or other rules. The first four such zones were established in 1979, and the number had expanded to 18 by 1984. The largest was Shenzhen (Shen-chen), adjacent to Hong Kong. By late 1984, it had attracted only $220 million of investment, mostly from Chinese residents in Hong Kong, to China's apparent disappointment.

A few Chinese companies began in July selling stock to the public — the first such capitalist venture since the Communists came to power in 1949. The stock sold quickly because it offered a better return than banks to those who had large savings.

Economic Problems. The Communist Party declared that the major targets of the 1981-1985 economic development plan had been fulfilled by the beginning of 1984. Deng said on October 22 this indicated that industrial and agricultural production could be quadrupled by the year 2000.

Problems continued to plague China's economy, however. Power shortages forced industries to work short hours in some areas, and transportation bottlenecks hindered development.

Exxon Corporation announced on September 17 that it had discovered oil east of Hainan (Hainan) Island in the South China Sea. The 30 other oil firms from nine countries that had signed contracts to drill off the China coast reported only discouraging results. With oil production declining and domestic use rising, China's ability to keep exporting oil — which earned one-fifth of its foreign exchange — was in question.

Environmental Pollution was another problem, a result of China's headlong industrialization. The Ministry of Construction and Environmental Protection said 5 billion metric tons (5.5 billion short tons) of industrial waste were discharged annually.

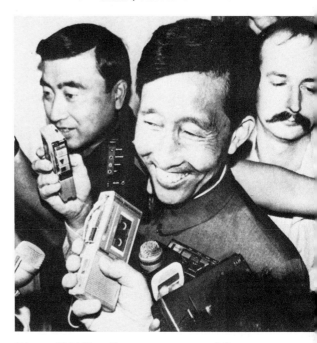

Chinese official Wang Zhenyu announces completion in September of an agreement for the transfer of Hong Kong from British to Chinese control in 1997.

Chinese cities were gray with soot, and the rate of lung cancer deaths in urban areas rose. Tap water had to be filtered and boiled to become safe to drink. A few cities began antipollution efforts.

The Armed Forces continued to receive a low economic priority so that limited resources could be devoted to consumer problems and investment. However, China talked to foreign countries about buying weapons. During Defense Minister Zhang Aiping's June visit to the United States, President Ronald Reagan made China eligible for military sales and assistance. No sales had been made by year-end, however.

China held its first military parade since 1959 on Oct. 1, 1984, to celebrate National Day, the 35th anniversary of the People's Republic of China. Deng reviewed the parade of some 500,000 soldiers and civilians in his capacity as commander of the country's armed forces and chairman of the Communist Party's Central Military Commission. The display included China's first unveiling of its nuclear missiles.

The military chief of staff, Yang Dezhi, announced to the National People's Congress on May 22, 1984, that military ranks would be restored. Mao had abolished them in 1965 as a step toward equality, but border fighting with Vietnam in 1979 had shown that it was difficult to operate without clear rankings. Military leaders also reportedly wanted the prestige of ranks and of medals, which were also restored.

In December, 40 high-ranking officers resigned. The resignations, China's largest military shakeup in years, allowed the army to replace aging veterans with young officers holding modern ideas.

Communist Party leaders continued to campaign against the effects of the Cultural Revolution, Mao's attempt to return China to a radical revolutionary course. The official press complained about "factional activities" of radical Maoist leftists, saying they obstructed reforms.

A Campaign Against Crime also continued in 1984. Authorities claimed that "the crime rate has dropped, and there has been a notable turn for the better in social order." The London-based human rights group Amnesty International said the number of crimes punishable by death had nearly doubled to 44, and thousands of people had been executed. Amnesty also said thousands of political prisoners were being mistreated in China.

Relations with the United States improved. Premier Zhao visited Washington, D.C., in January. He and President Reagan signed on January 12 an industrial and technological cooperation agreement. They also renewed a five-year accord on scientific exchanges.

Reagan visited China from April 26 to May 1, going to Shanghai and Xian (Sian) as well as Beijing (Peking). He and Zhao signed a bilateral tax agreement and a new cultural agreement. Reagan also concluded a long-pending nuclear cooperation pact permitting China to buy U.S. equipment for nuclear power plants. China wanted the technology but was reluctant to allow the normal international inspections to safeguard against converting nuclear materials into weapons. The United States Congress criticized the compromise reached by Reagan and held up nuclear sales to China.

Soviet Pacts. On December 28, China and the Soviet Union signed three economic agreements in Beijing. The most important of the pacts calls for the Soviets to help modernize dozens of Chinese factories built with their assistance in the 1950's. At the same time, the two nations announced that they would expand trade with each other by more than 25 per cent in 1985.

Scattered Fighting continued in 1984 with Vietnam. Chinese troops on April 6 seized two hilltops inside Vietnam's border and held them in bitter fighting. China and Vietnam said the attack was Chinese retaliation for Vietnamese attacks from Kampuchea into Thailand.   Henry S. Bradsher

See also ASIA (Facts in Brief Table); HONG KONG; TAIWAN. In WORLD BOOK, see CHINA.

CHURCHES. See EASTERN ORTHODOX CHURCHES; JEWS AND JUDAISM; PROTESTANTISM; RELIGION; ROMAN CATHOLIC CHURCH.

CISKEI. See AFRICA.

CITY. Urban leaders in the United States in 1984 labored to overcome a discouraging lack of concern at the national level in urban problems. The U.S. Conference of Mayors and other groups fought back with determination not to let cities deteriorate further. Realizing that progress depended on their helping themselves, many cities launched a number of innovative programs designed to reinvigorate local economic growth and provide care for the disadvantaged.

Politics. Neither President Ronald Reagan nor his Democratic challenger in the November election, Walter F. Mondale, made urban problems a campaign issue. And it seemed clear to many observers at year-end that the plight of U.S. cities was unlikely to get any more attention during President Reagan's second term than during his first. M. Carl Holman, president of the National Urban Coalition — a Washington, D.C.-based organization that seeks solutions for urban problems — suggested in May that the federal government's absence of sympathy for cities may reflect a lack of interest among the general population. "You say 'cities,' and people think, 'blacks, Hispanics, poor,' " Holman said.

Social Welfare. The U.S. Conference of Mayors in an October report, *A Plan to Rebuild America's Cities*, called on the federal government to take over the administration of welfare programs from the states. The recommendations by big-city mayors were part of the conference's blueprint for urban revitalization. Washington, D.C., Mayor Marion S. Barry, Jr., chairman of the subcommittee that drafted the report, acknowledged that the $9-billion proposal is unlikely to be adopted by the Reagan Administration in view of its stated policy of turning many federal welfare responsibilities over to state and local agencies. The report estimated that state and national welfare spending declined by 9 per cent from 1979 to 1984.

The report was careful to point out, however, that cities did not expect the federal government to assume all the costs of helping the poor. The government's primary responsibility, the mayors said, was to divide the cost of welfare programs equitably among all the nation's taxpayers.

Barry commented that the seemingly high cost of tackling poverty is cheaper than allowing urban areas to deteriorate further. "In 1979, the poverty rate was 11.7 per cent, and by the end of 1983 it was 15.2 per cent, an addition of 9 million people," he said. "The cost of not breaking the poverty cycle — in terms of unemployment compensation, public assistance, drug abuse treatment, family destruction, incarcerations, and the like — far outweighs the cost of building self-sufficiency."

Medical Care. The Conference of Mayors also recommended in its October report that the federal government pay all the health-care costs of the nation's poorest citizens. The report said the lack of adequate health care is a serious problem for many poor people. It estimated that 12 per cent of all Americans — 21 million adults and 7 million children, most of them urban dwellers — went without needed medical treatment in 1983 because they were unable to afford it. The report also recommended that Congress pass legislation increasing federal support for hospitals that treat uninsured patients. Hospital administrators would welcome such a move. Many urban medical centers have expressed concern about the difficulty of maintaining a high level of service and research due to increasing numbers of patients who cannot pay their bills.

Urban Hardship. A report on economic hardship in Chicago, issued in July by Northwestern University in Evanston, Ill., revealed that about 50 per cent of the people interviewed in a random-sample survey said their families were "worse off" than they had been in 1980. Moreover, nearly 25 per cent of the people interviewed said there had been at least one occasion in late 1983 or early 1984 when they could not afford to buy groceries. A study released in November by Harvard University in Cambridge, Mass., described hunger in Chicago and three other U.S. cities as "nothing less than a public-health emergency." The Harvard study, produced by a 22-member Physicians Task Force on Hunger in America, also reported that urban doctors are witnessing increases in malnutrition diseases such as those seen in developing countries and a general decline in the health of their low-income patients.

Crime Statistics published by the Federal Bureau of Investigation in October 1984 showed an overall decline in serious crimes in the United States for the third consecutive year. The total number of crimes for the first six months of 1984 was 5 per cent below the total for the same period in 1983, with decreases registered for murder, 5 per cent; robbery, 7 per cent; burglary, 8 per cent; and larceny-theft, 5 per cent. The decline was seen in cities of all sizes, in suburbs, in rural areas, and in every region of the country. However, there were increases in the rates for four crimes — rape, 6 per cent; aggravated assault, 1 per cent; motor vehicle theft, 1 per cent; and arson, 2 per cent. Most experts attributed the overall reduction in crime to the post-baby-boom decline in the number of 18- to 25-year-olds — the age group most prone to committing violent crimes.

Organized crime remains a persistent problem in many large cities. In October, the President's Commission on Organized Crime issued its first report, *The Cash Connection: Organized Crime, Financial Institutions and Money Laundering*, which proposed new legislation to curb the practice of *laundering* money — the use of financial institutions

50 Largest Cities in the World

Rank	City	Population
1.	Shanghai	11,859,748
2.	Mexico City	9,373,353
3.	Beijing (Peking)	9,230,687
4.	Seoul, South Korea	8,366,756
5.	Tokyo	8,349,209
6.	Moscow	8,275,000
7.	Bombay, India	8,227,332
8.	Tianjin (Tientsin), China	7,764,141
9.	New York City	7,086,096
10.	São Paulo, Brazil	7,033,529
11.	London	6,608,598
12.	Jakarta, Indonesia	6,503,449
13.	Cairo, Egypt	6,133,000
14.	Hong Kong	5,664,000
15.	Bangkok, Thailand	5,153,902
16.	Rio de Janeiro, Brazil	5,093,232
17.	Karachi, Pakistan	4,901,627
18.	Delhi, India	4,884,234
19.	Leningrad, Soviet Union	4,827,000
20.	Teheran, Iran	4,496,159
21.	Santiago, Chile	4,271,000
22.	Lima, Peru	3,968,972
23.	Calcutta, India	3,305,006
24.	Madras, India	3,276,622
25.	Madrid, Spain	3,201,234
26.	Pusan, South Korea	3,160,276
27.	Berlin (East and West), East and West Germany	3,038,689
28.	Los Angeles	3,022,247
29.	Chicago	2,997,155
30.	Baghdad, Iraq	2,969,000
31.	Rome	2,914,042
32.	Buenos Aires, Argentina	2,908,001
33.	Sydney, Australia	2,874,415
34.	Bogotá, Colombia	2,850,000
35.	Yokohama, Japan	2,773,822
36.	Lahore, Pakistan	2,707,215
37.	Osaka, Japan	2,648,158
38.	Melbourne, Australia	2,578,527
39.	Istanbul, Turkey	2,547,364
40.	Bangalore, India	2,476,355
41.	Ho Chi Minh City, Vietnam	2,441,185
42.	Shenyang (Shen-yang), China	2,411,000
43.	Dhaka, Bangladesh	2,365,695
44.	Alexandria, Egypt	2,320,000
45.	Singapore, Singapore	2,308,200
46.	Kinshasa, Zaire	2,242,297
47.	Taipei, Taiwan	2,200,427
48.	Hyderabad, India	2,187,262
49.	Paris	2,176,243
50.	Wuhan (Wu-han), China	2,146,000

Sources: 1982 Bureau of the Census estimates for cities of the United States; censuses and estimates from governments for cities of other countries.

50 Largest Cities in the United States

Rank	City	Population*	Per cent change in population since 1970	Mayor[†]
1.	New York City	7,086,096	+ 0.2	Edward I. Koch (D, 1/86)
2.	Los Angeles	3,022,247	+ 1.8	Thomas Bradley (NP, 6/85)
3.	Chicago	2,997,155	− 0.3	Harold Washington (D, 4/87)
4.	Houston	1,725,617	+ 8.2	Kathryn J. Whitmire (NP, 1/86)
5.	Philadelphia	1,665,382	− 1.4	W. Wilson Goode (D, 1/88)
6.	Detroit	1,138,717	− 5.3	Coleman A. Young (D, 1/86)
7.	Dallas	943,848	+ 4.3	A. Starke Taylor (NP, 5/85)
8.	San Diego	915,956	+ 4.6	Roger Hedgecock (R, 12/88)
9.	Phoenix	824,230	+ 4.3	Terry Goddard (D, 12/85)
10.	San Antonio	819,021	+ 4.0	Henry G. Cisneros (D, 4/85)
11.	Baltimore	774,113	− 1.6	William Donald Schaefer (D, 12/87)
12.	Indianapolis	707,655	+ 1.0	William H. Hudnut III (R, 12/87)
13.	San Francisco	691,637	+ 1.9	Dianne Feinstein (NP, 1/88)
14.	San Jose	659,181	+ 4.7	Thomas McEnery (D, 12/86)
15.	Memphis	645,760	− 0.1	Dick Hackett (I, 12/87)
16.	Washington, D.C.	633,425	− 0.8	Marion S. Barry, Jr. (D, 1/87)
17.	Milwaukee	631,509	− 0.8	Henry W. Maier (D, 4/88)
18.	Columbus, Ohio	570,588	+ 1.0	Dana G. Rinehart (R, 1/88)
19.	New Orleans	564,561	+ 1.2	Ernest N. Dutch Morial (D, 5/86)
20.	Boston	560,847	− 0.4	Raymond L. Flynn (D, 1/88)
21.	Cleveland	558,869	− 2.6	George V. Voinovich (R, 11/85)
22.	Jacksonville, Fla.	556,370	+ 2.9	Jake M. Godbold (D, 7/87)
23.	Denver	505,563	+ 2.6	Federico Peña (D, 6/87)
24.	Seattle	490,077	− 0.8	Charles Royer (NP, 1/86)
25.	Nashville	455,252	− 0.1	Richard H. Fulton (D, 9/87)
26.	Kansas City, Mo.	445,222	− 0.6	Richard L. Berkley (NP, 4/87)
27.	El Paso	445,071	+ 4.7	Jonathan W. Rogers (NP, 4/85)
28.	St. Louis	437,354	− 3.4	Vincent L. Schoemehl, Jr. (D, 4/85)
29.	Atlanta	428,153	+ 0.1	Andrew J. Young, Jr. (D, 1/86)
30.	Oklahoma City	427,714	+ 5.9	Andy Coats (D, 4/87)
31.	Pittsburgh	414,936	− 2.1	Richard S. Caliguiri (D, 1/86)
32.	Fort Worth	401,402	+ 4.2	Bob Bolen (NP, 4/85)
33.	Miami	382,726	+10.3	Maurice A. Ferre (D, 11/85)
34.	Cincinnati	380,118	− 1.4	Charles J. Luken (D, 11/85)
35.	Tulsa	375,300	+ 4.0	Terry Young (D, 5/86)
36.	Honolulu	374,302	+ 2.5	Eileen Anderson (D, 1/85)
37.	Long Beach	371,426	+ 2.8	Ernie Kell (D, 7/86)
38.	Minneapolis	369,161	− 0.5	Donald M. Fraser (D, 1/86)
39.	Austin	368,135	+ 6.4	Ron Mullen (NP, 4/85)
40.	Portland, Ore.	367,530	− 0.1	J. E. Clark (NP, 11/88)
41.	Tucson	352,455	+ 4.7	Lewis C. Murphy (R, 12/87)
42.	Toledo	350,565	− 1.1	Donna Owens (R, 12/85)
43.	Buffalo	348,035	− 2.7	James D. Griffin (D, 12/85)
44.	Oakland	344,652	+ 1.6	Lionel J. Wilson (D, 6/85)
45.	Albuquerque	341,978	+ 2.9	Harry E. Kinney (R, 12/85)
46.	Omaha	328,557	+ 0.3	Michael Boyle (NP, 6/85)
47.	Charlotte	323,972	+ 2.7	Harvey B. Gantt (D, 11/85)
48.	Newark	320,512	− 2.7	Kenneth A. Gibson (D, 7/86)
49.	Louisville	293,531	− 1.7	Harvey Sloane (D, 12/85)
50.	Birmingham	283,239	− 1.2	Richard Arrington, Jr. (NP, 11/87)

*1982 estimates (U.S. Bureau of the Census, except for Honolulu, which is a WORLD BOOK estimate).
†The letters in parentheses represent the mayor's party, with D meaning Democrat, R Republican, I independent, and NP nonpartisan. The date is when the mayor's term in office ends (National League of Cities; Municipal Yearbook 1984).
‡Estimates for autumn 1981 for Metropolitan Statistical Areas (U.S. Bureau of Labor Statistics). n/a = not available.

Average cost of living (family of 4)‡	Unemployment rate§	Revenue#	Gross debt outstanding#	Per capita income**	Sales tax rate††
$29,540	10.3	$19,912,568,000	$10,412,297,000	12,874	8.25%
25,025	9.5	3,346,262,000	2,814,629,000	13,080	6.5%
25,358	8.1	2,262,170,000	1,159,171,000	13,069	8%
23,601	7.1	1,025,066,000	1,519,127,000	14,128	6.125%
26,567	7.2	2,375,027,000	2,059,273,000	11,946	6%
25,208	10.5	1,720,848,000	946,859,000	12,092	4%
22,678	4.0	551,197,000	652,502,000	13,846	6.125%
24,776	6.6	488,605,000	134,914,000	11,638	5.75%
n/a	3.6	540,790,000	644,212,000	11,086	6%
n/a	5.3	804,199,000	1,369,110,000	10,131	5.625%
25,114	6.1	1,428,035,000	883,143,000	11,560	5%
n/a	6.5	472,579,000	296,637,000	11,236	5%
27,082	6.7	1,669,787,000	894,582,000	17,131	6.5%
25,598	5.2	330,317,000	157,394,000	14,998	6%
n/a	7.6	1,157,910,000	593,733,000	9,968	7.75%
27,352	4.2	2,602,251,000	1,776,700,000	14,960	6%
26,875	7.1	519,967,000	395,348,000	12,597	5%
n/a	6.8	346,327,000	677,659,000	10,629	6%
n/a	8.6	509,619,000	512,514,000	11,680	9%
29,213	3.7	1,032,873,000	531,913,000	13,087	5%
n/a	8.2	501,647,000	382,265,000	12,757	6.5%
n/a	5.8	751,318,000	738,900,000	10,483	5%
24,820	4.2	650,684,000	426,675,000	13,964	6.6%
25,881	7.4	593,899,000	509,490,000	13,239	7.9%
n/a	6.1	849,927,000	426,675,000	10,229	7.75%
24,528	5.2	400,021,000	267,264,000	10,994	5.125%
n/a	10.2	192,033,000	89,309,000	7,832	5%
24,498	7.7	453,033,000	206,182,000	12,338	6%
23,273	4.9	475,284,000	1,000,314,000	11,590	4%
n/a	4.8	247,190,000	355,467,000	12,776	5%
24,717	11.6	274,674,000	293,638,000	11,762	6%
22,678	4.0	214,094,000	243,026,000	11,923	5%
n/a	7.9	210,211,000	204,830,000	11,717	5%
25,475	7.8	397,800,000	184,702,000	11,224	5.5%
n/a	7.1	231,001,000	184,468,000	12,750	6%
31,893	5.5	446,662,000	248,559,000	12,130	4%
25,025	9.5	484,709,000	210,821,000	13,080	6%
25,799	5.0	410,252,000	825,912,000	12,811	6%
n/a	3.6	544,547,000	1,002,673,000	11,249	5%
n/a	7.9	253,288,000	354,909,000	11,793	—
n/a	3.9	209,974,000	195,683,000	9,969	7%
n/a	9.5	219,267,000	171,233,000	10,892	6%
26,473	9.0	517,037,000	246,748,000	11,160	7%
27,082	6.7	301,575,000	379,484,000	13,671	6.5%
n/a	6.4	221,801,000	425,864,000	10,626	4.625%
n/a	4.8	168,482,000	148,038,000	11,397	5%
n/a	5.2	175,859,000	234,050,000	10,323	4.5%
n/a	6.0	436,350,000	144,245,000	13,671	6%
n/a	8.8	178,786,000	383,276,000	10,579	5%
n/a	10.0	182,672,000	309,924,000	9,941	5%

§July 1984 figures for Metropolitan Statistical Areas (U.S. Bureau of Labor Statistics).
#1981-1982 figures (U.S. Bureau of the Census).
**1982 figures for Metropolitan Statistical Areas (U.S. Bureau of Economic Analysis).
††Total sales tax rate, including state, county, city, school district, and special district taxes (Tax Foundation, Inc.).

Opening-day visitors stream into the Louisiana
World's Exposition in New Orleans in May, but
attendance slumped and the fair went bankrupt.

by U.S. crime figures to disguise the origins of illegally gained money, thus making it easier to use.
An estimated $20 billion to $70 billion is laun-
dered annually. The commission recommended
fines of up to $1 million and 10-year prison terms
for drug dealers, mobsters, and dishonest business
owners who launder funds. Opponents of the proposed law expressed fears that it would lead to invasion of privacy by opening up many confidential
bank transactions.

Neediest Cities. A report on the nation's 53 largest cities, issued in October by a congressional
committee, listed the 10 neediest and the 10 least
needy cities in the United States. The ranking was
"based on the number of people living below the
poverty level, net change and real growth in per-
capita income from 1969 to 1979, and the 1980
unemployment rate." The 10 most needy cities
were Newark, N.J.; Detroit; Atlanta, Ga.; Cleveland; Baltimore; Buffalo, N.Y.; Philadelphia; New
York City; Chicago; and St. Louis, Mo. The cities
considered least needy were Tulsa, Okla.; San
Jose; Wichita, Kans.; Houston; Virginia Beach,
Va.; Seattle; Honolulu, Hawaii; Austin, Tex;
Charlotte, N.C.; and Denver.

Joblessness. Although the national unemployment rate hovered near 7.5 per cent for most of
1984, the figure was much higher in the major industrial cities of the United States. Furthermore,

within those cities, joblessness was much higher
for Hispanics and blacks, and especially for young
blacks. The official jobless rate in 1984 was 10.3
per cent in New York City and 8.1 per cent in Chicago. Analysts believed, however, that the actual
rate in these and other large cities was much
higher because the official figures did not include
"discouraged workers" — people who had been unemployed for more than six months and were no
longer looking for work.

Innovations. Despite declining federal government support for cities — or perhaps because of
it — local political and civic leaders, foundations,
social agencies, and community organizations initiated programs in 1984 that they hoped would
"make a difference." Although city hall politics remained the primary force in most major cities,
community groups and organizations played increasingly important roles. In Chicago, for example, Mayor Harold Washington announced in October an "Affirmative Information Program," by
which the city will provide neighborhood organizations with information — on such topics as hous-
ing-code violations and zoning regulations — that
they need in making plans for their areas. Previously, such information had been generally inac-
cessible to the public. Community groups in Chicago also began to assert their right to have a voice
in the planning of the World's Fair scheduled to
be held on the city's lakefront in 1992.

Citizens' groups throughout the United States
also took a more active part in trying to reduce the
level of violence in American cities. For example,
the National Alliance Against Violence, a New
York City group, trained police in four cities —
New York City; Chicago; Minneapolis, Minn.; and
Oakland, Calif. — to work with local organizations
in discouraging the possession and use of hand-
guns. In a program begun by a Boston physician
specializing in adolescent medicine, concerned
adults in several other cities took videotapes and
street-theater tactics into school classrooms to help
students learn nonviolent ways of expressing their
feelings. And in a Chicago suburb suffering from
gang activity, black parents formed an organization of "Co-pops and Co-moms" who work in
teams to monitor school hallways and local youth
hangouts.

These and other local efforts, though they may
seem to be too scattered and too limited to be effective, were taking place in hundreds of cities nationwide. They represented citizens' determination and optimism that the negative trends of the
past can be reversed. Urban experts said that, with
the prospect of little or no aid from the federal
government, local officials and civic leaders must
actively support such efforts.   Margaret T. Gordon

See also articles on individual cities. In WORLD
BOOK, see CITY and articles on individual cities.

CIVIL RIGHTS. Calling torture "an epidemic in the world," Amnesty International, an independent, worldwide human rights organization based in London, released its annual report on human rights in 117 countries on Oct. 24, 1984. According to the report, torture is practiced in 98 countries, especially in Latin America, Asia, and Africa, often as part of state policy. According to the report, among Latin-American countries, Colombia, Peru, El Salvador, Paraguay, and Chile ranked as the worst offenders. In addition, the organization reported allegations of the use of torture in some developed countries, such as Italy, and mentioned instances of police brutality in the United States. The report also noted that a large number of people had been attacked by their governments for calling attention to human rights abuses.

Latin-American Picture. On August 24, an agency of the Roman Catholic Church in El Salvador reported that Salvadoran military forces had killed 1,331 civilians during the first six months of 1984. The agency also reported that 185 civilians were killed by right wing death squads. On September 11, President Augusto Pinochet Ugarte of Chile marked the 11th anniversary of the military coup that brought him to power by refusing to step down before 1989, when elections are scheduled, and by threatening a new crackdown on opposition leaders who organize public protests.

On the brighter side, on May 6, in an El Salvador election that was remarkably free from guerrilla harassment and administrative snags, José Napoleón Duarte, a moderate, was elected president. And another moderate, Julio María Sanguinetti, was elected president in Uruguay on November 25 in preparation for ending 11 years of military rule.

Sakharov's Fast. In the Soviet Union, physicist Andrei D. Sakharov, a human rights advocate and winner of the 1975 Nobel Peace Prize, began a hunger strike in May to pressure authorities to allow his wife, Yelena G. Bonner, to go abroad for medical treatment. Later that month, Sakharov reportedly was taken to a hospital in the Russian city of Gorki, to which he had been exiled. Friends of the Sakharovs in September confirmed reports that Bonner had been sentenced to five years of exile in Gorki on a charge of anti-Soviet slander. In December, reports indicated that Sakharov's health was satisfactory.

African Problems. Nigeria's military government issued a law on April 17 empowering it to close newspapers and radio stations and to jail journalists. On August 9, the U.S. Department of State cited civil rights violations in Uganda, including massacres and the forced starvation of dissident ethnic groups, as abuses of human rights that were "among the most grave in the world."

Quota Reversal. The U.S. Commission on Civil Rights on January 17 reversed a policy and denounced the use of quotas in the hiring and promotion of blacks. In 1983, President Ronald Reagan and Republican leaders in Congress had agreed on replacing most members of the commission with people who support the Administration's views on affirmative action and busing. The new policy was announced in a statement deploring the use of quotas by the Detroit Police Department to promote blacks from sergeant to lieutenant.

Desegregation Agreement. On January 25, the Reagan Administration concluded an agreement with school officials to desegregate public schools in Bakersfield, Calif., without mandatory busing. Under the agreement, Bakersfield will seek to attract white students to predominantly black and Hispanic schools by establishing special programs. Although previous administrations supported the use of such programs, they also relied on court-ordered busing.

Black Gains, Setback. The number of black elected officials in the United States rose 8.6 per cent in 1983, from 5,160 to 5,606, according to a study released in January 1984 by the Joint Center for Political Studies, a political research organization. The gains reversed an eight-year decline in the number of blacks elected to public office.

A study released on July 30 by the National Urban League, an interracial community service organization, noted a steady decline in the number of black men who can support a wife and children. The study cited discrimination in education and employment as the chief causes of the drop.

Censorship Issues. In February, the Reagan Administration announced it was delaying plans to impose lifelong censorship on federal employees and expand the use of lie-detector tests to investigate unauthorized disclosures of classified information. In May, the Senate Committee on Foreign Relations uncovered a United States Information Agency blacklist of 95 persons who were banned from an overseas speaking program. On September 18, a conference sponsored by 39 organizations, including the American Civil Liberties Union and the American Association of University Professors, protested the Reagan Administration's practice of restricting, allegedly for ideological reasons, the visits of prominent Latin Americans and Europeans to the United States.

Sex Bias Decision. Women's rights advocates criticized a decision handed down by the Supreme Court of the United States on February 28 that narrowed the scope of a major federal antidiscrimination law. The court ruled that a 1972 federal law barring sex discrimination in schools and colleges that receive federal funds applies only to the specific departments or programs receiving those funds and not to the entire school. The decision came in a case involving Grove City College in Pennsylvania. Previous administrations had interpreted the law to mean that the entire school was subject to the antidiscrimination law if any department received federal funds. However, the Reagan Administration had argued that the law should be more narrowly interpreted.

In June, the Reagan Administration announced that it had closed discrimination investigations of 23 schools and colleges as a result of the Grove City decision. Legislation introduced into Congress to reestablish the broader interpretation of the antidiscrimination law failed to pass before Congress adjourned in October.

Wage Gap Widens. A study of data collected by the U.S. Bureau of the Census published in January 1984 strongly suggested that young white women entering the job market in 1980 faced greater wage discrimination than did those entering in 1970. The study reported that despite the growth of affirmative action and the education gains made by women, white women entering the job market in 1980 earned less, compared to white men, than did white women joining the labor force in 1970.

According to the study, white women entering the job market in 1980 made an average of $4.20 per hour, compared to an average of $5.04 per hour earned by white men joining the labor force. In 1970, new white female workers earned $4.38 per hour, compared to $5.11 per hour earned by new white male workers.

The researchers who conducted the study attempted to account for the growth in the earnings gap with such factors as education, type of job,. and place of residence. They concluded that up to 17 per cent of the earnings gap in 1980 could not be attributed to anything but wage discrimination. This figure was almost twice the amount of the wage gap that the researchers attributed to discrimination in 1970.

Other Women's Issues. Women's rights advocates in the United States applauded a Supreme Court ruling on May 22 that federal antidiscrimination laws apply to partnership decisions in law firms. Lawyer Elizabeth A. Hishon had sued an Atlanta, Ga., law firm, contending that she had been denied a partnership because of her sex. The law firm had argued that the selection of partners was not covered by antidiscrimination laws. On August 16, United States Jaycees, prodded by a Supreme Court ruling against them, overwhelmingly approved a resolution admitting women to full membership in the previously all-male organization. Louis W. Koenig

In the Special Reports section, see A REVOLUTION IN THE WORKPLACE. In WORLD BOOK, see CIVIL RIGHTS.
CLOTHING. See FASHION.

COAL. Members of the United Mine Workers of America (UMW) on Sept. 27, 1984, approved a new, 40-month contract with the soft-coal industry, averting a nationwide strike. It was the first time since 1964 that the union had approved a contract without a strike. The contract with the Bituminous Coal Operators' Association provided for wage increases of 10.25 per cent, better pension benefits, and new restrictions on companies that lease their mines to outside operators. Most of the 160,000 active members of the UMW are covered by the new contract.

Coal Records. The U.S. economic recovery was expected to result in both record production and record consumption of coal in the United States for all of 1984. The National Coal Association (NCA), the major organization of coal producers, predicted in June that U.S. coal consumption would reach 849 million short tons (770 million metric tons) in 1984. That would be an increase of 39 million short tons (35 million metric tons) over 1983 levels, and well above the record 839 million short tons (761 million metric tons) consumed in 1981. Production was expected to reach 853 million short tons (774 million metric tons), up from the 781 million short tons (709 million metric tons) produced in 1983 and exceeding the record 834 million short tons (757 million metric tons) produced in 1982.

Utah Disaster. Twenty-seven people died after a fire started on Dec. 19, 1984, in a coal mine near Orangeville, Utah. The 27, including 5 executives of the Emery Mining Company, were trapped about 1 mile (1.6 kilometers) below ground, and efforts to save them failed.

Coal Leasing Criticized. A report released on Feb. 8, 1984, found that the government's coal leasing program was mismanaged under Secretary of the Interior James G. Watt, who resigned in 1983. The Commission on Fair Market Value Policy for Federal Coal Leasing, appointed by Watt in 1983 at the request of Congress, reported that the government may have received tens of millions of dollars less than fair market value for the coal leases it sold in Wyoming and Montana in 1982.

The commission made 36 recommendations for improving the program, which leases federal land to private companies for coal production. Secretary of the Interior William P. Clark suspended all competitive leasing of government coal reserves until procedures recommended by the commission were instituted. On August 30, Clark announced that the Interior Department would prepare a new report on the environmental impact of leasing government coal reserves.

New Standards. The U.S. Environmental Protection Agency on May 2 proposed stricter standards to control the discharge of water containing acids and heavy metals from coal mines and coal-refuse piles. The standards would cover about 6,000 mines and 540 other coal facilities throughout the United States.

Pipeline Canceled. On August 1, Energy Transportation Systems Incorporated canceled plans it had made to build a $3.6-billion pipeline that would have carried coal slurry, a mixture of crushed coal and water, 1,800 miles (2,900 kilometers) from Wyoming to Louisiana. The coal would have been separated, dried, and then burned at electric utilities. The firm said that delays in obtaining rights-of-way and other clearances had made the pipeline, which would have been the world's largest, too expensive.

British Strike. A long coal strike began in Great Britain on March 12. With the strike five months old in August, the British government estimated that it had cost the national economy as much as $458 million. The strike began after the British government, which owns the coal industry, announced plans to close 20 unprofitable mines and lay off about 20,000 miners in an effort to make the industry profitable. At year's end, the strike dragged on, though more than 60,000 miners had defied the strike and returned to work. See GREAT BRITAIN.   Michael Woods

See also ENERGY; ENVIRONMENT; MINING. In WORLD BOOK, see COAL.

COIN COLLECTING. Olympic coin sales merited a gold medal of their own in 1984, contributing a substantial part of the income earned by the Los Angeles Summer Games. As of July 31, the commemorative coins had produced $48.6 million in profits, on gross sales of $209.7 million, for the United States and Los Angeles Olympic committees. That figure was second only to the $225 million paid by the American Broadcasting Companies for television rights to the Summer Olympics. Total profits from the coin sales were expected to reach $65 million.

The commemorative coins, which were minted in both gold and silver and priced at $352 and $32, respectively, were sold by the U.S. Department of the Treasury. The Treasury has been considerably less successful in selling its gold medallions. In 1984, the department terminated its agreement with J. Aron and Company, a private precious-metals firm that had contracted in 1983 to market the medallions.

Coin Sets. The U.S. Bureau of the Mint, which ceased issuing mint coin sets in 1982, resumed production of the sets in 1984. Sets — consisting of a cent, nickel, dime, quarter, and half dollar — were offered by the Philadelphia and Denver mints. The coins all bore P or D mint marks, except for the Philadelphia-made cent, which had

A new Chinese 1,000-yuan (about $360) gold coin depicts a giant panda on one side and the Temple of Heaven in Beijing (Peking) on the other.

no mint mark. Because the Susan B. Anthony dollar was no longer included in the sets, the price of a set was reduced from $11 to $7.

Mint officials announced that coins with accidentally missing mint marks will no longer occur because mint marks will now be part of the *hub*—the cylindrical piece of steel on which the coin design is carved and from which the dies are made. Previously, mint marks had been added to individual dies and were sometimes omitted by mistake.

Auctions. At an estate sale in New York City in January, an 1804 silver dollar sold for $180,000, an 1849 $10 gold piece brought $120,000, and a 1794 "Flowing Hair" silver dollar, thought to be the finest in existence, went for $240,000.

At Auction '84, held July 25 and 26 in Dearborn, Mich., more than 2,000 coins were sold, for a total of more than $10 million. Sales included $110,000 paid for an 1855 gold $50 proof coin and $85,000 paid for a 1794 silver dollar.

A coin from the ancient world—a gold medallion minted in A.D. 297 to honor the Roman Emperor Constantius I, father of Constantine the Great—sold for $75,000 at a May auction in Beverly Hills, Calif. At the same sale, a silver coin minted in 42 B.C. and bearing the likeness of Marcus Junius Brutus, one of Julius Caesar's assassins, fetched $45,000. Lee Martin

In WORLD BOOK, see COIN COLLECTING.

COLOMBIA. President Belisario Betancur achieved worldwide recognition in 1984 for his pragmatic and conciliatory peacemaking efforts. Domestically, Betancur negotiated a historic truce between the government and leftist guerrillas, virtually ending more than 30 years of political violence. Internationally, Betancur played a leading role in the Contadora Group, a coalition of four Latin-American nations that have proposed a Central American peace settlement.

Guerrilla Accords. On August 24, guerrillas belonging to the Movement of April 19 signed a peace pact with the Betancur administration, pledging to respect a six-month truce. The previous day, a less well-known rebel group, the Popular Liberation Army, signed a similar armistice. It was the first time that a Latin-American nation had successfully completed an armistice with leftist rebels.

The peace pacts capped a bold initiative that President Betancur had begun early in his administration, in November 1982, when he called for a "national dialogue" to end the internal fighting. On March 28, 1984, Colombia's oldest and largest guerrilla organization, the Armed Revolutionary Forces of Colombia (FARC), had set the process in motion by agreeing to a one-year truce, which began on May 28. Still in the field were the National Liberation Army—a small rebel group—and a

breakaway group from FARC, which refused any accord with the Colombian government.

Despite these holdouts, the agreements included nearly all of the estimated 30,000 guerrillas in Colombia and represented a significant step toward peace. The armistices provided for joint monitoring of a cease-fire, and the government agreed to seek amnesty for all guerrillas.

Drug Traffic. On March 10, Colombian police swept down in aircraft on a cocaine-processing center in the jungle to make the largest drug seizure in history. The police arrested 40 people and seized about 13.8 short tons (12.5 metric tons) of cocaine with a retail value of $1.2 billion.

Stung by such raids and facing extradition to the United States, seven Colombian drug dealers met secretly with Colombia's Attorney General Carlos Jimenez Gomez in Panama in May, it was revealed on July 5. The drug dealers were said to control 80 per cent of Colombia's illegal drug trade and to earn an estimated $2 billion annually. They sought amnesty in return for mending their ways and investing their profits in legal business ventures in Colombia. The government rejected the offer. Nathan A. Haverstock

See also LATIN AMERICA (Facts in Brief Table). In WORLD BOOK, see COLOMBIA.

COLORADO. See STATE GOVERNMENT.

COMMON MARKET. See EUROPE.

COMMUNICATIONS. The breakup of the American Telephone and Telegraph Company (AT&T) on Jan. 1, 1984, changed telephone service dramatically throughout the United States. The breakup stemmed from the 1982 settlement of an antitrust suit brought by the United States Department of Justice. AT&T agreed to combine its 22 local phone companies into seven independent regional firms. In exchange, the government agreed to lift a ban against AT&T's entering the computer field.

After the breakup, most of AT&T's 1 million employees—who made up the United States largest corporate work force—stayed on their jobs. The breakup had little immediate, obvious impact on telephone users, though it contributed to a rise in telephone bills for many customers.

Congress headed off even bigger price hikes in 1984, however. Telephone companies have to pay fees to hook up telephones to long-distance networks. In 1983, the Federal Communications Commission (FCC) had declared that it would allow telephone companies to pass along hookup costs to their customers by adding *access charges*, starting at $2 per month for residential users, to telephone bills. The FCC decision was to take effect on April 3, 1984.

Congressional opponents of the access-charge plan claimed that it would shift costs of telephone

The breakup of AT&T on Jan. 1, 1984, brought increasing competition from lower-priced long-distance services and other communications firms.

service from business users to residential users. The FCC allowed telephone companies to begin charging large businesses $6 per month in May 1984. On December 19, the FCC voted to allow a charge of $1 per month for residences and small businesses, beginning in June 1985. The charge would be allowed to rise to $2 in June 1986.

AT&T's efforts to establish itself in the computer field, once the ban on such activity was lifted, met with mixed success in 1984. It had trouble getting its own computer business off the ground, but it had improved its position in December 1983 by buying 25 per cent of Olivetti and Company, an Italian electronics firm.

More Competition. International Business Machines Corporation (IBM) intensified its competition in telecommunications, raising its stake in a long-distance services firm, Satellite Business Systems, from one-third to a controlling interest. IBM also said it would buy the 77 per cent of Rolm Corporation it did not already own. Rolm makes telecommunications equipment.

The spin-off companies from AT&T opened up a gigantic new U.S. market by purchasing an increasing amount of equipment from firms other than AT&T. Companies from other countries, such as NEC Corporation of Japan and Northern Telecom Canada Limited, took advantage of this opening. Competition in the long-distance field also intensified as local phone companies began a two-year process of making it easier for customers to hook up with long-distance competitors of AT&T.

Cable Television prospects in the United States improved on October 30 when President Ronald Reagan signed the nation's first major cable bill. Industry experts viewed the law as a positive development because it offered cable companies and investors a measure of certainty about the future of cable television. The bill ended a long debate on the roles of cable operators and city governments in setting rates. The bill ends local control of rates in two years. It also provides the first clear guidelines for cities to use in determining whether to renew cable franchises.

Direct Broadcast Satellites. The collapse on November 30 of a plan to merge the competing direct broadcast satellite (DBS) operations of Communications Satellite Corporation (COMSAT) and United Satellite Communications, Incorporated, raised questions about the future of DBS in the United States. Direct broadcast satellites relay programs from ground stations to small dish-type antennas on rooftops. United had begun DBS service in the spring of 1984.   Merrill Brown

See also TELEVISION. In WORLD BOOK, see COMMUNICATION.

COMOROS. See AFRICA.

COMPUTER technology continued to develop as a branch of the technology of information storage and movement in 1984, and the several branches of the larger technology continued to merge. For example, it became difficult in 1984 to discuss computer technology without mentioning the technology of the *integrated circuits* (*IC's*) that process data in computers and transmit information to and from computers in data-communications networks.

An IC is an assembly of electronic components built into a single piece of material by various etching and coating processes. Most commercially available IC's are built into silicon chips as small as a fingernail.

One extremely important kind of IC is the *microprocessor*, a virtually complete computer on a chip. Microprocessors have become so important because they perform the control, arithmetic, and logic operations of extremely popular — and extremely numerous — small computers. These machines include desktop computers used in business and industry, personal computers that perform business and some household functions, and home computers.

Microprocessor Research in 1984 moved computer technology closer to the development of the *engineering work station* — a desktop computer for product design, engineering, and manufacturing. Computer experts believe that eventually these three functions plus inventory maintenance and shipping control will be available from a system made up of engineering work stations, high-capacity memory units, and high-speed communication components.

The key to the development of engineering work stations is the *32-bit microprocessor*, which can process 32 *bits* simultaneously. (A bit is a 0 or 1 in the binary numeration system that computers use.) Present computers use 8- and 16-bit microprocessors. A typical 16-bit chip can carry out 500,000 to 1 million instructions per second. The 32-bit chip can handle 2 million to 3 million.

Supercomputers. United States and Japanese firms continued their struggle for world supremacy in *supercomputers* — machines that are much faster and store much more data than do ordinary computers. On the U.S. side of the competition were the two firms that once monopolized the high-speed, high-capacity computer business — Control Data Corporation and Cray Research, Incorporated, both of Minneapolis, Minn. Opposing them were three of the largest computer manufacturers in Japan — Fujitsu Limited, Hitachi Limited, and NEC Corporation. Also active were research and development laboratories taking part in Ja-

Drawing by Modell; © 1984, The New Yorker Magazine, Inc.

"It must be you. The computer, it so happens, is user-friendly."

pan's Fifth Generation Computer Project — a joint effort of government and industry — and similar projects in the European Community (EC or Common Market) and Great Britain. (Britain is a member of the EC but has its own project.)

More Memory. To keep up with the higher speeds of tomorrow's computers, manufacturers are increasing the amount of data their systems can store and are cutting *access time* — the time a computer needs to obtain information from them. In 1984, manufacturers of disk-type storage systems experimented with such exotic materials as cobalt chromium, tellurium, and selenium, which can store more information than the iron used in today's disks. Manufacturers slashed access time by improving recording and playback methods. One promising technique is *perpendicular recording*, which stores data on a disk in an unusual manner. An ordinary memory disk — a flexible unit called a *floppy disk* — stores data in regions of magnetism located on the disk surface. The rigid disk used in perpendicular recording, however, has magnetic storage regions that are perpendicular to the surface. Each perpendicular region uses less surface area than does a region on a floppy, so the rigid disk's scanning time is much shorter than that of the floppy disk.

One disadvantage of perpendicular recording is that the rigid disk is more expensive than a floppy disk. In 1984, researchers tried to work their way around this disadvantage by developing hybrid disks that combine the high-performance features of the rigid disk with the cheapness of the floppy.

Optical Fibers. Researchers continued to improve the ability of *optical fibers* — hair-thin strands of glass — to transmit information over long distances. Optical fibers transmit information in the form of extremely brief flashes of light at rates of tens of millions of light pulses per second. Such fibers can carry much more data than can copper cables of the same thickness, so the strands have tremendous potential as transmission lines in data-communications systems. Designers of data-communications systems want to use this potential in systems spread out over long distances. The major difficulty with transmitting signals through extremely long optical fibers is that the individual pulses tend to overlap, resulting in a loss of data.

In 1984, researchers improved the ability of a certain type of strand — the *single-mode fiber* — to transmit signals clearly over long distances. This type of fiber is made of two kinds of material — a core substance and a cladding. Experiments with various materials and techniques led to an increase in transmission distance from about 60 to 90 miles (100 to 150 kilometers).   Howard Wolff

See also ELECTRONICS. In WORLD BOOK, see COMPUTER.

CONGO. See AFRICA.

CONGRESS OF THE UNITED STATES. When the second session of the 98th Congress convened on Jan. 23, 1984, members immediately began grumbling about money — how much to spend and how much to borrow to keep the government functioning. And when Congress adjourned on October 12, it did so only after a spectacular battle over money that came close to stripping the government simultaneously of both spending and borrowing authority. It was an untidy wind-up to an election-year session that left more than half a dozen major legislative issues unresolved. Among postponed items of business were immigration reform, a strengthening of civil rights programs, banking and natural gas deregulation, and the financing of toxic-waste cleanup.

Few Major Confrontations Erupted during the year between the legislators and President Ronald Reagan. The President received less money than he wanted for defense, however, and was forced to let Congress defer until 1985 major decisions on producing the MX missile, financing antigovernment guerrillas in Nicaragua, and ratifying the Genocide Convention — a 36-year-old United Nations treaty outlawing *genocide* (the systematic extermination of a racial or cultural group).

The Senate also postponed considering the nomination of White House counselor Edwin Meese III to succeed William French Smith as attorney general of the United States. The Senate Judiciary Committee had held up the nomination after questioning Meese's finances. But a court-appointed investigator reported in September that he could find "no basis" for indicting Meese on any of the 11 charges raised by the committee.

School prayer continued to claim much of Congress's attention. Although the Senate in March rejected a proposed constitutional amendment to permit organized spoken prayer in public schools, both the Senate and House of Representatives later voted to permit "silent prayer" by students. Students obviously could pray silently with or without legislation, but the measure permitted lawmakers to claim they had voted for school prayer.

The session included several notable achievements. Congress approved a major expansion of wilderness areas, strengthened the health warnings on cigarette packs, overhauled federal criminal laws, gave women improved pension rights, revised the nation's bankruptcy laws, and encouraged states to raise the minimum drinking age to 21.

Money Was the Dominant Topic during the year. In his January 25 State of the Union message to Congress, Reagan called for a bipartisan effort to reduce the federal budget deficit by $100 billion over a three-year period. He said the reductions would represent a "down payment" on

Senator Jesse A. Helms (R., N.C.) celebrates his win over Governor James B. Hunt, Jr., in one of 1984's most costly and hard-fought Senate races.

the deficit, which economists predicted would total more than $500 billion by the end of 1987 if no effective action were taken.

Budget talks between White House officials and a bipartisan congressional delegation began on Feb. 8, 1984. James A. Baker III, White House chief of staff, proposed a three-year tax increase of $44.8 billion and spending cuts of $45.5 billion. He contended that such measures would keep interest rates from rising and save an additional $10 billion in interest payments on the national debt, thus achieving $100 billion in savings.

The need for action was underscored on February 22, when the nonpartisan Congressional Budget Office (CBO) estimated that deficits would increase from $192 billion in fiscal 1985 — which ends on Sept. 30, 1985 — to $248 billion in fiscal 1989. The CBO projection differed sharply from Reagan's claims that annual deficits would drop from $180 billion to $123 billion in the same period. Reagan's prediction, however, was based on his optimistic expectation that the United States would experience faster economic growth, continually declining inflation, and lower interest rates.

With many Congress members calling for a larger down payment on the deficit than the President had proposed, the bipartisan negotiations broke down on February 28 after four meetings. But Republican congressional leaders persisted

and, at a March 15 meeting, reached an agreement with Reagan on a revised budget that they said would pare deficits by $150 billion over three years.

Their plan called for tax increases totaling $48-billion and $83.4 billion in spending cuts, the latter to be achieved in part by limiting the annual growth of defense outlays to 7.5 per cent after inflation, down from Reagan's original request for a 13 per cent increase. In addition, lower interest rates were expected to save about $18 billion over the three years.

Speaker of the House Thomas P. (Tip) O'Neill, Jr. (D., Mass.), welcomed the package as "the first crack in the wall." Despite that apparent endorsement, the Democratic-controlled House rejected the proposal, and on April 5 it adopted its own plan to reduce the deficit by $182 billion over three years. The House measure reduced annual defense increases to 3.5 per cent after inflation. In the Republican-controlled Senate, a Democratic deficit-reduction plan was defeated in a 49 to 49 tie vote, and a modified version of the March 15 plan agreed on by Reagan and the Republican congressional leaders finally was adopted on May 17, 65 to 32. It called for a 7 per cent after-inflation increase in defense spending.

Both the Senate and House had proposed deficit-reducing tax increases of nearly $50 billion. With that in mind, Reagan told reporters at a June 14 news conference that he would want firm guarantees of spending cuts before signing a tax hike. Although the guarantees he sought were not forthcoming, Reagan on July 18, for the third time in four years, signed legislation incorporating major income tax revisions. The measure, called the Deficit Reduction Act of 1984, had been passed by large majorities of the House and Senate on June 27. It affected more than 200 provisions of the Internal Revenue Code and was designed to raise about $50 billion in taxes through 1987. In addition, the measure ordered $13 billion in spending cuts, mostly through changes in the Medicare and Medicaid health care programs for the elderly and the disabled. But cuts in other domestic programs and smaller increases in defense outlays were not included.

The Year's Second Money Battle erupted on two fronts as adjournment neared. Not only did Congress have to nail down the promised savings in defense and other programs, but the mounting deficits also made it necessary to boost the ceiling on the national debt.

Because Congress had not passed all the appropriations bills called for in the 1985 budget by October 1 — the start of the 1985 fiscal year — it began wrestling with a single *omnibus bill* (a bill that includes many things) to finance most federal departments and agencies, including the Depart-

Members of the United States Senate

The Senate of the first session of the 99th Congress consisted of 53 Republicans and 47 Democrats when it convened in January 1985. Senators shown starting their term in 1985 were elected for the first time in the Nov. 6, 1984, elections. Others shown ending their current terms in 1991 were reelected to the Senate in the 1984 balloting. The second date in each listing shows when the term of a previously elected senator expires.

State	Term	State	Term	State	Term
Alabama		**Louisiana**		**Ohio**	
Howell T. Heflin, D.	1979 — 1991	Russell B. Long, D.	1948 — 1987	John H. Glenn, Jr., D.	1975 — 1987
Jeremiah Denton, R.	1981 — 1987	J. Bennett Johnston, Jr., D.	1972 — 1991	Howard M. Metzenbaum, D.	1977 — 1989
Alaska		**Maine**		**Oklahoma**	
Theodore F. Stevens, R.	1968 — 1991	William S. Cohen, R.	1979 — 1991	David L. Boren, D.	1979 — 1991
Frank H. Murkowski, R.	1981 — 1987	George J. Mitchell, D.	1980 — 1989	Don Nickles, R.	1981 — 1987
Arizona		**Maryland**		**Oregon**	
Barry Goldwater, R.	1969 — 1987	Charles McC. Mathias, Jr., R.	1969 — 1987	Mark O. Hatfield, R.	1967 — 1991
Dennis DeConcini, D.	1977 — 1989	Paul S. Sarbanes, D.	1977 — 1989	Bob Packwood, R.	1969 — 1987
Arkansas		**Massachusetts**		**Pennsylvania**	
Dale Bumpers, D.	1975 — 1987	Edward M. Kennedy, D.	1962 — 1989	John Heinz, R.	1977 — 1989
David H. Pryor, D.	1979 — 1991	John F. Kerry, D.	1985 — 1991	Arlen Specter, R.	1981 — 1987
California		**Michigan**		**Rhode Island**	
Alan Cranston, D.	1969 — 1987	Donald W. Riegle, Jr., D.	1977 — 1989	Claiborne Pell, D.	1961 — 1991
Pete Wilson, R.	1983 — 1989	Carl Levin, D.	1979 — 1991	John H. Chafee, R.	1977 — 1989
Colorado		**Minnesota**		**South Carolina**	
Gary W. Hart, D.	1975 — 1987	David F. Durenberger, R.	1978 — 1989	Strom Thurmond, R.	1956 — 1991
William L. Armstrong, R.	1979 — 1991	Rudy Boschwitz, R.	1979 — 1991	Ernest F. Hollings, D.	1966 — 1987
Connecticut		**Mississippi**		**South Dakota**	
Lowell P. Weicker, Jr., R.	1971 — 1989	John C. Stennis, D.	1947 — 1989	Larry Pressler, R.	1979 — 1991
Christopher J. Dodd, D.	1981 — 1987	Thad Cochran, R.	1979 — 1991	James Abdnor, R.	1981 — 1987
Delaware		**Missouri**		**Tennessee**	
William V. Roth, Jr., R.	1971 — 1989	Thomas F. Eagleton, D.	1968 — 1987	James R. Sasser, D.,	1977 — 1989
Joseph R. Biden, Jr., D.	1973 — 1991	John C. Danforth, R.	1977 — 1989	Albert A. Gore, Jr., D.	1985 — 1991
Florida		**Montana**		**Texas**	
Lawton Chiles, D.	1971 — 1989	John Melcher, D.	1977 — 1989	Lloyd M. Bentsen, D.	1971 — 1989
Paula Hawkins, R.	1981 — 1987	Max Baucus, D.	1979 — 1991	Phil Gramm, R.	1985 — 1991
Georgia		**Nebraska**		**Utah**	
Sam Nunn, D.	1972 — 1991	Edward Zorinsky, D.	1977 — 1989	Edwin Jacob Garn, R.	1975 — 1987
Mack Mattingly, R.	1981 — 1987	J. James Exon, D.	1979 — 1991	Orrin G. Hatch, R.	1977 — 1989
Hawaii		**Nevada**		**Vermont**	
Daniel K. Inouye, D.	1963 — 1987	Paul Laxalt, R.	1975 — 1987	Robert T. Stafford, R.	1971 — 1989
Spark M. Matsunaga, D.	1977 — 1989	Chic Hecht, R.	1983 — 1989	Patrick J. Leahy, D.	1975 — 1987
Idaho		**New Hampshire**		**Virginia**	
James A. McClure, R.	1973 — 1991	Gordon J. Humphrey, R.	1979 — 1991	John W. Warner, R.	1979 — 1991
Steve Symms, R.	1981 — 1987	Warren Rudman, R.	1981 — 1987	Paul S. Trible, Jr., R.	1983 — 1989
Illinois		**New Jersey**		**Washington**	
Alan J. Dixon, D.	1981 — 1987	Bill Bradley, D.	1979 — 1991	Slade Gorton, R.	1981 — 1987
Paul Simon, D.	1985 — 1991	Frank R. Lautenberg, D.	1983 — 1989	Daniel J. Evans, R.	1983 — 1989
Indiana		**New Mexico**		**West Virginia**	
Richard G. Lugar, R.	1977 — 1989	Pete V. Domenici, R.	1973 — 1991	Robert C. Byrd, D.	1959 — 1989
Dan Quayle, R.	1981 — 1987	Jeff Bingaman, D.	1983 — 1989	John D. Rockefeller IV, D.	1985 — 1991
Iowa		**New York**		**Wisconsin**	
Charles E. Grassley, R.	1981 — 1987	Daniel P. Moynihan, D.	1977 — 1989	William Proxmire, D.	1957 — 1989
Tom Harkin, D.	1985 — 1991	Alfonse M. D'Amato, R.	1981 — 1987	Robert W. Kasten, Jr., R.	1981 — 1987
Kansas		**North Carolina**		**Wyoming**	
Robert J. Dole, R.	1969 — 1987	Jesse A. Helms, R.	1973 — 1991	Malcolm Wallop, R.	1977 — 1989
Nancy Landon Kassebaum, R.	1979 — 1991	John P. East, R.	1981 — 1987	Alan K. Simpson, R.	1979 — 1991
Kentucky		**North Dakota**			
Wendell H. Ford, D.	1975 — 1987	Quentin N. Burdick, D.	1960 — 1989		
Mitch McConnell, R.	1985 — 1991	Mark Andrews, R.	1981 — 1987		

Members of the United States House of Representatives

The House of Representatives of the first session of the 99th Congress consisted of 252 Democrats and 182 Republicans (not including representatives from American Samoa, the District of Columbia, Guam, Puerto Rico, and the Virgin Islands), with 1 seat being contested, when it convened in January 1985, compared with 267 Democrats and 167 Republicans, with 1 seat vacant, when the second session of the 98th Congress convened. This table shows congressional district, legislator, and party affiliation. Asterisk (*) denotes those who served in the 98th Congress; dagger (†) denotes "at large."

Alabama
1. H. L. Callahan, R.
2. William L. Dickinson, R.*
3. Bill Nichols, D.*
4. Tom Bevill, D.*
5. Ronnie G. Flippo, D.*
6. Ben Erdreich, D.*
7. Richard C. Shelby, D.*

Alaska
†Donald E. Young, R.*

Arizona
1. John S. McCain III, R.*
2. Morris K. Udall, D.*
3. Bob Stump, R.*
4. Eldon D. Rudd, R.*
5. Jim Kolbe, R.

Arkansas
1. Bill Alexander, D.*
2. Tommy Robinson, D.
3. John P. Hammerschmidt, R.*
4. Beryl F. Anthony, Jr., D.*

California
1. Douglas H. Bosco, D.*
2. Eugene A. Chappie, R.*
3. Robert T. Matsui, D.*
4. Vic Fazio, D.*
5. Sala Burton, D.*
6. Barbara Boxer, D.*
7. George Miller, D.*
8. Ronald V. Dellums, D.*
9. Fortney H. (Pete) Stark, D.*
10. Don Edwards, D.*
11. Tom Lantos, D.*
12. Edwin V. W. Zschau, R.*
13. Norman Y. Mineta, D.*
14. Norman D. Shumway, R.*
15. Tony Coelho, D.*
16. Leon E. Panetta, D.*
17. Charles Pashayan, Jr., R.*
18. Richard H. Lehman, D.*
19. Robert J. Lagomarsino, R.*
20. William M. Thomas, R.*
21. Bobbi Fiedler, R.*
22. Carlos J. Moorhead, R.*
23. Anthony C. Beilenson, D.*
24. Henry A. Waxman, D.*
25. Edward R. Roybal, D.*
26. Howard L. Berman, D.*
27. Mel Levine, D.*
28. Julian C. Dixon, D.*
29. Augustus F. (Gus) Hawkins, D.*
30. Matthew G. Martinez, D.*
31. Mervyn M. Dymally, D.*
32. Glenn M. Anderson, D.*
33. David Dreier, R.*
34. Esteban E. Torres, D.*
35. Jerry Lewis, R.*
36. George E. Brown, Jr., D.*
37. Alfred A. McCandless, R.*
38. Robert K. Dornan, R.

39. William E. Dannemeyer, R.*
40. Robert E. Badham, R.*
41. William D. Lowery, R.*
42. Daniel E. Lungren, R.*
43. Ronald C. Packard, R.*
44. Jim Bates, D.*
45. Duncan L. Hunter, R.*

Colorado
1. Patricia Schroeder, D.*
2. Timothy E. Wirth, D.*
3. Michael L. Strang, R.
4. Hank Brown, R.*
5. Kenneth B. Kramer, R.*
6. Daniel Schaefer, R.*

Connecticut
1. Barbara B. Kennelly, D.*
2. Samuel Gejdenson, D.*
3. Bruce A. Morrison, D.*
4. Stewart B. McKinney, R.*
5. John G. Rowland, R.
6. Nancy L. Johnson, R.*

Delaware
†Thomas R. Carper, D.*

Florida
1. Earl Hutto, D.*
2. Don Fuqua, D.*
3. Charles E. Bennett, D.*
4. Bill Chappell, Jr., D.*
5. Bill McCollum, R.*
6. Kenneth H. (Buddy) MacKay, D.*
7. Sam M. Gibbons, D.*
8. C. W. Bill Young, R.*
9. Michael Bilirakis, R.*
10. Andy Ireland, R.*
11. Bill Nelson, D.*
12. Thomas F. Lewis, R.*
13. Connie Mack III, R.*
14. Daniel A. Mica, D.*
15. E. Clay Shaw, Jr., R.*
16. Lawrence J. Smith, D.*
17. William Lehman, D.*
18. Claude D. Pepper, D.*
19. Dante B. Fascell, D.*

Georgia
1. Lindsay Thomas, D.*
2. Charles F. Hatcher, D.*
3. Richard B. Ray, D.*
4. Pat Swindall, R.
5. Wyche Fowler, Jr., D.*
6. Newt Gingrich, R.*
7. George Darden, D.*
8. J. Roy Rowland, D.*
9. Edgar L. Jenkins, D.*
10. Doug Barnard, Jr., D.*

Hawaii
1. Cecil Heftel, D.*
2. Daniel K. Akaka, D.*

Idaho
1. Larry Craig, R.*
2. Richard Stallings, D.

Illinois
1. Charles A. Hayes, D.*
2. Gus Savage, D.*
3. Marty Russo, D.*
4. George M. O'Brien, R.*
5. William O. Lipinski, D.*
6. Henry J. Hyde, R.*
7. Cardiss Collins, D.*
8. Dan Rostenkowski, D.*
9. Sidney R. Yates, D.*
10. John Edward Porter, R.*
11. Frank Annunzio, D.*
12. Philip M. Crane, R.*
13. Harris W. Fawell, R.
14. John E. Grotberg, R.
15. Edward R. Madigan, R.*
16. Lynn M. Martin, R.*
17. Lane A. Evans, D.*
18. Robert H. Michel, R.*
19. Terry L. Bruce, D.
20. Richard J. Durbin, D.*
21. Melvin Price, D.*
22. Kenneth J. Gray, D.

Indiana
1. Peter J. Visclosky, D.
2. Philip R. Sharp, D.*
3. John Patrick Hiler, R.*
4. Dan R. Coats, R.*
5. Elwood H. Hillis, R.*
6. Danny L. Burton, R.*
7. John T. Myers, R.*
8. contested
9. Lee H. Hamilton, D.*
10. Andrew Jacobs, Jr., D.*

Iowa
1. Jim Leach, R.*
2. Thomas J. Tauke, R.*
3. Cooper Evans, R.*
4. Neal Smith, D.*
5. Jim Ross Lightfoot, R.
6. Berkley Bedell, D.*

Kansas
1. Pat Roberts, R.*
2. James C. Slattery, D.*
3. Jan Meyers, R.
4. Dan Glickman, D.*
5. Bob Whittaker, R.*

Kentucky
1. Carroll Hubbard, Jr., D.*
2. William H. Natcher, D.*
3. Romano L. Mazzoli, D.*
4. M. G. (Gene) Snyder, R.*
5. Harold (Hal) Rogers, R.*
6. Larry J. Hopkins, R.*
7. Carl C. (Chris) Perkins, D.

Louisiana
1. Robert L. Livingston, R.*
2. Corinne C. (Lindy) Boggs, D.*
3. W. J. (Billy) Tauzin, D.*
4. Charles Roemer, D.*
5. Thomas J. (Jerry) Huckaby, D.*
6. W. Henson Moore, R.*
7. John B. Breaux, D.*
8. Gillis W. Long, D.*

Maine
1. John R. McKernan, Jr., R.*
2. Olympia J. Snowe, R.*

Maryland
1. Roy P. Dyson, D.*
2. Helen Delich Bentley, R.
3. Barbara A. Mikulski, D.*
4. Marjorie S. Holt, R.*
5. Steny H. Hoyer, D.*
6. Beverly B. Byron, D.*
7. Parren J. Mitchell, D.*
8. Michael D. Barnes, D.*

Massachusetts
1. Silvio O. Conte, R.*
2. Edward P. Boland, D.*
3. Joseph D. Early, D.*
4. Barney Frank, D.*
5. Chester G. Atkins, D.
6. Nicholas Mavroules, D.*
7. Edward J. Markey, D.*
8. Thomas P. O'Neill, Jr., D.*
9. John Joseph Moakley, D.*
10. Gerry E. Studds, D.*
11. Brian J. Donnelly, D.*

Michigan
1. John Conyers, Jr., D.*
2. Carl D. Pursell, R.*
3. Howard E. Wolpe, D.*
4. Mark D. Siljander, R.*
5. Paul B. Henry, R.
6. Bob Carr, D.*
7. Dale E. Kildee, D.*
8. Bob Traxler, D.*
9. Guy Vander Jagt, R.*
10. Bill Schuette, R.
11. Robert W. Davis, R.*
12. David E. Bonior, D.*
13. George W. Crockett, Jr., D.*
14. Dennis M. Hertel, D.*
15. William D. Ford, D.*
16. John D. Dingell, D.*
17. Sander M. Levin, D.*
18. William S. Broomfield, R.*

Minnesota
1. Timothy J. Penny, D.*
2. Vin Weber, R.*
3. Bill Frenzel, R.*
4. Bruce F. Vento, D.*
5. Martin O. Sabo, D.*
6. Gerry Sikorski, D.*
7. Arlan Stangeland, R.*
8. James L. Oberstar, D.*

Mississippi
1. Jamie L. Whitten, D.*
2. William W. Franklin, R.*
3. G. V. (Sonny) Montgomery, D.*
4. Wayne Dowdy, D.*
5. Trent Lott, R.*

Missouri
1. William L. (Bill) Clay, D.*
2. Robert A. Young, D.*
3. Richard A. Gephardt, D.*
4. Ike Skelton, D.*
5. Alan D. Wheat, D.*
6. E. Thomas Coleman, R.*
7. Gene Taylor, R.*
8. Bill Emerson, R.*
9. Harold L. Volkmer, D.*

Montana
1. Pat Williams, D.*
2. Ron Marlenee, R.*

Nebraska
1. Doug Bereuter, R.*
2. Hal Daub, R.*
3. Virginia Smith, R.*

Nevada
1. Harry M. Reid, D.*
2. Barbara F. Vucanovich, R.*

New Hampshire
1. Robert C. Smith, R.
2. Judd Gregg, R.*

New Jersey
1. James J. Florio, D.*
2. William J. Hughes, D.*
3. James J. Howard, D.*
4. Christopher H. Smith, R.*
5. Marge Roukema, R.*
6. Bernard J. Dwyer, D.*
7. Matthew J. Rinaldo, R.*
8. Robert A. Roe, D.*
9. Robert G. Torricelli, D.*
10. Peter W. Rodino, Jr., D.*
11. Dean A. Gallo, R.
12. Jim Courter, R.*
13. H. James Saxton, R.
14. Frank J. Guarini, D.*

New Mexico
1. Manuel Lujan, Jr., R.*
2. Joe Skeen, R.*
3. William B. Richardson, D.*

New York
1. William Carney, R.*
2. Thomas J. Downey, D.*
3. Robert J. Mrazek, D.*
4. Norman F. Lent, R.*
5. Raymond J. McGrath, R.*
6. Joseph P. Addabbo, D.*
7. Gary L. Ackerman, D.*
8. James H. Scheuer, D.*
9. Thomas J. Manton, D.
10. Charles E. Schumer, D.*
11. Edolphus Towns, D.*
12. Major R. Owens, D.*
13. Stephen J. Solarz, D.*

14. Guy V. Molinari, R.*
15. Bill Green, R.*
16. Charles B. Rangel, D.*
17. Ted Weiss, D.*
18. Robert Garcia, D.*
19. Mario Biaggi, D.*
20. Joseph D. DioGuardi, R.
21. Hamilton Fish, Jr., R.*
22. Benjamin A. Gilman, R.*
23. Samuel S. Stratton, D.*
24. Gerald B. Solomon, R.*
25. Sherwood L. Boehlert, R.*
26. David O'B. Martin, R.*
27. George C. Wortley, R.*
28. Matthew F. McHugh, D.*
29. Frank Horton, R.*
30. Fred J. Eckert, R.
31. Jack Kemp, R.*
32. John J. LaFalce, D.*
33. Henry J. Nowak, D.*
34. Stan Lundine, D.*

North Carolina
1. Walter B. Jones, D.*
2. Tim Valentine, D.*
3. Charles O. Whitley, D.*
4. William W. Cobey, Jr., R.
5. Stephen L. Neal, D.*
6. Howard Coble, R.
7. Charlie Rose, D.*
8. W. G. (Bill) Hefner, D.*
9. J. Alex McMillan III, R.
10. James T. Broyhill, R.*
11. William H. Hendon, R.

North Dakota
†Byron L. Dorgan, D.*

Ohio
1. Thomas A. Luken, D.*
2. Willis D. Gradison, Jr., R.*
3. Tony P. Hall, D.*
4. Michael G. Oxley, R.*
5. Delbert L. Latta, R.*
6. Bob McEwen, R.*
7. Michael DeWine, R.*
8. Thomas N. Kindness, R.*
9. Marcy Kaptur, D.*
10. Clarence E. Miller, R.*
11. Dennis E. Eckart, D.*
12. John R. Kasich, R.*
13. Donald J. Pease, D.*
14. John F. Seiberling, D.*
15. Chalmers P. Wylie, R.*
16. Ralph Regula, R.*
17. James Traficant, Jr., D.
18. Douglas Applegate, D.*
19. Edward F. Feighan, D.*
20. Mary Rose Oakar, D.*
21. Louis Stokes, D.*

Oklahoma
1. James R. Jones, D.*
2. Mike Synar, D.*
3. Wesley W. Watkins, D.*
4. Dave McCurdy, D.*
5. Mickey Edwards, R.*
6. Glenn English, D.*

Oregon
1. Les AuCoin, D.*
2. Robert F. Smith, R.*

3. Ron Wyden, D.*
4. Jim Weaver, D.*
5. Denny Smith, R.*

Pennsylvania
1. Thomas M. Foglietta, D.*
2. William H. (Bill) Gray III, D.*
3. Robert A. Borski, Jr., D.*
4. Joseph P. Kolter, D.*
5. Richard T. Schulze, R.*
6. Gus Yatron, D.*
7. Bob Edgar, D.*
8. Peter H. Kostmayer, D.*
9. E. G. (Bud) Shuster, R.*
10. Joseph M. McDade, R.*
11. Paul E. Kanjorski, D.
12. John P. Murtha, D.*
13. Lawrence Coughlin, R.*
14. William J. Coyne, D.*
15. Don Ritter, R.*
16. Robert S. Walker, R.*
17. George W. Gekas, R.*
18. Doug Walgren, D.*
19. William F. Goodling, R.*
20. Joseph M. Gaydos, D.*
21. Thomas J. Ridge, R.*
22. Austin J. Murphy, D.*
23. William F. Clinger, Jr., R.*

Rhode Island
1. Fernand J. St. Germain, D.*
2. Claudine Schneider, R.*

South Carolina
1. Thomas F. Harnett, R.*
2. Floyd Spence, R.*
3. Butler Derrick, D.*
4. Carroll A. Campbell, Jr., R.*
5. John McK. Spratt, D.*
6. Robert M. (Robin) Tallon, D.*

South Dakota
†Thomas A. Daschle, D.*

Tennessee
1. James H. Quillen, R.*
2. John J. Duncan, R.*
3. Marilyn Lloyd, D.*
4. James H. Cooper, D.*
5. William H. Boner, D.*
6. Bart Gordon, D.
7. Donald K. Sundquist, R.*
8. Ed Jones, D.*
9. Harold E. Ford, D.*

Texas
1. Sam B. Hall, Jr., D.*
2. Charles Wilson, D.*
3. Steve Bartlett, R.*
4. Ralph M. Hall, D.*
5. John W. Bryant, D.*
6. Joe Barton, R.
7. Bill Archer, R.*
8. Jack Fields, R.*
9. Jack Brooks, D.*
10. J. J. (Jake) Pickle, D.*
11. J. Marvin Leath, D.*
12. James C. Wright, Jr., D.*
13. Beau Boulter, R.
14. Mac Sweeney, R.
15. Eligio (Kika) de la Garza, D.*
16. Ronald Coleman, D.*
17. Charles W. Stenholm, D.*

18. Mickey Leland, D.*
19. Larry Combest, R.
20. Henry B. Gonzalez, D.*
21. Tom Loeffler, R.*
22. Tom DeLay, R.
23. Albert G. Bustamante, D.
24. Martin Frost, D.*
25. Michael A. Andrews, D.*
26. Richard Armey, R.
27. Solomon P. Ortiz, D.*

Utah
1. James V. Hansen, R.*
2. David S. Monson, R.
3. Howard C. Nielson, R.*

Vermont
†James M. Jeffords, R.*

Virginia
1. Herbert H. Bateman, R.*
2. G. William Whitehurst, R.*
3. Thomas J. (Tom) Bliley, Jr., R.*
4. Norman Sisisky, D.*
5. Dan Daniel, D.*
6. James R. Olin, D.*
7. D. French Slaughter, R.
8. Stanford E. (Stan) Parris, R.*
9. Frederick C. Boucher, D.*
10. Frank R. Wolf, R.*

Washington
1. John Miller, R.
2. Al Swift, D.*
3. Don Bonker, D.*
4. Sid Morrison, R.*
5. Thomas S. Foley, D.*
6. Norman D. Dicks, D.*
7. Mike Lowry, D.*
8. Rod Chandler, R.*

West Virginia
1. Alan B. Mollohan, D.*
2. Harley O. Staggers, Jr., D.*
3. Robert E. Wise, Jr., D.*
4. Nick J. Rahall II, D.*

Wisconsin
1. Les Aspin, D.*
2. Robert W. Kastenmeier, D.*
3. Steven Gunderson, R.*
4. Gerald D. Kleczka, D.*
5. Jim Moody, D.*
6. Thomas E. Petri, R.*
7. David R. Obey, D.*
8. Toby Roth, R.*
9. F. James Sensenbrenner, Jr., R.*

Wyoming
†Dick Cheney, R.*

Nonvoting Representatives
American Samoa
Fofo I. F. Sunia, D.*

District of Columbia
Walter E. Fauntroy, D.*

Guam
Ben Blaz, R.

Puerto Rico
Baltasar Corrada, D.*

Virgin Islands
Ron de Lugo, D.*

261

ment of Defense. Because Election Day was drawing near, the lawmakers offered dozens of politically popular amendments to the bill, many representing legislation that otherwise would have died when Congress adjourned.

On October 4, as the wrangling continued, two-thirds of the government was—technically, at least—out of money. Reagan sent half a million federal workers home at midday, claiming there was no money to pay them. "You can lay this right on the majority [Democratic] party of the House of Representatives," he said. But Democrats were quick to point out that it was the Republican-controlled Senate that had missed the deadline for adopting a stopgap spending-authorization bill. By nightfall, Congress passed the temporary measure, and the government was back in business while the big money battle continued.

Complicating consideration of the omnibus appropriation was a Reagan threat to veto any measure that included $100 million for 39 so-called pork-barrel water projects, such as a dam and locks on the Columbia River in Washington state, that eventually would have cost $18 billion. House Democratic leaders reluctantly abandoned the popular projects, and the Administration, in turn, agreed to stop all aid to antigovernment guerrillas in Nicaragua for at least five months.

On October 11, the money bill, now totaling $370 billion, was passed by the House, 252 to 60. Senate approval came later that day, 78 to 11. The bill provided for an after-inflation hike of about 5 per cent in defense spending and restored some earlier Administration cuts in social welfare programs.

The bill was so laden with amendments that it weighed about 10 pounds (4.5 kilograms). Included in it was a major revision of federal criminal statutes that provides stiffer penalties for drug dealing, permits pretrial detention of some defendants, and makes the use of the insanity defense in a criminal trial more difficult.

Debt Limit Raised. With the amended spending bill out of the way, raising the debt limit by $251 billion to $1.824 trillion was all that remained to be done before adjournment. The House had approved the higher debt ceiling on October 1, and it was expected that the Senate would pass it routinely on October 12. But then a snag developed. Senate Democrats, still smarting from Republican criticism for having raised the debt limit in earlier administrations, decided to force their political opponents to bear responsibility for the new hike. Demanding a roll-call vote in the early morning hours of October 12, after many Republican senators had left Washington, D.C., Democrats took the lead in rejecting the higher debt limit, 46 to 14.

Soon after dawn, the White House dispatched

Maryland Republican Helen Delich Bentley gives the "thumbs up" sign after being elected to the U.S. House of Representatives in November.

Air Force jets to pick up some absent Republican senators, while others scrambled to book commercial flights to the capital. By afternoon, 41 Republicans were on hand. Thirty-seven voted for the higher limit, while the other 4 joined all 26 Democrats present in voting against the measure.

The Senate then cast aside its rule against applause and, before adjourning, gave a standing ovation to its retiring majority leader, Howard H. Baker, Jr., of Tennessee. Baker, 58, will head the Washington, D.C., office of a Texas law firm while considering a try for the 1988 GOP presidential nomination. Another notable 1984 retiree was Senator Jennings Randolph (D., W. Va.), 82, the longest-serving member of Congress, with 52 years on Capitol Hill.

Other Events. Spring saw an unusual battle between Speaker O'Neill and a group of Republican conservatives, led by Representative Newt Gingrich of Georgia. At the end of each day's session, the conservative group denounced House Democrats in speeches that were broadcast live by cable television to an estimated 17 million U.S. households. Because House rules required TV cameras to focus on the rostrum, viewers were unaware that speakers were addressing an empty chamber. O'Neill ordered camera operators to show the empty room. Addressing the House on May 15, O'Neill accused Gingrich of "the lowest thing that

I've heard in my 32 years here" because Gingrich had attacked Democrats who were not present. Representative John Joseph Moakley (D., Mass.), who was presiding temporarily, formally rebuked O'Neill for his language and stopped the televising of the empty chamber.

Despite the year's wrangling over money matters, the members of Congress agreed on one thing: They would get a $2,500 pay increase on Jan. 1, 1985, hiking their annual salary from $72,600 to $75,100. They assured themselves of the raise by doing nothing to change a salary recommendation made in August 1984 by Reagan.

On July 31, the House reprimanded Representative George Hansen (R., Idaho), for submitting false financial disclosure statements. The 354 to 52 action was the least severe punishment possible under House rules. Hansen had appealed an April 2 felony conviction for the same offense, for which he was sentenced to 5 to 15 months in prison and fined $40,000. Hansen was the first congressman convicted under the Ethics in Government Act of 1978.   Frank Cormier and Margot Cormier

See also UNITED STATES, GOVERNMENT OF THE; PRESIDENT OF THE UNITED STATES. In the Special Reports section, see LOBBYING THE LAWMAKERS. In WORLD BOOK, see CONGRESS OF THE UNITED STATES.

CONNECTICUT. See STATE GOVERNMENT.

CONSERVATION leaders in the United States in 1984 launched the most ambitious political campaign in the history of the U.S. environmental movement. Rafe Pomerance, president of Friends of the Earth, began the campaign at an acid rain conference in New Hampshire on January 8. Pomerance called President Ronald Reagan's environmental policy a "lemon." The League of Conservation Voters, a political action committee, said in February that environmental issues cut across party lines and would be crucial to any successful effort to beat Reagan. Marion B. Edey, executive director of the league, said on April 10 that environmental groups planned to spend $2-million—twice as much as in any past election—on the presidential and congressional races.

Reagan Defended his commitment to the environment. In a speech at the National Geographic Society in Washington, D.C., on June 19, the President charged that some conservationists had attempted to politicize the environmental movement. In July, the President went on the road to praise his Administration's environmental record, touring Maryland's Chesapeake Bay, Kentucky's Mammoth Cave, and Theodore Roosevelt Island in the Potomac River. Reagan contended that he had restored "energy and vision" to the conservation movement. Angry conservationists renewed their criticism of his environmental policies.

Conservationists showed up in record numbers at the Democratic National Convention and for the first time organized their own caucus. They cheered the environmental plank in the platform adopted on July 17. The plank called for a 50 per cent reduction in sulfur dioxide emissions to decrease acid rain, a substantial budget increase for the Environmental Protection Agency (EPA) and its effort to clean up hazardous wastes, and a strengthening of the nation's clean-air and clean-water laws. On September 19, the Sierra Club departed from its 92-year tradition of remaining nonpartisan in presidential races, endorsing Democratic candidate Walter F. Mondale.

Burford Nomination. President Reagan's efforts to build bridges to moderate environmental groups were undermined on July 2 by the announcement that he had appointed Anne M. Burford to head a national advisory committee on the environment. Burford had resigned under fire from her post as EPA administrator in March 1983 amid allegations of political manipulation and mismanagement. Following lopsided votes by both houses of Congress calling on the President to withdraw her appointment, President Reagan accepted Burford's withdrawal on August 1.

Campaign Fails. The difficulties facing anti-Reagan environmentalists were underlined in New Jersey, which has more dangerous toxic-waste dumps than any other state. Residents rated toxic-waste cleanup as their main domestic concern. Nevertheless, a League of Conservation Voters poll of 400,000 New Jersey voters showed that most voters scarcely considered environmental concerns in deciding on their presidential choice.

Although the campaign against Reagan failed, two-thirds of the candidates backed by the league won House and Senate races. One of their two main targets, Senator Roger W. Jepsen (R., Iowa), was defeated; but the other, Senator Jesse A. Helms (R., N.C.), won.

Energy Leasing Slows. The Department of the Interior announced on August 30 that it would prepare a new environmental impact statement for leasing federally owned coal, perhaps delaying the resumption of leasing until July 1985. Also on August 30, Interior Secretary William P. Clark suspended coal leasing until the department adopted procedures that a special study commission was developing.

The Supreme Court of the United States ruled on January 11 that states cannot veto decisions of the federal government to issue offshore oil leases, even if state officials expect oil drilling to cause environmental damage to their coasts. On March 27, representatives of coastal states opened a bipartisan drive in Congress to overturn the ruling. On August 2, the House of Representatives approved a one-year extension of a moratorium on

A black rhinoceros is captured in South Africa for removal to a Texas ranch for breeding in an effort to save the species, which is endangered.

offshore oil and gas drilling within 20 miles (32 kilometers) of much of the southern California coastline. The moratorium, which was attached to the 1985 Interior Department appropriations bill, also protected waters off central and northern California and portions of the Georges Bank fishing area off the Massachusetts coast. Reagan signed the bill on October 12.

The Interior Department canceled a massive sale of offshore oil leases on the Georges Bank on September 25 after only the environmentalist group Greenpeace bid on the tracts. On the same day, U.S. District Court Judge David Mazzone granted an injunction against the sale of 149 environmentally sensitive tracts totaling about 840,000 acres (340,000 hectares) in the Georges Bank.

Statue of Liberty Renovation. Officials of the $230-million fund-raising drive for the renovation of the Statue of Liberty in New York Harbor and neighboring Ellis Island announced on August 18 that almost $100 million had been raised. The elevators and stairways at the statue were closed on May 29, and on July 4 the torch was lowered. The goal of the campaign is to renovate the Statue of Liberty and the Great Hall in the registry building on Ellis Island by July 4, 1986.

Grizzly Bear Attacks on people in Glacier and Yellowstone national parks highlighted what Na-tional Park Service Director Russell E. Dickenson said was "the number-one current resource-management issue in the National Park Service." On July 26, a grizzly mauled a woman hiking in Glacier National Park. In Yellowstone National Park, a grizzly killed a woman backpacker on July 30, and a boy was mauled on August 5.

Wetlands Protection. Seven environmentalist groups urged the Reagan Administration on July 19 to seek Supreme Court review of a ruling that threatens to drastically reduce protection of ecologically fragile wetlands. On March 7, the Sixth U.S. Circuit Court of Appeals had found that, to receive protection under the Clean Water Act, wetlands must be "frequently flooded by waters from adjacent streams." Led by the National Wildlife Federation, the environmental coalition said that "millions of acres of currently regulated wetlands throughout the United States do not meet" the requirement of frequent flooding.

In December, a five-year study by the EPA and the Interior Department found that water quality in U.S. rivers and streams had improved slightly since 1979. The study also reported that bass, trout, and other sport fish were thriving in 73 per cent of such waterways. Andrew L. Newman

See also ENVIRONMENT. In the Special Reports section, see PRESERVING OUR PRAIRIE HERITAGE. In WORLD BOOK, see CONSERVATION.

CONSTITUTION OF THE UNITED STATES. A constitutional amendment that would have permitted organized spoken prayer in public schools was defeated in the U.S. Senate on March 20, 1984. The vote was 56 to 44 in favor of the measure, 11 votes short of the two-thirds majority needed for an amendment.

The amendment would have allowed public school pupils to pray individually or in groups but stipulated that "no person shall be required to participate in prayer." Despite that provision, the amendment's opponents in the Senate — 26 Democrats and 18 Republicans — said the legislation violated the principle of separation of church and state established in the First Amendment.

In 1984, three more states — Delaware, Iowa, and Louisiana — approved an amendment that would give the District of Columbia voting representation in Congress. This brought to 16 the number of states that had passed the amendment.

No additional states in 1984 approved a resolution calling for a constitutional convention to write an amendment requiring balanced federal budgets. In 1983, Missouri had become the 32nd state to vote for the measure. Thirty-four states must pass such a resolution before a constitutional convention can be held.   David L. Dreier

In WORLD BOOK, see CONSTITUTION OF THE UNITED STATES.

CONSUMERISM. The United States experienced another year of moderate price increases in 1984. By year's end, the government's Consumer Price Index (CPI) — the most widely used measure of inflation — stood about 4 per cent higher than a year earlier. Consumer purchasing power dropped by 4 per cent during the same period because income failed to keep pace with prices and taxes.

Cost increases for health care also moderated. This trend had begun even before government-imposed ceilings on hospital charges for Medicare patients took effect in October 1983. Medicare is a federal health insurance program for the elderly and the disabled. The annual increase in medical costs was 10.3 per cent in 1983, the lowest rate of increase in 10 years.

Part of the savings came from a decline in hospital use. From October 1983 to July 1984, the average length of stay in hospitals serving Medicare patients dropped 22 per cent, from 9.6 days to 7.5 days. This drop caused some health insurers to reduce premiums for the first time in many years. In addition, the American Medical Association, an organization of physicians, voted in February for a voluntary one-year freeze on doctors' fees.

Communication Costs, however, took some large jumps, with more hikes likely in 1985. The split-up of the American Telephone and Telegraph Company (AT&T) on Jan. 1, 1984, left many customers with sharply higher monthly telephone bills. Some of the increases affected calls within the same state and installation and repair charges, especially for small businesses. Long-distance rates charged by AT&T and its competitors came down approximately 5 per cent. But the reductions did not offset the increases in other telephone services.

Private companies began to offer a variety of electronic mail services that delivered messages far faster than routine postal service. Federal Express Corporation, for example, launched ZAPMail, a service that promised to speed a five-page photographic image called a *facsimile letter* cross-country in two hours for $35. Its major competition came from MCI Mail, a service offered by MCI Communications Corporation, which claimed it could send the same letter in four hours for $25. Western Union Corporation said it could deliver a computerized letter within two hours to a recipient who had no computer terminal. And it maintained that it could send a money order to an authorized delivery point in only 15 minutes if the sender paid cash; or in 30 minutes if the sender used a credit card. However, not all of these services were available in all parts of the United States.

As competition heated up, the U.S. Postal Service offered to send a facsimile letter for only $5 per page from several U.S. cities to points abroad by means of INTELPOST. It promised overnight delivery via Express Mail of packages weighing 2 pounds (0.91 kilogram) or less throughout the United States for $9.35. Express Mail also served 34 other countries. For speed, however, none of these services could beat electronic messages sent from one computer terminal to another.

The Federal Trade Commission (FTC) — the chief government watchdog of the market place — adopted new regulations designed to eliminate abuses in the funeral industry. The rules, which took effect on April 30, prohibited funeral directors from certain practices, including embalming a body without permission, requiring a casket for cremation, and requiring the purchase of other unwanted products or services. The new rules also ordered funeral homes to provide itemized price lists and to give this information over the telephone or in writing when requested.

In July, the FTC adopted a new rule for used-car dealers. The dealers were told to disclose the terms of any warranty or else to explain that the automobile was sold "as is," without a warranty. The new rule provoked criticism from consumer groups because the FTC had voted down a proposal that required used-car dealers to disclose an automobile's known defects as well.

The Food and Drug Administration (FDA) ended a long wrestling match with the food industry over disclosure of sodium (salt) content. A voluntary

Counterfeit watches go under a steamroller in Tokyo in June as an executive of Cartier, maker of the expensive originals, helps smash the fakes.

system for such disclosure had failed to win the compliance of all manufacturers. The FDA, therefore, ordered sodium content disclosed by July 1, 1985, on the labels of all products that claimed to have nutritional benefit. Products with 35 milligrams (0.54 grain) or less of sodium could be labeled "very low sodium" and those with 140 milligrams (2.2 grains) or less, "low sodium."

In July, the FDA published a food industry request for approval to use radiation for killing insects and microbes on fruits and vegetables. The agency said the process could extend shelf life and would not make food radioactive or change nutritional values. Spice manufacturers already had government permission to use low-dose radiation. By fall, the FDA was weighing about 4,000 comments from the public before making a final decision on the rule.

New Laws Affecting Consumers included a law signed in September by President Ronald Reagan to reduce the cost of drugs. The new law called for quick approval of low-cost generic versions of many widely used medications after the expiration of patents that protect the more costly brand-name versions of these drugs. Sponsors of the measure estimated that consumers would save approximately $1 billion over 10 years. The new law also gave drug manufacturers extended patent protection on drugs they had developed.

A law passed in June made it more difficult for consumers to wipe out their debts by declaring bankruptcy. The new law prevents individuals who have enough income for necessities and for partial payment of their financial obligations from escaping those obligations by pleading Chapter 7 of the Bankruptcy Code of 1978. Under Chapter 7, a person's assets were sold to pay debts, but income was never touched. The new law forces individuals to pay their debts. It also allows debtors to keep some of their assets—up to $4,000 in household goods and up to $7,500 per family member in home equity. The law took effect in October 1984.

The Supreme Court of the United States came down on the side of consumers and against the Reagan Administration in an antitrust decision in March. The decision preserved the right of retailers to price products below manufacturers' suggested levels. The case was won by a distributor who had cut prices of a pesticide manufactured by Monsanto Company. The court ruled that Monsanto had illegally cut off the distributor from further supplies. The Reagan Administration had asked the court to overturn an earlier ruling, which had held that agreements between manufacturers and distributors about minimum resale prices were an automatic violation of the Sherman Antitrust Act.   Arthur E. Rowse

In WORLD BOOK, see CONSUMERISM.

CONTÉ, LANSANA (1934?-), became president of Guinea in April 1984. Conté, an army colonel, seized power in a bloodless coup just a few days after the death of Ahmed Sékou Touré, Guinea's president since 1958. The new chief executive vowed to bring progress to the impoverished west African country. See GUINEA.

Conté was born in Guinea and educated at French-sponsored military schools in Ivory Coast and Senegal. He later served with the French Army in Africa and Vietnam. After Guinea won its independence from France in 1958, he became a member of the Guinean Army and held several top posts, including chief of staff.

In 1970, Conté played a leading role in defeating Guinean rebels who invaded the country with the help of Portuguese soldiers. He also fought against Portugal in the neighboring country of Guinea-Bissau during its 11-year independence struggle, which ended in 1974.

After he became president, Conté and his fellow coup leaders formed a Military Committee for National Rectification, headed by Conté. In a radio address to the nation, Conté said he would try to "banish all the harm Touré has done."

Conté is a Muslim and has made a pilgrimage to the city of Mecca in Saudi Arabia. He and his wife have two teen-age sons.   David L. Dreier

COSTA RICA. See LATIN AMERICA.

COURTS AND LAWS. In a rebuff to the United States, the International Court of Justice at The Hague, in the Netherlands, decided unanimously on May 10, 1984, that the United States should cease its attempts to mine or blockade Nicaragua's ports. The United States had fought the nonbinding ruling on procedural grounds and had earlier attempted to withdraw itself from the jurisdiction of the 15-member judicial body — an agency of the United Nations (UN) often called the World Court — over Nicaragua's complaint.

In another significant decision, the World Court in October settled a 20-year-old territorial dispute by awarding about five-sixths of the Georges Bank fishing area to the United States and the remainder to Canada. See FISHING INDUSTRY.

Genocide Treaty. Led by Senator Jesse A. Helms (R., N.C.), conservatives in the U.S. Senate again blocked ratification of a 35-year-old UN treaty outlawing *genocide,* the systematic extermination of a racial or cultural group. However, on October 11, the Senate, by a vote of 87-2, approved a compromise resolution calling for ratification of the treaty in 1985. Although Helms voted for the resolution — presumably to allow the Senate to move on to other business — he and other conservative senators vowed continued opposition to the treaty. Opponents of the treaty object to placing American citizens under international law. The United

States in 1984 was the only major country that had not ratified the measure.

Federal Judges in Trouble. In November, the U.S. Eighth Circuit Court of Appeals criticized U.S. District Judge Miles W. Lord of Minneapolis, Minn., for unjudicial conduct. On February 29, as he approved a $4.6-million civil settlement against A. H. Robins Company Incorporated for health problems resulting from the use of its Dalkon Shield birth-control device, Lord delivered an extraordinary lecture to three of the pharmaceutical company's top executives. He called the Dalkon Shield "an instrument of death, mutilation, and disease" and accused the officials, who were not defendants in the lawsuit, of putting profits above the health of women who used the shield.

In Reno, Nev., on August 10, U.S. District Judge Harry E. Claiborne was found guilty of two counts of income tax evasion. He was sentenced to two years in prison and a $10,000 fine. Claiborne, who was accused of concealing $104,000 in fees he received after assuming the federal judgeship in 1978, was the first federal judge convicted of a crime while still on the bench.

Burger Lambastes Legal System. Chief Justice of the United States Warren E. Burger continued to make headlines in 1984 with his criticisms of the American judicial system. In a speech to the

Automaker John Z. De Lorean and his wife, Cristina, are all smiles after De Lorean was acquitted of drug-trafficking charges in Los Angeles in August.

Science Outruns the Law

In April 1983, a Los Angeles couple, Mario and Elsa Rios, died in a plane crash in Chile. Their death led to an international controversy because they left behind two tiny embryos — fertilized eggs — frozen in liquid nitrogen at a Melbourne, Australia, medical center. After the existence of the Rios embryos became widely known in June 1984, legal experts, together with physicians and religious leaders, hotly debated the embryos' fate. Should they be implanted in *surrogate* (substitute) mothers and given the chance to develop, or should they be destroyed?

The technique of freezing human embryos takes the creation of "test-tube" babies one step further. In the usual procedure, several of a woman's egg cells are surgically removed and fertilized in the laboratory with the sperm of the woman's husband or of an anonymous donor. After the cells have developed into embryos of usually eight cells each, they are implanted into the woman's uterus in the hope that pregnancy will result.

In the freezing technique, pioneered at Melbourne's Queen Victoria Medical Centre, one or more embryos are stored in liquid nitrogen at a temperature of –385° F. (–196° C). These can be thawed and implanted later.

Unable to conceive a child by natural means, the Rios couple turned in 1981 to the laboratory-fertilization program at the Melbourne medical center. Doctors there fertilized a number of Elsa Rios' egg cells, using donated sperm. Several of the resulting embryos were implanted, and two were frozen.

Although Elsa Rios did not become pregnant at that time, the couple postponed having the frozen embryos thawed and implanted. While the embryos remained in their state of suspended animation, Elsa and Mario Rios died.

The problem of what to do with the "orphaned" embryos centered on the question of whether a frozen embryo has the same legal rights as a human being, particularly the right to life. The fate of the embryos remained undecided while a committee appointed by the state government of Victoria — where Melbourne is located — debated legal questions raised by laboratory fertilization and embryo freezing. The committee of legal experts, church leaders, and scientists recommended in August 1984 that frozen embryos be destroyed if couples die or divorce without specifying in writing what should be done with the embryos.

In October, the Victorian Parliament passed an amendment calling for the Rios embryos to be implanted in surrogate mothers. However, physicians at the Melbourne medical center said that the embryos, which had been frozen while the technique was still being refined, had almost no chance of survival.

Even so, the controversy surrounding the Melbourne embryos pointed out once again how far the law is lagging behind science and technology. As scientists devise ever newer ways of manipulating life, the world's lawmakers will be hard pressed to keep pace. David L. Dreier

Embryos are frozen in liquid nitrogen at Queen Victoria Medical Centre.

American Bar Association (ABA) in Las Vegas, Nev., on February 12, Burger declared that "our system is too costly, too painful, too destructive, and too inefficient for a truly civilized people." In another speech to ABA officials, on August 5 in Chicago, Burger warned of unprofessional advertising by lawyers and criticized attorneys who demand a *contingency fee* — a percentage of a victim's monetary award — in cases where there is little or no doubt that the defendant is liable.

Bankruptcy Law. After two years of debate, President Ronald Reagan signed a new law on July 10 to reform the nation's bankruptcy court system, clogged at year-end with 600,000 pending cases. The law placed federal bankruptcy judges under the jurisdiction of federal district courts, with 14-year terms of office.

Trials. The year's most celebrated criminal trial ended on August 16 with the acquittal in Los Angeles of former automaker John Z. De Lorean, who had been accused of conspiring to distribute 55 pounds (25 kilograms) of cocaine to raise money for his ailing automobile company. De Lorean was secretly videotaped several times in 1982 during a "sting" operation conducted by the Federal Bureau of Investigation (FBI). One tape showed him looking at a suitcase filled with cocaine and saying it was "better than gold." Federal prosecutors charged that De Lorean took an active part in the drug transaction, but De Lorean's attorneys argued that he had been the victim of overzealous FBI agents.

In San Angelo, Tex., Henry Lee Lucas, who claimed to have killed some 360 people as he drifted around the United States, was sentenced to death on April 13 for the 1979 murder of a female hitchhiker. Lucas was already serving time in a Texas prison for two other murders.

A sensational rape trial in Fall River, Mass., resulted in guilty verdicts for four men in March. The four were convicted of raping a woman on a pool table in a New Bedford, Mass., tavern. The four received prison sentences ranging from 6 to 12 years. Two other defendants were acquitted.

In October, what promised to be a landmark libel trial opened in the U.S. District Court in New York City, as General William C. Westmoreland, the former commander of U.S. forces in Vietnam, sued the CBS television network for $120 million. Westmoreland charged that CBS libeled him in a 1982 documentary in which he was accused of lying to his superiors about enemy troop strength in Vietnam. The trial focused close attention on television news-gathering techniques, and some news officials feared the outcome could accelerate a trend toward stricter legal controls on the press in its coverage of public officials.   David C. Beckwith

See also CRIME; SUPREME COURT OF THE UNITED STATES. In WORLD BOOK, see COURT; LAW.

CRIME. Terrorism in support of political objectives continued to plague governments throughout the world during 1984. The most serious incident was the assassination on October 31 of India's Prime Minister Indira Gandhi by two of her bodyguards in New Delhi, India's capital city. Great Britain's Prime Minister Margaret Thatcher was the target of a Provisional Irish Republican Army bomb blast at a hotel in Brighton, England, on October 12. The blast killed five people, including a member of the British Parliament.

Pope Plot. On October 26, an Italian magistrate announced that he had indicted three Bulgarians and four Turks for conspiracy in the 1981 assassination attempt on Pope John Paul II in Rome. Italy had only three of the seven in custody by the end of 1984. The magistrate apparently based the indictments largely on the testimony of Mehmet Ali Agca, a Turk already convicted for the assassination attempt. Agca, who shot the pope, said that the Bulgarian secret service had a part in the plot. Defense attorneys charged that Agca had changed his story several times.

Child Abuse. In the United States, attention focused on sexual and other physical abuse of children. Police throughout the country made arrests as public awareness of such abuse increased. Prosecutions met with mixed results, however, partly because of the unreliability of testimony of young alleged victims. On March 22, seven people connected with the Virginia McMartin Pre-School in Manhattan Beach, Calif., were indicted on 115 counts of molesting children at the school. On May 24, 93 counts were added. And on August 2, the state closed a nearby nursery school. Investigators said that, since 1979, children had been taken from the McMartin school to the nursery school where they "were physically and sexually abused." See CHILD WELFARE (Close-Up).

Religious communes in Island Pond, Vt., and The Dalles, Ore., were targets of police action after complaints about possible child abuse. Another well-publicized case involved day-care centers in New York City.

The strangest allegations were made in rural Jordan, Minn., where authorities arrested 24 adults on charges of maintaining a sex ring involving more than 40 children, aged 2 to 17. Only one defendant pleaded guilty. Two defendants were acquitted on September 19. Scott County Attorney Kathleen Morris then dropped all charges against the remaining defendants. She said that she did not want to traumatize child witnesses or to jeopardize other investigations. The Minnesota Bureau of Criminal Apprehension and the Federal Bureau of Investigation (FBI) were looking into allegations that children had been murdered. On November 14, the investigators announced that they had found no evidence of murder. They then

A police officer at a cocaine-processing plant in Colombia in March
stacks bags of the narcotic seized in the largest drug raid in history.

shifted their attentions to allegations of sexual abuse and pornography involving children.

Mass Killings. On July 18, a recently fired security guard suddenly started shooting employees and patrons at a McDonald's restaurant in San Ysidro, Calif., near San Diego. He killed 21 people and wounded 19 others in the largest mass murder on a single day in U.S. history. A San Diego police sharpshooter killed the gunman, 41-year-old James Oliver Huberty, 77 minutes later.

A bloody episode of sex crimes ended on April 13, when a state trooper shot and killed 39-year-old Christopher B. Wilder at a Colebrook, N.H., gas station. Authorities linked Wilder to at least 11 kidnappings and 4 murders of young women in a crime odyssey that ranged from Florida to California, Indiana, and New York. Wilder, who was born in Australia, posed as a photographer, but he was really a rich electrical contractor.

Allegations of White-Collar Crime reached high levels of the federal government during 1984. On August 10, U.S. District Court Judge Harry E. Claiborne, 67, of Nevada, was convicted on two counts of income tax evasion and later sentenced to two years in prison. On October 1, the indictment of U.S. Secretary of Labor Raymond J. Donovan was announced in New York City. Donovan was charged on 137 counts involving the falsification of business records. He took an unpaid leave of absence to fight the charges. Both events were historic firsts: Claiborne was the first sitting federal judge ever convicted of a crime, and Donovan the first incumbent Cabinet member ever indicted.

R. Foster Winans, a former columnist for *The Wall Street Journal*, and two alleged accomplices were indicted on August 28 on multiple counts of fraud and conspiracy. Authorities charged that Winans was paid for information about the stock market in advance of publication in the *Journal*. The indictments were based in part on the controversial principle that reporters have a duty to disclose personal gain from information gathered in the course of their work. Press groups objected, saying that application of the principle could lead to government supervision of news operations.

Major Crime in the United States continued to decline in 1984. The FBI reported a 2 per cent drop in reported violent crimes and a 5 per cent decline in property crimes for the first half of 1984. Rape increased by 6 per cent, however; aggravated assault, 1 per cent; motor vehicle theft, 1 per cent; and arson, 2 per cent. Murder declined by 5 per cent; robbery, 7 per cent; burglary, 8 per cent; and larceny-theft, 5 per cent. The FBI also reported that serious crime had dropped a record 7 per cent in 1983.   David C. Beckwith

See also COURTS AND LAWS. In WORLD BOOK, see CRIME.

CUBA. President Fidel Castro marked the 25th anniversary of the Cuban revolution on Jan. 2, 1984, with a speech that bitterly attacked the Administration of United States President Ronald Reagan and the 1983 U.S. invasion of Grenada. Castro called U.S. leaders "Nazi-fascist barbarians," but later in the year, as Reagan's reelection seemed assured, Castro adopted a more conciliatory tone toward the United States.

Jackson Visit. Castro appeared eager to influence the U.S. presidential contest. In June, he laid out the welcome mat for Democratic presidential candidate Jesse L. Jackson, who had been sharply critical of the U.S invasion of Grenada. As a gesture to Jackson's visit, Castro on June 27 approved the release of 22 U.S. citizens and 26 Cubans from Cuban jails. Most of the U.S. prisoners had been held on drug charges.

Cuban Refugees. In December, U.S. and Cuban negotiators, meeting in New York City, agreed that 2,746 criminals and mental patients, who came to the United States during the 1980 boat lift and ended up in federal penal or mental institutions, would be returned to Cuba. In exchange, the United States agreed to resume processing Cuban immigrants.

U.S. Relations. On July 26, the anniversary of the 1953 attack that launched the 1959 Cuban revolution, Castro said that Cuba genuinely sought better ties with the United States. A U.S. Department of State official replied that better ties were unlikely unless Cuba made fundamental changes in its foreign policy. The changes, according to the official, would have to include withdrawing Cuban troops and advisers from Angola, Ethiopia, and Nicaragua, and ending support for Third World revolutionary movements.

In October, visitors to Cuba observed civil defense preparations throughout the island-nation, including the digging of trenches around schools and hospitals. Cubans were reportedly being told to prepare for a possible U.S. invasion that might coincide with a U.S. invasion of Nicaragua.

Soviet Relations. Events in 1984 continued to confirm Cuba's economic dependence on the Soviet Union, as well as the close political ties between the two nations. Soviet naval units made use of Cuban ports in March and April while the Soviets conducted war games in the Gulf of Mexico. Cuba grew increasingly dependent on the sale of its sugar crop to the Soviet Union at the enormously subsidized price of 50 cents per pound ($1.10 per kilogram).   Nathan A. Haverstock

See also LATIN AMERICA (Facts in Brief Table). In WORLD BOOK, see CUBA.

CYPRUS. See EUROPE.

Jesse Jackson enjoys a Havana cigar with Cuban President Fidel Castro after Castro agreed in June to release 48 U.S. and Cuban prisoners.

CZECHOSLOVAKIA

CZECHOSLOVAKIA remained the Communist bloc's chief advocate of the hard-line approach in 1984. In March, the Czechoslovak Communist Party daily newspaper *Rudé Právo* (Red Justice) attacked Communist states that sought "one-sided" advantage from the West, adopted "narrow" attitudes in the face of temporary economic difficulties, or praised their own economic "models." Political observers interpreted this attack as a criticism of East Germany, Hungary, and Romania. The Soviet Union weekly magazine *Novoye Vremya* (New Times) reprinted the article in April, giving the impression that the Soviet government supported the attacks. *Rudé Právo* returned to the attack in April, criticizing attempts to "modernize" Marxism-Leninism, particularly such efforts by the Communist parties of Italy and Yugoslavia.

In January, the Soviet Union announced that its soldiers were stationed at new missile bases in Czechoslovakia. In February, more than 1,000 Czechoslovaks signed a petition protesting the presence of Soviet missiles in their country. In the same month, *Rudé Právo* admitted receiving many letters expressing concern about the missiles.

Church and State. Relations with the Roman Catholic Church remained tense throughout 1984. Frantisek Cardinal Tomasek, the archbishop of Prague, announced in April that he had invited Pope John Paul II to visit Czechoslovakia in April 1985 to celebrate the 1,100th anniversary of the death of Saint Methodius, who helped introduce Christianity to Moravia, a region in Czechoslovakia. The government said the visit would be "inopportune." The government-controlled press attacked the pope throughout the year. More than 150,000 pilgrims visited two Catholic shrines in July—one in Moravia and the other in Slovakia.

In July, it was reported that the government planned to set up an independent Catholic Church. This church would be aligned with the Russian Orthodox Church, which the Soviet government closely controls.

National Income Grew by 3.2 per cent in the first half of 1984, compared with the first half of 1983. Industrial output rose by 4.1 per cent and productivity by 3.4 per cent, but investment fell by 15 per cent. The trade surplus with the West increased by 21 per cent to $609 million.

Dissidents. Miklos Duray, a geologist and writer, was arrested in May for championing the linguistic and other rights of the 600,000 ethnic Hungarians living in Slovakia. In October, Jaroslav Seifert, an 83-year-old Czech poet, won the 1984 Nobel Prize for literature. Seifert had been in trouble with the government for supporting Charter 77, a dissident organization. Chris Cviic

See also EUROPE (Facts in Brief Table); NOBEL PRIZES. In WORLD BOOK, see CZECHOSLOVAKIA.
DAM. See BUILDING AND CONSTRUCTION.

DANCING. If any one person dominated dance in the United States in 1984, it was Twyla Tharp. This modern-dance choreographer not only had astoundingly successful engagements with her own company, but she also made important inroads into the ballet establishment. Once considered a knotty, intellectual choreographer, Tharp in 1984 solidified her position as a popular artist, playing to capacity audiences throughout the United States.

The Twyla Tharp Dance Company's season from January 24 to February 12 at the Brooklyn Academy of Music in New York City was a mixture of old and new works, with the new pieces showing an extraordinary range of style and sub-

Members of the Martha Graham Dance Company
perform *The Rite of Spring*, Graham's new
work set to music by Igor Stravinsky, in March.

ject. The all-out hit was *Nine Sinatra Songs*, set to
recordings by singer Frank Sinatra. Frankly romantic and sexy in mood, the work's lush outpouring of lyrical movement swept audiences off
their feet. In direct opposition was *Fait Accompli*, a
harsh indictment of an overmechanized society
that was also exhilarating for its driving energy.
Fait Accompli was also notable for bringing Tharp
back to the stage as a dancer. A third new dance,
Telemann, was one of Tharp's most balletlike
dances. It was seen as a brave, if not altogether
successful, attempt to investigate ballet style and as
a tribute to the versatility of the Tharp dancers.

Other Tharp Works. Since 1976, Tharp has
worked from time to time with the American Ballet Theatre (ABT) in New York City. In 1984, the
ABT presented all-Tharp programs, causing
many observers to consider her the ABT's unofficial resident choreographer. Tharp's programs
were especially popular because they showcased
Russian-born dancer Mikhail Baryshnikov, who
danced in few other works in 1984. The Tharp-
Baryshnikov collaboration received wide exposure
on October 5 when "Dance in America," a series
televised by the Public Broadcasting Service, fea-

Give Us a Break!

Crowds gathered on sidewalks to watch it, young people spent hours practicing it, Hollywood made movies about it, dance studios began teaching it, and summer days seemed designed for it. In 1984, break dancing, a popular form of dance that began on the streets of New York City, spread across the United States and Canada. Although likely a fad, soon to fade, it was nevertheless a fixture of youth culture.

Break dancing is a catchall term for a variety of unique athletic dance styles that combine elements of gymnastics, martial arts, mime, and disco. Among many of the most common movements, the break dancer seems to spin effortlessly around a central axis — the axis being the dancer's hand, knee, shoulder, or even head — while the suspended legs perform various twisting gyrations, all to the accompaniment of a powerful beat.

Another dance style, the Electric Boogie, is performed to a syncopated rhythm and uses mime to create robotlike movements. A step called the Moon Walk makes the dancer's feet appear to float along the ground. Other styles include the Tick, the Wave, and the King Tut.

Unlike most popular dances, break dancing is not exactly sociable. Dancers, mostly young

males, usually perform solo, and occasional partners are usually of the same sex — even at night spots that cater to break dancers. The dancing is an activity in itself, rather than a way to meet people of the opposite sex.

Almost all accounts agree that break dancing began in New York City's South Bronx, an area of extreme poverty where hundreds of abandoned and burned-out buildings recall the bleak devastation of European cities at the end of World War II. Break dancing allegedly began as a "break" from fighting among gangs. Instead of fighting, a gang sent its best dancers to engage in a break-dance competition with a rival gang. The site might have been a playground or sidewalk with a piece of cardboard as the dance floor.

Out of these beginnings, break dancing developed its own language and style. For example, a *battle* is a break-dance competition; *burned* is losing a battle; *wacked* is making an incorrect move; and *bite* is stealing another dancer's move. Break dancers form groups called *crews*, and many have adopted names such as Funky Frank, Mr. Fresh, and Freakazoid.

Some observers see break dancing as part of a larger cultural movement among ghetto youth, who have distilled their own unique styles of dance, music, and art. Besides break dancing, these include *rapping*, a kind of rhythmic talking set to a musical beat; *deejay* music, in which musical sounds are mixed; and *graffiti* art, which uses the city itself — and especially subway cars — as its canvas.

This movement has inspired at least four motion pictures — *Wild Style, Breakin', Breakin' 2: Electric Boogaloo,* and *Beat Street* — which have in turn done much to spread the popularity of break dancing. In *Breakin',* two street dancers face hostility from the professional dance world until given a chance to prove their talents. "Street People" and "There's No Stopping Us," two popular songs from the movie, echo the film's theme that ghetto youth can win respect and recognition for what they have created out of their own experience, rather than by imitating what is considered acceptable.

Break dancing gained wide acceptance among professional dancers in 1984. *Dance* magazine devoted an entire issue to it; the respected Spoleto Festival U.S.A. in Charleston, S.C., featured it; dancer Gene Kelly highlighted it in a new film, *That's Dancing*; and a classical dance promoter planned a 40-city tour of break dancers and ballet dancers for 1985.

About the only discouraging note came from physicians who warned that neck and spinal injuries can result if certain moves, particularly head spins, are not practiced carefully.   Rod Such

A young break dancer shows off his talent.

tured Baryshnikov in Tharp's *Push Comes to Shove*, *The Little Ballet*, and *Sinatra Suite*.

Tharp further deepened her roots in the ballet world by collaborating with American choreographer Jerome Robbins on a new dance for the New York City Ballet. Robbins and Danish-born dancer Peter Martins are joint ballet masters in chief of the company. The Tharp-Robbins collaboration, called *Brahms/Handel*, premiered on June 6 during the troupe's annual two-month spring season at the New York State Theater in New York City. It proved to be a spectacular showcase for the City Ballet dancers. However, critics generally felt that the identities of the choreographers were lost in the process of collaboration.

The New York City Ballet produced other new ballets — by Martins and by other company members as well. The company's outstanding production of 1984, however, was by Russian-born choreographer George Balanchine, the cofounder of the New York City Ballet, who died in April 1983. The production was a revival on May 9, 1984, of Balanchine's 1960 masterpiece, *Liebeslieder Walzer*. Because of the ballet's intimacy and depth of feeling, dance experts believed the work was impossible to produce well without Balanchine's personal supervision. Yet, as restored by Karin von Aroldingen, the revived production of this hourlong waltz ballet was as dramatically vivid as it was when it had last been danced.

Dance from Other Countries. Modern dance has long been considered the special domain of the United States, but within the last 10 years, the art form has been revitalized in Europe and has even seeped into the traditional dance forms of Japan and India. One of the most exciting dance events of 1984 was the American debut of avant-garde choreographer Pina Bausch's Dance Theater from Wuppertal, West Germany. The company opened the Olympic Arts Festival in Los Angeles on June 1 and then performed at the Brooklyn Academy of Music and the Toronto Arts Festival in Canada.

Bausch's original way of combining dance, visual art, and speech in an expressionist form of theater powerfully impressed American audiences. Although some American critics declined to hail her as a pioneer of a new art form, as Europeans have done, most found her work, especially the autobiographical *1980*, provocative. Although her themes are pessimistic, dealing primarily with the impossibility of love, Bausch's theater pieces had enough humor and stunning visual effects to round out, if not soften, the social message.

The American Dance Festival in Durham, N.C., has recently become an important showcase for European dance in the United States. Celebrating its 50th anniversary in 1984, the festival continued its import policy. From June 10 to July 21, it presented modern dance groups from India and the

Philippines, the London Contemporary Dance Theater, the Susan Buirge Project from Paris, and Group Emile Dubois from Grenoble, France. The festival also honored American modern dance by commissioning dances by Merce Cunningham, Tharp, Alwin Nikolais, and the Pilobolus Dance Theater.

NEA Awards. The National Endowment for the Arts (NEA), a federal arts agency, awarded two grants of unusual interest in 1984. The first, sponsored in conjunction with the Rockefeller Foundation and the Exxon Corporation, gave funds to eight dance groups, enabling them to work with choreographers whose dances are not in their repertories. Announced in May, the grant is a major attempt to promote an exchange between modern dance and ballet.

The eight groups and choreographers are the Boston Ballet and Elisa Monte; the Dance Theatre of Harlem (New York City) and David Gordon; the José Limón Dance Company (New York City) and Heinz Poll; the North Carolina Dance Theater (Winston-Salem) and Nina Wiener; the Pennsylvania Ballet (Philadelphia) and Merce Cunningham; the Chicago Repertory Dance Ensemble and Ze'eva Cohen; the Louisville (Ky.) Ballet and Lynne Taylor-Corbett; and the Oakland (Calif.) Ballet Company and Tandy Beal.

On July 18, the NEA announced a grant of $250,000 to the Martha Graham Dance Company for the purpose of filming several of founder Martha Graham's masterpieces. In addition, the funds were to be used to finance voice-over commentaries by Graham on the technical and thematic content of 10 of her dances that have already been filmed.

Personnel Changes. On June 24, Violette Verdy resigned as artistic director of the Boston Ballet after a bitter dispute with the board of directors over artistic control and financial policy. Bruce Wells, the company's resident choreographer, was named temporary artistic director. On August 29, the San Francisco Ballet's Board of Trustees did not renew its contract with co-artistic director Michael Smuin. The trustees claimed that Smuin had resigned. Smuin contended that he had been fired. On September 21, he was rehired, but his status beyond May 1985 was uncertain.

In another major administrative change, John Taras, a long-time ballet master of the New York City Ballet, was appointed associate artistic director of the ABT on September 1. Kenneth MacMillan, codirector of Great Britain's Royal Ballet, became an artistic adviser of the ABT. The company produced his popular version of *Romeo and Juliet* during a three-week season at the John F. Kennedy Center for the Performing Arts in Washington, D.C., in December. Nancy Goldner

In WORLD BOOK, see BALLET; DANCING.

DEATHS

DEATHS of notable persons in 1984 included those listed below. Those listed were Americans unless otherwise indicated. An asterisk (*) indicates the person is the subject of a biography in THE WORLD BOOK ENCYCLOPEDIA.

*Adams, Ansel (1902-April 22), photographer, noted for his majestic landscapes of the American West.

Adler, Luther (1903-Dec. 8), star of stage and screen whose Broadway roles included Tevye in *Fiddler on the Roof.*

Aiken, George D. (1892-Nov. 19), Republican senator from Vermont from 1941 to 1975.

*Aleixandre, Vicente (1898-Dec. 13), Spanish poet who won the 1977 Nobel Prize for literature.

Alston, Walter (1911-Oct. 1), manager who led the Brooklyn (later Los Angeles) Dodgers baseball team to eight National League pennants and four World Series championships from 1953 to 1976.

*Andropov, Yuri Vladimirovich (1914-Feb. 9), general secretary of the Communist Party of the Soviet Union since 1982 and chairman of the Presidium of the Supreme Soviet since 1983. See RUSSIA (Close-Up).

Ashton-Warner, Sylvia (1908-April 28), New Zealand writer.

Astor, Lord Gavin (1918-June 28), former chairman of *The Times* of London.

Atkinson, Brooks (Justin Brooks Atkinson) (1894-Jan. 13), influential drama critic for *The New York Times* from 1925 to 1960.

J. B. Priestley,
British author.

Ethel Merman, vivacious star
of Broadway musicals.

Truman Capote,
noted writer and wit.

Raymond A. Kroc, founder of
McDonald's hamburger chain.

Barghoorn, Elso S. (1915-Jan. 28), geologist whose research pushed back estimates of the origin of life on earth to more than 3.4 billion years ago.

Barry, Jack (1918-May 2), television producer and star of game shows.

Barzini, Luigi (1908-March 30), Italian author and member of parliament from 1958 to 1972. He was best known for his book *The Italians* (1964).

Basehart, Richard (1914-Sept. 17), actor who played Admiral Nelson in the TV series "Voyage to the Bottom of the Sea" in the 1960's.

*Basie, Count (William Basie) (1904-April 26), jazz pianist and bandleader, a key figure in the "swing" era in the 1930's.

Bell, Ricky (1955-Nov. 28), University of Southern California football star who played six years in the National Football League.

Bentley, Max (1920-Jan. 19), Canadian ice hockey player inducted into the Hockey Hall of Fame in 1966.

Berlinguer, Enrico (1922-June 11), Italian politician who advocated Eurocommunism — a Westernized brand of Communism.

*Betjeman, Sir John (1906-May 19), Great Britain's poet laureate since 1972. His verse celebrated the life of Britain's middle class.

Bloom, Ursula (1883-Oct. 29), prolific British author of some 560 romantic novels.

Boylston, Helen Dore (1895-Sept. 30), author of the popular series of books about nurse Sue Barton.

Bratteli, Trygve (1910-Nov. 21), Norway's prime minister in 1971 and 1972 and from 1973 to 1976.

Brautigan, Richard (1935-reported Oct. 26), poet and novelist whose books included *Trout Fishing in America* (1967) and *The Tokyo-Montana Express* (1980).

Bricktop (Ada Beatrice Queen Victoria Louise Virginia Smith) (1894-Jan. 31), singer and entertainer in Europe's café society for 40 years.

Buckler, Ernest (1908-March 4), Canadian writer best known for *The Mountain and the Valley* (1952), a classic regional novel about life in Nova Scotia.

Bunker, Ellsworth (1894-Sept. 27), U.S. diplomat, ambassador to South Vietnam during the Vietnam War.

Burton, Richard (Richard Jenkins) (1925-Aug. 5), noted Welsh actor who performed in plays ranging from *Hamlet* (1953) to *Equus* (1976) and starred in more than 40 films, including *Cleopatra* (1963) and *Who's Afraid of Virginia Woolf?* (1966).

Byers, Lord (Charles Frank) (1916-Feb. 6), British politician, leader of the Liberal Party in Britain's House of Lords since 1967.

Caldwell, Millard F. (1897-Oct. 23), Democratic congressman from Florida from 1933 to 1941, and governor of that state from 1945 to 1949.

Campbell, Clarence S. (1905-June 24), Canadian president of the National Hockey League from 1946 to 1977.

*Capote, Truman (1924-Aug. 25), provocative writer whose best-selling books included *Breakfast at Tiffany's.*

Church, Frank F. (1924-April 7), Democratic senator from Idaho from 1957 to 1980.

*Clark, Mark W. (1896-April 17), last surviving top United States Army commander during World War II.

Coogan, Jackie (John Leslie Coogan) (1914-March 1), actor whose role as the foundling in *The Kid* (1920) made him the first child star in Hollywood.

Cooper, Tommy (1922-April 15), British stage and television comedian who turned a klutzy conjuring act into a hit comic performance.

*Cori, Carl F. (1896-Oct. 20), Czechoslovak-born biochemist, winner of the 1947 Nobel Prize for physiology or medicine with his first wife, Gerty, who died in 1957.

Cortázar, Julio (1914-Feb. 12), Argentine writer, born in Belgium, best known for his novel *Rayuela,* published in English as *Hopscotch* (1963).

Coxe, George Harmon (1901-Jan. 30), author of more than 60 mystery novels.

Crankshaw, Edward (1909-Nov. 29), British author, an expert on Soviet affairs.

Cronin, Joe (Joseph Edward Cronin) (1906-Sept. 7), baseball shortstop, a member of baseball's Hall of Fame.

Culver, Roland (1900-Feb. 29), British actor who played such impeccable characters as the Duke of Omnia in the BBC-TV series "The Pallisers."

Dart, Justin (1907-Jan. 26), drugstore executive and outspoken member of President Ronald Reagan's "kitchen cabinet."

David (1972-Feb. 22), a victim of severe combined immunodeficiency since birth. He spent all but the last 15 days of his life in a sterile plastic bubble.

Deacon, Richard (1922-Aug. 8), comic actor who played Lumpy Rutherford's father in the TV series "Leave It to Beaver" and the overbearing producer Mel Cooley in "The Dick Van Dyke Show."

Delmar, Kenny (1911-July 14), actor who played the very Southern Senator Beauregard Claghorn on Fred Allen's radio show in the 1940's.

*Dirac, Paul A. M. (1902-Oct. 20), British physicist, co-winner of the 1933 Nobel Prize for physics.

Dors, Diana (1931-May 4), Britain's blonde bombshell of the 1950's.

Dragon, Carmen (1915-March 28), composer and conductor who won an Oscar in 1944 for his score for the musical film *Cover Girl.*

Eckstein, Otto (1927-March 22), German-born economist who served as an adviser to President Lyndon B. Johnson from 1964 to 1966.

Egan, William A. (1914-May 6), first governor of Alaska from 1958 to 1966. He served again from 1970 to 1974.

Evins, Joe L. (1910-March 31), Democratic congressman from Tennessee from 1947 to 1977.

Farrar, Margaret (1897-June 11), pioneering crossword-puzzle editor for *The New York Times* from 1942 to 1969.

Ferencsik, Janos (1907-June 12), one of Hungary's foremost conductors.

Fixx, James F. (1932-July 20), writer and fitness enthusiast who spurred the jogging craze with his best-selling book *The Complete Book of Running* (1977).

Flowers, Walter (1933-April 12), Democratic congressman from Alabama from 1969 to 1977.

Forbush, Scott E. (1904-April 4), geophysicist who discovered the Forbush effect—a decrease in cosmic rays bombarding the earth.

Foreman, Carl (1914-June 26), writer, film producer, and director.

Forsythe, Edwin B. (1916-March 29), Republican congressman from New Jersey since 1970.

Foucault, Michel (1926-June 25), French philosopher and historian whose writing explored the relationship between society and social deviance.

Frere, Alexander S. (1893-Oct. 3), British publisher who influenced the careers of many writers.

*Galarza, Ernesto (1905-June 22), Mexican-American historian and civil rights leader.

*Gallup, George H. (1901-July 26), statistician who pioneered in public opinion polling. See Close-Up.

*Gandhi, Indira P. (1917-Oct. 31), prime minister of India from 1966 to 1977 and from 1980 until her death. See ASIA (Close-Up).

Garner, Peggy Ann (1931-Oct. 16), child actress of the 1940's who won a special Oscar in 1945 for her performance in *A Tree Grows in Brooklyn.*

Gaye, Marvin (1939-April 1), singer who blended the soul music of the city with the beat of gospel music.

Gaynor, Janet (1906-Sept. 14), Hollywood actress who in 1929 won the first Oscar ever given for best actress for her roles in three silent films—*Sunrise* (1927), *Seventh Heaven* (1927), and *Street Angel* (1928).

Lillian Hellman, major American playwright.

Richard Burton, noted Welsh actor.

Clarence M. Mitchell, lawyer and long-time NAACP lobbyist.

Frank F. Church, Democratic senator.

Geoffrey-Lloyd, Lord (1902-Sept. 12), British Cabinet minister who devised the English Channel pipelines that supplied fuel to Allied invasion forces in World War II.

Gobbi, Tito (1915-March 5), Italian operatic baritone, noted for his portrayal of Scarpia in Puccini's *Tosca.*

Goodman, Steve (1948-Sept. 20), composer and folk singer, known for his witty observations on human nature. He wrote the hit song "City of New Orleans."

Grunwald, Josef (1902-Aug. 10), Hungarian-born Hasidic rabbi who brought his congregation from Pupa, Hungary, to New York City after World War II.

Harden, Cecil Murray (1894-Dec. 5), Republican congresswoman from Indiana from 1949 to 1959.

Harris, Sir Arthur T. (1892-April 5), commander of Great Britain's Royal Air Force Bomber Command in World War II.

Hauser, Gayelord (1895-Dec. 26), German-born advocate of natural foods to assure good health.

*Hellman, Lillian (1905-June 30), playwright whose works included *The Children's Hour* (1934), *The Little Foxes* (1939), and *Toys in the Attic* (1960).

Hexum, Jon-Erik (1958-Oct. 19), actor in the TV series "Cover-Up."

Hill, Lister (1895-Dec. 20), former Democratic senator from Alabama who wrote the bill that established the Tennessee Valley Authority in 1933.

Himes, Chester B. (1909-Aug. 27), writer who dealt with racial themes but is best known for his crime novels.

Holst, Imogen (1907-March 9), British musician and composer, the daughter of composer Gustav Holst.

DEATHS

James Mason, actor for almost 50 years.

Ansel Adams, photographer of the majestic American West.

Count Basie, noted jazz bandleader.

Andy Kaufman, comedian who played in the TV series "Taxi."

Hoyt, Waite (1899-Aug. 25), baseball player, top pitcher for the New York Yankees in the 1920's. He was elected to baseball's Hall of Fame in 1969.

Hughes, Richard (1906-Jan. 4), Australian journalist and historian.

Hunter, Alberta (1895-Oct. 17), songwriter and blues singer of the 1920's who made a comeback in her 80's after working as a practical nurse for 20 years. She wrote "Down-Hearted Blues" (1923), singer Bessie Smith's first recording.

Hurd, Peter (1904-July 9), artist noted for his dramatic paintings of the American Southwest.

Hutton, Ina Ray (1916-Feb. 19), one of the first female bandleaders in the 1950's and 1960's.

Jacoby, Oswald (1902-June 27), contract bridge expert and long-time columnist.

Jaffe, Sam (1891-March 24), character actor whose performances ranged from the film *Gunga Din* (1939) to the 1950's TV series "Ben Casey."

Jenkins, Gordon (1910-May 1), composer and conductor perhaps best known for "Manhattan Tower" (1945) and "It Was a Very Good Year" (1965).

John, Sir Caspar (1903-July 11), Great Britain's First Sea Lord (commander of the Royal Navy) from 1960 to 1963. He was the son of artist Augustus John.

Johnson, Uwe (1934-March 13), German novelist whose novels about life in East Germany included *Two Views* (1965) and *Speculations About Jakob* (1959).

*Kapitsa, Pyotr L. (1894-April 8), Russian physicist, winner of the 1978 Nobel Prize for physics.

Kastler, Alfred (1902-Jan. 7), French physicist, winner of the 1966 Nobel Prize for physics.

Kaufman, Andy (1949-May 16), comedian who played the shy immigrant mechanic in the TV series "Taxi."

Keating, Tom (1917-Feb. 12), British painter who claimed to have forged more than 2,000 works of such geniuses as Rembrandt and Pierre Auguste Renoir.

Kelly, George (High Pockets) (1895-Oct. 13), baseball player who batted .296 over 16 major-league seasons. He was elected to baseball's Hall of Fame in 1973.

Kennedy, Jimmy (1903-April 6), Irish songwriter whose hits included "Red Sails in the Sunset" (1935) and "I'm Going to Hang Out My Washing on the Siegfried Line" (1939).

King, Martin Luther, Sr. (1899-Nov. 11), Baptist clergyman, father of civil rights leader Martin Luther King, Jr.

Knopf, Alfred M. (1892-Aug. 11), prestigious publisher of modern literature ranging from Thomas Mann's *Death in Venice* (1912) to John Hersey's *Hiroshima* (1946).

Krasna, Norman (1909-Nov. 1), playwright who won an Oscar in 1943 for his screenplay for *Princess O'Rourke*.

Krasner, Lee (Lee Krasner Pollock) (1908-June 19), abstract expressionist painter.

Kroc, Raymond A. (1902-Jan. 14), founder of McDonald's Corporation fast-food empire.

Laskin, Bora (1912-March 26), chief justice of Canada since 1973.

Laszlo, Ernest (1899-Jan. 6), Hungarian-born cinematographer who won an Oscar for *Ship of Fools* (1965).

Lawford, Peter (1923-Dec. 24), British-born motion picture and television actor.

Lee, William A. (1895-June 16), president of the Chicago Federation of Labor since 1940.

Loewenstein-Wertheim-Freudenberg, Prince Hubertus (1906-Nov. 28), German historian, an early opponent of Adolf Hitler.

Lonergan, Bernard J. F. (1904-Nov. 26), Canadian Jesuit philosopher and theologian.

Losey, Joseph (1909-June 22), film director blacklisted in the 1950's. His many major films included *The Servant* (1963) and *The Go-Between* (1971).

Low, George M. (1926-July 17), Austrian-born engineer who guided the U.S. astronaut program from 1949 to 1976.

Lynch, Sir Phillip R. (1933-June 19), Australian politician, former leader of the Liberal Party.

MacEntee, Sean (1889-Jan. 9), Irish politician, a leader in the founding of the Irish Republic.

Macmillan, Maurice (Viscount of Ovenden) (1921-March 10), British publishing giant and a Conservative member of Parliament since 1966.

Malik, Adam (1917-Sept. 5), Indonesian politician, president of the United Nations General Assembly in 1971 and 1972.

Manahan, Anna A. (1901-Feb. 12), Russian-born woman who claimed to be the Grand Duchess Anastasia, daughter of Russia's Czar Nicholas II.

Manne, Shelly (1920-Sept. 26), jazz drummer and composer who played with the Les Brown, Stan Kenton, and Woody Herman bands in the 1940's.

Mason, James (1909-July 27), British-born actor noted for his suave roles in more than 100 films.

*Mays, Benjamin E. (1895-March 28), educator and early champion of the civil rights movement.

McFarland, Ernest W. (1894-June 8), Democratic senator from Arizona from 1941 to 1953 and governor of that state from 1955 to 1959.

Mercer, Mabel (1900-April 20), cabaret singer for nearly 30 years. Her hits included "Fly Me to the Moon" and "Little Girl Blue."

Merman, Ethel (1909-Feb. 15), musical comedy star who belted out songs in such hit shows as *Call Me Madam* (1950) and *Gypsy* (1959).

The Pioneer of Polling

George H. Gallup, who died at his summer home in Switzerland on July 26, 1984, pioneered and popularized methods of polling public opinion. These methods have become standard in much of the world through the Gallup Organization affiliates that he established in 35 countries. Dedicated to the principle that what the public thinks is both important and newsworthy, Gallup played a crucial role in establishing polling as a credible feature of political reporting. The reliance of political leaders on Gallup's methods for measuring voting preferences and for analyzing public opinion has reshaped the electoral process in almost every country that holds free elections.

Central to Gallup's work was a conviction that sample surveys provide a powerful key to understanding, and even predicting, human behavior. Ever the practical man uninterested in abstract theory, he constantly experimented with new applications for surveys. Although best known for preelection polls, Gallup also used the survey method for investigating other topics, including: What makes advertising effective? How large an audience will a motion picture attract? And even: What are "the secrets of old age"?

Gallup believed in the essential rightness of public opinion and in the obligation of national leaders to pay attention to that opinion. In his view, polls enable political and nonpolitical leaders alike to keep in touch with the public's needs, hopes, and fears and to act intelligently on the basis of that knowledge. He used polls to test the public's receptivity to new proposals for legislation, for consumer products, and for entertainment.

George Horace Gallup was born in Jefferson, Iowa, on Nov. 18, 1901. He earned a Ph.D. in psychology from the University of Iowa in Iowa City in 1928. His thesis, "A New Technique for Measuring Reader Interest in Newspapers," reflected a lifelong interest in journalism. Gallup taught journalism briefly at several universities and organized Quill and Scroll, an honor society for high school journalists.

In 1932, Gallup became research director for Young & Rubicam, an advertising agency in New York City. He held that position until 1947. The Gallup Poll was founded in Princeton, N.J., in 1935 to provide newspapers with information about public opinion and national trends. The poll's success was assured when it correctly predicted that President Franklin D. Roosevelt would defeat Kansas Governor Alfred M. Landon in the 1936 presidential election. The then-prestigious *Literary Digest* magazine poll had forecast a Landon victory.

Audience Research, a firm founded by Gallup in 1939, developed methods for testing what makes a motion picture successful. The movie industry came to rely on these methods in selecting story ideas, casts, and titles. Gallup and Robinson, which was organized in 1948, served advertisers by testing the effectiveness of their advertising.

In 1948, the Gallup Poll, along with most other polls, incorrectly forecast that New York Governor Thomas E. Dewey would defeat President Harry S. Truman. The prediction cast doubt upon the accuracy of preelection polling. Changes in Gallup Poll methods, beginning with the 1952 election, have resulted in accurate predictions ever since. The changes included the use of probability sampling, the use of techniques for screening out nonvoters and for dealing with undecided voters, and the continuation of polling until close to Election Day to measure last-minute trends.

The Gallup Poll introduced such polling staples as public approval ratings of a President's performance in office; "trial heats" and "open primaries" to measure a potential candidate's strength long before an election; and gauging confidence in a political party's ability to handle important problems. Candidates have learned to rely on such measures of public opinion in preference to traditional measures of grassroots opinion — such as reports from local party organizations. Today, polls using methods popularized by Gallup guide the determination of campaign strategy and tactics and at times, even the selection of candidates.   Irving Crespi

George H. Gallup (1901-1984)

DEATHS

Middleton, Ray (1907-April 10), a leading baritone in films, TV, and top Broadway musicals for 30 years.

Mitchell, Clarence M., Jr. (1911-March 18), lawyer, lobbyist for the National Association for the Advancement of Colored People from 1950 to 1978.

Moore, Ray S. (1905-Jan. 13), cocreator of "The Phantom" comic strip.

Morecambe, Eric (1926-May 28), British entertainer, half of the comedy team Morecambe & Wise, popular on British television in the 1970's.

Motley, Arthur H. (Red) (1901-May 30), publisher of *Parade* magazine, a Sunday newspaper supplement, from 1946 to 1978.

Muhi al-Din, Ahmad Fuad (1926-June 5), prime minister of Egypt since 1982.

*Naguib, Muhammad (1901-Aug. 28), prime minister of Egypt in 1953 and 1954.

Niemöller, Martin (1892-March 6), German Protestant clergyman and theologian who opposed Adolf Hitler and the Nazi Third Reich. He survived eight years in concentration camps.

*O'Flaherty, Liam (1896-Sept. 7), Irish writer, best known for his novel *The Informer* (1926).

Oqirhuyakt (1900-reported in *Time*, July 30), Mongolian warlord, the last known lineal descendant of Genghis Khan.

Overstreet, David (1959-June 24), football player, running back with the Miami Dolphins.

Owings, Nathaniel A. (1903-June 13), architect who pioneered in the design of skyscrapers.

Sir John Betjeman,
British poet laureate.

Estelle Winwood, character
actress for almost 90 years.

James F. Fixx,
expert on running.

Prince Souvanna Phouma,
former prime minister of Laos.

Parks, George A. (1883-May 11), governor of the territory of Alaska from 1925 to 1933.

Parsons, Johnny (1918-Sept. 8) race-car driver who won the Indianapolis 500 race in 1950.

Partch, Virgil F., II (1916-Aug. 10), cartoonist whose work appeared in *The New Yorker* magazine. He also created the "Big George" comic strip.

Peccei, Aurelio (1908-March 14), Italian business executive who in 1968 founded the Club of Rome, a group of scientists and economists who studied problems of industrialization.

Peckinpah, Sam (1925-Dec. 27), motion picture director who made such films as *Ride the High Country* (1962) and *The Wild Bunch* (1969).

*Peerce, Jan (1904-Dec. 15), opera tenor who also sang Tevye in *Fiddler on the Roof* on Broadway and had a best-selling popular hit, "The Bluebird of Happiness."

Perkins, Carl D. (1912-Aug. 3), Democratic congressman from Kentucky since 1949 and a force in liberal social legislation.

*Petrillo, James C. (1892-Oct. 23), colorful president of the American Federation of Musicians from 1940 to 1958.

Petrosian, Tigran V. (1929-Aug. 14), Russian chess grand master, world champion from 1963 to 1969.

Pidgeon, Walter (1897-Sept. 28), Canadian-born actor known for his courtly performances in such films as *How Green Was My Valley* (1941) and *Mrs. Miniver* (1942).

Pillsbury, Philip W. (1903-June 14), industrialist who built one of the largest diversified food-product firms in the United States.

Pocock, Philip E. (1906-Sept. 6), Roman Catholic archbishop of Toronto, Canada, from 1971 to 1978.

Pollack, Jack Harrison (1915-Sept. 30), writer whose books included *Dr. Sam: An American Tragedy* (1972), an analysis of the Sam Sheppard murder trial.

Powell, William (1892-March 5), Hollywood star of the 1930's and 1940's who played the sophisticated leading man in the "Thin Man" films with Myrna Loy.

*Priestley, J. B. (John Boynton Priestley) (1894-Aug. 14), British author, playwright, and literary critic, best known for his novel *The Good Companions* (1929).

*Raskin, Ellen (1928-Aug. 8), writer and illustrator who won the 1979 Newbery Medal.

Reard, Louis (1897-Sept. 17), French automobile engineer who designed the bikini swimsuit in 1946.

Reed, Arthur (1860-April 15), said to be the oldest man in the United States. He farmed cotton until he was 98 and worked as a watchman until he was 116.

Reeves, Rosser (1909-Jan. 24), advertising executive who advocated the hard sell in his popular book *Reality in Advertising* (1961).

Renault, Gilbert (Colonel Rémy) (1905-July 29), a leader of the French Resistance in World War II.

Robson, Dame Flora McK. (1902-July 7), leading British actress whose 50-year career included performances in 60 films and more than 100 plays.

Rock, John (1890-Dec. 4), codeveloper of the birth-control pill.

Romanov, Semyon F. (1922-May 22), Russian military leader, chief of staff of the Soviet air defense forces in 1983 when a Soviet fighter plane shot down Korean Air Lines flight 007.

Rose, Leonard (1918-Nov. 16), distinguished cellist, teacher at the Juilliard School of Music.

Rossiter, Leonard (1927-Oct. 5), British actor who starred in the TV series "The Fall and Rise of Reginald Perrin."

Rowe, James H. (1909-June 17), lawyer, an adviser to President Franklin D. Roosevelt, and a backroom power in Democratic politics for 40 years.

Ryle, Sir Martin (1918-Oct. 14), British astrophysicist, co-winner of the 1974 Nobel Prize for physics.

Schacht, Al (1892-July 14), baseball-player-turned-clown who entertained millions of fans at many World Series and All-Star games.

Schwartz, Arthur (1900-Sept. 3), composer for Broadway shows whose sophisticated hits included "Dancing in the Dark" (1931).

Seton-Watson, Hugh (1916-Dec.19), one of Great Britain's foremost historians.

***Shaw, Irwin** (1913-May 16), prolific author of such acclaimed stories as "The Girls in Their Summer Dresses" and "Sailor Off the Bremen." His best-selling novels included *The Young Lions* (1948) and *Rich Man, Poor Man* (1970).

***Shehan, Lawrence Joseph Cardinal** (1898-Aug. 26), Roman Catholic archbishop of Baltimore from 1961 to 1974. He was appointed cardinal in 1965.

***Sholokhov, Mikhail A.** (1905-Feb. 21), Russian author, winner of the Nobel Prize for literature in 1965. His books included the four-volume historical novel *The Quiet Don* (1928-1940).

Sinclair, Gordon (1900-May 17), Canadian journalist who became a folk hero to many Americans after his 1973 broadcast describing them as being "the most generous and possibly the least appreciated people in all the world."

Slipyj, Josyf Cardinal (1892-Sept. 7), Ukrainian Roman Catholic, major archbishop of the Ukrainian Catholic Church. He was appointed cardinal in 1965 after his release from 18 years in Soviet prisons.

Smith, John C. (1903-Jan. 15), Canadian-born theologian, a president of the World Council of Churches from 1968 to 1975.

Souvanna Phouma, Prince (1901-Jan. 10), prime minister of Laos for much of the time from 1951 to 1975.

Speidel, Hans (1897-Nov. 28), German general who plotted to kill Hitler and who commanded the North Atlantic Treaty Organization's land forces from 1957 to 1963.

Stern, Philip Van Doren (1900-July 31), novelist, best known for *The Greatest Gift* (1943), a Christmas fantasy that became the popular motion picture *It's a Wonderful Life* (1947).

***Stuart, Jesse H.** (1907-Feb. 17), poet laureate of Kentucky and author of the best-selling book *Taps for Private Tussie* (1943).

Taylor, Glen H. (1904-April 28), Democratic senator from Idaho from 1945 to 1951 and the Progressive Party's candidate for Vice President in 1948.

Teagarden, Charles E. (1913-Dec. 10), jazz trumpeter known as "Little Tea."

Touré, (Ahmed) Sékou (1922-March 26), president of Guinea since 1958.

***Truffaut, François** (1932-Oct. 21), French motion-picture director whose films ranged from *The 400 Blows* (1959) to *The Wild Child* (1970).

Tubb, Ernest (1914-Sept. 6), country music singer and composer whose hits included "I'm Walking the Floor over You" and "Try Me One More Time."

Ustinov, Dimitri F. (1908-Dec. 20), the Soviet Union's defense minister since 1976.

Voorhis, Jerry (1901-Sept. 11), Democratic congressman from California from 1937 to 1947. He lost his seat to then-novice Republican Richard M. Nixon.

Wallace, Lila Acheson (1889-May 8), cofounder of *Reader's Digest* magazine.

Waring, Fred M. (1900-July 29), musician, a big band conductor for six decades, especially known for his familiar theme "Dream, Dream, Dream." He also invented the Waring blender.

Webster, Paul F. (1907-March 22), Hollywood lyricist who won Oscars for "Secret Love" (1953), "Love Is a Many-Splendored Thing" (1955), and "The Shadow of Your Smile" (1965).

Marvin Gaye, singer who blended soul and gospel music.

François Truffaut, French film director.

Irwin Shaw, writer of acclaimed short stories and novels.

General Mark W. Clark, World War II leader.

Weissmuller, Johnny (1904-Jan. 20), Olympic champion of the 1920's who set 67 swimming records and became Hollywood's definitive Tarzan.

Werner, Oskar (1923-Oct. 23), Austrian actor best known for his roles in the motion pictures *Jules and Jim* (1961) and *Ship of Fools* (1965).

***West, Jessamyn** (1907-Feb. 23), writer, best known for her stories about Quakers, including *The Friendly Persuasion* (1945).

Willson, Meredith (1902-June 15), writer, composer, and lyricist whose hit shows included *The Music Man* (1957), and *The Unsinkable Molly Brown* (1960).

Wilson, Charles H. (1917-July 21), Democratic congressman from California from 1963 to 1980.

Winwood, Estelle (1883-June 20), British actress who appeared in 40 Broadway plays and 20 films.

Wolff, Karl (1900-July 16), Nazi SS general who negotiated the surrender of German troops in Italy to the Allied forces in 1945.

Yadin, Yigael (1917-June 28), Israeli military hero and archaeologist who led the 1963-1965 team that found the ruins of ancient Masada.

Yarbrough, LeeRoy (1938-Dec. 7), the top driver in stock car racing in 1969.

Young, Stephen M. (1889-Dec. 1), Democratic senator from Ohio from 1959 to 1971.

Zivic, Fritzie (1913-May 16), world welterweight boxing champion in 1940 and 1941.   Irene B. Keller

DELAWARE. See STATE GOVERNMENT.

DEMOCRATIC PARTY. The United States general election, held on Nov. 6, 1984, marked the second successive landslide defeat of a Democratic presidential ticket. The loss was made less painful, however, by a Democratic gain of 2 seats in the Republican-controlled U.S. Senate.

The Presidential Results. The Democratic presidential candidate was Walter F. Mondale, Vice President in the Administration of President Jimmy Carter. Mondale was swamped by the tidal wave of votes for President Ronald Reagan, who won reelection with about 59 per cent of the popular vote to Mondale's 41 per cent. Reagan carried 49 states, and Mondale prevailed only in his home state of Minnesota and the District of Columbia. The Democratic ticket of Mondale and U.S. Representative Geraldine A. Ferraro of New York — the first woman ever nominated for Vice President by a major political party — received a paltry 13 electoral votes compared to a record 525 for Reagan and Vice President George H. W. Bush.

Mondale was at a disadvantage from the outset of the campaign because of the credit given Reagan for peace and prosperity, and a feeling of renewed national pride among many Americans. Polls taken by television's ABC News of voters leaving polling places showed Reagan had the support of 62 per cent of the men voting, 54 per cent of women, 56 per cent of Roman Catholics, and 63 per cent of whites. Mondale was supported by 89 per cent of blacks, 69 per cent of Jews, and 54 per cent of union households. The polls also showed that President Reagan swept the South, winning the votes of 71 per cent of Southern whites. Mondale received the votes of 90 per cent of Southern blacks.

The Road to the Nomination. Democratic prospects for victory may also have been hampered by the long and sometimes bitter struggle for the party's presidential nomination. Contenders who dropped out of the race during the long primary season were Senator Alan Cranston of California, former Florida Governor Reubin O'D. Askew, Senator Ernest F. Hollings of South Carolina, Senator John H. Glenn, Jr., of Ohio, and former Senator George S. McGovern of South Dakota.

Among the contestants who stayed in the race was Jesse L. Jackson, a black civil rights leader from Chicago and the first major black candidate for the presidential nomination. But Mondale's principal rival for the nomination was Senator Gary W. Hart of Colorado, a dark horse contender who emerged as the surprise winner of New Hampshire's Democratic primary on February 28. Hart gained a clear advantage in early primaries. In the end, Hart won 12 primaries, Mon-

Democratic presidential hopefuls, from left, Walter F. Mondale, Jesse L. Jackson, and Gary W. Hart join CBS's Dan Rather, back to camera, for a debate in March.

Geraldine Ferraro and Walter Mondale wave to well-wishers in St. Paul, Minn., in July after Mondale named Ferraro as his running mate.

dale won 11, and Jackson won 2. But Mondale went to the party's July national convention in San Francisco with 2,191 delegates to 1,200.5 for Hart and 458.5 for Jackson. Mondale was nominated by acclamation on July 18.

Mondale's choice of Ferraro, a three-term House member, electrified the political scene and gave the Democrats a temporary lift. But soon there was controversy over disclosure of Ferraro's family finances and a divisive fight over an attempt by Mondale to oust Democratic National Chairman Charles T. Manatt.

Congressional Races. In House races, a 14- or 15-seat gain by Republican (GOP) candidates did not represent a great ideological change. The balance remained much the same because, in some cases, conservative Republicans defeated equally conservative Democrats. One Indiana race was still being contested as Congress convened in January 1985.

In the Senate, Democrats reduced the Republican majority from 10 to 6 — the new breakdown is 53 to 47 — after defeating two GOP incumbents who were Reagan loyalists. United States Representative Tom Harkin of Iowa, a liberal Democrat, defeated Senator Roger W. Jepsen, and Democratic U.S. Representative Paul Simon of Illinois bested Senator Charles H. Percy. The only Democratic senator to be defeated was Kentucky's

Walter D. Huddleston. This loss was offset by the election in Tennessee of Democratic U.S. Representative Albert A. Gore, Jr., to the seat vacated by retiring Senate Majority Leader Howard H. Baker, Jr.

State Races. Democrats lost one governorship as gains in North Dakota, Washington, and Vermont were more than offset by Republican gains in Utah, Rhode Island, North Carolina, and West Virginia. But Democrats still held an edge in governorships, 34 to 16. The number of state legislatures in which both houses were controlled by Democrats was reduced from 33 to 27. Republicans retained solid control in 11 states.

Leadership. In December, House Democrats reelected Thomas P. (Tip) O'Neill, Jr., of Massachusetts as Speaker and James C. Wright, Jr., of Texas, as majority leader. In the Senate, they reelected Robert C. Byrd of West Virginia as minority leader. Among Democrats seen as potential 1988 presidential candidates were Hart; Governors Mario M. Cuomo of New York, Mark White of Texas, and Michael S. Dukakis of Massachusetts; and Senators Bill Bradley of New Jersey, Joseph R. Biden, Jr., of Delaware, and Dale Bumpers of Arkansas. Frank Cormier and Margot Cormier

See also ELECTIONS; FERRARO, GERALDINE A.; MONDALE, WALTER F.; REPUBLICAN PARTY. In WORLD BOOK, see DEMOCRATIC PARTY.

DENMARK. The Conservative-led minority coalition government of Prime Minister Poul Schlüter narrowly won a general election on Jan. 10, 1984. At first, they seemed to have lost. But eight days after the vote, a miscount was discovered in the constituency of Frederiksværk. The seat, which had been awarded to the opposition Social Democrats, went instead to Deputy Prime Minister Henning Christophersen of the Liberal Party. The switch gave the ruling coalition 77 seats in the 179-seat Folketing (parliament). The coalition's seats and 13 seats held by coalition allies gave the coalition a potential of 90 votes, a majority.

Danish voters went to the polls again on June 14 to elect candidates to the European Parliament, a largely advisory body of the European Community (EC or Common Market), and to decide whether the country would remain in the EC. A slate of candidates known as the People's Movement Against the Common Market won only 20.8 per cent of the vote.

Campaigns from Prison. Mogens Glistrup, founder of the antitax Progress Party, campaigned for the Folketing from a public telephone in a prison. He had been imprisoned since August 1983, when he received a 3-year sentence for tax fraud. After winning his old seat in Copenhagen, he escaped from prison but was recaptured. On February 6, the Folketing expelled him, as it had in 1983.

DENTISTRY

Austerity Moves. On April 26, Schlüter proposed austerity measures that he hoped would lead to a reduction in Denmark's 10.7 per cent unemployment rate and a decrease in the nation's $1.3-billion balance-of-payments deficit. The proposals included a $142-million cut in government spending, higher taxes on tobacco and beer, and the extension until 1987 of a measure that held down wage increases.

Defense Cuts. After four months of negotiation, the government and the Social Democrats agreed on July 1 to maintain defense expenditures at their present level of about $1 billion per year until 1989. On May 10, the Folketing voted to withhold the balance of its agreed share of the cost of the installation of Pershing and cruise missiles in North Atlantic Treaty Organization (NATO) countries. (Denmark is a member of NATO, but that organization did not plan to install any of the missiles in Denmark.)

Three days later, the Folketing ordered the government to work toward a Nordic nuclear-free zone recognized by the United States and the Soviet Union. No nuclear weapons would be allowed in this zone, which would include Denmark, Finland, Norway, and Sweden. The Conservatives abstained from both votes.   Kenneth Brown

See also EUROPE (Facts in Brief Table). In WORLD BOOK, see DENMARK.

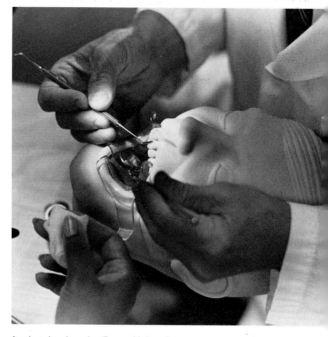

A robot developed at Emory University in Atlanta, Ga., proves to be a willing patient on which dental students can practice.

DENTISTRY. Dental researcher Ralph Rawls of Louisiana State University School of Dentistry in New Orleans reported in April 1984 that he had developed a new plastic sealant material that is longer lasting than existing tooth coatings. Sealants, which have been available for more than 10 years, are applied to protect the chewing surfaces of teeth by preventing decay-causing bacteria from lodging in the teeth's grooves. Long-term studies have shown a reduction of more than 90 per cent in the tooth-decay rate in children treated with conventional sealants. The protection lasts about five years. However, fluoride, a chemical that helps teeth resist decay, when added to the conventional sealant materials caused the sealant to wear down more quickly. Furthermore, researchers found that there was no steady absorption of fluoride by the tooth enamel.

Rawls reported that his new sealant material releases a steady level of fluoride that can benefit both the sealed tooth and neighboring teeth as well — and the sealant does not break down more quickly even though fluoride is added. Additional laboratory studies will be needed to determine the new sealant's effectiveness in human beings.

Biofeedback May Help people who habitually clench or grind their teeth, according to dentist Calvin J. Pierce of the State University of New York School of Dentistry in Buffalo. Pierce reported in mid-1984 on his study of 72 *bruxers,* as teeth-grinders are called. He found that they are not more anxious and are only slightly more depressed than people who do not have this destructive habit, contrary to popular belief.

Bruxism is usually treated with plastic dental splints, which separate opposing tooth surfaces, thus making it more difficult for bruxers to grind their teeth in their sleep. But Pierce's study showed that biofeedback may be beneficial in helping bruxers overcome the habit. Other effective techniques may include relaxation exercises or *mass practice,* a technique that involves deliberate clenching of the teeth several times daily for set periods of time.

Bruxism is a widespread condition. "While we have no accurate figures as to how many people in the general population brux," said Pierce, "a conservative estimate would be some 20 per cent."

Dentist in Space. The proposed three-month tour of duty for future space station crew members has raised the possibility that the astronauts may develop dental problems while in space. For that reason, the National Aeronautics and Space Administration has included an area for dental work in its planned earth-orbiting space station. At least one space station crew member would be trained in dental skills.   Lou Joseph

In WORLD BOOK, see DENTISTRY; TEETH.

DETROIT. The Detroit Tigers' victory over the San Diego Padres in the 1984 World Series — the Detroit baseball team's first championship since 1968 — lent an air of optimism and cheer to this recession-ravaged city in October. See BASEBALL.

Another factor adding to the city's mood of renewed hope was the continued resurgence of the automobile industry. Car and truck production by the Detroit-based "Big Three" automakers — General Motors Corporation (GM), Ford Motor Company, and Chrysler Corporation — rose by a projected 17 per cent over 1983 levels.

High Unemployment. Despite the upturn in the auto industry, however, unemployment in Detroit remained at around 11 per cent — nearly 4 percentage points higher than the rate for the United States as a whole. That meant continuing fiscal problems for Detroit Mayor Coleman A. Young, who proposed a 1984-1985 city budget of almost $1.6 billion, with a built-in deficit of $39 million.

The budget dilemma grew even worse in July, when a federal judge ordered Young to rehire 656 black police officers who were laid off during fiscal crises in 1979 and 1980. But Young said the city could not spend the $30 million required to rehire the officers without financial help from the court.

The mayor ordered increased police patrols around Detroit schools in February 1984, after 47 schoolgirls reported that they had been sexually attacked since September 1983. After the heightened patrols began, only four more schoolgirl assaults were reported during the school year.

Street crime also marred the city's image on the night of October 14, after the Tigers won the World Series. Accompanying the victory celebration in downtown Detroit were a fatal shooting, three reported sexual assaults, more than 100 injuries, and assorted muggings, purse snatchings, and acts of vandalism. Two weeks later, vandals set more than 500 fires in Detroit on "Devil's Night," October 30, and Halloween, October 31.

On November 27, Young announced that the city would take steps to reduce the amount of violent crime in Detroit. He said more police officers would be hired in 1985 and up to 1,000 more officers would be assigned to patrol the streets.

Bribery Conviction. In October 1984, Charles Beckham, the city's former director of water and sewers, was sentenced to three years in prison after being convicted on bribery and fraud charges. Federal prosecutors said that in 1982 Beckham took a bribe of $16,000 to steer a multimillion-dollar sludge-hauling contract to a private company. Although he quit his city job, Beckham said he was innocent and would appeal his conviction.

On a trade mission to Kenya in May, Detroit Mayor Coleman A. Young surveys the Masai Mara Game Reserve from an open-topped vehicle.

Another city department head, Detroit Institute of Arts Director Frederick J. Cummings, resigned in January 1984. Cummings' critics charged that he had appointed his friends to executive positions at the institute and had used the museum's funds improperly. A city audit disclosed no illegal conduct by Cummings or other institute executives.

Construction. Federal officials blocked Detroit's plans to enlarge Cobo Hall, which is part of the city's Civic Center, by extending it some 360 feet (110 meters) over the Detroit River. After the U.S. Army Corps of Engineers said that the $81-million proposal would cause environmental and safety hazards, city developers decided to build the addition on land.

The city broke ground in March on the Millender Center, a $71-million downtown complex consisting of a hotel, an apartment tower, and new retail, office, and parking space. The center was scheduled to be completed in 1985.

But an even larger downtown development project, the People Mover transit system, faced mounting economic and construction problems. Cost overruns pushed the estimated price of the project — a computer-controlled rail system designed to loop around downtown Detroit — from $135 million to $170 million. David Kushma

See also CITY. In WORLD BOOK, see DETROIT.

DICKSON, BRIAN (1916-   ), became chief justice of Canada on April 19, 1984, succeeding Bora Laskin, who died on March 26. Dickson had been a member of the Supreme Court of Canada since 1973. As a Supreme Court justice, he was noted for his sensitivity to the rights of the individual.

Robert George Brian Dickson was born on May 25, 1916, in Yorkton, Sask. He graduated from the University of Manitoba and in 1938 received a law degree from the university's law school.

Dickson served in the Royal Canadian Artillery from 1940 until 1945, during World War II. In 1944, he lost most of his right leg in combat. He practiced law with Aikins, MacAulay & Company in Winnipeg, Man., from 1945 until 1963 and was a lecturer at the University of Manitoba law school from 1948 until 1954. In 1963, he was appointed to Manitoba's Court of Queen's Bench, which hears all the province's major civil and criminal cases. In 1967, he was named to the Court of Appeal, Manitoba's highest court.

From 1960 to 1971, Dickson served as chancellor of the Diocese of Rupert's Land for the Anglican Church of Canada. From 1971 to 1973, he was chairman of the Board of Governors of the University of Manitoba.

Dickson and his wife, Barbara, have one daughter and three sons. Jay Myers

DISARMAMENT. See ARMED FORCES.

DISASTERS. The death toll from natural disasters is rising, and many disasters attributed to nature are actually caused or made worse by human activity. These were the conclusions reached by a study called *Natural Disasters: Acts of God or Acts of Man?* released in July 1984.

The study, sponsored by the Swedish Red Cross, was done by Anders Wijkman, head of the Swedish Red Cross, and Lloyd Timberlake, an official of a London-based environmental organization called Earthscan. Wijkman and Timberlake analyzed data from the 1960's and 1970's provided by the United States government and the International Red Cross. During the 1970's, natural disasters — defined as floods, droughts, earthquakes, hurricanes, and volcanic eruptions — caused six times as many deaths as in the previous decade. Much of the increase in disaster fatalities occurred in the developing countries of Africa, Asia, and Latin America.

Wijkman and Timberlake attributed the increase in deaths to several factors, all related to poverty. For example, rural families who cannot afford good farmland may be forced to live on low-lying areas prone to flooding or on steep hillsides where the risk of landslides is great. Overgrazing and the destruction of forests, which are common in developing countries, make the land susceptible to drought and flooding. In cities, poverty leads to the growth of shantytowns — crowded sections of substandard housing — where storms, earthquakes, and fires cause many deaths.

Such disaster-prone urban areas were the sites of two of 1984's worst disasters. In February, leaking gasoline from a pipeline ignited in a shantytown on the outskirts of Cubatão, Brazil. It set off a fire storm that quickly destroyed many of the town's flimsy shacks. The blaze burned at temperatures above 1800° F. (980° C), so hot that many of the dead were completely incinerated. Only 86 bodies were recovered, but official investigators placed the death toll at a minimum of 508 and perhaps more than 700.

In November, a series of explosions rocked a liquefied natural gas storage site in Tlalnepantla, near Mexico City. Balls of fire shot into the air, and fiery debris rained down on a slum neighborhood surrounding the gas-storage facilities. More than 20 square blocks turned into a blazing inferno where at least 490 people died.

Poverty also contributed to the worst industrial accident in history, a poison-gas leak in Bhopal, India, in December. Deadly methyl isocyanate gas from a pesticide plant spread over the city during the night, killing at least 2,500 people. Most of the dead were poor slumdwellers given land near the plant by the government.

Disasters that resulted in 30 or more deaths in 1984 included the following:

Fire fighters search the remains of a shantytown near Cubatão,
Brazil, where at least 508 people died in a gasoline-fed fire in February.

Aircraft Crashes

Jan. 10 — Sofia, Bulgaria. A Bulgarian airliner carrying 50 people crashed in snowy weather, killing all aboard.

Aug. 5 — Dhaka (formerly spelled Dacca), Bangladesh. A Bangladesh passenger plane plunged into a marsh while trying to land at the Dhaka airport during a rainstorm. All 49 people on board died.

Sept. 18 — Quito, Ecuador. An Ecuadorean Airlines cargo jet crashed in a residential neighborhood, killing 60 people — 54 of them on the ground.

Oct. 28 — Kabul, Afghanistan. About 240 Soviet soldiers died when their plane crashed shortly after take-off.

Bus and Truck Crashes

Jan. 30 — Ropar, India. About 80 people died after their bus swerved to avoid a bicyclist, broke through the railings of a bridge, and plunged into a canal.

Early May — Delhi, India. Thirty-five bus passengers were electrocuted when bicycles on the roof of the bus touched roadside electric wires.

June 9 — La Grita, Venezuela. A school bus struck a bridge, rolled over, and caught fire, killing 33 students.

Aug. 1 — Malda, India. At least 41 people died after their bus blew a front tire and hurtled into a canal.

Sept. 1 — Damagum, Nigeria, near Potiskum. About 40 people died after a bus collided with an oil tanker truck.

Oct. 31 — Buenos Aires, Argentina. Forty-three bus passengers were killed after a train slammed into their bus.

Dec. 24 — South Africa. A bus carrying workers from Cape Town to Transkei hurtled over a cliff, killing 45 people.

Explosions and Fires

Jan. 14 — Pusan, South Korea. Fire broke out in a sauna at a tourist hotel, killing at least 38 people.

Feb. 25 — Cubatão, Brazil. At least 508 people burned to death in a gasoline pipeline fire.

Mid-May — Severomorsk, Soviet Union, near Murmansk. A huge explosion tore through a naval ammunition depot, killing 200 to 300 people.

Nov. 2-3 — Ad Dahriyah, Egypt. At least 50 people died in a fire that began in a kitchen and was carried from house to house by strong winds and burning rats.

Nov. 19 — Tlalnepantla, near Mexico City. Explosions at a liquefied natural gas storage site sparked a fire storm that destroyed a slum area, killing at least 490 people.

Dec. 2 — Tbilisi, Soviet Union. At least 100 people were killed in a gas explosion that tore through an apartment building.

Floods

Jan. 29-Feb. 2 — Mozambique, Swaziland, and South Africa. More than 100 people died in floods caused by heavy rains from Cyclone Domoina.

Mid-May to mid-June — Bangladesh and northeastern India. Monsoon floods and landslides left about 200 dead.

Early September — South Korea. Heavy rains caused severe flooding that killed about 190 people.

Mid-September — Nepal. A heavy downpour brought floods and landslides that caused more than 150 deaths.

Mid-November — Andhra Pradesh and Tamil Nadu states, India. More than 393 people were killed in floods caused by a cyclone that struck on November 14.

Hurricanes, Tornadoes, and Other Storms

March 28 — North and South Carolina. A string of tornadoes killed at least 60 people.

June 9 — Western Soviet Union. A series of tornadoes caused at least 400 deaths, most of them near Ivanovo.

Aug. 29 — Philippines. Tropical Storm June battered the Philippines, killing 53 people.

Sept. 2-3 — Philippines. Typhoon Ike left more than 1,360 people dead and more than 500 others missing.

Late October — Philippines. Tropical Storm Warren triggered floods and landslides that killed 42 people.

Nov. 5 — Philippines. Typhoon Agnes pounded the central Philippines, killing at least 515 people.

Mine Disasters

Jan. 18 — Off Kyushu island, Japan. A fire in an undersea coal mine killed 83 miners.

April 21 — Resavica, Yugoslavia, near Belgrade. Thirty-three coal miners died in a gas explosion.

June 20 — Southeast of Taipei, Taiwan. An explosion triggered by a fire in a coal transport car killed 74 miners at the Hai-shan coal mine.

July 10 — Northeast of Taipei, Taiwan. Fire swept through the Mei-shan coal mine, killing 103 miners in Taiwan's second mine disaster in less than a month.

Dec. 5 — Southwest of Taipei, Taiwan. An explosion and cave-in at the Hai-shan Yikeng coal mine killed at least 93 miners.

Shipwrecks

Jan. 22 — Off Tawitawi Island, Philippines. A ferry capsized, drowning at least 50 people.

April 17 — Near Dhaka, Bangladesh. As many as 150 passengers drowned after two motor launches collided on a river, sinking one of the boats.

Aug. 13 — Off the coast of Sabah state, Malaysia. Nearly 200 Indonesians, most of them lumber workers, apparently drowned after a ferry capsized.

Aug. 16 — Off the coast of Brazil. At least 40 oil workers drowned after a rescue boat carrying them was swamped by the shock wave from an exploding offshore oil rig.

Mid-September — Rapti River, Nepal. An overcrowded boat capsized in the Rapti River near the border between Nepal and India, drowning nearly 100 passengers.

Oct. 14 — Western Nigeria. A river ferry on the way to Lagos sank, drowning more than 100 passengers.

Oct. 28 — Off Marinduque Island, Philippines. More than 100 people were missing and believed drowned after a ferryboat sank in stormy seas.

Late November — Barisal, Bangladesh. More than 100 people drowned after a boat turned over on a river.

Trainwrecks

Feb. 10 — Near New Delhi, India. One train slammed into the rear of another, killing at least 43 people.

June 18 — Central Angola. At least 50 people died after a speeding passenger train derailed and crashed.

July 14 — Divača, Yugoslavia, near Koper. A freight train crashed into the rear of a holiday express train that was halted on a siding, killing at least 36 people.

Aug. 16 — Near Balaghat, Madhya Pradesh state, India. At least 56 and perhaps as many as 100 people died after a bridge collapsed, plunging railroad cars into a river.

Other Disasters

May 27 — Dongchuan, China. A landslide triggered by heavy rains killed about 100 people.

Nov. 7 — Munnar, Kerala state, India. About 125 schoolchildren were missing and feared dead after a rope bridge — where they had been standing to watch a helicopter land — collapsed and plunged them into a stream.

Dec. 3 — Bhopal, India. Deadly methyl isocyanate gas, leaking from a Union Carbide Corporation pesticide plant, spread over the city of Bhopal. The gas killed at least 2,500 people and countless animals in the worst industrial accident in history.

Mid-December — Leninsk-Kuznetskiy, Soviet Union. Several hundred people died in an accident of undisclosed nature at a defense plant.   Sara Dreyfuss

DJIBOUTI. See Africa.

DOG. The Westminster Kennel Club held its 108th annual show in February 1984 at New York City's Madison Square Garden. A black Newfoundland, Champion Seaward's Blackbeard, was selected best-in-show. The dog is owned by Elinor Ayers of Manchester Center, Vt.

The American Kennel Club (AKC) registered 1,085,248 dogs during 1983. Cocker spaniels replaced poodles at the top of the list. Labrador retrievers advanced to third place, followed by Doberman pinschers, German shepherd dogs, golden retrievers, beagles, miniature schnauzers, dachshunds, and Shetland sheepdogs.

The AKC celebrated its 100th anniversary in 1984. The highlight of the centennial was a two-day dog show and obedience trial held in November in Philadelphia, where the AKC was founded. Champion Covy Tucker Hills Manhattan, a German shepherd dog owned by Shirlee Braunstein and Jane Firestone of Lyndonville, N.Y., was judged the top winner. The highest-scoring dog in the obedience trial was an English springer spaniel, Amity's Lord Maxwell CDX, owned by Steven McCrorie of Souderton, Pa.   Roberta Vesley

In WORLD BOOK, see DOG.

DOMINICAN REPUBLIC. See LATIN AMERICA; WEST INDIES.

DROUGHT. See AFRICA; WATER; WEATHER.

Champion Braeburn's Close Encounter, a Scottish terrier owned by Alan Novick, became the top winner in U.S. dog show history after an April success.

DRUGS. The United States Food and Drug Administration (FDA) on May 18, 1984, approved a new nonprescription drug for the relief of pain. The medication, ibuprofen, appeared on pharmacy and supermarket shelves under the brand names Advil and Nuprin. Both are intended for the temporary relief of headache, other aches and pains, and menstrual cramps; and for reducing fever. A high-dose form of ibuprofen had been available by prescription since 1974 under the brand names Motrin and Rufen. The FDA's approval of ibuprofen gave Americans access to their third over-the-counter pain reliever. Acetaminophen, the ingredient in Tylenol and Datril, and aspirin are the two other over-the-counter drugs.

A panel of scientific experts convened by the National Institutes of Health (NIH) in Bethesda, Md., on February 29 warned against extended, heavy use of nonprescription drugs that combine aspirin and acetaminophen. The panel concluded that heavy use of such combination pain-relievers could cause kidney damage. It said consideration should be given to banning these combinations.

New Drugs. A new group of oral prescription drugs for the treatment of Type II, or adult-onset, diabetes was approved by the FDA on May 10. The drugs are glipizide and glyburide. They are stronger and have fewer side effects than existing oral medicines for this milder form of diabetes, which does not require insulin injections. But the FDA cautioned on April 11 that the use of oral drugs in the treatment of diabetes is associated with increased risk of death from heart attack and stroke. The agency ordered that all such drugs carry a warning label telling prospective users about this risk.

On September 5, the FDA approved the first drug proved effective for the treatment of *intermittent claudication,* a painful impairment of blood circulation in the legs. The new medication, pentoxifylline, will be sold under the brand name Trental.

On December 11, the U.S. government announced changes in FDA regulations designed to speed the approval of new drugs. Among other changes, the new rules permitted use of clinical studies done in other countries to prove a drug's safety.

Generic Drugs. On September 24, U.S. President Ronald Reagan signed into law a bill to speed the introduction of generic drugs, making more of these low-cost prescription medications available to consumers. The bill's supporters said it would double the number of generic drugs available in the United States.

The new law allows generic-drug firms to begin marketing generic versions of brand-name drugs as soon as the patent has expired, without having to duplicate the lengthy testing for safety and effectiveness already performed on the original drugs. The law also provides big drug companies with additional patent protection for their products beyond the 17 years of exclusive marketing rights previously available. Firms have up to five additional years of patent protection to offset time spent in meeting FDA requirements for testing a new drug.

Vaccine Developments. Major advances in the development of new and more effective vaccines occurred in 1984. In August, two research teams — one at New York University Medical Center in New York City, the other consisting of scientists at the NIH and Walter Reed Army Institute of Research in Bethesda — announced that they had made progress toward developing a vaccine against malaria. The researchers used genetic-engineering techniques to isolate and reproduce genes from the parasite that causes malaria. Malaria affects about 220 million people and kills more than 1 million each year in Africa alone.

Successful testing of another genetically engineered vaccine — this one against hepatitis B — was reported on June 1 by scientists at the Merck Sharp & Dohme Research Laboratories in West Point, Pa. The researchers said the vaccine offers the first chance for worldwide elimination of this serious liver disease, caused by the hepatitis virus. Hepatitis B, also known as serum hepatitis, is responsible for about 200 million cases of liver damage, primarily in Africa and Asia.

A vaccine against chicken pox, licensed from Japanese researchers, was further developed by the Merck laboratories. Scientists at the University of Pennsylvania in Philadelphia tested the vaccine on a group of children and in May reported that it was effective in preventing chicken pox.

Scientists at the NIH in March reported progress toward developing a more effective influenza vaccine. The new vaccine can be administered by nose drops rather than by injection.

On June 13, Wyeth Laboratories Incorporated, in Wayne, Pa., one of two major U.S. producers of whooping cough vaccine, announced it was stopping further production and sale of the vaccine. The firm cited lawsuits arising from rare side effects of the vaccine. On December 11, Canadian-based Connaught Laboratories Incorporated withdrew its vaccine because of the high cost of liability insurance. The firms' actions created concern about a potential vaccine shortage. On December 19, Connaught offered to provide enough vaccine to avert a shortage if the U.S. government would assume liability for any lawsuits. On June 19, the U.S. Centers for Disease Control in Atlanta, Ga., had issued a public assurance about the safety of the vaccine.   Michael Woods

In the Special Reports section, see Don't Gamble with Your Heart. In World Book, see Drug.

DUARTE, JOSÉ NAPOLEÓN (1926-   ), became president of El Salvador on June 1, 1984, after winning a runoff election in May against Roberto D'Aubuisson, an extreme right wing candidate. Duarte, a moderate, thus became president for the second time, but this was the first time he was elected by popular vote. See EL SALVADOR.

Duarte was born on Nov. 23, 1926, in San Salvador, the capital of El Salvador. His father was a tailor. Duarte attended the University of Notre Dame in South Bend, Ind., and after graduating in 1948, he returned to El Salvador to work as a civil engineer. Duarte's interest in politics began in 1960, when he helped found the Christian Democratic Party. In 1964, he was elected mayor of San Salvador. In 1972, he ran for president of El Salvador and was narrowly defeated. Suspecting vote fraud, Colonel Benjamín Mejía led a coup attempt on Duarte's behalf, but it was routed. Duarte was jailed, beaten, and then exiled. He spent seven years in Venezuela.

After a military coup in 1979, Duarte returned to El Salvador in March 1980 to become a member of a civilian-military junta. In December 1980, the junta named him president, but after elections for the Constituent Assembly in March 1982, a new government came to power.

Duarte married Maria Inés Durán in 1949. They have six children.   Rod Such

DUVALL, ROBERT (1931-   ), received the Academy of Motion Picture Arts and Sciences Award for best actor on April 9, 1984. He won the Oscar for his performance in *Tender Mercies* as a down-on-his-luck country singer who turns his life around. Duvall had been nominated for an Oscar in 1972, 1979, and 1981, for his acting in *The Godfather, Apocalypse Now,* and *The Great Santini.*

Duvall, the son of a rear admiral in the United States Navy, was born in San Diego on Jan. 5, 1931. He graduated from Principia College in Elsah, Ill., in 1953 with a bachelor's degree in drama. In 1955, after serving in the U.S. Army, he moved to New York City to study acting.

Duvall got his first professional break in 1957 in a one-night stage production of Arthur Miller's *A View from the Bridge.* His performance led to television parts and eventually to movies. In 1965, Duvall won an Obie Award for his performance in the same role in another production of Miller's play. Duvall has also appeared in stage productions of *Wait Until Dark* and *American Buffalo.*

Duvall made his motion-picture debut in 1963 as the spooky neighbor in *To Kill a Mockingbird.* His other films include *M*A*S*H* (1970), *The Great Northfield Minnesota Raid* (1972), *The Seven-Per-Cent Solution* (1976), and *Network* (1977).

Duvall married his second wife, actress Gail Youngs, in 1982.   Barbara A. Mayes

EASTERN ORTHODOX CHURCHES. Unity remained an elusive goal at the 1984 meeting of the Roman Catholic-Eastern Orthodox Theological Commission. The commission has met every two years since 1980 to discuss ways of resolving the disagreements that have divided the Eastern and Western churches since their *schism* (split) in 1054. The 1984 talks centered on the nature of baptism, the Eucharist, and confirmation. Although agreement was reached on many points, the dialogue failed to produce a joint statement.

The Movement Toward Unity, known as ecumenism, received support in other meetings during 1984. On June 12, Pope John Paul II, leader of the world's Roman Catholics, visited the Western European headquarters of the Orthodox Church in Geneva, Switzerland. The pope assured Metropolitan Damaskinos, the leader of the Orthodox Church in Switzerland, that the Roman Catholic Church wanted to remove obstacles to healing the split between the churches. On June 29, representatives of the patriarch of Constantinople, the spiritual leader of the Eastern Orthodox churches, participated in the Feast of the Throne of Rome at St. Peter's Church in Rome.

A statement issued in 1983 by the World Council of Churches (WCC), an organization of Eastern Orthodox and Protestant churches, continued to

Jimmy Carter leads tributes to Archbishop Iakovos, who in April celebrated 25 years as head of the Greek Orthodox Church of North and South America.

provoke discussion in 1984. The statement expressed basic agreement on baptism, the Eucharist, and ministry. But it failed to win full approval from many Orthodox churches.

In Greece, tensions lessened between the Greek Orthodox Church and the Socialist government. Church and state had long been closely connected in Greece. But since coming to power in 1981, the government of Prime Minister Andreas Papandreou has legalized abortion, established civil marriage, simplified the divorce procedure, and passed other laws opposed by the church. In 1984, however, each side moderated its attacks against the other.

In the United States, Archbishop Iakovos celebrated his 25th anniversary as primate of the Greek Orthodox Diocese of North and South America. A service held on April 1 brought together Orthodox, Roman Catholic, and Protestant leaders — a testimony to the archbishop's dedication to ecumenism.

John Meyendorff was installed as dean of St. Vladimir's Orthodox Theological Seminary in Crestwood, N.Y., in May. Meyendorff succeeded Alexander Schmemann, who died in December 1983. The seminary serves the Orthodox Church in America. Stanley Samuel Harakas

In WORLD BOOK, see EASTERN ORTHODOX CHURCHES.

ECONOMICS. The United States economy grew briskly during the first half of 1984 and then slowed significantly in the second half. The net gain in the gross national product — after adjusting for inflation — was 6 per cent for the year, the most rapid rate since 1977. The actual level was just short of $3.6 trillion.

Unemployment dropped from its average 1983 level of 9.5 per cent to 7.2 per cent at the end of 1984. The total civilian labor force increased by some 2 million people during the year. More than 105 million people were at work, a net job creation of 3.8 million for the year.

Inflation in 1984 was about 4 per cent, as measured by the Consumer Price Index. Along with slightly longer work hours, this meant that the real average earnings of employed workers (after adjusting for inflation), rose by nearly 2 per cent. This equaled the increase in 1983.

Productivity (output per labor hour) continued to rise in 1984, in part because of increased investment in new plants and equipment, but mainly because the large number of workers who entered the labor force in the late 1970's and early 1980's were becoming more experienced at their jobs and, therefore, more productive. Along with modest increases in wages and relaxed work rules, this allowed manufacturers to hold labor costs per unit of output to less than a 1 per cent increase.

The Deficit. Despite these favorable developments, a number of problems remained unsolved at year-end, and some seemed likely to plague the economy well into the future. Chief among these was the size of the annual federal deficit. Although it dropped to $175.3 billion in the fiscal year ending Sept. 30, 1984, the slower growth rate and rising expenditures projected for 1985 promised to push the annual deficit near $200 billion. Only substantial expenditure cuts or increased taxes could lower the deficit below this level.

The size of the deficit greatly concerns many economists because it tends to keep interest rates high. During 1984, interest rates rose during most of the year and then fell in the third and fourth quarters to the levels of the first quarter. By historical standards, however, these rates were still well above normal. If government demand for borrowed funds could be significantly reduced, interest rates could be expected to fall and thus encourage continued growth in the economy.

Tax Plan. On November 27, Secretary of the Treasury Donald T. Regan unveiled the long-awaited tax-simplification plan that would substantially revise the current Internal Revenue Code. The proposal called for reducing the current 14 income tax brackets for individuals to 3 and the top corporate tax bracket from 46 per cent to 33

Treasury Secretary Donald T. Regan unveils the department's income tax reform proposal during a press briefing in November in Washington, D.C.

The leaders of the seven largest industrial democracies attend the opening
session of a three-day economic summit conference in London in June.

per cent. The new system would keep government
revenues at approximately their present levels but
would shift more of the total income tax burden
to corporations.

Under the plan, individual exemptions would
nearly double. The three tax brackets would call
for taxation at 15, 25, and 35 per cent, depending
on income. In addition, numerous minor changes
were made in individual income tax deductions.

The most notable was a limit placed on interest
deductions to $5,000 in excess of the total invest-
ment income reported, except for interest on
owner-occupied home mortgages, which would
continue to be fully deductible. For example, if an
individual earned $1,000 in interest from a sav-
ings account, that individual would be able to
deduct only an additional $5,000 in interest pay-
ments on other types of loans, such as a second-
home mortgage, a personal loan, or automobile
loan, for a total interest deduction of $6,000. De-
ductions for state and local taxes would be eliminated, and charitable deductions would be permitted only to the extent that they exceeded 2 per
cent of adjusted gross income.

The average taxpayer would save approximately
8.7 per cent through these and other changes, but
results would differ significantly among individuals, depending upon their particular financial circumstances and their geographic location. For ex-

ample, taxpayers living in states with high state
and local taxes might find themselves worse off as
a result of being unable to deduct these taxes from
their gross income, which could offset the generally lower tax rates. By the same token, taxpayers
living in areas with low state and local taxes would
reap larger benefits.

The Most Significant General Effect would be
that taxpayers at the low end of the income scale
would find their tax bill completely eliminated.
For example, under the present system, a family
of four pays taxes on all income over approximately $8,900. Under the Treasury plan, a family
of four would pay no taxes until income was more
than $11,800. Neither example takes into account
special circumstances that would move the nontax-
able income even higher.

Under the proposal, the tax rate on corporate
profits would drop from 46 per cent to 33 per
cent. For many companies, however, this would be
offset by the elimination of accelerated depreciation and the investment tax credit — benefits that
many corporations now use.

The Treasury Department's purpose was to ensure that all profitable companies pay approximately the same rate of tax. Under the present tax
system, many corporations have had to pay no income taxes at all. The initial response to the proposal, judging from a sharp drop in transactions

on the stock market in the days immediately following its announcement, suggested that this aspect of the road to tax reform and simplification would not be an easy one.

Most analysts agreed that the plan represented an attempt to treat people with equal incomes with greater evenhandedness and to remove some of the inequities that presently exist. No tax action, however, was likely to have any immediate impact on the federal deficit. And it was unlikely that the plan would be approved by Congress exactly as presented by Regan.

The Generally High Interest Rates that prevailed during 1984 did not appear to discourage U.S. consumer spending or investment in new plants and equipment. On the other hand, there were some less fortunate consequences.

The high interest rates attracted a steady flow of investment in the United States from other countries, especially from Europe. This investment kept the value of the U.S. dollar at record levels by comparison with the British pound, West German mark, French franc, Canadian dollar, and Japanese yen, among other currencies.

The strong dollar increased the price of U.S. exports and reduced the price of foreign imports, a combination that had two results. The foreign competition held down prices in the United States,

but U.S. exports became increasingly difficult to sell. The net result in 1984 was a trade deficit of more than $125 billion. Particularly hard hit in the United States were the steel and high-technology machine-tool industries, as well as the foreign market for U.S. farm produce.

All of this added to the number of unemployed people in those basic industries in 1984 and created strong pressures for government action to protect hard-hit industries from foreign imports. For example, shipments of Japanese automobiles to the United States have been under voluntary quotas for four years, and the quota agreement may be extended. Steel and textiles are other industries in which such agreements are either already in place or are under serious discussion.

Economists are almost unanimous in their agreement that such limitations on the free flow of goods and services serve only to reduce the total output of the world — make a smaller pie — and thus prevent many people from rising out of poverty. The fact remains, however, that unhampered trade hurts particular industries and countries. Because this situation prevails throughout much of Western Europe and in specific industries in the United States, economists in 1984 saw renewed pressure for trade limitations on the free flow of goods and services.

"I'm afraid we don't yet have a medical term for the fear of high interest rates."

Martin J. Bucella, *Changing Times*

Selected Key U.S. Economic Indicators

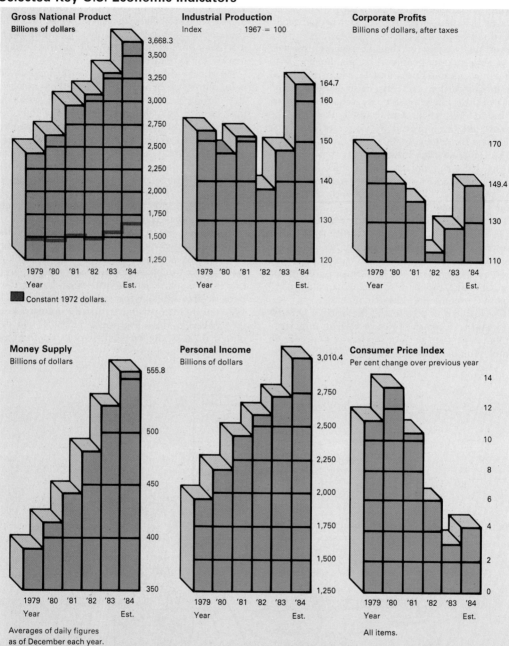

Gross National Product
Billions of dollars

3,668.3
3,500
3,250
3,000
2,750
2,500
2,250
2,000
1,750
1,500
1,250

1979 '80 '81 '82 '83 '84
Year   Est.

Constant 1972 dollars.

Industrial Production
Index   1967 = 100

164.7
160
150
140
130
120

1979 '80 '81 '82 '83 '84
Year   Est.

Corporate Profits
Billions of dollars, after taxes

170
149.4
130
110

1979 '80 '81 '82 '83 '84
Year   Est.

Money Supply
Billions of dollars

555.8
500
450
400
350

1979 '80 '81 '82 '83 '84
Year   Est.

Averages of daily figures
as of December each year.

Personal Income
Billions of dollars

3,010.4
2,750
2,500
2,250
2,000
1,750
1,500
1,250

1979 '80 '81 '82 '83 '84
Year   Est.

Consumer Price Index
Per cent change over previous year

14
12
10
8
6
4
2
0

1979 '80 '81 '82 '83 '84
Year   Est.

All items.

The most comprehensive measure of the nation's total output of goods and services is the gross national product (GNP).
The GNP represents the dollar value in current prices of all goods and services plus the estimated value of certain other
outputs, such as the rental value of owner-occupied dwellings. Industrial production is a monthly measure of the
physical output of manufacturing, mining, and utility industries. Corporate profits are quarterly profit samplings from
major industries. Money supply measures the total amount of money in the economy in currency and checking account
deposits. Personal income is current income received by people (including nonprofit institutions and private trust funds)
before taxes. The consumer price index (CPI) is a measure of changes in the prices of selected goods and services
consumed by urban families and individuals.
All 1984 figures are *Year Book* estimates.

Communist World. A fascinating economic development in the Communist world in 1984 was China's decision to grant a limited degree of independence to plants and businesses located in cities, ending rigid, centralized control by the state. The reforms enabled these state-owned companies to price their products at market rates and to retain a portion of the profits. Most observers believed that this departure from centralized planning, though limited in scope, was the result of the success of similar policies adopted in agriculture in the 1970's, which allow farmers to sell their produce on the open market after delivering a certain portion of their output to the state. The result has been a tremendous increase in agricultural production and rural prosperity. Although the 1984 economic reforms heralded a growing flexibility on the part of China's Communist government to experiment with market-oriented forces, it was a minor step in the direction of what the Western world recognizes as capitalism. See CHINA, PEOPLE'S REPUBLIC OF.

The Soviet Union suffered another shortfall in its planned grain production in 1984. This did not result, however, in an immediate increase in Soviet grain purchases from the United States.

Foreign Debt. Early in 1984, a significant number of developing nations appeared to be on the verge of defaulting on their foreign debts. Argentina, Brazil, Mexico, and the Philippines were most prominently mentioned. They owed substantial interest and principal payments but lacked the foreign exchange earnings necessary to make those payments and also continue importing necessary products. By September 1984, however, they had received substantial assistance from the International Monetary Fund, an agency of the United Nations, in return for promises to carry out austerity measures that would reduce their budget deficits.

Raging inflation was the main cause of Argentina's difficulties. Mexico was affected adversely by lower receipts for oil exports as the Organization of Petroleum Exporting Countries (OPEC) was forced to lower oil prices to $29 per barrel. Even that price was being significantly discounted by some OPEC members. See PETROLEUM AND GAS.

Stock Prices. Uncertainties about the impact of the deficit and the rate of growth in the U.S. economy were at least partially reflected in the level of stock prices on the New York Stock Exchange. Stock prices were approximately 10 per cent lower at the close of 1984 than they had been in late 1983. *Warren W. Shearer*

See also FARM AND FARMING; INTERNATIONAL TRADE AND FINANCE; MANUFACTURING; STOCKS AND BONDS; and individual country articles. In WORLD BOOK, see ECONOMICS.

ECUADOR. See LATIN AMERICA.

EDUCATION. A record number of students registered for the 1984-1985 school year at the approximately 3,000 colleges and universities in the United States. Enrollment reached 12.6 million, up from 1983's record enrollment of 12.5 million. Fewer high school graduates went directly on to college in 1984 than in previous years, but enrollments swelled because more adults started college late or returned to finish a degree in their late 20's or early 30's.

Test Scores. The year 1984 saw a modest increase in test scores. About half the U.S. colleges and universities require that applicants take either the Scholastic Aptitude Test (SAT) or American College Testing Program (ACT). The average SAT scores began to drop in 1963 and continued to drop in 17 of the next 20 years. The ACT average began to fall in 1975. This decline caused many educators to conclude that the quality of high school education was slipping and that colleges and universities were admitting increasingly less qualified students to fill their classrooms and dormitories.

The highest possible score on the SAT, which measures verbal and mathematical ability, is 800, and the lowest possible score is 200. Between 1963 and 1983, the average verbal score fell 53 points, and the average math score dropped 34 points. In 1984, the verbal average registered a tiny 1-point gain to 426, and the math average rose 3 points to 471. The ACT saw a gain from 1983 to 1984 of two-tenths of a percentage point.

Only about 25 per cent of all U.S. high school students take the SAT — presumably the better students who plan to attend a college that requires the tests. Also, the number of test takers varies widely from state to state, from a high of 69 per cent in Connecticut to a low of 3 per cent in Iowa, Mississippi, North Dakota, and South Dakota. Because of this, it is impossible to generalize accurately about a nationwide improvement in high school education from a small gain in SAT scores.

After the Reports. In 1983, a presidential commission issued a devastating indictment of U.S. public schools in *A Nation at Risk*. The report warned that a "rising tide of mediocrity" engulfed the school system and threatened the future of the United States. It was followed by other reports critical of teaching and learning in U.S. schools.

Despite disagreement on where to place the blame and on which solutions to initiate, significant changes took place in U.S. schools during 1984. For example, 48 states enacted or contemplated stiffer high school graduation requirements. Four states — Arkansas, Florida, New Jersey, and New York — began minimum competency tests for high-schoolers. Thirty other states had such tests under consideration.

Some 30 states permitted teachers to earn cred-

High-schoolers from Wheelersburg, Ohio, defeated a team from Jordan High in Durham, N.C., to win the National Academic Championship in Dallas in May.

its for certification at colleges and universities other than schools of education. Thus, the legislators put the emphasis on academic instruction. Discussion continued about subjecting both new and veteran teachers to examinations on the subjects they teach and to outside evaluation of their classroom performance. Other issues under discussion were merit raises for outstanding teachers and the use of "master" teachers to train and guide new teachers. Teachers' organizations, however, have rejected both of these suggestions, which they claim pit teacher against teacher.

Teachers issued their own recommendations for improving the schools at the June 1984 meeting of the National Education Association (NEA), the largest teachers' organization in the United States. The NEA report rejected the idea of peer reviews and master teachers. Instead, it called for a restructuring of the schools that would give teachers greater decision-making powers. It also called for better training of teachers and higher pay. In addition, the NEA proposed that schools require students to master subjects, not just to pass them.

Secretary of Education Terrel H. Bell termed the changes in public education resulting from 1983's reports "a tidal wave of reform." But some educators, including Theodore R. Sizer, former dean of Harvard University's Graduate School of Education, argued that the changes failed to at-

tack the central problems of the schools. Sizer argued for more flexible schooling in *Horace's Complaint: The Dilemma of the American High School.* The "Horace" of the title is a composite of veteran teachers who were interviewed and observed by Sizer. Horace, Sizer contended, must balance a desire to give students individual instruction with his own limited energy and available time.

Sizer's study called for making high school voluntary after a student completes basic courses and for granting a diploma after a student has mastered certain material. The report also recommended giving teachers authority to make meaningful decisions about teaching and more time to work individually with students.

Paying for the Reform. The American Association of School Administrators, an organization of school superintendents and other school executives, estimated that public school funding would have to rise at least 25 per cent for schools to stem the "rising tide of mediocrity." Much of the increased expenditure, the association said, should go into teachers' salaries.

The legislatures of nearly every state considered some scheme to secure more funding for public schools in 1984. Illinois, for example, instituted a plan to give its best teachers merit raises, and state legislators worked on an entirely new funding scheme for introduction in 1985. California, Florida, South Carolina, and Tennessee changed formulas for granting aid to school districts in an attempt to equalize school spending across the state.

Teaching the Teachers. Some of the reports criticizing the state of U.S. education put the major share of the blame on the quality of training received by teachers. Such criticism affected many institutions that train teachers. Among the changes instituted in 1984 were tighter evaluation standards of future teachers and more rigorous courses in subject matter.

Of the 130,000 degrees in education conferred in 1984, more than 42,000 went to students who specialized in secondary school education, 30,000 to those who specialized in elementary school education, and 15,000 to those in special education. Of concern was the small number of teachers who specialized in mathematics, science, and foreign languages. In 1984, only 2,311 degrees were granted to teachers of sciences, 2,078 to teachers of mathematics, and 1,058 to teachers of foreign languages.

The Rand Corporation, a nonprofit research organization, warned in a report issued in August that a severe teacher shortage might undermine school reform. Warning signals of the coming shortage included a sharp drop in the number of college students majoring in education and a predicted surge in the number of children attending elementary school through 1992. The report added that many able teachers were leaving the field because of low pay and lack of opportunities for advancement.

The Concern over Quality struck mainly high schools in 1983, but in 1984, colleges and universities came under fire. In October, a report issued by the National Institute of Education, the research branch of the Department of Education, warned of a decline in the quality of undergraduate education. The report, called *Involvement in Learning: Realizing the Potential of American Higher Education,* found that only half the students who enter college obtain a degree. It also stated that from 1964 to 1982, average scores declined in 11 out of 15 subject areas tested by the Graduate Record Examination and taken by college seniors who intend to enter graduate school.

Among the reasons for the decline, according to the report, were excessively vocational undergraduate curriculums and the granting of college credits for too many "soft" courses. The report stated, "Liberal education seems to have fallen out of favor over the past two decades, particularly with parents and students who have come to believe that the best insurance in a technological society is a highly specialized education that will lead to a specific job." The report recommended higher salaries for college professors and greater emphasis on the liberal arts.

Secretary of Education Terrel H. Bell, who resigned at year-end, discusses a government report on school violence and discipline in January.

In November, a panel of the National Endowment for the Humanities charged that United States colleges and universities fail to give their students "an adequate education in the culture and civilization of which they are members." The report said, "Most of our college students remain shortchanged in the humanities — history, literature, philosophy, and the ideals and practices of the past that have shaped the society they enter." As an example, the report pointed out that "a student can obtain a bachelor's degree from 75 per cent of all American colleges and universities without having studied European history [and] from 72 per cent without having studied American . . . history."

The Public's Attitude toward public schools in the United States improved in 1984, according to the 16th annual Gallup Poll. From 1976 to 1983, the Gallup Poll recorded a decline in confidence in public schools. In 1983, only 31 per cent of those polled gave a grade of A or B to public schools. But in 1984, 42 per cent gave the schools high grades, a jump of about 35 per cent.

For the first time, a Gallup Poll was taken of teachers' attitudes toward public schools. The poll asked teachers to rate public schools in general and their own school in particular. Two-thirds of the teachers gave schools as a whole a grade of A or B, and more than 70 per cent of the teachers gave top marks to the schools in which they teach.

For a number of years, Gallup Poll respondents have cited discipline as the "most important problem facing the public schools." That view persisted in 1984. Discipline was followed, in order of importance, by drug abuse, low standards, and the difficulty of finding and keeping good teachers.

Teachers, when asked to rate the problems of the schools, disagreed with the public. The teachers cited the parents' lack of interest and support as the most important problem. They ranked discipline fourth in importance, after funding and the pupils' truancy and lack of interest.

The poll also asked whether all high school students should have to pass a standard nationwide test before receiving a diploma. Only 44 per cent of high-school teachers approved of such a test, but 65 per cent of the public favored the idea. Sixty-three per cent of the teachers voted "yes" to a competency test for prospective teachers in the subjects they plan to teach. An overwhelming 89 per cent of the public favored such a test.

Secretary of Education Bell in November became the first Cabinet officer to resign after President Ronald Reagan's reelection. Bell, who left office on December 31, said he planned to teach in the Department of Education at the University of Utah in Salt Lake City.   Cynthia Parsons

In WORLD BOOK, see EDUCATION.

EGYPT. In 1984, President Hosni Mubarak continued to rebuild links broken between his country and other Arab states when Egypt signed a peace treaty with Israel in 1979. On Jan. 19, 1984, the 42-member Islamic Conference Organization, meeting in Casablanca, Morocco, voted to readmit Egypt as a member. Egypt and Morocco reopened diplomatic relations in February.

In September, Jordan followed up its 1983 trade pact with Egypt by announcing the resumption of full diplomatic relations between the two nations. When Jordan's King Hussein I visited Cairo in December 1984, however, he startled Mubarak by denouncing the 1979 Egypt-Israel treaty.

Mubarak's flexibility in foreign policy was underscored in July 1984, when ambassadors were exchanged with the Soviet Union for the first time since 1981. But Mubarak said relations between Israel and Egypt would remain "frozen" until Israeli forces withdrew from Lebanon.

Elections. A turning point for Egyptian democracy came on May 27, when elections were held for a new People's Assembly. Opposition parties took part, but only one, the center-right New Wafd, received the required 8 per cent of the popular vote to win seats in the Assembly. It won 58 seats. The overwhelming majority of the seats — 390 — went to candidates of Mubarak's ruling National Democratic Party. There was some violence

and charges of vote rigging, but the main problem was voter apathy. Only 5 million out of 12.6 million registered voters cast their ballots. In July, following the sudden death in June of Prime Minister Ahmad Fuad Muhi al-Din, President Mubarak named a new Cabinet headed by Kamal Hasan Ali, the former deputy prime minister and foreign minister.

The Economy. Revenues from Suez Canal tolls topped $1 billion for the first time in 1984. In April, Egypt began exporting rice, as production increases due to new seed strains reached 350,000 metric tons (386,000 short tons). The oil industry improved output to 830,000 barrels per day.

Despite optimism over the country's future, life for the average Egyptian remained difficult and costly. In September, the government increased prices of cooking oil, fuel oil, basic foodstuffs such as bread, and other necessities. Government subsidies for these commodities were also reduced by 18 per cent, and higher payroll deductions were levied for pensions. On October 1, after riots protesting the increases broke out in an industrial town near Alexandria, Mubarak ordered a price rollback. The riots were the first public protest against the regime since Mubarak took office in 1981.   William Spencer

See also MIDDLE EAST (Facts in Brief Table). In WORLD BOOK, see EGYPT.

ELECTIONS. Republican Ronald Reagan was reelected President of the United States with a record number of electoral votes on Nov. 6, 1984, defeating a Democratic ticket that included the first woman ever nominated for the vice presidency by a major political party. Reagan carried 49 states and received about 54.45 million popular votes, or 59 per cent of the total, in piling up an unprecedented 525 electoral votes. Democratic nominee Walter F. Mondale, who had been Vice President in the Administration of President Jimmy Carter, carried only the District of Columbia and his home state of Minnesota for a scant 13 electoral votes. Mondale's popular vote was 37.57 million, or 41 per cent of the total cast.

Republican joy at Reagan's triumph was tempered, however. The GOP lost 2 seats in the Senate, reducing its majority to 53 to 47, and pared only 14 or 15 seats from the lopsided Democratic majority in the House of Representatives. The new Democratic margin of 252 House seats to 182, with 1 seat still being contested, meant that Republicans fell well short of restoring the control they exerted, with conservative Democrats, before losing 26 seats in the 1982 elections.

Why Mondale Lost. At a November 7 news conference, Mondale summarized reasons for his defeat: "I was running against an incumbent President who was very popular personally, who was very well liked, in the midst of what is perceived as good economic times, and with diminished international tensions — I think of a temporary nature, but perceived as such — and with an electorate that understandably was anxious for some continuity."

Polls taken by ABC News of voters leaving polling places showed Reagan had the support of 62 per cent of the men voting, 54 per cent of the women, 66 per cent of Protestants, 56 per cent of Roman Catholics, and 63 per cent of whites. Mondale had the support of 89 per cent of blacks, 69 per cent of Jews, and 54 per cent of union households.

The Presidential Campaign. Reagan and his backers faced two periods of uncertainty en route to victory. The first came following the July 19 Democratic nomination for the vice presidency of Representative Geraldine A. Ferraro, 48, of New York, a two-term House member, mother of three, Roman Catholic, and daughter of Italian immigrants. National public opinion polls in late July indicated the Mondale-Ferraro ticket had narrowed the gap with Reagan and Vice President George H. W. Bush. Whatever strength Ferraro brought to the ticket was dissipated in August, however, during days of controversy over disclosing her family's finances.

A second period of uncertainty for Reagan followed a televised debate with Mondale in Louisville, Ky., on October 7. Mondale emerged as the surprise winner, with Reagan at times hesitant and seeming to lose his train of thought. This gave Mondale a boost in the polls and prompted serious public discussion of Reagan's age, health, and vigor. A second Reagan-Mondale debate, in Kansas City, Mo., on October 21, was viewed as a virtual tie. Reagan, when asked about the age issue, scored heavily by responding jokingly, "I am not going to exploit for political purposes my opponent's youth and inexperience."

Changes in the Senate meant that Reagan would face an altered ideological line-up as he sought support for his programs in his second term. Two Republicans who had given him strong support in the past were defeated by moderate to liberal Democrats. In Illinois, three-term Senator Charles H. Percy, chairman of the Senate Foreign Relations Committee, lost to U.S. Representative Paul Simon, who had been a House member for 10 years. In Iowa, another five-term House member, Representative Tom Harkin, defeated Senator Roger W. Jepsen.

Only one incumbent Democratic senator, Walter D. Huddleston of Kentucky, was defeated, by Addison M. (Mitch) McConnell, a Jefferson County (Louisville) judge. The loss of Huddleston's seat

The 1984 Electoral College Vote

was offset, however, by the victory in Tennessee of Democratic Representative Albert A. Gore, Jr., who claimed the seat being vacated by retiring Senate Majority Leader Howard H. Baker, Jr.

Four other Senate races claimed national attention. The most costly Senate contest, at about $25-million, saw Republican Senator Jesse A. Helms of North Carolina, a bedrock conservative, defeat Democratic Governor James B. Hunt, Jr. Three races were lively battles to succeed retiring senators. In Texas, Republican Representative Phil Gramm replaced Republican John G. Tower. In Massachusetts, Democratic Lieutenant Governor John F. Kerry, onetime leader of protests by Vietnam Veterans Against the War, succeeded Democrat Paul E. Tsongas. And in West Virginia, Democratic Governor John D. (Jay) Rockefeller IV spent a reported $7 million of his own money in claiming the seat of Democrat Jennings Randolph, who retired.

Ten women sought Senate seats, but the only winner was the lone incumbent in the group, Senator Nancy Landon Kassebaum (R., Kans.). The only other woman senator is Paula Hawkins (R., Fla.), who faces reelection in 1986.

GOP Gains in the House. The Republicans' modest gain of 14 or 15 House seats was viewed as increasing the likelihood of a partisan stalemate in that chamber. This was thought possible even though the ideological shift was less than 14 or 15

Election winners in 1984 included Madeleine M. Kunin, *top left,* Vermont's new Democratic governor; and senators-elect, *clockwise,* Phil Gramm, a Texas Republican; John D. (Jay) Rockefeller IV, a West Virginia Democrat; and Paul Simon of Illinois, also a Democrat.

seats because conservative Republicans defeated equally conservative Democrats in some races.

Representative James R. Jones (D., Okla.), a six-term incumbent and chairman of the House Budget Committee, who presented himself as a conservative, narrowly won reelection in his Tulsa district. Five important subcommittee chairmen were not so fortunate. Defeated were Democrats Clarence D. Long of Maryland and Joseph G. Minish of New Jersey, both 11-term House members; Elliott H. Levitas of Georgia; Jerry M. Patterson of California; and Donald J. Albosta of Michigan.

Republicans made the strongest showings in the South, picking up eight seats in Texas, Georgia, and North Carolina, where politically minded Christian fundamentalists were active. In Texas and North Carolina, exit polls indicated many votes were polarized along racial lines.

The new House that convened in January 1985 included 19 blacks, 1 fewer than before because of the primary-election defeat of freshman Representative Katie Hall (D., Ind.). Women still held 22 House seats, offsetting Hall's loss and the retirement of Representative Ferraro with gains elsewhere. Hispanics increased their numbers in the House from 9 to 10.

Two members who had been disciplined by the House in 1983 were defeated. Republican Representative Daniel B. Crane, censured for having sexual relations with a teen-age female page, lost his Illinois seat. Republican Representative George Hansen, reprimanded by his colleagues and appealing a prison sentence for filing false financial-disclosure reports, was narrowly defeated in Idaho. But in Massachusetts, Representative Gerry E. Studds, censured for having sexual relations with a teen-age male page, won reelection.

In State Races, Republicans captured four governorships from Democrats but made a net gain of only one because Democrats won three GOP-held seats. Democrats still held a gubernatorial edge of 34 to 16. Republicans elected their first governor in Utah (Norman H. Bangerter) in 20 years, their first in Rhode Island (Edward D. Di-Prete) in 16 years, and their first in North Carolina (James G. Martin) in 12 years. They also won a governorship in West Virginia, where Arch A. Moore, Jr., was elected. Democrats succeeded Republican governors in North Dakota (George Sinner), Washington (Booth Gardner), and Vermont, where Madeleine M. Kunin became the state's first woman governor.

In contests for state legislatures, Republicans wrested control of both houses from Democrats in Connecticut and North Dakota but lost control of the Vermont and Alaska legislatures. Thus they continued to control both legislative houses in 11 states. Republicans also took control of the Ohio Senate, the Minnesota House, and the Delaware House in reducing from 33 to 27 the number totally controlled by Democrats.

More than 200 state and local ballot issues faced voters, and gambling initiatives fared well. State lotteries were approved in California, Oregon, Missouri, and West Virginia.

But voters in California, Michigan, Nevada, and Oregon turned down proposals to curb state taxing authority, blunting the national "tax revolt" that began in 1978 when California voters adopted the big tax cuts of a ballot initiative called Proposition 13. Howard Jarvis, the leader of the Proposition 13 fight, lost in 1984 as Californians voted 55 per cent to 45 per cent against his Proposition 36, aimed at closing loopholes in the 1978 initiative. Californians also defeated a proposal to trim $3 billion from the state's $12 billion in welfare spending. In Michigan, a proposal to roll back some taxes to 1981 levels was defeated. Voters in Nevada narrowly rejected a constitutional amendment that would have made it more difficult to raise taxes. Frank Cormier and Margot Cormier

See also CONGRESS OF THE UNITED STATES; DEMOCRATIC PARTY; REPUBLICAN PARTY; STATE GOVERNMENT. In the Special Reports section, see LOBBYING THE LAWMAKERS. In WORLD BOOK, see ELECTION; ELECTION CAMPAIGN.

ELECTRIC POWER. See ENERGY.

ELECTRONICS. Digital electronics continued to make news in 1984, though the hectic pace of growth of recent years slowed somewhat. Instead, digital technology began to move into established fields of electronics. (Digital components process data in *bits* — the 0's and 1's of the binary numeration system. Computers are digital machines, as are pocket calculators and various timing devices such as the clocks on microwave ovens.)

One promising digital product, the digital television receiver, made its way to the United States market from Europe, where it has been available for several years. Digital receivers convert the incoming TV signal into bits and then manipulate the bits to produce an extremely sharp picture. The price of digital TV receivers was still in the $1,200 range, however, a figure that must come down before the sets turn up in most homes.

The Unhappy Experience of some manufacturers of personal computers and video games, forced out of the business after suffering huge losses, had shown that the consumer is soon bored with a product that cannot be used in everyday life. The dream of putting a computer into every home became a nightmare of swollen inventories and price wars. As a result, the frenzy over advanced technology that became the hallmark of consumer products in the early 1980's gave way to a wait-and-see attitude. Chastened manufacturers sat back and tried to figure out exactly what the technology offers their customers and whether the customers really want and need it.

Semiconductor Chip Technology continued to advance in 1984. A semiconductor chip is a piece of material — usually silicon — into which are built complete electronic circuits. A typical chip is about the size of a fingernail and contains many thousands of circuits. For example, memory chips used in most personal computers made in 1984 had about 64,000 special circuits called *memory cells*, each capable of storing 1 bit. But during the year, three Japanese manufacturers — Hitachi Limited, NEC Corporation, and Nippon Telegraph and Telephone — and the United States computer giant International Business Machines Corporation (IBM) announced that they had developed chips that would store more than 1 million bits.

Tape Beats Disc. In April, RCA Corporation announced that it would no longer make the Selecta Vision VideoDisc Player. The company had expected to sell 500,000 players a year, but only 550,000 were sold since the product's introduction in 1981. Most consumers preferred video-cassette recorders (VCR's) to videodisc machines, because a VCR can record broadcasts as well as play prerecorded tapes. RCA planned to continue making videodiscs for at least three years.   Howard Wolff

In WORLD BOOK, see ELECTRONICS.

EL SALVADOR. José Napoleón Duarte of the Christian Democratic Party was elected president of El Salvador on May 6, 1984, following two years of transitional rule. Duarte won 54 per cent of the vote in a special runoff election against his only opponent, Roberto D'Aubuisson of the right wing Nationalist Republican Alliance, who captured 46 per cent of the vote. See DUARTE, JOSÉ NAPOLEÓN.

Duarte was inaugurated on June 1, while D'Aubuisson's supporters charged that the United States Central Intelligence Agency (CIA) had won the election for Duarte. The CIA had reportedly funneled $2.1 million to parties opposing the election of D'Aubuisson, who has been linked to right wing death squads.

Duarte seemed to bring renewed vigor to El Salvador's leadership along with a will to bring the five-year-old civil war to a conclusion. With a stepped-up flow of war equipment and with training provided by U.S. military officers at a special camp in Honduras, Salvadoran troops appeared to operate more effectively on the field of battle.

With a stronger military footing, President Duarte — during a speech on October 8 to the United Nations General Assembly in New York City — made a surprise offer to meet with his rebel foes. On October 15, the meeting took place in the village of La Palma in El Salvador.

Duarte met face to face with a rebel delegation headed by Guillermo Manuel Ungo, who had been Duarte's vice presidential running mate during the 1972 elections. The talks resulted in the establishment of a joint commission to work toward a peaceful resolution of the conflict. Both sides met again on November 30, but by then, negotiating positions appeared to have hardened.

Only days after the first meeting, government forces had launched an offensive aimed at the rebel stronghold in Morazán province. The price of the offensive was the death of Lieutenant Colonel Domingo Monterrosa, considered El Salvador's most effective combat commander.

The rebels responded to the attacks by launching an offensive in the northern part of the country on November 9. The fighting at Suchitoto involved three battalions of rebels and government forces, the largest encounter since June.

Land Reform. The Constituent Assembly, dominated by the right wing, voted on June 28 not to extend the third phase of the nation's controversial land reform program. Under this phase, more than 60,000 peasant farmers bought tracts of land up to 17.5 acres (7 hectares) in size. Salvadoran leaders and some members of the U.S. Congress were quick to denounce the move. "The land reform program in this country is now formally paralyzed," remarked Deputy Agriculture Minister Jorge Camacho. "Land will go back to the owners, and the people will be kicked off."

Human Rights. El Salvador appeared to make progress in 1984 toward ending human-rights abuses, though death-squad activity continued, as did reports of massacres by the military. On May 24, five former members of the National Guard were convicted of homicide in the 1980 deaths of four U.S. churchwomen. Salvadoran judges said it was the first time a jury had convicted a member of the armed forces in a murder case with political overtones. Human-rights groups applauded the prosecutions, but some said that high-ranking officers were being protected.

In another case, which involved the 1981 slayings of two United States labor advisers and the head of the Salvadoran Institute for Agrarian Reform, the Salvadoran Supreme Court on November 19 ruled that a lieutenant accused of ordering the murders could not be tried. Two National Guard soldiers confessed to the murders and said they were acting under the lieutenant's orders, but the court ruled that the testimony of convicted murderers was inadmissible. On November 28, Duarte ordered the lieutenant dismissed without pension.   Nathan A. Haverstock

See also LATIN AMERICA (Facts in Brief Table). In WORLD BOOK, see EL SALVADOR.

EMPLOYMENT. See ECONOMICS; LABOR; SOCIAL SECURITY; WELFARE.

ENDANGERED SPECIES. See CONSERVATION.

ENERGY. A milestone in the development of the United States synthetic fuels industry was marked on July 28, 1984, when the Great Plains coal gasification project near Beulah, N. Dak., began selling natural gas made from coal. The gas was pumped through an interstate pipeline to customers in the Midwest and East. The $2.8-billion facility is the nation's first plant capable of making synthetic natural gas for commercial use. It was designed to produce 137 million cubic feet (4 million cubic meters) of natural gas per day from lignite, a low-quality grade of coal. The project was built with federal government loan guarantees. The U.S. Synthetic Fuels Corporation agreed to subsidize the price of the gas.

The Synthetic Fuels Corporation was created by Congress in 1980 with $20 billion to speed development of synfuels projects. But in August 1984, Congress took away all but about $8 billion of the corporation's money. The corporation's problems began on April 27 when its president, Victor M. Thompson, Jr., resigned in a controversy over his relationships with synfuels businesses. At that time, there were three vacancies on the corporation's seven-member board of directors. His resignation left the board without the number of directors necessary to conduct business. Another director resigned on May 16. President Ronald

Reagan refused to appoint new directors until Congress reduced the corporation's funding. Congress agreed to the cuts, and on October 10, President Reagan nominated two new directors to give the corporation a working board once again.

Energy-Use Increase. The U.S. Department of Energy (DOE) reported on September 1 that during the first half of 1984, U.S. energy consumption increased for the first time since 1979. Total energy consumption for the first six months of 1984 was about 8 per cent higher than during the same period in 1983. Coal consumption was up 12.6 per cent; natural gas, 7.7 per cent; and petroleum, 6.0 per cent. The DOE said improved economic conditions caused the increase. In an annual report completed on May 30, the DOE predicted that future energy prices would increase only moderately.

Imported Electricity raised concerns after a heat wave sent demand for electricity soaring along the East Coast in June. On June 11, electricity demand reached record levels from New England to the Chesapeake Bay, forcing many utilities to undertake voltage reductions or "brownouts." Electric utilities in New England were forced to import huge amounts of power from Canada to prevent serious disruptions in supply to the utilities' customers. Utilities serving the New England States

Generators stand uncompleted in Indiana's Marble Hill nuclear power plant after the Public Service Company of Indiana abandoned the project in January.

on June 19 signed a preliminary agreement with a Canadian utility for imports of $2.5 billion worth of electricity in the 1990's.

On September 6, the DOE expressed concern about the increasing reliance on imports of high-priced electricity by utilities in the Northeast. The DOE said that imports of electricity have increased sixfold since 1970 and will at least double from present levels by 1990. Although imports account for only about 2 per cent of all electricity used in the United States, some states have grown heavily dependent. Among these are New York state and much of New England. The DOE said that in 1983 U.S. utilities spent $1 billion for Canadian electricity. The department questioned whether utilities could better serve their customers by investing in new generating stations or by building new transmission lines to areas of the United States with a surplus of electricity.

The congressional Office of Technology Assessment on September 5 released a study of the effects of future foreign oil cutoffs. It concluded that other energy sources could be substituted for 75 per cent of current U.S. oil imports within five years after any cutoff of foreign oil supplies. It would cost $40 billion per year to convert oil-fired boilers to natural gas and other fuels. The United States would also have to produce an additional 2 trillion cubic feet (57 billion cubic meters) of natural gas, and 110 million short tons (99.8 metric tons) of coal and wood to replace the 3.6 million barrels of foreign oil lost each day.

Solar Assistance. The Department of Housing and Urban Development (HUD) on March 16 issued final regulations on distribution of funds from its Solar Energy and Energy Conservation Bank. The bank provides loans and grants for solar energy and energy conservation projects. Under the new rules, HUD will provide assistance to families of all income levels, rather than only to low- and middle-income families, as originally planned. Assistance also will go to owners of apartment buildings and commercial and industrial properties.

Nuclear Problems. The financially troubled U.S. nuclear power industry experienced new setbacks during 1984. Huge cost overruns and construction delays forced electric utilities to abandon a number of partially completed nuclear plants. Public Service Company of Indiana announced on January 16 that it was suspending work on its Marble Hill nuclear power plant near Madison. The utility had invested $2.5 billion in the plant. On April 18, Public Service Company of New Hampshire suspended any further construction on its Seabrook Nuclear Power Station after investing $2.5-billion in the project. Consumers Power Company in Jackson, Mich., announced on July 16 a halt to further work on its $4-billion Midland nuclear

plant, located 100 miles (160 kilometers) northwest of Detroit. Directors of the Tennessee Valley Authority on August 29 voted to abandon four partially completed generating units at two nuclear power plants in Mississippi and Tennessee.

Three Ohio utilities in January halted construction on the Zimmer Nuclear Power Station southeast of Cincinnati. On August 1, the utilities announced that they would spend $1.7 billion to convert the plant to coal. It was the first such conversion attempted at a big nuclear plant.

The possibility of construction flaws led the Nuclear Regulatory Commission (NRC) on January 13 to deny an operating license for the $3.4-billion Byron Nuclear Power Station being built by the Commonwealth Edison Company near Rockford, Ill. The agency on November 2 granted a full-power operating license for the Unit 1 reactor of Pacific Gas & Electric Company's Diablo Canyon nuclear plant near San Luis Obispo, Calif. The application had been pending since 1973. Environmentalists opposed the plant because it is located near an earthquake-prone geologic fault.

On April 9, the NRC acknowledged for the first time that its emphasis on repeated inspections and requirements for mounds of paperwork from utilities may be contributing to the nuclear power industry's problems. In a report to Congress, the NRC criticized itself for failing to screen utilities for their ability to manage nuclear power plants before granting permission to build the plants.

Engineers unbolted the top of the damaged nuclear reactor at the Three Mile Island Nuclear Power Station near Harrisburg, Pa., on July 27, a crucial step in efforts to clean up after the 1979 accident. The action cleared the way for removal of damaged and highly radioactive fuel in the core of the reactor.

Energy Abroad. The United States and China on April 30 initialed an agreement that would allow U.S. firms to compete for contracts to help build some of the nuclear power plants planned by the Chinese over the next 16 years.

Swiss voters on September 23 defeated proposals that would have halted construction of new nuclear plants. Egyptian officials announced on September 3 that financial problems would delay an ambitious government program to complete eight nuclear power plants by the year 2000.

The International Atomic Energy Agency, a United Nations agency that is based in Vienna, Austria, on September 24 predicted a worldwide decline in the growth of nuclear power because of financing difficulties and political problems. The agency also cited a slowing in worldwide demand for electricity.   Michael Woods

See also COAL; PETROLEUM AND GAS. In WORLD BOOK, see ENERGY SUPPLY.

ENGINEERING. See BUILDING AND CONSTRUCTION.

ENGLAND. British coal miners began a strike on March 12, 1984, in an attempt to prevent multiple mine closures and massive job losses. The strike had dramatic effects in England. Picket-line violence between police and strikers filled the news. Negotiations to settle the dispute made little progress, and, at year's end, most of the workers were still on strike (see GREAT BRITAIN).

Local Government. In 1984, the Conservative central government came one step closer to realizing its plans to abolish England's metropolitan councils and divide their functions among borough and district councils. England's six metropolitan counties, like the metropolitan area of Greater London, are governed by metropolitan councils controlled by the Labour Party. Since 1979, the councils have resisted central government policy aimed at reducing public spending. In 1984, the government attempted to cancel scheduled elections for the councils and to replace elected members with temporary appointees. Parliament blocked this move in June but extended the life of the elected councils only until 1986.

Religious Affairs. On March 14, David Jenkins, professor of theology at Leeds University since 1979, was appointed Bishop of Durham. The appointment aroused controversy because of Jenkins' view that doubts about the virgin birth and the Resurrection of Jesus Christ are not obstacles to Christian faith. Archbishop John S. Habgood of York received many letters opposing Jenkins' appointment but continued to support him and officiated at his consecration at York Minster cathedral on July 6.

On July 9, lightning struck the cathedral, causing a fire that damaged its southern part. Estimates of repair costs for the building, which dates from the 1200's, amounted to about 1 million pounds ($1.3 million).

The International Garden Festival, held in Liverpool from May 2 to October 14, was England's greatest tourist attraction in 1984. The festival was held on formerly derelict land and provided 600 temporary jobs in an area of high unemployment. Exhibitors included 26 countries that designed special gardens illustrating their national characteristics. Theme gardens ranged from a Japanese garden in the style of the 1600's to a Beatles maze.

Sports. Nottingham ice skaters Jayne Torvill and Christopher Dean captured the hearts of the English people with their sensational ice dancing performances in 1984. They won the European ice dancing championship, a gold medal at the Winter Olympic Games, and their fourth consecutive world championship.   William James Gould

See also GREAT BRITAIN. In WORLD BOOK, see ENGLAND.

Fire fighters hose down smoldering rubble in the south part of England's York Minster cathedral after a fire caused by lightning in early July.

ENVIRONMENT. William D. Ruckelshaus, administrator of the United States Environmental Protection Agency (EPA), resigned unexpectedly on Nov. 28, 1984, effective on Jan. 5, 1985. He had taken over as EPA chief in May 1983, two months after Anne M. Burford resigned the post amid controversy involving charges of manipulation, mismanagement, and conflict of interest within the agency. Ruckelshaus was credited with restoring the morale of the EPA staff.

Political observers speculated that Ruckelshaus stepped down because of a disagreement over EPA funding. Earlier in the month, Ruckelshaus had asked that the Administration of President Ronald Reagan spare the EPA budget cuts it was considering, but he faced strong opposition within the Administration.

Ruckelshaus said he resigned because of a "whole lot of personal things." He said, "I decided I had accomplished what I could accomplish, so I decided now is the time to make the break."

On Nov. 29, 1984, Reagan named Lee M. Thomas, manager of the EPA's toxic-waste program since March 25, 1983, to succeed Ruckelshaus. Thomas, like Ruckelshaus, had taken his earlier post amid controversy. Thomas' predecessor, Rita M. Lavelle, had been fired on Feb. 7, 1983, after refusing Burford's request to resign. On Jan. 9, 1984, Lavelle was sentenced to prison

A French freighter carrying radioactive cargo lies on its side off the coast of Belgium after colliding with a passenger ferry in August.

and fined for perjury and for impeding congressional investigations.

An Environmental Disaster occurred on December 3 when methyl isocyanate (MIC) poison gas escaped from a Union Carbide Corporation pesticide plant in Bhopal, India, a city of about 672,000 people. The gas formed by evaporation when liquid MIC overheated in a tank. Two safety systems intended to neutralize the gas or to burn it upon release failed for reasons not immediately known. The resulting cloud of gas left at least 2,500 people dead and thousands injured.

Pesticide Banned. On February 3, the EPA prohibited the use of the pesticide ethylene dibromide (EDB) on grain products and set guidelines for grain and foods already contaminated with EDB. The chemical had been used as a pesticide since 1948. In the 1970's, it was identified as a cause of cancer in laboratory animals. In September 1983, the EPA barred use of EDB fumes as a soil disinfectant or pesticide.

In December 1983 and January 1984, state and federal investigators found EDB residues in such foods as muffin and pancake mixes. In California, high levels of EDB were discovered in imported citrus pulp. As a result of these discoveries, individual states pressured the EPA to ban EDB.

On March 2, 1984, the EPA restricted the use of the chemical on fruit. The agency set a deadline of September 1 for eliminating the use of EDB on imported citrus fruits, mangoes, and papayas and on U.S.-grown citrus fruit sold abroad. (The chemical was not used on fruit grown in the United States for domestic consumption.)

The Acid-Rain Battle between environmentalists and the Reagan Administration grew in intensity throughout 1984. Environmentalists launched a drive in January for legislation to bring about a 50 per cent reduction in sulfur emissions from power plants. (Acid rain comes from sulfur dioxide and other pollutants emitted by coal-burning power plants and other sources. The pollutants change chemically as they travel through the atmosphere and fall to earth as acid rain or snow.)

The environmentalists failed to change the Reagan Administration's opposition to taking significant action on the problem until more evidence was gathered. On September 4, however, a panel of experts commissioned by President Reagan's Office of Science and Technology recommended an immediate start on "cost-effective" steps to reduce the pollution that causes acid rain.

Ruckelshaus said on August 26 that the acid rain panel exceeded its authority when it recommended immediate federal action. The Administration position was that the government needs more research to determine the exact cause and effects of acid rain, Ruckelshaus said.

On March 21, environmental and health ministers from nine European countries and Canada signed an agreement in Ottawa, Canada, committing their governments to reducing sulfur emissions by at least 30 per cent by 1993. The *30% Club*, as the group called itself, urged other nations to adopt similar measures.

The acid rain issue played a part in the 1984 presidential campaign. Vice President George H. W. Bush, campaigning in Illinois on September 24, said that the Reagan Administration would not adopt any proposal to control acid rain that might put coal miners out of work. Democratic presidential nominee Walter F. Mondale had called for a 50 per cent reduction in sulfur emissions over the next decade, Bush noted. Bush said that Mondale's plan would put a lot of miners out of work.

Superfund Increase. On August 10, the U.S. House of Representatives passed a bill that would increase the superfund for toxic-waste cleanup sixfold. The House leadership hurried the bill along even though the 1980 superfund law was not scheduled to expire until September 1985. The sponsors of the bill contended that the law should be renewed immediately because the nation's hazardous waste problems proved to be larger than Congress had foreseen in 1980.

On April 27, the EPA had revealed that more than 71 billion gallons (270 billion liters) of hazardous wastes are generated in the United States each year. The figure is 60 per cent higher than the agency estimated in August 1983.

The House measure, which would have extended the law through 1990, would have raised more than $10 billion for the superfund over the next five years and put the EPA on a strict timetable for cleaning up the worst dumps. The Reagan Administration argued that there would be plenty of time to renew the superfund in 1985. The proposed extension of the superfund died in the Senate on October 2.

Congress passed only one major piece of legislation in 1984 dealing with the cleanup of hazardous waste. The legislation tightened regulations governing the disposal of hazardous waste. Reagan signed the bill on November 9.

The EPA on October 2 added 244 sites to the priority list for superfund cleanup, bringing to 786 the number of toxic-waste sites the agency believes are an imminent threat to public health.

Controversy. William P. Clark, who succeeded James G. Watt as secretary of the interior on Nov. 21, 1983, received mixed reviews from conservationists and the press in 1984. Critics gave Clark high marks for shunning the public feuding that made Watt a political liability. They charged, however, that he delayed or avoided many tough decisions about the development of coal and oil.

Ruckelshaus also encountered criticism. Shortly after succeeding Burford, he had improved the EPA's relationships with Congress, environmentalists, and the press. By April 1984, however, lawmakers and environmental groups began to accuse the EPA's leadership of being too concerned about the costs of stringent pollution controls. Ruckelshaus became increasingly disturbed by what he believed were politically motivated attacks by conservation leaders.

Wilderness Additions. In 1984, Congress approved the establishment of 8.6 million acres (3.5 million hectares) of federal wilderness in 21 states, bringing the total area protected to 88.8 million acres (36 million hectares), of which 56.5 million acres (22.9 million hectares) are in Alaska. Congress approved more wilderness legislation in 1984 than it had in any other year since 1964.

The House of Representatives voted overwhelmingly on September 12 to protect 3.2 million acres (1.3 million hectares) in California as wilderness. This vote, confirming similar Senate action on August 9, provided the largest single addition to the National Wilderness System since the passage of the Alaska National Interest Lands Conservation Act of 1980.   Andrew L. Newman

See also CONSERVATION. In the Special Reports section, see PRESERVING OUR PRAIRIE HERITAGE. In WORLD BOOK, see ENVIRONMENTAL POLLUTION.
EQUATORIAL GUINEA. See AFRICA.

ETHIOPIA in 1984 suffered from devastating famine caused by chronic drought, loss of soil fertility by erosion, and the disruption of food distribution by civil war. Rebel guerrillas seeking secession or regional self-government operated in four drought-stricken provinces. Most famine relief supplies were distributed through government channels, but Ethiopia's relief administrators were unable or unwilling to help famine victims in rebel-controlled areas.

On October 24, the Ethiopian government appealed to other countries for massive help to save the estimated 6.4 million people facing starvation. Great Britain, the Soviet Union, the United States, West Germany, and other countries provided food, medicine, and transport planes to help distribute relief supplies. Such efforts, however, were not enough to prevent large numbers of deaths. Before the year ended, as many as 900,000 people may have died in Ethiopia.

On September 10, the Workers Party of Ethiopia — a Communist party — was launched as the country's sole legal party. Elected to lead the party was an 11-member Politburo headed by the party's General Secretary, Mengistu Haile-Mariam, head of state and government since 1977.   J. Dixon Esseks

See also AFRICA (Facts in Brief Table). In the Special Reports section, see AFRICA — THE TROUBLED CONTINENT. In WORLD BOOK, see ETHIOPIA.

EUROPE

Western Europe continued its climb out of recession in 1984 against a background of labor problems and international discord. The nearly bankrupt European Community (EC or Common Market) added to the difficulty by creating quotas and rules that turned country against country.

All attempts at détente between East and West failed. Some European leaders blamed United States President Ronald Reagan for the failure of détente, claiming that he had no spare energy in the election year to pursue a softer policy with the Soviets. And a change of leadership in the Soviet Union did not ease the bitterness that followed Russia's withdrawal from arms talks in 1983. In November 1984, however, the two sides announced that talks would resume in January 1985.

The North Atlantic Treaty Organization (NATO) set up Pershing 2 ballistic missiles and cruise missiles in Great Britain, Italy, and West Germany during 1984. Meanwhile, the Soviets *deployed* (installed) additional SS-20 missiles capable of hitting Western Europe.

Long Strikes. Great Britain, West Germany, and France suffered from labor problems. In Great Britain, management threats to close an unspeci-

On June 6, leaders of eight nations observe
the 40th anniversary of the D-Day invasion
of Europe on the beaches of Normandy in France.

fied number of coal mines led to a strike that began in March and was still unresolved at year's end. Pickets and police fought at the mines. A dock strike in July and another in August and September threatened British industry. Strikes closed all of West Germany's automobile plants, and steelworkers led the unrest in France. Quarrels over delays in allowing trucks to pass through border points and dissatisfaction over the EC's agricultural policies—particularly those allowing the

importation of lamb and beef—led truckers to blockade roads around the Alps mountain system.

The EC's Struggle to survive financially was hindered by a bitter, long-standing struggle with Great Britain over a promised budget rebate. The Commission—the EC's executive branch—warned on January 9 that the EC faced "the certainty of bankruptcy" if member states could not agree on "urgent and painful reforms" of the Common Agricultural Policy (CAP), which fixes production targets and price supports.

On January 13, the Commission told member states that they would have to cut some support prices and freeze the remainder to prevent the EC from collapsing. The EC overspent its budget by $2.2 billion in the first two months of 1984.

Discord Within the EC increased in early 1984. The EC claimed that Great Britain had received $585 million too much in milk subsidies in 1983, and asked Britain to repay the full amount. And France broke EC rules by curbing meat imports.

The EC dropped the claim against Britain in March. British Prime Minister Margaret Thatcher immediately began to press for a promised rebate of $594 million for 1983. She threatened to withhold British contributions to the EC if the EC did not pay by March 31, 1984. On March 1, the Commission asked the Council of Ministers to raise its spending limit by $10.8 billion per year to keep the EC from going broke.

EC Leaders Met in Brussels, Belgium, in March to discuss spending cuts. West Germany's Foreign Minister Hans-Dietrich Genscher called Thatcher "unrepentant and inflexible," setting the stage for arguments and accusations that continued through the summer. The EC froze the British rebate, and Thatcher refused the requests of the other nine countries to contribute generously to the EC. The meeting broke up in disarray.

Thatcher Agreed to a budget deal at a June 26 summit meeting at Fontainebleau, France. The EC guaranteed Great Britain an annual rebate in return for Britain's allowing an annual increase in the EC budget. However, Great Britain did not get the promised rebate of $594 million for 1983. On July 27, 1984, the European Parliament voted not to pay the rebate until the member countries agreed on a supplementary budget for 1984. Thatcher said such a budget was unnecessary and illegal, but the other nine countries supported it.

After more hard bargaining in Brussels, Britain agreed on September 7 to help the EC pay its bills in 1984 if the EC met a list of British demands, including paying the rebate. On September 12, the European Parliament agreed that Britain could have its rebate when the EC found funds.

In jeopardy throughout the budget discussions was $1.4 billion budgeted to help unemployed workers in the member countries and to subsidize

Representatives of NATO and the Warsaw Pact
meet in Vienna, Austria, in March to discuss
reducing armed forces in central Europe.

economically depressed regions. Commission President Gaston Thorn warned that the EC might have to use this money for farm subsidies.

Reforms Urged. EC leaders meeting in Dublin, Ireland, in December considered a committee report calling for major reforms in EC structure. The report recommended that the leaders meet in 1985 to draft a treaty establishing "a true political entity." The most important change would end the practice of allowing a member country to veto any measure that it considers vital to its interests. Britain, Denmark, Greece, and Ireland criticized the report.

Huge Surplus. On March 13, the EC agriculture ministers ordered dairy farmers to cut milk production from 110 million metric tons (121 million short tons) in 1984 to 98 million metric tons (108 million short tons) in 1985, and to drop another 1 million metric tons (1.1 million short tons) over the next four years. The EC told the farmers not to produce more than 1 per cent more milk than they supplied in 1981, and said that farmers who overproduced would have to pay extra taxes.

Overproduction increased the EC's reserves of butter — the so-called butter mountain — to more than 1 million metric tons in 1984. Farmers in the EC harvested 128 million metric tons (141 million short tons) of grain, topping the target of 116 million metric tons (128 million short tons).

EC Elections. Only 57 per cent of the 191 million voters in the EC went to the polls in June to elect candidates to the European Parliament. The election resulted in continuation of the center-right majority, but the Socialists gained strength.

There were some surprises. The French extreme right National Front party and its counterpart, the Italian Social Movement, won enough seats to bring them recognition as a political group for the first time. The West German antinuclear and environmentalist party, the Greens, won seven seats, their first ever. The major West German parties and the British Conservatives lost ground. The Greek Panhellenic Socialist Movement remained its country's leading party.

On July 24, the European Parliament chose Pierre Pflimlin, a French Christian Democrat, to be its president. He had been prime minister of France in 1958. Pflimlin defeated Pieter Dankert, a Dutch Socialist, who had been president of the European Parliament for 2½ years.

NATO Tried to increase the unity among its 16 member countries. Talks began in January on ways to implement Belgian Foreign Minister Leo Tindemans' call for a review of NATO policies toward the East and a determination of a common course of action. The Soviet Union had withdrawn from the medium-range missile talks in Geneva, Switzerland, on Nov. 23, 1983, and European members called for quick action to get the discussions going again. But the United States maintained that resumption should not be made too easy for the Soviets.

A May 1984 report by the International Institute for Strategic Studies — an independent organization based in London — noted the difference of opinion between European NATO members and the United States and said that East-West relations were worse than at any time since 1962. The institute called for improvement in these relations to lower the risk that miscalculation or "dangerous posturing" would lead to war. It criticized equally the "hostile rhetoric" of the United States and the aggressive actions of the Kremlin.

On Nov. 22, 1984, however, the United States and the Soviet Union announced that they had agreed to resume arms talks in January 1985. U.S. Secretary of State George P. Shultz and Soviet Foreign Minister Andrei A. Gromyko would meet in Geneva to discuss "the entire complex of questions concerning nuclear and space weapons."

Deterrent Defenses. NATO foreign ministers meeting in Washington, D.C., at the end of May 1984 reaffirmed the organization's determination to maintain strong defenses in Europe while seeking a peaceful long-term dialogue with the Soviet Union. They also emphasized the need to improve NATO's conventional forces to reduce NATO's reliance on nuclear weapons. NATO continued to

Facts in Brief on European Countries

Country	Population	Government	Monetary Unit*	Foreign Trade (million U.S. $) Exports†	Imports†
Albania	3,049,000	Communist Party First Secretary Enver Hoxha; People's Assembly Presidium Chairman Ramiz Alia; Prime Minister Adil Çarçani	lek (8.3 = $1)	106	111
Andorra	38,000	The bishop of Urgel, Spain, and the president of France	French franc & Spanish peseta	no statistics available	
Austria	7,525,000	President Rudolf Kirchschläger; Chancellor Fred Sinowatz	schilling (21.8 = $1)	15,431	19,364
Belgium	9,888,000	King Baudouin I; Prime Minister Wilfried A. E. Martens	franc (62.5 = $1)	51,929 (includes Luxembourg)	54,278
Bulgaria	9,069,000	Communist Party General Secretary & State Council Chairman Todor Zhivkov; Prime Minister Georgi Stanchev Filipov	lev (1 = $1)	11,428	11,527
Czechoslovakia	15,618,000	Communist Party General Secretary & President Gustáv Husák; Prime Minister Lubomir Strougal	koruna (13 = $1)	16,507	15,800
Denmark	5,150,000	Queen Margrethe II; Prime Minister Poul Schlüter	krone (11.2 = $1)	16,029	16,256
Finland	4,844,000	President Mauno Koivisto; Prime Minister Kalevi Sorsa	markka (6.4 = $1)	12,550	12,847
France	54,613,000	President François Mitterrand; Prime Minister Laurent Fabius	franc (9.5 = $1)	90,632	105,302
Germany, East	16,756,000	Communist Party Secretary General & State Council Chairman Erich Honecker; Prime Minister Willi Stoph	mark (2.9 = $1)	23,793	21,524
Germany, West	61,085,000	President Richard von Weizsäcker; Chancellor Helmut Kohl	Deutsche mark (3.1 = $1)	168,050	151,031
Great Britain	55,681,000	Queen Elizabeth II; Prime Minister Margaret Thatcher	pound (1 = $1.19)	91,653	100,083
Greece	9,942,000	President Constantine Karamanlis; Prime Minister Andreas Papandreou	drachma (125.2 = $1)	4,459	9,632
Hungary	10,769,000	Communist Party First Secretary Janos Kadar; President Pal Losonczi; Prime Minister Gyorgy Lazar	forint (50.5 = $1)	8,696	8,503
Iceland	240,000	President Vigdis Finnbogadottir; Prime Minister Steingrimur Hermannsson	krona (33.3 = $1)	751	815
Ireland	3,597,000	President Patrick J. Hillery; Prime Minister Garret FitzGerald	pound (punt) (1 = $1)	8,612	9,182
Italy	56,753,000	President Sandro Pertini; Prime Minister Bettino Craxi	lira (1,920 = $1)	72,681	80,367
Liechtenstein	28,000	Prince Hans Adam; Prime Minister Hans Brunhart	Swiss franc	no statistics available	
Luxembourg	368,000	Grand Duke Jean; Prime Minister Jacques Santer	franc (60.6 = $1)	51,929 (includes Belgium)	54,278
Malta	378,000	President Agatha Barbara; Prime Minister Carmelo Mifsud Bonnici	pound (1 = $2.09)	363	733
Monaco	27,000	Prince Rainier III	French franc	no statistics available	
Netherlands	14,531,000	Queen Beatrix; Prime Minister Ruud Lubbers	guilder (3.48 = $1)	65,662	61,573
Norway	4,158,000	King Olav V; Prime Minister Kaare Willoch	krone (9 = $1)	17,979	13,500
Poland	37,424,000	Communist Party First Secretary & Council of Ministers Chairman Wojciech Jaruzelski; President Henryk Jablonski	zloty (125.4 = $1)	10,951	9,931
Portugal	10,081,000	President António dos Santos Ramalho Eanes; Prime Minister Mário Soares	escudo (165 = $1)	4,608	8,245
Romania	23,184,000	Communist Party General Secretary & President Nicolae Ceausescu; Prime Minister Constantin Dascalescu	leu (22.4 = $1)	11,714	9,836
Russia	277,465,000	Communist Party General Secretary & Supreme Soviet Presidium Chairman Konstantin U. Chernenko; Council of Ministers Chairman Nikolay Aleksandrovich Tikhonov	ruble (1 = $1.17)	91,331	80,267
San Marino	23,000	2 captains regent appointed by Grand Council every 6 months	Italian lira	no statistics available	
Spain	38,865,000	King Juan Carlos I; President Felipe González Márquez	peseta (173.4 = $1)	19,735	29,196
Sweden	8,353,000	King Carl XVI Gustaf; Prime Minister Olof Palme	krona (8.8 = $1)	27,441	26,100
Switzerland	6,398,000	President Leon Schlumpf	franc (2.6 = $1)	25,595	29,117
Turkey	49,728,000	President Kenan Evren; Prime Minister Turgut Ozal	lira (400 = $1)	5,694	9,348
Yugoslavia	23,239,000	President Veselin Djuranovic; Prime Minister Milka Planinc	dinar (185 = $1)	9,038	11,104

*Exchange rates as of Dec. 1, 1984, or latest available data.   †Latest available data.

Prince Franz Josef II of Liechtenstein, right, grants his son, Crown Prince
Hans Adam, executive power in the tiny European principality in August.

carry out its 1979 decision to deploy 572 nuclear-armed Pershing 2 ballistic missiles and cruise missiles in Belgium, Britain, Italy, the Netherlands, and West Germany. However, Belgium and the Netherlands postponed until 1985 their decisions on whether to accept missiles.

In December, U.S. Secretary of Defense Caspar W. Weinberger told NATO ministers in Brussels that the Soviets had deployed nine additional SS-20 intermediate-range missiles capable of hitting Western Europe. The addition brought the number of SS-20's deployed to 387, each with three warheads. On December 6, NATO ministers agreed to spend more on conventional forces.

New Secretary-General. Joseph M. A. H. Luns retired after 13 years as secretary-general of NATO. He was succeeded by former British Foreign Secretary Lord Carrington on June 25. On September 4, the supreme allied commander of NATO, U.S. General Bernard Rogers, called for a 7 per cent annual increase in defense spending for the rest of the 1980's. He said the increase would provide "a reasonable prospect of frustrating a Soviet conventional attack." The increase was needed because most NATO countries had not fulfilled their pledge to boost defense spending by 3 per cent per year.

COMECON Summit. On June 12, Soviet leader Konstantin U. Chernenko opened the first summit

meeting of the Council for Mutual Economic Assistance (COMECON) since the early 1970's in Moscow. The three-day conference of the 10-nation group was held in secret. A declaration at the end of the meeting accused the United States of jeopardizing "the very existence of mankind," risking nuclear war, and persistently using economic penalties against the Soviet bloc "even in the food trade." The national leaders adopted a long-term economic cooperation program, stressed the need for industrial modernization, and called for a 20-year program of increased research in electronics and other technologies.

There was reported disagreement over the Soviet Union's demand that its East European allies supply it with "foodstuffs, consumer goods, and machinery of high quality," rather than selling such goods to Western countries for much-needed hard currency. Another area of discord was the high prices that the Soviets charged their satellite nations for oil. Observers said the summit did little to satisfy the insistence of Hungary, Poland, and East Germany on more trade with the West.

Trade Barriers Lifted. Seventeen European nations established a free trade area for industrial goods on Jan. 1, 1984. The area included the 10 EC countries — Belgium, Denmark, France, Great Britain, Greece, Ireland, Italy, Luxembourg, the Netherlands, and West Germany — and the 7 members of the European Free Trade Association—Austria, Finland, Iceland, Norway, Portugal, Sweden, and Switzerland. The 17 countries have a combined market of 310 million consumers.

Gas Pipeline. The Soviet Union's $9.1-billion pipeline from Siberia to Western Europe began supplying gas to France on January 1. However, energy experts said it would be years before the line would operate at full capacity.

Homage to War Dead. On June 6, King Baudouin I of Belgium, Prime Minister Pierre Elliott Trudeau of Canada, President François Mitterrand of France, Queen Elizabeth II of Great Britain, Grand Duke Jean of Luxembourg, Queen Beatrix of the Netherlands, King Olav V of Norway, and President Reagan of the United States traveled to the beach at Normandy, on the English Channel coast of France. The leaders paid homage to Allied servicemen who died there during the World War II invasion of Europe on D-Day, June 6, 1944. On Aug. 24, 1984, old Sherman tanks rolled down the streets of Paris as the city celebrated its liberation from Germany 40 years earlier. Belgium held a similar celebration later, on September 3. Kenneth Brown

See also the various European country articles. In WORLD BOOK, see EUROPE.

EXPLOSION. See DISASTERS.

FARM AND FARMING. United States farm families continued to experience economic and social stress in 1984. Many began to realize that family farms may no longer provide an adequate living.

The problems facing U.S. farmers in 1984 included low prices for their crops; declining farm exports due to a combination of a strong U.S. dollar, weak economic conditions abroad, and aggressive foreign competition; high production costs, especially interest charges and energy prices; and the declining value of farmland. Many farmers experienced cash-flow problems, which made repayment of loans difficult or impossible. U.S. farm programs seemed to help big farms more than family farms. On top of all this, consumers complained about high food prices and generally seemed less sympathetic toward farmers.

Debates about new U.S. government farm programs to replace programs set to expire in 1985 gave little comfort to farmers. Many people both in and out of government questioned the need, cost, and effectiveness of these programs.

U.S. Farm Production was up sharply in 1984, exceeding 1983 levels by about 16 per cent. The number of crop acres planted rose more than 10 per cent, and yields were up by about the same percentage, chiefly because of better weather. Corn production was up 80 per cent; sorghum, 68 per cent; wheat, 6 per cent; soybeans, 21 per cent;

rice, 42 per cent; potatoes, 8 per cent; cotton, 71 per cent; and tobacco, 28 per cent. Oats were down slightly. Livestock production was down about 1 per cent, with beef and veal down about 4 per cent and lamb and mutton, 12 per cent. Pork remained essentially unchanged. Turkeys and broilers rose about 5 per cent. Milk increased 1 per cent, and eggs were up about 2 per cent.

Prices Received by U.S. farmers in 1984 increased about 6 per cent above 1983 levels. Crop prices overall increased about 7 per cent, and overall livestock prices rose about 4 per cent. This price improvement came during the second half of 1984, chiefly because of slightly reduced meat supplies. Overall, farm prices in 1984 were helped by a relatively strong consumer demand.

World Production. World crop output was stimulated by sharply higher production in the United States, the European Community (EC or Common Market), and China. These larger crops more than offset the smaller crops in the Soviet Union, Canada, and Australia. Record production occurred outside the United States for wheat, coarse grains, rice, soybeans, and cotton. World sugar production was also up. World wheat production exceeded 500 million metric tons (551 million short tons) for the first time. The record world coarse grain production was 96 million pounds (43 million kilograms) above that of 1983. The world rice crop set a record for the fifth consecutive year, despite a sharp drop in Thailand's rice harvest.

The 15 per cent increase in world cotton production over 1983 levels resulted partly from continued increases in China and a sharp rebound in Pakistan. Several other countries, including Mexico, Brazil, and India, also had increases.

Agricultural Trade. The United States continued to be the world's largest agricultural exporter in 1984. American farmers depended upon export markets for 66 per cent of their wheat sales, 50 per cent of their soybean crop, and 40 per cent of their rice and cotton crops. The U.S. farm export volume of 144 million short tons (130.6 million metric tons) was down about 1 per cent from 1983 levels. The dollar value of U.S. farm exports, however, rose from $34.8 billion to $38.0 billion, reversing a two-year slump in dollar value that followed 12 consecutive years of increases. Exports of wheat in 1984 were up 14 per cent; cotton, 24 per cent; and rice, 1 per cent. Corn was essentially unchanged, and soybeans were down 22 per cent.

On September 11, President Ronald Reagan announced that the Soviet Union would be permitted to buy an extra 10 million metric tons (11 million short tons) of U.S. grain during the fiscal year ending Sept. 30, 1985. The decision allowed the Soviets, who suffered their sixth poor grain harvest in a row in 1984, to buy as much as 22 million metric tons (24 million short tons) of U.S. grain.

A laborer in a lettuce patch at a truck farm near Phoenix balances a stack of corrugated containers made specially to protect farm produce.

Farm imports in 1984 increased 16 per cent to $18.9 billion. Imports of fruits and nuts were up 21 per cent; sugar, 25 per cent; coffee, 18 per cent; and vegetables, 24 per cent. Meats were down 9 per cent. The U.S. agricultural trade surplus of $19.1 billion represented a 4 per cent increase and made a significant contribution to an otherwise unfavorable overall U.S. trade balance.

U.S. Farm Finances. Outlays for production expenses in 1984 increased over those of 1983, more than offsetting the slight increase in receipts from crop sales. As a result, net cash income fell for the first time since 1981, sliding about 10 per cent from U.S. farmers' record $40.1-billion net cash income for 1983. Crop inventories grew in 1984 and more than offset the $11.7-billion downturn in 1983 that resulted from low crop production. Interest and energy charges in 1984 were up over 1983 costs. Off-farm income earned by farmers was up about 7 per cent over the $41 billion earned in 1983 and continued to exceed net cash farm income.

Farm Policy was the topic of hundreds of discussion meetings and government hearings in 1984 due to the 1985 expiration date for nearly all farm price and income legislation established in the Agriculture and Farm Act of 1981. Most experts recommended substantial changes to improve farm incomes, make U.S. exports more competitive, prevent the death of family farms, reduce public subsidies to agriculture, and keep adequate supplies of food available at reasonable prices.

United States government outlays for price support programs, which had risen from less than $3 billion in fiscal year 1980 to nearly $19 billion in fiscal year 1983, moderated to about $6 billion in 1984. Nevertheless, they still made substantial contributions to farm income.

Government Programs. On Feb. 15, 1984, U.S. Secretary of Agriculture John R. Block announced that support levels for peanuts would remain unchanged from those in 1983. The Agricultural Programs Adjustment Act of 1984, signed into law by President Reagan in April, affected the wheat, feed grains, cotton, and rice programs. It also provided additional funds for economic emergency loans in fiscal year 1984.

Target prices for wheat were reduced to $4.38 per bushel. (The target price is the minimum price set by Congress for a commodity. If farmers cannot sell their crops for at least that price, the government buys the crops for that amount.) The target price for corn was reduced to $3.03 per bushel and frozen for rice at $11.90 per hundredweight (26.2 cents per kilogram) and for upland cotton at 81 cents per pound ($1.78 per kilogram). The government also offered modest crop-reduction programs, including acreage-reduction payments and the Payment-in-Kind (PIK) program. Under the PIK program, the government offered government stocks of certain crops to farmers who idled a portion of their cropland.

On September 14, Block announced the provisions of the 1985 government crop program. The target prices for corn, rice, and upland cotton remained the same. The market price of grain sorghum rose to $2.88 per bushel; barley to $2.60; and oats to $1.60 a bushel. The U.S. sugar import quota for the 1985 quota year (Oct. 1, 1984, to Sept. 30, 1985) was set at 2.6 billion short tons (2.4 billion metric tons), raw value.

On July 31, the Farmers Home Administration, an agency of the U.S. Department of Agriculture that offers credit to small-farm owners, announced that 31 per cent of its borrowers were behind in their payments. On September 18, President Reagan announced that his Administration would defer payments on some Farmers Home Administration loans for five years and offer banks and other commercial lenders $630 million in federal loan guarantees to reduce the value of the loans such lenders have made to farmers facing bankruptcy.

On November 19, Block and Mexico's Secretary for Agriculture and Water Resources Eduardo Pesqueira signed an agreement to extend a joint soil-conservation project and a new memorandum of understanding for cooperation in forestry.

Small Farm Increase. The U.S. Bureau of the Census reported in September that the number of small farms — farms of less than 50 acres (20 hectares) — in the United States soared 17 per cent between 1978 and 1982, to 637,000. During that period, the number of such farms rose in every state but North Carolina. The Census Bureau pointed out, however, that such farms are usually operated by people who earn most of their income from nonfarm sources. The bureau also reported an increase in the number of large farms — farms of at least 2,000 acres (800 hectares).

Citrus Comeback. Despite the outbreak of a devastating citrus canker that led to the destruction of millions of Florida citrus trees, the Florida citrus crop for the 1984-1985 season was expected to top the previous year's total. On August 24, citrus canker, a bacterium that attacks the leaves and limbs of citrus trees, was discovered in a citrus nursery near Avon Park in south central Florida. Harmless to human beings and animals, the canker can be destroyed only by burning the affected trees. The bacterium was later discovered at four other citrus nurseries.

On September 13, the U.S. Department of Agriculture banned the shipment of all citrus fruit from Florida. On November 7, the government lifted the ban except on shipments to five citrus-producing states. By December, more than 6.7 million citrus trees had been burned.

Agricultural Statistics, 1984

World Crop Production
(million units)

Crop	Units	1983-1984*	1984-1985*†	% U.S. 1984-1985†
Corn	Metric tons	350	438	44
Wheat	Metric tons	489	507	14
Rice (rough)	Metric tons	451	459	1
Barley	Metric tons	170	171	8
Oats	Metric tons	46	45	15
Rye	Metric tons	32	33	2
Soybeans	Metric tons	78	90	57
Cotton	Bales‡	67	82	16
Coffee	Bags§	92	94	1
Sugar (centrifugal)	Metric tons	96	98	6

*Crop year. †Preliminary.
‡480 pounds (217.7 kilograms) net.
§132.3 pounds (60 kilograms).

Output of Major U.S. Crops
(millions of bushels)

Crop	1962-1966*	1983-1984†	1984-1985†‡
Corn	3,876	4,166	7,498
Sorghum	595	479	807
Oats	912	477	472
Wheat	1,229	2,420	2,570
Soybeans	769	1,636	1,972
Rice (rough)§	742	997	1,412
Potatoes#	275	332	359
Cotton**	140	78	133
Tobacco††	2,126	1,357	1,740

*Average. †Crop year. ‡Preliminary.
§100,000 hundredweight (4.54 million kilograms).
#1 million hundredweight (45.4 million kilograms).
**100,000 bales (50 million pounds) (22.7 million kilograms).
††1 million pounds (454,000 kilograms).

U.S. Production of Animal Products
(millions of pounds)

	1957-1959*	1983-1984†	1984-1985†‡
Beef	13,704	23,477	22,575
Veal	1,240	466	385
Lamb and mutton	711	363	320
Pork	10,957	14,586	14,575
Eggs§	5,475	5,695	5,820
Turkey	1,382	2,546	2,660
Total milk#	1,230	1,361	1,373
Broilers	4,430	12,947	13,550

*Average. †Crop year. ‡Preliminary.
§1 million dozens.
#100 millions of pounds (45.4 million kilograms).

On November 28, the canker was found for the first time in a mature citrus grove, adjacent to the nursery where the outbreak was first reported. Florida officials estimated that as many as 1 million more trees might have to be destroyed.

The canker was the second blow to the Florida citrus industry in less than a year. In December 1983, a freeze damaged or destroyed hundreds of thousands of acres of citrus trees. Despite these problems, Florida growers expected to harvest 119 million boxes of citrus fruits, 3 million boxes more than in the 1983-1984 season.　　　Charles E. French

See also FOOD. In WORLD BOOK, see AGRICULTURE; FARM AND FARMING.

FARM MACHINERY. See MANUFACTURING.

FASHION

FASHION. The man-tailored look for women was dramatically introduced in Milan, Italy, by the Italian designer Giorgio Armani in his spring 1984 collection. By fall, the menswear theme had affected fashion collections everywhere.

The Masculine Look. Armani's presentation was striking not only for the severely tailored clothes but also for the austere look of the models and their accessories. Vivid makeup and elaborate hairdos were banished. Jewelry was limited to an inconspicuous stickpin. The models sometimes wore ties with tailored shirts, and their shoes were flat-heel oxfords. On the last day of the spring shows, Armani received the Golden Eye award from the international fashion press. The award cited him for best representing "the spirit of today's fashion."

The tailored look was based on slightly over-sized coats and slouchy jackets, which were worn with trousers or calf-length skirts. It turned up later in the French and British spring collections.

By the time the fall collections were shown, the masculine look dominated women's fashion. It appeared in full strength in the United States in clothes designed by Calvin Klein, Ralph Lauren, Donna Karan and Louis Dell'Olio for Anne Klein, and Perry Ellis for Portfolio, his new moderately priced line. The menswear concept provided a clean, uncomplicated way for women to dress in their professional lives and in their leisure hours.

Many of the American clothes were longer and fuller than their European counterparts. In keeping with the tradition of American sportswear, the designs were based on the theory of interchangeable separates. Sweaters could be substituted for blouses; jackets could be worn with skirts or trousers; and big overcoats could go over everything.

Other Options. Of course, a countertrend soon developed. Some women objected to the masculine look and chose instead to wear clinging, ultra-feminine designs that hugged the body and left little to the imagination.

The Japanese look, which had such a strong impact on fashion in the early 1980's, seemed to recede in 1984. For a while, it had appeared that the loose, formless clothes of such leading Japanese designers as Rei Kawakubo, Mitsuhiro Matsuda, and Yohji Yamamoto would change the way Western women dressed. The black and gray shades used by these designers did indeed influence the collections of European and American designers. But by the fall of 1984, bright, searing colors — including hot pink, chartreuse, and citron yellow — began to show up in coats, suits, and dresses.

The reaction to Japanese design came in part from Great Britain. London, which had sparked the youth revolution in fashion in the 1960's, staged a fashion comeback in 1984. In March, British Prime Minister Margaret Thatcher invited

A sports jacket, trousers, and big overcoat by U.S. designer Anne Klein exemplify the menswear look that dominated women's fashion during 1984.

leading retail executives from many parts of the world to a reception at her official residence at 10 Downing Street. The celebration honored Britain's new crop of fashion designers as well as such established designers as Zandra Rhodes and Jean Muir. By fall, designs in cheerful colors from such newcomers as Katharine Hamnett, Body Map, and Jasper Conran turned up in American stores alongside clothes by French and Italian designers. Great Britain was back on the world fashion map.

By the end of 1984, it became clear that there was no single fashion look. Hemlines ranged from knee-baring lengths for the ultrafeminine styles to ankle-grazing lengths for some of the mannish coats. Women had their choice of a wide palette of bright or muted colors. They could wear tight or easy clothes. Fashion seemed to be growing up.

Coty American Fashion Critics' Awards were presented on Sept. 24, 1984. Sportswear designer Adrienne Vittadini received the women's fashion award known as the Winnie. Andrew Fezza won the award in the menswear category. Women's fashion designers awarded special citations were Donna Karan and Louis Dell'Olio for Anne Klein, Ralph Lauren, and Perry Ellis. Ellis and Alexander Julian received citations for menswear. Special awards went to M & J Savitt for jewelry and to Barry Kieselstein-Cord for belts.   Bernadine Morris

In WORLD BOOK, see FASHION.

FEBRES-CORDERO, LEÓN (1931-   ), leader of the Social Christian Party, was elected president of Ecuador on May 6, 1984. He represented the conservative National Reconstruction Front, a six-party coalition, in defeating Rodrigo Borja Cevallos of the Democratic Left Party. The outgoing president was Osvaldo Hurtado Larrea.

Febres-Cordero was born on March 9, 1931, in Guayaquil, Ecuador. He was educated in the United States, where he studied at Charlotte Hall Military Academy in Maryland and at Mercerberg Academy in Pennsylvania. He graduated in 1953 with a degree in mechanical engineering from Stevens Institute of Technology in Hoboken, N.J.

After returning to Guayaquil, Febres-Cordero worked as a mechanical engineer for a brewery and an electric company and then as an executive manager in the flour, paper, and textile industries. From 1966 to 1970, he served in Ecuador's Congress, but he became better known as a business leader. For most of the 1970's, he was president of the Ecuadorean Federation of Industrial Chambers, an association of business leaders and industrialists. In 1979, Febres-Cordero was again elected to Congress as a leader of the Social Christian Party and became a critic of the left-of-center government then in power.

Febres-Cordero is married to the former Eugenia Cordovez.   Rod Such

FERRARO, GERALDINE ANNE (1935-   ), was Democrat Walter F. Mondale's running mate in the 1984 United States presidential election. Ferraro, a member of the New York delegation in the U.S. House of Representatives, was the first woman ever nominated for Vice President by a major U.S. political party. She and Mondale were defeated in the election. See ELECTIONS.

Ferraro was born on Aug. 26, 1935, in Newburgh, N.Y. When her father died eight years later, she and her older brother, Carl, were taken by their mother to New York City to live.

After graduating from Marymount Manhattan College in New York City in 1956, Ferraro taught at one of the city's public elementary schools while attending evening classes at Fordham University School of Law. She graduated in 1960 and married John A. Zaccaro, a real estate developer, but continued to use her maiden name professionally. She and Zaccaro have three grown children.

Ferraro had her own law practice until 1974, when she was appointed assistant district attorney for the New York City borough of Queens. Four years later, she was elected to Congress.

Ferraro's personal finances became an issue during the campaign. A House of Representatives committee investigating her financial disclosure statements ruled on December 4 that she had unintentionally violated the law.   David L. Dreier

FINLAND. The Finnish Communist Party fired party leader Jouko Kajanoja in 1984 and dismissed other members of its extremist Stalinist faction who held leading party positions. Arvo Aalto, leader of the moderate Eurocommunists, replaced Kajanoja.

The Eurocommunists used their majority at a three-day party congress in May to force the changes. The moves ended 20 years of internal discord that had cost the party half its public support. The split also had caused Social Democrat Prime Minister Kalevi Sorsa to exclude Communists from his coalition government, which came to power after general elections in May 1983.

Doctors Strike. Sorsa made long-term pay offers to several sectors of workers during the year in an attempt to cut unemployment and inflation while encouraging exports. The offers angered many workers. Doctors struck for seven weeks after being offered increases of up to $1,120 per month for 2½ years. The strike ended on May 20. On March 9, 100,000 office and technical workers struck for one day after rejecting a similar offer.

Export Problems. Exports, which amounted to 32 per cent of the Finnish national product, did not benefit much in 1984 from the two devaluations of the currency in 1983. Only the wood-processing industry increased its exports sharply — by 6 per cent — in 1983. Total imports were up by

11.4 per cent, leaving a trade deficit of $254 million at the beginning of 1984. The Soviet Union stabilized Finland's trade balance by purchasing 25 per cent of Finland's exports with oil.

"Prisoner of Conscience." President Mauno Koivisto made an unprecedented decision to pardon a conscientious objector on March 24. He freed Perti Haaparanta, a 29-year-old political scientist, who had been serving a nine-month prison term for refusing duty in the armed forces. Amnesty International, an international human-rights group based in England, had called Haaparanta Finland's first "prisoner of conscience." The organization hoped that the pardon would ease the plight of 30 other conscientious objectors facing nine-month prison terms in Finland. This prison sentence is mandatory for any able-bodied man who fails to convince a government-appointed committee that his antimilitary convictions are strong enough to warrant his serving in a civilian job rather than in the armed forces.

Budget Proposal. In September, Sorsa proposed a 1985 budget of $14.6 billion, a 10 per cent increase over 1984. The government hoped the new budget would drive down both the inflation and unemployment rates to 5 per cent.   Kenneth Brown

See also EUROPE (Facts in Brief Table). In WORLD BOOK, see FINLAND.

FIRE. See DISASTERS.

FISHING. Rick Clunn of Montgomery, Tex., won the first prize of $40,000 in the 14th annual Bass Anglers Sportsman Society Masters Classic tournament held in August 1984 on the Arkansas River near Pine Bluff, Ark. Clunn set a record for the event—a total catch of 75 pounds 9 ounces (34.27 kilograms).

In October 1984, Vojai Reed of Broken Bow, Okla., won the Bass N'Gal Classic at Elephant Butte Reservoir near Truth or Consequences, N. Mex. Her total catch of bass, weighing 15 pounds 7 ounces (7.00 kilograms), won her a fully rigged bass boat and cash totaling $20,000.

Striped Bass. Controversy surrounding the striped bass fishery off the Atlantic Coast continued. According to fisheries experts, the catch of striped bass, a premier game and food fish, has declined by nearly 90 per cent there since 1973.

On Oct. 30, 1984, President Ronald Reagan signed the Atlantic Striped Bass Conservation Act, calling for a 55 per cent reduction in the catch from North Carolina to Maine by July 1, 1985. The bill also authorizes the secretary of commerce to ban striped bass fishing in the waters of any state that fails to enforce the reduction.

The United States Fish and Wildlife Service says that acid rain is one culprit in the striped bass decline. In April 1984, aquatic toxicologist Lenwood Hall of Johns Hopkins University in Baltimore,

Md., found that 90 per cent of striped bass larvae placed in the Nanticoke River on the eastern shore of Chesapeake Bay died after four days. At the same time, only 25 per cent of larvae kept in clean alkaline water died. Hall said that the acidity of the Nanticoke made the difference.

Big Fish. In Arizona on September 17, Johnny Adkins of Yuma caught a tilapia weighing 4 pounds 5⅓ ounces (1.97 kilograms), the largest ever taken by hook and line. Adkins caught the fish with a Fat Rap lure at Mittry Lake near the Colorado River. The National Fresh Water Fishing Hall of Fame lists the only record for this species, a fish weighing 3 pounds 7½ ounces (1.57 kilograms) taken in 1973 from the Salinity Canal in Arizona by Ted Hughes. Adkins' tilapia, if verified, would become the new all-tackle record.

A 1,649-pound (748-kilogram) Pacific blue marlin, which would have beaten the current all-tackle world record by 273 pounds (124 kilograms), was denied by the International Game Fish Association (IGFA). The association, in a letter to angler Gary Merriman of Atlanta, Ga., claimed that certain parts of Merriman's fishing line exceeded the maximum limits allowed by IGFA rules. In March 1984, Merriman spent 2 hours 35 minutes landing the marlin off Kailua Kona on the island of Hawaii.   Tony Mandile

In WORLD BOOK, see FISHING.

FISHING INDUSTRY. A dispute between the United States and Canada over a boundary in the Gulf of Maine was settled in October 1984 by the International Court of Justice (World Court), a United Nations agency in The Hague in the Netherlands. The Gulf of Maine lies between Massachusetts and Nova Scotia and includes the Georges Bank off Cape Cod, one of the world's most productive fishing areas. The court drew an ocean boundary that gave five-sixths of the Georges Bank to the United States and one-sixth to Canada. The United States had asked for all of the Georges Bank, and Canada had asked for half.

The ruling required U.S. and Canadian fishing boats to leave each other's waters by October 16. The boundary change denied the United States access to an area of the Georges Bank rich in scallops, haddock, and cod.

Fishing industry officials in both the United States and Canada expressed disappointment with the ruling. U.S. officials predicted a drop in the supply of fish and a rise in the price, and Canadian officials feared a loss of jobs.

Overfishing in the Georges Bank has dealt a nearly fatal blow to fish stocks there, especially haddock. The overfishing crisis developed after the United States and Canada in 1977 extended their jurisdiction over fishing rights from 12 nautical miles (22 kilometers) off their coasts to 200

The World Court's Fishing Line

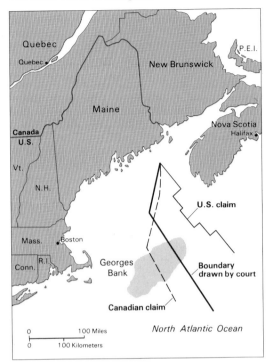

The World Court's Fishing Line

North Atlantic Ocean

nautical miles (370 kilometers). Banking on reduced competition from abroad, U.S. and Canadian fishing industries expanded and modernized. As the two countries increased their shares of the fish caught in the Georges Bank, the fish stocks became depleted.

Ban on Soviets Ends. In July, President Ronald Reagan lifted a ban barring Soviet fishing boats from U.S. waters. As a result, the Soviets were allowed to catch about 50,000 metric tons (55,000 short tons) of fish per year in U.S. waters off the Pacific coast. The ban had been imposed by President Jimmy Carter in January 1980 after the 1979 Soviet invasion of Afghanistan.

The United States Fish Catch totaled 6.4 billion pounds (2.9 billion kilograms) of edible and industrial fish and shellfish in 1983, according to statistics released in 1984. The landings were up about 71 million pounds (32 million kilograms) from 1982 and fell just shy of the 1980 record of 6.5 billion pounds (2.95 billion kilograms). A poor salmon catch off the west coast of the United States and bad weather off the east coast combined to boost fish prices in 1984. In March, the price of fish increased 30 per cent. Andrew L. Newman

In WORLD BOOK, see FISHING INDUSTRY.

FLOOD. See DISASTERS.

FLORIDA. See STATE GOVERNMENT.

FLOWER. See GARDENING.

FOOD. The United States food industry continued to improve during 1984. A good harvest helped to hold food prices to a moderate 3.7 per cent increase, which was lower than the 4 per cent price gain for all items in the government's Consumer Price Index — the most widely used measure of inflation. Americans spent only 15.2 per cent of their disposable income — money available for spending or saving after taxes are paid — on food, one of the lowest rates in the world.

Generally, 1984 was a good year for most developed nations. However, the story was mixed for developing countries. Fewer of the 67 poorest nations of the world required some sort of food aid during 1984. But the number of countries identified by the United Nations as suffering some degree of famine increased to 27. Most of these nations are in the region of Africa south of the Sahara. A drought that has lasted several years has turned previously fertile areas of eastern Africa into desert wasteland. See AFRICA.

Agriculture. United States crop production rose 26 per cent in 1984, with feed grains showing a gain of almost 80 per cent. The 1984 corn crop was almost double the 1983 crop, which was damaged by drought. The wheat crop was the third largest on record. Although livestock production was lackluster, adequate supplies were available.

EDB Ban. On February 3, the Environmental Protection Agency (EPA) banned the use of the pesticide ethylene dibromide (EDB) on grain. The EPA took action after detectable levels of EDB were found in grain-based products, such as cake and muffin mixes, on grocery shelves. Several states had ordered the products removed from stores. On March 2, the EPA banned the use of EDB on citrus fruit after Sept. 1, 1984.

Eating Out accounted for 28 per cent of total food spending in the United States in 1984. Sales in all eating and drinking establishments were up about 9 per cent. Because restaurant costs rose just over 4 per cent, restaurants experienced a real growth of 5 per cent. Higher disposable income in the hands of consumers was the main reason for the strong growth.

Full-menu restaurants had sales gains of 7 per cent, while limited-menu operators, primarily fast-food restaurants, had a 14 per cent sales growth. Ethnic fast-food restaurants, such as Mexican restaurants, were the fastest growing.

Grocery-Store Sales were up more than 6 per cent, while food prices rose only 3.7 per cent. The larger food store chains had an average sales growth of 5.5 per cent. The smaller chains and independent stores reported sales increases of more than 7 per cent. Convenience stores had the highest growth rate of all food stores.

Warehouse Supermarkets. During 1984, the number of warehouse supermarkets grew to about

10 per cent of all supermarkets. These stores compete with conventional supermarkets by charging prices that are 10 to 15 per cent lower than those at conventional supermarkets, eliminating customer services, cutting overhead, and having fewer specialty departments.

Superwarehouse stores, which first appeared in 1983, also continued to increase in number. These stores, which are usually about 60,000 square feet (5,600 square meters) in area, are twice as large as warehouse supermarkets and three times larger than conventional supermarkets. Superwarehouse stores can ring up more than $1 million a week in sales — 5 to 10 times more than warehouse and conventional supermarkets. Because superwarehouse stores buy from wholesalers in huge quantities and have low overhead, they can offer customers extremely low prices. Although only 50 to 100 of these superstores exist in the United States, they have begun to have a major impact on food buying.

The Federal Trade Commission, the United States government agency that protects competition, held hearings in several cities during 1984 to examine the effect of warehouse and superwarehouse food stores on other food retailers. Operators of conventional supermarkets and smaller food stores expressed fears that the larger stores would drive them out of business because they would not be able to match the larger stores' low prices. However, consumers would benefit from the lower prices.

Consumption. The improved U.S. economy and lower rate of unemployment caused American consumers to "trade up" in 1984. The market share of low-priced generic or nonbrand products and store brands fell, while the share of nationally advertised brands rose. Many higher-priced products — such as expensive cuts of meat, gourmet and imported foods, bakery and delicatessen items, and salad bars — had wider acceptance.

Consumer concerns about health and nutrition helped spur an increase in the number of low-salt and low-cholesterol products on the market. Sales of caffeine-free soft drinks exploded at the expense of drinks containing caffeine. Sales of so-called natural foods and foods sold in bulk or out of bins also increased.

Packaging Developments. Aseptic packaging of fruit drinks and milk increased rapidly in 1984. An aseptic package is a foil-paper combination that is lighter and often cheaper than a metal can. Aseptic packages also significantly increase food-storage time. For example, milk processed at very high temperatures and sealed in aseptic packages requires no refrigeration and stays fresh for months.   Walter H. Heller

See also FARM AND FARMING; NUTRITION. In WORLD BOOK, see FOOD; FOOD SUPPLY.

FOOTBALL. Controversy marked professional and college football in the 1984 season and overshadowed the triumph of the San Francisco 49ers, who defeated the Miami Dolphins in the 1985 Super Bowl. Controversy even dogged the unofficial national college champion, Brigham Young University of Provo, Utah.

USFL. The decision of the two-year-old United States Football League (USFL) to switch from a spring to a fall season in 1986 stunned many people, including many in the established National Football League (NFL). In 1983, the USFL began as a springtime professional league. Although it made an impact by outbidding the NFL for such outstanding college players as quarterback Steve Young and Heisman Trophy-winning running backs Mike Rozier and Herschel Walker, most of its players were not up to NFL standards.

Neither was the USFL's television income. In 1984, while each NFL team collected more than $14 million from CBS Inc., the National Broadcasting Company (NBC), and the American Broadcasting Companies (ABC) for network television rights, the USFL's television contracts with ABC and the Entertainment & Sports Programming Network (ESPN) on cable television paid each team only $1 million.

The USFL played with 18 teams in 1984, up from 12 in 1983. Although attendance and TV ratings were modest but acceptable, the league said it lost more than $100 million over two years.

Donald Trump, a New York City realtor who had purchased the New Jersey Generals franchise, urged that the USFL play in the fall rather than in spring and summer. Eddie Einhorn, the new owner of the Chicago Blitz franchise, agreed. On August 22, the USFL club owners voted to switch to a fall schedule, starting in 1986. Einhorn then tried to negotiate a network television schedule.

The networks showed little interest. All were televising NFL games, and CBS and ABC were also showing college football games. Its quest for a new TV package frustrated, the USFL on October 17 filed an antitrust suit against the NFL that sought damages totaling $1.32 billion. The suit accused the NFL of conspiring to monopolize professional football. The USFL asked the courts to invalidate the NFL's contracts with the three major networks and force the NFL to divide into two competing 14-team leagues, each limited to a contract with one major network.

The USFL then attempted to reduce its costs for 1985, when it expected to play its last spring season. It consolidated to 14 teams by merging the Michigan Panthers with the Oakland Invaders, the Pittsburgh Maulers with the Philadelphia Stars, and the Oklahoma Outlaws with the Arizona Wranglers; and by allowing the Chicago Blitz to sit

National Football League Final Standings

American Conference

Eastern Division

	W.	L.	T.	Pct.
Miami Dolphins	14	2	0	.875
New England Patriots	9	7	0	.563
New York Jets	7	9	0	.438
Indianapolis Colts	4	12	0	.250
Buffalo Bills	2	14	0	.125

Central Division

	W.	L.	T.	Pct.
Pittsburgh Steelers	9	7	0	.563
Cincinnati Bengals	8	8	0	.500
Cleveland Browns	5	11	0	.313
Houston Oilers	3	13	0	.188

Western Division

	W.	L.	T.	Pct.
Denver Broncos	13	3	0	.813
Seattle Seahawks	12	4	0	.750
Los Angeles Raiders	11	5	0	.688
Kansas City Chiefs	8	8	0	.500
San Diego Chargers	7	9	0	.438

National Conference

Eastern Division

	W.	L.	T.	Pct.
Washington Redskins	11	5	0	.688
New York Giants	9	7	0	.563
St. Louis Cardinals	9	7	0	.563
Dallas Cowboys	9	7	0	.563
Philadelphia Eagles	6	9	1	.406

Central Division

	W.	L.	T.	Pct.
Chicago Bears	10	6	0	.625
Green Bay Packers	8	8	0	.500
Tampa Bay Buccaneers	6	10	0	.375
Detroit Lions	4	11	1	.281
Minnesota Vikings	3	13	0	.188

Western Division

	W.	L.	T.	Pct.
San Francisco 49ers	15	1	0	.939
Los Angeles Rams	10	6	0	.625
New Orleans Saints	7	9	0	.438
Atlanta Falcons	4	12	0	.250

Individual Statistics

Leading Scorers, Touchdowns

	TDs.	Rush.	Rec.	Ret.	Pts.
Marcus Allen, L.A. Raiders	18	13	5	0	108
Mark Clayton, Miami	18	0	18	0	108
Pete Johnson, San Diego-Miami	12	12	0	0	72
Steve Largent, Seattle	12	0	12	0	72
Louis Lipps, Pittsburgh	11	1	9	1	66
John Stallworth, Pittsburgh	11	0	11	0	66

Leading Scorers, Kicking

	PAT	FG	Longest	Pts.
Gary Anderson, Pittsburgh	45-45	24-32	55	117
Norm Johnson, Seattle	50-51	20-24	50	110
Tony Franklin, New England	42-42	22-28	48	108
Nick Lowery, Kansas City	35-35	23-33	52	104

Leading Quarterbacks

	Att.	Comp.	Yds.	TDs.	Int.
Dan Marino, Miami	564	362	5,084	48	17
Tony Eason, New England	431	259	3,228	23	8
Dan Fouts, San Diego	507	317	3,740	19	17
Dave Krieg, Seattle	480	276	3,671	32	24

Leading Receivers

	No. Caught	Total Yds.	Avg. Gain	TDs.
Ozzie Newsome, Cleveland	89	1,001	11.2	5
John Stallworth, Pittsburgh	80	1,395	17.4	11
Todd Christensen, L.A. Raiders	80	1,007	12.6	7
Steve Largent, Seattle	74	1,164	15.7	12

Leading Rushers

	No.	Yds.	Avg. Gain	TDs.
Earnest Jackson, San Diego	296	1,179	4.0	8
Marcus Allen, L.A. Raiders	275	1,168	4.2	13
Sammy Winder, Denver	296	1,153	3.9	4
Greg Bell, Buffalo	262	1,100	4.2	7

Leading Punters

	No.	Yds.	Avg.	Longest
Jim Arnold, Kansas City	98	4,397	44.9	63
Reggie Roby, Miami	51	2,281	44.7	69
Rohn Stark, Indianapolis	98	4,383	44.7	72
Steve Cox, Cleveland	74	3,213	43.4	69

Individual Statistics

Leading Scorers, Touchdowns

	TDs.	Rush.	Rec.	Ret.	Pts.
Eric Dickerson, L.A. Rams	14	14	0	0	84
John Riggins, Washington	14	14	0	0	84
Gerald Riggs, Atlanta	13	13	0	0	78
James Wilder, Tampa Bay	13	13	0	0	78
Roy Green, St. Louis	12	0	12	0	72

Leading Scorers, Kicking

	PAT	FG	Longest	Pts.
Ray Wersching, San Francisco	56-56	25-35	53	131
Mark Moseley, Washington	48-51	24-31	51	120
Neil O'Donoghue, St. Louis	48-51	23-35	52	117
Paul McFadden, Philadelphia	26-27	30-37	52	116
Mike Lansford, L.A. Rams	37-38	25-33	50	112

Leading Quarterbacks

	Att.	Comp.	Yds.	TDs.	Int.
Joe Montana, San Francisco	432	279	3,630	28	10
Neil Lomax, St. Louis	560	345	4,614	28	16
Steve Bartkowski, Atlanta	269	181	2,158	11	10
Joe Theismann, Washington	477	283	3,391	24	13

Leading Receivers

	No. Caught	Total Yds.	Avg. Gain	TDs.
Art Monk, Washington	106	1,372	12.9	7
James Wilder, Tampa Bay	85	685	8.1	0
Roy Green, St. Louis	78	1,555	19.9	12
James Jones, Detroit	77	662	8.6	5

Leading Rushers

	No.	Yds.	Avg. Gain	TDs.
Eric Dickerson, L.A. Rams	379	2,105	5.6	14
Walter Payton, Chicago	381	1,684	4.4	11
James Wilder, Tampa Bay	407	1,544	3.8	13
Gerald Riggs, Atlanta	353	1,486	4.2	13

Leading Punters

	No.	Yds.	Avg.	Longest
Brian Hansen, New Orleans	69	3,020	43.6	66
Greg Coleman, Minnesota	82	3,473	42.4	62
Bucky Scribner, Green Bay	85	3,596	42.3	61
Michael Horan, Philadelphia	92	3,880	42.2	69

United States Football League Final Standings

Western Conference

Central Division

	W.	L.	T.	Pct.
Houston Gamblers	13	5	0	.722
Michigan Panthers	10	8	0	.556
San Antonio Gunslingers	7	11	0	.389
Oklahoma Outlaws	6	12	0	.333
Chicago Blitz	5	13	0	.278

Pacific Division

	W.	L.	T.	Pct.
Los Angeles Express	10	8	0	.556
Arizona Wranglers	10	8	0	.556
Denver Gold	9	9	0	.500
Oakland Invaders	7	11	0	.389

Eastern Conference

Atlantic Division

	W.	L.	T.	Pct.
Philadelphia Stars	16	2	0	.889
New Jersey Generals	14	4	0	.778
Pittsburgh Maulers	3	15	0	.167
Washington Federals	3	15	0	.167

Southern Division

	W.	L.	T.	Pct.
Birmingham Stallions	14	4	0	.778
Tampa Bay Bandits	14	4	0	.778
New Orleans Breakers	8	10	0	.444
Memphis Showboats	7	11	0	.389
Jacksonville Bulls	6	12	0	.333

Individual Statistics

Leading Scorers

	TDs.	FG	Att.	1XP	Att.	Pts.
Toni Fritsch, Houston	0	21	26	67	69	130
Herschel Walker, New Jersey	21	0	0	0	0	128*
David Trout, Philadelphia	0	26	40	49	53	127
Gary Anderson, Tampa Bay	21	0	0	0	0	126

*Includes one 2-point conversion.

Leading Quarterbacks

	Atts.	Comp.	Yds.	TDs.	Int.
Jim Kelly, Houston	587	370	5,219	44	26
Chuck Fusina, Philadelphia	465	302	3,837	31	9
Cliff Stoudt, Birmingham	366	212	3,121	26	7
John Reaves, Tampa Bay	544	313	4,092	28	16

Leading Receivers

	No. Caught	Total Yds.	Avg. Gain	TDs.
Richard Johnson, Houston	115	1,455	12.7	15
Ricky Sanders, Houston	101	1,378	13.6	11
Joey Walters, Washington	98	1,410	14.4	13
Trumaine Johnson, Arizona	90	1,268	14.1	13

Leading Rushers

	No.	Yds.	Avg. Gain	TDs.
Joe Cribbs, Birmingham	297	1,467	4.9	8
Kelvin Bryant, Philadelphia	297	1,406	4.7	13
Herschel Walker, New Jersey	293	1,339	4.6	16
Buford Jordan, New Orleans	214	1,276	6.0	8

Leading Punters

	No.	Yds.	Avg.	Longest
Jeff Gossett, Chicago	85	3,598	42.3	60
Larry Swider, Pittsburgh	90	3,778	42.0	65
Stan Talley, Oakland	110	4,569	41.5	89
Frank Corral, Arizona	69	2,856	41.4	58

The 1984 College Football Season

1984 College Conference Champions

Conference	School
Atlantic Coast	Maryland
Big Eight	Nebraska-Oklahoma (tie)
Big Sky	Montana State
Big Ten	Ohio State
Ivy League	Pennsylvania
Mid-American	Toledo
Missouri Valley	Tulsa
Ohio Valley	Eastern Kentucky
Pacific Coast	Nevada-Las Vegas
Pacific Ten	Southern California
Southeastern	Florida
Southland	Louisiana Tech
Southwest	Houston-Southern Methodist (tie)
Southwestern	Alcorn State
Western Athletic	Brigham Young
Yankee	Boston University-Rhode Island (tie)

Major Bowl Games

Bowl	Winner	Loser
Aloha	Southern Methodist 27	Notre Dame 20
Amos Alonzo Stagg (Div. III)	Augustana (Ill.) 21	Central (Ia.) 12
Bluebonnet	West Virginia 31	Texas Christian 14
Blue-Gray	Gray 33	Blue 6
California	Nevada-Las Vegas 30	Toledo 13
Cherry	Army 10	Michigan State 6
Cotton	Boston College 45	Houston 28
Fiesta	UCLA 39	Miami (Fla.) 37
Florida Citrus	Florida State 17 (tie)	Georgia 17 (tie)
Freedom	Iowa 55	Texas 17
Gator	Oklahoma State 21	South Carolina 14
Hall of Fame	Kentucky 20	Wisconsin 19
Holiday	Brigham Young 24	Michigan 17
Hula	East 34	West 14
Independence	Air Force 23	Virginia Tech 7
Liberty	Auburn 21	Arkansas 15
Orange	Washington 28	Oklahoma 17
Palm (Div. II)	Troy State (Ala.) 18	North Dakota State 17
Peach	Virginia 27	Purdue 24
Rose	Southern California 20	Ohio State 17
Senior	South 23	North 7
Sugar	Nebraska 28	Louisiana State 10
Sun	Maryland 28	Tennessee 27
NCAA Div. I-AA	Montana State 19	Louisiana Tech 6
NAIA Div. I	Carson-Newman (Tenn.) 19 (tie)	Central Arkansas 19 (tie)
NAIA Div. II	Linfield (Ore.) 23	Northwestern (Ia.) 22

All-America Team (as picked by AP)

Offense

Tight end — Mark Bavaro, Notre Dame
Wide receivers — Eddie Brown, Miami; David Williams, Illinois
Tackles — Lomas Brown, Florida; Bill Fralic, Pittsburgh
Guards — Dan Lynch, Washington State; Del Wilkes, South Carolina
Center — Mark Traynowicz, Nebraska
Quarterback — Doug Flutie, Boston College
Running backs — Keith Byars, Ohio State; Kenneth Davis, Texas Christian
Place kicker — John Lee, UCLA

Defense

Tackles — Leslie O'Neal, Oklahoma State; Bruce Smith, Virginia Tech
Middle guard — Tony Casillas, Oklahoma
Linebackers — Gregg Carr, Auburn; Jack Del Rio, Southern California; James Seawright, South Carolina; Larry Station, Iowa
Defensive backs — David Fulcher, Arizona State; Jerry Gray, Texas; Kyle Morrell, Brigham Young; Tony Thurman, Boston College
Punter — Ricky Anderson, Vanderbilt

Player Awards

Heisman Trophy (best player) — Doug Flutie, Boston College
Lombardi Award (best lineman) — Tony Degrate, Texas
Outland Award (best interior lineman) — Bruce Smith, Virginia Tech

out the 1985 season. In addition, it approved franchise moves of Philadelphia to Baltimore; Washington, D.C., to Orlando, Fla.; and New Orleans to Portland, Ore.

Among the relocated teams was the Philadelphia Stars (16-2), which had the best record in the 1984 regular season. Philadelphia won the USFL championship with a 23-3 victory over the Arizona Wranglers (10-8) on July 15 in Tampa, Fla.

NFL Season. The 49ers (15-1) had the best record and became the first NFL team to win 15 games in a regular season. Of the league's 28 teams, the 49ers and nine others advanced to the play-offs.

The conference championships were decided on Jan. 6, 1985. In the National Conference, the 49ers shut out the Chicago Bears, 23-0, in San Francisco, though the Bears were thought to have the better defense. In the American Conference, the Dolphins beat the Pittsburgh Steelers, 45-28, in Miami, Fla., as Dolphin quarterback Dan Marino connected on four touchdown passes, an American Conference championship-game record.

That put the 49ers and the Dolphins in Super Bowl XIX on Jan. 20, 1985, in Palo Alto, Calif. The 49ers won, 38-16, as quarterback Joe Montana passed for three touchdowns and ran for a fourth. The 49ers' defense harassed Marino and held him to one touchdown pass.

Marino was named Player of the Year by *The Sporting News*. He set NFL one-season passing records of 362 completions, 5,084 yards (4,649 meters), 48 touchdowns, and four 400-yard (370-meter) games. Mark Clayton, one of Marino's receivers, set an NFL record of 18 touchdown catches in one season.

Two major rushing records fell in 1984. Running back Walter Payton of Chicago broke Jim Brown's career record of 12,312 yards (11,258 meters), raising it to 13,309 yards (12,170 meters). Running back Eric Dickerson of the Los Angeles Rams, with 2,105 yards (1,925 meters) in 16 games, bettered O. J. Simpson's 1973 one-season record of 2,003 yards (1,832 meters) in 14 games.

Other Pro Football. The Baltimore Colts, unhappy with their aging stadium, moved to Indianapolis on March 29 without NFL permission. The NFL took no action against the move because of its pending appeal in the case of the Raiders' earlier move from Oakland, Calif., to Los Angeles. On November 5, the Supreme Court of the United States refused to hear the NFL's appeal, which challenged the Raiders' move, meaning the team could stay in Los Angeles.

The Pro Football Hall of Fame in Canton, Ohio, added four retired players in 1984 — wide receiver Charley Taylor, cornerback Willie Brown, offensive tackle Mike McCormack, and defensive tackle Arnie Weinmeister.

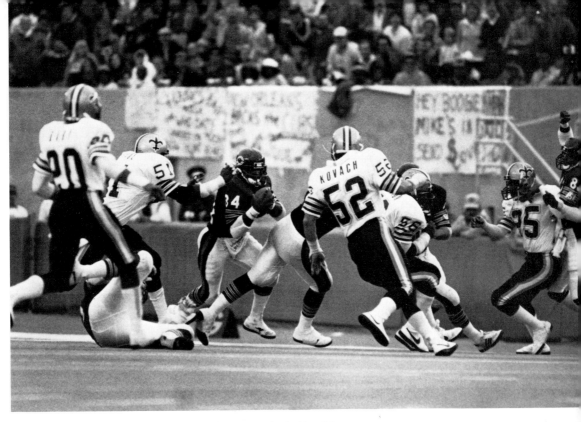

Chicago Bears running back Walter Payton, number 34, gets by the New Orleans defense on a run that broke Jim Brown's career rushing record in October.

In the nine-team Canadian Football League, the regular-season leaders were the British Columbia Lions (12-3-1) and the Winnipeg Blue Bombers (11-4-1) in the Western Division and the Toronto Argonauts (9-6-1) in the Eastern Division. Winnipeg routed the Hamilton Tiger-Cats, 47-17, in the Grey Cup championship game on Nov. 18, 1984, in Edmonton, Canada.

College. Of the 105 colleges that played football in the National Collegiate Athletic Association (NCAA) Division I-A, only Brigham Young (12-0) finished the regular season undefeated. The other leaders included Washington (10-1), South Carolina (10-1), Florida (9-1-1), Oklahoma (9-1-1), Nebraska (9-2), Boston College (9-2), Oklahoma State (9-2), Ohio State (9-2), Southern Methodist (9-2), Louisiana State (8-2-1), and Virginia (7-2-2).

After the regular season, the weekly polls of writers and broadcasters for the Associated Press and coaches for United Press International ranked Brigham Young first and Oklahoma second. Barry Switzer, the Oklahoma coach, was among many who contended that Brigham Young played a relatively weak schedule and therefore should not be considered the national champion.

There was still the matter of bowl games. As champion of the Western Athletic Conference, Brigham Young was committed to the Holiday Bowl on December 21 in San Diego. Although its opponent was Michigan (6-5), not an especially strong team, Brigham Young struggled. But with 83 seconds left, Brigham Young quarterback Robbie Bosco, despite ankle and knee injuries, threw a touchdown pass that won the game, 24-17.

Oklahoma hoped that an impressive victory over Washington in the Orange Bowl on Jan. 1, 1985, in Miami would earn it the national championship. Instead, Washington won, 28-17. The next day, the final wire-service polls placed Brigham Young first, Washington second, and Oklahoma sixth.

Flutie. One of the year's most exciting players was Doug Flutie of Boston College. At 5 feet 9¾ inches (177 centimeters), Flutie was an undersized but highly talented quarterback. He made a spectacular play during a nationally televised game when he threw a desperation 48-yard (44-meter) touchdown pass on the last play of the game that gave Boston College a 47-45 victory over the University of Miami on November 23 in Miami.

Flutie led major-college quarterbacks in passing efficiency and became the first college player to exceed 10,000 yards (9,100 meters) passing in his career. He won the Heisman Trophy as the outstanding player in the United States.   Frank Litsky

In the Special Reports section, see COLLEGE SPORTS: BIG MONEY ON CAMPUS. In WORLD BOOK, see FOOTBALL.

323

FORD, GERALD RUDOLPH

FORD, GERALD RUDOLPH (1913-   ), the 38th President of the United States, barnstormed actively during the 1984 election campaign for Republican candidates. Ford made several dozen appearances, paid for by the Republican National Committee and the Republican campaign committees for the Senate and House of Representatives.

Half the fees the former President received were earmarked for the Gerald Ford museum in Grand Rapids, Mich., and the Ford presidential library in Ann Arbor, Mich. The rest went to the Betty Ford alcohol and drug rehabilitation center in Rancho Mirage, Calif., where a number of celebrities, such as actress Elizabeth Taylor, have been treated.

In August, Ford attended the Republican National Convention in Dallas. In an address to the delegates, he was sharply critical of the policies of former President Jimmy Carter, who defeated him in the 1976 presidential election.

On April 9, Ford had a reunion in Washington, D.C., with President Ronald Reagan and former President Richard M. Nixon, whose resignation in 1974 propelled then-Vice President Ford into the White House. The three met at an anniversary dinner of the Chowder and Marching Society, an organization of Republicans in the House of Representatives.   Frank Cormier and Margot Cormier

In WORLD BOOK, see FORD, GERALD R.

Fire fighters clear a strip of forestland
to stop the spread of blazes that destroyed
forests and rangeland in Montana in August.

FOREST AND FOREST PRODUCTS. The United States Congress on Oct. 1, 1984, approved legislation sought by timber firms in the Pacific Northwest. The legislation enabled the firms to partially buy out of government timber contracts. Timber companies had bid high prices for future purchases of federal timber during an inflationary period in the late 1970's. At that time, they expected a housing boom to inflate timber prices. But the boom failed to appear because of a recession and high interest rates, and the price of timber fell.

Industry sources said that more than 100 timber firms faced a combined loss estimated at $1.5 billion from the contracts. As a result of the legislation, timber companies may spend about $250 million in penalties to buy out of the contracts. The legislation also called for a cap on timber sales in the Pacific Northwest to ensure that timber firms there do not gain a competitive advantage over firms in the rest of the United States.

The Administration of President Ronald Reagan had opposed the bill. Richard E. Lyng, deputy secretary of agriculture, told Congress on June 27, 1984, that an Administration plan granting five-year interest-free extensions of the contracts should be given a chance to work.

Tree Growth Declines. Evidence of a "pronounced decline" in tree growth, possibly caused by air pollution, over a wide range of forests in the Eastern United States was reported to Congress on March 30 by William D. Ruckelshaus, administrator of the Environmental Protection Agency. Ruckelshaus said that early studies do not point to acid rain as an important cause of the forest damage, though some scientists think such pollution may be to blame. See BOTANY.

Although scientists were uncertain about the causes of the problem, they expressed concern that the growth decline could be an early warning of the sort of catastrophe that has killed vast areas of European timber. One-third of West Germany's forests have been afflicted by slow growth since 1979, costing that nation's lumber industry an estimated $200 million annually.

Forest Destruction. The earth each year loses nearly 4.6 million acres (1.9 million hectares) of tropical forests — an area about the size of Pennsylvania — according to a congressional study. The study found that tropical forests are being steadily destroyed by people in developing countries who are desperate for firewood and farmland.

A chain of forest and prairie fires destroyed nearly 230,000 acres (93,000 hectares) of Montana timber in late August. Heavy rains finally brought the fires under control.   Andrew L. Newman

In WORLD BOOK, see FOREST; FOREST PRODUCTS; FORESTRY.

FOUR-H CLUBS. See YOUTH ORGANIZATIONS.

FRANCE. After six months of industrial unrest, strikes, and blockades, Socialist Prime Minister Pierre Mauroy resigned on July 17, 1984, ending 27 months of stormy alliance with the Communists. Since 1981, Mauroy's support in public opinion polls had plunged from 70 to 20 per cent.

Minister for Industry Laurent Fabius, 37, succeeded Mauroy immediately. On July 19, the new prime minister named a cabinet of 16 ministers, none of them Communist. The Communists said they would give the Fabius government "partial support without participation." On July 20, Fabius cut taxes by $8.7 billion and slashed government spending by about twice that amount.

Direct Vote Proposal. On July 12, President François Mitterrand said he would ask Parliament to change the Constitution to allow the government to call *referendums*—direct votes of the people—on questions involving civil liberties. The government's opponents in Parliament had demanded a referendum on a long-running dispute over a plan to increase government control of private schools. The government, favoring the additional control but fearing defeat in a referendum, had said it would be unconstitutional. On June 24, at least 850,000 people had demonstrated against the plan in Paris. This was the largest demonstration in France in 40 years.

Mitterrand said that if Parliament gave him the power to call referendums on civil liberties issues, he would use the power only when he considered a referendum "useful and in the interests of the country." On August 9, the opposition-controlled Senate rejected a bill to grant him this power.

Chad Affair. A troop-withdrawal agreement hurt Mitterrand politically in November. In August 1983, France had sent troops to Chad to prevent a take-over there by Chadian rebels and Libyan soldiers. In September 1984, France and Libya agreed to a simultaneous pullout from Chad.

France announced in mid-November that the withdrawal was complete. The United States Department of State, however, revealed that about 3,000 Libyan troops remained in Chad. The French press described the handling of the Chad affair as the worst foreign policy error of Mitterrand's presidency.

Meat Wars. The year began with a quarrel over imports of lamb from Belgium, Denmark, Great Britain, and West Germany. On January 11, French farmers hijacked three British trucks in Normandy and held the drivers hostage. Mitterrand called the farmers "violators of the public order," but the hijackings continued.

Economic Problems caused unrest among civil servants, steelworkers, miners, and shipyard workers, all of whom faced job losses. On March 1, bank workers, wine growers, and public service workers began a series of strikes. On March 29,

About 35,000 French workers march in Paris in April to protest against a government plan to eliminate jobs in the steel industry.

the government said it planned to eliminate 25,000 jobs in the hard-hit steel industry by 1987. Steelworkers reacted with anger and violence. However, Mitterrand refused to change his plans. On April 13, 35,000 steelworkers and sympathizers marched through Paris in protest. Peace did not return to the industry until July, when unions and management agreed there would be no forced layoffs.

Blockades. On February 16, thousands of truckdrivers began to blockade roads and railroads to protest transportation delays caused by a strike of French and Italian customs officials. Talks between Minister of Transport Charles Fiterman and union leaders failed to resolve the issue and, on February 21, French truckers blocked all traffic between Paris and Charles de Gaulle Airport. Eventually, 6,300 trucks became involved in 240 blockades. Traffic snarls hampered industry, tourism, and the shipment of food. On February 24, the government offered to discuss all the strike issues, and the blockades ended.   Kenneth Brown

See also EUROPE (Facts in Brief Table). In WORLD BOOK, see FRANCE.

FUTURE FARMERS OF AMERICA (FFA). See YOUTH ORGANIZATIONS.

GABON. See AFRICA.

GAMBIA. See AFRICA.

GAMES AND TOYS. The toy industry had one of its best years ever in the United States in 1984. For the first 11 months of the year, manufacturers' shipments were 52 per cent higher than during the same period in 1983, and orders were up 69 per cent. By year's end, retail sales of traditional toys were expected to be more than 15 per cent higher than in 1983. Reasons for this dramatic growth included a strong economy, low inventories in retail stores as the year began, and the rising number of children.

Dolls. Among the star performers of 1984 were dolls, including male action figures. Licensed products based on commercially created characters continued to predominate among new toys. The most successful was the Rainbow Brite line of dolls produced in a collaborative effort by Mattel, Incorporated, and Hallmark Cards, Incorporated. Mattel Toys expected to ship $110 million worth of Rainbow Brite merchandise by the end of the year, surpassing the $65 million worth of Cabbage Patch Kids shipped in 1983. The Kids, however, held onto their overwhelming popularity, and finding a Cabbage Patch Kid to "adopt" was still difficult in 1984. Coleco Industries, Incorporated, expanded the Kids line by introducing infant dolls called Preemies and pet animal dolls called 'Koosas.

A few twists and turns change this helicopter into a robot, one of a line of action figures called GoBots that became best-selling toys in 1984.

Trivia Games. Another phenomenally successful product from 1983 still going strong in 1984 was Trivial Pursuit. The Baby Boomer and Young Players' editions were the newest add-on card sets for the games. Since the success of Trivial Pursuit, rival manufacturers have issued more than a dozen other trivia games, including Entertainment Tonight and Ripley's Believe It or Not.

Robots. The most innovative product of 1984 was the robot toy—most notably GoBots from Tonka Corporation and Transformers from Hasbro Bradley Incorporated. With a twist and a turn, these dual-purpose, die-cast toys can be changed from a robot to a car, truck, or plane, and then back to a robot again. Like such male action figures as G.I. Joe and Masters of the Universe, these robot characters represent the forces of good in their struggle against the forces of evil.

Two toy companies marketed programmable robots in 1984. CBS Inc. produced the Maxx Steele robot, and Tomy Toys introduced a trio of robots called Ding-bot, Ver-bot, and Omni-bot.

Merger. In September, Hasbro Industries, the sixth-largest toy company in the United States, acquired the fifth-ranked Milton Bradley Company. The resulting company, Hasbro Bradley Incorporated, is one of the biggest toy companies in the United States. Donna M. Datre

In WORLD BOOK, see DOLL; GAME; TOY.

GANDHI, RAJIV (1944-   ), became prime minister of India on Oct. 31, 1984. He succeeded his mother, Indira Gandhi, who had been assassinated only hours before. Rajiv, whose grandfather Jawaharlal Nehru was the nation's first prime minister, thus became the third generation of his family to lead India. See INDIA.

Gandhi was born on Aug. 29, 1944, in Allahabad, India. His father was Indian politician Feroze Gandhi, no relation to independence leader Mohandas K. Gandhi. As a boy, Rajiv attended the Doon School, one of India's leading private schools, and then went to Great Britain to further his education. He received a degree in mechanical engineering from Cambridge University in 1965.

Gandhi became a pilot for Indian Airlines, while his younger brother, Sanjay, entered politics and seemed likely to become his mother's successor. In 1980, however, Sanjay was killed in a plane crash, and Rajiv abandoned his career as a pilot to run for his brother's parliamentary seat. Rajiv won by a wide margin in June 1981.

In February 1983, Gandhi became one of five general secretaries of his mother's Congress-I Party. The Indian press nicknamed him Mr. Clean for his efforts to end corruption in the party.

Gandhi and his wife, Sonia—who is Italian-born—have a son and daughter. Gandhi operates a ham radio in his spare time. Sara Dreyfuss

GARDENING. In October 1984, Gardens for All, a national organization that promotes gardening, announced the findings of a Gallup Poll on interest and activity in gardening in the United States. The poll showed that gardening continued to hold its lead in 1984 as the nation's number-one outdoor leisure activity. According to the survey, gardening was more popular than bicycling, golf, jogging, swimming, or tennis. The survey found that 80 per cent of households in the United States were involved in at least one form of indoor or outdoor gardening.

Disease-Resistant Elms. As of May 1984, scientists had identified more than 20 varieties of elm that are resistant to Dutch elm disease. Among them are three resistant varieties of American elm that have been developed. The three are named Delaware II, Iowa State, and NPS 3. The resistant elm varieties are not immune to Dutch elm disease, but they can survive it with little damage.

Plant Conservation. On March 21, the World Wildlife Fund announced an international plant conservation program. Many other international conservation organizations and botanic gardens were expected to join in this effort to improve public awareness, conserve plant genetic material, and protect wild plants. Scientists warn that 40,000 of the 250,000 known species of flowering plants could become extinct by the mid-2000's unless emergency action is taken.

Horticulturalist Honored. In 1984, the Arthur Hoyt Scott Garden and Horticulture Award of Swarthmore College, one of gardening's highest prizes, was presented to Thomas H. Everett of the New York Botanical Garden. Everett was honored for his many contributions to horticulture, including his 10-volume *New York Botanical Garden Illustrated Encyclopedia of Horticulture* (1982).

Prize-Winning New Plants. In October 1984, All-America Selections, an organization that evaluates new seed varieties, awarded its prizes for 1985 to seven new garden plants. Prize-winning flowers were Century Mixed, a mixture of brightly colored celosia; Mini-Star Tangerine, a tangerine-colored gazania; Rose Diamond, an early geranium with multiple flower heads; Trinidad, an upright, rose-colored verbena; and Yellow Marvel, a zinnia that blooms over a long season. Vegetables chosen were Red Sails, an early, red leaf lettuce; and Sunburst, the first yellow scalloped squash.

The 1985 All-America Rose Selections winner was Showbiz, a brilliant scarlet floribunda rose that produces many blossoms. Showbiz, a cross between the Dream Waltz and Marlena varieties, was developed by Mathias Tantau, a West German rose breeder. Phil Clark

In WORLD BOOK, see FLOWER; GARDENING.

GAS AND GASOLINE. See ENERGY; PETROLEUM AND GAS.

GEOLOGY

GEOLOGY. In May 1984, the first direct measurements of the movement of the earth's continents were reported by scientists at the National Aeronautics and Space Administration's (NASA) Goddard Space Flight Center in Greenbelt, Md. The scientists found that North America and Europe are drifting apart by as much as ⅔ inch (17 millimeters) per year.

The NASA scientists charted the movement of the continents by beaming laser signals at an orbiting satellite, then measuring the time it took the signals to return to tracking stations around the world. They also clocked the arrival time of radio waves from space at the tracking stations.

Mapping the Interior. In April 1984, scientists produced the first three-dimensional maps of the interior of the earth. Two teams — led by geophysicists Robert N. Clayton and Don L. Anderson of the California Institute of Technology in Pasadena and Adam M. Dziewonski of the Massachusetts Institute of Technology in Cambridge, Mass. — produced the maps by analyzing the speed of shock waves from earthquakes recorded by a worldwide network of recording stations. Earthquake waves travel through the earth at various depths and speeds, speeding up in cooler, rigid rock and slowing down in hotter, more fluid rock.

One of the mapmakers' findings was that the continents may extend deeper into the *mantle* — the layer between the earth's outer crust and the core — than scientists had believed. For example, Africa and South America, which were once joined at the surface, appear to be still united 300 miles (480 kilometers) below the surface.

In May, geophysicists K. C. Creager and Thomas H. Jordan of Scripps Institution of Oceanography in La Jolla, Calif., using a similar technique, reported evidence that some lithospheric plates — segments of the earth's crust on which the continents and oceans ride — penetrate at least 620 miles (1,000 kilometers) below the surface.

This research, along with the new maps of the interior, may help geologists determine whether the currents of partially melted rock that fuel the movement of the plates are present only in the upper mantle. Some scientists believe the currents also exist in the lower mantle. The new evidence suggests that if the plates penetrate so deeply, the currents must also exist at great depths.

Ancient Plate Movement. Research published in 1984 provided new evidence of large-scale movement of the earth's lithospheric plates 2 billion years ago. Previously, geologists had direct evidence of such movement only for the past 200 million years.

In February, geologists Paul F. Hoffman of the Geological Survey of Canada and Samuel A. Bowring of the University of Kansas in Lawrence reported finding evidence of continental breakup and collision in 1.9-billion-year-old sedimentary rocks in Canada. These rocks are similar to sedimentary rock found along known plate boundaries where two continents are pulling apart. The scientists also found changes in the rocks similar to those in rocks at plate boundaries where two continents are colliding.

In September, geologists led by Tullis C. Onstott of Princeton University in New Jersey combined two techniques for the first time to determine how far rocks from Africa and South America had moved in relation to each other between the time that they formed — 2 billion years ago — and 1 billion years ago. The scientists first determined the age of the rocks by measuring the ratio of two forms of argon in the rocks. One form of argon is formed by the decay of potassium over time at a fixed rate.

Onstott and his co-workers then determined the position of the rocks when they formed by measuring the rocks' magnetic orientation, and compared this position to the rocks' location 1 billion years ago. The scientists discovered that the rocks were as much as 620 miles farther apart then than they were when they formed.   Eldridge M. Moores

See also PALEONTOLOGY. In WORLD BOOK, see GEOLOGY.

GEORGIA. See STATE GOVERNMENT.

Mauna Loa on the island of Hawaii, the world's largest active volcano, erupts in March for the first time since 1975.

GERMANY, EAST. A desire to improve relations with West Germany led Communist Party Secretary General and State Council Chairman Erich Honecker to suggest in March 1984 that he should make his first official visit to West German Chancellor Helmut Kohl in the fall. The news of this suggestion sparked a verbal attack on West Germany by the Soviet Union and strenuous Soviet efforts to dissuade Honecker. By defying Moscow, Honecker risked the worst split with the Soviet Union since the Communist German state was established in 1949.

On August 2, a major article in the East German Communist Party newspaper *Neues Deutschland* (New Germany) defended economic and political contact with West Germany by referring to the Helsinki agreement—an agreement signed by 35 Eastern and Western nations in Helsinki, Finland, in 1975. The agreement included a pledge to increase security, cooperation, and mutual understanding in Europe. The Soviet Union's Communist Party newspaper, *Pravda* (Truth), criticized "West German attempts to put political pressure on East Germany and undermine Communism." Soviet pressure intensified, and Honecker announced on September 4 that he would not go.

Moscow Also Criticized a $333-million loan that West Germany made to East Germany. The Soviets said that West Germany was using the loan to "disturb East German stability with the eventual aim of reunification." West Germany had approved the private bank loan in July in return for easing of restrictions on travel from East to West.

Asylum Plea. Both East and West Germany were embarrassed in February when Ingrid Berg, niece of East German Prime Minister Willi Stoph, took refuge in the West German Embassy in Prague, Czechoslovakia, with her husband, two children, and mother-in-law, and sought asylum in West Germany. After a week's negotiations, the East Germans promised the family visas. They crossed to West Germany on March 20.

Mission Incident. Fifty-five East Germans sought refuge in the West German diplomatic mission in East Berlin on June 29. It took more than a month to get all the East Germans out of the mission with promises that they would not be punished and that they would receive emigration visas later.

Trade between East and West Germany developed rapidly during 1984. In the first six months, East Germany's exports rose by 2 per cent to $1.4-billion. With oil deliveries from the Soviet Union cut, Honecker became more dependent on his Western neighbor. 　　　　　　　Kenneth Brown

See also EUROPE (Facts in Brief Table). In WORLD BOOK, see GERMANY.

East German immigrants enter a camp in West Germany. More than 15,000 were allowed to leave East Germany between January and April 1984.

GERMANY, WEST

GERMANY, WEST. Three scandals and a long period of industrial unrest made 1984 a difficult year for West German Chancellor Helmut Kohl. The first scandal began on Dec. 31, 1983, when Defense Minister Manfred Wörner dismissed General Günter Kiessling as deputy supreme commander of North Atlantic Treaty Organization (NATO) forces. Wörner said that Kiessling's reported homosexuality posed a "security risk." Wörner told a defense committee on January 12, however, that he "no longer had trust in him [Kiessling]," but that Kiessling's alleged visits to homosexual bars in Cologne were not the reason for the forced retirement. Kiessling denied being a homosexual.

Kohl's opponents in parliament attacked his handling of the affair and called for Wörner's resignation. On February 1, Kohl reinstated Kiessling and said that Kiessling had not engaged in homosexual activities. However, Kohl refused to accept Wörner's resignation. Kiessling retired with full military honors on March 26.

Flick Scandals. The Kohl administration was badly shaken by a second scandal when Otto Lambsdorff resigned as minister of economics on June 26. He faced trial on charges of corruption over alleged bribes paid to him by the giant Flick group of companies in return for tax concessions. Kohl quickly replaced Lambsdorff with Martin Bangemann.

The third scandal led to the resignation of Rainer Barzel as speaker of the Bundestag (the more powerful of the two houses of parliament) on October 25. Barzel had been accused of taking bribes from Flick in return for surrendering the leadership of the Christian Democratic Union to Kohl in 1973. Barzel denied taking the bribes. Philipp Jenninger was elected speaker of the Bundestag on November 5, replacing Barzel.

On November 7, Kohl faced a parliamentary committee investigating a report that Flick paid Kohl $125,000. Kohl admitted receiving cash from Flick, but denied any wrongdoing.

Labor Conflict disturbed West Germany's normally calm industrial scene in 1984. Early in March, there were scattered strikes by metalworkers demanding that the 40-hour workweek be reduced to 35 without a cut in pay. On April 17, after talks with industry leaders failed, the metalworkers' union said it would take a strike vote in May. Metalworkers in the automobile and engineering industries, along with printers, voted for national strikes, and — on May 14 — strikes began at 14 automobile parts factories. By the fifth week of the strike, about 440,000 workers were off the job.

On June 28, metalworkers accepted a compromise proposed by an eight-member arbitration panel, and they returned to work on July 2. The printers won a similar settlement on July 6.

West German metalworkers strike in May to press their demand for a shortening of the 40-hour workweek to 35 hours.

East-West Relations. Kohl's *Ostpolitik* policy of seeking *détente* (easing of tensions) with the East received a setback on September 4, when East German leader Erich Honecker — apparently because of pressure from the Soviet Union — canceled a visit to West Germany scheduled for September 26. A further blow came on September 9, when Todor Zhivkov, Bulgarian Communist Party general secretary, also canceled a visit to Bonn.

In October, however, Romania's President Nicolae Ceausescu visited Bonn. Romania is a Warsaw Pact member, but it has at times acted independently of the Soviet Union.

New President. Richard von Weizsäcker, 64, a liberal Christian Democrat, was elected president of West Germany on May 23. He defeated a candidate of the Greens — an antinuclear and environmentalist party — 832 votes to 68. Von Weizsäcker was sworn in on July 1. See VON WEIZSÄCKER, RICHARD.

Economic Scene. In September, Finance Minister Gerhard Stoltenberg said the inflation rate was 1.7 per cent, down from 5.4 per cent two years earlier. The unemployment rate was still about 9 per cent, however. The 1985 budget, approved in December, called for spending about $83.4 billion, a 2 per cent increase from 1984.   Kenneth Brown

See also EUROPE (Facts in Brief Table). In WORLD BOOK, see GERMANY.

GHANA. The government of Ghana foiled an attempted coup in 1984. On March 23 and 24, one group of armed rebels entered Ghana from Ivory Coast and another from Togo. According to Ghanaian officials, the infiltrators were quickly defeated. This was the fifth known plot against the military government of Chairman Jerry John Rawlings since he seized power in 1981.

In early July 1984, the Rawlings government announced that it was planning to return the country to civilian rule. In mid-July, two civilian members were added to the ruling Provisional National Defense Council.

Ghana's cacao industry continued to decline in 1984. Annual harvests formerly exceeded 500,000 metric tons (550,000 short tons). In the 1983-1984 crop year, however, Ghana harvested only about 158,000 metric tons (174,000 short tons). The decline has resulted from farmers planting more profitable food crops, a scarcity of agricultural laborers, drought, and poor transportation. In 1984, the World Bank and the African Development Fund gave $54 million in loans to rehabilitate cacao farming in Ghana.   J. Dixon Esseks

See also AFRICA (Facts in Brief Table). In the Special Reports section, see AFRICA — THE TROUBLED CONTINENT. In WORLD BOOK, see GHANA.

GIRL SCOUTS. See YOUTH ORGANIZATIONS.
GIRLS CLUBS. See YOUTH ORGANIZATIONS.

GOLF. Tom Watson became the Professional Golfers' Association of America (PGA) Player of the Year in 1984 for a record sixth time. The title was decided at the Pensacola (Fla.) Open from October 25 to 28, the final official tournament of the 10-month PGA Tour.

At the start of the tournament, Tom Watson and Denis Watson (no relation) of South Africa were tied for Player of the Year, each with 54 points. Each had won three tournaments during the year. The Player of the Year award involves a complicated scoring system that incorporates tournament victories and the season standings for earnings and stroke average. Denis Watson played at Pensacola and finished far back. Tom Watson did not play at Pensacola, but when Mark O'Meara and Andy Bean failed to qualify for the final 36 holes there, Watson was assured of the money-winning title with $476,260. And when Bruce Lietzke shot a 72 on the final round at Pensacola, it meant that Watson passed him in the season scoring average. Watson thus gained the two points that decided the award, 56 points to 54.

All three major professional tours paid record prize money in 1984 — $19.5 million for the 44 tournaments on the PGA Tour, $7.9 million for the 38 stops on the Ladies Professional Golf Association (LPGA) tour, and $5.4 million for the 26 tournaments on the PGA seniors tour.

PGA Tour. The four Grand Slam tournaments were won by Ben Crenshaw, Frank (Fuzzy) Zoeller, Severiano (Seve) Ballesteros of Spain, and Lee Trevino. It was the sixth major victory for Trevino, the fourth for Ballesteros, the second for Zoeller, and the first for Crenshaw.

The Grand Slam tournaments began with the Masters, played from April 12 to 15 in Augusta, Ga. Crenshaw sank a 60-foot (18-meter) birdie putt on the final round, and his 72-hole score of 277 beat Tom Watson by two strokes.

In the United States Open, played from June 14 to 18 in Mamaroneck, N.Y., Greg Norman of Australia sank a 40-foot (12-meter) putt on the 72nd hole. That tied him with Zoeller at 276, five strokes ahead of their nearest pursuer, Curtis Strange. The next day, in an 18-hole play-off, Zoeller sank a 68-foot (21-meter) birdie putt on the second hole, and Norman took a double-bogey. Zoeller went on to finish with a 67 that beat Norman by eight strokes.

In the British Open, held from July 19 to 22 in St. Andrews, Scotland, Ballesteros and Tom Watson were tied for the lead. Then Watson bogeyed the next-to-last hole, and Ballesteros' 276 beat Watson and Bernhard Langer of West Germany by two strokes. Watson had won the two previous British Opens.

The PGA championship was played from August 16 to 19 at Shoal Creek near Birmingham, Ala. The seven-year-old course, designed by Jack Nicklaus, was the newest course ever used for a major championship. Despite an ailing back that limited his practice, Trevino shot 273 and defeated Gary Player of South Africa and Lanny Wadkins by four strokes.

The LPGA Tour. Patty Sheehan and Amy Alcott each won four tournaments on the LPGA tour in 1984. Ayako Okamoto of Japan and Betsy King each won three. King led the tour in earnings ($266,771) and Sheehan in low stroke average (71.40). King was named the LPGA Player of the Year.

Sheehan gained the LPGA championship, held from May 31 to June 3 in Kings Island, Ohio, near Warren, with a record score of 272 and a record margin of 10 strokes. Hollis Stacy rallied in the final round from five strokes back and won by a stroke the women's U.S. Open, held from July 12 to 15 in Peabody, Mass.

Seniors. The 53-year-old Miller Barber and 54-year-old Don January were the stars of the PGA seniors tour for professionals 50 and older. January won four tournaments from March to September. In June and July, Barber won four tournaments, including the seniors U.S. Open, in which he defeated 54-year-old Arnold Palmer by two strokes.   Frank Litsky

In WORLD BOOK, see GOLF.

GREAT BRITAIN

British coal miners walked off the job on March 12, 1984, beginning a strike of marathon proportions, even by British standards. The strike developed into a gargantuan struggle between the National Union of Mineworkers (NUM), led by left wing firebrand Arthur Scargill, and the Conservative government of Prime Minister Margaret Thatcher. Attempts to negotiate an agreement failed, and at year's end, the strike dragged on, though more than 60,000 miners had defied the strike and returned to work.

The union claimed that the National Coal Board, which runs Great Britain's coal mines, was planning to close 20 mines, leading to the loss of 20,000 jobs and the ruin of entire mining communities. It accused the government of refusing to compromise and of seeking to destroy the unions. The government claimed that Scargill's aim was to bring down the Conservative administration.

Nearly the whole British population took sides in the dispute, the debate being fueled by daily televised scenes of violence at mine entrances. The strike split the traditionally solid mineworkers' union and set family against family in the mining villages. About one-fourth of the miners defied union orders and continued to work, particularly those in the more prosperous coal fields not threatened by closures. The police tried to keep mine entrances open for the miners who wanted to work. "Flying pickets," mobile teams of strikers organized by the NUM, appeared at mines to confront police brought in from all around Britain.

Moderate miners won several court actions against the NUM. On September 28, a court declared the strike unofficial because no national ballot of the miners had been called. The union was ordered to stop sending pickets outside their own area of employment and to stop threatening working miners with expulsion from the union. On October 10, the NUM was fined 200,000 pounds (about $260,000) for ignoring the court.

Assassination Attempt. On October 12, a skillfully planted bomb went off shortly before 3 A.M. in the hotel in which members of the government were staying during the annual Conservative Party conference at the English coastal resort of Brighton. The Irish Republican Army said that it had planted the bomb. Five people were killed, and 33 others were injured. The dead included one Con-

Police clash with British coal miners near Dover, England, in September during a long and violent strike by the National Union of Mineworkers.

A section of the Grand Hotel in Brighton, England, shows damage from a bomb attack on Conservative Party conventioneers in October that killed five people.

servative member of Parliament (MP) and the wife of another. Thatcher escaped uninjured but narrowly missed death. Two minutes before the blast, she had been in her bathroom, which was badly damaged.

Political Events. Within the government, Thatcher reigned supreme. The only moderate remaining in the Cabinet was Secretary of State for Energy Peter Walker. Opposition, however, came from Thatcher's own *backbenchers* (members of Parliament who are not party leaders). Francis Pym, a former foreign secretary, criticized Thatcher's style of leadership and some of her economic policies in speeches designed to make himself the flagbearer of traditional Tory values.

Labour's fortunes revived as the party won a parliamentary special election at Chesterfield, England, on March 1 and did well in elections for the European Parliament on June 14. But the honeymoon for Labour's new leader, Neil G. Kinnock, ended when party members returned to their habit of fighting among themselves. Internal strife broke out when Kinnock attempted to change the party's rules for *reselection* — deciding whether Labour MP's should run for reelection or not. Kinnock wanted to allow local party caucuses to permit all local party members to have a say in reselecting Labour MP's. But his proposal was voted down at Labour's annual conference on October 1.

Controversy arose over the sinking of the Argentine cruiser *General Belgrano* by a British submarine during the Falkland Islands conflict in 1982. Thatcher and other ministers said that the *Belgrano* had been sailing toward the British task force when the British government ordered it to be sunk. However, after persistent questioning by Labour MP Tam Dalyell, the government admitted that it had misled the House of Commons and had secretly changed its own rules of engagement to sink the *Belgrano*. A senior Ministry of Defence official, Clive Ponting, was accused of supplying Dalyell with documents relating to the sinking.

Government Secrets. On March 23, Sarah Tisdall, a Foreign Office clerk, was sent to prison for six months for leaking details to a newspaper about the arrival of U.S. cruise missiles in Britain. Also in 1984, Ray Williams, a Ministry of Defence official, faced trial on charges of selling documents about defense spending to a newspaper.

On April 16, Michael J. Bettaney, a British intelligence officer, was found guilty of spying and sentenced to 23 years in prison. Bettaney was accused of offering the Soviet Union a detailed account of the operations of British intelligence. On May 22, Britain announced that it had expelled Arkadi V. Gouk, security officer at the Soviet Embassy, who had been named in the Bettaney trial. In response, the Soviet Union expelled John Burnett, security officer at the British Embassy in Moscow.

The biggest dispute concerning government secrets occurred when, on January 25, the government announced it was abolishing the right of employees at Government Communications Headquarters (GCHQ) to belong to unions. The government said it feared breaches of security through strikes at GCHQ, where foreign government communications are monitored. The government offered the 5,000 employees 1,000 pounds (about $1,300) each to give up their union rights. Almost all accepted.

Libyan Embassy Shooting. Britain broke off diplomatic relations with Libya on April 22 after a London policewoman was killed by machine-gun fire from a window in the Libyan embassy. The shooting took place on April 17, during a demonstration against Libyan leader Muammar Muhammad al-Qadhafi. It led to a 10-day "siege" of the embassy by British police. Diplomatic privilege finally compelled the British to allow the Libyans in the building, including the unidentified gunman, to leave the country on April 27.

Kidnap Attempt. In a bizarre episode on July 5, Umaru Dikko, a former Nigerian minister of transport living in exile in London, was kidnapped and found drugged in a wooden crate about to be flown to Lagos, Nigeria. Dikko had been accused of corruption by Nigeria's military rulers. Four men, one Nigerian and three Israelis, were later charged with the kidnapping. Britain told the Nigerian ambassador, who was in Lagos, not to return to London and deported two other Nigerian diplomats. Nigeria responded by expelling two British diplomats.

Economy and the Budget. The government budget for the year beginning April 1, 1984, was announced in March. It projected a deficit of about 15 billion pounds ($20 billion). Economic growth was expected to hold steady at 3 per cent and inflation to drop half a point to 4.5 per cent. Revised figures in November showed 4.9 per cent inflation. The government blamed a drop in the growth rate to 2.5 per cent on the effects of the long coal strike. Unemployment stood at 12.7 per cent in December.

A Royal Birth. On September 15, to widespread delight, Princess Diana gave birth to her second child — a boy. He was named Henry Charles Albert David. Prince Harry, as he immediately became known, is third in line to the throne.

Currency Changes. On March 29, the Royal Mint ceased production of halfpennies, and the coin was removed from circulation on Dec. 31, 1984 — more than 700 years after it had been in-

A London policewoman lies dying from a shot fired from the Libyan embassy during a demonstration against Libyan leader Muammar Qadhafi in April.

Young Prince Harry — Henry Charles Albert David — born on September 15, goes home from the hospital with his parents, Prince Charles and Princess Diana.

troduced. For several years, the halfpenny had cost more than its face value to mint.

The Bank of England issued the last one-pound note on Dec. 31, 1984. The note will be replaced by the one-pound coin introduced in 1983. The new coin is expected to have an average circulation life of 40 years, compared with 10 months for the note, making the coin more economical.

Education. On June 20, Secretary of State for Education and Science Sir Keith Joseph announced a new 16-plus examination for English and Welsh schools. Beginning in September 1986, the exam, called the General Certificate of Secondary Education, will replace the existing General Certificate of Education (Ordinary Level) and the Certificate of Secondary Education.

Proposed cuts in government aid to university students met a storm of protest late in 1984. For 22 years, the government has paid students' tuition and given them grants for food, housing, and transportation. Secretary Joseph had proposed eliminating the grants for wealthy students and requiring their parents to pay part of the tuition. Following demonstrations by thousands of middle-class students and their parents, however, Joseph rescinded the proposed tuition aid cuts on December 5. Ian J. Mather

See also ENGLAND; IRELAND; SCOTLAND; WALES. In WORLD BOOK, see GREAT BRITAIN.

GREECE continued its verbal battle with Turkey throughout 1984. This conflict crippled operations of the North Atlantic Treaty Organization (NATO) in the eastern Mediterranean Sea. Greece and Turkey are NATO members, but they refused to cooperate in military exercises in the eastern Mediterranean. The Greeks feared that the presence of Turkish armed forces in this region would put some Greek islands, especially Limnos and Lesbos, at risk.

Base Blocked. On July 8, about 1,600 striking Greek employees blocked access to a United States Air Force base near the Athens airport because, they said, the Americans refused to accept a ruling of a Greek labor court. The ruling would have linked wages to inflation, upgraded pay scales, and reduced the workweek to 37½ hours.

One day later, Greece accused the United States of trying to interfere in Greece's domestic affairs. Greece also warned that operations at all four of the bases that the United States operates in Greece could be affected if Turkey continued to receive an "overt" supply of U.S. military aid. Tensions eased on July 11, when Prime Minister Andreas Papandreou met with U.S. Ambassador Monteagle Stearns. But on September 1, Greece's Foreign Undersecretary Yiannis Kapsis protested the dismissals of Greek workers at the U.S. air base in Athens.

Cyprus Hopes. In January, President Spyros Kyprianou of Cyprus presented to the United Nations (UN) a framework for a settlement that could lead to the unification of Cyprus. (Cyprus is inhabited mostly by ethnic Greeks and ethnic Turks. In November 1983, the Turkish Cypriots declared their part of the island an independent republic.) Turkish Cypriot leader Rauf R. Denktaş responded to Kyprianou's proposal by offering him a nonaggression pact.

UN Secretary-General Javier Pérez de Cuéllar flew to Famagusta, the Turkish Cypriots' capital city, on March 26 to propose that the Turkish Cypriots place the Greek section of the city under UN supervision. Denktaş turned down this proposal. On May 13, the UN Security Council censured Turkey for "secessionist actions" in Cyprus.

Weak Economy. The 24-nation Organization for Economic Cooperation and Development (OECD) in 1984 described the Greek economy as "weak." The OECD blamed Greece's 1981 entry into the European Community (EC) and a large fall in agricultural output. The OECD blamed the continuing rise in personal income for Greece's inflation rate of about 20 per cent. _Kenneth Brown_

See also EUROPE (Facts in Brief Table). In WORLD BOOK, see CYPRUS; GREECE.

GRENADA. See WEST INDIES.

GUATEMALA. See LATIN AMERICA.

GUINEA. Ahmed Sékou Touré, Guinea's president since the country became independent in 1958, died on March 26, 1984, at the age of 62. Touré, who had ruled longer than any other African head of state, fell ill while on a diplomatic mission in Saudi Arabia. He was rushed by plane to the Cleveland (Ohio) Clinic in the United States, where he died during heart surgery.

Military Takes Over. After Touré's funeral on March 30, leaders of Guinea's ruling Democratic Party scheduled a meeting to choose his successor. However, on April 3, members of the Guinean armed forces seized power in an apparently bloodless coup. The coup's leader, Colonel Lansana Conté, was named Guinea's president (see CONTÉ, LANSANA). Another colonel, Diarra Traore, became prime minister. Conté and his fellow officers justified the take-over on the grounds that under continued civilian rule, Guinea's decrepit economy would have deteriorated further and there would have been a fierce and disruptive struggle for power among factions of the Democratic Party.

The new government, which called itself the Military Committee for National Rectification, consisted of 41 members, all but 8 of whom were from the military. One of the government's first actions was to change the country's official name from the Popular and Revolutionary Republic of Guinea to, simply, the Republic of Guinea. In an-

Mourners in Conakry, Guinea, kneel before the coffin and portrait of their president, Ahmed Sékou Touré, who died on March 26.

other step away from the radical socialist posture of the Touré regime, the military leaders promised to encourage private enterprise. They hoped to attract new foreign investment to Guinea.

Debt Refinanced. To help Guinea pay its approximately $1.2-billion foreign debt, Western nations offered easier payment terms and more than $100 million in new credits. The West hoped the easing of financial pressure would enable Guinea to revive its export-crop industry, thereby earning the money to pay its debts. For various reasons, including Touré's policy of compelling farmers to sell to government buyers at artificially low prices, farming had badly declined.

To increase the supply of skilled workers, the new government restored the legality of private schools. Touré's regime had closed all such schools, including 60 Roman Catholic schools.

The military rulers expressed the hope that many returning Guineans, forced into exile by Touré, would have the skills needed to rebuild the economy. By August, an estimated 200,000 exiled Guineans were back in the country.   J. Dixon Esseks

See also AFRICA (Facts in Brief Table). In WORLD BOOK, see GUINEA.

GUINEA-BISSAU. See AFRICA.

GUYANA. See LATIN AMERICA.

HAITI. See LATIN AMERICA.

HANDICAPPED. Disabled persons emerged as a political force in the United States in 1984, as Republicans and Democrats alike courted their support in the November elections. Edward M. (Teddy) Kennedy, Jr. — the son of Senator Edward M. Kennedy (D., Mass.) — who lost a leg to cancer, appeared before the Democratic National Convention in July to appeal for a new awareness of disability issues. A massive drive brought thousands of new disabled voters into the political process.

Baby Doe Rules. Controversy over the 1982 death of the severely disabled infant boy known as "Baby Doe" continued in 1984. Baby Doe's parents, physicians, and an Indiana court had agreed to withhold food and medical treatment, allowing the infant to die. This prompted President Ronald Reagan to propose regulations for protecting the lives of severely disabled newborns. But the medical community feared that the rules would cause too much government interference with a physician's practice. A compromise was reached when Congress approved legislation that would outlaw the withholding of treatment for disabled infants, except when such treatment would be inhumane or prolong dying. President Reagan signed the bill into law on Oct. 9, 1984.

Disability and Discrimination. Overwhelming negative public reaction spurred Secretary of

Canadian businessman Andre Viger on April 16 crosses the finish line of the Boston Marathon to win its first official wheelchair division race.

Health and Human Services Margaret M. Heckler to stop disability benefit cutoffs in April 1984. Since 1980, when Congress ordered the Social Security Administration (SSA) to review the cases of individuals receiving federal disability benefits, nearly half a million people had been dropped from the rolls. In September 1984, Congress passed legislation ordering the SSA to prove that a disabled person has improved medically before benefits can be cut off and to continue benefits during the appeal process. President Reagan signed the legislation on October 9.

A February decision by the Supreme Court of the United States affected disabled people as well as women, minority groups, and the elderly. The court ruled that the law barring sex discrimination in schools was restricted to specific programs receiving federal funds rather than all the school's programs. The same principle would apply to federal laws forbidding discrimination against disabled persons.

Summer Olympics. The 1984 Summer Olympic Games, held in Los Angeles in July and August, included two official exhibition events for disabled athletes — a women's 800-meter and a men's 1,500-meter wheelchair race.   Michael E. Landwehr

In WORLD BOOK, see HANDICAPPED.

HARNESS RACING. See HORSE RACING.

HAWAII. See STATE GOVERNMENT.

HEALTH AND DISEASE. Major advances in the international scientific effort to understand the mysterious disease known as acquired immune deficiency syndrome (AIDS) were reported in 1984. On April 23, U.S. Secretary of Health and Human Services Margaret M. Heckler announced the discovery of a virus thought to be the "probable cause" of AIDS, which disables the body's disease-fighting mechanisms and makes victims vulnerable to many infections and certain forms of cancer. The virus, named HTLV-3, is a close relative of the human T-cell leukemia virus.

A research team headed by virologist Robert C. Gallo of the National Cancer Institute in Bethesda, Md., identified the virus after months of intensive work. Only two days before Heckler's announcement, scientists at the U.S. Centers for Disease Control in Atlanta, Ga., confirmed that French researchers had discovered an AIDS-related virus. The French group, working at the Pasteur Institute in Paris, named their suspected AIDS virus the LAV virus. Gallo said he believed that both the French and the U.S. discoveries were of the same virus.

Scientists then began to develop a test for use in blood banks to identify any donated blood contaminated by the HTLV-3 virus. Although most AIDS cases occur among intravenous drug abusers and promiscuous male homosexuals, a small

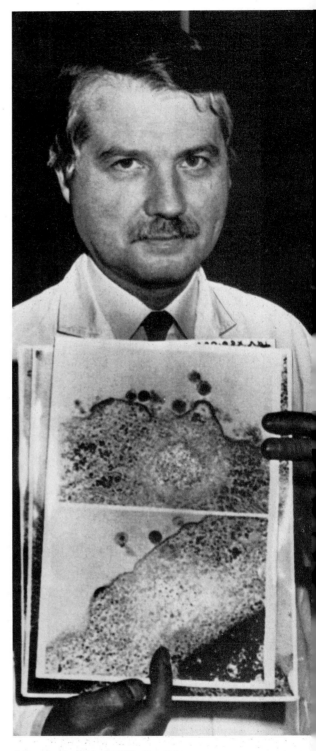

A French scientist in April displays pictures showing similarities between an AIDS virus he helped discover and one found by U.S. researchers.

number of cases are spread through transfusions of blood or blood products. Other biomedical researchers in October began investigations of the test to determine whether it was accurate enough for general use.

War on Smoking. Surgeon General of the United States C. Everett Koop on May 23 opened a new chapter in the long-standing dispute over the effects of cigarette smoke on nonsmokers. In releasing a 515-page report on smoking and health, Koop said the federal government has evidence that nonsmokers can suffer lung diseases as a result of exposure to cigarette smoke. The Tobacco Institute, the research and lobbying arm of the tobacco industry, challenged the contention.

Congress on September 26 approved a bill to strengthen the health warning labels that appear on cigarette packages and in cigarette advertisements. The new labels would cite the relationship between cigarette smoking and heart disease, lung cancer, and emphysema. In addition, they would warn pregnant women that cigarette smoking can damage the fetus and may result in premature birth.

Life Style and Cancer. There was growing emphasis during the year on the role of diet and life style in the prevention of cancer. The American Cancer Society (ACS) on February 10 issued its first guidelines for an "anticancer diet." The diet calls for reduced consumption of fat and salt-cured and smoked foods as well as moderation in the consumption of alcohol. The guidelines also recommend that people eat more fiber along with more yellow vegetables and other foods rich in vitamin A and beta-carotene, a compound related to vitamin A. The ACS stressed that people should watch their weight, because statistics show that cancer rates are higher among obese individuals.

On March 6, the Department of Health and Human Services urged that Americans make a series of life-style changes that could reduce the cancer death rate by 25 per cent by the year 2000. These changes included an anticancer diet, quitting smoking, and avoiding overexposure to the sun and to medical X rays.

Alzheimer's Disease, which causes progressive memory loss and mental deterioration, was the focus of increased research efforts during 1984. On September 14, scientists at the University of Iowa in Iowa City reported that damaged brain cells in Alzheimer's disease victims are confined to a small area of the brain. Physicians previously believed that the entire brain was involved.

In October, scientists at Dartmouth Medical School in Hanover, N.H., reported success in treating four Alzheimer's victims with a drug that

U.S. Surgeon General C. Everett Koop in May releases a report blaming smoking for 90 per cent of deaths caused by chronic lung diseases.

mimics acetylcholine, a chemical deficient in the brains of Alzheimer's victims. The Dartmouth scientists used a system that injected the drug directly into the patients' brains. Dosage was controlled by a pump implanted in their abdomens.

Exercise Hazards? The debate over the risks and benefits of strenuous exercise intensified following the death on July 20 of jogging enthusiast Jim Fixx, author of *The Complete Book of Running* (1977). Fixx died of a heart attack while jogging. A major study designed to help resolve the debate was released on October 4. It stated that jogging, wood chopping, swimming, and other intense exercise can both protect against and cause sudden death from a heart attack. The study, conducted at the University of Washington in Seattle, found that the risk of sudden death from cardiac arrest is greater during vigorous exercise. But it also showed that the risk of dying at any time from cardiac arrest is about 60 per cent lower among men who exercise regularly than among men who seldom exercise.   Michael Woods

See also MEDICINE; NUTRITION. In the Special Reports section, see DON'T GAMBLE WITH YOUR HEART. In WORLD BOOK, see HEALTH; DISEASE.

HIGHWAY. See BUILDING AND CONSTRUCTION; TRANSPORTATION.

HOBBIES. See COIN COLLECTING; GAMES AND TOYS; STAMP COLLECTING.

HOCKEY. The Edmonton Oilers, the highest-scoring team in National Hockey League (NHL) history, won the Stanley Cup as the NHL champions in 1984. They defeated the New York Islanders, 4 games to 1, in the play-off finals, ending the Islanders' string of four straight championships.

The NHL's 21 teams each played 80 regular-season games from October 1983 to April 1984. The division winners were the Oilers with 119 points, the Islanders with 104 points, the Boston Bruins with 104 points, and the Minnesota North Stars with 88 points. They were among the 16 teams that advanced to the play-offs.

In the first three rounds of the play-offs, the Oilers eliminated the Winnipeg Jets, 3 games to 0; the Calgary Flames, 4 games to 3; and Minnesota, 4 games to 0. The Islanders beat the New York Rangers, 3 games to 2; the Washington Capitals, 4 games to 1; and the Montreal Canadiens, 4 games to 2.

That set up a rematch of the 1983 final, in which the Islanders overwhelmed the Oilers in four straight games. The Oilers won the first game of the best-of-seven series, 1 to 0. The Islanders won the second game, 6 to 1. Then, the Oilers won three straight, 7 to 2, 7 to 2, and 5 to 2. Mark Messier, an Edmonton center, was voted the Conn Smythe Trophy as the Most Valuable Player of the play-offs.

National Hockey League Standings

Prince of Wales Conference

Lester Patrick Division	W.	L.	T.	Pts.
New York Islanders	50	26	4	104
Washington Capitals	48	27	5	101
Philadelphia Flyers	44	26	10	98
New York Rangers	42	29	9	93
New Jersey Devils	17	56	7	41
Pittsburgh Penguins	16	58	6	38

Charles F. Adams Division				
Boston Bruins	49	25	6	104
Buffalo Sabres	48	25	7	103
Quebec Nordiques	42	28	10	94
Montreal Canadiens	35	40	5	75
Hartford Whalers	28	42	10	66

Clarence Campbell Conference

James Norris Division	W.	L.	T.	Pts.
Minnesota North Stars	39	31	10	88
St. Louis Blues	32	41	7	71
Detroit Red Wings	31	42	7	69
Chicago Black Hawks	30	42	8	68
Toronto Maple Leafs	26	45	9	61

Conn Smythe Division				
Edmonton Oilers	57	18	5	119
Calgary Flames	34	32	14	82
Vancouver Canucks	32	39	9	73
Winnipeg Jets	31	38	11	73
Los Angeles Kings	23	44	13	59

Scoring Leaders	Games	Goals	Assists	Points
Wayne Gretzky, Edmonton	74	87	118	205
Paul Coffey, Edmonton	80	40	86	126
Michel Goulet, Quebec	75	56	65	121
Peter Stastny, Quebec	80	46	73	119
Mike Bossy, New York Islanders	67	51	67	118
Barry Pederson, Boston	80	39	77	116
Jari Kurri, Edmonton	64	52	61	113
Bryan Trottier, New York Islanders	68	40	71	111
Bernie Federko, St. Louis	79	41	66	107
Rick Middleton, Boston	80	47	58	105
Dale Hawerchuk, Winnipeg	80	37	65	102

Leading Goalies (25 or more games)	Games	Goals against	Avg.
Pat Riggin, Washington	41	102	2.66
Tom Barrasso, Buffalo	42	117	2.84
Al Jensen, Washington	43	117	2.91
Doug Keans, Boston	33	92	3.10
Bob Froese, Philadelphia	48	150	3.14

Awards

Calder Trophy (best rookie) — Tom Barrasso, Buffalo
Hart Trophy (most valuable player) — Wayne Gretzky, Edmonton
Lady Byng Trophy (sportsmanship) — Mike Bossy, New York Islanders
Masterton Trophy (perseverance, dedication to hockey) — Brad Park, Detroit
Norris Trophy (best defenseman) — Rod Langway, Washington
Ross Trophy (leading scorer) — Wayne Gretzky, Edmonton
Selke Trophy (best defensive forward) — Doug Jarvis, Washington
Smythe Trophy (most valuable player in Stanley Cup) — Mark Messier, Edmonton
Vezina Trophy (most valuable goalie) — Tom Barrasso, Buffalo

Wayne Gretzky of the Edmonton Oilers hoists the Stanley Cup in celebration after the Oilers beat the New York Islanders in May.

Individual Stars. During the regular season, the Oilers scored 446 goals, breaking their year-old NHL record of 424. They had the most prolific scorer in Wayne Gretzky. Gretzky led the league with 87 goals, 118 assists, and 205 points. He scored a goal or an assist in each of the first 51 games of the season, breaking his record of 30 games. He won the Hart Trophy as Most Valuable Player for the fifth straight year.

Tom Barrasso of the Buffalo Sabres gained the Vezina Trophy as the best goaltender and the Calder Trophy as rookie of the year. Rod Langway of Washington received the Norris Trophy as the outstanding defenseman. The All-Star team consisted of Barrasso in goal, Ray Bourque of Boston and Langway on defense, Gretzky at center, and Michel Goulet of the Quebec Nordiques and Mike Bossy of the Islanders at wing.

International Competition. The six-nation Canada Cup competition took place from September 1 to 10. Canada surprisingly won the title after it had eliminated the favored Soviet Union by a score of 3 to 2 in overtime in the semifinals.

The United States team played well in the preliminary round before losing to Sweden, 9 to 2, in the semifinals. Canada then defeated Sweden, 5 to 2 and 6 to 5, in Edmonton, Canada, in the best-of-three-game finals.   Frank Litsky

In WORLD BOOK, see HOCKEY.

HONDURAS. Hondurans in 1984 became increasingly concerned about the presence of foreign troops, which appeared to place Honduras at center stage in the Central American conflict. Some Hondurans demanded an end to the United States military presence, while others sought only to moderate it.

Five Armies. During most of 1984, five different armed forces operated within Honduran borders. They were U.S. Army and Navy forces, which carried out large-scale land and naval maneuvers; a rebel army of U.S.-backed Nicaraguans, which used Honduran territory to stage operations against Sandinista forces in Nicaragua; Salvadoran troops, who received training from U.S. military advisers at a camp located in Honduras; elements of Nicaragua's army, which frequently violated Honduran borders to pursue their foes; and the army of Honduras itself, which U.S. advisers sought to build up as a bulwark against leftist forces.

U.S. Relations. On March 31, President Roberto Suazo Córdova ousted General Gustavo Alvarez Martínez, commander of Honduran military forces and an outspoken advocate of closer ties with the United States. Four other generals were also forced to resign. The ouster proved to be only the prelude to an increasing chill in U.S.-Honduran relations.

On September 27, the Honduran government banned all training of Salvadoran troops within Honduras. Relations between Honduras and El Salvador had been strained since the two countries fought a brief war in 1969. The presence of Salvadoran troops in Honduras was particularly irksome to Honduran public opinion. United States Army advisers had been training Salvadorans at a special center in Honduras since 1983, as a way of getting around U.S. congressional limitations on the number of U.S. military advisers permitted in El Salvador.

On October 8, Foreign Minister Edgardo Paz Bárnica complained that the United States had failed to reply to a Honduran request for a high-level commission to discuss a new relationship between the two countries. On November 29, however, senior Honduran officials concluded a week-long series of meetings with high-level officials of President Ronald Reagan's Administration in Washington, D.C. The Hondurans announced that the United States had agreed to establish the commission. Further, the Honduran officials said negotiations were underway to allow the United States to resume training Salvadoran soldiers at its center in Honduras. The Honduran officials made it clear that they were seeking increased U.S. military and economic aid.   Nathan A. Haverstock

See also LATIN AMERICA (Facts in Brief Table). In WORLD BOOK, see HONDURAS.

HONG KONG. On Dec. 19, 1984, China and Great Britain signed an agreement for the transfer of Hong Kong from British to Chinese control on July 1, 1997. Hong Kong consists of an area on the mainland of Asia, Hong Kong Island, and more than 235 other islands. Great Britain acquired ownership of Hong Kong Island by an 1842 treaty and added part of the mainland area by an 1860 treaty. In 1898, China leased the rest of Hong Kong, an area called the New Territories, to Britain on a 99-year lease that will expire on July 1, 1997. Because the rest of Hong Kong is inseparably tied to the New Territories, Britain decided to give up the entire colony when the lease expires.

The agreement outlined policies that China said it would follow in Hong Kong for 50 years after 1997. Hong Kong would become a special administrative region of China, directly controlled by Beijing (Peking) and enjoying "a high degree" of independence "except in foreign and defense affairs." Hong Kong would have its own executive, legislative, and judicial systems, with British-style laws remaining "basically unchanged." China would appoint a chief executive on the basis of elections or "consultations to be held locally." The capitalist system that had made Hong Kong prosperous would remain unchanged.   Henry S. Bradsher

In WORLD BOOK, see HONG KONG.

HORSE RACING. The first Breeders' Cup Series, held at Hollywood Park near Los Angeles, made Nov. 10, 1984, the richest day in thoroughbred racing history. Seven races offered total purses of $10 million.

The Breeders' Cup Series, which was designed to attract the best North American and European horses, was financed largely through fees paid by thoroughbred breeders. The largest purse was $3-million for the 1¼-mile Classic. It was won by Wild Again, a long shot, in a tight finish over two other horses.

The winner of the next-largest purse in the Breeder's Cup Series was Lashkari, from France. Lashkari won the $2-million Breeders' Cup Turf, a 1½-mile race on the grass, defeating All Along, the 1983 Horse of the Year.

The winners of other Breeders' Cup races, each worth $1 million, strengthened their bids for divisional honors. They included 2-year-old colt Chief's Crown, sprinter Eillo, and Princess Rooney, who took the 1¼-mile race for fillies and mares.

The eventful Breeders' Cup Series also saw the 4-year-old filly Royal Heroine tie the world record of 1 minute 32⅗ seconds for 1 mile on turf. Outstandingly was awarded victory in the 2-year-old filly race after Fran's Valentine was disqualified for interference.

Military helicopters hover above U.S. and Honduran soldiers during a ceremony in February to mark the end of joint military exercises.

Major Horse Races of 1984

Race	Winner	Value to Winner
Belmont Stakes	Swale	$310,020
Breeders' Cup Juvenile	Chief's Crown	450,000
Breeders' Cup Juvenile Fillies	Outstandingly	450,000
Breeders' Cup Sprint	Eillo	450,000
Breeders' Cup Mile	Royal Heroine	450,000
Breeders' Cup Distaff	Princess Rooney	450,000
Breeders' Cup Turf	Lashkari	900,000
Breeders' Cup Classic	Wild Again	1,350,000
Budweiser-Arlington Million	John Henry	600,000
Epsom Derby (England)	Secreto	319,321
Grand National Steeplechase (England)	Hallo Dandy	79,415
Jockey Club Gold Cup	Slew o' Gold	350,400
Kentucky Derby	Swale	537,400
Preakness Stakes	Gate Dancer	243,600
Prix de l'Arc de Triomphe (France)	Sagace	267,750
Rothmans International	Majesty's Prince	360,000
Santa Anita Handicap	Interco	298,650

Major U.S. Harness Races of 1984

Race	Winner	Value to Winner
Cane Pace	On the Road Again	$180,000
Hambletonian	Historic Freight	609,500
Little Brown Jug	Colt Fortysix	110,931
Meadowlands Pace	On the Road Again	646,500
Messenger Stakes	Troublemaker	189,671
Roosevelt International	Lutin d'Isigny	125,000
Woodrow Wilson Pace	Nihilator	1,080,500

Although the Breeders' Cup Series was intended to match the year's best horses, inevitably some did not compete. Missing was the 1981 American champion, John Henry, who was sidelined by an injury after a highly successful season in which the 9-year-old gelding earned $2,336,650. After winning stakes throughout the country in a strong bid to be grass champion for a third time, John Henry ended the year with career earnings of $6,597,947, about $2.7 million more than any other horse in history.

Also absent from the Breeders' Cup was Swale, winner of the Kentucky Derby at Churchill Downs in Louisville on May 5 and the Belmont Stakes at Belmont Park near New York City on June 9. On June 17, Swale collapsed and died after returning from a gallop. An extensive autopsy failed to disclose the exact cause of the 3-year-old colt's sudden death.

Harness Racing. Fancy Crown was named the 1984 Horse of the Year on December 11. The 3-year-old filly equaled the fastest trotting mile in history in 1984.

Quarter Horse Racing. Eastex won the $2.5-million All-American Futurity on September 3 at Ruidoso Downs, N. Mex. Eastex earned $1 million in the 440-yard race. Jane Goldstein

In WORLD BOOK, see HARNESS RACING; HORSE RACING.

HOSPITAL. The United States Department of Health and Human Services (HHS) in June 1984 announced that Medicare payments to hospitals during 1985 will increase by only 6 per cent, the smallest increase since Medicare began in 1965. Medicare is the federal health insurance program for elderly and disabled Americans. The biggest Medicare payment increase occurred in 1981, when hospital costs rose by 22 per cent.

Secretary of Health and Human Services Margaret M. Heckler credited the new Medicare system of paying hospitals on the basis of predetermined rates with helping to control hospital costs. That system, initiated in 1983, is based upon 467 categories of treatment called diagnosis-related groups (DRG's). If treatment costs exceed the set payment for a particular DRG, then the hospital must absorb the excess cost. If treatment costs are less, the hospital keeps the difference.

On Sept. 16, 1984, the American Hospital Association in Chicago said the DRG system had given U.S. hospitals a strong incentive to economize. As a result, hospital costs during the first half of 1984 increased by only 4.8 per cent, down from the 12.8 per cent increase during the same period in 1983.

Legal Matters. The Supreme Court of the United States on March 27 upheld a hospital's right to require patients to use the services of a specific group of anesthesiologists, radiologists, or pathologists. The court noted that patients are free to enter a hospital served by the anesthesiologist or other practitioner of their choice.

So-called Baby Doe regulations, designed to prevent hospitals from withholding treatment from severely handicapped infants, continued as a controversial issue during the year. Many doctors and hospitals opposed the rules on the grounds that they interfered with medical practice.

In October, President Ronald Reagan signed into law a Baby Doe amendment to the federal Child Abuse Prevention and Treatment Act of 1974. The amendment requires that states receiving federal child abuse funds investigate — and if necessary prosecute — any cases involving the withholding of "medically indicated treatment" from handicapped infants. But the new law does not require futile efforts that would only prolong a baby's dying.

A 47-Day Strike — mainly by orderlies, housekeepers, clerks, and technicians — at 30 hospitals and 15 nursing homes in New York City ended on August 29, when the 49,000 strikers agreed to a 5 per cent pay increase. On July 9, 6,300 nurses at 16 hospitals in the Minneapolis, Minn., area agreed to a new contract, ending the largest nurses' strike in U.S. history. Michael Woods

In WORLD BOOK, see HOSPITAL.

HOUSING. See BUILDING AND CONSTRUCTION.

HOUSTON continued in 1984 to wrestle with problems caused by the lingering effects of the worldwide crude-oil glut on the city's economy, which relies heavily on the energy industry. In June, Houston's leaders started a major effort to attract new businesses to the city. With the strong backing of Mayor Kathryn J. Whitmire, the Houston Chamber of Commerce collected $6.7 million in private donations to fund the Houston Economic Development Council. The council will lead the effort to bring more diversity to the city's economy.

Houston's unemployment rate dropped steadily during 1984. It reached 5.7 per cent in October 1984, down from 8.2 per cent a year earlier.

Building Slump. During the 1970's and early 1980's, Houston experienced a construction boom. The city's growth slowed dramatically, however, with the drop in oil prices in 1982. The amount of building, measured by building-permit applications submitted to Houston city officials, dropped from $558 million worth of construction in the second quarter of 1983 to $314 million during the same period in 1984. The number of building permits dropped about 44 per cent over the same period. The building slowdown reflected the high vacancy rate for the city's office buildings, which reached 25 per cent in the third quarter of 1984.

Housing starts in the Houston area sank to an annual rate of about 37,000 units in October 1984—about half the 1983 rate. In addition, between 50,000 and 70,000 existing houses were up for sale in the Houston area.

Public Works. During 1984, Houston's leaders worked to improve the city's roads, utilities, parks, and flood-control system, which had been unable to keep pace with the tremendous population growth accompanying the oil boom. On September 11, voters approved a $595-million bond issue to finance the construction of parks, libraries, and police and fire stations.

Also in September, construction began on a new $30-million police station on the west side of the city. Three more stations—in the northwest, northeast, and south sections of Houston—are planned in an effort to decentralize police operations.

With increased commitments of state funding, nearly all of Houston's freeways were being improved in 1984. Special *transitways*, lanes limited to buses and commuter vans, were opened along two major freeways during the year. In addition, construction began on a 21.6-mile (34.8-kilometer) toll road from north Harris County to near downtown Houston.

Construction also began on the Wortham Theater Center, a $70-million entertainment complex in downtown Houston that will be the home of the Houston Grand Opera and the Houston Ballet.

The center, which will have 2,300-seat and 1,100-seat theaters, is being built on city-owned land but is being funded by private donations.

City Government. One of the most emotional issues facing Houston in 1984 was the City Council debate on two measures protecting homosexuals from discrimination in employment in city government. The City Council amended existing laws to bar employment discrimination because of sexual orientation. But a group of conservative political and religious leaders mounted a petition drive that succeeded in forcing a public vote on the antidiscrimination measures. Enforcement of the amendments was delayed until after the vote on Jan. 19, 1985.

The City Council approved Mayor Whitmire's $1.15-billion operating budget. Councilors were disappointed, however, because the budget did not provide funding for such important city services as regular collection of heavy trash and increased demolition of dangerous buildings. Whitmire insisted that such services would require tax increases, which would be unwise because of the sluggish economy.

The City Council approved Mayor Whitmire's nomination of a new fire chief for Houston. Fire Chief Robert Swartout of Seattle replaced Houston's retiring fire chief, V. E. Rogers. William A. Mintz

See also CITY. In WORLD BOOK, see HOUSTON.

HUNGARY continued to reform its economy while maintaining good relations with Eastern bloc nations and the West in 1984. In April, Hungary's Communist Party Central Committee approved further decentralization of the economy, including a measure that allows workers to participate in the appointment of top managers of businesses.

In September, the party defended the establishment of *income differentials*—large differences in workers' pay based on worker productivity and on the value of the items produced or the services performed by the workers. Party officials said that income differentials stimulate the economy by rewarding superior work. Critics argued that income differentials are an element of a free-market economy inconsistent with Communism. Also in September, the government banned two free-market practices—reselling new automobiles, and buying food from producers for resale to retailers.

Environmental Issues. Early in the summer, an independent group called the Danube Circle circulated a petition against a plan to divert Danube River water for a hydroelectric plant and to build a second plant on the river itself. The project, which was already under construction, would provide cheap electricity and improve navigation and flood control. The protesters argued that the project would damage the environment and endanger the supply of drinking water for 8 million people.

HUNGARY

Margaret Thatcher, decorating a war memorial
in Budapest in February, pays the first
visit to Hungary by a British prime minister.

The Danube Circle gathered more than 6,000 signatures for their petition.

In June, Hungary and Austria signed the first environmental agreement between a Soviet-bloc nation and a non-Communist one. It calls for cooperation in waste disposal, noise abatement, air pollution control, and environmental research.

Three Western Leaders traveled to Hungary in 1984 — Great Britain's Prime Minister Margaret Thatcher in February, followed by Prime Minister Bettino Craxi of Italy in April and Chancellor Helmut Kohl of West Germany in June. Soviet Foreign Minister Andrei A. Gromyko visited Hungary in April and voiced approval of its policies.

Economy. Hungary borrowed $2 billion in 1984, including $450 million from the International Monetary Fund and a record $480 million in a package arranged by the World Bank and commercial banks. During the first half of 1984, Hungary's exports to the West increased by 0.8 per cent, compared with the first six months of 1983. Imports from the West fell by 2.5 per cent. Exports to Eastern European nations rose by 11.2 per cent, while imports dropped by 0.5 per cent. In the first nine months of 1984, industrial production increased by 2.9 per cent and productivity rose by 3.1 per cent.   Chris Cviic

See also EUROPE (Facts in Brief Table). In WORLD BOOK, see HUNGARY.

346

HUNTING. The deaths in 1984 of two bald eagles, the national bird of the United States, and a whooping crane, an endangered species, from ingested lead quickened efforts in the United States to ban the use of lead shot for waterfowl hunting. United States Fish and Wildlife Service officials targeted five counties in three states where lead shotgun pellets may not be used. Counties where the ban is due to take effect, starting in the 1985-1986 hunting season, include Siskiyou and Modoc counties in California, Klamath and Jackson counties in Oregon, and Holt County in Missouri.

The National Wildlife Federation blamed the use of lead shot for the deaths of thousands of waterfowl and other birds. The birds mistake the pellets for food, eat them, and die of lead poisoning. As a result of a campaign by the National Wildlife Federation, the use of lead shot in hunting may soon be prohibited throughout the United States.

Dove Season. In 1984, for the first time in 87 years, Indiana residents were permitted to hunt the mourning dove, despite opposition from antihunting groups. A resolution urging Director James M. Ridenour of the Indiana Department of Natural Resources to set a dove season was introduced during the spring session of the state legislature, where it passed easily.

Poaching Arrests. In predawn raids on October 4, heavily armed federal and state wildlife agents arrested more than 20 people accused of illegally killing numerous protected or endangered animals, including golden eagles, mountain lions, and bighorn sheep, in the area around Yellowstone National Park, which is centered in Wyoming. The raids, called Operation Trophykill by the U.S. Fish and Wildlife Service, were conducted in nine states, following a three-year investigation.

In all, warrants were issued for 34 people charged with the poaching and smuggling of protected animals and animal parts. Some of the animal parts, the agents said, were exported to South Korea and other Asian nations, where they are prized for their alleged medicinal powers.

Alligators. For the first time in 15 years, residents of Texas had an alligator hunting season in 1984. The Texas Parks and Wildlife Department placed the alligator on its endangered species list in 1969. In recent years, however, the reptiles have become a nuisance in some residential areas.

With an alligator population of over 100,000 animals in southeast Texas, wildlife biologists said that allowing hunters to kill about 800 alligators would not threaten their existence. Sidney Dupuy, a commercial hunter who sells the reptiles' hides, was high bidder to remove 80 alligators from a state-owned wildlife management area near Port Arthur.   Tony Mandile

In WORLD BOOK, see AMMUNITION; HUNTING.

ICE SKATING. Figure skaters Scott Hamilton of Denver and Katarina Witt of East Germany won gold medals in the Winter Olympic Games held in February in Sarajevo, Yugoslavia. The British team of Jayne Torvill and Christopher Dean won the Olympic gold medal in ice dancing.

The World Championships were held from March 19 to 24 in Ottawa, Canada, and there these Olympic medalists won again. Hamilton's world championship was his fourth straight. Torvill and Dean also won their fourth straight title.

The only Olympic champions who lost in the world championships were the Soviet pairs team of Elena Valova and Oleg Vasiliev. They finished second to Barbara Underhill and Paul Martini of Canada. Caitlin (Kitty) and Peter Carruthers of Burlington, Mass., Olympic silver medalists, missed the world championships because Kitty had tendinitis.

The United States Championships and Olympic trials took place from January 18 to 22 in Salt Lake City, Utah. Hamilton won his fourth consecutive men's title, and Rosalynn Sumners of Edmonds, Wash., her third straight women's championship. The Carruthers sister-brother team won their fourth straight pairs championship; and Judy Blumberg of Tarzana, Calif., and Michael Seibert of Washington, Pa., got their fourth straight title in dance.

After the Olympics, Hamilton, Torvill and Dean, the Carrutherses, and Sumners turned professional. The best singles skaters who remained amateur were Brian Orser of Canada, second in the Olympics, and Tiffany Chin of Toluca Lake, Calif. Chin, fourth in the Olympics, missed the world championships because of injury.

Speed Skating. Karin Enke of East Germany was the year's most successful speed skater. She won two gold and two silver medals in the four Olympic races for women. She won the world overall championship for women held on January 28 and 29 in Deventer, the Netherlands. Enke also swept the four women's races in the world sprint championship held on March 3 and 4 in Trondheim, Norway.

Gaetan Boucher of Quebec City, Canada, won two golds and one bronze in the men's Olympic races. He won the world sprint championship by beating Sergei Khlebnikov of the Soviet Union by 0.01 second in the final 1,000-meter race.

The world overall championship for men was held on February 25 and 26 in Göteborg, Sweden. Oleg Bogiev became the first Soviet skater in 22 years to win the title.   Frank Litsky

See also OLYMPIC GAMES. In WORLD BOOK, see ICE SKATING.

ICELAND. See EUROPE.

IDAHO. See STATE GOVERNMENT.

ILLINOIS. See CHICAGO; STATE GOVERNMENT.

Scott Hamilton of Denver skates to victory, winning the Olympic gold medal in figure skating at the Winter Games in Sarajevo, Yugoslavia, in February.

347

IMMIGRATION. Congress adjourned on Oct. 12, 1984, without taking final action on the most sweeping overhaul of United States immigration laws in nearly two decades. The House of Representatives had joined the Senate in passing a controversial immigration bill. However, because there were important differences between the House and Senate bills, congressional conferees labored in vain in search of a compromise on the legislation. Called the Simpson-Mazzoli bill, the measure was named for its chief sponsors — Senator Alan K. Simpson (R., Wyo.) and Representative Romano L. Mazzoli (D., Ky.). During a seven-year effort to fashion new immigration policies, the Senate passed legislation in 1982 and 1983, but the House did not approve a bill of its own until June 20, 1984.

Pressure for Action stemmed from concern about a flood of illegal aliens from Latin America, especially Mexico. Before the House vote, President Ronald Reagan contended, "The simple truth is that we've lost control of our own borders, and no nation can do that and survive."

With both parties wooing Hispanic voters in the 1984 election campaign, the strenuous objections of many Hispanic political leaders to some provisions of the legislation were a major factor in the congressional debate on the Simpson-Mazzoli bill. Walter F. Mondale, the 1984 Democratic presidential nominee, strongly opposed the measure.

One area of Senate-House disagreement involved the broad amnesty proposed for illegal immigrants, who are estimated to number at least 2 million and perhaps as many as 10 million. The House version of the bill would have legalized the presence of all aliens who moved to the United States before 1982. The Senate version, favored by Reagan, would have given legal status to those who established U.S. residence before 1980.

Penalties for Violators. Both versions would have made it unlawful for an employer to knowingly hire an illegal alien, and both would have provided civil fines of up to $2,000 for violators. In addition, the Senate bill would have provided criminal penalties, including six-month jail terms, for employers who repeatedly hired illegal immigrants. Hispanic opposition to the legislation focused on fears that employers would avoid hiring any Hispanics, even U.S. citizens.

Raids Allowed. On April 17, the Supreme Court of the United States ruled, 7 to 2, that the Immigration and Naturalization Service can conduct "factory surveys," its term for surprise raids on businesses that might be hiring illegal aliens. The high court overturned an appeals court ruling that the surprise raids constituted unreasonable searches of private property.   Frank Cormier and Margot Cormier

In WORLD BOOK, see IMMIGRATION.

INCOME TAX. See ECONOMICS; TAXATION.

INDIA was rocked in 1984 by the assassination of Prime Minister Indira Gandhi on October 31 and the worst industrial accident in history on December 3. Gandhi was shot by two of her own bodyguards as she walked from her residence to her office in New Delhi, India's capital. The two guards were members of the Sikh religious community. One of them, Beant Singh, was killed by other bodyguards. The other, Satwant Singh, confessed on December 3 to a plot in which vows to kill Gandhi had been taken in the Sikhs' holiest shrine, the Golden Temple at Amritsar in Punjab state.

The Golden Temple had been seized by the Indian Army on June 5 to 7 on Gandhi's order. She ordered the seizure to try to quell violence by Sikh extremists who sought a separate Sikh state. The leader of the extremists, Sant (Holy Man) Jarnail Singh Bhindranwale, used the temple as a sanctuary from which to send teams to kill moderate political leaders and others. From August 1982, when the violence began, until the army took control of the Punjab on June 3, 1984, 410 people were killed and over 1,180 others injured.

During the two-day battle for the Golden Temple, the army also cleared extremists from 41 other Sikh temples. The Indian government officially reported that the combined death toll was 92

Sikhs in April march past the Golden Temple, which in June became the scene of a clash between Sikh extremists and the Indian Army.

India's new prime minister, Rajiv Gandhi (in white hat), watches as his mother's body is cremated in a traditional Hindu funeral ceremony in November.

soldiers and 554 extremists. Indian news media gave much higher counts, saying as many as 200 soldiers and 800 Sikhs died at the Golden Temple alone. Bhindranwale himself died there during the army's assault.

Many Sikhs, including those who opposed Bhindranwale's violence, were outraged by the attack on the Golden Temple. Gandhi's associates warned her of the danger of a revenge attack, but she rejected suggestions that all Sikhs be removed from her security guard. She said such action would violate her policy of no religious discrimination. See ASIA (Close-Up).

The Assassination touched off four days of rioting against Sikhs. Home Minister P. V. Narasimha Rao said 1,277 people died in the riots.

Gandhi's son, Rajiv, succeeded her as prime minister hours after the assassination. His succession was not challenged by older politicians. See GANDHI, RAJIV.

The Worst Industrial Accident in history occurred on December 3 in Bhopal, capital of Madhya Pradesh in central India. Fumes of methyl isocyanate, a poisonous gas used in making pesticides, escaped during the night from a factory and spread over part of the sleeping city. More than 2,500 people were reported killed, and many more were sickened and temporarily blinded. See CHEMICAL INDUSTRY.

Elections. Rajiv Gandhi called elections for Parliament on December 24, 27, and 28 in all but two states, Punjab and Assam, where no voting was to be held because the states were torn by violence. The two states will not be represented in Parliament until they have elections.

Opposition parties, suddenly deprived of Indira Gandhi as a target against whom they could rally voters, failed to overcome their differences and present a united front. As a result, the new prime minister's Congress-I Party (I for Indira) won at least 401 of the 508 parliamentary seats at stake, though it received only about 50 per cent of the popular vote. Winning the huge parliamentary majority gave Rajiv Gandhi a solid base of support on which to govern for the next five years.

Opposition Parties had tried before the assassination to unify against Indira Gandhi's manipulation of state governments. She used the figurehead governors of Sikkim, Jammu and Kashmir, and Andhra Pradesh—whom she appointed—to oust elected leaders. One of those ousted was the top elected official of Andhra Pradesh, Chief Minister Nadamuri T. Rama Rao, a former film star whose party had upset Congress-I in 1983 state elections. Rama Rao was reinstated on Sept. 16, 1984, a month after the governor deposed him on the false grounds that he no longer had the support of a majority in the state legislature. During the intervening month, dozens of people died in rioting over the ouster.

Strife Between Hindus and Muslims, which has flared up from time to time in India's villages, erupted into mob frenzy in Bombay and adjacent areas in mid-May. Rioters burned people alive in Bhiwandi, near Bombay, and officials called in the army to restore order after the violence spread to Bombay. More than 250 people died.

Relations with India's Neighbors in 1984 were troubled. Indian officials accused Pakistan of training and arming Sikh extremists, which Pakistan denied. In the summer and early fall, soldiers of the two countries skirmished along the 1949 cease-fire line dividing the disputed Kashmir area, two-thirds of which makes up Jammu and Kashmir state.

India in April began building a 1,600-mile (2,600-kilometer) fence to try to keep out immigrants from Bangladesh. Bangladesh denounced the action. After several small clashes, India in May halted construction indefinitely. Sri Lanka accused India of training and arming Sri Lankan guerrillas, but India denied the charges. From September 17 to 22, India and China held a fifth round of talks on their border dispute but made no progress. Henry S. Bradsher

See also Asia (Facts in Brief Table). In World Book, see India.

INDIAN, AMERICAN. Indian leaders, federal officials, and natural resource developers met in Washington, D.C., on June 19, 1984, to try to ease the growing conflict over the West's scarce water resources. Assistant Secretary of the Interior for Indian Affairs Kenneth L. Smith urged negotiated settlements of the more than 50 lawsuits being waged over Indian water rights. However, Elmer M. Savilla, executive director of the National Tribal Chairmen's Association (NTCA), argued that, to most Indian leaders, negotiation means "outright denial of rights."

Several court decisions have established Indian rights to water, but most have not clarified just how much water is involved. In a 1906 ruling known as the Winters Doctrine, the Supreme Court of the United States declared that Indians have federally reserved rights to water that passes through their reservations. In 1963, the Supreme Court set the entitlement of the tribes in the lower Colorado River Basin at enough water to irrigate the arable portion of the tribes' land. The Western Governor's Association has estimated that applying this standard to Indian lands in 11 Rocky Mountain and West Coast states would grant Indians more than three times the total annual flow of the Colorado River. About 80 per cent of the available surface water in the Rocky Mountain and West Coast states is already being used.

Settlement of the disputes will have a tremendous effect on the future development of the West. Ralph F. Cox, an executive of the Atlantic Richfield Company, one of the largest U.S. oil companies, claimed in June that the national defense and the stability of the U.S. economy are closely linked to continued development of Western resources. This development, in turn, depends upon "the most precious resource of all: water," he argued.

BIA Criticized. In March 1984, Representative Sidney R. Yates (D., Ill.), charged that the Bureau of Indian Affairs (BIA) has not properly protected the water, land, and mineral rights of Native Americans. In November, a presidential commission described the BIA's management of these tribal resources as "incompetent" and said that the present system "thrives on the failure of Indian tribes." The commission recommended replacing the BIA with a new federal agency and reducing the dependence of Indians on the federal government.

Politics. At the midyear conference of the National Congress of American Indians (NCAI) in May, Executive Director Suzan Shown Harjo said the Administration of President Ronald Reagan had stubbornly avoided addressing the problems of Indians. However, Harjo said she was hopeful that the treatment of Indians would improve under Secretary of the Interior William P. Clark, who assumed the post in November 1983 after the resignation of James G. Watt. Both the NCAI and the NTCA had called for Watt's resignation, saying that he failed to understand the plight of Native Americans.

Bingo Boom. On June 19, 1984, Deputy Assistant Secretary of the Interior John W. Fritz expressed the Administration's concern that bingo gambling on Indian reservations might attract organized crime. In 1984, about 80 tribes operated, or planned to operate, bingo games on their lands. Several courts have ruled that reservations are not subject to state gambling laws that limit bingo jackpots. As a result, thousands of people flock to reservation bingo games, drawn by prizes ranging up to $50,000.

Indian Fugitive Surrenders. On September 13, Dennis Banks, a founder of the American Indian Movement, surrendered to police in Rapid City, S. Dak., ending nine years as a fugitive. Banks said that he had fled after his 1975 conviction for assault and rioting because he feared for his life in prison. Banks's lawyers explained that he surrendered because he was tired of living the life of a fugitive. On October 8, Banks was sentenced to three years in prison. His lawyers planned to appeal the sentence. Andrew L. Newman

In World Book, see Indian, American.
INDIANA. See State Government.

INDONESIA recorded steady economic growth during 1984. Western aid givers and the World Bank, a United Nations agency that loans funds for development, at a meeting in June praised Indonesia's "decisive and timely measures" to cope with economic problems. They noted that inflation and the balance-of-payments deficit had been reduced. The meeting pledged $2.45 billion in new aid for the year that began on April 1, 1984, up 11 per cent from the previous year's aid.

Indonesia's Fourth Five-Year Plan for economic development began on April 1. Hoping to increase revenues from sources other than oil and liquefied natural gas, the country's main export earners, government planners gave new emphasis to such traditional exports as rubber, palm oil, and coffee.

The head of Pertamina, Indonesia's state-owned oil company, Brigadier General Judo Sumbono, was dismissed in June. The government had become unhappy about lagging revenues and about management problems at the company. Major General Abdulrachman Ramli, who had headed a state-owned tin company, took over Pertamina.

The 1984-1989 development plan also called for more than 4 million people to move from Java to outlying islands. Java has only 7 per cent of Indonesia's land but 60 per cent of its people.

The Army's Role. President Suharto asserted on August 16 that the armed forces would continue to have a role in Indonesia's political development until the year 2000. He said that military participation was not incompatible with democracy. However, a group of prominent citizens charged that liberties were being eroded as power became concentrated in the hands of the armed forces and of Suharto himself, a former general.

Religious Tensions. Under government pressure, the United Development Party, a Muslim political coalition, adopted Suharto's state doctrine, called Pancasila, as the sole foundation of its beliefs. However, some Muslims argued that the doctrine conflicted with Islam.

On the night of September 12-13, Muslims in Jakarta's port district clashed with security forces, and 18 people were killed. But the riot was not clearly related to religious tensions.

Border Clashes on the ground and violations of Indonesia's airspace were reported from the border with Papua New Guinea. The clashes apparently occurred as Indonesian troops fought rebels of the Free Papua Movement on the island of New Guinea, which is divided between Indonesia and Papua New Guinea.   Henry S. Bradsher

See also ASIA (Facts in Brief Table). In WORLD BOOK, see INDONESIA.

President Suharto hits a gong in January to open a conference in Jakarta of nonaligned nations – those allied with neither the East nor the West.

INSURANCE. Property and casualty insurance companies in the United States registered a net loss in their operations in 1984. It was the first such loss since 1906, when an earthquake and subsequent fire devastated San Francisco.

The insurance industry does two kinds of business. First, it *underwrites* (sells protection against financial loss to individuals and businesses), and second, it invests the premiums it collects. For the fourth year in a row, problems arose with the first kind of business because companies paid out far more in claims for financial losses than they collected in premiums. In 1984, this underwriting loss was estimated at $21.0 billion. It exceeded 1983's underwriting loss of $13.3 billion by an astounding 58 per cent. At year's end, industry sources said that the combined underwriting loss for 1983 and 1984 was greater than the total underwriting deficit for the preceding 25-year period.

Before 1984, investment earnings had pulled the industry through. Even though investment income was up from $16.0 billion in 1983 to an estimated $17.3 billion in 1984, the increase failed to offset the underwriting loss. Putting together investment gains and underwriting losses, U.S. property and casualty companies in 1984 showed a pretax net loss estimated at $3.7 billion, compared with a pretax net gain of $2.7 billion in 1983.

The Financial Results demonstrated that underwriting losses have finally caught up with investment gains. Since the figures represented industry averages, some insurers at the lower end of the scale clearly faced problems with solvency. In mid-1984, insurance examiners reported that 319 of some 4,500 U.S. property and casualty insurers were in sufficient danger to require suggested operating and management changes from their state insurance regulators.

Many insurance companies sought to improve their condition by increasing the rates they charged for coverage, in some cases by more than 100 per cent. In addition, they sharply reduced the number and kinds of risks they would underwrite. Premium dollars generated in 1984 came to an estimated $117.1 billion, compared with $108.4 billion in 1983.

The best overall measure of industry performance was the *combined loss ratio* (CLR) — the amount that insurance companies pay out in claims and expenses for every dollar of premium income. The CLR reached 117.1 per cent in the first half of 1984, meaning that insurers paid out $1.17 for every $1 they received in premiums. The CLR for the similar period in 1983 was 109.36 per cent. Industry analysts predicted that the CLR for all of 1984 would rise to about 118 per cent, up from 112 per cent in 1983.

Catastrophes. Record losses resulted from hurricanes and other catastrophes in the first half of 1984, according to the Property Claim Services division of the American Insurance Association, a trade organization. Losses from catastrophes — that is, losses totaling $5 million or more — moderated in the third quarter of 1984 despite Hurricane Diana, which struck North and South Carolina in mid-September and caused an estimated $36 million in insured losses. The total nine-month payout came to $1.39 billion, compared with $1.27 billion for the same period of 1983.

Legislation. The federal crime insurance program expired on Sept. 30, 1984, and was reinstated retroactively by legislation signed by President Ronald Reagan on October 12. The program provides federally sponsored burglary and theft insurance in economically deprived urban areas. Most of the coverage has been written for homes and businesses in New York City.

Other Developments. The Department of Transportation said in July that automobile manufacturers would have to provide airbags or automatic seat belts on all new cars by 1989. However, the ruling would not go into effect if states that had a total of two-thirds of the U.S. population passed laws requiring the use of seat belts. Several insurance companies and industry trade groups filed a suit that challenged the legality of leaving the decision to the states. Emanuel Levy

In WORLD BOOK, see INSURANCE.

INTERNATIONAL TRADE AND FINANCE. The world economy gained further momentum in 1984, largely because of an unusually vibrant United States economy, which grew by more than 6 per cent, the highest rate since the 1950's. Japan and Canada also registered strong economic growth, in the 4 to 5 per cent range. But West European nations had only moderate growth, generally less than 3 per cent.

Although unemployment in the United States fell further — to 7.2 per cent in December — it continued to rise in Western Europe. Joblessness in the 10-nation European Community (EC or Common Market) was estimated at 11 per cent.

Developing nations, on the whole, posted their best growth rate since 1979, as their combined gross national product (GNP) — the total value of goods and services produced — increased by almost 4 per cent. Most of the growth occurred in Asia. Growth was negligible in Latin America.

Inflation in the industrial nations declined to about 4.5 per cent, the lowest average level in more than a decade. Inflation in the United States remained at about 4 per cent. Most developing countries also reduced their rates of inflation, but Argentina, Bolivia, Brazil, Israel, and Peru suffered rates of more than 200 per cent.

Rescheduling Debts. The debt problem of a number of developing nations was a major issue at

WORLD BANKING

THIRD WORLD LOANS

Ken Alexander, *San Francisco Examiner*

the economic summit held in London from June 7 to 9. Leaders of Canada, France, Great Britain, Italy, Japan, the United States, and West Germany endorsed the concept of multiyear, or long-term, rescheduling by commercial banks and governments of the debts of developing nations that undertake effective economic reforms. The leaders also pledged to reduce interest rates, partly to help the developing countries pay their foreign debts. Multiyear scheduling, which eliminates the need to negotiate debts annually, helps debtor nations by giving them more certainty in their planning. It also provides for lower interest rates.

Two high-debt countries — Mexico and Venezuela — negotiated tentative multiyear debt rescheduling with commercial bank creditors in 1984. On September 7, $48.5 billion of Mexican debt due between 1982 and 1990 was tentatively rescheduled for payment between 1986 and 1998. The banks also agreed to reduce the interest on the debt. Venezuela reached a similar agreement on September 22 with its main creditor banks on a debt of almost $21 billion, some of it already overdue. Argentina and Brazil were among other countries seeking multiyear rescheduling, but they had no immediate success.

Crisis Eased. The worst of the developing countries' debt crisis seemed to be over, many of the world's finance ministers agreed at the annual

meeting of two United Nations agencies — the International Monetary Fund (IMF), which assists countries with large international payments deficits, and the World Bank, which lends money for development projects. The meeting was held from September 24 to 27 in Washington, D.C.

The combined international payments deficit of the developing countries was estimated at $50 billion, the smallest in four years. Much of the improvement reflected substantially greater exports by the developing countries.

Moreover, because the foreign reserves of a number of developing countries grew substantially during 1984, their borrowing demands on the IMF diminished. The IMF approved about $5.2-billion in new loans to help developing countries with severe payments problems, a far smaller amount than that approved in 1983, and India said it no longer needed IMF credit. Still, the developing countries' total debt in 1984 edged past $800 billion.

To help the economic improvement, some international aid agencies expanded their resources in 1984. The World Bank's capital was increased by $8.4 billion, and wealthy nations granted an additional $9 billion to the bank's International Development Association, which makes interest-free, 50-year loans to the poorest nations. In September, however, the IMF voted to put a limit on

353

Workers at Tokyo's foreign exchange market flash hand signals on March 8 as the U.S. dollar rebounds after hitting a 26-month low the day before.

loans to nations already deeply in debt after Jan. 1, 1985. Many developing countries protested.

World Trade. The volume of world trade in 1984 soared after four years of little or no growth, rising by about 8 per cent. A major factor in the rise, the sharpest advance since 1976, was the strong U.S. economy. Imports into the United States increased by about 30 per cent, creating a merchandise trade deficit of $125 billion, by far the largest U.S. trade deficit ever.

Quotas, Free Trade. Major U.S. industries reacted to the import surges by asking the Administration of President Ronald Reagan for import quotas. Quota requests from the copper and footwear industries were denied, but the Administration in December negotiated "voluntary" restraints on steel exports from Brazil, Japan, South Korea, Spain, and other nations. On November 29, the Administration banned the import of steel pipes and tubes from the EC into the United States until year's end. The Reagan Administration also tightened existing controls on textile and apparel imports in October, despite protests from foreign suppliers and U.S. retailers.

In an attempt to promote freer world trade, the Reagan Administration backed a trade bill passed by Congress in October that authorized the President to negotiate a free-trade agreement with Israel. This agreement would permit the United States and Israel to exempt each other's goods from import duties. If negotiated, the agreement would be the first of its kind between the United States and another country. The bill conditionally authorized the Administration to negotiate similar agreements with other countries. As part of the same trade bill, Congress voted to renew for 8½ years a duty-free program for thousands of products imported from developing countries.

U.S.-Japanese Economic Relations appeared to worsen during 1984 because of Japan's record $35-billion trade surplus with the United States. Prodding by the United States led Japan to agree in May to allow its unit of currency, the yen, to be used more freely in international markets. Japan also eased restrictions on foreign banks operating in Japan and pledged to remove ceilings on domestic interest rates to attract more foreign investment. Such actions were expected to increase eventually the value of the yen, making Japanese goods more expensive for other countries to buy and, therefore, less competitive on world markets.

Japan had agreed in November 1983 to extend through March 31, 1985, controls on the export of automobiles to the United States. However, the export quota, now in its fourth year, was increased to about 1.9 million cars. Richard Lawrence

In WORLD BOOK, see INTERNATIONAL TRADE.
IOWA. See STATE GOVERNMENT.

IRAN in February 1984 marked the fifth anniversary of the revolution that overthrew Shah Mohammad Reza Pahlavi with the regime of Ayatollah Ruhollah Khomeini in full control. The principal opposition leaders, former President Abol Hasan Bani-Sadr and Massoud Rajavi, head of the anticlerical *Mujahedeen-i-Khalq* (Fighters for the Faith), remained in exile. In March, friction between the two led to Bani-Sadr's resignation from the National Resistance Council for Liberation and Independence (NRC), which they had organized in 1981. Bani-Sadr opposed Rajavi's position that the NRC stood a better chance of overthrowing Khomeini by aligning itself with Iraq.

Opposition to the Khomeini regime in Iran was minimal, due to the exile of these key opposition leaders and ruthless measures to curb dissent. In February and March, 179 members of the Communist Tudeh (Masses) party received prison terms of up to 10 years for plotting to overthrow the government. The Tudeh had been outlawed in 1983 and its members charged with spying for the Soviet Union. The relative leniency of the sentences reflected Iran's desire to mend its fences with the Soviet Union, which had bitterly criticized the trials.

Military News. Despite huge expenditures of personnel and equipment, Iran failed to win any significant advantages in its war with neighboring Iraq. Iranian forces launched a major offensive in southern Iraq in March against the Iraqi port of Basra. The advance took the Iranians 25 miles (40 kilometers) inside Iraq before an Iraqi counterattack drove the invaders back.

Thereafter, the conflict shifted to one of air attacks on shipping in the Persian Gulf and the Strait of Hormuz. Iranian ground troops launched another offensive in October in hilly terrain along the border east of Baghdad, Iraq's capital, and succeeded in occupying several ridges overlooking the Iraqi border town of Mandali.

Government forces in August also attacked Kurdish rebels in the mountains of northwestern Iran. The rebels have demanded self-rule for Iran's Kurdish population since the revolution.

Elections were held on April 15 for the second Majlis (parliament) to take office since the revolution. Approximately 60 per cent of Iran's 25 million eligible voters—including women—participated. The elections were marred by charges of fraud and balloting irregularities, however, and a number of the leading candidates failed to receive the necessary 51 per cent majority.

A second election was held on May 17, and the new Majlis finally convened on May 28. About 100 of its 270 seats were won by members of the dom-

Iran's Ayatollah Ruhollah Khomeini casts his vote in April during elections for the second parliament to take office since the 1979 revolution.

inant Islamic Republican Party. The remaining winners ran as independents. The only opposition deputies in the outgoing Majlis — five deputies led by former Prime Minister Mehdi Bazargan — boycotted the elections.

In contrast to the first Majlis, the new parliament had fewer religious leaders as deputies. Ayatollah Hossein Ali Montazeri, Khomeini's chief lieutenant and probable successor, urged voters to choose candidates familiar with national needs and problems. He warned against too much clerical influence in politics.

Rejected Ministers. The new parliament served notice early that it would not be a rubber stamp. On August 15, Prime Minister Hosein Musavi-Khamenei presented his Cabinet for approval. But the Majlis rejected five of the ministers, replacing them with three ministers of their own. The dismissed ministers were charged with giving political jobs to their relatives, inefficiency, and ties with Hodjatieh, a group dedicated to the establishment of a strict Islamic social system in Iran. In September, Musavi himself took over the two remaining posts.

The Iranian Economy surged forward despite the drain caused by the war. Oil production in August reached 2.4 million barrels per day.   William Spencer

See also IRAQ; MIDDLE EAST (Facts in Brief Table). In WORLD BOOK, see IRAN.

IRAQ, despite some minor setbacks, improved its position significantly in 1984 in its war with neighboring Iran, which began in September 1980. Advanced weaponry, strong defensive positions, and an improved military command structure gave Iraq a clear margin of superiority.

In February 1984, the Iranians captured the Majnoon Islands northeast of the Iraqi port city of Basra. The islands have more than 50 oil wells and a 7-billion-barrel oil reserve. In October, Iranian forces mounted an offensive in the hilly Mandali border area east of Iraq's capital of Baghdad, capturing several ridges overlooking Iraqi positions.

However, in late February and early March, Iraqi forces halted a major Iranian offensive on the southern front, near Basra. And by June, the Iraqis had recaptured a major portion of the Majnoon Islands.

Elsewhere, Iraqi counterattacks, supported by effective air cover, drove the Iranians back to the border with heavy casualties. The Iraqis' performance showed that they could probably thwart any large-scale Iranian move into the country's flat eastern region.

Despite the economic strains caused by the war and the high casualty rate — nearly every family in Iraq has suffered the death of at least one member — Iraqis were strongly united in support of the conflict. In April, sales of special government

bonds issued to finance the war reached a total of $238 million.

U.S. Relations. On November 26, Iraq and the United States announced the restoration of formal diplomatic relations between the two countries. Iraq had severed relations in 1967 in retaliation for United States support of Israel during the Six-Day War.

Bailout. Although the country remained geared for war, there was some progress toward a return to the economic boom years of the late 1970's. One reason was a shift from a cash to a credit financing system. Previously, Iraq had paid cash for nearly all its imports. But the war and the shutdown by Syria in 1982 of the pipeline that carried Iraqi oil through Syria to ports on the Mediterranean Sea forced the government to use its cash reserves to finance imports. As a result, Iraq began falling behind in its payments to foreign contractors, shippers, and governments.

Concern that economic rather than military reasons might force Iraq to surrender to Iran encouraged Iraq's European creditors and suppliers to bail out the Iraqi economy. In February, Italy agreed to reschedule Iraq's debts of $180 million, owed mostly for Italian equipment and work done by Italian contractors. France, Iraq's largest supplier of military equipment ($4.9 billion since the start of the war), agreed in March to lend Iraq an additional $500 million to help Iraq pay its debts to French contractors. The Soviet Union provided $1 billion in economic aid, plus new weapons.

Iraq compensated in part for the shut-down of the Syrian pipeline by opening new sections of a pipeline across Turkey in February. The enlarged pipeline boosted capacity to 900,000 barrels per day. Turkey also agreed to supply trucks to haul 1 million short tons (907,000 metric tons) of Iraqi oil overland to European markets.

Development Projects. In January, a pharmaceutical plant opened in Baghdad. The plant will meet a large part of domestic demand for drugs. New cement and brick factories went into production in March. Their output of 8 million short tons (7.3 million metric tons) of cement and 600 million bricks per year will meet all domestic needs.

Another promising development was the growth of mixed-sector companies — companies that are managed by the government but financed with private capital. Although the ruling Baath party is committed to state-controlled socialist development, mixed-sector companies were seen as a way to attract new capital, both domestic and foreign, into the economy. During 1984, the companies' production of such items as television sets, radios, air conditioners, and soft drinks increased by 22 per cent over 1983 levels.   William Spencer

See also IRAN; MIDDLE EAST (Facts in Brief Table). In WORLD BOOK, see IRAQ.

IRELAND. The most significant political event of 1984 in Ireland was the release of the New Ireland Forum report on May 2. This 38-page document represented 11 months of effort by Ireland's main political parties to solve the problem of political violence in Northern Ireland. The report had been prepared by Ireland's ruling coalition parties, Fine Gael (Gaelic People) and the Labour Party; the opposition Fianna Fáil (Soldiers of Destiny); and Northern Ireland's Roman Catholic Social Democratic and Labour Party (SDLP).

The main conclusion of the report was that a united Irish state stood the best chance of bringing peace, but that reunification could be achieved only with the consent of all, including the Protestant majority in Northern Ireland. In addition, the report stressed that the rights of minority groups should be guaranteed in any new constitution. Fine Gael and Labour were willing to consider the options of federalism, with two parliaments, and joint British and Irish sovereignty over Northern Ireland. Fianna Fáil argued for a united Ireland.

The report aroused much hostility in Northern Ireland. The Protestant Official Unionist Party, the Protestant Democratic Unionist Party, and Sinn Féin (Ourselves Alone), the political wing of the outlawed Irish Republican Army (IRA), denounced the report.

President Ronald Reagan is escorted to a ceremony at University College, Galway, Ireland, where he received an honorary degree during a June visit.

In November, Ireland's Prime Minister Garret FitzGerald met with Great Britain's Prime Minister Margaret Thatcher to discuss the report. Thatcher rejected the possibility of Irish unification, federation, or joint British sovereignty.

Economic Plan. On October 2, Prime Minister FitzGerald announced a three-year program aimed at solving Ireland's economic problems. The country was burdened with heavy foreign debts and an unemployment rate of 16.9 per cent — the highest in Europe. FitzGerald's most controversial proposal was a land tax that would double the taxes paid by farmers. Public service workers were told that they would get no raises before 1987. The government also announced the establishment of a national lottery, longer hours for *public houses* (taverns) to encourage tourism, and a cut in the price of whiskey to help eliminate smuggling from Northern Ireland.

Weapons Seizure. On September 29, Irish security forces seized the trawler *Marita Anne,* which was carrying 7 metric tons (7.7 short tons) of arms destined for the IRA. It was one of the biggest arms hauls in Irish history. On December 12, three IRA members were sentenced to 10 years in prison for their part in the smuggling. Ian J. Mather

See also NORTHERN IRELAND. In WORLD BOOK, see IRELAND.

IRON AND STEEL. See STEEL INDUSTRY.

ISRAEL. National elections held on July 23, 1984, produced a political deadlock that underscored the deep divisions among Israelis on domestic and foreign policy issues. The divisions were accentuated by the costly and apparently fruitless occupation of southern Lebanon. And as if these problems were not enough, Israel in 1984 faced the worst economic crisis in its history.

Elections for the Knesset (parliament) were not scheduled until fall 1985. But the lack of success by Prime Minister Yitzhak Shamir and the ruling Likud bloc in dealing with runaway inflation and a huge budget deficit, coupled with dissatisfaction with the government's Lebanon policy, accelerated the timetable. Several motions of no confidence in the Likud bloc's policies, introduced by the opposition Labor Party in the Knesset in January, were barely defeated. Shamir then agreed to advance the election date to July.

Shimon Peres was unopposed in his bid for leadership of the Labor Party (see PERES, SHIMON). But Shamir had to beat back a challenge from former Defense Minister Ariel Sharon.

Israel's already fragmented political system was divided even further on June 28 when the Supreme Court allowed two extremist parties to enter the elections. They were the Kach party, headed by Meir Kahane, which advocates the expulsion of all Arabs from Israel, and the Progressive List for Peace (PLP), which supports the establishment of a Palestinian state on the West Bank.

Stalemate and Negotiation. The elections on July 23 resulted in a political stalemate. Labor won 44 seats to Likud's 41. The remainder went to smaller parties, which picked up a total of 35 seats, with Ezer Weizman's new Yahad Party receiving 3 seats; the PLP, 2; and Kach, 1. Since neither of the major blocs had a majority in the 120-seat Knesset, President Chaim Herzog named Peres acting prime minister, with a 42-day deadline to form a government of national unity that would include both major blocs.

Weeks of political maneuvering followed as Labor and Likud also negotiated with the smaller parties to assemble the 61 seats necessary to form their own coalition government. However, both parties' attempts to put together a coalition failed, despite a 21-day deadline extension. Finally, on September 13, Peres and Shamir agreed to establish a government of national unity with 97 Knesset seats.

The agreement specified that Peres would serve as prime minister for the first 25 months of the 50-month term, and Shamir would serve as deputy prime minister and foreign minister. During the second 25 months, the two men would reverse

positions. The Cabinet was enlarged to 25 ministers, with 12 posts allotted to each major party. The 25th post went to the head of the National Religious Party. To win Likud's participation, Peres accepted Sharon as minister of industry and trade and agreed not to oppose the construction of 5 or 6 of the 27 new settlements on the West Bank already planned. Construction of the remaining settlements would have to be approved by a majority vote of an "inner Cabinet" consisting of five members from Labor and five from Likud.

Both leaders committed themselves to an Israeli withdrawal from southern Lebanon. But there was little consensus as to when or how withdrawal would be accomplished.

Economic Crisis. By the time the new coalition government took office, the Israeli economy had reached a state requiring emergency surgery. Among the problems was a soaring inflation rate — which reached 400 per cent in July — a budget deficit of $2.5 billion, and a drop in foreign currency reserves to $700 million.

In September, the government announced austerity measures, including cutbacks in food and fuel subsidies, a freeze on civil service hiring, and cuts in defense expenditures. Following Peres' visit to the United States in October, the U.S. Congress converted $2.6 billion in U.S. loans to Israel to

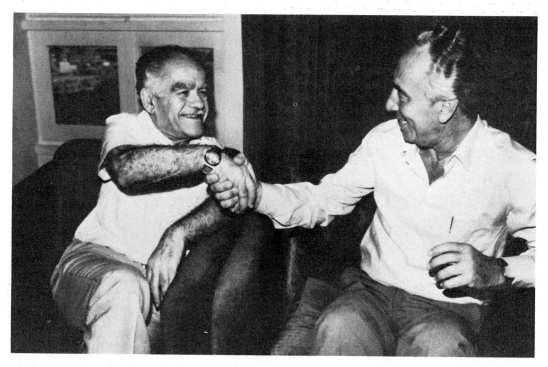

Israeli leaders Yitzhak Shamir, left, and Shimon Peres meet in September during talks that led to the formation of a government of national unity.

grants. In November, with inflation now at 800 per cent, the Israeli government and organized labor and employers' organizations agreed to a three-month wage and price freeze.

Jewish, Arab Terrorism. In April, Israeli security forces foiled a plot by an underground network of Jewish extremists to blow up Arab-owned buses in Jerusalem. In May, 25 Jews, many of them highly respected Israeli citizens, were charged with belonging to a terrorist organization that planned or conducted at least six violent attacks on Arabs. These attacks included the attempt to blow up the buses, the 1980 bombings of the cars of Arab mayors on the West Bank, and a 1983 raid on the Islamic College in Hebron, in which three Arab students were murdered. In June, Israeli courts sentenced five Jewish terrorists to prison terms.

Israeli security forces also came down hard on Palestinian terrorists. On April 12, four Palestinians hijacked a bus on a highway south of Tel Aviv-Yafo, Israel's largest city, taking 34 hostages. The security forces stormed the bus, killing one of the hostages and two terrorists, and then clubbed the two surviving terrorists to death. After an official inquiry into the affair, the Israeli Ministry of Defense censured the commander of the Israeli Army in southern Israel.   William Spencer

See also MIDDLE EAST (Facts in Brief Table). In WORLD BOOK, see ISRAEL.

Italy's Prime Minister Craxi shakes hands with a Vatican official in February after signing a pact reducing the church's privileges in Italy.

ITALY. Socialist Prime Minister Bettino Craxi's five-party coalition government was in difficulty in the first seven months of 1984 as opposition to his anti-inflation program intensified. Craxi proposed on February 14 to cut automatic wage hikes that compensated for inflation, freeze rents for one year, limit the prices of certain basic articles and services temporarily, improve family allowances, take severe measures against tax evasion, and decrease interest rates. He claimed this package would reduce inflation from the 1983 level of 15 per cent to 10 per cent in 1984, and to 7 and then 5 per cent in succeeding years. However, the proposal to cut the automatic wage hikes jeopardized his government.

Workers Split. Labor unions disagreed on Craxi's program. Communist unions opposed it; but Socialists, Roman Catholics, and Social Democrats in three union confederations representing about 60 per cent of the country's workers accepted it.

Demonstrations against the proposal disrupted rail and air traffic throughout Italy. In the Chamber of Deputies — one of the two houses of Italy's Parliament — Craxi's opponents offered 3,233 amendments to the proposal, giving it little chance of being passed in 60 days, as required by law. Time ran out on the proposal on April 15. However, the government survived a vote of confidence on the issue by 360 votes to 236.

Craxi Reintroduced the anti-inflationary package on April 17. Again, Craxi sought votes of confidence. He won the first vote — in the Chamber of Deputies — on May 24, 329 to 256. He won the second in the other house of Parliament — the Senate — on June 8, 172 votes to 12, after Communist senators walked out. Parliament approved the proposal by the June 16 deadline.

Coalition Difficulties. Repercussions from a 1981 scandal involving Propaganda Two (P-2), a secret Masonic lodge, threatened Craxi's coalition. (Secret organizations are illegal in Italy.) Charges were made that Christian Democrat Foreign Minister Giulio Andreotti was the power behind P-2. The Christian Democrats called on the Socialists to distance themselves from the charges. However, Craxi did not do so.

In July, a parliamentary investigating commission found that Budget Minister Pietro Longo, a Social Democrat, was a P-2 member. On May 10, Craxi had refused to accept the resignation of Longo after his name appeared on what was reported to be a list of 962 members of P-2. On July 12, Longo resigned after admitting that he had met Licio Gelli, the leader of P-2, when the lodge was active.

The coalition suffered further setbacks before the summer recess. Parliament defeated bills that would have renewed an investment program for the poor southern part of Italy, allowed regional governments to use money collected by the national government, and granted permanent employment to thousands of health workers.

Indictments in Pope Plot. On October 26, investigating magistrate Ilario Martella indicted three Bulgarians and four Turks for complicity in the 1981 attempt to assassinate Pope John Paul II in Rome. Martella also ordered another trial for a fifth Turk, Mehmet Ali Agca, who already had been convicted of the assassination attempt. Martella charged Agca with complicity in importing the weapon with which he shot the pope.

Police Arrested 97 people on December 11 as part of a nationwide crackdown on the Mafia. The crackdown began with the issuing of 366 arrest warrants in September, following confessions by Tomasso Buscetta, a former Mafia leader.

Italy Recovered from a recession in 1983. However, the 24-nation Organization for Economic Cooperation and Development (OECD) warned in May 1984 that the government's tight financial policies might cut the recovery short. The OECD said that Italy's chief economic problems were a low level of economic activity, high unemployment, and high inflation.   Kenneth Brown

See also EUROPE (Facts in Brief Table). In WORLD BOOK, see ITALY.

IVORY COAST. See AFRICA.

JACKSON, MICHAEL (1958-   ), won an unprecedented eight Grammy Awards at the National Academy of Recording Arts and Sciences annual presentation ceremony in February 1984. The album of the year award went to Jackson's *Thriller,* the all-time best-selling album. Jackson's other awards included record of the year and best male vocalist in three categories. A 14-minute video of the song "Thriller" also won for best video.

Jackson and four of his brothers opened a multi-city "Victory" tour in July 1984. Some aspects of the tour, such as the $30 ticket price, drew criticism. Jackson later announced that he would donate his share of the profits to charity.

Michael Joseph Jackson, whose widely appealing music and exuberant dancing have made him one of the world's most popular entertainers, was born in Gary, Ind., on Aug. 29, 1958. He began performing with his brothers when he was only 5.

In 1968, Jackson and his older brothers, calling themselves the Jackson Five, signed with Motown Records and quickly rose to the top of the music charts. His first solo album, *Got to Be There,* was released in 1972. Jackson became firmly established as a solo performer in 1979 with the disco-oriented album *Off the Wall.*   Barbara A. Mayes

In the Special Reports section, see THE SIGHTS AND SOUNDS OF MUSIC VIDEOS.

JAMAICA. See LATIN AMERICA.

JAPAN seemed to enter a period of new political stability and continuity in 1984. Prime Minister Yasuhiro Nakasone easily won reelection on October 28 to the presidency of the ruling Liberal Democratic Party (LDP), which despite its name is basically conservative. Reelection as head of the party ensured that Nakasone — who took office on Nov. 26, 1982 — would continue as prime minister, becoming the first Japanese leader since 1972 to remain in office for longer than two years. His strong position was bolstered by unusually high approval ratings — up to 58 per cent — in public opinion polls taken in October 1984.

On October 31, Nakasone named his new Cabinet, changing most posts as is customary in Japan. In an effort for continuity, however, he retained two of the top Cabinet ministers — Foreign Minister Shintaro Abe and Finance Minister Noboru Takeshita. The new Cabinet also included the first woman since 1962, Director-General of the Environment Agency Shigeru Ishimoto.

World Affairs. With little change in domestic politics, attention focused on Japan's international relations during much of 1984. In policy speeches before the Diet (parliament) on February 6, Prime Minister Nakasone and Foreign Minister Abe emphasized the need for Japan to strengthen its role in world affairs. The prime minister said that Japan's peace and prosperity are dependent on the world's. The foreign minister said that Japan has "a major international role to play commensurate with our economic might."

The prime minister attended an economic summit conference in London from June 7 to 9, joining the leaders of six other industrial nations — Canada, France, Great Britain, Italy, the United States, and West Germany. The seven leaders pledged efforts to strengthen the world economy, to assist the developing countries, to solve the international debt crisis, and to cooperate on environmental problems. Japan also supported the summit's call for a settlement of the Iran-Iraq conflict, which threatens to interrupt the vital flow of oil to Japan. Prior to the London meeting, Nakasone declared in an interview that Japan — the only one of the seven powers to have good relations with both Iran and Iraq — would make "positive efforts" to end the conflict. But no progress had been made by year's end.

President Chun Doo Hwan of South Korea paid an official visit to Japan from September 6 to 8, the first such visit by a South Korean president. The highlight of the visit was a statement by Emperor Hirohito that the "unfortunate past" between the two countries was "regrettable," a reference to Japan's colonial domination of Korea from 1910 to 1945. Nakasone, in support of the emperor, issued a statement expressing regret for the "error" of Japan's past actions in Korea.

Chun and Nakasone discussed at length the relationship between North Korea, which is a Communist nation, and South Korea, which is strongly anti-Communist. In a joint statement issued at the end of their meeting, Nakasone supported South Korea's call for a "direct dialogue" between the two Koreas to settle their differences.

Nakasone visited China in March and Pakistan and India in May. He offered China a $2-billion loan through 1991 to assist its modernization program — the largest foreign-aid package Japan had ever given. In Pakistan, Nakasone and President M. Zia-ul-Haq called for an end to the conflict in Afghanistan, where rebel guerrillas are fighting Soviet troops and a puppet government installed by the Soviet Union.

Japan-U.S. Relations seemed to rest on a firm basis of popular support during 1984. A January Gallup Poll of Americans revealed that 57 per cent regarded Japan as a dependable ally, the highest percentage recorded on this issue. In Japan, a Foreign Ministry survey in mid-1983 showed that 72 per cent of those answering believed that the United States was the "most friendly" of the world's nations to Japan.

The United States continued to press Japan to increase its defense spending. The Japanese Cabinet recommended on January 25 about $12.6 billion in military expenditures for the fiscal year starting April 1, 1984, a 6.55 per cent increase over the 1983 budget. On Dec. 29, 1984, the Cabinet approved a 1985 budget that included $12.6-billion for the armed forces — about the same amount as in 1984 in U.S. dollars but a 6.9 per cent hike calculated in yen because of the yen's declining value. Both the 1984 and 1985 figures were less than 1 per cent of the gross national product — a self-imposed limit the government has observed since 1976 — and substantially less than many U.S. government officials would like.

The United States continued during 1984 to suffer a serious deficit in its trade with Japan, though some progress was made on the problem. Between January and June, Japan recorded its largest six-month surplus in trade with the United States, $14.5 billion. This surplus helped establish a record $13.35-billion surplus in Japan's overall trade for the six months. During the period, Japan's exports to the United States were $27.9 billion and its imports $13.4 billion.

The two governments announced in Washington, D.C., on April 7 that Japan had agreed to increase its quotas for importing beef and citrus fruit from the United States for the next four years. Of potentially greater impact, however, was a complex financial agreement announced on May 29. It was designed to increase international use of the yen, Japan's unit of money, driving up the yen's value on world markets and thus making

Japan's Prime Minister Yasuhiro Nakasone delivers a speech on federal policy at the opening of the 101st session of the Diet (parliament) in February.

Japanese exports more expensive for other nations to buy.

The agreement also included measures to open Japanese financial markets more widely to foreign firms. One measure was the removal of interest-rate ceilings to attract more foreign investment. Another provision permitted non-Japanese banks in Japan to trade Japanese government securities.

Healthy Economy. The Japanese government predicted on September 20 that the gross national product — the total of all goods and services produced — would grow 5.3 per cent in 1984 after adjustment for inflation. Earlier, the government had predicted growth of only 4.1 per cent.

On November 1, the Bank of Japan issued new 1,000-, 5,000-, and 10,000-yen bank notes. The new notes feature a special ink to make counterfeiting more difficult and marks that enable the blind to read a bill's denomination by touch.

Candy Crimes. Three major Japanese candy makers, the Ezaki Glico, Morinaga, and Marudai Ham companies, became the targets of bizarre crimes during 1984. On March 18, the president of Ezaki Glico was kidnapped and held for $4.3-million ransom, but he escaped unharmed three days later. In May, major news organizations received letters stating that packages of the company's candy had been poisoned and placed on store shelves. No tainted candy was found, but Glico sales plummeted. In July, the culprits sent more letters to newspapers saying that they had become bored with the affair, had destroyed the poisoned candy, and were leaving for a vacation in Europe.

In October, boxes of poisoned Morinaga candy appeared in stores. Newspapers again received letters demanding more than $400,000 from the candy company, which refused to pay. Both companies suffered severe financial losses due to lost sales, though no deaths or injuries were reported.

In November, the letter-writers demanded $250,000 from the Marudai Ham Company, which refused to pay. Japanese police began the biggest criminal investigation in their history, but by year's end, they had not solved the crime.

Other Developments. A series of rockslides on the southwestern face of Mount Fuji, Japan's tallest and most famous peak, threatened to destroy the mountain's beauty. In September, the government began construction of a concrete barrier wall designed to slow the slides.

Construction continued on Tsukuba Science City, a new town created 40 miles (64 kilometers) northeast of Tokyo as a center for scientific research. The town will open to visitors as part of Expo '85, a world's fair of science and technology, in March 1985. The fair's organizers expect more than 20 million visitors.   John M. Maki

See also ASIA (Facts in Brief Table). In WORLD BOOK, see JAPAN.

JEWS AND JUDAISM. The major issues of concern to Jews in the United States in 1984 focused on the presidential campaign. For the first time in recent years, anti-Semitism, the role of Jewish voters, and public policy questions of a religious nature all became election issues.

The Presidential Campaign. Black candidate Jesse L. Jackson's bid for the Democratic presidential nomination added a significant dimension to these issues. Relations between Jackson and the Jewish community had often been strained in the past because of Jackson's criticism of Israel and questions about his attitudes about Jews.

In February, a reporter revealed that Jackson had used the derogatory term "Hymies" in referring to Jews and had called New York City, which has a large Jewish population, "Hymietown." Although Jackson denied that he had intended any ethnic slur by such remarks and apologized for them, Jewish leaders expressed concern about such behavior on the part of a presidential candidate. Emotions became further inflamed by the public alliance between Jackson and Louis Farrakhan, the leader of the Nation of Islam, a Black Muslim sect. Farrakhan made anti-Jewish statements on several occasions during the campaign and referred to Judaism at one point as a "gutter religion." Jackson's failure to repudiate this alliance caused dismay in American Jewry.

The role and concerns of Jewish voters also emerged as a campaign issue. Both Democratic presidential candidate Walter F. Mondale and incumbent Republican President Ronald Reagan sought Jewish support by issuing assurances of their support for the state of Israel.

A prominent concern of many U.S. Jews was the growing influence of fundamentalist Christian groups in the Republican Party. The 1984 Republican Party platform reflected the positions of these groups in favor of organized prayer in the public schools and against abortion. Such positions raised issues of the separation of church and state and of the role of religion in politics. Both candidates addressed the Jewish service organization B'nai B'rith in September and pledged their support for religious freedom and the separation of church and state.

In the end, many Jewish voters felt the need to choose between their traditional support for the liberal social principles of the Democratic Party and a popular perception that the Republican candidates were stronger in both their support of Israel and their condemnation of anti-Semitism. Although polls indicated that Jews intended to vote for the Republican ticket in record numbers, post-election estimates revealed that about 65 per cent of Jewish voters cast their ballots for Mondale.

Tensions Between Jews and Blacks in the United States were underscored by Jackson's relationship with the Jewish community. During the campaign, Jewish and black leaders met together and made public calls for restraint and a reaffirmation of the historic ties that have bound blacks and Jews since the civil rights movement of the 1960's. After the election, leaders of both communities continued to discuss means of overcoming mutual prejudice and misunderstandings.

Religious Developments. Controversies continued to surface within the Jewish community in 1984, reflecting divisions between traditionalists and liberals on matters of religious law and practice. American Judaism's most liberal branch, the Reform movement, continued to reach out to prospective converts and to Jews and non-Jews who have intermarried. The Jewish Theological Seminary of America in New York City, which serves the Conservative movement, admitted its first women rabbinical students. Orthodox Judaism, the most traditional branch of Judaism, continued to oppose these developments.

In Israel in July, Orthodox religious parties in the Knesset (parliament) proposed a change in Israeli law that would prevent the government from recognizing conversions performed by Reform and Conservative rabbis. A coalition of American Jewish organizations protested what they considered a divisive and offensive action. Howard A. Berman

In WORLD BOOK, see JEWS; JUDAISM.

Jordan's King Hussein I greets Queen Elizabeth II of Great Britain as she arrives at the airport in Amman on March 26 for her first visit to Jordan.

JORDAN. King Hussein I broke ranks with other Arab leaders on Sept. 25, 1984, by announcing the restoration of full diplomatic and trade links with Egypt. Jordan severed relations in 1979 after Egypt signed a peace treaty with Israel. Hussein acted after Syria and Libya blocked earlier efforts to convene an Arab summit conference on reconciliation with Egypt. Hussein's move reflected his belief that no unified Arab effort toward a peace settlement with Israel was possible without Egyptian participation.

Parliament Reconvened. On Jan. 9, 1984, Hussein reconvened the National Assembly, which was dissolved in 1974. The first action of the House of Representatives, the elected lower chamber of the Assembly, was to amend the Jordanian Constitution to allow separate elections for vacant seats from the East Bank, Jordanian territory east of the Jordan River. The amendment also allows the members to appoint new representatives from the Israeli-occupied West Bank.

On January 10, the king appointed a new Cabinet. The Cabinet's 20 members included 9 Palestinians. These moves were seen as attempts by the king to broaden his popular base and improve his position as spokesman for the Palestinians.

Elections to fill eight vacant House seats from the East Bank and one West Bank seat were held on March 12. For the first time in national elec-

tions, women were permitted to vote. The winning candidates included three Islamic fundamentalists and two Christians.

Debate on Terrorism. Evidence that Hussein's popularity was not a guarantee against criticism from Islamic extremists emerged in May during a parliamentary debate on terrorism. The debate centered on the arrest on May 17 of Islamic student militants who were charged with attempting to bomb public buildings in Jordan. Some deputies accused Jordanian security forces of denying the students' civil rights.

The Economy continued to improve dramatically, underscoring an observation that Jordan seemed to be the most prosperous of the developing countries in the Middle East. New phosphate sales contracts with India, Japan, South Korea, and Poland boosted phosphate exports by 1.45 million short tons (1.3 million metric tons) to 6.4 million short tons (5.8 million metric tons).

But there were danger signs. The worst drought in 40 years reduced wheat production. And only $600 million in aid from other Arab states was forthcoming.   William Spencer

See also MIDDLE EAST (Facts in Brief Table). In WORLD BOOK, see JORDAN.

JUDAISM. See JEWS AND JUDAISM.

JUNIOR ACHIEVEMENT (JA). See YOUTH ORGANIZATIONS.

KAMPUCHEA. The Vietnamese-backed government of Kampuchea (formerly known as Cambodia) said that fighting with a coalition opposing it escalated during 1984. Guerrilla attacks were officially reported in 15 of Kampuchea's 19 provinces in midyear. Defense Minister Bou Thang said on August 16 that this was the most intense series of attacks since 1979. He said the enemy "succeeded in a number of attempts" to disrupt official plans, build up its guerrilla bases, and win over government soldiers. But he claimed that in the first half of 1984 more than 10,000 opposition guerrillas had been killed, wounded, or captured — more than three times as many as in 1983.

Kampuchea's Armed Forces apparently grew to some 30,000 or more troops under control of the Vietnamese army, and they increasingly fought enemies based along Kampuchea's border with Thailand. On June 20, the Vietnamese army reported its third annual withdrawal of troops from Kampuchea, saying that 10,000 were leaving.

The Coalition opposing the Vietnamese-backed regime in Phnom Penh remained torn by conflict. It was composed of Communists who had ruled Kampuchea from 1975 to 1979, and two anti-Communist groups. One of the anti-Communist groups was the Khmer People's National Liberation Front (KPNLF), headed by former Premier Son Sann. It reportedly grew stronger in 1984 with help from the Association of Southeast Asian Nations (ASEAN) — Brunei Darussalam, Indonesia, Malaysia, the Philippines, Singapore, and Thailand. As a result, the Communists in the coalition sometimes attacked the KPNLF.

The coalition leader and head of the other anti-Communist group, former Cambodian head of state Prince Norodom Sihanouk, sought a settlement of the war. ASEAN leaders supported his efforts. But after Sihanouk arranged through a French diplomat to meet representatives from Vietnam and Phnom Penh secretly in November, the Communists in his coalition and their Chinese backers opposed the meeting and prevented it.

On December 25, Vietnam launched an offensive against four KPNLF resistance camps. At year-end, heavy fighting continued at the largest camp, Rithisen — also called Nong Samet.

Angkor Wat Damaged. Experts from India reported that the ruins of Angkor Wat, a magnificent temple built in the 1100's in northwestern Kampuchea, had weathered almost into collapse. Various armies added to the natural damage by looting statues and other artifacts.   Henry S. Bradsher

See also Asia (Facts in Brief Table). In World Book, see Cambodia or Kampuchea.
KANSAS. See State Government.

Vietnamese refugees at a camp in Kampuchea perform a traditional dragon dance in January to celebrate Tet, the Vietnamese lunar New Year festival.

KARAMI, RASHID (1921-   ), was named prime minister of Lebanon for the 10th time on April 26, 1984 (see LEBANON). Karami, a Sunni Muslim and the political leader of the northern Lebanese city of Tripoli, was also appointed minister of foreign affairs. Under the Lebanese political system, the prime minister must be a Sunni Muslim.

The appointment of Karami, who is pro-Syrian, was strongly backed by Syria's President Hafiz al-Assad. In return for Karami's appointment, Syria reportedly promised to pressure its Lebanese Muslim allies to cooperate with the Lebanese government.

Rashid Abdul Hamid Karami was born in 1921 in Tripoli (Tarabulus), where his family has been prominent in politics for many years. He received a law degree from Fuad al-Awal University in Cairo, Egypt, in 1947. During the next three years, Karami practiced law in Beirut, Lebanon.

In 1951, Karami was elected to the National Assembly (parliament) and, in 1955, at the age of 34, he became the youngest prime minister in Lebanese history. Since then, he has served eight other terms as prime minister, most recently in 1975 and 1976. In addition, he has at various times served as minister of economy and social affairs, minister of the interior, and minister of finance and defense.   Barbara A. Mayes

KENTUCKY. See STATE GOVERNMENT.

KENYA in 1984 signed a cooperation agreement with its neighbor and former enemy Somalia. Previous Somali governments had claimed a section of northern Kenya where Somali-speaking people live. In the 1960's, Somalia supported a guerrilla movement that fought to detach that area from Kenya. However, the current president of Somalia, Mohamed Siad Barre, renounced claims to the area. On July 25, the two nations committed themselves to economic cooperation.

The agreement was signed despite reports that in February, Kenyan security forces massacred an estimated 900 members of a Somali-speaking ethnic group, the Degodia. Kenya's government admitted to the deaths of only 57 Degodia people and said they had been killed in a conflict over land rights with another ethnic group, the Ajuran. According to the government, police and military units intervened in the dispute because the Degodia refused to cease their attacks on the Ajuran.

Kenya was one of many African countries south of the Sahara afflicted by serious drought in 1984. Crop yields plummeted, and thousands of cattle had to be slaughtered prematurely.

In March, Hezekiah Ochuka, the leader of an unsuccessful 1982 coup, was found guilty of treason. He was sentenced to death.   J. Dixon Esseks

See also AFRICA (Facts in Brief Table). In WORLD BOOK, see KENYA.

KOREA, NORTH. President Kim Il-song of Communist North Korea sought during 1984 to improve relations with his neighbors, especially anti-Communist South Korea. Kim said in September that he wanted to end confrontation with South Korea and with the United States soon.

North Korea gave South Korea $12 million worth of cement, rice, clothing, and medicine as flood relief in September. The supplies were the first goods to cross the demilitarized zone separating the two countries in more than three decades. On November 15, the two governments held their first talks since 1980 on economic cooperation. Further talks were postponed until January 1985 after the defection of a Russian led to a shooting incident in the demilitarized zone.

Kim also sought better relations with the Soviet Union. He made a 46-day railroad journey in May and June to Moscow and several East European capitals. In his absence, his son, Kim Chong Il, presided over the government. Radio Pyongyang declared on August 6 that the son was "the sole successor" to the president — indicating an unprecedented Communist dynasty. The Supreme People's Assembly (parliament) passed a law on September 8 permitting foreign investment for the first time.   Henry S. Bradsher

See also ASIA (Facts in Brief Table); KOREA, SOUTH. In WORLD BOOK, see KOREA.

KOREA, SOUTH. President Chun Doo Hwan of South Korea moved to allow broader political participation during 1984 in preparation for National Assembly elections due in 1985. On Feb. 25, 1984, Chun removed a ban on the political activity of 202 dissidents, and he lifted the ban on 84 others on November 30. He left 15 opposition politicians under the ban, which was imposed in 1980.

Chun also removed in March 1984 some restrictions on students, who have traditionally opposed his regime. He released about 300 student activists from jail and reinstated 1,400 students who had been expelled from their universities. In addition, Chun barred riot police from campuses unless they were asked in by university authorities. Despite this, students continued to agitate against the government. They accused it of drafting student leaders to punish dissent and of preventing media reporting of opposition political activities.

To celebrate South Korea's August 15 Independence Day, Chun restored the civil rights of 714 newly freed political prisoners. He also freed from prison and sent to Taiwan six Chinese who had hijacked a Chinese airliner in May 1983.

Opposition Leaders. The country's two most prominent opposition political leaders, Kim Dae Jung and Kim Young Sam, dropped their rivalry and joined others to form on June 15 a Council for the Promotion of Democracy. Although the council was technically illegal, the government tolerated it.

Kim Dae Jung announced in September that he wanted to return from exile in the United States. He had been serving a 20-year prison sentence in South Korea on charges of trying to overthrow the government, but Chun allowed him to go abroad for medical treatment in 1982. The South Korean government said on Sept. 21, 1984, that Kim had violated the terms of his permission to go abroad by political activities and later warned that he would be sent back to prison if he returned home.

Chun fired the chairman of his ruling Democratic Justice Party, Jung Nae Hiuk, on June 25 after press charges that Jung had acquired a fortune by corrupt means. Both Jung and his successor, Kwon Ik Hyun, were retired generals.

Relations with Other Asian Nations. Heavy rains caused the worst flooding in years in early September. The floods killed about 190 people and left 200,000 homeless. After some wrangling, South Korea — which is strongly anti-Communist — agreed in mid-September to accept relief supplies from Communist North Korea.

Talks between North and South Korea on April 9 about sending a joint team to the 1984 Summer Olympic Games quickly broke down. The two nations began talks on economic cooperation on November 15. But North Korea postponed further talks until January 1985 after an exchange of gunfire on Nov. 23, 1984, in the demilitarized zone separating the two Koreas. One South Korean and three North Koreans died in the shooting, which was sparked by a Soviet defector dashing across the zone to South Korea.

From September 6 to 8, Chun made the first visit by a South Korean president to Japan. Referring to Japan's 35-year colonization of Korea, which ended in 1945, Japanese Emperor Hirohito expressed regret for "an unfortunate past" between their countries.

Pope John Paul II visited South Korea from May 3 to 7. Before a crowd of more than 800,000 in Seoul, the pope *canonized* (recognized as saints) 103 martyrs executed in the 1800's for spreading Catholicism in Korea.

Economic Growth continued in 1984, but some sectors of South Korea's economy ran into trouble. The state-owned steel plant at Pohang, one of the most productive in the world, faced foreign import restrictions. The nation's shipbuilding industry gained few new orders in 1984.

The Finance Ministry announced on April 21 a phased removal of limitations on foreign banking in South Korea. On July 1, the government lifted import bans on 344 items.   Henry S. Bradsher

See also Asia (Facts in Brief Table). In World Book, see Korea.

KUWAIT. See Middle East.

LABOR. Unemployment in the United States fell from 8.2 per cent of the civilian labor force in December 1983 to 7.2 per cent in December 1984, after registering a sensational drop of nearly three percentage points the year before. The labor force, which grew by only 1 million workers during 1983, posted a gain of 2 million workers during 1984. The expanding labor force, coupled with a sputtering economy in the second half of 1984, slowed improvement in the jobless rate. Job growth remained strong, however. By December, more then 3 million jobs had been added, for a total of 7.2 million new jobs since the economic recovery began in December 1982.

Collective Bargaining agreements yielded mixed results during 1984, despite the economic expansion. Settlements negotiated in contracts affecting 1,000 or more workers resulted in annual increases averaging 2.8 per cent over the life of the contract, compared with an annual average increase of 7.2 per cent in 1981 and 1982. Construction contracts reached during the first nine months of 1984, which covered about 420,000 workers, averaged an even lower annual increase of 1.2 per cent over the life of the contract. One factor contributing to the moderate increases was the relatively low rise in consumer prices of about 4 per cent during the year.

An Oil Industry Agreement between Gulf Oil Corporation and the Oil, Chemical and Atomic Workers International Union was widely expected to set the industry pattern after its announcement in January. The agreement, however, turned out to be the pattern only after some hard bargaining and strikes at other companies.

The Gulf Oil pact provided pay increases of 20 cents an hour in the first year and 35 cents an hour in the second year, and it increased employer payments for family health care by $15, to $166.50 a month. Employee contributions to family health plans jumped from $22.50 a month to $50.50, reflecting a trend toward making workers pay more of the cost of health care.

Automobile Industry workers shared in the first payouts under profit-sharing plans set up in 1982 bargaining at General Motors Corporation (GM) and Ford Motor Company. Some 531,000 union and nonunion employees at GM shared $322 million. At Ford, about 158,000 union and nonunion workers shared almost $70 million in profits. The bonuses had been written into contracts to limit or replace specific wage and benefit increases.

After GM and Ford offered no specific wage increase for 1984, the United Automobile Workers (UAW) struck selected GM factories from September 14 to 21. The final settlement provided smaller wage and benefit increases than autoworkers had received in the 1970's and earlier. First-year increases ranged from 50 cents an hour for skilled workers to 9 cents an hour for janitors. The agreement also called for special payments and bonuses.

The 1984 negotiations focused on job security. Under the new contract, GM agreed to set up and fund a "job opportunity bank." The bank would enroll workers, under certain conditions, who had at least a year's seniority and had been displaced by automation or shifts in production to other places. It would pay the displaced workers for a year or until they found another job and would, in some cases, retrain them. Dissatisfaction with the contract became apparent when only 58 per cent of GM workers approved it.

The Ford agreement reached in October generally followed the GM contract. One key difference was Ford's agreement to a moratorium on plant closings over the duration of the three-year contract.

In October, a strike by about 38,000 workers at GM plants in Canada shut down GM assembly plants in the United States and idled about 52,000 U.S. workers. In the past, Canadian autoworkers accepted contracts patterned on U.S. contracts. In 1984, however, the Canadians sought increased pay and benefits rather than improved job security because Canada's inflation rate outpaced that of the United States. The strike ended after two

weeks with some improvements in the wage package. Later, Ford workers in Canada accepted a package similar to that received by GM workers.

On December 10, the Canadian UAW announced that it would split from the parent union. The latter had refused the Canadians' demands to run many of their own affairs, including calling strikes and handling contract negotiations with employers in Canada.

Coal Miners overwhelmingly approved a new contract with soft-coal companies on September 27, just three days before the expiration of their previous contract. The United Mine Workers of America (UMW) thus narrowly averted a strike under the union's "no contract, no work" rule. The agreement increased pay by $1.40 an hour over the contract's 40-month life, resulting in a new top daily rate of $124.52.

This was the first contract negotiated by the UMW without a strike in 20 years. In preparation for an expected strike, the mineworkers had raised a fund of about $45 million. Despite "give-backs" by other unions during 1982 and 1983, the mineworkers entered the negotiations vowing "not one step backward."

On the Waterfront. Another industry with a history of tumultuous bargaining settled peacefully on a new three-year contract. In August, the In-

Striking workers picket Disneyland in Anaheim, Calif., in October to protest the "Mickey Mouse contract" they claim they were offered.

ternational Longshoremen's and Warehousemen's Union reached an agreement with the Pacific Maritime Association. The agreement would increase wages 80 cents an hour in the first year and 85 cents an hour in each of the two following years. It covered 10,000 workers on the Pacific Coast.

Early in 1984, the International Longshoremen's Association (ILA) ratified an agreement that covered some 50,000 workers in ports on the Atlantic and Gulf of Mexico coasts. The union had agreed in 1983 to the contract's financial terms, which raised wages $1 an hour in 1983, 1984, and 1985. The union had refused, however, to approve the agreement after the Federal Maritime Commission, a regulatory agency, sought a federal injunction to prevent shipping companies from applying rules regarding containerized cargo. The rules, which were designed to protect ILA jobs, required that containerized cargo under most circumstances be loaded and unloaded only by ILA members. After the injunction was denied, the union ratified the contract.

In the Air. A battle between McDonnell Douglas Corporation and the UAW ended in February, when aerospace workers voted to end a strike that had dragged on for four months. After the company threatened in January to replace strikers, half of the 4,800 strikers crossed the picket line. The contract provided 3 per cent bonuses and hourly increases ranging from 8 cents to 72 cents.

Settlements at Republic Airlines and Northwest Orient Airlines illustrated the variety of terms agreed upon in the troubled airline industry. At Republic, six unions agreed to extend through March 1986 a 15 per cent salary cut that they had taken in September 1983. In exchange, Republic agreed to place employee representatives on its board of directors and to establish employee stock ownership and profit-sharing plans. At Northwest, workers belonging to the Airline, Aerospace, and Allied Employees union accepted a six-month freeze on wages through June 1984. But a 6 per cent increase took effect on July 1, and additional pay increases were scheduled to come in 1985 and 1986.

Other Bargaining. Just before the major-league baseball play-offs began in October, umpires went on strike over postseason play. To end the walkout, the Major Leagues Umpires Association and the two baseball leagues agreed to submit to binding arbitration by Peter V. Ueberroth, the newly named baseball commissioner. Ueberroth supported the umpires on the establishment of a system of pooled compensation whereby all umpires would receive pay for postseason work, not just those who officiated.

United Auto Workers President Owen Bieber (wearing glasses) and union negotiators announce an accord with General Motors, ending a strike on September 21.

Changes in the United States Labor Force

	1983	December 1984*
Total labor force	112,646,000	116,162,000
Armed forces	1,671,000	1,698,000
Civilian labor force	110,975,000	114,464,000
Total employment	101,277,000	107,971,000
Unemployment	11,369,000	8,191,000
Civilian unemployment rate	10.1%	7.2%
Change in real earnings of production and nonsupervisory workers (private nonfarm sector)†	+2.4%	−1.0%
Change in output per employee hour (private nonfarm sector)‡	+3.5%	+2.3%

*December 1984 labor force, employment, and unemployment data are seasonally adjusted; armed forces data are not.

†Constant (1977) dollars; 1983 change from December 1982 to December 1983; 1984 change from October 1983 to October 1984 (preliminary data).

‡Annual rate for 1983; for 1984, change is from third quarter 1983 to third quarter 1984 (preliminary data).

Source: U.S. Bureau of Labor Statistics.

In September, more than 1,500 clerical and technical workers at Yale University in New Haven, Conn., went on strike for increased pay and benefits. Many of the strikers were women, who claimed that the university paid men more for comparable work. Blue-collar workers at the university honored the white-collar picket lines. The strike was interrupted in December, when strikers returned to work to collect holiday pay.

Government Policies. In July 1984, President Ronald Reagan signed legislation that modified the effect of a February 1984 decision of the Supreme Court of the United States. The court decision, which grew out of the bankruptcy filing of the Bildisco Manufacturing Company, allowed companies that reorganized under bankruptcy petitions to cancel collective bargaining agreements only after the courts determine that the contracts would threaten the firm's continued existence. Spokespersons of both labor and management expressed approval of the modification.

On November 5, the Department of Labor issued regulations that permit certified employers to hire knitters who work at home. Labor unions and some firms had argued against lifting the ban on industrial home knitting. The government had banned several kinds of work at home during the 1940's to prevent employers from getting around child-labor and minimum-wage laws.

Unions. Lynn R. Williams, a Canadian, won a March election for the presidency of the United Steelworkers of America (USWA). Williams, the acting president, defeated Frank McKee, the union treasurer, in a hard-fought election. See WILLIAMS, LYNN R.

The Supreme Court wrote an apparent final chapter to the 1981 strike of the Professional Air Traffic Controllers Organization (PATCO). In October, the high court refused to review appeals court decisions that upheld Reagan's authority as President to fire more than 11,000 striking controllers in August 1981.

Secretary of Labor Raymond J. Donovan became the first U.S. Cabinet member to be indicted while holding office. A Bronx County, New York, grand jury on Sept. 24, 1984, charged Donovan and nine others with grand larceny and falsifying records in a $186-million New York City subway project. Before joining the Reagan Administration, Donovan had been an executive of the company that supervised the project. Donovan pleaded not guilty to the indictment and vowed to clear his name. He was granted a leave of absence from his post as secretary. Robert W. Fisher

See also ECONOMICS. In the Special Reports section, see A REVOLUTION IN THE WORKPLACE. In WORLD BOOK, see LABOR FORCE; LABOR MOVEMENT.

LANGE, DAVID RUSSELL (1942-   ), leader of New Zealand's Labour Party, became that country's 32nd prime minister on July 26, 1984. He succeeded Sir Robert D. Muldoon of the National Party as prime minister after a Labour victory in July elections. Lange also assumed the post of foreign minister. See NEW ZEALAND.

Lange (pronounced *LAHNG ee*) was born in Auckland on Aug. 4, 1942. He attended local schools and received law degrees from the University of Auckland in 1968 and 1970. Thereafter, Lange spent six years in private law practice.

Lange was first elected to Parliament in 1977 as member from Mangere, a working-class suburb of Auckland. He rose quickly through Labour Party ranks and held a succession of posts in the party's shadow cabinets from 1979 to 1983. In 1979, Lange became deputy leader of the Labour Party. He was elected party leader in 1983.

Lange is a moderate socialist. He favors some private and some government ownership of industries. In foreign policy matters, he supports greater independence from Great Britain and the United States. During the election campaign, Lange called for the exclusion from New Zealand waters of all nuclear-powered or nuclear-armed ships.

Lange married Naomi Joy Crampton in 1968. They have three children. Robie Liscomb

LAOS argued with Thailand over three border villages in 1984, and the quarrel led to exchanges of gunfire. Although the dispute involved only about 1,800 people and 1,000 acres (400 hectares), it soured relations between the two countries.

The Three Villages — Sawang, Klang, and Mai — lie along the border of Thailand's Uttaradit province and the Laotian province of Sayaboury. In March, Thai workers began building a road into the area near the villages, and Laotian troops reportedly objected. Laos claimed that the villages were in its territory, but Thailand said a 1907 map showed that it owned the area.

Both sides sent in soldiers. Laotian troops held the villages for a time, and each side accused the other of using artillery fire to back its claim. On June 6, Thai reinforcements seized the villages.

A propaganda war then escalated. Laos charged on September 19 that external forces were encouraging Thai *expansionism* — a policy of trying to add to its territory. Thailand accused Laos' Vietnamese backers of trying to drive a wedge between Thailand and Laos to distract attention from Vietnamese policy in Kampuchea (formerly Cambodia), occupied by Vietnamese forces.

Human Rights Issues. A deputy foreign minister of Laos, Khampai Boupha, said in October that the "reeducation camps" set up after the Communists won control of Laos in 1975 had been closed. But others said some former inmates might still be living under restrictions. About 20 camps reportedly held 15,000 political prisoners in 1980.

The number of refugees fleeing from Laos into Thailand increased in 1984. United Nations officials at one refugee camp said that 3,200 refugees had arrived in 1982, but in the first seven months of 1984, the total was 6,200. Poor economic conditions in Laos, forced transfer of property from individual to state ownership, compulsory enlistment in the armed forces, and other problems caused new refugees to join thousands who had fled Laos since the Communists came to power.

Anti-Communist Guerrillas continued to strike at the government and its Vietnamese backers. Swedish workers on a forestry project reported that their truck convoy was ambushed northeast of the Laotian capital of Vientiane on March 22, with three Laotians killed. In May, a military convoy was reported ambushed in southern Laos, with 32 Vietnamese and 8 Laotian Communists killed. Radio Vientiane complained on May 19 that some Laotian military units failed to report resistance activities and even cooperated with the enemy.

New Constitution. The Laotian government announced on May 22 that a 15-member commission would write a new national constitution. No deadline was reported.   Henry S. Bradsher

See also ASIA (Facts in Brief Table). In WORLD BOOK, see LAOS.

LATIN AMERICA

Latin-American countries made progress in 1984 in restoring democracy and returning to civilian rule. Many of the new civilian governments and the remaining military regimes in the region, however, were hard-pressed to maintain order in the face of economic austerity measures that drew sharply negative reactions from labor unions and peasant farmers.

Restoring Democracy. Three newly elected civilian presidents took office in Latin America in 1984 — in Ecuador, El Salvador, and Panama. A fourth, who will take office in 1985, was elected in Uruguay. In addition, the military regimes of Brazil and Guatemala promised a return to civilian rule in 1985. But still, those Latin Americans who continued to live under military regimes were impatient, particularly in Chile, where elections are not scheduled until 1989.

Perhaps the most massive popular campaign for democracy in Latin-American history unfolded in Brazil in the first half of 1984. Millions of Brazilians repeatedly thronged the streets of major cities to express their support for direct popular election of their next president. Although they did not achieve the objective of direct elections, the military government agreed to restore civilian rule through elections by an electoral college in 1985.

Peace Hopes. The promise of eventual peace in El Salvador commanded world attention on October 15, when for the first time in that country's five-year-old civil war, rebel and government leaders met face-to-face. The meeting, which took place at La Palma, a rural village in El Salvador, failed to achieve a cease-fire or any other concrete measure to end a war that has caused 50,000 deaths. But the two sides agreed to establish a joint commission for working toward a peaceful resolution of the conflict. The two sides met again on November 30.

Financial Problems. One Latin-American country after another was rescued from the brink of bankruptcy in 1984. The International Monetary Fund (IMF), an agency of the United Nations, worked closely with overseas banks that held Latin-American loans. By late 1984, some two-thirds of Latin-American nations underwent the strains of cuts in governmental expenditures in return for IMF assistance.

The ongoing stagnation of foreign investment in Latin America heightened the severity of un-

A crippled woman holds a peace flag she made out of plastic as she tries to crawl to the peace talks in La Palma, El Salvador, in October.

A U.S. Army helicopter prepares to remove a bullet-riddled helicopter that was downed in January by Nicaraguan soldiers near the Honduran border.

employment. Economists raised doubts about the area's ability to create enough jobs in future years. The Inter-American Development Bank, an international agency that makes long-term development loans to Latin-American nations, estimated that Latin America's population will double from 400 million to 800 million within 40 years, creating an accelerating demand for jobs.

Latin-American hopes in 1984 for a quick economic recovery were stymied by continued depressed prices for major commodities, including sugar, coffee, and oil. In June, the economic and foreign ministers of 11 Latin-American nations met in Cartagena, Colombia, to discuss the region's worsening economic situation and ways to refinance foreign debts. Quickly dubbed the Cartagena Group, the ministers met again in September in Mar del Plata, Argentina. Several ministers criticized protectionist trade practices among industrialized nations, particularly the United States. In 1984, U.S. companies won a number of disputes that resulted in higher tariffs on Latin America's manufactured exports to the United States on the grounds that Latin-American products benefited from government subsidies.

New Development. In 1984, Latin America began to reap the rewards of enormous investments over the past decade in the development of highways, hydroelectric plants, and port facilities. In

October, the presidents of Brazil and Paraguay threw a switch to turn on the turbines at the gigantic hydroelectric dam at Itaipú on the Paraná River. A joint project of the two nations, the Itaipú Dam, when fully operational, will be the world's largest source of hydroelectric power.

Elsewhere in Latin America, construction moved ahead on projects that demonstrated impressive engineering skill, as nations joined forces to tap rich resources of natural gas as well as to exploit hydroelectric potential. South American nations have begun to develop the resources of the vast interior of the continent, evidenced by increased commerce on South America's principal river systems, the Amazon and Orinoco. Due to improvements in ports and cargo-handling facilities and to an improved highway system, intraregional trade has steadily increased.

Sugar Quota Reductions. Ambassadors from a dozen Caribbean nations protested the U.S. government's decision on October 1 to cut their countries' shares of U.S. sugar imports by 16 per cent. The quota reductions more than offset gains achieved through President Ronald Reagan's Caribbean Basin Initiative, designed to encourage trade from pro-U.S. Caribbean nations by allowing duty-free treatment for many products.

The Dominican Republic, which relies on sugar exports to the United States for nearly 40 per cent of its earnings, was faced with the dismal prospect of selling its sugar on world markets at a considerable loss. The news came hard on the heels of a decision by Gulf & Western Industries, Incorporated, a New York City-based corporation with branches in several countries, to sell its holdings in the Dominican Republic. The holdings include sugar-producing lands that employ 37,000 people at the peak of the sugar harvest.

U.S. Relations. The U.S. flag was lowered for the last time at Fort Gulick in Panama on September 30. Under the 1977 Panama Canal treaties, the fort was turned over to Panama. The U.S. Army had used the fort to train Latin-American military personnel since World War II.

The United States was roundly denounced in Latin America after U.S. officials said on April 7 that U.S. citizens under contract to the U.S. Central Intelligence Agency (CIA) had directly supervised the mining of Nicaraguan harbors as part of a campaign to hamper trade and weaken Nicaragua's economy. It marked the first acknowledgment by the Reagan Administration of a direct U.S. role in military operations against the Sandinista regime.

The revelation drew sharp rejoinders from the U.S. Congress, as well as from other countries. Senator Barry Goldwater (R., Ariz.), chairman of the Senate Intelligence Committee, when apprised of the action through newspaper accounts, wrote an angry letter to CIA Director William J. Casey. It read in part: "I don't like this. I don't like it one bit from the President or from you."

On April 8, the U.S. Department of State took the unusual step of announcing that the United States would not accept the jurisdiction of the International Court of Justice (World Court) for the next two years in disputes involving the United States and Central America. Editorial reaction in Latin America ranged from shock to dismay. It was the first time that the United States had refused to be bound by the World Court. On April 9, Nicaragua asked the World Court to order the United States to stop the mining and cease aiding attacks on Nicaragua. See COURTS AND LAWS.

In the wake of the revelation about the U.S. role in mining Nicaragua's harbors, growing numbers of Latin Americans criticized the Reagan Administration for placing too much emphasis on military solutions to problems. On May 15, some 20,000 to 30,000 Costa Ricans marched through the streets of San José, the capital, in support of their country's neutrality in Central American affairs. "Peace yes, war no!" the marchers chanted, waving banners that blamed the United States for fanning the flames of war in Central America.

A number of Latin-American observers also expressed concern in 1984 that the Reagan Administration failed to take seriously the efforts of the

Nearly 1 million Brazilians gather in downtown Rio de Janeiro in April to press their demand for direct presidential elections.

Facts in Brief on Latin American Political Units

Country	Population	Government	Monetary Unit*	Foreign Trade (million U.S. $)	
				Exports†	Imports†
Antigua and Barbuda	81,000	Governor General Sir Wilfred Ebenezer Jacobs; Prime Minister Vere C. Bird	dollar (2.7 = $1)	31	137
Argentina	29,474,000	President Raúl Alfonsín	peso Argentino (148.6 = $1)	7,116	4,099
Bahamas	256,000	Governor General Sir Gerald C. Cash; Prime Minister Lynden O. Pindling	dollar (1 = $1)	6,546	7,014
Barbados	263,000	Governor General Sir Hugh Springer; Prime Minister J. M. G. Adams	dollar (2 = $1)	338	617
Belize	159,000	Governor General Minita Gordon; Prime Minister Manuel Esquivel	dollar (2 = $1)	60	132
Bolivia	6,402,000	President Hernán Siles Zuazo	peso (5,000 = $1)	789	514
Brazil	133,121,000	President João Baptista de Oliveira Figueiredo	cruzeiro (2,814 = $1)	21,366	16,311
Chile	12,168,000	President Augusto Pinochet Ugarte	peso (119 = $1)	3,840	2,775
Colombia	31,393,000	President Belisario Betancur	peso (96.2 = $1)	3,001	4,471
Costa Rica	2,487,000	President Luis Alberto Monge Alvarez	colón (44.4 = $1)	867	995
Cuba	9,976,000	President Fidel Castro	peso (1 = $1.15)	5,536	6,293
Dominica	82,000	President Clarence Seignoret; Prime Minister Mary Eugenia Charles	dollar (2.7 = $1)	25	47
Dominican Republic	6,168,000	President Salvador Jorge Blanco	peso (1 = $1)	811	1,282
Ecuador	9,803,000	President León Febres-Cordero	sucre (92.6 = $1)	2,203	1,465
El Salvador	5,536,000	President José Napoleón Duarte	colón (2.5 = $1)	792	986
Grenada	117,000	Governor General Sir Paul Godwin Scoon; Prime Minister Herbert A. Blaize	dollar (2.7 = $1)	19	56
Guatemala	6,776,000	Head of State Oscar Humberto Mejía Víctores	quetzal (1 = $1)	1,120	1,388
Guyana	880,000	President Forbes Burnham; Prime Minister Hugh Desmond Hoyte	dollar (3.7 = $1)	256	283
Haiti	5,601,000	President Jean-Claude Duvalier	gourde (5 = $1)	154	461
Honduras	4,372,000	President Roberto Suazo Córdova	lempira (2.6 = $1)	654	712
Jamaica	2,356,000	Governor General Sir Florizel Glasspole; Prime Minister Edward Seaga	dollar (4.4 = $1)	738	1,518
Mexico	76,590,000	President Miguel de la Madrid Hurtado	peso (211 = $1)	21,399	8,136
Nicaragua	3,216,000	3-member Government of National Reconstruction Junta headed by Daniel Ortega Saavedra	córdoba (200 = $1)	406	776
Panama	2,116,000	President Nicolás Ardito Barletta Vallarina	balboa (1 = $1)	304	1,412
Paraguay	3,303,000	President Alfredo Stroessner	guaraní (240 = $1)	262	506
Peru	20,240,000	President Fernando Belaúnde Terry; Prime Minister Sandro Mariategui Chiappe	sol (4,643 = $1)	3,230	3,787
Puerto Rico	3,188,000	Governor Carlos Romero Barceló	U.S. $	8,888	8,167
St. Christopher and Nevis	46,000	Governor General Clement Arrindell; Prime Minister Kennedy Alphonse Simmonds	dollar (2.7 = $1)	19	45
St. Lucia	129,000	Governor General Sir Allen Montgomery Lewis; Prime Minister John Compton	dollar (2.7 = $1)	42	118
St. Vincent and the Grenadines	133,000	Governor General Sir Sydney Gunn-Munro; Prime Minister James Mitchell	dollar (2.7 = $1)	32	61
Suriname	402,000	Acting President L. F. Ramdat-Misier; Commander-in-Chief of the National Army Desi Bouterse	guilder (1.8 = $1)	429	511
Trinidad and Tobago	1,136,000	President Ellis Emmanuel Innocent Clarke; Prime Minister George Chambers	dollar (2.4 = $1)	2,387	2,558
Uruguay	3,000,000	President Gregorio C. Alvarez	peso (58 = $1)	1,105	647
Venezuela	16,298,000	President Jaime Lusinchi	bolívar (12.2 = $1)	15,924	6,667

*Exchange rates as of Dec. 1, 1984, or latest available data. †Latest available data.

Contadora Group — Colombia, Mexico, Panama, and Venezuela — to bring peace to Central America. Nicaragua's acceptance of a draft peace treaty proposed by the Contadora Group appeared to make the Reagan Administration even more uncomfortable with the Contadora process.

Inter-American Relations. On November 29, Chile and Argentina settled a century-old dispute regarding territorial rights over the Beagle Channel in Tierra del Fuego at the southernmost tip of South America. The foreign ministers of the two countries signed a treaty in Rome, where officials of the Vatican had helped mediate the accord. Under the treaty, Chile will control three islands at the Atlantic Ocean entrance to the Beagle Channel, but Chile's maritime rights in the area will be limited.

Brazilian Heads OAS. Little fanfare greeted the announcement in Washington, D.C., on March 12 that João Clemente Baena Soares was elected secretary general of the Organization of American States (OAS). Baena Soares, a 52-year-old career diplomat from Brazil, pledged himself to renewing support for the OAS, a body characterized by his predecessor as "increasingly irrelevant." The same day the OAS admitted to membership the tiny Caribbean island-nation of St. Christopher and Nevis (St. Kitts-Nevis).

Urban Crime. Crime continued to plague some of Latin America's big cities in 1984. General Ramón Mota Sanchez, the police chief of Mexico City, advised citizens "to provide for their own self-defense." He candidly acknowledged that corruption was still rife in the police force he commands, even though he fired several thousand police officers. Complaints of major crime in Mexico City were up more than 40 per cent in 1984, and the murder rate was 25 per cent higher than that of New York City.

The former police chief of Mexico City, Arturo Durazo Moreno, fled the country when it was alleged that he had amassed a multimillion-dollar fortune on a salary equal to that of a cabdriver. He was placed under custody in June by U.S. authorities in Los Angeles while awaiting extradition to face charges of tax fraud in Mexico.

Miami Goes Latin. Miami, Fla., has become a Latin-American-style city because so many tens of thousands of Latin Americans have settled there or go there to visit. To serve them and also Latin Americans who wish to avoid currency devaluations in their own countries, a number of Latin-American banks have opened branches in Miami. The advantages to Latin Americans of doing business in a city where 70 per cent of the population speaks Spanish are obvious. And visitors from Latin America can combine business with pleasure by arranging deals with the hundreds of Miami-based export companies that have made the city a

sort of "business capital" for Latin America, while packing off their families to Florida tourist attractions. Latin Americans now have at least $10 billion invested in Miami banks and at least $5 billion invested in real estate in the fast-growing Miami area, according to some estimates.

Major-League Baseball. Latin Americans continued to increase their numbers on U.S. major-league baseball teams. The city of San Pedro de Macorís on the south coast of the Dominican Republic, with a population of 100,000, now boasts 11 of its native sons on U.S. teams.

Maya Tomb. U.S. and Guatemalan archaeologists made a significant discovery in the remote jungles of northern Guatemala in May 1984. They found the first intact painted tomb to be discovered in the Maya Indian lowlands since the 1960's. The tomb, said to be more than 1,500 years old, was discovered in near-perfect condition near the village of Río Azul. The tomb was found still sealed, unlike others in the area, which have been looted. See ARCHAEOLOGY.   Nathan A. Haverstock

See also articles on the various Latin-American countries. In the WORLD BOOK SUPPLEMENT section, see SAINT CHRISTOPHER AND NEVIS. In WORLD BOOK, see LATIN AMERICA and articles on the individual countries.

LAW. See CIVIL RIGHTS; COURTS AND LAWS; CRIME; SUPREME COURT OF THE UNITED STATES.

LEBANON. Prospects for the reconciliation of warring factions and an end to civil war glimmered fitfully in Lebanon in 1984, like a dim light at the far end of a dark tunnel. By early February, continued fighting between the Lebanese Army and Muslim militias along with growing Muslim criticism of the leadership of Lebanese President Amin Gemayel led to the disintegration of Gemayel's coalition government. On February 5, as fighting intensified, Lebanon's Muslim Prime Minister Shafiq al-Wazzan and his Cabinet resigned.

Gemayel attempted to restore order by sending the Lebanese Army to disband the various militias. But the army split along sectarian lines, with Shiite and Druse soldiers, in particular, refusing to fight against members of their own faction.

On February 6 and 7, Shiite and Druse militias, in what was described as the worst fighting in Beirut since the 1975-1976 civil war, seized control of West Beirut, plunging the city into chaos. Almost overnight, Lebanon's capital again became a divided city, separated into a Christian East and a Muslim West by a barricade 5 miles (8 kilometers) long called the Green Line.

Unity Attempts. In an attempt to restore national unity, Gemayel, under pressure from Muslim leaders, on March 5 canceled a troop-withdrawal agreement signed with Israel in May 1983. The action came after a conference between

Lebanese Muslim militiamen celebrate their take-over of the U.S. Marine base at the Beirut airport following the withdrawal of U.S. forces in February.

Gemayel and Syria's President Hafiz al-Assad, whose negotiators had been working behind the scenes for months to reconcile Lebanese leaders. However, unity talks, held in Switzerland by the warring factions, broke down on March 20.

After weeks of talks, a new Cabinet headed by veteran politician Rashid Karami took office in May (see KARAMI, RASHID). The Cabinet included the leaders of the other major factions.

The Gemayel government took another hesitant step forward on June 23, when, with Syrian help, it hammered out an agreement with opposition leaders to restructure the Lebanese Army. The new organization would allow for greater participation by Shiite Muslims and Druse in the officer corps, where they have been underrepresented.

The agreement also provided for a new national security agency, headed by a Shiite officer, which would have the responsibility for coordinating intelligence and security activities both within and outside Lebanon. The army's chief of staff, Major General Ibrahim Tannous, a Maronite Christian, was replaced by Major General Michel Aoun, another Maronite officer, whose powers were limited. Tannous had been bitterly criticized by Muslim officers for favoring Christian units.

The two halves of Beirut were reunited in July when army units took over the Green Line, removed checkpoints, and began disbanding Shiite and Druse militias. The airport and port of Beirut were reopened to traffic.

In August, army units began fanning out along the major highways out of Beirut and into the nearby Shouf Mountains southeast of Beirut, the scene of fierce factional strife in 1983. The plan was to eventually bring Lebanese forces to the Awwali River, the limit of Israeli control in southern Lebanon. On December 20, the Lebanese Army took control of the northern port city of Tripoli (also called Tarabulus) from Muslim militias. It was the first time the Lebanese Army had assumed control of the mostly Muslim city since civil war broke out in Lebanon in 1975.

Redistributing Power. Ultimately, peace and national unity in Lebanon depended not on army reorganization or troop-withdrawal agreements, but on a redistribution of political power. It would have to be one acceptable to all factions.

In September, the Cabinet began discussing the formation of a new National Assembly, which would draw up a power-sharing agreement. The parliament would have 39 members—8 members each from the Maronite, Sunni Muslim, and Shiite Muslim factions, plus 4 Druse, 4 Greek Orthodox, 4 Greek Catholic, and 2 Armenian members, and 1 member representing all other minorities. If finally accepted, the realignment would be the first reallocation of seats in the parliament since 1932.

Fundamentalist Threat. In addition to rivalries and personal feuds among Lebanese leaders, the rise of Islamic fundamentalism also threatened Lebanese national unity. Shiite militants belonging to the pro-Iranian extremist group Holy War carried out terrorist attacks, including the September 20 bombing of the U.S. Embassy in Aukar, near Beirut, in which at least 14 people were killed. The Holy War group advocates an Islamic state in Lebanon organized under traditional Islamic law. But the real danger was that the Holy War terrorists would split the Shiite community, headed by Minister for Southern Lebanon Nabih Berri, leader of the majority Amal (Hope) militia and a moderate.

The Economy limped along. Any serious efforts at reconstruction were delayed pending a political resolution. In June, the Lebanese pound dropped to a low of 6 = U.S. $1, and the national debt reached $2 billion. The amount of money sent back home by Lebanese workers abroad, which usually provides 35 per cent of national income, dropped to $1 billion. The 1984 budget called for expenditures of $2 billion, but no one knew where the money would come from.   William Spencer

See also MIDDLE EAST (Facts in Brief Table). In WORLD BOOK, see LEBANON.

LESOTHO. See AFRICA.

LIBERIA. See AFRICA.

LIBRARY. Legislation signed into law by President Ronald Reagan in September 1984 authorized the construction of a facility to give new life to old books. Utilizing a process patented by chemists at the Library of Congress in Washington, D.C., the treatment will neutralize the acid that causes paper to become brittle and deteriorate over time. The process could add 400 to 600 years to the life of books made from wood-pulp paper.

According to Librarian of Congress Daniel J. Boorstin, "One of the most pressing problems facing libraries today is the rapid deterioration of their collections because of the unstable quality of paper produced since around 1850." The preparation used in modern papermaking to stiffen and coat paper contains a chemical that gradually breaks down, producing sulfuric acid. The new process involves treating the books with diethyl zinc to neutralize the acid.

A survey of the Library of Congress collection, completed in March 1984, indicated that 75 per cent of the library's 80 million holdings — books, manuscripts, documents, and other printed materials — would benefit from the process. The rest of the collection can be preserved only by transferring the documents to microfilm or other forms of storage, which will be much more costly. The library plans to build the $11.5-million deacidification facility at Fort Detrick in Frederick, Md. The facility will be able to deacidify at least 500,000 books and other library materials per year.

New Buildings. The new $39-million, eight-story main library building of the Broward County Library System in Fort Lauderdale, Fla., was dedicated on April 29, 1984. The 256,000-square-foot (23,800-square-meter) building will also serve Florida Atlantic University in Boca Raton, Florida International University in Miami, and Broward Community College in Fort Lauderdale. A huge atrium links the interior areas of the building. The new $22-million Walter Royal Davis Library at the University of North Carolina in Chapel Hill provides shelving for 1.8 million volumes.

Reagan Library. Plans to locate the Ronald Reagan presidential library on the campus of Stanford University in Palo Alto, Calif., were announced on February 14. A museum will also be located there.

Conferences. The International Federation of Library Associations and Institutions' 50th general conference was held in Nairobi, Kenya, from August 19 to 25. The 39th annual conference of the Canadian Library Association was held in Toronto, Ont., from June 7 to 12. The 103rd annual conference of the American Library Association was held in Dallas June 23 to 28.   Robert J. Shaw

See also AMERICAN LIBRARY ASSOCIATION; CANADIAN LIBRARY ASSOCIATION. In WORLD BOOK, see LIBRARY.

LIBYA. An attempt to overthrow Leader of the Revolution Muammar Muhammad al-Qadhafi on May 8, 1984, underscored growing internal opposition to the Libyan leader. Fifteen guerrillas attacked Qadhafi's military headquarters in Tripoli, but they were all killed by loyal army units and youthful members of the Revolutionary Committees, who are Qadhafi's strongest supporters. The National Front for the Salvation of Libya, a group of Libyan exiles based in Cairo, Egypt, claimed responsibility for the attack.

Following the coup attempt, some 3,000 people were arrested in a "reign of terror" as Qadhafi cracked down on the opposition. Between June 3 and June 7, seven alleged "enemies of the state" were publicly hanged without a trial. Most of those arrested were later released.

London Violence. The increasing division between Libyans for and against Qadhafi spread to Great Britain in 1984. Bomb attacks on public places frequented by Arabs in London and Manchester in March caused several dozen casualties.

On April 17, machine-gun fire from a window of the Libyan embassy in London, which had been taken over in February by revolutionary Libyan zealots, wounded 10 Libyan students demonstrating against Qadhafi and killed a British policewoman. The London police laid siege to the embassy, and Britain broke diplomatic relations with

Libya on April 22. On April 27, the 30-member embassy staff was allowed to return to Libya under diplomatic immunity. On the same day, the staff of the British Embassy in Tripoli returned to Great Britain.

Despite Such Incidents, Qadhafi's isolation, internationally and in the Arab world, lessened in 1984. The Libyan border with Egypt reopened on April 2, and airline flights were resumed between the two countries. On August 13, Qadhafi unexpectedly signed an agreement establishing a "union of states" with King Hassan II of Morocco. Almost as surprising was a Libyan agreement with France in September for the joint withdrawal of Libyan and French troops from the war-torn African country of Chad. Both sides announced on November 10 that they had pulled their forces out, but intelligence sources estimated that up to 3,000 Libyans remained in Chad.

Red Sea Mines. During July, August, and September, a number of cargo ships in the Red Sea were damaged by exploding mines. Libya denied involvement, but a Libyan freighter, the *Ghat*, became the prime suspect in the minelaying. On August 22, France seized the *Ghat* in Marseille, where it was docked for repairs.   William Spencer

See also AFRICA (Facts in Brief Table). In WORLD BOOK, see LIBYA.

LIECHTENSTEIN. See EUROPE.

LITERATURE. Although a number of interesting and well-crafted novels were published in the United States in 1984, few works of fiction seemed to meet the acid test of literature: Is it worth rereading? The handful that passed the test included Gore Vidal's 19th novel, *Lincoln: A Novel,* a well-researched book about United States President Abraham Lincoln and his political circle, and Joan Didion's *Democracy,* a provocative tale of political idealism gone sour.

Joseph Heller's fourth novel, *God Knows,* a satire based on the life of the Biblical King David, proved highly controversial. Some critics admired its dark humor. But others deplored its repetitive excesses. Alice Adams' *Superior Women* was a melodrama from a highly respected writer. Norman Mailer's *Tough Guys Don't Dance,* a gloomy attempt at a murder mystery, was more stylish than engrossing. John Updike's *The Witches of Eastwick* was a quirky, unconvincing erotic novel.

Several younger writers offered more encouraging work. *Half Moon Street* by Paul Theroux presented two well-crafted short novels. Rosellen Brown wrote a fine novel, *Civil Wars,* about a husband and wife in the civil rights movement in the South. Marge Piercy contributed *Fly Away Home,* a romance set against a backdrop of social issues.

The year's most impressive first novel was *Machine Dreams* by Jayne Anne Phillips. A story about

the dissolution of an American family, the work was remarkable for re-creating a time and place. *". . . And Ladies of the Club"* — which represented a 50-year effort by its 88-year-old author, Helen Hooven Santmyer — described life in a small Ohio town during the late 1800's and early 1900's. Harriet Doerr, at the age of 73, contributed her first novel, *Stones for Ibarra,* which told of an American couple living in a Mexican village.

Other important novels came from Michael J. Arlen, Frederick Barthelme, Jack Fuller, William Kennedy, Alison Lurie, William McPherson, William Wharton, and Richard Yates. Praiseworthy collections of short stories included Saul Bellow's *Him with His Foot in His Mouth and Other Stories,* E. L. Doctorow's *Lives of the Poets,* and Lynne Sharon Schwartz's *Acquainted with the Night.*

Fiction from Abroad. Works from Great Britain included *The Life and Loves of a She-Devil* by Fay Weldon, a remarkable novel of revenge, and *The Only Problem* by Muriel Spark, a witty tale whose central metaphor came from the Bible's Book of Job. South Africa's Nadine Gordimer offered *Something Out There,* a novella and a collection of meticulously crafted short stories. Her countryman J. M. Coetzee wrote *Life and Times of Michael K,* a tale of suffering seen through the eyes of a simpleton. An Australian writer, David Malouf, offered *Harland's Half Acre,* a partly realistic, partly dreamlike study of life in Australia.

Several fine novels came from Latin America. Argentine novelist Manuel Puig set the fantasy *Blood of Requited Love* in Brazil. Peruvian writer Mario Vargas Llosa based *The War of the End of the World* on events in South America at the end of the 1800's. Chilean writer José Donoso spun a fantastic tale of a wealthy family surrounded by cannibals in *A House in the Country.*

Milan Kundera, a Czechoslovak writer in exile, contributed *The Unbearable Lightness of Being.* The novel told of love under a Communist regime.

A new edition of Irish novelist James Joyce's masterpiece *Ulysses* corrected nearly 5,000 omissions, transpositions, and other errors in earlier editions. The errors were introduced mainly by friends who typed Joyce's manuscript and by French typesetters who prepared the first edition. The new edition, brought out by Garland Publishing in June, took seven years to prepare.

Essays and Criticism. Few books were published in this category during 1984, but they included some notable efforts. *The Essays, Articles and Reviews of Evelyn Waugh* added to that writer's vast body of work. Leon Edel discussed the craft of biography in *Writing Lives.* Alfred Kazin assessed U.S. writers from Ralph Waldo Emerson to F. Scott Fitzgerald in *An American Procession.* Paul Zweig reassessed a poet's relation to his culture in *Walt Whitman: The Making of the Poet.*

Helen Hooven Santmyer, aged 88, autographs a copy of her 1,300-page novel — ". . . And Ladies of the Club" — which became a best seller in 1984.

Literary Biography. One of the most fascinating lives of American writers to appear in many years was Elinor Langer's *Josephine Herbst*. The book revived an almost-forgotten novelist who had once been ranked with the American writers Ernest Hemingway and John Dos Passos.

William H. Pritchard concentrated on Robert Frost's work and reputation as a poet in *Frost: A Literary Life Reconsidered*. Laurence Bergreen examined the tormented life of a gifted writer in *James Agee: A Life*. In *Home Before Dark*, Susan Cheever compassionately discussed the long battle of her novelist father, John Cheever, with homosexuality and alcoholism.

James R. Mellow's *Invented Lives* dispassionately examined the writings of Fitzgerald and his wife, Zelda, and their self-destructive lives. *Solzhenitsyn* by Michael Scammell was a powerful life of the Russian novelist. Other significant literary biographies included Scott Elledge's *E. B. White*, Virginia Spencer Carr's *Dos Passos*, Ann Thwaite's *Edmund Gosse*, A. N. Wilson's *Hilaire Belloc*, and Ernst Pawel's *The Nightmare of Reason: A Life of Franz Kafka*.

General Biography. Two vastly different but complementary lives of anthropologist Margaret Mead appeared during 1984. Mary Catherine Bateson's *With a Daughter's Eye* took a close look at her mother's personal life, while Jane Howard's *Margaret Mead* attempted a broader view of Mead's life and work. Another biography of a scientist, Andrew Hodges' *Alan Turing: The Enigma*, told of an eccentric British mathematician who played an important role in the development of the computer.

Political biographies included *Eisenhower: The President*, the second volume of Stephen E. Ambrose' life of the 34th U.S. President. Richard Norton Smith tried to restore Herbert Hoover's reputation in *An Uncommon Man*. Robert V. Remini produced another authoritative presidential biography, *Andrew Jackson and the Course of American Democracy, 1833-1845*. Peter Collier and David Horowitz presented an unflattering but well-researched portrait of a powerful political family in *The Kennedys: An American Drama*.

Two lives of a famous anarchist who became a feminist heroine appeared during 1984. They were Candace Falk's *Love, Anarchy, and Emma Goldman* and Alice Wexler's *Emma Goldman: An Intimate Life*. Patricia Bosworth's *Diane Arbus* was a fine biography of the photographer of freaks and misfits who killed herself in 1971. Bob Woodward's *Wired*, a powerful and disturbing biography of the late entertainer John Belushi, won both praise and condemnation for its emphasis on Belushi's drug use.

Autobiography and Letters. Eudora Welty's *One Writer's Beginnings*, which told of her childhood in Mississippi, became a surprise best seller. V. S. Naipaul contributed *Finding the Center*, two autobiographical narratives. The first dealt with his origins as a Hindu in Trinidad and his professional development in London. The second described a visit to Ivory Coast, in West Africa.

The Belgian mystery writer Georges Simenon offered an intense but loosely written self-examination in *Intimate Memoirs*. The exiled Soviet soprano Galina Vishnevskaya ably and warmly described life as one of Moscow's favorite prima donnas in *Galina: A Russian Story*. John Edgar Wideman's *Brothers and Keepers* explored the social pressures and personal responses that made him a respected black novelist and put his brother behind bars as a murderer. The distinguished foreign correspondent William L. Shirer produced *The Nightmare Years: 1930-1940*, the second volume of his memoirs.

Rosalynn Carter told of her life as the President's wife in *First Lady from Plains*. Autobiographies appeared from two famous anthropologists. They were Mary Leakey's *Disclosing the Past* and her son Richard E. Leakey's *One Life*. Composer Aaron Copland described his life from his birth in 1900 to 1942 in *Copland*.

Contemporary Affairs. Strobe Talbott subjected President Ronald Reagan's conduct of nuclear disarmament talks with the Soviet Union to highly

Studs Terkel in 1984 came out with a best-selling collection of reminiscences about the World War II years entitled *"The Good War."*

critical scrutiny in *Deadly Gambits*. Peter Matthiessen's *Indian Country* criticized U.S. policy toward Native Americans. Michael Harrington's *The New American Poverty* discussed President Lyndon Johnson's War on Poverty and argued that an attack on the problem must continue. Kristin Luker's *Abortion and the Politics of Motherhood* ably explored a growing American controversy.

Jane Jacobs' *Cities and the Wealth of Nations*, the most interesting book on economics in 1984, argued that national policies the world over harm cities and those who live in them. Freeman Dyson's *Weapons and Hope* was a heartening attempt to find a workable political solution to the threat posed by nuclear weapons. Robert Sam Anson's *Exile* examined Richard Nixon's career since his resignation from the presidency. The book concluded that although Nixon has remained publicly visible, he has had little influence on U.S. policy.

Southeast Asia continued to provide material for important books. Wallace Terry's *Bloods* presented the recollections of black soldiers who served in the Vietnam War. Joe Klein's *Payback* followed a group of former marines through their personal post-Vietnam upheavals. *Long Time Passing: Vietnam and the Haunted Generation* by Myra MacPherson captured the complexity and diversity of the lives led by soldiers after the war. *The Quality of Mercy* by William Shawcross indicted

many nations for ignoring the atrocities committed by Khmer Rouge Communists in Cambodia (Kampuchea).

Joan Peters' *From Time Immemorial* explored the origins of the conflict between Arabs and Jews over Palestine and challenged the claims of the Palestine Liberation Organization to the territory. In *Religion in the Secular City*, Harvey Cox viewed the worldwide resurgence of fundamentalist religions as a revolt against the modern world.

History. The most memorable book of 1984 in this category was *The Chronicle of the Łódź Ghetto, 1941-1944*, edited by Lucjan Dobroszycki. It told the story, largely through diaries and documents, of the Nazi destruction of the Jewish ghetto in Łódź, Poland, during World War II. Studs Terkel's thoughtful book — *"The Good War"* — related memories of people who experienced World War II. *The Discoverers* by Daniel J. Boorstin explored the circumstances surrounding major discoveries. Barbara W. Tuchman's *The March of Folly* examined famous instances of misgovernment.

George F. Kennan's *The Fateful Alliance*, an examination of the origins of World War I, had pointed lessons for the present. *The Perspective of the World* was the third and final volume of French historian Fernand Braudel's masterly trilogy, *Civilization and Capitalism*. Joel Williamson investigated the history of bigotry and segregation in the United States in *The Crucible of Race*. Martin E. Marty told the story of religious faiths and sects in the United States in *Pilgrims in Their Own Land: 500 Years of Religion in America*.

Best Sellers. Among the top best sellers of 1984 were *The Talisman*, by Stephen King and Peter Straub; *The Fourth Protocol*, by Frederick Forsyth; *Love and War*, by John Jakes; *Strong Medicine*, by Arthur Hailey; *The Aquitaine Progression*, by Robert Ludlum; *What They Don't Teach You at Harvard Business School*, by Mark H. McCormack; *The One Minute Sales Person*, by Spencer Johnson and Larry Wilson; *Eat to Win*, by Robert Haas; *Mary Kay on People Management*, by Mary Kay Ash; and *Loving Each Other*, by Leo F. Buscaglia.

Among the leading paperback best sellers in 1984 were Stephen King's *Pet Sematary*, Erma Bombeck's *Motherhood: The Second Oldest Profession*, James A. Michener's *Poland*, Ken Follett's *On Wings of Eagles*, Thomas J. Peters and Robert H. Waterman, Jr.'s *In Search of Excellence*, Danielle Steel's *Changes*, Joe McGinniss' *Fatal Vision*, Jackie Collins' *Sinners*, Judith Krantz's *Mistral's Daughter*, and Dan Kiley's *The Peter Pan Syndrome*.   Henry Kisor

See also AWARDS AND PRIZES (Literature Awards); CANADIAN LITERATURE; LITERATURE FOR CHILDREN; POETRY; PUBLISHING. In WORLD BOOK, see LITERATURE.

LITERATURE, CANADIAN. See CANADIAN LIBRARY ASSOCIATION; CANADIAN LITERATURE.

LITERATURE FOR CHILDREN. Books for children aged 6 months to about 3 years flourished in 1984. Pop-up books and picture books remained popular. Strong characterization highlighted books for older readers, the realism often lightened by touches of humor. Informational books continued to be published on various subjects.

Some outstanding books of 1984 were:

Picture Books

The Story of Jumping Mouse, by John Steptoe (Lothrop, Lee & Shepard Bks.). This finely illustrated American Indian legend tells of a mouse who seeks to learn more about life. Ages 5 to 9.

Fix-It, by David McPhail (Dutton). Emma is upset when the television set stops working, but Mother Bear finds a solution. Ages 2 to 5.

Buffalo Woman, by Paul Goble (Bradbury Press). An American Indian legend that shows the kinship between Indian and buffalo is movingly told and magnificently illustrated. Ages 5 and up.

What Next, Baby Bear!, by Jill Murphy (Dial Press). Baby bear goes to the moon in a richly illustrated, imaginative tale. Ages 3 to 7.

The Man Who Could Call Down Owls, by Eve Bunting, illustrated by Charles Mikolaycak (Macmillan). Wonderful drawings capture the mood and action of this haunting tale. Ages 5 to 9.

Animal Alphabet, by Bert Kitchen (Dial Press). Many unusual creatures appear in this beautiful, informative book. All ages.

Small Cloud, by Ariane, illustrated by Annie Gusman (Dutton). This original tale is fine for reading aloud, and the vivid paintings are a delight. Ages 3 to 6.

The Miser Who Wanted the Sun, by Jürg Obrist (Atheneum Pubs.). A miser tricks a tailor and is tricked in return. Lavish paintings highlight and extend the tale. Ages 5 to 8.

The Rose in My Garden, by Arnold Lobel, illustrated by Anita Lobel (Greenwillow Bks.). Exuberantly illustrated flowers almost conceal a variety of creatures. Ages 4 to 8.

Jimmy's Boa Bounces Back, by Trinka Hakes Noble, illustrated by Steven Kellogg (Dial Press). Hilarious illustrations capture odd events as Jimmy's pet snake goes to a Garden Club meeting. Ages 4 to 8.

The Winter Wren, by Brock Cole (Farrar, Straus, & Giroux). Simon and his little sister set out in search of spring. Ages 5 to 8.

Hansel and Gretel, by the Brothers Grimm, retold by Rika Lesser, illustrated by Paul O. Zelinsky (Dodd, Mead). Rich paintings capture the mood and content of a familiar tale. Ages 8 to 12.

Boxes! Boxes!, by Leonard Everett Fisher (Viking Press). Excellent paintings accompany the rhymed text that shows some of the shapes and uses of boxes. Ages 4 to 7.

The Glorious Flight: Across the Channel with Louis Blériot by Alice and Martin Provensen won the 1984 Caldecott Medal for children's picture books.

Babushka, by Charles Mikolaycak (Holiday House). This Russian Christmas tale is simply retold and richly illustrated. Ages 5 to 8.

The Mysteries of Harris Burdick, by Chris Van Allsburg (Houghton Mifflin). Readers are invited to make up their own stories to accompany the captioned illustrations in this intriguing book. Ages 8 and up.

The Quilt, by Ann Jonas (Greenwillow Bks.). A little girl's quilt takes her to imaginary places in this finely illustrated book. Ages 3 to 6.

Is It Rough? Is It Smooth? Is It Shiny?, by Tana Hoban (Greenwillow Bks.). Color photographs reveal a variety of textures including eggs, hay, and a beard. All ages.

The Crack-of-Dawn Walkers, by Amy Hest, illustrated by Amy Schwartz (Macmillan). Drawings enhance the walk taken by Sadie and her grandfather. Ages 4 to 7.

Poetry and Songs

Cold Stars and Fireflies: Poems of the Four Seasons, by Barbara Juster Esbensen, illustrated by Susan Bonners (Crowell). Fresh language and pictures describe children's activities. Ages 8 to 12.

Waiting to Waltz: A Childhood, by Cynthia Rylant, illustrated by Stephen Gammell (Bradbury Press). A small town is vividly brought to life through the eyes of a young girl. Ages 9 to 12.

Old MacDonald Had a Farm, by Tracey Campbell Pearson (Dutton). Extra verses and exuberant water colors expand on the familiar song. Ages 3 to 7.

The New Kid on the Block, by Jack Prelutsky, illustrated by James Stevenson (Greenwillow Bks.). Humor and nonsense fill the pages. Ages 8 and up.

If There Were Dreams to Sell, compiled by Barbara Lalicki, illustrated by Margot Tomes (Lothrop, Lee & Shepard Bks.). This colonial-style alphabet book includes lines from Mother Goose, English poets, and others. Ages 4 to 8.

Secrets of a Small Brother, by Richard Margolis, illustrated by Donald Carrick (Macmillan). A young boy's feelings about his older brother are expressed in words and drawings. Ages 5 to 8.

Grandparents' Houses: Poems About Grandparents, selected by Corrine Streich, illustrated by Lillian Hoban (Greenwillow Bks.). Fifteen poems from a variety of cultures each celebrate a grandparent. Ages 8 to 12.

Fantasy

The Beggar Queen, by Lloyd Alexander (Dutton). The final book of the Westmark trilogy brings Mickle, Theo, and others together for high adventure. Ages 11 and up.

The Candlemaker and Other Tales, by Victoria Forrester, illustrated by Susan Seddon Boulet

Theodor Seuss Geisel (Dr. Seuss), who won a special Pulitzer Prize in 1984 for his contributions to children's literature, signs a new book in March.

(Atheneum Pubs.). Four delightful tales are combined with expressive illustrations. Ages 8 and up.

Building Blocks, by Cynthia Voigt (Atheneum Pubs.). Brann gains new understanding when he goes back in time and spends a day with his father, aged 10. Ages 10 to 13.

Skinny Malinky Leads the War for Kidness, by Stanley Kiesel (Dutton). Unusual characters help Skinny try to restore kidness in this satiric tale. Ages 8 to 12.

Heart's Blood, by Jane Yolen (Delacorte Press). This sequel to *Dragon's Blood* is full of action and drama. Ages 12 and up.

The Memory String, by Chester G. Osborne (Atheneum Pubs.). An absorbing tale set 30,000 years ago tells of a boy's coming of age as he reluctantly learns the mysteries of becoming a shaman. Ages 12 and up.

Giant Cold, by Peter Dickinson, illustrated by Alan E. Cober (Dutton). A family outing becomes a haunting quest. Ages 9 to 12.

Fiction

One-Eyed Cat, by Paula Fox (Bradbury Press). The gift of an air rifle sets off a chain of events in this beautifully written book. Ages 12 and up.

The Serpent's Children, by Laurence Yep (Harper & Row). Set in China many years ago, the story tells of one child's determination to become his own person. Ages 12 and up.

The Present Takers, by Aidan Chambers (Harper & Row). Lucy tries to handle bullies. Ages 9 to 11.

Tracker, by Gary Paulsen (Bradbury Press). John goes hunting without his dying grandfather and learns of life and death. Ages 11 to 13.

Him She Loves?, by M. E. Kerr (Harper & Row). When Henry and Valerie fall in love, her father causes problems. Ages 12 and up.

The Island on Bird Street, by Uri Orlev, translated by Hillel Halkin (Houghton Mifflin). Alex awaits the return of his father, who was taken away by Nazis in 1945. Ages 11 and up.

Sugar Blue, by Vera Cleaver (Lothrop, Lee & Shepard Bks.). Amy Blue, 11, takes care of her 4-year-old niece, Ella, whom she comes to love and lose. Ages 9 to 11.

A Place to Come Back To, by Nancy Bond (Atheneum Pubs.). Oliver's world is shattered when the great-uncle he lives with dies. Ages 12 and up.

The Way to Sattin Shore, by Philippa Pearce (Greenwillow Bks.). Kate, 10, uncovers a mystery about her father, who is missing and assumed to be dead. Ages 8 to 10.

Fly Free, by C. S. Adler (Coward, McCann & Geoghegan). Shari, an abused 13-year-old, begins to understand her mother better after a family secret is revealed. Ages 12 and up.

Night Cry, by Phyllis Reynolds Naylor (Atheneum Pubs.). A stranger and a kidnapping worry

Ellen, who is frequently left by herself. Ages 12 and up.

S.O.R. Losers, by Avi (Bradbury Press). An unwilling 7th-grade soccer team responds to losses in an unusual way. Ages 9 to 12.

Who Is Carrie?, by James Lincoln Collier and Christopher Collier (Delacorte Press). Carrie, a black girl in New York City in the 1700's, tries to find out who her parents are. Ages 12 and up.

US and Uncle Fraud, by Lois Lowry (Houghton Mifflin). When Uncle Claude visits Louise and Marcus' family, everything changes. Ages 10 to 14.

Ramona Forever, by Beverly Cleary (Morrow). Ramona's mother is pregnant, and Ramona and Beezus show how capable they are. Ages 8 to 12.

The Kite Song, by Margery Evernden (Lothrop, Lee & Shepard Bks.). Jamie's shattered self-image is gradually restored with the help of caring adults. Ages 12 and up.

The Slopes of War: A Novel of Gettysburg, by N. A. Perez (Houghton Mifflin). Fictional and real characters reveal the horrors of war. Ages 12 and up.

Unclaimed Treasures, by Patricia MacLachlan (Harper & Row). Twins Willa and Nicholas spend a memorable summer with Horace. Ages 10 to 12.

Show Me No Mercy: A Compelling Story of Remarkable Courage, by Robert Perske (Abingdon Press). A loving family is struck by a tragedy. Ben, who has Down's syndrome, provides the motivation for recovery. Ages 12 and up.

Animals, People, Places, and Projects

Kids Are Baby Goats, by Janet Chiefari (Dodd, Mead). An interesting text and expressive photos explain all about raising goats. Ages 7 to 10.

Building a House, by Ken Robbins (Four Winds Press). A simple text and clear photos demonstrate the process of building a house. Ages 5 to 9.

One Day in the Alpine Tundra, by Jean Craighead George, illustrated by Walter Gaffney-Kessell (Crowell). Clear prose and fine illustrations describe tundra life during daytime. Ages 10 to 12.

The Moon, by Seymour Simon (Four Winds Press). Excellent photographs enhance this fascinating book about the moon. Ages 7 to 11.

The Elephant Book, by Dennis Pepper (Oxford Univ. Press). Here are poetry, fantasy, fiction, and firsthand stories about elephants. Ages 6 to 10.

As the Waltz Was Ending, by Emma Macalik Butterworth (Four Winds Press). The author tells of her childhood in Vienna, Austria, before and during World War II. Ages 12 and up.

Hands Up!, by Ruth Goode, illustrated by Anthony Kramer (Macmillan). This interesting account of what hands can do provides games, sign language, puppets, and more. Ages 7 to 10.

Water World, by Mary Lee Settle (Dutton). This fascinating book describes the role of water in our lives. Ages 10 to 14.

Beverly Cleary's *Dear Mr. Henshaw* won the 1984 Newbery Medal. It reveals a boy's reactions to his parents' divorce through letters and a diary.

The Animal Shelter, by Patricia Curtis, photographs by David Cupp (Dutton). A fine history describes past and present shelters. Ages 10 to 14.

Puffin, by Naomi Lewis, illustrated by Deborah King (Lothrop, Lee & Shepard Bks.). Glowing pictures help tell the interesting life story of the puffin, a sea bird. Ages 8 to 12.

Being Adopted, by Maxine B. Rosenberg, illustrated by George Ancona (Lothrop, Lee & Shepard Bks.). Three adopted children reveal their feelings and problems. Ages 5 to 9.

Gorilla, by Robert McClung, illustrated by Irene Brady (Morrow). A story about gorilla life also tells of destruction by poachers. Ages 9 to 12.

Awards in 1984 included:

The Newbery Medal for "the most distinguished contribution to American literature for children" was awarded to Beverly Cleary for *Dear Mr. Henshaw.* The Caldecott Medal for children's picture books went to Alice Provensen and Martin Provensen for *The Glorious Flight: Across the Channel with Louis Blériot.* The Mildred L. Batchelder Award cited Viking Press for publishing *Ronia, The Robber's Daughter,* by Astrid Lindgren. Marilyn Fain Apseloff

See also CANADIAN LITERATURE; LITERATURE; POETRY. In WORLD BOOK, see CALDECOTT MEDAL; LITERATURE FOR CHILDREN; NEWBERY MEDAL.

LIVESTOCK. See FARM AND FARMING.

LOS ANGELES

LOS ANGELES saw a busy 1984 in which it hosted the Summer Olympic Games for the first time since 1932, moved ahead of Chicago as the second most populous city in the United States, and revamped plans to construct a subway system.

The Olympic Torch burned atop the Los Angeles Memorial Coliseum as the city hosted the Summer Games from July 28 through August 12 (see OLYMPIC GAMES). On September 13, the Los Angeles Olympic Organizing Committee reported a $150-million surplus. That enabled Los Angeles to abide by a city charter amendment requiring that no public funds be spent on the games.

New Second City. The United States Bureau of the Census reported on April 7 that the estimated population of Los Angeles rose from 2,968,579 in 1980 to 3,022,247 in 1982 — an increase of 1.8 per cent. Thus Los Angeles officially replaced Chicago as the second-largest U.S. city. According to the Census Bureau, Chicago's population fell during the same period from 3,005,072 to 2,997,155.

Metro Rail, a proposed 18-mile (29-kilometer) subway that will link downtown Los Angeles with the suburban San Fernando Valley, ran into funding problems in 1984. Because of those difficulties, the start of construction was delayed.

Local officials were still saying that the system will begin operating during the 1990's. But the Southern California Rapid Transit District, which will construct and operate the line, admitted that there is a shortage of federal funds for Metro Rail. On June 4, the transit district submitted a revised plan that calls for the subway to be built in phases, beginning with a 4-mile (6.4-kilometer) segment.

Police Spying Suit. The City Council on February 22 gave final approval to a $1.8-million settlement in a lawsuit against the Los Angeles Police Department for alleged spying. The American Civil Liberties Union, representing 144 plaintiffs, sued the police department in 1979, claiming that the department had spied on law-abiding citizens. The settlement, which the council said was made to avoid a lengthy lawsuit, also established strict curbs on police intelligence-gathering activities. On November 18, a study ordered by the city accused the police chief and his top aides of trying to cover up improper intelligence activities.

Homes for the Homeless. The Los Angeles County Board of Supervisors voted on Aug. 14, 1984, to acquire surplus government buildings that can be renovated and then leased to private groups to provide inexpensive housing for the county's homeless people. The move came after Los Angeles' homeless poor won two court victories on August 2. The judges in the cases ruled that the county must try harder to house the

Balloons soar into the sky over Los Angeles Memorial Coliseum during the opening ceremonies of the 1984 Summer Olympic Games on July 28.

needy and that the city must stop harassing homeless people forced to sleep on sidewalks or in parks.

A Long-Standing Feud over water rights in the Owens River Valley, 200 miles (320 kilometers) north of Los Angeles in Inyo County, ended on April 18 when the City Council signed an agreement with the Inyo County Board. The pact gives the county an equal say with the city in how much water can be pumped from the valley — the source of 80 per cent of Los Angeles' water.

Municipal and County Elections on June 5 saw incumbents retain their offices in nearly every race. The only exception was in the race for district attorney, in which Robert H. Philibosian, who had been appointed to that office in 1982, was defeated by Los Angeles City Attorney Ira Reiner.

Budgets. On May 23, the City Council approved a $1.9-billion budget for 1984-1985, balancing it by continuing a $127.2-million increase in taxes and fees imposed in 1983. The County Board of Supervisors on June 29 adopted a $6.1-billion spending program that, for the first time in seven years, called for no layoffs or serious reductions in county programs. Victor Merina

See also CITY. In WORLD BOOK, see LOS ANGELES.

LOUISIANA. See STATE GOVERNMENT.

LUMBER. See FOREST AND FOREST PRODUCTS.

LUSINCHI, JAIME (1924-   ), took office as president of Venezuela on Feb. 2, 1984, succeeding Luis Herrera Campíns, after winning the biggest electoral majority in 25 years of Venezuelan democracy. He promised to impose austerity measures to help relieve Venezuela's foreign debt, estimated at $27.5 billion. See VENEZUELA.

Lusinchi was born on May 25, 1924, in Clarines in Anzoátegui state. He studied at the Central University of Venezuela in Caracas, graduating as a doctor of medicine in 1947. As a student, he became head of the university chapter of the Democratic Action Party (AD).

After a 1948 military coup, Lusinchi became a member of the AD's underground resistance to the dictatorship. In April 1952, he was arrested, tortured, and expelled to Argentina. During six years in exile, he lived in Chile, where he became a pediatrician, and in the United States, where he worked at Bellevue Hospital in New York City.

In 1958, after the military dictatorship was ousted, Lusinchi returned to Venezuela and was elected to the Chamber of Deputies. For the next 25 years, he served as the AD's parliamentary leader.

Lusinchi is married to the former Gladys Castillo, who is also a pediatrician. They have five children. Rod Such

LUXEMBOURG. See EUROPE.

MACLAINE, SHIRLEY (1934-   ), received the Academy of Motion Picture Arts and Sciences Award for best actress on April 9, 1984. She won the Oscar for her performance as a demanding mother in *Terms of Endearment*. MacLaine had been nominated five times before, including once for a documentary film on China she produced.

Shirley MacLaine was born Shirley MacLean Beaty on April 24, 1934, in Richmond, Va. She won her first part in a Broadway musical in 1950 at age 16. Her rapid rise in show business began in 1954 when she stepped into the leading role in a Broadway production of *The Pajama Game* after the star of the show was injured.

Her success on Broadway led to her motion-picture debut in *The Trouble with Harry* (1956). Since then, MacLaine has starred in about 40 other films, including *The Apartment* (1960) and *The Turning Point* (1977), for both of which she received Academy Award nominations.

An outspoken feminist, MacLaine has also been active in many political and social causes. In 1973, she led the first delegation of United States women to visit China since 1949. MacLaine has written three books, including the autobiographical best seller *Out on a Limb* (1983).

MacLaine was married to Steve Parker. They have a daughter, Stephanie Sachiko. Barbara A. Mayes

MADAGASCAR. See AFRICA.

MAGAZINE advertising revenues in the United States increased in 1984 by about 18 per cent over 1983's record high, reaching nearly $4.75 billion, and the number of pages of advertising grew by about 8 per cent. The combined circulation per issue of all consumer magazines surveyed by the Audit Bureau of Circulations (ABC) in the United States climbed to a record high of 312 million during the first six months of 1984, up 2.2 per cent over the same period in 1983. The ABC is an organization that issues circulation figures, verified by auditors, for magazines and other publications.

A survey conducted by the Magazine Publishers Association (MPA) and Price Waterhouse & Company indicated that magazines were more profitable in 1983 than in 1982. The magazines' net income for 1983 was 5.88 per cent of revenue.

According to a survey by Mediamark Research, Incorporated, 94 per cent of U.S. adults read magazines, and these people read an average of 9.6 magazine issues per month. The survey indicated that the average magazine reader is 37 years old with at least a high school education.

Awards. The MPA named Walter H. Annenberg, president of Triangle Publications, Incorporated, as the 1984 recipient of the Henry Johnson Fisher Award, the industry's most prestigious honor. The American Society of Magazine Editors presented its National Magazine Awards in April.

"I have this terrible fear of a world run by computer magazines."

Among the winning publications were *Esquire* for single-topic issue; *House & Garden* for design; *The New Republic* for essays and criticism; *New York* for service to the individual; *The New Yorker* for public service; *Seventeen* for fiction; and *Vanity Fair* for reporting. In the category of general excellence, which is presented in four groups according to circulation size, the winners were *The American Lawyer* (under 100,000); *Outside* (100,000 to 400,000); *House & Garden* (400,000 to 1 million); and *National Geographic* (more than 1 million).

New Magazines. Among the magazines introduced in 1984 was *National Geographic Traveler*, a quarterly published by the 96-year-old National Geographic Society and available only to its members. The *Traveler* features stories and photographs about both popular and less well-known places accessible to visitors. The first issue appeared in March.

New England Monthly, introduced in April, is published for residents of Connecticut, Maine, Massachusetts, New Hampshire, Rhode Island, and Vermont. The magazine contains articles on New England business, politics, sports, food, and gardening.

Changes. *U.S. News & World Report* and Boston real estate developer Mortimer B. Zuckerman announced on June 11 that Zuckerman had bought the magazine and the other properties of the company that owned it for $163 million. Zuckerman also owns and publishes *The Atlantic.* The purchase was completed in October.

In June, an investor group including Paul Dietrich, president of the National Center for Legislative Research, and bankers David Simpson and Jerry Green of Kansas City, Mo., bought *Saturday Review* from Jeffrey M. Gluck. The estimated purchase price was $300,000. Gluck publishes the *St. Louis Globe-Democrat.*

In March, Historical Times, Incorporated, acquired *Blair & Ketchum's Country Journal* for an undisclosed eight-figure price. In November, CBS Inc. announced the purchase of 12 magazines, including *Car and Driver* and *Popular Photography*, from Ziff-Davis Publishing Company for $362.5-million, believed to be the highest price ever paid for a group of magazines. Also in November, Australian publisher Rupert Murdoch bought Ziff-Davis' 12 technical and travel publications, including 8 magazines, for $350 million. *The New York Review of Books* was sold in December to Rea Hederman, former executive editor of *The Jackson* (Miss.) *Clarion-Ledger.* The sales price reportedly was about $5 million.   Gloria Ricks Dixon

See also PUBLISHING. In WORLD BOOK, see MAGAZINE.

MAINE. See STATE GOVERNMENT.
MALAWI. See AFRICA.

MALAYSIA. On Feb. 9, 1984, the sultans who reign over 9 of Malaysia's 13 states elected Mahmood Iskandar Al-Haj Ibni Almarhum Sultan Ismail, the sultan of Johor, to be the country's king. Under Malaysia's unique system of rotating kingship, the sultans elect one of their number to be king for five years. Mahmood was the most senior of those who had not yet held that office.

Prime Minister Mahathir bin Mohamed lobbied against Mahmood, who had opposed his efforts to limit the power of the king. Mahathir's efforts ended in failure on January 9 and 10, when revision of the Constitution let the king retain more authority than the prime minister liked.

The Constitutional Amendments give the king 30 days to consider legislation passed by Parliament. He can send back bills he dislikes, delaying their passage. However, bills can become law without the king's signature if they are repassed by a two-thirds vote of Parliament. The king also retains the power to declare national emergencies, which Mahathir wanted for the prime minister.

Mahathir won a strong endorsement on May 25 from his party, the United Malays National Organization. Those who had opposed him in the struggle to curb the king's powers were dropped from the party's 27-member council.

Deputy Prime Minister Musa Hitam won another term as Mahathir's deputy party leader, defeating Finance Minister Razaleigh Hamzah. On July 14, Mahathir moved Razaleigh to the less important post of minister of trade and industry. The new finance minister was Daim Zainuddin, a wealthy lawyer and property developer with little previous political experience. Ahmad Rithauddeen bin Ismail replaced veteran Foreign Minister Muhammad Ghazali bin Shafie.

Efforts to Tighten Control of the press continued with passage on March 28 of a law permitting the government to ban the printing, distribution, and possession of any publication considered harmful to the nation's interest. The move reflected Mahathir's belief that the press had reported the constitutional crisis and other issues unfairly.

Economic Problems surfaced during 1984, though Malaysia's domestic production continued to increase faster than the world average, and inflation remained low. Finance Minister Daim announced on September 14 that the largest Malaysian bank, which had lost money in Hong Kong property, was being bought by the national oil company. Daim said he wanted to reduce large government deficits by turning more government enterprises over to private business. Henry S. Bradsher

See also ASIA (Facts in Brief Table). In WORLD BOOK, see MALAYSIA.

MALDIVES. See ASIA.

MALI. See AFRICA.

MALTA. See EUROPE.

MANITOBA. Premier Howard Pawley's New Democratic Party government in February 1984 was forced to abandon its effort to pass a bill restoring language rights to Manitoba's 60,000 French-speaking citizens. Progressive Conservative Party members of the provincial legislature blocked passage of the measure by walking out of 12 consecutive legislative sittings. Premier Pawley reluctantly announced the end of the 14-month legislative session on February 27. This left no possibility of a provincial settlement of the issue.

On February 24, the federal Parliament had passed a resolution repeating its October 1983 request that Manitoba restore French-language rights, which had been revoked in 1890. On April 5, the federal government referred the matter to the Supreme Court of Canada, asking the court to declare invalid all Manitoba laws that had been passed only in English. The Supreme Court began to hear arguments in the case on June 11.

The Pawley government announced on June 14 a hydroelectric power sale to Northern States Power Company of Minnesota. The agreement, subject to approval by the National Energy Board, provides for power sales worth $3.2 billion (Canadian dollars; $1 = U.S. 76 cents as of Dec. 31, 1984) between 1993 and 2004. David M. L. Farr

See also CANADA. In WORLD BOOK, see MANITOBA.

MANUFACTURING in the United States continued to recover in 1984 from the recession that ended in 1982. Production and profits surpassed even the most optimistic projections, especially in the first half of 1984. The gross national product — total goods and services produced — expanded at a dizzying 10.1 per cent annual rate in the first quarter, and at a 7.1 per cent annual rate in the second quarter, before slowing substantially to a 1.6 per cent annual rate in the third quarter. Although the rate of growth slowed, declining interest rates pointed to sustained growth for the fourth quarter of 1984 and on into 1985. "This has been the strongest recovery in the postwar period," exulted Secretary of Commerce Malcolm Baldrige.

Unemployment, which had been at a post-depression high of 10.8 per cent in December 1982 and was 8.2 per cent in December 1983, dropped to 7.2 per cent in December 1984. Manufacturing employment, however, was still more than 600,000 jobs below the prerecession pace it had achieved in July 1981, according to the Department of Labor. The biggest growth in jobs was in trade and service industries, which were not hampered by foreign competition and swings in inventory, unlike manufacturing.

One indication of the changing face of manufacturing was the emergence of electronics and re-

Technicians prepare a weather satellite for testing inside a special
chamber opened by RCA Astro-Electronics in East Windsor, N.J., in May.

lated industries as the largest manufacturing employers. An estimated 2.3 million people worked
at 2,700 electronics companies, according to the
American Electronics Association. Manufacturing
employment in electronics was up 10 per cent in
1983 alone. Transportation equipment is the second biggest manufacturing employer, with just
under 2 million jobs.

Business Inventories were up for manufacturers, wholesalers, and retailers. Inventories rose 0.8
per cent in October 1984 to $565.3 billion, accord-
ing to the Department of Commerce. That followed a 0.9 per cent increase in inventories in September. The ratio of inventories to sales for all
businesses continued to rise during 1984, from
1.32 in June to 1.38 in October. This ratio reflects
the amount of unsold goods on retail shelves and
in warehouses. The higher the number, the more
unsold goods are tied up in factory inventories.
Late in 1984, as the economy slowed, producers
built inventory more slowly than earlier in the
year, when they increased production in anticipation of greater consumer demand for their goods.

New Factory Orders fell 2.5 per cent in October,
the steepest decline since April, to a seasonally adjusted $185.08 billion, a sign of a slowing econ-
omy. The drop was the third in as many months.
Included in the decline was a 9.3 per cent drop in
orders for nondefense capital goods — buildings,

machinery, and tools — which indicated a reduction in business investment for new plants and
equipment.

Orders for durable goods — products that are
intended to last more than three years, such as automobiles, furniture, and machinery — dropped
3.5 per cent during October to $95.21 billion. The
biggest decline was in machinery, with orders for
electrical machinery off 14.6 per cent, mainly due
to weak demand for communications equipment
and electronics parts. Orders for transportation
equipment slipped 1.3 per cent, after an 11.9 per
cent drop in September. The only increase was in
primary metals, which were up 2.5 per cent, notably because of an increased demand for steel.
Orders for nondurable goods — such as clothing,
chemicals, paper, and food — were down 1.4 per
cent to $89.86 billion.

Capital Spending Plans normally pick up when
an economic recovery gathers steam, and 1984 fit
this scenario perfectly. Capital investments, as
measured in 1972 dollars, totaled $144.66 billion
after adjusting for inflation, shattering the previous record high of $141.35 billion in 1981. Sec-
retary of Commerce Baldrige called the 13.3 per
cent increase over 1983 the largest annual increase
since a 15.2 per cent spurt in 1966. Capital spending had fallen by 3.6 per cent in 1983 and 6.2 per
cent in 1982, after adjusting for inflation.

Consumer 'demand for products resulted in strong sales volumes, and that, in turn, gave companies money to invest in capital equipment. Liberal tax incentives for capital spending through the Economic Recovery Tax Act of 1981, which allowed for faster depreciation of equipment, was also a factor in the upturn. Much of the investment in 1984 was in equipment that would modernize plants and reduce production costs. An example was General Electric Company's $100-million investment in automated production lines to build dishwashers, which reduced production costs by10 per cent.

U.S. Factories ran at 81.9 per cent of capacity in November, down from a peak of 82.7 per cent in July and 82.6 per cent in August, according to the Board of Governors of the Federal Reserve System. The average rate for 1984 was 82 per cent, up considerably from the 75 per cent average in 1983.

Production gains, which had been greatest early in 1984, slowed in August. Overall production fell 0.6 per cent in September, the first monthly decline since November 1982. Defense production remained steady throughout 1984, rising at an annual rate of 12 per cent in real terms.

Productivity — output per hours worked — has become an increasingly important factor in manufacturing, as labor costs rise. Nonfarm productivity dropped 0.7 per cent in the third quarter, the first quarterly decline in more than two years. Overall productivity for 1984, however, was up 2.5 per cent over 1983.

Productivity normally rises in the early stages of a recovery and slacks off as more workers are hired. With increasing automation in factories, manufacturing productivity has outpaced other industries in the last two years, increasing at an annual 5.1 per cent average, compared with the overall 2.8 per cent average. Some economists noted that the United States has closed the gap in manufacturing output costs against foreign competitors. Output costs in U.S. manufacturing are now only 10 per cent higher than Japan's and 15 per cent higher than those of continental Europe.

Wages continued to rise at a slow rate in 1984, as inflation remained under control. Unionized workers averaged $17.02 per hour, including benefits and cost-of-living adjustments, versus $12.44 for nonunion workers, according to the American Federation of Labor and Congress of Industrial Organizations (AFL-CIO). Raises through September averaged a relatively low 4.1 per cent for union and 5.2 per cent for nonunion workers.

Research and Development (R & D) outlays increased about 2.9 per cent to $96.9 billion in 1984, compared with $94.2 billion in 1983, according to the National Science Foundation and Battelle Columbus Laboratories, an independent research concern. Since 1973, real R & D has increased an average of 3.71 per cent a year.

Machine Tool builders improved their situation in 1984, after experiencing the worst year in the industry's modern history in 1983. Business in 1984 was strong but not booming. Orders were up 83 per cent in the first three quarters to $2.16 billion. Orders for October 1984 stood at $283.5 million, down 0.9 per cent from September's $286.2-million, but up from $202.6 million in October 1983. Domestic orders were still far below early 1980 levels, which averaged more than $500 million per month.

Imports continued to hurt the machine tool industry. They represented 42 per cent of U.S. consumption. Many U.S. machine tool companies are moving some manufacturing operations to other countries. Employment in the industry, which was about 120,000 before the recession began in 1981, dropped to about 60,000 in 1984.

Rubber. The automobile industry was back in a big way in 1984, but the good times did not spill over to the rubber industry. Sales for tire makers were flat due to strong competition in the domestic replacement-tire market and weaknesses in the farm equipment and large construction machinery markets. Low-priced tire imports meant that U.S. tire makers kept their prices low to remain competitive. Nevertheless, Firestone Tire & Rubber Company reported third-quarter profits of 55 per cent over the same period in 1983, as did B. F. Goodrich Company, 81 per cent; Uniroyal Incorporated, 82 per cent; and Goodyear Tire & Rubber Company, 4 per cent. Many of these companies have diversified to include chemicals, fabrics, and other products to avoid sole reliance on the auto industry for their business.

Electrical Equipment sales enjoyed a real overall increase of 9.9 per cent in 1984, a return to pre-recession levels, according to the National Electrical Manufacturers Association. The strong economic recovery pushed sales well ahead of last year's 1.9 per cent growth rate. The largest gains were made in sales of industrial electrical equipment, which were up 14.4 per cent, and of wire and cable, up 14.3 per cent.

Paper and Paperboard sales were up 7 per cent in 1984 over the previous record high, which was established in 1983. Paper and forest products companies' sales and profits finally rebounded in 1984 after four years of decline. The industry's third-quarter profits were up 68 per cent over the same period in 1983.   Ronald Kolgraf

In WORLD BOOK, see MANUFACTURING.
MARINE CORPS, U.S. See ARMED FORCES.
MARYLAND. See STATE GOVERNMENT.
MASSACHUSETTS. See STATE GOVERNMENT.
MAURITANIA. See AFRICA.
MAURITIUS. See AFRICA.

MEDICINE

MEDICINE. There were two major developments in heart surgery in 1984. On October 26, surgeons at Loma Linda University Medical Center in California transplanted a baboon heart into a 15-day-old girl born with a fatal heart defect. The infant, known as Baby Fae, weighed about 5 pounds (2.3 kilograms) when she was born three weeks prematurely. Loma Linda doctors said she was the smallest human being ever to get a heart transplant. Baby Fae, who died on November 15 — 21 days after the transplant — was the longest-surviving human recipient of an animal heart. The operation stirred much controversy. Some critics opposed using animals for transplants into human beings. Some medical researchers questioned the ethics of performing such a highly experimental operation on a human being.

On November 25, William J. Schroeder, aged 52, became the second human being to receive a permanent artificial heart. The surgery was performed by a 17-member team headed by William C. DeVries at the Humana Heart Institute International in Louisville, Ky. DeVries had performed the first artificial heart implant at the University of Utah in Salt Lake City in December 1982 on Barney B. Clark, who lived for 112 days after the surgery. Both hearts were designed by bioengineer Robert K. Jarvik, also of the University of Utah.

A Boston plastic surgeon in August holds up a sample of "test-tube" skin grown in laboratory culture to provide grafts for burn victims.

DeVries had left the university earlier in 1984, claiming there was too much "red tape" involved in trying to get permission to do artificial heart implants. Humana, a private institution, promised to underwrite the cost of about 100 such operations.

"Test-Tube" Skin. Doctors at Massachusetts General Hospital in Boston on August 15 reported the first successful use of a dramatic new technique for saving victims of extensive burns, one of the most difficult of all medical conditions to treat. The new technique involves covering burned areas of the victim's body with sheets of "test-tube skin," grown in the laboratory from tiny patches of unburned skin removed from the patient. Plastic surgeon G. Gregory Gallico III, who heads the project, said the test-tube skin saved two children who faced almost certain death from burns covering 97 per cent of their bodies.

The boys — 7-year-old Glen Selby and his 6-year-old brother, Jamie, of Casper, Wyo. — were burned while using a solvent to remove paint they had playfully smeared on their bodies. Realizing that the boys had no other chance for survival, Gallico and his team removed tiny pieces of unburned skin from each brother and, in the laboratory, used cell culture techniques to grow about 1 square yard (0.84 square meter) of new skin for each boy. The new skin then was grafted onto the boys in a series of surgical operations that took several months. Physicians said the technique could substantially improve the care of the roughly 15,000 Americans who suffer extensive burns each year. The new technique also may be used in the treatment of accident victims and others needing large skin grafts to cover wounds.

Taming Tests. The Blue Cross and Blue Shield Association on June 13 announced new guidelines to discourage unnecessary use of costly medical diagnostic tests. The tests include X rays, computerized X-ray scans known as CT scans, thermograms, ultrasound scans, and other procedures that produce images of structures inside the body. Bernard R. Tresnowski, president of Blue Cross and Blue Shield, said physicians ordered about 200 million diagnostic images during 1983 at a cost of $7 billion. In 1985 — after a yearlong educational program to convince physicians not to overuse such diagnostic methods — Blue Cross and Blue Shield will begin refusing to pay for X rays and other imaging procedures that do not meet the new guidelines.

Research Advances. The head of the American Diabetes Association (ADA) on September 13 told millions of diabetics not to expect immediate benefits from highly publicized research in which scientists cured diabetes in dogs. The research was done at the University of Miami School of Medicine in Florida, where doctors transplanted islet cells to diabetic dogs. Islet cells are insulin-produc-

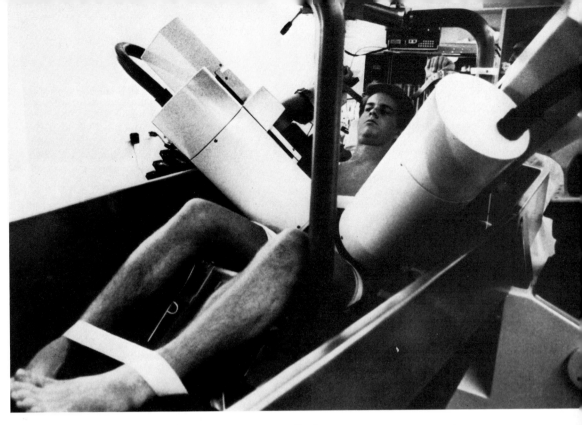

A kidney stone patient undergoes shock-wave treatment, approved by the FDA in December, that shatters the stone without damaging tissue.

ing cells in the pancreas. Karl E. Sussman, president of the ADA, said that many scientists around the world were working on islet cell transplantation. But he said much additional research will be necessary to determine whether the technique holds any promise for human diabetics.

The first treatment to prevent or suppress recurring attacks of genital herpes was announced on June 13 by medical researchers with the National Institute of Allergy and Infectious Diseases in Bethesda, Md., an agency of the National Institutes of Health (NIH). The new treatment involves daily administration of acyclovir, a drug already being used to treat acute attacks of the sexually transmitted disease. Researchers said the treatment is expected to primarily benefit patients with severe cases of genital herpes who are troubled by frequent outbreaks of sores.

Researchers at Boston University in October reported the discovery of a substance that seems to make blood vessels grow. Stimulating growth of new blood vessels could limit damage from heart attacks and strokes and aid in the healing of injuries.

Ultrasound and Blood Warnings. An expert advisory panel convened by the NIH on February 8 warned against the routine use of ultrasound scans to produce images of the fetus in pregnant women. The panel said that ultrasound scans should be performed only when there is a specific medical reason. Because the safety and benefits of ultrasound have not been established, the NIH panel advised doctors to avoid making ultrasound scans a routine part of prenatal care. The 14 experts on the panel emphasized that there is no direct evidence that ultrasound harms the fetus, but they added that lingering uncertainties about the technique's safety and effectiveness demand restrictions on its use.

Another NIH advisory panel on September 26 recommended that federal health officials act to limit the growing use of transfusions of fresh-frozen plasma. The panel found that about 700,000 patients now receive transfusions of fresh-frozen plasma each year. Plasma is the pale-yellow fluid that makes up most of the volume of blood. It is separated from other blood components and frozen for storage and later use. Authorities said about 90 per cent of fresh-frozen plasma transfusions are unwarranted. About 10,000 patients each year develop hepatitis and other diseases from unnecessary plasma transfusions. According to the panel, the greatest number of such unnecessary transfusions are given during heart surgery.   Michael Woods

See also DRUGS; HEALTH AND DISEASE; HOSPITAL. In the Special Reports section, see DON'T GAMBLE WITH YOUR HEART. In WORLD BOOK, see MEDICINE.

MENTAL ILLNESS. Results of the most comprehensive survey of mental illness ever conducted in the United States were released on Oct. 2, 1984, by the National Institute of Mental Health (NIMH) in Bethesda, Md. The study, which cost $15 million and surveyed nearly 10,000 people, concluded that almost 20 per cent of U.S. adults — about 29.4 million people — suffer mental disorders. One of the most surprising findings was that psychiatric problems occur with about equal frequency among men and women. The study did determine that certain mental disorders, such as phobias and depression, occur more often among women. But it found that other psychiatric problems, such as drug and alcohol abuse and antisocial behavior, are more frequent among men.

Psychiatrist Darrel A. Regier, who headed the study, said it also revealed that Americans suffer from a surprisingly high incidence of anxiety disorders, which include common anxiety, phobias, panic attacks, and compulsive behavior. The study found that anxiety disorders affect about 8.3 per cent of all U.S. adults.

The next most common mental disorder identified in the NIMH study was drug and alcohol abuse, affecting about 6.4 per cent of all U.S. adults. Mood disorders, including major depression and manic depression, affect about 6 per cent of the adult population. Schizophrenia, a severely disabling form of mental illness, affects about 1 per cent of American adults.

Street People. The American Psychiatric Association (APA) in Washington, D.C., on September 12 urged establishment of a nationwide system to care for homeless mentally ill men and women cast adrift in society as a result of efforts to discharge patients from state mental hospitals. The APA said the practice of moving mentally ill patients out of institutions and into community treatment programs — called *deinstitutionalization* — is basically sound. But a major study sponsored by the APA found that communities have not carried out deinstitutionalization properly. As a result, mentally ill patients have been left without adequate treatment.

According to the APA report, so many of these patients lack such basic necessities as proper food, clothing, and shelter that the situation is "a major societal tragedy." The study estimated that up to 1 million mentally ill people in the United States are homeless — drifting from city to city, sleeping in alleys or on heating grates.

The Risks of Grief. A panel of authorities on death reported on September 19 that the psychological impact of the death of a close family member may increase the risk of mental and physical

"There's nothing I can do for you – you *are* a duck."

Noel Ford in *Punch*

illness among the 8 million Americans who experience such bereavement each year. The panel was organized by the Institute of Medicine of the National Academy of Sciences, the agency that advises the federal government on science, technology, and health. The panel found that mental and physical distress caused by bereavement is long-lasting. Symptoms of depression, for example, may persist for a year or longer. Men who have lost their wives face a sharply higher risk of death from accident, heart attack, stroke, and infectious disease during the following year. The increased risk may persist for up to six years among widowers who do not remarry.

The study recommended that doctors and nurses learn more of the counseling skills used by mental health professionals, provide more emotional support for bereaved people, and watch for symptoms that may require professional mental health care.

Insanity Plea. On September 18, the U.S. House of Representatives rejected a bill curbing use of the insanity defense in federal courts. The bill, which had received Senate approval, was introduced in response to John W. Hinckley's acquittal on grounds of insanity in 1982 of attempting to murder President Ronald Reagan.   Michael Woods

See also PSYCHOLOGY. In WORLD BOOK, see MENTAL ILLNESS.

MEXICO. Mexico's President Miguel de la Madrid Hurtado continued to cope in 1984 with growing frustration among Mexican workers who were struggling under an economic austerity program. Prior to the Mexican president's visit to Washington, D.C., on May 14, demonstrators protested against the austerity program. On May 2, during a May Day parade in front of the National Palace in Mexico City, two Molotov cocktails exploded near de la Madrid, but he was not injured.

Labor Opposition. Mexican labor unions, which had been supporters of the de la Madrid administration, were disillusioned with the economic program, which they said was not working. Having accepted wage settlements that failed to keep pace with the cost of living, Mexican workers suffered a further erosion of their real take-home pay as inflation continued to rage. It reached 60 per cent, considerably higher than the government's target of 40 per cent for 1984.

The atmosphere for the Mexican president's visit to Washington was soured on May 15 when syndicated columnist Jack Anderson published allegations that President de la Madrid had amassed a huge personal fortune while in office. The Mexican president's visit to the United States was also marked by a clash with President Ronald Reagan over U.S. policy toward Central America. Reagan sought to stress the threat to the region posed by Communist expansionism. De la Madrid expressed fear that such an attitude could increase conflicts in Central America. During welcoming ceremonies at the White House on May 15, de la Madrid called for a rejection of "interventionist solutions of any kind" and urged use of "the principles and rules of international law." He told a joint session of Congress on May 16 that the conflict in Central America was rooted in poverty and the struggle for social justice.

Conflicts in Central America spilled over into Mexico in 1984. On May 30, the Mexican government announced that it had begun to resettle 46,000 Guatemalan refugees in a single planned community in the Valley of Edzna in Campeche state. The refugees, who fled a crackdown on leftist guerrillas, had been placed in some 80 camps near the Guatemalan border, where they were vulnerable to attack. One of the camps was attacked in April by 200 gunmen wearing Guatemalan Army uniforms. Refugees have reported massacres by the Guatemalan Army, though the Guatemalan government denies the charges.

On May 30, Mexico's leading investigative columnist, Manuel Buendía, was killed by a gunman in Mexico City. Buendía, whose column was published in some 200 newspapers, was shot in the back at point-blank range. It was widely believed that he was slain for one of his many exposés. Shortly before his assassination, Buendía had been writing about alleged corruption within the Mexican Petroleum Workers Union and by the former Mexico City police chief and the former director of Mexico's state-owned oil company. He had also written a book, published in early 1984, called *The CIA in Mexico,* which named U.S. intelligence agents.

Trade Relations. During 1984, the Mexican government pushed for a trade agreement with the United States. The agreement would make it necessary for U.S. companies to prove that Mexican exports harm sales of U.S. products before the U.S. government could impose additional duties that raise the prices of Mexican goods sold in the United States. Mexico also pushed for continued special tariff treatment from the United States, arguing that it still ranks as a developing nation.

Companies based in the United States continued to be reluctant to invest in Mexico during 1984. Many also scaled back their Mexican operations. The exception was the Ford Motor Company, which announced on January 10 that it would invest $500 million to build a factory at Hermosillo in northern Mexico, near the U.S. border. The new plant will produce 100,000 subcompact cars annually.   Nathan A. Haverstock

See also LATIN AMERICA (Facts in Brief Table). In WORLD BOOK, see MEXICO.

MICHIGAN. See DETROIT; STATE GOVERNMENT.

MIDDLE EAST

The evacuation of United States Marine Corps units from Beirut, Lebanon, in February 1984 to ships off the Lebanese coast marked the end of direct American involvement in that country and a return to the customary U.S. role as a liaison between the Arab states and Israel. The evacuation also symbolized the inability of outside forces, particularly the superpowers, to decisively influence the course of events in the Middle East without massive military intervention. And such intervention was an option neither the United States nor the Soviet Union was prepared to exercise. With the United States preoccupied with the 1984 elections and Israel equally preoccupied with internal political and economic problems, there was little momentum among Arab leaders to revive the negotiating process. Any new Middle East peace initiative, they felt, would have to come from the United States after the elections.

War in Lebanon. The departure of the Marines from Beirut, followed by the withdrawal of most of the French, British, and Italian units of the multinational peacekeeping force, became inevitable when the government of Lebanon's President Amin Gemayel proved incapable of knitting the country together under a unified national army. The U.S. Marines in particular became identified in the Lebanese mind with an unrepresentative Christian Maronite government that refused to share power with other groups and sects. After the Lebanese Army split along sectarian lines in early February, the U.S. contingent found itself under fire from Druse, Shiite Muslim, and even some Sunni Muslim militias.

The withdrawal of the last of the multinational peacekeeping units on March 31 still left Syrian and Israeli forces in Lebanon. The Israelis occupied southern Lebanon, and the Syrians held the eastern Bekaa Valley, near the Lebanon-Syria border. Prodded by Syrian negotiators, Gemayel on March 5 unilaterally canceled the May 1983 Lebanese-Israeli troop withdrawal "agreement" arranged by U.S. Secretary of State George P. Shultz. Gemayel said the pact had been made under duress and violated the Arab policy of refusing to deal directly with Israel.

Lebanese-Israeli Talks. One of the conditions set by Gemayel's political opponents for an end to sectarian strife was that Israeli troops be withdrawn

With Iraqi tanks burning behind them, Iranian soldiers push through barbed wire during their assault on Iraq's Majnoon Islands in 1984.

Scene of Conflicts

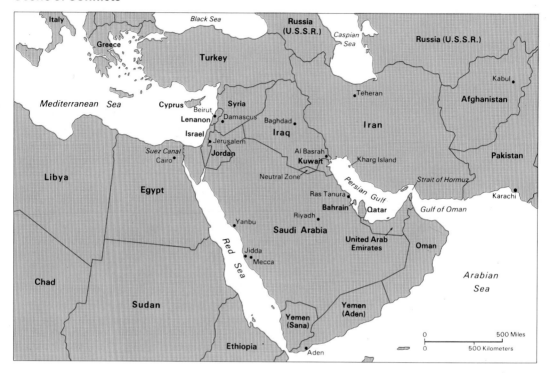

from Lebanon. Negotiations began on November 8 between Lebanese and Israeli military representatives in the south Lebanese village of Naqura. Although both sides were eager to end the Israeli occupation, their negotiating positions were far apart. Lebanon demanded $10 billion in war reparations and full Lebanese Army control of south Lebanon, with the Israelis to withdraw in stages. Israel insisted that south Lebanon be controlled by the Lebanese South Army, an Israeli-trained and Israeli-financed militia in southern Lebanon.

Anti-Americanism. The Marines and the heavy-handed U.S. policy they seemed to represent encouraged a backlash of terrorism directed at U.S. installations and civilians in Lebanon. The president of the American University of Beirut, Malcolm H. Kerr, was murdered on January 18; a number of American residents were kidnapped; and on September 20, the relocated U.S. Embassy in Aukar, near Beirut, was blown up by a suicide truck-bomber, killing at least 14 people. A shadowy, reportedly pro-Iranian group called Holy War claimed responsibility for the bombing. The embassy staff was reduced to about 30 people after the attack, and U.S. President Ronald Reagan admitted that incomplete security arrangements had been a factor in the bombing.

The Iran-Iraq War entered its fifth year in September 1984 with no progress toward a settlement

in sight. Radio broadcasts beamed between the two neighbors indicated their uncompromising positions. Iranian broadcasts referred to Iraq's President Saddam Hussein as "the tyrant of Baghdad." Iraq, in turn, described Iran as a "nest of charlatans and jugglers." Each side accused the other of heresy against Islam.

Ground action in the war was limited to two Iranian offensives, in February and October. In the first offensive, Iranian commandos seized the Majnoon Islands, the site of an important Iraqi oil field, north of Basra. But a lack of airpower, along with effective Iraqi resistance, kept Iran from exploiting its success. Iraq's arsenal, on the other hand, was strengthened with the addition of Soviet SS-12 missiles, plus new Soviet tanks and fighter aircraft.

Gulf Attacks. Iraq's new weaponry and the deadlock on the ground prompted Iraq to raise the stakes in late February. It blockaded Iranian ports and staged a series of missile attacks on ships in the Persian Gulf and the Strait of Hormuz going to and from Iranian oil terminals. The Iraqis hoped to cut off Iran's oil-exporting ability, discourage tanker traffic to Iranian ports, and, presumably, force Iran to negotiate. Iran responded by attacking neutral ships off the coasts of Saudi Arabia and Kuwait.

By September, 45 tankers had been damaged,

and Iranian exports were down 50 per cent. In July, Iraq temporarily called off the attacks and threatened to destroy the main Iranian oil export terminal at Kharg Island. The threat was not carried out. In October, Iranian forces attacked Iraqi positions north of Baghdad, Iraq's capital. In December, Iraq resumed attacks on Iran-bound tankers.

U.S.-Iraq Relations. An interest in winning additional allies and aid for its hard-pressed economy led Iraq on November 26 to announce the resumption of diplomatic relations with the United States after a 17-year break. Iraq hoped that renewed relations would ensure U.S. help for a proposed pipeline that would carry Iraqi oil across Jordan to the Gulf of Aqaba.

Soviet Gains. The Soviet Union was no more successful than the United States in influencing regional affairs directly. But the way the Reagan Administration handled the situation in Lebanon, along with the strong U.S. commitment to Israel, enabled the Soviets to make some political gains. In March, the Soviets agreed to help Syria build that country's first nuclear power plant and to provide an electronic defense system to match a satellite-aided communications network provided to Israel by the United States. The number of Soviet advisers in Syria rose to 7,000.

In July, Egypt resumed full diplomatic relations with the Soviet Union for the first time since 1981. Egyptian President Hosni Mubarak declared that the Soviets should be included in any Middle East settlement conference. Kuwait ordered $327 million in Soviet weapons in August. The deal included 10 Soviet training advisers, the first such advisers to be sent to Kuwait. In October, the Soviets signed a 20-year friendship treaty with Yemen (Sana), where in July oil was found for the first time.

The War in Afghanistan between the government of Revolutionary Council President Babrak Karmal and its Soviet allies and Afghan *mujahedeen* (fighters for the faith) ground on in 1984, though the Soviet occupation seemingly did not affect Soviet relations with various Muslim Arab governments. Some 15,000 to 20,000 Soviet troops carried out a major offensive in April in the Panjshir Valley northeast of the Afghan capital of Kabul, the base of the most effective mujahedeen commander, Ahmad Shah Massoud. Soviet forces occupied the lower parts of the valley but were unable to destroy Massoud's forces, which regrouped in the high mountains and resumed their guerrilla tactics.

Although stopping short of all-out support for the mujahedeen, the United States denounced the Soviet occupation and criticized the Soviet Union

Americans and Lebanese view the damage to the U.S. Embassy near Beirut after a terrorist bomb in September killed at least 14 people.

Facts in Brief on Middle Eastern Countries

Country	Population	Government	Monetary Unit*	Foreign Trade (million U.S. $) Exports†	Imports†
Bahrain	401,000	Amir Isa bin Sulman Al-Khalifa; Prime Minister Khalifa bin Sulman Al-Khalifa	dinar (1 = $2.65)	3,789	3,614
Cyprus	652,000	President Spyros Kyprianou (Turkish Republic of Northern Cyprus: Acting President Rauf R. Denktaş)	pound (1 = $1.62)	494	1,219
Egypt	47,395,000	President Hosni Mubarak; Prime Minister Kamal Hasan Ali	pound (1 = $1.27)	3,120	9,078
Iran	44,255,000	President Ali Khamenei; Prime Minister Hosein Musavi-Khamenei	rial (92.6 = $1)	12,587	12,549
Iraq	15,463,000	President Saddam Hussein	dinar (1 = $3.22)	9,795	10,761
Israel	4,267,000	President Chaim Herzog; Prime Minister Shimon Peres	shekel (586 = $1)	4,931	8,386
Jordan	3,568,000	King Hussein I; Prime Minister Ahmed Obeidat	dinar (1 = $2.48)	579	3,030
Kuwait	1,798,000	Amir Jabir al-Ahmad al-Sabah; Prime Minister & Crown Prince Saad Al-Abdullah Al-Sabah	dinar (1 = $3.32)	16,298	6,969
Lebanon	2,929,000	President Amin Gemayel; Prime Minister Rashid Karami	pound (7.7 = $1)	560	3,052
Oman	1,038,000	Sultan Qaboos bin Said	rial (1 = $2.89)	4,058	2,492
Qatar	287,000	Amir & Prime Minister Khalifa bin Hamad Al-Thani	riyal (3.6 = $1)	3,384	1,456
Saudi Arabia	10,818,000	King & Prime Minister Fahd ibn Abd al-Aziz Al Saud	riyal (3.6 = $1)	79,118	40,654
Sudan	21,191,000	President & Prime Minister Gaafar Mohamed Nimeiri	pound (1.3 = $1)	624	1,354
Syria	10,835,000	President Hafiz al-Assad; Prime Minister Abd al Ra'uf al-Kassem	pound (3.9 = $1)	2,026	4,015
Turkey	49,728,000	President Kenan Evren; Prime Minister Turgut Ozal	lira (400 = $1)	5,694	9,348
United Arab Emirates	1,263,000	President Zayid bin Sultan Al-Nahayyan; Prime Minister Rashid ibn Said al-Maktum	dirham (3.7 = $1)	16,836	9,419
Yemen (Aden)	2,267,000	Supreme People's Council Presidium Chairman & Council of Ministers Chairman Ali Nasir Muhammad	dinar (1 = $2.91)	740	1,449
Yemen (Sana)	6,531,000	President Ali Abdallah Salih; Prime Minister Abdel Aziz Abdel Ghani	rial (5.8 = $1)	47	1,758

*Exchange rates as of Dec. 1, 1984, or latest available data.   †Latest available data.

for using brutality and terror tactics against Afghan civilians. The bombing of villages and strafing of refugee caravans drove some 3 million Afghan refugees into neighboring Pakistan. For the fiscal year beginning Oct. 1, 1984, the Congress of the United States authorized $280 million in aid to the mujahedeen, for a total of $625 million since the Soviets invaded Afghanistan in 1979.

The Israeli-Occupied West Bank remained a back-burner issue during 1984, largely because of the disarray of the Palestine Liberation Organization (PLO) and Israel's preoccupation with elections. One encouraging sign was the willingness of the Israeli government to prosecute alleged Jewish terrorists for violence against Palestinians living on the West Bank. In May, Israeli security forces charged 25 Jews with belonging to an underground terrorist organization that had staged car-bombing attacks on West Bank Arab mayors in 1980 and other acts of violence.

Weakened PLO. Despite its continued appeal to Palestinians, the PLO was largely ineffective as a political organization during 1984. During the year, some PLO members drifted back to Lebanon, from which the organization had been expelled in 1982. But the majority remained scattered in various Arab countries. The largest group, 12,000 members, was in Syria under Syrian command, with another 4,000 in Syrian-controlled territory in eastern Lebanon.

A further difficulty was caused by fighting among various PLO groups. PLO leader Yasir Arafat, after many delays, convened a meeting in November of the Palestine National Council, the PLO's policymaking body. The meeting was boycotted by Syrian-backed factions, but a majority of the delegates voted to continue backing Arafat.

Red Sea Mines. In July, August, and September, mysterious attacks on ships in the Red Sea threatened to disrupt traffic through the Suez Canal. About 20 ships were damaged by what were thought to be underwater mines. In early August, the United States sent minesweeping helicopters to help Egypt clear the Red Sea. France, Great Britain, Italy, and the Soviet Union also joined in the effort. In mid-September, the British and French reported finding two unmarked minelike devices. No other mines were found.

At first, Egypt blamed Libya and Iran for the incident. After Iranian leader Ayatollah Ruhollah Khomeini denounced the attacks, however, Egypt backed away from its charges of Iranian involvement and laid the blame solely on Libya.

The Islamic extremist group Holy War claimed responsibility for the explosions, saying they were intended to punish "imperialists" for their support of Iraq. Because the attacks caused no serious damage, there was speculation they were intended chiefly to disrupt traffic through the Suez Canal, a major source of income for Egypt.

Libyan Fence-Mending. With the United States and Israel both absorbed in domestic issues, the Arab states did some fence-mending. Despite accusations about Libya's role in the Red Sea mining, Libya's Muammar Muhammad al-Qadhafi was the most active Arab leader. Libya's border with Egypt was reopened in April, and diplomatic relations with Jordan, broken off in February when the Jordanian Embassy in Tripoli, Libya's capital, was set afire, were restored in September.

The most surprising Qadhafi action was an agreement with King Hassan II of Morocco, announced in August, to unify their two states. Under the agreement, both states would retain their separate governmental institutions but work toward an eventual joint legislative council.

In September, Qadhafi and French President François Mitterrand agreed on a joint withdrawal of Libyan and French troops from Chad. But the Libyan leader failed to live up to the agreement. As of December, 3,000 Libyan troops were still in Chad.   William Spencer

See also KARAMI, RASHID; PERES, SHIMON; and articles on the various Middle Eastern countries. In WORLD BOOK, see MIDDLE EAST and individual Middle Eastern country articles.

Egypt's President Mubarak, right, reviews Jordanian troops with King Hussein in October during the first trip to Jordan by an Egyptian leader since 1979.

MINING. President Ronald Reagan on Sept. 6, 1984, refused to impose import restrictions or raise tariffs to protect United States copper-mining companies from financial damage caused by low-priced imported copper. The International Trade Commission, a federal agency that oversees U.S. trade laws, recommended such protection. The commission found that the U.S. copper-mining industry had been damaged by copper imported from such countries as Chile, Peru, and Zaire, where mines receive government subsidies.

In announcing Reagan's decision, William E. Brock, U.S. special trade representative, said U.S. import restrictions could reduce the ability of other countries to buy goods from the United States. He also said that such restrictions would raise the price of copper goods in the United States, causing the loss of more factory jobs than would be saved in copper mines. The decision caused dismay in the copper-mining industry.

Production Cutbacks. Phelps Dodge Corporation, one of the largest copper producers in the United States, announced on August 6 that it was suspending operations for at least three months at its mine in Ajo, Ariz. The company cited low copper prices and overproduction by countries with government-owned copper mines as reasons for the cutback. The action idled about 500 miners. On August 7, the Arizona Mining Association in Phoenix said that about half of all copper miners in that state had lost their jobs since 1981. Kennecott Corporation, the largest U.S. copper producer, cut production at its huge Bingham Canyon mine in Utah by two-thirds on July 1.

Strip-Mining Agreement. The U.S. departments of Justice and the Interior on October 16 agreed to speed up the collection of overdue fines totaling as much as $150 million from strip-mine operators who violated environmental protection laws. The agreement settled a lawsuit brought by environmental groups who charged that the Interior Department had failed to fully enforce strip-mining laws. The department said on April 6 that it would take over enforcement of strip-mining laws and inspection of strip mines in Tennessee and Oklahoma because state enforcement was inadequate.

Cobalt from Copper. The U.S. Bureau of Mines reported on February 28 that it had identified a potential new source of cobalt, a mineral critical for the production of high-strength alloys with a variety of industrial and military uses. Scientists have discovered that when copper ore is treated with acid solutions to dissolve the copper, cobalt in the ore is also dissolved. The bureau said valuable amounts of cobalt can be extracted from such acid solutions, helping reduce U.S. dependence on other countries for the mineral.

New Ventures. Pechiney, a French-owned metals company that is the fourth largest aluminum producer in the West, and its partners in the United States and Canada announced an agreement on March 16 to build a $1.2-billion aluminum smelter in Bécancour, Canada. The South Australia Ministry of Mines on June 12 said that Western Mining Corporation and British Petroleum Australia — the two partners in a big mining project at Roxby Downs — had decided to proceed with development of the $900-million project to produce uranium and copper. On July 10, delegates to the ruling Australian Labor Party's policy-making conference reversed a policy forbidding new uranium mines and approved the project.

Pullout in Jamaica. Reynolds Metals Company on March 5 announced that it would no longer mine bauxite, the ore used to make aluminum, in Jamaica. The Jamaican government said the pullout would disrupt its plans for economic growth.

Diamond Dumping. The American Diamond Industry Association said on October 19 that the Soviet Union was flooding world markets with low-priced diamonds. The association reported that the Soviets were selling diamonds in huge numbers to earn the money needed to buy foreign grain after a poor harvest. Michael Woods

In WORLD BOOK, see MINING.

MINNESOTA. See STATE GOVERNMENT.

MISSISSIPPI. See STATE GOVERNMENT.

MISSOURI. See STATE GOVERNMENT.

MONDALE, WALTER FREDERICK (1928-   ), was the presidential candidate of the Democratic Party in the United States in 1984. Mondale hammered hard against President Ronald Reagan's huge budget deficit and alleged lack of sympathy for the poor, but Reagan easily defeated Mondale in the election. See ELECTIONS.

Mondale made political history on July 12 when he chose Representative Geraldine A. Ferraro as his running mate. She was the first woman ever named to the presidential ticket of a major U.S. political party (see FERRARO, GERALDINE A.).

After surviving a strong challenge from Senator Gary W. Hart (D., Colo.) in the primary race, Mondale won nomination on the first ballot at the Democratic National Convention in San Francisco on July 18. In his acceptance speech, Mondale said that if elected president, he would raise taxes to reduce the federal budget deficit.

In the fall campaign, Mondale faced Reagan in two national televised debates. Mondale's standing in the political polls improved somewhat after the debates, but not enough to affect the outcome of the election.

Mondale was a senator from Minnesota from 1964 to 1976. From 1976 to 1980, he was Jimmy Carter's Vice President. David L. Dreier

MONGOLIA. See ASIA.

MONTANA. See STATE GOVERNMENT.

MONTREAL began to reverse four years of economic decline in 1984. Two major construction projects were announced for the downtown area. They are a controversial $140-million concert hall and commercial center to be built on the southern end of McGill College Avenue and a $50-million project at the avenue's northern end. (All monetary amounts in this article are Canadian dollars, with $1 = U.S. 76 cents as of Dec. 31, 1984.) The projects include an avenue about 100 feet (30 meters) wide bordered by landscaped gardens and walkways where parking lots and shabby storefronts once stood.

Construction on the northern project, known as the Industrial Life Tower, began in July and was expected to be finished in early 1986. Construction on the southern project was to begin in 1985.

Debate on the southern project pitted Mayor Jean Drapeau and the developers, Cadillac Fairview Corporation, against urban planners, the local chamber of commerce, and the academic community. The developers wanted to build on both sides of the avenue, leaving a narrow street under a walkway linking the two sides. A storm of protest led to public hearings, which resulted in planning a wider street. At year's end, however, the fate of the southern project was still unresolved.

A section of Montreal Central Station lies in ruins after a bomb exploded there on September 3, killing 3 people and injuring 29 others.

At year's end, another development project inspired spirited debate in Montreal. This project was a plan to dam the St. Lawrence River at the Lachine Rapids and build a combined park and hydroelectric project called Archipel. Environmentalists had long opposed the plan, but city planners argued that it would provide both energy and recreation opportunities and help keep Montreal's population from declining further.

Defense Contract. Good economic news came to Montreal in the form of a contract to build six destroyers for the Royal Canadian Navy. This contract created about 1,000 new jobs in 1984 and could eventually bring as many as 10,000 new jobs and $10 billion to industries in the area.

The new jobs were welcome in Montreal, which has seen unemployment rates climb above 15 per cent in recent years. In 1984, however, the jobless rate fell to around the national average of 12 per cent of the labor force.

City Government. A month-long strike by city transit workers ended in mid-November with a wage increase and shorter workweek for transit employees. City councilors in September appropriated $547 million to upgrade civic buildings and streets, especially in industrial areas.

It was widely believed that 1984 would be Jean Drapeau's last full year as mayor. Drapeau has served as mayor of Montreal since 1954, except for a three-year interruption from 1957 to 1960. The mayor, frail and enfeebled by a stroke, is not required to call new elections until 1986. However, there were indications in late 1984 that he would step down before then.

If elections are called, Drapeau's Civic Party probably will continue to dominate local politics. Roger D. Landry, publisher of Montreal's largest French daily newspaper, *La Presse,* announced his desire to succeed Drapeau as mayor. Opposing the Civic Party is the left-leaning Montreal Citizens Movement led by lawyer Jean Dore.

Business Scandal. On May 11, Robert Harrison, former president of the Montreal Board of Trade, was arrested on charges of fraud. Harrison fled to Paraguay but returned to face the charges in September. By year's end, his testimony had implicated senior political figures and business leaders, though no charges against them had been proved.

Bomb Blast. On September 3, a bomb exploded in Montreal Central Station, killing 3 people and injuring 29 others. The bombing was thought to be linked with an impending visit by Pope John Paul II, who arrived in Montreal on September 10. Thomas Brigham, a mentally disturbed U.S. veteran who had made threats against the pope, was charged with the attack.   Kendal Windeyer

See also CANADA; QUEBEC. In WORLD BOOK, see MONTREAL.

MOROCCO

MOROCCO. Government-ordered price increases of up to 67 per cent for basic foodstuffs set off a week of rioting in Morocco in January 1984. The increases had been required by the International Monetary Fund, an agency of the United Nations, as a condition for loans to stabilize the economy.

But the price hikes fell heaviest on the poor. The worst violence erupted in the disadvantaged northern region. Officials called in army units to restore order. Casualties were estimated at 60 dead and hundreds injured. In a speech on January 22 announcing that the price increases would be rescinded, King Hassan II accused leftists and followers of Iranian leader Ayatollah Ruhollah Khomeini of provoking the riots.

Underlying Problems. Morocco's food riots underscored a number of underlying social and economic problems. These problems included an unemployment rate of 25 per cent, large foreign trade deficits, and declining world prices for phosphates, one of Morocco's leading exports.

One of the biggest drains on the economy, however, was the war in Western Sahara. During 1984, Morocco gained ground in its struggle against the Polisario Front guerrillas, who have been fighting for independence since Morocco annexed the territory in 1976. In February, Morocco's sand wall, a 9-foot (2.7-meter) wall of sand, stone, barbed wire, and minefields protecting the main towns and phosphate mines of Western Sahara, was extended to the Mauritanian border.

On November 12, Morocco withdrew from the Organization of African Unity to protest that group's 1982 decision to seat delegates claiming to represent the Sahara Arab Democratic Republic in Western Sahara.

Libyan Connection. Hassan also acquired unexpected political support in 1984. On August 13, he signed a pact with Libyan leader Muammar Muhammad al-Qadhafi establishing a union of the two countries. The agreement was approved by a Moroccan national referendum on September 2. As part of the agreement, Libya promised to renounce its support for the Polisario Front. The union would not affect Morocco's sovereignty or change its existing political institutions.

Elections to choose two-thirds of the 306 members of the National Assembly were held on September 14. The promonarchist Constitutional Union won 55 seats, followed by the centrist National Independence Assembly with 38, and the opposition Socialist Union of Popular Forces with 34. Other parties also won seats. The remaining Assembly members are elected by local governments and professional associations. All parties supported the Libyan union and Hassan's Saharan policy.   William Spencer

See also AFRICA (Facts in Brief Table); LIBYA. In WORLD BOOK, see MOROCCO.

MOTION PICTURES

After years of concentrating on urban themes, the motion-picture industry in the United States demonstrated a renewed interest in the American heartland in 1984. Hollywood released three films in as many months that centered on the plight of small farmers. Robert Benton's critically acclaimed *Places in the Heart* featured Sally Field in a film derived from Benton's own memories of growing up in Waxahachie, Tex., during the Great Depression of the 1930's. *Country* and *The River* had contem-

Ghostbusters — starring Bill Murray, left, and Dan Aykroyd, center — earned over $200 million to become the most successful U.S comedy ever.

porary settings. In *Country*, Jessica Lange and playwright-actor Sam Shepard fought to save their Iowa farm from foreclosure. In *The River*, Sissy Spacek and Mel Gibson tried to keep their Tennessee homestead from being taken over by the government.

Comebacks and Failures. One of the most publicized films of 1984 was Francis Ford Coppola's *The Cotton Club*, which had a final budget of $47-million. The motion picture, about a celebrated jazz club in New York City's Harlem, starred Richard Gere. Critics considered *The Cotton Club* Coppola's chance to redeem his reputation as a director following the failures of *One from the Heart* (1982), *The Outsiders* (1983), and *Rumble Fish*

(1983). By early December, the movie looked like a commercial hit and a middling critical success.

Italian director Sergio Leone was less fortunate. Leone's *A Fistful of Dollars* (1964) and *The Good, the Bad, and the Ugly* (1966) had been critical and popular successes. In 1984, he created a massive gangster epic, *Once upon a Time in America*. But the studio cut the film drastically and released it to an indifferent audience response. Critics considered an uncut version, released later, to be superior.

Harrison Ford stars in *Indiana Jones and the Temple of Doom,* a sequel to
Raiders of the Lost Ark (1981) and the second most successful film of 1984.

John Avildsen, who had been floundering since directing 1976's *Rocky*, redeemed himself commercially in 1984 with *The Karate Kid*. The surprise hit closely followed the *Rocky* formula, with the sentimental appeal of rooting for the underdog.

Meanwhile, Sylvester Stallone, the star of all three Rocky movies and the director of *Rocky II* (1979) and *Rocky III* (1982), had one of 1984's most resounding flops with *Rhinestone*. He co-starred with Dolly Parton in the tired comedy.

Director George Roy Hill, whose *Butch Cassidy and the Sundance Kid* (1969) and *The Sting* (1973) rank among Hollywood's most profitable and fondly remembered features, also suffered a setback. He adapted to the screen John le Carré's complicated 1983 best seller *The Little Drummer Girl*. Diane Keaton starred as an actress trained as a terrorist. Despite the novel's reputation, the movie flopped.

Screen Versions of Serious Literature were some of 1984's most successful motion pictures. Czechoslovak-born director Milos Forman enjoyed his first success since 1975's *One Flew over the Cuckoo's Nest* with *Amadeus*. The film was an adaptation of Peter Shaffer's complex, compelling 1979 play about the rivalry between composers Wolfgang Amadeus Mozart and Antonio Salieri.

Director Norman Jewison scored a popular and critical hit with *A Soldier's Story*, based on Charles Fuller's 1983 Pulitzer Prize-winning drama *A Soldier's Play*. The film told a story of racial tensions at an Army base in the U.S. South during World War II. *A Soldier's Story* bore strong resemblances to Jewison's most famous film, *In the Heat of the Night* (1967), which also dealt with racial friction.

Veteran director John Huston, a favorite of many critics since 1941's *The Maltese Falcon*, returned to the top of his form with a relentless adaptation of Malcolm Lowry's 1947 novel *Under the Volcano*. Too depressing to find a wide audience, the film provided new proof of Huston's brilliant sense of atmosphere. The director obtained splendid performances from Albert Finney and Jacqueline Bisset.

Director Barry Levinson gave a glossy treatment to Bernard Malamud's baseball novel *The Natural* (1952). Levinson turned the film into an old-fashioned star vehicle for Robert Redford.

British director David Lean made a highly praised film version of E. M. Forster's 1924 novel *A Passage to India*. The movie, Lean's first since 1970's *Ryan's Daughter*, dealt with the clash between British and Indian culture.

The Year-End Films included several science-fiction offerings. The producers of the eagerly awaited film version of Frank Herbert's 1965 novel *Dune* kept the movie shrouded in secrecy until only a few days before it opened in mid-December. Similar mystery surrounded *2010*, a sequel to Stanley Kubrick's revered 1968 classic, *2001: A Space Odyssey*. Kubrick, however, had no hand in the sequel, which was written, produced, and directed by Peter Hyams. John Carpenter's *Starman* was a gentle and engaging romance between a friendly alien and a young widow. It mixed science-fiction traditions with trappings of old-fashioned "road pictures" like Frank Capra's *It Happened One Night* (1934).

Beverly Hills Cop, another of the year-end films, was not a science-fiction movie, though its hero did find himself in an alien world. Eddie Murphy starred as a tough Detroit detective who travels to posh Beverly Hills to solve a murder.

Ghostbusters emerged unexpectedly as the most commercially successful film of the year, with a gross profit in the United States alone in excess of $200 million. Directed by Ivan Reitman, the film recalled the good-natured goofiness of a Bud Abbott and Lou Costello comedy of the 1940's. Bill Murray's performance as an oversexed scientist who becomes an exorcist propelled him to the top ranks of box-office stars.

Ghostbusters, which also loomed as a smash hit in its first overseas engagements, became the most successful comedy ever released in the United States. The term *busters* became part of American pop culture, appearing in advertising for insecticides ("Roachbusters"), cigarette warnings ("Smokebusters"), and other products.

Gremlins, despite protests over its violence, became the third most popular film of 1984, behind *Ghostbusters* and *Indiana Jones and the Temple of Doom*. It also became a merchandiser's dream. At least 50 manufacturers received licenses from Warner Brothers to make and sell articles bearing likenesses of the creatures in the film. *Gremlins* merchandise included sleepwear, video games, beach towels, greeting cards, and watches.

However, the merchandising bonanza had aftereffects. Warner Brothers eventually had to file a petition with the United States International Trade Commission (ITC), a federal agency that deals with world trade, to bar importation of bogus *Gremlins* articles, many of which were produced in Asia. In an unprecedented move for a film company, the studio asked the ITC to take action against 32 manufacturers, importers, and distributors of unlicensed merchandise using the copyrighted likenesses of the movie's gremlins.

New Rating. The Motion Picture Association of America added a new rating in 1984 for the first time since the advent of the ratings system in 1968. The new PG-13 rating, introduced on July 1, falls between PG (parental guidance suggested)

Sally Field plays a widowed mother who struggles to keep her family's home in *Places in the Heart,* one of 1984's most acclaimed films.

and R (restricted), which prohibits children under 17 from being admitted unless accompanied by a parent or adult guardian. The PG-13 rating is only advisory, but it serves to warn parents that a film includes violence or other content that might be unsuitable for children under the age of 13.

A Public Outcry over Violence in two family-oriented blockbusters, *Indiana Jones* and *Gremlins*, prompted the PG-13 rating. Ironically, Steven Spielberg, the brilliant young director whose films have long championed children, was involved in both. He directed *Indiana Jones* and produced *Gremlins*. Before *Indiana Jones* was released in Great Britain, the studio shortened some of the violent scenes, including the most controversial one, in which a heart is pulled from the chest of a sacrificial victim. British viewers did not see the hand enter the chest and extract the organ.

The biggest public outcry against violence in cinema, however, came at the holiday season. The horror film *Silent Night, Deadly Night* featured a crazed mass murderer in a Santa Claus costume who stabbed his victims while reciting verses of " 'Twas the Night Before Christmas." Opening in the United States just before Thanksgiving, the film drew such an immediate negative response that the studio pulled it from release.

A Record Year at the Box Office brought ticket sales of more than $4 billion in the United States during 1984. The winter months early in the year had proved mildly disappointing, with only 1983's *Terms of Endearment* and *Sudden Impact* emerging as true heavyweights. The spring was unexpectedly profitable, however, with healthy returns coming from *Footloose, Police Academy, Romancing the Stone,* and *Splash.* Summer proved a bonanza with *Ghostbusters, Gremlins,* and *Indiana Jones,* followed by *The Karate Kid, Purple Rain, Red Dawn, Star Trek III: The Search for Spock,* and *Tightrope.*

Feature film production in the United States was up 40 per cent over 1983's pace, with independent productions having a big surge. American film distributors predicted that more than 400 films would be released by the end of 1984.

The Overseas Box-Office Outlook was not as cheerful as that in the United States. In Scandinavia, the scene was strangely mixed. Ticket sales dropped more than 20 per cent in Norway, but film production was up in Denmark, with 15 Danish features expected to premiere during 1984.

Australian box-office results also were disappointing for the entire year, with summer being a particularly bleak period. A lengthy rail strike hurt box-office business, and 10 drive-in theaters closed in Sydney and Melbourne. Ironically, 1984 was the second busiest year ever for Australian film production, with 24 feature films receiving financing under new tax laws that encouraged investment in motion pictures.

Box-office receipts also were disappointing during the first half of 1984 in West Germany. West German exhibitors believed, however, that the year's end would bring an increase in revenue.

Deaths. The death of French director François Truffaut on October 21 was mourned worldwide. Truffaut, the creator of *The 400 Blows* (1959), *Jules and Jim* (1961), and *Stolen Kisses* (1968), was one of the most influential filmmakers of his generation. Such American directors as Spielberg and Robert Benton openly acknowledged their debt to him. Coincidentally, Austrian actor Oskar Werner, who played Jules in *Jules and Jim*, died just two days after Truffaut.

The death of Welsh actor Richard Burton on August 5 rekindled debates regarding celebrity versus artistry. Some critics felt that Burton's notoriety as a high-living, highly paid movie star had detracted from his worth as an artist. Nevertheless, he left behind a legacy of first-rate work.

Another much noted loss was that of director Joseph Losey. His death on June 22 robbed the international film scene of one of its angriest voices.   Philip Wuntch

See also AWARDS AND PRIZES (Arts Awards); DU-VALL, ROBERT; MACLAINE, SHIRLEY. In the Special Reports section, see THE SIGHTS AND SOUNDS OF MUSIC VIDEOS. In WORLD BOOK, see MOTION PICTURE.

MOZAMBIQUE. On March 16, 1984, the government of President Samora Moisés Machel signed a peace treaty with South Africa, its former enemy. The pact stated that neither country would attack the other or allow its territory to be used by forces rebelling against the other.

Since achieving independence in 1975, Mozambique had granted sanctuary to the African National Congress (ANC), the largest black nationalist movement opposing white rule in South Africa. In response, South Africa since 1980 had supported a rebel force, the Mozambique National Resistance (MNR), dedicated to overthrowing the Machel government. By mid-1984, the MNR had an estimated 10,000 troops operating in Mozambique. The MNR's attacks on power stations, railroads, and other targets had weakened the government's ability to provide essential services.

Rebels' Homes Raided. To uphold its half of the treaty, the Machel government on March 25 and 26 raided ANC houses and offices to confiscate weapons. ANC members were given the choice of leaving Mozambique or entering refugee camps. About 800 rebels had reportedly left Mozambique by year-end.

Under the terms of the agreement, South Africa was supposed to take similar steps against the MNR. But MNR attacks continued, and on August 13 Mozambique complained that the rebels were still receiving supplies from South Africa. Tensions eased on October 3, however, when the South African government announced that, with its help, the Machel government and the MNR had negotiated a cease-fire. The agreement provided for recognition of Machel as Mozambique's head of state and for South African troops to police the cease-fire.

Economic Ties. Mozambique also sought to improve its economic relations with South Africa. In a pact signed on May 1, South Africa agreed to buy large quantities of electric power from Mozambique's Cabora Bassa power station and to help protect that installation from MNR sabotage. And an August 13 agreement provided for a $6-million South African loan to develop the harbor at the Indian Ocean port of Maputo.

Mozambique hoped that the cease-fire with the MNR would lead to improved distribution of food in drought-stricken areas of the country. In early June, United Nations officials estimated that about 1.5 million Mozambicans out of a total population of 14 million depended totally on relief supplies for their food. But getting those supplies to the people who needed them had been hindered by MNR attacks on truck convoys, bridges, and food-distribution centers.   J. Dixon Esseks

See also AFRICA (Facts in Brief Table). In WORLD BOOK, see MOZAMBIQUE.

MULRONEY, MARTIN BRIAN (1939-   ), was sworn in as prime minister of Canada on Sept. 17, 1984. He came to office as a result of the landslide victory of his Progressive Conservative Party (PC) in elections on September 4. Mulroney succeeded John N. Turner of the Liberal Party, who had served as prime minister since June 30, when he succeeded Pierre Elliott Trudeau. See CANADA.

Mulroney (pronounced *muhl ROO nay*) was born on March 20, 1939, in Baie-Comeau, Que. He received a bachelor's degree in political science from St. Francis Xavier University in Antigonish, N.S., and a law degree from Laval University Law School in Quebec City, Que.

From 1965 to 1976, Mulroney specialized in labor law with the Montreal law firm of Ogilvy, Renault. In 1974, he was appointed to a commission that investigated crime in Quebec's construction industry. In 1976, he lost his first bid for the PC leadership. He then joined the Iron Ore Company of Canada as vice president and became president and a director of the company in 1977.

Mulroney was elected leader of the PC on June 11, 1983, succeeding former Prime Minister Charles Joseph Clark. On Aug. 29, 1983, Mulroney was elected a member of the House of Commons from central Nova Scotia.   Robie Liscomb

In the WORLD BOOK SUPPLEMENT section, see MULRONEY, MARTIN BRIAN.

MURDOCH, RUPERT (1931-   ), is an Australian publisher who owns about 90 newspapers and magazines in Australia, Great Britain, and the United States. He is known for buying financially struggling papers and turning them into money-makers — often, critics charge, by emphasizing stories about crime and sex.

Keith Rupert Murdoch was born on March 11, 1931, in Melbourne, Australia. His father, Sir Keith Murdoch, was a wealthy newspaper executive. Rupert was educated at Oxford University in Britain, where he earned an M.A. degree in 1953. In 1954, Murdoch took charge of the Adelaide, Australia, *News,* inherited from his father, and soon began to buy other publications.

Murdoch's most extensive holdings are in Australia, where he owns more than 25 newspapers, 2 television networks, a record company, and other concerns. In Britain, his publications range from the respected *Times* of London to the sensational *News of the World.* In the United States, he owns *The Boston Herald,* the Chicago *Sun-Times,* the *New York Post,* and several other papers.

In 1967, Murdoch married Anna Maria Torv, a reporter on one of his Australian papers. They have three children, and Murdoch has one child by a previous marriage. He has lived mainly in the United States since 1974, at homes in New York City and near Albany, N.Y.   Sara Dreyfuss

MUSIC, CLASSICAL. Music's harmonies, enjoyed throughout the world, were interrupted by discord from time to time in 1984. The New York Philharmonic, on a tour of the Far East in August, planned to play Ernest Bloch's *Schelomo,* or *Solomon,* written for cello and orchestra, in Malaysia, a predominantly Muslim country. The Malaysian government objected, however, because of the Jewish theme of the work. The orchestra's management agreed to remove the piece from the program. Then New York City government officials and Jewish organizations objected, so the orchestra asked permission to reinstate the Bloch piece. After Malaysia denied the request, the New York Philharmonic canceled its concerts in Malaysia and performed in Bangkok, Thailand, instead.

In November, a jury in Boston awarded actress Vanessa Redgrave $100,000 in damages, agreeing with her claim that the Boston Symphony Orchestra was guilty of breach of contract for canceling her appearance as the narrator for Igor Stravinsky's *Oedipus Rex* in 1982. But the jury rejected her claim that the orchestra had called off her appearance because of her support for the Palestine Liberation Organization.

Variations on Themes. There was also considerable discord about what mischievously creative directors were doing to traditional operatic masterpieces. Giuseppe Verdi's *Rigoletto* became a

Philip Glass's opera *Akhnaten,* which premiered in March in Stuttgart, West Germany, tells the story of the first Egyptian pharaoh to worship one god.

favorite target. In Jonathan Miller's version, performed by the English National Opera on a tour of the United States, the action shifted from the northern Italian city of Mantua in the 1500's to New York City's "Little Italy" neighborhood in the early 1950's.

At the Florence, Italy, opera house, Soviet expatriate director Yuri Lyubimov dressed the jester, Rigoletto, as a circus clown. And at an East Berlin opera house, *Rigoletto* was performed inside a huge, split-open angel on a turntable. The heroine was seen floating heavenward on wires, and choristers played tennis as they sang.

At the New York City Opera, which celebrated its 40th birthday in 1984, director Frank Corsaro moved the story of Georges Bizet's *Carmen* to 1936 during the bitter Spanish Civil War. In November, producer Joseph Papp introduced an altered *La Bohème,* which composer Giacomo Puccini might not recognize, starring pop singer Linda Ronstadt and country singer Gary Morris at the New York Shakespeare Festival.

Special Events of 1984. Morton Subotnick's staged tone poem *The Double Life of Amphibians* helped open the Olympic Games in Los Angeles.

A previously unknown opera named *Elizabeth* by Gaetano Donizetti, an Italian composer of the 1800's, was discovered by *The New York Times* music critic Will Crutchfield in the basement of

London's Royal Opera House, Covent Garden, and at the National Library in Paris. In June, Wolf Trap Park for the Performing Arts outside Washington, D.C., the home of a summer music festival, opened the new Filene Center.

In December, Christoph Wolff, chairman of the music department at Harvard University in Cambridge, Mass., discovered 33 previously unknown compositions by Johann Sebastian Bach at the Yale University library in New Haven, Conn. The pieces, all for organ, increased the number of Bach's organ works by about 25 per cent.

Musical Chairs. In September 1984, Christoph von Dohnányi took over as musical director of the Cleveland Orchestra. Gunther Herbig began his conducting duties at the Detroit Symphony Orchestra, and Sergiu Comissiona took the top post at the Houston Symphony Orchestra.

Carlo Maria Giulini announced his retirement as music director of the Los Angeles Philharmonic for health reasons. André Previn, musical director of the Pittsburgh (Pa.) Symphony Orchestra, announced in May that he would be replacing Giulini in January 1986. Lorin Maazel became music consultant to the Pittsburgh orchestra after resigning, 2½ years before his contract expired, as director of Austria's Vienna State Opera. Maazel withdrew following increasing criticism of his management and style from the Viennese press and public. Italian Claudio Abbado was named to replace Maazel.

Commemorations honoring the 300th anniversary of the birthdays of Bach and George Frideric Handel in 1685 began in 1984, a year early. The San Francisco Symphony Orchestra, for example, held a three-week Bach celebration in October and November, and New York City's Carnegie Hall opened its Handel Opera Festival in November with *Orlando*. Another important anniversary was the 50th birthday of Great Britain's Glyndebourne Festival Opera.

Opera Premieres included: *Akhnaten* by Philip Glass (Stuttgart, West Germany) in March; *The Damast Drum* by Paavo Heininen (Helsinki, Finland); P. D. Q. Bach's parody *The Abduction of Figaro* (Minneapolis, Minn.) and Conrad Susa's *The Love of Don Perlimplin* (San Francisco) in April; and *Samstag* by Karlheinz Stockhausen (Milan, Italy) and Paul Earl's *Icarus, A Sky Opera* (Boston) in May. Other premieres included *Raleigh's Dream* by Iain Hamilton (Durham, N.C.) and *X* (about the life of black leader Malcolm X) by Anthony Davis (Philadelphia) in June; *The King Goes Forth to France* by Aulis Sallinen (Hélsinki) in July; Sergei Rachmaninoff's unfinished *Monna Vanna* (Saratoga Springs, N.Y.) in August; and William Grant Still's *Minette Fontaine*, finished in 1958 (Baton Rouge, La.), in October. Robert Wilson's epic of world history and the future, *The CIVIL warS: a tree is best measured when it is down*, had three more sections premiered during 1984—in Cologne, West Germany; Rome; and Minneapolis.

New Orchestral Works. It was also a busy year for new orchestral works. Among those introduced by U.S. symphonies were: Charles Wuorinen's Third Piano Concerto (Albany, N.Y.); John Harbison's Symphony Number 1 and Michael Tippett's *The Mask of Time* (Boston); Jonathan Kramer's *Moments in and out of Time* and Ira Taxin's *Concerto for Brass Quintet and Orchestra* (Cincinnati, Ohio); Wuorinen's *Movers and Shakers* (Cleveland); Robert Rodriguez' *Oktoechos* (Dallas); Ellen Taaffe Zwilich's Celebration for Orchestra (Indianapolis); Interplay by William Kraft (Los Angeles); Concerto for Orchestra by Stephen Paulus and Lloyd Ultan's Violin Concerto (Minnesota); George Crumb's *Haunted Landscape* and George Rochberg's Oboe Concerto (New York); *Prismatic Variations* by Donald Erb (St. Louis, Mo.); and Louis Andriessen's *Velocity* (San Francisco). Michael Colgrass' Viola Concerto premiered in Toronto, Canada.

A noteworthy special event was a weeklong celebration of sacred music by American composers presented by the Milwaukee Symphony Orchestra in September. The orchestra performed the works of more than 30 composers.   Peter P. Jacobi

In WORLD BOOK, see CLASSICAL MUSIC; OPERA.

Christoph von Dohnányi, who became musical director of the Cleveland Orchestra in September, conducts the orchestra at a concert.

MUSIC, POPULAR. Business boomed for the United States popular music industry in 1984. Cassette and album sales were up. Merchants reported an increase in new store openings. Compact disks (CD's) and CD players went down in price and up in sales. And music videos emerged as a major income-producer in the growing home-video market.

Black Music, having grown steadily more popular in the early 1980's, played a major role in the pop-music scene in 1984. Michael Jackson's *Thriller*, which was released in 1983 and continued to top the charts into April 1984, became the largest-selling album in history — it sold more than 30 million copies. Jackson won a record eight Grammy Awards in February. And the Jacksons' Victory Tour, with its $30 ticket price, was a huge success.

Lionel Richie's album *Can't Slow Down* was also a top seller in 1984. Other successful albums were Luther Vandross' *Busy Body* and Tina Turner's energy-packed, rock-oriented album, *Private Dancer*. The year also produced a major new black star — Prince — whose motion picture *Purple Rain* was a box-office smash. The sound-track album and hit singles from *Purple Rain* gave Prince the number-one slot on several record-industry sales charts in August. Also in August, 6 of the top 10 pop album

slots were occupied by black performers — Prince, Turner, the Jacksons, Richie, the Pointer Sisters, and Ray Parker, Jr. Stevie Wonder collected his eighth number-one pop hit in October with "I Just Called to Say I Love You," 21 years after his first number-one hit, "Fingertips."

Dance Music was back in a big way in 1984 as many new high-tech video dance clubs opened. Some of the performers of dance-club hits were Laid Back, Art of Noise, Shannon, Prince, Sheila E., and Diana Ross. The widespread popularity of the dance craze was shown by the number of mainstream rockers who had dance-oriented hits — Bruce Springsteen, ZZ Top, Kenny Loggins, Van Halen, David Bowie, Daryl Hall and John Oates, Cyndi Lauper, and Huey Lewis and the News. Rap music — a kind of rhythmic talking set to a musical beat — and break dancing continued to grow, earning the name "hip hop" (see DANCING [Close-Up]). Many rap-music artists emphasized uplifting themes, such as peace and respect for law, in their songs.

Rock Music rocked on, but without any notable new trends or performers. In July, 9 of the top 10 pop singles were by performers who started in earlier decades, including 6 who started in the 1960's — the Jacksons, Turner, Rod Stewart, Elton John, ZZ Top, and the Pointer Sisters. Artists who reunited to go on tour or cut reunion albums included the Everly Brothers, Deep Purple, Aerosmith, and three members of the original Yardbirds under the name Box of Frogs.

Many solo albums were by artists who gained fame as part of a group, including Christine McVie of Fleetwood Mac, Grace Slick of Jefferson Starship, and Barry Gibb of the Bee Gees. Yoko Ono, the widow of Beatle John Lennon, released *Milk and Honey*, an album she cut with John before his death in 1980. Another Beatle, Paul McCartney, wrote, starred in, and supervised a movie musical, *Give My Regards to Broad Street*.

The two biggest-selling rock albums to premiere in 1984 were The Cars' fifth, *Heartbeat City*, and Springsteen's seventh, *Born in the U.S.A.* Springsteen's album contains stories of the problems and dreams of small-town Americans. Albums issued in 1983 but still big in 1984 were Van Halen's *1984*, the British group Culture Club's *Colour by Numbers*, and Lauper's *She's So Unusual*.

Politics Was Important in the music of a growing number of rockers. Bonnie Raitt and Jackson Browne teamed up at a rally opposing U.S. military involvement in Central America, a concern also expressed in Little Steven's *Voice of America* and Jefferson Starship's video for "Layin' It on the Line," from their new album *Nuclear Furniture*. Jerry Dammers of Great Britain's Special AKA had a top-10 hit in Britain with "Free Nelson Mandela," which referred to a man being held as a po-

Backed up by her band, rock star Cyndi Lauper belts out a tune. Lauper's 1983 album *She's So Unusual* remained a hit in 1984.

Led by superstar brother Michael Jackson, second from left, the Jacksons open their Victory Tour on July 6 in Kansas City, Mo.

litical prisoner in South Africa. And in the video for "Two Tribes," British band Frankie Goes To Hollywood depicted the leaders of the United States and the Soviet Union fighting in a ring.

Women continued to play a growing role in rock. Those in the spotlight, in addition to performers already mentioned, included Rickie Lee Jones, Laurie Anderson, Patty Smyth of Scandal, Madonna, and the female groups The Bangles, Bananarama, and the extremely popular Go-Go's.

Music Video, more important than ever in 1984, was the focus for two awards ceremonies and an international festival in 1984. The popularity of the 24-hour music video channel Music Television (MTV) led to the creation of three other such channels, all of which planned to begin broadcasting in late 1984 or early 1985: Discovery Music Network, Ted Turner's music video network, and a second channel by the owners of MTV. The three newcomers said they would program for an older audience — 25 to 49 — and play more varied kinds of music, including pop, rock, black, and country. In November, Turner, an Atlanta, Ga.-based broadcasting executive, announced that he was canceling his music channel.

Discovery Music Network brought a restraint-of-trade suit against MTV for its exclusivity agreements with record companies. At least six major record companies agreed to let MTV air certain

video clips for 30 days before anyone else was allowed to show them. Three trends on MTV were more contests and giveaways, more complicated and sophisticated video special effects, and more guitar-oriented "heavy metal" music.

Movie Sound-Track Albums did very well in 1984. There had been only two *platinum* (million-selling) sound tracks in each of the previous three years, but 1984 had at least eight: *Breakin', Hard to Hold, Footloose, The Big Chill, Two of a Kind, Yentl, Purple Rain,* and *Ghostbusters.*

Jazz. Trumpeter Wynton Marsalis, 23, won Grammies for the best jazz and classical albums, an unprecedented achievement. Herbie Hancock was the big winner in the MTV Music Video Awards when his hip-hop song "Rockit" won in five categories. Other performers whose albums topped the jazz charts were Earl Klugh, Miles Davis, David Sanborn, and Spyro Gyra. The continued popularity of jazz was demonstrated when more than 30,000 people — a record turnout — attended Europe's North Sea Jazz Festival. Attendance at all jazz festivals was up an average of 15 per cent from 1983 attendance. Many jazz titles appeared on CD's, which can reproduce the finer shadings of jazz musicians' phrasing and tone with near-perfection.

Country Music climbed onto the video bandwagon. The major Nashville record companies an-

411

Menudo, a teen-age rock group from Puerto Rico,
struts its stuff at Radio City Music Hall in
New York City during a concert in February.

swered the growing demand for country video by producing a number of high-quality clips.

The blurring of distinctions among pop styles, which has produced various forms of fusion music, such as jazz-rock, progressed in country music as well. Rockers Richie, Bob Seger, Sheena Easton, and Neil Young were on the country charts, and country great Ronnie Milsap appeared on MTV. Some of the year's best-selling country albums in a more traditional vein were by Alabama, the Oak Ridge Boys, George Strait, Hank Williams, Jr., Willie Nelson, Merle Haggard, and Ricky Skaggs, whose hit "Uncle Pen" with bluegrass pioneer Bill Monroe showed that the older country styles were still popular. Another hit — but one to be played on a card table rather than a turntable — was Louise Mandrell's Country Music Trivia Game.

Deaths. Some of pop music's greats died in 1984: cabaret singer Mabel Mercer, country veteran Ernest Tubb, soul singers Jackie Wilson and Marvin Gaye, British blues artist Alexis Korner, blues "shouter" Willie Mae "Big Mama" Thornton, folk singer Steve Goodman, and jazz pianist and bandleader Count Basie.   Jerry M. Grigadean

See also AWARDS AND PRIZES (Arts Awards); JACKSON, MICHAEL. In the Special Reports section, see THE SIGHTS AND SOUNDS OF MUSIC VIDEOS. In WORLD BOOK, see COUNTRY MUSIC; JAZZ; POPULAR MUSIC; ROCK MUSIC.

NAMIBIA. South Africa, which has administered Namibia — formerly called South West Africa — since 1920, announced on Jan. 31, 1984, that it was pulling its approximately 5,000 troops out of a large area of southern Angola. For more than two years, South African forces had been fighting Namibian nationalist guerrillas based in Angola.

As a condition for South Africa's total withdrawal, Angola's government agreed on February 16 that it would keep the guerrillas — members of the South West Africa People's Organization (SWAPO) — from reestablishing bases in the area that the South Africans were vacating. The South African troops withdrew to a point about 25 miles (40 kilometers) from the Angola-Namibia border but refused to pull back any farther.

At Two Conferences during the year, South Africa and SWAPO tried to negotiate a cease-fire as a prelude to independence for Namibia. Prior to the first meeting, held in May in Lusaka, Zambia, the government of South Africa said that if the Namibian political parties in attendance — SWAPO and six others, called the Multiparty Conference — could agree on a formula for independence, South Africa would accept the agreement.

But SWAPO and the Multiparty Conference, which SWAPO contended was controlled by South Africa, could not agree. The Multiparty Conference rejected the SWAPO position that Namibia's independence should be achieved through United Nations (UN) intervention, as provided for in a UN Security Council resolution passed in 1978.

On another critical point of disagreement, two of the Multiparty Conference member groups supported the South African position that Namibian independence be conditional on the withdrawal of approximately 23,000 Cuban troops stationed in neighboring Angola. However, Angola said it needed the Cubans as protection against rebel guerrillas — as well as against South Africa — and it refused to remove them. See ANGOLA.

The Second Conference. On July 25, leaders of SWAPO and South Africa met in Cape Verde for unprecedented direct talks. In previous meetings, South Africa had sent only low-ranking representatives. South Africa offered SWAPO a cease-fire and the right to participate in elections to be held in Namibia. SWAPO continued to insist on implementation of the 1978 UN plan.

On June 6, South Africa offered to hand over Namibia's administration to Canada, France, Great Britain, West Germany, or the United States if one or more of those countries would bear the financial costs and ensure the withdrawal of Cuban troops from Angola. However, none of the Western countries took up the offer.   J. Dixon Esseks

See also AFRICA (Facts in Brief Table). In WORLD BOOK, see NAMIBIA.

NATIONAL PTA (NATIONAL CONGRESS OF PARENTS AND TEACHERS) in 1984 recorded its second consecutive increase in membership, after almost 20 years of decline. The increase reflected a nationwide concern for quality education and greater parent involvement in education. A National PTA project, "Looking In on Your School," encourages parents to take a more active role in school policymaking.

To boost membership further, the National PTA selected Phyllis George Brown as the 1984-1986 honorary membership chairman. Brown, one of the first woman sportscasters in the United States, said in accepting the post that because so many families have two working parents, "It is more difficult for us to be aware of our schools and what is happening in them. . . . But we must take the time [to find out] to ensure that the quality of our children's education remains high."

In honor of its cofounder, the National PTA in 1984 established the Phoebe Apperson Hearst Outstanding Educator of the Year Award with a grant from the William Randolph Hearst Foundation. The first award was presented to Leonard L. Diggs, a music teacher at O'Connell Junior High School in Lakewood, Colo.   Joan Kuersten

In WORLD BOOK, see NATIONAL CONGRESS OF PARENTS AND TEACHERS; PARENT-TEACHER ORGANIZATIONS.

NAVRATILOVA, MARTINA (1956-), became one of only five tennis players in the sport's history to win the grand slam when she captured the French Open in June 1984. To achieve a grand slam, a player must win the four major tennis tournaments in succession — Wimbledon, the United States Open, the Australian Open, and the French Open. Navratilova not only claimed these titles but she also won all four tournaments in the doubles category — with Pam Shriver — becoming the only player ever to accomplish this feat.

Navratilova was born on Oct. 18, 1956, in Prague, Czechoslovakia. At the age of 15, she entered Czechoslovakia's national championship tournament as a relatively unknown player. She won, and held the national title for the next three years. She began to compete in international events, and in 1975, while playing at the U.S. Open in Forest Hills, N.Y., she said she was defecting. In 1981, she became a U.S. citizen.

In September 1983, after winning her first U.S. Open singles title, Navratilova's career earnings amounted to $6,113,756, more than any other tennis player. In January 1984, the Associated Press named her "female athlete of the year." Navratilova resides in Dallas.   Rod Such

NAVY. See ARMED FORCES.

NEBRASKA. See STATE GOVERNMENT.

NEPAL. See ASIA.

NETHERLANDS. Mounting public pressure led the Dutch government on June 1, 1984, to postpone the installation of United States nuclear cruise missiles in the Netherlands. In 1979, the North Atlantic Treaty Organization (NATO) had decided to place 572 nuclear-armed Pershing 2 balistic missiles and cruise missiles in five European countries — Belgium, Great Britain, Italy, the Netherlands, and West Germany. NATO was to deploy 48 cruise missiles in the Netherlands in 1986 and 1987. By the end of 1984, Belgium and the Netherlands had not yet agreed to take the missiles.

On May 20, Prime Minister Ruud Lubbers called for a "crisis alternative." The Netherlands would prepare the missile site that it had selected in January 1983, but the missiles would be taken to the site only if an East-West crisis developed.

On June 1, 1984, the government decided to deploy the cruise missiles by the end of 1988 unless Moscow agreed to freeze the number of SS-20 missiles aimed at Western Europe. The government would make its final decision, based on Soviet actions, in 1985. The government survived a debate on the issue in parliament on June 13 and 14, 1984. Six deputies from small right wing parties helped the government survive.

Rising Unemployment. The volume of private consumption declined in 1984, the first year most

413

Dutch protesters demonstrate in June against the North Atlantic Treaty
Organization's plan to place cruise missiles in the Netherlands.

workers did not receive wage increases to make up
for inflation. Economists predicted that unemployment would reach 900,000 — 17 per cent of the
work force — by the end of 1984.

No Tax Increase. A new budget outlined on September 18 — the first day of the legislative year —
called for a tax freeze and a reduction in social
security premiums. The government expected
these measures to boost purchasing power by 1 to
2 per cent and to lower the growth of unemployment. Proposed cuts in public spending totaling
$2.8 billion would affect mainly the salaries of
workers employed by the state, social security benefits, and public health expenditures.

The government said that it would give police
and courts more money. Defense spending would
rise by 2 per cent in 1985. The government promised that it would meet the NATO requirement of
a 3 per cent annual increase in military spending
by 1987. The 24-nation Organization for Economic Cooperation and Development (OECD) reported in February that weak responses to market
forces in the labor field, higher energy prices, and
rapid growth of government spending had caused
poor economic growth in the Netherlands for five
consecutive years.   Kenneth Brown

See also EUROPE (Facts in Brief Table). In
WORLD BOOK, see NETHERLANDS.

NEVADA. See STATE GOVERNMENT.

NEW BRUNSWICK. Plans for a government-backed
French-language newspaper to be published in
New Brunswick failed to bear fruit in 1984. However, a private daily, *L'Acadie nouvelle* (New Aca-
dia), began publication on June 7.

New Brunswick received more than 40 per cent
of its revenue in the form of transfer payments
from the federal government for fiscal year 1984-
1985. The projected provincial deficit for the fiscal
year was $97.5 million (Canadian dollars; $1 =
U.S. 76 cents as of Dec. 31, 1984). The lack of
funds caused the Progressive Conservative government of Premier Richard B. Hatfield to cancel
three promises it had made during the 1983 election campaign: kindergartens for all New Brunswick children, an income supplement for senior
citizens, and a mortgage-payment insurance plan.

On October 26, Hatfield was charged with possession of marijuana after police in Fredericton
found a small amount of the drug in his suitcase.
Hatfield said that the drug was not his and that he
had no idea how it got into his luggage. His trial
was to begin on Jan. 28, 1985.   David M. L. Farr

See also CANADA. IN WORLD BOOK, see NEW
BRUNSWICK.

NEW HAMPSHIRE. See STATE GOVERNMENT.

NEW JERSEY. See STATE GOVERNMENT.

NEW MEXICO. See STATE GOVERNMENT.

NEW YORK. See NEW YORK CITY; STATE GOV'T.

NEW YORK CITY. A historic redevelopment plan for Times Square received the approval of the Board of Estimate, New York City's highest legislative body, on Nov. 9, 1984. The West 42nd Street block of Times Square, long known as the "Crossroads of the World" — and in recent years a symbol of urban blight — will be razed and rebuilt at a cost of $1.6 billion. Four office towers designed by noted New York City architect Philip Johnson will anchor the corners of Broadway, Seventh Avenue, and 42nd Street. A merchandise mart and a luxury hotel will stand on the Eighth Avenue and 42nd Street corners.

The plan also called for razing the old Times Tower, a focal point for New Year's Eve celebrations, and renovating 9 of the area's 13 motion-picture theaters. The rehabilitated movie houses will be reopened as Broadway theaters. Construction is expected to begin in late 1985.

Work began in late November on a $500-million computer data center and office facility in lower Manhattan for Shearson Lehman/American Express, Incorporated. The administration of Mayor Edward I. Koch agreed to defer $83 million in real estate taxes and provide low-cost electricity for the facility to keep the company from moving its operations to a site in Jersey City, N.J.

Also in November, the landmark S. Klein department store was razed. Construction began on a $150-million retail and residential complex that will change the face of the 14th Street-Union Square section of Manhattan.

New York's Economy continued to show strength in 1984, benefiting from a projected record year in the rental of Manhattan office space; strong growth in the construction, financial, and service industries; high levels of tourism; and rising retail sales. Air traffic at the region's three airports climbed a record 14.7 per cent in the first six months of 1984.

The city adopted an $18-billion budget in June and, for the second fiscal year in a row, ended the period with a surplus of more than $500 million. Negotiations between the city and unions representing more than 200,000 city workers, whose contracts expired on June 30, were deadlocked in November. To break the stalemate, the administration asked for state-sanctioned arbitration.

Commuter Boom. The United States Bureau of Labor Statistics reported in May that the number of workers commuting into the city each day increased by 46,000 between 1970 and 1980. Surveys by the Port Authority of New York and New Jersey found that traffic on the Hudson River bridges between New York and New Jersey increased by 20 per cent over the same period.

Because building more bridges would be too expensive, the Port Authority, the New York City Planning Commission, and the New Jersey De-

New York City's Mayor Edward I. Koch shows China's Premier Zhao Ziyang how to view a glass engraving of the city seal given Zhao in January.

partment of Transportation began studying the feasibility of restoring commuter ferry service between the two states and within the city. In February, the city announced it was buying two new ferries, at a cost of $3.5 million, to provide service between Manhattan and Staten Island.

Subway Gunman. On December 22, four teenagers demanded $5 from a man on a New York City subway. He said, "Yes, I have $5 for each of you," drew a gun, and shot them. New Yorkers flooded authorities with calls praising the gunman. Bernhard H. Goetz, who surrendered to police on December 31, admitted the shootings.

New Archbishop. John J. O'Connor, the former Roman Catholic bishop of Scranton, Pa., was installed as head of the New York Archdiocese on March 19. He succeeded Terence Cardinal Cooke, who died in October 1983.

School Chief Resigns. Anthony J. Alvarado resigned as chancellor of the New York City school system on May 11 after he was declared "unfit" for his position by the Board of Education. A city investigation had found that Alvarado misused his authority while serving as the superintendent of an East Harlem school district. He was succeeded by Nathan Quinones, director of the board's division of high schools.   Owen Moritz

See also CITY. In WORLD BOOK, see NEW YORK CITY.

NEW ZEALAND

NEW ZEALAND. In a general election on July 14, 1984, voters decisively rejected the conservative National Party government headed by Prime Minister Sir Robert D. Muldoon, which had held power since 1975. The moderate left Labour Party headed by David R. Lange won, with 56 of the 95 seats in Parliament. The National Party received 37 seats, and the Social Credit Party won 2. A significant feature of the election was the strong showing by the newly formed right wing New Zealand Party, which advocated less government intervention in the economy. Although the new party failed to win any seats in Parliament, it received 12.3 per cent of the vote.

Lange, the new prime minister, appointed a 21-member Cabinet that included 2 women and 2 Maoris — members of New Zealand's Polynesian race. Lange also assumed the post of foreign minister. In November, the National Party chose James K. McLay as its leader, replacing Muldoon. McLay, a 39-year-old lawyer, had served as deputy party leader under Muldoon.

Economy. The four-week election campaign was called four months ahead of schedule and was fought amid a growing economic crisis. The crisis included a rapidly expanding foreign debt, an outflow of funds from New Zealand, and a rapidly growing budget deficit. At the end of June, for-

eign debt was estimated at $15 billion (New Zealand dollars; $NZ1 = U.S. 63 cents on June 29, 1984). The budget deficit for the year ending March 31 was $NZ2.6 billion. The National Party government's tight controls over wages and prices had reduced inflation to 3.5 per cent. But the business community was unhappy with the tight control of financial markets and interest rates.

Immediately following the election, the Lange government devalued the New Zealand dollar by 20 per cent, eased controls on financial markets, and introduced a temporary wage and price freeze. Both inflation and the budget deficit increased during the second half of 1984.

Relations with the United States were affected by the new government's policies of banning nuclear-powered or nuclear-armed warships from New Zealand waters, and seeking the establishment of a nuclear-free zone in the South Pacific. In a visit to the United States in September, Lange sought to allay fears that New Zealand wished to withdraw from its alliance with the United States. Nevertheless, the Lange government's policies created complications for ANZUS, a defense treaty formed in 1951 by Australia, New Zealand, and the United States.   David A. Shand

See also Asia (Facts in Brief Table); LANGE, DAVID R. In WORLD BOOK, see NEW ZEALAND.

A fleet of protesters demonstrating against nuclear-armed and nuclear-powered ships surrounds the U.S. submarine *Queenfish* in Auckland in March.

NEWFOUNDLAND received a stunning blow on March 8, 1984, when the Supreme Court of Canada ruled that the central government, not the province, owns and controls the rich Hibernia oil fields off Newfoundland's coast. However, the Progressive Conservative (PC) government of Newfoundland Premier Brian Peckford received some consolation in June when the federal PC leader, Brian Mulroney, said that the offshore area should be treated as if it were Newfoundland soil, which would allow the province to set and collect oil and natural gas royalties. Mulroney's Conservatives swept to victory in September's general election, and his statement on the issue was translated into a formal agreement on December 12.

The provincial budget introduced on March 20 forecast a deficit drastically reduced from that of the previous year as a result of cuts in public spending. However, the budget promised no quick drop in Newfoundland's 18 per cent unemployment rate—the highest in Canada.

The crews of Newfoundland's 61 deep-sea trawlers began a strike in July that dragged on through 1984. The crews wanted higher wages and more time on shore between fishing trips. The strike led to the closing of fish-processing plants in the province.   David M. L. Farr

See also CANADA. In WORLD BOOK, see NEW-FOUNDLAND.

The *St. Louis* (Mo.) *Evening News* appeared briefly and unsuccessfully in the spring, making its bow in April and bowing out in May.

NEWSPAPER. Advertising revenues of United States newspapers increased, and 13 of the 20 largest daily newspapers in the country grew in circulation in 1984. The U.S. newspaper industry was encouraged by the surprising success of *USA Today.* Its first official audit in June showed an average circulation of 1,138,030 during the three months ending on Dec. 31, 1983, making it the third-largest daily, behind *The Wall Street Journal*— also a national paper—and the *New York Daily News.* For the first time in several years, not a single major metropolitan daily newspaper closed down, though a new daily in St. Louis lasted only a month.

However, 1984 was not a good year for United Press International (UPI), the nation's second-largest wire service. The company had lost $13-million in 1983 and predicted that it would lose $7 million in 1984. On Aug. 23, 1984, UPI laid off more than 100 workers and cut the wages of all remaining employees by 25 per cent.

Last One in the Pool. On October 10, the U.S. Department of Defense presented a plan for press coverage of U.S. combat operations that might occur on short notice. The Pentagon proposed to form a pool, or group, of 11 journalists to cover such operations. The plan did not specify individual journalists, but it designated media and types of journalists. The Pentagon list did not include newspaper reporters. After sharp protests from newspapers, the Pentagon agreed the next day to include one newspaper reporter.

Newspapers Were Shaken by the allegation in March that *Wall Street Journal* columnist R. Foster Winans had provided a group of brokers and investors with advance information about columns that could affect stock prices. On August 28, a federal grand jury indicted Winans on criminal charges. The jury based part of the indictment on a legal principle—untested in the courts—that reporters have a legal duty to their employers and readers to reveal any financial interest they have in stocks they discuss. Press groups claimed that this could give the government dangerous power over the press. On October 10, the U.S. Department of Justice said it was withdrawing all charges based on the untested doctrine.

Technology's Impact on newspapers increased. Computers enabled editors to lay out pages on video screens rather than on paper. And some newspapers, including *The Washington* (D.C.) *Post, The* (Providence, R.I.) *Journal,* and the *New York Daily News,* experimented with *flexography,* a printing process that eliminates the most frequent reader complaint about newspapers—ink rubbing off onto the hands. Flexography ink is water-based, rather than oil-based.   Mark J. Fitzgerald

In WORLD BOOK, see NEWSPAPER.

Nicaraguans mark the anniversary of the death of their national revolutionary hero, Augusto César Sandino, in February in Managua.

NICARAGUA. Daniel Ortega Saavedra, as expected, was elected president of Nicaragua in the Nov. 4, 1984, elections, the first elections held in Nicaragua since the Sandinista National Liberation Front came to power in 1979. However, the victory margin of 63 per cent was smaller than predicted by Ortega, who had headed the ruling Sandinista junta since 1981.

A total of 1.1 million Nicaraguans, or about 75 per cent of registered voters, went to the polls. Seven parties were on the ballot, but three parties refused to take part, citing unfair election procedures, and a fourth withdrew after ballots had been printed. Negotiations to delay the election to ensure the participation of the main opposition leader, Arturo José Cruz, broke down in October. The opposition charged that the Sandinistas did not want an open vote, and the Sandinistas countercharged that the United States, knowing that Cruz would lose, did not want him to legitimize the elections.

U.S. Relations. The elections did little to improve relations with the Administration of United States President Ronald Reagan, which maintained its hard-line stance toward the Sandinista regime. However, in a surprise visit on June 1, U.S. Secretary of State George P. Shultz met with Ortega at the airport in Managua, the capital, to "figure out a way to bring peace to the region."

In April, the U.S. Central Intelligence Agency (CIA) said U.S. citizens hired by the CIA had been directly involved in the mining of Nicaraguan harbors. It was the first report of a direct U.S. role in a military operation against Nicaragua.

In October, the CIA was again at the center of a controversy, over a manual that was distributed to rebels fighting the Sandinistas. The handbook, which became an issue in the U.S. presidential election, advised rebels on how to kidnap and kill Sandinista officials. Reagan Administration officials disowned the manual, which they said they had not approved.

Relations between the two countries became most tense in November when the Sandinistas put their armed forces on combat alert, charging that the United States was going to invade. Reagan Administration officials denied that an invasion was planned but warned the Sandinistas not to obtain advanced Soviet jet fighters.

Nicaragua's Economy continued to deteriorate. In October, Ortega acknowledged the problem, blaming the situation on the high cost of defending the nation from U.S.-backed guerrillas. He said the government was forced to spend 25 per cent of its budget on defense.   Nathan A. Haverstock

See also LATIN AMERICA (Facts in Brief Table). In WORLD BOOK, see NICARAGUA.

NIGER. See AFRICA.

NIGERIA. Following their successful coup of Dec. 31, 1983, Nigeria's military leaders established a government headed by Major General Muhammadu Buhari. He presided over a 19-member policymaking body, the Supreme Military Council, consisting of other military officers. On Jan. 18, 1984, Buhari appointed an 18-member cabinet made up of 11 civilians and 7 military officers (see Buhari, Muhammadu).

The new government accused the regime of ousted President Shehu Shagari of unbridled corruption. By February, 282 former government officials, including the vice president and 18 state governors, were in prison awaiting trial, and Shagari was under house arrest. The first corruption trials began in May, with the defendants tried in secret by military courts. By mid-October, 11 former governors had been sentenced to prison.

London Kidnapping Thwarted. The new government particularly wanted to prosecute Umaru Dikko — Shagari's brother-in-law and the former minister of transport. Dikko, accused of illegally amassing a huge personal fortune while in office, fled to Great Britain after the coup. On July 5, he was seized by Nigerian agents on a London street, drugged, and placed in a shipping crate. But before the crate could be smuggled onto a plane bound for Nigeria, British police found and re-

leased him. Four men — one Nigerian and three Israelis — were later charged with the kidnapping.

Nigeria's Growing Foreign Debt was another major concern of the new government. Particularly serious was the country's inability to pay for current imports. In March, Nigeria had an estimated $5.6 billion in overdue import bills. By October, the total had climbed to about $7 billion. The government tried to curb unnecessary imports, but the controls contributed to shortages of food, raw materials, and other goods.

Oil Policy. The main cause of Nigeria's mounting debt was a large drop in earnings from its major export, crude oil. Petroleum revenues declined from some $24 billion in 1980 to about $10 billion in 1983. At the July 1984 summit meeting of the Organization of Petroleum Exporting Countries (OPEC), Nigeria obtained permission to increase its daily oil production in September.

In its pricing policy, however, Nigeria acted without OPEC approval. On October 18, it lowered the price for its main grade of oil from the OPEC-set level of $30 per barrel to $28. Nigerian authorities justified this action on the grounds that Great Britain had lowered its price for the same kind of oil. J. Dixon Esseks

See also Africa (Facts in Brief Table). In World Book, see Nigeria.

Muhammadu Buhari, head of Nigeria's military government — standing at the right in the car — reviews his troops on Army Day in July in Lagos.

NIXON, RICHARD MILHOUS (1913-   ), 37th President of the United States, emerged anew as a public figure in 1984 — lecturing, having a new book published, starring in television interviews, and exchanging thoughts with world leaders.

Premier Zhao Ziyang of China made a special visit to Nixon's New York City office during a January visit to the United States. Another January visitor was George S. McGovern, the 1972 Democratic presidential nominee whom Nixon defeated in a landslide just two years before becoming the first U.S. President to resign. McGovern praised Nixon's latest book, *Real Peace* (1984).

In the spring, Nixon was the subject of filmed interviews broadcast by the CBS television network, for which CBS reportedly paid $500,000. On March 13, the former President addressed the Economic Club of New York, and on May 5 he spoke at the Washington, D.C., meeting of the American Society of Newspaper Editors.

Because Nixon's wife, Pat, had suffered a stroke earlier, the Nixons planned to move from Upper Saddle River, N.J., to a $1.8-million New York City apartment. They canceled their plans in February after a resident of the building objected. Mrs. Nixon was hospitalized twice for the treatment of lung infections. Frank Cormier and Margot Cormier

In WORLD BOOK, see NIXON, RICHARD M.

NOBEL PRIZES in peace, literature, economics, and the sciences were awarded in 1984 by the Norwegian Storting (parliament) in Oslo and by the Royal Academy of Science, the Caroline Institute, and the Swedish Academy of Literature, which are in Stockholm, Sweden.

The Peace Prize was awarded to Bishop Desmond Mpilo Tutu, 53, general secretary of the South African Council of Churches, for his nonviolent efforts to end that country's policy of racial segregation, called apartheid. The Nobel committee said its award should be seen as "recognition of the courage and heroism shown by black South Africans in their use of peaceful methods in the struggle against apartheid." In naming Tutu, the committee for the second straight year selected a champion of human rights for its peace award. The 1983 winner was Poland's Lech Walesa. In November, Tutu was appointed Anglican bishop of Johannesburg, South Africa.

The Literature Prize went to poet Jaroslav Seifert, 83, of Czechoslovakia, who was little known outside of his own country. Although 30 volumes of his poetry have been published, only 2 have been translated into English — *The Plague Monument* (1980) and *The Casting of Bells* (1983). Considered his country's national poet, Seifert has been tolerated in recent years by the Communist gov-

Former President Richard M. Nixon is interviewed in April by his former speech-writer Frank Gannon for a videotaped program later televised by CBS.

Bishop Desmond Tutu, winner of the 1984 Nobel Peace Prize, is greeted at the airport in Johannesburg in October on his return to South Africa.

ernment, though he criticized the Soviet Union's invasion of Czechoslovakia in 1968 and was a signer of Charter 77, a human rights petition.

The Chemistry Prize was awarded to R. Bruce Merrifield, 63, professor of biochemistry at Rockefeller University in New York City, for his work in developing a method for making proteins by assembling amino acids into chains called peptides. His discovery was cited for its practical importance, "both for the development of new drugs and for gene technology."

The Economics Prize went to Sir Richard Stone, 71, a retired professor of economics at Cambridge University in England, for his pioneering work in creating a standard accounting model for the world's nations. Stone's model, developed following World War II, made it possible to compare one nation's economic progress with another's.

The Physics Prize was shared by physicists Carlo Rubbia, 50, of Italy and Simon van der Meer, 59, of the Netherlands for their roles in discovering three subatomic particles during experiments conducted at the European Organization for Nuclear Research (CERN) — now the European Laboratory for Particle Physics — near Geneva, Switzerland. The discovery of the long-sought particles confirmed the prediction of a theory that unites two of nature's fundamental forces — electromagnetism and the weak force. For years, physicists felt it was too costly to build a particle accelerator powerful enough to discover these particles. Rubbia broke the stalemate by realizing that the required high energies could be achieved with an existing accelerator at CERN by causing collisions between protons and antiprotons. Van der Meer, a senior engineer at CERN, devised a key technique that made these collisions possible.

The Physiology or Medicine Prize was shared by three men who provided new insights into the human immune system. The winners were Argentine-born British scientist César Milstein, 57, of the Medical Research Council's Laboratory of Molecular Biology in England; West German researcher Georges J. F. Köhler, 38, of the Basel Institute of Immunology in Switzerland; and British-born Danish researcher Niels K. Jerne, 72, a retired professor at the institute. Milstein and Köhler were recognized for their discovery in 1975 of a laboratory technique for producing monoclonal antibodies, which are used for research, diagnosis, and treatment of diseases. Jerne was cited as "the leading theoretician in immunology during the last 30 years." Rod Such

In WORLD BOOK, see NOBEL PRIZES.

NORTH ATLANTIC TREATY ORGANIZATION (NATO). See EUROPE.

NORTH CAROLINA. See STATE GOVERNMENT.

NORTH DAKOTA. See STATE GOVERNMENT.

NORTHERN IRELAND. Hopes for a solution to the continuing political violence in Northern Ireland were focused on a November 1984 meeting between Great Britain's Prime Minister Margaret Thatcher and Prime Minister of the Republic of Ireland Garret FitzGerald. However, Thatcher flatly rejected three possible solutions proposed by the New Ireland Forum, a group of Ireland's major political parties (see IRELAND).

British Cabinet Replacement. On September 10, the expected replacement of James Prior as Britain's secretary of state for Northern Ireland was announced. His replacement was Douglas Hurd, a former diplomat, a Foreign Office minister, and a writer of political novels. Hurd was received with suspicion by Protestant politicians in Northern Ireland because, five years earlier, he had met with Gerry Adams, president of Sinn Féin (Ourselves Alone), the political wing of the outlawed Irish Republican Army (IRA).

Police Attack. An international furor broke out after 1 man was killed and 20 people injured in a confrontation with police in Belfast on August 12. Members of the Royal Ulster Constabulary (RUC), Northern Ireland's predominantly Protestant police force, rushed into a crowd of demonstrators, firing plastic bullets and waving their batons. They were seeking Martin Galvin, an American IRA supporter who had been banned from Northern Ireland. The incident occurred during an appearance by Galvin, publicity director of the Irish Northern Aid Committee (Noraid), which raises money in the United States for IRA causes. Seconds after he appeared, the police struck.

The police action provoked widespread violence in Northern Ireland and criticism of the RUC. The government of the Republic of Ireland criticized Galvin, accusing him of being "responsible for death and destruction in Northern Ireland."

Terrorism. The IRA admitted planting a bomb that exploded on October 12, killing 5 people and injuring 33 others at a hotel in Brighton, England. Prime Minister Thatcher and members of her Cabinet were staying at the hotel.

On March 22, Paul Kavanagh, a Belfast man, appeared before a London court charged with planting a bomb at Harrods department store. Six people were killed and 94 injured when the bomb went off on Dec. 17, 1983. Kavanagh entered no plea, and the case was continued.

The largest trial of anti-British terrorist suspects in Northern Ireland ended on December 18 with the acquittal of all 35 defendants. They had been charged with murder, attempted murder, and other crimes. The case against them was based on the word of one informer, whose testimony was described by the judge as "entirely unworthy of belief."   Ian J. Mather

In WORLD BOOK, see NORTHERN IRELAND.

NORTHWEST TERRITORIES. The first major Inuit (Eskimo) land-rights agreement in Canada's North was enacted by the federal Parliament on June 29, 1984, and went into effect a month later. The agreement gave the Inuit of the western Arctic about $45 million in 1977 Canadian dollars to be paid in installments by 1997. In addition, a $17.5-million (Canadian dollars; $1 = U.S. 76 cents as of Dec. 31, 1984) economic and social development fund will be set up for 2,500 Inuit in six communities. The Inuit will become owners of about 11,000 square kilometers (4,250 square miles) of land around their villages, including gas, mineral, and oil rights. They will receive an additional 78,000 square kilometers (30,000 square miles) of land without mining rights.

Richard Nerysoo, a 30-year-old Dene (Indian), was elected leader of the executive committee of the Northwest Territories government on January 11. He became the first native person to hold the post — the territories' highest elective office.

Construction began in January on a controversial pipeline to carry oil from Norman Wells, N.W. Ter., to Zama, Alta. Indian groups had long opposed the pipeline, arguing that it complicated their land-rights claims.   David M. L. Farr

See also CANADA. In WORLD BOOK, see NORTHWEST TERRITORIES.

Construction of a controversial oil pipeline in the Northwest Territories proceeds in early 1984, despite the objections of Indian leaders.

A Norwegian reproduction of a centuries-old Viking ship stops in New York City in September during a voyage around the world.

NORWAY and Great Britain discussed a $26-billion natural gas deal in 1984. But the deal fell through when the two countries failed to decide which one would take the tax benefits from the pipeline that would carry the gas from Norwegian deposits under the North Sea to Britain.

The British government was lukewarm toward the deal because the purchase of gas would affect Britain's balance of payments negatively. On July 3, Great Britain agreed in principle to take 1 million cubic feet (28,000 cubic meters) of gas per day during the 1990's, but final agreement depended upon solving the tax problem. On October 15, Norway upset the Organization of Petroleum Exporting Countries (OPEC) by unilaterally cutting its oil price from $30.10 to $29.00 per barrel. In December, Norway suspended its official oil-pricing system and began negotiating with customers on the basis of free-market prices.

More Oil. On November 4, the Energy Ministry and Statoil, the state-owned oil company, announced that the Haltenbanken oil field off the country's central coast may contain as much oil as Norway's largest producing North Sea field, Statfjord. Statoil said that it had made a major oil discovery at Haltenbanken in October.

Spy Denounced. Prime Minister Kaare Willoch denounced Arne Treholt as a Soviet spy on January 23. Treholt, deputy press secretary at Nor-

way's foreign office, had been arrested as he was about to leave Norway on January 20. Foreign Minister Svenn Stray said that Treholt might have given Soviet agents information on Norway's negotiating position before talks with the Soviets on fishing rights and on the division of undersea areas containing oil and gas deposits.

Strike Called Off. On May 29, the government decided to use compulsory arbitration to prevent a strike by 500,000 state and municipal employees. The strike would have paralyzed communications throughout Norway. The workers wanted more money and greater job security.

Herring Problem. A European Community (EC or Common Market) decision reached on May 24 threatened to end Norway's cooperation with the EC countries on fishing in the North Sea. Norway and the EC had failed to agree on how to split a total of 230,000 metric tons (254,000 short tons) of fish that probably would be caught during the year. Nevertheless, the EC assigned rights to 155,000 metric tons (171,000 short tons) to those of its member countries whose fishing fleets operate in the North Sea. The 24-nation Organization for Economic Cooperation and Development reported in July that Norway would have a record surplus of $2 billion in 1984. Kenneth Brown

See also EUROPE (Facts in Brief Table). In WORLD BOOK, see NORWAY.

NOVA SCOTIA. The Progressive Conservative government of Premier John Buchanan was reelected by a wide margin on Nov. 6, 1984. It was the third consecutive victory for Buchanan's government, in power since 1978. The Progressive Conservatives won 42 seats in the legislature, a gain of 4; the Liberals won 6, a loss of 7; the New Democrats won 3, a gain of 2; and the Cape Breton Labor Party retained its 1 seat.

The spraying of herbicides, always controversial in forested Nova Scotia, received provincial government approval in 1984. In late summer, wood lots were sprayed to prevent hardwood brush from choking out young softwood trees. A two-year court battle by a group of Cape Breton landowners failed to block the use of 2,4,5-T and 2,4-D — the ingredients of the defoliant Agent Orange — on property adjoining their own.

North America's first tidal-power plant, designed to harness the awesome 10-meter (33-foot) tides of the Bay of Fundy, began generating electricity on August 25 in Annapolis Royal. This experimental facility will generate 20,000 kilowatts of power. The complete project, which will take a decade to build, will produce 4 million kilowatts of electric power.   David M. L. Farr

See also CANADA. In WORLD BOOK, see NOVA SCOTIA.

NUCLEAR ENERGY. See ENERGY.

NUTRITION. A 10-year study released in January 1984 by the National Heart, Lung, and Blood Institute in Bethesda, Md., was the first to demonstrate conclusively that reducing blood cholesterol can help prevent heart disease in susceptible people. Heart disease kills more than 500,000 Americans each year and is the major cause of death and disability in the United States and other industrialized nations. Cholesterol is produced by the body and also found in such foods as meat, eggs, and dairy products.

The $150-million study tested whether lowering blood cholesterol reduced the risk of heart disease in middle-aged men with high blood-cholesterol levels. The 3,806 study participants followed a moderate cholesterol-lowering diet. Those whose blood cholesterol was lowered by a drug — cholestyramine — had 24 per cent fewer heart disease deaths and 19 per cent fewer nonfatal heart attacks than a group receiving a *placebo* (a substance containing no medication) instead of the drug.

The researchers recommended that men and women with high blood-cholesterol levels — about 230 to 240 milligrams per deciliter and up — try to reduce them. They stressed that the preferred way is with diet — reducing total fat, particularly animal fat, and cutting down on foods high in cholesterol. In the Special Reports section, see DON'T GAMBLE WITH YOUR HEART.

Diet and Cancer. In February 1984, the American Cancer Society (ACS) said Americans should change their eating habits to reduce their risk of cancer. The dietary guidelines focused on avoiding obesity. Research supported by the ACS has found a marked increase in cancers of the uterus, gall bladder, kidney, stomach, colon, and breast associated with obesity. The ACS also urged that people reduce total fat intake to lower the risk of breast, colon, and prostate cancer, and eat less salt-cured, smoked, and nitrite-cured food, such as bacon and ham. Other recommendations included eating more high-fiber foods, such as fruits, vegetables, and whole grain foods; foods rich in vitamins A and C, such as carrots, tomatoes, spinach, apricots, cantaloupes, sweet potatoes, peppers, and citrus fruits; and foods in the cabbage family, such as broccoli, Brussels sprouts, and cauliflower. The guidelines also urged moderation in the consumption of alcoholic beverages to reduce the risk of cancers of the mouth, larynx, and esophagus. See HEALTH AND DISEASE.

Sodium on Food Labels. The Food and Drug Administration announced in April 1984 that food companies will have to disclose the sodium content of a product if the company makes nutritional claims about the product. Starting in July 1985, manufacturers that fortify their foods or make any health claims will have to list the milligrams of sodium contained in the product along with the calories, protein, carbohydrates, and other information on the label.

Secretary of Health and Human Services Margaret M. Heckler said this ruling is "of special importance to many Americans with high blood pressure, which can lead to stroke and heart attack," and noted that "many individuals can lower their blood pressure by sodium restriction and weight reduction."

The Food and Nutrition Board of the National Research Council in Washington, D.C., has estimated that a daily intake of 1,100 to 3,300 milligrams of sodium is safe and adequate for adults. Many Americans consume 5,000 to 7,000 milligrams, much more than they need.

World Hunger. In February 1984, the U.S. House of Representatives Select Committee on Hunger was established and charged with making a comprehensive study of hunger and malnutrition in the United States and throughout the world. Committee Chairman Mickey Leland (D., Tex.) said special attention would be given to infant mortality, a key indicator of hunger throughout the world. In September, the committee opened hearings on the food crisis in Africa, where more than 150 million people in 1984 were facing starvation.   Jean Weininger

See also AFRICA; FOOD. In WORLD BOOK, see DIET; FOOD; NUTRITION.

424

OCEAN. In July, United States President Ronald Reagan signed a proclamation declaring the period from July 1, 1984, to July 1, 1985, the Year of the Ocean. This nationwide celebration of the United States ocean heritage concentrates on the many uses of the ocean and the resources that lie within the U.S. 200-nautical-mile (370-kilometer) limit. In 1983, Reagan had proclaimed a U.S. 200-nautical-mile exclusive economic zone (EEZ), claiming all fishing and other rights in that area.

World Court Boundary Decision. On October 12, a special five-judge panel of the International Court of Justice (World Court) at The Hague in the Netherlands settled an ocean boundary dispute between Canada and the United States. At stake was the rich fishing area of the Georges Bank in the Gulf of Maine. The court awarded Canada about one-third of the gulf, including about one-sixth of the Georges Bank. Canada's portion includes about half the valuable scallop fishery and areas rich in cod, haddock, and lobster. Many fishing communities in New England and in Nova Scotia depend heavily upon the catch from the Georges Bank for their livelihood. Fishing industry representatives in both countries expressed disappointment with the decision, saying that it would lead to job losses. The Georges Bank has also attracted interest as a possible area of petroleum deposits. See FISHING INDUSTRY.

Scientific Ocean Drilling. In 1984, a 10-year international Ocean Drilling Program (ODP) was launched to explore the continental margins — the region of the earth's crust between the continental shelf and the deep ocean abyss. *Sedco/BP 471* was selected as the drilling vessel. It has a computer-controlled positioning system that keeps the ship over a specific location while drilling. *Sedco/BP 471* can drill in waters as deep as 27,000 feet (8,200 meters) with a rig that can handle up to 30,000 feet (9,000 meters) of drill pipe. The ODP will receive guidance from the Joint Oceanographic Institutions for Deep Earth Sampling (JOIDES), representing Canada, France, Great Britain, Italy, Japan, the Netherlands, Norway, Sweden, Switzerland, the United States, and West Germany.

Discoveries on the Ocean Floor. A summer expedition off the U.S. Pacific Northwest discovered exotic life forms and potentially important ore deposits. Scientists, led by oceanographer Alexander Malahoff of the National Oceanic and Atmospheric Administration, found active hydrothermal vents and 5-foot (150-centimeter) worms like those found surrounding hot vents near Ecuador's Galapagos Islands. Color photographs and videotapes taken from the submersible research craft *Alvin* showed colonies of yellow bacteria that depend on chemosynthesis rather than photosynthesis for their existence. These bacteria exist on hydrogen sulfide and serve as food for other ocean creatures.

Minerals rich in zinc sulfide were gathered on the Gorda Ridge, some of which lies beyond the United States EEZ off northern California and Oregon. Samples from the more active Juan de Fuca Ridge, the northern part of which lies within Canada's 200-nautical-mile economic zone, were mainly copper sulfide.

In December, two Smithsonian Institution botanists announced the discovery of plant life living far deeper in the ocean than had been thought possible. They found a new species — a purple coralline algae of the seaweed family — thriving in 884 feet (269 meters) of water on the Atlantic Ocean floor off the Bahamas. The plants need little light to survive. The finding of the algae indicated the existence of much more plant life on the ocean floor than scientists had expected.

Oil Spill. In late July and early August, a major spill of about 2 million gallons (7.6 million liters) of crude oil threatened beaches on the east end of Galveston Island, Texas. The spill came from the British tanker *Alvenus*, which ran aground in the Gulf of Mexico 11 miles (17.7 kilometers) off the Louisiana coast. Most of the oil either dissipated or washed ashore on the island's west end.

Seabed Pact. Eight industrialized countries signed an agreement on August 3 aimed at avoiding disputes among mining companies over potential mineral-mining sites in the seabed. The accord — signed by Belgium, France, Great Britain, Italy, Japan, the Netherlands, the United States, and West Germany — followed a 1983 agreement among six international industrial groups to avoid overlapping one another's sites when mining manganese nodules from the Pacific Ocean. Such mining will not begin before 1988.

Advisory Committee Controversy. On July 2, 1984, President Reagan appointed Anne M. Burford, the controversial former head of the U.S. Environmental Protection Agency (EPA), to chair the National Advisory Committee on Oceans and Atmosphere (NACOA). However, in a surprise move, Burford withdrew on August 1, just hours before she was scheduled to be sworn in. Her withdrawal followed a storm of protest capped by overwhelming votes in the Senate and House of Representatives in favor of a resolution requesting Reagan to withdraw her appointment. Burford had resigned as EPA head in 1983 amid charges of mismanagement and political favoritism.

In July 1984, NACOA issued a report entitled *Nuclear Waste Management and the Use of the Sea.* The report recommended that the prohibition against disposing of low-level radioactive waste in the oceans should be revised.   Arthur G. Alexiou

In WORLD BOOK, see OCEAN.

OHIO. See STATE GOVERNMENT.

OKLAHOMA. See STATE GOVERNMENT.

OLD AGE. See SOCIAL SECURITY.

OLYMPIC GAMES

Despite a boycott by the Soviet Union and 13 allied nations of the XXIII Olympic Summer Games and a severe snowstorm that disrupted Alpine skiing at the XIV Winter Games, the 1984 Olympics were considered a rousing success. The Winter Olympics were held from February 8, the day of the opening ceremony, to February 19 in Sarajevo, Yugoslavia, with a record number of nations (49) and athletes (1,510). The Summer Olympics were held from July 28 to August 12 in Los Angeles with nearly 8,000 athletes from a record 140 nations.

Boycotts have never affected the Winter Olympics, and every nation with winter sports took part in Sarajevo. However, boycotts have affected all of the Summer Olympics since 1976. In 1980, the United States and more than 40 other nations withdrew from the Olympics in Moscow to protest the 1979 Soviet invasion of Afghanistan. Their absence diminished the quality of the competition.

In 1984, though fewer nations boycotted, competition was weakened in many sports that are usually dominated by Soviet-bloc nations. The boycotters included East Germany, Czechoslovakia, Poland, Hungary, Bulgaria, and Cuba — all among the world's leading sports nations. Of the Warsaw Pact members, only Romania competed.

The Soviet Union, East Germany, and the United States had been expected to win the most medals. Without the Soviets and the East Germans, the United States won by far the most.

The Summer Olympics encompassed 25 medal sports and two demonstration sports (baseball and tennis). The United States won medals in everything except soccer, rhythmic gymnastics, and team handball in accumulating 83 gold, 61 silver, and 30 bronze medals. It won more than four times as many gold medals as its nearest rival, Ro-

mania, which had 20 gold medals. The U.S. total of 174 medals was almost three times that of West Germany, which had the next highest with 59.

The United States won 21 gold medals in swimming, 16 in track and field, 9 in boxing, 9 in wrestling, 5 in gymnastics, 4 in cycling, 3 in equestrian events, 3 in shooting, 3 in yachting, 2 in basketball, 2 in diving, 2 in rowing, 2 in synchronized swimming, 1 in archery, and 1 in volleyball. Altogether, the United States won 40 medals in track and field, 34 in swimming, 16 in gymnastics, 13 in wrestling, 11 in boxing, 9 in cycling, 8 in diving, and 8 in rowing.

All seven U.S. divers won medals. Greg Louganis of Mission Viejo, Calif., who was entered in

Olympic gold medalists display their form: Great Britain's Daley Thompson clears a hurdle on his way to winning the decathlon; Canada's Gaetan Boucher wins the 1,500-meter speed-skating race for one of his two golds; Greg Louganis of the U.S. executes one of the dives that won him two golds; U.S. skier Debbie Armstrong wins the giant slalom; Canada's Alex Baumann, who won two golds, celebrates his win in the 200-meter medley; and Carl Lewis of the U.S. takes the long jump to win one of his four gold medals.

both men's diving events, won both. All seven U.S. yachts won gold or silver medals. Of the 12 U.S. boxers, 11 won medals. United States athletes won Olympic medals for the first time in volleyball, field hockey, Greco-Roman wrestling, equestrian team jumping, women's individual gymnastics, and women's rowing.

Heroes. The United States also supplied many of the heroes. None received more attention than Carl Lewis, who duplicated Jesse Owens' feat in the 1936 Olympic Games of winning gold medals in the 100-meter dash, 200-meter dash, 400-meter relay, and long jump.

Lewis was raised in Willingboro, N.J., and lived in a luxurious home in Houston. He could afford that home because the liberalized rules of amateurism allowed him to earn about $1 million a year and still compete as an amateur.

Edwin Moses of Laguna Hills, Calif., repeated his 1976 Olympic victory in the men's 400-meter hurdles, and his annual earnings were expected to exceed $900,000. In November, Mark Breland of New York City, the 147-pound (66.7-kilogram) boxing champion, began a professional career expected to earn him millions of dollars. Michael Jordan of Wilmington, N.C., star of the Olympic men's basketball champions, signed a multimillion-dollar contract with the Chicago Bulls.

Mary Lou Retton, 16 years old, of Fairmont, W. Va., who won five medals including the gold

Official Results of the 1984 Olympic Games

Winners of the Winter Olympics in Sarajevo, Yugoslavia, in February

Event	Winner	Country	Mark
Men's Skiing			
Downhill	Bill Johnson	U.S.A.	1:45.59
Giant slalom	Max Julen	Switzerland	2:41.18
Slalom	Phil Mahre	U.S.A.	1:39.41
15-kilometer cross-country	Gunde Svan	Sweden	41:25.6
30-kilometer cross-country	Nikolai Zimyatov	U.S.S.R.	1:28:56.3
50-kilometer cross-country	Thomas Wassberg	Sweden	2:15:55.8
40-kilometer cross-country relay	Wassberg, Svan, Kohlberg, Ottosson	Sweden	1:55:06.3
70-meter jump	Jens Weissflog	E. Germany	215.2 pts.
90-meter jump	Matti Nykaenen	Finland	231.2 pts.
Nordic combined	Tom Sandberg	Norway	422.595 pts.
Women's Skiing			
Downhill	Michela Figini	Switzerland	1:13.36
Giant slalom	Debbie Armstrong	U.S.A.	2:20.98
Slalom	Paoletta Magoni	Italy	1:36.47
5-kilometer cross-country	Marja-Liisa Hamalainen	Finland	17:04.0
10-kilometer cross-country	Marja-Liisa Hamalainen	Finland	31:44.2
20-kilometer cross-country	Marja-Liisa Hamalainen	Finland	1:01:45
20-kilometer cross-country relay	Berit Aunli, Brit Pettersen, Inger Nybraaten, Anne Jahren	Norway	1:06:49.7
Ice Hockey		U.S.S.R.	
Men's Speed Skating			
500 meters	Sergei Fokichev	U.S.S.R.	38.19
1,000 meters	Gaetan Boucher	Canada	1:15.80
1,500 meters	Gaetan Boucher	Canada	1:58.36

Event	Winner	Country	Mark
5,000 meters	Tomas Gustafson	Sweden	7:12.28
10,000 meters	Igor Malkov	U.S.S.R.	14:39.9
Women's Speed Skating			
500 meters	Christa Rothenburger	E. Germany	41.02*
1,000 meters	Karin Enke	E. Germany	1:21.61*
1,500 meters	Karin Enke	E. Germany	2.03.42†
3,000 meters	Andrea Schöne	E. Germany	4:24.79*
Biathlon			
10-kilometer event	Eirik Kvalfoss	Norway	30:53.8
20-kilometer event	Peter Angerer	W. Germany	1:11:52.7
30-kilometer relay	Shalna, Kachkarov, Bouliguin, Vasiliev	U.S.S.R.	1:38:51.7
Bobsledding			
Two-man	Wolfgang Hoppe, Dietmar Schauerhammer	E. Germany	3:25.56
Four-man	Hoppe, Wetzig, Schauerhammer, Kirchner	E. Germany	3:20.22
Figure Skating			
Men's singles	Scott Hamilton	U.S.A.	3.4‡
Women's singles	Katarina Witt	E. Germany	3.2
Pairs	Elena Valova, Oleg Vasiliev	U.S.S.R.	1.4
Ice dancing	Jayne Torvill, Christopher Dean	Great Britain	2.0
Men's Luge			
Singles	Paul Hildgartner	Italy	3:04.258
Doubles	Hans Stangassinger, Franz Wembacher	W. Germany	1:23.62
Women's Luge			
Singles	Steffi Martin	E. Germany	2:46.57

Winners of the Summer Olympics in Los Angeles in July and August

Event	Winner	Country	Mark
Archery			
Men	Darrell Pace	U.S.A.	2,616 pts.*
Women	Seo Hyang-Soon	S. Korea	2,568 pts.
Boxing			
Light flyweight	Paul Gonzales	U.S.A.	
Flyweight	Steve McCrory	U.S.A.	
Bantamweight	Maurizio Stecca	Italy	
Featherweight	Meldrick Taylor	U.S.A.	
Lightweight	Pernell Whitaker	U.S.A.	
Light welterweight	Jerry Page	U.S.A.	
Welterweight	Mark Breland	U.S.A.	
Light middleweight	Frank Tate	U.S.A.	
Middleweight	Joon-Sup Shin	S. Korea	
Light heavyweight	Anton Josipovic	Yugoslavia	
Heavyweight	Henry Tillman	U.S.A.	
Super heavyweight	Tyrell Biggs	U.S.A.	
Canoeing, Men			
500-meter kayak singles	Ian Ferguson	New Zealand	1:47.84
500-meter kayak tandems	Ferguson, MacDonald	New Zealand	1:34.21
500-meter Canadian singles	Larry Cain	Canada	1:57.01
500-meter Canadian tandems	Ljubek, Nisovic	Yugoslavia	1:43.67
1,000-meter kayak singles	Alan Thompson	New Zealand	3:45.73
1,000-meter kayak tandems	Fisher, Morris	Canada	3:24.22
1,000-meter kayak fours	Bramwell, Ferguson, MacDonald, Thompson	New Zealand	3:02.28

Event	Winner	Country	Mark
1,000-meter Canadian singles	Ulrich Eicke	W. Germany	4:06.32
1,000-meter Canadian tandems	Potzaichin, Simionov	Romania	3:40.60
Canoeing, Women			
500-meter kayak singles	Agneta Andersson	Sweden	1:58.72
500-meter kayak tandems	Andersson, Olsson	Sweden	1:45.25
500-meter kayak fours	Constantin, Ionescu, Marinescu, Stefan	Romania	1:38.34
Cycling, Men			
Individual road race	Alexi Grewal	U.S.A.	4:59:57
Sprint 1,000-meter time trial	Mark Gorski, Freddy Schmidtke	U.S.A. W. Germany	1:06:10
4,000-meter individual pursuit	Steve Hegg	U.S.A.	4:39:35
4,000-meter team pursuit	Grenda, Nichols, Turtur, Woods	Australia	4:25.99
100-kilometer team time trial	Vandelli, Bartalini, Giovannetti, Poli	Italy	1:58:29
50-kilometer points race	Roger Llegems	Belgium	37 pts.
Cycling, Women			
79-kilometer road race	Connie Carpenter-Phinney	U.S.A.	2:11:14
Equestrian			
Three-day event, individual	Mark Todd	New Zealand	51.60 pts.
Three-day event, team	Plumb, Stives, Fleischmann, Davidson	U.S.A.	186.00 pts.

*New Olympic record. †New world record. ‡New scoring system for 1984.

428

Event	Winner	Country	Mark
Dressage, individual	Reiner Klimke	W. Germany	1,504 pts.
Dressage, team	Klimke, Sauer, Krug	W. Germany	4,955 pts.
Show-jumping, individual	Joe Fargis	U.S.A.	4 pts.
Show-jumping, team	Fargis, Burr, Homfeld, Smith	U.S.A.	12 pts.

Fencing, Men

Event	Winner	Country	Mark
Individual foil	Mauro Numa	Italy	
Team foil	Borella, Cerioni, Cipressa, Numa, Scuri, Vitalesta	Italy	
Individual epee	Philippe Boisse	France	
Team epee	Borrmann, Fischer, Heer, Nickel, Pusch	W. Germany	
Individual sabre	Jean-François Lamour	France	
Team sabre	Dallabarba, Giovanni, Meglio, Arcidiacono, Marin	Italy	

Fencing, Women

Event	Winner	Country	Mark
Individual foil	Luan Jujie	China	
Team foil	Weber, Hanisch, Bischoff, Funkenhauser	W. Germany	

Gymnastics, Men

Event	Winner	Country	Mark
All-around	Koji Gushiken	Japan	118.700 pts.
Vault	Lou Yun	China	19.950 pts.
Pommel horse	Li Ning; Peter Vidmar (tie)	China U.S.A.	19.950 pts.
Horizontal bar	Shinji Morisue	Japan	20 pts.
Parallel bars	Bart Conner	U.S.A.	19.950 pts.
Rings	Koji Gushiken; Li Ning (tie)	Japan China	19.850 pts.
Floor exercise	Li Ning	China	19.925 pts.
Team	Gaylord, Conner, Vidmar, Daggett, Hartung, Johnson	U.S.A.	591.40 pts.

Gymnastics, Women

Event	Winner	Country	Mark
All-around	Mary Lou Retton	U.S.A.	79.175 pts.
Balance beam	Simona Pauca; Ecaterina Szabo (tie)	Romania Romania	19.800 pts.
Uneven parallel bars	Julianne McNamara; Ma Yanhong (tie)	U.S.A. China	19.950 pts.
Vault	Ecaterina Szabo	Romania	19.875 pts.
Floor exercise	Ecaterina Szabo	Romania	19.975 pts.
Rhythmic	Lori Fung	Canada	57.950 pts.
Team	Szabo, Agacag, Cutina, Grigroas, Stanulet, Pauca	Romania	392.20 pts.

Judo

Event	Winner	Country	Mark
132 pounds (60 kg)	Shinji Hosokawa	Japan	
143 pounds (65 kg)	Yoshiyuki Matsuoka	Japan	
157 pounds (71 kg)	Byeung-Keun Ahn	S. Korea	
172 pounds (78 kg)	Frank Wieneke	W. Germany	
190 pounds (86 kg)	Peter Seisenbacher	Austria	
209 pounds (95 kg)	Hyoung-Zoo Ha	S. Korea	
Over 209 pounds	Hitoshi Saito	Japan	
Open weight	Yasuhiro Yamashita	Japan	

Modern Pentathlon

Event	Winner	Country	Mark
Individual	Daniele Masala	Italy	
Team	Masala, Massullo, Cristofori	Italy	

Rowing, Men (all distances 2,000 meters)

Event	Winner	Country	Mark
Single sculls	Pertti Karppinen	Finland	7:00.24
Double sculls	Lewis, Enquist	U.S.A.	6:36.87
Four sculls	Hedderich, Hormann, Widenmann, Dursch	W. Germany	5:57.55
Pairs without coxswain	Iosub, Toma	Romania	6:45.39
Pairs with coxswain	C. Abbagnale, G. Abbagnale, Di Capua	Italy	7:05.99
Fours without coxswain	O'Connell, O'Brien, Robertson, Trask	New Zealand	6:03.48

Event	Winner	Country	Mark
Fours with coxswain	Cross, Budgett, Holmes, Redgrave, Ellison	Great Britain	6:18.64
Eights with coxswain	Turner, Neufield, Mark Evans, Main, Steele, Mike Evans, Crawford, Horm, McMahon	Canada	5:41.32

Rowing, Women (all races 1,000 meters)

Event	Winner	Country	Mark
Single sculls	Valeria Racila	Romania	3:40.68
Double sculls	Popescu, Oleniuc	Romania	3:26.75
Four sculls with coxswain	Taran, Sorohan, Badea, Corban, Oancia	Romania	3:14.11
Pairs without coxswain	Arba, Horvat	Romania	3:32.60
Fours with coxswain	Lavric, Fricioiu, Apostol, Bularda, Ioja	Romania	3:19.30
Eights with coxswain	O'Steen, Metcalf, Bower, Graves, Flanagan, Norelius, Thorsness, Keeler, Beard	U.S.A.	2:59.80

Shooting, Men

Event	Winner	Country	Mark
Skeetshooting	Matthew Dryke	U.S.A.	198 pts.
Trapshooting	Luciano Giovannetti	Italy	192 pts.
Free pistol	Xu Haifeng	China	566 pts.
Rapid-fire pistol	Takeo Kamachi	Japan	595 pts.
Small-bore rifle, prone	Edward Etzel	U.S.A.	599 pts.
Small-bore rifle, three positions	Malcolm Cooper	Great Britain	1,173 pts.
Rifle, running game target	Li Yuwei	China	587 pts.
Air rifle	Philippe Herberle	France	589 pts.

Shooting, Women

Event	Winner	Country	Mark
Air rifle	Pat Spurgin	U.S.A.	393 pts.
Small-bore rifle, three positions	Wu Xiaoxuan	China	581 pts.
Sport pistol	Linda Thom	Canada	585 pts.

Swimming and Diving, Men

Event	Winner	Country	Mark
100-meter freestyle	Ambrose Gaines IV	U.S.A.	49.80*
200-meter freestyle	Michael Gross	W. Germany	1:47.44†
400-meter freestyle	George DiCarlo	U.S.A.	3:51.23
1,500-meter freestyle	Michael O'Brien	U.S.A.	15:05.20
100-meter backstroke	Rick Carey	U.S.A.	55.79
200-meter backstroke	Rick Carey	U.S.A.	2:00.23
100-meter breaststroke	Steve Lundquist	U.S.A.	1:01.65†
200-meter breaststroke	Victor Davis	Canada	2:13.34†
100-meter butterfly	Michael Gross	W. Germany	53.08†
200-meter butterfly	Jon Sieben	Australia	1:57.04†
200-meter medley	Alex Baumann	Canada	2:01.42*
400-meter medley	Alex Baumann	Canada	4:17.41†
400-meter medley relay	Carey, Lundquist, Morales, Gaines	U.S.A.	3:39.30†
400-meter freestyle relay	Cavanaugh, Heath, Biondi, Gaines	U.S.A.	3:19.03†
800-meter freestyle relay	Heath, Larson, Float, Hayes	U.S.A.	7:15.69†
Platform diving	Greg Louganis	U.S.A.	710.91 pts.
Springboard diving	Greg Louganis	U.S.A.	754.41 pts.

Swimming and Diving, Women

Event	Winner	Country	Mark
100-meter freestyle	Carrie Steinseifer; Nancy Hogshead (tie)	U.S.A. U.S.A.	55.92
200-meter freestyle	Mary Wayte	U.S.A.	1:59.23
400-meter freestyle	Tiffany Cohen	U.S.A.	4:07.10*
800-meter freestyle	Tiffany Cohen	U.S.A.	8:24.95*
100-meter backstroke	Theresa Andrews	U.S.A	1:02.55
200-meter backstroke	Jolanda De Rover	Netherlands	2:12.38

Event	Winner	Country	Mark
100-meter breaststroke	Petra Van Staveren	Netherlands	1:09.88*
200-meter breaststroke	Anne Ottenbrite	Canada	2:30.38
100-meter butterfly	Mary T. Meagher	U.S.A.	59.26
200-meter butterfly	Mary T. Meagher	U.S.A.	2:06.90*
200-meter medley	Tracy Caulkins	U.S.A.	2:12.64*
400-meter medley	Tracy Caulkins	U.S.A.	4:39.24
400-meter freestyle relay	Torres, Steinseifer, Johnson, Hogshead, Andrews, Caulkins	U.S.A.	3:43.43
400-meter medley relay	Meagher, Hogshead	U.S.A.	4:08.34
Synchronized swimming (solo)	Tracie Ruiz	U.S.A.	198.467 pts.
Synchronized swimming (duet)	Ruiz, Costie	U.S.A	195.584 pts.
Platform diving	Zhou Jihong	China	435.51 pts.
Springboard diving	Sylvie Bernier	Canada	530.71 pts.

Track and Field, Men

Event	Winner	Country	Mark
100 meters	Carl Lewis	U.S.A.	9.99
200 meters	Carl Lewis	U.S.A.	19.80*
400 meters	Alonzo Babers	U.S.A.	44.27
800 meters	Joaquim Cruz	Brazil	1:43.00*
1,500 meters	Sebastian Coe	Great Britain	3:32.53*
5,000 meters	Said Aouita	Morocco	13:05.59*
10,000 meters	Alberto Cova	Italy	27:47.54
110-meter hurdles	Roger Kingdom	U.S.A.	13.20*
400-meter hurdles	Edwin Moses	U.S.A.	47.75
3,000-meter steeplechase	Julius Korir	Kenya	8:11.80
Marathon	Carlos Lopes	Portugal	2:09.21
400-meter relay	Graddy, Brown, Smith, Lewis	U.S.A.	37.83†
1,600-meter relay	Nix, Armstead, Babers, McKay	U.S.A.	2:57.91
20-kilometer walk	Ernesto Canto	Mexico	1:23:13*
50-kilometer walk	Raul Gonzalez	Mexico	3:47:26*
High jump	Dietmar Moegenburg	W. Germany	7 ft. 8½ in. (2.35 m)
Long jump	Carl Lewis	U.S.A.	28 ft. ¼ in. (8.54 m)
Triple jump	Al Joyner	U.S.A.	56 ft. 7½ in. (17.26 m)
Pole vault	Pierre Quinon	France	18 ft. 10¼ in. (5.75 m)
Discus throw	Rolf Danneberg	W. Germany	218 ft. 6 in. (66.60 m)
Javelin throw	Arto Haerkoenen	Finland	284 ft. 8 in. (86.76 m)
Shot-put	Alessandro Andrei	Italy	69 ft. 9 in. (21.26 m)
Hammer throw	Juha Tiainen	Finland	256 ft. 2 in. (78.08 m)
Decathlon	Daley Thompson	Great Britain	8,797 pts.*

Track and Field, Women

Event	Winner	Country	Mark
100 meters	Evelyn Ashford	U.S.A.	10.97*
200 meters	Valerie Brisco-Hooks	U.S.A.	21.81*
400 meters	Valerie Brisco-Hooks	U.S.A.	48.83*
800 meters	Doina Melinte	Romania	1:57.60
1,500 meters	Gabriella Dorio	Italy	4:03.25
3,000 meters	Maricica Puica	Romania	8:35.96*
100-meter hurdles	Benita Fitzgerald-Brown	U.S.A.	12.84
400-meter hurdles	Nawal El Moutawakel	Morocco	54.61*
400-meter relay	Brown, Bolden, Cheeseborough, Ashford	U.S.A.	41.65
1,600-meter relay	Leatherwood, Howard, Brisco-Hooks, Cheeseborough	U.S.A.	3:18.29*
High jump	Ulrike Meyfarth	W. Germany	6 ft. 7½ in.* (2.02 m)
Long jump	Anisoara Stanciu	Romania	22 ft. 10 in. (6.96 m)
Discus throw	Ria Stalman	Netherlands	214 ft. 5 in. (65.36 m)
Javelin throw	Tessa Sanderson	Great Britain	228 ft. 2 in.* (69.56 m)

Event	Winner	Country	Mark
Shot-put	Claudia Losch	W. Germany	67 ft. 2¼ in. (20.48 m)
Marathon	Joan Benoit	U.S.A.	2:24.52
Heptathlon	Glynis Nunn	Australia	6,390 pts.*

Weight Lifting

Event	Winner	Country	Mark
Flyweight	Zeng Guoqiang	China	518 lbs. (235 kg)
Bantamweight	Wu Shude	China	589 lbs. (267.5 kg)
Featherweight	Chen Weiqiang	China	623 lbs. (282.5 kg)
Lightweight	Yao Jingyuan	China	705 lbs. (320 kg)
Middleweight	Karl-Heinz Radschinsky	W. Germany	749½ lbs. (340 kg)
Light heavyweight	Petre Becheru	Romania	782 lbs. (355 kg)
Middle heavyweight	Nicu Vlad	Romania	865 lbs.* (392.5 kg)
First heavyweight	Rolf Milser	W. Germany	848 lbs. (385 kg)
Second heavyweight	Norberto Oberburger	Italy	859 lbs. (390 kg)
Super heavyweight	Dean Lukin	Australia	909 lbs. (412.5 kg)

Wrestling (Freestyle)

Event	Winner	Country	
Paperweight (106 lbs. or less)	Bobby Weaver	U.S.A.	
Flyweight (115 lbs. or less)	Saban Trstena	Yugoslavia	
Bantamweight (126 lbs. or less)	Hideaki Tomiyama	Japan	
Featherweight (137 lbs. or less)	Randy Lewis	U.S.A.	
Lightweight (149 lbs. or less)	In Tak Yoo	S. Korea	
Welterweight (163 lbs. or less)	Dave Schultz	U.S.A.	
Middleweight (181 lbs. or less)	Mark Schultz	U.S.A.	
Light heavyweight (198 lbs. or less)	Ed Banach	U.S.A.	
Heavyweight (220 lbs. or less)	Lou Banach	U.S.A.	
Super heavyweight (Over 220 lbs.)	Bruce Baumgartner	U.S.A.	

Wrestling (Greco-Roman)

Event	Winner	Country	
Paperweight	Vincenzo Maenza	Italy	
Flyweight	Atsuji Miyahara	Japan	
Bantamweight	Pasquale Passarelli	W. Germany	
Featherweight	Weon-Kee Kim	S. Korea	
Lightweight	Vlado Lisjak	Yugoslavia	
Welterweight	Jouko Salomaki	Finland	
Middleweight	Ion Draica	Romania	
Light heavyweight	Steven Fraser	U.S.A.	
Heavyweight	Vasile Andrei	Romania	
Super heavyweight	Jeffrey Blatnick	U.S.A.	

Yachting

Event	Winner	Country	Mark
Finn class	Russell Coutts	New Zealand	34.70 pts.
Tornado class	Sellers, Timms	New Zealand	14.70 pts.
470 class	Doreste, Molina	Spain	33.70 pts.
Soling class	Haines, Trevelyan, Davis	U.S.A.	33.70 pts.
Flying Dutchman	McKee, Buchan	U.S.A.	19.70 pts.
Star class	Buchan, Erickson	U.S.A.	29.70 pts.
Windglider	Stephan Van Den Berg	Netherlands	27.70 pts.

Team Sports

Event		Country	
Basketball (men)		U.S.A.	
Basketball (women)		U.S.A.	
Field hockey (men)		Pakistan	
Field hockey (women)		Netherlands	
Handball (men)		Yugoslavia	
Handball (women)		Yugoslavia	
Soccer (men)		France	
Volleyball (men)		U.S.A.	
Volleyball (women)		China	
Water polo (men)		Yugoslavia	

medal in women's all-around gymnastics, received many endorsement offers. So did the six men who upset China and gave the United States its first gold medal in team gymnastics.

The Soviets Objected to this capitalization on Olympic fame. They had spent perhaps $10 billion to stage the 1980 Olympics, and they objected to what they called the "commercialization" of the Los Angeles Olympics, the first ever financed privately. They also charged that the security provisions in Los Angeles were inadequate. And they complained about what they called anti-Soviet attitudes and actions by the U.S. government.

These were among the reasons given by the Soviets for their boycott. However, many organizing officials felt the main reason was revenge for the U.S. boycott of the Moscow Olympics.

Four days after the Olympics ended, the Soviet bloc opened the Friendship '84 Games in six nations. This multisport competition had all the Olympic trappings, including torchlight, medals, and anthems. The Soviets were quick to point out when Friendship '84 performances surpassed those of the Los Angeles Olympics, and that happened frequently.

The Level of Competition in many Olympic sports and events suffered because of the absent athletes. Every gold medalist in weight lifting would have been an underdog to the Soviets or Bulgarians. Half of the gold medalists in boxing might have lost to Cubans. East Germans and Soviets would have dominated women's track and field, and runner Valerie Brisco-Hooks of Los Angeles, who won three gold medals, might have won none. The 11 U.S. gold medals in women's swimming might have numbered only 6.

The results likely would have been different in canoeing, rowing, team handball, and rhythmic gymnastics. The boycotters would have done well in gymnastics, basketball, fencing, cycling, soccer, shooting, and Greco-Roman wrestling.

But not everything would have changed. Lewis would still have won his four gold medals. Moses would have won his hurdles final. Joan Benoit of Freeport, Me., would have won the first Olympic women's marathon. No one from a boycotting nation would have prevented British gold medalists Sebastian Coe (men's 1,500-meter run) or Daley Thompson (decathlon) from repeating their 1980 Olympic triumphs.

Louganis would still have won both gold medals in diving. Tracie Ruiz of Bothell, Wash., would still have won both gold medals in synchronized swimming. Darrell Pace of Hamilton, Ohio, would still have won the gold medal in men's archery.

The winners of the greatest number of medals were gymnasts. Li Ning of China won six medals. Retton, Ecaterina Szabo of Romania, and Koji Gushiken of Japan captured five each. Had the

Jayne Torvill and Christopher Dean of Great Britain dance their way to a gold medal at the Olympic Winter Games in February.

Soviets competed, those numbers might have been smaller.

In swimming, the most impressive winners were Michael Gross of West Germany and Alex Baumann of Sudbury, Canada, each with two gold medals and a world record. The United States won 20 of the 29 events and had five triple gold-medal winners—Ambrose (Rowdy) Gaines IV of Winter Haven, Fla.; Rick Carey of Mount Kisco, N.Y.; Mary T. Meagher of Louisville, Ky.; Tracy Caulkins of Nashville, Tenn.; and Nancy Hogshead of Jacksonville, Fla.

There were moments to remember—the bumping between Mary Decker of Eugene, Ore., and Zola Budd of Great Britain in the final of the women's 3,000-meter run that knocked Decker out of the race; the staggering finish of the dehydrated Gabriela Andersen-Schiess of Switzerland in the women's marathon; and the emotional victories by the United States in team gymnastics and the 800-meter freestyle swimming relay.

Organization. The Los Angeles Olympic Organizing Committee raised $619 million, mostly from television rights, commercial sponsorships, and ticket sales. After the games, the committee donated most of its surprisingly large surplus of $215 million to amateur sports.

The costs were low for an Olympics because existing facilities were used for most sports. The new swimming and diving pools, cycling velodrome, and shooting range were donated by sponsors. The Los Angeles Memorial Coliseum, site of the track and field events and the opening and closing ceremonies, was refurbished by a sponsor.

Winter Olympics. For the Yugoslav organizers, these first Winter Olympics in a Communist nation were an unqualified success. The Yugoslavs were so well organized that even when it snowed for four days without interruption, the 20 inches (50 centimeters) of snow that fell on the city was carried off almost instantly.

For U.S. athletes, the results were mixed. United States athletes remembered the euphoria of the 1980 Winter Olympics in Lake Placid, N.Y., where they won six gold medals — five by Eric Heiden in speed skating and one by an inspired hockey team. Still, their Sarajevo achievement of four gold and four silver medals was respectable.

But the U.S. athletes were disappointed because they had expected more medals. They were also disappointed because their eight medals had come in only two sports — Alpine skiing and figure skating.

The leading medal winners were the Soviet Union (25), East Germany (24), Finland (13), Norway (9), the United States (8), and Sweden (8). The leaders in gold medals were East Germany

(9), the Soviet Union (6), the United States (4), Finland (4), and Sweden (4).

The Soviet hockey team, with seven victories in seven games, was awesome in winning the gold medal. The U.S. team lost its first two games, tied its third, and finished seventh overall.

In speed skating, Karin Enke of East Germany won a medal in every women's race, finishing with two golds and two silvers. Gaetan Boucher of Quebec City, Canada, won two gold medals and a bronze in men's speed skating; Gunde Svan of Sweden won two gold medals, one silver, and one bronze in men's cross-country skiing; Marja-Liisa Hamalainen of Finland won three gold medals and one bronze in women's cross-country skiing; and Wolfgang Hoppe of East Germany won the two gold medals in bobsledding.

Alpine Skiing. Until three weeks before the Olympics, when he won a World Cup downhill race in Wengen, Switzerland, 23-year-old Bill Johnson of Van Nuys, Calif., had impressed few people. But the cocky Johnson boasted that he would win the Olympic gold medal — and he did. No male U.S. skier had ever before won an Olympic gold medal in Alpine skiing or any Olympic downhill medal.

U.S. skiers finished first, second, and fourth in the women's giant slalom. Debbie Armstrong of

Gymnast Mary Lou Retton, who won a gold medal in women's all-around, soars above the balance beam at the Olympic Summer Games in August.

Seattle won the gold, and Christin Cooper of Sun Valley, Idaho, won the silver. Tamara McKinney of Squaw Valley, Calif., finished fourth.

The final Alpine event, on the last day of the Olympics, was the men's slalom. The field included Phil and Steve Mahre, 26-year-old identical twins from White Pass, Wash. Phil had won the World Cup men's overall titles for the three previous years and the silver medal in the 1980 Olympic slalom. Steve, six minutes younger than Phil, was the 1982 world champion in giant slalom. But neither had been skiing well of late, and they were looking forward to retirement within a month. After the slalom began and favorite after favorite fell on the treacherous course, however, the Mahres were at their best. Phil won the gold medal, and Steve won the silver.

Ice Skating. In figure skating, the United States had medal contenders in all four events. They had hoped that for the first time since David Jenkins and Carol Heiss won in 1960, they would take both the men's and women's gold medals. Instead, they settled for one gold medal and two silvers in the four events.

The gold went to 25-year-old Scott Hamilton of Denver, a heavy favorite among the men, though he disappointed himself by not skating his best. Rosalynn Sumners of Edmonds, Wash., like Hamilton a world champion, took the women's silver medal behind Katarina Witt of East Germany. Sumners probably would have won the gold had she not omitted two difficult jumps toward the end of her free-skating program. The other U.S. medalists were Caitlin (Kitty) and Peter Carruthers of Burlington, Mass., who trained in Wilmington, Del. They placed second among the pairs.

Judy Blumberg of Tarzana, Calif., and Michael Seibert of Washington, Pa., who trained in Monsey, N.Y., were crestfallen after their fourth-place finish in ice dancing. They were scored unusually low by judges who seemed uncomfortable with their untraditional interpretive style. Jayne Torvill and Christopher Dean of Great Britain, with a similar approach, received 19 perfect scores en route to the gold medal.

Other Sports. In 1980, led by Heiden, the United States won eight Olympic medals in speed skating. This time, the best U.S. finishes were fourth places by Dan Jansen of West Allis, Wis., and Nick Thometz of Minnetonka, Minn.

The fifth-place finish by a U.S. team headed by Jeffrey Jost of Malone, N.Y., in four-man bobsledding was unexpectedly high. Jost's original sled was not competitive with those of the East Germans and Soviets. Only three days before the race, Jost obtained a new sled from a Swiss driver angry he had not been chosen to compete. Frank Litsky

In WORLD BOOK, see OLYMPIC GAMES.
OMAN. See MIDDLE EAST.

ONTARIO. William G. Davis, premier of Canada's most populous province for 13 years, announced on Oct. 8, 1984, that he was stepping down from that post. The Progressive Conservative Party leader said he was retiring to make room for new leaders with new ideas. A party convention was to be held in early 1985 to select his successor.

In 25 years in politics, Davis gave cautious but respected leadership, helping build Ontario's Progressive Conservative Party into an effective political force. Earlier, Davis had served as minister of education at a time of unprecedented growth in the province's schools and universities.

Private School Funding. Davis took a historic step on June 12 when he announced that Roman Catholic schools in Ontario will be granted status and financing equal to that of the province's public schools. In the past, Catholic school boards received public funds for their elementary grades, but, beginning in the fall of 1985, they will also get funds for their 30,000 secondary school students, who have had to pay tuition fees.

Language Rights. The right of French-speaking Ontarians to obtain education in their own language was affirmed in 1984. On June 26, the province's Court of Appeal ruled that parts of Ontario's Education Act were unconstitutional because they denied basic rights to French-speaking citizens. The court said that the new Canadian constitution overrides restrictions in the Education Act, which offered French-language education only "where numbers warrant."

The Davis government immediately introduced legislation guaranteeing students' language rights regardless of the number of French-speaking students in a school district. Ontario has 94,000 French-speaking students, about 5 per cent of the total number of students.

A law passed on April 24 made French an official language in Ontario's courts. Already available to French-speaking people in the criminal courts, French is now also allowed in family, county, and provincial courts.

The Provincial Budget for 1984-1985, announced on May 15, was based on the assumption of strong economic growth. Public spending was to rise by 7.4 per cent to $26.8 billion (Canadian dollars: $1 = U.S. 76 cents as of Dec. 31, 1984). A deficit of just over $2 billion was projected. The budget increased Ontario Health Insurance Plan premiums by 4.9 per cent and confirmed the 1984 termination of a 5 per cent surcharge on personal income taxes begun in 1983. However, there was little immediate relief in the budget for the province's 421,000 unemployed people. David M. L. Farr

See also CANADA. In WORLD BOOK, see ONTARIO.
OPERA. See MUSIC, CLASSICAL.
OREGON. See STATE GOVERNMENT.

PACIFIC ISLANDS. Relations between Indonesia and Papua New Guinea were strained for much of 1984. Members of the Free Papua Movement staged an unsuccessful uprising against Indonesian rule of Irian Jaya, the western half of New Guinea, in February. After the rebels failed to capture Jayapura, the capital of Irian Jaya, more than 10,000 refugees fled across the border to Vanimo, Papua New Guinea. Although in sympathy with the refugees' struggle against Indonesian rule, Papua New Guinea negotiated to send them back. Papua New Guinea's Foreign Minister Rabbie Namaliu complained in October to the United Nations (UN) General Assembly that Indonesia had sent military aircraft across the border, destroying a village, and had built a highway that crossed the border at several places.

In New Caledonia, the Melanesians were increasingly restless over their country's slow progress toward independence from France. Because France rejected demands that New Caledonia become independent in 1986, most Melanesians boycotted elections for the Territorial Assembly on November 18. French settlers opposed to independence won 34 of the 42 Assembly seats. The Melanesians reacted with a campaign of civil disorder, blocking roads, burning homes, and taking hostages. Several people were shot dead. After a provisional Melanesian government was set up on December 1, France sent a special envoy to try to restore peace and find a formula for the country's political future. A referendum on its future had previously been planned for 1989.

Nuclear Testing by France at Mururoa Atoll in French Polynesia was roundly condemned at home and abroad. In Tahiti, the biggest protest marches since 1973 were held in February and March. Gaston Flosse, vice president of the council of government of French Polynesia, said he would ask the French government to hold a referendum on whether the tests should continue. In August, at a meeting in Tuvalu of the South Pacific Forum—an organization of 14 South Pacific nations—leaders discussed a proposal for a nuclear-free South Pacific. Despite continued protests, however, France said that nuclear arms testing would continue.

New Leaders. Sergio Rapu, the first Easter Islander to become governor of his home island since Chile annexed it in 1888, took office on Jan. 24, 1984. Rapu, aged 34, who speaks Spanish, English, and Rapanui, the language of Easter Island, retained his post as director of the local museum.

In the Cook Islands, a constitutional crisis was averted in August when the Democratic Party of Prime Minister Sir Thomas Davis formed a coali-

Facts in Brief on Pacific Island Countries

Country	Population	Government	Monetary Unit*	Exports†	Imports†
Australia	15,661,000	Governor General Sir Ninian Martin Stephen; Prime Minister Robert Hawke	dollar (1.2 = $1)	20,651	19,349
Fiji	691,000	Governor General Sir Penaia Ganilau; Prime Minister Sir Kamisese Mara	dollar (1.1 = $1)	233	484
Kiribati	62,000	President Ieremia Tabai	Australian dollar	4	22
Nauru	7,000	President Hammer DeRoburt	Australian dollar	75	11
New Zealand	3,177,000	Governor General Sir David Stuart Beattie; Prime Minister David R. Lange	dollar (2 = $1)	5,272	5,279
Papua New Guinea	3,405,000	Governor General Sir Kingsford Dibela; Prime Minister Michael Thomas Somare	kina (1 = $1.08)	734	974
Solomon Islands	271,000	Governor General Sir Baddeley Devesi; Prime Minister Sir Peter Kenilorea	dollar (1.3 = $1)	66	76
Tonga	108,000	King Taufa'ahau Tupou IV; Prime Minister Prince Fatafehi Tu'ipelehake	pa'anga (1.1 = $1)	5	47
Tuvalu	7,000	Governor General Sir Fiatau Penitala Teo; Prime Minister Tomasi Puapua	Australian dollar	0.1	2
Vanuatu	136,000	President Ati George Sokomanu; Prime Minister Walter H. Lini	vatu (96 = $1)	31	64
Western Samoa	161,000	Head of State Malietoa Tanumafili II; Prime Minister Tofilau Eti Alesana	tala (1.6 = $1)	16	51

*Exchange rates as of Dec. 1, 1984. †Latest available data.

Pope John Paul II blesses islanders who presented him with gifts during a Mass he celebrated in the central highlands of Papua New Guinea in May.

PAKISTAN was disturbed by religious controversies during 1984. President M. Zia-ul-Haq proclaimed in April a law banning Pakistan's Ahmadiyya religious sect from calling itself Muslim. The Ahmadis accept most Muslim teachings but recognize their founder, Mirza Ghulam Ahmad, as a prophet. Orthodox Muslims believe there has been no prophet since Muhammad and therefore consider the Ahmadis to be heretics.

Zia's Islamization Program, the process of bringing Pakistani life into conformity with Islam, continued. On July 26, the 310-member Federal Advisory Council, an advisory group hand-picked by Zia, approved a law applying Islamic rules of justice to certain offenses. It used the principle of "an eye for an eye" in cases of murder, for which the punishment is death or the payment of "blood money" to the dead person's family. The law set compensation for a murdered woman or a non-Muslim man at only half that for a Muslim man, as well as giving their legal testimony only half the value. About 20 council members walked out to protest the inequalities.

Zia announced, on August 14, a new network of prayer wardens to ensure that Pakistanis prayed five times a day, as required of Muslims. He said the wardens would "reinforce morality."

A *referendum* (direct vote of the people) held on December 19 asked whether Pakistani voters approved of Zia's drive to Islamize the country's laws. About 98 per cent of the voters — who are overwhelmingly Muslim — voted yes. Before the referendum, Zia had announced that he would interpret a "yes" vote as a public call for him to stay in power five more years.

Opposition to Zia flared in Karachi, Pakistan's largest city, and in nearby areas in October. At least five students were killed by police in a clash on October 17. The main opposition group, an alliance of 10 banned political parties called the Movement for Restoration of Democracy, held a secret meeting in August. The movement appealed for a return to parliamentary democracy.

Foreign Relations were troubled. Afghan air and artillery units bombed and shelled border areas of Pakistan used by Afghan rebels, who were fighting the Soviet troops occupying their country and a puppet national government installed by the Soviet Union. The border strikes killed more than 50 people in August and September.

The Economy grew 4.6 per cent in the fiscal year that ended on June 30, the lowest growth rate since Zia took power but higher than that in most developing countries. One booming but illegal export was heroin. On April 12, Western countries offered Pakistan $1.82 billion in aid for the year beginning July 1.   Henry S. Bradsher

See also ASIA (Facts in Brief Table). In WORLD BOOK, see PAKISTAN.

tion government with the opposition Cook Islands Party of Geoffrey A. Henry. Henry became deputy prime minister. In the Solomon Islands, Sir Peter Kenilorea replaced Solomon Mamaloni as prime minister following elections on October 24.

Other Developments. The Fiji government airline, Air Pacific, was placed under the management of the Australian international airline, Qantas, in October. Air Pacific, which serves many islands in and around Fiji, had reportedly run up debts of about $24 million.

The United States and the Solomon Islands were at loggerheads over the Solomons government's seizure of the U.S. tuna-fishing vessel *Jeanette Diana* on June 26. The Solomons government claimed that the vessel, valued at $3.5 million, had been fishing illegally in Solomons waters. The United States contested the Solomons' right to seize the vessel.

On December 5, landowners of Kwajalein Atoll in the Marshall Islands filed suit to cancel an agreement allowing the U.S. Department of Defense to use the atoll for testing antimissile defense systems. The landowners claimed that the U.S. government had broken its promise to improve living conditions on the atoll.   Robert Langdon

See also AUSTRALIA. In WORLD BOOK, see PACIFIC ISLANDS.

PAINTING. See VISUAL ARTS.

PALEONTOLOGY. In March 1984, a group of scientists led by physicist Walter Alvarez of the University of California at Berkeley reported additional evidence supporting their theory that a mass extinction occurring 65 million years ago was caused by the collision of a giant meteor with the Earth. Dinosaurs were among the many groups of animals that disappeared at this time.

Alvarez' theory was based on the discovery of concentrations of the element iridium between sediments laid down at the end of the Cretaceous Period, when the extinctions occurred, and sediments laid down in the Tertiary Period that followed. Iridium is rarely found on Earth but is plentiful in meteors.

The scientists found iridium at the boundary between the Cretaceous and Tertiary periods at 48 places throughout the world. They also reported on studies showing that the fossil record of a number of groups of marine animals ends abruptly at the Cretaceous-Tertiary boundary.

A study of sediment layers at the Cretaceous-Tertiary boundary in the Hell Creek area of Montana, also published in March, revealed a similar pattern. Geologists J. Smit and S. van der Kaars of the University of Amsterdam in the Netherlands reported finding evidence that the fossil record of some animal groups ends abruptly at the iridium

Scientists from the Carnegie Museum in Pittsburgh, Pa., dig in the Wind River Basin in Wyoming, where 50-million-year-old fossils were found in September.

layer. Above the layer, the scientists found the fossils of different types of animals.

Extinction Pattern. One of the most exciting new theories about mass extinctions was published in February 1984 by David M. Raup and J. John Sepkoski, Jr., of the University of Chicago. While analyzing the fossil record of 567 families of marine animals, the two paleontologists found an apparent pattern of mass extinctions occurring about every 26 million years. The most recent took place 11 million years ago. Some of the other extinctions occurred about 38 million, 65 million, 219 million, and 248 million years ago.

Impact Craters. During 1984, scientists attempted to link Alvarez' explanation of the extinction 65 million years ago to these other periods of extinction. In April, Alvarez and physicist Richard A. Muller of the Lawrence Berkeley Laboratory in California reported on their analysis of 13 craters, formed by meteor impact between 5 million and 250 million years ago, whose ages were firmly established. They found an apparent cycle of crater formation lasting 28.4 million years. This cycle closely matches the cycle of mass extinction reported by Raup and Sepkoski. Another study by astronomers Michael R. Rampino and Richard B. Stothers of the Goddard Institute for Space Studies in New York City reported a similar cycle of crater formation lasting 31 million years.

A Common Cause. A number of theories were proposed to explain this apparently parallel cycle of extinctions and meteor impacts. In April, Rampino and Stothers suggested that the cause of the cycles may be a disturbance of the cloud of comets that surrounds the solar system. They proposed that as the solar system passes through the concentrations of dust and gas in the plane of the Milky Way Galaxy about every 33 million years, the orbits of the comets in the clouds are disrupted, triggering comet showers on Earth.

Also in April, two other teams of researchers proposed a different theory. Physicist Daniel P. Whitmire of the University of Southwestern Louisiana in Lafayette and Albert A. Jackson IV of Computer Sciences Corporation in Houston and a group consisting of astrophysicist Marc Davis of Berkeley, Piet Hut of the Institute for Advanced Study in Princeton, N.J., and Muller suggested that the sun has an as-yet-undiscovered companion star. According to this theory, the star, which has a highly elongated orbit, passes close to the cloud of comets about every 30 million years. As it does, it disturbs the comets' orbits, sending some of the comets crashing to Earth.

However, many scientists disputed this theory. In their opinion, a star with such a highly elongated orbit would soon be pulled off course by other stars and away from the sun. Ida Thompson

In WORLD BOOK, see PALEONTOLOGY.

PANAMA. On Oct. 11, 1984, Nicolás Ardito Barletta Vallarina took office as Panama's president. He pledged his administration to rebuilding the national economy, battling corruption, and keeping the military out of politics. See ARDITO BARLETTA VALLARINA, NICOLÁS.

The Panamanian economy was in dire straits after 16 years of military rule. Industrial output was stagnant, and unemployment ranged from 14 to 40 per cent in depressed areas of the country. Many Panamanians had expected that the country's economy would flourish with their eventual ownership of the Panama Canal, which they now operate in partnership with the United States. But in 1983 the canal showed an operating loss of $4-million, reflecting a global slump in shipping.

Among the new chief executive's first tasks was the framing of an austerity program to obtain continued financial assistance from the International Monetary Fund, an agency of the United Nations. To develop public support for unpopular measures, Ardito Barletta set about forming a government of "national conciliation" with representation from his opposition. Nathan A. Haverstock

See also LATIN AMERICA (Facts in Brief Table). In WORLD BOOK, see PANAMA.

PAPUA NEW GUINEA. See ASIA; PACIFIC ISLANDS.

PARAGUAY. See LATIN AMERICA.

PENNSYLVANIA. See PHILADELPHIA; STATE GOV'T.

PERES, SHIMON (1923-   ), was sworn in as prime minister of Israel on Sept. 14, 1984. Peres, the leader of the Labor Party, became the head of a government of national unity that included both his party and Israel's other major political group, the Likud bloc. See ISRAEL.

Peres was born Shimon Persky on Aug. 16, 1923, in Vishnevo, Poland, near Minsk (now in the Soviet Union). His family immigrated to Israel, then called Palestine, in 1934. In 1947, Peres joined the Haganah, an organization dedicated to establishing a Jewish state.

In 1950, two years after Israel declared its independence, Peres was sent to the United States as the head of an Israeli defense mission. While in the United States, he studied at New York University in New York City and at Harvard University in Cambridge, Mass. In 1952, he returned to Israel and was appointed deputy director of the ministry of defense. The following year, Peres was appointed director-general of that ministry.

Peres was elected to the Knesset (parliament) in 1959. In 1968, he helped found the reorganized Labor Party. From then until 1977, he held a number of government posts. Twice, in 1977 and 1980, he won the Labor Party's nomination for prime minister but lost in national elections.

Peres is married to the former Sonia Gelman. They have three children. Barbara A. Mayes

PERSONALITIES OF 1984 included the following:

Adams, Robert McCormick, 58, became the new secretary of the Smithsonian Institution in Washington, D.C., in September 1984. He is only the ninth person to hold that position in the institution's 138-year history and succeeds S. Dillon Ripley, who headed the Smithsonian for 20 years. Adams, a noted anthropologist and archaeologist, is a specialist in the agriculture and urban history of the Middle East and Mexico.

Ali, Muhammad, 42, came out swinging in September against an opponent more troublesome than all the boxers he has faced in the ring. In early September, Ali checked into the Columbia Presbyterian Medical Center in New York City for tests to determine the cause of symptoms, including slurred speech and a halting gait, that have plagued the former heavyweight champion since he retired from boxing in 1980. Ali's doctors decided the champ was suffering from Parkinson's syndrome, an umbrella term for a collection of symptoms associated with Parkinson's disease. However, they determined that Ali was not suffering from the disease itself. After a two-week stay at the hospital, doctors reported marked improvement. As for Ali himself, he met reporters at the door to the hospital, saying, "I came out to show you that I am still the greatest of all time."

Alliluyeva, Svetlana, 58, the daughter of Soviet dictator Joseph Stalin, returned to Russia in November, 17 years after defecting to the West. The Soviet government immediately restored her citizenship, which had been revoked in 1969. Alliluyeva, who defected in 1967 while visiting India, had been living in London with her 13-year-old daughter, Olga, the child of Alliluyeva's third husband, an American architect. Friends speculated that she had returned to her homeland because she had never really been comfortable with her life in the West and because she wanted to see her two children by her other marriages.

Blanc, Mel, 75, the man of a thousand voices, used his real voice to thank well-wishers at a ceremony at the Smithsonian Institution in March celebrating his 50 years in show business. Blanc, who said his real voice sounds a lot like that of Sylvester ("sufferin' succotash") the cat, also does all the talking for Bugs Bunny, Porky Pig, Daffy Duck, Yosemite Sam, Foghorn Leghorn, and Barney Rubble. At the Smithsonian, Blanc donated videotapes, movie posters, and figures of some of his most popular characters for inclusion in the museum's collection on U.S. entertainment history. Blanc wrapped up the press conference that followed the ceremony by quoting Porky Pig—"Th . . . th . . . th . . . that's all, folks!"

Craft, Christine, 39, a television anchorwoman, tried one more time in January and won $325,000 for her efforts. In 1983, Craft sued her former employer, a television station in Kansas City, Mo., for fraud and sex discrimination. Craft charged that although her employer claimed to have hired her for her journalistic abilities, she was demoted after viewers criticized her appearance. A jury awarded her $500,000 in damages. But a federal district judge later threw out the award, and ordered a new trial.

De Wilde, Eric, 16, stumbled over a bag of rocks and ended up in July a wealthy young man. While walking along a railroad track in Florida one day in 1983, De Wilde, an orphan, found a bag of what he thought was pretty costume jewelry. His aunt, however, recognized diamonds when she saw them and urged him to turn the stuff over to the police, which he did. Six months later, after no one else proved ownership of the 116 bracelets, brooches, rings, and unmounted stones, De Wilde took possession. In July 1984, auction houses began selling Eric's treasure. The value of his lucky find? More than $350,000.

Gish, Lillian, 90, who made her movie debut in 1912, was awarded the American Film Institute's Life Achievement Award in February 1984. Gish, who began acting on the stage when she was 6, became perhaps the finest actress of the silent film. Many of her films, including *The Birth of a Nation* (1915) and *The Wind* (1928), became clas-

Joe W. Kittinger, who completed the first solo balloon flight across the Atlantic Ocean, waves to a hometown crowd in Orlando, Fla., in September.

sics. Altogether, she has acted in 50 plays and more than 100 movies. Nor has her enthusiasm diminished over the years. Her latest movie was scheduled for release in spring 1985.

Johnson, Sonia, a feminist from Sterling, Va., became the Citizens' Party's candidate for President of the United States in August. Johnson first gained national attention in 1979 when she was excommunicated from the Church of Jesus Christ of Latter-day Saints (the Mormon Church) for supporting the proposed Equal Rights Amendment to the U.S. Constitution.

In all, Americans had 18 presidential candidates to choose from in 1984. Besides Johnson, they included Gus Hall of the Communist Party of the United States — running for the third time; David P. Bergland of the Libertarian Party; Dennis Serette of the Independence Alliance; and Mel Mason of the Socialist Workers Party.

Kittinger, Joe W., 56, of Orlando, Fla., floated up, up, and away and into the record books in September. In *Rosie O'Grady* — his 10-story-high, helium-filled balloon — Kittinger completed the first solo balloon flight across the Atlantic Ocean and set a world distance record for a solo balloon flight. His historic journey, which began in Caribou, Me., ended 3,535 miles (5,689 kilometers) and nearly 84 hours later near Savona in northwestern Italy when Kittinger slammed into trees on a mountainside in heavy winds and rain. During his landing, Kittinger, who has set other world flight records, broke an ankle but proclaimed that it was a small price to pay for the triumph.

Peller, Clara, about 80, a diminutive former beauty-shop owner from Chicago, became the most quoted woman in the United States in 1984. Her words were on the lips of children and adults alike, and were even repeated by presidential candidates. Those famous words — "Where's the beef?" — were spoken in a commercial for Wendy's hamburgers. Peller played one of three women outraged by receiving a tiny hamburger patty dwarfed by a huge bun.

Peller, who repeated her line in several other Wendy's commercials during 1984, quickly became a star. She appeared on television talk shows, and her picture or her famous question showed up on T-shirts, mugs, and greeting cards. There were even Clara Peller dolls, one of which asked (what else), "Where's the beef?"

Santmyer, Helen Hooven, 88, finally saw her 50-year effort to rebut author Sinclair Lewis pay off in August. Santmyer, angered at Lewis' unflattering portrait of small-town America in *Main Street* (1920), began writing her own book in the late 1920's to contradict him. Santmyer set her book on small-town life in Ohio during the period from 1868 to 1932, focusing on the members of the local women's literary club. Unfortunately, when the

With Daisy looking on, Clarence Nash, Donald Duck's voice, congratulates the foul-tempered duck, who celebrated his 50th birthday in 1984.

book—titled *". . . And Ladies of the Club"*—was finally published in 1982, it sold only a few hundred copies. In August 1984, however, Santmyer's book was republished, chosen as the main selection of a major book club, and bought for adaptation into a television miniseries. Although some reviewers criticized the book as tedious and elitist, it soon became a best seller.

Senghor, Leopold-Sédar S., 77, a poet and former president of the northwest African nation of Senegal, became the first black member of the French Academy in March. Founded in 1635 by the French statesman Cardinal Richelieu, the Academy is an organization of scholars and writers who work to preserve the French language and culture. Its 40 members, who are elected for life, are known as The Immortals. Senghor's most significant intellectual accomplishment has been his elaboration of the concept of *negritude*, the idea that the black peoples of Africa share a common cultural and spiritual heritage.

Shinwell, Lord Emanuel, was honored in October for becoming the first member of either house of the British Parliament to sit in that legislative body on his 100th birthday. An 81-year member of the Labour Party, Shinwell, who became a member of the House of Lords in 1970 at the age of 85, was first elected to the House of Commons in 1935. He won a reputation for his acrid tongue

and outrageous behavior. The son of a tailor from Poland, Shinwell once slapped another member of the Commons who, during a debate, suggested that Shinwell "go back to Poland." He also spent four months in prison for incitement to riot. Throughout, he remained a champion of British labor, once saying that he did not give a "tinker's cuss" for anybody but organized workers.

Torvill, Jayne, 26, and **Christopher Dean,** 25, swept the crowd off its feet as they skated to a triumphant victory in the ice dancing competition at the Winter Olympic Games in Sarajevo, Yugoslavia, in February. The two skaters from Nottingham, England, earned perfect scores for artistic interpretation with a slow, sensuous performance to Maurice Ravel's *Bolero*. Their stunning and innovative program also gave Great Britain its only gold medal in the Winter Games. Afterward, the two acknowledged their debt to their hometown, whose city council has helped finance their training. The excited folks back home also proclaimed the pair Freemen of Nottingham, an ancient honor that entitles them to herd their sheep across the town square.

Uemura, Naomi, 44, a Japanese mountain climber, became on February 12 the first person to reach the summit of Mount McKinley in Alaska alone in winter. Tragically, Uemura disappeared shortly afterward. He was presumed dead after an

Vietnamese-born Chi Luu, who spoke no English on his 1979 U.S. arrival, graduated first in his class at City University of New York in 1984.

eight-day search failed to find him. Uemura had climbed the highest peak on every continent except Antarctica and was the first person to reach the North Pole alone.

Williams, Vanessa, 21, the first black woman to become Miss America, became, on July 23, the first Miss America to resign her title. Pageant officials requested her resignation after *Penthouse* magazine announced it would publish nude photographs of her taken in 1982. Williams said that the photographer had assured her the pictures would remain confidential and that she had not signed a release permitting their publication.

Although at that time nothing in a Miss America's contract with the pageant forbade posing nude for photographs, pageant officials decided that Williams must resign to prevent "irrevocable" damage to the Miss America program. Williams was replaced by first runner-up Suzette Charles of Mays Landing, N.J., who is also black.

Wittkowski, Michael E., 28, of Chicago found in September that 2, 3, 10, 26, 30, and 43 equal 40 — $40 million, that is. Wittkowski, a printer, won $40 million in the Illinois State Lottery. It was the largest prize ever awarded to a single winner in North America and, perhaps, the world. Under a special arrangement, Wittkowski, his father, brother, and sister will share $2 million per year for 20 years.   Barbara A. Mayes

PERU. During 1984, President Fernando Belaúnde Terry presided over an economic crisis that seemed to deepen with every day he spent in office. Peru's future appeared bleak as the country headed toward national elections to choose a new president and a new legislature on April 14, 1985.

Peru's economy in 1984 was mired in what economists called the worst crisis of this century. On the one hand, the International Monetary Fund (IMF), an agency of the United Nations, demanded new austerity measures. On the other, workers and farmers protested those measures and their declining standard of living, while Belaúnde Terry attempted a delicate balancing act.

Terrorist Activity. Meanwhile, in the countryside, Sendero Luminoso (Shining Path) guerrillas continued to stage attacks on government installations, particularly in their stronghold area of Ayacucho. They were joined in 1984 by a second group of terrorists, who called themselves the Tupac Amaru Revolutionary Movement.

Civil Unrest. From March 1 to 3, more than 1 million farmers protested continued depressed prices for their crops and new, higher taxes on consumer goods. The farmers blocked highways at key locations to prevent shipments of food from reaching the cities.

In a vain effort to forestall a nationwide strike

A Peruvian policeman in Lima grabs a protester by the hair during a crackdown on a one-day general strike called by unions in March.

by Peru's workers, which was scheduled for March 22, President Belaúnde Terry on March 19 accepted the resignation of his finance minister, who was an open advocate of the IMF austerity program. Then, on March 21, he declared a three-day national state of emergency and the suspension of civil rights. Finally, he offered Peruvians a bonus of $1 each — the equivalent of a half-day's pay — if they would ignore the strike. But to little avail. Union leaders proclaimed the one-day general strike a success, though the government said 60 per cent of the work force did not participate.

More political resignations followed. In April, Prime Minister Fernando Schwalb López Aldana resigned in protest against economic policies that he said ran counter to IMF demands. On June 8, another state of emergency and suspension of civil rights was declared in reaction to the country's largest civil service strike. Most schools and hospitals closed as most of Peru's 600,000 civil servants walked briefly off their jobs on June 5, demanding a wage increase of 150 per cent. In November, there was still another nationwide strike and another state of emergency. The restoration of order and economic recovery would be important issues in the 1985 election. Nathan A. Haverstock

See also LATIN AMERICA (Facts in Brief Table). In WORLD BOOK, see PERU.

PET. See CAT; DOG.

PETROLEUM AND GAS. A persistent world over-supply of crude oil led Statoil, Norway's state-owned oil company, on Oct. 15, 1984, to cut official prices for oil produced in its rich North Sea fields. The action triggered similar price cuts by bigger producers, raising hopes for a general worldwide decline in petroleum prices. On October 17, the British National Oil Corporation reduced its prices. Nigeria followed the next day, becoming the first member of the Organization of Petroleum Exporting Countries (OPEC) to openly defy the official pricing structure established by the 13-nation oil cartel in 1983. On October 31, after an emergency meeting in Geneva, Switzerland, OPEC members agreed to cut oil production in an effort to keep prices at the official level of $29 per barrel. On December 29, OPEC members announced a new pricing agreement that raised the price of heavy crude oil and lowered the price of light crude. Nigeria and Algeria refused to endorse the agreement.

The oil glut and price declines occurred despite concerns earlier in 1984 that an escalation in the long war between Iran and Iraq could lead to a worldwide oil shortage. Beginning in April, both Iran and Iraq attacked oil tankers in the Persian Gulf. Oil-importing countries feared the attacks might halt oil shipments through the gulf.

Oil Consumption. In its annual review of United States petroleum consumption published on April 30, the U.S. Department of Energy (DOE) said that oil imports in 1983 declined for the sixth straight year, reaching their lowest level since 1971. The agency said oil imports averaged 4.2 million barrels per day (bpd) in 1983, with only about 12 per cent of the total coming from OPEC countries. In 1984, U.S. dependence on OPEC oil declined for the sixth consecutive year.

On September 11, the DOE predicted that U.S. petroleum demand during 1984 would increase for the first time since 1978 but would then stabilize during 1985. Economic expansion during 1984 was expected to raise demand to an average of 15.9 million bpd, up about 4 per cent over 1983 levels. The DOE said U. S. oil imports would rise by 16 per cent, reaching 5.0 million bpd.

Choice at the Pumps. More than 50,000 gasoline service stations affiliated with a specific brand of gasoline were permitted to sell more than one brand of gas under an agreement reached on September 21 and 24 by 13 major oil companies. The agreement, which was to last for five years, came in a settlement of a 1971 lawsuit filed by operators of franchised service stations, who accused the oil companies of restraining trade in the sale of gasoline. Some oil industry authorities said the agreement would reduce gasoline prices by allowing service station operators to shop for the cheapest gasoline.

PETROLEUM AND GAS

Mergers. A number of mergers between big oil companies were proposed in 1984. On March 5, the Standard Oil Company of California announced that it would buy Gulf Oil Corporation for $13.3 billion in the largest corporate merger in U.S. history. Mobil Corporation on March 11 announced an agreement to purchase Superior Oil Company for $5.7 billion. The Federal Trade Commission on July 10 gave final approval to Texaco Incorporated's purchase of the Getty Oil Company for $10.1 billion. Marathon Oil Company said on March 29 that it would buy Husky Oil Company for $505 million.

The rash of oil company mergers led the Senate to consider temporarily halting further mergers involving the 50 largest U.S. oil firms. But the Senate rejected the bill on March 28.

Pollution Controls. The petroleum industry agreed on April 17 to adopt tougher controls on the discharge of pollutants from oil refineries into rivers and lakes. The agreement settled a lawsuit brought by the U.S. Environmental Protection Agency and the Natural Resources Defense Council, an environmental group.

The U.S. Department of the Interior on March 15 halted the subdivision of oil and gas leases into small parcels, many of which were sold at inflated prices to people who believed they contained val-

uable energy resources. The department said that many of the parcels were so small that they were unattractive to potential oil producers.

Gas Production, Consumption. United States production of natural gas totaled 10.2 trillion cubic feet (289 billion cubic meters) during the first seven months of 1984, the DOE reported on September 1. Production for the period was about 12 per cent higher than during 1983. The American Gas Association, a natural gas industry group, said on September 13 that the amount of new natural gas discovered during 1983 had almost equaled the amount of gas consumed. It was the fourth consecutive year in which additions to natural gas reserves almost equaled or exceeded consumption. United States consumption of natural gas during the first seven months of 1984 totaled 10.6 trillion cubic feet (300 billion cubic meters), about 8.4 per cent more than during the same period in 1983.

Price Controls. The DOE on July 2 assured Congress that natural gas prices would not rise sharply after Jan. 1, 1985, when price controls were to expire on about half of all natural gas produced in the United States. The DOE predicted a price increase of only about 2.5 per cent when partial price decontrol takes place under the provisions of the Natural Gas Policy Act of 1978. Concern over the possibility of major price increases in 1985 led

Only a blasted landscape remains after a pipeline carrying natural gas from the Soviet Union to Western Europe exploded in March in West Germany.

Smoke billows from the Saudi oil tanker *Safina al-Arab* in the Persian Gulf in April, one of many oil-carrying vessels attacked in the war zone in 1984.

the Energy and Commerce Committee of the House of Representatives to approve on April 12, 1984, legislation extending price controls until 1987. But Congress took no further action on the measure.

Canada on July 13 eased its price controls on natural gas exported to the United States, a step expected to reduce gas prices paid by some U.S. consumers. Under the new Canadian policy, natural gas could be sold to U.S. companies for 30 per cent less than the minimum price previously set by the Canadian government. The new pricing policy was established to prevent further declines in exports of gas to the United States. Canadian gas exports have declined by about 29 per cent since 1979.

Leasing Bids. United States oil companies on July 18 submitted bids totaling $945.7 million for oil and natural gas prospecting rights in the western Gulf of Mexico. On August 22, the oil industry bid $877.1 million for offshore oil exploration rights in the Diapir Basin of Alaska's Beaufort Sea.

Oil Discoveries. Exxon Corporation on September 17 said it had discovered oil off the coast of China, bolstering hopes that the area could become a major new source of petroleum and natural gas. The well, drilled about 75 miles (120 kilometers) east of Hainan (Hai-nan) Island in the South China Sea, was the first site with commercial potential found since China opened its offshore waters to exploration by Western oil companies in 1983. Hunt Oil Company on July 9, 1984, announced the discovery of an oil field in Yemen (Sana), the first such discovery in that Arab state on the Red Sea.

The Occidental Petroleum Corporation on August 23 estimated that a major oil discovery in Colombia could produce almost 100,000 bpd by 1986. Occidental also announced the award of a $171-million contract for the construction of a new 184-mile (296-kilometer) pipeline from its Colombian oil fields over the Andes to Cúcuta.

Stormy Weather Rig. The first movable offshore oil platform capable of operating year-round in stormy water completed its first successful winter of operation in 1984. The French-built platform, named the *Glomar Labrador-1*, drilled continuously in the North Atlantic Ocean about 300 miles (480 kilometers) east of Halifax, Canada, despite 50-foot (15-meter) waves and winds of 100 miles (160 kilometers) per hour. Oil industry authorities said the new platform represents an important advance over traditional offshore drilling platforms, which must be anchored in port from November through April to prevent damage by winter storms.   Michael Woods

In WORLD BOOK, see GAS; PETROLEUM.

PHILADELPHIA. In one of the biggest scandals in the history of the Philadelphia Police Department, 20 former officers by the end of 1984 had been convicted on bribery charges or had pleaded guilty to such charges, and 14 of them had been sentenced to prison.

Fifteen officers were indicted on March 8 by a federal grand jury on charges of taking bribes totaling $350,000 from illegal gambling operations in the city. Ten of those officers were convicted, three pleaded guilty, and two were acquitted. On September 24, 10 of the guilty officers received prison terms. They included the two highest-ranking Philadelphia police officials ever convicted of corruption charges: former Deputy Police Commissioner James J. Martin, the number-two officer on the force, who was sentenced to 18 years in prison; and former Chief Inspector Joseph De-Peri, who received a 15-year sentence. Five other officers received prison terms ranging from 3 to 15 years, and three more officers were convicted on November 23. In addition, seven officers had been convicted and sentenced to prison in 1983.

In another corruption probe, a Philadelphia County grand jury on October 23 accused 12 current and former employees of the Philadelphia Traffic Court and 3 private citizens of participating in a scheme to fix hundreds of thousands of dollars worth of traffic tickets.

Mob Warfare. The body of Salvatore Testa, 28, considered a rising figure in Philadelphia organized crime, was found on September 14 in New Jersey. He had been shot to death execution-style. His father, Philip, was killed in 1981 in a mob-related explosion outside the Testa home. By late 1984, warfare among Philadelphia mobsters had resulted in 22 killings and attempted killings.

City Budget. On May 30, the City Council unanimously approved Mayor W. Wilson Goode's $1.5-billion operating budget, which provided funding for 200 more police officers, 125 additional fire fighters, and 120 more sanitation workers. The council approved the budget after the state legislature passed new business tax measures that were considered essential for a balanced city budget. The new business taxes will provide an estimated $105 million for the city and its public schools during the fiscal year that began on July 1. On December 2, Mayor Goode announced plans to cut 1,200 workers from the city payroll by mid-1986.

On May 31, the Pennsylvania Commonwealth Court ruled that Philadelphia's two-tiered wage tax — 4.96 per cent for city dwellers and 4.31 per cent for nonresidents — violated the state constitution. Although a uniform wage tax was supposed to be established by August, the two-tiered tax remained in effect at year-end while the city filed an appeal with the state Supreme Court.

Other Council Actions. On October 4, the City Council approved a $441.9-million convention center by passing a series of bills that carved out a new urban-renewal area at the proposed site in downtown Philadelphia. Construction of the center is expected to begin in 1986 and to be completed by fall 1989. The council had been reluctant to create the urban-renewal area because some 150 businesses will be forced to relocate.

On October 19, the city and the municipal court system agreed on a plan to end overcrowding in the city's jails by 1988. This will be accomplished through construction of a long-debated criminal-justice complex, which will contain court offices and prisoner cells, and the speedy completion of a 650-cell jail in northeast Philadelphia.

Railroad Tunnel. Philadelphia's commuter rail systems were linked on November 12 with the opening of the long-awaited $330-million Center City Commuter Tunnel. The 1.7-mile (2.7-kilometer) tunnel, which had been under construction for six years, combined the 12 Reading and Pennsylvania Central railroad lines into 7 routes and enabled the landmark Reading Terminal rail station to be closed. According to city transit officials, the railroad network is the first totally unified regional rail system in North America.   Jan Schaffer

See also CITY. In WORLD BOOK, see PHILADELPHIA.

PHILIPPINES. Political and economic aftershocks from the 1983 murder of opposition leader Benigno S. Aquino, Jr., kept the Philippines in turmoil throughout 1984. Aquino was killed at the Manila airport minutes after returning from the United States.

Aquino Inquiry. A government-appointed, five-member commission investigated the murder and issued its report on Oct. 23, 1984. The panel agreed that Aquino had not been killed by Rolando Galman y Dawang, who military leaders said was hired by Communists to kill Aquino and who was himself killed moments later. Instead, Aquino had been murdered in a military plot.

The panel did not agree, however, on the extent of the conspiracy. The chairman, Corazon J. Agrava, said a general and six soldiers conspired to kill Aquino. The other four commission members said 25 military men and 1 civilian were in the plot, including General Fabian C. Ver, the chief of staff of the Philippine armed forces. Ver is a cousin and close friend of President Ferdinand E. Marcos. A three-member panel of investigators reported in late November that they had found "probable cause" to prosecute all 26 men.

Aquino's younger brother, Agapito, expressed doubt that the case would get a fair hearing in a judicial system controlled by Marcos. Since his brother's death, Agapito had become the leader of the political opposition. He said demonstrations against the president would continue.

Elections on May 14 filled 183 National Assembly seats. Opposition candidates won 62 seats, up from 13 in the previous legislature, and charged that only fraud kept them from more. Voting on January 27 reinstated the office of vice president, which Marcos had abolished in the 1970's. Amid reports of his poor health, Marcos said in November that he planned to run for reelection in 1987.

Financial Rescue. Aquino's murder caused a decline in confidence in the Philippines by foreign bankers, hurting the nation's economy. The inflation rate soared from about 10 per cent when Aquino died to 40 or 50 per cent in 1984, and unemployment rose to 25 per cent.

Marcos announced on October 13 that he had reached agreement on a rescue plan with the International Monetary Fund (IMF), an agency of the United Nations. The IMF called for austerity measures, including higher taxes on petroleum products, in return for a loan of $630 million.

Guerrilla Surge. United States government officials estimated in September that the New People's Army, a Communist rebel group, had doubled its activities since 1983.　　Henry S. Bradsher

See also ASIA (Facts in Brief Table). In WORLD BOOK, see PHILIPPINES.

PHOTOGRAPHY. Cameras got "smarter" than ever in 1984 as manufacturers continued to refine the computerization of lens-opening and shutter-speed controls. In January, two "multiprogrammed" 35-millimeter (mm) single-lens reflex (SLR) cameras were introduced—the Canon T70 and the Ricoh XR-P. These models surpassed the capabilities of previous programmed cameras by allowing the photographer to pre-set the camera's program to favor high shutter speeds for stopping fast action, small lens openings for most depth of focus, or a compromise between the two.

Compact, Non-SLR 35-mm Cameras continued to be popular with amateur photographers. Many of the new models had controls that automatically set the film speed, using the DX system originated in 1983 by the Eastman Kodak Company. One of the most interesting cameras in this category was the Fuji DL-200, the only camera of its kind with a through-the-lens light meter. The DL-200's most novel feature is a film "prewinding" system. As soon as a roll of film is loaded into the camera, the film automatically advances completely onto the take-up reel. Then, as each photo is taken, the camera rewinds the film—one frame at a time—back into the cassette. This system is designed to prevent the fogging of exposed frames if the camera is opened accidentally.

The Small Wonder, a color video camera weighing just slightly more than 2 pounds (0.9 kilogram), was unveiled by RCA Corporation in January.

Filmless Electronic Cameras showed up in the hands of professional photographers for the first time in 1984. At the Summer Olympics in Los Angeles in July and August, photographers for two Japanese newspapers took pictures with prototype video cameras made by the Sony and Canon corporations of Japan. These cameras focus an image onto a *charge-coupled device,* a light-sensitive component that converts the image into an electronic signal. The signal is recorded on a magnetic disk, which can be inserted into a playback device to display encoded photographs on a television screen. After reviewing their pictures in this way, the Japanese photographers transmitted selected shots to Tokyo over telephone lines.

In October at *photokina,* the biennial trade show in Cologne, West Germany, Nikon exhibited a device that would enable photojournalists to view conventional negatives on a TV set and then transmit them by telephone. And Fuji demonstrated a device that converts conventional negatives, prints, or slides into electronic signals and records those signals on magnetic disks like the ones used in video cameras. When the disk is inserted into a home player, the pictures can be displayed on a TV set.

Video Action. The marketing of video motion-picture equipment surged in 1984, with companies introducing a wide variety of compact cameras, portable recorders, and combined "camcorders." Excellent high-fidelity stereophonic sound became available in many VHS Hi-Fi video recorders, joining the Beta Hi-Fi models already on the market. In the fall, Kodak became the first company to sell video equipment in the long-awaited 8-mm format, which some electronics experts predicted would become the standard, though other experts doubted it.

Fast Films. Several very-high-speed color films were introduced in 1984. Kodak issued Ektachrome transparency film that could be developed at either 800 or 1,600 ISO speed and an improved version of its Kodacolor VR 1000 (ISO 1,000) print film. Agfa-Gevaert, a West German company, introduced Agfachrome 1000 RS slide film and Agfacolor XRS print film (both ISO 1,000). And two Japanese companies—Fuji and Konica—marketed ISO 1,600 slide films. Konica also introduced a 1,600-speed print film.

Deaths. A number of prominent photographers died during 1984, most notably Ansel Adams, the dean of American landscape photographers, who died in April. Others included Hungarian-born French photographer Brassaï, in July; American photojournalist Garry Winogrand, in March; and Albanian-born American photographer Gjon Mili, who pioneered the use of electronic flash, in February.   Steve Pollock

In WORLD BOOK, see CAMERA; PHOTOGRAPHY.

PHYSICS. Experiments on dense and highly energetic matter provided technical progress and major discoveries in 1984. In July, physicists led by Ronald Parker at Massachusetts Institute of Technology (M.I.T.) in Cambridge published details of passing a milestone in the study of hot gases called plasmas. One reason to study plasmas is the prospect of developing *fusion reactors.* These devices would compress a plasma so much that atomic nuclei in the plasma would *fuse,* or combine. This would release more energy than required to heat and compress the plasma. The extra energy would be used to generate electricity.

In 1957, British nuclear physicist John D. Lawson described mathematically the conditions under which the power output of a fusion reactor would exceed the power needed for heating and compression. Lawson said that the plasma temperature and a certain number, which came to be called the *Lawson product,* must reach certain values. (The Lawson product equals the amount of material in a given volume of plasma multiplied by the length of time the fusion reactor holds the material in place.)

The M.I.T. physicists announced that, in November 1983, a fusion reactor called the Alcator C Tokamak had become the first device in which a plasma reached the critical value of the Lawson product. In fact, the plasma surpassed this value by 30 per cent. This achievement suggested that larger devices being built in 1984 may well be able to surpass the critical value while achieving the temperature needed to reach the point at which energy gains and losses are equal.

Superdense Matter. In April, a team of physicists headed by Arthur M. Postkanzer of Lawrence Berkeley Laboratory (LBL) in Berkeley, Calif., and Hans H. Gutbrod and Hans-Georg Ritter of the Institute of Heavy Ion Research in Darmstadt, West Germany, reported that they had compressed *nuclear matter*—a substance made up of tightly packed protons and neutrons. The physicists accelerated nuclei of the chemical element niobium to high energy in the Bevalac accelerator at LBL, and then smashed them into other niobium nuclei in a thin metal target. Particles flying from the collisions of nuclei struck more than 800 electronic detectors mounted in a sphere 4 feet (1.2 meters) in diameter almost surrounding the target. The detectors sent information about the particles to computers and recording devices. Analysis of the recorded results revealed that the nuclear matter appeared to be compressed during the collisions and then to break up in a way never before observed.

Top Quark. Particles such as protons and neutrons are themselves made up of even tinier particles called *quarks.* At the European Laboratory for Particle Physics (CERN—formerly the Euro-

A special plastic that bends light will be
used in a device being built to detect light
emitted by collisions of high-energy particles.

pean Organization for Nuclear Research) near Geneva, Switzerland, a huge machine called the Super Proton Synchrotron accelerates a beam of protons and a beam of *antiprotons* — antimatter opposites of protons — to high energies in opposite directions and causes the beams to collide head-on. In the collisions, quarks within the beams annihilate one another and new particles form. The detection of some of the new particles reveals the nature of matter at the most basic level.

In 1983, two teams of experimenters at CERN reported the first observations of a particle called the W. Since then, a team of 151 physicists from nine nations has analyzed data from about 1 million proton-antiproton collisions detected by a huge electronic particle detector named UA-1. Painstaking sifting of data revealed records of 81 reactions that produced a W. In July 1984, the UA-1 team announced that six of the W's seemed to break up into particles that included a previously undiscovered quark, called the *top*, or *t*, quark. Scientists had long suspected the existence of the t quark, because it was needed to complete a set of six kinds of quarks that, according to theory, form *hadrons* — a group of objects that includes protons and neutrons. Thomas O. White

In World Book, see European Organization for Nuclear Research; Particle Accelerator; Physics; Plasma; Quark.

POLAND. The government of General Wojciech Jaruzelski continued its struggles with the underground labor union Solidarity and the Roman Catholic Church in 1984. Poland's relations with the West improved, and its economy grew.

Solidarity's appeal for a boycott of local elections on June 17 was a moderate success. About 75 per cent of the eligible voters cast ballots, compared with a reported turnout of 98.87 per cent in the previous election, held in 1980. The 1984 election had a unique feature besides the boycott. For the first time since the establishment of Communist rule in the late 1940's, there were two candidates for each seat, rather than one.

National elections had been scheduled for 1984. In November, however, the Sejm (parliament) postponed them until 1985.

Amnesty for Activists. On July 13, four Solidarity activists went on trial on charges of planning to overthrow the government. The trial was suspended on July 18 in anticipation of a government amnesty; and, on July 21, the four defendants were granted amnesty. The pardon was part of a general amnesty marking the 40th anniversary of the establishment of the Polish Committee of National Liberation, which evolved into Poland's present government. The government granted amnesty to 652 political prisoners and about 35,000 criminals serving short sentences.

Priest Slain. On October 19, members of the secret police kidnapped Jerzy Popieluszko, a Roman Catholic priest from Warsaw and an outspoken supporter of Solidarity. On October 30, the priest's body was found in a reservoir. The government arrested four suspects and set their trial date for late December. Some 250,000 people attended Popieluszko's funeral on November 3.

The trial began on December 27. The prosecutor said the priest was a victim of a "well-prepared, willful murder." Two of the defendants allegedly said that an order to kill Popieluszko came from "a high level" of the government.

Crosses Removed. Relations with the church had become strained in March when students at a college in Mietne protested against the removal of crucifixes from the walls of their classrooms. On April 6, the government and the church reached a compromise permitting crucifixes in the library and dormitories but not in the classrooms.

Student Beating. On July 16, the government announced the verdicts in the trial of six people charged in connection with the death of Grzegorz Przemyk, a student. Przemyk had died in May 1983 as a result of mistreatment by the police. The court found two policemen not guilty. Two ambulance drivers were found guilty of negligence, and two doctors were convicted of accidental negligence. The drivers were sentenced to prison, but the doctors were granted amnesty.

Flowers adorn a photo of missing pro-Solidarity priest Jerzy Popieluszko in Warsaw on October 28, two days before he was found murdered.

Western Visitors. The October visit of Austria's Foreign Minister Leopold Gratz was the first of a series of trips to Poland by officials of non-Communist countries. Other October visitors were Greece's Prime Minister Andreas Papandreou and Finland's Foreign Minister Paavo Vayrynen.

Malcolm L. Rifkind, minister of state in the British Foreign Office, caused controversy during his November visit by laying a wreath at Popieluszko's grave. And West Germany's Foreign Minister Hans-Dietrich Genscher canceled a November visit on short notice because of disagreements over his plan to visit Popieluszko's grave and the tomb of a German soldier, and because Poland refused to grant a visa to a West German reporter.

IMF Ban Lifted. On December 14, the United States dropped its objection to Poland's joining the International Monetary Fund (IMF), a specialized agency of the United Nations. The United States had kept Poland out of the IMF to punish it for imposing martial law in December 1981.

The lifting of the ban came at a time when Poland needed a great deal of financial help. At the end of 1984, Poland owed $21 billion to Western nations.   Chris Cviic

See also EUROPE (Facts in Brief Table). In WORLD BOOK, see POLAND.

POLLUTION. See ENVIRONMENT.

POPULAR MUSIC. See MUSIC, POPULAR.

POPULATION. In mid-1984, the population of the world stood at nearly 4.8 billion — 30 per cent more people than in 1970 and 59 per cent more than in 1960, according to the United States Bureau of the Census. If the current rate of annual increase — 1.7 per cent — were to continue, the world's population would double within 40 years. However, because the world growth rate has been dropping — the rate of annual increase was 2.2 per cent in 1974 — total world population is expected to stabilize at about 10.5 billion by the year 2110.

Growth Rates. The population of the industrialized nations, which now hold less than 25 per cent of the world's people, has increased by just 0.6 per cent annually in recent years. The population of developing nations, however, has been rising by 2.3 per cent per year. Those nations will probably have more than 80 per cent of the world's population by the turn of the century.

Africa, with some 530 million people and an annual rate of increase of 3 per cent, had the fastest-growing population in the world. Latin America, with 397 million people and a growth rate of 2.4 per cent, also grew more rapidly than the world as a whole. Asia, whose 2.8 billion people accounted for about 60 per cent of the world's population, had a growth rate of 1.8 per cent.

On the other hand, the slow growth rates of North America (0.7 per cent) and Europe (0.3 per cent) indicate that those two regions will continue to decline in their shares of world population. By the turn of the century, experts estimate, North America will have only 5 per cent, and Europe only 7 per cent, of the world's people.

China, the nation with the largest population, had more than 1 billion people in 1984, but its growth rate — 1.3 per cent — is now lower than that of the world as a whole. India, the second most populous country with 739 million people, continued to grow at 2 per cent per year. At that rate, India's population may exceed China's by the year 2050. The Soviet Union, with 277 million people, and the United States, with 236 million, were third and fourth in population. Both countries had growth rates below the world average — 1.0 per cent and 0.7 per cent, respectively.

Life Expectancy continued to increase in most parts of the world in 1984, while death rates, particularly infant mortality rates, continued to decline. Life expectancies at birth were 75 years or more in Iceland, Norway, and Sweden, as well as in Australia, the Netherlands, and Switzerland. On the other hand, life expectancy was only a little more than half that long in Afghanistan and some areas of Africa. Jeanne C. Biggar

In WORLD BOOK, see POPULATION.

Life Expectancy at Birth

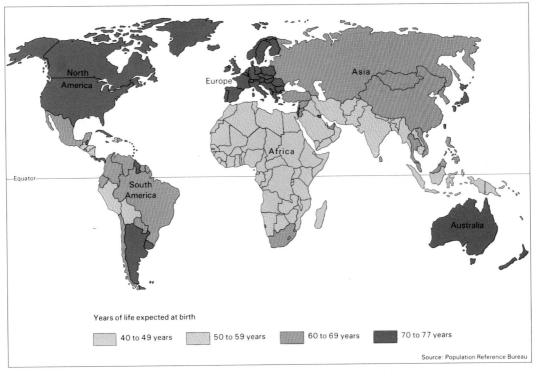

Years of life expected at birth

40 to 49 years | 50 to 59 years | 60 to 69 years | 70 to 77 years

Source: Population Reference Bureau

PORTUGAL. A devaluation of the currency and the adoption of severe financial measures in 1983 produced a dramatic drop in Portugal's balance-of-payments deficit in 1984. The balance fell from $3 billion in 1982 to $1.3 billion in 1984. However, the country's standard of living also declined.

The two-party coalition government of Socialist Prime Minister Mário Soares tried to improve the condition of 51 government-owned companies that were in deep financial trouble. "Losses in Portugal's public sector can endanger the entire economy," José da Silva Lopes, a former finance minister, told a gathering of the European Center of Public Enterprises — an organization of government-owned businesses — in Lisbon in June.

At the end of 1983, state-owned firms owed half of Portugal's $15-billion foreign debt. On May 22, Soares announced plans to raise capital by offering public land for sale to private farmers, selling companies that had been nationalized in 1975, and selling stock in other state-owned companies.

Failure to Pay Employees of state-owned firms led to massive demonstrations. Riot police dispersed 4,000 shipyard workers blocking a bridge in Lisbon on February 9. On March 30, police arrested 220 workers demonstrating outside the prime minister's office. The demonstrators said they represented 150,000 men who had not been paid for a year. Labor unions said that 457 companies owed workers $156 million in back wages.

Into the EC. British Prime Minister Margaret Thatcher visited Lisbon on April 17 to tell Soares that Great Britain wanted to welcome Portugal into the European Community (EC or Common Market) by January 1986. She said that the EC should reform to provide for a fairer distribution of burdens and benefits before Portugal's entry. President François Mitterrand of France delivered a similar message in Lisbon on June 27. The news of impending acceptance by the EC cheered Soares because 60 per cent of Portugal's exports go to EC countries.

Security Law. Parliament passed a controversial security law on July 27, 138 votes to 79. The law allows searches and arrests without warrants, phone tapping, and other surveillance. Soares said the law was necessary to protect the state against terrorism and organized crime.

In a roundup of suspected terrorists on June 20, Otelo Saraiva de Carvalho, an ultraleftist and a leader of the 1974 coup that established democracy in Portugal, was among 36 people arrested. The government said those arrested were suspected of being members of the Popular Forces of the 25th of April, a group responsible for several bank robberies and 12 killings.   Kenneth Brown

See also EUROPE (Facts in Brief Table). In WORLD BOOK, see PORTUGAL.

POSTAL SERVICE, UNITED STATES. The Postal Rate Commission recommended on Sept. 7, 1984, that first-class mail rates be raised in 1985 from 20 cents to 22 cents for the first ounce (28 grams). This was part of a $2.2-billion package of rate increases, which would be the first general hike in the cost of postage since 1981. However, the commission's proposal fell far short of what the U.S. Postal Service had sought.

The rate commission called for an average 9 per cent rate increase for all classes of mail, which would yield about $1.5 billion less per year than the 15.4 per cent hike sought by the service. The Postal Rate Commission is an independent, five-member panel appointed by the President to recommend postal rates to the Board of Governors of the Postal Service, which can accept or reject them. On December 12, the board announced that it had agreed to the higher rates, including the 22-cent first-class stamp, effective Feb. 17, 1985.

Wage and Benefits Contracts covering 600,000 unionized postal workers expired on July 20, 1984, after negotiators failed to agree on new contract provisions. The Postal Service demanded a three-year pay freeze for current employees and lower pay for newly hired workers. It contended that the average postal worker, who makes $23,000 per year plus benefits, was overpaid.

On July 25, the Postal Service announced that, effective August 4, new employees would be hired at pay levels 23 per cent below the wages of previously hired employees and would also receive fewer benefits. However, on August 10, Congress voted to bar the service from implementing any pay and benefit cuts not agreed on in negotiations.

In September, independent federal *arbitrators* (officials who help settle labor disputes) said the Postal Service should grant its workers a $2,000 wage increase over three years and abandon its plan to pay lower wages to newly hired employees. In October, the Postal Service and the unions entered into *binding arbitration* — contract negotiations by arbitrators whose decision must be accepted by both sides. In December, the arbitrators granted postal workers a 2.7 per cent annual pay increase for the next three years and cut starting salaries by an average of 25 per cent.

Electronic Mail Zapped. On June 6, the Postal Service Board of Governors voted to end a money-losing electronic mail service for businesses called E-COM, started in 1982. By mid-1984, only 54 businesses had converted to the E-COM system.

New Postmaster. Paul N. Carlin of Chicago, postmaster of the Postal Service's central region, on November 14 was named postmaster general, effective Jan. 1, 1985. Carlin succeeded William F. Bolger, who retired.   Frank Cormier and Margot Cormier

In WORLD BOOK, see POST OFFICE; POSTAL SERVICE, UNITED STATES.

PRESIDENT OF THE UNITED STATES Ronald Reagan devoted much of his time in 1984 to election-year politics as well as to national-security and foreign-policy concerns. With his popularity buoyed by a low rate of inflation and a strong economic upturn, Reagan won reelection by a landslide over Democratic challenger Walter F. Mondale in the November election. But even as he coasted toward that easy victory, Reagan's dominance of foreign and military affairs seemed to be eroding.

The Lebanon Dilemma. The continued presence of more than 1,500 U.S. Marines in Lebanon as part of an international peacekeeping force threatened to jeopardize Reagan's candidacy. On February 1, Democrats who controlled the U.S. House of Representatives, led by Speaker of the House Thomas P. (Tip) O'Neill, Jr. (D., Mass.), adopted a resolution calling for a "prompt and orderly" withdrawal of the Marines. Senate Democrats adopted a similar resolution the next day.

In a February 3 interview with *The Wall Street Journal,* Reagan responded that O'Neill "may be ready to surrender, but I'm not." The President said, "If we get out, that means the end of Lebanon." On February 7, however, the White House announced in Reagan's name that the Marines would be moved to Navy ships offshore. The "redeployment" was to be coupled with increased authority for the Navy to use air strikes and naval bombardment to retaliate against gun emplacements firing on Beirut. Within days, it became known that Reagan had made a tentative withdrawal decision on January 21 — more than a week before the passage of the congressional resolutions that supposedly had so aroused his scorn.

In the days following Reagan's announcement of the Marine pullout, the recommissioned World War II-era battleship *New Jersey* repeatedly shelled the hills above Beirut. On February 12, after the *New Jersey* had fired scores of shells from its 16-inch guns, Syria said it would abandon "self-restraint" if the bombardment continued.

At about the same time that U.S. forces were leaving Beirut — an operation that was concluded on February 26 — Italy and Great Britain were also withdrawing their peacekeeping troops from Lebanon. French forces left in March. On March 30, Reagan informed Congress that U.S. military involvement in Lebanon had ended. During the peacekeeping mission, which began in 1982, 264 U.S. servicemen were killed and 137 wounded.

Two more Americans, along with at least a dozen Lebanese citizens, died in a Sept. 20, 1984, suicide bombing at the U.S. Embassy annex in Aukar, near Beirut. The attack — the third successful truck-bombing of a U.S. installation in Lebanon in

Whistle-stopping in Ohio in October on the train President Harry S. Truman used in his 1948 campaign, Reagan addresses a crowd in Ottawa.

17 months — brought renewed charges from many members of Congress that the Administration had been negligent in beefing up security in Lebanon to protect American lives.

March saw the collapse of two Reagan peace initiatives in the Middle East. On March 5, the shaky government of Lebanese President Amin Gemayel canceled a U.S.-sponsored pact with Israel that had called for a withdrawal of all foreign troops from Lebanon. And on March 14, Jordan's King Hussein I said in a *New York Times* interview that he was abandoning an effort to revive Reagan's September 1982 proposal for a Mideast settlement. Hussein spoke just one day after Reagan, addressing a Jewish group, had called publicly for Israel to support his suggestion that a Palestinian homeland be created in the Israeli-occupied West Bank and Gaza Strip in "association with Jordan." Hussein said the United States was losing its credibility as a Middle East mediator because of its steadfast support of Israel.

U.S. Policy in Central America emerged anew in April as a major point of contention between Reagan and Congress. Reacting to press reports that the Central Intelligence Agency (CIA) had directed the mining of ports in Marxist Nicaragua, the Republican-controlled Senate on April 10 adopted, by a vote of 84 to 12, a resolution con-

demning the operation. Two days later, the House passed a similar resolution by a margin of 281 to 111. On April 11, the Reagan Administration announced that the mining had ended.

Prior to those congressional actions, on April 8, the U.S. Department of State announced that, for a two-year period, the United States would not accept the jurisdiction of the International Court of Justice (World Court) in cases relating to United States involvement in Central America. The unprecedented action was aimed at blunting Nicaragua's expected appeal the next day to the court.

As the State Department had anticipated, Nicaragua on April 9 requested that the court command the United States to end the mining and to cease giving assistance to *contra* rebels seeking to overthrow the Nicaraguan government. On May 10, the World Court ruled unanimously that the United States should halt any moves to blockade or mine Nicaraguan ports. Although the court made no mention of the *contras*, it issued a second decision — adopted by a 14 to 1 vote — saying that Nicaragua's national sovereignty should be "fully respected" by the United States.

United States policy in Central America, and especially the question of CIA military support for the *contras*, continued to be a friction point between President and Congress throughout 1984.

Children at a kindergarten in Shanghai entertain the President and first lady in May during the Reagans' six-day trip to China.

Reagan and Democratic presidential nominee Walter F. Mondale face off in their first televised debate, held on October 7 in Louisville, Ky.

On May 24, the House voted 241 to 177 against any further aid to the *contras*, called "marauders, murderers, and rapists" by Speaker O'Neill. The Senate favored continued financing for the guerrillas and remained stalemated with the House. Finally, on October 11 — the day before adjournment — Senate-House conferees agreed on a compromise: Assistance to the *contras* during the 1985 fiscal year would be limited to $14 million, none of which could be used until March 1, 1985, and then only with the approval of both the House and the Senate.

A fresh controversy involving the *contras* erupted in mid-October, when it was learned that the CIA had distributed a terrorist manual to the Nicaraguan rebels. The 89-page booklet recommended, among other things, "selective violence" to "neutralize" Nicaraguan government officials — an apparent violation of a 1981 Reagan executive order prohibiting even indirect American participation in assassinations. The ensuing furor led to the disciplining of some mid-level CIA employees.

El Salvador had been another ongoing bone of contention between the President and Capitol Hill. Congress initially rejected an Administration request for $117 million in additional military aid in fiscal 1984 for the government of El Salvador, which for several years has been battling leftist guerrillas. The House and Senate later reversed

themselves, however, and approved $70 million in added assistance.

Defense Spending. Congress forced Reagan to settle for an increase of about 5 per cent (after adjusting for inflation) in the Pentagon budget for fiscal 1985, far short of the 9.3 per cent hike he had requested. The President had also asked for money to produce 40 MX intercontinental ballistic missiles, but Congress cut that number to 15 — and even those could be built only with the approval of the Senate and House in 1985.

U.S.-Soviet Relations. With a U.S. presidential election looming in late 1984, continuing prickly relations with the Soviet Union took on added political significance. Reagan repeatedly professed a willingness to be flexible in discussing a wide range of common concerns with the Soviets, including the arms-control negotiations abandoned by Moscow in 1983 after the placement in Western Europe of U.S. Pershing 2 and cruise missiles by the North Atlantic Treaty Organization (NATO).

On June 29, the Soviets proposed holding talks in September aimed at banning weapons in space. The United States agreed but emphasized that it also wanted to talk about limiting nuclear missiles, a response the Soviets termed "totally unsatisfactory." Their initial proposal presumably reflected Soviet concern about the proposed "star wars" system to protect the United States against enemy missiles. Reagan first suggested the project in March 1983, and in January 1984 he ordered that research to develop it be started. Although critics contended that the star wars defense — which would use lasers and particle-beam weapons to destroy hostile missiles in flight — would be impractical and prohibitively expensive, Congress appropriated $1.4 billion for research on the system.

On September 28, barely five weeks before the presidential election, Reagan conferred at the White House with Soviet Foreign Minister Andrei A. Gromyko — the first meeting between the President and a top Soviet official. Afterward, both Reagan and Gromyko gave relatively upbeat assessments of the meeting, but there was no indication that they had made any real progress toward easing the tensions between Washington and Moscow. In November, however, the United States and the Soviet Union agreed to meet in Geneva, Switzerland, in January 1985 to discuss the entire complex of questions concerning nuclear and space weapons.

Reagan Made Two Overseas Trips in 1984. From April 26 to May 1, he was in China, drawing large, enthusiastic crowds wherever he went. And in June, Reagan made a trip to Europe, visiting the hometown of his Irish great-grandfather, attending a seven-nation economic summit in London, and speaking at ceremonies in France marking the 40th anniversary of the D-Day invasion of Normandy in World War II. Camera crews hired by the Republican National Committee accompanied the President everywhere, shooting film for campaign commercials. On the way home from China, Reagan met briefly in Fairbanks, Alaska, with Pope John Paul II, who was bound for South Korea. Eager for the approval of the 26 million Roman Catholic voters in the United States, the President on January 10 had renewed diplomatic relations with the Vatican after a 117-year break.

The Mounting Deficit in the federal budget, which Reagan had downplayed during the election campaign, became an important item on his agenda as the year drew to a close. On December 5, he proposed a list of spending cuts, including a 5 per cent pay cut for federal employees, that would save a total of $34 billion in the fiscal 1986 budget. The President told his Cabinet and the heads of major federal agencies to look for more ways to reduce spending. Congressional critics said that unless Reagan also agreed to substantial cuts in military spending, his proposed budget would stand little chance of being approved. Reagan said he would accept only limited military reductions.   Frank Cormier and Margot Cormier

See also CABINET, UNITED STATES; CONGRESS OF THE UNITED STATES; REAGAN, RONALD W.; UNITED STATES, GOVERNMENT OF THE. In WORLD BOOK, see PRESIDENT OF THE UNITED STATES.

PRINCE EDWARD ISLAND. A new headquarters building for the federal Department of Veterans Affairs was opened on June 28, 1984, in Charlottetown, the capital of this island province. The Department of Veterans Affairs is the only federal public service department headquartered outside Ottawa, Ont., Canada's national capital. The $20-million (Canadian dollars: $1 = U.S. 76 cents as of Dec. 31, 1984) building was named for Daniel J. MacDonald, former minister of veterans affairs.

The legislature of Canada's smallest province began its 1984 session on March 6. The Progressive Conservative government, headed by Premier James M. Lee, announced a revised development strategy based on a more competitive approach to introduce the province's agricultural and fisheries products to new international markets.

The province's budget for the 1984-1985 fiscal year, announced on April 10, predicted a reduction in the deficit without an increase in taxes. Expenditures were estimated to be $440 million, and revenues, $432 million.

In spring, more than 1,000 people in Canada's Atlantic Provinces were affected by food poisoning. The poisonings, caused by salmonella bacteria, were traced to unsanitary conditions on a dairy farm on Prince Edward Island.   David M. L. Farr

See also CANADA. In WORLD BOOK, see PRINCE EDWARD ISLAND.

PRISON. The incidence of serious crime dropped in the United States in 1984, for the fourth consecutive year. The prison population, however, continued to rise. A survey by the Bureau of Justice Statistics, a unit of the U.S. Department of Justice, indicated that a record 454,136 inmates were housed in state and federal prisons at midyear, up from the previous record of 438,830 at the end of 1983. In addition, a record 223,551 prisoners were serving time in local jails.

A report issued by the bureau on April 8 showed how severely prisons were overcrowded. In 1983, more than 21,000 prisoners in 15 states were released early because of cell congestion, 24 states had at least part of their penal system under court orders to relieve overcrowding, and only 7 states were operating at less than 100 per cent of listed capacity.

Prison expenditures were running at more than $6 billion per year. Operating expenses had risen by 44 per cent over the past four years. For the first time in recent years, there were no major outbreaks of rioting or violence in prisons in the United States in 1984.

Death Penalty. The pace of executions stepped up markedly as 21 convicts were put to death, bringing to 32 the number executed since the Supreme Court of the United States allowed the resumption of capital punishment in 1976. The death total included the first woman executed since 1962, convicted murderer Margie Velma Barfield, 52, who died on Nov. 2, 1984, of a lethal injection in a Raleigh, N.C., prison.

At the end of 1984, more than 1,400 inmates awaited execution, many with legal appeals running out. On January 23, the U.S. Supreme Court had moved to short-circuit some of those appeals by ruling, 7 votes to 2, that a state does not have to ensure that a death sentence is proportional to or comparable with punishment for similar crimes in the state.

Restrictions. Two Supreme Court rulings that were announced on July 3 restricted the privileges of prisoners. In a 5 to 4 decision, the high court rejected a Virginia inmate's claim that his constitutional rights were violated when guards destroyed personal property while searching his cell. The court declared that constitutional protections against unreasonable search and seizure do not apply to prisoners. In a 6 to 3 decision, the court also decided that prison officials could prohibit physical contact during visits by family members and friends if reasonable security needs seemed to demand that step.   David C. Beckwith

In WORLD BOOK, see PRISON.

PRIZES. See AWARDS AND PRIZES; CANADIAN LIBRARY ASSOCIATION; CANADIAN LITERATURE; NOBEL PRIZES.

PROTESTANTISM. Black Protestant churches in the United States made news during the 1984 presidential primary season by openly supporting Democratic candidate Jesse L. Jackson. Although political observers said it was the strongest public endorsement ever made by a large group of churches, black religious leaders described their support as consistent with a tradition of political activity within black Protestant churches.

Politics and Religion. Blacks were not alone in mixing politics with religion. White Protestant fundamentalists and some more-moderate evangelicals gave explicit support to the Republican Party platform, which many observers felt they had helped to shape. The Protestant conservatives also made clear their support for President Ronald Reagan and their opposition to any candidate who did not agree with their rejection of abortion under any circumstances.

Reagan made headlines in 1984 by appearing at gatherings of evangelical groups, where he expressed support for a proposed school prayer amendment and other issues of interest to evangelical Christians. Reagan's remarks led many to believe he implicitly called for a Christian United States. Reagan later modified his position, especially after Jewish groups expressed displeasure.

Vatican Ties Protested. The United States established full diplomatic relations with the Vatican on January 10. Although Protestants had long opposed such ties, criticism was generally muted when President Reagan appointed an ambassador to the Holy See. In September, however, a broad coalition of Protestant groups filed a lawsuit to nullify the diplomatic exchange between the United States and the Roman Catholic Church as a violation of constitutional guarantees of the separation of church and state. The National Council of Churches (NCC), which represents 31 Protestant and Orthodox groups, linked up with a number of other Protestant denominations and evangelical organizations to bring the suit.

Conservative Gains in the United States. The United Methodist Church observed the 200th anniversary of U.S. Methodism in 1984. Church leaders used the year to commemorate the anniversary and to try to bring new coherence to the denomination. The troubled 9.5-million-member church body has suffered membership losses in recent years. In May, the Methodists held their quadrennial general conference in Baltimore, where the first U.S. Methodist denomination was organized. Conservative Methodist congregations put their energies into opposing issues supported by the more liberal Methodist Federation for Social Action. Among other actions, the conference firmly stated its opposition to the ordination of "self-avowed, practicing" homosexuals. The church's Judicial Council upheld the ban on the ordination of homosexuals in October.

The largest Protestant body in the United States, the Southern Baptist Convention, held its annual meeting in Kansas City, Mo., in June. The militantly conservative faction continued to make gains. These gains included the election of fundamentalist pastor Charles F. Stanley of Atlanta, Ga., as president. The conservatives worked to restrict or eliminate seminary professors and leaders who do not agree with their interpretation of the Bible as free from error. In addition, the Southern Baptists passed a resolution opposing the ordination of women. However, the resolution cannot prevent local churches from continuing such ordinations. About 250 women have been ordained in the denomination.

The General Assembly of the Presbyterian Church (U.S.A.), which met in Phoenix in June, joined the United Methodists in opposing the ordination of practicing homosexuals. Several other resolutions passed by the assembly also were interpreted as victories for the denomination's more conservative elements. In what many regarded as a surprise, the Presbyterians elected James E. Andrews of Atlanta as its first *stated clerk* (chief administrator). Andrews, leader of the church's southern branch, defeated the favored William P. Thompson. Long a powerful Protestant figure, Thompson was leader of the church's northern

United Methodist Church delegates gather in Baltimore in May to observe the 200th anniversary of the founding of U.S. Methodism in that city.

branch. The church's northern and southern branches merged in 1983.

The Reorganized Church of Jesus Christ of Latter Day Saints bucked the conservative trend and joined the growing number of churches that permit the ordination of women. The action came after a written revelation, presented by church president Wallace B. Smith, and a convention vote at the body's World Conference in April. The Reorganized Church is considered closer to Protestantism than is the Church of Jesus Christ of Latter-day Saints, also known as the Mormon Church.

In Other U.S. News, the NCC elected Arie R. Brouwer, a pastor of the Reformed Church in America, general secretary in November. Moderately conservative in theological matters, Brouwer was to lead the NCC at a time when its social activism was under attack.

A major step toward Protestant unity was taken in November, when nine large denominations reached an accord on such key issues as baptism and ministry, paving the way for an eventual merger. The denominations have a combined membership of 23 million, including Methodists, Presbyterians, Episcopalians, and Disciples of Christ. The agreement was to go to member churches for study.

International News. Billy Graham, the senior statesman of the Protestant evangelical movement, avoided election-year politics. Instead, he took his crusade to bring people to Christ to Great Britain in late spring and the Soviet Union in late summer. Graham reported a significant response in Britain, where church attendance has traditionally been low. Having been criticized in 1982 for playing down Soviet religious persecution, he was careful to avoid such disputes in 1984.

In June, 266 American church leaders visited the Soviet Union under the sponsorship of the National Council of Churches. In Moscow, the group confronted signs held up by Baptists who protested the persecution of their religion. At other churches, the visitors also saw evidence of spiritual vitality. The Soviet press covered the visit enthusiastically, but the American press and many members of the delegation remained wary. On balance, however, most participants agreed that such visits had religious and political value.

The World Council of Churches elected Emilio Castro, a Methodist from Uruguay, general secretary at its July meeting in Geneva, Switzerland. The council is made up of about 300 Protestant, Anglican, and Eastern Orthodox churches. The election of a moderate Latin American was seen in part as an effort to bring together activist Third World churches and the more traditional denominations in Europe and North America. Many Third World churches have pursued policies denounced as supportive of Marxist revolutionaries by segments of the European and U.S. press.

At a summer meeting in Budapest, Hungary, the Lutheran World Federation expelled two South African churches that accepted their government's apartheid policy of racial segregation. The All Africa Lutheran Consultation asked for the action. Many Lutherans opposed the expulsion, which they feared would harden the attitudes of apartheid supporters.

The General Synod, the governing body of the Church of England, voted on November 15 in favor of ordaining women. But a complex approval process, including a vote of the British Parliament, had to be completed before women would become priests in the Church of England.

A visit to China in late 1983 by Robert Runcie, archbishop of Canterbury, drew attention throughout 1984 to the state of Protestantism in China. Of particular interest were the degrees of religious freedom permitted and the vitality of the surviving churches there. Ding Guangxun, official leader of China's Protestants, recognized 3 million Protestants in his country. Outside observers believe there are at least 20 million, due to the many Chinese who worship at home.   Martin E. Marty

See also RELIGION. In WORLD BOOK, see PROTESTANTISM and articles on Protestant denominations.

PSYCHOLOGY. Developments during 1984 continued to link psychology to neuroscience, the study of the biology and biochemistry of the brain and nerve cells. One example of how neuroscience is related to psychology involves anxiety. People given drugs called beta-blockers lose their anxiety. Victims of stage fright calm down and improve their performance, for example. At the 1984 Summer Olympic Games in Los Angeles, beta-blockers were found in the urine of a majority of athletes competing in the pentathlon after the pistol-shooting event. Consequently, beta-blockers are on the list of banned drugs for the 1988 Olympics.

However, the same drug that represents an unfair advantage in athletic events may be a breakthrough in the treatment of the severe irrational fears called phobias and other disabling anxiety states. In the past, psychologists explained anxiety states in psychological terms, such as being the result of traumatic events in early childhood. Some modern psychologists acknowledge that such events might be the cause of later anxiety, but increasingly they focus on reducing the physical symptoms of anxiety. Physically, anxiety is associated with excessive or inappropriate release of certain substances in the nervous system. Preventing the release of these substances with beta-blockers relieves the anxiety and often makes "mental" problems approachable and solvable.

"Split" Personality. Patients with surgically disconnected left and right halves, or hemispheres, of the brain have separate centers of consciousness in each half. In early 1984, scientists at the University of Southern California School of Medicine in Los Angeles reported in *Neuropsychologia,* a journal devoted to research on brain-behavior relationships, that they had found a subject with normally connected hemispheres who can "switch on" either hemisphere at will.

The patient was a 31-year-old woman. From an early age, she noticed two distinct patterns of mood and activity in herself. Each state was best suited for different types of tasks. At the age of 16, she learned to control the states, voluntarily switching into one or the other. The patient called one of the states "me" and the other "it."

The doctors used an electroencephalograph (EEG), a device that measures the electrical activity of the brain, to show that when she made a switch, the focus of her brain activity went from one hemisphere of her brain to the other. Left-hemisphere activity correlated with "me" and was better for such tasks as planning, writing, arithmetic, reading for information, or confronting new situations and meeting people. The patient called this her "businesswoman" side.

The other state correlated with right-hemisphere activity. The woman referred to "it" as her "gardening" personality. When "it" was dominant, she had more ability at drawing, sports, playing music, map reading and other spatial tasks, and socializing with friends. Some scientists now wonder whether ordinary people could use biofeedback techniques to boost activity in one hemisphere or the other.

Sexual Abuse of Children. Seldom has an issue risen so quickly from obscurity to national prominence as did the topic of the sexual abuse of children in the United States in 1984. On October 3, the U.S. Department of Justice reported that as many as 25 per cent of girls under age 13 may have been fondled or forced into sexual acts. Many incidents of sexual abuse involve incest—sex between relatives. According to a report in the May 1984 issue of *Psychology Today,* there are 15 million victims of incest in the United States alone. Typically, such sexual exploitation occurs between father and daughter, begins when the daughter is between ages 6 and 11, and lasts an average of two years.

In the past, guilt feelings and disbelieving family members prevented many victims of sexual exploitation from disclosing it. Experts in 1984 tried to bring the topic into the open with publicity campaigns that stressed the theme, "It's OK to tell." See CHILD WELFARE (Close-Up).   Russell A. Dewey

See also MENTAL ILLNESS. In WORLD BOOK, see PSYCHOLOGY.

PUBLISHING

PUBLISHING houses in the United States registered solid sales gains in almost all book categories in 1984. Publishers were especially pleased by the increased sales of hard-cover books. That gain was not surprising in a year when some critics hailed the "return of serious fiction," novels with both literary and entertainment value. Serious writers hitting best-seller lists for fiction included John Updike with *The Witches of Eastwick*, Saul Bellow with *Him with His Foot in His Mouth and Other Stories*, Gore Vidal with *Lincoln: A Novel*, Joseph Heller with *God Knows*, and Norman Mailer with *Tough Guys Don't Dance*.

Romance. With the renewed popularity of serious fiction came a decline in the profitability of romance novels, which had made big money in recent years. Publishers blamed the decline on increased competition from a glut of romance novels. The competitive situation eased somewhat on August 1, when Harlequin Enterprises Limited, the biggest publisher of romance novels, acquired Simon & Schuster, Incorporated's, Silhouette publishing division, also a leading romance publisher.

Controversy dogged several best-selling nonfiction books. Author Bob Woodward and publisher Simon & Schuster were sued on May 25 by Judith Jacklin Belushi, who objected to *Wired: The Short Life and Fast Times of John Belushi*, a biography of her comedian husband, who died of a drug overdose in 1982 at age 33. Members of the Kennedy family objected to *The Kennedys: An American Drama* by Peter Collier and David Horowitz. In July, Richardson & Snyder recalled from bookstores *God's Broker*, a biography of Pope John Paul II by Antoni Gronowicz. The author had claimed falsely to have based the book on extensive conversations with the pope.

On November 6, the Supreme Court of the United States began to hear arguments on whether *The Nation* magazine violated copyright laws when it published excerpts from *A Time to Heal*, a book of memoirs by former President Gerald R. Ford, without permission of the book's publisher, Harper & Row. *Time* magazine had bought exclusive rights to publish parts of the book. A court had ruled in 1983 that information in the book was news of public interest and therefore not protected by copyright laws.

Mergers. In a joint announcement on Nov. 26, 1984, Gulf & Western Industries, Incorporated, revealed that it would buy Prentice-Hall Incorporated for $705 million, and that the two firms would merge to form the largest book-publishing house in the United States. Gulf & Western already was a major publisher through its ownership of Simon & Schuster. In another book-publishing merger, in May, Macmillan Incorporated bought Scribner Book Companies.   Mark J. Fitzgerald

In WORLD BOOK, see PUBLISHING.

PUERTO RICO. Rafael Hernández Colón, leader of the Popular Democratic Party, defeated incumbent Carlos Romero Barceló in the Nov. 6, 1984, election to win the post of governor of Puerto Rico. Hernández Colón pledged to resolve the economic problems of the island, hit hard by federal cuts in welfare and tax incentives.

Hernández Colón said that one of his first acts as governor would be the naming of a special prosecutor to investigate the 1978 deaths of two pro-independence activists. The case was a major issue in the election because Barceló was governor at the time of the incident, when police officers allegedly ambushed the militant activists and beat them to death. On February 6, 10 former and current police officers were indicted on federal charges of having covered up the murders.

Puerto Rico's unemployment rate hovered around 20 per cent during 1984, and the very low wages offered for existing jobs provided little incentive for Puerto Ricans to seek work. An estimated 70 per cent of the work force received some kind of federal welfare assistance. About 10 per cent of the people lived in U.S. government-funded housing projects.   Nathan A. Haverstock

See also LATIN AMERICA (Facts in Brief Table). In WORLD BOOK, see PUERTO RICO.

PULITZER PRIZES. See AWARDS AND PRIZES.

Rafael Hernández Colón, embracing a voter during a campaign trip to the municipality of Toa Baja, was elected governor of Puerto Rico in November.

Two Inuit (Eskimos) drag a caribou carcass from northern Quebec's
Caniapiscau River, where thousands of the animals drowned in September.

QUEBEC. Eighty tall sailing ships from 18 countries visited Quebec City for five days in June 1984. The visit was the highlight of a celebration of the 450th anniversary of French explorer Jacques Cartier's first voyage to the Gulf of St. Lawrence in 1534.

Murderous Attacks. On May 8, a Canadian soldier, dressed in army fatigues, opened fire with a submachine gun in the Quebec National Assembly in Quebec City, killing 3 government workers and wounding 13 other people. The man, identified as Corporal J. P. L. Denis Lortie, was captured and charged with three counts of first-degree murder.

On September 3, a bomb exploded in Montreal's Central Station, killing 3 people and injuring 29 others. The incident was believed to be linked with the impending visit of Pope John Paul II to Montreal the following week. Thomas Brigham, a mentally disturbed United States citizen who had threatened the pope, was taken into police custody following the blast and charged with first-degree murder.

Caribou Disaster. In Quebec's Arctic region east of Hudson Bay in late September, about 10,000 caribou drowned while attempting to cross the swollen Caniapiscau and Koksoak rivers during their annual migration. Inuit (Eskimos) from villages in the region removed the carcasses from the rivers to prevent contamination of the water.

Electric Power. Prime Minister René Lévesque on May 27 opened La Grande 4, the last generator in the huge James Bay hydroelectric project. The new generator will double the capacity of the project and will add to the province's electric power surplus.

Lévesque sought to reduce the surplus on July 25 by arranging a power sale to Vermont. The sale will provide Vermont with 150,000 kilowatts of power for the next decade. An agreement in principle on a sale of power to the New England Power Pool was announced on June 19. Hydro-Québec will supply New England with 2 million kilowatts of power beginning in 1990.

Politics. The Parti Québécois (PQ), in power since 1976, lost three seats in the provincial assembly to the Liberal Party in elections on June 18. Dwindling public support for the PQ's commitment to independence for Quebec led to intraparty conflict late in 1984. Seven PQ cabinet ministers resigned in late November and early December, protesting Lévesque's intention to stress economic issues rather than independence in the next election campaign.   David M. L. Farr

See also CANADA; MONTREAL. In WORLD BOOK, see QUEBEC.

RACING. See AUTOMOBILE RACING; BOATING; HORSE RACING; ICE SKATING; OLYMPIC GAMES; SKIING; SPORTS; SWIMMING; TRACK AND FIELD.

RADIO. The most important event on radio in the United States in 1984 may have been a remark not heard over the air. Shortly before a radio address in August, President Ronald Reagan jokingly said, "My fellow Americans, I'm pleased to tell you today that I've signed legislation that will outlaw Russia forever. We begin bombing in five minutes." Although Reagan made the remark as part of a routine microphone check before the actual broadcast, it was heard by journalists and reported around the world. The Soviet Union's news agency, Tass, called the Reagan joke "unprecedentedly hostile toward the U.S.S.R." It was later learned that the Soviet Union had briefly put its military on special alert.

FM Domination, and the declining popularity of AM radio, was the biggest problem in the radio industry in 1984. In November, the National Association of Broadcasters, a trade organization, reported that FM stations drew 68 per cent of the total listening audience in 1984, even though AM stations slightly outnumber FM stations.

Increasingly in 1984, FM stations in large and medium-sized cities made efforts to identify specific radio audiences. They paid particular attention to defining the kind of rock music that appealed to each age group. As the baby boom generation in the United States has grown older, stations that play "hard rock" have lost listeners to what the radio industry calls "contemporary hit radio" or "CHR." In 1984, CHR was the hottest format in radio.

A 51-year-old Chicago disk jockey, Leo Rengers, won an age discrimination lawsuit in November in a decision the radio industry felt could have long-term implications. Rengers claimed he had been fired from WCLR-FM in 1980, when the station changed its format from "beautiful music," which appeals to older listeners, to "adult contemporary," appealing to younger listeners.

AM Stereo. Rock stations have proliferated on FM primarily because FM transmission in stereophonic sound produces truer sound reproduction than AM transmission does. During 1984, several AM stations began to experiment with broadcasts in stereo. The outcome of this effort was not expected to become clear for several years. Radio manufacturers, including those who make automobile radios, have thus far been reluctant to market AM stereo receivers aggressively.

National Public Radio (NPR), which ran up a $7-million debt in 1983, struggled successfully in 1984 to pay back some of the loans it received from the federally funded Corporation for Public Broadcasting. Although an NPR board member called the situation "fragile," member stations and NPR management appeared to have turned the corner toward solvency.   P. J. Bednarski

In WORLD BOOK, see RADIO.

RAILROAD companies in the United States enjoyed a sharp profit rise in 1984. The Association of American Railroads reported that U.S. railroads earned $2.17 billion in the first nine months of 1984, up 79 per cent from their $1.21-billion profits during the same period in 1983.

Rail freight traffic, measured in ton-miles, climbed 10.7 per cent through Dec. 22, 1984. Mergers eliminated some duplication of facilities, and railroads became more efficient, mainly due to employee cuts during the recession. On National Railroad Passenger Corporation (Amtrak) trains, ridership increased in 1984 for the second consecutive year. The number of passengers had risen 3.1 per cent by the end of November.

Sales and Mergers. The Department of Transportation (DOT) in 1984 strove to sell Consolidated Rail Corporation (Conrail), the big federally owned railroad serving the Northeast and Midwest. Once a money loser, Conrail had operating profits of $387.9 million in the first nine months of 1984, up 117 per cent from the same period in 1983. The DOT in September narrowed a list of bidders for Conrail to three, each offering about $1.2 billion. They were Alleghany Corporation, a holding company; the Norfolk Southern Corporation railroad; and a group headed by hotel executive J. Willard Marriott, Jr. Congress must approve the sale. Some members of Congress opposed it, saying the bids were too low and that the bidders might not keep the system intact.

The Interstate Commerce Commission (ICC) on July 24 approved the acquisition of American Commercial Lines, Incorporated, a barge line, by CSX Corporation, owner of the Chessie Systems, Incorporated, and Seaboard Coast Line Railroad. At year's end, both the Soo Line Railroad and the Chicago & North Western Transportation Company were competing to buy the 3,100-mile (5,000-kilometer) core of the bankrupt Milwaukee Road. The Rock Island Railroad emerged from nine years of bankruptcy on June 1.

Deregulation Backlash. Shippers unhappy with rate increases for railroad freight asked Congress to roll back a 1980 deregulation law. Coal companies and electric utilities urged a stronger ICC hold on rates. In June, ICC and court decisions derailed deregulation of boxcar shipments.

Secretary of Transportation Elizabeth Hanford Dole on June 6 proposed rules designed to curb alcohol and drug abuse by railroad crews. Federal investigators had cited alcohol and drug use as a factor in at least 45 train accidents between 1975 and 1983. A series of accidents involving Amtrak trains in July and August 1984 killed 11 people. This prompted the Federal Railroad Administration to conduct a safety investigation of the entire Amtrak system.   Albert R. Karr

In WORLD BOOK, see RAILROAD.

REAGAN, RONALD WILSON (1911-), 40th President of the United States, hit few bumps along the road to a reelection landslide in 1984. But one bump was a tooth rattler that threatened, if only briefly, to derail his drive toward a second term. In a televised debate from Louisville, Ky., on October 7, Reagan's Democratic rival, Walter F. Mondale, emerged as the surprise winner over the President — who had come to be known, because of his television skills, as the "Great Communicator." At times during the debate, Reagan was hesitant and seemed to lose his train of thought, which for the first time prompted serious public discussion of his age, health, and vigor. At 73, he was the oldest man ever to seek the U.S. presidency.

On October 10, the White House felt compelled to issue a statement by Navy Captain W. W. Karney, a physician who supervised a thorough physical examination of Reagan on May 18. Karney described the President as "a mentally alert, robust man who appears younger than his stated age." At the time of the exam, a team of seven doctors pronounced Reagan in "very exceptional physical condition," and Karney said all tests were "entirely normal." However, the doctors discovered, and partially removed, a small noncancerous growth in Reagan's large intestine.

Many observers viewed the second and final Reagan-Mondale debate, in Kansas City, Mo., on October 21, as a virtual tie. Asked about the age issue by one of the journalists who questioned the candidates, the President responded jokingly, "I am not going to exploit for political purposes my opponent's youth and inexperience." The quip helped to still speculation about Reagan's age and health, and the debate itself did little or nothing to boost Mondale's prospects.

Disclosure Statement. Reagan's annual financial disclosure statement, released on May 17, 1984, revealed that he and his wife, Nancy, accepted gifts worth $8,800 during 1983. The gifts included a pair of cowboy boots, a leather jacket, the hearing aid that Reagan began wearing in 1983 — reported at the time to have been paid for personally by the President — and cash donations from friends of $5,500 to help finance the purchase of a Jeep for use at the Reagans' California ranch.

On April 13, the Reagans made public their income tax returns for 1983, showing they paid $128,639 in federal income taxes on a combined income of $422,834. Their income had dropped sharply from $741,253 in 1982, when they had reported a $256,978 capital gain from the sale of their home in Pacific Palisades, Calif. The Reagans also had some financial reverses during 1983 in

The Reagans join daughter Patti Davis and son-in-law Paul Grilley at the young couple's wedding in Los Angeles on August 14.

Arriving at the Shannon airport with his wife, Nancy, on a June visit to Ireland, Reagan is presented with a plaque of his coat of arms.

RELIGION made news in 1984 through violent clashes in India and other parts of the world and through political skirmishes in the United States.

The Sikh Revolt was the most violent religious conflict of 1984. Sikhs form a majority in the state of Punjab in northwestern India and have persistently campaigned there for greater religious and political independence. (The Sikh religion split from both Hinduism and Islam during the early 1500's. It retains elements of both faiths but has a military aspect as well.)

In June 1984, Sikh extremists gathered in the holiest Sikh shrine, the Golden Temple in the city of Amritsar in Punjab. Under their militant leader, Jarnail Singh Bhindranwale, they set out to declare Punjab's independence. Indian soldiers, assigned the task of clearing them out, stormed the sacred area but tried to leave the temple itself unharmed. About 800 Sikhs and 200 soldiers were killed. Among the dead was Bhindranwale.

Through the military action, the government of India's Prime Minister Indira Gandhi hoped to crush Sikh efforts to form an independent state called Khalistan (Nation of the Pure). Even many of India's 13 million Sikhs privately supported the government. Although Gandhi risked driving moderate Sikhs into the extremist camp, she could count on support for the military action from the

the trust fund set up after Reagan became President. The fund had a net capital loss of $11,425. The Reagans claimed $15,307 in charitable contributions.

Presidential Library. White House officials and the trustees of Stanford University in California agreed on Feb. 14, 1984, to establish a Reagan presidential library and museum on the Stanford campus after he leaves office.

Reagan's Family. In a freak accident on November 4, Nancy Reagan hit her head in a bedroom fall. She complained of dizziness for several days but recovered quickly.

The Reagans' daughter, Patti Davis, 31, was married on August 14 to Paul Grilley, a 25-year-old yoga instructor, in a private ceremony in the garden of a Los Angeles hotel. Maureen Reagan, 43, the President's daughter by actress Jane Wyman, his first wife, spent 1984 campaigning for her father among women voters.

Son Ronald P. Reagan, 25, began doing radio features for the National Broadcasting Company and covered both national political conventions as a free-lance writer. Adopted son Michael Reagan, 39, set a powerboat endurance record in July in a run up the California coast from Long Beach to San Francisco.   Frank Cormier and Margot Cormier

See also PRESIDENT OF THE UNITED STATES. In WORLD BOOK, see REAGAN, RONALD WILSON.

The Dalai Lama, a Buddhist leader and exiled ruler of Tibet, meets with Robert Runcie, archbishop of Canterbury, in London in July.

vast majority of Indians. After the fighting, Sikhs honored those who fell as martyrs. Observers expected more such deaths to come, and later events proved them right.

On October 31, Gandhi was assassinated by two of her bodyguards. The gunmen, members of the Sikh religion, sought revenge for Gandhi's actions against the Sikhs. About 1,280 Indians were killed during the violent aftermath of the assassination, as Gandhi's Hindu followers sought revenge against Sikhs. See INDIA.

In the United States, most religious conflict is verbal. It usually involves controversy over issues of church and state or debates about "civil religion," the faith that links the citizens of the nation "under God." Most of the controversy in 1984 concerned the propriety of politicians' appeals for religious support and of the participation of religious groups in political campaigns.

In mid-September, a *New York Times*-CBS News poll found that only 22 per cent of those polled believed that candidates should discuss religion in a campaign; that only 15 per cent believed clergy should cite religion in political endorsements; and that 42 per cent believed that politicians in 1984 were misusing religion. Undeterred, clerics and politicians allied as they seldom had in recent United States history.

After some sharp confrontations early in the campaign, the focus on religion began to lessen. Still, support by Roman Catholic bishops and Protestant fundamentalists for legislation banning abortion dogged "pro-choice" candidates, many of them Democrats. Aggressive Protestant conservatives added other issues to their support for President Ronald Reagan and the Republican Party platform, which they dominated in the drafting stage. Chief among these issues was a proposed constitutional amendment permitting voluntary prayer in the public schools. Moderate religious leaders of both political parties protested the frequent invocation of religious symbols, even by candidates they otherwise favored.

Black Muslims also made news through political campaigns, due to support from Muslim leader Louis Farrakhan for Democratic presidential candidate Jesse L. Jackson in the primary elections. Farrakhan heads the small Nation of Islam, which split from the much larger American Muslim Mission in 1977. American Jews protested remarks by Farrakhan that they found repugnant, including the statement that Nazi dictator Adolf Hitler was a great man. Jackson's reluctance to dissociate himself from Farrakhan worried Jews, as did the refusal by so many blacks to condemn Farrakhan outright.
Martin E. Marty

See also EASTERN ORTHODOX CHURCHES; JEWS AND JUDAISM; PROTESTANTISM; ROMAN CATHOLIC CHURCH. In WORLD BOOK, see RELIGION.

U.S. Membership Reported for Religious Groups with 150,000 or More Members*

Group	Members
African Methodist Episcopal Church	2,210,000
African Methodist Episcopal Zion Church	1,134,179
American Baptist Association	225,000
American Baptist Churches in the U.S.A.	1,637,099
American Lutheran Church	2,343,412
Antiochian Orthodox Christian Archdiocese of North America	280,000
Armenian Apostolic Church of America	350,000
Armenian Church of America, Diocese of the	450,000
Assemblies of God	1,992,754
Baptist Missionary Association of America	234,142
Christian and Missionary Alliance	215,857
Christian Church (Disciples of Christ)	1,145,918
Christian Churches and Churches of Christ	1,043,642
Christian Methodist Episcopal Church	718,922
Christian Reformed Church in North America	218,659
Church of God (Anderson, Ind.)	182,910
Church of God (Cleveland, Tenn.)	493,904
Church of God in Christ	3,709,661
Church of God in Christ, International	200,000
Church of Jesus Christ of Latter-day Saints	3,602,000
Church of the Brethren	164,680
Church of the Nazarene	507,574
Churches of Christ	1,600,000
Community Churches, International Council of	173,500
Conservative Baptist Association of America	225,000
Episcopal Church	2,794,690
Free Will Baptists	226,422
General Association of Regular Baptist Churches	300,839
Greek Orthodox Archdiocese of North and South America	1,950,000
International Church of the Foursquare Gospel	164,688
Jehovah's Witnesses	649,697
Jews	5,728,075
Lutheran Church in America	2,925,008
Lutheran Church-Missouri Synod	2,630,947
National Baptist Convention of America	2,688,799
National Baptist Convention, U.S.A., Inc.	5,500,000
National Primitive Baptist Convention	250,000
Orthodox Church in America	1,000,000
Polish National Catholic Church in America	282,411
Presbyterian Church in America	155,988
Presbyterian Church (U.S.A.)	3,122,213
Progressive National Baptist Convention	521,692
Reformed Church in America	344,526
Reorganized Church of Jesus Christ of Latter Day Saints	192,830
Roman Catholic Church	52,392,934
Salvation Army	428,046
Seventh-day Adventists	623,563
Southern Baptist Convention	14,178,051
Unitarian Universalist Association	169,168
United Church of Christ	1,701,513
United Methodist Church	9,405,164
United Pentecostal Church, International	465,000
Wisconsin Evangelical Lutheran Synod	414,199

*A majority of the figures are for the years 1983 and 1984.
Source: National Council of Churches, *Yearbook of American and Canadian Churches* for 1985.

Beneath his own TV image, President Reagan on August 23 accepts nomination for reelection at the Republican National Convention in Dallas.

REPUBLICAN PARTY. Republicans had mixed fortunes in the United States national elections held on Nov. 6, 1984. The Republican Party (GOP) retained the White House with a landslide, but lost two important Senate seats and gained only 14 or 15 seats in the U.S. House of Representatives — well short of the number needed for ideological control. The GOP picked up one governorship and scored moderate gains in state legislatures.

The Republican standardbearer, President Ronald Reagan, fared best of all. He was reelected with a record electoral vote, establishing himself as probably the best-liked President since Dwight D. Eisenhower three decades earlier.

The Presidential Race. The President struck one of the most appealing themes of his still-unannounced candidacy in his State of the Union message to Congress on Jan. 25, 1984, declaring, "America is back — standing tall, looking to the 1980's with courage, confidence, and hope." Four days later, he dispelled all doubts by formally declaring his candidacy for reelection and announcing his choice of Vice President George H. W. Bush as his running mate. A mid-January Gallup Poll indicated that 54 per cent of those polled approved of Reagan's performance in office. Springtime polling, however, suggested that the presidential election might be close, and that Reagan might even lose.

Some of the President's early campaigning was done in other countries, with GOP camera crews at his elbow filming political commercials. Reagan was photographed on the Great Wall of China, paying tribute to World War II heroes in France, and mingling with pub patrons in Ballyporeen, Ireland, home of one of his great-grandfathers.

Reagan and his associates were not in complete control as delegates to the Republican National Convention in Dallas in August drafted a party platform. The solidly conservative platform, adopted by voice vote without debate, included a ban on "any attempts to increase taxes." Reagan had said he would favor higher taxes only as a last resort to curb federal deficits and had wanted the platform to allow for greater flexibility. The platform served as a focus of early competition between conservative and moderate Republicans as potential 1988 presidential candidates jockeyed for position. The party's most conservative elements were the clear winners as the 1984 platform scorned the Equal Rights Amendment, called for military superiority over the Soviet Union, urged Reagan to nominate for federal judgeships only candidates who support "the sanctity of innocent human life," and endorsed proposed constitutional amendments to make abortion a crime and to require a balanced federal budget. Reagan accepted renomination on August 23.

Reagan was the leader in public opinion polls

throughout the fall campaign. He stumbled only briefly after his Democratic opponent, former Vice President Walter F. Mondale, was widely judged to be the winner of the first of two televised debates, held October 7 in Louisville, Ky. In the balloting on November 6, Reagan received 59 per cent of the popular vote to Mondale's 41 per cent. Reagan garnered a record 525 electoral votes to 13 for Mondale, who carried only his home state of Minnesota and the District of Columbia.

Congressional Races. In U.S. Senate races, two Republican incumbents who had been reliable Reagan supporters were defeated. The Republican losers were Senator Roger W. Jepsen of Iowa and Charles H. Percy of Illinois, chairman of the Senate Foreign Relations Committee. Republican Addison Mitchell (Mitch) McConnell, a Kentucky county judge, narrowly defeated incumbent Democratic Senator Walter D. Huddleston. But that GOP gain was offset by the loss in neighboring Tennessee of the seat vacated by retiring Senate Majority Leader Howard H. Baker, Jr.

In the House, the modest Republican gain of 14 or 15 seats was about average for the party of a reelected President. The result of the race in Indiana's Eighth Congressional District still was not final when Congress convened in January 1985. Among the defeated Republicans were two incumbents who had been disciplined by the House. They were Daniel B. Crane of Illinois, censured in 1983 for having had sexual relations with a teenage female page, and George Hansen of Idaho, reprimanded after receiving a federal prison sentence for filing false financial-disclosure reports.

State Races. In governors' races, Republicans took over four governorships from Democrats — in North Carolina, Rhode Island, Utah, and West Virginia — but had a net gain of only one as Democrats succeeded Republican governors in North Dakota, Vermont, and Washington. After the balloting, Democrats had 34 governorships to the Republicans' 16.

In contests for state legislatures, Republicans took control of both houses in Connecticut and North Dakota. They lost control of legislatures in Vermont and Alaska. The GOP emerged with control of both legislative houses in 11 states, reducing from 33 to 27 the number of legislatures controlled by Democrats. Republicans also won the Ohio Senate, the Minnesota House, and the Delaware House.   Frank Cormier and Margot Cormier

See also DEMOCRATIC PARTY; ELECTIONS; REAGAN, RONALD W. In WORLD BOOK, see REPUBLICAN PARTY.

RHODE ISLAND. See STATE GOVERNMENT.

RHODESIA. See ZIMBABWE.

ROADS. See TRANSPORTATION.

Vice President Bush passes a bowl of soup as he lunches with the residents of a center for the elderly in Bangor, Me., in September.

ROMAN CATHOLIC CHURCH. The appropriate place of religion in politics became a major issue for Roman Catholics in the United States during the 1984 election campaign. Representative Geraldine A. Ferraro (D., N.Y.), the Democratic vice presidential candidate, had attended Roman Catholic schools and regularly worshiped with her family in her neighborhood parish in New York City. As a congresswoman, however, she supported efforts to use public funds to provide abortions to poor women. Ferraro said that although she personally thought abortion wrongfully took human life — a view held by the Catholic Church — she could not impose her religious beliefs upon others by her public actions.

Private Belief and Public Policy became a highly visible issue after the archbishop of New York City, John J. O'Connor, said at a press conference in June that he could not understand how a Catholic could remain loyal to personal values while supporting public policy that allowed abortion on demand. The discussion that followed drew comparisons between the archbishop's view and the views of Ferraro, New York Governor Mario M. Cuomo, and other prominent Catholic politicians. Cuomo had stated that he was sworn to uphold a 1973 ruling by the Supreme Court of the United States that struck down restrictive abortion laws.

In response to the public discussion, Ferraro

and Cuomo reasserted their positions. Both had private discussions with O'Connor. Another well-known Catholic politician, Senator Edward M. Kennedy (D., Mass.), publicly supported the views of Ferraro and Cuomo.

Among the bishops who questioned those views was James W. Malone of Youngstown, Ohio, the president of the National Conference of Catholic Bishops. On August 9, he issued a statement to clarify church policy. Malone said that U.S. Catholic bishops sought a "consistent ethic of life." That ethic, he said, involved not only abortion but also other "sanctity of life" issues, including nuclear arms, full employment, and adequate care for poor Americans. He added that it was "not logically tenable" for political candidates to state that "their personal views should not influence their public policy decisions."

Debate on Public Policy among Catholics continued after the election. In November, a committee of the National Conference of Catholic Bishops issued the first draft of a pastoral letter called *Catholic Social Teaching and the U.S. Economy*. The bishops condemned the gap between rich and poor as "morally unacceptable." They called for new policies and attitudes that would provide the poor with greater dignity and increased opportunity. They termed the welfare system "woefully inade-quate" and criticized the channeling of resources into the arms race.

The bishops withheld the 120-page statement, which many people viewed as an implicit criticism of President Ronald Reagan's Administration, until after the presidential election in November. The draft was prepared under the direction of Archbishop Rembert G. Weakland of Milwaukee. A final version was to appear in 1985.

Internal Church Discipline became an important issue on two occasions in 1984. The first occasion saw the church's seal of approval, called an *imprimatur*, removed from two books. On the second occasion, the Vatican addressed liberation theology, a doctrine that justifies church involvement in political struggles in developing countries.

The imprimatur, which a bishop is empowered to grant a book, attests that a work does not deviate from Roman Catholic doctrine. Without it, a book cannot be used in Catholic education.

The works that lost their imprimatur in 1984 were Anthony J. Wilhelm's best-selling *Christ Among Us: A Modern Presentation of the Catholic Faith* (1975) and *Sexual Morality: A Catholic Perspective* (1977) by Philip S. Keane. The Paulist Press, run by the Paulist religious order, had published both books and removed them from sale. In each case, a bishop had been instructed to withdraw his im-

William A. Wilson, the first U.S. ambassador to the Vatican in 117 years, presents his credentials to Pope John Paul II in a ceremony on April 9.

primatur by the Sacred Congregation for the Doctrine of the Faith, a Vatican body that safeguards faith and morals.

Some Catholic Church leaders applauded the Vatican action. They said that neither book truly represented Catholic teaching and that both books had in fact disputed it. Other Catholics criticized the decisions. They held that customary church processes had been ignored and that the action taken by the Vatican would restrict legitimate theological discussion among Catholics.

Liberation Theology. On September 3, the Vatican's Sacred Congregation published a lengthy document on liberation theology. The document denounced any theology that relies on "concepts uncritically borrowed from Marxist ideology" as incompatible with Catholicism. The document referred to efforts by some nuns and priests, especially in Latin America, to combine Catholic teachings with the ideas of Karl Marx, the founder of Communism. It warned against viewing Marxist analysis of the class struggle as a solution to social injustice.

At the same time, the document acknowledged that there was a valid theology of liberation. That theology, however, did not place liberation from material poverty above liberation from sin and greed. Rather it understood freedom in the Biblical sense as liberation from spiritual slavery, which occurs as a consequence of human sin. The document forcefully reaffirmed church commitment to human rights and expressed the urgent need to address imbalances between rich and poor throughout the world. Pope John Paul II approved the statement before its release.

On September 7, Leonardo Boff, a Franciscan friar and leading liberation theologian of Brazil, was called to Rome for questioning. Two Brazilian cardinals accompanied Boff in a gesture of support. Afterward, Boff described his meeting with Joseph Cardinal Ratzinger, head of the Sacred Congregation, as congenial and constructive.

Vatican-U.S. Ties. On January 10, the United States and the Vatican established full diplomatic relations for the first time in 117 years. President Reagan named William A. Wilson, a California businessman, U.S. ambassador to the Holy See, and the Senate confirmed the appointment on March 7 by a vote of 81 to 13. Archbishop Pio Laghi, the apostolic delegate to the United States, became the Vatican's acting ambassador to the United States.

Some Protestant, Jewish, and civil liberties groups in the United States objected to the diplomatic ties as a violation of the constitutional separation of church and state. In September, a coalition of Protestant groups filed suit to cancel the exchange of ambassadors. Catholic leaders took no part in the debate.

Pope John Paul II closes the holy door of St. Peter's Church in Rome on April 22 to end the Holy Year as more than 300,000 people look on.

Pope John Paul II made a number of good-will trips in 1984. They included visits to South Korea, Thailand, the Pacific Islands, Canada, and Spain.

The pope repeatedly spoke about birth control in discussions of moral issues during the summer. He reemphasized the view expressed by Pope Paul VI in 1968 that artificial contraception, even if achieved by birth control pills, violates natural law. John Paul stressed that the dignity of human life and the importance of human love must govern all sexual relations and any natural means of family planning, such as the rhythm method. The pope firmly denounced government policies that attempted to regulate births. He said that any decision to limit family size belongs solely to the individuals within the sexual union.

Other Developments. In January, John Paul named bishops to two major U.S. archdioceses. Bernard F. Law, bishop of the Springfield-Cape Girardeau, Mo., diocese, was appointed archbishop of Boston. He succeeded Humberto Cardinal Medeiros, who died in 1983. Bishop John J. O'Connor of Scranton, Pa., was named to follow Terence Cardinal Cooke, who also died in 1983, as archbishop of New York City. On October 15, the Vatican said it would permit celebration of the Latin Mass, banned since 1963.   Owen F. Campion

In WORLD BOOK, see ROMAN CATHOLIC CHURCH.

ROMANIA continued to pursue a foreign policy independent of the Soviet bloc in 1984. At home, the family of President Nicolae Ceausescu increased its power as a growing number of his relatives were given high government posts.

The country's major political event was the Communist Party congress, held from November 19 to 22 in Bucharest, Romania's capital. Delegates at the congress reelected Ceausescu as party leader for another five years, reelected his wife, Elena, to the Politburo — the party's policymaking body — and made his son Nicu a full member of the Central Committee. Ceausescu's brother Ilie and daughter-in-law Poliana Cristescu were also elected to the Central Committee. In December, the party reduced the Politburo's size from 13 members to 8. The only new member was Manea Manescu, Ceausescu's brother-in-law.

Overthrow Celebrated. On August 23, Romania celebrated the 40th anniversary of the overthrow of the government during World War II. After the overthrow, Romania switched sides in the conflict, leaving the German cause to join the Allies.

Under ordinary circumstances, the celebration would have been a major event in the Communist world, attended by leaders of all of Romania's fellow members of the Soviet bloc. Less than a month earlier, however, Romania had offended the bloc by becoming the only Eastern European nation to participate in the Summer Olympic Games in Los Angeles. In protest, all but one of the Soviet satellite nations sent officials of only middle rank to the celebration. The lone exception was East Germany, which was represented by its leader, Erich Honecker.

Soviet Relations. Soviet Foreign Minister Andrei A. Gromyko visited Bucharest in January, and Ceausescu went to Moscow in June. But Ceausescu continued to deviate from the Kremlin line. He broke a Soviet quarantine by visiting West Germany in October after Honecker and another Soviet bloc leader — Bulgaria's Todor Zhivkov — had canceled September visits to West Germany under pressure from Moscow. At the party congress in November, Ceausescu announced that Romania would extend its membership in the Warsaw Pact — the bloc's military alliance — but he added the qualifying phrase, "under certain conditions."

Canal Opens. On May 26, the Danube-Black Sea Canal opened. This 40-mile (64-kilometer) waterway connects the Danube River port of Cernavodă with the Black Sea port of Constanța. The canal eliminates the need for about 250 miles (400 kilometers) of travel along the Danube.   Chris Cviic

See also EUROPE (Facts in Brief Table). In WORLD BOOK, see ROMANIA.

ROWING. See OLYMPIC GAMES; SPORTS.

RUBBER. See MANUFACTURING.

RUSSIA. Soviet leader Yuri V. Andropov, 69, died on Feb. 9, 1984, after only 15 months in office (see Close-Up). On February 13, Konstantin U. Chernenko succeeded Andropov in the top post of the Soviet Communist Party — general secretary of the Central Committee. On April 11, he became head of state as chairman of the Presidium of the Supreme Soviet, the national legislature. For much of 1984, Chernenko appeared to be in poor health. During the summer, he was absent from public view for 53 days, finally reappearing on September 5. See CHERNENKO, KONSTANTIN U.

Mikhail S. Gorbachev, 53, a member of the Central Committee's Politburo — the Soviet Union's most powerful body — emerged as a possible successor to Chernenko. But Gorbachev's chief rival, Grigory V. Romanov, also a Politburo member, got much exposure. After the ailing Minister of Defense Dmitri F. Ustinov, 76, failed to appear at a November 7 military parade, Romanov was rumored to be in line to succeed him.

Ustinov died on December 20, and Romanov was named head of his funeral commission, again fueling speculation that Romanov would become minister of defense. But on December 22, First Deputy Defense Minister Sergei L. Sokolov, 73, succeeded Ustinov.

Human Rights. Jewish emigration from the Soviet Union slowed to a trickle in 1984. Between

July and October, the government cracked down on the teaching of Hebrew in private homes and on other Jewish cultural activities.

Physicist and Nobel Peace Prize laureate Andrei D. Sakharov went on a hunger strike in May to protest against the Soviet authorities' refusal to allow his wife, Yelena G. Bonner, to travel to the West for medical treatment. In June, Soviet authorities announced that Sakharov had stopped his hunger strike, but because he lives in exile in Gorki, there was no independent confirmation of his or Bonner's condition.

Word of Sakharov's health finally reached the West in December. Friends of Sakharov said that two Soviet physicists had visited him early that month. According to the friends, Sakharov's health seemed satisfactory.

Defectors. At least 20 people defected from the Soviet Union in the first eight months of 1984. They included Yuri Lyubimov — until March 6, 1984, the director of the Taganka Theater in Moscow; and Andrei Tarkovsky, a film director.

But defector Oleg Bitov, a former journalist for a Moscow weekly magazine, returned to the Soviet Union. Bitov had defected to Great Britain in 1983. On Sept. 18, 1984, at a press conference in Moscow, he claimed that Western intelligence agents had forced him to defect. And in November, Svetlana Alliluyeva, daughter of Soviet dictator Joseph Stalin, returned to the Soviet Union with her U.S.-born 13-year-old daughter. She said she had not been free in the West and had missed her two children who lived in the Soviet Union. Alliluyeva had defected to the West in 1967 and had been stripped of her Soviet citizenship.

The Economy. Russia harvested an estimated 170 million metric tons (187 million short tons) of grain in 1984, 70 million metric tons (77 million short tons) short of the production goal. The harvest was the smallest since 1981, and the second smallest since the disastrous 1975 crop.

Industrial production increased by 4.4 per cent in the first 10 months of 1984, compared with 1983. Productivity increased by 4.1 per cent.

Railroad Completed. On September 29, workers laid the last segment of track for the 3,012-kilometer (1,872-mile) Baikal-Amur Mainline (BAM) railroad in Siberia. The track took 10 years to lay. The cost may reach $10 billion. The BAM will help the Soviets exploit mineral deposits and timberlands in southeastern Siberia.

Space Feats. On July 25, cosmonaut Svetlana Savitskaya became the first woman to walk in space. On August 8, Soviet spacemen Leonid Kizim and Vladimir Solovyov set a record of 22 hours 50 minutes for the longest time spent space-

Frigid U.S.-Soviet relations thaw slightly in September when President Reagan meets with Soviet Foreign Minister Gromyko at the White House.

Pallbearers at the funeral of Soviet leader Yuri V. Andropov in February include his successor, Konstantin U. Chernenko, second from left.

walking on one mission. And on October 2, the two men and Oleg Atkov returned to earth after a record 237 days in space.

Arms Talks. On November 22, the Soviet Union and the United States agreed tentatively to hold arms talks early in 1985. This agreement was reached almost exactly a year after the Soviets broke off talks on strategic and intermediate-range nuclear missiles. The Soviets ended the discussions because the North Atlantic Treaty Organization (NATO) began to install United States Pershing 2 and cruise missiles in Western Europe.

Through much of 1984, the Soviets had insisted that they would resume talks only if NATO withdrew the missiles. Hopes for talks brightened on September 26, when Soviet Foreign Minister Andrei A. Gromyko met with U.S. Secretary of State George P. Shultz in New York City. Gromyko visited U.S. President Ronald Reagan at the White House on September 28.

Gorbachev discussed arms control with Great Britain's Prime Minister Margaret Thatcher for nearly 5½ hours on December 16 during a weeklong visit to Britain. British sources said that the talks were "very constructive."

Olympic Boycott. In May, the Soviet Union declared that it would boycott the Olympic Games in Los Angeles in July and August. The Soviets had sought assurances that the United States would

hand back any Soviet athlete who defected. Because the U.S. government refused to grant these assurances, the Soviets withdrew. The Soviets said they were pulling out because security arrangements were inadequate for Soviet and other Communist-bloc nations. In August, the Communist bloc staged its own games, the Friendship '84 sports festival. See OLYMPIC GAMES.

Satellite Nations. The Soviet Union tried during 1984 to strengthen cooperation within its trading bloc, the Council for Mutual Economic Assistance (COMECON). COMECON held its first summit meeting since the early 1970's in Moscow in June, and prime ministers of COMECON nations met in Havana, Cuba, in October. These meetings revealed sharp differences over such issues as pricing policy and joint investments.

In Afghanistan, Russia mounted what looked like a successful offensive against the Afghan rebels in April and May. Later, however, the rebels launched successful counterattacks against the Soviets and forces of the Afghan government.

China Pacts. On December 28, the Soviet Union and China signed three economic agreements in Beijing (Peking). The most important of the pacts calls for the Soviets to help modernize plants and other projects they helped to build in the 1950's.

The signing climaxed a diplomatic effort that began with preliminary, lower-level talks in Mos-

Too Little Time for Change

Yuri V. Andropov, the 69-year-old leader of the Soviet Union, died on Feb. 9, 1984, after only 15 months in office—not enough time to carry out his ambitious plans for change. Poor health had limited his effectiveness during the greater part of this period. Andropov suffered from diabetes and chronic kidney disease, and was not seen in public during the last six months of his life.

Andropov's plans for change were a result of the policies of his predecessor, Leonid I. Brezhnev, who had come to power in 1964 with a demand for stability. Brezhnev owed his rise to power to the belief of his colleagues in the Politburo—the policymaking body of the Communist Party—that he would be more cautious than his predecessor, Nikita S. Khrushchev, and that he would have more respect for the interests of various groups that made up the Soviet ruling establishment.

The Politburo's belief turned out to be justified. However, under Brezhnev, stability became stagnation. Economic growth rates declined, but Brezhnev refused to embark on significant economic reforms. Furthermore, there was a widespread public belief that corruption and other forms of crime were increasing. By the time of Brezhnev's death on Nov. 10, 1982, an important segment of the Soviet ruling group had decided that the time had come for bolder leadership.

Ill health caused Soviet leader Andropov, right, chatting with Foreign Minister Andrei Gromyko, to drop out of public view in August 1983.

For a while, Andropov seemed to provide it. He became general secretary of the Communist Party two days after Brezhnev's death and consolidated his position with remarkable speed. Within seven months, he acquired the same titles of power that Brezhnev had taken 13 years to attain. He became head of state as chairman of the Presidium of the Supreme Soviet, the national legislature. And he assumed the leadership of the armed forces as chairman of the Defense Council. Andropov used his power to give new vigor to the party and the government. Significant changes in personnel were made under Andropov's leadership. New appointees included one-fourth of the voting members of the Politburo; more than one-sixth of the country's top leadership team (voting and nonvoting members of the Politburo plus secretaries of the Communist Party Central Committee); more than one-third of the heads of departments of the Central Committee; and more than one-fifth of the Moscow-based ministers of the Soviet government. Most of the appointees were considerably younger than the people they replaced.

Andropov encouraged far-reaching economic reforms at home and abroad. For example, he favored Hungary's experimental program extending the authority of managers of private and state-owned businesses.

Within days of becoming party leader, Andropov launched a campaign against "breaches of party, state, and labor discipline." And on Aug. 7, 1983, the government published a labor decree that was much more strict than Brezhnev's decree of December 1979, his last on the subject. At the same time, the government increased its pressure on dissidents.

In foreign policy, Andropov continued Brezhnev's cautious approach. However, the role of Soviet military leaders showed signs of increasing in importance.

Andropov's highest priority in foreign policy was arms control. The Soviets directed their main diplomatic effort toward encouraging opposition to United States arms control and defense policies, particularly opposition among West Europeans. The effort's primary goal was to stop the installation of United States nuclear-armed cruise and Pershing 2 missiles in Western Europe. The Soviets conducted their effort skillfully, but it failed.

Andropov's successor, Konstantin U. Chernenko, had been a close ally of Brezhnev. Political analysts looked for little change in Soviet foreign policy under Chernenko, but they wondered whose example Chernenko would follow in domestic affairs—Brezhnev's, for stability; or Andropov's, for change.   Chris Cviic

cow in March 1984. The Soviets called off a May trip to China by Ivan V. Arkhipov, a first deputy prime minister, because of Vietnamese complaints against Chinese "aggressive acts" on China's border with Vietnam.

In September, Gromyko met in New York City with China's Foreign Minister Wu Xueqian. And in October, Soviet Deputy Foreign Minister Leonid F. Ilyichev held talks with Chinese ministers in Beijing. These talks failed because China insisted that any improvement in relations must be preceded by a Soviet pullout from Afghanistan, a reduction in Soviet forces on China's frontier, and an end of Soviet support for Vietnam's occupation of Kampuchea (Cambodia).

The Soviets met none of China's demands, but nevertheless Arkhipov went to China in December to negotiate the cooperation agreements. He became the highest-ranking Soviet official to visit that country since 1969.

As important as the agreements were, they apparently did not herald an overall improvement in relations between the two Communist powers. As 1984 drew to a close, the Soviet Union and China remained far short of their goal of restoring normal political relations. Chris Cviic

See also EUROPE (Facts in Brief Table). In WORLD BOOK, see RUSSIA.

RWANDA. See AFRICA.

SAFETY. After dropping for three years in a row, the traffic death toll in the United States began to rise in 1984. In March, the Department of Transportation (DOT) reported that in 1983 the number of motor-vehicle deaths hit its lowest level in 10 years — 42,584. Estimates showed that the number would increase in 1984 to about 43,800. The number of deaths for every 100 million miles traveled, however, fell slightly from 2.58 in 1983 to 2.54 in 1984, the lowest rate ever recorded in the United States.

Secretary of Transportation Elizabeth Hanford Dole had given credit for the drop in highway fatalities to vehicle-safety laws and to campaigns aimed at keeping drivers who drink off the highways. Many states raised the minimum drinking age to 21 and stiffened penalties for drunken driving, spurred by a new law reducing federal highway funds to states that failed to make 21 the minimum drinking age. At the same time, the law increased federal highway funds to states that tightened the penalties for drunken driving.

Business people — especially owners of restaurants, bars, and convenience stores — also grew increasingly concerned about the problem of drunken drivers. Under the leadership of Richard Berman, head of a nationwide chain of restaurants, a coalition called Beverage Retailers Against Driving Drunk was formed. The group was moti-

vated in part by recent court decisions holding that people who served alcohol to customers who were drunk and allowed those customers to drive were partially liable for accidents caused by the drunken drivers.

The coalition, along with other groups, conducted training sessions to help tavern personnel spot problem drinkers, cut off service, and prevent such drinkers from driving. Some establishments began paying taxi fares to get such patrons home safely. Partly as a result of these efforts, sales of alcoholic beverages in restaurants and bars dropped 12 per cent from 1982 to 1983, according to the trade journal *Nation's Restaurant News*.

A long-awaited decision on automobile safety was announced on July 11, 1984, by Secretary Dole. The decision would force manufacturers to install airbags or automatic seat belts in some new cars by September 1986 and in all new cars by 1989, unless states representing two-thirds of the U.S. population pass laws requiring the use of seat belts.

The ruling disappointed many advocates of highway safety, who wanted airbags made mandatory. Several major insurance companies filed suit in September, charging that the DOT plan violated "congressional requirements that national safety standards be uniform."

Secretary of Transportation Elizabeth Hanford Dole in July announces a plan aimed at getting airbags or seat belts installed in all new cars.

Smoking Restrictions. Health problems attributed to smoking received renewed attention in September when Congress passed a law requiring manufacturers to provide more explicit warnings on cigarette packages. Meanwhile, a growing number of states and communities adopted laws designed to protect the rights of nonsmokers. The most sweeping law took effect in San Francisco on March 1. It requires employers to adopt a company policy on smoking and to designate smoking areas if any worker objects to smoking. In Los Angeles, a similar measure went into effect on December 15.

Cigarette sales declined 6 per cent in the United States in 1983. It was the second consecutive year to show a decrease in sales.

Consumer Safety. The Consumer Product Safety Commission (CPSC), an independent government agency that has been rebuffed by Congress many times in recent years, finally won a few legal battles in 1984. One new law gave the CPSC power to act faster in taking unsafe toys off the market. Another law restored some of the agency's authority over amusement parks, following widespread publicity about fatal accidents on thrill rides. An earlier Congress, responding to pressure from the amusement park industry, had curbed CPSC power to inspect the rides.

Judicial rulings shifted the focus on formaldehyde from the CPSC to the Environmental Protection Agency (EPA). A 1983 court ruling had blocked the CPSC from banning the use of formaldehyde in foam insulation. A May 1984 decision ordered the EPA to undertake "an accelerated review" of evidence that the chemical harms people. The decision forced the EPA to reverse an earlier policy, which claimed that evidence showing formaldehyde caused cancer in laboratory animals was not sufficient evidence of a health risk to human beings.

A nationwide scare caused the EPA in February to impose new curbs on the use of ethylene dibromide (EDB), a pesticide that has caused cancer in laboratory animals. EDB had been widely used to kill fungus on citrus fruits, grains, and other foods. The scare occurred after detectable levels of EDB were found in flour, cereals, and other products made from grain.

New protections were also established for users of such devices as heart pacemakers, X-ray machines, and artificial joints. In September, the U.S. Food and Drug Administration ordered that manufacturers report all deaths and serious injuries resulting from use of the devices. The new regulations were scheduled to take effect on Jan. 14, 1985. Previously, such reporting had been largely voluntary. Arthur E. Rowse

In WORLD BOOK, see SAFETY.

SAILING. See BOATING; OLYMPIC GAMES.

SASKATCHEWAN. The Progressive Conservative Party, led by Premier Grant Devine, lost a seat in the Legislative Assembly in April 1984 when Bill Sveinson quit the party and crossed the floor to sit as a Liberal. The defection left the Conservatives with 55 seats, faced by 8 New Democrats and 1 Liberal. In December, however, the leader of Saskatchewan's Liberals asked that Sveinson be thrown out of the party, saying that he was disappointed with Sveinson's behavior in the legislature.

The province's budget for fiscal year 1984-1985 was announced on March 21. It called for a 20 per cent reduction in the deficit—to $267.2 million (Canadian dollars; $1 = U.S. 76 cents as of Dec. 31, 1984)—and offered a tax-credit plan for investors. The 10 per cent corporate income tax paid by small businesses was abolished.

Saskatchewan's production of synthetic crude oil was expected to increase substantially due to a June 5 announcement that Husky Oil Limited of Calgary, Alta., would build a $3.2-billion heavy oil upgrading plant near Lloydminster, Sask. The plant will produce about 50,000 barrels per day of synthetic crude oil. It will be the largest new energy project in western Canada in more than five years. David M. L. Farr

See also CANADA. In WORLD BOOK, see SASKATCHEWAN.

Saskatchewan Premier Grant Devine, confronted in March by unemployed workers, lends a sympathetic ear but explains that his hands are tied.

SAUDI ARABIA moved briefly into the front lines of regional conflict in 1984 through its direct involvement in the Iran-Iraq war. On March 27, a supply ship from the Arabian American Oil Company, a Saudi-owned oil company, was sunk by an Iraqi missile in the Persian Gulf. A few days later, a Saudi tanker was attacked by Iranian missiles in Saudi waters. Saudi vessels were hit again by Iraqi missiles in late April and in May. On June 5, Saudi Arabia's customarily cautious policy toward the conflict was abandoned as Saudi fighter aircraft shot down an Iranian jet in Saudi airspace over the Persian Gulf.

Low Profile. Generally, however, the Saudi government stayed in the background on regional and inter-Arab issues. The Saudis refrained from publicly criticizing Jordan for its decision in September to reestablish diplomatic relations with Egypt. In addition, Saudi Arabia continued to provide Jordan with subsidies, as it has since 1978.

In April, the government lent $3 billion to the International Monetary Fund, an agency of the United Nations (UN), to support its assistance to developing countries. Saudi Arabia also gave $4-million to the UN Relief and Works Agency for Palestine Refugees in the Middle East.

U.S. Relations. Concern over the inability of the United States to arrange an Arab-Israeli peace settlement, along with strong U.S. support for Israel, caused the Saudis to continue to back away from their close relationship with the United States during 1984. The changing relationship was underlined on January 15, when the Saudis agreed to purchase a $4-billion low-altitude air-defense system from France. The system was designed to complement the high-altitude defense system and Airborne Warning and Control System reconnaissance planes bought from the United States.

Economic News. Declining oil revenues and reduced production affected the Saudi economy more in 1984 than in previous years. Oil production reached a low of 3.6 million barrels per day. The Saudi unit of currency, the riyal, was devalued several times. The 1984 budget, approved in April by the Council of Ministers, set expenditures at $74.3 billion, about the same as in 1983. The budget was held in abeyance, however, pending clear estimates of income.

The year brought some encouraging signs, however. In June, a methanol plant opened in the new Saudi industrial complex at Al Jubayl. As a sign of good times to come, the kingdom also established its first automated bank teller machines and issued the first Arab credit card in October. William Spencer

See also MIDDLE EAST (Facts in Brief Table). In WORLD BOOK, see SAUDI ARABIA.

King Fahd of Saudi Arabia salutes the honor guard on his arrival at the Islamic Conference in Casablanca, Morocco, in January.

SAUVÉ, JEANNE MATHILDE (1922-), was sworn in as Canada's 23rd governor general on May 14, 1984. She is the first woman to serve as governor general, the representative of the British monarch in Canada. Sauvé succeeded Edward R. Schreyer in the largely ceremonial post.

Jeanne Mathilde Benoit was born in Prud'homme, Sask., on April 26, 1922. She was educated in Canada at Notre Dame du Rosaire Convent — an affiliate of the University of Ottawa — and in France at the University of Paris. In 1951, Sauvé became assistant to the director of the Youth Section of the United Nations Educational, Scientific and Cultural Organization (UNESCO) in Paris. For 20 years, she worked as a print and broadcast journalist in Canada.

Sauvé was first elected to Canada's House of Commons in 1972. Prime Minister Pierre Elliott Trudeau appointed her minister of state for science and technology in 1972, minister of the environment in 1974, and minister of communications in 1975. She served as Speaker of the House of Commons from 1980 to 1984. Sauvé was the first woman to be elected to this post.

She married Maurice Sauvé in 1948. They have one son.   Robie Liscomb

See also CANADA. In WORLD BOOK, see CANADA, GOVERNMENT OF.

SCHOOL. See CIVIL RIGHTS; EDUCATION.

SCOTLAND. The elections to the European Parliament on June 14, 1984, gave a boost to the Scottish Labour Party's morale when the party won five seats, three of them from the Conservative Party. In the most spectacular result, the Scottish National Party held the Highlands seat with a greatly increased majority. This left the Conservatives with two European seats in Scotland, and the Social Democratic Party/Liberal Party Alliance with none.

Labor Issues. Unemployment in Scotland continued to run at a higher rate than in England and Wales. The Scottish unemployment rate for December was 14.5 per cent of the working population, compared with 12.7 per cent for Great Britain as a whole. BL Limited (formerly British Leyland) announced in May that it would close its Bathgate truck plant by 1986. The Bathgate plant had already dismissed 4,500 workers in recent years, and the loss of an additional 1,800 jobs will be a blow to central Scotland, where unemployment runs at 21 per cent.

Transportation. Air travel was encouraged by the arrival of such new carriers as British Midland Airways Limited and Air UK to provide more national and international routes to Scotland. The continuing debate as to whether Glasgow Airport should take over from Prestwick as Scotland's transatlantic airport was given a new twist by Prest-

A snowbound passenger train lies stranded in northwest Scotland as blizzards sweep across the British Isles in late January.

wick's designation in February as one of six free ports — areas where no customs duties are collected — to be opened in 1984 and 1985 in Great Britain.

British Rail suffered one of its worst disasters on July 30 when an Edinburgh-to-Glasgow commuter train crashed at Polmont, killing 13 people and injuring 44 others. British Rail's Advanced Passenger Train (APT) began service between Glasgow and London in September.

Other Developments. In May, the General Assembly of the Church of Scotland caused a storm of controversy by two decisions. It allowed a convicted murderer to train for the ministry. Also, it decided not to consider a report on the Motherhood of God prepared by a joint committee of the Panel on Doctrine and the Woman's Guild.

On October 10, two Glasgow men, Thomas Campbell and Joseph Steele, were sentenced to life imprisonment for murdering James Doyle, four of his children, and one grandchild. The two men had burned the Doyle house in "the ice cream war," a campaign of violence against rival ice cream vendors.   Doreen Taylor

See also GREAT BRITAIN. In WORLD BOOK, see SCOTLAND.

SCULPTURE. See VISUAL ARTS.

SENEGAL. See AFRICA.

SEYCHELLES. See AFRICA.

SHIP AND SHIPPING. "World shipping and ship-building are experiencing the worst economic recession in the last 50 years," *Lloyd's Register of Shipping* reported in March 1984. The publication announced that world shipping fleet volume shrank in 1983 for the first time since 1945. Worldwide, 1,573 merchant ships were under construction on June 30, 1984, down 11 per cent from a year earlier. Orders, including ships being built, dropped from 2,845 to 2,657. Tonnage of the larger vessels on order rose to 31.2 million gross tons, 5 per cent above the mid-1983 level. Recession, overly ambitious purchases of vessels, and continued low petroleum demand combined to prolong a surplus of ship tonnage and low ocean-shipping rates.

United States Shipbuilders held orders of about $13 billion in 1984. The Maritime Administration of the Department of Transportation (DOT) said that commercial ship orders were valued at $639-million on October 1, down from $863 million in October 1983. Eight major shipyards closed in the United States in 1984. However, plans for achieving a 600-ship United States Navy by 1989 caused a surge in vessel orders in November.

Running the Gauntlet. Oil tankers in the Persian Gulf suffered numerous warship and warplane attacks in 1984 arising from the Iran-Iraq war. Iraqi planes attacked tankers bound for Iran's main oil-loading facility at Kharg Island. Iranian aircraft retaliated with attacks on ships elsewhere in the gulf. Responding to escalating attacks during May, Lloyd's of London, the insurance exchange, temporarily boosted war-risk insurance premiums for tankers bound for two Iranian ports from 1 per cent of a ship's value to 7.5 per cent.

Government Regulation. The U.S. Congress enacted legislation in March reducing the authority of the Department of Justice to restrict shipping lines that jointly set rates and divide cargoes. The law also limited the Federal Maritime Commission's power to reject rate increases.

Companies that operate government-subsidized tankers flying the U.S. flag awaited at year's end a DOT decision that could allow such ships to carry oil from Alaska to other states. In the United States, domestic shipping is not eligible for federal subsidies. Companies that took subsidies to build or operate tankers originally meant for foreign trade cannot use the ships for domestic runs. A 1983 proposal, if approved, would allow the tankers to compete in the Alaskan oil trade if the subsidies were repaid. Albert R. Karr

In WORLD BOOK, see SHIP.

SHOOTING. See HUNTING; SPORTS.

SIERRA LEONE. See AFRICA.

High and dry, the Maltese freighter *Eldia* attracts an audience on Nauset Beach, Orleans, Mass., where it ran aground during a storm on March 29.

SINCLAIR, IAN McCAHON (1929-   ), was elected leader of the opposition National Party of Australia on Jan. 17, 1984. He had served as the party's deputy leader under Douglas Anthony since 1971.

Sinclair was born in Sydney, Australia, on June 10, 1929. He earned bachelor of arts and bachelor of laws degrees from the University of Sydney and was admitted as a barrister of the Supreme Court of New South Wales in 1952.

Sinclair entered political life in 1962 as a member of the New South Wales Legislative Council. The following year, he was elected to represent New England, New South Wales, in Australia's House of Representatives, a seat he has held ever since. At various times between 1965 and 1983, Sinclair was minister for social services, minister assisting the minister for trade and industry, minister for shipping and transport, minister for primary industry, minister for communications, and minister for defense. After the Labor Party election victory in March 1983, Sinclair became opposition spokesman for defense and opposition leader in the House of Representatives.

Sinclair married Rosemary Fenton in 1970. He has two sons and two daughters.   Robie Liscomb

SINGAPORE. See ASIA.

SKATING. See HOCKEY; ICE SKATING; OLYMPIC GAMES; SPORTS.

SKIING. Pirmin Zurbriggen and Erika Hess of Switzerland won the 1984 overall titles in World Cup Alpine skiing. Each had to fight off a previous champion in the final week of the season.

The World Cup season ran from December 1983 to March 1984 in Europe, the United States, and Canada, with time out in February for the Winter Olympic Games in Sarajevo, Yugoslavia.

The 21-year-old Zurbriggen scored in every phase of the men's competition, though he was not strong in the slalom. He accumulated 256 points to 230 for Ingemar Stenmark of Sweden. Only Stenmark's refusal to ski in the downhill kept him from winning his fourth title in nine years.

The 21-year-old Hess entered the final race of the season, a slalom, on March 24 in Oslo, Norway, with a 9-point lead over Hanni Wenzel of Liechtenstein. After Wenzel missed a gate and was disqualified, Hess—who finished fourth in the race—became champion with 247 points to 238 for Wenzel.

The United States Alpine Skiers had more depth among women than men. That was evident in March, when 1983 World Cup champion Tamara McKinney of Squaw Valley, Calif., won giant slaloms on Whistler Mountain in Canada and in Zwiesel, West Germany, and a slalom in Oslo. In 1984, she finished third in World Cup competition. Debbie Armstrong of Seattle took the Olym-

Phil Mahre of White Pass, Wash., sweeps down the slalom course to win the Olympic gold medal at the Winter Games in Sarajevo, Yugoslavia, in February.

pic gold in the giant slalom. Christin Cooper of Sun Valley, Idaho, won the Olympic silver medal as well as a giant slalom in Lake Placid, N.Y. Holly Flanders of Deerfield, N.H., won a downhill in Ste.-Anne-de-Beaupré, Canada.

The leading American man in the overall standings, Bill Johnson of Van Nuys, Calif., finished 14th with 87 points. The 23-year-old Johnson, a brash and fearless downhill racer, surprisingly won a World Cup race on January 15 in Wengen, Switzerland. Then he won the Olympic downhill and three successive World Cup downhills.

Phil Mahre of White Pass, Wash., took the Olympic gold in the slalom, and his twin brother, Steve, won the silver. Both skiers retired from competition a month later. Neither won a race on the World Cup circuit, though it took a technicality to stop them. On January 10 in Parpan, Switzerland, Steve Mahre finished first and Phil was sixth in a World Cup slalom. However, because of a mix-up, Steve was wearing Phil's number and Phil was wearing Steve's. Both were disqualified.

Nordic Skiing. World Cup competitions were won by Jeff Hastings of Norwich, Vt., in jumping and Kerry Lynch of Granby, Colo., in Nordic combined. Lynch retired after the season and underwent knee surgery.   Frank Litsky

See also OLYMPIC GAMES. In WORLD BOOK, see SKIING.

SOCCER

SOCCER. Professional soccer in the United States and Canada fought for survival in 1984. The year was one of continuing disappointment for the sport, which seemed on the verge of success in the late 1970's.

The North American Soccer League (NASL) had only nine teams as the 1984 season opened, down from 24 in 1980. Most of the teams struggled financially. The San Diego Sockers reported losses of $10 million since 1978. The Tulsa Roughnecks reported losses of $8 million since 1980.

The NASL Lost two more teams at the end of the 1984 outdoor season. In August, Tulsa, the NASL champion in 1983, went out of business. In September, the Chicago Sting, the NASL champion in 1984, joined the Major Indoor Soccer League (MISL), the only other professional soccer league in the United States or Canada.

The MISL, which played a scaled-down and action-filled version of the game indoors, appeared to generate more excitement in some cities. Better attendance at the indoor games was one reason that Chicago quit the NASL to play exclusively in the MISL. The NASL gave permission to three of its members to play indoors in the MISL for the 1984-1985 season. The three were the Sockers, the Minnesota Strikers, and the New York Cosmos.

The NASL indoor season and play-offs ran from November 1983 to April 1984. The outdoor season ran from May to October 1984. Each of the NASL's nine teams played 32 games indoors and 24 games outdoors. The MISL's 14 teams each played 48 games between November 1983 and June 1984.

San Diego won the NASL indoor regular-season competition and the play-offs. In the NASL's outdoor play-off finals, the Sting swept the Toronto Blizzard, 2 to 1 and 3 to 2, winning the second game on October 3. The victory gave Chicago its second NASL crown in four years. In the MISL play-off series in June, the Baltimore Blast defeated the St. Louis Steamers, 4 games to 1.

International. Liverpool won the European Champions Cup in 1984 for the fourth time in eight years, the English League title for the third straight year, and the English Milk Cup. Everton, which came from Liverpool, won the English Football Association Cup. It also defeated Liverpool, 1 to 0, to win the Charity Shield. Aberdeen, top team in the Scottish League Premier Division, won the Scottish Football Association Cup. Shrewsbury took the Welsh Cup.

Tottenham Hotspur of England defeated Anderlecht of Belgium to take the UEFA Cup. Juventus of Italy won the European Cup Winners Cup, defeating Porto of Portugal. Frank Litsky

In WORLD BOOK, see SOCCER.

SOCIAL SECURITY. Trustees of the United States social security system reported on April 5, 1984, that programs providing monthly benefits for retirees, survivors, and the disabled were in good financial health. The trustees credited the improved economy and payroll tax increases, as well as other revisions adopted by Congress in 1983, for the bright financial picture. Even if a pessimistic economic forecast is used, the report predicted, the Old-Age and Survivors Insurance (OASI) Trust Fund should be able to meet its commitments "well into the next century."

Once again, however, the trustees said the Hospital Insurance Trust Fund, which finances Medicare health benefits for the aged, will run out of money by 1989 at the earliest and 1995 at the latest unless Congress reins in the program's mounting costs. Although Congress approved some Medicare cost-containment moves in 1984, it put off major changes until after the 1984 election.

Eligibility Review. Congress did grapple with the four-year-old controversy of reviewing disability-payment recipients for eligibility, however. Many legislators contended that the Administration of President Ronald Reagan had been overly zealous in reducing the disability rolls in an effort to pare federal spending. Since 1981, the government had reviewed 1.2 million disability cases, informing 490,000 beneficiaries that they would lose their benefits. Reacting to complaints, the Administration on April 13 suspended eligibility reviews until Congress enacted new disability legislation.

On September 19, both houses of Congress voted unanimously to make it more difficult to cancel disability benefits. The measure, signed by Reagan, provides that, in most cases, the Social Security Administration must prove that an individual's medical condition has improved before the agency can end benefits. It also requires eligibility examiners to take into account the cumulative effects of multiple ailments that, considered separately, might not be severely disabling.

Payroll Deductions. Effective Jan. 1, 1985, earnings subject to social security payroll taxes were to increase to $39,600, up from $37,800 in 1984. This was in line with a national increase in average wages. The maximum tax an individual would have to pay was to rise to $2,791.80, from $2,532.60 in 1984. Also effective Jan. 1, 1985, social security benefits were to increase by 3.5 per cent as a cost-of-living allowance (COLA). Under the 1983 social security revision, no COLA is due in years when inflation is less than 3 per cent. It was not clear in mid-1984 whether inflation for the year would be high enough to make a COLA due in 1985, but Congress voted in October to pay the COLA anyway. Frank Cormier and Margot Cormier

In WORLD BOOK, see SOCIAL SECURITY.

SOMALIA. See AFRICA.

SOUTH AFRICA. The white-minority government of South Africa won significant concessions in 1984 from two of its black-ruled neighbors. On February 16, Angola agreed to prevent Namibian nationalist guerrillas who had been fighting South African rule in Namibia from maintaining military bases in southern Angola. In return, South Africa agreed to withdraw its troops from Angola.

On March 16, South Africa and Mozambique signed a nonaggression treaty. Mozambique agreed to stop allowing South African black nationalists to launch attacks on South African targets from Mozambique. South Africa agreed to stop supplying aid to the rebel Mozambique National Resistance.

Civil Disorders. From early September to early October, an estimated 80 blacks were killed and more than 400 injured in conflicts with government security forces in black residential townships near Johannesburg. On October 23, about 7,000 soldiers conducted raids in three townships, searching for weapons and arresting suspected rioters—the first time since 1960 that army troops were used against civilians. Some of the disorders grew out of strikes by black workers. In September, nearly 90,000 gold miners struck for higher pay, and on November 5 and 6 up to 500,000 black workers in various industries walked off the

job. On November 14 and 15, some 2,300 black workers in the township of Sebokeng were arrested for various minor reasons.

Elections. Among the other immediate causes of the black unrest were elections in August for a restructured national Parliament that includes separate chambers for members of the country's Colored (mixed-race) and Asian minorities but excludes blacks, who constitute about 70 per cent of the population. At the urging of black, Colored, and Asian leaders, many voters boycotted the elections because the country's majority racial group had been excluded. On September 5, Prime Minister Pieter Willem Botha was elected the country's first state president.

White Party Opens Door. In November, the Progressive Federal Party, a white liberal opposition group, opened its membership to all races. It thus challenged the authority of the ruling National Party to enforce the prohibition against black participation in the government.   J. Dixon Esseks

See also AFRICA (Facts in Brief Table); NAMIBIA. In WORLD BOOK, see SOUTH AFRICA.

SOUTH AMERICA. See LATIN AMERICA and articles on Latin-American countries.

SOUTH CAROLINA. See STATE GOVERNMENT.

SOUTH DAKOTA. See STATE GOVERNMENT.

SOUTH WEST AFRICA. See NAMIBIA.

South African Coloreds—persons of mixed race—vote for representatives to a new Colored chamber of the restructured national Parliament in August.

SPACE EXPLORATION

SPACE EXPLORATION. Space shuttle missions launched by the United States in 1984 dramatically illustrated the triumphs and troubles involved in developing the first reusable space transportation system. Problems and progress began on February 3 with the perfect liftoff of the orbiter *Challenger,* the fourth flight of this shuttle. Once in orbit, the five-member crew launched the *Westar 6* communications satellite — owned by Western Union Corporation — from the cargo bay. However, the satellite did not go into its intended orbit. Three days later, the crew deployed another communications satellite — *Palapa B-2,* owned by Indonesia. It also failed to achieve a working orbit.

On the positive side, the crew, commanded by Vance D. Brand, successfully used *manned maneuvering units,* jet-powered backpacks that enable astronauts to fly free of the spacecraft. On February 7, Bruce McCandless II and Robert L. Stewart became the first persons to fly in space without a safety line. Brand and pilot Robert L. Gibson landed the *Challenger* on February 11.

Space Repair. *Challenger* blasted off again on April 6 with a crew of five commanded by Robert L. Crippen. They caught up with the *Solar Maximum Mission Observatory* (*Solar Max*) satellite, which had been launched in February 1980 and stopped functioning properly in November 1980. On April

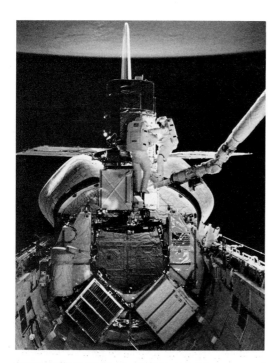

Astronauts from the shuttle *Challenger* work in April on *Solar Max,* the first satellite to be captured in space, repaired, and relaunched.

8, 1984, mission specialist George D. Nelson, wearing the jet backpack, flew over and tried to hook a line onto the satellite, causing it to spin wildly. The next day, ground controllers sent radio control signals to the satellite, slowing its spin, and on April 10, mission specialist Terry J. Hart snared it with the shuttle's 16-meter (50-foot) robot arm. He swung the satellite into the cargo bay. There, mission specialists Nelson and James D. van Hoften replaced malfunctioning controls and instruments. The crew then returned *Solar Max* to orbit, completing the first retrieval, repair, and relaunching of a satellite.

This mission also carried 3,300 honeybees and 100 kinds of seeds, including 12.5 million tomato seeds. The bees were part of an experiment designed by college student Dan M. Poskevich when he was in high school in Waverly, Tenn. The purpose of the experiment was to see how honeycombs built under weightless conditions compare with those constructed under normal gravity. The seeds were left aboard an orbiting container called a Long Duration Exposure Facility (LDEF). Astronauts were to retrieve the LDEF in February 1985. The seeds will then be distributed to schools for experiments to determine how plants grown from them differ from those grown from seeds not exposed to weightlessness and other conditions in space. *Challenger* landed on April 13.

Two Flights in One. The National Aeronautics and Space Administration (NASA) scheduled the first flight of the orbiter *Discovery* for June 25. However, a computer failure followed by the failure of a fuel valve caused an indefinite delay. NASA then combined this mission with another scheduled for August. *Discovery* finally lifted off on August 30. The crew of six, commanded by Henry W. Hartsfield, Jr., included the first commercial passenger, Charles D. Walker. McDonnell Douglas Corporation paid about $85,000 to send Walker into space with equipment designed to use reduced gravity to purify a hormone.

Astronauts on this mission launched three communications satellites and successfully tested an array of solar cells 31 meters (102 feet) long. Hartsfield and pilot Michael L. Coats landed *Discovery* at Edwards Air Force Base in California on September 5.

Woman Spacewalker. *Challenger* lifted off again on October 5 carrying the largest crew ever launched in a single spacecraft. The seven astronauts included Sally K. Ride, making her second space flight; Kathryn D. Sullivan, who became the first American woman to walk in space; and Marc Garneau, the first Canadian astronaut. The crew used the mechanical arm to launch a satellite designed to measure the sun's effect on Earth's weather. They also operated a radar camera, a mapping camera, and other sensors to get images

Astronaut Bruce McCandless II, wearing a jet-powered backpack, in February becomes the first person to fly free in space without a safety line.

of Earth never before obtained from space. *Challenger* landed at Cape Canaveral on October 13.

Satellite Salvage. *Discovery* flew again on November 8 with a crew of five astronauts led by Frederick H. Hauck. The crew launched a communications satellite on November 9 and another the next day. On November 12, *Discovery* caught up with the satellite *Palapa B-2*. Mission specialist Joseph P. Allen flew out to the satellite in a jet backpack and brought it under control so that mission specialist Anna L. Fisher could place it in the orbiter with the robot arm.

When the arm swung the satellite to the cargo bay, mission specialist Dale A. Gardner was supposed to attach a bracket to the satellite so that it could be locked into position within the bay. Gardner was unable to attach the bracket, so he and Allen had to maneuver the 3-meter (9-foot) satellite by themselves. On November 14, the crew retrieved the *Westar 6* satellite. *Discovery* landed at Cape Canaveral on November 16 with the two satellites on board. These were the first satellites ever brought back to Earth from space. Insurance underwriters paid NASA $5.5 million to recover them. After being repaired, they may be put into orbit again.

Soviet Records. United States space experts suspect that the Soviet Union plans to build a large station by linking several spacecraft. Since April 1982, groups of two and three cosmonauts and unpiloted freighters and tankers have been traveling back and forth to a small orbiting space station, *Salyut 7*. On Feb. 8, 1984, a spacecraft carrying Leonid Kizim, Vladimir Solovyov, and Oleg Atkov left Earth. The craft docked with *Salyut 7* the next day. In April, they were visited by three more cosmonauts, including Rakesh Sharma, India's first cosmonaut. Three more visitors in July included Svetlana Savitskaya, who became the first woman to walk in space and to go into space twice.

Kizim and Solovyov ventured outside *Salyut 7* six times. On August 8, they set a record for the most time spacewalking on one mission — 22 hours 50 minutes. On October 2, they and Atkov returned to Earth after a record 237 days in space.

Ariane. The space shuttle faced strong competition in the launch-for-a-fee business from *Ariane* rockets launched by the European Space Agency (ESA), an organization of West European countries. The ESA launched its first commercial payload on May 22. An *Ariane-1* rocket blasted off from Kourou Space Center, French Guiana, and put a communications satellite into orbit for GTE Corporation, a U.S. communications company. On August 4, an *Ariane-3* rocket — *Ariane-1*'s more powerful successor — launched two other commercial satellites.   William J. Cromie

In WORLD BOOK, see SPACE TRAVEL.

SPAIN. Commitment to the North Atlantic Treaty Organization (NATO) and Spain's proposed entry into the European Community (EC or Common Market) dominated Spanish politics in 1984. Spain had joined NATO in May 1982 and had immediately started preparing to link its armed forces with NATO's. When the Socialist Workers' Party came to power in October 1982, however, the government stopped the preparations. On June 3, 1984, more than 500,000 anti-NATO demonstrators rallied in Madrid. But Prime Minister Felipe González Márquez warned, "Withdrawal from NATO is no guarantee of peace." At its national meeting in December, the Socialist Workers' Party voted to keep Spain in NATO.

EC Membership. Spain discussed its entry into the EC in Madrid and at EC headquarters in Brussels, Belgium. Spain was concerned that its entry — scheduled for January 1986 — might increase its cost of living and its value-added tax, a kind of sales tax. The EC worried about a flow of cheap agricultural produce from Spain.

Serious Strikes followed the failure of employers and unions to fix wage increases for the country's workers for 1984. The government continued to restructure the steel, shipbuilding, and electrical industries. Workers protested against the restructuring program because it eliminated jobs.

However, González said the workers faced a choice between losing 20 to 25 per cent of the jobs in the three industries or forcing firms to close.

On October 9, González and representatives of employers and unions signed a two-year agreement on labor relations and salaries. The pact set wage hikes below the inflation rates expected in 1985 and 1986.

A Growing Crime Wave forced the government to reconsider its plan to enact reforms. The number of murders and armed robberies in major cities, along with reports of increased drug abuse, led Minister of the Interior José Barrionuevo to say on March 22 that the government would "rectify its mistakes." It would end tolerance of so-called soft drugs and ban bail concessions for people awaiting trial for serious offenses.

Terrorism Vote. Voters in the Basque region, a semi-independent area in the north, chose members of the regional parliament on February 26. The Basque Nationalist Party won 43 per cent of the vote, and the Socialists took 25 per cent. The turnout was almost 10 per cent higher than in the previous general election. Political observers said that the increase represented a protest against terrorism by the Basque Homeland and Liberty (ETA) organization. Kenneth Brown

See also EUROPE (Facts in Brief Table). In WORLD BOOK, see SPAIN.

King Juan Carlos I of Spain rides to a reviewing stand on May 27 to watch a parade honoring the nation's armed forces.

SPORTS. The athletic programs of many major universities and colleges in the United States came under close scrutiny in 1984. A number of college presidents attempted to gain a greater voice in the National Collegiate Athletic Association (NCAA), the major governing body of college sports, but they only partly succeeded. Walter Byers, the NCAA's executive director since 1951 and the most important administrator in college athletics, abandoned his traditional defense of the system and issued a warning that rules violations and unethical practices had got out of hand. As if to support his contention, the NCAA on October 23 placed the University of Florida in Gainesville on probation for three years for 59 rules violations. In the Special Reports section, see COLLEGE SPORTS: BIG MONEY ON CAMPUS.

College Sports. The NCAA's membership of 791 four-year universities and colleges included all the major athletic powers. The organization was controlled by athletics directors and faculty representatives from the individual colleges. As a result, many college and university presidents felt they did not have an effective voice inside the NCAA. In 1984, they attempted to change that situation.

The American Council on Education, a lobbying group for universities and colleges, urged the NCAA to set up a board of college presidents that would have veto power over NCAA rules governing academic standards and financial integrity. The NCAA voted down the proposal at its annual convention in January in Dallas, but it established a Presidents' Commission, made up of 44 college presidents and chancellors, to review and propose rules. The new commission said it hoped to have proposals ready for the NCAA's 1985 summer meeting.

In October, the NCAA's Byers told a reporter for *The New York Times* that illegal payments and other violations had become commonplace. He proposed that a convention of university presidents be called to establish stiffer penalties. He said the penalties should include dismissal of coaching staffs, suspension of team schedules for one or more years, and loss of more athletics scholarships.

Byers charged that some colleges had given individual athletes $20,000 or more a year in illegal payments. The problem, he said, "is much worse than I thought."

The NCAA's Division I-A consisted of 278 colleges with major programs in at least one sport. Byers said that he thought 10 per cent of these colleges were "chronic violators" of NCAA rules and another 10 to 15 per cent were likely to "turn their head" at violations.

Cases before the NCAA in recent years showed

The opening ceremony of the Friendship '84 Games, the Soviet bloc's alternative to the Olympics, gets underway in August in Moscow.

that illegal payments were made by coaches and boosters, mostly to football and basketball players. The payments took many forms, including cash, gifts, meals, clothing, automobiles, airplane tickets, summer-school tuition, and pay for nonexistent jobs.

The 59 charges in the University of Florida case included spying on opponents' football practices, maintaining a slush fund, and giving money and gifts to athletes and recruits. Early in the football season, as a result of the NCAA investigation, Florida fired Charlie Pell, its coach since 1979. Florida's three-year probation meant that its football team was barred from bowl games and television appearances during that time. The association also took away 20 of Florida's 95 football scholarships. The university appealed the punishment, calling it excessive.

The Sullivan Award, given annually by the Amateur Athletic Union to the top amateur athlete in the United States, in 1984 went to Edwin Moses, the world recordholder in the 400-meter hurdles and an Olympic gold medalist in 1976 and 1984. In 1984, Moses extended his winning streak in the 400-meter hurdles to 109 races.

Among the Winners in 1984 were the following:

Fencing. Peter Westbrook of New York City, the only United States fencing medalist in the Summer Olympics, also won his eighth United States sabre championship. Vincent Bradford of San Antonio won both United States women's titles — in foil and epee.

Gymnastics. Before Mary Lou Retton of Fairmont, W. Va., won the women's all-around gold medal in the Olympics, she won the United States championship, the United States Olympic trials, the American Cup, and the American Classic. The men's all-around winners included Peter Vidmar of Los Angeles in the United States Olympic trials and the American Cup and Mitch Gaylord of Van Nuys, Calif., in the United States and NCAA championships.

Rowing. Great Britain's Olympic eight-oared crew, representing the Leander and London clubs, defeated the University of Washington in Seattle by three lengths on July 1 for the Grand Challenge Cup at the Henley Royal Regatta in Great Britain. In U.S. college competition, Washington won the Cincinnati Regatta and the Pacific Coast championship. The U.S. Naval Academy in Annapolis, Md., won the Intercollegiate Rowing Association Regatta, and Brown University in Providence, R.I., won the Eastern sprints.

Marathon. Steve Jones of Great Britain won the America's Marathon/Chicago on October 21 and set an unofficial world record of 2 hours 8 minutes 5 seconds. Geoff Smith of Great Britain won the Boston Marathon, and Orlando Pizzolato of Italy won the New York City Marathon. The respective women's winners were Rosa Mota of Portugal, Lorraine Moller of New Zealand, and Grete Waitz of Norway.

Weight Lifting. Bulgaria defeated the Soviet Union for the team title in the European championships, which ended on May 1 in Vitoria, Spain. The Bulgarians won the six lightest weight classes, and the Soviets won the four heaviest. Anatoli Pisarenko of the Soviet Union, the world champion, won the super heavyweight title.

Wrestling. The Soviet Union defeated the United States, 6-4, to win the six-nation World Cup freestyle

Cheryl Miller, left, and Anne Donovan head downcourt as the U.S. Olympic women's basketball team takes on South Korea in August in Los Angeles.

competition, held on March 31 and April 1 in Toledo, Ohio. The title was the Soviets' 10th in 12 years. Dan Gable, the United States Olympic wrestling coach, led the University of Iowa in Iowa City to a record-tying seventh straight team title in the NCAA wrestling championships, which were held from March 8 to 10 in East Rutherford, N.J.

Other Champions. *Archery,* U.S. champions: men, Darrell Pace, Hamilton, Ohio; women, Ruth Rowe, McLean, Va., *Badminton,* All-England champions: men, Morten Frost, Denmark; women, Li Lingwei, China; U.S. champions: men, Rodney Barton, Tempe, Ariz.; women, Cheryl Carton, San Diego. *Biathlon,* World Cup champion: Frank-Peter Roetsch, East Germany; U.S. champions: men, Josh Thompson, Ashford, Wash.; women, Julie Newman, Mercer Island, Wash. *Billiards,* world 3-cushion champion: Nobuaki Kobayashi, Japan. *Boardsailing,* U.S. women's champion: Kathy Steele, Annapolis, Md. *Bobsledding,* U.S. champions: two-man, Brent Rushlaw, Saranac Lake, N.Y.; four-man, Jeffrey Jost, Burke, N.Y. *Canoeing,* world international 10-square-meter champion: Stephen Clark, Bristol, R.I. *Casting,* U.S. allaround champion: Steve Rajeff, San Francisco. *Court tennis,* U.S. Open champion: Chris Ronaldson, Great Britain. *Croquet,* U.S. champion: Jim Bast, Phoenix, Ariz. *Cross-country,* world champions: men, Carlos Lopes, Portugal; women, Maricica Puica, Romania. *Curling,* world champions: men, Eigil Ramsfjell, Norway; women, Connie Laliberte, Winnipeg, Canada. *Cycling,* world women's champions: sprint, Connie Paraskevin, Detroit; pursuit, Rebecca Twigg, Seattle. *Darts,* world champion: Eric Bristow, Great Britain. *Equestrian,* jumping champions: World Cup, Mario Deslauriers, Bromont, Canada; U.S. open, Conrad Homfeld, Petersburg, Va. *Field hockey,* U.S. college women's champion: Old Dominion. *Frisbee,*

world champions: men, Scott Zimmerman, Pasadena, Calif.; women, Judy Horowitz, Forest Hills, N.Y. *Gaelic sports champions:* football, Kerry; hurling, Cork. *Handball,* U.S. four-wall champions: men, Naty Alvarado, Hesperia, Calif.; women, Rosemary Bellini, New York City. *Hang gliding,* world champion: Steve Moyes, Australia. *Horseshoe pitching,* world champions: men, Jim Knisley, Bremen, Ohio; women, Tari Powell, Rankin, Ill. *Iceboating,* world DN Class champion: Tait Haagma, Soviet Union. *Judo,* U.S. open champions: men, Dewey Mitchell, New Port Richey, Fla.; women, Heidi Bauersachs, New York City. *Karate,* world men's team fighting champion: Great Britain. *Lacrosse,* U.S. college champion: Johns Hopkins University. *Lawn bowling,* U.S. open champions: men, Cappy Njus, Honolulu; women, Toni Mercer, New York City. *Luge,* U.S. champions: men, Tim Nardiello, Lake Placid, N.Y.; women, Bonnie Warner, Mount Baldy, Calif. *Modern pentathlon,* U.S. champions: men, Mike Storm, Arlington, Va.; women, Kim Dunlop, Tallahassee, Fla. *Motorcycle racing,* U.S. road-racing champion: Mike Baldwin, Stamford, Conn. *Paddle tennis,* U.S. champions: men, Mark Rifenbark, Santa Monica, Calif.; women, Kathy May Paven, Santa Monica, Calif. *Paddleball,* U.S. champions: men, Steve Wilson, Flint, Mich.; women, Carla Teare, Clarkston, Mich. *Parachute jumping,* world champions: men, Ronald Eilenstein, East Germany; women, Barbara Harzbecker, East Germany. *Polo,* Gold Cup champion: White Birch Farm, Palm Beach, Fla. *Racquetball,* U.S. champions: DP men's nationals, Mike Yellen, Southfield, Mich.; Ektelon men's nationals, Bret Harnett, Las Vegas, Nev.; women, Heather McKay, Toronto, Canada. *Racquets,* U.S. open champion: William Boone, Great Britain. *Rodeo,* U.S. all-around champion: Dee Pickett, Caldwell, Ida. *Roller skating,* world artistic champions: men, Michele Biscerni, Italy; women, Tina Kneisley, Maumee, Ohio; world speed champions: men, Bobby Kaiser, Salem, Va.; women, Stephania Ghermandi, Italy. *Rugby,* U.S. club champion: Dallas Harlequins. *Sambo,* U.S. unlimited champion: Ron Carlyle, Quantico, Va. *Shooting,* U.S. small-bore rifle (3-position) champion: Lones Wigger, Fort Benning, Ga. *Skateboarding,* U.S. national series champion: Tony Hawk, San Diego. *Sled dog racing,* world champion: Douglas McRae, Rhinelander, Wis. *Snowmobile racing,* world champion: Jim Dimmerman, White Bear Lake, Minn. *Softball,* U.S. fast-pitch champions: men, California Coors Kings, Merced, Calif.; women, Los Angeles Diamonds. *Squash racquets,* U.S. champions: men, Mark Talbott, Atlanta, Ga.; women, Alicia McConnell, New York City. *Squash tennis,* U.S. champion: Loren Lieberman, New York City. *Surfing,* Ocean Pacific pro champions: men, Tommy Curren, Santa Barbara, Calif.; women, Freida Zamba, Miami Beach, Fla. *Synchronized swimming,* U.S. champion: Tracie Ruiz, Bothell, Wash. *Table tennis,* world champions: men, Jiang Jialiang, China; women, Branka Batinic, Yugoslavia. *Tae kwon do,* U.S. heavyweight champions: men, Naim Hasan, Portland, Ore.; women, Lynnette Love, Detroit. *Team handball,* U.S. champions: men, California Heat, Hayward, Calif.; women, California West, Resada, Calif. *Triathlon,* Ironmen champions: men, Dave Scott, Davis, Calif.; women, Sylviane Puntous, Montreal, Canada. *Tumbling,* world champions: men, Steve Elliott, Lincoln, Nebr.; women, Jyll Hollenbeak, Rockford, Ill. *Volleyball,* U.S. champions: men, Nautilus Pacifica, Long Beach, Calif.; women, Carlson Chrysler, Palo Alto, Calif. *Water polo,* world women's champion: Australia. *Water skiing,* U.S. champions: men, Sammy Duvall, Windemere, Fla.; women, Deena Brush, Leesburg, Va.   Frank Litsky

See also OLYMPIC GAMES and articles on the various sports. In the WORLD BOOK SUPPLEMENT section, see BASKETBALL. In WORLD BOOK, see articles on the various sports.

SRI LANKA groped unsuccessfully in 1984 for a solution to the strife between its Sinhalese Buddhist majority and Tamil Hindu minority. The government continued to reject Tamil demands for the creation of a separate Tamil state. Tamil guerrilla attacks and savage reactions by Sri Lankan troops battered the northern, Tamil part of the island.

Political Efforts to find a compromise that would satisfy the Tamils made little headway. On July 23, President J. R. Jayewardene proposed creation of a second legislative chamber representing Sri Lanka's 24 districts to handle "legislation affecting fundamental rights and language rights." But many Tamils saw his offer as insufficient, and the government dropped the plan in December.

Guerrilla Attacks on government facilities and representatives in the north were carried out by eight small, separate Tamil guerrilla movements. The guerrillas ambushed soldiers, dynamited police stations, and massacred Sinhalese settlers in the north. In retaliation, Sri Lankan troops burned houses and shops and killed scores of people. The government said 33 soldiers faced court-martial for unnecessary brutality. The violence escalated near the year-end, leaving more than 400 people dead in late November and December.

More than 30,000 Tamil refugees fled to India. On August 2, a suitcase marked for a Sri Lankan flight exploded at the airport of Madras, capital of India's Tamil Nadu state, killing 32 people, including 24 Sri Lankans.

Antiterrorist Efforts. Indian news media reported that, despite Indian government denials, Tamil guerrillas were trained and based in Tamil Nadu state. The state, just across the Palk Strait from Sri Lanka, has many Tamils who support the Tamil separatists. The press in Colombo, Sri Lanka, said Sri Lanka had accused India's intelligence agency of training Tamil terrorists. Other sources reported that the Palestine Liberation Organization helped train the terrorists.

In May, after Great Britain and the United States rejected requests to train counterterrorists to help its army, Sri Lanka engaged about 25 Israeli advisers. The navy stepped up patrols of the Palk Strait to try to cut off guerrilla supplies. Jayewardene named Lalith Athulathmudali as minister of national security to lead the fight against terrorism.

Damage to Sri Lanka's Economy due to the strife continued. Efforts to increase employment by luring foreign investors had little result, and tourism slumped. However, higher world prices for Sri Lanka's main export, tea, kept the balance of payments in surplus.　　　Henry S. Bradsher

See also ASIA (Facts in Brief Table). In WORLD BOOK, see SRI LANKA.

STAMP COLLECTING. Young stamp collectors were invited to enter the United States Postal Service's new YES (Youths Exhibiting Stamps) competition in 1984. Participants, judged on the quality of their collections, competed for prizes at local, regional, and national levels. Entries were to close on March 1, 1985, with winners to be announced prior to October—National Stamp Collecting Month. The top six national winners were to receive all-expenses-paid trips for themselves and two family members to the AMERIPEX international stamp collectors' exhibition, to be held from May 22 to June 1, 1986, in Chicago.

The Postal Service honored a group of distinguished Americans on 20-cent commemorative stamps in 1984. They included businessman Horace A. Moses, founder of the Junior Achievement organization; Herman Melville, author of *Moby Dick;* silent-film actor Douglas Fairbanks, Sr.; baseball player and humanitarian Roberto Clemente; and Jim Thorpe, the famous American Indian athlete of the early 1900's.

Collectors voting in a poll conducted by *Linn's Stamp News* chose the $9.35 eagle-and-moon booklet stamp as the most popular stamp issued in 1983. The postal card getting the most votes was the 13-cent Olympic yachting card, and the most popular commemorative was the block of four 20-cent stamps honoring ballooning.

Sri Lanka's President J. R. Jayewardene in June presents a baby elephant to President Reagan for the National Zoological Park in Washington, D.C.

STAMP COLLECTING

Auction Sales. Two noted world rarities were sold on March 29 and 30 at an auction in Zurich, Switzerland. A one-of-a-kind Swedish 1855 stamp known as the 3-skilling-banco orange-yellow error sold for 977,500 Swiss francs (about $455,000) — the second highest price ever paid for an individual stamp issued by a government. Only the famed 1856 British Guiana 1-cent magenta, which changed hands in 1980 for $850,000, brought a higher price. A Swedish schoolboy originally found the orange-yellow error in 1885 on a letter belonging to his grandmother. The stamp, which should have been blue-green, was mistakenly printed in the orange-yellow color of another stamp being issued at the time, the 8-skilling-banco stamp. The error is thought to have been caused by a 3-skilling-banco design being included in an 8-skilling-banco printing.

At the same auction in Zurich, one of the two surviving Finland 1850 20-kopeck envelopes sold for 138,000 Swiss francs (about $64,000), the highest price ever paid for a piece of postal stationery. This envelope plus another in the Finnish Postal Museum are all that survive from the original issue of 3,500 20-kopeck envelopes.

A U.S. 1869 Pictorial Issue 2-cent brown stamp accidentally printed on both sides went on sale for the first time on April 14 at the Robert A. Siegel Auction Galleries' Rarities of the World Sale in New York City. This unique stamp, found by a collector in 1969, went for $5,250.

In November 1983, an American collector discovered a second *invert* (upside down) error in the series of British Commonwealth stamps issued from 1940 to 1950 in the African countries of Kenya, Uganda, and Tanganyika (now Tanzania). The used 30-cent stamp, printed with an *ultramarine* (deep blue) frame containing an inverted picture of Uganda's Owen Falls Dam in black, is similar to the 5-cent invert discovered by a New Jersey boy several years ago. The 5-cent error was valued at 10,000 pounds (about $13,000) by the British *Stanley Gibbons Stamp Catalogue*.

New Stamps. On May 23, Australia released a set of four stamps featuring tall clipper ships. These ships, including the renowned *Cutty Sark*, which is depicted on one of the stamps, transported cargo and passengers between Europe, Australia, and the Far East during the late 1800's.

On September 21, the United Nations Postal Administration issued its fifth series of sixteen 20-cent stamps picturing the flags of member nations.

The newly established Marshall Islands postal service issued its first commemorative stamps on June 19. The set of four 40-cent stamps featured reproductions of stamp designs used from 1897 to 1901 when the Pacific islands were under German colonial rule.   Paul A. Larsen

In WORLD BOOK, see STAMP COLLECTING.

486

STATE GOVERNMENT. Forty-three state legislatures held regular sessions in 1984, and Oregon and Texas conducted special sessions but no regular session. In addition, there were some 200 statewide referendum measures on ballots in 44 states in the November 6 elections.

Taxes. A combination of spending cuts, new taxes, and an economic recovery in 1983 left many state treasuries bulging with surpluses. As a result, in 1984, seven states reduced personal income taxes, and Ohio mailed rebates to taxpayers. Only 15 states increased taxes, and of these, Vermont alone raised personal income taxes. Only Vermont and New Hampshire had deficits in the 1984 fiscal year. Many of the states that cut taxes were in the Snow Belt of Northern states. Tax hikes were mainly in the Sun Belt in the South and West.

The tax revolt fell short at the polls on November 6. Voters in California, Michigan, Nevada, and Oregon rejected initiatives intended to roll back or limit taxes. The stakes were especially high in California, where the government would have had to refund $1.7 billion in property taxes. The Michigan measure would have repealed all tax hikes since Dec. 31, 1981. Voters in California, Missouri, Oregon, and West Virginia approved the establishment of state-run lotteries.

South Carolina and Tennessee hiked sales taxes 1 cent per dollar to fund educational reforms. Louisiana and Oklahoma increased their sales taxes to balance their budgets. Eight states raised gasoline taxes. Texas doubled its gas tax to 10 cents per gallon (3.8 liters) to finance highway and educational improvements. Eight states raised vehicle taxes to fund road improvements.

In March and June, Louisiana approved loans of $27.5 million so that the 1984 Louisiana World Exposition — a world's fair in New Orleans — could open on May 12 and then remain open until its scheduled closing date of November 1. The fair closed with a deficit, having fallen short of expected attendance, and filed for bankruptcy on November 6.

Education. A survey by the United States Department of Education found that more than 275 state-level task forces were examining public education by April 1984. More than half the states increased their aid to education in 1984.

Alabama, Kentucky, South Carolina, Tennessee, and Texas enacted major reforms, with new funding in the latter three states. Reforms included merit pay for teachers, standard tests for students and for teachers, smaller classes, tougher requirements for graduation from high school, and improved training for teachers.

On April 10, Nebraska's Governor Robert Kerrey signed a bill designed to settle a dispute over state control of church-run schools. The new law regulates the certification of people who teach in private schools. Such individuals no longer have to receive teaching certificates from the state. Instead, they may teach if they pass an examination designed to test their competence as teachers or if they receive a favorable evaluation from Nebraska's Department of Education.

Drinking and Driving. Twenty-eight states passed tough laws aimed at curbing drunken driving. The laws require stiffer fines, provide for the loss or suspension of drivers' licenses, make jail sentences mandatory, and raise the drinking age.

Five states raised the drinking age to 21, bringing the total to 23 states. Two other states raised the minimum age for drinking beer and wine to 19. Congress passed a law in June that would cut federal highway funds to states failing to raise the legal drinking age to 21. The reductions would begin in fiscal 1986. South Dakota filed a suit challenging this law.

Automobiles. Nine states passed laws requiring children in vehicles to be in safety restraint seats, leaving Wyoming as the only state without a restraint law. In July, New York became the first state to require adult passengers in the front seats of vehicles to use seat belts, effective on December 1. New Jersey and Illinois passed similar laws that were to take effect in 1985. Twelve states in 1984 passed *lemon laws* requiring motor vehicle manufacturers to repair or replace defective new vehicles.

Children. A sharp focusing of national attention on the plight of missing and exploited children led to increased action at the state level. Florida, Illinois, Kentucky, and Minnesota authorized databanks on missing children. Washington began a statewide identification program for children. Other states increased penalties for child pornography and sexual abuse, enacted new child-abuse laws, and made it a felony for a parent who does not have custody of a child to take the child by force. Several states required child-care centers to check workers for criminal records. Five states passed measures aimed at curbing domestic abuse. Kansas and Tennessee raised the marriage fee to fund shelters for abused spouses and children.

More states passed laws easing the collection of child support payments. California became the first to require courts to set child support payments at a level at least equal to state welfare payments.

Medical Issues. Eight states enacted so-called right-to-die laws. These measures forbid doctors to use life-support machinery and other extraordinary means to keep a patient alive if the patient has signed a document stating that, under certain circumstances, he or she would not want to be kept alive by such means.

Health costs remained a major concern, with a dozen states passing laws to control them. Arizona took over its privately run experimental alterna-

tive to Medicaid after the firm operating it ran into financial problems. On November 6, Arizona voters turned down ballot proposals for other programs that would have curbed health costs.

Jobs and Pay. Michigan financed a conservation corps, and Minnesota and Pennsylvania enacted other jobs programs. Wisconsin and Massachusetts provided aid for workers affected by plant closings. On November 6, voters in New Jersey approved a $90-million bond issue to finance the establishment of high-technology centers.

The debate over pay discrimination against women continued into 1984, after a federal judge in December 1983 ordered the state of Washington to give money to 15,500 female employees to compensate for past discrimination. By October 1984, Iowa, Minnesota, New Mexico, and Washington had begun to implement plans to reduce the pay gap between men and women who work for the state. Another 30 states were undertaking studies to evaluate pay equity. California, Florida, Missouri, and Nebraska, however, defeated pay equity bills in 1984.

Environment. Tennessee allocated $1.4 billion for a sewer project, and Maryland and Virginia funded a cleanup of Chesapeake Bay. Several states, including Illinois, Iowa, Kansas, and Minnesota, approved funds for cleaning up toxic

John W. Carlin of Kansas, left, succeeds James R. Thompson of Illinois, right, as head of the National Governors' Association in August.

Selected Statistics on State Governments

State	Resident population*	Governor†	Legislature† House (D)	(R)	Senate (D)	(R)	State tax revenue‡	Tax revenue per capita§	Public school enrollment#	Public school expenditures per pupil**
Alabama	3,959	George C. Wallace (D)	88	12††	12	4††	$ 2,341	$ 595	722	$2,177
Alaska	479	Bill Sheffield (D)	21	18‡‡	9	11	2,046	4,487	98	7,325
Arizona	2,963	Bruce E. Babbitt (D)	22	38‡‡	12	18	2,061	702	503	2,524
Arkansas	2,328	Bill Clinton (D)	90	10	31	4	1,338	577	432	1,971
California	25,174	George Deukmejian (R)	47	33	25	15	22,260	894	4,231	2,733
Colorado	3,139	Richard D. Lamm (D)	18	47	11	24	1,743	563	542	3,171
Connecticut	3,138	William A. O'Neill (D)	64	87	12	24	2,538	813	478	3,636
Delaware	606	Michael Castle (R)	19	22	13	8	639	1,064	91	3,456
Florida	10,680	Bob Graham (D)	78	42	32	8	6,225	588	1,496	2,680
Georgia	5,732	Joe Frank Harris (D)	154	26	47	9	3,504	619	1,051	2,169
Hawaii	1,023	George R. Ariyoshi (D)	40	11	21	4	1,151	1,189	162	3,239
Idaho	989	John V. Evans (D)	17	67	14	28	620	631	206	2,052
Illinois	11,486	James R. Thompson (R)	67	51	31	28	7,420	648	1,853	3,100
Indiana	5,479	Robert D. Orr (R)	39	61	20	30	3,195	576	984	2,414
Iowa	2,905	Terry E. Branstad (R)	60	40	29	21	2,014	694	497	3,095
Kansas	2,425	John W. Carlin (D)	49	76	16	24	1,566	653	405	3,058
Kentucky	3,714	Martha Layne Collins (D)	74	26	28	10	2,602	707	647	2,100
Louisiana	4,438	Edwin W. Edwards (D)	89	16	38	1	3,011	683	782	2,739
Maine	1,146	Joseph E. Brennan (D)	85	66	24	11	780	687	210	2,458
Maryland	4,304	Harry R. Hughes (D)	124	17	41	6	3,468	815	683	3,445
Massachusetts	5,767	Michael S. Dukakis (D)	126	34	32	8	5,156	896	879	3,378
Michigan	9,069	James J. Blanchard (D)	57	53	18	20	7,023	775	1,736	3,307
Minnesota	4,144	Rudy Perpich (DFL)	65	69	42	25	4,319	1,043	705	3,085
Mississippi	2,587	Bill Allain (D)	116	6	49	3	1,538	599	468	1,849
Missouri	4,970	John Ashcroft (R)	108	55	22	12	2,640	533	795	2,468
Montana	817	Ted Schwinden (D)	50	50	28	22	514	633	154	3,289
Nebraska	1,597	Robert Kerrey (D)	49	(unicameral, nonpartisan)			987	623	267	2,984
Nevada	891	Richard H. Bryan (D)	17	25	13	8	779	887	150	2,613
New Hampshire	959	John H. Sununu (R)	102	298	6	18	329	345	159	2,750
New Jersey	7,468	Thomas H. Kean (R)	44	36	23	17	6,128	823	1,148	4,007
New Mexico	1,399	Toney Anaya (D)	43	27	21	21	1,163	842	270	2,901
New York	17,667	Mario M. Cuomo (D)	94	56	26	35	16,208	919	2,675	4,686
North Carolina	6,082	James G. Martin (R)	83	37	38	12	4,028	674	1,090	2,162
North Dakota	680	George Sinner (D)	41	65	24	29	526	786	117	2,853
Ohio	10,746	Richard F. Celeste (D)	59	40	15	18	6,734	627	1,827	2,676
Oklahoma	3,298	George P. Nigh (D)	69	32	34	14	2,627	805	591	2,805
Oregon	2,662	Victor G. Atiyeh (R)	34	26	18	12	1,784	671	447	3,504
Pennsylvania	11,895	Dick Thornburgh (R)	103	100	23	27	8,430	709	1,738	3,329
Rhode Island	955	Edward D. DiPrete (R)	78	22	39	11	726	765	136	3,570
South Carolina	3,264	Richard W. Riley (D)	97	27	37	9	2,113	660	605	2,017
South Dakota	700	William J. Janklow (R)	13	57	10	25	325	468	123	2,486
Tennessee	4,685	Lamar Alexander (R)	62	37	23	10	2,246	482	822	2,027
Texas	15,724	Mark White (D)	97	53	25	6	9,019	579	2,990	2,731
Utah	1,619	Norman H. Bangerter (R)	16	59	6	23	974	604	379	2,013
Vermont	525	Madeleine M. Kunin (D)	72	78	18	22	358	682	90	3,051
Virginia	5,555	Charles S. Robb (D)	65	34	32	8§§	3,478	645	966	2,620
Washington	4,300	Booth Gardner (D)	53	45	27	22	4,191	988	736	3,211
West Virginia	1,965	Arch A. Moore, Jr. (R)	76	24	29	5	1,470	749	371	2,764
Wisconsin	4,751	Anthony S. Earl (D)	52	47	19	14	4,297	905	774	3,237
Wyoming	514	Ed Herschler (D)	18	46	11	19	736	1,443	101	4,045

*Number in thousands, 1983 estimates (U.S. Bureau of the Census).
†As of January 1985 (Council of State Governments; National Conference of State Legislatures).
‡1983 figures in millions (U.S. Bureau of the Census).
§1983 figures (U.S. Bureau of the Census).
#Number in thousands, fall 1983 (National Center for Education Statistics).
**1982-1983 per pupil in average daily attendance (National Center for Education Statistics).
††5 Independents in the House, 3 in the Senate.
‡‡1 Libertarian in the House.
§§1 Independent in the Senate.

wastes. New York passed a law aimed at reducing sulfur dioxide emissions and, thereby, also reducing the amount of acid rain.

Other Measures. Five states enacted laws to protect the rights of crime victims. Hawaii passed a bill requiring witnesses of crimes to come to the aid of victims. A new law in Wisconsin requires witnesses to report crimes. Four states tightened requirements for insanity defenses.

Wisconsin passed the Uniform Marital Property Act. This model legislation recognizes the economic equality of spouses in marriage.

Connecticut approved a 10-year, $5.5-billion program to repair roads and bridges, spurred by a bridge collapse in June 1983 that killed three people. Alabama and Texas approved $400-million highway programs in 1984.

Mississippi and South Dakota authorized lethal injections for executions. Connecticut and Oklahoma approved the release of inmates to relieve prison overcrowding.

South Dakota passed legislation requiring drug dealers to buy licenses and to pay taxes on the sale of illegal narcotics. Seven states adopted laws against the unauthorized use of a computer to contact and operate other computers, usually over telephone lines.   Elaine Stuart Knapp

See also ELECTIONS. In WORLD BOOK, see STATE GOVERNMENT and articles on the individual states.

STEEL INDUSTRY. The United States steel industry made progress during 1984 in its long battle against cheap imported steel that had been flooding the U.S. market, contributing to plant closings and loss of jobs. On September 18, President Ronald Reagan ordered measures intended to limit imports of most forms of steel to 18.5 per cent of U.S. annual consumption. The restrictions involved voluntary agreements with steel-exporting countries and stricter enforcement of laws against unfair trade practices. Reagan rejected more far-reaching import restrictions recommended on July 11 by the United States International Trade Commission. On December 19, the Reagan Administration announced it had reached agreements with Japan and six other leading steel-exporting countries to reduce their shipments to the United States by 30 per cent in 1985.

According to the American Iron and Steel Institute, a steel industry organization based in Washington, D.C., 12.5 million short tons (11.3 million metric tons) of steel were imported in the first half of 1984, more than during any other six-month period. The institute reported that 24 million short tons (22 million metric tons) had been imported during the first 11 months of 1984, 57 per cent more than in the same period in 1983.

American steel production increased early in the year but began a steady decline in June. Production during the first eight months of 1984 was 65.7 million short tons (59.6 million metric tons), up from 54.2 million short tons (49.2 million metric tons) during the same period in 1983.

The Institute of Scrap Iron and Steel announced that a record amount of U.S. iron and steel scrap was available for recycling during 1984. The supply, almost 744 million short tons (675 million metric tons), was sufficient to meet all foreseeable needs until the year 2003.

Deals and Mergers. Steel companies in other countries increased their investments in U.S. mills during 1984. On April 24, Nippon Kokan K.K., Japan's second-largest steel company, agreed to buy 50 per cent of National Steel Corporation for $292 million. National, a subsidiary of National Intergroup Incorporated, is the seventh-largest U.S. steel firm. The U.S. government approved the purchase on June 12. On July 16, Kawasaki Steel Corporation agreed to buy a 25 per cent share in a new firm that will own and operate Kaiser Steel Corporation's mill in Fontana, Calif. Kawasaki is Japan's third-largest steel company. Vale do Rio Doce, an iron ore firm owned by the Brazilian government, also will own part of the new firm, to be called California Steel Industries, Incorporated.

On March 9, United States Steel Corporation and National Intergroup Incorporated called off a $575-million merger proposal because they expected opposition from the U.S. Department of Justice, which felt the merger might violate antitrust laws. The Justice Department on March 21 ended its opposition to the merger of Republic Steel Corporation and LTV Corporation, which owns Jones & Laughlin Steel Corporation. Shareholders approved the $770-million merger on May 18. The new firm, LTV Steel Corporation, is second in size to United States Steel.

Labor Relations. On March 29, the United Steelworkers of America elected Lynn R. Williams as their new union president. He succeeded Lloyd McBride, who died in 1983. Williams had been acting president of the union and became its first Canadian president. See WILLIAMS, LYNN R.

Negotiators reached an agreement on June 28 in a metalworkers strike that had idled 440,000 workers in West Germany, and the strikers returned to work on July 2. The strike, Germany's longest since 1957, cost the metal industry $3.2-billion.

In France, a government plan to eliminate 25,000 jobs from the country's financially troubled steel industry led to protests during March and April. Workers throughout Lorraine, where many steel mills are located, blocked highways and railroads with coils of sheet steel, held protest marches, and battled riot police.   Michael Woods

In WORLD BOOK, see IRON AND STEEL.

STOCKS AND BONDS. Although the United States stock market hit its high for 1984 only six days into the new year, the news from the securities market during the rest of the year was not all bad. The Dow Jones industrial average (the Dow), the most widely watched index on the stock market, began the year at 1252.74 and hit the year's high of 1286.64 on January 6. The index fell steadily through the rest of January and early February. Large fluctuations in March widened in May, before the market dived to 1101.24 on May 29. The Dow plunged to 1086.90 on June 15, then bobbed up to around 1130 in late June.

New Records. By July 23, the Dow had fallen below 1100 once again. On July 24, it hit the year's low of 1086.57. But then came the excitement. On Friday, July 27, the Dow closed out the week at 1114.62. The mild activity that opened the market on the following Monday, July 30, turned into a stampede by Thursday. On Friday, August 3, the Dow closed at 1202.08 with 236.6 million shares traded, setting two records—one for the largest weekly price gains in history and another for one-day trading volume. The following week, the market showed no great price change, but 754,608,744 shares changed hands, setting a new weekly volume record.

The Dow hovered between 1200 and 1240 during the rest of August, then dipped below 1200 on September 11. During the rest of the year, the index generally stayed just above 1200 with occasional closes in the 1180's or 1190's. The bouncing Dow ended the year at 1211.57.

The Broader Market, as measured by the S&P 500, Standard & Poor's index of 500 common stocks, showed the same kind of movement as did the Dow. The S&P 500 opened 1984 at 164.36 and bounced around in the 150's and 160's before hitting the year's low of 147.82 on July 24. It rose in August to 162 and remained in the low and mid-160's until year-end, finishing at 167.24.

Bond Market. In contrast, the bond market in 1984 was a much more orderly place. Long-term corporate AAA bonds—the highest rated bonds—yielded 12.5 per cent at the beginning of the year, fell to under 12 per cent at the end of January, then began a sustained rise to 13.6 per cent in late June. They dipped to just under 12 per cent in early August and ended 1984 at 12.2 per cent.

Five-year Treasury bonds began the year at 11.5 per cent and peaked at 13.8 per cent in late June. By late October, they were back at 11.5 per cent and finished the year at 11.0 per cent.

A noteworthy event in late summer was the continued rise in short-term Treasury rates after long-term rates had started to fall. The three-month Treasury bill rate, for example, rose from 9.8 per cent to its yearly high of 10.6 per cent during July and August.

The Dow Dips and Recovers

Dow Jones Industrial Average

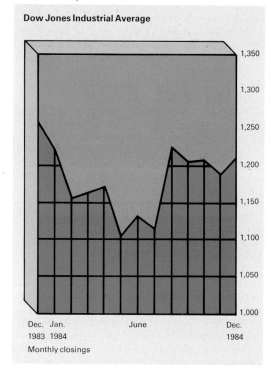

Dec. Jan.   June   Dec.
1983 1984   1984
Monthly closings

High interest rates and flat stock prices usually dampen corporate incentive to issue new securities. But continued economic expansion during 1984, which required new investment in plants and equipment, provided the necessary impetus. New corporate bonds were issued in 1984 at an average rate of $4.5 billion per month, compared with a monthly average of $3.9 billion in 1983. But new stock issues fell to $1.9 billion per month in 1984 from $4.3 billion per month in 1983.

Municipal Bonds (munis) issued by state and local governments usually pay lower interest rates than corporate or Treasury bonds because muni bondholders do not pay federal income tax on the interest they earn. Muni rates were somewhat higher in 1984 than in 1983, beginning January at 9.6 per cent, peaking at 11.0 per cent in early June, then hovering around 10 per cent for the rest of the year.

The municipal bond market waited nervously during 1984 for the effect of the 1983 default of the Washington Public Power Supply System, which was the largest tax-free bond default in history. But the effect on the market seemed to be remarkably slight. New municipal bond issues in 1984 declined by only $1 billion per month, to $5 billion. Donald W. Swanton

In WORLD BOOK, see BOND; INVESTMENT; STOCK, CAPITAL.

SUDAN. President and Prime Minister Gaafar Mohamed Nimeiri came under increasing attack in 1984 from opponents of his 1983 plan to divide the semi-independent southern Sudan into three provinces. Southern Sudanese, most of whom are Christian or practice local religions, also violently opposed Nimeiri's decision to establish Islamic law throughout the country.

Beginning in February, antigovernment groups staged attacks on government projects in the South to pressure Nimeiri into reversing his decision. On February 2, the Anyanya II guerrilla group attacked the United States-operated Chevron Oil Company exploration camp at Bentiu, killing three workers. On February 11, rebels attacked the main construction camp for the Jonglei Canal, a vital irrigation project. A military-civilian coalition movement, the Sudan Peoples' Liberation Movement, was organized in the South in March with the aim of overthrowing Nimeiri.

Emergency Decree. Nimeiri declared a national state of emergency on April 29. All strikes and public meetings were banned, and emergency courts with special powers were set up to deal with violators. On September 29, Nimeiri lifted the state of emergency and reversed his decision to divide the South into three provinces.   William Spencer

See also AFRICA (Facts in Brief Table). In WORLD BOOK, see SUDAN.

SUPREME COURT OF THE UNITED STATES. Moving to limit the rights of criminal suspects, the Supreme Court of the United States in 1984 carved out a wide loophole in the long-standing "exclusionary rule," which prohibits the use of illegally obtained evidence at a criminal trial. The ruling highlighted an exceptional year for the court, both on and off the bench. In the view of numerous observers, the court's rulings became markedly more conservative during the. term, and future Supreme Court appointments became a major issue in the U.S. presidential election campaign.

The court was badly split throughout the year, deciding an unusually high 29 of 150 opinions by 5 to 4 votes. The court's liberals were often the losers. In a speech, liberal Justice Thurgood Marshall suggested that under the influence of its conservative majority, the court has been inattentive to the rights of individuals — an attitude he said was "eroding faith" in the U.S. legal system. Justices John Paul Stevens and William J. Brennan, Jr., also publicly denounced the court, claiming it had been overstepping its authority in an effort to hand down rulings favorable to the government. Justice Harry A. Blackmun delivered the hottest blast of all, saying the court was disregarding past Supreme Court opinions and reaching decisions "by hook or by crook." Burt Neuborne, legal director of the American Civil Liberties Union,

called the court's term "genuinely appalling" and said the institution had become "a cheerleader for government."

By year's end, five of the nine justices were at least 76 years of age, and only one, Sandra Day O'Connor, was under 60. In the presidential campaign, Democratic candidate Walter F. Mondale warned that individual rights in the United States are in a "precarious state." And he noted that, because of the justices' ages, the next President would probably be able to make several new appointments to the court that would affect the court's outlook well into the next century.

Exclusionary Rule. The court's decisions in four exclusionary-rule cases were widely regarded as the most important of the term. For 70 years, trial courts have strictly enforced the Fourth Amendment's prohibition against illegal searches and seizures by refusing to allow any evidence turned up by police using illegal methods to be used in a criminal trial. In a 6 to 3 decision, however, the Supreme Court ruled on July 5 that evidence obtained by the police "in good faith" can be used.

The main case involved a narcotics raid based on a search warrant that was later judged to have been improperly issued. Justice Byron R. White complained that strict adherence to the rule had caused substantial "social costs" and stated, "Particularly when law enforcement officers have acted in objective good faith or their transgressions have been minor, the magnitude of the benefit conferred on such guilty defendants offends basic concepts of the criminal justice system." Justice Stevens' dissent called the majority decision "the product of constitutional amnesia."

Criminal defendants and prisoners also lost every other major case in 1984. The court on January 23 ruled that a state may execute a condemned prisoner without first conducting a special review to ensure that the prisoner's sentence is in line with other sentences handed down in the state for similar crimes. On June 4, the court decided that juveniles charged with being delinquents may be held before trial to keep them from committing more crimes. A July 3 ruling said prisoners have no constitutional right to freedom from unreasonable searches of their cells, and another ruling the same day said criminal suspects have no right to pretrial visits, with physical contact, from friends and relatives. In addition, the court established a new exception to the Miranda Rule, which requires that suspects be informed of their rights before being questioned. In a 5 to 4 decision on June 12, the court ruled that "the need for answers to questions in a situation posing a threat to the public safety outweighs the need" for protection against self-incrimination.

Discrimination. The court handed down several important decisions involving discrimination. In

The Supreme Court ruled in March that a city may use public funds to erect a Nativity scene, such as this one in Pawtucket, R.I.

unanimous rulings, the court held on May 22 that law firms must avoid sex discrimination in making partnership decisions and on July 3 that states can require the Jaycees to admit women members. Two other cases were more controversial, and in both the court's rulings supported views expressed by the Administration of President Ronald Reagan. On February 28, the court declared that the law prohibiting sex discrimination by schools and colleges receiving federal funds applies only to the specific departments or programs receiving the aid. And on June 12, the court ruled that the financially pressed Memphis city government could lay off recently hired black fire fighters while protecting the jobs of whites who had been with the fire department for a longer time. This decision may put limits on affirmative action programs, which impose racial quotas in new hiring to correct earlier patterns of discrimination.

Several Key Decisions in 1984 affected the press and broadcasting. The court ruled on June 27 that the National Collegiate Athletic Association's (NCAA) domination over college football television programming constituted a violation of federal antitrust laws — laws prohibiting business agreements that eliminate competition. The decision dissolved a contract between the NCAA and two television networks — the American Broadcasting Companies (ABC) and CBS Inc. — and opened the way for individual colleges to negotiate coverage of their football games.

The court ruled, in a 5 to 4 decision on January 17, that home videotaping of TV programs does not violate federal copyright laws. The ruling represented a major victory by electronics manufacturers over the motion-picture industry. In a decision that was applauded by the press, the justices on April 30 ordered lower courts to insist that malice, and not just falsity, be proved before granting a libel award.

Other Important Cases included:

■ A 5 to 4 ruling, on March 5, that constitutional requirements of separation of church and state do not prevent a city from using public funds to erect a Christmas Nativity scene representing the birth of Christ.

■ A 6 to 2 ruling, on July 5, that male students who are seeking government financial aid may be first required to certify they have registered for the draft.

■ A 5 to 4 ruling, on January 23, that federal judges may not instruct state officials on how to interpret state laws.   David C. Beckwith

See also COURTS AND LAWS. In WORLD BOOK, see SUPREME COURT OF THE UNITED STATES.

SURGERY. See MEDICINE.

SURINAME. See LATIN AMERICA.

SWAZILAND. See AFRICA.

SWEDEN worried about whether Soviet submarines were patrolling Swedish waters during the first half of 1984. On February 27, the Swedish Navy hurled hand grenades and fired machine guns into the water inside the Karlskrona naval base near the southern tip of Sweden after receiving "signals of underwater activity." Later, officials said that "several" frogmen had attempted to land on an island near the base but were driven back by machine-gun fire and depth charges. The Soviet newspaper *Iszvestia* (News) said the Swedes were suffering from "periscope sickness." Swedish opposition leaders criticized Prime Minister Olof Palme on April 6 for failing to protest strongly to the Soviet Union. However, the Swedish Navy's report on the Karlskrona incident fell short of naming Russia as the aggressor.

On August 9, a Soviet jet fighter pursued a Swedish airliner with 276 passengers on board into Swedish airspace. Defense officials in Stockholm said the airliner probably was mistaken for a target plane taking part in a Warsaw Pact military exercise. The Soviet fighter plane was the same kind that shot down a South Korean airliner in September 1983, killing 269 people.

Wage Restraint. Palme called on the unions to continue their wage restraint when he presented his 1984 budget on January 9. The budget projected a deficit of $8.70 billion, down from a $9.49-billion deficit in fiscal year 1983.

Finance Minister Kjell-Olaf Feldt said that the Socialist government's policies had made it possible for Sweden to work and save itself out of its economic crisis. He added, however, that inflation would have to come down from 9 per cent to 4 per cent in 1984. At midyear, it was about 7 per cent. Feldt pointed out that unions might ease their pressure for higher wages because they could use new *wage-earner funds* to buy shares in private companies. The unions receive these funds from special taxes on corporate revenues and employee pay. Both industry and the government's political opponents said that the budget makers were too cautious.

Queen Silvia Clashed with the Socialists over plans to cut private medical care. The government backed local plans to close four nursing schools in Stockholm because it was concerned about private inroads into public health care. The queen was supported by the king's sister, Princess Christina, who is honorary chairman of the Sofia Home, a private hospital in Stockholm.

New Road. On September 27, King Carl XVI Gustaf and King Olav V of Norway opened a 177-kilometer (110-mile) road linking their countries in the north. Built-in devices would blow the road up in the event of an invasion.   Kenneth Brown

See also EUROPE (Facts in Brief Table). In WORLD BOOK, see SWEDEN.

SWIMMING. In August 1984, at the Summer Olympic Games in Los Angeles, the United States swimming team won gold medals in 20 of 29 events. In those 20 events, 17 gold medals were won by six U.S. swimmers who finally got their chance to compete in the Olympic Games after being members of the 1980 United States team that boycotted the Olympics in Moscow to protest the Soviet invasion of Afghanistan in 1979. The gold medalists were Rick Carey of Mount Kisco, N.Y.; Tracy Caulkins of Nashville, Tenn.; Ambrose (Rowdy) Gaines IV of Winter Haven, Fla.; Nancy Hogshead of Jacksonville, Fla.; Steve Lundquist of Jonesboro, Ga.; and Mary T. Meagher of Louisville, Ky.

The U.S. men won 9 of their 15 Olympic events. The other gold medalists were Alex Baumann and Victor Davis of Canada, Michael Gross of West Germany, and Jon Sieben of Australia. These four men broke world records at the Olympic events. World records also were set by Lundquist; Carey; Pablo Morales of Santa Clara, Calif.; John Moffet of Costa Mesa, Calif.; and four U.S. relay teams, though only those by Lundquist and three relay teams survived the year.

Although the U.S. women won 11 of their 14 Olympic events, they broke no world records during the year. But in 1984's only meeting between U.S. swimmers and the powerful East Germans, at the United States Swimming International in January in Austin, Tex., the U.S. women performed well. Caulkins and Meagher each won twice in that meet. Each won twice in Olympic individual finals as well.

Record Breakers. During the year, world records fell in 11 of the 16 events for men, but only 5 of the 16 for women.

Among the world recordholders was 23-year-old Lundquist, who suffered a separated right shoulder in September 1983 in a water-skiing accident. He recovered in time to win the Olympic gold medal in the 100-meter breaststroke in 1 minute 1.65 seconds, regaining the world record.

There was heartbreak for Matt Gribble of Miami, Fla., and for Moffet. During the U.S. Olympic trials, Gribble lost his world record in the men's 100-meter butterfly, and in the Olympics, slowed by back problems, he did not make the final. Moffet set a record for the 100-meter breaststroke at the U.S. Olympic trials, then injured a muscle in the Olympics and finished fifth.

Diving. Greg Louganis of Mission Viejo, Calif., won Olympic gold medals for men in springboard and platform diving. He also won two of the three U.S. indoor titles and all three outdoor titles. His lifetime total of 29 national championships broke Cynthia Potter's record of 28.   Frank Litsky

See also OLYMPIC GAMES. In WORLD BOOK, see DIVING; SWIMMING.

SWITZERLAND. Swiss voters rejected five major proposals in 1984. On February 26, 64 per cent of the voters who went to the polls turned down a proposal that young men should be allowed to choose civilian work as an alternative to service in the armed forces. On May 20, 73 per cent of the voters decided against a relaxation of the banking secrecy law. A proposal to prohibit foreigners who were not permanent residents of Switzerland from buying residential property in Switzerland lost, 875,519 votes to 837,754, on the same day. On September 23, voters rejected a proposal to halt the building of nuclear power plants and a measure calling for energy conservation.

Woman Executive. On October 2, the Federal Assembly (parliament) elected Elisabeth Kopp to the Federal Council, a seven-member cabinet that serves in place of a single chief executive. Kopp became the first woman member of the council. She had been the mayor of Zumikon, a suburb of Zurich.

UN Vote. The lower house of the Federal Assembly voted on March 15 in favor of Switzerland's joining the United Nations, and the upper house followed suit on December 13. A referendum on membership was expected in 1986 or later.   Kenneth Brown

See also EUROPE (Facts in Brief Table). In WORLD BOOK, see SWITZERLAND.

Elisabeth Kopp takes the oath of office in October and becomes the first woman to serve in Switzerland's seven-member chief executive body.

SYRIA. President Hafiz al-Assad returned to active leadership of the ruling Baath Party and the Syrian government in early 1984 after reportedly spending several months recuperating from a heart attack suffered in 1983. In Assad's absence, a power struggle had developed between Assad's younger brother, Rifaat, and other members of the Baath Party hierarchy.

The struggle came to a head in early March, when Rifaat deployed units of the elite Special Defense Forces, which he commands, in Syria's capital city of Damascus in a showdown with his rivals. Prime Minister Abd al Ra'uf al-Kassem then resigned.

Assad returned to Damascus and ordered the Special Defense Forces to disband. On March 11, he shuffled the Cabinet, reappointing Kassem as prime minister, and named three vice presidents. The three—Rifaat, Deputy Prime Minister and Foreign Minister Abdel Halim Khaddam, and Zuheir Masharqa, assistant secretary-general of the Baath Party—were to have equal responsibilities and relieve Assad of day-to-day administrative duties, easing his workload. Reports of infighting and military confrontations between rival factions continued, however.

In May, Rifaat went on a mission to Moscow and did not return to Syria. In July, Assad sentenced him and his chief rivals to permanent exile, and the Special Defense Forces were reduced. But in November, Rifaat returned to Syria, was pardoned, and was named vice president for national security. His rivals were also pardoned by President Assad.

Foreign Policy Setbacks. In March, Syrian mediators helped to form a cabinet representing all warring factions in Lebanon. But the coalition unraveled during the summer.

A more serious blow was Jordan's decision on September 25 to restore diplomatic relations with Egypt. Relations had been severed in 1979 after Egypt signed a peace treaty with Israel. Assad warned other Arab states of harsh measures if they followed Jordan's example, but he took no formal action against Jordan.

The Syrian Economy clearly would have benefited from more successes in foreign policy and the return of stability to the Middle East. The cost of military preparedness, including weapons purchases and the maintenance of Syrian forces in Lebanon, remained high. The budget, issued in May, called for $10.6 billion in expenditures, with 58 per cent earmarked for defense. New oil finds in August in the Dayr az Zawr area promised some improvement in Syria's oil production, down to 8.4 million short tons (7.6 million metric tons) in 1984.   William Spencer

See also MIDDLE EAST (Facts in Brief Table). In WORLD BOOK, see SYRIA.

TAIWAN moved toward younger, locally trained leadership in 1984 after being ruled since 1949 by an aging group of refugees from mainland China. President Chiang Ching-kuo was elected by parliament on March 21 to a second six-year term.

Chiang was 74 years old, and his health was poor. His selection of a vice president was therefore important. Chiang replaced 77-year-old Shieh Tung-min with the provincial governor of the island, 61-year-old Lee Teng-hui. Lee is an American-educated economist with broad governmental experience. Earlier political leaders in Taiwan had been educated in mainland China before the Communist take-over in 1949. Chiang's choice of Lee was regarded as a continuation of a slow process of turning control of the island over to ethnic Taiwanese rather than mainland Chinese.

Prime Minister Sun Yun-hsuan suffered a stroke and underwent brain surgery on February 26. His cabinet resigned on May 15. Sun was made a senior adviser to Chiang, and parliament approved Yu Kuo-hwa as prime minister on May 25. Yu, 70 years old, was educated in the United States and Great Britain and worked for international organizations. He had headed the powerful Council for Economic Planning and Development since 1977.

Yu's cabinet, appointed by Chiang and sworn in on May 31, was described by the government news service as "the youngest in living memory and probably having the highest credentials in terms of education background." Seven of the 19 members were Taiwanese.

Relations with China. China's Premier Zhao Ziyang said on September 30 that the agreement for the transfer of Hong Kong from British to Chinese control in 1997 opened the possibility of unification with Taiwan. China's top leader, Deng Xiaoping, said the plan for Hong Kong to continue its capitalist system showed that Taiwan could also maintain a separate economic system after joining mainland China. Taiwan rejected these advances. Its foreign minister, Chu Fu-sung, said on October 4 that China's idea of "two [economic] systems in one country" was a deception.

Economic Growth continued so strongly — an estimated 11 per cent for 1984 — that Taiwan found itself with embarrassing trade surpluses. The United States, which was expected to buy $10-billion more in goods from Taiwan than it sold to Taiwan in 1984, pressed Taiwan to lower tariffs and purchase more U.S. products. In the third quarter of 1984, however, the U.S. demand for Taiwanese goods slowed, causing overall exports to grow only 17.6 per cent.   Henry S. Bradsher

See also ASIA (Facts in Brief Table); CHINA, PEOPLE'S REPUBLIC OF. In WORLD BOOK, see TAIWAN.

TANZANIA. See AFRICA.

TAXATION. On July 18, 1984, President Ronald Reagan signed into law the Deficit Reduction Act of 1984. The measure, which revised more than 200 income tax provisions and also raised liquor taxes and extended an excise tax on telephone bills, was designed to raise about $50 billion over a three-year period. In addition, it ordered $13-billion in spending cuts, mostly through changes in the Medicare and Medicaid health care programs for the elderly and the disabled. The new law was regarded by Congress as a "down payment" on a continuing effort to pare federal budget deficits that had been projected to total more than $500 billion by the end of 1987.

The House of Representatives passed the bill on June 27 by 268 to 155, with Democrats overwhelmingly in favor and a slight majority of Republicans voting against it. The Senate added its approval later in the day, 83 to 15, with nine Republicans and six Democrats opposed. Reagan signed the legislation without ceremony, perhaps because he had said earlier that he would not sign a tax increase during the election year unless Congress promised to make significant spending cuts. Major provisions in the bill included:

■ The 3 per cent excise tax on telephone bills, due to expire after 1985, will be extended through 1987. The excise tax on liquor will be increased, effective Oct. 1, 1985 — the first hike since 1951. The cost of a fifth (0.7 liter) of 85-proof whiskey or other spirits will rise by about 34 cents, but taxes on beer and wine will remain unchanged.

■ It will be more difficult, starting in 1985, for individuals who enjoy a large jump in earnings or a financial windfall to lower their tax liability by averaging their income. Henceforth, taxpayers may average their income if their taxable income for the year is 40 per cent more than their average taxable income for the previous three years. The old threshold was 20 per cent more than the average of the previous four years.

Federal Tax Receipts and other revenues rose to $666.5 billion in the 1984 fiscal year, compared with $600.6 billion in fiscal 1983. Individual income tax receipts were $295.96 billion, and corporations paid income taxes of $56.89 billion.

Tax Simplification. During the presidential election campaign, Reagan promised to support a deficit-cutting tax hike only as "a last resort." After being reelected, however, he began to talk about the possibility of simplifying federal income tax laws to broaden the tax base and raise revenues. At year-end, Congress was considering a proposal to eliminate most income tax loopholes and reduce the 14 tax brackets for individuals to 3 — 15, 25, and 35 per cent.   Frank Cormier and Margot Cormier

See also CONGRESS OF THE UNITED STATES; ECONOMICS; PRESIDENT OF THE UNITED STATES. In WORLD BOOK, see INCOME TAX; TAXATION.

TELEVISION

TELEVISION. Network television in the United States in 1984 was punctuated by events that take place only every four years — the Olympic Games and the U.S. presidential election. Television coverage of both events drew some criticism and some raves.

The Olympics. The American Broadcasting Companies (ABC) paid Olympic organizers $91.3-million for the rights to carry the Winter Games held in Sarajevo, Yugoslavia, from February 8 to 19. A combination of circumstances, however, contributed to weak ratings, as measured for the industry by the A. C. Nielsen Company. Yugoslavia's weather proved, if anything, too wintry even for winter games, forcing postponement of some major events. And the United States hockey team, which in 1980 had captured U.S. attention by winning an unexpected gold medal, played poorly in 1984. After the games were over, ABC was forced to give rebates or compensatory commercial time to advertisers who had been promised larger viewing audiences.

The Summer Games were played in Los Angeles in July and August. Doubters expected that ABC's record 168 hours of coverage — for which the network paid $225 million — would overwhelm viewers. ABC stations and affiliates scheduled Olympics programming on most days from 9 A.M.

until late at night, with few interruptions for other programs.

Shortly before the Summer Olympics began, the Soviet Union and most other countries in the Soviet bloc pulled out of the games. The absence of so many top contenders, it was presumed, would badly affect viewership. But it did not work out that way. ABC's ratings surpassed expectations.

On the field, as expected, U.S. athletes dominated the competition. In fact, they set an Olympic record by winning 83 gold medals. Many TV viewers, and even the International Olympic Committee, criticized ABC's coverage for U.S. viewers, which concentrated on the performances of U.S. athletes and seemed biased at times. (ABC also provided TV broadcasters in other countries with full coverage from which they could select what to show their own viewers.)

The Presidential Campaign. Television coverage of the Democratic and Republican national conventions and the election caused more brows to furrow. Because the presidential nominee of each party was virtually assured by the time of the convention, the networks trimmed convention coverage. Only the National Broadcasting Company (NBC) elected to air a promotional film extolling the virtues of President Ronald Reagan that was shown at the Republican convention.

One of the biggest new hits of the 1984-1985 television season was NBC's "The Cosby Show," a situation comedy starring veteran comic Bill Cosby.

Reagan and Democratic challenger Walter F. Mondale debated on television twice. Mondale's faltering campaign gained some momentum after Reagan appeared uncertain and ill-at-ease during the first debate on October 7. By the second meeting, on October 21, Reagan's talent for looking good on television had reemerged. Mondale's running mate, Representative Geraldine A. Ferraro, confronted Vice President George H. W. Bush in a TV debate on October 11.

On election night, CBS Inc. announced at 8 P.M. Eastern Standard Time that Reagan had won the presidential race, based on the network's exit polls and other surveys. ABC reported Reagan the winner at 8:11 P.M., and NBC followed at 8:30 P.M. These results were announced several hours before the polls closed in the West. As in 1980, there was criticism that the early projections could have affected voter turnout in states where polling places were still open and that this, in turn, could have affected the outcome of local or statewide races.

Congress earlier had passed nonbinding resolutions asking the networks to refrain from "characterizing" races. But network executives argued that it was not their business to withhold news. Afterward, the Committee for the Study of the American Electorate, a nonpartisan group, said that in 19 of the 25 states where network projections were broadcast before polls closed, voters turned out in lower numbers than in 1980.

The Prime-Time Audience of the three major commercial networks — ABC, CBS, and NBC — continued to erode in 1984, as independent stations and cable television picked up viewers. During the fall season, the networks drew 78.2 per cent of the television audience, a drop of 2 per cent. Even so, they remained the dominant source of prime-time television entertainment.

The 1983-1984 season ended in April, with NBC mourning its worst showing in 20 years and its ninth consecutive year as the least-watched network. But as the 1984-1985 season got underway in September 1984, NBC seemed to be in firm command of second place in the Nielsen ratings. It ranked ahead of ABC but behind CBS. Helping NBC was a new situation comedy, "The Cosby Show," starring Bill Cosby. The failure of most of ABC's new series also helped NBC.

Continuing a trend that began in 1983, the networks turned increasingly to serious made-for-television motion pictures on controversial topics in 1984. NBC's *The Burning Bed* was the true story of a woman who torched the bed in which her abusive husband lay sleeping. CBS's *Silence of the Heart* focused on the tragedy of teen-age suicide. NBC's *Fatal Vision* was based on a book about Green Beret Captain Jeffrey MacDonald, who was convicted of killing his wife and two children.

The new season emphasized violence and police action shows. In fact, the National Coalition on Television Violence, an organization committed to reducing TV violence, claimed that violent acts were being depicted at "record levels."

Tragically, on October 12, Jon-Erik Hexum, the 26-year-old co-star of a new CBS adventure series called "Cover-Up," accidentally shot himself on the set of the show while playing with a gun loaded with blanks. He died a week later.

Among noteworthy new Public Broadcasting Service (PBS) series were the nine-part "Heritage: Civilization and the Jews" and a prime-time series for children, "Wonderworks." In December, PBS began to air a much-heralded, 14-part saga about the twilight of British rule in India, "The Jewel in the Crown." It was based on *The Raj Quartet* by British author Paul Scott.

The Growth of Pay Television slowed in 1984. Home Box Office, Incorporated (HBO), the largest pay-movie channel, changed management and laid off employees, partly because of the lagging pace of new subscriptions. Pay-movie services faced increasing challenges from rentals of movies to owners of video-cassette recorders, a group that grew by 50 per cent in 1984.

Television and the Courts. Much of what made television news in 1984 took place in courts of law.

Top-Rated Television Series

The following were the most-watched television series for the 31-week regular season — Sept. 18, 1983, through April 15, 1984 — as determined by the A. C. Nielsen Company.

1. "Dallas" (CBS)
2. "Dynasty" (ABC)
3. "The A-Team" (NBC)
4. "60 Minutes" (CBS)
5. "Simon & Simon" (CBS)
6. "Magnum, P.I." (CBS)
7. "Falcon Crest" (CBS)
8. "Kate & Allie" (CBS)
9. "Hotel" (ABC)
10. "Cagney and Lacey" (CBS)
11. "Knots Landing" (CBS)
12. (tie) "ABC Sunday Night Movie" (ABC)
       "ABC Monday Night Movie" (ABC)
14. "TV Bloopers and Practical Jokes" (NBC)
15. "AfterMASH" (CBS)
16. "The Fall Guy" (ABC)
17. "The Love Boat" (ABC)
18. "Riptide" (NBC)
19. "The Jeffersons" (CBS)
20. "Scarecrow and Mrs. King" (CBS)

Angela Lansbury turns sleuth and tries to get a parrot to squeal in the new mystery series "Murder, She Wrote," which started in the fall on CBS.

The most notable case was the $120-million libel suit brought against CBS by retired General William C. Westmoreland, who commanded U,S. forces in Vietnam between 1964 and 1968. In a 1982 documentary, *The Uncounted Enemy: A Vietnam Deception,* CBS claimed Westmoreland had conspired to underestimate North Vietnamese troop strength in an effort to make it appear that the United States was winning the war. At the trial, which opened in October, Westmoreland bitterly denied the CBS charges.

In June, the Supreme Court of the United States ruled that the National Collegiate Athletic Association, which administers intercollegiate sports, had violated antitrust laws by holding exclusive rights to arrange televised broadcasts of football games between member schools. The decision opened the way for individual colleges and conferences to strike their own television deals. Although some collegiate football powers had fought for the ruling, the result was chaotic. Ratings dropped for TV broadcasts of college football games, as did TV viewership of professional football games, which led some observers to conclude that the sport had been overexposed.   P. J. Bednarski

See also AWARDS AND PRIZES. In the Special Reports section, see THE SIGHTS AND SOUNDS OF MUSIC VIDEOS. In WORLD BOOK, see TELEVISION.

TENNESSEE. See STATE GOVERNMENT.

TENNIS. Martina Navratilova of Dallas became the most successful tennis player of 1984 by sweeping the three most important tournaments for women — the United States Open, Wimbledon, and the French Open. She defeated Chris Evert Lloyd of Amelia Island, Fla., in those three finals, and she also defeated Lloyd in three other important title matches — the U.S. Indoor, the Virginia Slims final, and the Women's Tennis Association final. See NAVRATILOVA, MARTINA.

John McEnroe of New York City was almost as dominant among the men. He won the U.S. Open, Wimbledon, Volvo Masters, World Championship Tennis final, Tournament of Champions, and the U.S. Pro Indoor championship. He advanced to the final of the French Open but lost to Ivan Lendl of Czechoslovakia.

Women. The 27-year-old Navratilova, like McEnroe a left-hander, routed Lloyd, 6-3, 6-1, in the French Open final on June 9 in Paris. She earned a $1-million bonus from the International Tennis Federation for having won the grand slam. To achieve a grand slam, a player must win the Wimbledon, the U.S. Open, the Australian Open, and the French Open in succession.

On July 7, in the London suburb of Wimbledon, Navratilova won her fifth singles title at the All England Lawn Tennis Championships. It was also her third straight title there.

The Wimbledon victory did not come easily. Lloyd took a 3-0 lead in the first set with two service breaks, but Navratilova rallied to win, 7-6, 6-2. Lloyd was impressed, saying, "She is playing the best she has ever played."

At the U.S. Open final on September 8 in Flushing Meadows, N.Y., Navratilova defeated Lloyd, 4-6, 6-4, 6-4, in perhaps the best match of the 61 they had played against each other. It was Navratilova's 13th straight win over Lloyd in two years and gave her a 31-30 lead in their rivalry.

Navratilova's victory over Lloyd in the U.S. Open final was her 55th straight. No one knew it at the time, but that victory tied the record winning streak set 10 years before by Chris Evert. The record had been carried for years as 56 matches, but research showed that one victory was a default, and it was dropped from the streak.

Navratilova became the sole recordholder when she beat Melissa Brown of Scarsdale, N.Y., 6-1, 6-2, on September 21 in Fort Lauderdale, Fla., capturing her 56th consecutive victory in singles. By then, Navratilova and Pam Shriver of Lutherville, Md., had won 70 straight doubles matches, another record. Navratilova's winning streak in singles ended at 74 matches when she was defeated in a semifinal match of the Australian Open by Helena Sukova, 19, of Czechoslovakia.

Men. In 1984, the 25-year-old McEnroe won Wimbledon for the second straight year and the third time in four years. He also won his fourth U.S. Open.

At Wimbledon, McEnroe routed Jimmy Connors of Belleville, Ill., 6-1, 6-1, 6-2, on July 8. It was the most one-sided men's singles final at Wimbledon since Don Budge defeated Bunny Austin in 1938 and allowed Austin only four games.

In the U.S. Open on September 8, McEnroe won a bruising five-set semifinal from Connors in a match that lasted 3 hours 45 minutes and ended at 11:13 P.M. The next afternoon, McEnroe whipped Lendl, 6-3, 6-4, 6-1, in the final. That extended McEnroe's record for the year to 66-2.

It was the third straight defeat for Lendl in a U.S. Open final. The two previous defeats were at the hands of Connors. On June 10 at the French Open in Paris, however, Lendl came from behind to beat McEnroe, 3-6, 2-6, 6-4, 7-5, 7-5, in a four-hour final. That was Lendl's first title in a grand slam tournament.

Sweden won the Davis Cup by defeating the U.S. team — led by McEnroe and Connors — 4 matches to 1 in the best-of-five-match event held in December in Göteborg, Sweden.   Frank Litsky

In WORLD BOOK, see TENNIS.

TEXAS. See HOUSTON; STATE GOVERNMENT.

Martina Navratilova shows the form that carried her to a Wimbledon singles title in July, her third straight at Wimbledon and her fifth there overall.

THAILAND during 1984 found itself drawn into the continuing war in Kampuchea (formerly Cambodia), where a coalition of Communists and anti-Communists was fighting Vietnamese occupation forces and a puppet government installed by Vietnam. Thailand channeled aid to the groups fighting the Vietnamese, some of which were based along the Thai border with Kampuchea.

Thailand charged that Vietnamese army battalions penetrated 2 miles (3.2 kilometers) into Thai territory on March 24 while trying to encircle a guerrilla base of Khmer Rouge Communists. The Thai army used artillery and air strikes to push the Vietnamese back, and the Vietnamese also used artillery. In another raid on November 6, four Thai soldiers were killed.

Prime Minister Prem Tinsulanonda obtained promises of more United States military equipment during a visit to Washington, D.C., on April 12 and 13. Prem visited the United States again in September for a medical examination after suffering heart trouble. The 64-year-old Prem returned home on September 26 with a clean bill of health. But three days later he was hastily hospitalized with a blood clot in one lung and stayed in the hospital until October 12.

Prem has been in office since 1980, making him the longest serving head of a civilian administration since the Thai government changed from an absolute monarchy to a constitutional monarchy in 1932. Thailand has had about 15 military coups during that period.

Pressures on Prem were strong to agree to greater military participation in government. The army had lost an effort in 1983 to change the Constitution to permit active duty officers to serve in the cabinet. A new campaign for the change was blocked when parliament voted 371 to 76 on Sept. 3, 1984, to postpone consideration of the change.

The supreme military commander, General Arthit Kamlang-ek, maneuvered to succeed Prem. Arthit sought agreement that he would be exempt from normal military retirement when he reached the age of 60 in 1985. Prem put off a decision. Arthit renewed pressure on Prem by denouncing a devaluation of the baht, Thailand's unit of currency, by 17.3 per cent, effective on Nov. 5, 1984. The devaluation meant that the armed forces will have to pay more for some weapons and aircraft they planned to buy from the United States.

Economic Policies. The government sought to promote exports and reduce fuel imports. The devaluation, which will make Thai products cheaper for other countries, was part of this effort. Thailand also tried to lure more foreign investment to high-technology industries.   Henry S. Bradsher

See also Asia (Facts in Brief Table). In World Book, see Thailand.

THEATER. In an interesting reversal of entertainment trends, the Broadway theater during the 1984 season was dominated by serious drama and revival productions, instead of the usual comedies and lavish musicals. A revival of Arthur Miller's *Death of a Salesman* (1949), starring Dustin Hoffman as the tragic Willy Loman, proved to be one of the most significant theater events of 1984. Other important revival productions of the season included Eugene O'Neill's drama *A Moon for the Misbegotten* (1945), starring British actress Kate Nelligan; Tennessee Williams' moving family play *The Glass Menagerie* (1945), with Jessica Tandy; and George Bernard Shaw's *Heartbreak House* (1919), starring Rex Harrison.

American Works. Two of the most popular new plays on Broadway were written by American playwrights. *Glengarry Glen Ross*, which won David Mamet both the Pulitzer Prize for drama and the New York Drama Critics Circle Award for best new American play, is a slice-of-life study of a group of cutthroat Chicago real-estate salesmen who make their living by swindling people eager to buy a piece of the "American dream." The play's strong language shocked some audience members, but most theatergoers found the play's energy exhilarating.

In *Ma Rainey's Black Bottom*, black playwright August Wilson focused on a Chicago jazz recording session in the 1920's to show audiences how the American music industry exploited black performers. Charles S. Dutton won critical attention for his performance as a musician whose frustration triggers violence.

The most notable drama off Broadway proved to be David Rabe's *Hurlyburly*, about a group of Hollywood agents and actors whose self-indulgent lives reflect their lack of values. The Mike Nichols production, which starred William Hurt, Sigourney Weaver, and Christopher Walken, later moved to Broadway.

Dramatic Imports. British playwright Tom Stoppard won both the Antoinette Perry (Tony) Award and the New York Drama Critics Circle Award for best play for *The Real Thing*, a witty domestic drama about the nature of love and fidelity in a modern marriage. Stars Jeremy Irons and Glenn Close won Tonys of their own for their portrayals of an arrogant playwright and the wife who humbles him by having an affair.

Great Britain's Royal Shakespeare Company staged two productions on Broadway, William Shakespeare's *Much Ado About Nothing* and Edmond Rostand's *Cyrano de Bergerac*, both starring Derek Jacobi and Sinead Cusack. Italian dramatist Dario Fo, barred from the United States in 1980 for his leftist views, was allowed to attend the Broadway opening of his political drama, *Accidental Death of an Anarchist* starring Jonathan Pryce.

Actors in the Broadway hit *Sunday in the Park with George* re-create the painting *La Grande Jatte* by Georges Seurat, the subject of the musical.

Musicals. There were few musicals on Broadway in 1984. A short-lived youth-oriented production of the 1844 Alexandre Dumas classic *The Three Musketeers* featured teen idol Michael Praed as the dashing D'Artagnan, who rode to his adventures onstage on a live horse. Also appealing to young people was *The Tap Dance Kid* starring Hinton Battle, who won a Tony for his performance in this musical about a talented black youngster who must defy his lawyer-father if he wants to become a dancer. The parents-and-children theme was also pursued in *The Rink*, another short-lived musical, starring Liza Minnelli and Chita Rivera as a daughter and mother who battle over the sale of the family business, a skating rink.

The only new musical of 1984 that really made an impact on Broadway was Stephen Sondheim's *Sunday in the Park with George*. Considered by many critics to be highly innovative in form and content, the show centered on the life of Georges Seurat, a French painter of the 1800's, who was played by Mandy Patinkin. The musical, which also starred Bernadette Peters, tried to capture the distinctive pointillist painting technique invented by Seurat in both its musical style and visual concept.

The Business Picture. In analyzing the overall 1983-1984 theater season, *Variety*, the show-business newspaper, reported an impressive financial picture. Total box-office receipts rose to a new high of $432.6 million, split fairly evenly between Broadway productions and those produced in professional theaters throughout the United States.

The report also made it clear, however, that the number of Broadway productions had dropped substantially — to only 36 presentations — and that the year's attendance total of 7.9 million was the lowest since the 1975-1976 season. High ticket prices were credited with the healthy-looking box-office figures. *La Cage aux Folles*, for example, raised its top ticket price to $47.50 on July 2, making it the most expensive show on Broadway.

Small Theater Experiment. In November, a Broadway producer announced an experimental plan that some industry leaders hoped would reduce ticket prices and production costs in the commercial theater. Morton Gottlieb, the producer of a new drama called *Dancing in the End Zone*, negotiated with labor unions, artists' representatives, and the owner of the Ritz Theater to establish a special "small theater" category of production.

By agreeing to use only 499 seats of the 954-seat theater and to charge no more than $30 for a ticket, Gottlieb won financial concessions from the playwright, creative artists, union personnel, and theater management. If the experiment results in respectable profits, the new small theater category may find wider application on Broadway.

Beyond Broadway. The health of the many fine regional theaters in the United States was best illustrated by Chicago's Steppenwolf Theatre Company, whose productions of plays by David Mamet, Lanford Wilson, and others have often moved to New York City. In July, the company held a special press conference to reassure Chicagoans that the acclaim given to such individual ensemble members as John Malkovich had only strengthened the company's resolve to keep its operation based in Chicago. Explaining the decision, company member Tom Irwin said Chicago was "a place where we can be free to experiment."

Another heartening sign of life beyond Broadway was the resurgence of the Guthrie Theater in Minneapolis, Minn., for 20 years the leading classical repertory company in the United States. During the 1983 season, art director Liviu Ciulei announced that a $600,000 deficit had forced the theater to abandon its resident acting company. By May 1984, the Guthrie Theater had wiped out the deficit, increased its subscription list to 20,000, and announced plans to reinstate the acting ensemble.

Other Theater News. Other issues involving the theater industry in 1984 included a settlement of the seven-year management dispute over the Vivian Beaumont Theater at Lincoln Center for the Performing Arts in New York City. John V. Lindsay, a former mayor of New York City, was named chairman of the theater in September.

In June, the mayor's Theater Advisory Council recommended a series of zoning proposals designed to protect the 44 legitimate theaters that constitute Broadway from, among other things, demolition by real-estate developers. At year's end, the New York City Council had not yet acted on the recommendations.

Still unresolved, also, were criticisms aimed at the selection process for Tony Awards nominations. Controversy ran especially high in May, when the 1984 nominations were announced, because many important stars were not nominated.

Deaths. During 1984, the Broadway theater observed the deaths of some of its brightest artistic talents, including Ethel Merman, often considered the "queen of the musical"; playwright Lillian Hellman, author of *The Children's Hour* (1934) and other important American dramas; and actor Richard Burton. Other deaths included those of director Alan Schneider and composer Meredith Willson, who wrote the musical *The Music Man* (1957). Marilyn Stasio

See also AWARDS AND PRIZES (Arts Awards). In WORLD BOOK, see DRAMA; THEATER.

TIMOR. See ASIA.

TOGO. See AFRICA.

TORNADO. See DISASTERS; WEATHER.

TOYS. See GAMES AND TOYS.

TRACK AND FIELD. Carl Lewis of the United States, Sergei Bubka of the Soviet Union, and Uwe Hohn of East Germany were among the most successful track and field athletes of 1984. The Summer Olympic Games in Los Angeles provided Lewis with a prime forum to display his talents, an outlet denied to Bubka and Hohn because of the Soviet-bloc boycott of the games.

Lewis, of Houston, won four Olympic gold medals — in the 100-meter dash, 200-meter dash, 400-meter relay, and long jump. Lewis' best performance of the year was an unofficial world indoor record in the long jump on January 27 in New York City. Despite a short runway, he jumped 28 feet 10¼ inches (8.79 meters), matching his outdoor best. The world outdoor record is still Bob Beamon's 29 feet 2½ inches (8.90 meters), set at the 1968 Mexico City Olympics.

Pole Vault. In January and February 1984, Bubka set three indoor records in the pole vault — 19 feet ¾ inch (5.81 meters), 19 feet 1 inch (5.82 meters), and 19 feet 1½ inches (5.83 meters). Outdoors, between May and August, he set world records four times, bettering himself each time until, finally, he set the world record of 19 feet 5¾ inches (5.94 meters). His indoor record vanished when Thierry Vigneron of France vaulted 19 feet 2¼ inches (5.85 meters).

Losing her balance, Mary Decker falls after she collides with Zola Budd during the 3,000-meter race in August at the Summer Olympic Games.

World Track and Field Records Established in 1984

Men

Event	Holder	Country	Where set	Date	Record
10,000 meters	Fernando Mamede	Portugal	Stockholm, Sweden	July 2	27:13.81
20-kilometer walk	Ernesto Canto	Mexico	Bergen, Norway	May 5	1:18:40
400-meter relay	Sam Graddy, Ron Brown, Calvin Smith, Carl Lewis	U.S.A.	Los Angeles	Aug. 11	:37.83
High jump	Zhu Jianhua	China	Eberstadt, W. Ger.	June 10	7 ft. 10 in. (2.39 m)
Pole vault	Sergei Bubka	U.S.S.R.	Rome	Aug. 31	19 ft. 5¾ in. (5.94 m)
Javelin throw	Uwe Hohn	E. Ger.	East Berlin	July 20	343 ft. 10 in. (104.80 m)
Hammer throw	Yuri Sedykh	U.S.S.R.	Cork, Ireland	July 3	283 ft. 3 in. (86.34 m)
Decathlon	Jürgen Hingsen	W. Ger.	Mannheim, W. Ger.	June 8–9	8,798 points
Marathon	Steve Jones	Great Britain	Chicago	Oct. 21	2:08:05

Women

Event	Holder	Country	Where set	Date	Record
100 meters	Evelyn Ashford	U.S.A.	Zurich, Switz.	Aug. 22	:10.76
200 meters	Marita Koch	E. Ger.	Potsdam, E. Ger.	July 21	:21.71*
1 mile	Natalia Artemova	U.S.S.R.	Moscow	Aug. 6	4:15.8
2,000 meters	Tatyana Kazankina	U.S.S.R.	Moscow	Aug. 4	5:28.72
3,000 meters	Tatyana Kazankina	U.S.S.R.	Leningrad, U.S.S.R.	Aug. 26	8:22.62
5,000 meters	Ingrid Kristiansen	Norway	Oslo, Norway	June 28	14:58.89
10,000 meters	Olga Bondarenko	U.S.S.R.	Kiev, U.S.S.R.	June 24	31:13.78
400-meter hurdles	Margarita Ponomaryeva	U.S.S.R.	Kiev, U.S.S.R.	June 22	:53.58
1,600-meter relay	Gesine Walther, Sabine Busch, Dagmar Rübsam, Marita Koch	E. Ger.	Erfurt, E. Ger.	June 3	3:15.92
3,200-meter relay	Nadezhda Olizaryenko, Lyubov Gurina, Ludmilla Borisova, Irina Podyalovskaya	U.S.S.R.	Moscow	Aug. 5	7:50.17
High jump	Ludmila Andonova	Bulgaria	East Berlin	July 20	6 ft. 9½ in. (2.07 m)
Shot-put	Natalia Lisovskaya	U.S.S.R.	Sochi, U.S.S.R.	May 27	73 ft. 11 in. (22.53 m)
Discus throw	Zdenka Silhava	Czech.	Nitra, Czech.	Aug. 26	244 ft. 7 in. (74.56 m)
Heptathlon	Sabine Paetz	E. Ger.	Potsdam, E. Ger.	May 5–6	6,867 points

m = meters; *ties record; †unofficial record.

Billy Olson of Abilene, Tex., became the first U.S. 19-foot (5.79-meter) vaulter when he cleared 19 feet ¼ inch (5.80 meters) indoors. Outdoors, the U.S. record was raised between May and July from 18 feet 11 inches (5.77 meters) by Mike Tully of Encino, Calif., to 19 feet ¼ inch (5.80 meters) by Earl Bell of Jonesboro, Ark., to 19 feet ¾ inch (5.81 meters) by Tully, and then finally to 19 feet 1¼ inches (5.82 meters), again by Tully.

Hohn's Long Throw. On July 20, in East Berlin, East Germany's Hohn threw the javelin 343 feet 10 inches (104.80 meters), shattering the world record of Tom Petranoff of Northridge, Calif., by a startling 16 feet 8 inches (5.08 meters). The throw was so long that the nervous officials first measured it incorrectly, then measured it correctly with a cloth tape, and then remeasured it the next day when they located the steel tape required to measure a world-record throw.

Zola Budd. No track and field athlete created more interest than Zola Budd, a skinny teen-ager from South Africa who ran barefoot. On January 5 in Stellenbosch, South Africa, Budd ran 5,000 meters in 15:01.83, bettering the 1982 world record of 15:08.26 set by Mary Decker of Eugene, Ore. But Budd's performance was not recognized because South Africa was banned from international track and field, a result of its racial policies.

In March, the Budd family moved to Great Britain. Because Budd's grandfather was a British citizen, Zola was eligible to become a citizen and run for Great Britain in the Olympics.

She was leading in the Olympic women's 3,000-meter final, barely ahead of Decker, when the two women made contact. Decker fell, injured a hip, and did not finish. Budd finished seventh.

Other Stars. Evelyn Ashford of Los Angeles won the Olympic 100-meter gold medal for women. Then, on August 22 in Zurich, Switzerland, she beat her East German archrival, Marlies Göhr, and lowered her world record to 10.76 seconds.

Edwin Moses of Laguna Hills, Calif., won his second Olympic gold medal in eight years. Later, in Europe, he extended his seven-year winning streak in the 400-meter hurdles to 109 races, consisting of 94 finals and 15 preliminaries.

Between June and August, Joaquim Cruz dominated the men's 800-meter run. He won the National Collegiate Athletic Association title for the University of Oregon. Then he set an Olympic record and won a gold medal for Brazil during the Summer Games, and also came within four-hundredths of a second of Sebastian Coe's world record. In August, Johnny Gray of Santa Monica, Calif., broke the U.S. 800-meter record three times in seven days. Frank Litsky

See also OLYMPIC GAMES. In WORLD BOOK, see TRACK AND FIELD.

Happy throngs welcome San Francisco's cable cars back into full service on June 21 after a 20-month absence for renovation work.

TRANSIT systems in the United States continued to pull ahead in 1984. Ridership rose, service additions outpaced reductions, and cities moved ahead with new projects, especially the modern trolley lines called *light rail*. Federal and local financing held steady. But the overall transit deficit continued to climb.

The American Public Transit Association reported that ridership on urban mass-transit systems increased for the second consecutive year. The systems carried 6.7 billion passengers in the first 10 months of 1984, up 2.6 per cent. San Francisco's Bay Area Rapid Transit system set ridership records as patronage rose 9.2 per cent through October 1984. But total passengers fell 1.3 per cent in New York City and 1.8 per cent in Portland, Ore.

Service Expansions revived in 1984 after efforts to curb deficits in previous years had led to cutbacks. Chicago-area systems made a sharp turnaround and restored some service in 1984. Some also cut fares, and ridership through October rose 4.6 per cent. The restructured Chicago-area Regional Transportation Authority (RTA) trimmed costs after getting a $75-million annual state subsidy late in 1983. In April, the RTA repaid the last installment of a $100-million bank loan it had received in 1982.

The recently expanded Los Angeles system and the Portland, Ore., system scrapped service-reduction plans. Los Angeles instead added nearly 50 buses. The Transit Authority of Northern Kentucky in April 1984 boosted bus service into downtown Cincinnati, Ohio. Systems in Pittsburgh, Pa., and Ann Arbor, Mich., also added service. New special services such as trips to zoos or recreational areas, and vans for the disabled, were offered in Tulsa, Okla.; Atlanta, Ga.; and New Jersey. San Francisco's famed cable cars returned to service in June after a 20-month rehabilitation.

Miami, Fla., opened its new, 11-mile (17.7-kilometer) rapid transit line on May 20 and added 4 more miles (6.4 kilometers) on December 17. The Washington, D.C., Metro reached deeper into Maryland with the opening of new subway segments in August and December totaling 13.7 miles (22 kilometers). The Chicago Transit Authority's 7.9-mile (12.7-kilometer) rapid transit extension to O'Hare International Airport opened on September 3. On December 15, a 9-mile (15-kilometer) addition to Atlanta's rapid transit system extended service to the city's northern suburbs. Los Angeles, with new federal aid, planned its first rapid transit line. Boston expanded its commuter-rail system for the first time since 1975.

Many cities, wanting rail transit and facing hefty subway costs, turned to light-rail systems, or considered doing so. Such lines were under construction in Buffalo, N.Y.; Portland; Pittsburgh; San

Jose and Sacramento, Calif; and Santa Clara County, California, in 1984.

Fares and Funds. Transit systems in Pittsburgh and in Charlotte, N.C., lowered fares. On the other hand, systems in Los Angeles; Washington, D.C.; and elsewhere raised fares. The Port Authority Trans-Hudson rail system linking New York City and New Jersey boosted fares from 50 cents to 75 cents on June 3 to finance improvements — the second fare hike in two years.

The Administration of President Ronald Reagan again sought to limit spending on transit systems in 1984. However, Congress kept operating subsidies at an annual level of $875 million. The Administration proposed cost-effectiveness ratings of new transit-construction projects as a means of deciding which projects should receive money. Congress, however, said the ratings should be advisory rather than binding.

Transit Vehicle Purchases. Buses produced by non-U.S. companies were bought by many American transit systems in 1984. Several U.S. systems also purchased Canadian or Japanese rapid transit or light-rail cars. A 400-bus order by the Los Angeles-area system in June, however, helped revive General Motors Corporation's bus production, which had been suspended in January. Albert R. Karr

In WORLD BOOK, see TRANSPORTATION.

TRANSKEI. See AFRICA.

TRANSPORTATION companies in the United States benefited greatly from the economy's expansion during 1984. Airlines had combined record profits as more carriers registered traffic increases, improved earnings, and reduced labor costs. Railroads extended gains derived from improved productivity and deregulation-spurred flexibility. But shipping lines were still plagued with surplus capacity and lagging demand, and shipyard business continued to slump. Truck firms adjusted further to deregulated freight rates and increased competition. Mass-transit systems expanded. Long-distance bus lines lost more customers to automobile travel and airlines.

Frank Smith of Transportation Policy Associates, a consulting firm, estimated U.S. transportation revenues at $706 billion for 1984, up 8.4 per cent from 1983. Mainland intercity freight, measured in ton-miles, rose 10 per cent, with railroad freight up 10 per cent, truck freight up 7 per cent, air freight up 14 per cent, and pipeline volume up 8 per cent. Great Lakes traffic climbed 20 per cent, and river and canal traffic was up 15 per cent. Intercity passenger traffic increased 4.6 per cent. Automobile travel was up 5 per cent; air travel, 3 per cent; and railroad passenger traffic, 6 per cent. Bus traffic fell again, by 1 per cent.

Congress, in an effort to reduce highway fatalities from drunken driving, enacted a law in June aimed at forcing states to raise their minimum drinking age to 21. The law would withhold some federal highway funds from states that do not raise the minimum drinking age to 21.

Interstate highway construction delays were threatened when Congress adjourned in October without releasing $7.7 billion in federal road funds. A dispute over road projects favored by several members of the House of Representatives and the Senate caused the funding deadlock.

The Regulators. Members of the Interstate Commerce Commission (ICC) — a federal agency that regulates commercial transportation across state lines — squabbled over policy for much of the year. Three new members appointed by President Ronald Reagan took office in September and seemed to leave the seven-member board with a narrow majority backing railroad and truck deregulation.

The Civil Aeronautics Board (CAB) on May 31 voted to prohibit smoking on short flights. The next day, however, it reversed this action and upheld a March decision against the ban instead. Under the provisions of a 1978 deregulation law, the CAB was abolished at the end of 1984, and its remaining duties were transferred to the U.S. Department of Transportation.

Airbags and Safety Belts. Secretary of Transportation Elizabeth Hanford Dole on July 11 announced that, starting with the 1987 model year, automakers will have to phase in airbags, automatic safety belts, or other effective passive-restraint systems. If states representing two-thirds of the U.S. population enact laws requiring motorists to wear seat belts, however, the airbags or other devices would not be required. On July 12, New York became the first state to enact a buckle-up law. The legislatures of New Jersey and Illinois passed similar laws in November and December, respectively.

Auto Recalls. A trial began in Washington, D.C., in March as part of the government's attempt to force General Motors Corporation (GM) to recall 1.1 million 1980 X-cars. The Department of Justice contended that the cars have defective brakes. In a separate matter, GM, Ford, and Chrysler Corporation agreed in November to recall more than 4 million vehicles for safety checks.

In Canada, the new government of Prime Minister Brian Mulroney, who took office in September, continued the airline and trucking deregulation policies of its predecessor. The new minister of transport, Donald Frank Mazankowski, pledged to restore some previously discontinued passenger-train service on VIA Rail Canada, Canada's national rail passenger system. Albert R. Karr

See also AUTOMOBILE; AVIATION; RAILROAD; SHIP AND SHIPPING; TRANSIT; TRUCK AND TRUCKING. In WORLD BOOK, see TRANSPORTATION.

TRINIDAD AND TOBAGO. See LATIN AMERICA.

TRUCK AND TRUCKING. United States trucking firms moved forward in 1984 as the economy improved. The American Trucking Associations (ATA) estimated in November that trucks would haul about 830 million short tons (750 million metric tons) in 1984, up 10 per cent from 1983. Revenues were estimated at about $52 billion, up 12 per cent, and net income at $1.23 billion, up 10 per cent.

The shakeout of truck companies caused by a 1980 deregulation law eased a bit in 1984, with more stability for larger, more profitable carriers. The Interstate Commerce Commission (ICC) — the federal agency that regulates truckers traveling between states — allowed general freight-rate increases ranging from 1.5 to 8 per cent between April and October. But competitive rate-cutting continued among many firms. Looking toward labor negotiations with the Teamsters Union to replace contracts due to expire on April 1, 1985, many small and medium-sized trucking firms left the industry bargaining group, Trucking Management Incorporated, late in 1984. These firms, facing competition from new, nonunion trucking companies, wanted to negotiate on their own to obtain contract concessions that would cut labor costs.

Deregulation. A total-deregulation bill drafted by the Administration of President Ronald Reagan in 1983 stayed on the shelf because of Teamsters opposition. The bill would end all protection from antitrust prosecution when truck firms jointly set rates. Antitrust immunity for some forms of joint rate-setting expired by law on July 1, 1984.

In April, Norfolk Southern Corporation, a big railroad, agreed to buy North American Van Lines from PepsiCo Incorporated. This deal, made possible by ICC deregulation, prompted industry calls for keeping some ICC controls.

Large Trucks. A federal judge ruled in March that the Department of Transportation (DOT) must set standards for deciding which federal-aid roads — besides those in the interstate highway system — are safe for the use of the new wider and longer trucks. Congress in October enacted legislation to allow big twin trailers and wide trucks to use federal-aid roads with lanes narrower than 12 feet (3.7 meters), if the DOT determines that such use does not pose a safety hazard.

Taxes. Congress in June scaled back the annual road-use tax on the heaviest trucks to $550 from the $1,900 high that they would have had to pay beginning in mid-1988. But the federal tax on truck diesel fuel was raised from 9 cents to 15 cents per gallon (3.8 liters).   Albert R. Karr

See also TRANSPORTATION. In WORLD BOOK, see TRUCK.

Striking European truckdrivers blockade the Brenner Pass in the eastern Alps, paralyzing traffic between Austria and Italy in mid-February.

TRUDEAU, PIERRE ELLIOTT (1919-   ), stepped down as Canada's prime minister on June 30, 1984, after more than 15 years in the post — from 1968 to 1979 and from 1980 to 1984. Although Trudeau did not leave enjoying the warm popularity of his early years in office, he remained the dominant presence on the Canadian political scene until the day of his resignation.

Trudeau continued his peace mission, begun in 1983, by which he hoped to reduce East-West tensions and bring about arms negotiations between the superpowers. The mission carried him to Western Europe, three Eastern European countries, and the Soviet Union in 1984. Always independent in his views, Trudeau publicly expressed doubts about the credibility of the nuclear strategy of the North Atlantic Treaty Organization. Trudeau's assessment of his "peace crusade" was that it had helped to revive East-West dialogue. On November 13, in Washington, D.C., Trudeau received a $50,000 award from the Albert Einstein Peace Prize Foundation for his efforts toward world disarmament and peace.

After his resignation, Trudeau and his three sons — all born during his time in office — moved to Montreal. There, he joined a law firm specializing in corporate, tax, and labor law. David M. L. Farr

See also CANADA (Close-Up). In WORLD BOOK, see TRUDEAU, PIERRE ELLIOTT.

TUNISIA. Dissatisfaction with the economic policies and general leadership of Prime Minister Mohamed Mzali's government produced an explosion of violence in Tunisia in January 1984. The immediate cause of the riots was an increase of from 80 to 110 per cent in the price of bread and other basic commodities.

The government had hoped to cut its budget deficit by reducing subsidies paid to grain producers to keep prices low. But the public reacted violently. Riots began in the far south, Tunisia's poorest region, and spread to northern cities and urban areas. The government declared a state of emergency on January 3 and called out army units to deal with the rioters. On January 6, President Habib Bourguiba rolled back the increases. However, in February and again in July, the government raised the price of bread and other grain products by about 10 per cent with little public outcry.

Bourguiba also dismissed Interior Minister Idris Guiga, who was later charged with treason. In June, Guiga was sentenced, in his absence, to 10 years at hard labor. The former minister, living in Rome, denied any guilt.

In April, an inquiry into the riots listed 88 dead and more than 900 wounded, including 348 members of the security forces. On July 27, 36 members of the outlawed Islamic Tendency Movement were tried and imprisoned for provoking the riots. But most were released in an August 1 amnesty.

Shortly after the riots, the government began a shakeup of police and internal security forces. Many officials were charged with negligence, bribery, drug smuggling, and incompetence.

Underlying Problems. The "Bread Riots" underlined broader economic and social problems, including 20 to 25 per cent unemployment, which was worst among young people; economic disparity among regions; and protests by Islamic fundamentalist groups over the secularization and Westernization of Tunisian life.

Public concern also centered on the question of who would succeed the 80-year-old Bourguiba, who has been named president for life. His great popularity disturbed many Tunisians, particularly young people, but Prime Minister Mzali, the heir apparent, aroused little enthusiasm.

The Economy showed few bright spots. One was the opening on May 21 of a 120-kilometer (75-mile) canal from the Majardah River to Cape Bon. The canal will divert water from the north to the arid northeast region. The resolution of a border incident with Libya resulted in July in Libyan grants of $60 million for road and electricity networks in southern Tunisia. William Spencer

See also AFRICA (Facts in Brief Table). In WORLD BOOK, see TUNISIA.

TURKEY. Prime Minister Turgut Ozal received firm public support in 1984, both for his political leadership and his programs designed to solve Turkey's long-time economic problems. The results of local elections held on March 25 for mayors and other municipal officials confirmed Ozal's support among voters. His party won 45 per cent of the vote. The opposition Social Democracy Party, which was excluded from elections held in November 1983, received 23.4 per cent.

Political Stability. In general, Turkey had a remarkably peaceful year. The Turkish government lifted martial law in 13 of the country's 67 provinces on March 1 and in an additional 13 provinces on June 28 for the first time since the military coup in 1980.

Several trials of people implicated in the violence that led to the 1980 coup were held during 1984. In the most important one, in May, 13 members of the leftist Dev Yol (Revolutionary Path) group were sentenced to death, and 94 other members received long prison terms.

Rebel Activity in eastern Turkey, a region populated mainly by Kurds, continued to disturb the general tranquillity, however. In April and May, 31 Kurdish nationalists were sentenced to death, and about 400 were given prison terms, for attempting to form a separate Kurdish state. Nevertheless, Kurdish guerrillas continued to raid

Turkish military posts. In October, the army launched "Operation Sun" in the rugged Hakkari region along the Iraqi border and scattered the guerrillas.

Mediation Attempt. Turkey, which has good relations with both Iran and Iraq, attempted without success to mediate in the Iran-Iraq war. In February, expansion of the pipeline that carries Iraqi oil across Turkey to the Mediterranean Sea was completed. Ozal visited Teheran, Iran's capital, in May and agreed to an $800-million increase in exports to Iran. In return, Iran agreed to provide $2.9 billion in oil to meet Turkish needs.

Ozal's Economic Reforms included devaluation of Turkey's unit of currency, the lira, in January and a 49 per cent increase in interest rates to encourage savings and combat inflation, which ran at 40 per cent. A March law permitted foreign companies to invest in any sector of the economy.

Initial responses were encouraging. In March, the Islamic Development Bank, which provides funds for economic development, provided $750-million in stand-by credits, and the International Monetary Fund, an agency of the United Nations, lent Turkey $238 million in April. The United States came through in September with $900 million in military and economic aid.   William Spencer

See also MIDDLE EAST (Facts in Brief Table). In WORLD BOOK, see TURKEY.

TURNER, JOHN NAPIER (1929-   ), a Liberal, served briefly as prime minister of Canada in 1984. He was sworn in on June 30, succeeding Pierre Elliott Trudeau, who retired after more than 15 years in office. On September 17, Turner was replaced by Brian Mulroney, leader of the Progressive Conservatives. See CANADA.

Turner was born on June 7, 1929, in Richmond, England. His father died when Turner was 2 years old. Shortly after that, his mother, an economist, moved the family to Canada.

Turner graduated from the University of British Columbia in 1949, received a degree in jurisprudence from Oxford University of England in 1951 and a civil-law degree at Oxford in 1952. In 1954, he joined a law firm in Montreal, Que.

Turner was first elected to the House of Commons in 1962. Beginning in 1965, he held a series of Cabinet positions. He became minister of finance in 1972 but resigned that post in 1975. He resigned from Parliament in 1976 to practice law.

Turner married Geills McCrae Kilgour in 1963. They have a daughter and three sons.   Jay Myers

In the WORLD BOOK SUPPLEMENT section, see TURNER, JOHN NAPIER.

UGANDA. See AFRICA.

UNEMPLOYMENT. See ECONOMICS; LABOR.

UNION OF SOVIET SOCIALIST REPUBLICS (U.S.S.R.). See RUSSIA.

UNITED NATIONS (UN) meetings in 1984 helped pave the way for disarmament negotiations between the Soviet Union and the United States, and for peace negotiations between El Salvador's government and Salvadoran rebels by bringing government officials together at UN Headquarters. The officials were on hand for the 39th annual session of the UN General Assembly, which opened on September 18.

The Assembly elected Zambia's Ambassador Paul J. F. Lusaka president by unanimous consent. In his opening address, Lusaka expressed deep regret at "the present low ebb in the relationship between the two superpowers."

Gromyko and Reagan. The Soviet Union's foreign minister, Andrei A. Gromyko, had skipped the 1983 Assembly amid friction over the shooting down of a South Korean airliner by a Soviet plane on Sept. 1, 1983. He attended the 1984 session and was present on September 24 when President Ronald Reagan of the United States opened the annual round of policy speeches.

Reagan proposed what came to be called "umbrella talks" on disarmament. He said, "We need to extend the arms control process, to build a bigger umbrella under which it can operate," and pronounced the United States "ready for constructive negotiations" with the Soviet Union. He urged that the two powers consult with each other periodically at the cabinet level on regional problems and on ways "to reduce the vast stockpiles of weapons in the world."

Gromyko told the Assembly on September 27 that the Soviet Union wanted talks on limiting nuclear arms in Europe, reducing strategic arms throughout the world, and heading off a nuclear arms race in outer space. But he said there would be no talks because the United States did not want them. In fact, the Soviets had broken off the last rounds of nuclear arms talks. In November 1983, they left talks in Geneva, Switzerland, on intermediate-range nuclear missiles when the North Atlantic Treaty Organization (NATO) placed such missiles in Western Europe. And when a round of discussions on long-range strategic missiles ended in December 1983, the Soviets refused to set a date for resuming meetings.

On Sept. 28, 1984, Gromyko met with Reagan in the White House for 3½ hours. Neither reported any agreement. But on November 22, the Soviet Union and the United States announced that they had agreed "to enter into new negotiations with the objective of reaching mutually acceptable agreements on the whole range of questions concerning nuclear and outer space arms." The announcement said Shultz and Gromyko would meet in Geneva on Jan. 7 and 8, 1985, "to reach a common understanding as to the subject and objectives of such negotiations."

A United Nations delegation examines a bomb in Iran in March to check Iran's claim that Iraq is using chemical weapons in the war between the two countries.

El Salvador. Meanwhile, on Oct. 8, 1984, President José Napoleón Duarte of El Salvador made a bid for peace with leftist guerrillas who had been fighting since the late 1970's to topple the government of that country. Speaking before the General Assembly, Duarte invited the guerrilla leaders to meet him on October 15 in La Palma, a village in northern El Salvador. He proposed to meet them unarmed and in the presence of clergy and Salvadoran and foreign journalists.

The meeting took place as Duarte proposed. In a 4½-hour discussion, the two sides agreed to set up a commission to seek "humanization of the armed conflict" and eventual peace.

Nicaragua. Daniel Ortega Saavedra, head of the government of Nicaragua, told the Assembly on October 2 that the United States was planning military action to prevent Nicaraguan elections scheduled for November 4. He said that U.S. mercenary forces were "already concentrated" in neighboring Honduras and Costa Rica. The United States ignored the charge.

On April 4, the United States had vetoed a UN Security Council resolution to condemn — and call for an immediate end to — minelaying in Nicaraguan ports. Great Britain abstained from the vote. Voting for the resolution were the other 13 Council members: China, Egypt, France, India, Malta, the Netherlands, Nicaragua, Pakistan, Peru, the Soviet Union, the Ukraine, Upper Volta (Burkina), and Zimbabwe. (The Ukraine is part of the Soviet Union, but it has a separate seat in the United Nations.) Nicaraguan Ambassador Javier Chamorro Mora blamed the minelaying on the United States, and others mentioned the U.S. Central Intelligence Agency. United States delegate José S. Sorzano did not reply directly to the charge, but he remarked, "Apparently the only crime against the peace that the Security Council is concerned with is mining."

On May 10, in a case brought by Nicaragua, the International Court of Justice (World Court) in The Hague, the Netherlands, unanimously ordered the United States to stop immediately "any action restricting, blocking, or endangering access to or from Nicaraguan ports." The order by the 15-judge UN affiliate gave the court time to work on a definitive ruling on the case. On November 26, the court ruled that it had jurisdiction to make a final decision. The court's U.S. member, Judge Stephen M. Schwebel, dissented from this decision. The case remained on the court docket.

Fishing Rights. On October 12, the court settled a boundary dispute between the United States and Canada over the Georges Bank, a fishing area in the Gulf of Maine. The decision gave five-sixths of the Georges Bank to the United States and one-sixth to Canada. See FISHING INDUSTRY.

UNITED NATIONS (UN)

Dropping Out. On November 17, Poland gave notice that it was withdrawing from the International Labor Organization (ILO), a UN agency in Geneva. Stanislaw Turbanski, Polish representative at the UN office in Geneva, wrote ILO Director-General Francis Blanchard that Poland was leaving the organization because some segments of the ILO had a "tendentious [one-sided] and hostile" attitude toward Poland. He cited a decision that had been made the previous day by the ILO governing body to take note of the report of a commission that had looked into a complaint about Poland's observance of ILO agreements on freedom of association, collective bargaining, and the right to strike. This decision had the effect of acknowledging that the complaint might have been justified.

Great Britain announced in November that it would quit the United Nations Educational, Scientific and Cultural Organization (UNESCO) at the end of 1985 unless that agency reformed its management and spending practices. In December, Singapore gave notice that it would withdraw from UNESCO because membership was not a matter of high priority to Singapore. That country's ambassador to France, David Marshall, said the decision to leave was "totally independent" of the approaching withdrawal of the United States from UNESCO. The United States had said in 1983 that it would leave at the end of 1984.

Drought and Hunger in Africa were the subjects of a three-day General Assembly debate in early November. UN Secretary-General Javier Pérez de Cuéllar, who visited Africa repeatedly in 1984, issued a report saying that 27 African countries had abnormal food shortages, that almost 1 million Ethiopians faced the prospect of starving to death, and that 2,000 people had already starved to death in Chad. The UN Children's Fund (UNICEF), the Food and Agriculture Organization, and the World Food Program arranged to help the stricken countries.

New Member. On September 21, the General Assembly voted unanimously to admit Brunei Darussalam to UN membership, raising the number of members to 159. The new member, located on the island of Borneo, became independent of Great Britain on Dec. 31, 1983. In the WORLD BOOK SUPPLEMENT section, see BRUNEI.

Other Major Votes. In the Security Council on February 29, the Soviet Union vetoed a French resolution that would have created a new UN peacekeeping force in Beirut, Lebanon, after the withdrawal of the last contingent of the current force. Only the French contingent remained of a force that also had included troops from Great Britain, Italy, and the United States. The vote was 13-2, with the Soviet Union and the Ukraine voting no. On September 6, the United States vetoed a Lebanese resolution that would have demanded that Israel lift all restrictions on the movements of civilians in the parts of Lebanon under Israeli occupation. The other 14 countries voted for the resolution.

On September 28, the General Assembly condemned South Africa's new Constitution by a 137-0 vote with the United States and Britain abstaining. The Constitution granted parliamentary representation to ethnic Indians and *Coloreds* — people of mixed race — but not to blacks.

On October 26, the Assembly called unanimously for a speed-up in Central American peace talks.

An October 30 vote renewed earlier calls for withdrawal of foreign troops from Vietnamese-occupied Kampuchea (Cambodia). The vote was 110 to 2, with 18 abstentions.

On November 1, on a vote of 119 to 20 with 14 abstentions, the Assembly requested new talks between Britain and Argentina on the Falkland Islands. The two countries had fought an undeclared war over the islands in 1982.

On November 15, the Assembly voted 119 to 20 with 14 abstentions to call for withdrawal of foreign troops from Afghanistan. Soviet troops had invaded Afghanistan in December 1979 and have been fighting rebels there ever since. William N. Oatis

In WORLD BOOK, see UNITED NATIONS.

UNITED STATES, GOVERNMENT OF THE. The government of the United States produced few surprising initiatives in 1984, sticking largely to its essential chores while setting aside difficult problems until after the election year. Continued concern about the federal budget deficit, however, prompted Congress and the Administration of President Ronald Reagan to work together in an effort to increase revenues and restrain spending.

The budget deficit for the 1984 fiscal year, which ended on September 30, was $175.3 billion, second only to the fiscal 1983 record of $195.4 billion. On January 25, in his State of the Union message to Congress, Reagan called for a bipartisan search for ways to pare $100 billion from the $500 billion or more in budget deficits projected by the end of 1987. Bipartisan budget talks began on Feb. 8, 1984, but they ended later that month after just four meetings.

Despite the breakdown of the talks, Congress and Reagan subsequently agreed on a program expected to pare more than $100 billion from the three-year deficits. Part of that program was the Deficit Reduction Act of 1984, which the President signed into law on July 18. The measure, incorporating the third major revision of federal income tax laws in four years, was designed to raise about $50 billion in taxes over three years. In addition, it specified $13 billion in spending cuts,

Federal Spending

United States Budget for Fiscal 1984

Billions of dollars

National defense.	227.4
International affairs.	13.3
General science, space, and technology.	8.3
Energy.	2.5
Natural resources and environment	12.7
Agriculture.	12.2
Commerce and housing credit	5.2
Transportation	24.7
Community and regional development	7.8
Education, training, employment, and social services	26.6
Health	30.4
Social security and Medicare	235.8
Income security	96.7
Veterans benefits and services	25.6
Administration of justice	5.6
General government	4.8
General purpose fiscal assistance	6.6
Interest	111.0
Undistributed offsetting receipts.	−15.5
Total budget outlays	**841.8**

U.S. Income and Outlays

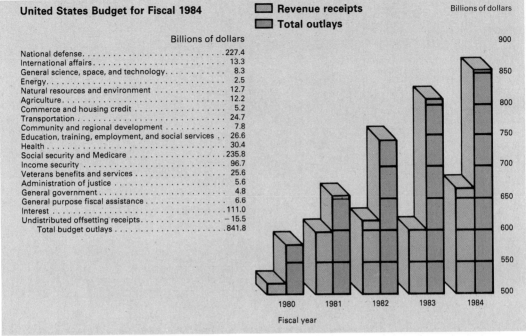

- ▢ Revenue receipts
- ▢ Total outlays

Billions of dollars

Fiscal year

Source: U.S. Department of the Treasury.

mainly through changes in the Medicare and Medicaid health-care programs for the elderly and the disabled. Reagan and Congress later agreed to hold after-inflation increases in defense spending to about 5 per cent, down sharply from the President's initial request for a 13 per cent hike.

The Grace Commission. Another blueprint for federal economizing was unveiled on January 12, when the President's Private Sector Survey on Cost Control, headed by industrialist J. Peter Grace, announced the findings of its 18-month study. The report by the survey panel — called informally the Grace Commission — recommended 2,478 cost-cutting measures that it claimed would produce three-year savings of $424.4 billion. The proposals included revising federal pension plans, closing unneeded military bases, and eliminating wasteful public works projects. Few of the suggestions had been adopted by year-end, and critics contended that implementing the plan on a large scale was unlikely as long as Congress and the Administration continued to give in to special-interest groups.

Before Congress Adjourned on October 12, a noisy battle over increasing the national debt limit and passing a comprehensive spending bill led on October 4 to a brief situation in which two-thirds of the government was technically out of cash. Reagan sent 500,000 federal workers home for

half a day, saying there was no money to pay them. Congress quickly passed a stopgap spending bill, and the government employees returned to work.

Several major legislative issues were left pending at adjournment, including immigration reform, a strengthening of civil rights programs, banking and natural gas deregulation, and financing for toxic-waste cleanup. In addition, several important national-security decisions, including whether to produce the MX ballistic missile and whether to fund antigovernment guerrillas in Marxist Nicaragua, remained unresolved.

New Postmaster. On November 13, the Board of Governors of the U.S. Postal Service announced the selection of Paul N. Carlin, postmaster of the 13-state Chicago region, to succeed Postmaster General William F. Bolger on Jan. 1, 1985. The independent board ignored last-minute White House efforts to replace the retiring Bolger with Edward J. Rollins, director of Reagan's reelection campaign.

Wick Controversies. Charles Z. Wick, one of Reagan's personal friends, retained his post as director of the United States Information Agency (USIA) but was twice involved in controversy. On January 9, Wick apologized for secretly taping telephone conversations, including one with former President Jimmy Carter.

Major Agencies and Bureaus of the U.S. Government*

Executive Office of the President

President, Ronald Reagan
  Vice President, George H. W. Bush
  White House Chief of Staff, James A. Baker III
  Presidential Press Secretary, James S. Brady
  Central Intelligence Agency — William J. Casey, Director
  Council of Economic Advisers — vacant
  Council on Environmental Quality — A. Alan Hill, Chairman
  Office of Management and Budget — David A. Stockman, Director
  Office of Science and Technology Policy —
    George A. Keyworth II, Director

The Supreme Court of the United States

Chief Justice of the United States, Warren E. Burger
  Associate Justices

William J. Brennan, Jr.	Lewis F. Powell, Jr.
Byron R. White	William H. Rehnquist
Thurgood Marshall	John Paul Stevens
Harry A. Blackmun	Sandra Day O'Connor

Department of State

Secretary of State, George P. Shultz
  U.S. Representative to the United Nations — Jeane J. Kirkpatrick

Department of the Treasury

Secretary of the Treasury, Donald T. Regan
  Bureau of Alcohol, Tobacco, and Firearms —
    Stephen E. Higgins, Director
  Bureau of Engraving and Printing — Robert J. Leuver,
    Director
  Bureau of the Mint — Donna Pope, Director
  Comptroller of the Currency — C. T. Conover
  Internal Revenue Service — Roscoe L. Egger, Jr., Commissioner
  Treasurer of the United States — Katherine Davalos Ortega
  U.S. Customs Service — William von Raab, Commissioner
  U.S. Secret Service — John R. Simpson, Director

Department of Commerce

Secretary of Commerce, Malcolm Baldrige
  Bureau of the Census — John G. Keane, Director
  Economic Development Administration —
    J. Bonnie Newman, Administrator
  National Bureau of Standards — Ernest Ambler, Director
  National Oceanic and Atmospheric Administration —
    John V. Byrne, Administrator
  Minority Business Development Agency —
    James H. Richardson Gonzales, Director
  Patent and Trademark Office —
    Gerald J. Mossinghoff, Commissioner

Department of Labor

Acting Secretary of Labor, Ford B. Ford
  Bureau of Labor Statistics — Janet L. Norwood, Commissioner
  Employment and Training Administration —
    Frank C. Casillas†, Administrator
  Employment Standards Administration —
    Susan R. Meisinger, Administrator
  Labor-Management Services Administration — vacant
  Mine Safety and Health Administration —
    David A. Zegeer, Administrator
  Occupational Safety and Health Administration —
    Robert A. Rowland, Administrator
  Women's Bureau — Lenora Cole-Alexander, Director

Department of Health and Human Services

Secretary of Health and Human Services, Margaret M. Heckler
  Administration for Children, Youth and Families —
    Dodie Truman Livingston†, Commissioner
  Administration on Aging — Lennie-Marie P. Tolliver,
    Commissioner
  Alcohol, Drug Abuse, and Mental Health Administration —
    Donald Ian Macdonald†, Administrator
  Centers for Disease Control — James O. Mason, Director
  Food and Drug Administration —
    Frank E. Young, Commissioner
  Health Care Financing Administration —
    Carolyne K. Davis, Administrator
  Health Resources and Services Administration —
    Robert Graham, Administrator

National Institutes of Health — James B. Wyngaarden, Director
Office of Consumer Affairs — Virginia Knauer, Director
Public Health Service — C. Everett Koop, Director
Social Security Administration — Martha A. McSteen, Acting
  Commissioner

Department of Defense

Secretary of Defense, Caspar W. Weinberger
  Joint Chiefs of Staff — General John W. Vessey, Chairman
  Secretary of the Air Force — Verne L. Orr
  Secretary of the Army — John O. Marsh, Jr.
  Secretary of the Navy — John F. Lehman, Jr.

Department of Justice

Attorney General, William French Smith
  Bureau of Prisons — Norman A. Carlson, Director
  Drug Enforcement Administration —
    Francis M. Mullen, Jr., Administrator
  Federal Bureau of Investigation — William H. Webster, Director
  Immigration and Naturalization Service —
    Alan C. Nelson, Commissioner
  Office of Justice Assistance, Research, and Statistics —
    Lois H. Herrington, Acting Director
  Solicitor General — Rex E. Lee

Department of the Interior

Secretary of the Interior, William P. Clark
  Assistant Secretary for Indian Affairs — Kenneth L. Smith
  Bureau of Land Management — Robert F. Burford, Director
  Bureau of Mines — Robert C. Horton, Director
  Bureau of Reclamation — Robert Olson, Acting Commissioner
  Geological Survey — Dallas L. Peck, Director
  National Park Service — Russell E. Dickenson, Director
  Office of Territorial and International Affairs —
    Richard T. Montoya, Director
  U.S. Fish and Wildlife Service — Robert A. Jantzen, Director

Department of Agriculture

Secretary of Agriculture, John R. Block
  Agricultural Economics — William Gene Lesher, Director
  Agricultural Marketing Service — Vern Highley, Administrator
  Agricultural Stabilization and Conservation Service —
    Everett G. Rank, Administrator
  Farmers Home Administration — Charles W. Shuman,
    Administrator
  Federal Crop Insurance Corporation — Merritt Sprague, Manager
  Food and Consumer Services — Mary C. Jarratt, Administrator
  Food and Nutrition Service — Robert Leard, Administrator
  Forest Service — R. Max Peterson, Chief
  Rural Electrification Administration — Harold V. Hunter,
    Administrator
  Soil Conservation Service — Peter C. Myers, Chief

Department of Housing and Urban Development

Secretary of Housing and Urban Development, Samuel R. Pierce, Jr.
  Community Planning and Development —
    Alfred C. Moran, Administrator†
  Federal Housing Commissioner — Maurice L. Barksdale
  Government National Mortgage Association —
    Robert W. Karpe, President

Department of Transportation

Secretary of Transportation, Elizabeth Hanford Dole
  Federal Aviation Administration — Donald D. Engen, Administrator
  Federal Highway Administration — Ray A. Barnhart, Administrator
  Federal Railroad Administration — John H. Riley,
    Administrator
  Maritime Administration — Harold E. Shear, Administrator
  National Highway Traffic Safety Administration —
    Diane K. Steed, Administrator
  U.S. Coast Guard — Admiral James S. Gracey, Commandant
  Urban Mass Transportation Administration —
    Ralph L. Stanley, Administrator

Department of Energy

Secretary of Energy, Donald Paul Hodel
  Economic Regulatory Administration — Rayburn D. Hanzlik,
    Administrator
  Energy Information Administration — J. Erich Evered,
    Administrator

Federal Energy Regulatory Commission —
  Raymond J. O'Connor, Chairman
Office of Energy Research — Alvin W. Trivelpiece, Director

Department of Education
Secretary of Education, vacant
  National Institute of Education — Manuel J. Justiz, Director

Congressional Officials
President of the Senate pro tempore — Strom Thurmond
Senate Majority Leader — Robert J. Dole
Senate Minority Leader — Robert C. Byrd
Speaker of the House — Thomas P. O'Neill, Jr.
House Minority Leader — Robert H. Michel
Architect of the Capitol — George M. White
Comptroller General of the U.S. — Charles A. Bowsher
Congressional Budget Office — Rudolph G. Penner, Director
Librarian of Congress — Daniel J. Boorstin
Office of Technology Assessment — John H. Gibbons, Director
Public Printer of the U.S. — Ralph E. Kennickell, Jr.†

Independent Agencies
ACTION — Thomas W. Pauken, Director
Commodity Futures Trading Commission — Susan M. Phillips,
  Chairman
Consumer Product Safety Commission —
  Nancy Harvey Steorts, Chairman
Environmental Protection Agency — William D. Ruckelshaus,
  Administrator
Equal Employment Opportunity Commission —
  Clarence Thomas, Chairman
Export-Import Bank — William H. Draper III, President
Farm Credit Administration — Donald E. Wilkinson, Governor
Federal Communications Commission — Mark S. Fowler, Chairman
Federal Deposit Insurance Corporation — William M. Isaac,
  Chairman
Federal Election Commission — Lee Ann Elliott, Chairman
Federal Emergency Management Agency — Louis O. Giuffrida,
  Director
Federal Home Loan Bank Board — Edwin J. Gray, Chairman
Federal Maritime Commission — Alan Green, Jr., Chairman
Federal Mediation and Conciliation Service — Kay McMurray,
  Director
Federal Reserve System — Paul A. Volcker,
  Board of Governors Chairman
Federal Trade Commission — James C. Miller III, Chairman
General Services Administration — Jack L. Courtemanche†,
  Administrator
Interstate Commerce Commission — Reese H. Taylor, Jr.,
  Chairman
National Aeronautics and Space Administration —
  James M. Beggs, Administrator
National Endowment for the Arts — Frank Hodsoll, Chairman
National Endowment for the Humanities — William J. Bennett,
  Chairman
National Labor Relations Board — Donald L. Dotson, Chairman
National Mediation Board — Helen M. Witt, Chairman
National Railroad Passenger Corporation (Amtrak) —
  W. Graham Claytor, Jr., President
National Science Foundation — Erich Bloch, Director
National Transportation Safety Board — James E. Burnett, Jr.,
  Chairman
Nuclear Regulatory Commission — Nunzio J. Palladino, Chairman
Occupational Safety and Health Review Commission —
  Elliott R. Buckley, Chairman
Office of Personnel Management — Donald J. Devine, Director
Peace Corps — Loret Miller Ruppe, Director
Securities and Exchange Commission — John S. R. Shad,
  Chairman
Small Business Administration — James C. Sanders, Administrator
Smithsonian Institution — Robert McC. Adams, Secretary
Synthetic Fuels Corporation — Edward E. Noble, Chairman
Tennessee Valley Authority — Charles H. Dean, Jr., Chairman
U.S. Arms Control and Disarmament Agency —
  Kenneth L. Adelman, Director
U.S. Commission on Civil Rights —
  Clarence M. Pendleton, Jr., Chairman
U.S. Information Agency — Charles Z. Wick, Director
U.S. International Development Cooperation Agency —
  M. Peter McPherson, Acting Director
U.S. International Trade Commission — Alfred Eckes, Chairman
U.S. Postal Service — Paul N. Carlin, Postmaster General
Veterans Administration — Harry N. Walters, Administrator

*As of Jan. 1, 1985.   †Nominated but not yet confirmed.

A month later, Wick was further embarrassed when *The Washington* (D.C.) *Post* reported that his agency had blacklisted 95 prominent Americans from speaking abroad under USIA auspices. They included broadcaster Walter Cronkite, Senator Gary W. Hart (D., Colo.), and civil rights activist Coretta Scott King. The blacklist was abandoned.

Investigations. An investigation into widely publicized allegations that the 1980 Reagan campaign had used stolen private papers of then-President Carter to prepare Reagan for a televised debate with Carter was set aside in 1984. On May 23, a House of Representatives subcommittee said "the better evidence" was that William J. Casey, later director of the Central Intelligence Agency, was the recipient of the so-called Debategate papers. The subcommittee recommended that the Department of Justice name an independent counsel to look into possible violations of criminal law in the incident. The Justice Department, however, stuck to its position that there was "no credible evidence" of a crime and "no evidence that the material was stolen."

Two other investigations led to more serious — and unprecedented — consequences for federal officials. In Reno, Nev., U.S. District Judge Harry E. Claiborne was sentenced on October 3 to two years in prison for income tax evasion. Claiborne, who appealed the sentence, was the first federal judge ever convicted of a crime while still serving on the bench. On the same day, special agent Richard W. Miller of the Federal Bureau of Investigation (FBI) was arrested in San Diego on charges of selling classified documents to agents of the Soviet Union. Miller was the first FBI agent ever accused of spying for a foreign power.

Banking and Foreign Trade. One of the most significant federal actions of 1984 was the bailout of the Continental Illinois National Bank and Trust Company of Chicago, which held some $5 billion in problem loans. Federal banking regulators pledged their full support on May 17, but the touchy situation was not resolved until July 26, when the Federal Deposit Insurance Corporation took over $4.5 billion in questionable loans "to avoid general instability in the financial system."

As the election approached, Reagan had to deal with two politically sensitive trade disputes. On September 6, the President declined to impose import quotas or higher tariffs on copper produced in other countries. And on September 18, he announced that he would seek "voluntary" restraints on steel imports, rejecting the quotas or higher tariffs sought by the U.S. steel industry. On December 19, the Administration concluded pacts with Brazil, Japan, South Korea, and four other nations putting limits on steel imports.

Reagan and Gromyko Meet. On September 28, Reagan conferred for 3½ hours at the White

UNITED STATES CONSTITUTION

House with Soviet Foreign Minister Andrei A. Gromyko. It was the first time the President had met with a top-level Soviet official, and some critics said Reagan agreed to the meeting simply to give his reelection campaign a boost. One apparent result, however, was a joint U.S.-Soviet announcement in November that the two nations would meet in Geneva, Switzerland, in January 1985 to discuss nuclear and space weapons.

The Courts. On September 18, Justice Harry A. Blackmun of the Supreme Court of the United States, in a supposedly off-the-record talk at a Washington club, described the court as weary and overworked and "moving to the right" in its rulings. On January 2, Chief Justice of the United States Warren E. Burger said that too few federal judges and too many lawyers were pushing the judiciary to "the verge of collapse." He called for the creation of 75 new federal judgeships.

On July 10, Reagan signed a bill overhauling the bankruptcy court system and creating 85 new federal judgeships.   Frank Cormier and Margot Cormier

See also CABINET, UNITED STATES. In the Special Reports section, see LOBBYING THE LAWMAKERS. In WORLD BOOK, see UNITED STATES, GOVERNMENT OF THE.

UNITED STATES CONSTITUTION. See CONSTITUTION OF THE UNITED STATES.

UPPER VOLTA. See AFRICA.

URUGUAY. Uruguay's military leaders followed through on their pledge to return the country to civilian rule by holding national elections on Nov. 25, 1984. Julio María Sanguinetti, a 48-year-old lawyer and the candidate of the Colorado Party, was elected president with 38.8 per cent of the vote over two other contenders. The voting was the first national election in Uruguay since 1971. When Sanguinetti is inaugurated on March 1, 1985, Uruguay will have a civilian government for the first time since the military took power in 1973.

The elections were marred by the government's refusal to allow two opposition groups to select their first choices for presidential candidates. The Blanco Party's first choice would have been Wilson Ferreira Aldunate, who was jailed in 1984 after he returned from exile. The Broad Front would have selected General Liber Seregni, who was released in February after nine years in prison on trumped-up charges. Instead, both parties ran lesser-known candidates.   Nathan A. Haverstock

See also LATIN AMERICA (Facts in Brief Table). In WORLD BOOK, see URUGUAY.

UTAH. See STATE GOVERNMENT.

UTILITIES. See COMMUNICATIONS; ENERGY; PETROLEUM AND GAS.

VANUATU. See PACIFIC ISLANDS.

VENDA. See AFRICA.

VENEZUELA. In February 1984, Venezuela's newly inaugurated President Jaime Lusinchi, with his Democratic Action Party (AD) in control of the National Congress, announced an austerity program designed to trim public expenditures and a bloated bureaucracy. The Lusinchi administration also mounted a campaign against corruption and brought officials from past administrations before the courts.

Economic Problems. The new president faced a tough challenge. Earnings from oil continued to be depressed because of an oil glut on world markets. To keep foreign exchange earnings at home, thereby stimulating productivity and creating jobs, Lusinchi refused to allow most private sector companies to make interest payments on their overseas debts. He thus continued in the direction set by his predecessor in office, Luis Herrera Campíns, who had suspended principal payments on both government and private debts in early 1983 in a vain attempt to make his Social Christian Party (COPEI) popular with voters.

When Lusinchi's AD party was the overwhelming victor in municipal elections on May 27, 1984, it became apparent that his government had the public support necessary to handle renegotiating Venezuela's foreign debt. Final results from the May election gave the AD 60 per cent of the vote; COPEI, 28 per cent; and the left wing Movement Toward Socialism, 12 per cent.

The two opposition parties had sought to characterize the elections as a test of support for Lusinchi's economic policies. Following the AD victory, the National Congress formally approved a bill on June 20 granting Lusinchi special emergency powers to do whatever he might deem necessary to restructure Venezuela's foreign debt — without first consulting the National Congress.

By then, Venezuela was overdue in making payments on both government and private sector debts. Bank regulators in the United States had classified Venezuela's debts as "substandard," meaning that they had to be written off as losses by those U.S. banks that held them. In September, however, the Venezuelan government announced that it had reached an agreement to refinance $20.75 billion of its $27.5-billion foreign debt. The agreement was similar to one that gave Mexico extended time to repay its debts, though Venezuela did not require a loan from the International Monetary Fund, an agency of the United Nations.

Bank Failure. On June 5, the Venezuelan government closed down the state-owned Banco Nacional de Descuento, after efforts to save the ailing institution failed.   Nathan A. Haverstock

See also LATIN AMERICA (Facts in Brief Table); LUSINCHI, JAIME. In WORLD BOOK, see VENEZUELA.

VERMONT. See STATE GOVERNMENT.

VETERANS. United States District Court Judge Jack B. Weinstein announced on Sept. 25, 1984, his tentative approval of a $180-million settlement in an Agent Orange case. The case was a class-action lawsuit brought by some 16,000 Vietnam War veterans against seven manufacturers of the herbicide Agent Orange, used to defoliate Vietnamese jungles. The veterans claimed that exposure to dioxin, a chemical in the herbicide, had caused them serious health problems. The seven chemical companies contended that no scientific proof linked dioxin with harm to human beings.

Weinstein said that "at best the evidence is inconclusive" concerning any relationship between specific health problems and dioxin. He added that a veteran would have difficulty proving exposure to dioxin and identifying the manufacturer of the product. The judge withheld final approval, pending a plan to distribute the funds.

The Veterans of Foreign Wars elected Billy Ray Cameron of Sanford, N.C., commander in chief at their annual convention in August. He is the first Vietnam War veteran to hold a top position in the organization.   Frank Cormier and Margot Cormier

In WORLD BOOK, see VETERANS ADMINISTRATION; VETERANS' ORGANIZATIONS.

VICE PRESIDENT OF THE UNITED STATES. See BUSH, GEORGE H. W.

VIETNAM forged closer ties with the Soviet Union in 1984. In mid-April, the Vietnamese and Soviets held their first-ever joint military exercises. The maneuvers apparently were stimulated by a Chinese attack along Vietnam's northern border earlier in April. China attacked to retaliate for Vietnamese offensives against Chinese-backed guerrillas opposing Vietnam's occupation of Kampuchea (formerly Cambodia). Localized fighting along the border continued for most of 1984.

Visits to Other Countries. Vietnam's Defense Minister Van Tien Dung visited Moscow for talks on May 16 and June 26 with Soviet Defense Minister Dmitri F. Ustinov. Vietnam sought more and better Soviet weapons, but its economic problems and inability to pay apparently made Moscow reluctant to provide arms. In November, Foreign Minister Nguyen Co Thach visited Moscow.

Vietnam's top leader, Communist Party General Secretary Le Duan, visited India from September 21 to 26. It was his first trip to a non-Communist country. His talks focused on economic cooperation.

Economic Changes. At a meeting from July 3 to 10 of the Communist Party's Central Committee, Le Duan won approval for an extension of the system of economic incentives that had improved Vietnam's agricultural production since 1979. Al-

A Vietnam War veteran—the only known American casualty still unidentified—is buried in May in the Tomb of the Unknowns in Arlington, Va.

though not as sweeping as the economic reforms adopted by China in 1984, the changes stirred controversy in Vietnam. The country's second most important leader, Chief of State Truong Chinh, reportedly opposed them as un-Communist. Possibly because of that dispute, he was not left in charge when Le Duan went to India. Instead, the fifth-ranked party official, Le Duc Tho, handled affairs.

Guerrilla Resistance to Communist rule continued in Vietnam. The Vietnamese army newspaper said on April 4 that 45 clashes had occurred in the Dak Tô area in western Vietnam between Vietnamese troops and a people called Montagnards.

Refugee Problems. Vietnam said on June 25 that the United States acceptance of only 1,000 Vietnamese refugees per month had created a backlog of 28,000 people waiting with exit visas. U.S. Secretary of State George P. Shultz said on September 11 that the United States was willing to take up to 10,000 political prisoners and families who were still in Vietnamese "reeducation camps." Official talks began on the refugee backlog and on bringing to the United States an estimated 5,000 to 15,000 children of U.S. soldiers and Vietnamese mothers. Henry S. Bradsher

See also ASIA (Facts in Brief Table). In WORLD BOOK, see VIETNAM.

VIRGINIA. See STATE GOVERNMENT.

VISUAL ARTS. Several lavish exhibitions honored leading European painters during 1984. From June to September, the National Gallery of Art in Washington, D.C., in cooperation with the Grand Palais in Paris, presented "Antoine Watteau 1684-1721" on the 300th anniversary of the birth of that French rococo painter. From October to December, the Metropolitan Museum of Art in New York City held "Van Gogh in Arles," covering the most productive period of Dutch-born painter Vincent Van Gogh. The Philadelphia Museum of Art organized a show called "Masters of 17th Century Dutch Genre Painting" from March to May.

Current Art was displayed in several important exhibitions. From September to November, the St. Louis (Mo.) Art Museum summarized the fiery career of German painter Max Beckmann. The Guggenheim Museum in New York City presented "Picasso: The Last Years, 1963-1973" from March to May. The Metropolitan Museum of Art in New York City gave exhibitions in February and March for both American painter Charles E. Burchfield and the puzzling Polish-born painter known as Balthus.

The Museum of Modern Art in New York City held a huge show called " 'Primitivism' in 20th Century Art: Affinity of the Tribal and the Modern" from September 1984 to January 1985 to celebrate its reopening after a four-year renovation and construction program. In May, the museum opened its new west wing, which occupies the first six floors of a 44-story residential tower designed by American architect Cesar Pelli.

Photography continued to appear in important exhibitions. They included a retrospective of the work of American photographer Irving Penn at the Museum of Modern Art from September to November and "Photography in California: 1945-1980," in the spring at the San Francisco Museum of Modern Art.

Other news included the largest museum acquisition in the history of photography. The J. Paul Getty Museum in Malibu, Calif., purchased 18,000 photographs from nine private collections in June for about $20 million.

Romantic Art. A number of exhibitions focused on the romantic artists of the late 1800's. "The Orientalists: Delacroix to Matisse" appeared at the National Gallery of Art. From June to September, the Museum of Fine Arts in Montreal, Canada, presented paintings by Adolphe William Bouguereau, a French academic artist of the 1800's now newly appreciated.

American Painting was seen in several exhibitions. At the Museum of Fine Arts in Springfield, Mass., "Erastus S. Field, 1805-1900" showed the work of Field, an American primitive painter. The brutal images of war, death, and torture painted by Leon Golub appeared in a retrospective of his work organized by the New Museum in New York City. Museumgoers could experience the urgency of urban life in the early 1900's in the work of American painter Robert Henri at the Delaware Art Museum in Wilmington.

Large Outdoor Sculpture continued to intrigue the American public. In Chicago, a sculpture 40 feet (12 meters) tall, *Monument with Standing Beast* by French artist Jean Dubuffet, was dedicated in November at the new State of Illinois Center. In Philadelphia, a work by American sculptor Isamu Noguchi called *Bolt of Lightning: A Memorial to Benjamin Franklin,* a stainless steel sculpture 102 feet (31 meters) tall, was unveiled at a plaza adjacent to the Franklin Bridge. American sculptor Robert Graham designed two monumental works for the entrance to the Los Angeles Memorial Coliseum, where the Summer Olympic Games took place in July and August. They were a male and a female torso, each 25 feet (7.6 meters) tall.

A Modigliani, Maybe. One of the year's strangest stories involved the Italian artist Amedeo Modigliani. Legend says that the artist, disgusted with his work, threw a wheelbarrow full of sculpture into a canal in Leghorn, Italy, in 1909. In July 1984, the Leghorn city council dragged the canal and recovered two stone heads, apparently by Modigliani. In September, however, three Italian university students claimed they had made one of the heads

A seascape by British painter J. M. W. Turner sells in London in July for about $10 million, by far the most ever paid at auction for a picture.

as a prank. The origin of the sculptures remained unclear at year's end as experts studied them.

New Museums both large and small opened in 1984. In January, the Dallas Museum of Art began operation in a $53-million, 210,000-square-foot (19,500-square-meter) structure designed by American architect Edward Larrabee Barnes. The Art Institute of Chicago announced the construction of a new $20-million south wing and — with a $5.5-million grant from the Regenstein Foundation — the construction of the largest special exhibitions center in the United States.

The residents of Stockbridge, Mass., where American artist Norman Rockwell lived and painted for 25 years, voted in May to allow construction of a new $3.3-million gallery devoted to his works. In Miami, Fla., the $6-million Center for the Fine Arts opened in January as part of a $24-million arts complex. In New York City, the American Craft Museum will move to the first two floors of a new CBS Inc. headquarters to be erected at the museum's former location. The museum swapped its site for four times as much space in the new building. The Center for African Art opened in New York City in September.

In Canada, the National Gallery in Ottawa began construction of its first permanent building. The huge structure — 320,000 square feet (29,700 square meters) — will use natural light.

The World's Wealthiest Museum, Malibu's J. Paul Getty Museum, became even richer in January after the Getty Trust, which operates the museum, sold its Getty Oil Corporation holdings for $4.6 billion. The sale increased the museum's endowment income to over $100 million yearly.

Important Museum Acquisitions in 1984 included 249 abstract geometric works given to the Museum of Modern Art in March. The McCrory Corporation, which operates clothing and other retail stores, donated the works. In Norfolk, Va., art collector Walter P. Chrysler, Jr., gave the museum that bears his name 10 paintings valued at $10 million, together with $4.1 million for expansion. In February, the Los Angeles Museum of Contemporary Art bought 80 abstract-expressionist and pop art works for $11 million from an Italian collector, Count Giuseppe Panza di Biumo. And in May, the Mark Rothko Foundation gave most of its 1,000 works by Rothko, a leading American artist who died in 1970, to 19 museums in the United States and other countries. The National Gallery of Art received a group of 285 paintings described as the core of the collection.

Auction Sales. One of the largest sums ever paid at a single auction session went for the Duke of Devonshire's collection of 70 drawings by old masters, which sold for $28.5 million in July. A record price for a drawing was set at the same auction when $4.7 million was paid for *Study of a Man's Head and Hand* by the great Italian Renaissance painter Raphael.

A new auction record for the work of French painter Paul Gauguin was achieved in May when his 1892 painting *Mata Mira* sold for $3.8 million. At the same sale, a 24-foot (7.3-meter) metal mobile by American sculptor Alexander Calder called *Big Crinkly* established a record price both for his works and for American sculpture when it sold for $852,500. In November, Modigliani's 1917-1918 painting *The Dreamer* fetched $4.6 million at auction, the highest price ever paid for that artist's work. A record corporate art purchase was announced in February by the Equitable Life Assurance Society, which bought a 10-panel mural by American painter Thomas Hart Benton, *America Today* (1931), for $3.1 million for display in their new headquarters in New York City. The highest price for a living artist's work was achieved in November when *Two Women,* painted in 1953 by Dutch-born painter Willem de Kooning, sold for $1.98 million. *Seascape: Folkestone* by British painter J. M. W. Turner was auctioned in July for about $10 million, far more than had ever been paid at auction for any picture. Joshua B. Kind

In WORLD BOOK, see ART AND THE ARTS; PAINTING; SCULPTURE.

VITAL STATISTICS. See CENSUS; POPULATION.

VON WEIZSÄCKER, RICHARD (1920-), was elected president of West Germany on May 23, 1984. He succeeded Karl Carstens, who did not seek reelection. Von Weizsäcker had been mayor of West Berlin since 1981.

Von Weizsäcker was born in a family castle in Stuttgart, Germany, on April 15, 1920. His father was a diplomat who rose to the position of chief state secretary in the foreign office in 1938 and was named ambassador to Vatican City in 1943. Richard von Weizsäcker studied in Oxford, England, and Grenoble, France, before joining the German army. He took part in the invasion of Poland at the beginning of World War II.

After the war, von Weizsäcker interrupted his law studies at Göttingen University in West Germany to help defend his father at the war crimes trials in Nuremberg. The elder von Weizsäcker was sentenced to five years imprisonment but was released after 18 months. The future president returned to the study of law, receiving a degree in 1954, and went into business and politics.

Von Weizsäcker was elected to Parliament in 1969. In 1974, he was the Christian Democrat candidate for president. He lost the election to Walter Scheel, a Free Democrat.

Von Weizsäcker's favorite hobbies are chess and hiking. He and his wife, Marianne, have three sons and a daughter. Jay Myers

WALES. Industrial problems dominated events in Wales throughout 1984. Most notable was the impact of the British coal miners' strike. Despite votes against the strike at most mines, all 20,000 miners in the South Wales coal field joined the dispute during March, and mining at all pits in the area was halted. Miners in one of the two mines in northern Wales continued to work, but those in the other joined the strike.

During the spring, police clashed with miners attempting to stop production at the two big southern Wales steelworks at Port Talbot and Llanwern, near Newport. The National Union of Mineworkers in southern Wales used pickets to stop trucks taking coke from Port Talbot. This action led to the union being fined 50,000 pounds ($65,000) on July 31 for contempt of court. When the union refused to apologize to the court, their funds of 700,000 pounds ($915,000) were impounded. The strike had been provoked by fear of mine closures at a time of record and growing unemployment. In December, more than 170,000 people in Wales were out of work—an unemployment rate of 16 per cent.

On November 30, David Wilkie, a 35-year-old taxi driver, was killed as he drove one of South Wales's few working miners to work. Wilkie died after a concrete post hit his taxi. Two striking miners were charged with his murder.

Political Changes. Ioan Evans, Labour Party member of Parliament (MP) for Cynon Valley (formerly the Aberdare constituency) for 10 years, died on Feb. 10, 1984. In an election on May 3, he was succeeded by Ann Clwyd, also of the Labour Party, who became the first woman MP in Wales since 1970. Clwyd gave up her seat as one of the four Welsh members of the European Parliament when elections for that body were held on June 14. Three of the European Parliament seats were won by Labour, and the other was held by the Conservative Party. Dafydd Wigley, the president of Plaid Cymru, the Welsh nationalist party, resigned on October 27. He was succeeded by Dafydd Elis Thomas.

Other Developments. A long, dry summer brought restrictions on the use of water. Much of Wales suffered a severe drought. Rain arrived in early September, just in time to prevent rationing of water for up to 17 hours per day.

The Royal National Eisteddfod of Wales, a festival promoting Welsh culture, was held in Lampeter in August, and the chair—the premier poetry prize—went to Aled Rhys Wiliam. Large crowds attended a memorial service for actor Richard Burton, held on August 11 in his home village of Pont-rhyd-y-fen. Patrick Hannan

See also GREAT BRITAIN. In WORLD BOOK, see WALES.

WASHINGTON. See STATE GOVERNMENT.

WASHINGTON, D.C. Federal law officials in 1984 conducted several investigations into the administration of Washington Mayor Marion S. Barry, Jr. A probe of alleged drug use by district employees led in June to the conviction of Karen K. Johnson, a city worker, on charges of possessing and selling cocaine. Barry had testified about the case before a federal grand jury in January and later acknowledged having had a personal relationship with Johnson. Johnson was sentenced to a jail term of up to 18 months for refusing to answer the grand jury's questions.

At year-end, a second grand jury was investigating the suspected misuse of federal funds at Washington's Bates Street housing redevelopment project, which Barry had hoped would be a model project in the heart of the city's rundown Shaw area. Another investigation sought to determine whether district employees and a private contractor for the Department of Employment Services had used city funds to purchase personal items.

Home Rule. Serious problems with Washington's authority to govern itself were resolved during the final days of the 98th Congress. The problems resulted from a 1983 ruling by the Supreme Court of the United States invalidating the so-called legislative veto. The veto enabled Congress, under the district's 1973 Home Rule Charter, to overturn Washington City Council ordinances. With its veto power taken away, Congress was forced to go to court to challenge district actions it did not approve of. Under the corrective legislation, signed by President Ronald Reagan in October, City Council ordinances can be overturned by a vote of Congress and the agreement of the President.

Mental Hospital. Washington reached an agreement with the U.S. government in 1984 on a long-standing dispute over when and how St. Elizabeth's Hospital should be transferred from federal to city jurisdiction. Congress approved legislation allowing the district to take over operation of the huge mental institution in October 1987 and to receive federal subsidies until 1991.

Elections. Democratic presidential candidate Jesse L. Jackson won a decisive victory in Washington's May 1 presidential primary, receiving 67 per cent of the vote. In November, more than 85 per cent of Washington voters cast their ballots for Democratic presidential nominee Walter F. Mondale, making the district the only jurisdiction besides his home state of Minnesota to choose him.

The Homeless. Washington residents also voted overwhelmingly in November for an initiative requiring the district to provide adequate overnight shelter for the homeless. The initiative was the first such measure approved anywhere in the United States.

Only days before, President Reagan agreed to use federal funds to renovate an 800-bed shelter

Two veterans of the Vietnam War examine the statue *Three Servicemen,* which was added to the Vietnam Veterans Memorial in Washington, D.C., in November.

for the homeless near the Capitol. The shelter's director, Mitch Snyder, ended a 51-day hunger strike when federal officials told him of the President's decision.

Cable TV. The Washington City Council in December voted to award a 15-year cable-television franchise to District Cablevision Incorporated. The company promised to install a 79-channel residential cable network and a separate institutional network.

Officers' Club Bombed. An early-morning explosion on April 20 severely damaged the officers' club at the Washington Navy Yard, but no one was injured. The Federal Bureau of Investigation (FBI) said a group calling itself the Guerrilla Resistance Movement had claimed responsibility for the blast. A tape-recorded message played over the telephone to newspapers and broadcasting stations on the night of the bombing said the act was an expression of solidarity with a leftist guerrilla group in El Salvador. The message also called for independence and socialism in Puerto Rico.

Rhodes Tavern, a 185-year-old brick-and-stucco structure, was demolished in September. The razing of the historic tavern ended a seven-year battle between preservationists and the owner of the site, Oliver T. Carr, one of the city's major real estate developers.   Sandra Evans

In WORLD BOOK, see WASHINGTON, D.C.

WATER. On July 31, 1984, the United States Senate voted to continue selling at cost electric power generated at the Hoover Dam in Nevada. Lawmakers rejected demands to raise the price to normal market rates. The legislation guaranteed inexpensive power to customers in Arizona, southern California, and Nevada for 30 years.

Senator Howard M. Metzenbaum (D., Ohio) led the opposition to the bill, contending that it could cost U.S. taxpayers $6 billion over the next decade and even more in later years. Western senators who led the fight to keep the rates low argued that users have repaid the government's cost for the power and should not be forced to pay higher rates merely to add to government revenue. The President signed the bill on August 17.

Garrison Diversion Project Compromise. On June 6, conservationists and Western development interests broke a decades-long impasse over the proposed $1.2-billion Garrison Diversion water project in North Dakota. The bitterly contested water project is designed to irrigate North Dakota farmland with Missouri River water. Opponents included environmentalists who warned that the project would destroy wildlife habitats; the Canadian government, which contended that it would threaten fish in Manitoba; and critics who charged that the project was unnecessary and wasteful.

The compromise endorsed the Administration's proposed appropriation of $53.6 million for Garrison but prohibited spending it until a presidential commission studied alternatives to the project. In November, the panel issued a preliminary report calling for a scaled-down version of the project that eliminated a large dam and reservoir — the most controversial part of the plan. The commission filed its final report in December.

Floods and Drought. A heavy snowmelt in June and July produced a record runoff in the Colorado River. More than 100 dwellings along the lower Colorado were isolated by the high waters. In 1984, there was more storage space available in the system of dams along the river than in 1983, when high waters caused millions of dollars in damage. As a result, damage was less severe.

Heavy rains across the Midwest in June caused unusually long-lasting floods along the Missouri River and its tributaries. Floodwaters caused damage estimated at $1 billion in loss of crops, eroded soil, and harm to small-town economies in Iowa, Kansas, Missouri, Nebraska, and South Dakota.

Record rainfalls in May caused the worst flooding to hit the Northeast in decades. Flooding in Connecticut, Massachusetts, New Hampshire, New Jersey, and New York forced thousands from their homes and caused millions of dollars in damage. In late October, torrential rains led to the worst flooding in southern Louisiana in 20 years.

In Texas, a two-year drought, the worst since the 1950's, cost farmers and ranchers an estimated $1 billion in 1984. By the end of July, 67 cities had imposed voluntary or mandatory restrictions on use of municipal water. In west Texas, where the drought had lasted four years, many farmers were forced to sell their breeding stocks at a loss.

Water Quality and Supply Threatened. Concern rose in 1984 that pollution and shortages may soon end the era of cheap and plentiful water in the United States. In January, a U.S. Geological Survey report warned that, in some areas, groundwater supplies are being used faster than they can renew themselves.

The U.S. Environmental Protection Agency (EPA) reported in January that about half of the 181,000 ponds or other surface water areas containing toxic wastes in the United States pose a threat to ground-water supplies. A study by the congressional Office of Technology Assessment issued in April and an EPA document made public in October concluded that the EPA program to protect ground water from contamination was not working. On August 30, the EPA announced plans to coordinate efforts to keep ground water pure. However, some legislators and environmentalists criticized the plan because it imposed no mandatory standards on the states. Andrew L. Newman

In WORLD BOOK, see WATER.

WEATHER. The abnormal global weather of 1982-1983 gave way to normal conditions in 1984. Rainfall was abnormally low in most parts of Africa, however, worsening a drought that began in the early 1970's in some areas (see AFRICA). Most other agricultural regions had good growing seasons, though dry weather damaged the corn crop of southern Africa and the wheat crops of Algeria, Argentina, Canada, and Morocco.

In the United States, the record-breaking cold wave of the 1983 Christmas season gave way to a rapid warming of the eastern two-thirds of the nation in early January 1984. However, two outbreaks of severe cold set low-temperature records of $-20°F.$ $(-29°C)$ in Toledo, Ohio, and $-7°F.$ $(-22°C)$ in Baltimore. A large *anticyclone* — a system of winds rotating clockwise in the Northern Hemisphere — dominated the West, keeping it unusually cold. Storms were generally deflected far to the north across Canada.

February was unusually warm in the Eastern United States. Two major winter storms in the West brought heavy snow to the Rocky Mountains, the plains of Nebraska, much of the Midwest, and the Northeast. Because of the warm weather, however, there was little or no snow cover in the Great Plains.

March came in like a lamb, but soon a parade of storms rampaged like lions across the United

A tornado reduced Barneveld, Wis. (population 579), to rubble in about 20 seconds as a storm system swept across the Midwest on June 7-8.

States from southwest to northeast. The storms brought many tornadoes to the Mississippi Valley, and a record temperature of 106°F. (41°C) to Brownsville, Tex. Tornadoes in the last storm killed about 60 people in North and South Carolina on March 28.

April and May saw hot, dry weather from western Texas to California. Phoenix recorded its hottest May on record. Through July and August, temperatures were over 100°F. (38°C) as far north as Washington and Idaho.

During June, the upper Mississippi and Missouri river valleys had a period of severe weather and heavy precipitation. On June 15, the Missouri River below Omaha, Nebr., was at its highest level in 32 years. On June 18, 50 tornadoes were recorded in the area.

June marked the beginning of a long hot, dry spell in the northwestern Great Plains. It was most severe in Montana and southern Alberta in Canada. The drought damaged crops and led to widespread forest fires that finally yielded to rain in September.

Warm, humid air from the Pacific Ocean brought abnormally heavy rains to the inland Southwest during July and most of August. In July, the total rainfall in Phoenix was 5.1 inches (13 centimeters) — more than six times normal. Mud slides closed roads in Zion National Park in southwest Utah. Rainfall was also unusually heavy from the Carolinas to northern Florida.

A heat wave in the central United States lasted through most of August as a large anticyclone hung over the East. Temperatures in Kansas and surrounding areas soared to 110°F. (43°C).

The Rocky Mountain states were abnormally cold through October, while the weather was unusually mild in the East. Record early winter storms brought up to 15 inches (38 centimeters) of snow to the Denver area and 24 inches (61 centimeters) to parts of Utah. The pattern reversed in November, with chilly weather in the East and milder conditions in the West.

The year ended warm in the East and South. Many records for December high temperatures were set the last four days of the year.

***GOES* Goes.** At the beginning of 1984, the United States had two advanced weather satellites called *Geostationary Operational Environmental Satellites* (*GOES*) in orbit. Each satellite hovered above a fixed location on the equator, with its camera observing the weather over about a quarter of the globe. A major use of these satellites has been the tracking of hurricanes. On July 29, one of the satellites — called *GOES East* — failed. The National Oceanic and Atmospheric Administration (NOAA) moved the other satellite — *GOES West* — to a position above the Galapagos Islands, so that it could observe most of the continental United States and adjacent oceanic areas. In November, NOAA moved *GOES West* westward to track Pacific cyclones.

Nuclear Winter. Scientists use computers to predict weather changes. The computers manipulate data based on simplified numerical descriptions of the global atmosphere called *models*.

During 1984, several scientists used computer models to predict how a nuclear war would affect the global climate. In October 1983, five U.S. researchers had reported that their computer study predicted a drastic effect. The researchers fed computers information on the large amounts of soot and smoke that fires caused by nuclear explosions would throw into the atmosphere. The computers showed that these materials would absorb a great deal of energy from the sun's rays. Much of this energy normally would reach Earth and would help heat its surface. But, as a result of the absorption, the surface would become several tens of degrees colder, perhaps for months. The predicted period of abnormal coldness has been named *nuclear winter*. Computers have indicated that a nuclear winter would be worldwide and probably would disrupt the world's food supply catastrophically. Alfred K. Blackadar

In WORLD BOOK, see METEOROLOGY; WEATHER.
WEIGHT LIFTING. See OLYMPIC GAMES; SPORTS.

WELFARE. No major changes were made in United States social welfare programs during 1984. But there was no shortage of election-year talk about the adequacy of existing programs.

Poverty. On February 23, the Bureau of the Census gave some support to claims by the Administration of President Ronald Reagan that poverty statistics are overstated. A bureau study showed that the number of people living below the poverty level would have been as much as 33 per cent lower in 1982 had noncash government benefits been added to income. Such benefits include food stamps, subsidized school lunches, and subsidized housing and medical care. The government does not include noncash benefits when it calculates the number of Americans living in poverty. The poverty level in 1982 was defined as a cash income of $9,862 for a family of four.

When noncash benefits are counted, the number of poor Americans in 1982 dropped from 34.4 million to between 22.9 million and 31.4 million, depending on the formula used to place a value on benefits. Although the study found the Administration theory correct for 1982, it found the theory incorrect over a longer period. From 1979 to 1982, the number of poor Americans increased by between 7.8 million and 8.9 million even when noncash income was included.

Using the traditional measure of cash income

only, the Census Bureau reported on Aug. 2, 1984, that the number of poor had increased from 34.4 million in 1982 to 35.3 million in 1983. The national poverty rate reached 15.2 per cent of the total population, the highest rate since the mid-1960's. (The poverty level for 1983 was set at a cash income of $10,178 for a family of four.)

In reaction to the report, Thomas P. (Tip) O'Neill, Jr. (D., Mass.), Speaker of the House of Representatives, said, "Today, we have the smoking gun of Reagan unfairness. Under Reagan, the poor are getting poorer." The White House argued that the increased poverty rate was caused by the recession of the early 1980's, which it blamed on the Administration of President Jimmy Carter.

Hunger. On January 9, a government Task Force on Food Assistance reported that although "there is hunger in America . . . there is no evidence that widespread undernutrition is a major health problem in the United States." On January 10, 42 national religious and antipoverty groups contended that the panel's recommendations "would make this tragic problem worse."

The task force's most controversial recommendation would permit states to drop out of federal food-assistance programs, other than the food stamp program, and to receive block grants for their own programs. Critics noted that this policy would eliminate nationwide uniformity of benefits and of eligibility requirements.

Homeless by Choice? In a televised interview on January 31, Reagan commented on the report on hunger: "One problem that we've had, even in the best of times . . . is the people who are sleeping on the [heating] grates [in large cities], the homeless, who are homeless, you might say, by choice." The White House later said the President probably referred to "some studies" showing that "perhaps as many as 25 per cent of all the homeless are homeless for other than economic reasons."

On May 1, the Department of Housing and Urban Development estimated the number of homeless Americans at between 250,000 and 350,000. According to the report, about half of the homeless suffer from alcoholism, drug addiction, or mental illness. Some private groups have estimated that 2 million to 3 million Americans are homeless.

The U.S. Conference of Mayors, in a 66-city survey released on June 14, reported a serious shortage of housing for the poor in major cities. The mayors found that low-income families wait an average of nearly two years to obtain public and subsidized housing, and that 61 per cent of the cities had closed their waiting lists. The Reagan Administration has denied that any such shortage exists and has virtually halted federal housing construction. Frank Cormier and Margot Cormier

In WORLD BOOK, see WELFARE.

WEST INDIES. The Caribbean economy was in the doldrums during 1984, according to a report issued on May 22 by the Caribbean Development Bank based in Barbados. Prospects for relief were not on the horizon, said the bank report, which blamed the worsening economic situation on depressed world market prices for export commodities of the West Indies.

Unemployment in the islands was high. With shortfalls in earnings, most of the nations in the area were unable to generate capital for job-producing activities. United States companies were slow to invest in the region, despite incentives offered by President Ronald Reagan's Caribbean Basin Initiative.

Dominican Republic. "Never before have we seen such bad times," said President Salvador Jorge Blanco on October 11, in welcoming Pope John Paul II on a visit to commemorate Christopher Columbus' first voyage to the New World. In April, food riots left 64 people dead. And on October 1, the U.S. government reduced its sugar imports by 16 per cent — a tremendous blow for sugar producers in the Dominican Republic.

Haiti. Food riots also occurred in Haiti in May. People from the port city of Cap-Haïtien staged a 15-mile (24-kilometer) protest march that ended with a raid on a food warehouse operated by CARE, the U.S. relief program. Reacting to the riots, Haiti's President Jean-Claude Duvalier made a sweeping reorganization of his Cabinet.

Guadeloupe. Pro-independence terrorists disturbed the tranquillity of Guadeloupe in 1984 to protest the island's colonial status as an overseas department of France. In April, the Caribbean Revolutionary Alliance set off 15 bombs that damaged a number of buildings. On May 3, the government outlawed the group.

Grenada. About 250 U.S. troops were still occupying Grenada on October 25, the first anniversary of the U.S. invasion of the tiny island nation. On October 28, Grenada's international airport was formally opened. The $19 million the United States spent on completing the airport was the largest single item in a foreign aid program that totaled nearly $60 million.

On December 3, Herbert A. Blaize, a moderate who was backed by the United States, easily won election for prime minister over Eric Gairy, a former prime minister. Gairy was overthrown in 1979 by Maurice Bishop, whose murder in October 1983 by ultraleftists helped touch off the U.S. invasion. Nathan A. Haverstock

See also BLAIZE, HERBERT A.; LATIN AMERICA (Facts in Brief Table). In WORLD BOOK, see WEST INDIES.

WEST VIRGINIA. See STATE GOVERNMENT.

WILLIAMS, LYNN RUSSELL (1924-   ), was elected president of the United Steelworkers of America (USWA) on March 29, 1984. He had become acting president in November 1983 after the death of Lloyd McBride, union president since 1977. Williams, the first Canadian to hold the top position in the USWA, will serve out McBride's term, which ends in March 1986. Williams defeated Frank McKee, union treasurer.

Williams was born on July 21, 1924, in Springfield, Ont. The son of a minister, he grew up in small industrial towns. Williams graduated from McMaster University in Hamilton, Ont., in 1944. He joined the USWA in 1947, after taking a job in a Toronto factory. Within a few months, he became an organizer for the Canadian Labour Congress, a federation of labor unions.

Williams joined the staff of the USWA in 1956 and helped boost union membership. In 1965, he moved to USWA District 6 Headquarters in Toronto. He became director of District 6 in 1973. From 1977 until his election as union president, Williams served as secretary of the USWA. He and his wife, Audrey, live in Pittsburgh, Pa. They have four children. Karin C. Rosenberg

WISCONSIN. See STATE GOVERNMENT.

WYOMING. See STATE GOVERNMENT.

YEMEN (ADEN). See MIDDLE EAST.

YEMEN (SANA). See MIDDLE EAST.

Herbert A. Blaize, Grenada's new prime minister, waves to crowds in Point Salines on his way to his inaugural ceremony in December.

YOUTH ORGANIZATIONS.

YOUTH ORGANIZATIONS. The Boy Scouts of America (BSA) launched several new programs in 1984. "Cub Scouts Sports" encourages 7-year-old boys in the Tiger Cubs program to learn and play 14 sports, ranging from soccer and archery to marbles. "Varsity Scouting" emphasizes "high adventure" activities for boys aged 14 through 17 who are not involved in other Scouting programs. "Youth's Frontier" is designed to help young people make ethical decisions.

In January, the State Commission on Human Rights and Opportunities in Connecticut ruled that the BSA was guilty of sex discrimination in refusing to allow Catherine Pollard, a 65-year-old mother of two Eagle Scouts, to become the first woman Scoutmaster in the United States. The BSA, which appealed the case, contended that only men should be Scoutmasters because boys aged 11 through 14 need male role models.

Boys Clubs of America (BCA) in 1984 launched "Target Outreach," a delinquency-intervention program funded by the Office of Juvenile Justice and Delinquency Prevention of the United States Department of Justice. The program's activities are designed for delinquent youths in urban areas. The BCA also introduced the new Boys Clubs slogan: "The Club That Beats the Streets."

The BCA held its annual national conference in Kansas City, Mo., from April 6 to 10. In September, Anthony Agtarap, 18, of Edmonds, Wash., was named National Youth of the Year.

Camp Fire introduced in 1984 a new self-reliance program called "I Can Do It!" It teaches second- and third-grade girls and boys about safety, handling of emergencies, and family responsibilities. Camp Fire also launched "Save Our Statue," a project to help restore the Statue of Liberty and Ellis Island, an island in New York Harbor that was a U.S. immigration station. Another new program was "Friendship Across the Ages," designed to promote friendship between Camp Fire members and adults over the age of 55.

4-H Clubs, in cooperation with the U.S. Department of Agriculture, in 1984 produced a 17-minute film called *Get the Message?* intended to discourage drug and alcohol use among preteens. In June, 4-H celebrated the 25th anniversary of the National 4-H Center in Chevy Chase, Md., where young people from around the world attend leadership training programs. About 1,600 4-H members attended the 62nd National 4-H Congress held in Chicago from November 27 to December 1.

Future Farmers of America (FFA). Nearly 22,000 FFA members and supporters attended the 57th annual national convention held from November 8 to 10 in Kansas City, Mo. Larry O. Nielson, 21,

President Reagan helps Stephanie Dashasor of Danville, Wash., center, and Marci Brown of Philadelphia celebrate 72 years of Girl Scouting in March.

of Tulare, S. Dak., was named Star Farmer of America. Rex Wichert, 20, of Fairview, Okla., was named Star Agribusinessman. Kevin Gingerich, 19, of Kokomo, Ind., won the first National Computers in Agriculture Award for the best use of computers in farming. In September, the Ag Ed Network, the first agricultural computer education system, began operation. It was established by the FFA Foundation and AgriData Resources, Inc.

Girl Scouts of the United States of America (GSUSA). Reports of cookies containing pins, needles, pieces of glass, and other objects temporarily halted sales of Girl Scout cookies in March at the height of the organization's annual cookie sale. More than 800 incidents of tampering were reported in 24 states.

In many areas, Scouts resumed selling the cookies after having cookie boxes X-rayed. Many Scout councils also held fund-raising drives to make up for lost sales. At year's end, the Federal Bureau of Investigation and the U.S. Food and Drug Administration were still investigating the cookie sabotage. The GSUSA announced that in 1985, a stronger glue would be used to seal cookie boxes.

In 1984, the GSUSA introduced Daisy Girl Scouts, a new program for 5-year-old girls. Girls must be at least 6 years old to join the Brownies.

Girls Clubs of America (GCA) received $800,000 for national and local sports programs for teenage girls for its participation in the 1984 Olympic Torch Relay Event. The money-raising relay, which began in New York City on May 8, ended on July 28 in Los Angeles at the torch-lighting ceremony that opened the Summer Olympic Games.

The GCA held its annual conference in Chattanooga, Tenn., from April 30 to May 3. The theme of the conference was "Girls: Engineering the Future." At workshops and seminars, GCA delegates discussed ways to help girls and young women prepare for careers in such fields as politics, medicine, business, and engineering.

Junior Achievement (JA) held its 10th annual National Business Leadership Conference and Business Hall of Fame induction ceremony in Chicago in March. About 2,000 JA executives attended. Among the laureates named to the Business Hall of Fame were William E. Boeing, founder of the Boeing Company, and Bernard Kilgore, the editor who transformed *The Wall Street Journal* into a successful national newspaper.

At the National Association of Junior Achievers Conference held in Bloomington, Ind., from August 5 through 10, Niki Tapantelias of Orlando, Fla., was named Outstanding Young Businesswoman. Michael Thompson of Minneapolis-St. Paul, Minn., was named Outstanding Young Businessman.   Barbara A. Mayes

In WORLD BOOK, see entries on the individual organizations.

YUGOSLAVIA struggled with economic and political problems in 1984. On July 7, workers at an abrasive-materials factory in Kratovo, Macedonia, struck because they feared that a proposed merger with another business enterprise would lead to a loss of jobs. The strike dragged on until September 14, when the government withdrew the plan. This was the longest strike since 1958, the year of the first strikes in Communist-ruled Yugoslavia.

Debt Deals. During the second half of 1984, Yugoslavia negotiated with the International Monetary Fund (IMF), a United Nations agency, to reschedule its debt to that agency. Yugoslavia's foreign debt was about $20 billion. The country owed about one-third of this amount to international institutions such as the IMF, one-third to Western governments, and the remainder to commercial banks in the West.

Yugoslavia asked the IMF to postpone payment dates and to relax certain requirements in the loan agreement. To obtain the loan, Yugoslavia had agreed to take steps to control its economy. Government negotiators said that some of these steps were causing economic and political difficulties.

On December 7, Western banks agreed in principle to reschedule four years of debt. The banks and Yugoslav officials agreed to meet in London

Resavica, Yugoslavia, says farewell to 33 miners who were killed on April 21 by an explosion of gas in a nearby coal mine.

during the week of Jan. 7, 1985, to work out the details of the rescheduling.

Dissidents Tried. On Nov. 5, 1984, six Serbian nationalists went on trial in Belgrade, Yugoslavia's capital, for conspiring to overthrow the government. On April 20, they had taken part in a private discussion attended by Milovan Djilas, Yugoslavia's best-known dissident.

Radomir Radovic, who also attended the meeting, was found dead under suspicious circumstances in May after questioning by the police. Still another at the meeting, Vojislav Seselj, was sentenced to eight years in prison by a court in Sarajevo. Later, the sentence was cut in half.

Olympics. Sarajevo played host to the XIV Winter Olympic Games from February 8 through 19. A record 49 nations sent 1,510 participants. The Sarajevo Olympic Organizing Committee announced on February 19 that the games would at least break even financially. See OLYMPIC GAMES.

Biggest Crowd. In August, about 300,000 people attended the national Eucharistic congress in Marija Bistrica, Croatia. This was the largest unofficial gathering in Eastern Europe, except for Poland, since 1945. Pope John Paul II had planned to attend the congress, but the Yugoslav government objected.   Chris Cviic

See also EUROPE (Facts in Brief Table). In WORLD BOOK, see YUGOSLAVIA.

YUKON TERRITORY. After 10 years of negotiation, the Canadian federal government and Yukon Indian leaders agreed in principle on Indian land claims in January 1984, only to see the accord collapse at year's end. Under the agreement, the Indians were to receive $540 million (Canadian dollars; $1 = U.S. 76 cents as of Dec. 31, 1984) over a 20-year period, as well as legal title and mineral rights for 20,000 square kilometers (7,700 square miles) of land. In return, they would give up their claims to the rest of the Yukon.

The agreement collapsed at year's end because the requirement that at least 10 of the 12 Yukon Indian bands ratify it was not met. At least one band refused to sign the agreement, and three bands reportedly rejected ratification. In voting on the agreement, Indians indicated their displeasure with its description of their giving up further land claims as "extinguishment of aboriginal rights." Some Indian leaders also wanted to renegotiate clauses on self-government and hunting and trapping rights.

Christopher Pearson, government leader in the Yukon since 1978, announced on October 16 that he would resign his post in 1985.   David M. L. Farr

See also CANADA. In WORLD BOOK, see YUKON TERRITORY.

ZAIRE. See AFRICA.

ZAMBIA. See AFRICA.

ZIMBABWE. On Aug. 11, 1984, delegates to a national congress of the Zimbabwe African National Union (ZANU), the nation's ruling political party, approved a draft constitution calling for the creation of a socialist one-party state. At that time, four different parties had representatives in Parliament, with ZANU holding 57 of the 100 seats in the House of Representatives.

The plan for constitutional change provided for a single legal party that would control all aspects of government. Leading the party would be a Politburo and Central Committee. On August 12, Prime Minister Robert Gabriel Mugabe, the head of ZANU, appointed the first Politburo. Seven of the 15 members were reported to be from Mugabe's own Zezuru clan of the Mashona people.

Let the People Decide. After the party congress, Mugabe announced that the ZANU proposal would be put to a public vote sometime in early 1985. Standing in the way of establishing a one-party state, however, were Zimbabwe's Constitution and the opposition parties, particularly the Zimbabwe African People's Union (ZAPU).

The Constitution, which went into effect in 1980 when Zimbabwe — then called Rhodesia — gained its independence from Great Britain, provided various forms of protection for minority interests. These safeguards included a provision that, until 1987, a major constitutional change such as the ZANU plan would require unanimous approval in Parliament. Although many Zimbabweans expressed doubts that Mugabe's government would respect that provision, the delegates at the party congress pledged that the transition to one-party rule would take place "in accordance with the law and the Constitution."

ZAPU, the Chief Opposition Party, was the other major obstacle to ZANU's constitutional plan. ZAPU is firmly based in Matabeleland province, the homeland of the Matabele people, who make up nearly one-fifth of the nation's population.

According to the government, the Matabele have supported ZAPU guerrillas who began an armed rebellion in 1982 after ZAPU's leader, Joshua Nkomo, was expelled from the Cabinet. To suppress that support, the government sent troops to Matabeleland in January 1983 and again in February 1984. During the second expedition, soldiers blocked shipments of food and other supplies that might have fallen into the hands of the rebels, but they also prevented those shipments from reaching civilians.

On April 6, Zimbabwe's seven Roman Catholic bishops accused government troops of brutally mistreating Matabeleland residents and causing widespread starvation. Normal food distribution resumed later that month.   J. Dixon Esseks

See also AFRICA (Facts in Brief Table). In WORLD BOOK, see ZIMBABWE.

ZOOLOGY. In the summer of 1984, zoologist Sydney Brenner, director of the Medical Research Council's Laboratory of Molecular Biology in Great Britain, reported on a 20-year research project investigating the complete embryological development of an animal. Brenner and his colleagues published their findings after completing the first major part of their monumental task.

The British scientists studied a 1-millimeter (1/25-inch) *nematode* — a class of roundworms — and found that the worm consisted of exactly 959 body cells, including 302 nerve cells. This research made it possible to report the complete history of each cell as the animal grew from a fertilized egg to an adult worm 3½ days later. The scientists learned how cells of the digestive tract, reproductive system, muscles, and other organs form and move into position in the embryo. The study was so precise that all of the 8,000 connections between the nematode's nerve cells were described. Such detailed work is impossible in a human being with trillions of body cells and 100 billion nerve cells.

Embryological development is surprisingly complex, the study revealed. About 20 per cent of the cells formed in the nervous system die almost as soon as they are formed. They are examples of what the scientists called programmed death or

A quarter horse mare at the Louisville, Ky., zoo nuzzles a Grant's zebra foal born in May from an embryo implanted in the mare nearly a year earlier.

"cell suicides." Another example of embryological complexity was seen in the forming of the right and left sides of the body. The two sides are not formed in identical ways, though they end up as mirror images of each other.

The ultimate goal of this massive project is to learn how the genes of a cell control embryological development. Toward that end, biologists have now carefully mapped the position of 500 of the worm's genes and discovered thousands of individual worms with genetic mutations. The mutants provide the researchers with a means of discovering which genes are responsible for controlling particular phases of the worm's development. The relative simplicity of nematode anatomy, though it took 20 years to work out, has given scientists a new and powerful experimental system.

Pandas. In January 1984, zoologist George B. Schaller, director of the Animal Research and Conservation Center of New York Zoological Society (Bronx Zoo) in New York City, reported on the status of the giant panda in China. Schaller estimated that about 250 of the approximately 1,000 giant pandas living in the wild were threatened with starvation as a result of the growth cycle of bamboo, the panda's exclusive food.

Bamboo plants flower in cycles, ranging from 45 to 100 years. When the plants flower, they form seeds and die. Entire stands of bamboo disappear. It takes many years before the seedlings grow into the mature plants that provide the pandas with their food. The flowering of arrow bamboo was threatening the panda with starvation during 1984. Schaller reported that it could take as long as five years for the bamboo forests to be restored.

To help meet the crisis, the Chinese government set up a program to relocate people away from areas where pandas live so that bamboo can be planted. The Chinese also set up rescue teams to seek out starving pandas and take them to emergency holding stations.

Mountain of the Mists. In April 1984, a group of United States and Venezuelan scientists reported finding many new plant and animal species in a remote region of a tropical rain forest in Venezuela. The team journeyed to Neblina (Mountain of the Mists), a 650-square-kilometer (250-square-mile) area in southern Venezuela. The mountain is actually a steep-sided mesa that climbs 1,800 meters (5,900 feet) above the rain forest. Once part of a vast plateau, the mesa has steep sides that were formed more than 100 million years ago by erosion. Because of its isolation from the rest of the rain forest, the plant and animal life on Neblina has evolved in its own unique way, providing scientists with a natural laboratory for testing theories of evolution. Clyde Freeman Herreid II

See also PALEONTOLOGY; ZOOS. In WORLD BOOK, see ZOOLOGY.

ZOOS in the United States made major progress in breeding endangered species during 1984. The most dramatic advances involved *embryo transfer* — placing a fertilized egg from one female into the womb of another. The procedure was successfully used to breed a wild member of the horse family for the first time. On May 17, a quarter horse mare at the Louisville (Ky.) Zoo gave birth to a male Grant's zebra foal. The zebra embryo had been implanted nearly a year earlier in the mare's womb. The Grant's zebra species is not endangered, but researchers will eventually try to use embryo transfer to increase the population of endangered zebra species.

Scientists also succeeded for the first time in transferring an embryo from one antelope species to a substitute mother from another antelope species. A team from the Cincinnati (Ohio) Wildlife Federation — a joint effort of the Cincinnati Zoo, Kings Island Wild Animal Habitat, and the University of Cincinnati College of Medicine — removed fertilized eggs from a rare African bongo at the Los Angeles Zoo, flew them to Cincinnati, and in August 1983 implanted them in the more common eland. Two bongo calves were born in June 1984. The experiment also marked the first cross-country embryo transfer. The Cincinnati team achieved another first in 1984. In October, a female eland calf was born — the result of the first transfer of a frozen embryo to a zoo animal. The eland embryo had been frozen for about 18 months before it was thawed and implanted in a substitute eland mother. Zoo officials hope someday to be able to ship frozen embryos regularly. Frozen embryo banks might prevent the extinction of some vanishing species.

Another Breeding Breakthrough took place at the Bronx Zoo in New York City. Like many temperate-zone reptiles, Chinese alligators need a seasonal drop in temperature to stimulate reproductive activity. In 1976, reptile experts at the Bronx Zoo sent their nonreproductive Chinese alligators to the Rockefeller Wildlife Refuge in southwestern Louisiana. The climate there is almost identical to that of the Yangtze River Valley in southern China, the natural habitat of the Chinese alligator. Since 1976, 25 young have hatched. This and other research helped the New York scientists simulate the required breeding environment at the Bronx Zoo. In August 1984, four Chinese alligators emerged from eggs, the first ever to hatch in a zoo.

Return to the Wild. The National Zoological Park in Washington, D.C., in 1973 launched a program to breed golden lion tamarins, tiny reddish-gold South American monkeys with manes. Only about 100 of the animals survive in their native Brazil, but some 250 of the monkeys have been born and raised in the Washington Zoo. In

A rare baby bongo antelope, born in June in the Cincinnati Zoo as the result of an embryo transplant, is guarded by its mother, an eland.

November 1983, the zoo sent 14 captive-born tamarins to the Rio de Janeiro Primate Center, where they were helped to adjust to life in the wild and taught to hunt for food. In June 1984, researchers released the tamarins in a reserve north of Rio. Although 3 monkeys disappeared soon after release, the 11 healthy survivors acted as if they had always lived in the Brazilian forest.

New Exhibits. Sea World, near Orlando, Fla., opened a killer whale display in August. The aquarium, which contains 5 million gallons (19 million liters) of artificially created seawater, is the largest marine animal habitat ever built. Its main section features a 5,200-seat stadium alongside a pool. The pool contains a sloping concrete island, on which the whales slide almost out of the water, enabling spectators to view them close-up. Sea World staff members will also use the facility to study killer whale biology and behavior.

The Brookfield Zoo near Chicago opened a South American Tropic World in June. Visitors enter through a cave and emerge in a tropical rain forest inhabited by golden lion tamarins and 5 other species of monkeys, a two-toed sloth, a Brazilian tapir, and 13 species of birds. "Thunderstorms" dampen the forest three times daily, just as they do in the African and Asian sections of Tropic World.   Eugene J. Walter, Jr.

In WORLD BOOK, see ZOO.

Answers to the Quiz

1. India's Prime Minister Indira Gandhi.

2. Race officials gave him a 16-hour credit because he detoured to help a competitor whose yacht had capsized.

3. President Jimmy Carter.

4. Martina Navratilova. She won the grand slam — consecutive victories in the four major tennis tournaments.

5. She became the first Miss America to resign.

6. The Georges Bank fishing area off Cape Cod.

7. Attorney General-designate Edwin Meese III was cleared. Secretary of Labor Raymond J. Donovan was indicted.

8. Michael Jackson.

9. d.

10. Chrysler Corporation.

11. Upper Volta.

12. Acquired immune deficiency syndrome (AIDS).

13. British Prime Minister Margaret Thatcher.

14. Georges Seurat.

15. Ray Meyer's career as DePaul's basketball coach ended with a loss to Wake Forest.

16. Guinea.

17. Dr. Seuss (Theodor Seuss Geisel).

18. Pierre Elliott Trudeau, John N. Turner, and Brian Mulroney.

19. Sugar Ray Leonard.

20. The transfer of Hong Kong from British to Chinese control.

21. James Joyce's *Ulysses*.

22. Libya.

23. Break dancing.

24. b.

25. Where's the beef?

26. Walter Payton of the Chicago Bears surpassed Jim Brown's career rushing record with the Cleveland Browns of 12,312 yards (11,258 meters).

27. East Germany's Erich Honecker, who — apparently acting on Soviet advice — canceled a September visit to West Germany.

28. He offered to meet with Salvadoran rebel leaders in an effort to end the country's five-year civil war.

29. The world championship of chess.

30. The Vatican. Some Protestant, Jewish, and civil liberties groups protested that the action was a violation of U.S. constitutional separation of church and state.

31. The Winter Olympic Games.

32. Continental Illinois National Bank and Trust Company.

33. Honduras.

34. A pain-relieving drug.

35. The temple is in Amritsar, India. Indian troops were fighting Sikh militants.

36. The rating PG-13, which warns parents that a motion picture has violence or other content unsuitable for children under the age of 13.

37. Carl Lewis.

38. The skin used was grown in a laboratory from tiny patches of the boys' own skin.

39. d.

40. J. M. W. Turner.

41. Minnesota. He also carried the District of Columbia.

42. The U.S. Bureau of the Census announced that Los Angeles had surpassed Chicago in population to become the second-largest city in the United States.

43. John Henry, a 9-year-old thoroughbred race horse.

44. China.

45. She became the longest surviving human recipient of an animal heart.

46. *USA Today.*

47. The second son of Prince Charles and Diana, Princess of Wales, born on September 15. He is third in line to the British throne.

48. The Maya.

49. The Statue of Liberty.

50. Shimon Peres, leader of Israel's Labor Party, and Yitzhak Shamir, leader of the Likud bloc. They agreed to share power, with Peres serving as prime minister the first half of the term, and Shamir succeeding him for the second half.

World Book Supplement

1984

To help WORLD BOOK owners keep their encyclopedias up to date, the following new or revised articles are reprinted from the 1985 edition of the encyclopedia.

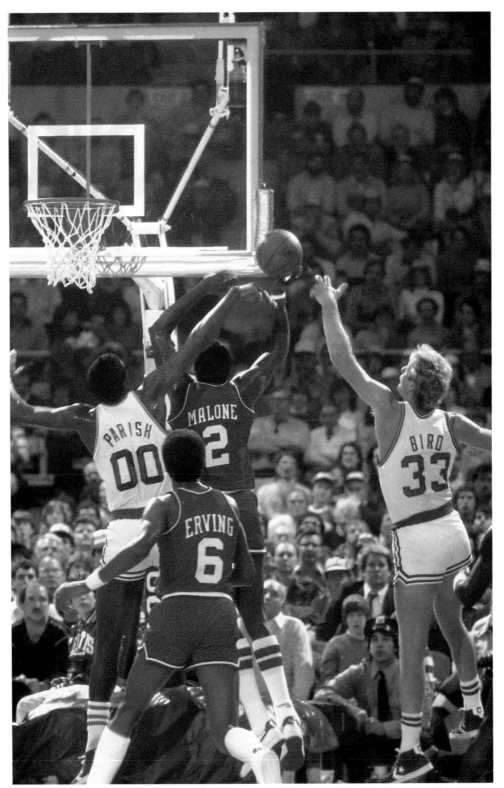

See "Basketball," page 544.

Detail of *Family and Court of Ludovico Gonzaga II* (1474), a fresco by Andrea Mantegna; Ducal Palace, Mantua (SCALA/Art Resource)

The Ruling Families of the Italian City-States strongly supported the Renaissance. Like the Gonzaga family of Mantua, *above,* they employed many leading artists and scholars at their courts.

RENAISSANCE

RENAISSANCE, *REHN uh sahns,* was a great cultural movement that began in Italy during the early 1300's. It spread to England, France, Germany, the Netherlands, Spain, and other countries in the late 1400's and ended about 1600.

The word *Renaissance* comes from the Latin word *rinascere* and refers to the act of being reborn. During the Renaissance, many European scholars and artists, especially in Italy, studied the learning and art of ancient Greece and Rome. They wanted to recapture the spirit of the Greek and Roman cultures in their own artistic, literary, and philosophic works. The cultures of ancient Greece and Rome are often called *classical antiquity.* The Renaissance thus represented a rebirth of these cultures and is therefore also known as the *revival of antiquity* or the *revival of learning.*

The Renaissance overlapped the end of a period in European history called the Middle Ages, which began in the 400's. The leaders of the Renaissance rejected many of the attitudes and ideas of the Middle Ages. For example, European thinkers in medieval times believed that people's chief responsibility was to pray to God and concentrate on saving their souls. They thought that so-

Painted terra-cotta statue (about 1485) by Andrea del Verrocchio; National Gallery of Art, Washington, D.C., Samuel H. Kress collection, 1939

Lorenzo de' Medici was the political and cultural leader of Florence when the city was the center of the Italian Renaissance in the 1400's. Lorenzo was called "the Magnificent" because of his many achievements as a ruler, supporter of the arts, and author.

Anthony Molho, the contributor of this article, is Professor of History at Brown University.

ciety was filled with evil temptations. Renaissance thinkers, on the other hand, emphasized people's responsibilities and duties to the society in which they lived. They believed that society could civilize people rather than make them wicked.

During the Middle Ages, the most important branch of learning was *theology* (the study of God). However, many Renaissance thinkers paid greater attention to the study of humanity. They examined the great accomplishments of different cultures, particularly those of ancient Greece and Rome.

Medieval artists painted human figures that looked stiff and unrealistic and which often served symbolic religious purposes. But Renaissance artists stressed the beauty of the human body. They tried to capture the dignity and majesty of human beings in lifelike paintings and sculptures.

The changes brought about by the Renaissance happened gradually and did not immediately affect most Europeans. Even at the height of the movement, which occurred during the late 1400's and early 1500's, the new ideas were accepted by relatively few people. But the influence of the Renaissance on future generations was to prove immense in many fields—from art and literature to education, political science, and history. For centuries, most scholars have agreed that the modern era of human history began with the Renaissance.

The Italian Renaissance

Political Background. Italy was not a unified country until the 1860's. At the beginning of the Renaissance, it consisted of about 250 separate states, most of which were ruled by a city. Some cities had only 5,000 to 10,000 people. Others were among the largest cities in Europe. For example, Florence, Milan, and Venice had at least 100,000 people each in the early 1300's.

At the dawn of the Renaissance, much of Italy was supposedly controlled by the Holy Roman Empire. However, the emperors lived in Germany and had little power over their Italian lands. The popes ruled central Italy, including the city of Rome, but were unable to extend political control to the rest of Italy. No central authority was thus established in Italy to unify all the states.

During the mid-1300's and early 1400's, a number of major Italian cities came under the control of one family. For example, the Visconti family governed Milan from the early 1300's until 1447, when the last male member died. Soon after, the Sforza family took control of Milan and governed the city until the late 1400's. Other ruling families included the Este family in Ferrara, the Gonzaga family in Mantua, and the Montefeltro family in Urbino.

The form of government established by the ruling families of the Italian cities was called the *signoria*, and the chief official was known as the *signore*. All power was concentrated in the signore and his friends and relatives. An elaborate court slowly grew up around each signorial government. At the court, the area's leading artists, intellectuals, and politicians gathered under the sponsorship of the signore.

Other Italian cities had a form of government known as *republicanism*. In republican cities, a ruling class controlled the government. Members of the ruling class considered themselves superior to the other residents of the

city. The most important examples of republican government were in Florence and Venice.

In the republican government of Florence, about 800 of the city's wealthiest families made up the ruling class. The members of these Florentine families intermarried and lived in large, beautiful palaces built by Renaissance architects. They paid for the construction of great religious and civic buildings and impressive monuments throughout Florence. They also supported artists and intellectuals. In addition, the ruling class encouraged the study of ancient Greek and Roman authors in the desire to have their society resemble the cultures of classical antiquity.

By the 1430's, the Medici family dominated the ruling class of Florence. The family controlled the largest bank in Europe and was headed by a series of talented and ambitious men. Under Medici domination, the government of Florence resembled a signorial government.

About 180 families controlled the republican government of Venice. All government leaders came from these families. A law passed in 1297 restricted membership in the Great Council, the principal governing body, to descendants of families that had already sat in the council. Like Florence, Venice became a leading center of Renaissance art under the support of the ruling class.

Humanism was the most significant intellectual movement of the Renaissance. It blended concern for the history and actions of human beings with religious concerns. The humanists were scholars and artists who studied subjects that they believed would help them better understand the problems of humanity. These subjects included literature and philosophy. The humanists shared the view that the civilizations of ancient Greece and Rome had excelled in such subjects and thus could serve as models. They believed that people should un-

WORLD BOOK map

Renaissance Italy consisted of about 250 states, most of which were ruled by a city. The Renaissance began during the 1300's in the *city-states* of northern Italy. Early centers of the Renaissance included the cities of Florence, Milan, and Venice.

RENAISSANCE

derstand and appreciate classical antiquity to learn how to conduct their lives.

To understand the customs, laws, and ideas of ancient Greece and Rome, the humanists had first to master the languages of classical antiquity. The Greeks had used a language foreign to Italians, and the Romans had used a form of Latin far different from that used in the 1300's and 1400's. To learn ancient Greek and Latin, the humanists studied *philology* (the science of the meaning and history of words). Philology became one of the two principal concerns of the humanists. The other was history, which the humanists saw as the study of great actions taken by courageous, noble, or wise men of classical antiquity.

The interest of the humanists in ancient Greece and Rome led them to search for manuscripts, statues, coins, and other surviving examples of classical civilization. For example, they combed monastery libraries throughout Europe, locating on dusty shelves long neglected manuscripts by classical authors. The humanists carefully studied these manuscripts, prepared critical editions of them, and often translated them.

Petrarch and Giovanni Boccaccio were the first Renaissance humanists. During the mid-1300's, the two friends recovered many important but long ignored ancient manuscripts. Petrarch discovered the most influential of these works. It was *Letters to Atticus*, a collection of letters on Roman political life by the statesman and orator Marcus Tullius Cicero.

As Petrarch and Boccaccio studied the rediscovered classical writings, they tried to imitate the styles of the ancient authors. They urged that people express themselves accurately and elegantly, characteristics they saw in classical literary style. Petrarch said, "The style is the man." He meant that careless expression reflected careless thought.

Petrarch became known for his poetry, and Boccaccio for his collection of stories called the *Decameron* (about 1349-1353). In their works, they tried to describe human feelings and situations that people could easily understand. Petrarch and Boccaccio insisted that the duty of intellectuals was to concentrate on human problems, which they believed were more important than an understanding of the mysteries of nature or of God's will. They thought that people could learn how to deal with their problems by studying the lives of individuals of the past.

The Ideal Courtier. Some Italian humanists spent most of their time in signorial courts. During the late 1400's, these humanists began to develop ideas about the proper conduct of *courtiers*—the noblemen and noblewomen who lived in a royal court. About 1518, an author and diplomat named Baldassare Castiglione completed *The Book of the Courtier.* Castiglione based the work on his experiences at the court of Urbino. It was translated into several European languages and influenced the conduct of courtiers throughout Europe. *The Courtier* also strongly influenced educational theory in England during the Renaissance.

Castiglione wrote that the ideal male courtier is re-

Detail of *The Madonna Enthroned with Angels* (about 1285), an oil painting on wood panel by Cimabue; Uffizi Palace, Florence, Italy (SCALA/Art Resource)

Detail of *The Small Cowper Madonna* (1505), an oil painting on wood panel by Raphael; National Gallery of Art, Washington, D.C., Widener collection, 1942

Medieval and Renaissance Art differed in the portrayal of the human figure. The medieval painting at the left has unlifelike figures that represent religious ideas, not flesh-and-blood people. The Renaissance painting at the right shows realistic figures in a natural setting.

fined in writing and speaking and skilled in the arts, sports, and the use of weapons. He willingly devotes himself to his signore, always seeking to please him. The courtier is polite and attentive to women. Whatever he does is achieved with an easy, natural style, which reflects his command of every situation. An ideal court woman knows literature and art and how to entertain the court. She exhibits the highest moral character and acts in a feminine manner.

The Fine Arts. During the Middle Ages, painters and sculptors tried to give their works a spiritual quality. They wanted viewers to concentrate on the deep religious meaning of their paintings and sculptures. They were not concerned with making their subjects appear natural or lifelike. But Renaissance painters and sculptors, like Renaissance writers, wanted to portray people and nature realistically. Architects of the Middle Ages

Bronze statue (1430's); Bargello, Florence, Italy (SCALA/Art Resource)

Donatello's *David* was the first large free-standing nude since classical antiquity. The sculptor's emphasis on the subject's physical beauty greatly influenced other Renaissance artists.

SCALA/Art Resource

The Pazzi Chapel in Florence, Italy, was one of the first buildings to be designed in the Renaissance style. The chapel was begun in 1429 and completed in 1461. The architect, Filippo Brunelleschi, incorporated arches, columns, and other elements of classical architecture into his design. Both the exterior, *above,* and the interior, *right,* have been praised for the beauty and harmony of their proportions.

SCALA/Art Resource

RENAISSANCE

designed huge cathedrals to emphasize the majesty and grandeur of God. Renaissance architects designed buildings on a smaller scale to help make people aware of their own powers and dignity.

Arts of the 1300's and Early 1400's. During the early 1300's, the Florentine painter Giotto became the first artist to portray nature realistically. He produced magnificent *frescoes* (paintings on damp plaster) for churches in Florence, Padua, and Assisi. Giotto attempted to create lifelike figures showing real emotions. He portrayed many of his figures in realistic settings.

A remarkable group of Florentine architects, painters, and sculptors worked during the early 1400's. They included the architect Filippo Brunelleschi, the painter Masaccio, and the sculptor Donatello.

Brunelleschi was the first Renaissance architect to revive the ancient Roman style of architecture. He incorporated arches, columns, and other elements of classical architecture into his designs. One of his best-known buildings is the beautifully and harmoniously proportioned Pazzi Chapel in Florence. The chapel, begun in 1429, was one of the first buildings designed in the new Renaissance style. Brunelleschi also was the first Renaissance artist to use *linear perspective*, a mathematical sys-

tem in which painters could show space and depth on a flat surface.

Masaccio's finest work was a series of frescoes he painted about 1427 in the Brancacci Chapel of the Church of Santa Maria del Carmine in Florence. The frescoes realistically show Biblical scenes of emotional intensity. Masaccio created the illusion of space and depth in these paintings by using Brunelleschi's mathematical calculations.

In his sculptures, Donatello tried to portray the dignity of the human body in realistic and often dramatic detail. His masterpieces include three statues of the Biblical hero David. In a version completed in the 1430's, Donatello portrayed David as a graceful, nude youth, moments after he slew the giant Goliath. The work, which is about 5 feet (1.5 meters) tall, was the first large free-standing nude created in Western art since classical antiquity.

Arts of the Late 1400's and Early 1500's were dominated by three men. They were Michelangelo, Raphael, and Leonardo da Vinci.

Michelangelo excelled as a painter, architect, and poet. In addition, he has been called the greatest sculptor in history. Michelangelo was a master of portraying the human figure. For example, his famous statue of the Israelite leader Moses (1516) gives an overwhelming impression of physical strength and spiritual power. These qualities also appear in the frescoes of Biblical and classical subjects that Michelangelo painted on the ceiling of the Sistine Chapel in the Vatican. The frescoes were painted from 1508 to 1512 and rank among the greatest achievements of Renaissance art.

Raphael's paintings are softer in outline and more poetic than those of Michelangelo. Raphael was skilled in creating perspective and in the delicate use of color. He painted a number of beautiful pictures of the Madonna (Virgin Mary) and many outstanding portraits. One of his greatest works is the fresco *School of Athens* (1511). The painting shows the influence of classical Greek and Roman models. It portrays the great philosophers and scientists of ancient Greece in a setting of classical arches. Raphael was thus making a connection between the culture of classical antiquity and the Italian culture of his time.

Leonardo da Vinci painted two of the most famous works of Renaissance art, the fresco *The Last Supper* (about 1497) and the portrait *Mona Lisa* (about 1503). Leonardo had one of the most searching minds in all history. He wanted to know the workings of everything he saw in nature. In more than 4,000 pages of notebooks, he drew detailed diagrams and wrote down observations. Leonardo made careful drawings of human skeletons and muscles, trying to discover how the body worked. Because of his inquiring mind, Leonardo has become a symbol of the Renaissance spirit of learning and intellectual curiosity.

The Renaissance Outside Italy

During the late 1400's, the Renaissance spread from Italy to such countries as France, Germany, England, and Spain. It was introduced into those countries by visitors to Italy, who included merchants, bankers, diplomats, and especially young scholars. The scholars acquired from the Italians the basic tools of humanistic study—history and philology.

Pen-and-ink drawing (about 1488); Bibliothèque Nationale, Paris (Art Resource)

The Drawings of Leonardo da Vinci reveal the inquiring mind of perhaps the greatest intellect of the Renaissance. Leonardo was fascinated by the possibility of human flight. He designed a flying machine that used revolving paddles, *above.*

Detail of a fresco (1510-1511); The Vatican, Rome (SCALA/Art Resource)

Raphael's *School of Athens* portrays an imaginary gathering of ancient Greek philosophers and scientists, including the mathematician Euclid, *bending forward, foreground.* The painting shows the Renaissance respect for classical culture.

A series of invasions of Italy also played a major role in the spread of the Renaissance to other parts of Europe. From 1494 to the early 1500's, Italy was repeatedly invaded by armies from France, Germany, and Spain. The invaders were dazzled by the beauty of Italian art and architecture and returned home deeply influenced by Italian culture.

In Italy, evidence of classical antiquity, especially Roman antiquity, could be seen almost everywhere. Ruins of Roman monuments and buildings stood in every Italian city. This link between the present and the classical past was much weaker elsewhere in Europe. In ancient times, Roman culture had been forced upon northern and western Europeans by conquering Roman armies. But that culture quickly disappeared after the Roman Empire in the West fell in the A.D. 400's.

The relative scarcity of classical art affected the development of European art outside Italy during the 1400's. Painters had few examples of classical antiquity to imitate, and so they tended to be more influenced by the northern Gothic style of the late Middle Ages. The first great achievements in Renaissance painting outside Italy appeared in the works of artists living in Flanders. Most of the Flanders region lies in what are now Belgium and France. Flemish painting was known for its precise details. The human figures were realistic but lacked the sculptural quality that was characteristic of Italian painting.

Political Background. During the Renaissance, the political structure of northern and western Europe differed greatly from that of Italy. By the late 1400's, England, France, and Spain were being united into nations under monarchies. These monarchies provided political

and cultural leadership for their countries. Germany, like Italy, was divided into many largely independent states. But Germany was the heart of the Holy Roman Empire, which tended to unify the various states to some extent.

The great royal courts supported the Renaissance in northern and western Europe much as the cities did in Italy. For example, the French king Francis I, who ruled from 1515 to 1547, tried to surround himself with the finest representatives of the Italian Renaissance. He brought Leonardo da Vinci and many other Italian artists and scholars to France. In England, the House of Tudor became the most important patron of the Renaissance. The Tudors ruled from 1485 to 1603. Henry VII, the first Tudor monarch, invited numerous Italian humanists to England. These men encouraged English scholars to study the literature and philosophy of ancient Greece and Rome.

Christian Humanism. Renaissance scholars in northern and western Europe were not as interested as the Italians in studying classical literature. Instead, they sought to apply humanistic methods to the study of Christianity. These scholars were especially concerned with identifying and carefully editing the texts on which Christianity was based. These texts included the Bible, the letters of Saint Paul, and the works of such great early church leaders as Saint Ambrose, Saint Jerome,

Oil painting on wood panel (about 1460);
Uffizi Palace, Florence, Italy (SCALA/Art Resource)

Mythological Subjects were popular with Italian artists. Antonio del Pollaiuolo painted the Greek hero Hercules killing a monster called the Hydra, *above.* His realistic portrayal of the human body in vigorous action inspired many other Renaissance artists.

Detail of *The Madonna and Child with Chancellor Rolin* (about 1436), an oil painting on wood panel; the Louvre, Paris (SCALA/Art Resource)

A Northern Renaissance Painting by the Flemish artist Jan van Eyck emphasizes lighting, perspective, and precise details. Van Eyck was one of the first major Renaissance artists outside Italy.

and Saint Augustine. The scholars became known as *Christian humanists* to distinguish them from those humanists who were chiefly involved with the study of classical antiquity.

Desiderius Erasmus and Saint Thomas More were the leading Christian humanists. They were close friends who courageously refused to abandon their ideals.

Erasmus was born in the Netherlands. He was educated in Paris and traveled throughout Germany, England, and Italy. He was an excellent scholar, with a thorough knowledge of Latin and Greek.

Erasmus refused to take sides in any political or religious controversy. In particular, he would not support either side during the Reformation, the religious movement of the 1500's that gave birth to Protestantism. Both Roman Catholics and Protestants sought Erasmus' support. He stubbornly kept his independence and was called a coward by both sides. However, Erasmus did attack abuses he saw in the church in a famous witty work called *The Praise of Folly* (1511). In this book, Erasmus criticized the moral quality of church leaders. Erasmus also accused them of overemphasizing procedures and ceremonies while neglecting the spiritual values of Christianity.

Saint Thomas More was born in England and devoted his life to serving his country. He gained the confidence of King Henry VIII and carried out a number of important missions for him. In 1529, the king appointed More lord chancellor, making him England's highest judicial official.

Throughout his career, More dedicated himself to the principles that had inspired Erasmus. Like Erasmus, he believed it was important to eliminate the abuses, inequalities, and evils that were accepted as normal in his day. More's best-known work is *Utopia* (1516). In this book, More described a society in which the divisions between the rich and the poor and the powerful and the weak were replaced by a common concern for the health and happiness of everyone.

More's strong principles finally cost him his life. He objected to Henry VIII's decision to divorce the queen, Catherine of Aragon, and remarry. More then refused to take an oath acknowledging the king's authority over that of the pope. In 1535, More was beheaded for treason.

The Heritage of the Renaissance

The Renaissance left an intellectual and artistic heritage that still remains important. Since the Renaissance, scholars have used Renaissance methods of humanistic inquiry, even when they did not share the ideas and spirit of the Renaissance humanists. In literature, writers have tried for centuries to imitate and improve upon the works of such Renaissance authors as Petrarch and Boccaccio.

The influence of Renaissance painters, sculptors, and architects has been particularly strong. The artists of Florence and Rome set enduring standards for painting in the Western world. For hundreds of years, painters have traveled to Florence to admire the frescoes of Giotto and Masaccio. They have visited Rome to study the paintings of Raphael and Michelangelo. The works of Donatello and Michelangelo have inspired sculptors for generations. The beautifully scaled buildings of Brunelleschi and other Renaissance architects still serve as models for architects.

Since the Renaissance, people have also been inspired by the intellectual daring of such men as Petrarch and Erasmus. Leaders of the Renaissance seemed to be

Detail of an oil painting on wood panel (about 1523) by Hans Holbein the Younger; the Louvre, Paris (Art Resource)

Desiderius Erasmus, a Dutch priest and scholar, became a leading Christian humanist during the Renaissance. Erasmus often attacked religious superstition and abuses he saw in the church.

breaking out of intellectual boundaries and entering unknown territories.

Perhaps it is no accident that some of the greatest explorers of the late 1400's and early 1500's were Italians exposed to the traditions of the Renaissance. Christopher Columbus was a sailor from Genoa and an expert navigator. For his voyage to the New World, Columbus consulted the same scientist who taught mathematics to the architect Filippo Brunelleschi. Columbus—like such other Italian explorers as John Cabot, Giovanni da Verrazano, and Amerigo Vespucci—was willing to take enormous risks to achieve results that people had never dreamed of. In a sense, Columbus' arrival in America in 1492 was one of the greatest achievements of the Renaissance.   ANTHONY MOLHO

Related Articles in WORLD BOOK include:

ARCHITECTS

Alberti, Leon Battista	Jones, Inigo
Bramante, Donato	Palladio, Andrea
Brunelleschi, Filippo	

PAINTERS

Bellini	Holbein, Hans, the Younger
Botticelli, Sandro	Lippi
Bruegel, Pieter, the Elder	Mantegna, Andrea
Campin, Robert	Masaccio
Caravaggio, Michelangelo	Michelangelo
Merisi da	Piero della Francesca
Da Vinci, Leonardo	Pollaiuolo, Antonio del
Dürer, Albrecht	Raphael
Fra Angelico	Tintoretto
Ghirlandajo, Domenico	Titian
Giorgione	Uccello, Paolo
Giotto	Van der Weyden, Rogier
Greco, El	Van Eyck, Jan
Grünewald, Matthias	Veronese, Paolo
Holbein, Hans, the Elder	

POLITICAL LEADERS

Borgia	Machiavelli, Niccolò
Francis (I, of France)	Medici

SCULPTORS

Cellini, Benvenuto	Ghiberti, Lorenzo	Pisano
Della Robbia	Goujon, Jean	Verrocchio,
Donatello	Michelangelo	Andrea del

WRITERS

Ariosto, Ludovico	Petrarch
Boccaccio, Giovanni	Rabelais, François
Castiglione, Baldassare	Ronsard, Pierre de
Cervantes, Miguel de	Shakespeare, William
Du Bellay, Joachim	Spencer, Edmund
Erasmus, Desiderius	Surrey, Earl of
Marlowe, Christopher	Tasso, Torquato
Marot, Clement	Vega, Lope de
Montaigne, Michel de	Wyatt, Sir Thomas
More, Saint Thomas	

OTHER RELATED ARTICLES

See the section on the Renaissance in the various articles on national literatures, such as ITALIAN LITERATURE (The Renaissance). See also the following articles:

Architecture	Florence
Classical Music	Fresco
Clothing	Furniture
Dancing	Humanism
Democracy (Development)	Italy (History)
Drama	Jewelry
Education (The Renaissance)	Literature
Elizabethan Age	Mathematics
Exploration (The Great Age	Mural
of European Discovery)	Painting

Perspective	Science
Philosophy	Sculpture
Poetry	World, History of the
Reformation	

Outline

I. The Italian Renaissance
  A. Political Background
  B. Humanism
  C. The Fine Arts
II. The Renaissance Outside Italy
  A. Political Background
  B. Christian Humanism
  C. Desiderius Erasmus and Saint Thomas More
III. The Heritage of the Renaissance

Questions

What was the most significant intellectual movement of the Renaissance?

What is meant by *classical antiquity*?

How did the Renaissance spread from Italy?

What are some lasting achievements of the Renaissance?

How did many attitudes and ideas of the Renaissance differ from those of the Middle Ages?

What three men dominated Italian arts during the late 1400's and early 1500's?

How did the signorial and republican governments of the Italian cities promote the Renaissance?

Why was *philology* studied during the Renaissance?

What was *The Book of the Courtier* and why was it important?

Who were the *Christian humanists*?

Reading and Study Guide

See *Renaissance* in the RESEARCH GUIDE/INDEX, Volume 22, for a *Reading and Study Guide*.

Additional Resources

Level I

GAIL, MARZIEH. *Life in the Renaissance.* Random House, 1968.

GRANT, NEIL. *The Renaissance.* Watts, 1971.

MEE, CHARLES L. *Lorenzo de' Medici and the Renaissance.* American Heritage, 1969.

MIQUEL, PIERRE. *The Age of Discovery.* Silver Burdett, 1980.

PRICE, CHRISTINE. *Made in the Renaissance: Arts and Crafts of the Age of Exploration.* Dutton, 1963.

SHAPIRO, IRWIN. *The Golden Book of the Renaissance.* Golden Press, 1962. An adaptation for younger readers of *The Horizon Book of the Renaissance.*

Level II

BURCKHARDT, JACOB. *The Civilization of the Renaissance in Italy.* 2 vols. Washington Square, 1966. First published in 1860. The first important analysis of the Renaissance as a historical period.

CHAMBERLIN, ERIC R. *Everyday Life in Renaissance Times.* Putnam, 1965. *The World of the Italian Renaissance.* Allen & Unwin, 1982.

GILBERT, CREIGHTON. *History of Renaissance Art: Painting, Sculpture, Architecture Throughout Europe.* Abrams, 1973.

GOLDSTEIN, THOMAS. *Dawn of Modern Science.* Houghton, 1980. A history of the reawakening of scientific thought in the Renaissance.

HALE, JOHN R. *Renaissance.* Time, Inc., 1965. *A Concise Encyclopedia of the Italian Renaissance.* Oxford, 1981.

HARTT, FREDERICK. *History of Italian Renaissance Art: Painting, Sculpture, Architecture.* Abrams, 1969.

HAY, DENYS. *The Italian Renaissance in Its Historical Background.* 2nd ed. Cambridge, 1976.

The Horizon Book of the Renaissance. Doubleday, 1961.

MARTINDALE, ANDREW. *Man and the Renaissance.* McGraw, 1966.

The Portable Renaissance Reader. Ed. by James B. Ross and M. M. McLaughlin. Rev. ed. Viking, 1958.

SETTON, KENNETH M., and others. *The Renaissance: Maker of Modern Man.* National Geographic Society, 1970.

Basketball Is a Fast-Paced Sport that requires teamwork, speed, and endurance. Millions of fans each year attend games in arenas and gymnasiums to cheer for their favorite teams. The finest male players in the world compete as professionals in the National Basketball Association, *above*.

Peter Read Miller, Focus West

BASKETBALL

BASKETBALL is a fast, exciting, and entertaining sport played between two teams, each consisting of five players. A team wins games by scoring more points than the opposing team. Players score by shooting a large inflated ball into a raised goal, called a *basket*, at one end of a basketball court. A player can advance the ball toward the basket only by *dribbling* (bouncing the ball) or by passing to a teammate. Each team also tries to prevent the other team from scoring.

Basketball was invented in the United States in 1891. By the mid-1900's, it had become the world's most popular indoor sport. Today, millions of fans crowd into gymnasiums and arenas to watch their favorite teams. Millions more watch games on television. In the United States, thousands of elementary schools, high schools, and colleges and universities sponsor amateur teams for male and female players. The finest male players in the world compete as professionals in the National Basketball Association (NBA).

Basketball is a popular form of recreation as well as an organized team sport. Park districts, religious organiza-

tions, and youth centers sponsor recreational leagues. Most schools sponsor intramural competition. Both young people and adults enjoy playing on neighborhood playgrounds, in backyards, in alleys, and on driveways. As few as two players can play; all they need is a ball, a basket, and a level surface that can serve as the court.

Basketball requires teamwork, quick reactions, and endurance. Tall players have an advantage because they can reach closer to the basket or above other players to shoot and rebound. But smaller players also make important contributions to their teams as shooters and ball handlers.

This article deals chiefly with basketball as played in the United States. The game differs somewhat in other countries. The section *International Competition* describes some of the differences.

How to Play Basketball

The Court. A regulation basketball court measures 94 feet (29 meters) long and 50 feet (15 meters) wide. Courts for high school games may be 84 feet (26 meters) long. Most courts are made of wood. Various lines, 2 inches (5 centimeters) wide, mark off the court into sections. For the names of these lines and the sizes and

John R. Thompson, Jr., the contributor of this article, is Head Basketball Coach at Georgetown University in Washington, D.C.

Peter Read Miller, Focus West

Women's Basketball has become a popular college sport. Basketball also ranks among the major girls' sports in high school. The rules for women's and men's competition are basically the same.

Basketball Terms

Assist is a pass by an offensive player that leads directly to a basket.

Backcourt is the defensive team's half of the court.

Blocked Shot occurs when a defensive player legally hits a shot with the arm or hand before the ball reaches the basket.

Dunk is a field goal made by slamming the ball through the basket from above the rim.

Front Court is the offensive team's half of the court.

Goaltending is illegally interfering with the flight of a field goal attempt when the ball is above the basket. If goaltending is called on the defense, the shot is scored as a field goal. If goaltending is called on the offense, the defensive team is awarded possession of the ball and no points are scored.

Held Ball is a ball in the possession of a player from each team at the same time. In high school and college games, one team gains possession of the ball after a held ball is called. The other team gets possession following the next held ball. In the NBA, possession is determined by a jump ball between the two players.

Lay-Up is a shot taken close to the basket.

Rebound is a ball that bounces back off the backboard or rim after a shot has been missed.

Steal occurs when a defensive player legally takes possession of the ball from the offense, such as by intercepting a pass.

Tip-In is a field goal made by tipping a rebound into the basket, usually with the fingers of one hand.

Turnover occurs when the offensive team loses possession of the ball without taking a shot.

Diagrams of a Court and Backboards A basketball court is a rectangle divided into halves by a division line. Other lines further divide the court into sections. A backboard and basket hang over each end of the court. High school teams use fan-shaped or rectangular backboards. College and professional teams use rectangular ones.

WORLD BOOK diagrams

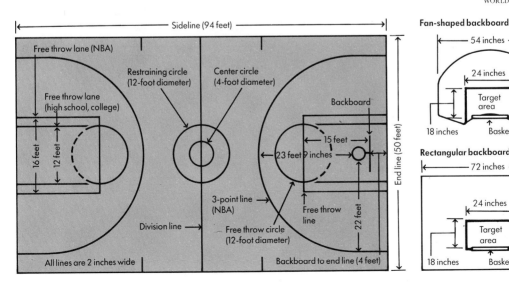

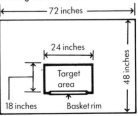

BASKETBALL

The Basketball is round and made of orange or brown leather with a pebble grain. The ball shown above is used for boys' and men's games. Girls and women play with a slightly smaller ball.

names of the sections, see the diagram of a court in this article.

A *basket* and a *backboard* hang over each end of the court. Each backboard must be 4 feet (122 centimeters) inside the end line. The basket consists of a rim, net, and backboard support. The rim is a cast-iron hoop 18 inches (46 centimeters) in diameter and not more than $\frac{5}{8}$ inch (16 millimeters) thick. The rim is attached to a metal plate shaped like an upside-down L that is bolted to the backboard so it is parallel to the floor and 10 feet (3 meters) above it. Backboards are made of clear fiberglass or metal. High school teams use fan-shaped or rectangular backboards. In college and NBA games, rectangular backboards are used. The cotton or synthetic fabric net is attached to the rim and has a hole in the bottom large enough for the ball to drop through.

Equipment. Basketball is played with a round brown or orange inflated leather ball. The ball for boys' and men's games weighs between 20 and 22 ounces (567 to 624 grams) and is about 30 inches (75 centimeters) in circumference. Girls and women use a ball that weighs between 18 and 20 ounces (510 to 657 grams) and is about 29 inches (74 centimeters) in circumference.

The standard basketball uniform consists of a sleeveless shirt, shorts, white socks, and lightweight canvas or leather shoes with rubber soles. The shirt and shorts are made of lightweight cotton or polyester. Each jersey has a number on the front and back so the player can be easily identified by the officials and spectators. Many college and all professional players have their last name on the back of the jersey with the name of the team printed on the front. The home team usually wears light-colored jerseys and shorts and the visiting team wears a uniform of some darker color.

The Players. The five players on a team play both offense and defense. When their team has the ball, they are *on offense;* when their opponents have the ball, they are *on defense*. Because possession of the ball can change rapidly, all players must be alert so they can quickly switch between offense and defense.

Normally, a team consists of two guards, two forwards, and a center. However, players can move anywhere on the court at any time, no matter what their position. A team can also vary the positions at any time, for example, playing three guards and two forwards. This section describes the role of each position on offense.

The guards are usually the smallest and quickest players. They normally play farther from the basket than the forwards or center. Guards should be good dribblers and passers. They direct the offense and start most of the plays. Some teams have a *point guard*, who has the major ballhandling responsibilities. The other guard is called the *shooting guard* and is often the best shooter on the team.

Forwards are generally taller and stronger than guards. Forwards usually play in the area from the base line to the free throw lane. They should be good rebounders and be able to maneuver for shots close to the basket. The center is usually the team's tallest player and best rebounder. Center is the most important position on the team. A center who is a good rebounder and scorer can dominate a game.

The Coach is a basketball team's teacher. Most college and professional teams have one or more assistant coaches who help the coach work with the team. Together, they make up the *coaching staff*.

The coach organizes practice sessions to prepare the team for each game. He or she selects the players who will start the game. During the game, the coach substitutes players, trying to use those players who perform best in certain situations. The coach decides when the team needs a time out, and determines what type of offense and defense will be most effective.

The Coaching Staff prepares a team for each game and determines offensive and defensive strategy during the game. The coach shown above is giving instructions during a time out.

A coach must analyze the opposing team, determining its strengths and weaknesses. Often an assistant coach will *scout* (watch) a game involving an upcoming opponent and report back to the coach on the best strategy for playing the team.

The Officials consist of a referee, one or two umpires, one or two scorekeepers, and one or two timekeepers.

The referee is in charge of the game. The referee and umpires operate on the court to ensure that the game is played by the rules. They both can call any foul or violation they see anywhere on the court. Usually, one official operates near the offensive team's basket and the other near the division line. The officials reverse positions when the teams move to the other end of the court. If a second umpire is used, he or she stands near a sideline. To call a violation or foul, the official blows a whistle to stop play and the clock. The official explains the violation or foul, usually with a hand or arm signal, and enforces the penalty. The game then resumes.

The scorekeepers and timekeepers sit at a table behind one of the sidelines. One scorekeeper operates the electronic scoreboard. The other scorekeeper keeps the official scorebook, recording all the field goals, free throws, fouls, and time outs. One timekeeper operates the electric game clock. A second timekeeper operates the shot clock if the rules call for each team to shoot within a given time limit. Players entering the game must first report to the scorekeeper in charge of the scorebook. The timekeeper must stop the clock every time the referee or umpire blows the whistle. One of the officials will signal the timekeeper when to restart the clock.

Playing Time. High school games last 32 minutes. They are divided into two 16-minute halves, each consisting of two 8-minute quarters. The teams take a 1-minute break at the end of the first and third quarters and a 10-minute break between halves. College teams play two 20-minute halves, with a 15-minute break between halves. NBA teams play four 12-minute quarters. They take a $1\frac{1}{2}$-minute break between quarters and a 15-minute break between halves. A game clock located above the court shows the time remaining in a half or quarter.

If the score is tied at the end of regulation time, teams play as many overtime periods as needed to determine a winner. High school teams play 3-minute overtimes. College and professional teams play 5-minute overtimes.

Play is stopped if an official calls a foul or violation, if the ball goes out of bounds, and if a team calls a time out. The game may also be stopped if a player is injured or if the officials determine that spectators are interfering with the normal progress of the game.

High school teams are permitted four time outs during a game. College teams may call five time outs, plus one additional time out for each overtime period. If a college game is televised, each team is permitted only four time outs during regulation play. In addition, at least three time outs may be called for TV commercials. The NBA permits seven 90-second time outs during a game. Each team is also allowed one 20-second time out each half. However, a pro team may call no more than four time outs during the fourth quarter.

Scoring. A team scores points by making field goals and free throws. A field goal may be attempted from anywhere on the floor by any offensive player while the

Peter Read Miller, Focus West

A Jump Ball starts a basketball game. The referee tosses the ball into the air. A player from each team jumps inside the center circle and tries to tap the ball to a teammate.

game clock is running. In high school and most college games, field goals are worth 2 points. In a few college conferences and in the NBA, field goals count 3 points if the shot is taken from behind a 3-point line. Other field goals count 2 points.

A free throw counts 1 point and is taken as a penalty after certain fouls. A player attempts a free throw from behind the free throw line and inside the free throw circle. Players have 10 seconds to shoot after the official hands them the ball.

Richard Mackson, Focus West

Dribbling is an important offensive skill. A good dribbler can move past a defender for an easy shot or set up a teammate for a shot. A team's guards generally do most of the dribbling.

The Jump Shot is the most common shot in basketball. The shooter jumps straight up and releases the ball at the peak of the jump. The shot can be released quickly and is difficult to block.

The Dunk is one of basketball's most exciting shots. The shooter slams the ball through the basket from above the rim. Many dunks are unguarded shots that come at the end of a fast break.

Playing the Game. A game starts with the center jump. Four players from each team stand outside the re-straining circle. The fifth player, usually the center, stands inside the center circle. The official tosses the ball into the air above the two players, who jump up and try to tap it to a teammate. The game clock starts as soon as a player touches the ball.

Once it gains possession of the ball, the offensive team advances the ball into the front court. The team can dribble the ball or pass it. If the offensive team scores,

the opposing team immediately takes the ball out-of-bounds from behind the base line and tries to move the ball to the basket at the other end of the court. It becomes the offensive team and the team that just scored becomes the defensive team. Action continues in this manner until the clock is stopped.

If a player misses a shot, both teams try to gain possession of the ball by catching the rebound. All missed field goal attempts and most missed free throw attempts result in rebounds. Rebounding is a vital part of the game.

Rebounds occur after missed field goal attempts and most missed free throws. Players try to capture rebounds by positioning themselves close to the basket with opponents behind them.

A Free Throw is shot from behind a line in the free throw circle. Players from both teams line up along the free throw lane. They cannot step into the lane until the shooter releases the ball.

544

Most teams miss at least 50 per cent of their shots. Therefore, a strong rebounding team can control the ball more than its opponent and has more scoring opportunities.

Offensive Strategies try to free a player for a good scoring opportunity. The offense may run plays that require a number of passes and constant movement by the five players. A successful play will produce a good shot or cause a defender to commit a foul. Players may set a *screen* or *pick* to free a teammate for a shot. In a screen or pick, an offensive player legally blocks a defensive player with his or her body so the defensive player cannot guard the player with the ball. That player can then take an open shot.

The *fast break* is designed to score quickly after the offensive team gains possession of the ball. The offense tries to get at least one of its players ahead of the defense for an easy shot before the defenders can move into proper position.

The *delay* is an offensive strategy that is primarily designed to use up time, rather than to score. Teams often use a delay to protect a lead late in the game, passing and dribbling to keep the ball away from the other team.

Defensive Strategies. There are two types of team defense, *zone* and *man-to-man*. In a zone defense, each player is assigned a particular area of the front court to defend. In man-to-man defense, each player guards a particular offensive player on all parts of the court. The zone defense is prohibited in the NBA.

One variation of the two defenses is the *press*. The press is designed to put defensive pressure on the offensive team all over the court. The press tries to force the offensive team into a *turnover* (losing possession of the ball). Pressing defenses often use a tactic called the *trap* or *double-team*. In a trap, two defensive players suddenly converge on the player with the ball, trying to force that player into making a turnover.

Fouls are called by officials. Players may commit either a *personal foul* or a *technical foul*.

The more common type of foul is the personal foul. Most personal fouls occur when a player holds, pushes, or charges into an opponent, or hits the arm or body of an opponent who is in the act of shooting. A player

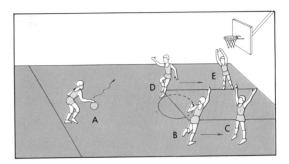

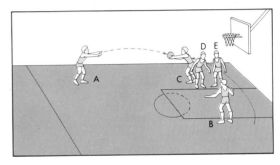

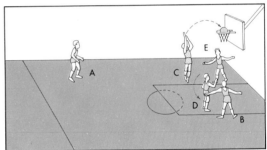

WORLD BOOK illustrations by Bill and Judie Anderson

Offensive Plays are often designed to create a good shot for a particular player. The play shown above is intended to free player C for a shot. Player A dribbles to his left and passes the ball to player C, who has moved across the free throw lane.

WORLD BOOK illustrations by Bill and Judie Anderson

Defensive Systems include the zone defense, *left,* and the man-to-man defense, *right.* The zone is designed to give each defensive player a certain area of the court to guard. In a man-to-man defense, defensive players are assigned specific opponents and follow them anywhere in the forecourt.

BASKETBALL

Richard Mackson, Focus West

The Trap is a defensive maneuver in which two defenders closely guard the ballhandler. The trap is designed to force the offensive player to make a bad pass or to commit a turnover.

fouled in the act of shooting gets two free throws if the shot was missed and one if it was made. If the fouled player is on the offensive team but not shooting, his or her team retains possession of the ball. A team goes into the *penalty situation* after committing a certain number of personal fouls in a quarter or half. The fouled team then shoots one or two free throws after every foul for the rest of that quarter or half.

In high school games, the fouled player is awarded a free throw beginning with the fifth foul committed by the opposing team each half. If the player makes the free throw, a second shot is awarded. This situation is called the *one-and-one*. In college games, the one-and-one begins with the seventh foul on the opposing team. In any competition, if an official determines that a foul was committed intentionally, the fouled player will receive two free throws. At any time, if a foul is committed by an offensive player, the defensive team gets possession of the ball and no free throws are taken.

In the NBA, the fouled player shoots two free throws beginning with the opposing team's fifth foul in each quarter. In addition, a fouled player gets two free throws if the offending team has committed more than one foul in the last two minutes of a quarter.

A high school or college player is disqualified from a game after committing five personal fouls. In the NBA, disqualification comes after six personal fouls.

A technical foul may be called on any player or coach. Most technical fouls are called for unsportsmanlike conduct toward officials. After a high school or college

Officials' Signals   Officials use a variety of hand signals to inform players and spectators of fouls and violations during a game. Any official on the court can call a foul or violation and give the signal. Most signals are the same in high school, college, and professional games. The most common ones are shown below.

WORLD BOOK illustrations by Bill and Judie Anderson

Start Clock	Jump Ball	Personal Foul	Technical Foul	Holding	Blocking	Traveling

Player Control Foul	Illegal Use of Hands	Illegal Dribble	3-Second Violation	Over and Back, Carrying the Ball	5-Second Violation

Direction Signal	No Score	Goal Counts or Is Awarded	Points Scored, (1 or 2 Fingers)	Bonus Free Throw

player is charged with a technical foul, the opponent gets one free throw and possession of the ball. If the technical foul is against a coach, the opposing team gets two free throws and possession of the ball. A player or coach called for three technical fouls is disqualified from the game. In the NBA, one free throw is awarded for a technical foul and the team with the ball at the time of the foul retains possession. Two technicals against a coach or player result in disqualification.

Violations are usually committed by the offensive team. The penalty for most violations is loss of possession of the ball. The most common violations result from ball-handling errors. For example, an official calls a violation for an illegal dribble when the player bounces the ball with both hands at the same time, or stops dribbling and then starts again.

A number of violations result from time restrictions. For example, a team must get the ball in play from out-of-bounds within 5 seconds and must move the ball across the division line within 10 seconds or a violation is called. Officials also will call a violation if any offensive player stands in the front court free throw lane for more than 3 seconds. In high school and college games, the offensive team commits a violation if a closely guarded player has the ball in the front court for more than 5 seconds without shooting or passing to a teammate.

In some competition, a team commits a violation if it fails to shoot within a certain number of seconds. A special shot clock at each end of the court keeps track of the time. NBA teams must shoot within 24 seconds. In women's college basketball, the limit is 30 seconds. Some men's college conferences also have such rules, but each conference sets its own limit.

Basketball Competition

High School Competition. More high schools in the United States participate in basketball than in any other sport. About 17,000 high schools sponsor boys' teams and about 16,500 high schools sponsor girls' teams.

Some states divide their high schools into classes based on school enrollment. For example, Maryland has four classes: AA, A, B, and C. The AA schools have the largest enrollments and C schools the smallest. Schools in each class compete in a separate state championship tournament held after the regular season. Indiana is a state that has no class system. All of the state's nearly 600 high school teams compete in a single state championship tournament at the end of the regular season. In a few states, private schools and public schools conduct separate championship tournaments. Some large cities, such as Philadelphia and Chicago, hold their own championship tournaments.

College Competition. Most U.S. colleges and universities belong to the National Collegiate Athletic Association (NCAA). About 750 schools in the NCAA sponsor men's basketball teams and about 550 sponsor women's teams. The teams with the largest enrollment compete in Division I. The smaller schools compete in Division II or Division III. About 500 other schools with small enrollments belong to the National Association of Intercollegiate Athletics (NAIA), which conducts both men's and women's basketball competition.

Most schools in the NCAA and NAIA belong to one of the more than 100 college conferences. Most confer-

NCAA Basketball Champions

Men

1938-1939	Oregon	1962-1963	Loyola (Ill.)
1939-1940	Indiana	1963-1964	UCLA
1940-1941	Wisconsin	1964-1965	UCLA
1941-1942	Stanford	1965-1966	Texas Western
1942-1943	Wyoming	1966-1967	UCLA
1943-1944	Utah	1967-1968	UCLA
1944-1945	Oklahoma A&M	1968-1969	UCLA
1945-1946	Oklahoma A&M	1969-1970	UCLA
1946-1947	Holy Cross	1970-1971	UCLA
1947-1948	Kentucky	1971-1972	UCLA
1948-1949	Kentucky	1972-1973	UCLA
1949-1950	CCNY	1973-1974	North Carolina State
1950-1951	Kentucky		
1951-1952	Kansas	1974-1975	UCLA
1952-1953	Indiana	1975-1976	Indiana
1953-1954	La Salle	1976-1977	Marquette
1954-1955	San Francisco	1977-1978	Kentucky
1955-1956	San Francisco	1978-1979	Michigan State
1956-1957	North Carolina	1979-1980	Louisville
1957-1958	Kentucky	1980-1981	Indiana
1958-1959	California	1981-1982	North Carolina
1959-1960	Ohio State	1982-1983	North Carolina State
1960-1961	Cincinnati		
1961-1962	Cincinnati	1983-1984	Georgetown

Women

1981-1982	Louisiana Tech
1982-1983	Southern California
1983-1984	Southern California

ences consist of teams in the same geographical area. A number of these conferences are also major football conferences (see FOOTBALL [table: Major College Football Conferences]).

The NCAA championships are determined by a round of play-offs that begin after the end of the regular season. Sixty-four teams are selected to compete in the men's Division I tournament. The men's Division II and Division III championships begin with 32 teams. The NCAA women's championship has 32 teams for Division I and III and 24 in Division II. The NAIA also holds a national tournament.

The Metropolitan Intercollegiate Basketball Association of New York City sponsors the annual National Invitation Tournament (NIT) in March. The association selects Division I teams from throughout the United

National Basketball Association

EASTERN CONFERENCE

Atlantic Division	Central Division
Boston Celtics	Atlanta Hawks
New Jersey Nets	Chicago Bulls
New York Knickerbockers	Cleveland Cavaliers
Philadelphia 76ers	Detroit Pistons
Washington Bullets	Indiana Pacers
	Milwaukee Bucks

WESTERN CONFERENCE

Midwest Division	Pacific Division
Dallas Mavericks	Golden State Warriors
Denver Nuggets	Los Angeles Clippers
Houston Rockets	Los Angeles Lakers
Kansas City Kings	Phoenix Suns
San Antonio Spurs	Portland Trail Blazers
Utah Jazz	Seattle SuperSonics

BASKETBALL

States who are not participating in the NCAA tournament.

Almost 500 junior colleges sponsor men's teams and about 400 sponsor women's teams. The National Junior College Athletic Association holds an annual championship tournament.

Professional Competition. The National Basketball Association is the world's leading professional basketball league. The NBA consists of 23 teams divided into two conferences and four divisions. Each team plays an 82-game schedule. After the regular season ends, the eight teams in each conference with the best records qualify for the championship play-offs.

NBA teams obtain new players through an annual draft of former college players. The teams with the poorest records pick first, and the NBA champion picks last.

A professional league called the Continental Basketball Association (CBA) also operates in the United States. Most of the players are former college stars hoping for a chance to play in the NBA.

International Competition. Basketball has become a popular amateur and professional sport in countries throughout the world. Both men's and women's basketball are sports in the Summer Olympic Games.

International rules are basically the same as American rules. However, there are a few important differences. For example, teams must shoot within 30 seconds after gaining possession of the ball. Teams go into the penalty situation after committing seven personal or technical fouls in a half. Until a team reaches the penalty situation, the opponents receive possession of the ball after being fouled. Beginning with the 11th foul, the fouled team has the choice of shooting two free throws or gaining possession of the ball. In addition, markings on the court are somewhat different in international competition.

The History of Basketball

Beginnings. James A. Naismith invented basketball in 1891. Naismith was a physical-education instructor at the School for Christian Workers (now Springfield College) in Springfield, Mass. Luther H. Gulick, head of the school's physical-education department, asked Naismith to create a team sport that could be played indoors during the winter.

For his new game, Naismith decided to use a soccer ball because it was large enough to catch easily. He then asked the building superintendent for two boxes he could use as goals. The superintendent had no boxes, but he did provide two peach baskets. The baskets were attached to a gymnasium balcony railing 10 feet above the floor. The first game took place between members of Naismith's physical-education class in December 1891.

After the first experimental game, Naismith drafted the original 13 rules of the game. They were published in the *Triangle*, the school newspaper, on Jan. 15, 1892. The sport immediately caught on. Soon basketball was being played by YMCA teams, high school and college teams, and professional teams throughout the United States and Canada.

Changes in the Game. Soon after Naismith invented basketball, changes were adopted to improve the sport. In 1893, metal hoops with net bags attached replaced the wooden baskets. Officials pulled a cord attached to the net to let the ball drop out. Baskets with bottomless nets came into general use about 1913. The backboard was introduced in 1894. That year, larger balls replaced soccer balls.

In 1932, the *10-second* rule was adopted. This rule stated that the offensive team must advance the ball across the division line within 10 seconds or lose possession. Once the ball crossed the line, the offensive team lost possession if a player took the ball back over the line. This rule eliminated stalling with the ball in the backcourt. Until 1937, a center jump was held after every field goal. Beginning in 1937, the defensive team received the ball out-of-bounds after a field goal.

In 1935, a rule was adopted that prohibited any offensive player from standing in the free-throw lane for more than three seconds. In 1955, the foul lane was widened to 12 feet (3.7 meters) from the previous 6 feet (1.83 meters). These changes resulted in more offensive movement and less rough physical contact near the basket.

Early basketball had little scoring. Players basically used two shots, the lay-up and a two-handed set shot. Hank Luisetti revolutionized the game by popularizing a one-handed shot. Luisetti was a star for Stanford University from 1935 to 1938. His one-handed shot could be released quicker than the two-handed shot and was more difficult to defend.

The one-handed shot was the most popular shot in basketball until Joe Fulks popularized the *jump shot*. Fulks played for the Philadelphia Warriors of the NBA from 1946 to 1954. When he wanted to shoot, Fulks jumped up and released the ball at the peak of his jump. The jump shot was even more accurate and difficult to defend against than the one-handed shot. The jump shot became the most popular shot in basketball and greatly increased scoring.

UPI/Bettmann Archive

The First Important Intersectional Game was played in 1934 in New York City. More than 16,000 spectators watched New York University defeat Notre Dame, 25-18.

The History of College Basketball. The first college game using five-player teams took place in Iowa City, Iowa, on Jan. 16, 1896. The University of Chicago defeated the University of Iowa, 15-12.

During the game's early days, colleges played teams in their own area. Travel was too difficult and too expensive to allow frequent games between schools from different sections of the country. Instead, teams in a region formed conferences. The Ivy League, the oldest conference still in existence, was established for the 1901-1902 season. By 1905, more than 40 colleges had intercollegiate basketball teams.

The first important intersectional game took place in 1934. The University of Notre Dame played New York University in Madison Square Garden in New York City as part of a double-header that attracted more than 16,000 fans and marked the beginning of intersectional basketball on a regular basis. The first national tournament, the NIT, was held at the end of the 1937-1938 season. Temple University won the first title. The University of Oregon won the first NCAA tournament, held after the 1938-1939 season.

After the end of World War II in 1945, a number of developments helped spread the popularity of college basketball. Schools built large arenas for games, increasing attendance. Many games were televised. The revenue from greater attendance and from television enabled schools to offer athletic scholarships to players. Many young athletes turned to basketball in the hope of winning a scholarship.

Until about 1950, college basketball was a largely segregated sport. Gradually, black players were allowed to play on previously all-white college teams. By the mid-1960's, a large percentage of the players on major college teams were black.

The University of California at Los Angeles (UCLA) dominated college basketball in the 1960's and 1970's. The UCLA teams, coached by John Wooden, won 10 NCAA titles between 1964 and 1975.

The History of Professional Basketball. The first professional basketball league was the six-team National League, formed in 1898. It lasted for five seasons. The Buffalo Germans, founded in 1895, dominated early professional basketball. The team won 111 straight games from 1908 to 1910. The most famous professional team of the early 1900's was the Original Celtics of New York City, founded in 1918. The team won 720 of 795 games from 1921 to 1928.

The American Basketball League was formed in 1925 with teams from the East and Midwest. The league disbanded in 1931 and re-formed in 1933 with teams concentrated in the East. A primarily Midwestern league called the National Basketball League (NBL) was organized in 1937. The Basketball Association of America (BAA) was formed in 1946. The NBL and BAA merged in 1949 to form the National Basketball Association.

During the 1920's and 1930's, two all-black professional teams dominated their competition. The teams were the New York Renaissance Big Five, called the Rens, and the Harlem Globetrotters. Because professional leagues were segregated, the Rens and Globetrotters were forced to travel across the country playing exhibition games. The Globetrotters still play today.

In 1950, Chuck Cooper signed with the Boston Celt-

National Basketball Association Champions

	Eastern Division	Western Division	Play-Off Champions
1946-1947*	Washington Capitols	Chicago Stags	Philadelphia Warriors
1947-1948*	Philadelphia Warriors	St. Louis Bombers	Baltimore Bullets
1948-1949*	Washington Capitols	Rochester Royals	Minneapolis Lakers
1949-1950†			Minneapolis Lakers
1950-1951	Philadelphia Warriors	Minneapolis Lakers	Rochester Royals
1951-1952	Syracuse Nationals	Rochester Royals	Minneapolis Lakers
1952-1953	New York Knickerbockers	Minneapolis Lakers	Minneapolis Lakers
1953-1954	New York Knickerbockers	Minneapolis Lakers	Minneapolis Lakers
1954-1955	Syracuse Nationals	Fort Wayne Pistons	Syracuse Nationals
1955-1956	Philadelphia Warriors	Fort Wayne Pistons	Philadelphia Warriors
1956-1957	Boston Celtics	St. Louis Hawks	Boston Celtics
1957-1958	Boston Celtics	St. Louis Hawks	St. Louis Hawks
1958-1959	Boston Celtics	St. Louis Hawks	Boston Celtics
1959-1960	Boston Celtics	St. Louis Hawks	Boston Celtics
1960-1961	Boston Celtics	St. Louis Hawks	Boston Celtics
1961-1962	Boston Celtics	Los Angeles Lakers	Boston Celtics
1962-1963	Boston Celtics	Los Angeles Lakers	Boston Celtics
1963-1964	Boston Celtics	San Francisco Warriors	Boston Celtics
1964-1965	Boston Celtics	Los Angeles Lakers	Boston Celtics
1965-1966	Philadelphia 76ers	Los Angeles Lakers	Boston Celtics
1966-1967	Philadelphia 76ers	San Francisco Warriors	Philadelphia 76ers
1967-1968	Philadelphia 76ers	St. Louis Hawks	Boston Celtics
1968-1969	Baltimore Bullets	Los Angeles Lakers	Boston Celtics
1969-1970	New York Knickerbockers	Atlanta Hawks	New York Knickerbockers
	Eastern Conference	**Western Conference**	**Play-Off Champions**
1970-1971	Baltimore Bullets	Milwaukee Bucks	Milwaukee Bucks
1971-1972	New York Knickerbockers	Los Angeles Lakers	Los Angeles Lakers
1972-1973	New York Knickerbockers	Los Angeles Lakers	New York Knickerbockers
1973-1974	Boston Celtics	Milwaukee Bucks	Boston Celtics
1974-1975	Washington Bullets	Golden State Warriors	Golden State Warriors
1975-1976	Boston Celtics	Phoenix Suns	Boston Celtics
1976-1977	Philadelphia 76ers	Portland Trail Blazers	Portland Trail Blazers
1977-1978	Washington Bullets	Seattle SuperSonics	Washington Bullets
1978-1979	Washington Bullets	Seattle SuperSonics	Seattle SuperSonics
1979-1980	Philadelphia 76ers	Los Angeles Lakers	Los Angeles Lakers
1980-1981	Boston Celtics	Houston Rockets	Boston Celtics
1981-1982	Philadelphia 76ers	Los Angeles Lakers	Los Angeles Lakers
1982-1983	Philadelphia 76ers	Los Angeles Lakers	Philadelphia 76ers
1983-1984	Boston Celtics	Los Angeles Lakers	Boston Celtics

*Basketball Association of America champions.
†The NBA had three division champions: Eastern Division, Syracuse Nationals; Central Division, Minneapolis Lakers; Western Division, Indianapolis Olympians.

BASKETBALL

The Harlem Globetrotters, an all-black professional team, was founded in 1927. The team has entertained fans throughout the world with its blend of comedy and basketball skills.

ics, becoming the first black player in the NBA. In a short time, black players were on teams throughout the NBA. Most of the outstanding NBA players of the 1950's and 1960's were such former black college stars as Bill Russell, Wilt Chamberlain, Oscar Robertson, and Elgin Baylor. Russell led the Boston Celtics to 11 NBA titles from 1957 to 1969.

In 1967, a professional league called the American Basketball Association was formed. It merged with the NBA in 1976, forming a 22-team league.

Basketball Today. During the 1970's and 1980's college basketball greatly increased in popularity. Much of this popularity came from the frequent regional and national televising of games. The NCAA Division I men's championship tournament now ranks among the major sports events of the year.

Professional basketball is suffering from economic problems. These problems have been largely caused by high player salaries and low attendance in some cities. However, large crowds still attend many NBA games to watch such stars as Julius Erving and Moses Malone of the Philadelphia 76ers, Larry Bird of the Boston Celtics,

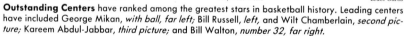

Outstanding Centers have ranked among the greatest stars in basketball history. Leading centers have included George Mikan, *with ball, far left;* Bill Russell, *left,* and Wilt Chamberlain, *second picture;* Kareem Abdul-Jabbar, *third picture;* and Bill Walton, *number 32, far right.*

Great NBA Scorers included Elgin Baylor, *in dark uniform, far left;* John Havlicek, *with ball, left;* Jerry West, *in dark uniform, third picture;* and Oscar Robertson, *far right.* All four also gained recognition for their all-around team play during their professional careers.

AP/Wide World

AP/Wide World

Stars of the 1980's in the National Basketball Association include forwards Julius Erving, *in dark uniform,* and Larry Bird, *number 33, left;* and center Moses Malone, *with ball, right.*

Earvin (Magic) Johnson of the Los Angeles Lakers, and Ralph Sampson of the Houston Rockets.

There has been an enormous increase in the popularity of women's basketball at both the high school and college levels. Women's basketball became an Olympic sport in 1976. The NCAA held its first national tournament for women's teams in 1982.   JOHN R. THOMPSON, JR.

Modern Women's Basketball gained international popularity in the 1970's and became an Olympic sport in 1976. During the 1976 games, the United States played Canada, *above.*

Canapress

Outline

I. How to Play Basketball
    A. The Court
    B. Equipment
    C. The Players
    D. The Coach
    E. The Officials
    F. Playing Time
    G. Scoring
    H. Playing the Game
    I. Offensive Strategies
    J. Defensive Strategies
    K. Fouls
    L. Violations
II. Basketball Competition
    A. High School Competition
    B. College Competition
    C. Professional Competition
    D. International Competition
III. The History of Basketball

Questions

What contributions did Hank Luisetti and Joe Fulks make to basketball?

How many high schools sponsor girls' basketball teams?

What is meant by the *one-and-one?* The *penalty situation?*

How long is a high school game? A college game? A professional game?

How does the NCAA determine its annual champions?

Who invented basketball? When was the first game played?

What is a *technical foul?*

How long is a basketball court?

What are the duties of the scorekeepers?

What is the difference between a *man-to-man defense* and a *zone defense?*

Additional Resources

Level I

CLARK, STEVE. *Illustrated Basketball Dictionary for Young People.* Harvey, 1977.

DEVANEY, JOHN. *The Story of Basketball.* Random House, 1976.

ISAACS, NEIL D., and MOTTA, DICK. *Sports Illustrated Basketball.* Harper, 1981.

SULLIVAN, GEORGE. *Better Basketball for Boys.* Rev. ed. Dodd, 1980.

YOUNG, FAYE, and COFFEY, WAYNE. *Winning Basketball for Girls.* Facts on File, 1984.

Level II

DEVENZIO, DICK. *Stuff! Good Players Should Know.* Fool Court Press, 1983.

HOENIG, GARY, and SHAUGHNESSY, DAN. *Courtside: The Fan's Guide to Pro Basketball.* Vanderbilt Press, 1984.

HOLLANDER, ZANDER, ed. *The Modern Encyclopedia of Basketball.* 2nd ed. Doubleday, 1979.

ISAACS, NEIL D. *All the Moves: A History of College Basketball.* Rev. ed. Harper, 1984.

NCAA Basketball. National Collegiate Athletic Assn. Published annually.

Official NBA Guide. The Sporting News. An annual publication.

STERN, ROBERT. *They Were Number One: A History of the NCAA Basketball Tournament.* Leisure Press, 1983.

WIELGUS, CHUCK, JR., and WOLFF, ALEXANDER. *The In-Your-Face Basketball Book.* Everest House, 1980.

The Contribution of the Negro to American Democracy (1943), a tempera painting on plaster by Charles White; courtesy of Hampton Institute, Hampton, Va.

The History of Black Americans is largely the story of their struggle for equality and freedom. This mural of noted blacks includes slave leader Nat Turner (with torch), Revolutionary War hero Peter Salem (below Turner), bearded abolitionist Frederick Douglass, agricultural researcher George Washington Carver (with test tube), and singer Marian Anderson, *far right center.*

BLACK AMERICANS

BLACK AMERICANS are Americans mostly or partly of African descent. More than 28 million blacks live in the United States. They account for 12 per cent of the nation's total population and make up the largest minority group. About half of all black Americans live in the Southern States. Most of the rest live in large cities in the East, Midwest, and West.

Black Americans belong to the African geographical race. This race consists of dark-skinned peoples who live—or whose ancestors lived—south of the Sahara, the vast desert that stretches across northern Africa. In addition to dark brown skin, most members of this race have brown eyes, dark woolly or curly hair, and thick lips. For a discussion of how races are classified, see the WORLD BOOK article RACES, HUMAN. The article also tells how races developed and changed.

Most black Americans have used five terms to refer to themselves. The terms *Negro* (which means *black* in Spanish and Portuguese) and *colored* were commonly

Alton Hornsby, Jr., the contributor of this article, is Chairman of the Department of History at Morehouse College and editor of The Journal of Negro History.

used until the mid-1960's. Since then, most black Americans have chosen to express deep pride in their color or origin by calling themselves *blacks, Afro-Americans,* or *African-Americans.*

The majority of American blacks trace their origin to an area in western Africa that was controlled by three great and wealthy black empires from about the A.D. 300's to the late 1500's. These empires—Ghana, Mali, and Songhai—thrived on trade and developed efficient governments. During the early 1500's, European nations began a slave trade in which blacks from western Africa were brought to European colonies in the Americas. For about the next 300 years, millions of enslaved black Africans were shipped across the Atlantic Ocean to what are now the United States and Latin America.

The history of black Americans is largely the story of their struggle for freedom and equality. From the 1600's until the Civil War (1861-1865), most black Americans worked as slaves throughout the South. They did much to help Southern agriculture expand. At the same time, free blacks helped develop industry in the North. After 1865, when slavery was finally abolished in the nation, black Americans briefly gained their civil rights during a period called Reconstruction. But after Reconstruction, they again lost those rights and suffered from widespread segregation and poverty. The determined efforts of black Americans to achieve equality and justice led to the start of a strong civil rights movement in the 1950's.

The lives of black Americans have improved since the 1950's. However, many of them still suffer from segregation and poverty, discrimination in jobs and housing, and other problems. At the same time, more and more blacks are making important contributions in all areas of American life.

This article describes the African background of black Americans and traces their history from their arrival in North America to the present. The section at the end of the article includes a listing of the many related articles in WORLD BOOK.

The African Background

The Cultural Heritage. The ancestors of most American blacks came from an area of Africa known as the Western Sudan. This area was about as large as the United States, not including Hawaii and Alaska. It extended from the Atlantic Ocean in the west to Lake Chad in the east and from the Sahara in the north to the Gulf of Guinea in the south.

From about the A.D. 300's to 1591, three highly developed black empires, in turn, controlled all or most of the Western Sudan. These empires were Ghana, Mali, and Songhai. Their economy was based on farming, on mining gold, and on trade with the Arabs of northern Africa.

Ghana ruled much of the Western Sudan from the 300's to the mid-1000's. The Ghanaians became the first people in western Africa to smelt iron ore. They made

arrows, swords, and other weapons of iron, which helped them conquer nearby nations.

In 1235, the Malinke people of Mali began to develop the second great black African empire of the Western Sudan. By 1240, they controlled all Ghana. The Mali Empire's most famous ruler was Mansa Musa, who reigned from 1312 to about 1337. Mansa Musa encouraged the practice of Islam, the religion of the Muslims. Under his rule, Mali reached its height of wealth, political power, and cultural achievement.

Beginning in the 1400's, the Songhai Empire gained control of most of northwestern Africa south of the Sahara, including much of Mali. Under Askia Muhammad, who ruled Songhai from 1493 to 1528, the empire had a well-organized central government and excellent universities in such cities as Timbuktu and Jenne. Like Mansa Musa, Askia encouraged his people to practice the Islamic faith. Invaders from Morocco conquered Songhai in 1591.

Some ancestors of black Americans lived in smaller nations in the Western Sudan. These nations included Oyo, Benin, Dahomey, and Ashanti. Their economies also depended on farming, trade, and gold mining. For more details on the major black African empires, see GHANA EMPIRE; MALI EMPIRE; SONGHAI EMPIRE.

Beginning of the Slave Trade. Africans had practiced slavery since ancient times. In most cases, the

The North American Slave Trade

The map at the right shows the route ships used to carry slaves from western Africa to North America. On the map below, the red type indicates the groups from which most slaves were taken. The groups that captured the most Africans for European and American slave traders are shown in bold black type.

WORLD BOOK maps

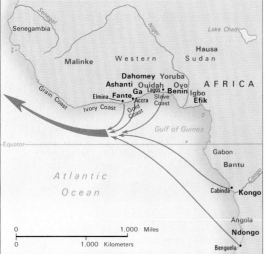

Granger Collection

Africans Marched Captured Enemies, *above,* to coastal slave markets. The cutaway drawing below shows the *tight packing* system used on many ships to deliver the slaves to North America.

Schomburg Collection, New York Public Library

slaves had been captured in warfare and sold to Arab traders of northern Africa. Portugal and Spain became increasingly involved in the African slave trade during the early 1500's, after they had established colonies in the Americas. Portugal acquired African slaves to work on sugar plantations that its colonists developed in Brazil. Spain used slaves on its sugar plantations in the West Indies. During the early 1600's, the Netherlands, France, and England also began to use African slaves in their American colonies.

The Europeans obtained slaves from black Africans who continued to sell their war captives or trade them for rum, cloth, and other items, especially guns. The Africans needed the guns for use in their constant warfare with neighboring peoples.

The slave trade took several triangular routes. Over one route, ships from Europe transported manufactured goods to the west coast of Africa. There, traders exchanged the goods for slaves. Next, the slaves were carried across the Atlantic Ocean to the West Indies and sold for huge profits. This part of the route was called the *Middle Passage*. The traders used much of their earnings to buy sugar, coffee, and tobacco in the West Indies. The ships then took these products to Europe.

On another triangular route, ships from the New England Colonies carried rum and other products to Africa, where they were exchanged for slaves. The ships then transported the slaves to the West Indies to be sold. The slave traders used some of their profits to buy sugar and molasses, which they took back to New England and sold to rum producers.

The slave trade was conducted for profit. The captains of slave ships therefore tried to deliver as many healthy slaves for as little cost as possible. Some captains used a system called *loose packing* to deliver slaves. Under that system, captains transported fewer slaves than their ships could carry in the hope of reducing sickness and death among them. Other captains preferred *tight packing*. They believed that many blacks would die on the voyages anyway and so carried as many slaves as their ships could hold.

Most slave ship voyages across the Atlantic took several months. The slaves were chained below deck all day and all night except for brief periods of exercise. Their crowded conditions led to the chief horrors of the Middle Passage—filth, stench, disease, and death.

The Atlantic slave trade operated from the 1500's to the 1800's. No one knows how many Africans were enslaved during this period. The most reliable estimates range from 10 million to 20 million blacks. Of this total, North America received from 400,000 to 1,200,000.

The Years of Slavery

Some scholars believe that the first blacks in America came with the expeditions led by Christopher Columbus, starting in 1492. Black slaves traveled to North and South America with French, Portuguese, and Spanish explorers throughout the 1500's.

The best-known black to take part in the early explorations of North America was a slave named Estevanico. In 1539, he crossed what are now Arizona and New Mexico on an expedition sent by Antonio de Mendoza, ruler of Spain's colony in America.

Colonial Times. The first blacks in the American Colonies were brought in, like many lower-class whites, as *indentured servants*. Most indentured servants had a contract to work without wages for a master for four to seven years, after which they became free. Blacks brought in as slaves, however, had no right to eventual freedom. The first black indentured servants arrived in Jamestown in the colony of Virginia in 1619. They had been captured in Africa and were sold at auction in Jamestown. After completing their service, some black indentured servants bought property. But racial prejudice among white colonists forced most free blacks to remain in the lowest level of colonial society.

The first black African slaves in the American Colonies also arrived during the early 1600's. The slave population increased rapidly during the 1700's as newly established colonies in the South created a great demand for plantation workers.

By 1750, about 200,000 slaves lived in the colonies. The majority lived in the South, where the warm climate and fertile soil encouraged the development of plantations that grew rice, tobacco, sugar cane, and later cotton. Most plantation slaves worked in the fields. The

Granger Collection

Slave Trading became increasingly profitable throughout the South from the time the first slaves arrived in the early 1600's. Buyers often paid more than $1,000 for a skilled, healthy slave. Many slaves were sold at auctions like this one in Virginia.

Granger Collection

Crispus Attucks, *center,* was a leader of the patriot mob that was fired upon by British troops in the Boston Massacre of 1770. Attucks and many other free blacks who lived in the North opposed British rule in the American Colonies.

others were craftworkers, messengers, and servants.

Only 12 per cent of slaveowners operated plantations that had 20 or more slaves. But more than half of all the country's slaves worked on these plantations. Most of the other slaveowners had small farms and only a few slaves each. Under arrangements with their masters, some slaves could hire themselves out to work for other whites on farms or in factories or other city jobs. Such arrangements brought income to both the slaves and the masters.

The cooler climate and rocky soil of the Northern and Middle colonies made it hard for most farmers there to earn large profits. Many slaves in those colonies worked as skilled and unskilled laborers in factories, homes, and shipyards and on fishing and trading ships.

During the mid-1600's, the colonies began to pass laws called *slave codes*. In general, these codes prohibited slaves from owning weapons, receiving an education, meeting one another or moving about without the permission of their masters, and testifying against white people in court. Slaves received harsher punishments for some crimes than white people. A master usually received less punishment for killing a slave than for killing a free person for the same reason. Slaves on small farms probably had more freedom than plantation slaves, and slaves in urban areas had fewer restrictions in many cases than slaves in rural areas.

By 1770, there may have been 40,000 or more free blacks in the American Colonies. They included runaway slaves, descendants of early indentured servants, and black immigrants from the West Indies. Many free blacks opposed British rule. One of the best-known black American patriots was Crispus Attucks, who died in the Boston Massacre of 1770 while mocking the presence of British soldiers.

During the Revolutionary War in America (1775-1783), most blacks probably favored the British. They believed that a British victory would offer them their earliest or best chance for freedom. But about 5,000 blacks fought on the side of the colonists. Most of them were free blacks or slaves from the Northern and Middle colonies. Black heroes of the war included Peter Salem and Salem Poor of Massachusetts, who distinguished themselves in the Battle of Bunker Hill in 1775.

The Growth of Slavery. By the early 1800's, more than 700,000 slaves lived in the South. They accounted for about a third of the region's people. Slaves outnumbered whites in South Carolina and made up over half the population in both Maryland and Virginia.

Slavery began to develop even deeper roots in the South after Eli Whitney of Massachusetts invented the cotton gin in 1793. This machine removed the seeds from cotton as fast as 50 people working by hand and probably contributed more to the growth of slavery than any other development. The cotton gin enabled farmers to meet the rapidly rising demand for cotton. As a result, the Southern cotton industry expanded, and cotton became the chief crop in the region. The planters needed more and more workers to pick and bale the cotton, which led to large increases in the slave population. The thriving sugar cane plantations of Louisiana also used many slaves during the first half of the 1800's. By 1860, about 4 million slaves lived in the South.

Numerous slaves protested against their condition. They used such day-to-day forms of rebellion as destroying property, running away, pretending illness, and disobeying orders. Major slave protests included armed revolts and mutinies. The most famous of about 200 such revolts was led by Nat Turner, a slave and preacher. The revolt broke out in 1831 in Southampton County in Virginia. The rebels killed about 60 white people before being captured. The best-known slave mutiny occurred in 1839 aboard the *Amistad*, off the coast of Cuba. A group of Africans, led by Cinqué, brought the vessel to Long Island in New York. The slaves were given their freedom soon afterward.

Slaves received beatings or other physical punishment for refusing to work, attempting to run away, or participating in plots or rebellions against their owners. Some slaves were executed for rebelling.

Free Blacks. The Revolutionary War helped lead to new attitudes about slavery, especially among whites in the North. The war inspired a spirit of liberty and an appreciation for the service of the black soldiers. Partly for this reason, some Northern legislatures adopted laws during the late 1700's that provided for the immediate

The Production of Cotton increased rapidly in the South after the invention of the cotton gin, *left,* in 1793. This machine removed the seeds from cotton as fast as 50 people working by hand and helped planters meet the growing demand for cotton. More and more workers were needed on cotton plantations, *right,* which led to a tremendous growth in the slave population.

or gradual end of slavery. Another reason for such laws was simply that slaves had no essential role in the main economic activities of the North.

The Census of 1790 revealed that the nation had about 59,000 free blacks, including about 27,000 in the North. By the early 1800's, most Northern states had taken steps to end slavery. Besides former slaves freed by law, free blacks included those who had been freed by their masters, who had bought their freedom, or who had been born of free parents.

After the Revolutionary War, numerous free blacks found jobs in tobacco plants, textile mills, and other factories. Some worked in shipyards, on ships, and later in railroad construction. Many free blacks became skilled in carpentry and other trades. Some became merchants and editors. The best-known editors were Samuel Cornish and John Russwurm, who helped start the first black newspaper, *Freedom's Journal*, in 1827.

Most whites treated free blacks as inferiors. Many hotels, restaurants, theaters, and other public places barred them. Few states gave free blacks the right to vote. The children of most free blacks had to attend separate schools. Some colleges and universities, such as Bowdoin and Oberlin, admitted black students. But the limited number of admissions led to the opening of black colleges, including Lincoln University in Pennsylvania in 1854 and Wilberforce University in Ohio in 1856.

In both the North and the South, churches either banned blacks or required them to sit apart from white people. As a result, some blacks set up their own churches. In 1816, Richard Allen, a black Philadelphia minister, helped set up the African Methodist Episcopal Church, the first black denomination in the country.

The rising number of free blacks alarmed many whites and led to further restrictions on their activities. In parts of New England, free blacks could not visit any town without a pass. They also needed permission to entertain slaves in their homes. In the South, free blacks could be enslaved if caught without proof that they were free. Fears that free blacks would lead slave revolts encouraged almost all states to pass laws severely limiting the right of free blacks to own weapons.

Increasing concern over the large number of free blacks led to the founding of the American Colonization Society in 1817. The society was sponsored by well-known supporters of slavery, including U.S. Representatives John C. Calhoun of South Carolina and Henry Clay of Kentucky. Their plan was to lessen "the race problem" by transporting free blacks on a voluntary basis to Africa. In 1822, the society established the black American colony of Liberia on the continent's west coast. In 1847, Liberia became the first self-governing black republic in Africa. Although they suffered from discrimination, most free blacks felt that the United States was their home. As a result, only about 12,000 of them had volunteered to settle in Liberia by 1850.

In spite of their inferior position, a number of free blacks won wide recognition during the late 1700's and early 1800's. For example, Jupiter Hammon and Phillis Wheatley gained fame for their poetry. Newport Gardner distinguished himself in music. Benjamin Banneker, a mathematician, published outstanding almanacs. Notable black ministers included Absalom Jones in the

North and George Liele and Andrew Bryan in the South. Paul Cuffe and James Forten acquired great wealth in business.

By 1860, the nation had about 490,000 free blacks. But most of them faced such severe discrimination that they were little better off than the slaves.

The Antislavery Movement. Many white Americans, particularly Northerners, felt that slavery was wicked and violated the ideals of democratic government. However, plantation owners and other supporters of slavery regarded it as natural to the Southern way of life. They also argued that Southern culture introduced the slaves to Christianity and helped them become "civilized." Most white Southerners held such beliefs by 1860, though less than 5 per cent of them owned slaves and only about half the slaveowners had more than five slaves. In addition, Southern farmers insisted that they could not make money growing cotton without cheap slave labor.

The Southern States hoped to expand slavery as new states were admitted to the Union. However, the Northern States feared they would lose power in Congress permanently if more states that permitted slavery were admitted. The North and the South thereby became increasingly divided over the spread of slavery.

The slavery issue created heated debate in Congress after the Territory of Missouri applied for statehood in 1818. At the time, there were 11 *slave states*, in which slavery was allowed, and 11 *free states*, in which it was prohibited. Most Missourians supported slavery, but many Northern members of Congress did not want Missouri to become a slave state. In 1820, Congress reached a settlement known as the Missouri Compromise. This measure admitted Missouri as a slave state, but it also called for Maine to enter the Union as a free state. Congress thus preserved the balance between free and slave states at 12 each.

New, aggressive opponents of slavery began to spring up in the North during the 1830's. Their leaders included William Lloyd Garrison, Lucretia Mott, Lewis Tappan, and Theodore Dwight Weld. During the 1830's and 1840's, these white abolitionists were joined by many free blacks, including such former slaves as Frederick Douglass, Henry Highland Garnet, Harriet Tubman, and Sojourner Truth.

Most of the abolitionist leaders attacked slavery in writings and public speeches. Garrison began to publish an antislavery newspaper, *The Liberator*, in 1831. Douglass, the most influential black leader of the time, started an abolitionist newspaper called the *North Star* in 1847. Tubman and many other abolitionists helped Southern slaves escape to the free states and Canada. Tubman returned to the South 19 times and personally led about 300 slaves to freedom. She and others used a network of routes and housing to assist the fleeing blacks. This network became known as the *underground railroad*.

The Deepening Division over Slavery. After 1848, Congress had to deal with the question of whether to permit slavery in the territories that the United States gained from Mexico as a result of the Mexican War (1846-1848). The territories covered what are now California, Nevada, Utah, and parts of four other states. Following angry debates among the members of Congress, Senators Henry Clay of Kentucky and Daniel Webster of Massachusetts helped work out a series of measures that became known as the Compromise of 1850. The Compromise allowed slavery to continue but prohibited the slave trade in Washington, D.C. A key measure in the Compromise admitted California to the Union as a free state. Another agreement gave the residents in the other newly acquired areas the right to decide for themselves whether to allow slavery. The Compromise included a federal fugitive slave law that was designed to help slaveowners get back runaway slaves.

The Compromise of 1850 briefly ended the heated arguments in Congress over the slavery issue. However, the abolitionist movement and the hostility between the North and the South continued. The publication of Harriet Beecher Stowe's antislavery novel *Uncle Tom's Cabin* (1851-1852) greatly increased the tensions between Northerners and Southerners. In addition, attempts by Northerners to stop enforcement of the fugitive slave law further angered Southerners.

The quarrel over slavery flared again in Congress in 1854, when it passed the Kansas-Nebraska Act. This law created two federal territories, Kansas and Nebraska, and provided that the people of each territory could decide whether to permit slavery. Most Nebraskans opposed slavery. However, bitter, bloody conflicts broke out between supporters and opponents of slavery in Kansas. In 1856, for example, the militant abolitionist John Brown led a raid against supporters of slavery in a small settlement on Pottawatomie Creek in Kansas. Brown's group killed five men and focused the nation's attention on the conflict in the territory, which became known as "Bleeding Kansas." In the end, Kansas joined the Union as a free state in 1861.

Supporters of slavery won a major victory in 1857, when the U.S. Supreme Court issued its ruling in the case of *Dred Scott v. Sandford*. In the Dred Scott Decision, the court denied the claim of Scott, a slave, that his residence in a free state and territory for a time made him free. The court also declared that no black—free or slave—could be a U.S. citizen. In addition, it stated that Congress had no power to ban the spread of slavery.

Tension in the South increased again in 1859, when John Brown led another abolitionist group in seizing the United States arsenal at Harpers Ferry in Virginia (now West Virginia). Federal troops quickly captured Brown,

and he was executed later that year. But his raid helped convince many Southerners that the slavery issue would lead to fighting between the North and the South.

The End of Slavery

Slavery became a major issue in the U.S. presidential election of 1860. Many Democrats in the North opposed the spread of slavery, but Democrats in the South favored it. Each group nominated its own candidate for President, thereby splitting their party. Most Republicans opposed the expansion of slavery. They chose Abraham Lincoln of Illinois as their presidential candidate. In November 1860, he was elected President.

The Civil War. Southerners feared that Lincoln would limit or end slavery. On Dec. 20, 1860, South Carolina *seceded* (withdrew) from the Union. Early in 1861, six other Southern states seceded. The seceded states took the name Confederate States of America. On April 12, 1861, Confederate troops attacked Fort Sumter, a U.S. military base in South Carolina, and the Civil War began. Four more slave states joined the Confederacy soon afterward. Four other slave states—Missouri, Kentucky, Maryland, and Delaware—remained loyal to the Union.

At the start of the Civil War, Lincoln's chief concern was to preserve the Union, not to end slavery. He therefore refused requests of blacks to join the Union Army. He felt that their participation in the war could lead more slave states to secede. Lincoln also knew that many Northerners were hostile toward blacks and so might oppose the use of black troops.

A number of developments gradually persuaded Lincoln to make the war a fight against slavery. For example, some Union military commanders, without the President's consent, had freed the slaves in areas they had conquered. Furthermore, abolitionists and black leaders urged that the war be fought to end slavery, and they demanded the use of black troops. Most importantly, the war was going badly for the Union. By fighting against slavery, Lincoln hoped to strengthen the war effort in the North and weaken it in the South.

In March 1862, Lincoln gave Congress a plan for the

UPI/Bettmann Archive

Frederick Douglass, *right,* was the most influential black leader in the United States during much of the 1800's. He started an abolitionist newspaper, the *North Star,* in 1847 and advised government leaders on the problems of free blacks in the North.

Schomburg Collection, New York Public Library

Bloody Conflicts broke out during the 1850's between supporters and opponents of a proposal to allow slavery in the Territory of Kansas. Because of shootings like this one, which occurred in 1858, the territory became known as "Bleeding Kansas."

BLACK AMERICANS

gradual freedom of slaves. The plan included payment for the slaveowners. In April, the President approved legislation that abolished slavery in the District of Columbia and provided funds for any of the freed slaves who wished to move to Haiti or Liberia. In June, Lincoln signed into law a bill that abolished slavery in all federal territories.

By July 1862, Lincoln was ready to accept blacks in the Union Army. In September, he issued a preliminary order to *emancipate* (free) the slaves. It declared that all slaves in areas or states in rebellion against the United States on Jan. 1, 1863, would be forever free. The order excluded areas still loyal to the Union, meaning that they might retain slaves. The order had no immediate effect in the Southern-controlled areas, but it meant that each Union victory brought the end of slavery another step closer. The final order was issued on Jan. 1, 1863, as the Emancipation Proclamation. Black Americans referred to that day as the Day of Jubilee. Bells rang from the spires of most Northern black churches to celebrate the day.

More than 200,000 blacks fought on the side of the Union. They were discriminated against in pay, assignments, and rank. Nevertheless, many of them contributed greatly to the war effort. Robert Smalls of South Carolina, a harbor pilot, was one of the first black heroes. In 1862, he sailed a Confederate ship, the *Planter,* out of Charleston Harbor and turned it over to the Union. Smalls then joined the Union Navy.

In 1863, black regiments played an important role in the attack on Port Hudson, La. The fall of Port Hudson helped the Union gain control of the Mississippi River. Altogether, 24 blacks won the Medal of Honor, the nation's highest military award, for heroism during the Civil War.

The Confederate States did not decide to use blacks as soldiers until 1865, the last year of the war. About 40,000 black troops—nearly all of them Union troops—died during the war. In April 1865, the main Southern army surrendered. In December 1865, the adoption of the 13th Amendment to the U.S. Constitution officially ended slavery throughout the nation.

The First Years of Freedom. The period of rebuilding that followed the Civil War became known as Reconstruction. A major concern during Reconstruction was the condition of the approximately 4 million *freedmen* (freed slaves). Most of them had no homes, were desperately poor, and could not read and write.

To help the freed slaves and homeless whites, Congress established the Bureau of Refugees, Freedmen, and Abandoned Lands. The agency, better known as the Freedmen's Bureau, operated from 1865 until 1872. It issued food and supplies to blacks; set up more than 100 hospitals; resettled more than 30,000 people; and founded over 4,300 schools, which enrolled about 200,000 students. Some of the schools developed into outstanding black institutions, such as Atlanta University, Fisk University, Hampton Institute, and Howard University.

In spite of its achievements, the Freedmen's Bureau did not solve the serious economic problems of black Americans. Most of them continued to live in poverty. They also suffered from racist threats and violence and from laws restricting their civil rights. All these problems cast a deep shadow over their new freedom.

The legal restrictions on black civil rights arose in 1865 and 1866, when many Southern state governments passed laws that became known as the *black codes.* These laws were like the earlier slave codes. Some black codes prohibited blacks from owning land. Other codes established a nightly curfew for blacks. A number of codes permitted states to jail blacks for being jobless.

The black codes shocked a powerful group of Northern congressmen called Radical Republicans. These senators and representatives won congressional approval of the Civil Rights Act of 1866. The act gave blacks the rights and privileges of full citizenship. The 14th Amendment to the Constitution, adopted in 1868, further guaranteed the citizenship of blacks. However, most Southern whites resented the new status of blacks. The whites simply could not accept the idea of former slaves voting and holding office. As a result, attempts by Southern blacks to vote, run for public office, or enjoy other civil rights were met by increasing violence from whites in the South. In 1865 and 1866, about 5,000 Southern blacks were murdered. Forty-six blacks were

Harriet Tubman, *left,* was the most famous leader of the *underground railroad,* which helped slaves flee to freedom.

The Emancipation Proclamation, issued on Jan. 1, 1863, freed the slaves in Confederate areas. Advancing Union troops told slaves they were free.

Black American Troops made important contributions to the Union victory in the Civil War. Over 200,000 blacks served in segregated Northern units, such as the 2nd U.S. Colored Artillery, *above.*

killed when their schools and churches were burned in Memphis, Tenn., in May 1866. In July, 34 blacks were killed during a race riot in New Orleans.

In some instances, law enforcement officers encouraged or participated in assaults on blacks. But lawless groups carried out most of the attacks. One of the largest groups was the Ku Klux Klan. It was organized in 1865 or 1866 in Pulaski, Tenn. Bands of hooded Klansmen rode at night and beat and murdered many blacks and their white sympathizers. The Klan did much to deny blacks their civil and human rights throughout Reconstruction.

The federal government tried to maintain the rights of blacks. In 1870 and 1871, Congress passed laws authorizing the use of federal troops to enforce the voting rights of blacks. These laws were known as the Enforcement Acts or the Ku Klux Klan Acts. In addition, President Ulysses S. Grant signed a proclamation demanding respect for the civil rights of all Americans.

Temporary Gains. The policies of the Radical Republicans enabled blacks to participate widely in the nation's political system for the first time. Congress provided for black men to become voters in the South and called for constitutional conventions to be held in the defeated states. Many blacks attended the conventions held in 1867 and 1868. They helped rewrite Southern state constitutions and other basic laws to replace the black codes drawn up by whites in 1865 and 1866. In the legislatures elected under the new constitutions, however, blacks had a majority of seats only in the lower house in South Carolina. Most of the chief legislative and executive positions were held by Northern white Republicans who had moved to the South and by their white Southern allies. Angry white Southerners called the Northerners *carpetbaggers* to suggest that they could carry everything they owned when they came South in a *carpetbag*, or suitcase.

Blacks who won election to important posts during Reconstruction included U.S. Senators Hiram R. Revels and Blanche K. Bruce of Mississippi and U.S. Representatives Joseph H. Rainey of South Carolina and Jefferson Long of Georgia. Others were Oscar J. Dunn, lieutenant governor of Louisiana; Richard Gleaves and Alonzo J. Ransier, lieutenant governors of South Caro-

lina; P. B. S. Pinchback, acting governor of Louisiana; Francis L. Cardozo, secretary of state and state treasurer of South Carolina; and Jonathan Jasper Wright, an associate justice of the South Carolina Supreme Court. Most of these blacks had college educations.

By the early 1870's, Northern whites had lost interest in the Reconstruction policies of the Radical Republicans. They grew tired of hearing about the continual conflict between Southern blacks and whites. Most Northern whites wanted to put Reconstruction behind them and turn to other things. Federal troops sent to the South to protect blacks were gradually withdrawn. Southern whites who had stayed away from elections to protest black participation started voting again. White Democrats then began to regain control of the state governments from the blacks and their white Republican associates. In 1877, the last federal troops were withdrawn. By the end of that year, the Democrats held power in all the Southern state governments. For more details on the Reconstruction era, see RECONSTRUCTION.

The Growth of Discrimination

During the Late 1800's, blacks in the South increasingly suffered from segregation, the loss of voting rights, and and other forms of discrimination. Their condition reflected beliefs held by most Southern whites that whites were born superior to blacks with respect to intelligence, talents, and moral standards. In 1881, the Tennessee legislature passed a law that required railroad passengers to be separated by race. In 1890, Mississippi adopted several measures that in effect ended voting by blacks. These measures included the passing of reading and writing tests and the payment of a poll tax before a person could vote.

Several decisions of the U.S. Supreme Court enabled the Southern States to establish "legal" segregation practices. In 1883, for example, the court declared the Civil Rights Act of 1875 to be unconstitutional. That act had guaranteed blacks the right to be admitted to any public place. In addition, the Civil Rights Act of 1866 and the 14th Amendment to the Constitution, ratified in 1868, had forbidden the states to deny equal

Schools for Blacks were established by the Freedmen's Bureau during Reconstruction, the period of rebuilding after the Civil War. Some of the schools the bureau opened became outstanding black colleges.

Ku Klux Klan Members were white terrorists who tried to deny blacks their rights after the Civil War.

Black Voters helped the Republican Party win control of all the state governments in the South during the Reconstruction period.

rights to any person. But in 1896, the Supreme Court ruled in the case of *Plessy v. Ferguson* that a Louisiana law requiring the separation of black and white railroad passengers was constitutional. The court argued that segregation in itself did not represent inequality and that separate public facilities could be provided for the races as long as the facilities were equal. This ruling, known as the "separate but equal doctrine," became the basis of Southern race relations. In practice, however, nearly all the separate public facilities provided for blacks and whites in the South were unequal. Black schools, places of recreation, and other facilities were typically far inferior to those of whites.

In spite of the increasing difficulties for black Americans, a number of them won distinction in various fields during the late 1800's. For example, Samuel Lowery started a school for blacks in Huntsville, Ala., in 1875 and won prizes at international fairs for specimens of silk made at the school. In 1883, Jan E. Matzeliger invented a revolutionary shoe-lasting machine that shaped the upper part of a shoe and fastened it to the sole. Jockey Isaac Murphy won the Kentucky Derby in 1884, 1890, and 1891—the first rider to win the Derby three times. Mary Church Terrell helped found the National Association of Colored Women in 1896 and advised government leaders on racial problems. Charles Waddell Chesnutt published *The Conjure Woman* in 1899. He became the first major black American novelist and short-story writer.

During the Early 1900's, discrimination against Southern blacks became even more widespread. By 1907, every Southern state required racial segregation on trains and in churches, schools, hotels, restaurants, theaters, and other public places. The Southern States also adopted an election practice known as the *white primary.* The states banned blacks from voting in the Democratic Party's primary elections by calling them "private affairs." However, the winners of the primary elections were certain of victory in the general elections. Their victories were assured because Republican and independent candidates received little support from whites and rarely ran for office. By 1910, every Southern

state had taken away or begun to take away the right of blacks to vote.

The Ku Klux Klan also attempted to keep blacks from voting through an increased use of threats, beatings, and killings. The Klan and members of similar groups had lynched more than 3,000 blacks during the late 1800's, and they lynched hundreds more throughout the South during the early 1900's.

Blacks had little opportunity to better themselves economically. Some laws prohibited them from owning saloons, teaching, and entering certain other businesses and professions. Large numbers of blacks had to take low-paying jobs as farm hands or servants for white employers. Many other blacks became sharecroppers or tenant farmers. They rented a small plot of land and paid the rent with money earned from the crops. They had to struggle to survive, and many ran up huge debts to their white landlords or the town merchants.

The Rise of New Black Leaders. By the early 1900's, the educator Booker T. Washington had become the most influential black leader in the United States. Washington, a former slave, had been principal of Tuskegee Institute since 1881. He urged blacks to stop demanding political power and social equality and to concentrate, instead, on economic advancement. Washington especially encouraged blacks to practice thrift and to respect hard labor. He asked whites to help blacks gain an education and make a decent living. Washington believed his program would lead to progress for blacks and would keep peace between the races.

Many blacks throughout the United States agreed with Washington's ideas. But many others strongly rejected them. The chief opposition came from W. E. B. Du Bois, a sociologist and historian at Atlanta University. Du Bois's reputation rested on such works as *The Suppression of the African Slave-Trade to the United States of America, 1638-1870* (1896) and *The Souls of Black Folk* (1903).

Du Bois argued that Washington's approach would not achieve economic security for blacks. Instead, Du Bois felt that Washington's acceptance of racial segregation and the rest of his program would strengthen the beliefs that blacks were inferior and could be treated unequally. As evidence for their position, Du Bois and his

Library of Congress

George Washington Carver, *center,* won worldwide fame for agricultural research. He taught at Tuskegee (Ala.) Institute.

Historical Pictures Service

Booker T. Washington, principal of Tuskegee Institute, was the most influential U.S. black leader of the early 1900's.

From *A Pictorial History of the Negro in America,* by Langston Hughes and Milton Meltzer

W. E. B. Du Bois, *second from right,* a sociologist and historian, helped lead the black struggle for equality during the early 1900's. He directed the publications of the NAACP from 1909 until 1934.

supporters pointed to the continuing lynching of blacks and to the passage of additional segregation laws in the South. In 1905, Du Bois and other critics of Washington met in Niagara Falls, Canada, and organized a campaign to protest racial discrimination. Their campaign became known as the Niagara Movement.

Bitter hostility toward blacks erupted into several race riots during the early 1900's. Major riots broke out in Brownsville, Tex., and Atlanta, Ga., in 1906 and in Springfield, Ill., in 1908. The riots alarmed many white Northerners as well as many blacks. In 1909, a number of white Northerners joined some of the blacks in the Niagara Movement to form the National Association for the Advancement of Colored People (NAACP). The NAACP vowed to fight for racial equality. The organization relied mainly on legal action, education, protests, and voter participation to pursue its goals.

The Black Migration to the North. The efforts of new black leaders and of the NAACP did little to end the discrimination, police brutality, and lynchings suffered by Southern blacks during the early 1900's. In addition, Southern farmers had great crop losses because of floods and insect pests. All these problems persuaded many Southern blacks to move to the North.

During World War I (1914-1918), hundreds of thousands of Southern blacks migrated to the North to seek jobs in defense plants and other factories. The National Urban League, founded in New York City in 1910, helped the newcomers adjust to city life. More than 360,000 blacks served in the armed forces during World War I. They were organized into all-black units.

Between 1910 and 1930, about a million Southern blacks moved to the North. Most of them quickly discovered that the North did not offer solutions to their problems. They lacked the skills and education needed for the jobs they sought. Many of them had to become laborers or servants and thus do the same kinds of work they had done in the South. Others could find no work at all. Numerous blacks were forced to live crowded together in cheap, unsanitary, run-down housing. Large all-black slums developed in big cities throughout the North. The segregated housing promoted segregated schooling. Poverty, crime, and despair plagued the black communities, which became known as *ghettos*.

After World War I, race relations grew increasingly tense in the Northern cities. The hostility partly reflected the growing competition for jobs and housing between blacks and whites. In addition, many black veterans, after fighting for democracy, returned home with expectations of justice and equality. The mounting tension helped the Ku Klux Klan recruit thousands of members in the North. In the summer of 1918, 10 people were killed and 60 were injured in racial disturbances in Chester and Philadelphia, Pa. A series of riots erupted in the summer of 1919. A black poet named James Weldon Johnson described this violent period as "the Red Summer." By the end of the year, 25 race riots had broken out across the country. At least 100 people died and many more were injured in the riots.

The Garvey Movement offered new hope for many blacks deeply disturbed by the race riots of 1918 and 1919 and the economic and social injustice they encountered. The movement had begun when Marcus Garvey founded the Universal Negro Improvement Association in Jamaica in 1914. In 1917, Garvey brought the movement to Harlem, a black community in New York City. By the mid-1920's, he had established more than 700 branches of the association in 38 states.

Garvey tried to develop racial pride among blacks. But he doubted that their life in the United States would ever be much improved. As a result, Garvey urged the establishment of a new homeland in Africa for dissatisfied black Americans. His plans collapsed, however, when he was sent to prison in 1925 after having been convicted of using the mails to commit fraud.

The Harlem Renaissance and Other Achievements. The Harlem Renaissance was an exceptional outpouring of black literature chiefly in Harlem during the 1920's. It demonstrated that some blacks had acquired talents within American society which whites as well as blacks could appreciate.

The writers drew their themes from the experiences of blacks in the Northern cities and the rural South. The best-known writers included James Weldon Johnson, Langston Hughes, Nella Larsen, Claude McKay, Countee Cullen, and Jean Toomer.

© 1969 by James Van Der Zee

Marcus Garvey founded the Universal Negro Improvement Association, which worked to create a new homeland in Africa for black Americans. He wore a plumed hat for this parade in 1924.

Schomburg Collection, New York Public Library

Langston Hughes contributed to the Harlem Renaissance, an outpouring of black literary works in the 1920's.

UPI/Bettmann Archive

Duke Ellington, playing the piano in this scene from the movie *Cabin in the Sky* (1943), became one of the greatest jazz musicians.

561

BLACK AMERICANS

Black musicians also gained increasing fame among whites as well as blacks during the early 1920's. A black bandleader named W. C. Handy, who had composed "St. Louis Blues" in 1914, became known as the father of the blues. Jazz grew out of black folk blues and ballads. Two black bandleaders, Louis Armstrong and Duke Ellington, became the country's leading jazz musicians.

Another noted black of the early 1900's was the great agricultural researcher George Washington Carver. Carver created hundreds of products from peanuts, sweet potatoes, and other plants and revolutionized Southern agriculture. Other famous blacks of the early 1900's included labor leader A. Philip Randolph, journalist Ida Wells-Barnett, singer Paul Robeson, dancer Bill Robinson, U.S. Representative Oscar DePriest of Illinois, runner Jesse Owens, and heavyweight boxing champions Jack Johnson and Joe Louis.

The Great Depression. In October 1929, a sudden, sharp drop in the value of stocks in the United States marked the beginning of a worldwide business slump known as the Great Depression. The depression brought hard times for most Americans, but especially for blacks. Blacks became the chief victims of job discrimination. They adopted the slogan "Last Hired and First Fired" to express their situation.

To help ease the poverty in the ghettos, blacks organized cooperative groups. These groups included the Colored Merchants Association in New York City and "Jobs for Negroes" organizations in such places as St. Louis, Chicago, Cleveland, and New York City. The groups bought food and other goods in large volume to get the lowest prices. They boycotted stores that had mostly black customers but few, if any, black workers.

Most black Americans felt that President Herbert Hoover, a Republican, had done little to try to end the depression. In the elections of 1932, some black voters deserted their traditional loyalty to the Republican Party. They no longer saw it as the party of Abraham Lincoln the emancipator but of Hoover and the depression. In 1936, for the first time, most blacks supported the Democratic Party candidate for President, Franklin D. Roosevelt, and helped him win reelection.

Roosevelt called his program the New Deal. It included measures of reform, relief, and recovery and benefited many blacks. A group of blacks advised Roosevelt on the problems of black Americans. This group, called the Black Cabinet, included William H. Hastie and Mary McLeod Bethune. Hastie served as assistant solicitor in the Department of the Interior, as a U.S. district court judge in the Virgin Islands, and as a civilian aide to the secretary of war. Bethune, founder of Bethune-Cookman College, directed the black affairs division of a federal agency called the National Youth Administration. As a result of the New Deal, black Americans developed a strong loyalty to the Democratic Party.

Blacks deeply admired President Roosevelt's wife, Eleanor, for her stand in an incident in 1939 involving the great concert singer Marian Anderson. The Daughters of the American Revolution (DAR), a patriotic organization, denied the singer permission to perform at Constitution Hall in Washington, D.C., because she was black. Eleanor Roosevelt then resigned from the DAR and helped arrange for Anderson to sing, instead, at the Lincoln Memorial on Easter Sunday. More than 75,000 blacks and whites attended the concert.

During the early 1940's, the NAACP began to step up its legal campaign against racial discrimination. The campaign achieved a number of important victories, including several favorable rulings by the U.S. Supreme Court. In 1941, for example, the court ruled that separate facilities for white and black railroad passengers must be significantly equal. In 1944, the court declared that the white primary, which excluded blacks from voting in the only meaningful elections in the South, was unconstitutional.

Besides taking legal action, blacks used new tactics to attack segregation in public places. In 1943, for example, the Congress of Racial Equality (CORE) launched a *sit-in* at a Chicago restaurant. In this protest, blacks sat in places reserved for white people.

World War II (1939-1945) opened up new economic opportunities for black Americans. Like World War I, it led to expanding defense-related industries and encouraged many rural Southern blacks to seek jobs in Northern industrial cities. During the 1940's, about $2\frac{1}{2}$ million

© 1969 by James Van Der Zee

The Great Depression brought hard times for blacks. These children are receiving food from St. Mary's Convent in New York City.

UPI/Bettmann Archive

Marian Anderson, with the help of Eleanor Roosevelt, sang at the Lincoln Memorial in 1939 after the DAR would not let her sing in Constitution Hall.

Signal Corps Photo

During World War II, nearly a million black Americans served in the U.S. armed forces. Most were in such segregated units as the 92nd Division, *above.*

Southern blacks moved to the North. Discrimination again prevented many of them from getting work. In 1941, blacks led by A. Philip Randolph of the Brotherhood of Sleeping Car Porters threatened to march in Washington, D.C., to protest job discrimination. President Roosevelt then issued an executive order forbidding racial discrimination in defense industries.

Nearly a million blacks served in the U.S. armed services during World War II, mostly in segregated units. In 1940, Benjamin O. Davis became the first black brigadier general in the U.S. Army. His son, Benjamin O. Davis, Jr., later became the first black lieutenant general in the Air Force. Desegregation of the armed forces began on a trial basis during the war. It became a permanent policy in 1948 under an executive order issued by President Harry S. Truman.

The Civil Rights Movement

The Beginning. After World War II, three major factors encouraged the beginning of a new movement for civil rights. First, many blacks had served with honor in the war. Black leaders pointed to the records of these veterans to show the injustice of racial discrimination against patriots. Second, more and more blacks in the urban North had made economic gains, increased their education, and registered to vote. Third, the NAACP had attracted many new members and received increased financial support from whites and blacks. It also included a new group of bright young lawyers.

Rulings by the U.S. Supreme Court during the late 1940's and early 1950's brought major victories for blacks. In several decisions between 1948 and 1951, the court ruled that separate higher education facilities for blacks must be equal to those for whites—or the facilities would have to be integrated. Largely because of federal court rulings, laws permitting racial discrimination in housing and recreation also began to be struck down. Many of these rulings came in cases brought by the NAACP. An increasing number of blacks began to move into all-white areas of Northern cities. Many whites then moved out of the cities to the suburbs, and the cities became increasingly black.

The NAACP won a historic victory in 1954. That year, the U.S. Supreme Court ruled in the case of *Brown*

v. Board of Education of Topeka that segregation in the public schools was in itself unequal and thus unconstitutional. The suit had been filed because the school board had not allowed a black student named Linda Brown to attend an all-white school near her home. The court's decision rejected the separate but equal ruling of 1896 and inspired blacks to strike out boldly against other examples of discrimination, particularly in public places.

Rosa Parks, a seamstress in Montgomery, Ala., became a leading symbol of blacks' bold new action to attain their civil rights. In 1955, she was arrested for disobeying a city law that required blacks to sit or stand in the back of buses. Montgomery's blacks protested her arrest by refusing to ride the buses. Their protest lasted 382 days, ending when the city abolished the bus law. The boycott became the first organized mass protest by blacks in Southern history. It also focused national attention on its leader, Martin Luther King, Jr., a Montgomery Baptist minister.

Many Southern communities acted slowly in desegregating their public schools. Governor Orval E. Faubus of Arkansas symbolized Southern resistance. In 1957, he defied a federal court order to integrate Little Rock Central High School. Faubus sent the Arkansas National Guard to prevent black students from entering the school, but President Dwight D. Eisenhower used federal troops to enforce the court order.

The Growing Movement. In 1957, King and other black Southern clergymen formed the Southern Christian Leadership Conference (SCLC) to coordinate the work of civil rights groups. King urged blacks to use only peaceful means to achieve their goals. In 1960, a group of black and white college students organized the Student Nonviolent Coordinating Committee (SNCC) to help in the civil rights movement. They joined with young people from the SCLC, CORE, and the NAACP in staging sit-ins, boycotts, marches, and *freedom rides* (bus rides to test the enforcement of desegregation in interstate transportation). During the early 1960's, the combined efforts of the various civil rights groups ended discrimination in many public places, including restaurants, hotels, theaters, and cemeteries.

UPI/Bettmann Archive

Jackie Robinson of the Brooklyn Dodgers became the first black player in modern major league baseball in 1947. He helped break down racial barriers in professional sports.

Carl Iwasaki,
Life magazine, © Time Inc.

Linda Brown was the focus of a 1954 case in which the U.S. Supreme Court outlawed segregation in public schools.

AP/Wide World

Rosa Parks refused to move to the back of a bus in Montgomery, Ala., in 1955. Her arrest led to a black boycott of the bus system.

BLACK AMERICANS

Numerous cities and towns were unaffected by the civil rights movement because sit-ins and other local protests could not be carried out everywhere at once. Black leaders therefore felt the United States needed a clear, strong federal policy that would erase all remaining discrimination in public places. To attract national attention to that need, King and such other leaders as A. Philip Randolph, Roy Wilkins of the NAACP, James Farmer of CORE, and Whitney M. Young, Jr., of the Urban League organized a march in Washington, D.C., in August 1963. More than 200,000 people, including many whites, took part in what was called the March on Washington.

A high point of the March on Washington was a stirring speech by King. King told the crowd that he had a dream that one day all Americans would enjoy equality and justice. Afterward, President John F. Kennedy proposed strong laws to protect the civil rights of all U.S. citizens. But many people, particularly Southerners, opposed such legislation.

Kennedy was assassinated in November 1963, and Vice President Lyndon B. Johnson became President. Johnson persuaded Congress to pass Kennedy's proposed laws in the Civil Rights Act of 1964. This act prohibited racial discrimination in public places and called for equal opportunity in employment and education. King won the 1964 Nobel Peace Prize for leading nonviolent demonstrations for civil rights.

Black celebrities not directly involved with civil rights groups also contributed to the growing civil rights movement. Author James Baldwin criticized white Americans for their prejudice against blacks. Other noted blacks who promoted civil rights causes included gospel singer Mahalia Jackson, dancer Katherine Dunham, artist Charles White, singer Harry Belafonte, and comedian Dick Gregory.

Political Gains. In the South, many elected officials and police officers refused to enforce court rulings and federal laws that gave blacks equality with whites. In some cases, this opposition extended to the right to vote.

In 1965, a major dispute over voting rights broke out in Selma, Ala. King had gone there in January to assist blacks seeking the right to vote. He was joined by many blacks and whites from throughout the country. In the next two months, at least three people were killed and hundreds were beaten as opposition to the protests increased. But authorities continued to deny blacks their voting rights. Finally, in late March, King led about 30,000 people, guarded by federal troops, on a trip from Selma to the State Capitol in Montgomery. There, before about 50,000 supporters, he demanded that blacks be given the right to vote without unjust restrictions.

Largely as a result of the activities in Selma, Congress passed the Voting Rights Act of 1965. The act banned the use of a poll tax as a requirement to vote and forbade major changes in Southern voting laws without approval of the Department of Justice. In addition, it provided for federal officials to supervise voter registration wherever the right to vote had been unjustly denied. The act gave the vote to thousands of Southern blacks who had never voted and led to a huge increase in the number of black elected officials.

Blacks began to take an increasingly important role in the national government during the mid-1900's. In 1950, U.S. diplomat Ralph J. Bunche became the first black person to win the Nobel Peace Prize. In 1966, Robert C. Weaver became the first black Cabinet member as secretary of housing and urban development. In 1967, Thurgood Marshall became the first black justice on the Supreme Court. In 1969, Shirley Chisholm of New York became the first black woman to serve in the U.S. House of Representatives.

Economic and Social Progress. In 1965, President Johnson declared that it was not enough simply to end *de jure* segregation—that is, separation of the races by law. It was also necessary to eliminate *de facto* segregation—that is, racial separation in fact and based largely on custom. Johnson called for programs of "affirmative action" that would offer blacks equal opportunity with whites in areas where discrimination had a long history and still existed. Many businesses and schools then began to adopt affirmative action programs. These programs, some of which were ordered by the federal government, gave hundreds of thousands of blacks new economic and educational opportunities.

The new economic opportunities enabled many

Larry Obsitnik,
Arkansas Gazette

United States Troops enforced a federal court order to integrate Little Rock Central High School in Arkansas in 1957.

Pictorial Parade

Martin Luther King, Jr., spoke to over 200,000 civil rights demonstrators after a march in Washington, D.C., in 1963. His appeal for racial equality won wide support for the civil rights movement.

United Press Int.

Author James Baldwin became a leading critic of racial discrimination in the United States during the mid-1900's.

black Americans to increase their incomes significantly during the mid-1900's. This development, in turn, greatly expanded the black middle class. Some middle-class blacks moved from crowded city communities to suburbs, and a number of largely black middle-class suburbs formed throughout the nation.

Racial barriers fell in several professional sports and in the arts during the mid-1900's. In 1947, Jackie Robinson of the Brooklyn Dodgers became the first black player in modern major league baseball. He had an outstanding career and became a national hero. Other black sports heroes of the mid-1900's included Willie Mays, Henry Aaron, and Frank Robinson in baseball; Jim Brown and Gale Sayers in football; and Oscar Robertson, Bill Russell, and Wilt Chamberlain in basketball.

In the arts, Gwendolyn Brooks became the first black to win a Pulitzer Prize. She received the award in 1950 for a collection of poems titled *Annie Allen*. In 1955, Marian Anderson became the first black to sing a leading role with the Metropolitan Opera in New York City. In 1958, Alvin Ailey formed one of the nation's finest dance companies. Sidney Poitier became the first black to win an Academy Award for best actor. He won the 1963 award for his work in *Lilies of the Field*.

Unrest in the Cities. Since the start of the civil rights movement, various court decisions, laws, and protests had clearly removed the great legal injustices long suffered by black Americans. But many blacks continued to be discriminated against in jobs, law enforcement, and housing. They saw little change in the long-held racist attitudes of numerous white Americans.

During the 1960's, unrest among ghetto blacks exploded into a series of riots that shook the nation. The first riot occurred in Harlem in the summer of 1964. In August 1965, 34 people died and almost 900 were injured in an outburst in the black ghetto of Watts in Los Angeles. During the next two summers, major riots erupted in numerous cities across the nation.

The race riots puzzled many people because they came at a time when black Americans had made tremendous gains in the campaign for full freedom. In 1967, President Johnson established a commission headed by Governor Otto Kerner of Illinois to study the causes of the outbreaks. In its March 1968 report, the Kerner Commission put much of the blame on racial prejudice of whites. It stated that the average black American was still poorly housed, clothed, paid, and educated and still often suffered from segregation, police abuse, and other forms of discrimination. The commission recommended vast programs to improve ghetto conditions and called for greater changes in the racial attitudes of white Americans.

Less than a month after the Kerner Commission report was issued, race riots broke out in at least 100 black communities across the nation. The rioting followed the assassination of Martin Luther King, Jr., on April 4 in Memphis, Tenn. James Earl Ray, a white drifter, was convicted of the crime and sentenced to 99 years in prison. King's murder helped President Johnson persuade Congress to approve the Civil Rights Act of 1968. This law, also known in part as the Fair Housing Act of 1968, prohibited racial discrimination in the sale and rental of most of the housing in the nation.

Black Militancy. During the height of the civil rights movement, some blacks had charged that it was almost impossible to change white racial attitudes. They saw the civil rights movement as meaningless and urged black Americans to live apart from whites and, in some cases, to use violence to preserve their rights. The main groups promoting these ideas included the Black Muslims, the Black Panthers, and members of the Black Power Movement.

The Black Muslims had been led since 1934 by Elijah Muhammad, who called whites "devils." He also criticized racial integration and urged formation of an all-black nation within the United States. But the most eloquent spokesman for the Black Muslims during the 1950's and 1960's was Malcolm X. Malcolm wanted to unite black people throughout the world. He was assassinated in 1965 after forming a new organization to pursue his goal. Three black men, at least two of whom were Black Muslims, were convicted of the murder.

The Black Panther Party was founded in Oakland, Calif., in 1966. Its two main founders, Huey P. Newton and Bobby Seale, had been inspired by Malcolm X. At

Black Muslim Leaders of the 1950's and the 1960's included Malcolm X, *left,* and Elijah Muhammad, *right.*

AP/Wide World

A Riot in Watts, a black neighborhood in Los Angeles, shocked the nation in 1965. The California National Guard, *above,* helped curb the outburst, which led to 34 deaths and about $40 million in damage.

John Malmin, *Los Angeles Times*

Thurgood Marshall became the first black associate justice of the Supreme Court of the United States in 1967.

United Press Int.

BLACK AMERICANS

first, the party favored violent revolution as the only way to end police actions that many blacks considered brutal and to provide opportunities for blacks in jobs and other areas. The Panthers supported the use of guns for self-defense, and members had frequent clashes with police and others. Later, the party became less militant and worked to achieve full employment for blacks, education related to the needs of black children, and other peaceful goals.

The Black Power Movement developed in 1966 after James H. Meredith, the first black student to attend the University of Mississippi, was shot by a sniper while on a civil rights march. The shooting and other racial violence caused Stokely Carmichael, H. Rap Brown, and other members of the Student Nonviolent Coordinating Committee to doubt the sincerity of white support for black rights.

Carmichael and other blacks called for a campaign to achieve "Black Power." They urged blacks to gain political and economic control of their own communities and to reject the values of whites and form their own standards. They also stressed that "black is beautiful" and suggested that black Americans no longer refer to themselves as *Negroes* or *colored people* but as *blacks*, *African-Americans*, or *Afro-Americans*.

Recent Developments

Achievements. Blacks have made great progress in many areas of American life since 1970. Gains in education have been especially significant. From 1970 to 1980, high school enrollments among blacks rose from about 1,800,000 to 2,200,000. During the same period, college enrollments among blacks increased from about 600,000 to more than a million. Part of the gains in higher education resulted from vigorous affirmative action programs by predominantly white colleges and universities. By 1984, more than half of all blacks 25 years of age or older had completed high school. About 8 per cent had finished college.

The number of black-owned businesses in the United States increased from about 185,000 to 235,000 during the 1970's. However, about 95 per cent of these companies were small, one-owner businesses.

A black studies movement emerged on college campuses throughout the nation during the 1970's and drew increasing attention to the heritage of black Americans. In addition, black musical and theater groups and African-American museums were established in almost every U.S. city with a fairly large black population.

The Voting Rights Act of 1965 led to the removal of restrictions on voting in most places. As a result, black Americans were able to help elect an increasing number of their fellow blacks and sympathetic whites to many public offices. In 1973, Thomas Bradley was elected the first black mayor of Los Angeles. That same year, Maynard H. Jackson was elected the first black mayor of a major Southern city, Atlanta, Ga.

Blacks gained considerable influence in the Administration of Jimmy Carter, a Democrat who served as President of the United States from 1977 to 1981. Under Carter, Andrew Young became the first black U.S. ambassador to the United Nations (UN). Carter named Patricia Roberts Harris secretary of housing and urban development. She thus became the first black woman to hold a Cabinet post.

Since 1970, more and more black Americans have won nationwide recognition in many fields besides politics. These blacks included sports heroes, such as football players O. J. Simpson and Walter Payton; basketball players Kareem Abdul-Jabbar, Earvin (Magic) Johnson, Julius (Doctor J) Erving, and Moses Malone; baseball star Reggie Jackson; and heavyweight boxing champion Muhammad Ali. In 1983, Guion S. Bluford, Jr., became the first black American astronaut to travel in space. Alice Walker won a Pulitzer Prize for her novel *The Color Purple* (1983). Singer Michael Jackson became a superstar in popular music. His album *Thriller* sold over 30 million copies—more than any other album in history—after its release in 1982.

Setbacks. Several developments that began during the late 1970's have lessened the hopes of many black Americans for continued economic and social progress. These developments included confusing court decisions and changing government priorities.

The confusing court decisions included some rulings by the U.S. Supreme Court, which appeared vague in its support of affirmative action. In 1978, the court ruled

From the United Artists release *Lilies of the Field*, © 1963 Rainbow Productions, Inc.

Sidney Poitier was the first black to win an Academy Award for best actor. He was honored for his role in *Lilies of the Field* (1963).

Bill Nation, Sygma

Thomas Bradley became the first black mayor of Los Angeles. He was elected mayor in 1973.

Eric Smith, Gamma/Liaison

Voter Registration became a chief goal among black American leaders during the mid-1980's. The NAACP and other black organizations sponsored many marches like this one to get blacks to register.

in *Regents of the University of California v. Allan Bakke* that racial quotas could not be used in admitting students to colleges and universities. But the next year, the court held that the Civil Rights Act of 1964 did not ban voluntary affirmative action programs even if the programs used a quota system. In 1984, the court ruled that employees hired under affirmative action programs had to be fired before employees with longer service.

Ronald Reagan, a Republican, succeeded Carter as President in 1981. During the early 1980's, blacks accused Reagan of retreating on affirmative action. They charged that the government's settlement of job discrimination complaints fell sharply under his Administration. Black leaders further criticized the President for reducing federal welfare programs, which they said especially hurt needy blacks. Reagan denied any retreat in the enforcement of civil rights laws. He also stated that the welfare cuts did not affect the truly needy.

A recession that struck the United States during the early 1980's contributed to the economic problems of many black Americans. The economy began to recover in 1983. By late 1984, however, the unemployment rate for blacks was still more than double the rate for whites. Furthermore, unemployment among black men aged 18 and 19 exceeded 40 per cent. The incomes of about a third of the nation's blacks fell below the government's official poverty line of about $10,000 for a family of four. In addition, about half of all black children lived in poverty-stricken families.

Black Politics Today. Many black leaders today stress the use of political means to solve the problems of blacks. They urge more blacks to vote and to run for public office. In 1984, blacks held more than 5,000 of the approximately 500,000 elective offices in the United States. No blacks served in the U.S. Senate, and only about 20 served in the U.S. House of Representatives.

The highlight of black politics since the 1960's has been the continuing increase in the number of black mayors of large U.S. cities. Major cities headed by blacks in 1984 included Atlanta, Ga.; Birmingham, Ala.; Chicago; Detroit; Los Angeles; Newark, N.J.; New Orleans; Philadelphia; Richmond, Va.; and Washington, D.C.

In 1984, Jesse Jackson, a black civil rights leader and Baptist minister, waged a strong campaign to register new black voters and win the Democratic presidential nomination. Jackson's bid for the nomination failed, but he became a hero to most blacks.   ALTON HORNSBY, JR.

Related Articles in WORLD BOOK include:

POLITICAL FIGURES

Bond, Julian	Hatcher, Richard G.
Bradley, Thomas	Jordan, Barbara C.
Brooke, Edward W.	Pierce, Samuel Riley, Jr.
Bruce, Blanche K.	Pinchback, P. B. S.
Chisholm, Shirley	Powell, Adam Clayton, Jr.
Coleman, William T., Jr.	Revels, Hiram R.
Duvalier, François	Stokes, Carl B.
Harris, Patricia R.	Washington, Harold
Hastie, William H.	Young, Andrew J., Jr.

ATHLETES AND SPORTS LEADERS

Aaron, Henry	Brown, Jim
Abdul-Jabbar, Kareem	Chamberlain, Wilt
Ali, Muhammad	Gibson, Althea
Ashe, Arthur	Johnson, Jack
Baylor, Elgin	Louis, Joe

Mays, Willie	Pelé	Robinson, Jackie
Owens, Jesse	Robertson, Oscar	Robinson, Ray
Paige, Satchel	Robinson, Frank	Russell, Bill

CIVIL RIGHTS LEADERS

Abernathy, Ralph D.	Malcolm X
Carmichael, Stokely	McKissick, Floyd B.
Du Bois, W. E. B.	Meredith, James H.
Evers (brothers)	Parks, Rosa Lee
Farmer, James L.	Randolph, A. Philip
Gregory, Dick	Rustin, Bayard
Hooks, Benjamin L.	Terrell, Mary Church
Jackson, Jesse L.	Wells-Barnett, Ida Bell
Jacob, John E.	White, Walter F.
Jordan, Vernon E.	Wilkins, Roy
King, Coretta Scott	Young, Whitney M., Jr.
King, Martin Luther, Jr.	

EDUCATORS AND SCHOLARS

Bethune, Mary McLeod	Mays, Benjamin E.
Cary, Mary Ann Shadd	Moton, Robert R.
Clark, Kenneth Bancroft	Nabrit, James M., Jr.
Franklin, John Hope	Quarles, Benjamin A.
Frazier, E. Franklin	Washington, Booker T.
Hope, John	Weaver, Robert C.
Johnson, Charles S.	Woodson, Carter G.
Locke, Alain L.	

JAZZ MUSICIANS AND SINGERS

Armstrong, Louis	Handy, W. C.	Lewis, John A.
Basie, Count	Hawkins,	Monk, Thelonious
Coltrane, John W.	Coleman	Parker, Charlie
Davis, Miles	Henderson,	Smith, Bessie
Ellington, Duke	Fletcher	Tatum, Art
Fitzgerald, Ella	Hines, Earl	Waller, Fats
Gillespie, Dizzy	Holiday, Billie	Young, Lester W.
Hampton, Lionel	Joplin, Scott	

OTHER SINGERS AND ENTERTAINERS

Ailey, Alvin	Jackson, Michael
Aldridge, Ira	Maynor, Dorothy
Anderson, Marian	Mitchell, Arthur
Belafonte, Harry	Poitier, Sidney
Berry, Chuck	Price, Leontyne
Burleigh, Harry T.	Robeson, Paul
Dunham, Katherine	Robinson, Bill
Hayes, Roland	Waters, Ethel
Horne, Lena	Wonder, Stevie
Jackson, Mahalia	

MILITARY FIGURES

Attucks, Crispus	Dessalines, Jean J.
Christophe, Henri	Miller, Dorie
Davis, Benjamin O., Jr.	Toussaint L'Ouverture
Delany, Martin R.	

SCIENTISTS

Banneker, Benjamin	Julian, Percy L.
Carver, George W.	Lawless, Theodore K.
Drew, Charles R.	Williams, Daniel Hale

WRITERS

Baldwin, James A.	Hamilton, Virginia
Baraka, Amiri	Hansberry, Lorraine
Bontemps, Arna	Harper, Frances E. W.
Brooks, Gwendolyn	Hughes, Langston
Bullins, Ed	Hurston, Zora Neale
Chesnutt, Charles W.	Johnson, James W.
Cleaver, Eldridge	McKay, Claude
Cullen, Countee	Taylor, Mildred
Dunbar, Paul L.	Toomer, Jean
Ellison, Ralph	Wheatley, Phillis
Giovanni, Nikki	Wright, Richard
Haley, Alex	

BLACK AMERICANS

Outline

I. The African Background
  A. The Cultural Heritage
  B. Beginning of the Slave Trade
II. The Years of Slavery
  A. Colonial Times
  B. The Growth of Slavery
  C. Free Blacks

  D. The Antislavery Movement
  E. The Deepening Division over Slavery
III. The End of Slavery
  A. The Civil War
  B. The First Years of Freedom
  C. Temporary Gains
IV. The Growth of Discrimination
  A. During the Late 1800's
  B. During the Early 1900's
  C. The Rise of New
    Black Leaders
  D. The Black Migration
    to the North
  E. The Garvey Movement
  F. The Harlem Renaissance
    and Other Achieve-
    ments
  G. The Great Depression
  H. World War II (1939-
    1945)
V. The Civil Rights Movement
  A. The Beginning
  B. The Growing
    Movement
  C. Political Gains
  D. Economic and
    Social Progress
  E. Unrest in the Cities
  F. Black Militancy
VI. Recent Developments
  A. Achievements
  B. Setbacks
  C. Black Politics Today

Questions

When did the first black African slaves arrive in the American Colonies?

What were the achievements of Harriet Tubman, George Washington Carver, and Thurgood Marshall?

How did the Voting Rights Act of 1965 help blacks?

What was the Emancipation Proclamation?

Why did black American leaders organize the March on Washington in 1963?

On slave ships, what was *loose packing? Tight packing?*

How did the cotton gin contribute to the growth of slavery in the United States?

How did the United States government help the freed slaves after the Civil War?

What was the "separate but equal doctrine"?

What was the Harlem Renaissance?

Reading and Study Guide

See *Black Americans* in the RESEARCH GUIDE/INDEX, Volume 22, for a *Reading and Study Guide.*

Additional Resources

Level I

JACKSON, FLORENCE. *Blacks in America, 1954-1979.* Watts, 1980.
MELTZER, MILTON, ed. *In Their Own Words: A History of the American Negro.* 3 vols. Harper, 1964-1967.
PETERS, MARGARET. *The Ebony Book of Black Achievement.* Rev. ed. Johnson Pub. Co., 1974.
STERLING, DOROTHY. *Tear Down the Walls! A History of the American Civil Rights Movement.* Doubleday, 1968.
STEVENS, LEONARD A. *Equal! The Case of Integration vs. Jim Crow.* Coward, 1976.

Level II

BERRY, MARY F., and BLASSINGAME, J. W. *Long Memory: The Black Experience in America.* Oxford, 1982.
DAVIS, CHARLES T. *Black Is the Color of the Cosmos: Essays on Afro-American Literature and Culture, 1942-1981.* Garland, 1982.
FONER, PHILIP S. *History of Black Americans.* 3 vols. Greenwood, 1975-1983.
FRANKLIN, JOHN HOPE. *From Slavery to Freedom: A History of Negro Americans.* 5th ed. Knopf, 1980.
GUTMAN, HERBERT G. *The Black Family in Slavery and Freedom, 1750-1925.* Pantheon, 1976.
HORNSBY, ALTON, JR. *The Black Almanac.* 4th ed. Barron's Educational Series, 1977.
HUGHES, LANGSTON, and others. *A Pictorial History of Blackamericans.* 5th ed. Crown, 1983.
KLUGER, RICHARD. *Simple Justice: The History of Brown v. Board of Education and Black America's Struggle for Equality.* Knopf, 1976.
LITWACK, LEON F. *Been in the Storm So Long: The Aftermath of Slavery.* Knopf, 1979.

Hughes Helicopters, Inc.

A Heavily Armed Attack Helicopter on a Mission

Doug Wilson, Black Star

A Helicopter Hovering over a Logging Site

Aerospatiale Helicopter Corp.

A Transport Helicopter Flying Supplies to an Oil Rig

Bell Helicopter Textron

A Business Helicopter Landing on a Downtown Rooftop

The Tasks of Helicopters include jobs that airplanes cannot do. Unlike planes, military *attack helicopters* can turn instantly to fire weapons in almost any direction. Helicopters can hover in midair and take off and land in small areas, such as forest clearings, drilling platforms, and rooftops.

HELICOPTER

HELICOPTER is an aircraft that is lifted into the air and kept aloft by one or two powerful whirling rotors. A helicopter rotor resembles a huge propeller that is parallel to the ground. However, the rotor is actually a rotating wing. The name *helicopter* refers to the rotor. It comes from the Greek words *helix*, meaning *spiral*, and *pteron*, meaning *wing*. Nicknames for the helicopter include "chopper," "eggbeater," and "whirlybird."

A helicopter can fly straight up or straight down, forward, backward, or sideways. It can even *hover* (stay in one spot in the air). Unlike most airplanes, helicopters need no runway. They can take off and land in very small space. In addition, helicopters can fly safely at much slower speeds and lower altitudes than airplanes. However, they cannot fly as fast as most planes. Most helicopters cannot exceed 200 miles (320 kilometers) per hour. At faster speeds, strong vibrations develop that could damage the rotor blades. Helicopters also use more fuel than airplanes to travel the same distance. In general, helicopters can fly only two to three hours—or less than 600 miles (970 kilometers)—without refueling.

Helicopters range in size from tiny, single-seat models

Floyd D. Kennedy, Jr., the contributor of this article, is coauthor of World Combat Aircraft Directory *and* Military Helicopters of the World: Military Rotary-Wing Aircraft Since 1917.

to huge transports that can carry two trucks in their cargo hold. The heaviest helicopter ever manufactured is the Soviet Union's Mil Mi-26. It weighs 31 short tons (28 metric tons) and can carry 22 short tons (20 metric tons) of cargo.

Uses of Helicopters

Helicopters can be used for many tasks because they are able to hover in midair and take off and land in small areas. They are particularly useful (1) for rescue missions, (2) for aerial observation, (3) for transportation and construction work, (4) for agricultural and forestry operations, and (5) for military missions.

For Rescue Missions. Many early developers of helicopters intended them to be used for saving lives. Over the years, many thousands of people have been rescued by these "angels of mercy." A helicopter can hover above the scene of a disaster. A sling or harness can then be lowered from the craft to endangered people below. They are then pulled up and flown to safety. Helicopters have been used to pluck people from burning skyscrapers, sinking ships, and rising floodwaters. They have flown stranded mountain climbers and injured skiers to safety. Serving as flying ambulances, helicopters can land near automobile or airplane crashes and rush the injured to hospitals. Helicopters are also used to deliver food and medicine to areas that cannot be reached by other vehicles because of earthquakes, floods, or storms.

For Aerial Observation. In many cities, police use helicopters to trail fleeing suspects and direct squad cars

569

on the ground. Law enforcement agents in helicopters look for lost people and escaped convicts. They also patrol national borders on the lookout for smugglers and illegal immigrants.

Many radio and television stations use helicopters to cover news events from the air. In large cities, helicopter pilots observe the flow of traffic and broadcast radio reports warning drivers of traffic jams. Motion-picture companies often film from helicopters to give audiences a bird's-eye view of a scene. Helicopter pilots fly low along pipelines, railroad tracks, and power lines to inspect them for damage.

Helicopters are used to explore wilderness areas, to survey land, and to help locate oil and other resources. From helicopters, scientists count wildlife populations and chart the migration routes of wild animals. Some fishing fleets use helicopters to spot schools of tuna.

For Transportation and Construction Work. Helicopter transportation is expensive. However, the convenience of helicopter flight makes "choppers" ideal transport vehicles for certain uses. The flexibility, security, and speed of helicopter travel have made it a major method of transportation for political leaders in many countries. Helicopter travel saves business executives time that they otherwise might waste in using slow-moving ground transportation. From *heliports* (airports for helicopters) atop downtown office buildings, business executives may fly directly to nearby cities for meetings.

Helicopter service is essential to many offshore oil-drilling operations. Numerous offshore wells are in rough ocean waters that make it hazardous to bring in replacement crews and supplies by ship. However, helicopters can land on the drilling platforms and so provide much faster and safer delivery than ships.

Helicopters are often used to transport cargo that is too large or awkward for other vehicles to haul. The cargo is carried in a sling hanging below the craft.

Powerful helicopters are used in construction work as "flying cranes." Workers in helicopters install antennas and huge air conditioners atop tall buildings and erect preassembled electric power transmission towers. Workers also use helicopters to pour concrete in hard-to-reach places and to put long bridge sections in position.

U.S. Coast Guard

Helicopter Rescue Missions have saved the lives of thousands of people. The United States Coast Guard helicopter above has picked up the crew members from a sinking ship.

For Agricultural and Forestry Operations. Farmers use helicopters to spread seeds, fertilizers, weedkillers, and insecticides over large areas. Instead of building roads, some companies that manufacture forest products depend on helicopters to transport logging crews into and out of forests and to carry out logs.

For Military Missions. In the armed forces, helicopters serve as flying ambulances and as troop transports. Powerful military helicopters carry artillery to key battle positions and fly jeeps, tanks, and other equipment wherever they are needed. Helicopters equipped with electronic gear pick up and disrupt enemy communications signals. The armed forces also use helicopters to observe the movements of enemy troops and ships. Many naval helicopters have devices to locate and track submarines. They may also be armed with depth charges, missiles, or torpedoes. Army *attack helicopters* may carry bombs, cannons, machine guns, or missiles. Their main targets are enemy tanks.

Types of Helicopters

Single-Rotor Helicopters are the most common type of helicopters. A single-rotor helicopter has one main rotor mounted above its body. Although such an aircraft is called a single-rotor helicopter, it also has a second, smaller rotor mounted on its tail. The main rotor may

Fred Ward, Black Star

Crop-Dusting by Helicopter enables farmers to spray agricultural chemicals exactly where they are needed. This specially equipped helicopter is being used to spray a field with insecticide.

Sikorsky Aircraft

An Antisubmarine Helicopter, armed with torpedoes, takes off from the deck of a U.S. Navy ship. Such helicopters carry electronic devices to locate and track submarines.

have from 2 to 8 blades. It provides the helicopter's lifting power. The tail rotor has from 2 to 13 blades. It is mounted vertically on either side of the tail and so spins at a right angle to the main rotor. The tail rotor is used to control direction. It also overcomes the tendency of the helicopter to spin around in the direction opposite to that of the main rotor.

Twin-Rotor Helicopters have two main rotors. The rotors turn in opposite directions and so eliminate the need for a tail rotor. Two basic types of twin-rotor helicopters are widely used: *tandem-rotor helicopters* and *coaxial-rotor helicopters*. A tandem-rotor helicopter has a main rotor mounted above each end of its body. A coaxial-rotor helicopter has one rotor above the other. The rotors are mounted above the middle of the helicopter's body. The shaft of the upper rotor turns inside the shaft of the lower rotor.

How Helicopters Fly

Lift is the force that causes an aircraft to overcome gravity, climb into the air, and stay aloft. Most aircraft rely on wings to produce lift. An airplane has *fixed* (immovable) wings that create lift as the airplane moves forward. Helicopter rotor blades are *rotary wings*. An engine turns the rotor, and the blades generate lift as they whirl through the air.

The special shape of wings helps them create lift. A wing's upper surface is curved, and its lower surface is less curved or flat. As a wing moves or whirls through the air, air flows over and under the wing. In the same amount of time, the air flowing over the curved upper surface travels farther than the air flowing under the wing. The air thus flows faster over the wing than under it. This difference in air speed creates a difference in air pressure above and below the wing. There is less pressure on the upper surface than on the lower surface. Because air is pushing more strongly against the bottom of the wing than against the top, lift is created. For additional information, see the article AERODYNAMICS (Principles of Aerodynamics).

Helicopter pilots, like airplane pilots, can control the amount of lift by changing the angle that the wings make with the airflow. This angle is called the *angle of attack*. You can demonstrate the relation between lift and the angle of attack by using a kite to serve as a simple wing. Hold the kite flat and point it into the wind. If you then slightly raise the front of the kite, you increase

Types of Helicopters

WORLD BOOK illustrations by Zorica Dabich

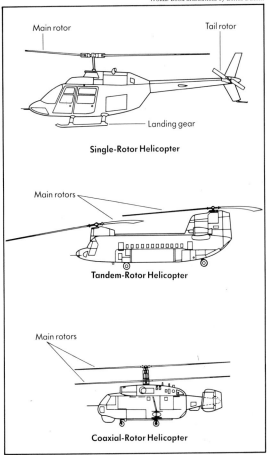

Single-Rotor Helicopter

Tandem-Rotor Helicopter

Coaxial-Rotor Helicopter

the angle of attack. You will feel a force trying to push the kite upward. This force is the lift created by the wind as it pushes against the bottom surface. If you decrease the angle of attack, the force becomes weaker.

Piloting a Helicopter. The pilot of a single-rotor helicopter operates three basic controls inside the cockpit. (1) The *collective pitch lever* makes the helicopter climb, hover, or descend. (2) The *control column*, also called the

How a Helicopter Rotor Produces Lift

WORLD BOOK illustrations by Zorica Dabich

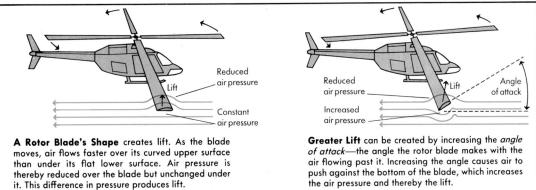

A Rotor Blade's Shape creates lift. As the blade moves, air flows faster over its curved upper surface than under its flat lower surface. Air pressure is thereby reduced over the blade but unchanged under it. This difference in pressure produces lift.

Greater Lift can be created by increasing the *angle of attack*—the angle the rotor blade makes with the air flowing past it. Increasing the angle causes air to push against the bottom of the blade, which increases the air pressure and thereby the lift.

HELICOPTER

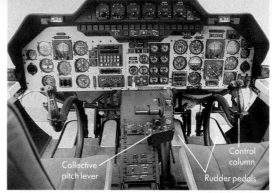

cyclic pitch control, causes it to fly forward, backward, or sideways. (3) The *rudder pedals* swing the tail around so that the helicopter can turn. Each control varies the *pitch* (angle) of the main rotor or tail rotor blades. A system of cables, rods, and other mechanical devices leads from the controls in the cockpit to the rotor blades.

Climbing, Hovering, and Descending. The pilot's left hand moves the collective pitch lever up and down. By raising the lever, the pilot increases the pitch of all main rotor blades equally. The increased pitch, in turn, increases the lift generated by the spinning rotor. When lift exceeds the force of gravity, the helicopter goes straight up. After reaching a particular altitude, the pilot may want to hover. The pilot then lowers the lever to decrease the pitch of the rotor blades and so reduce

Helicopter Controls. Moving the *collective pitch lever* makes the helicopter climb, hover, or descend. Tilting the *control column* causes forward, backward, or sideways flight. Pushing the *rudder pedals* controls the direction the helicopter points. This photo shows a craft with dual controls for the pilot and copilot.

Piloting a Helicopter   A pilot flies a helicopter by varying the *pitch* (angle) of the rotor blades. The lift of the main rotor counteracts gravity. The force of the tail rotor counteracts *torque*, a force that tends to spin the aircraft in the direction opposite that of the main rotor. In the diagrams below, the pitch of the blades is indicated by the thickness of the circles showing the area swept by the rotor.

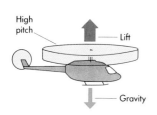

Climbing. Raising the collective pitch lever increases the pitch of the main rotor blades. Lift is increased, and the craft climbs.

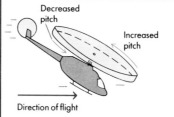

Forward Flight. Tilting the control column forward makes the pitch greatest as the blades approach the tail. The rotor tilts up in the rear and the craft flies forward.

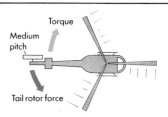

Pointing Straight. If neither rudder pedal is pushed, the tail rotor force balances the torque. The helicopter then points straight ahead.

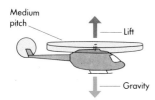

Hovering. Holding the collective pitch lever so the blades have medium pitch produces just enough lift to counteract gravity. The craft then hovers.

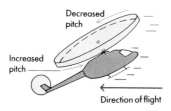

Backward Flight. Tilting the column back makes the pitch greatest as the blades approach the nose. The rotor tilts up in the front and the craft flies backward.

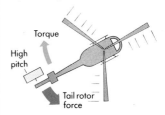

Turning Left. Pushing the left rudder pedal increases the pitch, and thus the force, of the tail rotor blades. The tail rotor force turns the craft left.

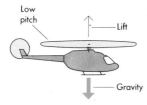

Descending. Lowering the collective pitch lever decreases the pitch. The blades create little lift, and gravity causes the helicopter to descend.

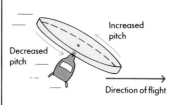

Sideways Flight. Tilting the column to one side makes the pitch greatest as the blades approach the opposite side. The craft then flies in the direction the column is tilted.

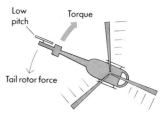

Turning Right. Pushing the right rudder pedal decreases the pitch, and thus the force, of the tail rotor blades. Torque then swings the craft to the right.

the amount of lift. When the rotor's lifting force has been reduced just enough to counteract the pull of gravity, the craft will maintain a constant altitude. To descend, the pilot lowers the collective pitch lever farther, thereby decreasing the lift. When lift becomes weaker than the force of gravity, the craft descends.

Flying Forward, Backward, and Sideways. The pilot's right hand operates the control column. The control column is a stick between the pilot's knees. It can be tilted in any direction. The helicopter moves in whatever direction the pilot tilts the column.

When the control column is tilted, the pitch of the main rotor blades alternately increases and decreases as they sweep through opposite sections of their circular path. To fly forward, the pilot pushes the column ahead. This causes the pitch to be greatest just before the blades pass over the tail. The blades have the least pitch just before they reach the nose. These changes in pitch cause the rotor blades to rise slightly in the rear. The rotor then tries to pull the helicopter both upward and ahead. Gravity counteracts the upward pull, however, and so the aircraft moves forward in level flight.

To fly backward, the pilot pulls back on the control column. This gives the blades the most pitch as they approach the nose and the least pitch as they approach the tail. The nose rises, the tail dips, and the helicopter flies backward. The aircraft can be made to fly sideways in a similar manner.

Turning. As a helicopter's main rotor spins in one direction, it creates a force that pushes against the body of the craft in the opposite direction. This twisting force is called *torque*. It must be overcome or the helicopter will be out of control and simply turn in circles.

The main rotor of a single-rotor helicopter spins in a counterclockwise direction, and so the push of the torque is clockwise. The pilot of a single-rotor craft uses the tail rotor to counteract torque and to change direction. The pilot controls the tail rotor by stepping on two rudder pedals. If neither pedal is depressed, the tail rotor blades spin at just the right pitch to produce exactly enough sideways force to counteract the torque. The helicopter then points straight ahead. To swing left, the pilot steps on the left rudder pedal, thereby increasing the pitch of the tail rotor blades. The increased force of the rotor pushes the tail in the direction opposite to the clockwise push of the torque. The helicopter then turns to the left. To turn right, the pilot depresses the right rudder pedal and so decreases the pitch—and thus the force—of the tail rotor blades. The torque itself then swings the tail in a clockwise direction, which turns the helicopter to the right.

On a twin-rotor helicopter, one main rotor turns clockwise and the other turns counterclockwise. As a result, the torque generated by one rotor cancels out that generated by the other. The pilot turns the craft by changing the pitch of the main rotors.

Development of the Helicopter

Early Designs and Experiments. The earliest known mention of a rotor-powered flying machine appears in a Chinese text written about A.D. 320. The design of this machine may have been based on a Chinese toy called the *flying top.* Such toys flew by means of feather rotors. In 1483, the great Italian artist and scientist Leonardo da Vinci sketched a design for a helicopter. It had a

Early Helicopters

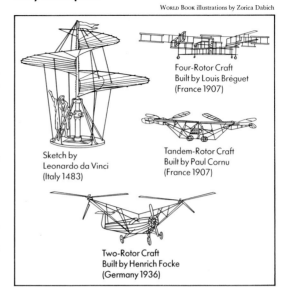

Sketch by
Leonardo da Vinci
(Italy 1483)

Four-Rotor Craft
Built by Louis Bréguet
(France 1907)

Tandem-Rotor Craft
Built by Paul Cornu
(France 1907)

Two-Rotor Craft
Built by Henrich Focke
(Germany 1936)

large screwlike wing made of starched linen. In 1784, two Frenchmen named Launoy and Bienvenu, built the first model helicopter in Europe that could fly. Based on the Chinese flying top, it had two rotors made of feathers. Throughout the 1800's, inventors in Europe and the United States experimented with model helicopters. The steam engines and electric motors of that time were too weak or too heavy to power a full-sized helicopter.

By the early 1900's, small, powerful gasoline engines had been developed that made manned helicopter flight possible. The first manned flight took place in 1907. The craft was a four-rotor helicopter built by Louis Bréguet, a French inventor. The helicopter lifted one of Bréguet's assistants 2 feet (61 centimeters) into the air for a minute. Assistants on the ground steadied the helicopter during the flight. Later in 1907, a French mechanic named Paul Cornu made the first free flight in a helicopter. He flew his tandem-rotor aircraft to a height of about 6 feet (1.8 meters) for about 20 seconds.

The First Practical Helicopters. Early helicopters were difficult to control, and their flight was wobbly. In 1935, Bréguet and another Frenchman, René Dorand, built a coaxial-rotor helicopter that was easier to control and flew far more steadily. In 1936, Henrich Focke, a German inventor, built a twin-rotor helicopter that was even further advanced. The following year, it reached a speed of 76 miles (122 kilometers) per hour and an altitude of about 8,000 feet (2,400 meters). It could stay aloft for 1 hour and 20 minutes.

The first flight of a practical single-rotor helicopter took place in the United States in 1939. The craft was built and flown by Igor I. Sikorsky, a Russian engineer who had moved to the United States in 1919. Both the British and the United States armed forces used an improved version of Sikorsky's helicopter during World War II (1939-1945).

Further Improvements. During the mid-1900's, the military use of helicopters began to increase greatly, which led to major improvements in their design. Helicopters had been used mainly for patrol and rescue mis-

HELICOPTER

Sikorsky Aircraft

The First Practical Single-Rotor Helicopter was built and flown by Igor Sikorsky. Its first flight, *above*, was in 1939.

James Pickerell, Black Star

Helicopters in Combat were first used on a massive scale by United States armed forces during the Vietnam War (1957-1975).

Sikorsky Aircraft

An Experimental Compound Helicopter has coaxial rotors to provide lift. However, it uses jet engines for forward movement. Such aircraft can fly much faster than regular helicopters.

sions in World War II. New tasks for the helicopter during the Korean War (1950-1953) included armed observation of enemy positions and strength and transporting troops and supplies to hard-to-reach areas. During the Vietnam War (1957-1975), thousands of armed U.S. attack helicopters flew combat missions.

The ever-expanding military use of helicopters encouraged the development of faster, larger, and more powerful craft. In the 1940's and 1950's, engineers adapted the jet engine for use in helicopters. Jet engines were lighter and more powerful than the previous engines used to turn the rotor shafts. They enabled helicopters to fly faster and higher and to carry heavier loads. In addition, the use of new construction materials

made helicopters lighter, safer, and stronger. For example, metal or wooden rotor blades were replaced by longer-lasting plastic blades. Such improvements also made helicopters suitable for more civilian uses.

Recent Developments include efforts by manufacturers to simplify the complicated operation of helicopters and to increase their speed. One manufacturer has developed a single-rotor helicopter that needs no tail rotor. Instead of a tail rotor, the craft uses jets of air to counteract torque and to change direction. Attempts to increase the speed of helicopters have led to the development of experimental *compound helicopters*. These vehicles do not depend entirely on rotors to provide forward movement as well as lift. Instead, they also have jet or propeller systems to help push or pull them ahead. One compound helicopter has reached the speed of 345 miles (555 kilometers) per hour. FLOYD D. KENNEDY, JR.

Related Articles in WORLD BOOK include:

Aerodynamics
Aircraft, Military
(Helicopters; picture)
Autogiro

Cayley, Sir George
Sikorsky, Igor I.
V/STOL

Outline

I. Uses of Helicopters
  A. For Rescue Missions
  B. For Aerial Observation
  C. For Transportation and Construction Work
  D. For Agricultural and Forestry Operations
  E. For Military Missions

II. Types of Helicopters
  A. Single-Rotor Helicopters   B. Twin-Rotor Helicopters

III. How Helicopters Fly
  A. Lift
  B. Piloting a Helicopter

IV. Development of the Helicopter

Questions

What kind of wings does a helicopter have?
How are helicopters used in the construction industry?
What is a *tandem-rotor helicopter*? A *coaxial-rotor helicopter*?
Who built and flew the first practical single-rotor helicopter?
What are some military uses of the helicopter?
Why does a single-rotor helicopter have a tail rotor?
What is a *compound helicopter*?
In what ways can a helicopter fly that an airplane cannot?
What happens when a helicopter pilot raises the collective pitch lever?
Why is helicopter service essential to many offshore oil-drilling operations?

Additional Resources

BERLINER, DON. *Helicopters.* Lerner, 1983. For younger readers.
FAY, JOHN. *The Helicopter: History, Piloting and How It Flies.* 3rd ed. David & Charles, 1977.
GABLEHOUSE, CHARLES. *Helicopters and Autogiros.* Rev. ed. Lippincott, 1969.
MCDONALD, JOHN J. *Flying the Helicopter.* TAB, 1981.
POLMAR, NORMAN, and KENNEDY, FLOYD D., JR. *Military Helicopters of the World: Military Rotary-Wing Aircraft Since 1917.* Naval Institute Press, 1981.
TAYLOR, MICHAEL J. and JOHN W. *Helicopters of the World.* 2nd ed. Scribner, 1978.

MARTIN BRIAN MULRONEY

Peter Bregg

Prime Minister of Canada
1984-

TRUDEAU	TURNER	MULRONEY
1980-1984	1984	1984-

MULRONEY, *muhl ROO nay,* **MARTIN BRIAN** (1939-), climaxed a remarkable rise to national prominence when he became prime minister of Canada in 1984. Mulroney had been chosen leader of the Progressive Conservative Party in June 1983. Before he became leader, he had been a lawyer and business executive and had never been elected to a public office. But he led the Conservatives to a landslide victory in the election of 1984 and succeeded John N. Turner as prime minister.

Brian Mulroney, as he preferred to be called, had been active in Progressive Conservative affairs since his college days in the late 1950's and early 1960's. During that period, he held many leadership positions in Progressive Conservative student groups. Mulroney later served on the finance committee of the Quebec Progressive Conservative Party. He became a candidate for the party's national leadership in 1976 but finished third in the race. Mulroney then developed a successful career as president of the Iron Ore Company of Canada. He held that position until he became party leader.

Mulroney was the second youngest prime minister in Canadian history. He was only 45 years old when he succeeded Turner. The youngest prime minister was Joe Clark, who was 39 years old when he was sworn into office in 1979. Friends knew Mulroney to be charming, confident, and decisive. Associates rated him as a superb administrator, negotiator, and organizer who at times was tough and cautious. Mulroney's favorite recreational activity was playing tennis.

When Mulroney became prime minister, Canada faced serious economic problems. A recession during the early 1980's had hurt the nation's businesses and caused severe unemployment. The business slump ended in 1983, but the economy had shown only a slight recovery, and the rate of unemployment remained high.

Early Life

Boyhood. Martin Brian Mulroney was born on March 20, 1939, in Baie-Comeau, Que. He was the third oldest of the six children of Benedict M. Mulroney and Irene O'Shea Mulroney. Brian's father was an electrician for a paper company in Baie-Comeau.

Brian became an excellent tennis player as a teen-ager and won the Baie-Comeau Junior Tennis Championship. He attended local schools until he was 13 years old. Then his parents sent him to St. Thomas College, a boys' school in Chatham, N.B.

College Education. In 1955, at the age of 16, Mulroney entered St. Francis Xavier University in Antigonish, N.S. He earned honors in political science and developed an interest in politics. Mulroney's parents had

Important Dates in Mulroney's Life

1939 (March 20) Born in Baie-Comeau, Que.
1959 Graduated from St. Francis Xavier University.
1959 Elected executive vice president of Progressive Conservative Student Federation.
1973 (May 26) Married Mila Pivnicki.
1974 Became member of Cliche Royal Commission.
1977 Became president of Iron Ore Company of Canada.
1983 Elected leader of Progressive Conservative Party.
1984 (Sept. 17) Became prime minister of Canada.

supported the Liberal Party. But Brian came to admire Robert L. Stanfield, leader of the Nova Scotia Progressive Conservative Party, and joined the Conservative club at the university. He became devoted to the club and was elected its leader in 1958. The next year, Mulroney received a Bachelor of Arts degree.

Mulroney then enrolled at Dalhousie University in Halifax, N.S., to study law. Later in 1959, he was elected executive vice president of the Progressive Conservative Student Federation of Canada. A year later, Mulroney transferred to Laval University Law School in Ste.-Foy, Que., and resumed his participation in student Conservative activities. In 1961, Mulroney became leader of the Progressive Conservative club at Laval. He received his law degree in 1963.

Early Business Career

Young Lawyer. After graduating from law school, Mulroney joined the Montreal law firm of Ogilvy, Renault. He specialized in labor law.

Mulroney's involvement with the Progressive Conservative Party continued to grow. He served on its policy committee from 1966 to 1971 and on the finance committee of the Quebec Progressive Conservative Party from 1966 to 1974.

On May 26, 1973, Mulroney married Mila Pivnicki (1953-) of Montreal. The Mulroneys had three children, Caroline (1974-), Benedict (1976-), and Robert Mark (1979-).

In May 1974, Mulroney was appointed to the Cliche Royal Commission, which was established to investigate violence in Quebec's construction industry. He frequently appeared on the evening television news and began to gain national prominence.

First Bid for Leadership. In 1975, Progressive Conservative leader Robert L. Stanfield announced his intention to retire. Mulroney's work on the Cliche commission had impressed influential members of the Progressive Conservative Party, and they urged him to become a candidate for the leadership. Mulroney accepted the challenge and ran a strong campaign.

The party met to choose its new leader in February 1976. Mulroney finished second on the first ballot behind Claude Wagner, a leading Conservative official

Crombie McNeil

The Mulroney Family in 1984. From left to right are Mulroney, son Robert Mark, Mrs. Mulroney, daughter Caroline, and son Benedict.

from Quebec. However, neither candidate received the required majority. Finally, on the fourth ballot, Joe Clark of Alberta won the election. Mulroney finished third in the balloting.

Business Executive. In June 1976, Mulroney joined the Iron Ore Company of Canada as executive vice president of corporate affairs. He had done some legal work for the company and was admired by its president, William Bennett. The company had its headquarters in Sept-Îles, Que., and offices in Montreal. In 1977, Bennett retired and Mulroney became president of the firm. The company had long been troubled by labor strikes and was deeply in debt. Mulroney settled the labor disputes and led the company to record profits.

Mulroney faced another challenge at the company during the early 1980's, when decreased demands for steel led to a sharp drop in iron ore prices. Iron ore is used to make steel, and the Iron Ore Company suffered large losses. As a result of these losses, the company closed its iron ore mine in Schefferville, Que., in 1982. Mulroney arranged a generous compensation and relocation program for the 285 employees who lost their jobs.

Career in Government

Election as Party Leader. Joe Clark had led the Progressive Conservative Party to power in the general election of 1979. But the Liberals regained control in a general election the next year. Opposition to Clark's leadership then began to grow.

A race for the leadership developed early in 1983 when Clark failed to win adequate support at a party congress. Clark then resigned and called a party convention for June to select a new leader. Mulroney became a major candidate for the leadership even though he had never won election to a public office. His supporters felt that his Quebec connections would help strengthen the party's prospects in that province, which was a traditional stronghold of the Liberal Party. Quebec had about a fourth of Canada's population.

Clark tried to regain his position at the convention, but Mulroney's fresh appeal and Quebec background helped carry him to victory. Mulroney was the first Progressive Conservative leader ever to win that position without any experience in an elected office. Two months later, he easily won election to the Canadian House of Commons from a district in Nova Scotia.

The 1984 Election. Prime Minister Pierre E. Trudeau decided to retire in 1984. He was succeeded in late June 1984 by John N. Turner, a Toronto lawyer who had held several Cabinet positions in the governments headed by Lester B. Pearson and Trudeau. Turner called a general election for Sept. 4, 1984.

At the time of the campaign, Canada's economy was slowly recovering from a recession. The country's rate of unemployment was still high, standing at 11 per cent of the labor force. Mulroney said a new Conservative government would create jobs, increase industrial productivity, and increase foreign investment in Canada.

In the election, Mulroney led the Conservatives to a tremendous victory. His party won 211 of the 282 seats in the House of Commons. It captured 58 of the 75 seats in Quebec, the most the Conservatives had ever won in that traditional Liberal stronghold. Mulroney took office as prime minister on September 17. KENDAL WINDEYER

JOHN N. TURNER

Prime Minister of Canada
1984

TRUDEAU
1980-1984

TURNER
1984

MULRONEY
1984-

TURNER, JOHN NAPIER (1929-   ), served as prime minister of Canada for 2½ months in 1984. Turner, a Liberal, succeeded Prime Minister Pierre E. Trudeau, who had resigned. Turner called for a general election shortly after he took office. But Brian Mulroney, the leader of the Progressive Conservatives, led his party to a landslide victory and replaced Turner as prime minister.

Turner had been a corporation lawyer before he entered politics. He first held office in 1962, when voters from Montreal elected him to the Canadian House of Commons. Turner later served as registrar general and minister of consumer and corporate affairs in the Cabinet of Prime Minister Lester B. Pearson. Trudeau succeeded Pearson in 1968. Under Trudeau, Turner served as solicitor general and as minister of justice and attorney general before becoming minister of finance.

Turner's silver hair, blue eyes, and athletic build made him an impressive figure. Turner liked to ski, go canoeing, and play squash and tennis. He also enjoyed music, especially opera, and reading biographies.

Early Life

Boyhood. John Napier Turner was born on June 7, 1929, in Richmond, England, near London. His father, Leonard Turner, was a British gunsmith. His mother, Phyllis Gregory Turner of Rossland, B.C., was an economist and the daughter of a miner. She was studying at the London School of Economics when she met her future husband, and they were married in England. John had a sister, Brenda, born in 1931.

When John was 2 years old, his father died. The family then moved to Canada, and John's mother in time got a job as an economist with the federal tariff board in Ottawa. Later, during World War II (1939-1945), she became federal administrator of oils and fats. Various ministers in the Cabinet of W. L. Mackenzie King often discussed government activities in the family home. Partly as a result of these meetings, John developed an interest in public service at an early age.

John attended schools in Ottawa. He went to Normal Model Public School, Ashbury College, and St. Patrick's College. He was a bright, popular student, and he was active in sports. In 1945, John's mother married Frank Ross, a Vancouver industrialist.

College Years. Turner graduated from St. Patrick's in 1945 and then entered the University of British Columbia. He was an outstanding student and won honors in political science. Turner also became a star sprinter on the track and field team. An injury ruined his chances to qualify for Canada's 1948 Olympic team. Turner received a Bachelor of Arts degree in 1949. He was named the most popular student in his class.

Turner also won a Rhodes Scholarship to study at Oxford University in England. He studied law there and received a bachelor's degree in jurisprudence in 1951 and a bachelor's degree in civil law in 1952. In 1952 and 1953, Turner took graduate courses in French civil law at the Sorbonne in Paris. He also became fluent in French. In 1954, Turner joined the Stikeman, Elliott law firm in Montreal.

Early Political Career

Entry into Politics. Turner's government career began in June 1962, when he was elected to the Canadian House of Commons. He had run as a Liberal from the Montreal riding of St. Lawrence-St. George.

In May 1963, Turner married Geills McCrae Kilgour

of Winnipeg, one of his campaign workers. Kilgour, the daughter of an insurance company president, had majored in mathematics and physics at McGill University in Montreal and had done graduate work in business administration at Harvard University. The Turners had four children, Elizabeth (1964-   ), Michael (1965-   ), David (1968-   ), and James (1971-   ).

Early Cabinet Posts. As a member of Parliament, Turner impressed Prime Minister Pearson. Pearson brought Turner into his Cabinet in December 1965 as minister without portfolio. In April 1967, Pearson appointed Turner registrar general. In December 1967, Turner became minister of consumer and corporate affairs.

Pearson resigned as party leader and prime minister in April 1968. Turner campaigned hard to succeed him. But the party chose Pierre E. Trudeau, a Montreal professor. Turner ran third in the balloting.

In Trudeau's Cabinet. In April 1968, Trudeau gave Turner the additional office of solicitor general. Later in 1968, Trudeau made Turner minister of justice and attorney general. In this position, Turner introduced changes in criminal law that guaranteed legal services and eased bail requirements for the poor. He also established the Law Reform Commission of Canada. Many reforms proposed by this agency have become part of Canada's civil and criminal law.

In 1969, Turner helped push the Official Languages Act through the House of Commons. This act required federal facilities to provide service in both French and English if 10 per cent of the people in a particular area speak either language. In 1970, a crisis arose when the *Front de Libération du Québec* (FLQ), a terrorist group, kidnapped two officials. Turner worked to win parliamentary permission to put the War Measures Act into effect. This act allows the government to suspend civil liberties. Trudeau felt the act was necessary to help police deal with the crisis.

In January 1972, Trudeau appointed Turner minister of finance. In 1974, Turner introduced inflation-indexed personal tax exemptions. This system allowed individuals to make income tax deductions that reflected increases in the rate of inflation.

Return to Private Life. Rapid inflation continued to trouble the economy. Early in 1975, Turner began an effort to persuade labor and business leaders to accept voluntary limits on wage and price increases. But he failed to obtain an agreement. In September 1975, Turner surprised the nation by resigning from his powerful position in the Cabinet.

Many political observers felt Turner resigned because

Important Dates in Turner's Life

1929 (June 7) Born in Richmond, England.
1949 Graduated from University of British Columbia.
1962 First elected to House of Commons.
1963 (May 11) Married Geills McCrae Kilgour.
1968 Appointed minister of justice and attorney general.
1972 Appointed minister of finance.
1975 Resigned as minister of finance.
1984 (June 30) Became prime minister.
1984 (Sept. 4) Liberals defeated in general election.

he opposed legislation planned by Trudeau to require limits on wage and price increases. But some officials argued that Turner supported the plan. Other observers believed that Turner asked Trudeau for a new government position or for a promise of future support for the leadership, but got neither. Both Turner and Trudeau refused to discuss Turner's action. In February 1976, Turner resigned from the House of Commons, and his once promising political career appeared to be finished.

Political Comeback

After ending his government service, Turner became a partner in the law firm of McMillan, Binch in Toronto. He greatly increased his personal wealth and was chosen to serve as a director by 10 large companies.

Canapress

The Turner Family. From left to right are son David, daughter Elizabeth, son James, Mrs. Turner, Turner, and son Michael.

Return to Politics. In February 1984, Trudeau announced his desire to resign as party leader and prime minister. Turner declared his candidacy for the leadership in March. He faced six opponents, all of whom were ministers in Trudeau's Cabinet. But Turner became the early favorite in the race. During the leadership campaign, he promised programs to strengthen the then stalled Canadian economy. In June, the Liberal Party leadership convention chose Turner on the second ballot. Turner became prime minister on June 30.

The 1984 Election. Early in July, Turner called a general election for Sept. 4, 1984. His rival party leaders were Brian Mulroney of the Progressive Conservative Party and Edward Broadbent of the New Democratic Party. In the campaign, Turner said his first major goal as prime minister would be to lower the unemployment rate, which stood at 11 per cent of the country's labor force. He proposed a plan to create jobs for unemployed youths. Mulroney and Broadbent charged that the Liberals did not know how to strengthen the economy.

In the election, the Liberals won only 40 of the 282 seats in the House of Commons—the worst defeat in their history. The Conservatives won 211 seats. Mulroney succeeded Turner as prime minister on September 17.   CHRISTINA MCCALL-NEWMAN

SAINT CHRISTOPHER AND NEVIS, *NEE vuhs* or *NEHV uhs*, is a country in the Caribbean Sea that consists of two islands. The islands are St. Christopher, commonly called St. Kitts, and Nevis. The islands lie about 190 miles (310 kilometers) east of Puerto Rico.

The country has a land area of 101 square miles (262 square kilometers). St. Kitts covers 65 square miles (168 square kilometers), and Nevis covers 36 square miles (93 square kilometers). St. Christopher and Nevis has a population of about 44,400. About 80 per cent of the people live on St. Kitts.

St. Christopher and Nevis became an independent nation in 1983, after being controlled by Great Britain since 1713. Basseterre (pop. 14,725) is the country's capital and largest city. The East Caribbean dollar is the basic unit of currency. For a picture of the country's flag, see FLAG (Flags of the Americas).

Government. St. Christopher and Nevis is a constitutional monarchy and a member of the Commonwealth of Nations (see COMMONWEALTH OF NATIONS). A prime minister heads the government and carries out its operations with the aid of a Cabinet. A one-house parliament makes the country's laws. It consists of 11 representatives and 3 senators. The people elect the representatives. The senators are appointed on the advice of the prime minister and the leader of the opposition political party. The head of the political party with the most seats in parliament usually serves as prime minister. Nevis has a large degree of control over its own government affairs. It has its own local legislature.

People. Almost all the people of St. Christopher and Nevis are descendants of black Africans. The people speak English, the official language. About two-thirds of the people live in rural villages scattered along the coasts. Most of the rural people work on small farms or sugar plantations. Most of the rest of the people live in urban areas. Basseterre, on St. Kitts, is the chief urban center. Charlestown is the main urban center of Nevis.

Most of the country's people live in houses made of concrete, stone or wood. They wear lightweight clothing similar to that worn in summer in the United States and other Western nations. Both islands have well-developed primary and secondary educational systems.

Land and Climate. The two islands lie about 2 miles (3.2 kilometers) apart. They are the tops of two volcanic mountains that rise out of the Caribbean Sea. The mountain that forms St. Kitts is called Mount Misery. It rises 3,792 feet (1,156 meters) above sea level. The peak of Nevis is 3,232 feet (985 meters) above sea level. Both islands have a narrow fringe of fertile plains along their coasts. Many beaches on the islands are formed by black volcanic sand. The islands receive about 55 inches (140 centimeters) of rain annually. The average temperature is 78° F. (25° C).

Economy. The economy of St. Christopher and Nevis is based on sugar and tourism. Sugar cane is raised on St. Kitts and is processed at a large government-owned sugar mill there. The fertile land of Nevis is divided into small farms that produce vegetables, fruits, and cotton. The country's beaches, scenery, and warm sunny climate attract many tourists. St. Kitts has an international airport. Ferryboats and small planes carry people between the two islands.

Unemployment is high on both islands, especially during periods when tourism and sugar production are slow. Each year, a number of young people leave the islands to look for work elsewhere.

History. Arawak Indians were the first inhabitants of the islands of St. Kitts and Nevis. They were followed by Carib Indians. Christopher Columbus sighted the islands in 1493 on his second voyage to the New World. In 1624, British and French people began settling on St. Kitts. Nevis was first settled in 1628 by British people. The European settlers brought African slaves to St. Kitts to work on sugar cane plantations.

Britain took complete control of St. Kitts in 1713. The British later ruled St. Kitts and Nevis, along with the island of Anguilla, as a single colony. In 1967, the colony became an associated state of Britain. Anguilla became a separate British dependency in 1980. St. Christopher and Nevis became an independent nation on Sept. 19, 1983.   THOMAS G. MATHEWS

BRUNEI, *BROO ny* or *BROO nay*, is a small country in Southeast Asia. It lies on the north coast of the island of Borneo. The people of Brunei enjoy a high standard of living, mainly because of the country's valuable offshore petroleum deposits. Brunei covers 2,226 square miles (5,765 square kilometers) and has a population of 277,000. Bandar Seri Begawan is its capital and largest city.

Brunei was a protectorate of Great Britain from 1888 to 1984, when it became an independent nation. The basic unit of money is the Brunei dollar. For a picture of Brunei's flag, see FLAG (Flags of Asia and the Pacific).

Government. Brunei's government is headed by a monarch called a sultan. The sultan is chosen for life by a council of succession. Sir Muda Hassanal Bolkiah, who has been the sultan since 1967, also serves as the country's prime minister, minister of finance, and minister of home affairs. Several members of his family hold high positions in the government.

Various advisory and legislative councils assist the sultan in operating the government. The sultan appoints council members. There are no political parties in Brunei.

Brunei is divided into four administrative districts for purposes of local government. Each has a district council. The sultan appoints the council members.

Brunei's highest court is the supreme court. It consists

St. Christopher and Nevis

⊛	National capital
•	Other city or town
+	Elevation above sea level
▬	Road

62° 40'West Longitude

Dieppe Bay
St. Christopher
(St. Kitts)
+Mt.Misery 3,792 ft. (1,156 m)
Sandy Point · Cayon
Old Road · GOLDEN ROCK AIRPORT
Basseterre
Great Salt Pond
Nags Head · The Narrows · Newcastle
17° 10'North Latitude · Nevis Peak 3,232 ft. (985 m) +
Charlestown · Zion Hill
Nevis

Caribbean Sea

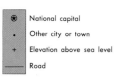

U.S. · Bahamas
North Atlantic Ocean
Cuba · Puerto Rico
Jamaica
ST. CHRISTOPHER AND NEVIS
Caribbean Sea
Colombia
Venezuela

0 ___ 10 Miles
0 ___ 10 Kilometers

WORLD BOOK map

BRUNEI

of a chief justice and several commissioners, who are appointed by the sultan.

People. About 65 per cent of Brunei's people live in urban areas, and about 35 per cent in rural areas. About two-thirds of the people are Malays. Chinese, the largest minority, make up about a fourth of the population. Most Bruneians speak Malay, the official language. But English and Chinese are also used. Nearly all the Malays are Muslims. Most of the Chinese are Christians, and a small percentage are Buddhists.

Most Bruneians in urban areas wear clothing similar to that worn by people in Western nations. However, many Muslim women wear outfits of long skirts and long-sleeved blouses. In rural areas, many men and women wear loose shirts and *sarongs*, which are long pieces of cloth worn as a skirt and tied at the waist. Many people in the cities live in modern houses or apartments made of brick or stone. Most houses in the rural areas are wooden and have thatched roofs.

Bruneians enjoy a high standard of living. There is relatively little unemployment. The government provides free schooling and medical services for citizens. Chinese people own most of the businesses. However, less than 10 per cent of the Chinese have been granted citizenship. Noncitizens cannot receive free education or medical care, and they are not allowed to own land.

Most Bruneian children complete elementary school and many go on to high school. Brunei has teachers colleges and vocational schools. Many Bruneians study at foreign universities. The government pays for their education.

Land and Climate. Brunei borders the South China Sea on the north. The rest of the country is surrounded by Malaysia. Most of Brunei is flat, and the interior is heavily wooded. The Brunei River flows through the capital.

Brunei has a tropical climate with average monthly temperatures of about 80° F. (27° C). There is little difference between summer and winter temperatures. Rainfall averages about 100 inches (250 centimeters) a year along the coast and about 125 inches (320 centimeters) inland.

Economy. Petroleum found beneath the coastal waters of Brunei has brought wealth to the country. Petroleum, petroleum products, and natural gas found with petroleum account for almost all the nation's exports. Brunei has small agricultural, fishing, forestry, and manufacturing industries.

The petroleum and gas industry employs only about 10 per cent of the country's labor force. More than 50 per cent of the labor force works for the government, the largest employer by far.

Brunei's petroleum and gas reserves are expected to last only until the early 2000's. The government owns part of the petroleum and gas industry and receives much revenue from it. When Brunei runs out of petroleum and gas, the government may not be able to afford to pay the large numbers of employees it now has. The government encourages the creation of more jobs in private businesses.

Brunei's chief trading partners include Great Britain, Japan, and the United States. Brunei is a member of the Association of Southeast Asian Nations (ASEAN), which also includes Indonesia, Malaysia, the Philippines, Singapore, and Thailand. Brunei trades with other ASEAN nations. See ASSOCIATION OF SOUTHEAST ASIAN NATIONS.

History. Brunei is mentioned in Chinese writings as early as the A.D. 600's. By then, it was an important trading center. The first sultan of Brunei came to power in the 1200's. During the 1400's and 1500's, Brunei was a powerful country that controlled most of the north coast of Borneo and parts of the southern Philippines. In the 1600's and 1700's, Brunei supported pirates who attacked European trading ships in Southeast Asia.

Great Britain took control of most of northern Borneo in the 1800's to protect its shipping lanes between China and India. Brunei lost much of its land and power. In 1888, Britain made Brunei a British protectorate. By then, Brunei had been reduced to approximately its present size.

The discovery of oil off the coast in 1929 brought wealth to Brunei. In the early 1960's, political unrest led the sultan to abolish political parties.

Brunei became an independent nation on Jan. 1, 1984. Although prosperous, it faces the need to build up other economic activities before its petroleum runs out. Tension between Chinese and non-Chinese Bruneians is another problem.   DAVID P. CHANDLER

Brunei

- International boundary
- Road
- ⊛ National capital
- • Other city or town
- + Elevation above sea level

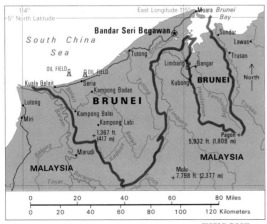

WORLD BOOK map

Dictionary Supplement

This section lists important words from the 1985 edition of THE WORLD BOOK DICTIONARY. This dictionary, first published in 1963, keeps abreast of our living language with a program of continuous editorial revision. The following supplement has been prepared under the direction of the editors of THE WORLD BOOK ENCYCLOPEDIA and Clarence L. Barnhart, editor in chief of THE WORLD BOOK DICTIONARY. It is presented as a service to owners of the dictionary and as an informative feature to subscribers to THE WORLD BOOK YEAR BOOK.

A a

am|bi|son|ic (am′bi son′ik), *adj.* having to do with recorded sound that simulates the directional qualities of the sound it reproduces: *Ambisonic master recordings are made in the full four-channel format* (New Scientist). [< Latin *ambi-* surrounding + English *sonic*]

ATM (no periods) or **A.T.M.,** automatic teller machine (an electronic machine that makes change, records deposits, etc.): *Most A.T.M. users are also shoppers . . . able to "bank" from 8 in the morning until 10 at night* (New York Times).

B b

ba|gel|i|no (bā′gə lē′nō), *n. U.S.* a cross between a bagel and a pretzel, usually covered with sesame seeds: *For those who follow the fashions in sidewalk vending, frozen yogurt and bagelinos made their debuts* (Marian Burros). [< *bagel* + *-ino,* as in *bambino*]

ba|sho (bā′shō), *n., pl.* **ba|sho.** a fifteen-match tournament in sumo wrestling: *Kitanoumi's growing dominance of the sport was strikingly evident when he won both the March and September basho* (Andrew M. Adams). [< Japanese *basho* matches, tournaments]

beltway bandit, *U.S. Slang.* a consultant or expert, often a former government employee, hired by a corporation to help secure government contracts: *Well-paying jobs in electronics and at national corporate headquarters are filled by "Beltway Bandits"* (New York Times). [< *beltway* that circles Washington, D.C., seat of the U.S. government]

birth, *adj.* related by birth or blood, not by adoption or the like; biological: *Parent Finders was started . . . to help adoptees find their birth relatives* (Maclean's).

break dancing, *U.S.* a style of dancing, often competitive, in which the dancers wriggle, spin on their backs, and perform other acrobatics: *They are young street dudes, nearly all of them black . . . and what they are doing is a new style of dancing known as "breaking" or "break dancing"* (New York Daily News).

build-down (bild′doun′), *n., v.,* **built-down, building-down.—***n.* a reduction of nuclear armament by eliminating existing weapons for new ones produced: *Some of the steam went out of . . . the so-called "build-down" scheme for reducing the superpower's nuclear arsenals* (Economist).**—***v.t.* to reduce (armaments) by a build-down: *President Reagan will . . . offer to "build-down" the USA's nuclear weapons when deadlocked strategic arms talks resume* (USA Today). [patterned on *build-up*]

C c

cattle show, 2 *U.S. Informal.* a public gathering of Presidential candidates running in a primary election campaign: *In a cattle show, national candidates are herded into a ballroom, which then becomes a kind of stockyard-showcase* (William Safire).

CD (no periods), **3** compact disk: *Because there is no groove in a CD, there are none of the mechanical problems involved in keeping a phonograph needle in a groove* (Suburbia Today).

chat|com (chat′kom), *n. U.S. Informal.* an interview program on television or radio that is informal, and usually humorous: *"Late Night" is . . . a chatcom whose mixture of the real and the surreal keeps the viewer agreeably off-balance* (Time). [< *chat*[1] + *com*(edy), patterned on *sitcom*]

compact disk or **disc, 1** a digital disk without grooves whose sounds are picked up by a laser: *Many see the compact disk as a potentially enormous growth area for the languishing consumer audio-electronics industry* (New York Times). **2 Compact Disc,** a trademark for such a disk. *Abbr:* CD (no periods).

com|put|er|ist (kəm pyü′tə rist), *n.* a person trained or skilled in the use of computers: *Pick up any "documentation" (called "instructions" in the real and ordinary world), and you are apt to be immediately bombarded by gibberish, at best intimidating to the neophyte and portentous to the versed computerist* (New York Times).

contact visit, a prison visit during which a prisoner is permitted to have physical contact with his visitors: *Following the ruling Spenkelink was allowed contact visits with his 67-year-old mother . . . and his fiancee* (New York Post).

cryp|to|zo|ol|o|gy (krip′tō zō ol′ə jē), *n.* the study of and search for legendary animals: *The formation . . . of the International Society of Cryptozoology (the study of "hidden" animals) confers a new respectability on scientists who study the likes of . . . Sasquatch, the Himalayan Yeti, and the Loch Ness Monster* (Pat Ohlendorf). [< *crypto-* + *zoology*] **—cryp′to|zo|o|log′i|cal,** *adj.* **— cryp′to|zo|ol′o|gist,** *n.*

D d

dan|cer|cise (dan′sər sīz), *n.* the practice of dancing, especially in a group, as a type of physical exercise: *Witnessing a performance of Les Ballets Jazz de Montréal is much like watching a "dancercise" class work itself into a . . . lather of shimmying, shaking, jiving, and high-kicking* (Maclean's). [blend of *dance* and (ex)*ercise*]

death squad, an organized group of killers, especially ones hired by a government to assassinate suspected political enemies: *Military regimes in Argentina, Brazil, Uruguay, Paraguay, Bolivia and Chile, augmented by plainclothes "death squads," have killed many guerrilla leaders and followers* (New York Times).

deek (dēk), *n. U.S. Slang.* a policeman: *The regulars long since recognized them as "deeks"—street slang for cops—but not because they had seen the policemen's snapshots or because they were white* (New Yorker). [probably alteration or variant of *dick*]

digital disk or **disc,** a sound recording whose sound is enhanced by processing with a digital computer: *The first fully digital discs, compact and metallic, gleaming with rainbow colors, their music free of all interference . . . will be tracked by a laser beam on a completely new kind of player* (Manchester Guardian Weekly).

dirty war, the use of terrorism, death squads, or other unorthodox means of waging war: *Argentina's Permanent Assembly for Human Rights documents more than 5,100 missing persons, victims of . . . a "dirty war" against leftist guerrillas* (Richard Boudreaux).

disk drive, the machinery of a computer that turns a disk to retrieve information stored on the disk: *In addition to floppy disk drives, there are hard disk drives, which rapidly spin hard, metal disks that store vastly greater amounts of information than do floppy disks* (New York Times).

diving reflex, a bodily reflex of mammals that takes place when the head is submersed in cold water slowing the heartbeat and diverting blood to the brain, heart, and lungs, to delay suffocation: *The diving reflex . . . is especially strong in younger persons* (Science News).

donor card, a card designating which organs may be used in transplant surgery upon the bearer's death: *If a person carries a donor card, . . . that should overrule any objections by the coroner unless there is a reason, such as damage to the body, why the organ should not be used* (London Times).

E e

edit *v.t.* **4** to alter (a gene) by genetic engineering: *For large genes it is probably more practical to isolate the natural gene and then, when necessary, merely "edit" the gene with chemically synthesized DNA* (Science).

eth|no|phar|ma|col|o|gy (eth′nō fär′mə kol′ə jē), *n.* the traditional use of medicinal substances by a particular culture; folk medicine: *The recent creation of the Journal of Ethnopharmacology attests to a growing interest in exploring medical use of plants among primitive peoples* (Science News).

eye, *n.* **12** the angle from which a graphic image is viewed on a computer screen: *In addition to three-dimensional manipulation of an object, the program offers separate but simultaneous manipulation of the "eye," the viewing point* (Popular Computing).

F f

fast-track (fast′trak′), *adj.* rapid; accelerated: *The Government has approved the use of fast-track planning procedures, which minimise the scope for public scrutiny and debate* (Manchester Guardian Weekly).

-flation, *combining form.* inflation: *slumpflation, hesiflation, stagflation. Armstrong said that when inflation hits the tax system—taxflation, he calls it—it penalizes the poor* (Memphis Press-Scimitar). *Oilflation breeds huge trade and balance-of-payments deficits* (New York Times). *Many parents undoubtedly believe that the problem of "kidflation" is child's play. . . . But many kids themselves feel quite harassed by increasing prices* (Wall Street Journal).

freeze|nik (frēz′nik), *n. U.S. Slang.* a person who supports a freeze on the production of nuclear weapons: *Having failed in a shabby effort to brand the freezeniks as dupes of the Kremlin, [he] now approaches arms control through the Gospel* (New York Times). [< *freeze, n.* + *-nik*]

fun run, a running race that acknowledges participation rather than performmance: *Her only other formal running had been done in another fun run a few months earlier* (London Times).

fuzz|i|fy (fuz′ə fī), *v.t.,* **-fied, -fy|ing.** *Informal.* to muddle or confuse: *While further blurring the already fuzzy categories of car size,* [the] *fuzzifying began in earnest ... when General Motors inaugurated the downsizing trend* (Time).— **fuzz′i|fi|ca′tion,** *n.*

G g

ganz|feld (gänts′felt), *n. Psychology.* a blank surface, used to prevent interference with internally produced visual imagery: *A ganzfeld can be a whitewashed wall or even, as in some experiments, halves of Ping-Pong balls taped over the eyes* (Marilyn Ferguson). [< German *Ganzfeld,* from *ganz* whole + *Field* field]

golden parachute, an employment contract guaranteeing continued salary and benefits when control of a company is transferred to new owners: *Martin Marietta also disclosed that it had given so-called golden parachutes ... to 29 key executives five days after it received the takeover bid from Bendix* (Raleigh News and Observer). [probably patterned after *golden handshake*]

H h

hack¹, *v.t.* **4** *U.S. Informal.* **b** to manipulate (computer programs), especially with skill: *For solitary entertainment, these young adults spend long hours hacking—inconsequentially toying with complex programs—at the terminals of university computers* (Charles M. Cegielski).

hack|er (hak′ər), *n.* **1** a person who hacks, especially a person who fools around to pass time. **2** *U.S. Informal.* a computer operator, especially one skilled in manipulation of computer programs: *Then came the movie War Games and a rash of long-distance, electronic break-ins by a group of computer-literate teenagers, or "hackers," from Milwaukee* (Inc.). [< *hack¹, v.t.,* def. 4 + *er¹*]

hu|ma|lin (hyü′mə lin), *n.* insulin made for humans through genetic engineering: *The Food and Drug Administration approved the marketing of "humalin"—human insulin made artificially from gene-splicing techniques* (Carol Bellamy). [< *huma*(n) + (insu)*lin*]

I i

IMINT (im′int), *n.* intelligence obtained through aerial photography: *The most solid evidence the U.S. has about events in Central America comes from IMINT* (Time). [< *im*(age) *int*(elligence)]

in|cre|men|tal|ism (in′krə men′tə liz′əm, ing′-), *n.* gradual change, especially in social behavior and attitudes or political policy, or government intervention: *In particular, the Bureau* [of the Budget] *had become central to the process of creeping government or incrementalism. ... Under the incremental approach, small programs expanded year by year in reach and cost until they became major items* (Atlantic).

in|fo|bit (in′fō bit′), *n.* an item of information in a databank: *Rights will be threatened in this new world of the 21st Century, property rights and copyrights in particular. Will the database owners track down and pay the originators of every "infobit" accessed?* (Library Journal). [< *info* + *bit⁴*]

J j

ju|di|care (jü′də kãr′), *n. U.S.* a government-sponsored program providing free legal services to the poor: *For all the arguments over the pros and cons of judicare, there is agreement that too many of the nation's poor still go without legal help* (Time). [< *judi*(cial) + *care,* patterned on *medicare*]

K k

K-point (kā′point′), *n.* the point in the landing area in ski jumping beyond which there is insufficient space for a safe landing: *If someone lands at the K-point, the starting gate is lowered to reduce speed* (Maclean's). [half-translation of German *K-Punkt,* short for *Kritischer Punkt* critical point]

K-Z syndrome, a group of symptoms in liberated prisoners of war, including anxiety, insomnia, memory lapse, and guilt for surviving: *It may be that all or part of the K-Z syndrome will show up in the returned Vietnam POW's, but the evidence is inconclusive so far* (Science News). [*K-Z,* from German *Konzentrationslager* concentration camp]

L l

laser disk or **disc,** = optical disk: *Today's videodiscs differ radically ... from one another. The most sophisticated is the optical disc, or laser disc* (Arthur Fisher).

lethal injection, injection of a lethal drug into the body of a person condemned to death: *... to receive a lethal injection in a Texas prison for a 1980 murder* (Milton Greenberg).

M m

mail center, *U.S.* a business establishment that provides mailboxes for patrons: *Storefront businesses ... sometimes called "mail centers"—began springing up in California* [in] *response to the shortage of boxes at United States Post Offices* (New York Times).

mal|il|lu|mi|na|tion (mal′i lü′mə nā′shən), *n.* a condition that arises from overexposure to artificial light: *Any excess of artificial light (particularly from a TV) leads to a syndrome—malillumination* (New Scientist).

mech|a|tron|ics (mek′ə tron′iks), *n.* the design, manufacture, and use of miniaturized components in electronic circuits: *Mechatronics ... combines the potentialities of mechanical and electronic engineering* (Japan Times). [< *mecha*(nics) + (elec)*tronics*]

mi|cro|fil|a|men|tous (mī′krō fil′ə men′təs), *adj.* consisting of microfilaments: *The actin and myosin of the microfilamentous system interacted with each other while floating just under the membrane* (New Scientist).

mi|cro|grav|i|ty (mī′krō grav′ə tē), *n.* a condition of very low gravity, especially approaching weightlessness: *In the past, some astronauts had a hard time getting used to microgravity and were nauseated for first few days in orbit* (The Space Shuttle Operator's Manual).

mouse, *n.* **5** a device to control a cursor or other image on a computer display screen: *Other ... features of the System One will be the availability of a "mouse," or hand-held control device* (Wall Street Journal).

my|o|ther|a|py (mī′ō ther′ə pē), *n.* the application of pressure to relieve muscular pain: *In myotherapy, once the offending trigger point has been located, pressure is applied to it with fingers, knuckles, or elbows for seven seconds* (Berkshire Sampler).

N n

neutralist, *n., adj.* **2** a geneticist who attributes genetic variation to random disappearance of different forms or stages of organisms: *Neutralists and selectionists have also diametrically opposed explanations for the mechanism by which genetic variability is maintained within a species, particularly in the form of ... coexistence in a species of two or more different forms of a protein* (Scientific American).

N.I.C. or **NIC** (no periods), newly industrialized country (a country that has begun to show rapid industrial development): *Nor have the higher rates in the N.I.C. ... brought appreciable change in the conditions of existence of the great mass of their people* (Scientific American).

O o

off-price (ôf′prīs′, of′-), *adj., adv. U.S.—adj.* offering merchandise below the retail price suggested by manufacturers. — *adv.* at a price lower than that suggested by manufacturers: *Mr. Syms, whose business is buying and selling merchandise off-price ("we are not discounters"), said that his personal exposure has helped the business* (New York Times).

om|ni|cide (om′nə sīd), *n.* the destruction of all life: *The subject of nuclear omnicide has proliferated in the pages of the Guardian* (Manchester Guardian Weekly). [< *omni-* + *-cide²*]

oral, *n.* **2** *U.S. Informal.* a secretly recorded conversation, not filmed or videotaped: *That was recorded in what the F.B.I. called an "oral," ... through a pair of microphones concealed at opposite ends of* [an] *office* (B.A. Franklin).

Pronunciation Key: hat, āge, cãre, fär; let, ēqual, tėrm; it, īce; hot, ōpen, ôrder; oil, out; cup, pút, rüle; child; long; thin; ᴛʜen; zh, measure; ə represents a in about, e in taken, i in pencil, o in lemon, u in circus.

orphan drug, a drug not manufactured because only a small number of patients might purchase it: *The 97th Congress . . . passed the Orphan Drug Act. The act offers hope to thousands of hopeless victims of rare diseases* (Tuscaloosa News).

Oz|y|man|di|an (oz′ə man′dē ən), *adj.* extremely large; huge: *It is those Ozymandian budget deficits that are soaking up private capital, driving the economy out of productive investment* (Time). [< *Ozymandias*, an ancient Egyptian king whose statue is said to have been the largest in Egypt, made famous in a sonnet by Shelley]

P p

passenger cell, a white blood cell that is accidentally implanted with an organ from a donor: *Organ culture must work by clearing away "passenger cells" that for some reason provoked rejection* (New Scientist).

pre|quark (prē′kwôrk′), *n. Nuclear Physics.* a hypothetical particle from which all quarks and leptons are made: *Each quark and lepton in the standard model would be accounted for as a combination of prequarks, just as each hadron can be explained as a combination of quarks* (H. Harari).

press opportunity, *U.S.* a brief news conference: *A "press opportunity" is on the schedule when the plane sets down in Omaha (whose media reach into Iowa)* (New Yorker). [patterned on *photo opportunity*]

pro-fam|i|ly (prō fam′ə lē, -fam′lē), *adj. U.S.* favoring large families rather than abortions; right-to-life: *It is possible that pressure from the Republican right could force the White House to undertake a major effort to push across "pro-family" legislation* (New York Times Magazine).

Q q

quality circle, *U.S.* a group of workers who meet regularly on behalf of the company to discuss ways to improve production: *"Quality circle" groups are blossoming at dozens of companies and others are making frankly financial appeals to their workers* (Newsweek).

quark|o|ni|um (kwôr kō′nē əm), *n. Nuclear Physics.* a hypothetical particle consisting of a quark and its antiparticle: *This quarkonium structure (a particular kind of quark bound to its antiquark) is also represented in the psi particles, which are held to be a charm quark plus its antiquark* (Science News). [< *quark* + *-onium*, as in *bottomonium, charmonium*]

R r

rad|waste (rad′wāst), *n.* radioactive waste material from industrial and medical processes: *the disposal of radwaste.*

rainbow coalition, *U.S.* a coalition for political action of disadvantaged groups of the country (originally in reference to the different colors represented by blacks, Hispanics, whites, American Indians, and Asians): *Unity among the white poor, minorities, and women will create a "Rainbow Coalition" that can have a significant impact on our process of gov-*

ernment (Alvin A. Poussaint). [popularized by the Reverend Jesse L. Jackson, an American civil rights leader]

ri|pog|ra|phy (ri pog′rə fē), *n. Informal.* the unauthorized photocopying of books, often in violation of copyright laws: *Canadian authors and publishers, for instance, rail against losses caused by . . . "ripography." Their targets are academic institutions that copy texts . . . in vast quantities for classroom use* (Maclean's). [blend of *rip-o(ff)* + *-graphy*, as in *xerography*]

rock-jock (rok′jok′), *n. Slang.* a mountain climber: *Scruffy "rock-jocks" . . . could mount challenges to the best British, Polish, and American climbers in the high peaks of Asia* (Thomas Hopkins). [< *rock¹* + *jock²*]

S s

scuzz (skuz), *n. U.S. Slang.* a dirty, shabby person or thing: *The CC, Eighth Avenue local, was described to me as "scuzz"—disreputable* (New York Times Magazine). [perhaps shortened and altered < *disgusting*]

skell (skel), *n. U.S. Slang.* a derelict living in a city subway system: *"Wolfman Jack" is a skell, living underground at the Hoyt-Schermerhorn station in Brooklyn, on the GG line. The police there give him food and clothes* (New York Times Magazine). [perhaps shortened < *skeleton*, in reference to the emaciated appearance of such a person or to his being "buried" underground]

sliver, *n.* 3 *U.S.* a tall and very narrow building: *By allowing skyscrapers to be wedged into the East Side, in allowing the sliver design . . . the City Planning Commission has abandoned part of its mission* (J. Melanowski).

space telescope, a telescope housed in an artificial satellite in space: *Space telescopes are . . . especially vital in the study of gamma rays, X rays, and ultraviolet rays that are blocked by the earth's atmosphere* (J.M. and N. Pasachoff).

stretch, *n.* 9 *U.S. Informal.* a long limousine: *This big Mercedes stretch . . . with the plush seats and the glass partition, with the uniformed chauffeur in front and the bar and radio in back* (Colette Dowling).

sun|choke (sun′chōk′), *n.* the edible tuber of the Jerusalem artichoke: *Whether or not the sunchoke, . . . will ever make the big time is still unclear. There was a flurry of activity a few years ago when the vegetable was renamed* (Marian Burros). [< *sun* + (arti)*choke*]

T t

tel|e|com|put|ing (tel′ə kəm pyü′ting), *n.* transmission of computerized data over a long distance, as by telephone or radio connection: *Those considering what it takes to get into telecomputing will appreciate his detailed lists of the necessary equipment* (Popular Computing).

tel|e|mat|ics (tel′ə mat′iks), *n.* the machinery and processes for transmission of computerized information: *What is delaying greater use of telematics in libraries? High costs and limited communication capabilities* (Library Journal). [< *tele*(communication) + (infor)*matics*; patterned on French *télématique*]

touch tablet or **panel**, a thin box or tablet connected to a computer and containing an electronic device that is heat sensitive. By the touch of a finger graphic material or images drawn on the tablet can be displayed on a computer screen: [The] *light pen lets you draw lines on the computer's display [screen] or select menu options by touch. The touch tablet performs a similar function except that you touch an electronic pad rather than a screen, giving higher resolution* (Popular Computing).

T-W (tē′ dub′əl yü), *n. U.S. Informal.* a three-wheeled motorcycle with balloon tires which allow it to traverse rough or soft terrain: *The three-wheelers' serious uses include farm haulage, tending vineyards, construction work, and herding cattle. But the T-W's principal allure is recreational* (Time). [< *t*(hree)-*w*(heeler)]

U u

ul|tra|light (ul′trə līt′), *n.* a small, usually open, airplane constructed of an aluminum frame with sailcloth wings and a small motor: *An ultralight may not weigh more than 254 pounds . . . must stay out of controlled airspace, and may not fly at night* (National Geographic).

understand, *v.t.* 10 to follow instructions in (a particular computer language): *Acorn has agreed to modify substantially the BASIC used by its current range of machines, called Atoms, so that other microcomputers can understand the language as well* (New Scientist).

us|er-friend|ly (yü′zər frend′lē), *adj.* designed to be easy to use: *I also was impressed by how "user-friendly" the software is* (ABA Banking Journal).—**us′er-friend′li|ness,** *n.*

W w

walk-on, *n.* 3 *U.S. Sports.* an athlete who is not drafted or awarded a scholarship: *Martinez has had to make do with New Mexico talent, including one player who did not even come to Highlands on a basketball scholarship—a category of athlete known in the trade as "walk-ons"* (New Yorker).

Z z

zoo event, an astronomical event of no known source or cause: *A White House panel of scientists issued a report . . . that concluded the flash was a "zoo event," a signal of unknown origin, possibly caused by the impact of a small meteoroid on the satellite* (Science News).

zy|de|co or **Zy|de|co** (zī′də kō), *n., pl.* **-cos.** *U.S.* a style of country music similar to bluegrass but with elements of rock, blues, and Latin-American music: *It is this concoction of musical styles that has helped make Zydeco popular, . . . with a big following in Europe* (Daily Argus).

Z-ze|ro (zē′zir′ō), *n. Nuclear Physics.* a hypothetical elementary particle, about 100 times the mass of the proton, thought to be a weakon, or carrier of the weak interaction: *Discovery of the Z-zero (so called because its electric charge is zero) would complete the roster of particles carrying the weak force* (Walter Sullivan).

Index

1984

How to Use the Index

This index covers the contents of the 1983, 1984, and 1985 editions of THE WORLD BOOK YEAR BOOK.

Each index entry is followed by the edition year and the page number, as:

VISUAL ARTS, 85-516, 84-515, 83-520

This means that information about visual arts begins on page 516 in the 1985 edition of THE YEAR BOOK.

An index entry that is the title of an article appearing in THE YEAR BOOK is printed in capital letters, as: **RUSSIA.** An entry that is not an article title, but a subject discussed in an article of some other title, is printed: **Music videos.**

The "See" and "See also" cross references are to other entries within the index. Clue words or phrases are used when two or more references to the same subject appear in the same edition of THE YEAR BOOK. These make it easy to locate the material on the page, since they refer to an article title or article subsection in which the reference appears, as:

Artificial heart: heart disease, Special Report, 84-64; medicine, 85-390, 84-400, 83-400

The indication "il." means that the reference is to an illustration only. An index entry in capital letters followed by "WBE" refers to a new or revised WORLD BOOK ENCYCLOPEDIA article in the supplement section, as:

RENAISSANCE: WBE, 85-532

INDEX

A

Abdul-Jabbar, Kareem: basketball, 85–216
Abortion: Ireland, 84–362; Roman Catholic, 85–465, 84–466; Spain, 84–479; Supreme Court, 84–490
Abu Bakar, Ahmad: Malaysia, 84–396
Academy of Motion Picture Arts and Sciences: awards, 85–208, 84–210, 83–207
Accelerator, Particle: physics, 85–447, 84–443
Access charges: communications, 85–254, 84–257
Accidents. See DISASTERS; SAFETY.
Accretionary plate tectonics: Special Report, 84–134
Acetylcholine: biochemistry, 85–219
Achievement test: testing, Special Report, 83–97
Acid rain: botany, 85–221; Canada, 85–233, 83–241; environment, 85–306, 84–310; Close-Up, 84–309, 83–313
Acquired immune deficiency syndrome. See AIDS.
Acreage allotment: farming, Special Report, 84–111
ACT test: education, 85–295; testing, Special Report, 83–100
Action for Excellence: education, 84–299; schools, Special Report, 84–71
Adams, Ansel: deaths, 85–276; il., 85–278
Adams, Gerry: Northern Ireland, 84–425
Adams, Robert McCormick: personalities, 85–437
Addiction: psychology, 84–454, 83–456
Aden. See Yemen (Aden).
Adler, Luther: deaths, 85–276
Adler, Mortimer J.: schools, Special Report, 84–69
Adoption Assistance Child Welfare Act: child welfare, 84–244
ADVERTISING, 85–174, 84–180, 83–178; consumerism, 84–270; magazine, 85–385, 84–395, 83–395; television, 83–499
Aegyptopithecus zeuxis: anthropology, Close-Up, 85–186
Aerospace industry. See AVIATION; SPACE EXPLORATION.
Afars and Issas, Territory of. See Djibouti.
Affirmative action: civil rights, 85–251, 84–254; Supreme Court, 85–492
AFGHANISTAN, 85–175, 84–181, 83–179; Asia, 85–196, 84–198, 83–197; Middle East, 83–408; Pakistan, 85–435
AFL-CIO: Democratic Party, 84–285, 83–289
AFRICA, 85–177, 84–183, 83–180; anthropology, 83–188; civil rights, 85–251; perspective, 85–165; population, 83–447; religion, 83–465; Special Report, 85–31. See also entries for specific countries.
African Methodist Episcopal Church: religion, 85–463, 84–462, 83–464
African Methodist Episcopal Zion Church: religion, 85–463, 84–462, 83–464
African National Congress (ANC): Mozambique, 85–406; South Africa, 84–477
Agca, Mehmet Ali: crime, 85–269
Agent Orange: chemical industry, 85–238, 84–240; veterans, 85–515, 84–514
Agricultural Programs Adjustment Act of 1984: farm, 85–314
Agriculture. See FARM AND FARMING.
AgRISTARS: *Landsat,* Special Report, 84–148
Agrobacterium tumefaciens: biochemistry, 84–221; botany, 84–223; gene-splicing, Special Report, 85–71
Ahidjo, Ahmadou: Cameroon, 85–227
Ahmadiyya Muslims: Pakistan, 85–435
Aid to Families with Dependent Children: city, 83–253; welfare, 84–520, 83–524
AIDS (Acquired Immune Deficiency Syndrome): health, 85–339, 84–350; public health, Close-Up, 84–455; West Indies, 84–522
Air Force. See ARMED FORCES.
Air pollution: chemical industry, 85–238; coal, 84–255; environment, Close-Up, 84–309. See also Pollution.
Air traffic controllers: aviation, 84–209, 83–205
Airbag: safety, 85–473, 83–473; transportation, 84–505, 83–508
Airline. See AVIATION.
Akhnaten: il., 85–408
Alabama: state govt., 85–488, 84–485, 83–488
Alaska: hunting, 84–352, 83–357; il., 84–132; petroleum, 83–439; state govt., 85–488, 84–486, 83–488

Alaska National Interest Lands Conservation Act: hunting, 84–352
ALBANIA, 85–182, 84–188, 83–185; Europe, 85–311, 84–315, 83–318
ALBERTA, 85–182, 84–188, 83–186; Canada, Special Report, 84–41
Albright, Ivan: deaths, 84–278
Albuquerque: city, 85–248, 84–250, 83–254
Alburt, Lev: chess, 85–239
Alcohol Traffic Safety Act: safety, 84–470
Alcoholism: mental illness, 84–402; psychology, 83–457
Alcott, Amy: golf, 85–331
Aleixandre, Vicente: deaths, 85–276
Aleksandrov, Aleksandr: space, 84–478
Alfalfa: farm, 84–320
ALFONSÍN, RAÚL RICARDO, 84–189; Argentina, 85–190; 84–194
ALGERIA, 85–183, 84–189, 83–186; Africa, 85–178, 84–184, 83–182
Ali, Muhammad: personalities, 85–437
Alicia, Hurricane: Houston, 84–350; weather, 84–519
Alien. See IMMIGRATION.
All-America Selections: gardening, 85–327, 84–332, 83–338
Alligator: hunting, 85–346; zoology, 83–529; zoos, 85–528
Alliluyeva, Svetlana: personalities, 85–437
Allison, Bobby: auto racing, 84–207, 83–205
Alpha Ridge: Northwest Territories, 84–426
Alpine Experiment (ALPEX): weather, 83–524
Alpine skiing: Olympics, 85–432; skiing, 85–477, 84–474, 83–477
Alumina: mining, 84–408
Alvarado, Anthony J.: New York City, 84–420
Alzheimer's disease: health, 85–340
Al Zulfikar: Pakistan, 83–431
AM radio: radio, 85–460
Amazon Project: Brazil, 83–224
America II: boating, 85–220
American Ballet Theatre: dancing, 85–273, 84–276, 83–281
American Baptist Association: religion, 85–463, 84–462, 83–464
American Baptist Churches in the U.S.A.: religion, 85–463, 84–462, 83–464
American Contract Bridge League: bridge, 85–223
American Dance Festival: dancing, 85–275, 84–277
American Indian. See INDIAN, AMERICAN.
American Institute of Architects: awards, 85–208, 84–210, 83–207
American Kennel Club: dog, 85–288, 84–291, 83–295
AMERICAN LIBRARY ASSOCIATION (ALA), 85–184, 84–189, 83–187
American Lutheran Church, The: Protestantism, 83–455; religion, 85–463, 84–462, 83–464
American Medical Association: health, 84–343; medicine, 83–401
American Motors Corporation: automobile, 84–205, 83–203; labor, 83–377
American Procession, An: literature, 85–378
American Red Cross: disasters, 84–288
Amino acids: obesity, Special Report, 83–154
Amniocentesis: medicine, 84–401
Amtrak: railroad, 85–460, 84–459, 83–462
Anabolic steroid: sports, 84–480
Ancient Evenings: literature, 84–386
". . . And Ladies of the Club": literature, 85–378
Anderson, Maxie: deaths, 84–278
Andorra: Europe, 85–311, 84–315, 83–318
Andrews, James E.: Protestantism, 85–455
ANDROPOV, YURI VLADIMIROVICH, 83–187; Close-Up, 85–471; Europe, 84–313; President, 84–448; Russia, 84–468, 83–470
Angina: drugs, 83–295; health, 84–343; heart disease, Special Report, 84–51
Angiocardiography: heart disease, Special Report, 84–56
Anglicans: Roman Catholic, 83–468. See also Episcopal Church, The.
ANGOLA, 85–184, 84–190, 83–188; Africa, 85–178, 84–184, 83–182; Namibia, 85–412, 84–418, 83–419
ANGUILLA: WBE, 83–570
Animal. See CAT; CONSERVATION; DOG; FARM AND FARMING; ZOOLOGY; ZOOS.
Anthony, Earl: bowling, 85–221, 84–223, 83–222
ANTHROPOLOGY, 85–185, 84–190, 83–188. See also ARCHAEOLOGY.
Antigen: biochemistry, 84–221; gene-splicing, Special Report, 85–68
Antigua and Barbuda: WBE, 83–569; Latin America, 85–374, 84–381, 83–384
Antiochian Orthodox Christian Archdiocese of

North America, The: Eastern Orthodox Churches, 83–297; religion, 85–463, 84–462, 83–464
Antitrust laws: consumerism, 85–266
Anxiety disorder: mental illness, 85–392; psychology, 85–457
ANZUS: Australia, 85–202; New Zealand, 85–416
Aparicio, Luis: baseball, 85–216
Apartheid: civil rights, 84–253; Protestantism, 85–457
Aphid: gardening, 84–332
Apolipoprotein A1: cholesterol, Special Report, 85–137
Aquariums. See ZOOS.
Aquino, Agapito: Philippines, 85–444
Aquino, Benigno S., Jr.: Philippines, 85–444, 84–440; Asia, 84–199
Arabia. See MIDDLE EAST; SAUDI ARABIA.
Arabs: Egypt, 83–306; Middle East, 83–407; Saudi Arabia, 83–474
Arafat, Yasir: ils., 84–275, 83–510; Middle East, 84–405, 83–407; Syria, 84–493
ARCHAEOLOGY, 85–187, 84–191, 83–189; Monticello, Special Report, 85–102. See also ANTHROPOLOGY.
Archery: sports, 85–484, 84–481, 83–483
ARCHITECTURE, 85–189, 84–192, 83–190; awards, 85–208, 84–210, 83–207. See also BUILDING AND CONSTRUCTION.
ARDITO BARLETTA VALLARINA, NICOLÁS, 85–190
ARGENTINA, 85–190, 84–194, 83–192; Alfonsín, Raúl, 84–189; Bignone, Reynaldo, 83–218; Canada, 83–233; Chile, 84–249; Falklands, 83–322; Latin America, 85–374, 84–381, 83–384; United Nations, 83–511
Argonne National Laboratory: il., 84–442
Ariane: space, 85–481
Arizona: state govt., 85–488, 84–485, 83–488
Arkansas: state govt., 85–488, 84–485, 83–488
ARMED FORCES, 85–192, 84–194, 83–193; il., 84–382; President, 84–449, 83–452; Robinson, Roscoe, Jr., 83–467; U.S. govt., 84–512; West Indies, 84–521. See also entries for specific continents and countries.
Armenian Church of America, Diocese of the: religion, 85–463, 84–462, 83–464
Arms-control negotiations: armed forces, 84–194, 83–193; Canada, 83–233; Europe, 85–310, 84–313; President, 85–453, 84–448, 83–451; Russia, 85–470; Trudeau, Pierre, 84–506; United Nations, 85–508
Armstrong, Debbie: il., 85–426
Army, U.S.: armed forces, 83–194; Robinson, Roscoe, Jr., 83–467
Arrington, Richard, Jr.: elections, 84–302
Art Institute of Chicago: visual arts, 85–517
Arthit Kamlang-ek: Thailand, 85–500, 84–499, 83–501
Artificial heart: heart disease, Special Report, 84–64; medicine, 85–390, 84–400, 83–400
Artificial sweetener: nutrition, 84–427
Arts: awards, 85–208, 84–210, 83–209. See also ARCHITECTURE; DANCING; LITERATURE; MOTION PICTURES; MUSIC, CLASSICAL; MUSIC, POPULAR; POETRY; THEATER; VISUAL ARTS.
Asbestos: courts, 83–275
ASEAN: Asia, 85–197, 83–196; Kampuchea, 84–371
ASIA, 85–194, 84–196, 83–195; population, 83–447; Russia, 85–470. See also entries for specific countries.
ASKEW, REUBIN O'DONOVAN, 84–200; il., 84–284
Aspartame: drugs, 84–292; nutrition, 84–427
Aspirin: drugs, 83–295; health, 84–343
Assad, Hafiz al-: Syria, 85–494, 84–493, 83–495
Assad, Rifaat al-: Syria, 85–494
Assam state (India): Asia, 84–199; India, 84–354
Assassination: Egypt, 83–305; Philippines, 84–440
Assemblies of God: religion, 85–463, 84–462, 83–464
Association of Evangelical Lutheran Churches: Protestantism, 83–455
Association of Southeast Asian Nations. See ASEAN.
Asthma: health, 84–344
Astronaut. See SPACE EXPLORATION.
ASTRONOMY, 85–199, 84–201, 83–198
AT&T (American Telephone and Telegraph Company): architecture, 85–190; communications, 85–254, 84–257, 83–262; consumerism, 85–265, 84–269
Atherosclerosis: cholesterol, Special Report, 85–134; heart disease, Special Report, 84–50

586

U

V

Acknowledgments

The publishers acknowledge the following sources for illustrations. Credits read from top to bottom, left to right, on their respective pages. An asterisk (*) denotes illustrations and photographs that are the exclusive property of THE YEAR BOOK. All maps, charts, and diagrams were prepared by THE YEAR BOOK staff unless otherwise noted.

3	NASA; Gamma/Liaison
9	NASA
10	© David Burnett, Contact
12	© Bill Nation, Sygma; © Randy Taylor, Sygma
13	© Sal di Marco, Black Star
14	© Sipa Press; © Sipa Press; © Max Scheler, Black Star
16	Diana Walker, Gamma/Liaison; Bob Nickelsberg, Woodfin Camp, Inc.; Focus on Sports
17	NASA; Bryson, Sygma
18	Stuart Franklin, Sygma; Gregg Vaughn, Black Star
19	UPI/Bettmann Archive; Tass from Sovfoto; © Dennis Brack, Black Star
20	Wilbur E. Garrett, © 1984 National Geographic Society; © Giannini Giansanti, Sygma; © Dennis Brack, Black Star
21	Steve Powell, *Sports Illustrated*; Baldev, Sygma; Pool, Gamma/Liaison
22	Traver, Gamma/Liaison; Sven Nackstrand, Gamma/Liaison; Sygma
23	Randy Taylor, Sygma; David Hume Kennerly, Gamma/Liaison
24	Peltier, Sipa Press; F. Reglain, Gamma/Liaison; Lord Snowdon, Sipa Press
25	Stuart Franklin, Sygma; Bill Lyons, Black Star; Roland Neveu, Gamma/Liaison
26	Sygma; NASA
27	Mahendra Sinh, Sipa Press
29	© Chuck Fishman, Woodfin Camp, Inc.
30	Peter Magubane, Black Star
31	J. Pickerell, Black Star
36	Robert Frerck
39	M. P. Kahl, Bruce Coleman Ltd.; Jim Fisher, Black Star
40	W. Campbell, Sygma; Peter Ward, Bruce Coleman Ltd.
42	Magnum; W. Campbell, Sygma
43	Susan Meiselas, Magnum; Chiasson, Gamma/Liaison
44	Kal Muller, Woodfin Camp, Inc.; Charles Henneghien, Bruce Coleman Inc.
46	David Muench
50	Patricia D. Duncan; David Muench
51	Patricia D. Duncan; Patricia D. Duncan; Susan Gibler, Tom Stack & Assoc.
52	Jim Brandenburg; Randy Bean, Living Prairie Museum; Pat Armstrong, Morton Arboretum
53	Jim Brandenburg; J. Gerlach, Tom Stack & Assoc.
54	John Shaw, Tom Stack & Assoc.; Patricia D. Duncan; Patricia D. Duncan
55	Rod Planck, Tom Stack & Assoc.; Patricia D. Duncan; Rod Planck, Tom Stack & Assoc.
56	Pat Armstrong, Morton Arboretum; Jim Brandenburg; Patricia D. Duncan
58	C. Godshalk, Morton Arboretum; Pat Armstrong, Morton Arboretum; Fermi National Laboratory
60	Erich Hartmann, Magnum
63	Trudy Rogers*; Jack Griffith, University of North Carolina
64	National Research Council
65	Dan McCoy, Rainbow
66	Trudy Rogers*; Biogen N.V.; Dan McCoy, Rainbow
67	Trudy Rogers*; Genentech, Inc.; Molecular Genetics Inc.; Molecular Genetics Inc.
68	University of California at Berkeley; Buck Miller
69	John Marmaras, Woodfin Camp, Inc.; R. L. Brinster and R. E. Hammer, School of Veterinary Medicine, University of Pennsylvania
70	Trudy Rogers*; J. E. Seegmiller, M.D., University of California at San Diego
71	Trudy Rogers*
74	From the video "Miss Me Blind" by Culture Club. © Epic Records
76	© Walt Disney Productions
77	© Epic Records
78	From the video "Eyes Without a Face" by Billy Idol. © Chrysalis Records
79	© Lynn Goldsmith, LGI; From the video "Rio" by Duran Duran. © Capitol Records
80	From the video "Catch Me I'm Falling" by Real Life. © Stephan Hopkins
82	© Susan Phillips, LGI; © Chuck Fishman, Woodfin Camp, Inc.; © Chuck Fishman, Woodfin Camp, Inc.
83	© Allan Tannenbaum, Sygma
84	© Allan Tannenbaum, Sygma, © Debra Trebitz, LGI; © Jim McHugh
86-97	Dean Mathews*
100	© Robert Llewellyn
101	William M. Kelso
103	William M. Kelso
104	Maryland Historical Society, Baltimore, Gift of Mrs. Frances C. Semmes
105	Massachusetts Historical Society; William M. Kelso; William M. Kelso
106	Benjamin Franklin Papers, Yale University Library
107	William M. Kelso
108	Greg Harlin*
110	Alice F. Dole
111	© Robert Llewellyn
112	William M. Kelso
113	Alice F. Dole
114-115	William M. Kelso
116	© Robert Llewellyn; Manuscripts Department, University of Virginia Library
118	© Charles Vioujard, Gamma/Liaison; UPI/Bettmann Archive
122	Windsor Publications Inc., FPG; © Lee Balterman, Marilyn Gartman Agency; © Peter Menzel, Stock, Boston
124	© Louis Fernandez, Black Star; © Christopher Morris, Black Star
125	© Michael Heron, Woodfin Camp, Inc.; © Michael Philip Manheim, Marilyn Gartman Agency
126	Official Airline Guides; © Cary Wolinsky, Stock, Boston
130	© Allan Tannenbaum, Sygma
132	Joe Rogers*
135	Lou Lainey, © *Discover* Magazine, Time Inc.; Trudy Rogers*
136	Data from the Lipid Research Clinics Coronary Primary Prevention Trial. Adapted from *The Journal of the American Medical Association*. (Trudy Rogers*)
137	© American Heart Association. Reproduced with permission. (Trudy Rogers*); By permission of Ancel Keys. (Trudy Rogers*)
138-142	Joe Rogers*
144	Dennis Brack, Black Star
147	Granger Collection
148	Dennis Brack, Black Star
150	Office of Senator Nancy Landon Kassebaum
152	Chick Harrity, *U.S. News & World Report*
155	AP/Wide World
156	Keith Jewell, U.S. House of Representatives
159	Newberry Library, Chicago
160	Newberry Library, Chicago; Granger Collection; Newberry Library, Chicago; Newberry Library, Chicago
162	Brown Bros.
163	Newberry Library, Chicago; Newberry Library, Chicago; UPI/Bettmann Archive; Newberry Library, Chicago; Thomas Nast, 1884
167	BBC Hulton from UPI/Bettmann Archive; Ann Ronan Picture Library; International Museum of Photography at George Eastman House; UPI/Bettmann Archive
168	The New York Historical Society, New York City, Weld Collection; UPI/Bettmann Archive
171	Canapress
172	UPI/Bettmann Archive; Steve Hopkins, Black Star
173	Jet Propulsion Laboratory; Gustavo Feinblatt, *Time* Magazine
174-176	AP/Wide World
180	Mark Peters, NYT Pictures
181	AP/Wide World
183	© United Press Canada
185	David Brill © 1984 National Geographic Society
186	William E. Sauro, NYT Pictures
188	Wilbur E. Garrett, © 1984 National Geographic Society
189	Andy Levin, Black Star
191-192	AP/Wide World
193	Drawing by Dana Fradon; © 1984 The New Yorker Magazine, Inc.
195-198	UPI/Bettmann Archive
200	Jet Propulsion Laboratory
201	News Ltd.
203	Chrysler Corporation
205	AP/Wide World
207	Nik Kleinberg, Picture Group
209-210	AP/Wide World
213-214	UPI/Bettmann Archive
216	AP/Wide World
219	George Tames, NYT Pictures
220	UPI/Bettmann Archive
225	© Andy Levin, Black Star

229	© Dilip Mehta, Contact
231	UPI/Bettmann Archive
236-238	AP/Wide World
240	Tass from Sovfoto
241	Val Mazzenga, *Chicago Tribune*
242	Derek Debono
244	UPI/Bettmann Archive
245	AP/Wide World
250	UPI/Bettmann Archive
253	AP/Wide World
255	Scott Thode, *U.S. News & World Report*
256	Drawing by Modell; © 1984 The New Yorker Magazine, Inc.
258	UPI/Bettmann Archive
262	*The* (Baltimore) *Sun*
264	Louise Gubb, Jullien
266-267	AP/Wide World
268	Outline
270-271	AP/Wide World
272	Martha Swope
274	Steve Hopkins, Black Star
276	AP/Wide World; UPI/Bettmann Archive; UPI/Bettmann Archive; UPI/Bettmann Archive
277	UPI/Bettmann Archive; UPI/Bettmann Archive; AP/Wide World; AP/Wide World
278	AP/Wide World; © 1984 Chuck Fishman, Contact; AP/Wide World; *New York Daily News*
279	Victor Schrager
280	AP/Wide World; UPI/Bettmann Archive; AP/Wide World; UPI/Bettmann Archive
281-282	AP/Wide World
283	UPI/Bettmann Archive
284	Emory University
285	AP/Wide World
287	Agencia O Globo, *Time* Magazine
288	Martin Booth
290	UPI/Bettmann Archive
291	Cynthia Johnson, *Time* Magazine
292	UPI/Bettmann Archive
293	Martin J. Bucella
296	Ben Weaver, Camera 5
297	AP/Wide World
300	UPI/Bettmann Archive; Phil Valasquez, © News Group Chicago Inc. 1984. Reprinted with permission of the Chicago *Sun-Times;* AP/Wide World; AP/Wide World
303	William Strode Assoc., *Time* Magazine
305	AP/Wide World
306	UPI/Bettmann Archive
308	Tim Graham, Sygma
310	AP/Wide World
312	UPI/Bettmann Archive
314-316	AP/Wide World
323-324	UPI/Bettmann Archive
325	AP/Wide World
326	Tonka Toys
328	Baron Sakiya, Contact from Woodfin Camp, Inc.
329	AP/Wide World
330	Sven Simon
332	AP/Wide World
334	Stuart Franklin, Sygma
335	Associated Newspapers Group Limited
336	© Tim Graham, Sygma
337-340	AP/Wide World
342	United Press Canada
343	AP/Wide World
346	© P. Jordan, Gamma/Liaison
347-348	AP/Wide World
349	© Baldev, Sygma
351	UPI/Bettmann Archive
353	Ken Alexander, Copley News Service
354-357	AP/Wide World
358	Gustavo Feinblatt, *Time* Magazine
359-368	AP/Wide World
371	José Moré, *Chicago Tribune*
372	UPI/Bettmann Archive
373-376	AP/Wide World
379	UPI/Bettmann Archive
380	Patrick E. Girouard
381	From *The Glorious Flight* by Alice and Martin Provensen. Copyright © 1983 by Alice and Martin Provensen. Reprinted by permission of Viking Penguin Inc.
382	AP/Wide World
383	Brent Jones*
384	© Jose Azel, Contact
386	© *Punch* from Rothco
388	RCA News & Information
390	AP/Wide World
391	UPI/Bettmann Archive
392	© *Punch* from Rothco
394	AP/Wide World
397	G. Hobeiche, Sygma
399-401	AP/Wide World
402	© 1984 Columbia Pictures
404	Keith Hamshere, © Lucasfilm Ltd.
405	Tri-Star Pictures
408	Horst Huber
409	Peter Hastings
410	© Debra Trebitz, LGI
411	UPI/Bettmann Archive
412-414	AP/Wide World
415	Jim Wilson, NYT Pictures
416-418	AP/Wide World
419	William Campbell, Sygma
420	AP/Wide World
421	Mark Peters, NYT Pictures
422	John Harquail, Toronto, courtesy of Interprovincial Pipe Line Limited
423	Keith Meyers, NYT Pictures
426	AP/Wide World
427	AP/Wide World; AP/Wide World; AP/Wide World; UPI/Bettmann Archive; Canapress
431	UPI/Bettmann Archive
432	© G. Rancinan, Sygma
435	UPI/Bettmann Archive
436	Leonard Krishtalka
438-439	AP/Wide World
440-441	UPI/Bettmann Archive
442-443	AP/Wide World
445	RCA Corporation
447	Argonne National Laboratory
448	AP/Wide World
451	© Dennis Brack, Black Star
452	UPI/Bettmann Archive
453	© Dennis Brack, Black Star
456	John Goodwin, United Methodist Church
458	Anne Nelson, NYT Pictures
459	Ryan Remiorz, United Press Canada
461	UPI/Bettmann Archive
462	AP/Wide World; UPI/Bettmann Archive
464	UPI/Bettmann Archive
465	AP/Wide World
466	UPI/Bettmann Archive
467	AP/Wide World
469	UPI/Bettmann Archive
470-471	AP/Wide World
472	UPI/Bettmann Archive
473	Canapress
474-475	UPI/Bettmann Archive
476	AP/Wide World
477	UPI/Bettmann Archive
479	William Campbell, Sygma
480-481	NASA
482	AP/Wide World
483	Tass from Sovfoto
484-494	AP/Wide World
496	National Broadcasting Company
498	Columbia Broadcasting System
499	UPI/Bettmann Archive
501	Martha Swope
502	Bruce Chambers, Gamma/Liaison
504-509	AP/Wide World
515	© Dennis Brack, Black Star
517	AP/Wide World
519	George Tames, NYT Pictures
521	Allen Fredrickson, Sipa Press
523-528	AP/Wide World
531	Dick Raphael

A Preview of 1985

January

		1	2	3	4	5
6	7	8	9	10	11	12
13	14	15	16	17	18	19
20	21	22	23	24	25	26
27	28	29	30	31		

1 **New Year's Day.**

5 **Twelfth Night,** traditional end of Christmas festivities during the Middle Ages.

6 **Epiphany,** 12th day of Christmas, celebrates the visit of the Three Wise Men to the infant Jesus.

15 **Martin Luther King, Jr.'s Birthday,** honoring the slain civil rights leader, celebrated on this day in several states and the District of Columbia.

20 **Super Bowl XIX,** the National Football League's championship game, in Palo Alto, Calif.

21 **Public Inauguration Ceremony** for the President of the United States. Private ceremony held January 20.

28 **Australia Day** marks Captain Arthur Phillip's landing in 1788 where Sydney now stands. The actual anniversary is January 26.

February

					1	2
3	4	5	6	7	8	9
10	11	12	13	14	15	16
17	18	19	20	21	22	23
24	25	26	27	28		

1 **Black History Month** through February 28.

2 **Ground-Hog Day.** Legend says six weeks of winter weather will follow if the ground hog sees its shadow.
Candlemas, Roman Catholic holy day, marks the presentation of the infant Jesus in the Temple.

6 **Tu B'Shebat,** Jewish arbor festival, observed by donating trees to Israel.

8 **Boy Scouts of America Birthday Anniversary** marks the founding of the organization in 1910.

12 **Abraham Lincoln's Birthday,** observed in most states.

14 **Valentine's Day,** festival of romance and affection.

18 **George Washington's Birthday,** according to law, is celebrated on the third Monday in February. The actual anniversary is February 22.

19 **Mardi Gras,** celebrated in New Orleans and many Roman Catholic countries, is the last merrymaking before Lent.

20 **Ash Wednesday,** first day of Lent for Christians, begins the period of repentance that precedes Easter.
Chinese New Year begins year 4683, the Year of the Ox, on the ancient Chinese calendar.

March

					1	2
3	4	5	6	7	8	9
10	11	12	13	14	15	16
17	18	19	20	21	22	23
24	25	26	27	28	29	30
31						

1-31 **Red Cross Month.**

7 **Purim,** Jewish festival commemorating how Esther saved the Jews from the tyrant Haman.

10-16 **Girl Scout Week** marks the group's 73rd birthday.

17 **St. Patrick's Day,** honoring the patron saint of Ireland.

17-23 **Camp Fire Birthday Week** marks the 75th anniversary of the group.

19 **St. Joseph's Day,** Roman Catholic feast day honoring the husband of the Virgin Mary.
Swallows Return to San Juan Capistrano, California, from their winter homes.

20 **First Day of Spring,** 11:14 A.M. E.S.T.

21 **Bach's Birthday,** 300th anniversary of the birth of German composer Johann Sebastian Bach in 1685.

25 **Academy Awards Night,** when the Academy of Motion Picture Arts and Sciences presents the Oscars.

31 **Palm Sunday** marks Jesus Christ's last entry into Jerusalem, where people covered His path with palm branches.

April

	1	2	3	4	5	6
7	8	9	10	11	12	13
14	15	16	17	18	19	20
21	22	23	24	25	26	27
28	29	30				

1 **April Fool's Day,** a traditional day for jokes and tricks.

4 **Maundy Thursday,** Christian celebration of Christ's commandment to love others.

5 **Good Friday** marks the death of Jesus on the cross. It is a public holiday in many countries and several states of the United States.

6 **Passover,** Jewish festival that celebrates the exodus of the Jews from bondage in Egypt.

7 **Easter Sunday,** commemorating the Resurrection of Jesus Christ.

14-20 **National Library Week.**

15 **U.S. Income Tax Day.**

24 **Professional Secretaries Day** acknowledges the contributions of secretaries in business, government, and other fields.

28 **Daylight-Saving Time** begins at 2 A.M.

30 **Walpurgis Night,** when witches gather, according to legend.

May

		1	2	3	4	
5	6	7	8	9	10	11
12	13	14	15	16	17	18
19	20	21	22	23	24	25
26	27	28	29	30	31	

1 **May Day,** observed as a festival of spring in many countries and as a holiday honoring workers in socialist and Communist countries.
Law Day U.S.A.

4 **Kentucky Derby,** thoroughbred horse race at Churchill Downs in Louisville, Ky.

5-12 **National Music Week.**

12 **Mother's Day.**

16 **Ascension Day,** or Holy Thursday, 40 days after Easter, celebrates the ascent of Jesus Christ into heaven.

18 **Armed Forces Day** honors all branches of the armed forces in the United States.

20 **Victoria Day,** in Canada, marks the official birthday of the reigning monarch.

21 **First Day of Ramadan,** the Islamic holy month, observed by fasting.

26 **Shavuot,** Jewish Feast of Weeks, marks the revealing of the Ten Commandments to Moses on Mount Sinai.
Pentecost, or Whitsunday, the seventh Sunday after Easter, commemorates the descent of the Holy Spirit upon the 12 disciples.
Stratford Festival, drama and music, through October 13 in Stratford, Canada.

27 **Memorial Day,** by law, is the last Monday in May.

June

						1
2	3	4	5	6	7	8
9	10	11	12	13	14	15
16	17	18	19	20	21	22
23	24	25	26	27	28	29
30						

2 **Trinity Sunday,** the eighth Sunday after Easter, honors the union of the Father, the Son, and the Holy Spirit.

5 **World Environment Day.**

6 **D-Day** commemorates the Allied landing in Normandy in 1944, during World War II.

13-16 **United States Open Golf Championship,** Birmingham, Mich.

14 **Flag Day.**

16 **Father's Day.**

21 **First Day of Summer,** 6:44 A.M. E.D.T.

23 **Midsummer Day,** summer celebration in many European countries.

July

	1	2	3	4	5	6
7	8	9	10	11	12	13
14	15	16	17	18	19	20
21	22	23	24	25	26	27
28	29	30	31			

1 **Canada Day,** in Canada, celebrates the confederation of the provinces in 1867.
4 **Independence Day,** in the United States, the anniversary of the day on which the Continental Congress adopted the Declaration of Independence in 1776.
9 **Baseball All-Star Game,** Minneapolis, Minn.
14 **Bastille Day,** in France, commemorates the uprising of the people of Paris against King Louis XVI in 1789 and their seizure of the Bastille, a hated Paris prison.
15 **St. Swithin's Day.** According to legend, if it rains on this day, it will rain for 40 more.
25 **Puerto Rico Constitution Day.**
28 **Tishah B'Ab,** Jewish holy day, marks the destruction of the first and second temples in Jerusalem in 587 B.C. and A.D. 70.

August

				1	2	3
4	5	6	7	8	9	10
11	12	13	14	15	16	17
18	19	20	21	22	23	24
25	26	27	28	29	30	31

6 **Hiroshima Day,** memorial observance for victims of the first atomic bombing in Hiroshima, Japan, in 1945.
8-11 **Professional Golfers' Association of America Championship,** Denver.
11-13 **Perseid Meteor Shower.**
15 **Feast of the Assumption,** Roman Catholic and Eastern Orthodox holy day, celebrates the ascent of the Virgin Mary into heaven.
19 **National Aviation Day** commemorates the birthday of pioneer pilot Orville Wright in 1871.
26 **Women's Equality Day** commemorates the enactment of the 19th Amendment in 1920 giving women the vote.
27 **United States Open Tennis Championship** through September 8 in Flushing Meadows, N.Y.

September

1	2	3	4	5	6	7
8	9	10	11	12	13	14
15	16	17	18	19	20	21
22	23	24	25	26	27	28
29	30					

2 **Labor Day** in the United States and Canada.
8 **National Grandparents Day** honors grandfathers and grandmothers.
13 **Friday the 13th,** widely believed to be an unlucky day. Also December 13.
15-16 **Mexico Independence Days.**
16 **Rosh Ha-Shanah,** or Jewish New Year, beginning the year 5746 according to the Jewish calendar.
17 **Citizenship Day** celebrates the rights and duties of U.S. citizens.
22 **First Day of Fall,** 10:08 P.M. E.D.T.
25 **Yom Kippur,** or Day of Atonement, the most solemn day in the Jewish calendar.
30 **Sukkot,** or Feast of Tabernacles, begins — Jewish festival that originally marked the harvest season. **End of the Fiscal Year** for the United States government.

October

		1	2	3	4	5
6	7	8	9	10	11	12
13	14	15	16	17	18	19
20	21	22	23	24	25	26
27	28	29	30	31		

6-12 **National 4-H Week. Fire Prevention Week. National Employ the Handicapped Week.**
7 **Shemini Atzeret,** the eighth day of Sukkot, marked with a special prayer for rain. **Child Health Day.**
8 **Simhat Torah,** Jewish festival of rejoicing in God's law, marks the end of the annual cycle of Scripture readings. **Baseball's World Series** begins.
11 **Pulaski Day** honors Casimir Pulaski, Polish general who fought in the American Revolution.
14 **Columbus Day** commemorates Christopher Columbus' landing in America in 1492. The actual anniversary is October 12. **Thanksgiving Day** in Canada.
19 **Sweetest Day,** when sweethearts exchange cards and gifts.
27 **Standard Time Resumes** at 2 A.M.
31 **Halloween. UN Children's Fund (UNICEF) Day. Reformation Day,** celebrated by Protestants, marks the day in 1517 when Reformation leader Martin Luther posted his Ninety-Five Theses.

November

					1	2
3	4	5	6	7	8	9
10	11	12	13	14	15	16
17	18	19	20	21	22	23
24	25	26	27	28	29	30

1 **All Saints' Day,** observed by the Roman Catholic Church.
2 **All Souls' Day,** observed by the Roman Catholic Church.
5 **Election Day** in the United States. **Guy Fawkes Day,** in Great Britain, marks the failure of a plot to blow up King James I and Parliament in 1605.
11 **Veterans Day** in the United States. **Remembrance Day** in Canada.
11-17 **Children's Book Week.**
17-23 **American Education Week.**
28 **Thanksgiving Day** in the United States.
30 **St. Andrew's Day,** feast day of the patron saint of Scotland.

December

1	2	3	4	5	6	7
8	9	10	11	12	13	14
15	16	17	18	19	20	21
22	23	24	25	26	27	28
29	30	31				

1 **Advent** begins, first of the four Sundays in the season before Christmas.
6 **St. Nicholas Day,** when children in many European countries receive gifts.
8-15 **Hanukkah,** or Feast of Lights, eight-day Jewish festival that celebrates the defeat of the Syrian tyrant King Antiochus IV in 165 B.C.
10 **Nobel Prize Ceremony** in Stockholm, Sweden. **Human Rights Day** marks the anniversary of the adoption of the Universal Declaration of Human Rights in 1948.
13 **St. Lucia Day,** in Sweden, celebrates the return of light after the darkest time of the year.
15 **Bill of Rights Day** in the United States marks the ratification of that document in 1791.
21 **First Day of Winter,** 5:08 P.M. E.S.T.
24 **Christmas Eve.**
25 **Christmas Day.**
26 **Kwanzaa,** black American holiday based on a traditional African harvest festival, through January 1. **Boxing Day** in Canada and Great Britain.
31 **New Year's Eve.**